Handbook of Learning Disabilities

A Multisystem Approach

JACK C. WESTMAN, M.D.

University of Wisconsin

ALLYN AND BACON
Boston   London   Sydney   Toronto

Library of Congress Cataloging-in-Publication Data
Westman, Jack C.
    Handbook of learning disabilities : a multisystem approach / Jack
C. Westman.
        p.   cm.
    Includes bibliographical references (p.   ).
    ISBN 0-205-12120-9
    1. Learning disabilities—Handbooks, manuals, etc.   2. Learning
disabled children—Education—Handbooks, manuals, etc.   I. Title.
LC4704.W47   1990
371.9—dc20   89-28184
                                                                  CIP

Printed in the United States of America
10 9 8 7 6 5 4 3 2 1   94 93 92 91 90

*To the children, parents, and teachers
who have shared their frustrations
and successes with me*

CONTENTS

PART V   THE CLINICAL APPROACH TO FUNCTIONAL DISABILITIES   *373*

PART VI   THE DIAGNOSIS OF FUNCTIONAL DISABILITIES   *429*

PART VIII   TREATMENT   *607*

PREFACE

Rarely does a child have difficulty learning in school for a single reason. Usually many factors in a particular child's internal and external worlds are involved. As a result a variety of mental health and health professionals have joined educators in their concern about children's problems with schoolwork. By the same token, the lack of cross-fertilization between these disciplines has led to disparate theories and practices that often fragment and interrupt the continuity of services intended to help these children.

From years of experience in schools and clinics, I am convinced that holistically trained professionals employing the clinical process are needed in schools. I also believe that clinicians need more awareness of schools and related clinical disciplines. I know that healing power for a particular child comes from the integration of a variety of professional approaches.

This book is an effort to assemble pertinent knowledge in a coherent theoretical framework so that clinicians and educators can have ready access to the many facets of the field. The greatest barrier to understanding children with problems in academic learning is our emphasis upon their surface behavior. Seldom do we talk with them. Consequently, I will shift our attention from performance on tests to the underlying difficulties these children face in doing schoolwork. I also will point out how failure in school may, or may not, lead to failure in adult life.

My experience as a child psychiatrist working with young people as they try to learn academic skills inspired me to undertake the formidable task of sifting through the vast literature pertaining to them. This endeavor revealed both new and old insights about why children founder in schoolwork. As a physician my orientation is to base practice on the foundation of basic sciences. This perspective helped me to find coherence in a field that suffers from fragmentation.

The broad scope of this book is for clinicians, researchers, and professionals related to special education. The essential points, however, are made for teachers and parents. My aim is that, through the adults closest to them, children will gain insights about themselves.

Whenever possible I have avoided the use of technical terms that obscure rather than illuminate. The inadequacies of language are major obstacles to uniting different branches of knowledge. Because communication among researchers, clinicians, administrators, and laypersons is so important, a common language is essential. The veil of mystery must be lifted from these children. Thus I have used the word thinking rather than programming and managerial system rather than ego. On the other hand, when technical terms reduce ambiguity, I employ them. So hyperkinesis is used as a more accurate term than hyperactivity and dyslexia as more precise than reading disability.

The early pages of this book will introduce terms that will be unfamiliar to some readers. Most will be explained in subsequent chapters; however, a glossary has been provided for the reader's convenience. The references I cite range from the early part of this century to the present time. This reflects the unfortunate fact that the problems in education in the United States are not new. Ideas for solving them have been around for decades but have not found their way into practice.

I have drawn upon clinical knowledge of both children and adults, because adults continue to be affected by their childhood learning difficulties, and because adult disorders demonstrate features more clearly than those of childhood. Still children and adults differ fundamentally so that generalizations between them must be made cautiously.

One of the risks of attempting this comprehensive view is that I cite studies that have been challenged. Yet the chances are that controversial ideas will be revitalized in more useful forms. I also am reassured by the fact that professional meetings always are rife with disagreements.

I know that integrating knowledge from the various disciplines concerned with children's learning problems is time consuming, wrenching, and beyond the grasp of a single person. That it can be done through team effort, however, has been dramatically illustrated by the space program, which united the physical, biological, and social sciences to place human beings on the moon. The pursuit of common goals can yield a similar result for children with learning problems. This does occur now for a few optimally served children. It is not beyond our grasp for other children as well.

In writing this book, it became evident that my task was to create a framework within which existing knowledge could make sense. In so doing I found that many controversies actually result from communication barriers between professional disciplines. I hope that this effort will contribute to surmounting them and help others to make connections that have eluded me.

Jack C. Westman, M.D.
Madison, Wisconsin

ACKNOWLEDGMENTS

During the late 1950s, the University of Michigan was alive with new ideas in the neural and social sciences. Under the leadership of Raymond Waggoner, the Mental Health Research Institute had just been created. In that setting I was exposed to the thinking of Ralph Gerard in neurophysiology, Anatole Rapaport in information theory, and James Grier Miller in the general theory of living systems. At the same time, the Institute for Social Research was established and provided me with contact with Ronald Lippitt, Jack R. P. French, Martin Gold, and Theodore Newcomb. I am indebted to these persons whose rigorous and inspirational thinking left an indelible impression on me.

In preparing a manuscript of this scope, I asked for critical reviews of parts of the manuscript by many colleagues. I particularly want to acknowledge the assistance of Peter Bergenske, O.D., Dennis P. Cantwell, M.D., Kate Hathaway, Ph.D., William McKinney, M.D., Charles Matthews, Ph.D., James Grier Miller, M.D., William C. Morse, Ph.D., Margaret B. Rawson, and Peter Tanguay, M.D.

I also appreciate the suggestions of the following mainstream and special educators: Carol Clark, Gretchen Daub Westman, Barbara Draigh, Dolores Lillge, and Sherry Sinclair. For the viewpoints of students and trainees, I am indebted to Laurie Applebaum, David Israelstam, James Killpack, John Phillips, Sandra Rakow, and Eric Westman.

I want to thank Patricia Grinyer for her creative labors in typing the manuscript and tables. Most of all I am grateful to my wife, Nancy, for her painstaking editorial assistance and without whose support and forebearance the entire undertaking would not have been possible.

INTRODUCTION

Why should children who fail in school need the attention of professionals outside of the field of education? This understandable question is raised by those who feel that if children were to try harder or be taught better, their problems would be resolved. In many instances, that is the case; however, it is not true for the almost one in five schoolchildren who encounters barriers to academic learning at a variety of levels and for whom more intense effort and usual teaching are not enough.

A look at the factors involved in academic learning levels reveals why learning problems in school are not as simple as one might think. First of all, in order to learn in school, a child must accept the authority of a teacher and be motivated to pay attention to and concentrate on a task. Then the child must be able to see, hear, and interpret stimuli as the teacher does. Most importantly, the child must be able to understand the task; know how to begin it, carry it out step by step, and finish it; be able to coordinate and communicate ideas about the task verbally and in writing; and recognize when errors are made and have the desire to correct them. All of this must be remembered and carried through to the next day, when something new will be added.

Furthermore, the process of education routinely confronts children with what they do not know and, unlike the work of adults, allows little opportunity for sustained mastery. Consequently, the attitudes, emotional states, and personalities of children strongly affect their schoolwork. In turn, the repeated experience of failure in school affects a child's character development.

From this bird's-eye view of academic learning, the many points at which interferences can occur become evident. There usually is not a single explanation or a simple solution for a particular child's learning problems. The difficulty usually has an extensive background. Strong feelings, also, are frequently encountered as to whether the learning problems are the fault of the child, parents, teachers, or school program. This results in significant misunderstandings on the parts of all of these people. Accordingly, surmounting blame, guilt, and despair is an important step toward helping each child and concerned adults.

Learning problems in school tend to fall into five general categories, with mixtures of all occurring in some children. The first consists of difficulties related to paying attention, concentration, movement, and motivation. The second relates to variations in the ways in which children perceive, understand, and remember information from their external and internal worlds. The third is comprised of language difficulties expressed through variations in speech, reading, spelling, and writing. The fourth includes problems children have in organizing, thinking about, carrying out, and obtaining recognition for their work. The fifth results from self-distortions that interfere with children's attitudes toward learning in school.

We are confronted, then, with problems in which no single factor is critical unless of extreme strength. In analyzing these problems, it is necessary to link surface manifestations with underlying processes that can become the focus of treatment. The approach of this book is to identify those key processes. It is based upon the experience of the University of Wisconsin Learning Disabilities Service, which draws upon the resources of a university hospital, particularly the disciplines of pediatrics, neurology, child psychiatry, neuropsychology, communicative disorders, social work, special education, and occupational therapy. Each of these disciplines evaluates particular aspects of a child's central nervous system functions. When their findings are combined, an understanding of a particular child's problem is formulated and a plan for treatment designed.

Our approach is to help a child and the parents become members of a team that identifies interferences with that child's schoolwork and what can be done about them. This involves discussions and demonstrations of our findings and varying degrees of therapeutic work with the child and family in order to unravel attitudes and relationships that stand in the way of effectively using educational techniques that can correct and compensate for factors that underlie the child's academic learning problems.

An introduction to a book of this scope serves the reader best by conveying its flavor. I will do this by describing its contents in capsule form. My orientation is that an understanding of disorder requires a background of basic knowledge. Accordingly I first review the history of professional approaches to children's learning problems and reframe the concept of learning disabilities. Then I point out the value of the general theory of living systems as a framework for handling the variety of relevant factors. This is followed by consideration of the important external influences on children from society, schools, families, peers, and classrooms, in addition to the internal influences of the central nervous system functions that comprise a child's character. A model for integrating all of these influences is proposed, with illustrations of the variety of academic learning problems and means of identifying them. Finally, the array of treatment approaches is outlined.

Historically the experience of two centuries can be brought to bear upon current conceptions of children's learning problems in school. In so doing in Chapter 1, I will trace four streams of thought and practice in the fields of special education, neurology, pediatrics, and psychoanalysis.

As public education evolved in the United States, special provisions were made for children identified as physically handicapped and mentally retarded. More recently, efforts have been made to define a group of children with learning disabilities. However, for a variety of theoretical, scientific, and pragmatic reasons, the terms educational disability and handicap have administrative and political advantages over the term learning disability. Furthermore, distinguishing between functional disabilities and educational disabilities and handicaps has merit, as shown in Chapter 2.

Research on children's learning problems has suffered because of the lack of coherent theoretical models. The advancement of knowledge inevitably sets aside past conceptions and adds new, at times revolutionary, insights. We are prepared to receive and apply these insights if our theoretical models are both comprehensive and adaptable. Understanding children's learning problems in school depends upon moving beyond assigning simple causes of behavior to the level of multifactorial determinants interacting over time. The general theory of living systems described in Chapter 3 offers a means of doing this. The key systems for our purposes are society, schools, classrooms, families, and the individual, with emphasis upon the brain as the organ of the mind. I deal with each of these system levels as they bear upon children's problems with schoolwork.

Chapter 4 addresses a number of social factors that play roles in producing educationally handicapped children. The genetic basis for satisfaction through mastery of oneself and the environment has been progressively undermined by contemporary social attitudes, so that children receive confusing messages about the value of work. Also overlooked in the United States is the responsibility adults have for sharing their wisdom with children. We seem to have imposed upon children the responsibility for determining their own futures. We have failed to impart our knowledge that trial and error learning is a necessary ingredient of competence in society. We have conveyed an image of instant success and have not shared the frustrations that each one of us has experienced with our children. Our failure to share our disappointments with the young has perpetuated the illusion that being an adult in itself brings success.

Our public schools suffer because of the discrepancy between their charge to meet the educational needs of all children and the limited means available to them to do so. Chapter 5 deals with the reasons for this state of affairs. School administrators are immersed in the management of their plants, personnel, and schedules, so that their bureaucracies tend to promote routines and to discourage the initiative of staffs and students. Above all, school administrators are hampered in their efforts to create and maintain working conditions that support professionalism in competent and dedicated teachers.

The greatest neglect in educational research is of how children actually learn in school classrooms, the topic of Chapter 6. The ecology and social atmosphere of the classroom supply the context for the interplay of relationships and activities among individual children, their teachers, and their peers. Although varying in size, composition, and significance from a single yearlong experience in the early grades to the multiple, circumscribed classes of high school, the classroom is the crucible within which a variety of key educational, adult–child, peer, and cultural experiences take place. The interaction between teachers and children is the fulcrum for academic learning. The peer audience before which they perform also affects teachers and children in both supportive and destructive ways.

The family establishes the foundation for academic learning through the communication and problem solving skills and trust that result from solid attachment bonds between parents and children. Children who do not have stable and dependable early life experiences are predisposed to difficulties with schoolwork. Chapter 7 illustrates why the family is central to the identification, management, and long-range course of children with educational disabilities and handicaps.

Because it is the seat of the mind and the source of behavior, I summarize current knowledge of the structural components of the central nervous system in Chapter 8. The mind is lodged in the cells, chemicals, and energy of the brain. It springs from the inheritance of genes and culture. Through its conscious and unconscious components, it struggles to create significance in its psychosocial and ecological context. Through communication it reaches out to other minds.

The central nervous system has two structural components. One is anatomical and consists of cells, as do other organs of the body. The other is chemical in the form of neuroregulators. Both of these components have genetic determinants and are influenced by life experiences. Situated within the cellular components, the chemical components are the substrate of learning. The interacting developmental determinants of central nervous system functioning then are its cellular components, life experience, and its action upon its own neural circuitry.

The anatomical subsystems of the central nervous system described in Chapter 9 are the sensory systems, visual-motor system, motor systems, cerebellar system, reticular activating system, autonomic nervous system, limbic system, language system, cortical associational systems, frontal lobe systems, and cerebral hemispheres. The relatively discrete anatomical nature of these systems corresponds to the progressive addition of each level in the evolution of animal forms.

The maturation of a child's central nervous system recapitulates the phylogenetic sequence of mammalian evolution. The tissue of the brain arises from and maintains a corresponding relationship to the skin, muscles, and viscera. The progressive development of mental and behavioral capacities outlined in Chapter 10 can be related to maturational events in the brain, which continue into the third decade of life.

Learning reflects the underlying processes of the central nervous system. The distinction between mind and body is no longer tenable, because the mind is a phase of the brain's activity. As such, an understanding of the enormously complicated brain requires models for relating mental functioning to its structure and processes. Our present knowledge justifies a model comprised of five major functional systems, as presented in Chapter 11. The state regulating system determines how we relate to the environment through its role in consciousness and the expression of appetitive and affective instincts. The information processing and storage system permits communication with others. The managerial system mediates the needs of the individual in the surrounding world. The self system provides the human qualities that link the present to the past and the future and monitors behavior in social contexts.

I propose a model of human behavior that employs general living systems theory as a setting for these five functional systems of the central nervous system, psychodynamic conceptions of character, and the sociological concepts of links between behavior and social context. The model draws attention to five corresponding areas of human functioning based upon findings emerging from child development and clinical research: temperament, cognition, language, personal management, and the self. This model offers the possibility of shifting from the ambiguous concept of learning disabilities to the level of identifying specific disabilities in these central nervous system functions.

As the reflection of the activity of the state regulating system, temperament refers to one's emotional state and disposition toward action. The determinants of temperament detailed in Chapter 12 lie in attentional and motivational mechanisms that are expressed through motor activity. The voluntary deployment of attention depends upon motivation arising from the appetitive and affective instinctual systems. The vicissitudes of resulting cravings and emotions play key roles in learning problems.

Cognition is a complex process through which personalized knowledge is acquired by blending information from our external and internal worlds. The stages of cognition that reflect the activity of the information processing and storage system are described in Chapter 13 as encoding, perception, imagery, imagination, and memory. A variety of cognitive styles can be described as they apply to acquiring knowledge in school.

Spoken language has been a human capacity long enough to become genetically programmed. It is likely that this extends to visual symbols as well, but not to words, since reading is such a recent evolutionary acquisition. As indicated in Chapter 14, the language system is both an integral part of character development and a reflection of that development.

As the vehicle for the mastery drives, the managerial system is devoted to fulfilling one's needs in the external world of people, places, and things. Chapter 15 shows how the managerial system straddles the state regulating and information processing systems, organizes itself around the language system, operates at the behest of the self, and also has a life of its own in the form of a vast reservoir of automatic mechanisms for negotiating the routines of life.

The self is the interface between the individual and society and provides a person's sense of continuity in time and coherence in space. The neurophysiological evidence cited in Chapter 16 supports the existence of a self that arises from the human capacity to represent ourselves in symbols and concepts, monitors how successfully we are living, holds our hopes for the future, offers the luxury of contemplating our existence, and provides the inspiration for scientific and artistic creativity.

The crucial system for understanding children with learning problems is the child at work in school. Accordingly I address the nature of learning generally, the specific learning of academic skills, and the development of competencies needed for schoolwork.

Learning takes place in conditioned, instrumental, and didactic forms, as explained in Chapter 17. Conditioned and instrumental learning that directly fulfill personal needs are essential aspects of living. Didactic learning, however, is without immediate benefit except as a child is motivated to please adults, enhance one's status, satisfy the mastery of challenge, or be excited by creativity. Although the glint of creativity is apparent during early childhood, the process of didactic teaching gradually tends to diminish or extinguish it.

Chapter 19 deals with acquiring the basic skills in reading and arithmetic in school. Reading is important to the fullness of human experience by allowing an appreciation of one's cultural heritage and enabling occupational success. Unlike speech, the ability to read has not been necessary for survival long enough to become genetically programmed and so must be learned. The teaching of reading in school has fluctuated between phonetic and meaning methods, creating problems for children who are weak in using the particular method in vogue. Writing is one of the most complicated actions of the central nervous system and is a form of creativity in itself. Mathematics draws on a different set of central nervous system functions and has received less attention than reading as a problem area for children.

All learning builds upon a developmental sequence of emerging capacities, so that children progress from an initial brittle state to increasing flexibility as they become articulate and skillful. Learning is the process of acquiring skills and knowledge through the modification of images, symbols, and concepts of the self, others, and the world. For children, the reward of learning is satisfaction from mastery in play, which forms the basis for work in an adult sense. Consequently, our current knowledge of child development, as summarized in Chapter 19, raises many questions about the relationship of variations in early development to academic learning problems.

A melange of barriers to understanding the special needs of children with learning problems results from the multitude of fragmented professional approaches to them. For this reason Chapter 20 devotes considerable attention to the clinical process that places a child at the center of diagnosis and builds outward to incorporate the critical systems impinging upon that child through teamwork. In so doing the clinical process draws upon a range of professional disciplines in developing an integrated treatment plan with continuity over the years required to obtain an optimal outcome.

The model of human behavior employed in this book permits a coherent understanding of interferences with academic learning. Chapter 21 treats variations in expressions of temperament that strongly influence the attention, movement levels, and moods of children in school in addition to playing a key role in their motivation to perform schoolwork. Although seemingly a simple matter, paying attention proves to be complex. Sitting still in classrooms is difficult for children with a variety of forms of hyperkinesis. Affective disorders also interfere with schoolwork.

The cognitive problems described in Chapter 22 range from those involving defects in the sensory organs themselves to obscure distortions caused by psychological defense mechanisms. The imagery from external and internal sources is the forum within which each child constructs personal knowledge in the form of symbols and concepts of oneself and the external world. The capacity for symbolization enriches and expedites that process but also can introduce malevolent phantoms into the classroom. The process of conceptualization makes it possible to move from concrete to abstract knowledge but may be incompletely developed.

Verbal language disabilities receive attention in Chapter 23 as factors contributing to problems with schoolwork. Speech disabilities are those of articulation, speaking resonance, and fluency. Internal language disabilities can be expressions of general developmental disability syndromes, specific language delays, interpersonal delays, developmental dysphasia, hearing deficits, and elective mutism.

Because of the central role of reading in education, the developmental dyslexias are emphasized in Chapter 24. They are found in a multifaceted group of children and adults who have difficulties with reading, writing, spelling, and arithmetic skills. Four general types of dyslexia have been described: vestibulo-cerebellar dysmetria, visual-spatial dysgnosia, auditory-linguistic dysphasia, and articulo-graphic dyspraxia.

Because they have not been the focus of psychological and educational testing, managerial functions are not given sufficient consideration in most approaches to children with schoolwork problems. The incomplete development of managerial functions mentioned in

Chapter 25, however, causes many children to need specific help in learning how to work in school and to relate effectively to adults and peers. They have impulse control disabilities, thinking disabilities, neurotic inhibitions of productivity, and pervasive developmental disorders.

The self system is the essence of a person, and its harmonious functioning is taken for granted. The disturbances in this functioning as described in Chapter 26, however, are reflected in distressful feelings of and about oneself. Failures and distortions in its development have devastating effects on one's ability to relate to other people and the world. The achievement of self-respect and self-confidence is an important sign of maturity denied to many children who fail in schoolwork. As a result their competence is further undermined.

Chapter 27 defines individual differences and pathology as helpful concepts in understanding the origins of educational disabilities and handicaps. The interplay of hereditary and experiential factors is highlighted. Chapter 28 more specifically outlines the ways in which functional disabilities become educational disabilities and handicaps through the mediating influences of learning and work styles, levels of self-development, and maladaptive personality patterns.

The management of children's learning problems involves a wide range of factors, from the broadest level of social policies to the most specific level of prescribing a medication.

The focus of Chapter 29 is on social policy, which plays a key role in the detection and management of children with learning problems. Society cannot afford to ignore them because of the high social and economic cost of caring for educational failures through later welfare, correctional, and mental health services. Since social and public policies are determined through the political process, professional and lay organizations can exert powerful influences upon school boards and legislators to provide needed services for their children. The federal Education for All Handicapped Children Act of 1975 was a major step toward ensuring that all children profitably pass through the educational system.

The operations of school systems can both contribute to and significantly resolve children's learning problems. Schools can extrude children or mold them to fit into peripheral subsystems—which, although presumably arranged to benefit children, actually reduce stress within the school system itself at the peril of affected children. On the other hand, school programs can be designed to prevent and manage educational disabilities once they become evident, as proposed in Chapter 30. Rather than classifying children on the basis of educationally unrelated diagnoses, such as mental retardation, emotional disturbance, and learning disability, it is more realistic to identify educational disabilities and levels of educational handicaps. When this is done, four levels of handicap emerge. There are children who need to learn how to care for themselves, those who need to learn basic academic skills, those who need to learn social skills, and those who need tutorial support.

The importance of teachers as models for children cannot be overestimated. To the extent that they are palpable persons with satisfactions and frustrations, teachers can facilitate mutually trusting relationships that motivate children to perform schoolwork. The teacher's management of a classroom is critical in creating and maintaining an atmosphere conducive to academic learning. Chapter 31 illustrates how children with learning problems can be aided in acquiring self-discipline, interpersonal skills, and self-confidence through the creative arts, structured group activities, and physical education.

Largely overlooked but of considerable potential significance is the role of the peer group in assisting children with learning problems. Peer attitudes toward special education can be shifted from disparagement to acceptance. Older children can model maturity for younger children and can play a direct role in tutoring. Peer attitudes can be influenced by a curriculum devoted to accepting individual differences, in addition to a teacher's leadership in promoting small group activities that stimulate constructive interaction in the classroom.

For children with weaknesses in the basic academic skills, group or individual remedial tutoring is required. A variety of effective specialized techniques developed for remedying reading, spelling, writing, and arithmetic difficulties are outlined in Chapter 32. Some children may need specifically designed language therapy.

Individual psychotherapy is a potent resource for changing the attitudes, character structures, and self-evaluations of children with academic learning problems. Psychotherapy as detailed in Chapter 33 is particularly useful in assisting children to recognize and accept their weaknesses and strengths and to ameliorate self-defeating and interpersonal manipulative patterns.

Psychoactive medications can play a role as adjuncts in the treatment of some children. They should not be used for behavioral control; however, they can be helpful in promoting a child's participation in classroom activities when employed as a carefully monitored component of an overall treatment program, as illustrated in Chapter 34.

Parents can gain the expertise needed to understand and interpret their child's needs as members of a team created to assist the child. Chapter 35 is devoted to ways in which professionals can foster this role by establishing alliances with parents, who can then understand the nature of their children's problems and desirable treatment approaches. Furthermore, therapeutic interventions with families can unravel pathological interactions, promote successful child-rearing techniques, and improve communication within families, so that parents can help their children more effectively.

In sum, the learning problems of children are reflections of the unsuccessful efforts of children to cope with socialization in an increasingly complex, ever-changing world. Most significantly, we have failed to appreciate that children who do not conform to our expectations of them in school are themselves the keys to meeting those expectations. Our failure to develop a child-centered approach to academic learning problems is the greatest barrier to resolving them. Professionals have neglected to integrate existing knowledge, and parents have been unaware of their crucial role in helping their own children. Professionals have retreated from the vast array of knowledge to the protection of their respective turfs. They also have not appreciated that human behavior is a reflection of brain functions that are products of genes, life experience, and each child's unique creations.

The clinical process offers an approach to a child through establishing a diagnosis and a treatment plan. Because the evaluation of children with learning problems usually is fragmented by the isolation of professional disciplines, the team concept is essential in evaluation procedures and for treatment plans with continuity. Most critically, parents and the child should be members of that team.

We need a sensible approach to the puzzling and frustrating problems of children who do not learn as expected in our schools. At one extreme there are children who are falsely regarded as mentally retarded. At the other extreme are gifted children who fail to realize their potentials.

At this time we vascillate between blaming them, their parents, or their schools for the difficulties children have in becoming contributing members of society. In fact, we are all responsible. Our children have varying degrees of academic talent, their parents have varying degrees of understanding, our educational system has limited capacities to meet their needs, and our society does not provide clear goals for them. The frustration all experience is best met not by each blaming the other, but by enlightened collaboration among professionals, parents, and children in a society that plans for the next generation. The following pages represent an effort to facilitate that collaboration.

I

The Situation

It is the great task of contemporary humans to invent solutions to problems that are largely unprecedented in the
history of the species. Science can help. But to be truly effective in meeting these novel human predicaments, science
must transcend its traditional boundaries and achieve a level
of mutual understanding, innovation, and cooperation among
disciplines rarely achieved in the past.

David A. Hamburg, 1983

A T LEAST 17 percent of
school-age children in
the United States have
significant difficulties in
performing schoolwork. The evidence ominously points to the persistence of these problems into adulthood unless effective interventions take place during childhood. As the learning difficulties children
encounter in school often are not outgrown, they warrant both professional and public attention.

Historically separate strands of thought have emerged about children's learning problems in the fields of special education, neurology,
pediatrics, and psychoanalysis. Each discipline has its own language
for describing these children. The time is ripe for drawing together
the accumulated knowledge of these fields for the benefit of educators, clinicians, and researchers.

The need for integration is particularly urgent because vested
interests have coalesced around diagnostic labels that carry implications regarding responsibility for a given child's difficulties. The labels
assign responsibility to a child's brain, personality, parents, school, or
society. At the broadest level, these labels channel funding from federal, state, local, and health-care sources. Most important, they influence a child's self-concept and carry forward through the person's
life.

In order to clarify the situation for each child, a useful distinction
can be made between variations in brain functions, educational disabilities, educational handicaps, and reactions to those disabilities and
handicaps. When this is done, treatment for a particular child can be
rationally planned and carried out.

The concept of learning disabilities has been useful in focusing attention on many children who founder in school. It is not scientifically, clinically, or educationally sound, however. This section will explicate the reasons for this conclusion and set the stage for the remainder of the book. The inescapable implication is that if optimal individualized education were available, and appropriate expectations held, for each child, there would be no educational handicaps.

A new way of thinking is required to understand children who have problems in school. Our failure to do so results from simplistic, linear, cause–effect thinking. The general theory of living systems offers a means of thinking about the many levels of factors involved when a child performs schoolwork in the social role of student. It permits conceptualization of the external and internal worlds of children as they are influenced by their society, schools, classrooms, peers, and families.

1

Historical Background

Life can only be understood backward but it must be lived forward.

Soren Kierkegaard, 1845

Four strands of thought lie behind current perspectives toward children's learning problems. The origins of these approaches can be traced to the "Wild Boy of Aveyron," stroke victims who could not read, brain-injured soldiers, encephalitis victims, and Sigmund Freud's visit to Clark University in 1908.

The first strand is the field of special education, which evolved from Jean Itard's work in the early 1800s with the feral "Wild Boy of Aveyron." The second is based upon the concept of dyslexia as derived from the neurological study of adult stroke victims later in the 19th century. The third arose from the linkage of hyperkinetic children with Kurt Goldstein's descriptions of brain-injured soldiers in World War I and of victims of the encephalitis epidemic of 1918. The fourth was the application of psychoanalysis to education during the second and third decades of this century.

Although interrelating at points, these strands evolved separately. This chapter traces each through the years and concludes with a summary of the findings of the Collaborative Perinatal Project, a large-scale study that demonstrated the validity of each of these approaches.

THE EVOLUTION OF SPECIAL EDUCATION

In the summer of 1800, Itard's groundbreaking work with Victor, the so-called "Wild Boy of Aveyron," established the field of special education. Itard brought Victor from a savage to a civilized level by teaching him the fundamentals of language (Itard, 1962; Lane & Pillard, 1978).

Based upon his work with Victor, Itard proposed that teaching should be individually tailored and should build progressively on a child's resources. He devised the first systematic method for teaching reading in small steps by breaking down complex performances into their component skills. Itard's approach to education gained breadth and momentum in the hands of his student, Edward Seguin, who went on to educate the mentally retarded. As he witnessed retarded children throughout the world benefit from his efforts, Seguin foresaw the application of lessons learned in the education of the handicapped to the education of all children. He ultimately came to the United States, where he served as head of the Pennsylvania Training School.

The tradition of special education in the United States was furthered by Howe, who worked with blind children at the Perkins Institute for the Blind; one of its teachers, Ann Sullivan Marcey, worked with Helen Keller. It was over 130 years ago that Howe moved the Massachusetts legislature to declare that all citizens should share in the blessings of education, thus foreshadowing U.S. Public Law 94-142, the "Right to Education" bill of 1975. In 1848 the Perkins Institute began to treat retarded children, and in 1887 that program was moved to Waltham, Massachusetts, where it became the Fernald State School.

Maria Montessori built upon Itard's methods in the early 20th century and emphasized children's abilities to teach themselves as well. She evolved six principles of education (Montessori, 1974). The first was that children are biologically programmed for self-education. The second called for a science of child development based upon observation. The third held that the school environment should be organized in direct relation to a child's internal organization. The fourth maintained that a child must be free to interact spontaneously with that prepared environment. The fifth was that programming must be oriented to each individual child. The sixth held that children should employ multiple senses in learning.

Montessori's methods drew upon an array of materials that engaged all of the senses except taste and smell. Many of her devices were derived from those previously used by Seguin and employed Itard's method of dwindling contrasts for stimulating sensory discrimination. Montessori particularly credited Itard with showing how perceptions and language could be associated.

In 1922, the coming of age of special education was signaled by the organization of the Council for Exceptional Children. At that time, Gates and Gray urged teachers to make systematic and detailed studies of the reading difficulties of children and to provide appropriate remedial instruction (Gates, 1922; Gray, 1922).

In 1932 Marian Monroe described her sensorimotor remedial program for severely retarded readers. She noted that many of these children had no observable deficits in their sensory organs and yet failed to discriminate the sounds of vowels or the spatial configurations of letters because of difficulties in central coordinating brain mechanisms (Monroe, 1932).

In the 1930s and 1940s, educators were influenced by Alfred Strauss's view that behavior could be interpreted as putative evidence of brain damage. The contemporary work of Orton and Critchley on specific language disabilities had little impact then, however.

Continuing the tradition of Itard and Montessori, in 1943 Grace Fernald, in *Remedial Techniques in Basic School Subjects,* described kinesthetic stimulation as a tool for teaching retarded readers. It involved the learning of words by tracing them repeatedly. Marianne Frostig studied the visual perception of children with learning problems and devised training programs that in themselves, however, did not improve performance in academic subjects (Frostig, 1964).

Jean Ayres developed a sensory integration program whose objective was to improve perception and motor planning through training involving postural reflexes, equilibrium reactions, the level of excitability of the nervous system, and a variety of sensory modalities through such activities as rubbing, swinging, spinning, hopping, and climbing (Ayres, 1972).

Language specialists contributed to special education in the 1950s and 1960s. Katrina DeHirsh, a psychologist and speech pathologist who directed the pediatric language disorder clinic at Columbia Presbyterian Medical Center in New York, developed formulations of reading disabilities that drew upon perceptual-motor and psychopathological material, as well as a model of language pathology. In the early 1950s, she described receptive and expressive language difficulties in complex linguistic processing, word finding, formulating of verbal output, and spatial and temporal concepts. She predicted later reading failure in preschoolers from a variety of perceptual-motor skill, body image, and language measures (de Hirsch, 1966).

Helmer Myklebust, another linguistically oriented professional, began his work with hearing-impaired and aphasic persons and ultimately became interested in the relationships between brain function and learning behavior (Johnson & Myklebust, 1967).

Samuel Kirk spent the early stages of his career in the field of mental retardation. He is known for his development of the Illinois Test of Psycholinguistic Abilities based on a theoretical model of language further expanded by Osgood for planning teaching strategies (Hallahan & Cruickshank, 1973). In the 1960s Kirk responded to the call of parents and suggested the term *specific learning disability* for the newly formed Association for Children with Learning Disabilities.

In 1961 William Cruickshank's Montgomery County Study concluded that structure was needed in classroom work with emotionally disturbed children. During the same year, Nicholas Hobbs introduced Project Re-ED as a model for educating emotionally disturbed children with an emphasis on the operation of the total social system of which the child is a part rather than on intrapsychic processes (Lewis, C., 1975).

During the mid-1960s, the influence of Skinner was felt in the application of learning theory to understanding and modifying behavior (Skinner, 1953). In 1968 Frank Hewett described a behavioral approach to teaching disturbed children in *The Emotionally Disturbed Child in the Classroom.*

The strength of the special education approach has been its focus on the cognitive stimulation of children. Its weakness has been its lack of influence on the multiple systems impinging upon children. The result is epitomized by the initial experiences of Itard with Victor and has been repeated over and over again since. Although brilliantly providing for the education of Victor, Itard isolated him from other children in a highly structured life, alternating between house and classroom (Lane & Pillard, 1978). Itard's focus on Victor's education in an adult context led him to overlook the importance of motivation, peer interactions, and psychosexual development in a growing child. Without consideration of these vital factors, simply teaching pupils still falls short of the goal of educating young people.

THE NEUROLOGICAL CONCEPT OF DYSLEXIA

The second strand of thought began over a century ago when European physicians realized that disease or injury of certain parts of the brain impaired reading ability. In 1676, Schmidt described the loss of reading ability, which Kussmaul named *alexia,* or word blindness, in 1877. In 1887 Berlin suggested the term *dyslexia* for the partial loss of reading ability. Even at that time Marie pointed out that there could be no single word center, because the brain could not have a center for a function that only recently appeared in evolution (Critchley, 1970).

In 1895 reports by a British physician, James Hinshelwood, of brain-damaged adults who had lost the ability to read stimulated W. Pringle Morgan to describe congenital word blindness in a 14-year-old boy, who was among the brightest in his school and had exceptional talents in mathematics. To account for his reading difficulty, Morgan suggested that there was underdevelopment of the angular gyrus of the parietal lobe. The notion of variation in the maturation of areas of the brain subserving reading thus was conceived. Several weeks before Morgan's paper appeared, another British physician, James Kerr, wrote an essay that also dealt with reading and writing difficulties in children who manifested no other cognitive difficulties.

Advancement of the idea of congenital word blindness was carried on by Hinshelwood (1917). He noted a family history of similar difficulties and found that with proper education these children usually could be taught to read. He used the term *congenital dyslexia* to refer to mild reading problems that could be distinguished from severe cases of congenital word blindness and suggested that both were the result of developmental anomalies of the angular gyrus region. At that time, however, some regarded reading and spelling difficulties as expressions of the low end of an endowment curve for those abilities rather than pathology (Hollingworth, 1923).

In the 1920s Samuel T. Orton, a psychiatrist, neurologist, and neuropathologist, sharpened thinking about the neurological basis of learning difficulties. At a mental hygiene clinic in Iowa City, Iowa, Orton saw many children who appeared to be bright but had difficulty with reading, writing, spelling, and speech. Many of these children also showed confusion in time, space, and directional orientation. They really were not word blind. They could see and copy words but were unable to understand their meanings. Orton thought that the fundamental problem lay in translating between heard and written words and proposed the term *strephosymbolia* (twisted symbols) to replace congenital word blindness (Goody, 1961; Orton, 1928).

Orton approached reading as a stage of language development, preceded by spoken language and later expressed in writing, which involved spelling. He looked upon language as a hierarchy of complex integrations in the nervous system, culminating in unilateral control by one of the two brain hemispheres. He worked during an era in which many left-handed children were being trained to be right-handed. He proposed that the cause of strephosymbolia was a failure in the development of a clearly dominant cerebral hemisphere with resulting indistinct image formation. He preferred the term *developmental* to *congenital* in order to take into account the interaction of heredity and environment in producing this state (Orton, 1937).

Although Orton originally worked at the University of Iowa, his major writing was done at the New York Neurological Institute. The application of his concepts to education was accomplished by Gillingham and Stillman, and stressed the simultaneous association of visual, auditory, and kinesthetic stimuli presented in small units, then expanded into larger and more complex wholes in the tradition of Montessori. Later in 1949 the Orton Society was established to further the understanding and treatment of dyslexia.

Through the years the association of spatial discrimination difficulties with dyslexia has been noted. In his review in 1956, Arthur Drew concluded that dyslexia was a hereditary disturbance of gestalt formation due to defective figure-ground recognition (Drew, 1956). Macdonald Critchley (1970) proposed parieto-occipital developmental discrepancies as the etiology. Knud Hermann (1970) called attention to the relationship between the spatial disorientation seen in some dyslexics and Gerstmann's syndrome, a disorder characterized by right–left disorientation, dyscalculia, dysgraphia, and finger agnosia. The significance of this relationship is unclear, however, because reading difficulty is not characteristic of Gerstmann's syndrome.

More recently, Norman Geschwind proposed that dyslexia may be the brain manifestation of a broader spectrum of immune disorders (Geschwind & Behan, 1984; Geschwind, 1985).

THE CONCEPT OF MINIMAL BRAIN DYSFUNCTION

The third strand of thought linked hyperkinetic and impulsive behavior to brain lesions and was initiated in England in 1902 by Still, a pediatrician. He described children with "defects of moral control" characterized by temper tantrums, disobedience, and impulsivity. Many of these children were assumed to have brain damage resulting from tumors, infectious diseases, or head injuries (Still, 1902). In 1908 Tredgold proposed that hyperkinetic children may have suffered mild brain injuries at birth.

As a result of his work with brain-injured soldiers in Europe during World War I, Kurt Goldstein was able to describe the severely brain-damaged adult as stimulus bound, perseverative, unable to deal with abstractions, incapable of differentiating between figure and ground, and prone to catastrophic emotional reactions. The application of these findings to children led to inferences, such as that extreme temper tantrums are attributable to catastrophic reactions (Goldstein, 1954; Ross, 1977).

In the United States, brain damage became an explanation of behavioral and educational problems in children following the epidemic of Von Economo's encephalitis in 1918. In its wake was a group of postencephalitic children who manifested restlessness, insomnia, irritability, distractability, and emotional lability. Although these behavioral disturbances diminished with the passage of time, many of the children never completely recovered. Hohman (1922) and Ebaugh (1923) described these postencephalitic children as antisocial, irritable, impulsive, and hyperkinetic. Kahn

and Cohen (1934) used the term *organic drivenness* to describe this behavior pattern, also found in children with no known brain damage. They presumed that hyperkinesis resulted from inadequate cortical inhibition of subcortical responses.

Two of Goldstein's students, Alfred Strauss and Heinz Werner, emigrated to the United States, where they worked in the Wayne County Training School, an institution for the mentally retarded in Michigan. They found figure-ground problems, difficulties in abstracting, stimulus-bound behavior and perseveration among mentally retarded children and inferred underlying brain damage. Later Strauss founded the Cove School in Racine, Wisconsin, and with Lehtinen in 1947, in their influential book *Psychopathology and Education of the Brain Injured Child,* defined a brain-injured child as one who, before, during, or after birth, had received an injury to or suffered an infection of the brain with resulting disturbances in perception that impeded learning. They emphasized the cardinal features of brain injury: hyperkinesis, impulsivity, distractibility, emotional lability, and perseveration. Perceptual disturbances and neurological abnormalities also were described. This clinical picture was widely construed as a *prima facie* indication of brain injury.

The influence of Strauss soon made itself felt in work with cerebral palsied children. Cruickschank played a central role in demonstrating that children with cerebral palsy displayed the kind of performance deficits observed by Strauss in his putatively brain-injured retarded children (Cruickshank, 1967). Since children with cerebral palsy benefited from exercise designed to improve their motor control, Newell Kephart, who also worked with Strauss, pursued the idea that perceptual motor exercises might help children with learning difficulties (Strauss & Kephart, 1955).

In 1937, Charles Bradley reported that

overactivity in children often responded favorably to stimulant medication. This was construed to confirm the existence of brain injury as the basis for hyperkinesis.

Arnold Gesell and Catherine Armatruda also found the concept of minimal cerebral injury useful in explaining an atypical developmental syndrome in children who showed speech difficulties, poorly defined cerebral dominance, motor incoordination, perceptual deficits, and difficulty in learning to read. They preferred the term maturational lag to brain injury, however (Gesell & Armatruda, 1974).

Gesell was a psychologist and physician who observed the usual developmental sequence of language, cognitive, motor, and adaptive behavior and identified lags in development, which could be accelerated by specific stimulation. Gesell believed that brain cells early in life retain a plasticity that responds not only to genetic maturation, but also to environmental stimulation.

Gesell's developmental rather than pathological perspective also was held by Harry and Ruth Bakwin, who called attention to a group of children they thought were constitutionally hyperkinetic from early life but did not pose management problems until entry into school, when their behavior interfered with their classroom adjustment and academic learning (Bakwin & Bakwin 1960).

Lauretta Bender was a student of Orton and Gesell with training in neuropathology. In the mid-1930s she became director of the Children's Service at Bellevue Psychiatric Hospital in New York City and saw the behavior problems following the influenza epidemic of 1918. She contributed to the neurological understanding of a variety of childhood disorders.

In the early 1960s, Benjamin Pasamanick and Hilda Knobloch advanced the concept of a continuum of reproductive casualty and postulated a range of vulnerability in early life, from death by spontaneous abortion of a grossly defective fetus to educa-tional problems in the later lives of prematurely born infants.

In 1975 Maurice Laufer reflected upon decades of research on hyperkinesis and favored the concept of syndromes of cerebral dysfunction. He pointed out that to know the hyperkinetic disorder is to know every aspect of child psychiatry, from the psychodynamic to the most specifically organic (Laufer, 1975). Laufer used the term *hyperkinetic impulse disorder*. He thought it resulted from a variety of causes, such as prenatal and perinatal maldevelopment, malformation, and malfunction. He proposed that the complex of symptoms was related to reticular activating system and diencephalic dysfunctions. The diencephalon serves to route, sort, and pattern impulses from peripheral and central receptors, not only diverting them to appropriate cortical areas, but also giving them significance, weight, and valence. In Laufer's view, when these centers are dysfunctional, the brain could be flooded with stimuli.

Paul Wender pointed out that the diagnosis of minimal brain dysfunction depends more on history than on psychological or neurological diagnostic techniques. For him the diagnosis was based upon dysfunction in the following areas: motor activity, attention, cognition, impulse control, motor coordination, physical development, electroencephalography, language development, emotional lability, thought, and self-identity. Wender proposed a biochemical abnormality to explain these behavioral phenomena (Wender, 1971).

In the context of vehement controversies, the pediatric literature of the 1960s reflected a cautious approach to the problem of the etiology, diagnosis, and treatment of school dysfunctions (Levine et al., 1980). Pediatricians were urged to consider the variety of physical, emotional, and social etiological factors. Revisions of pediatric textbooks reflected the rapidly changing terminologies by including such novel sections as "General Motor Restlessness," "Behavioral Patterns Associated with Minimal Cerebral Dysfunction," "The Syndrome of Nonmotor Brain Damage," "Cerebral Dysfunction (Brain Damage, Learning Disorders)," and "Central Auditory Defects." As psychopharmacology became a major factor in the practice of adult psychiatry, and as public pressure for a treatment for children with behavioral disorders in school increased, the use of medication for dysfunctioning schoolchildren became widespread. Drug treatment ranges from amphetamines across a wide range of pharmacologic agents, including major and minor tranquilizers, antidepressants, antihistamines, and anticonvulsants.

With the appearance of the *Diagnostic and Stastistical Manual of Mental Disorders-III* of the American Psychiatric Association, the diagnosis of attention deficit disorder with or without hyperactivity was recommended as a replacement for the terms *hyperkinetic syndrome* and *minimal brain dysfunction.*

Critique of the Minimal Brain Dysfunction Concept

The notion of minimal brain dysfunction represents a stage in an evolving effort to explain the behavior of a group of children who have difficulty in school. Because it implies a definitive cause within a child, the concept is deeply entrenched in medical and popular thinking.

From the scientific point of view, it is imperative that a direct relationship between brain lesions and behavior be established in order to validate this concept. Experimentation with animals and clinical knowledge of organic brain syndromes come very close to achieving this. At the same time, these are viable alternative explanations that can be derived from our knowledge of organic brain syndromes in adults and individual differences in children.

Animal Research

Animal research points to a definite brain-hyperkinetic behavior relationship. The findings from animal models may or may not directly bear upon humans, however, and must be interpreted with caution (Rajecki, 1983).

A symptom complex of minimal brain dysfunction, including decreased learning ability, hyperkinesis, and impulsivity, has been produced in kittens with midsagittal sections of the corpus callosum (Scheder et al., 1977). This suggests that the behavior of some children may be a consequence of faulty neural transmission across the corpus callosum, which plays a role in excitatory and inhibitory processes.

In another animal study, newborn rat pups were selectively depleted of brain dopamine by treatment with 6-hydroxydopamine. The pups displayed hyperkinesis, disturbed habituation, learning, and cognitive deficits, all of which were improved with stimulant medication (Alpert et al, 1978). Experimental interference with the maturation of the cerebellum and hippocampus in the rat also produces hyperactivity and learning difficulty related to attentional deficits (Gazzara & Altman, 1981).

Lesions in rat brains produced what has been described as the ventral tegmental syndrome, which consists of disorganized behavior resulting from the depletion of cortical dopamine and causing distractibility, increased purposeless activity, inaccurate interpretation of environmental cues, and disorganized behavior. This behavior was reversed by d-amphetamine (Grahame-Smith, 1978).

A "septal syndrome" has been described as an experimental animal model of behavioral propensities that could underlie "disinhibitory psychopathology" in humans. The syndrome includes poor impulse control, an inability to delay gratification, a high need for stimulation, and responsiveness to feared stimuli only when they are immediately at hand (Buck, 1984).

Human Organic Brain Syndromes

Discrete lesions of the frontal and prefrontal association areas appear to be associated with hyperkinesis in humans (Accardo, 1980). This may relate to reducing the inhibiting effect of the frontal lobes on the reticular activating system. In contrast, extensive frontal lobe damage produces passivity, inertia, and lack of motivation. Hyperkinesis may be a final common behavioral pathway for many disturbances in the modulation of lower centers by higher ones.

These observations should be placed in the context of our general knowledge of brain injury. The classic dysfunctions arising from brain injury in humans occur in the form of agnosias, which are failures in the recognition of things; aphasias, which are failures in understanding and using language; apraxias, which are failures in performing learned movements; and amnesias, which are losses in recent memory (Springer & Deutsch, 1981).

Chronic organic brain syndromes in children have been characterized by intellectual impairment, poor memory, perseveration, obsessive concern about details, limited ability to abstract, deficiencies of attention, weak impulse control, and hyper- or hypokinesis (Chess & Hassibi, 1978). The correspondence of these symptoms to those of minimal brain dysfunction provides support for the concept. On the other hand, children, especially under the age of eight, show remarkably complete recoveries from traumatic acute brain syndromes without significant long-range effects (Geschwind, 1979a). Furthermore, even when obvious damage occurs to the brain in adults, the behavioral symptoms actually result from the person's reaction to the cognitive and ideational deficits. These reactions to their deficits lead them to be at odds with their particular environments (Schain, 1977; Finger & Stein, 1982).

We do know that the destruction of cerebral tissue increases rather than decreases the activity of the brain through the release of inhibition and the impairment of modulation. The resulting behavior tends to be inappropriate to the circumstances because it is not appropriately modulated. The uninjured brain selectively rejects inappropriate responses from a pool of possibilities in order to produce only appropriate behavior. Rejection of an inappropriate response is based upon matching possible responses and outcomes to determine the appropriate fit (Williams, M., 1979). The disturbances reflecting cerebral damage actually result from the breakdown of this process and a poor fit between behavior and the person's environment and interpersonal relationships. For example, loss of memory means little in itself except as it impedes important activities. A misperception of reality is only significant when it interferes with work, play, or relating to people. Behavioral disturbances following demonstrable brain damage, therefore, are strongly influenced by life experience (Pond, 1960).

There are some human behavioral syndromes that have definite neuroanatomical pathological causes. Examples include: (1) the frontal lobe syndrome of apathetic indifference and relative release from social inhibitions; (2) the Kluver-Bucy syndrome, resulting from bilateral temporal lobe damage with hyperphagia, loss of fear of danger, indiscriminate sexual behavior, and marked distractability in addition to a memory disorder; (3) the hyperphagia, rage, and dementia accompanying a ventromedial hypothalamic neoplasm; and (4) the personality changes associated with temporal lobe epilepsy, consisting of grandiosity, perserverative preoccupation with detail, hypergraphia, and sexual behavioral changes (Waxman & Geschwind, 1975).

In spite of these possible continuations

of the concept of minimal brain dysfunction, Sameroff (1982) believes that only the most extreme cases of brain damage cause behavioral disturbances in children. For every other kind of disability, there is clear evidence that variations in life experience are crucial in producing variations in outcome. Individual adaptation is a consequence of the ability of caregivers to adapt to the needs of the developing child. There are many disabilities, especially in the sensory domain, for which the outcome is no different than for children without those disabilities. For example, a deaf or blind child may reach high levels of intellectual and social adjustment and achievement. In contrast children reared in socially impoverished environments show a behavioral syndrome of hyperkinesis similar to that seen in socially deprived experimental animals (Sahakian, 1981).

Most children receiving the minimal brain dysfunction or hyperkinesis diagnosis also show evidence of other psychiatric disorders, particularly affecting impulse control. Nearly all of the studies of children with those diagnoses have been of broad, ill-defined, and almost certainly heterogenous groups of restless, disruptive, and inattentive children who can be described in terms of other psychiatric diagnoses (Rutter, 1982).

The concept of minimal brain dysfunction, therefore, has been seriously questioned. It has been regarded as a dangerous, ill-defined notion that links too many behaviors to implied brain damage (Kalverboer, 1978); as an escape from making a diagnosis (Yule, 1978); and as a neuromythology to cover ignorance (Rutter, 1982). It may have been useful in drawing attention to a heterogenous group of developmental disorders, but its continuing usage is not scientifically sound, since it assumes a homogenous symptomatology and implies a known etiology. The hyperkinetic syndrome in pure form probably is not a commonly encountered clinical entity (Rutter, 1982). The evidence does suggest, however, that there is a group of children with pervasive hyperkinesis ascribable to either a traumatic or a genetic basis, or both (Thorley, 1984).

Our understanding of minimal brain dysfunction is at the stage of our understanding of heart disease hundreds of years ago (Gardner, 1979). Minimal brain dysfunction probably refers to a group of syndromes that have in common mild neurological disturbances. The term will fall into disuse as its various subcategories are defined. The syndromes are characterized by mild neuromuscular deficits, generally less intellectual impairment than in the mentally retarded, difficulties in accurately processing sensory information, and degrees of dysphasia, dysnomia, dyslexia, and dyspraxia.

In spite of these questions, the concept of minimal brain dysfunction as an explanation for children's behavior has become well established in the medical literature of the United States. In addition to its explanatory appeal, the syndrome implies the existence of a medical disorder compensable by health insurance carriers and treatable by medication. It is of interest that European pediatricians usually do not recognize the syndrome and infrequently use stimulant medications (Peters et al, 1975; Rutter & Hersov, 1986).

PSYCHOANALYSIS AND EDUCATION

The fourth strand was signaled when Sigmund Freud related psychoanalysis to education at Clark University in 1909. It was not until the 1920s, however, that his ideas began to influence education through child guidance clinics. Psychotherapy for children, guidance for parents, and education in psychoanalysis for teachers was recommended. The founding of the American

Orthopsychiatric Association in 1924 brought together a variety of mental health disciplines around the educational problems of children (Lewis, C., 1975).

In the 1930s and 1940s, the swing of the pendulum was toward emotional factors in learning problems. James Strachey's (1930) paper on psychological factors in reading disabilities stimulated psychoanalytic interest in academic learning problems. Through the years the improvement of children's school performance as a result of psychotherapy has been interpreted as evidence both for the learning difficulty's psychogenic etiology and for the alleviation of secondary emotional symptoms.

Leo Kanner described the psychopathology of early infantile autism in 1943 and attempted to clarify its etiology. In 1944 Bruno Bettelheim opened the Sonja Shankman Orthogenic School in Chicago, from which the term *therapeutic milieu* emerged. In 1945 Margaret Mahler described pseudoimbecility, which subsequently became known as learning impotence (Westman & Bennet, 1985).

In 1946 Abraham Blau highlighted the negativitism of children in school learning problems, and proposed that it played a key role in left-handedness as well (Blau, 1946). Blanchard reviewed the psychoanalytic literature on learning problems in the same year. Rosen (1955) highlighted the symbolic significance of integrating visual and auditory stimuli in an analysis of a case of dyslexia. Ralph Rabinovitch, in 1952, classified reading retardation in terms of primary (dyslexic), secondary (emotional), and organic brain syndrome etiologies.

The growth of the child guidance movement following World War II broadened the scope of mental health services for children. Two early programs designed to assist these children were the Pioneer House, under the direction of of Fritz Redl and David Wineman, in Detroit and the "600" schools in New York City. The ex-

perience of Redl and Wineman was described in *The Aggressive Child,* first published in 1957 (Redl & Wineman, 1960).

Fenichel opened the League School, a day school for schizophrenic children, in 1953, focusing education methods more specifically on emotionally disturbed children. In 1955 William Morse wrote about the skills teachers needed to work with emotionally disturbed children (Morse & Wingo, 1955; Morse, 1964). Also, in 1960, Eli Bower described research on the early identification of such children in school settings (Bower & Hollister, 1967; Bower, 1981).

In 1960 Berkowitz and Rothman wrote the first text, *The Disturbed Child,* to be devoted specifically to the education of the emotionally disturbed from a psychoanalytic perspective. A review of the literature in 1965 revealed extensive writings on emotional factors in learning problems (Westman et al, 1965). With the growing appreciation of family dynamics, attention was called in the 1960s to family contributions to learning disabilities (Miller & Westman, 1964).

Redl wrote extensively on the educational management of emotionally disturbed children. In 1962 Haring and Phillips dealt with educational strategies in their text, *Educating Emotionally Disturbed Children.* In 1965 Long, Morse, and Newman published their influential text, *Conflict in the Classroom,* which offered a number of techniques for the educational and behavioral management of disturbed children. Between 1961 and 1966, Morse developed a unique educational role for specialized teachers of emotionally disturbed children, the forerunner of present-day diagnostic-prescriptive and resource teachers (Lewis, C., 1975).

In 1970 Blom concluded that emotional determinants usually were not the primary cause of reading problems (Blom & Jones, 1970). Furthermore, an exclusive focus on psychotherapy could lead to a delay in providing the educational training children need to remedy skill deficits. Just as educators may unduly stress cognitive and language factors in learning problems, psychotherapists risk minimizing them and overemphasizing neurotic factors. Unfortunately the misunderstanding of psychoanalytic conceptions of parent-child relationships led to blaming parents and teachers for children's learning problems and obscured considering intrapsychic phenomena in children themselves. The misapplication of psychoanalytic insights in schools also has produced inappropriate permissiveness and an emphasis on self-determination beyond the capacities of many children. There also has been a tendency unduly to emphasize motivation and to overlook the importance of self-discipline in effective schoolwork. In more recent years, recognition of the contribution of cognitive and language deficits to affective and thinking disorders has set the stage for a more realistic blending of all of these factors.

EPIDEMIOLOGICAL STUDIES

Because of the combined weight of four extensive epidemiological studies, we now have a reasonably solid basis for estimating the extent and nature of children's behavior problems. Although these studies vary in methodology, in the aggregate they constitute an impressive body of knowledge.

The studies in question are the National Study in Great Britain (Davie & Butler, 1975), the Isle of Wight and London Studies (Rutter et al, 1970), the Kauai study in Hawaii (Werner et al, 1971), and the Collaborative Perinatal Project also in the United States (Nichols & Chen, 1981). These surveys support the clinical impression that academic learning difficulties, hyperkinetic behavior, and neurological disorders represent separate groups of

children. Furthermore, perinatal distress has proved to be far less important than socioeconomic factors in predicting later difficulties in school. Of even greater importance are family-related factors. All of these considerations express themselves through a particular child's personality in which managerial skills and self-concept loom as the critical factors in producing success or failure in the performance of schoolwork.

Of the four epidemiological studies, the Collaborative Perinatal Project is the most recent and pertinent to our interests and will be described in detail. This project, sponsored by the National Institute of Neurological and Communicative Disorders and Stroke, collected prospective data on 28,889 children followed from birth to the age of seven (Nichols & Chen, 1981). It provides detailed information on the nature and prevalence of academic learning, behavioral, and neurological problems in a general population sample.

Employing factor analysis, the project identified three clusters of symptoms: those described as learning difficulties (LD), those described as hyperkinetic-impulsive (HI), and those described as soft neurological signs (NS). Twenty-one percent of the total sample showed problems in one or more of these three areas: learning difficulties (6 percent), hyperkinetic-impulsive behavior (6 percent), soft neurological signs (6 percent), and combinations of the three (3 percent). The associations among these clusters were not strong, however. Only 15 percent of the hyperkinetic-impulsive group had learning difficulties and only 14 percent had soft neurological signs. Only 10 percent of those with soft neurological signs had learning difficulties, and only 13 percent were hyperkinetic-impulsive.

In a smaller scale survey, Silver also found that only a minority (26 percent) of children with learning difficulties were hyperkinetic. Conversely, however, most of his hyperkinetic children had learning problems. He also found emotional disturbances in 80 percent of both groups (Silver, A., 1981b).

Another epidemiological study disclosed that 3.75 percent of 9,293 children in a school system were candidates for the diagnosis of hyperkinesis. Seventy-five percent of those children had been treated with medication, usually as the only form of therapy (Bosco & Robin, 1980).

The prevalence of dyslexia has not been reliably established because of the lack of clarity of the diagnostic criteria. Critchley estimated that of the 10 percent of schoolchildren who are retarded readers, one-fifth are dyslexic boys, and one-twentieth are dyslexic girls (Critchley, 1974).

The Collaborative Perinatal Project findings suggest that a triadic minimal brain dysfunction syndrome of learning difficulties, hyperkinetic-impulsive behavior, and neurological "soft" signs is not commonly encountered. However, altogether more than 350 significant associations were found among the three groups and antecedent variables, suggesting an underlying common process. For example, the families of LD, HI, and NS children all tended to be of low socioeconomic status, to have moved frequently, to include retarded siblings, and to have nonprofessional or technically trained parents. The LD families tended to be large with two parents and low maternal education level and, as with HI families, on public assistance. The HI families tended to be small and without fathers. The NS families did not show characteristic family patterns.

From the point of view of pregnancy and delivery complications, all three groups tended to have histories of maternal illness and hospitalization during pregnancy and of maternal smoking. The LD mothers tended to have less intensive prenatal care and longer labors. The HI and NS infants tended to show more evidence of distress during delivery.

Preschool predictors were more strongly related to HI behavior than were earlier antecedents. Also implicated, however, were genetic, demographic, pregnancy, and infant development factors. Like the HI group, the NS group was more highly related to preschool performance than to perinatal complications. All three groups showed reduced cranial circumference. As infants, all three groups showed lower performance on the Bayley developmental scales. The HI and NS groups also showed delayed motor development. Compared with controls at age four, all three groups showed higher activity levels, less mature copying of a cross, and lower Porteus maze performance. The LD and HI groups had shorter attention spans. The HI group showed language problems. At age seven all groups showed right-left directional and ocular problems.

The Collaborative Perinatal Project revealed two essential points. First, learning disability, hyperkinetic-impulsive, and neurological-sign groups are distinct and generally separable at an early school age. However, these children do share a number of developmental characteristics that can be construed as reflecting compromised integrity of brain functioning. This means that there are intervening variables beyond prenatal, perinatal, and postnatal insult to the brain that determine whether or not children fall in the LD or HI category. The existence of the NS group without LD or HI suggested further that brain factors are not enough to produce clinical symptoms. This was confirmed by Carey, who did not find a characteristic temperament for children with neurological signs and academic learning and behavior problems (Carey et al, 1979). Shaffer et al (1985) also found no relationship between early soft neurological signs and attention deficit or conduct disorders.

The second essential conclusion from the Collaborative Perinatal Project is the overriding importance of demographic and family variables. The potent variables that make the critical difference in determining whether or not a child falls into the HI and LD groups are parent–child dyadic transactions, family dynamics, personal psychodynamics, and school peer factors.

The current evidence, then, suggest that the historical dyslexic and minimal brain dysfunction strands were dealing with substantially different children. For both of these groups of children, the critical factors that determine their success or failure in school are social, familial, and educational.

SUMMARY

The experience of two centuries can be brought to bear upon current conceptions of children's learning problems in school. In so doing four strands of practice and research in the evolving fields of special education, neurology, pediatrics, and psychoanalysis can be identified. This book will weave in additional strands; however, these four constitute the important traditions from which our current knowledge has been derived.

The work of Itard with the Wild Boy of Aveyron was continued by Seguin and Montessori, so that special techniques were brought into education. With the passage of time, the distinctions between mental retardation and other forms of learning difficulties have become blurred, and current attention is devoted to the specific factors that interfere with learning in school. The shift from institutionalizing to mainstreaming deviant children has resulted in the proliferation of special education personnel and programs in schools.

The concept of congenital dyslexia grew from the linkage of word blindness with brain lesions in adults in the late 19th century. Since that time, the accumulation of neurobiological and postmortem evidence has confirmed the role of genetic and developmental variations in the angular gyrus of the parietal lobe and cerebral lateralization in certain forms of reading difficulties.

Since the turn of the century, interest in the relationship of hyperkinetic, impulsive behavior and cerebral dysfunction has grown in the field of pediatrics. The striking phenomenon of "organic brain drivenness" seen following the encephalitic epidemic of 1918 focused attention upon Goldstein's experience with brain-injured soldiers in World War I. The experimental production of hyperkinesis and impulsivity in research animals and their response to stimulant medication verified clinical experience with chemotherapy in children with similar symptoms. The clinical adumbration of the frontal lobe syndrome manifested by social disinhibition and disorganization of behavior further suggests localization of the source of these behaviors. Further progress in the delineation of syndromes is needed to replace the ambiguous notion of minimal brain dysfunction.

The application of psychoanalytic insights to education has waxed and waned over the years with varying degrees of emphasis upon affective reactions to cognitive and language distortions. The focus of psychoanalysis on character and its social context has provided the entrée for including interpersonal and family dynamics in the diagnosis and management of children with learning difficulties. The theoretical models of psychoanalysis have provided useful tools, as well.

Epidemiological studies have verified the prevalence of children with difficulties in school as approximately 17 percent. More specifically, it has been possible to identify three groups of children: those with specific learning difficulties, those with hyperkinesis, and those with neurological signs. These findings support the dyslexic and hyperkinetic strands and reveal that a triad of learning difficulty, hyperkinesis, and neurological signs is not commonly encountered. Most important, the epidemiological studies point to the most potent variables in determining whether or not a child has school problems as related to parent–child, family, intrapsychic, and peer dynamics, as well as social and educational factors.

The time-honored entities of minimal brain dysfunction (a neurological concept), hyperkinesis (a behavioral concept), and learning disability (an educational concept) have produced a wealth of descriptive, experimental, theoretical, and therapeutic literature. Follow-up studies indicate also that these problems are not simply phenomena of childhood, but may involve lifelong interference with self-concept, vocational adjustments, social interactions, and family relationships. It is likely that they reflect maturational lags, permanent structural differences in the brain, and mixtures of both. Established groups of adherents to each of these concepts have become constituencies with political, and even commercial, reasons for maintaining them.

The study of children's learning problems in school requires the pooled resources at least of the disciplines of neurology, psychology, physiology, psychiatry, education, epidemiology, biochemistry, sociology, pediatrics, communicative disorders, optometry, and obstetrics. This book proposes models within which the evidence from these fields can be integrated.

2

Educational Disabilities and Handicaps

The manner in which we make our observations determines what we will see.

Ferdinand Schiller, 1917

The terms "disability" and "handicap" have a long history in the vocational rehabilitation field. They first were used for physically evident differences. Then they were extended to those who were obviously mentally retarded or developmentally disabled as federally defined. More recently they have been applied to children who founder in school.

Because disability and handicap have different connotations but often are used interchangeably, with resulting confusion, the distinction between them deserves special consideration (Neff, 1968; Krause, 1976; Hall, 1984). A *disability* is a person's condition whereas a *handicap* is an interference with a person's activity. More specifically, a disability is the functioning of an organ system in such a way that it does not meet a given health standard. For example, cerebral palsy may be expressed in the disability of a partial paralysis of one side of the body; lens cataracts may cause the disability of blindness. The diagnosis of the existence and degree of disability lies within the province of professionals trained to diagnose them.

A handicap exists when a disability significantly interferes with the performance of a personal or social activity and requires special consideration or advantage. For example, a cerebral-palsied child with the disability of partial paralysis may not be handicapped in walking but may be handicapped in riding a bicycle. A blind person may be handicapped in traveling, but not when assisted by a guide dog in familiar places. Color blindness is not a handicap unless one wishes to be an interior decorator. Thus the degree of a disability and its salience to important functions determine whether or not a disability constitutes a temporary or permanent handicap. The judgment of the existence and degree of handicap lies with those equipped to evaluate an individual's functional ability in particular social, educational, vocational, and recreational contexts.

A disability, then, is a distinguishing inherent characteristic of an individual and is susceptible to objective study. A handicap is a judgment of the effect a disability has upon a specific activity in a specific context. The definition of a handicap, then, depends upon both the diagnosis of disability and an assessment of functional impairment in a specific activity. One may have a disability without a handicap, but one cannot be handicapped without a disability, except in the instance of educational handicap, as we will see.

The judgment of the existence of a handicap has social and legal implications by determining whether or not an individual qualifies for exemption from responsibility, for special services, or for financial assistance. To make such judgments, professionals use legal standards to evaluate the degree of impairment of levels of functioning.

Limiting the term *disability* to altered functioning of an organ system and *handicap* to the effect of that disability upon an activity in a specific context has value for both practical and research purposes. Distinguishing between disability and handicap has particular value for children with learning problems in school. As background we first touch upon physical and developmental disabilities and handicaps.

PHYSICAL DISABILITIES AND HANDICAPS

Those in the field of physical rehabilitation have had extensive experience in working with the blind, deaf, and orthopedically handicapped. The diagnosis of these disabilities is relatively straightforward, and the nature and extent of the resulting functional handicaps are relatively obvious (Kirk & Gallagher, 1983). In these instances the optimal functioning of an organ system is known, and direct links can be traced between a pathological condition and behavioral manifestations.

Still, many individuals with diagnosed bodily disabilities may not regard themselves as handicapped or may not be handicapped according to social and legal definitions. From the physically handicapped we have learned that the attitude of the person with a disability plays an important role in determining whether or not that person is regarded as handicapped.

DEVELOPMENTAL DISABILITIES AND HANDICAPS

The situation is more complicated in the federally defined field of developmental disabilities, which primarily involves functions of the central nervous system. The spectrum of developmental disabilities includes cerebral palsy, mental retardation, epilepsy, certain language disorders, and infantile autism (Capute & Palmer, 1980).

An actual picture of the scope of developmental disabilities can be drawn from a survey of 41 university centers for the developmentally disabled (Urbano et al, 1984). The following groups were identified: (1) mental retardation, 28 percent; (2) specific learning disability, 16 percent; (3) general underachievement, 12 percent; (4) behavior disorders, 8 percent; (5) speech impaired, 7 percent; (6) severely emotionally disturbed, 6 percent; (7) orthopedically impaired, 4 percent; (8) sensory impaired, 3 percent; (9) autistic, 2 percent; (10) other, 14 percent. Even though these university centers tend to see the most complicated problems, the statistics demonstrate the lack of a clear-cut distinction between the developmentally disabled and learning disabled populations.

The complicated relationship between a developmental disability and handicap can be illustrated by the case of mental retardation. Although on the surface the situation appears simple, it actually is exceedingly complex, because mental retardation is but a symptom arising from many factors. For this reason the diagnosis of mental retardation is most appropriately made on clinical grounds that include an evaluation of overall development and levels of functioning in addition to psychological tests (see Figure 2-1).

Mental retardation is characterized by generalized disabilities that impede one in solving the problems of ordinary living (Grossman, 1983). The possibilities for the direct treatment of these disabilities lie in the potential for nerve cell regeneration in the central nervous system through grafting and transplants; pharmacological agents that enhance memory and learning; the cure of inborn errors of metabolism; early childhood stimulation; and chromosomal and genetic engineering (Menolascino et al, 1983).

By the time a child reaches school age, moderate or more pronounced mental retardation is evident; hence classical mental retardation syndromes are not found to be the primary cause of unanticipated learning failure in school. On the other hand, mild retardation may not become evident until the school years. Social, emotional, and educational factors themselves also contribute to the progressive development of the picture of mild mental retardation, as illustrated by the following case:

Larry was first seen by the University of Wisconsin Learning Disabilities Service at the age of 15½ because of his aggressiveness, inability to work in a special class for the educable mentally retarded, and fear that he would hurt someone. His school system was seeking residential placement for him.

The history disclosed that the onset of his speech was delayed. Upon enrollment in kindergarten at the age of four because of an October birthdate, testing disclosed visual-perceptual and motor coordination immaturity. In the first grade, he was tutored in reading, and his full-scale IQ was 86 with a verbal level of 100 and a performance of 74. In the second grade, a change of schools resulted in Larry's failure in a mainstream class. By the end of that year, his IQ had dropped to a full scale of 69 with a verbal of 84 and a performance of 58. He was then placed in a self-contained class for behaviorally disturbed children, where he remained until the sixth grade. At the age of 11, his full-scale IQ was 52 with a verbal of 67 and a performance of 45. He then was placed in a special class for the educable retarded, where he remained until the time of referral. Between the ages of 13 and 15½, he displayed increasing aggressiveness, a fascination with violence, and temper outbursts. He was apprehended by the police for fighting and shoplifting. He was unable to concentrate on schoolwork, admit mistakes, or accept the authority of teachers. At the age of 15, his IQ had stabilized at a full scale of 59 with a verbal of 70 and performance of 50. His reading and arithmetic skills were at the second grade level.

The medical history disclosed his mother had had a normal pregnancy, as were the birth and perinatal period. Larry had the first of six febrile seizures at the age of 12 months and the last at the age of seven years following a beesting when a borderline abnormal EEG was reported. He was placed on phenobarbital, which made him restless, and then dilantin, which was discontinued at the age of nine.

The family history did not include relatives with learning problems, mental retardation, or seizures. Two younger siblings were doing well in school. The parents sought the University Hospital evaluation, because they felt that Larry was a boy with normal potential who had been mishandled by the school. They had not seen aggressive behavior at home and regarded his arrests as resulting from peer goading. Through the years they maintained the belief that Larry could do the work if he wanted to, and they said they were unaware of his severely retarded reading and arithmetic skills.

The Learning Disabilities Service evaluation disclosed findings consistent with multiple dysgnosias manifested by visual-spatial dyslexia and Gerstmann's syndrome, which consists of finger agnosia, dysgraphia, dyscalcalia, and right–left disorientation. He also showed a mild verbal dyspraxia. He revealed grandiose fantasies, paranoid tendencies, poor social judgment, and weak impulse control. He expressed the feeling that killing someone was justified if that person sufficiently angered him.

During the course of Larry's treatment, which included outpatient individual and family psychotherapy, remedial reading, arithmetical tutoring, and vocational training, a picture emerged in which a combination of temperamental, cognitive, language, and managerial function problems combined with educational management and family relationship problems to contribute to the creation of a functionally mentally retarded person. Larry's self was split into an omnipotent "tough guy" and a helpless "baby" part; the former emerged whenever the latter was exposed. Larry and his mother were not completely individuated, so that each assumed the other knew what the other was thinking and feeling. Accordingly there was no direct exchange of ideas and emotions between them. Both parents took Larry's side in confrontations with the school and peers. Larry's placement with educationally handicapped children promoted his identification with them. He achieved recognition from antisocial peers through "tough guy" delinquent acts.

When Larry and his parents could express their rage and sadness to each other, he became able to face his helplessness and the "mess" he was making of his life. Both he and his parents then were able to assume responsibility for his failures rather than projecting responsibility for them upon others. He was then able to exert the diligent effort required to gain a functional level of reading and vocational skills. He finally was able to shed the label of mental retardation that he had carried through his later school years and had protested against through his aggressive, antisocial behavior.

The World Health Organization defines mental retardation on the basis of actual impairment in developing self-help skills, in academic learning, and in social adjustment in the home and community. 85 percent of the mentally retarded are mildly disabled (IQ 50–69) because of multiple biological, psychological, and social factors (Figure 2-1). 10 percent are moderately disabled (IQ 35–49), and 5 percent are severely (IQ 20–34) or profoundly disabled (IQ below 20) because of over 350 known conditions, such as cranial anomalies, genetic defects, tumors, trauma, infections, malnutrition, neurotropic poisons, progressive central nervous system deterioration, and inborn errors of metabolism (Menolascino et al, 1983). The mildly retarded can be educated and often later live independently. The moderately retarded can be trained for supervised living and sheltered workshop vocations. The severely and profoundly retarded require institutional care.

The prevalence of a handicap as a result of mental retardation varies with age, from 3 percent of the school-age population who require special education to 1 percent of the adult population who require special programs. This discrepancy occurs because most mildly retarded children become visible as educationally handicapped in school. Thus if measured intelligence is taken as a reflection of overall mental retardation or disability and impaired educational or vocational functioning as a handicap, only during the school years do they correlate highly (Grossman, 1983).

When thoroughly studied the distinctions between what are called developmental and learning disabilities often are found to be quantitative rather than qualitative. For this reason greater integration of research in each field is needed.

THE LEARNING DISABILITY CONCEPT

The inadequacy of the concept of learning disability becomes obvious when one looks

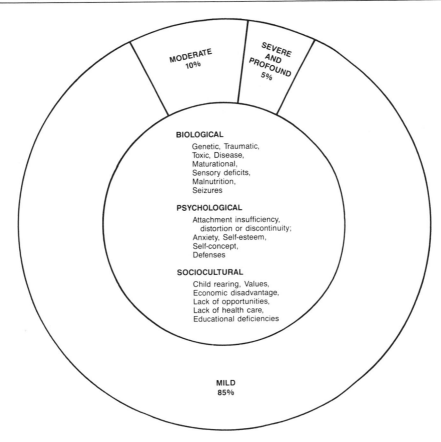

Figure 2-1. Multiple factors in developmental disabilities.

closely at the population of children in question. Much of the controversy and conceptual confusion surrounding this area are the result of insufficient knowledge of the children themselves, their backgrounds, and their schools. Unlike physical and most developmental disabilities, most learning disabilities are relative, not absolute, individual differences in functions of the brain rather than pathological conditions.

We first review the efforts that have been made to define learning disabilities and the political, administrative, and professional advantages of the concept. We then consider the scientific weaknesses of the learning disability concept based upon the collegiate orientation of U.S. school standards, studies of educationally handicapped populations, the weighting of social and cultural factors, and the current knowledge of brain development. We also examine the social disadvantages of the learning disability concept. Finally, the usefulness of substituting *educational* disability for *learning* disability is considered.

Definition of Learning Disabilities

As a reflection of its ambiguous nature, the definition of learning disabilities has been continually revised over the years. The human wish for an explanation for poorly understood phenomena is nowhere more apparent than in these efforts to explain the behavior of children with learning problems in school.

The term *learning disability* became popular when the Association for Children with Learning Disabilities was organized in 1963. Samuel Kirk appropriately suggested the term as preferable to causatively oriented labels, such as cerebral dysfunction and brain injury (Kirk & Kirk, 1983). A number of efforts to define learning disabilities have evolved since that time patterned after one formulated in 1969 by the Division for Children with Learning Disabilities of the Council for Exceptional Children (Haring & Bateman 1969):

> A child with learning disabilities is one with adequate mental ability, sensory processes, and emotional stability who has specific deficits in perceptual, integrative, or expressive processes which severely impair learning efficiency.

More recent definitions of learning disabilities have been influenced by the regulations for implementing Public Law 94-142 by the U.S. Office of Education (1979):

> A learning disability is a disorder in one or more of the basic psychological processes involved in understanding or using spoken or written language. A learning disability may be manifested in disorders of thinking, listening, talking, reading, writing, spelling, or arithmetic. It includes conditions which have been referred to as perceptual handicaps, brain injury, minimal brain dysfunction, dyslexia, and developmental aphasia. It does not include learning problems which are due primarily to visual, hearing or motor handicaps, mental retardation, emotional disturbance, or environmental disadvantage.

There has been a tendency both to include (Cruikshank, 1979) and exclude (Kronick, 1981) the mentally retarded from the ranks of the learning disabled. This has

been a particularly troublesome point because 85 percent of the mentally retarded are mildly disabled, and when their clinical states are carefully examined, many disclose histories of having been within learning disability definitions in the past (Bernstein & Menolascino, 1970; Menolascino, 1983; Perry, 1966; Webster, 1970).

Definitions of learning disability thus imply the presence of central nervous system dysfunction that is responsible for suboptimal academic learning (Kirk & Kirk, 1983). Most important, the resulting handicap is in learning specific academic subjects rather than in a child's general ability to learn. This distinction is essential because a specific problem in learning an academic subject need not imply impaired learning of nonacademic tasks. Moreover, the definitions do not require positive evidence of cerebral disorder; rather they are deduced from the exclusion of known causes of learning problems, such as emotional disturbance, environmental disadvantage, sensory deficits, or classical neurological disorders (Schain, 1977). A learning disability, then, has been construed to be a significant discrepancy between expected intellectual ability and actual academic performance without a social, educational, or emotional cause (Ohlson, 1978; Rudel, 1980).

Until recently the definitions of learning disabilities have narrowed the focus from the general population of children with learning problems to a presumed subgroup. In 1981 a more realistic definition was proposed by the National Joint Committee for Learning Disabilities (Hammill et al, 1981):

> Learning disabilities is a generic term that refers to a heterogeneous group of disorders manifesting by significant difficulties in the acquisition and use of listening, speaking, reading, writing, reasoning, or mathematical abilities. These disorders are intrinsic to the individual

QUALIFIER	AREA OF INVOLVEMENT	PROBLEM
SECONDARY	NERVOUS	DEFICIT
MINIMAL	BRAIN	DYSFUNCTION
MILD	CEREBRAL	DAMAGE
MINOR	NEUROLOGICAL	DISORDER
CHRONIC	NEUROLOGIC	DESYNCHRONIZATION
DIFFUSE	CNS	HANDICAP
SPECIFIC	LANGUAGE	DISABILITY
PRIMARY	READING	RETARDATION
DEVELOPMENTAL	PERCEPTUAL	DEFICIENCY
DISORGANIZED	IMPULSIVE	IMPAIRMENT
ORGANIC	VISUAL-MOTOR	PATHOLOGY
CLUMSY	BEHAVIOR	SYNDROME
FUNCTIONAL	PSYCHONEUROLOGIC	COMPLEX

Figure 2-2. Do-it-yourself terminology generator. Select any word from first column, add any word from second column, then add any word from third column. If you don't like the result, try again. It will mean about the same thing. (Based on E. Fry, "Do-It-Yourself Terminology Generator," *Journal of Reading, 11,* 1968, 428.)

and presumed to be due to central nervous system dysfunction. Even though a learning disability may occur concomitantly with other handicapping conditions (e.g., sensory impairment, mental retardation, social and emotional disturbance) or environmental influences (e.g., cultural differences, insufficient or inappropriate instruction, psychogenic factors), it is not the direct result of those conditions or influences.

The task of identifying learning disabilities has been undertaken by clinicians and educators. These pursuits have not led, however, to the discovery of precise markers that cause a functional disability in the same sense that cataracts cause visual disability. They have produced a melange of diagnosis, as illustrated in Figure 2-2. Each of these terms offers an explanation of a child's learning difficulty and the illusion of scientific understanding.

The more the concept of a disability departs from definable physical markers, the more difficult its detection becomes.

The notion of learning disabilities depends upon judgments regarding academic learning behavior. Thus a disability in learning is presumed to exist when a child's performance in school is lower than expected in a certain area. This actually means that an educational handicap is judged to exist without identifying the disability of the child. As a result many children are handicapped in school without known disabilities. At this time it is easier to identify educational handicap than disability. This loose terminology and failure to distinguish disability from handicap has created endless confusion. The issue really is whether or not a personal characteristic of a child in the form of a disability produces an educational handicap. If such a disability cannot be identified, the handicap still exists but most likely is the result of factors lying outside of the child.

For children with academic learning problems, disability is most appropriately used to connote an underlying functional characteristic of a child. Handicap then can be limited to an inability of that child to perform schoolwork because of a lack of knowledge and skills. Thus, a visual-spatial dyslexia is an example of a disability that can result in the educational handicap of reading retardation. The growing specificity in identifying such disabilities offers greater precision in defining mild educational disabilities and handicaps (Miller & Davis, 1982).

Advantages of the Learning Disability Concept

The benefits of the learning disability concept have been evident in the increased attention being paid to seeking reasons and remedies for children's learning difficulties in school (Rist & Harrell, 1982). It was conceived to call attention to children who were not defined as mentally retarded, deaf, blind, emotionally disturbed, crippled, or economically disadvantaged, but who had difficulty in learning to read, write, and cipher. The learning disability concept thus is less a clinical entity and more an administrative category for channeling funds into educational programs and has been politically and administratively useful (McLeod, 1978; Farnham-Diggory, 1980).

There are other pragmatic advantages in designating persons as having learning disabilities. For example, the College Entrance Examination Board and Educational Testing Service makes provisions for certified learning disabled students to be given extra time for working on standardized tests.

The concept of learning disabilities has generally strengthened the role of education in their management. When the causes of learning problems were presumed to be entirely emotional, the role of teachers was presumed to be one of patience and understanding. With a greater understanding of their educational implications, teachers can expect to contribute more to these children.

All of these advantages also inhere in the concepts of educational disability and handicap and are not dependent upon the term learning disability. In fact, the separation of disability and handicap offers the administrative advantage of providing for the early detection and remediation of the former and special educational planning for the latter.

The Scientific Weakness of the Learning Disability Concept

What we call learning disabilities are defined by educational standards and testing that subtly value certain capacities, such as verbal abilities that favor academic achievement more than others. The concept of learning disability places the onus totally on the child and runs the risk of subjecting that child to bias that favors academic achievement as defined by the educational system. It is appropriate, therefore, to examine educational standards closely.

The determination of success or failure in school depends upon the standards society creates for children. In English-speaking countries, these standards are influenced subtly by the doctrine of Cyril Burt, who reflected Plato's classification of children in "gold," "silver," and "lead" categories (Hearnshaw, 1980):

> The duty of the state, through its school service, is first to find out to what order of intelligence each child belongs, then to give him the education most appropriate to his powers, and finally . . . to place him in the particular type of occupation for which nature has marked him.

Following this doctrine, tests designed to measure the ingredients of intelligence are widely accepted for determining a child's overall intellectual abilities and the presence of learning disabilities. Most school psychological services were established to classify children intellectually and place them in auxiliary programs where they presumably would not suffer failure and discouragement. This testing approach does not consider the extent to which children can be taught to develop their intellectual powers, only their limitations. The philosophy does not take into account children who have educational disabilities but, because of instruction that builds upon their abilities and their effort, may not be defined as handicapped in academic achievement (Chalfant & Scheffelin, 1969).

The most compelling criticism of the learning disability concept is that it implies a generalized difficulty in all learning, but actually refers to academic learning as measured by normative tests. It also obscures academic learning that may be taking place in school but is not reflected in standard testing.

Furthermore, the learning disability concept is used without recognition that a range of value judgments lies behind it. It conceals the fact that these judgments are being made in particular educational settings using criteria determined by persons with a stake in their significance, such as removing a child from a classroom or gaining an additional special education student (Smith, M., 1982). Most critically, it glosses over the real distinctions between disability and handicap. A closer look at the determinants of educational standards and the children themselves brings out these points.

The Collegiate Bias of Academic Standards

Academic standards in the United States have been influenced strongly by collegiate values, even though educators have recognized that many children do not live up to these expectations. Among the population of children with academic learning

difficulties are many who will be more successful as adults in their vocations than as children in school. The ranks of the eminent are well represented by scholastic misfits who were impatient with classroom activities but loved other forms of learning (Goertzel & Goertzel, 1978). Adults have a vast range of occupations and avocations that allow for accommodations to individual strengths and weaknesses. Such custom fitting has not been available in public education (Coles, G., 1987). Figure 2-3 illustrates the way in which a childhood educational disability in attentional capacity may become a liability or an asset in adulthood, depending upon a child's fortune in encountering development facilitating or deterring experiences.

Certain brains seem particularly specialized for meeting all of the formal collegiate academic expectations of our society. Others may be well adapted to particular aspects of education. For example, some individuals may not rely on verbal thinking and instead become sophisticated in visual-spatial symbol processing with success in mathematics, as did Albert Einstein. Others may not learn well in competitive, test-regulated circumstances.

Still others function best in nonacademic areas. Not all young people are academically oriented. For those who are interested in farming, animal husbandry forestry, carpentry, plumbing, and auto mechanics, the academic thrust of schools, particularly high schools, may be frustrating. For such young people, school imposes chronic stress that leads to burnout and dropout (Elkind, 1981).

Our schools hold standards based upon values that are regarded as important for citizenship and vocational success in the United States. The role of these standards in defining disability and handicap is brought into sharp focus when we consider our attitude toward skills that are not necessary for independent functioning in our

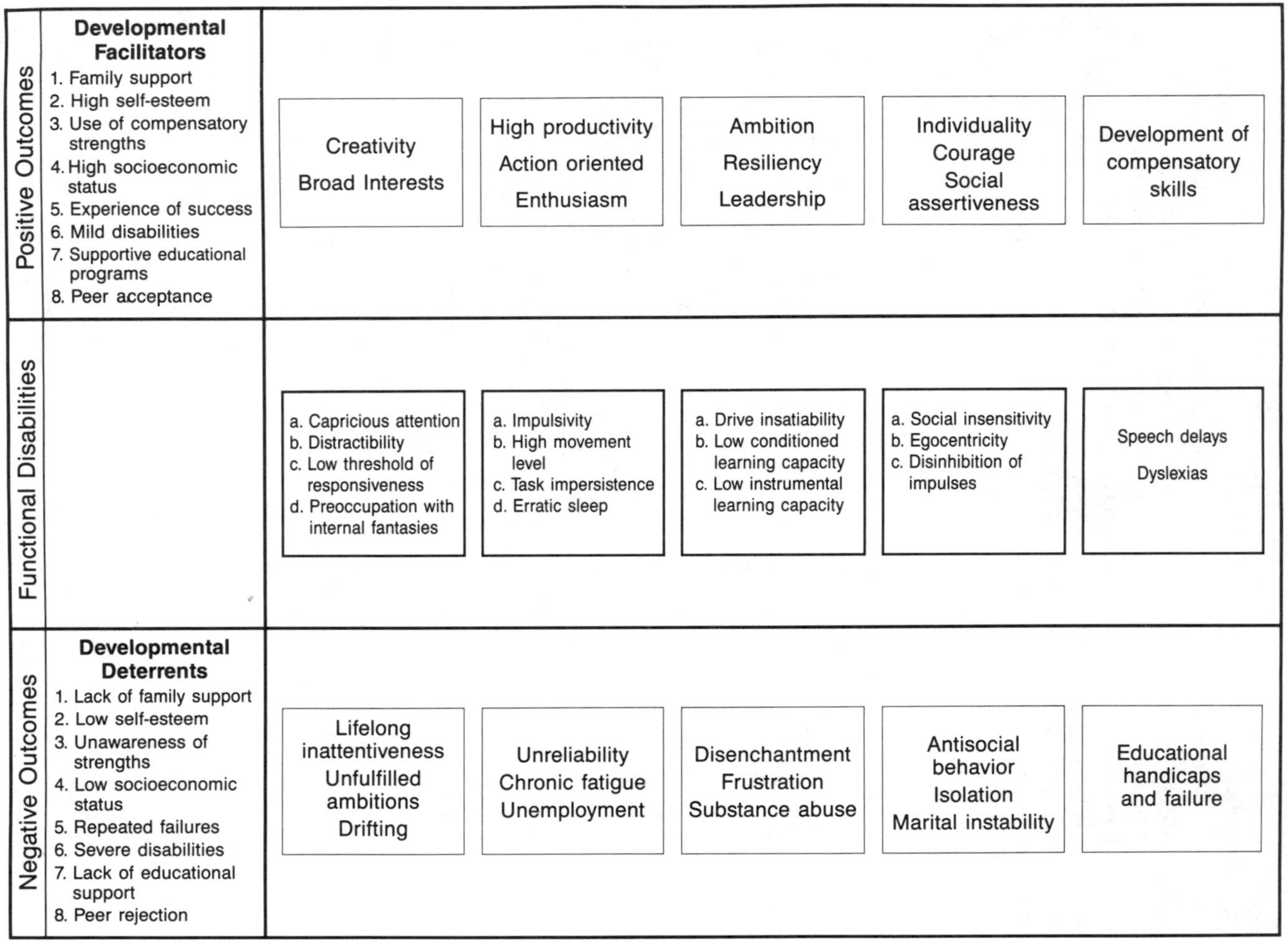

Figure 2-3 table (rotated layout):

	Developmental Facilitators				
Positive Outcomes	1. Family support 2. High self-esteem 3. Use of compensatory strengths 4. High socioeconomic status 5. Experience of success 6. Mild disabilities 7. Supportive educational programs 8. Peer acceptance	Creativity Broad Interests	High productivity Action oriented Enthusiasm	Ambition Resiliency Leadership	Individuality Courage Social assertiveness	Development of compensatory skills
Functional Disabilities		a. Capricious attention b. Distractibility c. Low threshold of responsiveness d. Preoccupation with internal fantasies	a. Impulsivity b. High movement level c. Task impersistence d. Erratic sleep	a. Drive insatiability b. Low conditioned learning capacity c. Low instrumental learning capacity	a. Social insensitivity b. Egocentricity c. Disinhibition of impulses	Speech delays Dyslexias
Negative Outcomes	**Developmental Deterrents** 1. Lack of family support 2. Low self-esteem 3. Unawareness of strengths 4. Low socioeconomic status 5. Repeated failures 6. Severe disabilities 7. Lack of educational support 8. Peer rejection	Lifelong inattentiveness Unfulfilled ambitions Drifting	Unreliability Chronic fatigue Unemployment	Disenchantment Frustration Substance abuse	Antisocial behavior Isolation Marital instability	Educational handicaps and failure

Figure 2-3. The rectangles at the top represent positive outcomes for childhood functional disabilities, while those at the bottom illustrate negative consequences. On the left-hand side are facilitators and deterrents of development. (Adapted from M. D. Levine, S. R. Brooks, and J. P. Shonkoff, *A Pediatric Approach to Learning Disorders*, copyright 1980 by John Wiley and Sons, New York.)

society. An example is the ability to play baseball. Some children possess innate talent and, with practice, learn expert pitching and batting skills. Even with exhaustive practice, however, other children cannot pitch or bat expertly. We do not regard those children as having ball-playing handicaps. If ball-throwing skills were vocationally essential, as they are for the professional pitcher, however, we could speak in terms of a ball-throwing disability producing a pitching handicap. If we did, ball players might find themselves regarded as either able or handicapped. Ball-playing skills could then be assessed and special help provided to those viewed as handicapped. From this perspective it is evident that our concern actually is not with learning but with educationally defined disabilities and handicaps in socially critical skills.

The Heterogeneity of Educationally Handicapped Populations

A realistic perspective on the learning disability concept can be gained from the study of populations of children with demonstrated educational handicaps. When this is done, a complicated picture emerges in which isolated disabilities in learning functions are rarely found in practice. More typically, educationally handicapped children show multiple problems in a variety of functions that are essential for the performance of work in school (Silver, A., 1979; Werner & Smith, 1979).

To illustrate this point, descriptions of children with problems in school that stem from the following sources are cited: (1) the historical view of Bronner, (2) current school-based literature, (3) a neuropsychological laboratory, (4) clinical classifications of children with educational handicaps, and (5) clinical pictures of dyslexic children.

Bronner's Classification. Over 60 years ago, concerns about children's school performance were voiced in virtually the same way

as today. Even at that time, however, there was awareness that disabilities resided in specific characteristics of children rather than in the process of learning itself.

In 1917 Bronner identified the following categories of children's educational disabilities that could produce educational handicaps in school: (1) special defects in language ability, especially in reading and spelling; (2) special defects in mental processes such as visual memory, slowness in speed of reactions, imagination, and inventive ability; (3) defects in self-control expressed through hyperactivity, poor impulse control, and extreme emotions; (4) difficulty in number work; and (5) mental subnormality with particular deficits in numbers, language, rote memory, or manual work (Bronner, 1917).

Current Classifications of Children's School Problems. Among examples of current classifications of children's school problems based upon an extensive array of publications are the following (Millman et al, 1980; Wallace & Kaufman, 1973): (1) classroom management problems, such as dishonest behavior, truancy, cursing, rowdy behavior, noncompliance, acting the class clown, temper tantrums, annoying others, out-of-seat behavior, and destructive behavior; (2) immature behaviors, such as hyperactivity, distractibility, inattentiveness, impulsivity, messiness, daydreaming, procrastination, dawdling, poor coordination, and crying; (4) habit disorders, such as poor academic skills, enuresis, encopresis, masturbation, thumb sucking, nail biting, speech disorders, substance abuse, and inappropriate sexual behavior; (5) disturbed peer relationships, such as aggressiveness, prejudice, shyness, withdrawal, and social isolation; and (6) disturbed teacher relationships, such as disruptiveness, defiance, shyness, and overdependency.

From this perspective the range of actually reported problems of children in school is wide and not easily related to the concept of learning disability. As a result the large numbers of children who fail to learn but do not answer to strict definitions of learning disabilities are being educationally neglected (Stott, 1978).

Neuropsychological Classification of the Educationally Handicapped. The neuropsychological findings in children with educational handicaps are in a variety of cognitive functions, such as visual perception, discrimination, and memory; auditory perception, discrimination, and memory; language processing, articulation, fluency, and vocabulary; motor processing in fine motor coordination, motor-spatial organization, and motor-temporal organization; and deficits in intermodal correspondence. The educationally handicapped tend either to perform as do younger children or to make the same but quantitatively more errors than their peers. Thus many of their handicaps appear to be delays in the developmental progression of skill mastery. An important area for study is distinguishing those findings that reflect earlier developmental stages from those that reflect brain lesions (Gaddes, 1980).

Several categories of children can be identified through neuropsychological testing (Matthews, 1985): (1) children with test evidence of impairment in many areas of psychological functioning, ranging in severity from frank mental retardation to borderline normal intelligence (the largest group); (2) those who show a test pattern compatible with mild impairment of left-hemisphere integrity reflected in language functions but who perform quite well on other aspects of the neuropsychological battery; (3) children who have essentially normal neuropsychological profiles but various mixtures of social and emotional determinants; and (4) those who have relatively normal neuropsychological profiles but are retarded in reading and have a family history of reading difficulty in male relatives.

The exclusion of mentally retarded children from the learning disability category has obscured the fact that many mildly retarded children come from the ranks of educationally handicapped children whose intelligence quotients have drifted downward through their school careers because of the cumulative effect of their educational failures. This exclusion also has inappropriately mandated that a primarily retarded child cannot be further handicapped by a compounding specific educational disability (Bryan & Bryan, 1975).

The absolute distinction made between developmental and learning disabilities has been artificially determined by administrative and political considerations. Even with the purest form of familial mental retardation, which reflects the lowest levels of intellectual ability on a Gaussian scale of intelligence distribution in a population, we are dealing with the performance of individuals at the lowest ends of continua of a variety of different functions.

The point has been made that learning disabilities refer to individuals with specific areas of weaknesses; however, areas of weakness and strength also can occur in well-defined syndromes of mental retardation. Children with Down syndrome, for example, show wide variations from moderate to mild handicap levels related to early stimulation and later educational encouragement from their families (Connolly, 1978; Gibson, 1978). Such children particularly tend to be stronger in visual-spatial than in auditory-verbal functions. They also have specific difficulties with short-term verbal memory (Marcell & Armstrong, 1982; Silverstein et al, 1982).

Although it usually results in moderate mental retardation, untreated phenylketonuria occurs with normal intelligence, behavior disturbances, and weaknesses in specific cognitive functions (Mabry & Podoll, 1963; Koch et al, 1982). These children dramatically illustrate the fallacy of sharply distinguishing developmental from learning disabilities.

The neuropsychological study of educationally handicapped children reveals disabilities in specific developmental characteristics rather than learning itself. Furthermore, the close scrutiny of the mildly retarded population discloses that these persons often have areas of specific functional disabilities. The evidence questions the validity of distinctions between developmental and learning disabilities. The obvious conclusion is that from the scientific point of view, whether or not the overall intelligence of individuals falls within, above, or below the average range should not determine whether or not they are regarded as educationally disabled.

Much can be learned from lifting the artificial distinctions between those persons regarded as developmentally and learning disabled. There may be pragmatic reasons for separating the two, but a more realistic view is that both of these categories are comprised of persons with educational disabilities and resulting handicaps. A latent prejudice against the mentally retarded probably has played a role in the preference for limiting the learning disability concept to children who are "bright" but underachieving in school.

Clinical Classifications of Educationally Handicapped Children. The Learning Disabilities Service of the University of Wisconsin demonstrates the complex nature of children who are regarded as having learning disabilities (Westman et al, 1987). The nature of the referral process to the service excludes those children who can be managed by the resources available within a particular school system.

Of 180 children followed by the Learning Disabilities Service, overlapping diagnoses, according to the American Psychiatric Association's *Diagnostic and Stastical Manual-III*, were as follows: (1) Personality disorders, 42 percent—oppositional, 7 percent; borderline, 16 percent; conduct disorders, 8 percent; and passive-aggressive; 11 percent. (2) Attention deficit disorder, 18 per-

cent—with hyperactivity, 15 percent, and without hyperactivity, 3 percent. (3) Developmental disorders, 9 percent —specific reading disorder, 5 percent; mixed, 5 percent; developmental language disorder, 4 percent; and mixed specific disorders, 5 percent. (4) Mental retardation, 12 percent—mild, 9 percent; moderate, 2 percent; and severe, 1 percent. (5) Neuroses, 15 percent—dysthymic disorder, 11 percent; overanxious disorder, 3 percent; and elective mutism, 1 percent. (6) Adjustment reactions, 2 percent. (7) Psychoses, 3 percent. (8) Organic brain syndromes, 6 percent. (9) Convulsive disorders, 7 percent.

The overlapping treatment recommendations were as follows: individual and family psychotherapy, 75 percent; specialized educational services, 63 percent; specific reading tutoring, 21 percent; medication, 15 percent; language therapy, 11 percent; and social services, 7 percent. This experience illustrates the fact that more precise diagnoses can be made on children with school learning problems, so that the broad term learning disability is not a useful clinical concept. It also highlights the range of treatment modalities employed in their treatment.

In another classification system designed especially for children with school learning problems, Kinsbourne and Caplan distinguish between academic underachievement, cognitive power, and cognitive-style disorders as more specific concepts than learning disabilities (Kinsbourne & Caplan, 1979). Underachievement represents generalized school failure resulting from motivational, instructional, and cultural factors. Cognitive-power disorders refer to selective failures in reading and arithmetic resulting from developmental lags and individual differences. This category covers children who have dyslexia, dyscalculia, and perceptual deficits. Cognitive-style disorders include overfocused or compulsive children who fail academically because of slowness in shifting attention from one activity to the next, and underfocused or impulsive and distractible children who fail because they shift attention too quickly.

Clinical Syndromes of Dyslexic Children. Since word blindness was first described (Morgan, 1896), many able children have been handicapped in school and in later life because their special educational needs were not recognized. Some, through their own efforts, have compensated for their educational handicaps. A few have been fortunate, and, with the understanding of their parents, special education, and therapeutic intervention, have been successful in school (Simpson, 1979).

Dyslexia has proved to be but one aspect, however, of a group of syndromes involving thinking, time-sense, spatial-orientation, and other problems, as illustrated by a composite history given by parents of dyslexic children (Rosner, 1979).

> He always seemed bright and interested in everything around him. He did not have the patience to sit in one place for very long and look at books, but there was no doubt he was capable of learning. We didn't think he had a problem until he entered school. He masters electronic and mechanical appliances. He learns the rules and fine points of games and may learn the batting averages of baseball players or the repertoires of popular musical groups.
>
> In the classroom, however, he tries for awhile but fails to catch on. He does not seem to be able to recognize any connection among his daily lessons that weave the information into cohesive, memorable patterns. He must memorize everything by rote as separate, unrelated pieces of information. Since this is impossible, he resorts to guessing. Ultimately he becomes so frustrated that he stops trying and adopts an "I don't care" attitude. His misbehavior leads to a confrontation between him and the school. The outcome may be an incorrigible youngster who refuses to follow the rules of society. If he

has a more passive nature, he still fails but is tolerated and receives social promotions until he finally finds work that does not require academic skills.

This typical clinical picture points out the fallacy of focusing exclusively upon a specific disability in situations that result from multiple functional disabilities. Dyslexic children particularly call attention to the inappropriate nature of the learning disability concept, because their disabilities lie in cognitive and language functions rather than in the capacity to learn. Their functional disabilities are in the educational realm. They also may show a general blocking of emotional expression in school. They may be easily frustrated and discouraged by failure. They may be distractible and show impaired concentration. They may have underlying low self-evaluations and neurotic symptoms (Hallgren, 1950; Missildine, 1963).

In summary, the study of educationally handicapped populations reveals that the exclusion of sensory deficits in the learning disability concept is contradicted by the presence of subtle but crucial sensorimotor problems in some of these children. The exclusion of mentally retarded children is contradicted by the complexity of that syndrome, the settling of children with educational disabilities into the mildly retarded range, and the presence of islands of specific educational disabilities within primarily mentally retarded persons. The exclusion of emotional disorders is contradicted by the vagueness of that category, the neuropsychological inseparability of affect and cognition, and the presence of personality problems in most of these children. Furthermore, the U.S. Supreme Court has affirmed the educationally handicapped status of emotionally disturbed children (*Honig v. Doe*, 1988).

The concept of learning disabilities actually turns out to be the result of a superficial view without sufficient breadth and continuity over time to give a clear picture of the actual characteristics and life courses of children so designated. Putting the complicated question of disability aside for the moment, these children can be more accurately seen as educationally handicapped in social, work, and academic skills.

Social Class Factors

The exclusion of social class and cultural factors from the concept of learning disability is particularly questionable. Judgments about behavior are made according to what is considered important at a given point in life by a particular culture and community. The judgment of disability is in the eye of the beholder, whether an adult or the children themselves. Disabilities expressed only through behavior thus tend to be defined by social norms, whereas physical disabilities are defined by pathological conditions of the body (Hassibi & Breuer, 1980).

The disproportionate incidence of students from minority and lower socioeconomic groups who are not performing well in academic work has been explained as the result of mutual incompatibility between the attitudes of school personnel and such groups (Adelman & Taylor, 1983). In the National Child Development Study, parental social class was the variable that related most strongly to reading attainment (Davie & Butler, 1975). The importance of social and ecological factors in the educational handicap of reading retardation was suggested further by the 3.5 percent prevalence on the Isle of Wight and 6 percent in London (Rutter et al, 1970).

At the same time, learning disabilities are more commonly identified in the middle and upper classes than among the disadvantaged, where similar children tend to be labeled as having behavior problems (Adelman et al, 1982; Ross, 1977). Some upper-class children receive remediation

and avoid being categorized as handicapped altogether. Furthermore, a study of boys categorized as either delinquent or educationally handicapped disclosed the same neurological maturational delay and neuropsychological impairment in both groups. They differed only in that the delinquents came from lower and the educationally handicapped from higher socioeconomic classes (Hurwitz et al, 1972).

Economically disadvantaged children may not have prerequisite skills for successful schoolwork, particularly reading readiness (May, 1973; Wallach & Wallach, 1976). For them the student role is unfamiliar. Some of these children are unable both to control themselves and to accept external controls. Because learning elicits curiosity, which is a blend of cautious fear and aggression, inner controls of these emotions and external control by teachers are required. The fear generated by the school situation thus may be unmanageable and evoke the defenses of withdrawal into fantasy, overactivity with destructive aggression, and the use of peers to effect distraction from schoolwork (Gardner, G.E., 1971). Furthermore, abstract models for motivating achievement are inappropriate for children who tend to learn only about things that have meaning in their daily needs and activities (Entwhisle, 1979).

Death at an Early Age (Kozol, 1967) vividly described the educational conditions in a segregated, overcrowded ghetto school in Boston during the academic year 1964–1965. The adverse effects of the interaction of racist teachers and resentful, alienated children on the personality, skill, and value development of the children were clearly demonstrated. Although written during the days of a particular period of social turmoil, the circumstances described remain relevant. No pedagogic techniques can succeed without a social and educational environment that promotes mutual respect and cooperation between teachers and students.

A noted black economist grew up in an environment that communicated to him that he was stupid and that little success could be expected of him (Sowell, 1980). He was a rebellious character, however, who did not internalize this belief in the form of helplessness as did many of his contemporaries. Because an attitude of helplessness is a central problem, repeated experience with success is necessary to break the cycle of poverty. It is crucial that these successes be perceived by the disadvantaged as resulting from their own skill and competence and not from the benevolence of others. Thus poverty is not only an economic problem, but a problem of individual mastery, dignity, and self-esteem (Seligman, 1975).

Malnutrition associated with poverty may cause damage to the brain; however, psychological impoverishment stemming from environments that do not stimulate children sufficiently also may produce a social deprivation syndrome characterized by concentration and learning difficulties that result in poor scholastic achievement (Valentine & Valentine, 1975). Some of the children so affected in extreme may be diagnosed as suffering from pituitary dwarfism or mental retardation, yet when rescued from their damaging environments, they may achieve normal development (Reinhardt & Brash, 1969).

Socioeconomic factors, then, are relevant to the concept of learning disabilities, both because learning disabilities tend to be diagnosed and remedied more in upper-class than lower-class families, and because lower-class children may lack early stimulation for the development of basic language skills. With these considerations in mind "educational" disability is a less socially biased term than "learning" disability.

Cultural Factors

The cultural bias of most standardized psychometric and educational testing has been amply demonstrated. Most immigrant groups score well below normal on intelligence tests in their early years of residence in this country, some low enough to be considered mildly retarded. In 1921 Italian Americas scored from 77 to 85 on IQ tests. Almost the same levels were found in the same period for Slovakian, Greek, Polish, Spanish, Portugese, and Jewish immigrants. Now all of these groups test at or above the national average. The current difference in black–white IQ scores of about 15 points is about the same as between immigrant and native American groups in the past. The upward economic mobility of blacks appears to increase IQ scores (Sowell, 1980).

Awareness of the potential cultural bias of intelligence tests has led to the development of scales, such as the System of Multicultural Pluralistic Assessment (Mercer, 1979). They are based upon the premise that comparisons must be made between children of comparable ethnic and socioeconomic backgrounds in assessing intelligence.

In English-speaking countries, the fact that children are learning to read a difficult language often is overlooked. Compared with other languages, written English is remarkably inconsistent and capricious in the way it looks and sounds. Centuries of usage have obfuscated the relationship between words and sounds of the English writing systems. Nevertheless, the learner's task still is to try to understand the intentions of those who created and modified the code of written English (Liberman, 1983).

England and the United States have created an artificial critical period, which does not allow all children sufficient time to mature cognitively, by initiating reading instruction between the ages of five and seven. In Sweden and Denmark, school does not begin until the age of seven. Consequently Swedish and Danish children are less likely to become educationally handicapped, because they grow out of this potential problem before they enter reading instruction; they also are given early support in learning to read, if needed (Downing, 1979).

Child-rearing and educational practices have been raised as possible explanations for the low incidence of reading problems reported in Chinese children. A study of Chinese children raised in Canada revealed the striking finding that 18 percent were retarded in ideographic Chinese and 15 percent in English (Kline & Lee, 1972). This finding flies in the face of the assumption that reading difficulty is greater for alphabetical than ideographic written symbols. A possible explanation is that Canadian Chinese families transplanted into a Western culture may not have carried through the clear expectations that their young children would exercise self-discipline, as is the case in Taiwan and the Republic of China.

The importance of cultural factors in school learning problems was highlighted by the 1975 North Atlantic Treaty Organization on the neuropsychology of learning disabilities. Because the concept of learning disability had different meanings in Europe than in North America, each country accordingly decided to work on its own definition (Gaddes, 1980).

Current Knowledge of the Brain and Development

The definitions of learning disabilities imply that separate parts of the brain are involved in academic learning, intelligence, emotions, and nonacademic behavior. These distinctions are incompatible with current knowledge of neuroanatomy and neurophysiology. Furthermore, the separation of nature and nurture has been replaced by an epigenetic understanding of the interplay of brain structure and environmental influences in the development of the brain as summarized by Adelman and Taylor in Figure 2-4.

In reality academic underachievement may result from a variety of disabilities that involve discrete areas of development critical for productivity in school, such as difficulties in language processing, visual–spatial orientation, directing attention, concentration, memory, and motor output (Levine & Melmed, 1982).

Social Disadvantages of the Learning Disability Concept

The learning disabled designation, which inherently connotes deviance, has negative consequences that deserve special consideration as they take place in school, family, and peer group.

Deviance is defined not by a person's qualities but by judgments applied by others. What is determined to be deviance also is influenced by who has the power to enforce such a determination. The end result is the social construction of a label. Furthermore, persons labeled as deviant may come to view themselves as irrevocably deviant so that systems, such as prisons, mental hospitals, training schools, and special classes, may foster rather than reverse deviant behavior (Rist & Harrell, 1982; Edgerton et al, 1984).

To complicate matters even further, it is in the nature of social systems to enhance ingroup solidarity by creating outgroups and maintaining a certain level of deviance in order to clarify group boundaries (Erikson, K., 1966). These deep-seated social phenomena color attitudes toward children who founder in school, often incisively expressed by school personnel and the peer group.

A relevant example lies in the situation of deaf children whose behavior may not be a necessary consequence of their hearing impairment but a result of social attitudes that magnify a child's differences and result in the isolation of the child. As a result deaf children tend to lack intellectual stimulation and fall behind developmentally and educationally (Furth, 1966).

	ENVIRONMENT	PERSON	INTERACTIONS AND TRANSACTIONS BETWEEN ENVIRONMENT AND PERSON
Levels of Focus	1. Primary (e.g., home, classroom) 2. Secondary (e.g., neighborhood, community) 3. Tertiary (e.g., national, international)	1. Molecular (e.g., synaptic transmission, genetic) 2. Molar activity of varying units (e.g., activity, manners, bodily mores)	Molecular or molar activity of the individual in the primary or secondary environment or with reference to tertiary environmental factors (physical activity in classroom, the value placed on education in society)
Areas of Focus	1. Physical (e.g., geographical, architectural) 2. Social (e.g., interpersonal, organizational socio-cultural, economic)	1. Internal-biological and psychological (e.g., thoughts, decision making, feelings) 2. Overt actions-motor and verbal (e.g., spoken language, facial expressions, activity level)	Internal or external activity of the individual with reference to the physical or social environment (the effect of architectural design on feelings and behavior)
Types of Instigating Factors	1. Insufficent stimuli (e.g., impoverished environs, deprivation of learning opportunities at home or school, inadequate diet) 2. Excessive stimuli (e.g., overly demanding pressure to achieve and contradictory expectations) 3. Intrusive and hostile stimuli (e.g., medical practices, conflict in home or faulty child rearing practices, migratory family, social prejudices)	1. Physiological "insult" (e.g., cerebral trauma or disease, endocrine dysfunctions) 2. Genetic anomaly (e.g., genes which limit, slow or lead to atypical development) 3. Cognitive and affective states (e.g., lack of basic cognitive strategies and ability to cope with emotions, low self-esteem) 4. Physical characteristics shaping contact with environment (e.g., visual, auditory, or motoric deficits; excessive or reduced sensitivity to stimuli; easily fatigued) 5. Deviant actions of the individual (e.g., excessive errors in reading and speech, high and low levels of activity)	1. Severe to moderate personal vulnerabilities and environmental defects and differences (e.g., person with slow development in a highly demanding, understaffed classroom) 2. Minor personal vulnerabilities not accommodated by the situation (e.g., person with auditory perceptual disability enrolled in phonetic reading program, very active student in quiet classroom) 3. Minor environmental defects and differences not accommodated by the individual (e.g., student excessively sensitive to racial or cultural minority status)

| Interactions of Variables within Categories | 1. Concurrent environmental transactions (e.g., overly punitive parent, demanding teachers)
2. Sequential environmental transactions (e.g., special school placement and negative expectations of others) | 1. Concurrent personal transactions (e.g., awareness of poor skills and of lack of ability to cope with anxiety, problems reading and speaking)
2. Sequential personal transactions (e.g., awareness of loss of basic cognitive coping skills, problems in doing school assignments) | |

Figure 2-4. Hypothesized causes of educational disabilities. (From *Learning Disabilities in Perspective* by Howard S. Adelman and Linda Taylor. Copyright © 1983 by Scott, Foresman and Company. Reprinted with permission.)

The same phenomenon obtains with the blind. Because they may be regarded as inferior to the sighted, blind persons' self-concepts and self-evaluations may suffer. Even systems of interventions for the blind have unintended adverse consequences for the persons they purportedly serve (Scott, 1969).

Schools and the Learning Disability Concept

The review of special education classification practices suggests that the labels assigned to children often are inaccurate. They may be used to remove children from classrooms and to justify specialized interventions that are administratively available only after a certain diagnosis is made (Adelman, 1978; Forness et al, 1984). For many children the label of learning disability means less positive classroom interaction with teachers, reduced levels of interaction of teachers with parents, and increased peer rejection (Rist & Harrel, 1982).

The learning disability label may crystallize the notion of a child's defectiveness, particularly since brain damage may be implied by the term. The internalization of the label can lead a child to feel defective and helpless. In addition, programs designed to identify and help children so labeled through early intervention can have negative effects by removing them from mainstream activities to participate in well-intentioned but harmful programs of remediation. Because it emphasizes weaknesses rather than strengths, the learning disability label risks a self-fulfilling prophecy (Levine et al, 1980; Rosenthal & Jacobson, 1968). Any ambiguous diagnosis can be misinterpreted to the detriment of a child.

An extreme example is a six-year-old boy who received the diagnosis of the Silver-Russell syndrome, which largely refers to short stature. In his school records, it was assumed to signify a mental retardation syndrome that accounted for his behavior problems in school. At the age of 13, after six years in an educable mentally retarded class, his superior intellectual abilities were discovered during an interdisciplinary clinical evaluation. The label of Silver-Russell syndrome, a benign genetic variation without mental retardation, had been misunderstood through the years, and the child had fulfilled the expectation of mental retardation.

On the other hand, children may be excused for willful misbehavior because of a learning disability that presumably is beyond their control. Euphemisms cannot conceal the fact that many of these children do provoke, lie, steal, defy, sabotage, and pose daily frustrations for adults through their manipulative behavior.

Ethical concerns mandate that decisions in education be made with awareness of whose interests are being served—those of a child, the school, the parents, or other children. Diagnostic procedures also must minimize errors, misprescriptions, violations of legal rights, negative repercussions of assessment processes, and inappropriate financial costs. Methodological concerns are of reliability, construct validity, predictive validity, content validity, biasing factors, norms, and standards, in addition to the utility of the procedures.

If these ethical and methodological requirements are not met, school diagnostic practices may invade a child's privacy and incorrectly label a child as deviant with negative consequences for self-esteem, motivation, and social status due to the tendency of tests to focus only on what is readily measurable. In general the reliance on the mechanistic evaluation and decision making of testing programs may infringe on essential freedoms (Adleman & Taylor, 1983).

Schools are more likely to recognize their ethical and methodological responsibilities for children with school learning problems if these are called educational disabilities rather than learning disabilities, which are more readily construed to be exclusively child centered.

Parents and the Learning Disability Concept

Parents naturally have idealized expectations for their children. A child, however, may not further the image a family wishes to promote and may reflect negatively on the family (Kronick, 1981). For example, the parents of a child who may be talented in art but who has difficulty in learning to read are faced with conflict. How they value each will determine whether they emphasize their child's assets or limitations. If they support their child's talent in art, the extra effort required in reading may come more easily than if the child feels both unappreciated in art and incompetent in reading.

Some parents are relieved when their child's unacceptable performance in school can be attributed to a learning disability. They feel more comfortable with a diagnostic label that implies physical rather than emotional problems and create pressure to make such a diagnosis (Gaddes, 1980). There is a strong need on the part of many adults to see a child's learning problems as being "organic" and not "emotional." Underlying this need is the question of where the blame for the child's problems lie. If the problem is based upon something "organic," neither the child, nor the parents, nor the educators can be blamed for it. A corollary is that if the problem is "organic," there is no deliberate element in the child's failure to learn, whereas if the problem is "emotional," then there is an intentional element.

The questions of who is to blame and whether or not the behavior is deliberate permeate most of the misunderstandings of the determinants of all behavior problems. Actually blame is not necessary to the understanding and resolution of a particular child's problems. Conscious, preconscious, unconscious, willed, and random elements are present in all forms of human behavior whether in the context of a cerebrovascular accident or a phobic neurosis. If the pejorative factors of blame and intent are removed from the situation, a disability can be understood as an intrinsic part of a child, just as are physical appearance and a sense of humor (Kronick, 1981).

For some parents a learning disability provides a preferable alternative to facing festering individual personality and family problems. For others a learning disability may signify something that the educational system can eliminate without involving them. For still others the quest for a cure for a specific disability may divert attention from painful realities.

The concept of educational disability offers relief to parents and children by focusing attention upon the child's performance in academic learning in school rather than by increasing the pressure to find something wrong with the child that does not aggravate parental guilt.

Peer Reactions to the Educationally Handicapped

The learning disability label does invite teasing from peers related to learning incompetence (Osman, 1982). The children find themselves called "dummy," "mental," and "stupid." Regardless of whether they are regarded as having learning or educational disabilities, educationally handicapped children are likely to be isolated and rejected by peers because of their personal qualities and special treatment (Bryan, 1974; Bryan et al, 1976). Peers accurately tend to view them as worried and frightened, as not appearing to have a good time, as being sad, and as ignored by other children (Graffagnino, 1966).

Some of the social problems of the educationally handicapped may result from their own avoidance of peer interaction, because they regard themselves as undesirables and find few opportunities to present themselves as competent. Children are not eager to befriend such a low-status person, nor are some educationally handicapped children eager to befriend other children who share low status. As long as children avoid friendships with those with similar problems, they can cling to the illusion that they are like everyone else (Kronick, 1981). Unlike the deaf, who can form the identity of a deaf person with the support of other people with a similar handicap, the educationally handicapped have few peer resources to draw upon (Higgins, 1980).

EDUCATIONAL DISABILITY AND HANDICAP CONCEPTS

The notion of learning disability falls short of the conceptual clarity so desperately needed in addressing the problems children experience in their school work (Fletcher & Taylor, 1984). Learning disability is too global a term for problems largely related to academic learning and ignores the fact that learning in other areas may be unimpeded, if not facile. It does not acknowledge sufficiently the fact that a child's difficulty lies in tasks carried out in the context of school-based education. It is not consistent with current knowledge of brain functions and development. It overlooks the often critical roles of economic disadvantage and cultural background that cannot be separated from a child's performance in school. It artificially excludes the mildly mentally retarded population, which is fed by a range of disabilities handled by separate professional groups to the detriment of scientific, clinical, and educational progress in each field. Its emphasis upon a vague deficit in a child does not logically lead to conceptualizations of educational handicaps and appropriate remediation. And finally, it tends to inculcate negative self-concepts and self-evaluations in the children so designated.

A more realistic and useful generic concept that covers the range of specific temperamental, cognitive, language, managerial, and self-system functional disabilities actually identified in children who experience difficulty in academic learning is educational disability. This concept acknowledges that the problems lie in the context of schoolwork. It does not imply that a child has general difficulties in learning. It encompasses all of the social and cultural factors that are relevant to success or failure in school. It acknowledges the children who fail because the curriculum does not meet their needs (Elkind, 1983). It acknowledges the overlap between the

traditional fields of developmental disabilities and learning disabilities. It does not
in itself foster generally negative self-concepts and self-evaluations. It does relate
directly to educational handicap as expressed in lack of knowledge, skill deficiencies, incompetencies in schoolwork,
and lacks in interpersonal skills. In this way
educational disability and educational
handicap have useful implications for
treatment by placing the emphasis on the
interaction between a child and the educational process. In so doing they acknowledge the collegiate value system that
influences school performance standards,
and they admit the possibility of adjusting
standards to the needs of specific children.
They also provide a rationale for administrative treatment and the deployment of
special education resources.

The concept of educational disability
recognizes that an academic learning problem may be caused primarily by variables
within a child, such as functional disabilities, or within a child's environment, such
as an unfavorable school experience. It also
encompasses the more common situation
in which variables in both a child and environment are critical (Adelman & Taylor,
1983). The concept of educational disability fosters individualized approaches to education, which optimally could erase
handicaps themselves (Summers, 1981).

A telling endorsement of the educational disability concept comes from children and adults who have lived with the
learning disability label. They know the
disadvantages of bearing a vaguely defined
personal sense that they cannot learn well.
They would prefer to view themselves and
to be regarded by others as having difficulty with academic subjects. For them educational disability is both more realistic
and acceptable.

The concept of learning disability served
the useful purpose of shifting the focus
from etiological terms such as brain injury.
The concept of functional disability permits greater precision in diagnosis and is

explicated in subsequent chapters. The
term functional has been used loosely to
connote a "nonorganic" or psychological
etiology. Here it refers to definable functions of the central nervous system. The
concept of educational disability offers the
advantage of shifting the focus from a
child's general learning capacity to those
central nervous system functions involved
in academic learning in school.

SUMMARY

As public education in the United States
evolved, the handicapping conditions of
blindness, deafness, orthopedic disorders,
and mental retardation were progressively
defined. More recently efforts have been
made to define a group of children who
have learning disabilities by those concerned with the funding of special education programs.

Inherent in the concept of learning disabilities is the assumption that there are
children who have learning problems that
are not related to their childhood experiences, their family lives, their socioeconomic statuses, their cultures, and their
races. That assumption implies that failure
to learn academic subjects can be solely related to a definable inborn defect, injury,
or disease unrelated to motivation, values,
personality, or opportunity. In practice
such an assumption excludes most children
who founder in school. It also ignores the
large number of children who manage to
become competent, if not eminent, adults
in spite of specific problems in learning
academic subjects, because they possessed
self-discipline and motivation that enabled
their passage through school without evident handicap.

The value of the learning disabilities
concept has been political, through its offering of the image of a learning disabled
child as a means of attracting attention and

funding action. The concept also has provided the educational system with administrative leverage for building specialized educational services. On the negative side, it has perpetuated the illusion that there are children who have simple disabilities in learning.

The belief has existed that a precise definition of learning disability is possible. The closer one gets to an understanding of the children themselves, however, the more the task of definition flies out of focus. There are important scientific weaknesses and social disadvantages in the learning disability concept. We are confronted squarely with the fact that most children who do poorly in school do so because of their total life experiences. The illusion that there is such a thing as a learning disability unrelated to life experience has been fostered by schools that disavow failure in identifying individual learning capacities, by parents who disavow involvement in their children's learning problems, and by a society that disavows responsibility for the economic, social, and cultural factors that impede the education of children. Furthermore, for a child to be identified as having a learning disability requires the attention of a school with resources and of parents who can be advocates for their child. For this reason children of middle class parents are the most likely to be identified as having learning disabilities. The economically disadvantaged are less likely to be identified as having learning disabilities because of the lack of access to diagnostic resources and because the current definitions of learning disability exclude them.

The quest for a disability in a child tends to absolve schools, parents, and society of their responsibilities to promote the development of children in the light of their unique individual differences in responding to the routines of schooling. These unique qualities can be more precisely defined as educational disabilities in temperament, cognition, language, managerial, and self characteristics. When these disabilities lead to significant impairment of schoolwork performance, the concept of educational handicap is useful in guiding treatment.

The fact is that children fail in school and later life because of their talents, personalities, families, and opportunities. Organizations committed to the term learning disabilities could profitably substitute the more cogent terms educational disability and educational handicap. The need really is to identify and assist children who are handicapped in performing their schoolwork. The large number of children who fail to learn but do not fit into the current strict definitions of learning disabilities are being overlooked and educationally neglected. Once a child is determined to be educationally handicapped in reading, arithmetic, or general task performance, specific attention can be devoted to the child's more precise disabilities that produce the handicap. School learning problems, thus, are but symptoms, a final common pathway, stemming from a multiplicity of possibilities involving the interaction of biological, psychological, social, educational, and opportunity factors.

Expecting competency in children and adults, except when there are clear-cut handicaps, is an important and laudable aim. When we expect competency in children, however, we also should expect competency in their parents and in the schools and social systems responsible for them. The quest for competency in children clearly raises questions about competency in parenting, educating, and governing.

The definition of educational handicap within itself has the seeds for its solution. Specifically it lends itself to an individualized approach to the identification and treatment of educational disabilities. If each child were viewed as a unique individual for whom realistic expectations were held and all education were individually oriented, there would be no educational handicaps.

3

The Multisystem Approach

A hypothesis or theory is clear, decisive and positive, but it
is believed by no one but the person who created it. Experimental findings, on the other hand, are messy inexact things
which are believed by everyone except the person who did
the work.

Harlow Shapley, 1935

Molière depicted a doctoral examination in which the can-
didate was asked why opium
puts people to sleep. The
triumphant answer was, "Because it contains a dormitive principle!" (Bateson, 1972).
Today the explanation that opium induces
sleep because it contains something that
induces sleep would be rejected by a fifth
grader. Yet the explanation that children
have difficulty learning in school because
they have learning disabilities, the equivalent of the dormitive principle, has mes-
merizing appeal. The psychological and
philosophical reasons for this bear close
examination.

From the psychological standpoint,
learning problems in children create confusion in those who try to understand and
remedy them. In the face of confusion, the
human tendency is to grasp for plausible
explanations (Hughes & Grieve, 1983;
Singer & Benassi, 1981). Research on problem solving shows that people have strong
tendencies to perceive order and causality
in random arrys of data. Furthermore,
they tend to perceive what seems correct

to them even when contradicted by facts
and consequently seek only confirmatory
evidence. Having thus managed to expose
themselves only to confirmation, people
tend to be fallaciously confident of the validity of their judgments. These human
tendencies help to explain why the concept
of learning disability provides a plausible
and reassuring explanation for many.

The appeal of discovering a learning
disability as the explanation for a child's
learning problems in school also springs
from scientific philosophy. Rooted in me-
dieval theology, which pictured the universe as carrying out the purposes of a
divine, human being-like God, science of
the Industrial Age has been dominated by
the Cartesian conception of the universe
as a machine comprised of clockwork
mechanisms. In this framework the Newtonian approach of science has been to attack a problem by taking it apart, studying
its parts, finding a defective part, replacing
it, and putting the parts back together
again to recreate the whole. The physical
sciences progressed long ago beyond this
view to holistic transactional conceptions

(Randall, 1926; Bohm, 1980). The social sciences, however, still employ Newtonian cause–effect models.

EDUCATIONAL RESEARCH

Academic research on learning began in the Newtonian model in German laboratories in the late 1800s and flowered in the 1930s in the work of Pavlov in Russia and Thorndike in the United States. After World War II, the emphasis on quantifiable research continued so that the quest for cures of educational problems has been based upon behavioral models that view a particular behavior as having its source in observable factors. Even when researchers warned that their approaches did not suggest it, single cause and treatment interpretations were given to their work (Mahoney, 1974). Thus the empirical techniques of experimental psychology and sociology have been unable to apprehend adequately the complexities of learning (Rossi, 1983).

Two decades ago, an exhaustive review of the literature on learning problems in children exposed the frustrations of research that focuses on one aspect of brain functioning to the exclusion of others (Chalfant & Scheffelin, 1969). For example, extensive studies disclosed that some children had difficulty in discriminating between the figure–ground relationships of sounds. Ignored in those studies was the factor of attention, which can be readily diverted by daydreaming or lack of motivation.

In particular, there has been little scholarly interest in what actually goes on in schools and classrooms in both the day-to-day and long-range management of children with academic learning problems. Educational researchers have opted for the Newtonian methods of the social sciences in which statistics are regarded as assuring objectivity and more discursive approaches are seen as unscientific. As a result pitifully little has been learned about what actually transpires in our schools (Phillips, 1960; Graubard, 1981). The resulting chasm between schools and educational research has created a destructive tension between practitioners and researchers. Educators and clinicians who work with children know that families, peers, schools, and society contribute to the problems children have in school and so are not satisfied with much of the educational research (Chalfant & Schefflin, 1969; Cruickshank, 1977).

More specifically, in educational research sample definitions vary widely and negate comparison. Proper controls often are not used. Furthermore, the role of the observer in making observations usually are not recognized. A common language for communicating the nature of research to others is lacking. Most critically, systematic research programs do not exist to follow up and refine findings (Torgesen, 1975). This lack of long-term data subjects education to current fads and fashions.

Educational research has contributed so little to educational practice, because it has not been forthcoming and because education is a complex effort to help humans learn how to live. Becoming educated is learning how to use experience and knowledge to enrich the gifts with which we start life. Egan (1983) put it well: "If we hope to talk sensibly about education, or enquire into it, or do research about it, then we need to be able to identify what accumulates in the process of becoming educated."

In a broad sense, the research produced in the Newtonian analytic framework dominates the 75,000 scientific and technical journals and the 60,000 books that appear annually. Experimenters unwittingly repeat the research of others, because the unsystematic arrangement of facts and the unclear relationships of theories make it difficult to retrieve earlier studies that are buried under the avalanche of new research (Miller, 1978). The accumulation of this myriad of findings has made life easier in some ways, but it also has diverted attention from the realities of human nature (Capra, 1982). There is nothing wrong with specialization as such. In fact, the dramatic progress made in recent decades in such fields as physics and surgery could not have happened without it. However, we pay a price for specialization. It isolates us from each other so that we become more and more unaware of what it feels like to work in another field, and we even become estranged (Redl, 1966).

The difficulties with research on learning problems in children are the result of these general conceptual and methodological problems that produce a literal tower of Babel. There is an urgent need for a common language. Psychological research has been restricted to small fragments of the three areas of individual psychology: cognition, emotion, and conation. Within these frameworks psychoanalysts have concentrated upon aspects of cognition and emotion, Piagetian psychologists on aspects of cognition, and behavioral psychologists upon the observable behavior of conation. Behaviorism, in particular, became an antitheoretical movement and lost its connection to brain functioning (Mandler, 1969).

Fundamental problems result from separating cognition, emotion, and conation. Not only are they functionally inseparable, but each encompasses too much. Cognition refers to the process of knowing, which ranges from perception to thinking. Emotion refers to psychophysiological states that are difficult to handle conceptually and depend upon cognition. Conation refers to actions that are influenced by both emotions and cognition.

All of these considerations make it evident that educational research requires the methods of both science and the humanities. The scientist seeks causes and predictibility in the form of natural laws. The humanist seeks order and reasons for events. Both kinds of understanding are necessary complements to each other (Kavale & Forness, 1985; Scruton, 1980).

THE MULTISYSTEM VIEW

The earliest roots of general systems theory can be traced at least as far back as 500 B.C. to Heraclites, the Greek philosopher who introduced the ideas of interacting and conflicting forces into explanations of the development of life and matter (Stokes, 1968). In ancient China the yin-yang principle embodied the same ideas.

At the turn of the century, William James recognized the limitation of the Newtonian analytic approach to human behavior. He threw into bold relief the holistic point of view in which any phenomenon could be understood only when considered in relation to other phenomena. Thereafter the individual could be seen as a part of the whole of nature, particularly human society, and as propelled by a nervous system functioning within the context of other organ systems of the body (Goldstein, 1963). The realization dawned that the universe only appears to have discrete parts because of human methods of abstracting it (Spiegel, 1971). Patterns of mental processes were found to be matters of form rather than substance through the discoveries of cybernetics and general systems theory (Bateson, 1972).

Before World War II, Vygotsky (1978) sought to reconstruct the series of changes in intellectual operations that unfold during the course of a child's development. For him child development was not merely the accumulation of changes, but a complex process characterized by periodicity, the unevenness in the development of different functions, the metamorphosis of one function into another, the intertwining of external and internal factors, and adaptive processes. He conceived of both evolutionary and revolutionary changes in the course of an individual's development. Beyond his contemporaries—Thorndike, Piaget, and Koffka—he envisioned the historically shaped and culturally transmitted psychology of human beings.

In the history of science, theories compete with each other over decades, if not centuries. The ultimate solution does not flow from the complete victory of one theory but from a synthesis of the best elements of several theories. The raw material for comparing and integrating the physical, biological, and social sciences is already available (Mayr, 1982). In particular this is the case in understanding children's learning problems.

For our purposes six theoretical positions stand out as useful: the psychoanalytic, which accounts for drives and emotions in a comprehensive theory of character development; the Piagetian, which focuses upon cognitive processes; the neuropsychological, which relates brain structures to function; the behavioral, which elaborates learning processes; the ethological, which draws upon commonalities with other animals; and general systems theory, which integrates them all. The material in this book is drawn from all of these sources, which bring unique perspectives to the same phenomena; without general systems theory, none explains them completely. Furthermore, the evidence cited as factual actually occurs on a continuum of more or less warranted statements and is subject to revision as new data emerge. For this reason completely impartial observation is never achieved (Mead, 1936; Spiegel, 1971).

With these combined theoretical tools, we can describe individual children in their particular societies and cultures, families, schools, peer groups, and classrooms as they employ their particular cognitive, temperamental, language, and managerial styles in the progressive development of their personal selves.

Research on human behavior should be conducted on three essential levels: (1) in search of facts that apply to all human beings; (2) in search of facts that are true for certain groups of people; and (3) in search of facts that explain the behavior of an individual. Quantitative multivariant research methods can be used to test hypotheses generated from the qualitative case method of studying individuals. Furthermore, the most powerful and useful information can be gained through the dialectic application of empirical methods and contrasting theoretical models (Rossi, 1983).

Interactional research is not useful, therefore, if it tries to parcel out how much of each factor is operating in a particular cross section of time, because life consists of sequences of time. The emphasis should be on studying multivariate sequences of interactions in the way in which they naturally unfold between persons over time (Cattell, 1980). The issues studied also should have functional significance. For this reason a practical clinical sense is important in determining what to study (Cantwell & Forness, 1982). Unfortunately much research has regarded the human being as comprised of mathematical, computer, and game theory models. Although very useful, these abstract models can take on a life of their own even though the answers fail to enhance understanding of practical problems (Wallach & Wallach, 1976).

At this time the insights of many disciplines cry out for integration. A myriad of significant but unappreciated findings constitute an enormous, fragmented body of knowledge. The lack of integrating theories has been responsible for the plethora of illusory, simplistic and ineffective efforts to help children with academic learning problems.

THE GENERAL THEORY OF LIVING SYSTEMS

The general theory of living systems as outlined by James Grier Miller (1978) employs the concepts that advanced the physical sciences to permit placing people on the moon. It offers the biological and social sciences the same potential for fitting facts together in a coherent way in order to attain desired objectives.

In contrast with closed nonliving systems, living systems are open and exchange information and matter with their surroundings. The terms stimulus and response obscure the fact that the human being processes both information and matter-energy, because they do not make clear whether, in a particular situation, the matter-energy or the informational aspect of a transmission, or both, are influencing the receiver (Miller, 1978). Systems theory divides stimuli and responses into matter-energy or information inputs and outputs. This distinction between matter-energy and information helps to resolve the ancient philosophical dilemma of what in an organism is matter and what is mind. That dilemma persists, however, in the wide breach between the biological and social sciences. Systems theory can unify these disparate disciplines in the study of the human being as a whole.

The information inherent in the matter-energy processed makes it possible for a living system to seek, obtain, and utilize necessary inputs. Within living systems subsystems produce useful or useless outputs as evaluated by a suprasystem. Suprasystems select useful outputs of their subsystems and reject useless outputs. Living systems that survive in evolution are those in which useful outputs exceed useless outputs (Berrien, 1968). Successful living systems process information and matter-energy in order to maintain themselves and survive. In so doing they follow a course of progressive development to higher levels of differentiation and organized complexity.

Seven hierarchical levels can be identified as living systems—the cell, organ, organism, group, organization, society, and

LEVEL

Cell

Organ

Organism

Group

Organization

Society

Supranational System

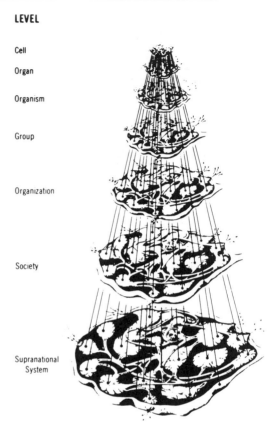

Figure 3-1. The living system is shown here at each level. The diagram indicates that the 19 subsystems at the level of the cell shred out to form the next more advanced level of system, the organ. This still has the same 19 subsystems, each being more complex. A similar shredding-out occurs to form each of the five more advanced levels—organism, group, organization, society, and supranational system. (From J. G. Miller, *Living Systems,* copyright 1978 by McGraw-Hill Book Company, New York. Reproduced with permission.)

supranational (Figure 3-1). As symbolized by the face of Janus, each system has a whole aspect and an aspect that is a part of another system (Koestler, 1978). The wholes are more than their parts, and each whole is simultaneously a part of another whole. Of the seven levels, our particular interest is in the organ, organism, group,

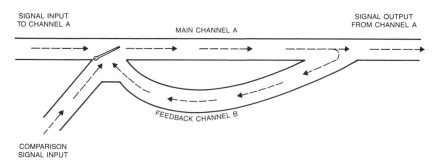

SIGNAL INPUT
TO CHANNEL A

SIGNAL OUTPUT
FROM CHANNEL A

MAIN CHANNEL A

FEEDBACK CHANNEL B

COMPARISON
SIGNAL INPUT

Figure 3-2. Negative feedback is the decrease and positive feedback the increase of input to channel A regulated by feedback from its output to correspond to an expected signal input. (From J. G. Miller, *Living Systems,* copyright 1978 by McGraw-Hill Book Company, New York. Reproduced with permission.)

organization, and society. Thus human beings are systems within systems. The human being is a dynamic open system that actively searches for stimulation rather than waiting passively to respond and has the capacity to modify the environment.

The word *system* derives from roots that mean "standing together." A system then is composed of *components* that together process inputs and produce outputs. Living systems have *boundaries* and are *self-regulating.* The basic property of a living system is a *boundary* between itself and its environment. The boundary of a system is defined by the relationships between components. The state of affairs inside the boundaries of a living system differs from the state of affairs in its environment and generally is more stable. The second property of a living system is *self-regulation.* A living system has mechanisms that adjust the state of the system relative to changes in its environment as it processes both matter-energy and information.

The trend of the universe is toward increasing entropy, or randomness, and death. In order to survive, living systems draw upon matter-information from the environment to counter entropy through ingestion, digestion, energy production, and the use of energy. Information and

entropy have an antithetical relationship that gives rise to tension between them in living systems. Information and entropy may be contrasted on the following dimensions: signal–noise, accuracy–error, form–chaos, regularity–randomness, order–disorder, heterogeneity–homogeneity, improbability–probability, and predictability–unpredictability (Miller, 1978).

Information is processed through sensory assimilation and accommodation of input with resulting output through motor activity. A living system is cybernetically self-regulating because not only does its input affect its output, but its output adjusts its input. The result is that the living system adapts homeostatically to its environment through positive and negative feedback.

Feedback takes place when two channels exist so that channel B loops back to the input of channel A and transmits some portion of the output of channel A so that it can be compared with an expected pattern (Figure 3-2). When the output is fed back in such a way that it increases the output of channel A from an expected steady state, positive feedback exists (Miller, 1978). Positive feedback enhances a particular form of behavior, as in the pleasure obtained from eating. Positive feedback can initiate system changes; however, it is po-

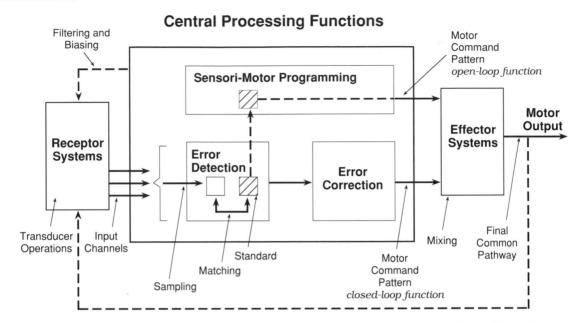

Figure 3-3. Flow diagram of a hypothetical system for controlling motor activity. (From R. A. Chase, "An Information-Flow Model of the Organization of Motor Activity," *Journal of Nervous and Mental Disease, 140,* 1965, 334–335. Copyright 1965 by the Williams & Wilkins Company, Baltimore MD. Reproduced with permission.)

tentially dangerous, because it can cause depletion of the input, exhaustion, or structural breakdown, as through extreme overeating.

Negative feedback decreases the output of channel A from an expected pattern and thereby maintains the steady state of the system. In the form of distress, negative feedback inhibits a particular form of behavior. For example, the discomfort of gastric distention causes the discontinuation of eating. Steady states in all living systems are controlled by negative feedbacks. When they fail, the system's survival is jeopardized.

The model depicted in Figure 3-3 contains the three basic parts of a feedback control system: a receptor system, central processing functions, and an effector system. The principal central processing functions are the error-detection and error-correction functions. The former matches the sensory feedback pattern against an expected pattern that is based on previous experience. Serious difficulty arises if one channel is placed out of step with the others, such as when conflicting information is received about the progress of skilled behavior (Chase, 1965).

In addition to boundaries and self-regulation, sophisticated living systems have the capacity to modify their environments. Thus feedback that suggests a passive organism-regulating output in a mechanistic way is not the whole story. There also are feed-forward loops that actively seek specific kinds of information and stimuli rather than simply taking whatever happens. We are programmed with images of what we seek, such as food, mates, and books. Thus the operation of both feed-forward and feedback systems guide the forecasting and execution of intentional behavior (Pribram, 1971). Out of the seemingly endless resources of our minds, we examine everything that presents itself to us, projecting its possibilities, rating probabilities, selecting among action alternatives, generating and executing plans of attack through feed-forward, changing both plans and attack according to feedback, practicing anew and advancing anew, always in movement into a future that either looms in doubt or dances tantalizingly before us (Loye, 1983).

Living systems have only a finite number of ways in which to behave when the usual responses fail. A system may alter itself by learning new skills or reorganizing itself so as to make new behaviors possible; may alter the environment; may withdraw from the environment and seek a more favorable one; or may alter definition of the internal steady state (Vickers, 1959).

The sociologist Talcott Parsons refers to a field of human action as composed of the cultural system, the social system, the personality system of the individual, and the person's behavioral system (Parsons, 1977). For him intelligence is anchored in the behavioral system, whereas affect is anchored in the social system. Therefore, the affective attachments of individuals to each other and to groups that comprise a social system are at the center of the moral order of a social system.

In sum, the theory of living systems encompasses the following principles in humans (Marmor, 1983):

1. The human being is an internally active as well as externally responsive open system capable of self-regulation with permeable boundaries that permit physical energy and information to pass from inside out and from outside in, and that enable a person to grow, learn, and reproduce over the course of time.

2. Character develops out of the interactions of the human biological substrate with matter, energy, and information from outside the biological system, that is, from the physical environment, the family, the school system, peer groups, the community, the nation, and the culture.

3. Tensions, conflicts, or difficulties within any of these interacting systems can induce ripple effects within any or all of the other systems.

Figure 3-4 is a schematic illustration of a living system. Within the boundaries of a living system are its interacting parts or *components*. The spatial relationships between these components are called *structures*, which are stable over time and under differing conditions. The *processes* of a living system are the stable patterns of change taking place within the structures over time. The *functions* of a living system regulate the internal state of the system and its relations with its environment.

This kind of analysis can be applied to any living system from the cell to the supranational. For our purposes the most completely understood living system is at the organ level, the central nervous system. At the same time, it is the essence of a human being as an organism, because it carries out critical organism functions in regulating the internal state of the body and relations with the human and ecological environments. Indeed, brain death is equated with the death of a person. It will be the focus of Part III of this book. In anticipation of that later discussion, the following systems analysis of the central nervous system can serve as a model for analyzing the group, organization, and societal levels. This promising task has yet to be definitively undertaken for children's learning problems in school.

In brief the central nervous system's components are subsystems composed of cells and chemical neuroregulators. Its boundaries are the perimeters of the brain and spinal cord. Its spatial structures are

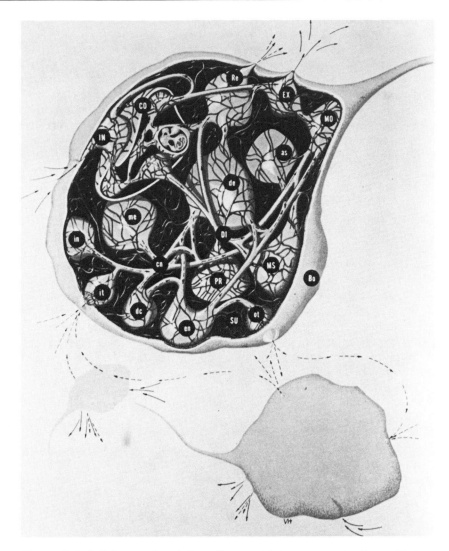

Figure 3-4. A living system interacting and intercommunicating with two others in its environment. Its subsystems which process both matter-energy and information are the Reproducer (Re) and Boundary (Bo). Its subsystems which process matter-energy are: Ingestor (IN); Distributor (DI); Converter (CO); Producer (PR); Matter-energy storage (MS); Extruder (EX); Motor (MO); Supporter (SU). Its subsystems which process information are: Input transducer (it); Internal transducer (in); Channel and net (cn); Decoder (dc); Associator (as); Memory (me); Decider (de); Encoder (en); Output transducer (ot). (From J. G. Miller, *Living Systems*, copyright 1978 by McGraw-Hill Book Company, New York. Reproduced with permission.)

three-dimensional arrangements of its components in neural circuits and can be conceptualized as the input transducer, internal transducer, channel and net, decoder, associator, memory, decider, encoder, and output transducer subsystems. Its basic temporal elements are its stable feedback processes that revolve around the assimilation and accommodation of information through the operations of schemes. Through assimilation information is transmitted in harmony with existing structures. Through accommodation structures are adjusted to harmonize with information entering the central nervous system. Positive and negative feedback maintain the steady state of the system. Its functions are expressed through the output of its major subsystems: the state regulating, information processing, language, managerial, and self systems.

As can be seen, the general theory of living systems suggests how to make observations and to conduct experiments on a wide range of phenomena with some assurance that they have relevance to each other. Without such a theory, a scientist does not know how to decide which of the overwhelming number of possible observations are worth making.

All of these considerations illustrate why general systems theory can be useful in understanding the needs of a specific child. A multisystem approach liberates us from the elusive quest for a single etiology for a child's problems. Attention to the multiple systems that impinge upon a child's performance in school provides a comprehensive basis for understanding that child's educational needs. Consequently children can be viewed in the context of their specific characters, families, peer groups, schools, communities, and societies. Morever, the concept of participant observer is useful in appreciating that the context of an interaction, particularly the behavior of the researcher or clinician, influences the person being observed. Even

the behavior of electrons depends upon the environmental context within which they exist (Bohm, 1980).

In the absence of systems thinking, three fallacies commonly are encountered (Marmor, 1983). They share a tendency to think of causation in linear, unifactorial, cause-and-effect terms rather than in terms of pluralistic, multifactorial dynamics. The first fallacy is biological reductionism, as when a single pill or cure is expected to be found for an educational disability. The second fallacy is psychological reductionism, as when behavior is explained on the basis of a single event in early life or faulty parenting. The third fallacy is sociological reductionism, as when school failure is explained simply by poverty. In the broadest sense, the failure to comprehend systems contributes to the disorder and antagonism in our society.

SUMMARY

The time has come for the social sciences to move beyond Newtonian to general systems thinking. Understanding learning problems in children depends upon transcending the linear assignment of simple causes of behavior to the level of multifactorial, transactional determinants interacting over time. This means a shift from vertical thinking of parallel but isolated pieces to horizontal thinking in which interrelationships between systems are recognized.

The general theory of living systems provides a framework for doing this, particularly for educational research. In contrast with closed nonliving systems, living systems are open and exchange information and matter with their surroundings. This book is concerned with living systems at the levels of cell, organ, organism, group, organization, and society. Within the boundaries of a living system are its components, its structures that are spatial relationships between components, and its processes that handle the input and output of information and matter-energy over time. The functions of a living system serve internal regulation and relations with the environment. As the essence of the human being, the central nervous system is the focal point of this book.

The relevance of systems thinking to problems in learning is evident, because they may be due to personal, interpersonal, educational, or social factors, or to varying mixtures of them. In addition to the essential factors that produce a problem in learning are reactions to learning failure itself.

The thesis of this book is that academic learning depends upon learning about two worlds—the outer and inner worlds of experience. Knowing about our outer world depends upon the ways in which we experience it. And our experiencing of the outer world depends upon our use and mastery of our inner world of sensations, images, and emotions that ultimately determine the degree to which we attend to and register stimuli from the outside world.

A coherent yet comprehensive approach to the learning problems children encounter in school is needed to provide a framework within which research can flow from theoretical models in which diagnosis can identify relevant characteristics that treatment can address.

In an effort to provide this framework, we first identify the social, school, classroom, and family factors that bear upon the development of the personal competencies children need to work in school. As a means of understanding the underlying factors that produce these competencies, we then describe our current knowledge of the structures and processes of the brain and the ways in which they function. Thereafter we trace the developmental stages of childhood as they pertain to learning the competencies needed for schoolwork.

II

The External World of Children

A report card on public education is a report card on the nation. Schools can rise no higher than the communities that surround them. It is in the public school that this nation has chosen to pursue enlightened ends for all its people.

Carnegie Foundation for the
Advancement of Teaching, 1983

THIS SECTION describes the critical systems that influence children— society, organizations, classrooms, peers, and families. Unless they are allied to support a particular child's efforts to succeed in school, they can pose significant barriers to that child's education.

A society usually corresponds to a nation. It is a self-sufficient system composed of organizations and lower levels of living systems. A culture is the fabric of a society, like the character of a person. It determines a society's modes of information processing, language, behavior, artifacts, and social structure. The pluralistic society of the United States is an expression of Judeo-Christian culture and many subcultures.

A society's view of children sets the tone for their education. An inherent ambivalence toward children in the United States leads to the waxing and waning of interest in education. To the extent that society values childhood as a preparation for adult responsibilities and productivity in work, attention is devoted to the quality of public education. To the extent that childhood is ignored, education suffers with the risk that the next generation of adults will be inadequately prepared to cope with the responsibilities of a democratic society. The ambivalence of many adults toward work is expressed in the public image of work as an economic necessity to be avoided when possible, rather than as a source of personal fulfillment. All of these factors contribute to confusion in children regarding the purposes of education.

Three institutions socialize children and transmit their cultural heritages. The first is the family, in which a child learns how to relate to people. The second is the peer culture through which children learn social relationships outside of the family. The third is the school in which children acquire skills and knowledge.

As an organization in terms of the general theory of living systems, a school system is composed of subsidiary organizations and groups, such as elementary schools and classrooms, and is part of community and societal suprasystems. Organizations are much like organs in their dependency upon suprasystems of which they are a part. There are no freestanding living organs, as there are organisms. For this fundamental reason, schools cannot be understood outside of the context of their communities and society.

In the United States, the public schools are instruments of public policies. Paradoxically, as schools are confronted with increasing expectations that they will socialize children, they encounter increasing constraints upon their capacities to do so. They have become industries in themselves preoccupied with the management of facilities and personnel in the context of federal, state, and local ideological and financial pressures. These considerations drain efforts to improve the professionalism of teachers. Most important, schools lack clear guidelines for evaluating the quality of their products—socially competent adults. Consequently schools are mired in the details of processing groups of children from yeaar to year with limited capacities to meet the needs of individual children over extended periods of time.

The classroom is the place in which schoolwork is performed. Thus the ecology and the atmosphere of the classroom play pivotal roles in the quality of education. It is the site of the critical interactions among teachers, students, and peers. It also is the arena in which power, revenge, and dependent motives are played out between children and teachers. Most important, it is the social field in which children learn the roles of students and how to relate to adults and peers. Mastering the role of student is a necessary prerequisite for successful schoolwork.

In their families children develop the basic foundations for academic learning: they learn how to trust others, solve problems, handle emotions, and assume responsibility for themselves. To the extent that parents are unable to impart these basic qualities, children are ill prepared to work in school. The influence of parents on character development has an impact upon the degree to which children become successful students. Family members also play key roles in the identification, management, and continuity of help for children with educational disabilities and handicaps.

A wealth of theoretical and experimental work on social and group processes has accumulated; however, most of it has been based on groups artificially brought together for experimental purposes. We need more applied knowledge about society and naturally occurring organizations and groups.

4

Society

There is a high correlation between school failure and low self-esteem or social failure. No society can long support the waste of talent and manpower that such failures represent.

Paul A. Kolers, 1968

Every society has formal and informal institutions charged with communicating its culture to each new generation. Because the United States is a pluralistic society with numerous subcultures, its process of socializing children is particularly varied and subject to evolutionary change.

The efforts of the United States to socialize children are intermingled with irrational and expedient elements. This is seen in the tendency of its social systems to recoil from crises rather than resolve them. Thus the relief of immediate discomforts is favored over long-range planning, which requires forebearance. As a result there is a vague awareness that day-to-day actions often fly in the face of social goals. This is particularly evident in society's attitude toward children. For a variety of reasons, the interests of children conflict with the short-term interests of adults. Whether in the form of child rearing for parents or school budgets for communities, children are burdensome. Because their value as contributing members of society is in the distant future, it is difficult to relate their parenting and schooling to their later productivity.

From a historical perspective, however, children in the United States have come a long way from the extremes of oppression to their current status in which even their legal rights are gaining recognition. Still, it is apparent that we have not accomplished enough for children to stave off the continued production of socially and educationally handicapped young people and adults through the cycle depicted in Figure 4-1. More specifically, some 17 percent of our children have emotional, social, educational, and physical handicaps, and another 21 percent probably are living in circumstances in which they are at risk of them. Identifying and helping these children are major challenges for society. The social consequences of not doing so are evident in crime, welfare dependency, and occupational failure (Westman, 1979a).

In particular, educational handicaps abound in delinquent youths. From one-half to three-quarters of delinquent populations have been reported to show at least two years' retardation in reading. Conversely, one-quarter of children with reading retardation display antisocial behavior (Lewis, D., et al, 1981; Robbins et al, 1983). Adults with schizophrenic and personality

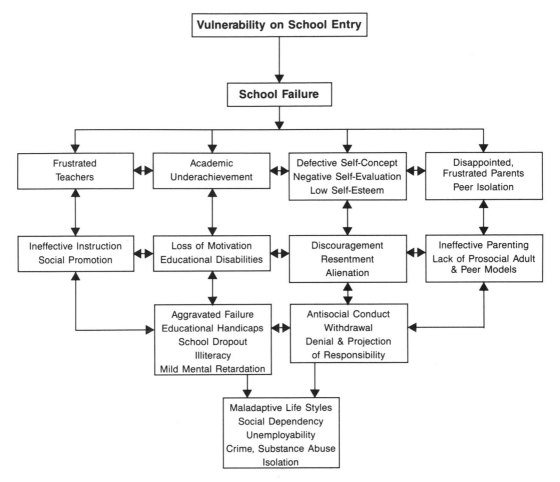

Figure 4-1. Social cost of school failure.

disorders also show deviance in their school backgrounds (Woerner et al, 1974; Knight & Bell, 1983).

Past efforts to help children have waxed and waned. A number of resistances to effective aid for children have resulted from the crisis–recoil nature of our society, as reflected in the tendency to deal with individual children by removing them from problem-generating situations in their homes and schools. Behind these practices lies the failure to plan for the long-range interests of children and their parents. As a result public policies that fragment fam-

ilies have been overdeveloped, and services that support and strengthen families are underdeveloped or nonexistent. Society has not been able to recognize effectively the link between a child's behavior in school and that child's family and life circumstances. For example, violence in homes, schools, and the streets instills chronic tension that interferes with the concentration of many children on their schoolwork (Bloch, 1978).

A more subtle factor that operates against the interests of children is the value judgment that only remuneration-gaining occupations are work. This has led to the degrading of homemaking, child rearing, and schoolwork, which are seen as less important than income-generating occupations. The financial value of these activities become apparent, however, as others are paid to care for one's children. Still, many children do not see an immediate reward from schoolwork and regard it as unimportant. This attitude is supported by a cultural value that prizes only remunerated productivity. In contrast, the superiority of elementary school Japanese and Chinese children in mathematics over children in the United States has been attributed to parental attitudes that support academic achievement and the involvement of both parents and children in schoolwork (Stevenson et al, 1986).

Early in this century, Maria Montessori (1974) called attention to what she termed universal prejudices against children. Akin to racism and sexism, agism is prejudice against the young and the old (Westman, 1979). Agism is evident in the attitude that adults always know what is best for children. As further examples, Montessori cited the false assumptions that children must be taught to learn, overlooking their innate thirst for learning; that children's minds are empty, overlooking their rich imaginations; and that young children do not work, overlooking the absorbing intensity of their play.

Thus agism and the association of valued work with remuneration have obscured the fact that children are working in their academic pursuits in school. Actually their work in school does have direct financial repercussions when seen as training for the work force in the light of the negative consequences of an inadequate education. If children's endeavors in school were regarded as work, public policy regarding education might be more realistic. If parenting were seen as having financial value, child rearing might be more highly valued.

To address these questions, a detailed examination of social attitudes toward work is in order. Specifically the personal qualities that make for success or failure at work in our society merit consideration. This will provide a background for understanding why social attitudes toward work influence whether or not children succeed in school.

THE NATURE OF WORK

Work can be defined as an activity carried out to maintain and advance the quality of life. Work also is subject to an array of overt and covert traditions, motivations, rewards, and sanctions. It connotes both pain and pleasure. There is an expectation in all societies that healthy members will perform some kind of work. Training in work habits accordingly is provided to some degree for children by every society (Neff, 1968).

Intriguingly, the motivations for work are both genetic and cultural. These two sources are anachronistic, however, as the evolutionary stage of our genes is at the level of our hunter–gatherer ancestors, and cultural values supporting work in the United States are derived from the last century.

We first consider the genetic aspects of work, which predestine an attraction to both personal competence and responsibility to other people. Then we assess the cultural values that permeate Western civilization, and specifically the United States. Finally, we consider the work style expected of children in school.

The Genetic Basis of Work

At the most fundamental level, in the terminology of physics, work is the expenditure of energy. Conversely, entropy is energy that is no longer capable of conversion into work. The total energy content of the universe is constant, and entropy is inexorably increasing—for example, birth death, value to waste, hot to cold, concentrated to dispersed, and order to disorder. In this sense life itself depends upon countering the universal trend toward entropy through the expenditure of energy, or work (Rifkin, 1980).

The grim fate of life on earth is illustrated by the fact that only about two dozen of the many thousands of species in existence at the beginning of the Mesozoic age have left any descendants, and almost all of the some 40,000 current species of vertebrate trace back to a handful of them (Wright, 1978). According to this perspective, the survival of our species depends upon actively working against a general trend toward extinction.

In evolutionary biology adaptation of a species is viewed as reproductive success of a population—keeping the genes of the population alive in future generations. Reproductive success of a population results from the reproductive success of its individual members. In turn the reproductive success of an individual depends upon effectively coping with the physical environment and guiding behavior according to the rules that are generally useful for the population in meeting its survival requirements and facilitating reproductive success. Such guidelines for behavior tend to be taught early in life, shaped by powerful rewards and punishments, and invested with strong emotions. Over long time spans, they prepare the young to fulfill the roles of adult life. In the course of mammalian, and especially primate, evolution, adaptive behavior that contributes to species survival confers a powerful selective advantage upon the more highly developed individuals (Hamburg et al, 1975).

Thus far homo sapiens has been eminently successful. Human beings became upright and began to use tools some three or four million years ago. One million years ago, humans probably had some form of

spoken language as they gathered food and hunted game. Fifty thousand years ago, Cro-Magnons were using blade tools and probably employed language as we now know it today. A mere 10,000 years ago, groups of people settled in villages and engaged in farming and the domestication of animals. About 5000 years ago, cities emerged, and human activities extended beyond farming. Subsequently the dramatic changes in human behavior during recorded history have been primarily due to cultural transmission rather than genetic factors (Fishbein, 1976).

Social learning by direct imitation or teaching by intimate associates is at the heart of cultural transmission. A skill such as language is acquired by simple inexpensive social learning, whereas academic skills are acquired through more costly didactic learning (Boyd & Richerson, 1985).

Nevertheless, our success as a species depends upon canalized orientations toward life (Wilson, 1980). Canalization is a genetic process in which genes compensate for, or collaborate with, each other to ensure that brain functions attain essential behavioral targets. Laddington (1962) considered the following targets as crucial elements in the successful adaptation of humans: (1) cooperative hunting, (2) food sharing, (3) tool manufacture, (4) husband–wife reciprocities, (5) symbolic communication, and (6) rule giving and following. Accordingly, genetic interaction occurred to ensure the canalization of the following behaviors essential to achieve those targets: (1) manual motor skills, (2) sustained attention and adaptible memory, (3) flexible spatial organization, (4) affiliative attachment bonding, (6) a drive for mastery, and (7) rewarding and inhibiting emotions.

Consequently, as a result of these innate capacities, homo sapiens has been described as the political, ethical, and cultural animal. The hallmark of humans is group life with reciprocal obligations.

Other animals show group cohesiveness; however, only human beings are fully genetically programmed to be reciprocally obligated, or responsible, to each other through lifelong attachment bonds. Together with the valuation inherent in pleasure and displeasure, these bonds form the biological basis for human values of basic goodness and badness (Simpson, 1949; Pugh, 1977).

Thus genetically based, human motivation is not only for individual survival but also to contribute to the survival of a group (Axelrod, 1984; Fishbein, 1976). From an evolutionary point of view, this necessitated a clear differentiation between the ingroup and the potentially dangerous outgroup, expressed in the form of foreigner, or stranger, anxiety (West, 1967). Individual goodness for the hunter– gatherer came from satisfaction through self-control subordinate to the interests of the group. Coupling of the affiliative and mastery drives led to a need for self-esteem dependent upon the approval of others. Goodness in the ingroup, then, was for one to become reciprocally obligated to other members of the ingroup; to be bad was to exert against a member of the ingroup behavior appropriate only toward the outgroup.

With the emergence of urban civilization, humans had to learn how to live closely with ingroup members and to deal with outgroup strangers. In order to do so elaborate cultural rules were needed to manage individual aggressive behavior (Burnet, 1978). To be good in the ingroup also meant to contribute to the collective welfare through work. In primitive cultures there is no clear distinction between work and leisure. Work is simply one of the conditions of existence. Through work humans domesticated animals, exploited the land, and learned to control many of the inimical forces of nature. Through work we also developed an efficient means of subjugating and killing fellow humans.

The survival of homo sapiens, for better or for worse, is the product of work. Without work we would not have become human at all (Neff, 1968).

Still, we are confronted with a conflict between society's aim of producing literate, competent citizens and evolution's single and only criterion of success—an increase in the number of individuals reproductively active as one generation succeeds another. Our social systems protect many individuals from survival-of-the-fittest natural selection. Because we foster the survival of maladapted individuals, there is a current downward trend in genetically determined intelligence. There is a negative correlation between family size and intelligence, and the less intelligent have more children than the more intelligent. Even if only made possible by financial aid from the state and the supervision of welfare workers, the reproductive success of the less intelligent marks them as biologically superior. Insofar as the relevant characteristics are genetic, they would be the sort of people to inherit the future, although productive workers would still be needed to provide the leadership and capital to support them; the balance between the productive and the nonproductive at some point becomes critical (Burnet, 1978).

The Cultural Basis for Work

The *Old Testament* tells us that one consequence of the expulsion from Eden was that people must earn their bread through the sweat of their brows. However, a stark counterpoint is the persistent human yearning to free ourselves from the need to work, as in the religious heavens, which are portrayed as workless utopias.

The work orientation of Western civilization is the result of trial and error. Much learning and relearning had to be done along the way before work in industrial countries enabled people to obtain more than mere subsistence wages for their labors. Ways of work and ways of living with it both had to be learned (Anderson, 1964).

In the industrial countries, many people have the proclivity for imposing work on themselves. In colonial times South Sea islanders asked, "Why does that mad dog of an Englishman go out in the noonday sun?" when they sought out the shade. The modern work ethic owes much to the Puritan attitude toward work in which "man works that he might have joy" and those who do not work may "fall into evil ways."

The regularity of Puritan life and its stern economy of time tended to produce persons of business capacity, ready for the management of affairs and the conduct of global undertakings. Puritanism accompanied commercial and industrial expansion and was the forerunner of the Industrial Revolution. This way of thinking came into full flower in America and spread westward with the nation's frontier. Work became part of the credo of success. People not only had to work, but they also had to be knowledgeable. If people did not do either, it was their fault. In the United States, personally motivated and disciplined work based upon self-control became prized objectives.

There is a cultural counterforce, however that bears upon self-control. The United States was born in circumstances that denied individual freedoms. It accordingly places a special value on such freedom. Consequently, there is a tension between the rights of individuals and their responsibilities to each other. The tension between freedom to express oneself and self-control may be expressed in ambivalence toward work. As an offshoot of the emphasis on individual freedom, a misguided emphasis on self-fulfillment also has produced unstructured classrooms filled with children who lack self-discipline (Etzioni, 1982).

The tension between self-expression and self-control is heightened by frontier values that nourish the fantasies of those who feel oppressed by puritanical values. Courageous risk-taking is a prominent frontier value that, in the extreme, is expressed through bravado and unbridled aggressiveness, as seen in heroes who get what they want when they want it. A result is the glorification of impulsiveness and magical wish gratification that subtly conveys the message that work is not a necessary component of success. As the United States became more urbanized and settled, many of the robust ways of asserting one's importance disappeared, although the need to prove one's worth in aggressive ways still exists as expressed in antisocial patterns of violence, drunkenness, and ruthless ambition (Mendelowitz, 1963).

Furthermore, self-determination is supported by puritanical and frontier values that encourage individuals to aspire to greater achievement and self-enhancement. But self-determination has a particularly devastating effect on children whose parents believe that they learn best for themselves and so permit them to follow their wishes without appropriate guidance. As a result these children have too much responsibility for themselves, and so their inevitable errors and miscalculations cause frustration and disappointment for both themselves and their parents.

Because imposing social controls on individuals is anathema in the United States, our society has a particular stake in promoting self-control in children. Without self-control children cannot achieve social competency and cope with the stresses of life, particularly schooling, and become competent adults, able to exercise the self-control and responsibility inherent in citizenship. The most evident academic competencies that children need to acquire are the basic skills of self-expression in the form of reading and ciphering, so that they ultimately can participate in a democratic society and provide for their own needs.

In the Western world, the increasing number of people who have been liberated from immediate concern with economic survival has elevated the importance of achievement in other areas: a sensitive and responsive marital relationship, challenging and significant work, the respect and approval of friends, identification with one's community, and a stimulating and fulfilling life.

Another social influence on children's attitudes toward work is the impact of television viewing upon their values, attitudes, and behavior (Berry & Mitchell-Kernan, 1982; Bryant & Anderson, 1983; Howe, 1983). The most powerful features of television viewing are the passive, non-participatory absorption of time and the reduction of spontaneity, conversational opportunities with other persons, free play, and reading. Dependency upon external stimulation and structure can be a result. Furthermore, for school-age children, unlike listening to the radio or records, viewing television is a strong distraction from studying.

Through the engaging and readily available media, our children are exposed to the problems of adult life and to the seductions of becoming consumers. Furthermore, the dramatization of hedonistic life-styles conflicts with exhortations that they should lead disciplined, productive lives. Many children, particularly the economically disadvantaged, are exposed to alluring images of adulthood without being assisted to place these in perspective and to understand how they were attained.

In the light of this background, work ordinarily is thought of as producing goods and services for an externally generated reward. This is not the whole story, however, because the creative process also constitutes work motivated by internally generated urges to achieve an objective, such as a musical skill, or to produce a product, such as a painting. Work also may relieve tension and boredom (Kramer, 1977). Work, therefore, need not be unpleasant. It can be creatively motivated and rewarded by the genetically based pleasure of mastery and fulfilling of reciprocal obligations to others in addition to fulfilling a culturally based sense of importance in one's group. It is the displeasure associated with work that has overwhelmed our genetic and cultural motivations to work. Fortunately counterbalancing technology can be used to reduce drudgery and encourage pleasure in work (Scott, 1970).

Work Styles

One's work style is a semiautonomous area of one's personality, which is a product of a prolonged period of the social learning of more or less enduring habits. Work difficulties then imply a deficiency in the development of one's work style (Neff, 1968).

The source of one's work style is in the genetically determined affiliative and mastery drives in addition to society's expectation that one should play a productive role. In its earliest form, children are confronted with the expectation of work when they enter school and begin to struggle with the expectation of achievement. They must learn to give up play for protracted periods of the day. They must become aware of time, meet schedules, and complete prescribed tasks. They must learn how to deal with authority. They, also, must find a place in their peer culture. At the same time, they are bombarded with messages about the virtues of working, many of which are contradictory.

Most children are confronted with external demands to achieve, which become internalized to varying degrees and in different forms. Once internalized, the expectation of work can become a stimulus for a range of feelings of pleasure, gratification, anxiety, guilt, or inadequacy. As a consequence coping behaviors appear and eventually consolidate into the particular work style of an individual. Some children may not have internalized society's valuation of productive roles. Some may have done so but be in conflict with other demands of the work situation in school, such as relating appropriately to peers and authority figures and meeting standards imposed by others. Many children's work styles are suitable only for certain kinds of tasks. For example, some can work better if a task is routine than if it requires innovation. For some children who have not found ways of being valued by others for their personal qualities, work provides a sense of importance. In the Western world, work has come to be one of the major components of self-evaluation and valuation by others (Neff, 1968).

Our knowledge of the responses of adults to work may be helpful in understanding children who identify with those adults. The factors involved in producing satisfaction in work for adults differ from those that lead to work dissatisfaction (Backer, 1973). Those that produce satisfaction are motivational factors related to personal growth: achievement, responsibility, possibility of advancement and recognition, and the nature of the work itself. Those that produce dissatisfaction are environmental factors related to the avoidance of discomfort: status; relationships with supervisors, peers and subordinates; employment policies and administration; job security; working conditions; personal life; and salary.

Five work styles appear to lead to adult failure in work (Neff, 1968). They characterize the following individuals:

1. People who do not value productive work and are dominated by impulse gratification. Their cultural background may not embrace the work ethic.
2. People who respond to the expectation of productivity with fear and anxiety so that they believe they are inept and incapable of being productive.

3. People who perceive work expectations as restrictive and hostile.
4. People who are dependent, lack initiative, and need continuous supervision.
5. Overprotected handicapped people who do not believe that usual performance standards apply to them.

As will be seen these factors are important in the ways children approach work as well. Children's work styles will be discussed in greater depth in Chapter 28.

SOCIAL VALUES AND CHILD REARING

Governments have well-established ways of responding to public needs for income, adequate housing, and health care. But they cannot cope with problems in human relationships and subjective states, such as alienation, boredom, job dissatisfaction, fear, loneliness, resentment, and other conditions that diminish the quality of people's lives. Governments do not have a clear sense of how widespread these problems are or of how to deal with them.

More specifically, the increasing tendency of government to assume parenting functions has blurred the question of whether families or government should assume ultimate responsibility for children, and especially children with special needs. As a result governments and families create unrealistic expectations of each other and distrust the competence of the other with disappointing results (Kronick, 1981).

The social values of Industrial Age societies are oriented toward things rather than people through the reinforcement of qualities that shape people as producers and consumers. Examples of valued characteristics are excellence, expertise, privacy, and conformity. Industrial Age values are based upon vertical, linear thinking in which each characteristic has a good, or high, and bad, or low, extreme. Success or failure is easily measured by external appearances of a characteristic on these scales. The vertical nature of the values, also, leaves an open end at each extreme so that in the absence of negative feedback, such as a saturated market, Industrial Age systems become uncontrolled through feedforward mechanisms. Thus these values can have untoward effects.

If the productivity and consumerism enhancing values of the Industrial Age are applied to parenting, the overindulgence of children in contemporary society can be seen as a logical outcome. Children have been afforded material affluence, and immediate gratification has been encouraged.

The pursuit of excellence places a premium upon being the best as assessed by standards reflecting quality and quantity. This value ensures that products will be competitive in the marketplace and motivates people to produce them. However, valuing excellence based upon external evidence of achievement sets an unattainable objective for most children and their parents.

Respect for expertise acknowledges that special knowledge and training enable the efficient achievement of excellence. Unfortunately, however, the inordinate reliance on expertise has deprived parents of confidence in their own intuitions for guidance in child rearing. The competence and success of parenting in what are regarded as primitive societies are ignored by many parents, who seek advice from experts, rather than relying on their own cultural customs and values.

Privacy is an important Industrial Age value that permits businesses and individuals to compete with each other by protecting their advantages. It also is a cherished protection of individuals against intervention from external quarters. On the other hand, privacy has reinforced the tendency of human beings to conceal their weaknesses and misadventures. Thus barriers to communication lead to alienation within family units, as they do in larger social systems.

Conformity originally ensured the dominion of royalty, and more recently of nations and corporations. At the level of nations, it has been important in deploying patriotism for economic and political purposes. In families, however, the parental expectation of unquestioning conformity, particularly of adolescents, obscures the reciprocal nature of parent–child relationships.

As an embodiment of the puritanical and frontier values of the Industrial Age, the ideal person has been a self-contained stoic man unmoved by pain, fear, or tenderness. He does not show evidence of enthusiasm or inspiration but gets what he wants when he wants it. He does this always for what is "right."

Fortunately, there is a contrasting set of values unique to the culture of the United States that promotes productivity in the context of individual freedom through teamwork. These values have made it possible for individuals to achieve material affluence through the advancement of common interests. The emphasis upon teamwork in competitive athletics and corporations provides a model for personal gain through the success of groups within organizations.

One of these values is personal competence so that social, academic, athletic, and work skills are prized qualities. Personal competence, also, provides an individual satisfaction through a sense of mastery. Personal pride is a quality particularly emphasized in the United States in terms of self-concept and self-esteem.

Adaptability to change is a positively valued quality characteristic of the United States, a nation that models maintaining solidarity in the face of challenge and ambiguity. The flexibility of national policies has permitted adaptation to changing national and international conditions. This capacity also is prized in individuals.

Justice is a value that underlies the impulse toward civil rights at the national level and reasonable child-rearing practices at the family level. An offshoot is equality of opportunity for a heterogeneous population and emphasis on commonalities among people. However, if indiscriminantly applied, these corollaries can blur appropriate distinctions between childhood and adulthood and between fathers and mothers.

Another factor that is increasingly affecting attitudes toward children is the so-called Information Age which has been ushered in by the efficient transmission of information that is removing barriers between individuals, nations, and continents. Television brings the world together through the vivid portrayal of events in the same way for everyone. Information about the world is permeating Western and Eastern societies, making it increasingly difficult to isolate oneself from others and world events. Individuals are increasingly confronted with their interdependence upon others, and the problems confronting children are receiving more attention.

The horizontal and multisystem information exposure of the Information Age reinforces values that support community relationships. This can foster awareness and acceptance of others. For many people the emphasis is shifting from being well off to well-being. For them success is measured not only by externally evident material criteria but also by the internal experience of purpose and meaning of life.

In a multisystem framework, the many levels of influence on children can be recognized (Brim, 1975). At the level of society, technology, law, media, and the economy can be seen as influencing children. At the organizational level, families, schools, and child-caring systems can be recognized as important to children. At the small-group level, those dyadic relationships in which children live can be appreciated as the actual mediators of influence on children. In this context the concept of child advocacy is helpful in focusing the attention of all of these systems upon realistically identifying and meeting the special needs of children (Westman, 1979a).

The multisystem view recognizes children as parts of family units. Thus the interests of children are served by policies that strengthen families, such as part-time employment for adults and adjustment of workplaces to families so that parents can care for their own children rather than remunerate others for such care.

SUMMARY

In the pluralistic, democratic society of the United States, the challenge is to maintain fundamental constancies that provide children with the opportunities and structure they need to develop reliable social skills and a positive outlook on life. This is important because our times are confusing for children. They are asked to take more responsibility for an increasing number of complex tasks as support for their families dwindles. They receive mixed messages about work. Moreover, our society's overwhelming emphasis on productivity, success, and excellence generates feelings of inadequacy in those who do not excel academically, athletically, or socially. A child may be affable, intelligent, creative, and cooperative, yet become discouraged in the atmosphere of our schools.

Our genes provide a biological basis for reciprocal obligations with other persons and personal mastery. When these human tendencies are drawn out through adequate parenting, personal satisfaction from mastery provides the basis for success in school. Because the expression of these genetically programmed capacities depends upon the formation of attachment bonds and learning academic and social skills, a large number of children, who are regarded as deviant, are products of inadequate child-rearing environments.

Equity in education will come not simply from legislation or funds. Our society must recognize the relationship between schooling and adult productivity and make a commitment to maximizing the educational success of our children. Then the knowledge of how to educate everyone, particularly those for whom academic success has been elusive in the past, can be realized (Graham, 1980). In so doing the delicate balance of doing things for people and helping them to do it for themselves is crucial. In extremes there are those who emphasize giving resources to people and those who emphasize expecting people to manage their own lives. Largely untapped is the possibility of ensuring for each child experiences that maximize the development of personal competency. The basic genetic and cultural factors generally impinging upon our children are in favor of success in school. At the same time, there are specific genetic and cultural factors that pose barriers to academic learning.

Children with learning problems in school cannot be realistically understood outside of their social contexts. Because they are susceptible to national problems, such as inflation, recession, unemployment, poverty, racial discrimination, workplace insensitivity to parenting, and ecological pollution, children require special consideration in the formulation of social and public policies.

Children are not only the objects of our hopes but also the recipients of our ambivalence. Because of our high hopes, we build child-care centers, schools, clinics, and universities. Because of our ambivalence, we deny children the best of their cultural heritages and the assurance of supportive child rearing. Because of adult anxieties, we model less than confidence in their futures.

No longer an economic asset, but now a cost, and no longer dependable support in old age, but a source of worry in the present, children are left without functions beyond those of providing affection and existential meaning for their parents and receptive adults. These functions, however, may be just what are needed by adults in a society afflicted by loneliness and lack of meaning. The greatest hope for our children lies in the recognition that they can enhance the quality of life for everyone now. In the long range, the survival of our society depends upon how we prepare our children for adulthood.

5

Schools

With all the huge amounts of money, time and effort thrown into the educational enterprise, we still find that pupils have to be coaxed, wheedled, commanded and forced to become the rational creatures we need to be.

Sydney Harris, 1983

At the beginning of this century, schools aspired to prepare children for vocations and citizenship. At the same time, the most obedient child was considered the best pupil. Mischievous and original children were martyrs. Only the easygoing could keep some of their own individuality and slip through school (Key, 1909). In certain fundamental ways, schools have not changed.

Schools are affected by locally elected school boards whose budgets are linked to taxation levels and ideological concerns of the times (Kinder, 1978). The economic pressures confronting schools tend to limit the focus of education to those students who can thrive in competitive, group-oriented environments. As a result most children with academic learning problems receive less than an adequate education (Adelman & Taylor, 1983; Tomlinson, 1987). They have no choice but to go to school, because laws mandate their attendance, but paradoxically, once they are enrolled in school, the responsibility for learning becomes theirs (Rosner, 1979).

Over the years, as schools have honored excellence that only a few children could hope to attain, most have felt less than successful and many have felt deeply wounded (Kagan, 1981). This feeling lingers in the ambivalent attitudes many adults have toward schools. More critically, an inherent tension has grown between the socializing and educational missions of the schools (Nyberg & Egan, 1981).

THE ROLE OF SCHOOLS IN SOCIALIZATION

Schools socialize children in two ways. The first is in the role of student. The second is more ambiguous socialization for later roles in society (Mercer, 1980; Selakovich, 1984). Schools are held responsible for ensuring that children accept the idea that they should be students, that they appreciate the importance of education, and that they cooperate actively in the educational process. Indeed, many of the learning difficulties children encounter in school are a result of failures to assume these elements of the role of student (Boocock, 1972). This makes it particularly difficult to develop the commitments and capacities prerequisite for adult vocational, citizenship, and family roles (Hills, 1976).

One of the factors that has detracted from the socialization of children in school is the teaching of science and the humanities as separate activities unrelated to contemporary living—which has been construed to mean that science and cultural heritage are unrelated. This has happened, in part, because the sciences originated outside of the religious tradition from which schools descended. As a result science tends to be seen as distinct from cultural values, so that facts are presented without a value system to provide them with meaning (Rifkin, 1980).

Many educated adults are unable to bring meaningful judgments to questions of science and technology. For example, in one study half of college sophomores tested did not realize that four-pound and two-pound lead weights fell at the same speed or that water in a tipped glass remains level (Singer & Benassi, 1981). Many believed that islands float in the ocean and that the moon is fixed in the sky and is visible only at night. These startling findings raise questions about the effectiveness of scientific education at the most elementary level. It appears that science has been taught as a set of compartmentalized facts to be acquired by rote methods so that students still rely on intuition when confronted with practical scientific issues.

There is a need to help students understand that science is not a collection of isolated facts but a unified and consistent view of the world (Saxon, 1982). By the same token, students need an appealing introduction to the humanities as an entrée into a life of enjoyment of the world of ideas and art.

Our schools were created for a different time and place, not our present information-rich society. The most important goals now are the mastery of basic communication skills, problem solving, the management of knowledge, and self-management (Anderson, 1973). Rather than bombard children with information about various subjects, it is important to teach them about themselves: how they listen, understand, recall, retain, and communicate. In essence, children need to learn how they learn and to maximize the products of their efforts.

The hidden curriculum of schools is society building itself (Richmond, 1973). The encouragement and refinement of human qualities actually are the most important goals of our culture—to be a good friend, to be a considerate mate, and to become a contributing citizen—yet we do not prepare our young people to be enjoyable and reliable persons (Smith, S.L., 1980).

Several social values undermine the education of children. Because of the strong anti-intellectual current in American frontier communities, brawn and bravado have seemed more important than brain and sensitivity. Moreover, the emphasis on the consumption of material goods suggests little use for the goals of education. Thus frontier bravado and consumerism have obscured the inclinations of many children toward creative activity as means of enhancing the quality of their lives (Mendelowitz, 1963; Rockefeller, 1983).

An even greater problem has been the way in which adults tend to teach children. Rather than building upon children's natural inclinations, we seek to supplant these with adult ways (Bettelheim, 1976). Many adults have lost the perspectives of their own childhoods. They expect children's minds to function as do their own and overlook the fact that a mature understanding of themselves and the world developed as slowly as their bodies. Since children lack the language to describe the uniqueness of their worlds, they have no choice but to accept the adult version while recognizing the disparity between the two.

This is illustrated, in particular, by adult views of what children's literature should be.

Children's literature is an important interface between the world of adults and that of children. It can strengthen the capacity for fantasy, stretch the imagination, and permit empathic identification with other persons and one's cultural heritage (Goldings, 1968; Mallet, 1984). The bulk of current children's literature, however, attempts to entertain or inform but fails to stimulate and nurture those resources children need most in order to cope with difficult human problems.

Some adults present children with their current social preoccupations in the belief that the toddler needs an early push into contemporary academic, artistic, and athletic activities and should develop an awareness of the grim intensity of adult life. Other adults believe that children should be exposed only to the sunny side of things. Unfortunately most believe that children must be diverted from what trouble them most: formless anxieties and frightening fantasies.

Adult-oriented television stimulates children's violent fantasies in realistic rather than imaginary life situations, consequently, children may be so preoccupied with television shows they watched the night before that they daydream about them in the classroom. Comic books also can undermine the interest of some children in the basic techniques of reading by conditioning them to look for pictures to explain the text. It seems it is more pleasant and less strenuous to daydream about what one has seen in pictures than to learn to read (Mosse, 1982).

For a story to hold a child's attention, it must entertain and arouse curiosity. But to enrich the child's life, it must also stimulate imagination, be attuned to anxieties and aspirations, and suggest solutions to perturbing problems (Bettelheim, 1976). To master the psychological problems of growing up, a child needs to have conscious awareness of the derivatives of unconscious fantasies. This awareness can be achieved less through rational comprehension of the nature and content of the unconscious and more by becoming familiar with it consciously through fantasizing about stories that resonate with unconscious urges. Subjected only to the rational teachings of others, young children bury their beliefs, which remain untouched by reality. When unconscious fantasies are denied entrance into awareness, a child's conscious mind may become crippled by rigid, defensive attempts to control them (Bettelheim, 1976).

For young children fairytales convey culturally tested messages that the struggle against difficulties is an intrinsic part of human existence. Evil and virtue are omnipresent and clearly presented. Young children gain more problem-resolution ability from fairytales and myths than from adult reasoning. They trust fairytales because the world view espoused there is in accord with their own magical, animistic thinking. The resurgence of interest in McGuffey's readers with their practical morality reflects this need.

Thus the purposes of education can be better served by integrating the teaching of the sciences, the humanities, and the arts into the context of our evolving cultural heritage at levels appropriate to the ages of children. Without the ability to comprehend education's short-range goals of developing personal coping skills and the ultimate goal of preparing them for adulthood, children wonder why they must endure schoolwork. Schools thus have a responsibility for developing children's values so that they can grasp the relationship between school and becoming educated members of society (Sugarman, 1973).

As we leave the Industrial Age and enter the Information Age, the Newtonian scientific view in which stocks of isolated facts are collected is being replaced by a view of the world as a web of interrelated phenomena. In this light academic learning is not a tool with which to carve up the world and fashion it into something else but a method to help us understand better how to live in it. The concept of "man against nature" is being replaced by the concept of "people in nature" (Rifkin, 1980).

THE QUEST FOR INDIVIDUALIZED EDUCATION

Although the history of education in the United States is studded with innovations, the basic problems of schooling relate to old issues: teacher–pupil ratios, classroom discipline, and the practical relevance of curricula. Foremost is the persistent inability of our schools to provide the individualized education called for in the early decades of this century. Lip service is paid to individualization, but implementation of this concept is ill-defined and differs vastly among classrooms and school systems (Sapir & Nitzburg, 1973). This can be attributed to the fact that schools are designed to process groups, not individuals, and must operate on a cost basis. Because of the size of classes, teachers cannot fully attend to each child's individuality. There also may be little tolerance for children who differ from the majority, as evident in the tendency to equate variance with abnormality (Torrance & Myers, 1972).

The wide range of abilities within each grade has been obvious for years. For example, the achievement scores of one group of seven-year-olds' ranged from first- to sixth-grade level, and for a group of ten-year-olds, the range was from first- to ninth-grade level. On the basis of age norms rather than grade norms, the range of educational ages in a group of children, all of whom had spent three and one-half years in school, was from six to 15 years. In other words, the child in the group with the lowest score knew no more than the average child just beginning school whereas the highest scorer was already at the high-school level (Hildreth, 1950). In view of such extremes, the barriers to individualizing education have been virtually insurmountable in graded schools.

PHILOSOPHIES OF EDUCATION

Three philosophies underlie the variety of approaches to education (Dobson & Dobson, 1981; Wolfgang & Glickman, 1980). The first is interventional, following the ideas of Watson, Thorndike, Skinner, and Engelmann. It assumes that children learn appropriate behavior as a result of environmental influences. A child is regarded as a receptacle of the knowledge, values, and skills of a culture in the tradition of Rousseau.

The second philosophy is interactional, following the ideas of Dewey, Lewin, Bruner, Piaget, Driekurs, and Glasser. It assumes that children learn skills best through experience and that each child discovers a personal reality in the world.

The third approach is noninterventional, following the ideas of Maslow, May, Perls, Rogers, Gordon, Berne, and Simon. It assumes that a student learns self-discipline through self-realization. The child is regarded as an observer who gains understanding through listening, watching, feeling, and speaking, in addition to being taught.

A melding of these philosophies can be productively applied to the educational issues of grading, classroom discipline, ability grouping, student motivation, the quality of teachers, and parental and community involvement in schools.

Ideological, bureaucratic, and economic influences, however, are much stronger than these educational philosophies in influencing educational practices

(Popkewitz et al, 1982). In general children are expected to listen to what is being taught, to note what is being said, to comprehend, to retain, to recall, and, finally, to display that knowledge in performance on tests, in essays, and in classroom responses. The expectations may be traditional rather than functional, such as through adherence to the Palmer method of cursive writing in spite of the advantages of printing and italic writing (Getty & Dubay, 1983). Throughout schooling it is assumed erroneously that children simply need to have information presented in order to be able to absorb and use it.

Curriculum innovations that do not take into account the traditions of schooling have been notoriously unsuccessful. The most dramatic example was the failure of "new math" following the 1957 orbiting of Russia's Sputnik. Although introduced to make learning mathematics easier and to point children in the direction of scientific careers, new math was taught traditionally by rote like the old math, and the children's level of consternation and perplexity remained the same (Sarason, 1971). Elementary school teachers, in particular, are the most comfortable when teaching the memorized intricacies of reading, writing, and arithmetic. It is the rare teacher who has training in how to tap the variety of children's learning styles (Dixon, 1983).

Modern information technology has great potential for innovative education. As different devices and systems are brought together to combine their effects, multipurpose systems can serve learners in many ways, both as individuals and as small groups (Hawkridge, 1983). Audiovisual devices and microcomputers offer advantages and also pose disadvantages. For example, talking computers can be used to teach three-year-olds to write before they can read and to type before they can spell. The increasing use of microcomputers offers the hope of more actively engaging children in the educational process (O'Neil,

1981). Care will be needed, however, to use them in ways that will expand upon rather than replace classroom teaching.

As a supplement to traditional schools, an educational utility is a delivery system for a vast array of software linked to desktop computers (Educational Utility Group). Learners also can interact with others via telephone lines and even satellites. Home computers can be plugged into the system for homework, adult learning, and information services, making schools community resource centers. The greatest advantage to the learner is self-pacing: the opportunity for remediation where needed without embarrassment and for acceleration where appropriate. This opens the way for the development of sophisticated technologies for teaching attentional and organizing skills that improve self-confidence and performance.

As we look ahead, it is likely that education in the future will apply the best of the three educational philosophies mentioned earlier through learning from practical experience. Apprenticeship may once again take on the importance it had in previous periods of history. Large, centralized schools may give way to learning environments, including home videotape centers. Going to school may mean going into the community to learn. Many institutions can teach in varied and powerful ways. An educational system could ally a cluster of these, so that the family, the college, the church collegium, the communications media, the workplace, and the larger community could contribute to children's educational interests (Martin & Harrison, 1972; Sizer, 1973).

BUREAUCRATIC PROBLEMS

Schools have become increasingly industrialized. Textbooks are standardized nationally, and testing has become mechanized.

This is not surprising, because mandatory schooling was introduced to prepare children for an industrialized society (Selakovich, 1984). Schools have reached full industrialization, however, at a time when it is becoming obsolete.

School systems have developed their own momentum, and the consumers, the children, are frequently overlooked in their operations. Schools are industries dominated as much by the management of their physical plants as by their educational mission (Dreeben, 1976). School administrators need systems analysis as an approach to planning, managing, and budgeting at least six sectors: students, academic production, nonacademic production, personal resources, physical facilities, and administrative control.

Schools suffer from the same ills as do traditional industries when workers are ignored. Children do poorly in school today, in part because they sense a lag between what and how they are learning in school and what is happening in the rest of the world. The result may be shoddy workmanship, absenteeism, and lack of commitment to the job of schooling (Elkind, 1981).

The leverage used to motivate students varies widely. For some children it may be maintaining self-respect in classrooms in which performance is publically evaluated. For others it may be achieving grades that will please parents or circumvent punishment (Dreeben, 1976). For other children, however, life outside of school is such that successful school performance has a low or nonexistent priority.

The most profound motivation to work comes from the sense of recognized personal growth and responsibility. Neither of these can flourish easily in bureaucratic situations (Herzberg et al, 1959). For the supervisor, or teacher, the opportunities to exercise personal judgment may be limited by a framework of rules in which authority is that of a position rather than of a person.

There can be little sense of achievement and little perception of growth in the exercise of authority according to "the book." For the subordinate, or the student—and in a bureaucracy everyone is a subordinate—the situation is as discouraging. The rules, as interpreted by the supervisor from "the book," determine not only what is to be done, but how it is to be done. The exercise of ingenuity and initiative is discouraged, and few rewards are offered for departures from rules.

The reaction of organizations to policy changes in the long run is often opposite to their reaction in the short run. Changing their performance is difficult, because adjustment processes that keep them in a steady state are powerful and difficult to counteract (Miller, 1978). Massive resistance to change in schools also is generated by government funding policies, credentialing procedures, and school board considerations; by personal investments of time, money, and prestige in current arrangements; and by the security of the status quo. Schools are under pressure to reduce problems and improve test scores. Thus many schools are more willing to try quick cures, especially the purchase of new hardware and materials, rather than to evaluate programs carefully in order to bring about significant and sustained change. Most problems between teachers, students, and parents result from management practices that do not incorporate human relations, child development, and organizational perspectives (Comer, 1980).

To overcome the problems of bureaucratization in schools, the public image of teachers must be clarified so that the professional stature of educators is recognized. The personal qualities necessary for teaching far exceed those required for technical occupations. Even with adroit accommodations and compromise, the work load of many teachers is still crushing, although they are paid less than peers in semiskilled blue-collar jobs and novices in other white-collar professions. As a result many highly motivated teachers have been exhausted by trying to reach and manage their students within the demands of their bureaucracies. Career ladders must be structured to increase the professional responsibilities of experienced teachers, whose salaries should be the same as middle managers in business (Graham, 1984).

The effective teacher avoids the pitfalls of bureaucratization through skills in interpersonal relations and because of a devotion to helping children learn and grow as human beings. Rather than being technicians who apply prescribed solutions to problems and are not expected to exercise judgment and evaluate results, teachers are professionals who need training in eclectic approaches for dealing with children in diverse classroom environments (Wolfgang & Glickman, 1980).

Teachers have not been adequately prepared to deal with children who have differing learning styles. They need solid training in theory, a broad exposure to methods and techniques, and supervised practicums under master teachers. They need training in child development and behavioral observation skills. Just as important, they need the support of administrators who convey a sense of excitement about the purposes and importance of education.

Requirements to pursue degrees rather than job-related skills pose problems for teachers. The bureaucratic requirement of a master's degree, for example, can negatively affect teaching when it places demands upon teachers' time without advancing teaching skills. In-service training and staff development programs, which may have more practical application than graduate education courses, often are not formally recognized as advancing professional status.

In their daily work, teachers need support from master teachers, supervisors, principals, and school administrators in dealing with frustrating children (Smith, S.L., 1980). They need someone to talk to about their concerns, materials, and lessons. The support of teachers determines the quality of education of children.

EVALUATING THE EFFECTIVENESS OF EDUCATION

Originally intended to prepare workers for an industrial society, schools have been charged with creating socially efficient citizens and more recently with enhancing self-fulfillment. With these vague objectives, measures of the success of schools usually have been based upon their tangible resources rather than their impact on graduates. The evidence we do have raises questions about the effectiveness of public schools.

Today's high-school diploma does not guarantee literacy or certify competence in science, geography, history or mathematics. Furthermore, 15 percent of white, 25 percent of black, and 35 percent of Hispanic students do not even graduate from high school. Public schools also are troubled by the loss of talented students, who are increasingly being placed in private schools by parents concerned about the uncertainties of public education (National Center for Educational Statistics, 1981). The use of the sight-meaning method in teaching reading, the separation of reading and writing, the lack of composition assignments, the use of uninteresting texts, the deemphasis on the basic rules of grammar, and automatic promotion to the next grade have contributed to inadequate reading skills in high-school graduates (Mosse, 1982).

The increase in reading problems has paralleled the increasing amount of time children go to school. In the past children at risk did not attend school or dropped out early. Children with reading problems have become more visible because of the greater role schooling plays in the lives of young people. However, for a variety of reasons, teenagers still reach high school without their reading handicaps being detected. Even if reading deficiency is noted, the false assumption is that a brief exposure to remedial classes will help (Kaluger & Kolson, 1969). Because of the variable rate at which children learn to read, sustained attention to reading in every subject is important. Teachers need more intensive training in teaching reading skills and access to reading consultants (Strang, 1962).

Recent research has shown that schools differ in how effective they are with comparable groups of children (Rutter et al, 1979; Joyce et al, 1983). In London, for example, the size of schools and their organization were found to be unrelated to differences in student outcomes (Coleman et al, 1982). Successful student outcomes were found when the overall pattern of schooling was one of order without excessive punishment, well-managed work-oriented lessons, concern for children's needs, appreciation of good work and behavior, an assumption that students will take a responsible part in their own schooling, and a pattern of teachers modeling cooperation. None of the other factors often associated with favorable education, such as modern facilities, continuity with individual teachers, and the punishment of unacceptable behaviors, were significantly associated with success. Thus when these London schools modeled high academic and behavior standards, their students showed higher achievement. This was more important than fiscal expenditures, physical facilities, and teachers' academic credentials.

When schools fail to educate a student, the child, not the school, is considered a failure. This profound disadvantage of children in situations controlled by adults breeds agism, a form of discrimination akin to racism and sexism. In fact, the competence of school administrators and teachers is directly related to children's success in school. Schools can do much to influence behavior and achievement, especially in disadvantaged areas. A study of first-grade classrooms disclosed that teachers who provided instruction at an appropriate level, used a phonic approach, and emphasized the importance of problem-solving thinking produced higher reading achievement in their pupils. Furthermore, teachers judged by their principals to be competent had fewer failures among their high-risk students than those judged to be incompetent (Chall, 1979).

All of these trends have fueled the demand for academic skill testing at the high-school level in the hope that this will press schools to evaluate their efforts and place more emphasis on remedial programs. School testing and evaluation evoke ambivalent feelings in contemporary society, however. On the one hand, normative testing is needed to ensure that schools are doing their job in educating children, and to identify children who need special help, as well. On the other hand, criterion-referenced testing and grading better serve the purpose of self-assessment for the student in achieving goals appropriate for that student and in motivating students by measuring the attainment of their personal objectives. Still there is a realistic need on the part of educational systems to identify and reward the outstanding so that the comparison of students in grading systems persists even though the competition thus engendered may be deplored. A national trend toward higher scores on standardized tests might increase public confidence and political support for increased funding in education. Without an increase in funding, a greater public emphasis on education could take funds away from special programs for the disadvantaged and handicapped.

Thus schools are confronted both appropriately and inappropriately with pressures to compare children with each other through tests. This situation requires careful interpretation. Some children fail in academic work but show progress in skills and knowledge on periodic achievement testing. In the final analysis, history is studded with examples of brilliant individuals who failed in school but later became learned people (Goertzel et al, 1978).

SUMMARY

Together with families and peer groups, schools introduce children to society and culture. In so doing, practical knowledge of science and the humanities is accomplished optimally through education about oneself and the world. The ever-present challenge is to bridge the worlds of adults and children so that the ministrations of adults are appropriate to children at various stages of their development.

The major problem for schools is the discrepancy between their charge to meet the needs of all children and the limited means available to them. As do children, schools occupy a secondary place in society's priorities in economic resources and prestige. Moreover, as an industry, schools are immersed in the management of their plants and personnel so that persistent effort is required to keep in focus their purpose—to produce educated children. Shifting ideological and economic pressures cause changes in educational philosophies from time to time, and place to place, from an emphasis on the extremes of classroom control to the self-realization of children.

The bureaucratic aspects of schools promote routine and the polarization of administration and teachers. Moreover, the existence of the third pole of parental influence complicates the team effort required to produce optimal educational milieus. The effectiveness of education also hinges on society's valuation of the professionalism of educators and the appropriate training, continuing education, and support of teachers.

The most important determinants of effective education are high academic and behavior standards in schools with modeling and reinforcement by administrators and teachers of work habits and cooperation. These factors appear to be more important than equipment, facilities, continuity with individual teachers, and firm discipline.

Because literacy is such a basic requirement of our society, the lack of easy engagement with reading and writing is a disability in Western civilization. Teaching reading skills should be a part of the entire educational experience. Books are our most important sources of information, and all educational learning depends upon the ability to read. The many vocationally successful dyslexic persons, however, illustrate that people can be appreciated for their human relations, teaching, and intellectual skills.

The struggle for control of America's public schools reflects deeply rooted and conflicting philosophies. Since the 1920s the approach to resolving these conflicts has been to make our schools provide something for everybody. The result of giving everyone a voice in running the schools often has been to fragment power to the point that no one seems to be in charge.

Schools cannot reorganize society, redistribute income, or provide the love and care that each child requires (Graham, 1984). They are having a difficult time insisting on their instructional roles amid the priorities of communities. Therefore, it is extremely important that there be community agreement about the fundamental purposes of schooling: to produce people who are numerate, literate, creative, able to communicate, and, above all, care about doing their jobs well. Such goals can best be achieved by nurturing and enhancing the thinking and reasoning of the young.

We now know more than ever before about how children learn and how teachers can be effective in aiding learning. The transmission of this research into practice is difficult and time consuming, but it can and must be done. Unless teachers possess specific competencies that are acknowledged and valued, it is impossible for them to claim professional status and to have that status recognized. Contemporary competing social and economic pressures require sophisticated political understanding and insight on the part of leaders in education.

Unfortunately those who control the public schools have not achieved the insight of wise teachers, who recognize the impact of their personal influence on their charges. It is through the personalities, commitment, and competence of individual teachers that schools make their imprint on the citizens of the future. The challenge for communities and school administrations is to maintain working conditions that inspire and support dedicated teachers. This is critical to the prevention, identification, and management of educational disabilities and handicaps.

CHAPTER

6

Classrooms

The problem exists not so much in learning itself, but in the fact that what the school imposes often fails to enlist the natural energies that sustain spontaneous learning—curiosity, a desire for competence, aspiration to emulate a model and a deep-seated commitment to the web of social reciprocity.

Jerome Bruner, 1966

The places and groups in which children do their schoolwork play a more important role in education than is usually recognized (Krasner & Krasner, 1987; Marx et al, 1985). The classroom group has two major socializing purposes. One purpose is to maintain a setting in which schoolwork can take place. It is carried out through the management of interpersonal relations and the development of social skills. The second purpose is the education of children. It is carried out through the assignment of tasks and the provision of necessary materials and equipment.

Classrooms vary in their characteristics, and classes range from a single group throughout the year in the early grades to multiple groups in high school. We will consider the ecology and atmosphere of classrooms, the interaction of children with their teachers and peers, and the typical roles of children with learning problems in classroom groups.

Before going further, two obvious factors that affect classroom behavior should be mentioned, because they frequently are overlooked. Prolonged or frequent absences from school take their toll on school achievement. Going to school, also, can set a negative tone for children. For example, some children arrive at school excited or weary after long rides in the stimulating environments of buses. Others may fear being victimized by other children on their ways to and from school.

CLASSROOM ECOLOGY

Classrooms should be comfortable and conducive to learning, and so optimal levels of sound and light level are important. If distracting stimuli impinge on them, many children have difficulty concentrating. Noise levels are particularly critical (Westman, 1981). Noisy classrooms may be a reflection of excited involvement in schoolwork, but they are not conducive to concentration, and for some children can be overwhelming.

The arrangements of classrooms often are reflections of teaching approaches.

The rectangular classroom in which pupils' desks are in straight rows with the teacher's desk in front conveys the image of learning only from the teacher. A classroom in which the pupils' desks are trapezoids, and can form a circle when placed next to one another, fits the image of learning from peers. An open classroom, featuring activity and resource centers with no desks, reflects the image of searching for novel, challenging experiences. Thus the organizations of a classroom is shaped by beliefs about how students learn. In turn, the arrangement of classroom furniture and traffic patterns can minimize disruptive classroom behavior (Adelman & Taylor, 1983).

Open and ungraded classrooms permit flexibility and individualization of instruction; however, they require exceptionally creative teachers and may not be comfortable for many teachers. Studies of the academic achievement, creativity, and social adjustment of children have not shown that open classrooms are particularly superior to traditional classrooms (Rosner, 1979).

Although it is administratively expedient and satisfies democratic principles, the grouping of children on the basis solely of chronological age ignores their differences in intelligence, talents, and social maturity. The talented are likely to be successful. The less talented, however, may not regard their comparatively inferior efforts as successful and so become discouraged. Thus mixing students of all levels of teachability has advantages and disadvantages. As an illustration, it may be helpful for children with learning difficulties to listen to the discussions of classmates in a heterogeneous social studies group. They may not be helped, however, through exposure to classmates who read in a way that they cannot begin to approximate, and they accordingly perform better in homogeneous reading groups (Rosner, 1979). A combination of heterogeneous and homogeneous student groupings probably is desirable so that the advantages of each can be enjoyed (Perkins, 1974). A merging of the models of the ungraded one-room country school and graded team teaching may produce the school of the future. The fact is that no single way works well for all children.

The scheduling of school activities should take into account the periods during the day when youngsters are receptive and when they are not preoccupied with competing urges to be active, to eat, or to rest. Unfortunately many school schedules evolve without consideration of these physical needs of children.

CLASSROOM ATMOSPHERE

In an ideal classroom atmosphere, the process of learning is absorbing and enjoyable for the students, feedback is prompt so that errors can be corrected, new learning is based upon previously acquired capabilities, children work at their own levels and paces with opportunities to learn from each other, sufficient time is allowed for new knowledge to be digested, learning situations are varied, and a personal relationship conducive to learning exists between the teacher and each student (Stott, 1978). These ideals are difficult to achieve because of covert forces inherent in groups that tend to block task performance. They are useful classroom objectives, however (Newman, 1974).

Under optimal circumstances, a classroom group of children undergoes four stages of development (Schmuck & Schmuck, 1971). The first stage is that of acceptance in which children seek a secure place in the peer group. The second is the stage of forming influence patterns during which students find their roles in the class. Third is the stage of productivity when trust and communication have developed so that students can work as a cohesive group with dialogue and feedback among members. Parenthetically, cohesiveness can work against a positive classroom climate, if the norms held by the peer group do not support schoolwork. The last stage is the stage of flexibility in which group norms allow for a variety of learning styles and are open to change. The role of the teacher is critical in maintaining a smooth flow of activities that stimulate student involvement in group activities (Brophey & Evertson, 1976).

A positive classroom atmosphere, then, is one in which the students democratically share high amounts of influence with each other and with the teacher; in which high levels of attraction exist for the group as a whole; in which norms are supportive of academic work, as well as for respecting individual differences, and in which communication is open (Schmuck & Schmuck, 1971).

A negative classroom atmosphere can develop rapidly when limits are not clearly maintained and peer distractions are prominent. The relationships between teachers and students take place with a peer group audience in a circular social process involving an individual child, classmates, and teacher. This social process may be negatively charged when a child is hostile or withdrawn and insensitive to feedback from others, when the peer group contributes rejection and isolation more than sympathy to a child regarded as deviant, and when a teacher fails to develop positive relationships with the students and does not support low-status students (Lippitt & Gold, 1959; White & Lippitt, 1960). More specifically, a laissez-faire policy leads to confusion and competition for power among the children. Autocratically led groups can be productive; however, as the center of the reinforcement system, the teacher disburses rewards and controls classroom behavior. The children accordingly bear little responsibility for controlling themselves. The resulting dependency upon the teacher fosters rivalry between the children and decreases the enjoyment children receive from teaching each other (Lewin et al, 1939).

The nature of group dynamics leads children and adults to cling to their own group views, right or wrong, rather than to change to something new and different. When threatened, groups tend to blame other groups and to become secretive or suspicious and avoid communication with other groups. Schools are particularly vulnerable to these group phenomena because they bring together groups of children, parents, teachers, administrators, and community factions (Newman, 1979).

Because organizational systems rely increasingly on it, teamwork has become as important as individual schoolwork skills. Thus classroom and smaller team projects help children learn how to research aspects of a problem, gain knowledge from others, and reach a larger goal by contributing to a group effort than they could individually. The totality of the members usually has had more relevant past experience, which may aid in learning. Moreover, groups profit from more error feedback since members can correct each other's errors. The opportunity to act in alternating leadership and collaborator roles can help children to see authority as a needed aspect of group process.

The challenge is how to use the classroom group to maximize the academic learning of individual children. The more the teacher performs the information-processing functions of the group, the less efficient is the learning of the children. The more each child personally performs the steps of information processing, the more efficient is that child's learning. The use of computer access to information has added a new dimension to the usual audiovisual and printed resource materials by permitting each child to gain personal information and bring it to the group.

Research on group dynamics points to

a five-person group as optimal for information-processing tasks (Miller, 1978). It appears to be large enough to permit members to express themselves freely, make efforts to solve problems even at the risk of antagonizing one another, and tolerate the loss of a member, and yet it is small enough so that there is regard for the feelings and needs of each person. Groups with an odd number of members are less likely than groups with even numbers to reach deadlock and show disagreement and antagonism.

TEACHER–CHILD INTERACTION

A teacher came to the frightening conclusion: I am the decisive element in my classroom. I have the power to make a child's life miserable or joyous. I can be a tool of torture or an instrument of inspiration. I can humiliate or humor, hurt or heal. (Ginott, 1972)

Children's relationships with their teachers during the early school years are crucial. Children are responsive to the styles of their teachers. Their attitudes toward teachers can be carried over to liking or disliking subject matter. A teacher, therefore, can enhance or restrict a child's academic experience (Stott, 1978).

Skillful individualized teaching without excessive pressure and with reinforcement and reassurances is the optimal teaching situation. Figure 6-1 depicts the critical variables in students and teachers and focuses attention on the importance of a student's perception of a task and the way in which a teacher handles it. This model also stresses the importance of feedback to both the student and the teacher. A teacher's expectations influence the treatment of a particular child. If a child does not actively

change those expectations, they in turn will shape the child's behavior so as to conform more closely to them.

Teachers' judgments about children whom they believe to have learning problems is based upon both first- and second-hand information. A student's prior performance, social status, sex, race, physical attractiveness, and neatness may be important factors, as may be the teacher's attitude toward the child's parents (Rist & Harell, 1982). If children do not learn as quickly and completely as teachers feel they should, they may be presumed to be lazy or intellectually limited. The prevailing bias is that children are not learning unless they can present visual evidence to the teacher that they are doing so. However, the evaluation of children based solely upon their written work obscures the achievement of some children who express themselves more efficiently through spoken language.

The importance of a teacher's attitude toward learners is illustrated at the most basic level in an experiment in which two groups of rats of equivalent ability were trained in running. One group was described as "rat geniuses" and the other as "stupid rats" to laboratory assistants who undertook to teach the two groups to run identical mazes by identical methods. The rats described as geniuses learned noticeably better than the rats that had been called stupid (Rosenthal & Fode, 1963).

There is a distinction between teacher expectation and teacher bias (Dusek, 1975). When teachers expect them to do more or less well, children are more or less likely to be successful in school (DeCharms, 1976). The biases teachers hold about behavior also may be fulfilled by children (Millman et al, 1980). This is particularly true when disruptive behavior and errors in schoolwork are categorically judged as "bad" rather than as mistakes in judgment or knowledge. For example, when a child cannot sit still, interrupts constantly, and messes up papers, an understandable reaction by

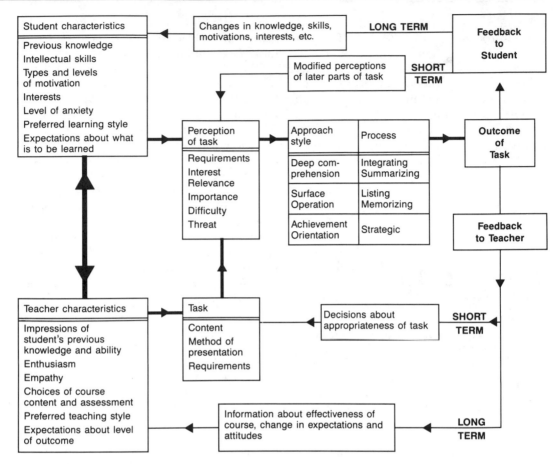

Figure 6-1. Model of factors influencing the academic learning process. (From D. R. Entwhisle, "The Child's Social Environment and Learning to Read," in T. G. Waller and G. E. MacKinnon, eds., *Reading Research: Advances in Theory and Practice: Vol. I.* Copyright 1979 by Academic Press, New York. Reproduced with permission.)

the teacher is that the child is willfully misbehaving, as illustrated by this quote:

> He won't listen to me. I can't teach or reach him. He takes all my time from other children. He does not belong in my class. Either he goes or I go.

Because of their vexing behavior, disruptive children can be treated cruelly. They may be humiliated by being seated in front of the class, having their work torn up, being called stupid, and being physically handled. A third-grade child may be sent to the first grade for reading. Children may be failed without preparation and support. Furthermore, some teachers are unable to provide the predictable structure needed for classroom work and inadvertently reinforce disruptive behavior by paying attention to it.

Unfortunately, many teachers believe that they are responsible when a child's performance improves, but not when it deteriorates, even though observers may see the reverse (Beckman, 1970). As a result, many children interpret difficulties with learning tasks as personal failures. The higher incidence of learning and behavior problems in boys than girls in elementary grades with predominantly female teachers calls attention to subtle discrimination against boys.

PEER INFLUENCES

A child's relationships with peers take up the largest share of the day, yet adults are prone to overlook them. For early adolescents peer-centered activities and concerns often take precedence over schoolwork (Everhart, 1983). Children in a classroom relate to each other informally and formally as they perform to their audience of peers. Children also may distract each other from schoolwork, because interacting with other children may be more important than doing schoolwork. The attitude of peers toward schoolwork, therefore, is of great importance. Children get into trouble in school for doing things that most of them enjoy: reading comics, talking to friends, flicking paper wads, mimicking the teacher, and chewing gum. A child who belongs to a peer group that supports such behavior will be less affected by a teacher's interventions than one who does not (Sugarman, 1973). Some boys view success in school as evidence of weakness. As one boy said:

> It doesn't pay to be smart in school. If you are, the other kids think you're the teacher's pet or cheating.

Interaction between students can further or impede the performance of schoolwork. We are only beginning to understand the positive contributions of the peer culture to children's capacities to relate to others, regulate emotional expression, and understand complex social events. We do know that the early experience of monkeys with agemates constitutes an important base for learning emotional control, and social skills (Suomi et al, 1978).

Children and adolescents live in two social worlds: that of their family and that of their peers. The family provides a child with the base for exploring the world of the peer culture. Behavior in each world bears the partial imprint of the other world, and values are integrated across these social systems. The interdependencies between the family and peer group are the most universal, essential, and elegant relationships in human development. The relationship between negative early peer interaction and later social maladaption has been established. For example, children evidencing poor peer relations are at significantly greater risk for adult psychopathology, antisocial behavior, and sexual disorders than individuals with positive peer relations (Campbell & Cluss, 1982; Hartrup, 1981).

The peer culture is composed of the patterns of belief, feeling, thinking, behaving, language, dress, activities, interests, and values that characterize a specific peer group (Asher & Gottman, 1981). Peer relationships are formed as the young child interacts and plays with agemates. The second grade in school, with its age-related changes in physical coordination and independence, marks the beginning of cliques and a true peer society. A cleavage of the two sexes is characteristic during this period, so that preadolescents are engrossed in activities and relationships within their own sex group. Interactions between the sexes become freer and more frequent as heterosexual activities emerge during adolescence.

Social interaction with peers is an important influence upon the development of social skills through learning how to engage in play and work routines. Children who do not have positive interactive experiences with peers, accordingly, may have difficulty developing concepts of co-operation, interpersonal sensitivity, and justice (Rubin & Ross, 1982; Rubin, 1980, 1983).

Peer friendships are conducive to realistic self-evaluation as one's needs and weaknesses, as well as capacities to help others, come to be recognized and accepted. Thus within friendships individuals feel they can be themselves without having to monitor their own behavior carefully. Principles acquired through friendship are transferable to other relations. An important element of a growth-promoting friendship is the immersion in a relationship of mutual respect without the loss of one's autonomy. Acts that promote the relationship simultaneously enhance self-interest and the interests of another person.

Winning the acceptance of peers is important to nearly all children and youth. Success or failure in these endeavors appears to be influenced by the compatibility of an individual with group purposes and goals, by the readiness and the extent of the individual's participation in and contributions to the group, and by personal qualities that influence the group. The extent to which an individual accepts and adheres to group codes, standards, and values is important, as well.

Some children do not hesitate to break the rules if it enables them to gain status with other children. Still, persons readily welcomed into most peer groups are likely to be those who have achieved some measure of personal security and self-esteem and are emotionally independent. Acceptance by peers is enjoyed by those who are able to play a nurturant role in satisfying the dependency needs of others (Perkins, 1974).

The ability to relate to peers depends upon an awareness of peer group norms and an inclination to respect them. Children must have a degree of sensitivity to the needs and feelings of others in addition to responsiveness to verbal and nonverbal communication (Kronick, 1981). Some children have difficulty expressing themselves verbally and comprehending the nuances of facial expressions, tone of voice, and gestures (Bryan, 1978). Thus the extent to which a child gains the respect of peers and what it takes to gain that respect affects that child's attitudes toward schoolwork and teachers.

Informal relationships in the peer group are often fraught with emotion. A student's evaluation of oneself is vulnerable to peer group influence. Each student's self-esteem is on the line in the classroom setting where informal peer relationships can be either threatening or supportive. The teasing, provoking, and bullying ridicule of the peer audience is indelibly stamped on the memories of many children with educational disabilities.

Early peer rejection most likely reflects a child's difficulties in social relationships; however, a child's particular classroom and neighborhood experience may loom as critical factors in determining whether social isolation is a consequence. Circumstances beyond a child's control, including placement in special programs with other children who lack social skills may play a key role in depriving that child of an opportunity to develop growth-facilitating peer relationships. This highlights the importance of considering the impact of any intervention by the school upon a child's opportunities for developing peer relationships.

Clique membership is influenced by physical proximity in the classroom, a feeling of similar group status, comparability of achievement in schoolwork, and a shared reluctance to "squeal" on each other to authority figures (Miller, 1978). Cliques are likely to be stronger in school settings that do not encourage opportunities for flexible student interactions.

The socioeconomic background of a child also must be taken into account. Disadvantaged children of average ability may not have the sophistication of peers from middle-class backgrounds. Such children, accordingly, may gravitate toward academically unsuccessful, antisocial peers, because educational and social expectations for them have been unrealistic.

Some children with academic learning problems have the social maturity to keep up with, and even lead, peers; they feel defeated in school but not in the neighborhood. This is an asset that should not be overlooked. Most, however, do not have the social maturity, physical agility, or communication skills to gain acceptance by peers and so are isolated (Smith, S.L., 1980).

Cultural factors have different effects on children's peer groups in different societies. Whereas in the Soviet Union youth groups may be used as instruments of adult society, in the United States opposition to adult values tends to color the power and autonomy of peer groups (Perkins, 1974). Instead of respect for institutions, a restless passion for change arises with each new generation. In the United States, schools fail to challenge the spirit of some young people, who seek the excitement of initiation into a peer group that is antisocially inclined. This can lead to skipping classes, watching videos, using drugs and alcohol, and engaging in casual sexual activities in the homes of absent parents (Welsh, 1986). Consequently, instead of being inspired by values of the community, many morally and sexually ambivalent young people are self-centered and dominated by impulses. This life-style exercises a powerful attraction and provides strong resistance to initiation into the responsibilities of adulthood. The peer group, like other social forces to which it is related, can enable or enslave.

TYPICAL COUNTERPRODUCTIVE CLASSROOM ROLES

To learn successfully in school, children must respond appropriately to instruction. Specifically, they must accept the work assigned by a teacher, complete the work in a reasonable time, work neatly and accurately, and be able to participate in group activities.

The primary motivation of some children, however, has little to do with performing schoolwork. These children strive for other goals, such as attention seeking, power seeking, revenge seeking, and using disability as an excuse. Because they conflict with educational objectives, these goals result in teacher–child conflicts that tend to elicit further misbehavior (Dreikurs et al, 1971). The dynamics of classroom groups fosters counterproductive roles.

Attention Seekers

Some children reverse the expected teacher–student relationship and attract the attention of the teacher instead of devoting their attention to the teacher (Wallace & Kauffman, 1973). These children have difficulty functioning in groups and cannot handle the give and take of competition. The attention their disruptive behavior attracts reinforces their attention seeking.

Behaviors most likely to attract the attention of the teacher include talking out of turn, moving about the room without permission, hitting other children, having temper tantrums, and crying. More subtle behaviors that are likely to attract a teacher's attention are irresponsibility, memory difficulties, lack of interest, laziness, impulsivity, and day dreaming.

Some children try to shift attention away from academic tasks by sulking, crying, or acting put upon. They deflect attention from their lack of skills through assuming a clowning role:

> They call me a freak; it's not because I really am one, but it's because I act like one. To prove it, I can turn it on when I want to.

Having been ridiculed when laughter was the opposite of what they sought, they act as if ridicule is what they want and seek the notoriety they actually fear they cannot escape (Gardner, 1968).

Some children inadvertently attract attention through their inability to integrate smoothly with the peer group, which makes them the focus of disruptive peer group behavior. Some children with visual–spatial processing difficulties believe verbal messages from others, because they don't recognize the body language that conveys the underlying intent of humor, doubt, or sarcasm. Their own body language may appear clumsy, constricted, or caricatured to others and elicit teasing. They also may not notice the nuances of clothing style and may miss cues denoting another's interest in friendship (Kronick, 1981). When they try to take part in group activities, they may be teased because of their awkwardness (Smith, S.L., 1980).

Power Seekers

Some children have an omniscient attitude that blocks awareness of lacks in their knowledge and skills, and they omnipotently engage the teacher in a power struggle with overt or covert resistance to schoolwork. The child refuses to submit to authority in an effort to control adults and other children (McWhirter, 1977). The peer group's latent resistance to authority can reinforce such a child's struggle with a teacher.

The importance of control issues between child and teacher is illustrated by the following comment by one boy:

> She can't tell me what to do. I know more than she does. She just wants to push me around.

Other children try to control the teacher because of a fear of the loss of self-bound-aries through depending on others. As one child said:

> I get mad when the teacher corrects me. I hate to depend upon others to get things right and just push them away.

Some children have narcissistic personalities and have little desire to please others. They are self-centered and unresponsive to the entreaties of parents and teachers. They must have their own way and either withdraw from or disrupt the class.

Revenge Seekers

Children whose goal is revenge often have concluded that they cannot maintain their position through obtaining attention or power. Their feelings have been hurt, and they want to hurt back. The experience of school failure intensifies their anger. They then resort to hurting others in the form of aggression, defiance, boisterousness, destructiveness, and hostility. Once the children believe that others are against them, they provoke actions from adults, which further justifies their revenge seeking (McWhirter, 1977).

Indirect revenge is taken by some children when parents subject them to excessively high expectations for achievement in school. They strike back in the way that hurts their parents the most—failing in schoolwork. Failure to perform may become a child's weapon to punish and worry parents. The peer group may reinforce the child's failure through scapegoating or admiration of rebel.

A child's envy of academically successful siblings and peers may lead to defensive behavior in which the importance of success in schoolwork is denigrated and the envied persons are disparaged. Spiteful school failure can be a child's way of acting as if success is not important and of avoiding revealing that the child actually does care about success but may be less able than an envied person (Daniels, 1964). This may be pertinent to cyclic underachievers, who give up after spurts of achievement because they cannot surpass an envied sibling. The following case illustrates the revenge motive:

> Jim was predisposed to educational disabilities because of an auditory–linguistic dyslexia and spatial disorientation in addition to reliance on the psychological defense of denial in fantasy. His educational disabilities had been misunderstood by school authorities and his parents. In the seventh grade, Jim was failing academically, because he either did not complete or turn in his assignments. He automatically took the opposite viewpoint from that of his parents and stubbornly clung to his views even when they were obviously false. He also denied errors and lack of knowledge.
>
> Jim harbored a fantasy world in which he was a David poised against a world of Goliaths. He felt mistreated by teachers and his parents. His underlying low self-esteem occasionally was evident when his depression and discouragement broke through. Generally, however, Jim felt justified in his campaign of vengeance against school and parental authority. He was indifferent to criticism because he was winning his righteous war: "They mistreated me. I will show them." He achieved revenge by failing to meet adult demands for performance in schoolwork.

Assumed Disability

School is the place in which children learn how helpless or effective they are (Seligman, 1975). It is important, therefore, to distinguish between actual disability and the apparent lack of ability assumed by a child (McWhirter, 1977). Some children hide behind a display of inferiority so that others expect little of them. An effective way to achieve this and still keep adults involved with them is to appear to have, or to exaggerate, a disability.

To these children every obstacle is a stop sign that is not sidestepped but embraced and leaned on for support. These children use their ingenuity to get through school without doing the work with a variety of excuses, as described by one teenager:

> It is easy to snow teachers. If you look like you are trying and don't disturb them, they leave you alone. I became schoolwise early in the game. I figured out that "not trying" makes teachers mad, so I come to school on time. I don't ask questions, and I am polite, and, of course, I am never caught not trying, so now they think I can't do the work (Ginott, 1972).

The role of assumed disability was illustrated by Kurt Goldstein's celebrated patient Schn, who was wounded in the head by shrapnel in World War I and was thought to have a selective impairment of his capacity to perceive forms. Years later he was found to be normal, but he had mastered a deviant way of behaving during the administration of certain tests. He appeared to have invested a significant part of his self-concept in the assumed role of a disabled patient (Gardner, 1976).

SUMMARY

As the site of schoolwork, the classroom exercises a crucial influence upon the education of children. Ecological considerations include the coming and going of children from school, the physical structure and stimulus level of the classroom, and the size and composition of a class.

The atmosphere of a classroom is influenced by the ecological factors; the policies, performance, and personality of the teacher; and the degree to which the class becomes a cohesive functioning group that supports the goals of academic learning. The classroom atmosphere most conducive to schoolwork is one in which the teacher attends to human relations, peer group process, and leadership in the context of democratic control.

The interaction between teacher and children is the fulcrum for academic learning. The expectations of the teacher set the tone for the educational process. When expectations are clear, realistic, and consistent, children function the most comfortably. Problems arise when teacher expectations lead to self-fulfilling prophesies of failure in children, when written measurements inaccurately reflect students' progress, when mistakes are regarded negatively, and when group reactions assign low-status children to and maintain them in deviant roles.

The peer culture shares with the family a key role in the social development of children. Particularly during the early adolescent years, the school is the center for engaging with the peer culture through specific peer groups. In the classroom children perform before a peer audience, which can profoundly affect them in both supportive and destructive ways. Children at the extremes in individual differences encounter difficulties in relating to peers and can assume isolated or disruptive roles in the classroom. The influence of the peer group inherently tends to be antiauthority,

self-indulgent, competitive, and denigrating, although the successful mastery of peer relations can facilitate competence, compassion, loyalty, and identification with group and social goals.

Some children cause problems for the classroom group through motives that run counter to group cohesiveness and the objectives of academic learning and adopt roles that are reinforced by group dynamics. Some children seek attention as a means of satisfying immature needs and masking their learning problems. Some children seek power because of underlying omnipotent and omniscient views that lead to struggles for control with authority figures and other children. Some children are driven by revenge motives based upon unrealistic perceptions of attitudes of others toward them. They seek revenge overtly through hostile behavior or covertly through sabotaging behavior. Other children use exaggerated helplessness because of disability as a means of excusing painful failures and avoiding assuming responsibility for themselves.

Although varying in size, composition, and significance from a single yearlong experience during the early grades to the multiple, circumscribed courses of high school, the classroom system is the crucible within which a variety of key educational, adult–child, peer, and cultural experiences take place. The classroom deserves more attention than it has received.

7

Families

We speak of families as though we all knew what families are. . . . The family is an introjected set of relations.

R. D. Laing, 1969

In the United States the variety of family life-styles has focused attention on the distinctions between the adult companionship and child-rearing functions of families. As a consequence there is increasing awareness that the interests of adults and children inherently conflict in family life.

Families are living systems related to external social and environmental and internal group and biological systems (Miller & Miller, 1980). Viewing them as systems focuses attention on both the interpersonal and material functions of families in addition to family boundaries and components. Many contemporary problems in family living arise simply from the struggle to define and maintain family systems.

At the most fundamental level, defining the components and boundaries of family systems is not easy when their forms vary from extended family to single parent households. Furthermore, the demands of working, school, and recreational schedules create conflicts around the flow of commodities through, and the economic maintenance of, households. Most conflicts within family systems are precipitated by how family members handle their responsibilities for maintaining a household, consuming commodities, and moving about from one place to another. These mundane, but critical, aspects of family life are often overlooked by researchers and clinicians, who focus on the information-processing functions of families.

In modern society the boundaries of families are becoming increasingly indistinct. Parents are confronted with unprecedented decisions about the exposure of their children to the public dissemination of information. In families without clear boundaries provided by parents, the broader social question of the exposure of children to information they are not prepared to handle is raised.

Within families the exchange of information is affected by the sensitivity to the feelings of other members and the ability to express one's own feelings. Moreover, parents may send messages of rejection over nonverbal channels while simultaneously verbalizing affection. Parents, also, vary in their effectiveness in helping their children to understand, or decode, information about the family and the outside world, as in learning how to give and take with peers and siblings.

A family's behavioral style may be generally withdrawn or outgoing, or antisocial or prosocial, depending upon the attitudes and values held by family members. The memories of a family and the degree to which they are valued and formally retained have much to do with cohesion of the family system. Of particular importance in the interaction of schools and families is the degree to which parents and children understand the family's internal state and can express it in language that can be understood by people outside of the family. Children who have difficulty talking about their families may be unaccustomed to dialog and confused about family relationships.

Families are integrated when they are under the control of a centralized decision-making process and work toward common goals. When the children are young, parents usually control the behavior of the children and coordinate family processes. As children grow older, an integrated family permits them to take part in decision making. The extent to which decision making involves all family members determines the extent to which each member assumes an appropriate degree of responsibility in contributing to the functions of the family. Some families are not well integrated, and members go their separate ways. In extreme situations children are neglected and components of a suprasystem, such as a department of social services, must intervene to protect them.

Families continually make adjustments through both internal and external positive and negative feedback loops. In an amusing example, under negative feedback a husband and wife with dual controls on their electric blanket can turn the heat up or down on each one's own side as desired. In a positive feedback situation, however, if the husband is cold, he turns up the heat on his wife's side of the bed, and she, becoming too warm, turns his control down. Family quarrels often have similar positive feedback effects that may escalate and even

result in breakup of the family. Similar interactions can occur between schools and families around reporting academic performance.

Against this backdrop and the growing knowledge about family dynamics and parent–child relationships, this chapter highlights the ways in which families contribute and react to children's learning problems in school.

FAMILY CONTRIBUTIONS TO LEARNING PROBLEMS

Children raised without human stimulation, such as the Wolf Boy of Aveyron (Itard, 1962) and Witmer's feral boy (Witmer, 1920), would be expected to be handicapped in academic learning. It may be difficult to understand, however, how learning problems in school can ensue from family life.

Nonetheless, epidemiological studies show that school learning problems are frequently related to family factors (Werner et al, 1971; Davie & Butler, 1975; Rutter et al, 1970). Most impressively, the Collaborative Perinatal Project, described in Chapter 1, strongly related learning difficulties to socioeconomic and demographic variables in addition to family patterns (Nichols & Chen, 1981).

There are three basic ways in which families play a role in the learning problems of children (Friedman, 1973). The first is through the impact of external stresses on families, the second is through the effects of parent–child relationships, and the third is through family dynamic patterns.

Social and Economic Factors

Major stresses for families are created by the conditions under which some ethnic minorities live, by poverty, and by parental work pressures (Marjoribanks, 1979). Aggressive antisocial youths who fail in school are examples of how these factors can distort the learning process when combined with the lack of parental commitment to long-range goals. In a family that disparages education, loyalty to family values often prevails, and the youngster remains in school solely to fulfill the law but drops out as soon as possible, with or without a job. Some boys in families with absent fathers view learning in school as feminine and as threatening their masculinity, since it is supported only by their mothers.

Even under disadvantaged circumstances, specific parental interaction with a child is crucial in determining outcome. For example, a study of poor, black urban families disclosed that the mothers of high achieving boys expressed ideals for their sons that emphasized self-motivated, active engagement with the world. The mothers of low achievers expressed ideals that emphasized constraint, isolation, and adult control (Scheinfeld, 1983). The potential for change even underdisadvantaged circumstances, therefore, can lie in improving the relationship of parents to their children and of adults to youths in their communities.

Parent–Child Factors

The interaction of early vulnerability in children and family instability leads to a high risk of school problems regardless of social class. The importance of early attachment bonds in later adaptation is illustrated by research on institutionally raised children, who tend to be attention seeking, restless, disobedient, and less socially adept than family-reared children in school. In contrast, foster children with a stable upbringing in a nuclear family tend to be more successful in school (Rutter, 1981a). The classic work of Skodak and Skeels demonstrated the dramatic differences between children regarded as mentally retarded in which home-reared children dramatically exceeded institutional children in later achievement (Skeels, 1966).

There is little doubt that the foundations for learning in school are laid in the context of the attachment bonding of early child–parent relationships (Bowlby, 1980). For example, secure attachment to a parent at 18 months predicts skill in problem solving and peer competence when a child is five (Sroufe, 1979; Arend et al, 1979). This, in turn, is related to competence displayed across a wide variety of contexts during the elementary school years (Block & Block, 1979). As will become evident later in this book, the perceptions of the quality of these relationships by a parent and child are critical.

Parents facilitate the learning of infants within the context of the mutual bonding process; however, babies are active contributors as well. Newborns are in a high state of alertness for their first meetings with their mothers. At birth babies orient and can follow human faces with their eyes, imitate facial gestures, and synchronize body movements to the rhythm of human voices (Field, 1983).

The amount of time taken by mothers to fall in love with their babies depends in part on the responsiveness of the baby and begins from before birth to the first few hours, or a week or longer. The early attachment between parents and babies has powerful effects that are discernible years later (Marono, 1981). The interdependence of the rhythms between infant and parent is at the root of attachment as well as attention and communication. Ideally a parent knows and responds to the rhythms of an infant. Bonding takes place through engagement and disengagement, with predictable matching so that the expectancies of each correspond to the other's behavior. Bonding, therefore, is both an integrative and a differentiating process. There is a reciprocal interaction between foreground disengagement over short time spans with background engagement over long time spans. When there is little coherence between engagement and disengagement, infants are at risk. Paradoxically, the capacity to be alone comes from being alone in the presence of someone, as in a baby's solitary play in a parent's presence (Sander, 1983).

Another important factor is a parent's sensitivity to an infant's method of controlling the amount of stimulation by looking away. A mother serves as a protective filter for her baby, screening out the background noise of the world, letting through only as much stimulation as the baby can handle and enlarging the exposure as the baby signals readiness for more before turning away. The persistence of this infantile dependency upon external regulation of environmental stimulation is seen in some older children with academic attention problems.

Thus infants learn about their environments and themselves. As they learn how to interact with and master their own physical needs, they free themselves to attend to their external world. Child rearing is not just a matter of taking care of a child but of supporting the child's efforts to care for oneself as well. The parents of children who cope well neither indulge them nor overprotect them. They facilitate children's abilities to ask for help by encouraging and rewarding their efforts, speaking directly to them, and offering reassurance at times of frustration and failure (Murphy & Moriarty, 1976; White et al, 1979).

Learning occurs when adults in a child's life effectively focus attention and interpret to the child the significance of objects, events, and ideas in the social surroundings. Thus parent-mediated interaction affects a child's capacity to use direct exposure to stimuli from early life on. A lack of mediated learning experience limits the meaning and significance of experienced events, which are only grasped in an episodic manner without being related to other events experienced by the individual (Feuerstein, 1980).

Individual differences between children must be taken into account in attempts to understand patterns of parent–child interactions, because children perceive and cope differently with experiences and the ways in which parents relate to them. These individual differences tend to show consistency over time and are implicated in the later development of learning problems in school. However, specific qualities, such as temperamental characteristics, do not reliably predict developmental outcome unless seen in the context of the vicissitudes of child development (Dunn, 1981).

As parents master the developmental tasks of child rearing, children acquire the capacity to relate to adults with affection and trust (Figure 7-1). This has obvious implications for later relationships with teachers. In settings of family disorganization and the absence of dependable sources of love and safety, children grow up with attitudes of distrust, hostility, and cynicism. Thus early experiences within the family may weigh more heavily in the long run in the educational achievement of children than does schooling itself (Erikson, 1950). As early as the first year of life, parents and children can enter a vicious cycle of increasing frustration for both.

Children, also, can learn maladaptive behavior from parents who are unaware of the effects of their own modeling. Thus the temper tantrums of parents may be replicated in their children. Parents who permit themselves to be manipulated by their children teach manipulative behavior, just as other parents teach dependency by overprotecting their children. If parents wish to change their children's behavior, they often must first change their own. Figure 7-2 lists a series of parental attitudes that can produce maladaptive responses in children. Later in life parental attitudes differentiate between youths with serious learning and behavior problems who im-

CHILD'S DEVELOPMENTAL TASKS		PARENTAL DEVELOPMENTAL TASKS	FAMILY DEVELOPMENT
Infant	Basic Trust	Learning the infant's cues	The marriage and disengagement from families of origin
			Create empathic marital relationship that deepens with addition of family members
Toddler	Autonomy	Accepting developing individuality of child; setting realist limits	Redefinition of roles with the birth of each child
Pre-school	Initiative	Learning to separate	Individuation of family members while promoting communication
School age	Industry	Fostering independence and self-discipline	Differentiation and consolidation of family roles; validation of individual members
Adolescence	Self-integration	Learning to accept diminishing importance to young person	Sustain integrated family life in the face of inter-generational value and dependency conflicts
Adulthood	Intimacy	Learning to build a new life	The integration of loss

Figure 7-1. Developmental tasks of children, parents, and families.

prove during adolescence and those who do not. Industriousness and persistence are the qualities most frequently found in the parents of youths who later improve (Werner & Smith, 1979).

Disturbed family relationships may exist in parental authority patterns that are dictatorial and punitive, permissive and indulgent, or ambiguous and inconsistent. The displacement of a child's attitudes and behaviors toward these parental authority patterns onto teachers may contribute to learning difficulties. On the other hand, some children perform successfully in school in order to express independence from their parents and realize their own goals (Strickler, 1969).

Family Dynamic Factors

A variety of forces within a family influence a child's performance in school. Thus faulty communication patterns impede the modeling of rational problem-solving techniques for children (Knapp & Kaye, 1980).

The stability of some families even depends upon their children's failure in school. Such families can be expected to resist or to react negatively to improvement in a child. Three family patterns merit particular mention.

The first is the family in which maternal overprotection and fear of the father promote school learning failure in a boy. This syndrome of learning impotence is de-

ATTITUDE	PARENTAL BEHAVIOR	CHILD'S USUAL RESPONSE
Oversubmission	Capitulation to child's immature whims and demands, without regard to parent's own rights and needs	Excessive demands, temper outbursts when demands are not met, impulsiveness, little consideration for others
Overcoercion	Direction and redirection of child's actions, without sufficient regard for child's rights to initiate own interests and activities	Undue reliance on outside direction, dawdling, daydreaming, forgetting, procrastination—active or passive resistance
Perfectionism	Withholding of acceptance until child's behavior is more mature than can be comfortably achieved at the current developmental level	Striving, overserious preoccupation with physical, intellectual, or social accomplishments, self-devaluation
Neglect	Little time for, consideration of, or awareness of child's right to interested assistance at each level of development	Relative incapacity to form and maintain close relationships with others or to get satisfaction from such relationships; often because has no close relationship to use for learning controls
Hypochondriasis	Morbid attention to body functions or organs that are objectively healthy, or anxious exaggeration of minor ailments and sensations	Excessive complaining and anxiety about body sensations, minor ailments, and organic functions
Overindulgence	Repeated showering of child with goods and services, without regard for child's needs	Boredom, blase behavior, lack of initiative, little capacity for persistent effort
Distrust	Anticipation of failure or inadequacy in child's character or performance	Self-belittling, tendency to gravitate toward characteristic that is the object of distrust
Rejection	Failure to give child a niche of acceptance in a family group	Bitter, hostile, anxious feelings of isolation, self-devaluation
Punitiveness	Excessive venting of personal aggressions on child, often thinking that this represents discipline; or parent from a family culture that insists that hurting children is part of the correct method of childrearing	Behavior that invites punishment, self-devaluation, longing for retaliation
Seductiveness	Conscious or unconscious stimulation of child's sexual feelings	Premature and excessive preoccupation with sex, hostility, guilt
Overresponsibility	Impositions of excessive and premature responsibility on child	Inability to enter into and derive enjoyment from play activities, assumption of excessive responsibility, often with hostility or self-belittling

Figure 7-2. Pathogenic parental attitudes. (Reprinted with permission of Ross Laboratories, Columbus, OH 43216, from W. H. Missildine, *Feelings*, Volume 25, No. 6, © 1983, Ross Laboratories.)

scribed in Chapter 26. Such a child wishes to remain infantile and dependent. To succeed in school means to grow up and become an adult and thereby lose the support of one parent and provoke fantasized retaliation from the other. As a result the child fails in school and gains attention and power through being helpless and inept.

In a second family pattern, one child is placed in the role of family scapegoat (McWhirter, 1977). Such a child adopts and lives out the role of a "black sheep," with consequent school failure and possible later antisocial behavior. Such a child may resent the superior ability of siblings and, rather than verbalize this concern, express it through indifference toward school. Under these circumstances an introverted child may withdraw and an extroverted child may become belligerent. Both dislike schoolwork.

In a third pattern, parental psychosis grossly distorts the meaning of a child to the parent. The child serves irrational purposes for the parent and consequently suffers a variety of developmental impairments. A child may be experienced by a parent as a part of the parent, as a fetish, as a transitional object, or as a parent to the parent. Psychotic parents may be chaotic, tantalizing, intrusive, fragmenting, harassing, victimizing, and unempathic, creating unpredictable confusion for their children. Although this is destructive for many, some of these children may adapt by functioning as parents to their parents.

In a more general sense, youngsters with divorced parents may have problems learning in school. Children of divorce often are caught in conflicts of loyalties, feelings of guilt, and feelings that they may have caused the divorce. When preoccupied with guilt and self-deprecatory feelings, these children have difficulty concentrating and attending to class work and doing homework. They may feel neglected, angry, and rejected. Their daydreams may be of such fantasies as their parents reuniting; however, they usually are unable to turn to their parents or siblings in order to clarify their wishes and resolve their feelings.

The preoccupation of parents with their own careers and personal problems detracts from their child-rearing abilities. As a result their children lack guidance and inspiration for performing successfully as students in school (Welsh, 1986).

FAMILY REACTIONS TO EDUCATIONAL DISABILITIES

Children with educational disabilities present a variety of problems for their families (Faerstein, 1981). When academic success is a high priority for a parent, a child who fails may constitute a blow to the parent's pride and start a chain reaction that tests the strengths of the family.

Unlike physically evident disabilities, those involving behavior and schoolwork do not permit clearly demarcated reactions and adjustments in the family. Even when there is a physically obvious disability, typical reactions are a stage of disbelief and denial; a stage of fear and frustration that may be associated with guilt or intensified strife in the family; and ultimately a stage of rational planning and accommodation to the disability (Anthony & Koupernik, 1973; Bicknell, 1983).

The families of children with educational disabilities are confronted with insidious and ambiguous situations in which the gamut of blame, failure, and frustration is run before the nature of their children's problems is identified. Even then the complex interactions of many variables make it impossible to point to a cause of an educational handicap.

Children who have appeared to be bright and responsive through their early years and yet fail to learn to read in school particularly disappoint their parents and teachers and feel bewildered and dismayed themselves. They may be told that they should try harder, because they could read if they would settle down to it. This is embarrassing and frustrating, when they already have been trying desperately to learn to read. Additional humiliation often is suffered at the hands of other children, who call them "dummies." Well-intentioned attempts by parents to help them read at that point may backfire, creating even more family tension. For the children, however, in later life the nagging question may remain: Why did not their parents detect their inability to read earlier in life?

The identification of a learning handicap may be greeted by a variety of parental reactions (Smith, S.L. 1980; Hartwig, 1984; Gargiulo, 1985). To know one's child is failing in school for reasons that are not understood can cause parents to feel drained, blamed, helpless, confused, hurt, anxious, attacked, or afraid. Guilt frequently occurs along with self-blame for their child's problem. Some parents react with denial in the form of disbelief that their child is having difficulty. That denial may result in a continual search for new professional opinions. Other parents may withdraw from the problem by ignoring it. The projection of blame on others may lead to a parent's anger toward the school, professionals, or spouse. Some parents give the appearance of being very certain when they feel uncertain. Others give the appearance of being very uncaring when they really feel helpless. Some simply blame the child for being lazy. Those who fear the consequences of academic failure for their child in later life are realistic. Optimally parents ultimately accept and take steps to resolve their children's problems. Before this occurs, however, denial, depression, anger, and guilt that foster parental defensiveness must be worked through (Perosa & Perosa, 1982). The following case illustrates how a child with a dyslexia can develop an omnipotent, omniscient attitude as a defense against awareness of an educational disability in a family that fosters grandiosity and denial:

At the age of 12, Jeff was failing in his school subjects and defiant of his teachers. He had a visual–spatial dyslexia and a severe reading handicap.

Jeff showed cognitive rigidity in his stubborn adherence to his ideas even when erroneous, and in habits, such as gazing at cracks in the walls of the classroom. He described himself grandiosely as a daredevil who wanted to have fun and see how much he could get away with. For him schoolwork did not matter, although he recalled being frustrated and confused in the early grades in school.

Jeff's home was in a state of chronic civil war in which family members were continually bickering and in conflict because of their rigid beliefs about the way things should be. The mother acted like a martyr but overindulged and adulated Jeff. She expected that he would become a university professor like herself. The father was aloof, haughty, and perfectionist. He thought that Jeff could excell in school if he wanted to. Both parents ignored the attempts of school personnel to call their attention to their son's educational problems.

In general one of the crucial problems for the parents of handicapped children is handling the dependence–independence dimensions of child rearing. Parents may differ in the degree to which they discourage or encourage a child's dependency. They also may differ in their perceptions of their child's limitations and capacities and in their sensitivities to social stigmata (Anthony & Koupernik, 1973). If the parental reaction extends into disruption of the marital relationship, a child is confronted with both personal and parental marital problems (Marcus, 1967).

Another common parental reaction is frustration resulting from counterproductive efforts to cope with a child's behavior and failure to do homework. The parents then may punish or reject the child who diminishes their self-evaluations as successful parents. The additional inconveniences of special education, tutoring, and treatment also pose burdens that add to parental frustrations.

An educationally handicapped child may provoke intense emotions in brothers and sisters and complicate their lives in ways that are resented. Important issues between siblings relate to rivalry, jealousy, and envy. Rivalry can be seen as competitive behavior among siblings for preferred care from the parent they share, in addition to possession of that person. Rivalry, therefore, is not a wish but an act. Jealousy is the emotion experienced toward a person who shares another person from whom one wishes the preferred love. Both rivalry and jealousy are defined in the context of triadic relationships. In contrast envy is dyadic and is the wish for the possession of attributes or possessions of another (Bank & Kahn, 1982; Neubauer, 1982, 1983).

Siblings may feel neglected when their parents devote time and attention to a handicapped child. This may lead to jealous aggressive behavior toward the handicapped child. Younger siblings may imitate a handicapped child's behavior. Older children may become frustrated with the handicapped child or develop overly self-sacrificing attitudes (Anthony & Koupernick, 1973). They may have to explain the child's invisible disabilities to other children. They may be held responsible by others for their sibling's behavior and feel resentful when asked to include that child in their play. They also may feel guilty because of their own ambivalent feelings toward that sibling (Smith, S.L., 1980).

SUMMARY

The family establishes a child's foundation for academic learning through its role in fostering a child's organizational, communication, and problem-solving skills. Interpersonal trust results from solid and mutually rewarding attachment bonds between parents and a child. When children do not have stable and dependable early-life experiences, they are predisposed to later difficulties in school.

The factors in family life that contribute to school learning problems may reflect broader social and economic conditions, although even then the relationships within the family unit are critical. As models for their children, parents teach much about handling emotions, relating to others, and being dependent or independent. Some families overprotect, and others scapegoat, an educationally handicapped child. Still others present a confusing, inconsistent atmosphere for their children.

The identification of an educationally handicapped child evokes a range of reactions in families, including denial, avoidance, withdrawal, guilt, anger, blame, fear, depression, and, optimally, acceptance, and realistic planning. The parents of an educationally handicapped child are confronted with new child-rearing challenges and negotiating the complicated pathways of special educational services and other diagnostic and treatment procedures. Siblings, also, must make adjustments to such a child at home, in school, and with their peers.

Because of their fundamental roles in the socialization of children, families are central in the identification, management, and long-range course of children with educational disabilities.

III

The Internal World of the Child

What we see, and where we see it, depends entirely upon the physiological functioning of our body.... Thus if we wish to understand the relation of our personal experience to the activities of nature, the proper procedure is to examine the dependence of our personal experiences upon our personal bodies.

Alfred North Whitehead, 1938

THIS SECTION IS written for clinicians and researchers who seek an exposition of current knowledge about the central nervous system (CNS). My intent is to portray the brain as the organ of the mind and the source of human behavior. In order to do this, a model of the CNS is proposed as a means of integrating clinical and research efforts. The chapters on the managerial system and the self are particularly relevant to clinicians and educators. For other readers the chapter summaries may well suffice.

In the course of evolution, two major networks of communication within the body have been the endocrine system and the nervous system. Both use chemical messengers and receptors to transmit information from cell to cell. Together the hormones and neurotransmitters of the two systems coordinate the activities of all body systems.

Neural scientists are beginning to trace the origins of basic emotions, drives, and behaviors from the level of genes and molecules to specific nerve circuits and brain systems. We carry coded instructions in our genes for CNS components, structures, and processes that influence the way we perceive the world and the way we feel, think, and act.

This section focuses on the internal world of the child as it is reflected in the CNS, of which the brain is our primary interest. The concept of the CNS resolves the dilemma of distinguishing among the brain, the mind, and behavior. The brain contains the cellular and chemical components that make up the three dimensional structures of the CNS. The mind is composed of these structures and the processes of the CNS. Thus brain, mind, and behavior are different facets of the CNS.

Strictly speaking, the brain itself is not a living system and, therefore, has no functions. It is made up only of cellular and chemical components organized in structures. Within these structures processes operate to form subsystems of the CNS. The outputs of these subsystems constitute the functions of a suprasystem. The central nervous system is the ultimate suprasystem that governs the other organ systems that join it to make up the individual organism.

The CNS comprises a myriad of component subsystems. Employing the terminology of the general theory of living systems, the structures of the CNS and their development are described in Chapters 8–10. These structures are related to its major functional systems in Chapter 11, and the specific processes and functions of the CNS are detailed in Chapters 12–16.

In addition to cellular and chemical components, the brain contains the neural circuit structures of the CNS that permit learning by storing memories of life experience. These components and structures are described in Chapter 8. Unlike other organ systems of the body, the CNS can act upon itself by regulating and modifying its own neural circuit structures.

The anatomical subsystems of the brain depicted in Chapter 9 operate together as structures of the central nervous system; however, they are sufficiently discrete to permit description of them as separate subsystems. The sensorimotor systems that relate to the external world are monitored by the cerebellum and those that relate to the internal world by the autonomic nervous system. As the powerhouse of the brain, the reticular activating system is the center of arousal. The limbic system mediates emotional responses and the storing of memories by assigning significance to stimuli from the external and internal worlds. The basal ganglia are the mediators of instincts and facilitators of sensorimotor activities, including focusing attention. The thalamus assists the cerebral cortex and plays a role in alert consciousness. The cerebral cortex analyzes and synthesizes stimuli under the supervision of the frontal lobes. The two cerebral hemispheres complement each other with differing emphases on space and time.

Chapter 10 outlines the development of the CNS as a recapitulation of the evolution of the species. Hence the maturational sequence underlying the stages of child development is reminiscent of the evolution of the brain in the hierarchy of animal forms. Furthermore, the migration of neurons in the maturation of the brain early in life causes a range of individual variations in brain components. At the same time, the maturing brain shows remarkable plasticity in its capacity to compensate for damage to its tissue.

In Chapter 11 an integrated model for relating the CNS to behavior is described in terms of five major functional systems—the state regulating, information processing, language, managerial, and self systems. This model is the centerpiece of the book.

The terms personality and character often are used synonymously, however, a useful distinction can be made between them. In essence personality refers to the kind of person an individual appears to be. It is the characteristic matter-energy and information output pattern of the organism. As the visible expression of character, one's personality can be observed by others through one's publicly displayed behavioral and bodily presentations. Personality traits, therefore, are individual differences in behavior attributed to a person by the observations of others. In contrast, one's character is made up of the functions of the CNS that underlie personality. As such, the elements of character are relatively stable feedback informational output loops of the five major subsystems of the central nervous system. Thus character is the complex of learned and innate CNS functions that determine the disposition, know-how, communication, and awareness of one's actions. Personality is the externally manifested output of the CNS, and, thereby, is a function of the person as a whole organism.

In Chapter 12 the behavioral manifestations of the state regulating system functions of arousal, consciousness, and motivation are expressed through temperament, which is the disposition of an individual to relate to the external world and an important determinant of one's personality. The involuntary and voluntary aspects of attention are defined. Motivation springs from the appetitive and adaptive instinctually programmed cravings and emotions, colored by the weighting of stimuli as pleasurable or distressing by the affective system. The details of this chapter illustrate the wealth of current knowledge and raise new questions about the internal wellsprings of behavior.

The output of the information processing system is manifested in cognitive functions, which personalize knowledge by blending information from the external and internal worlds. The basic information processing subsystems described in Chapter 13 are stimulus reception, perception, imaging, imagination, through which symbols and concepts are formed, and stored knowledge. Among the important dimensions upon which cognitive styles can be defined are rigidity versus flexibility, automatization, field dependence versus independence, and external versus internal locus of control.

Although it involves the other functional systems, language is sufficiently demarcated in structures and processes to warrant separate consideration in Chapter 14. Language has receptive, inner, and expressive processes. It also is expressed through both nonverbal and verbal forms.

Chapter 15 is devoted to the managerial system, which is based upon the mastery instincts and strives to fulfill the internal needs of an individual in the external world. Its adaptive functions are impulse control, information analysis, thinking, implementation of actions, and verification of actions. Its interpersonal functions transpire in role relationships through which affiliative and aggressive drive derivatives are expressed.

Chapter 16 is a unique effort to define, both broadly and specifically, the elusive notion of the self as a self system, which derives from the human capacity to represent oneself in symbols and concepts. It is the center of human experience of the external and internal worlds and is the interface between a person and society through social roles. It permits a sense of continuity in time and coherence in space. The basic subsystems of the self can be defined as self-awareness, self-esteem, self-concept, and self-evaluation, each of which develops in sequential stages.

8

Components of Central Nervous System Structures

Much harm has resulted from an artificially abrupt separation betwixt mind and body.

Hughlings Jackson, 1872

The central nervous system (CNS) has two kinds of components. One kind is anatomical and consists of cells. The other kind is chemical in the form of neuroregulators. The basic structures of the CNS are neural circuits consisting of interconnected neurons, whose communication is governed by neuroregulators. These neural circuits embody Piaget's schemes. The neuroregulators mediate CNS processes through the operations of these schemes.

In contrast with other organs, the brain has the remarkable capacity to modify its own structures. While the brain is forming during early life, its cellular components are influenced by experience (Chaudhari & Hahn, 1983). Beyond that the neural circuit of the brain is influence by experience throughout life and is the substrate of learning. Furthermore, the central nervous system's activity influences the brain's neuronal circuitry. This is dramatically illustrated by an epileptic person, who was able to inhibit the appearance of a full seizure first by smelling a certain aroma, and later by simply thinking of that odor (Efron, 1957). Thus, through continuous interaction with the environment, the CNS actually shapes the brain.

The three interacting developmental determinants of the CNS are the maturation of the brain, life experience, and its own action upon its neural circuitry. This fact precludes clear-cut distinctions between the effects of nature or nurture in development and between "organic" and "functional" disorders of the brain (Kandel, 1979).

The cellular components of the brain are neurons and neuroglia. Neural circuits are formed by junctions between neurons. These neuronal junctions are much more than way stations in the transmission of nerve impulses (Pribram, 1977). They embody electrochemical states that are acted upon by, and influence, nerve impulses.

CELLULAR COMPONENTS

Gross Anatomy of the Central Nervous System

The major anatomical distinction within the central nervous system is between lower

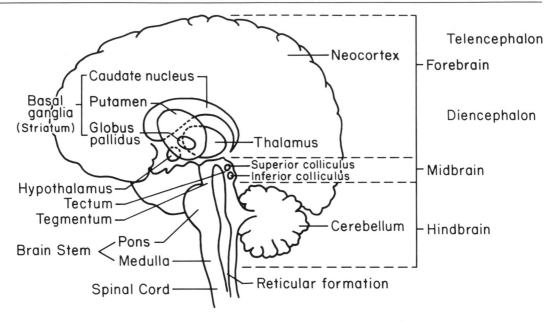

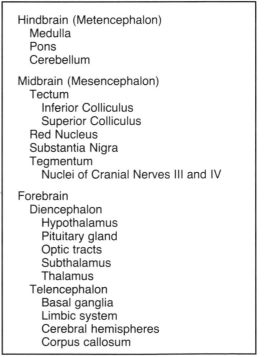

Figure 8-1. Schematic view of the major anatomical brain structures.

and higher centers (Figures 8-1 and 8-2). The spinal cord is the lowest and extends upward to the hindbrain, which includes the medulla, pons, and cerebellum. Next is the midbrain, which contains the colliculi, tectum, red nucleus, substantia nigra, and tegmentum. The highest level is the forebrain, which includes the diencephalon, composed of the hypothalamus, pituitary gland, optic tracts, subthalamus, and thalamus, and the telencephalon, which is constituted by the basal ganglia, the limbic system, the two hemispheres of the cerebral cortex, and the connecting corpus callosum.

Together the reticular activating system and the limbic system are the brain's powerhouse (Williams, 1979). The cerebral cortex is an outgrowth of the lower centers, particularly the thalamus. Thus, for each area of the cerebral cortex, there is a corresponding area of the thalamus. The structure of the cerebellum also corresponds to the structure of the cerebral cortex.

Hindbrain (Metencephalon)
    Medulla
    Pons
    Cerebellum

Midbrain (Mesencephalon)
    Tectum
        Inferior Colliculus
        Superior Colliculus
    Red Nucleus
    Substantia Nigra
    Tegmentum
        Nuclei of Cranial Nerves III and IV

Forebrain
    Diencephalon
        Hypothalamus
        Pituitary gland
        Optic tracts
        Subthalamus
        Thalamus
    Telencephalon
        Basal ganglia
        Limbic system
        Cerebral hemispheres
        Corpus callosum

Figure 8-2. Subdivisions of the brain.

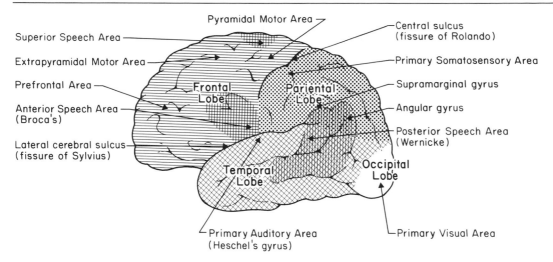

Figure 8-3. Lateral view of left cerebral hemisphere.

The two cerebral hemispheres are connected by a broad band of fibers, the corpus callosum. In most people the left hemisphere specializes in speech and language and the right in visual and spatial functions. Each hemisphere is divided into lobes that contain different functional regions of the cerebral cortex. The lower posterior (occipital lobe) aspects of the cortex in both hemispheres specialize in vision the upper posterior (parietal lobe) aspects in bodily sensations, the anterior (frontal lobe) aspects in foresight and anticipation, and the lateral (temporal lobe) aspects in hearing and communication (Figure 8-3).

Cellular Anatomy of the Central Nervous System

The brain is about three pounds of intricately woven tissue composed of some 10 billion highly specialized nerve cells called neurons and some 100 billion glial cells. The neurons are supported and nourished by the glial cells. The neurons' electrical signals can be detected, recorded, and interpreted, and many of their chemicals can be identified. Furthermore, the connec-

tions between neurons that constitute the brain's circuitry can be mapped (Hubel, 1979).

The fundamental cellular components of the central nervous system are the neurons and their interconnecting synapses. A typical neuron resembles a tree (see Figure 8-4). The branches of the tree are dendrites and the trunk is the axon, which may be from 0.1 mm to a meter in length.

The cerebral cortex contains a thin layer of neuron cell bodies, 1.5–4.5 mm thick, which cover the surface of all the convolutions of the brain and has a total area of about one quarter of a square meter. The remainder of the cerebral cortex consists largely of nerve fibers, which are the axons of neurons, and neuroglia. A tiny fraction, 0.02 percent, of all neurons are sensory or motor; all of the rest form a vast associational network between them (Nauta & Feirtag, 1979). The human brain has a far higher ratio of brain to body weight than that of other animals—hundreds of times higher than a rat and five to ten times higher than the apes. But what is crucial for human functioning is that so much of the human brain, and so little in other animals, is uncommitted to sensory and mo-

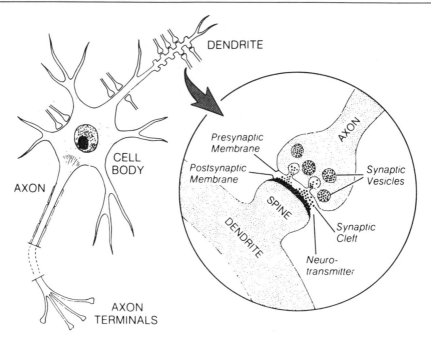

Figure 8-4. A central nervous system neuron and synapse. The enlargement shows the abutting of an axon against a dendritic spine. Neurotransmitters are released into the synaptic cleft from vesicles in the
presynaptic membrane and permit transmission of an impulse across
the junction. (From M. L. Batshaw and Y. M. Perret, *Children with Handicaps: A Medical Primer,* Paul H. Brooks Publishing Co., Baltimore MD.
Copyright 1981 by M. L. Batshaw and Y. M. Perret. Reproduced with
permission. Illustration by Elaine Kasmer.)

tor functions and, therefore, is available for higher mental processes (Hunt, 1982).

Glial cells outnumber neurons roughly ten to one in the human brain. The glial population increases as the brain matures. Glial cells may provide a protein known as nerve growth factor—vital for the growth and differentiation of neurons—and may modulate nerve-impulse transmission. Dopamine receptors have been found in glial cells, which suggests that they respond to the neuronal release of dopamine (Valzelli, 1981).

NEURAL CIRCUIT STRUCTURES

Most of the surface of a typical motor neuron is covered by some 2000 synaptic contacts on its body and some 8000 on its dendrites. Some 1000 trillion synapses are the key sites of the brain's activity. All information processing in the brain involves neurons "talking" to each other at synapses (Snyder, 1984b).

The two fundamental types of synapses are electrical and chemical. Electrical synapses permit the synchronous discharge of neurons by the current flow in one inducing field charges in its neighbor. Chemical synapses enable the amplification of signals and consist of clefts across which neurotransmitters pass under the influence of calcium ions.

Activation of one kind of synapse causes an increase in excitation along its axon. Activation of another type decreases excitation. The discharge of an impulse from a neuron occurs only when the summation of all synaptic influences exceeds its threshold of excitation and thus depolarizes the neuron. The resulting impulse triggers the release from presynaptic vesicles of a neurotransmitter, which travels across the synapse to influence another neuron's electrical activity (see Figure 8-4).

The signaling system in the brain is electrochemical in two forms: nerve impulses and neurotransmitters (Pribram, 1977). The signals generated by a neuron and transported along its axon are electrical impulses (see Figure 8-4). The signals transmitted between neurons are molecules of neurotransmitters that flow across a synapse between a supplier of information (an axon terminal or occasionally a dendrite end) and a recipient of information (a dendrite, a cell body, or occasionally an axon terminal).

The passage of a nerve impulse along an axon primarily involves sodium ions, which have a positive electrical charge. When a neuron is at rest, almost all of the sodium ions are outside the cell. Because of the negatively charged protein molecules inside of the neuron, there is a strong electrical force trying to pull the sodium ions into the neuron. The resulting voltage difference is nearly 0.1 volt. In the neuron membrane, sodium channels are closed at rest. They are electrically controlled and have a threshold of slightly less negative voltage than the inner surface of the membrane. A nerve impulse begins when the sodium channel gates in a particular region of the axon open briefly and sodium ions rush in. The sodium ions then build up inside the axon membrane under the adjacent closed gates, which makes the potential less negative there and triggers additional sodium channels to open. In this way the nerve impulse travels along the axon.

Inhibition is as important as excitation in the functioning of the central nervous system. Thus there are both excitatory and inhibitory neurons and neuroregulators.

Most neurons fire nearly continuously so that the brain is like an enormous powder keg that actually does explode in epileptic convulsions in the absence of inhibitory activity (Delgado, 1975).

The activity of a single neuron, then, is a tiny battle of excitation and inhibition that takes place against the modulating background of slow-acting inputs that are integrated by groups of neurons. This results in precisely summated outputs and ultimately in specific behavioral responses. The spatiotemporal pattern of signals in the normal brain is highly reliable and can give precise, predictable outputs throughout a lifetime. Thus the brain is built for reliability but at the same time can be highly flexible. Disturbances in the integration of neurons can cause disordered brain function. Consequently an understanding of the anatomical and neurochemical systems involved could lead to strategies to alleviate or abolish dysfunctions (Cotman & McGaugh, 1980).

Each neuron is fed by hundreds of thousands of other neurons, and, in turn, feeds into hundreds of thousands of still other neurons. Each neuron has the mathematical potential of some 10^{12} connections with other neurons. One-fifth of a second may elapse between a stimulus and consciousness of it as in a simple sensory experience. Since transmission between neurons takes 1/1000 second, there is time for 200 synaptic linkages to be achieved in 1/5 second. Because each neuron in the chain of 200 in turn is connected to thousands of its fellows, it is apparent that millions of electrical transactions are involved in the simplest sensation (Eccles, 1970). With this almost infinite complexity, the enormous redundant potential for flexibility of the brain is evident.

Neurons can be compared to notes on a musical scale, except that they are enormously more complicated and numerous. But just as the same notes in different combinations produce different melodies so neurons in different combinations produce different memories. These combinations of neurons correspond to Piaget's schemes. Moreover, immense numbers of groupings of schemes are ready for instant replay (Eccles, 1973).

Symbols and concepts are formed in the patterns of schemes, which provide meaning for perceptions (Schwartz & Wiggins, 1986). Whether such a pattern is rooted in the firing of neurons, the marching of ants, or the switching of silicon chips, the path to intelligence begins not with reasoning but with a level of randomness (Hofstadter, 1981). In an ant colony, for example, when carrying a piece of food from one part of a colony to another, no ant knows where the food is going. In fact, with all the random comings and goings of the individual ants, the whole original team may have long since scattered by the time the particle arrives at its destination. For ants we may substitute neurons or a mechanical equivalent.

The analogy of an ant colony is worth considering. An ant colony as a whole does have a kind of knowledge—how to grow, how to move, how to build—that is nowhere to be found in individual ants. The ant colony illustrates how a pattern of intelligence can emerge from the intertwining of different levels of activity. Like thoughts, signals between ants are sometimes orderly, sometimes erratic, but always changeable and fluid. When a piece of food moves two feet across a colony, an entomologist can describe that bit of behavior without any reference to the complicated underlying activity of scurrying ants. In the same way, some brain functions follow rules, such as the ability to manipulate numbers and to reason logically. These rules can be easily handled by computers. But the rules are the end of the story, not the beginning. To focus on them exclusively is to sacrifice the potential richness of human intelligence.

Beyond the rule-based intelligence of the ant colony the human brain is a clever combination of precise neural circuits. At the broadest level the brain coordinates representations of the world with movement in the world. This apparently is done through intricate transformations between four dimensional sensory and motor space representations (Churchland, 1986). The incredibly complex interconnections among neurons are not random, but are purposefully arranged in specific and general networks (Crick, 1979).

A specific network is organized so that within a small region, or module, everything is connected with everything else. The modules are vertical to the surface of the brain (Figure 8-5). Each of these columnar arrangements of up to 10,000 component neurons is a power unit that builds up energy so that its pyramidal neurons can generate discharges of impulses that act elsewhere in the central nervous system. At the same time a module exerts an inhibiting action on adjacent modules. A module, therefore, can be thought of as a unit that attempts to dominate other modules by virtue of its impulse discharges. Thus, in the early stage of signal processing within a specific network, some signals, such as one kind from the ear, do not relate to one another.

In a general network, signals proceed from one module to another so that the original mapping becomes more diffuse and abstract, and a signal is analyzed in successively more complex ways in association with signals from other modules. Each module acts upon hundreds of modules in other networks and itself receives excitatory and inhibitory inputs from other modules. A general network is broken down into many subnetworks, some parallel, others arranged serially. Moreover, the parcellation into subnetworks reflects both the structure of the external and internal worlds and the brain's relation to them. Seen in this way, the numerous functional areas of the brain and the many connections to each neuron take on a semblance

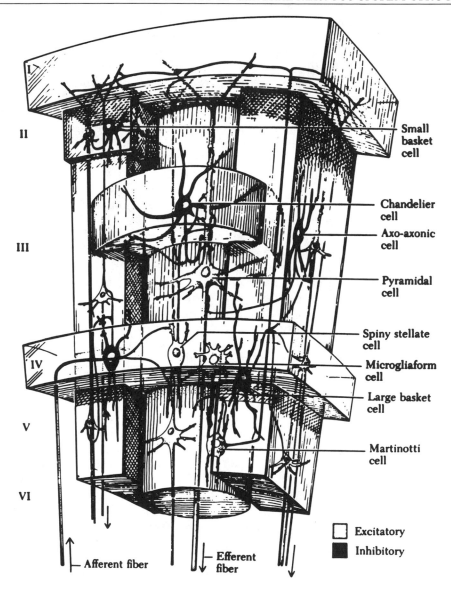

Figure 8-5. The cerebral cortex is made up of columnar modules of specialized neurons; this typical column is one-one hundredth of an inch in diameter. The boxlike structures are only diagrammatic. (From M. Hunt, *The Universe Within,* Simon & Schuster, Inc., New York. Copyright © 1982 by Morton Hunt. Reprinted by permission of Simon & Schuster, Inc.)

of order. The brain is not a collection of separate networks, however, as each neuron participates in a variety of networks.

The versatility of the brain is suggested under the microscope by the fact that each neuron appears to be different from its neighbors in form and in synaptic connections to other cells. Nonetheless consistent organization is imposed upon this diversity. One such organization is mapping. The axons that project from neurons in one region of the brain to neurons in another region generally reproduce neighboring relations. Another organization is the partitioning of a regionally mapped area of the brain into bands separating the types of information carried to that area. For example, the surface of the hand is represented in the somatic sensory cortex by a map of the hand consisting of alternating stripes representing different types of nerve endings, each of which brings a particular kind of information (Constantine-Paton & Law, 1982).

CHEMICAL COMPONENTS— NEUROREGULATORS

The processes of the central nervous system lie in the activity of neural networks. Although the pattern of interconnections in a network is largely genetically determined, the activities of synapses are mediated by neuroregulators that are responsive to life experience (Warburton, 1981). Identifying the nature and organization of neuroregulators is the crossroad of the cellular and behavioral neurosciences. The cellular approach requires knowledge of the nature of the neuroregulators in order to understand the mechanisms of synaptic transmission so that drugs can be identified to manipulate them selectively. The behavioral approach aims to understand more global functions and

depends upon knowledge of the organization of neuroregulator systems.

Neuroregulators are classified either as neuromodulators or as neurotransmitters. Neuromodulators fine-tune synaptic activity, such as by acting upon the reuptake mechanisms of neurotransmitters and prolonging the synaptic signal without altering the firing rate. Such substances probably are present in low concentrations and are metabolized quickly so that their study is difficult (Barchas et al, 1977a). Knowledge about neuromodulators is just beginning to accumulate.

In recent years, however, the knowledge of neurotransmitters has grown rapidly (Hoehn-Saric, 1982). Neurotransmitters may encourage or discourage the recipient neuron's firing, then disappear in a matter of milliseconds. It also may order a longstanding metabolic change in the receiving neuron, perhaps by switching on genes that produce new transmitters or receptors.

Neurotransmitters are distributed throughout the brain but are localized in specific neuronal circuits, which can be traced with precision as indicated in Figure 8-6. The superimposition of these diverse neurotansmitters on the complex neuronal circuitry of the brain provides the flexibility and specificity of the processes of the CNS.

The binding of neurotransmitters to specific receptors at synaptic junctions excites or inhibits neuronal firing. This neurotransmitter activation and inhibition can be related to behavior. The interaction of a neurotransmitter with its receptor site and the subsequent translation of this information into changes in ion movement or the formation of secondary messenger molecules are the keys to synaptic activity (Snyder, 1984a). The common origin of neurotransmitters and hormones is suggested by the fact that nerve cells make molecules that are secreted into the bloodstream and act as hormones at distant targets; morever, some hormones are made

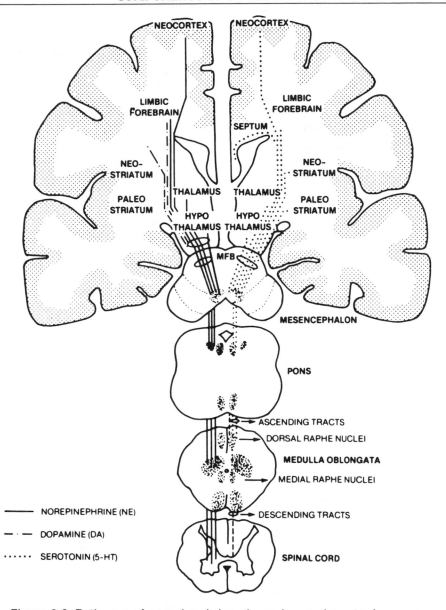

Figure 8-6. Pathways of norepinephrine, dopamine, and serotonin neurotransmitter systems. (Reproduced from C. Corfman, *Science Reports 1: Depression, Manic-Depressive Illness, and Biological Rhythms.* Division of Scientific and Public Information, National Institute of Mental Health, Rockville MD.)

in nerve cells, where they act as neurotransmitters. The action of neurotransmitters is influenced by hormones, as well. In these ways the brain is a complex gland (Bergland, 1986).

The diurnal pattern of neuroendocrine activity is tuned to daily problem-solving requirements (Harris, 1986). The relinquishing of a problem-solving focus at the threshold of sleep is associated with the serotonin inhibition of higher cortical functioning and the release of the catecholamine systems from energizing cortical functions. The uncoupling of the frontal system allows for a hierarchical regression in sleep to hypothalamic control of automatic regulatory processes. As norepinephrine production falls during the night, ACTH production rises and stimulates high morning cortisol levels for daytime problem-solving activity.

Synapses are the sites for modifying neuronal circuits that enable the brain to respond to the external world while monitoring and controlling the internal world. These neural junctions are much more than way stations in the transmission of nerve impulses. They compose, at any moment, a neural state that is influenced by arriving impulses (Pribram, 1977). At the synapse the transmitting nerve terminal has receptors listening to its own messages and to messages from the receiving nerve terminal. At the same time it may be intercepting chemical messages from the bloodstream and neighboring nerve endings. All of this feedback can change the activity of the transmitting cell as well as that of the receiving one.

It is now clear that different CNS processes are served by discrete neurotransmitter networks. These networks are regulators of general behavior patterns rather than specifiers of precise actions (Costa & Greengard, 1983; Lamble, 1981). For example, the norepinephrine network for eating controls the frequency and duration of eating but not the specific foods

that are sought and consumed. A dopamine network probably modulates behavioral excitation. A norepinephrine network seems to mediate mood states but not specific emotions. Descending cholinergic pathways control the nature of information processing but not the stimuli selected (Warburton, 1981).

Sensation seeking may be determined by levels of neurotransmitters and enzymes that regulate them. Thus the inheritance of psychological traits may depend upon the genetic transmission of the biochemical systems involved in sensitizing pleasure and arousal systems. For example, individual differences in monoamine oxidase levels might influence sensation seeking through influencing the levels of monoamine neurotransmitters (Zuckerman, 1983).

The important known neurotransmitters are monoamines, such as acetylcholine, dopamine, norepinephrine, serotinin, and histamine (Schwartz et al, 1980); amino acids, such as gamma aminobutyric acid, glutamic acid, glycine, and taurine; and neuropeptides (see Figure 8-7).

The monoamine systems have identifiable functions. For example, it has been proposed that the ascending norepinephrine systems are involved in focused attention, judgment, and feedback interaction with the environment; that the serotonin system is involved in dampening or reducing oscillations of general homeostatic processes; and that the dopamine systems are involved in nonspecific arousal (Hartmann, 1982). Agents that enhance neurotransmitter action are called agonists, those that impede it are called antagonists, and those that cause opposite effects are called inverse agonists.

The dopamine system has been equated with the psychoanalytic concept of libido because it readies the state of consciousness for consummatory behaviors, ranging from the quenching of thirst to sexual affection (Harris, 1986). In this view the norepi-

Neurotransmitters	Distribution in Central Nervous System	Precursors	Agonists	Antagonists	Postulated Functions
Acetylcholine	Somatic motor neurons; Preganglionic sympathetic and parasympathetic neurons; Postganglionic parasympathetic and sympathetic to sweat gland neurons	Choline	Physostigmine Nicotine	Cholinesterase Atropine	Voluntary and involuntary motor activity; visceral functioning; memory
Serotonin	Raphe nuclei of brainstem to hypothalamus, thalamus, cerebellum and spinal cord	Tryptophan	Monoamine oxidase inhibitor	Monoamine oxidase Lysergic acid diethylamide	Dampening of general homeostatic processes: temperature regulation, sensory perception, onset of sleep. Elevated in depression, enhances self-punishment, role in aggression
Histamine	Hippocampus, basal ganglia, thalamus; highest in hypothalamus; lowest in cerebellum and brainstem	Histadine	Reserpine	Mepyramine Anti-histamines	Inhibits noradrenergic neurovascular junctions; antihistamines sedate and impair motor performance; receptors blocked by antipsychotics and antidepressants
Catecholamines Dopamine	Substantia nigra, ventral tegmentum, reticular formation to corpus striatum, limbic and olfactory areas of frontal cortex.	Tyrosine Phenylalanine	L-DOPA Amphetamines	Monoamine oxidase Tyrosine	Nonspecific and pleasure arousal. Voluntary motor function. Matching response to stimuli. Overly active in schizophrenia. Underactive in Parkinsonism
Norepinephrine	Locus ceruleus, reticular formation, postganglionic sympathetic neurons (except sweat glands) to all parts of brain	Tyrosine Phenylalanine Dopamine	Amphetamine Tricyclic antidepressants	Monoamine oxidase Tyrosine hydroxylase	Focused attention, feedback, interaction with environment. Maintenance of arousal, REM sleep, mood regulation. Underactive in depression
Gamma aminobutyric acid (GABA)	All areas of brain	Glutamic Acid	Benzodiazepines Muscimol	Bicuculline Picrotoxinin	Principal inhibitory neurotransmitter; may inhibit anxiety, aggressive behavior, convulsions
Glutamic Acid	All areas of brain, especially cerebral cortex, cerebellum, nucleus accumbens especially	Glutamine	Kainic acid	L-glutamate diethylester	May be principal excitatory neuro-transmitter
Glycine	Substantia nigra, brainstem, spinal cord	Glucose		H-strychnine	Inhibition of nigrostriatal dopamine neurons
Taurine	Retina, lateral geniculate nuclei; corpus striatum	Cysteine	Beta-alanine	H-strychnine	Inhibition of neurotransmission; may inhibit aggression
Beta-endorphin	Hypothalamus to thalamus; pituitary (anterior and intermediate)	Glycoprotein	Opiates	Naloxone	Regulation of limbic excitability, pain perception, temperature of body, attentional and memory mechanisms
Enkaphalins	Widely distributed in pain pathways and limbic areas	Beta-lipotropin	Opiates	Naloxone	

Figure 8-7. Examples of the known neurotransmitters.

nephrine system is equated with the aggressive drive. The serotonin system then corresponds to the neutralizing agency that dampens dopamine- and norepinephrine-fueled drives.

Acetylcholine

Acetylcholine is involved in all preganglionic endings of the voluntary and autonomic nervous systems and at postganglionic endings of the parasympathetic system. Acetylcholine is inactivated by the neuromodulating enzyme cholinesterase, which splits it into its two major components, thus ceasing its stimulating effect. Acetylcholine antagonists, such as atropine, produce memory impairment associated with a disruption in access to information in semantic memory. Acetylcholine agonists tend to facilitate memory in some persons with senile dementia (Weingartner et al, 1983).

The acetylcholine facilitating system ascends through the reticular activating system and the reticular portion of the thalamus to turn on consciousness. Acetylcholine containing neurons in the cerebral cortex are thought to handle the complex information processing necessary for reflective thinking. Other acetylcholine containing neurons with axons extending throughout the cerebral cortex are located in the basal nucleus of Meynert.

Dopamine

As the central nervous system evolved, dopamine may have been the original catecholamine manufactured from phenylalanine, since it is found in the most primitive regions of the brain. The conversion of dopamine to norepinephrine made it possible to add new functions that were built upon those of dopamine. A further evolutionary step may have converted norepinephrine to epinephrine.

Neurons containing dopamine are concentrated in the substantia nigra and the ventral tegmentum regions of the midbrain. Many of the dopamine-containing neurons project their axons to the limbic and olfactory areas of the forebrain, where they are thought to be involved in regulating emotional responses. Other dopamine-containing fibers terminate in the corpus striatum where the degeneration of the fibers projecting into this region gives rise to the muscular rigidity and tremors of Parkinson's disease. The action of dopamine is terminated through its reuptake into neurons.

The stimulant amphetamine, a chemical analog of dopamine, triggers the release of dopamine, which also is associated with the arousal of the pleasure system. Sustained excessive levels of amphetamine can lead to disruption of thought processes, hallucinations, and delusions of persecution—symptoms similar to those found in some forms of schizophrenia. This and other evidence led to the hypothesis that overactivity in the brain dopamine systems or overresponsiveness to it might be related to schizophrenia. Although that has not been substantiated, it illustrates the heuristic value of testable hypotheses that are emerging from growing knowledge of the biochemistry of the brain. A variety of antipsychotic medications share the property of binding to dopamine receptors, thereby preventing dopamine from activating them.

Norepinephrine

Norepinephrine is the principle neurotransmitter at most sympathetic postganglionic endings. Norepinephrine and its derivative epinephrine also are secreted by the adrenal medulla. Norepinephrine is concentrated in the small cluster of neurons in the brain stem medulla known as the locus ceruleus, which produces approximately 70 percent of the brain's supply (Aston-Jones & Bloom, 1981; Hoehn-Saric, 1982). The axons of these neurons are highly branched and project to diverse regions, such as the hypothalamus, the cerebellum, and the forebrain. The norepinephrine system is involved in the maintenance of vigilance, focused attention, dreaming sleep, and modulation of mood. Norepinephrine tunes the cerebral cortex to the significance of external and internal stimuli by enhancing both inhibitory and excitatory synaptic activity.

Catecholamine antagonists, apparently of both dopamine and norepinephrine, produce interferences resembling those of clinical depression on tasks requiring concentration and episodic memory of events in time and place, but not on tasks that can be performed relatively automatically and are based upon semantic, or symbolic, memory. Catecholamine agonists, such as amphetamine, enhance these processes (Weingartner et al, 1983).

Serotonin

Serotonin is concentrated in a cluster of neurons in the region of the brain stem known as the raphe nuclei. Neurons of this center project to the hypothalmus, the thalamus, and many other brain regions. Serotonin is thought to be involved in temperature regulation, sensory perception, and the onset of sleep.

Amino Acids

Although amino acids are the precursors of neurotransmitters, they are widely distributed throughout the central nervous system, and it is likely that they also function in the general transmission of nerve impulses more than is currently known (DeFeudis & Mandel, 1981). Glutamic acid is an example of an amino acid that both excites neurons itself (Filer et al, 1979) and serves as the precursor for the major inhibitory neurotransmitter, gamma aminobutyric acid (Krogsgaard-Larsen et al, 1979). Glycine plays a role in regulating motor

functions through inhibiting nigrostriatal dopamine neurons. Taurine plays a role in the visual system.

Neuropeptides

The neuropeptides are an as yet incompletely understood class of neuroregulators found in the brain, endocrine glands, and gastrointestinal tract (Muller & Geenazzani, 1984). They have important physiological roles in stress responses, pain perception, regulation of appetite and sleep, and memory and learning. Almost 40 neuropeptides have been found in the brain, and the expectation is that hundreds ultimately will be identified. They link the nervous, endocrine, and immune systems.

Many neuropeptides function as hormones. Their biological activities in the central nervous system may be quite different from their properties as hormones when present in the systemic circulation. For instance, the antidiuretic hormone in the bloodstream is involved in water metabolism control but in the CNS facilitates memory and learning (Krieger & Martin, 1981).

Of the variety of brain peptides, the endorphins particularly are intriguing chemical messengers that occur naturally in the brain and bear a similarity to morphine (Krieger, 1983). Certain regions of the brain bind opiate drugs and endorphines with high affinity. These are centers involved in the perception and integration of pain and emotional experience.

There appear to be at least two separate endorphine systems. The enkephalins are widely distributed in the pain pathways and the limbic areas. The other system is comprised of beta-endorphins and originates in the hypothalamic areas; they also are found in the pituitary gland.

The neuropeptides may differ from the other neurotransmitters in that they appear to represent a global means of chemical coding for patterns of brain activity associated with particular functions, such as body fluid balance, sexual behavior, and pain or pleasure. These widely spread, overlapping, and independent systems of opioid peptides play roles as communicative agents between nerve cells and probably have additional multifaceted functions beyond pain suppression involving temperature regulation, memory, and attentional mechanisms (Bloom & Henriksen, 1981; Malick & Bell, 1982).

Prostaglandins

Another group of chemicals present in high levels in brain tissue are the prostaglandins, which have a variety of excitatory and inhibitory effects on neurons, playing neuromodulating rather than neurotransmitter roles (Greenberg et al, 1982). Prostaglandins may increase or decrease the amount of norepinephrine released from adrenergic nerve terminals and thus modify the function of smooth muscle in the blood vessels. Adrenergic neuronal activation promotes the synthesis of prostaglandins from fatty acids and triglycerides. Ibuprofen is a prostaglandin antagonist.

The central nervous system contains a number of different prostaglandins, particularly in the gray matter of the cerebral cortex and the reticular acrtivating system. These substances also are normal constituents of the cerebrospinal fluid. Their functions are unclear; however, a correlation exists between the release of prostaglandins from nervous tissue and the general level of neuronal activity. Prostaglandins play a key local feedback role in the regulation of the vascular bed. They also can reproduce inflammatory reactions and sensitize tissue to inflammatory agents.

Psychoactive Medications

There are two major categories of psychoactive drugs—those that occur naturally in the body, such as hormones and neurotransmitters, and those that are foreign to the body. The significance of this difference is that specific receptors have evolved that interact with naturally occurring drugs, whereas foreign drugs interact with a variety of cellular and extracellular constituents to produce their effects (Lamble, 1981).

All drugs that affect behavior presumably act by affecting synaptic transmission, by either mimicking or blocking the action of natural neurotransmitters. Drugs are classified as agonists if they activate receptors, thus mimicking the action of a neurotransmitter; as antagonists if they inactivate receptors; and as inverse agonists if they cause opposite effects. For example, a benzodiazepine agonist reduces anxiety, an antagonist prevents benzodiazepine reduction of anxiety, and an inverse agonist causes anxiety. Therapeutic actions of the antidepressants are thought to involve various aspects of norepinephrine disposition, as if depression might be associated with low, and mania with high, levels of norepinephrine.

The stimulant drug cocaine appears to work by blocking neurotransmitter synaptic reuptake. Hallucinogenic drugs bear a structural resemblance to natural transmitters. Mescaline is similar to norepinephrine and dopamine, and both d-lysergic acid and psilocybin are related to serotonin. Caffeine and theophylline exert a stimulant action on the brain by inhibiting the enzyme phosphodiesterase, which degrades cyclic adenosine monophosphate, thereby increasing the amount that accumulates in response to a neurotransmitter.

BRAIN METABOLISM

In the past the chemical intricacies of the brain have been difficult to unravel because of its relative inaccessability in the living state for structural and chemical studies (Karlsson, 1978; Ottoson, 1983). Advances in neuroradiological techniques, however, offer great promise in this respect.

Neurons share the biochemical machinery of all other living cells, such as generating energy from the oxidation of foodstuffs to maintain and repair themselves. The brain is the most active energy consumer of all body organs, as reflected in its rich blood supply and high oxygen uptake. Primate brains, as represented by the monkey, macaca mulatta, and homo sapiens generate a relatively higher proportion of the body metabolism (9 and 20 percent respectively) than do nonprimate brains, such as the cat and dog (4 to 6 percent). A major primate evolutionary adaptation appears to have been the allocation of a larger proportion of the body's energy supply for the brain (Armstrong, 1983).

Although the human brain comprises only 2 percent of the total body weight, there are several reasons why it accounts for 20 percent of the total resting body level of oxygen utilization. First, unlike other body cells neurons of the adult brain apparently must last a lifetime. Thus the continual replenishment of axonal components requires energy for transporting enzymes and other complex molecules manufactured in the region of the neuron body down the entire length of its axon. A second reason for the brain's relatively enormous expenditure of energy is to maintain membrane ionic gradients and chemical neurotransmitter levels upon which the conduction of impulses and synaptic communication depends. Third, there is no respite from the energy demand of the brain. The rate of brain metabolism is relatively constant day and night, and even increases somewhat during the dreaming phases of sleep. When placed in perspective, however, the total energy equivalent of brain metabolism still only approximates that of a 20-watt light bulb.

Whereas other body organs are able to use a variety of fuels, such as sugars, fats, and amino acids, neurons ordinarily use only glucose. Moreover, tissues such as muscle are able to function for short periods in the absence of oxygen, but the brain cannot. If the supply of oxygenated blood through the brain is interrupted, consciousness is lost within ten seconds, and permanent damage to the brain ensues after about seven minutes. Similar effects result from lowering of blood glucose, as when a diabetic takes an overdose of insulin. Accordingly, elaborate control mechanisms ensure that blood pressure remains stable and that there are constant levels of oxygen and glucose in the blood available to the brain.

Neurons also are exceedingly sensitive to chemical substances that find their way into the bloodstream and to small molecules that are normally present in the blood, such as amino acids. The brain, therefore, is protected from the general circulation by a filtration system composed of glial cells called the blood–brain barrier.

SUMMARY

Unlike other organs of the body, the brain has two components. One is anatomical and consists of cells. The other consists of chemical neuroregulators. The fundamental structures of the central nervous system are neural circuits that correspond to Piaget's schemes. The CNS has the remarkable capacity to modify the brain's neural circuitry in accordance with life experience. The three critical interacting development determinants of the CNS, therefore, are its innate cellular and neural circuitry components, life experiences, and its action upon its own neural circuitry.

The gross anatomy of the brain reflects the evolution of the species with the progressive addition of hindbrain, midbrain, and forebrain centers that provide for specialization and the more complex integration of behavior.

The fundamental cellular components of the CNS are some ten billion neurons and their some 1000 trillion interconnecting synapses in addition to some 100 billion neuroglia. Although each neuron differs from its neighbors, functional organization and mapping of the brain impose remarkable consistency upon them, producing the brain's incredibly versatile functional capacity.

The brain is an exceedingly clever combination of precise neural wiring arranged in specific formats of modules in which all neurons are interconnected and in general formats composed of parallel and serial modules. This arrangement permits the simultaneous localization and generalization of neural activity so that the brain functions both as a whole and from specific areas.

The brain is the most active energy consumer of all organs, accounting for 20 per-cent of the body's resting utilization of oxygen even though it constitutes only 2 percent of the body's weight. The brain is more vulnerable than other organs, because it ordinarily can metabolize only glucose, cannot function without oxygen, and must be protected from the chemicals present in the blood by the blood–brain filtration barrier.

The superimposition of neuroregulators at the synapses permits activation or suppression of neural circuits and the operation of CNS processes that modulate behavior. An increasing number of neuromodulators and neurotransmitters are being identified with specific interrelated functions, localization, antagonists, and agonists. Drugs that affect behavior presumably act through their influence on neuroregulators. Although further research will modify our understanding of neurotransmitters, an awareness of their significance in determining behavior is important for an appreciation of the neurophysiology of learning.

The Anatomical Subsystems of Central Nervous System Structures

The brain is an enchanted loom that weaves a dissolving pattern, always a meaningful pattern, although never an enduring one; a shifting harmony of subpatterns.

Sir Charles Sherrington, 1925

The anatomical subsystems of the central nervous system (CNS) structures are interconnected neural circuits that range from the receptors of sensory organs to the prefrontal cortex. They include (1) the special sensory systems, (2) the visual sensorimotor system, (3) the motor systems, (4) the cerebellum, (5) the autonomic nervous system, (6) the reticular activating system, (7) the limbic system, (8) the neuroendocrine system, (9) the thalamus, (10) the cortical receptive zones, (11) the frontal lobe systems, and (12) the cerebral hemispheres. In concert all of these subsystems constitute the anatomical basis of human behavior.

THE SPECIAL SENSORY SYSTEMS

The special sense systems begin with sensory end organs in the body, generally connected by nerve fibers to the thalamus, which distributes impulses to the primary sensory areas of the cerebral cortex.

The Olfactory System

Smell is the most primitive sense. In the course of evolution, it was the earliest source of distant information through which free-ranging animals could track food sources and distinguish their own species from others for recognition and sexual purposes. Its association with taste brings smell into alimentation.

The olfactory system is the only sensory system in which the primary neurons lie on the body surface and connect directly to the cerebral cortex. The transmission of smell signals is to the limbic system via the piriform cortex and the amygdala without the negotiating of complex pathways typical of the other sensory impulses. Olfaction, therefore, is simply a discriminator of intensity gradient and lacks the complexity inherent in the other sensory systems.

The Pain and Temperature Systems

The perception of pain and temperature is served by sensory fibers with nerve end-

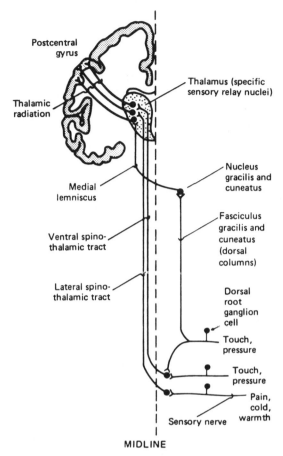

Figure 9-1. The touch, pressure, pain, and temperature pathways. (Reproduced, with permission, from W. F. Ganong, *Review of Medical Physiology,* 12th ed. Copyright 1985 by Lange Medical Publications, Los Altos CA.)

ings in the skin and cell bodies located in the dorsal root ganglia alongside the spinal cord (see Figure 9-1). These fibers enter the spinal cord, where they synapse with other nerves whose fibers cross the midline to form the lateral spinothalamic tracts, which end in the ventral posterolateral nuclei of the thalamus. From there fibers travel upward to terminate in the postcentral gyrus of the parietal lobe. Pain and temperature for the face are served separately by the fifth cranial nerve.

The Touch and Pressure Systems

The impulses of touch travel in relatively large fibers from nerve endings in and beneath the skin and around hair follicles. Receptors of pressure stimuli lie in the skin, connective tissue, and body cavity walls. They both enter the dorsal roots of the spinal cord via spinal ganglia and ascend and descend to give off collaterals for reflex connections (see Figure 9-1). They then cross to ascend the spinal cord via the ventral spinothalamic tract. At higher cervical levels, they may cross and join the medial lemniscus. They then are relayed to the postcentral parietal gyrus through thalamic nuclei.

The Proprioceptive System

The position sense of proprioception arises from nerve endings in muscles and tendons and is mediated by sensory fibers derived from neurons within the dorsal root ganglia that enter the posterior columns of the spinal cord and, without synapsing or crossing the midline, pass upward as the gracile and cuneate fasciculi to end in the gracile and cuneate nuclei of the medulla (see Figure 9-1). From there the fibers cross to the opposite side and end in the ventral posterolateral nuclei of the thalamus, and thence radiate to the postcentral gyrus of the parietal lobe. The integration of touch and proprioception is referred to as the haptic sense.

The Auditory System

The auditory system consists of three major components: a peripheral end organ (the inner ear), the eighth cranial nerve (the vestibulocochlear or acoustic nerve), and central structures (nuclei of the brain stem and the temporal lobe).

The external ear directs sound to the tympanic membrane, movements of which

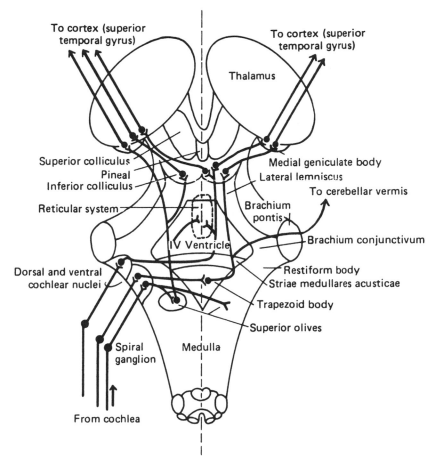

Figure 9-2. A simplified diagram of the main auditory pathways superimposed on a dorsal view of the brainstem. The cerebellum and cerebral cortex are not shown. (Reproduced, with permission, from W. F. Ganong, *Review of Medical Physiology,* 12th ed. Copyright 1985 by Lange Medical Publications, Los Altos CA.)

are transmitted by the ossicular chain of bones (malleus, incus, and stapes) to the perilymphatic fluid in the cochlea. In the cochlea the organ of Corti's hair cells respond to the fluid's movements and transmit impulses via the cochlear division of the acoustic nerve, which enters the brain stem and synapses with the cochlear nuclei of the medulla (see Figure 9-2). Fibers from the cochlear nuclei travel upward in the lateral lemniscus to the inferior colliculus of the midbrain and then to the medial

geniculate body of the thalamus. Fibers radiate from there to the superior gyrus of the temporal lobe (Heschl's gyrus).

The Vestibular System

The vestibular sensory organ transduces the forces associated with head acceleration and gravity into a neural signal. The control centers in the brain use this signal to develop a subjective awareness of the orientation of head position in relation to the environment and to mediate motor reflexes for equilibrium and locomotion (Baloh & Honrubia, 1979).

There are no commonly used words to designate the sensations of the vestibular system, which has the functions of controlling postural and eye movements and the conscious experiencing of space. The vestibule is an irregular sac filled with fluid and solid particles. Nerve endings in the wall of the vestibule register and transmit any shift in position of the solid particles in the contained fluid caused by postural changes from head movements and body position. Vestibular reflexes maintain the position of the eyes, head, and body in spite of movements of the head. These reflexes also maintain an upright position of the head in relation to gravity.

The vestibular division of the acoustic nerve passes to the posterior lobe of the cerebellum and to the vestibular nuclei of the midbrain from which they reach motor nuclei throughout the body, but chiefly those of the head, neck, and eye muscles through the medial longitudinal fasciculus and the lateral vestibulospinal tract.

When the vestibular system works normally, the pull of gravity generates a constant sensory flow. All other sensory inputs to the brain are superimposed upon that input from gravity receptors. Thus sensory integration of the vestibular system provides gravitational security—the primal trust that one is connected to the earth. The psychological aspects of the vestibular system are largely unexplored (Hubbard & Wright, 1985). Children spend much of their early life developing their relationship to gravity, from lifting their heads to picking up dropped objects (Ayres, 1979).

THE VISUAL SENSORIMOTOR SYSTEM

Because sight involves both sensory and motor components, it merits consideration separate from the other sensory systems. Phylogenetically the visual system preceded the auditory system. There are some one million fibers in the optic nerve and only some 30,000 fibers in the auditory nerve. Moreover, the amount of motor cortex representing vision equals that devoted to the rest of the body.

Sensory Aspects

The sensory component of vision involves a series of steps in the transmission of visual impulses from the eye to the brain (see Figure 9-3). Light first passes through the cornea, past pupillary accommodation to its intensity, and through the lens, which accommodates to focus, to the retina, where light-sensitive neurons, the rods and cones, are stimulated and transform light into neural impulses.

The retina processes light in a variety of ways and performs integrating functions in addition to adapting to light and dark by altering its level of sensitivity. The incessant automatic flicking movements of the eyes keep a visual image dancing upon the retinal receptors. These movements permit the synthesis of visual patterns from a myriad of point stimuli as does a television screen and enhance the clarity of the images. The steadiness of light is produced by flicker fusion that begins in the retina where the rods fuse flickers at lower frequencies than cones. Clear and precise vision is confined to the macula, the central two to three degrees of the retina, with discrimination of color and detail rapidly falling off so that peripheral vision is limited to discriminating movement only. In addition, structural variations in retinal cells are reflected in variations in their thresholds, latency responses, and channel capacities. The retinal cells also can expand upon or compress information.

From the retina visual information leaves the eye via the optic nerve fibers, which cross in the optic chiasm such that fibers

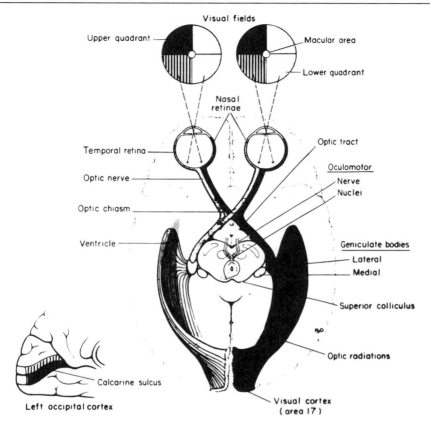

Figure 9-3. Diagram of the visual pathways viewed from the ventral surface of the brain. Light from the upper half of the visual field falls on the inferior half of the retina. Light from the temporal half of the visual field falls on the nasal half of the retina, while light from the nasal half of the visual field falls on the temporal half of the retina. Each macula is represented in a similar way. (From Truex and Carpenter, *Human Neuroanatomy,* © 1976, The Williams & Wilkins Co., Baltimore MD. Reprinted with permission.)

from the left half of each retina travel together in the left optic tract and from the right half of the retina in the right optic tract. Each optic tract is connected with a superior colliculus and the pretectal nuclei of the midbrain, which are involved in pupillary reactions to accommodation and light. From the lateral geniculate nuclei, fibers sweep around the walls of the lateral ventricles as the geniculocalcarine tract to terminate in the occipital cortex, where the visual fields are represented topographically in an upside-down and reversed fash-

ion. A similar pattern of cortical representation occurs for each macula.

Both hemispheres receive visual stimuli from both eyes so that ocular dominance does not indicate that only one hemisphere is functioning. Because there is a crossing of the optic nerve fibers in the optic chiasm from the nasal half of each retina, both hemispheres of the brain receive sensations from each eye from both the macula and peripheral retina. For example, the left hemisphere receives information from the left halves of the retina and macula of the left eye and the left halves of the retina and macula of the right eye. Thus eye dominance is a complicated matter.

The auditory and visual nervous systems can be contrasted in several ways that help to explain the greater fidelity of the visual system. The visual system involves frequency analysis much as does the auditory system but it concerns the frequency of light waves across space rather than sound vibrations over time (Pribram, 1977). No auditory fiber can reach its thalamic way station without synaptic interruption, because the auditory system is involved in alerting and startle reflexes that require intervening connections. In contrast, visual fibers go directly to the thalamus via the superior colliculus that connects both to the the thalamic lateral geniculate body, which projects to the visual cortex, and to the thalamic nucleus lateralis posterior, which projects to a nearby cortical region that is distinct from the visual cortex.

Thus the visual system has two channels for sending messages to the cerebral cortex and is capable of processing far more information with much greater rapidity than the auditory system, which has a relatively limited channel capacity and depends upon extracting meaning over a period of time rather than instantaneously as does vision. It is no wonder that a picture conveys more than 1000 words.

Motor Aspects

Beyond the sensory elements accurate vision depends upon a series of precisely coordinated eye movements (Berthoz & Jones, 1985). The first is the flicking nystagmus, or optokinetic nystagmus response (OKN), necessary for optimal retinal fixations. The mechanisms for these movements are not completely known at this time. Two brain mechanisms may exist that can produce flicking in response to visual stimulation. The first is the full-field OKN, which stabilizes the entire visually perceived environment on the retina when a person is in motion. It probably involves a short, direct brainstem pathway. The second, the partial-field OKN, stabilizes moving objects rather than the entire surround on the retina and probably involves elaborate cortical pathways in both the parietal and frontal lobes. Parenthetically, it is this form that has been reported to be abnormal in adult schizophrenic persons (Latham et al, 1981).

In addition to the flicking movements that keep a visual image on the macula, four motor systems are involved in sight: saccadic, pursuit, vergence, and vestibular. All of these movements are depicted in the following anecdote. A man is hunting ducks. When he hears sounds, his eyes make a rapid saccadic motion to fix on a flying duck and then follow the moving target with a pursuit movement. As he aims his rifle, the hunter's eyes converge in a vergence movement on the rifle sight. After he shoots, the boat begins to rock, and his vestibular system coordinates his resulting eye and head movements. In addition, as the duck flies away, optokinetic nystagmus is produced by the hunter's repeated fixations on the duck (Goldberg & Schiffman, 1983).

The first step in vision then is adjusting the aim and focus of the eyes upon an object through voluntary eye movements controlled by the frontal premotor cortex via the frontal optic tract to the pretectal area. In voluntary fixation, such as reading, the eyes are trained to scan across a page, making several saccadic movements of the eye for each line. The brain suppresses the visual images registered between saccadic fixation points so that one is unaware of the movement between points. The neural pathways for the control of eye movements include the medial longitudinal fasciculus, which connects the nuclei of the third, fourth, and sixth cranial nerves that reciprocally innervate the eye muscles (see Figure 9-4).

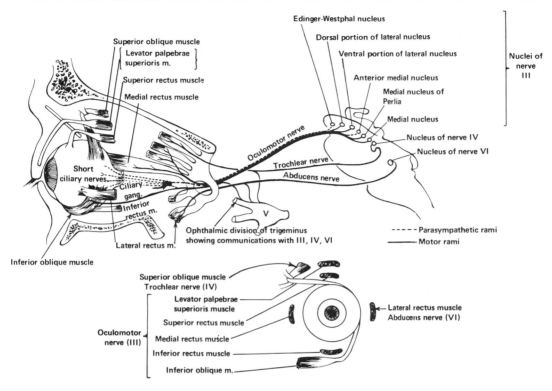

Figure 9-4. The oculomotor, trochlear, and abducens nerves, which comprise the motor aspects of the visual system. (Reproduced, with permission, from J. G. Chusid, *Correlative Neuroanatomy and Functional Neurology,* 19th ed. Copyright 1985 by Lange Medical Publications, Los Altos CA.)

Next, involuntary pursuit fixation controlled by the occipital cortex holds the eyes firmly on an object once it has been found. The occipital visual areas are connected to the pretectal and superior colliculus areas of the brainstem via the occipitotectal and occipitocollicular tracts. From both the pretectal and superior colliculus areas, oculomotor control signals then pass to the nuclei of the oculomotor nerves. Finally, strong signals are transmitted into the oculomotor system, which is closely interconnected to the cerebellum and the vestibular apparatus, by way of the medial longitudinal fasciculus for the coordination of eye and head movements (Guyton, 1977). Thus the frontal and occipital cerebral cortices,

in addition to the vestibulocerebellar system, are involved in eye movements.

Rapid eye movements are associated with dreaming and may play a role in stimulating dream imagery.

THE MOTOR SYSTEMS

Body movements are sensorimotor in nature and do not occur without concomitant sensory phenomena. Still it is useful to describe extrapyramidal and pyramidal motor systems. Furthermore, the extrapyramidal motor system is not really separate from the pyramidal motor system, since they both arise from the same regions of the frontal cortex (Brodal, 1963). The functional distinction, however, between involuntary extrapyramidal and voluntary pyramidal motor movements does warrant attention.

In both phylogenesis and ontogenesis, the involuntary extrapyramidal system preceded the voluntary pyramidal system in its appearance. In animals below mammals, the extrapyramidal system is the highest level of brain functioning and contains centers for instinctual behavior, such as feeding, mating, nesting, and migration. As the cerebral cortex evolved, however, the neurons of the extrapyramidal cortex projecting to the corpus striatum and lower centers were bypassed by direct connections from the frontal motor neurons to the body in the form of the pyramidal system (see Figure 9-5).

The Extrapyramidal Sensorimotor System

The extrapyramidal system actually is a sensorimotor correlation system that functions automatically to determine the interplay between muscles in influencing posture and movement (see Figure 9-5). In particular, the caudate-putamen and globus pallidus exercise control over both sensory input and motor output (Pribram, 1977). They are the core centers of sensorimotor schemes. They act as a clearinghouse that samples activities projected by the cerebral cortex and facilitates one and suppresses all others. Through their sensorimotor functions, they apparently are involved in focusing attention, spatial orientation, body image, and short-term memory (Bowen, 1976; Denny-Brown & Yanagisawa 1976). They enable movements across specific muscle groups.

The functions of the extrapyramidal system are nonspecifically involved with states of generalized muscular tonus, such as restlessness or placidity reflecting limbic system discharge, or with diffuse repetitive motor patterns, such as locomotion or swinging of the arms. The extrapyramidal system has three levels: lower, middle, and upper (see Figure 9-6).

The lower extrapyramidal system is located within the midbrain, pons, and medulla and is composed of the nuclei that affect the musculature of the head and thereby mediate the control of eye movements, mastication, and phonation. It also includes nuclei that affect extension, flexion, and rotation of the limbs and body trunk, as well as respiration (Weil, 1974).

The middle extrapyramidal system may be considered as a complex of genetically primitive reflex arcs mediated through the reticular formation; it lies in the tegmentum of the midbrain and includes the red nucleus, substantia nigra and medial longitudinal fasciculus. These nuclei involve the discharge of diffuse, repetitive, rhythmic motor reactions. For example, lesions of the substantia nigra as seen in Parkinsonism result in rhythmic resting tremors. This "primitive motor center" is maintained in an active state by its sensory input and is concerned with undifferentiated tonic, mainly postural, activity of the trunk muscles and the proximal muscles of the extremities. This primitive subconscious behavior is evinced in postural activity and in tonic facilitation of the voluntary motor apparatus and of vigilance (Bergstrom, 1963).

In addition to the premotor frontal cortex, the upper extrapyramidal system is located in the caudate nucleus, the putamen and the globus pallidus, which make up the corpus striatum, also known as the basal ganglia. These nuclei selectively facilitate and inhibit a number of middle extrapyramidal patterns of rhythmic movement. More significantly, they are sensorimotor correlational centers for instinctual behav-

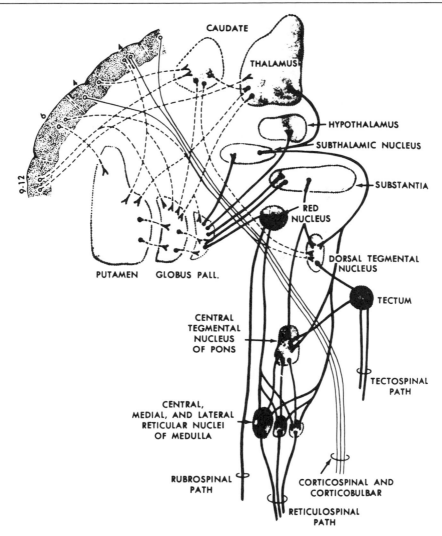

Figure 9-5. The afferent and efferent pathways of the extrapyramidal motor system surround the pyramidal system's corticospinal and corticobulbar pathways in the center. (From L. S. Woodburne, *The Neural Basis of Behavior,* Charles E. Merrill Publishing Co., Columbus OH. Copyright 1967 by Lloyd S. Woodburne. Reproduced with permission.)

ioral patterns. Lesions of the corpus striatum may cause disturbances in visual coordination and speech. Different parts of the body are spatially represented in this system, making possible both spatial and temporal coordination of middle extrapyramidal rhythms affecting different parts of the body (Weil, 1974). The basal ganglia automatically execute learned motor plans by selecting which behaviors will be carried out and suppressing unwanted ones (Lee, 1984).

The corpus striatum mediates genetically constituted forms of behavior in ani-

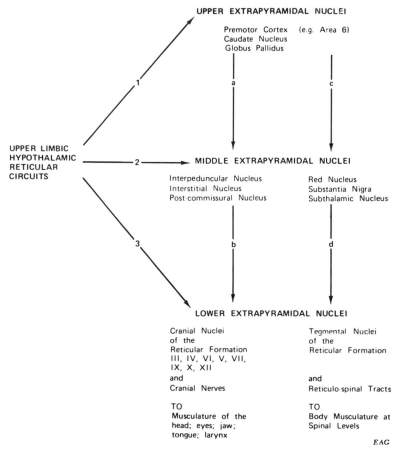

Figure 9-6. The extrapyramidal system. (From J. W. Weil, *A Neurophysiological Model of Emotional and Intentional Behavior,* 1974. Courtesy of Charles C. Thomas, Publisher, Springfield IL.)

mals, such as selecting a home site, establishing and defending territory, hunting, mating, homing, forming social hierarchies, and selecting leaders. In humans it may underlie repetitious, ritualistic, and imitative forms of behavior (Maclean, 1980). The educability of mammals is made possible by the cerebral cortex. Still the corpus striatum plays a continuous role in all behavior through its interplay with the sensorimotor cortex via the globus pallidus, substantia nigra, and thalamus. Its role in academic learning has not been fully appreciated.

The Pyramidal Motor System

The voluntary pyramidal motor system originates in the pyramidal neurons of the precentral motor cortex of the frontal lobe. This cortex is structured such that stimulation of a specific portion of the motor strip results in movement of a contralateral body part.

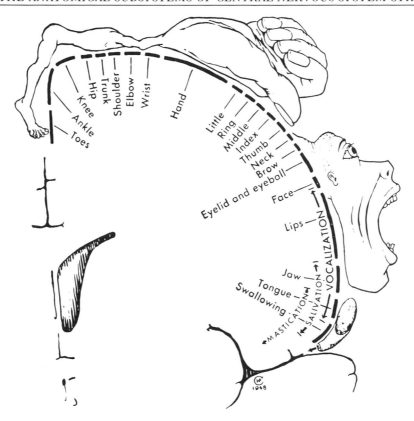

Figure 9-7. The proportional motor representation of the body in the precentral gyrus of the frontal lobe. (Reprinted with permission of Macmillan Publishing Co. from *The Cerebral Cortex of Man* by W. Penfield and T. Rasmussen. Copyright 1950 by Macmillan Publishing Co.; copyright renewed © 1978 Theodore Rasmussen.)

By means of electrical stimulation, it is possible to map the body regions on the precentral gyrus in a motor homunculus, as shown in Figure 9-7. There are two noteworthy aspects of this map. First, the representation of movements is inverted so that the feet are controlled by neurons located at the top of this gyrus and the face by neurons at the bottom. Second, the size of the cortical representation of each body part is proportional to the relative skill or precision with which a body part is used in voluntary movements. For example, the muscles involved in speech and in hand movements are highly represented in the

precentral gyrus. In contrast, a body part such as the back, which is subject to little discrete motor control, has a relatively small area devoted to it.

Pyramidal fibers travel through the diencephalon to the pons in the brain stem, where most cross over to the opposite side (see Figure 9-8). The pyramidal system continues in the spinal cord as the lateral corticospinal tracts that end in the anterior horn cells, which give rise to ventral roots that constitute the voluntary motor components of spinal nerves.

The control of voluntary movement is effected not directly by signals from the

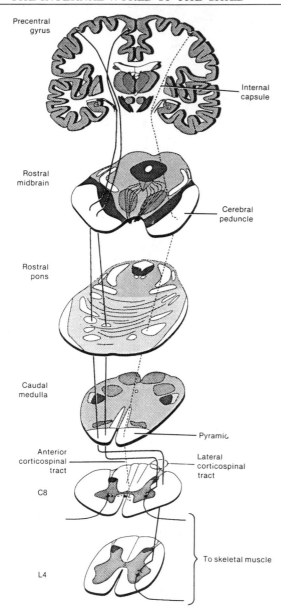

Precentral gyrus

Internal capsule

Rostral midbrain

Cerebral peduncle

Rostral pons

Caudal medulla

Pyramid

Anterior corticospinal tract

Lateral corticospinal tract

C8

L4

To skeletal muscle

Figure 9-8. Diagram of the essential connections of the pyramidal motor system. (Reproduced by permission from J. Nolte, *The Human Brain*, 2nd ed. St. Louis, 1988, The C. V. Mosby Co.)

cerebral cortex to the muscle fibers, but by focusing, intensifying, and adjusting background movement, usually that of maintaining postural muscle tonus, mediated by the basal ganglia and the anterior portion of the cerebellum (Pribram, 1977).

THE CEREBELLUM

The evolutionary growth of the cerebellum has matched that of the cerebrum because it plays major roles in the performance of all skilled actions and in conditioned learning. The cerebellum itself directs no body functions. It operates as a monitor of the brain's other centers and as a mediator between them and the rest of the body. The immense computational machinery of the cerebellum contains both sensory and motor neuronal connections that develop in relationship to learned skills so that it can learn from experience.

The various functions of the cerebellum take place in distinctly defined areas of its cortex. For example, the control of equilibrium is localized in the extreme front and rear surface areas. The proprioceptive areas appear as two distorted "homunculi" on the cerebellar cortex (see Figure 9-9).

Although its motor functions are usually emphasized, the cerebellum is basically a somatic afferent organ, the "head ganglia of proprioception." Of its afferent inputs, the spinocerebellar tracts are of particular importance. The tactile, auditory, and visual areas of the cerebellum project to the various sensory areas of the cerebrum via the sensory relay nuclei of the thalamus as well as the ascending reticular formation (Fields & Willis, 1970). Sensory neural stimulation reaches the cerebellum from the skin, muscles, tendons, joints, ears, and eyes, and from feedback of its own discharges to the cerebral cortex (Gaddes,

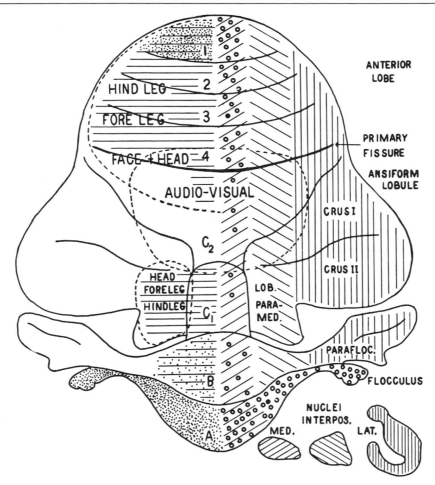

Figure 9-9. Diagram of the cerebellum showing regional specialization. (From S. W. Ranson and S. L. Clark, *The Anatomy of the Nervous System,* copyright 1959 by W. B. Saunders, Philadelphia PA. Reproduced with permission.)

1980). Thus the cerebellum plays a key role in modulating sensory input to the brain (Frick, 1982).

There is a high equivalence between the cerebral and cerebellar cortices based upon strong reciprocal connections between them. Practically every area of the central nervous system has two-way direct and indirect connections with the cerebellum. One-fifth of the internal capsule is composed of non-motor fibers projecting from frontal and temporal association areas to the cerebellum. The cerebellum, therefore, adds significantly to the integrational activity of the cerebral cortex.

The cerebellum verifies actions by comparing the intentions of the cerebral cortex with the performance of the body. If the body is not moving according to an intention, the discrepancy between the two is calculated by the cerebellum so that immediate appropriate correction can be made. The cerebellar feedback mechanism depicted in Figure 9-10 also helps the brain predict the future position of moving parts of the body. For example, the cerebellum detects from incoming proprioceptive signals the rate at which a limb is moving and then predicts from this the projected time course of its movement. A failure to control the distance that parts of the body move is called dysmetria, which simply means poor control of the distance of movement.

The rates of progression of auditory and visual phenomena also are predicted by the cerebellum. As an example, the cerebellum can predict from a changing visual scene how rapidly one is approaching an object by interpreting spatio-temporal relationships in incoming sensory information (Guyton, 1977). Thus the visual system is an important source of sensory input to the cerebellar flocculus (Noda, 1981). The flocculus of the cerebellum also plays a role in the visual modulation of the vestibulo-ocular reflex, which helps to keep an image stable on the retina. The vestibulo-cerebellar system coordinates balance and righting reflexes to promote postural stability and integrated actions. It also modulates autonomic activities that contribute to visceral homeostasis.

THE AUTONOMIC NERVOUS SYSTEM

Under the control of the hypothalmus, the autonomic nervous system is the mediator of the appetitive instincts controlled by the neuroendocrine system. Its parasympathetic component is concerned with life-maintenance processes, such as digestion, respiration, and blood circulation. Its sympathetic component mediates the defensive maneuvers of fight and flight.

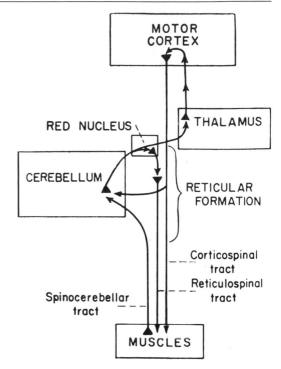

Figure 9-10. The pathways for cerebellar control of voluntary movements. (From A. C. Guyton, *Textbook of Medical Physiology,* 6th ed., copyright 1981 by W. B. Saunders, Philadelphia PA. Reproduced with permission.)

In general the actions of the two divisions of the autonomic nervous system are mutually antagonistic so that they equilibrate each other. The sympathetic division prepares one for emergency reactions in response to pain, rage, and fear. It accelerates the heart rate, increases blood pressure, and provides extra blood glucose as a source of energy. The distressing sympathetically mediated emotions of rage, fear, and disgust tend to ward off or decrease stimulating conditions.

In contrast, the parasympathetic division generally does the opposite. It slows the heart rate, lowers the blood pressure, neutralizes excess blood glucose, facilitates digestion and the disposal of body wastes, and activates the tear glands. It is generally calming and cathartic. The pleasurable emotions that tend to maintain or increase stimulating conditions are associated with the parasympathetic division. Most sympathetic postganglionic elements are adrenergic; most parasympathetic postganglionic elements are cholinergic. Rage has been called the most adrenergic and love the most cholinergic reaction.

The viscera receive a dual autonomic supply (see Figure 9-11). In most cases, the two sets of nerves antagonize each other; however, some autonomic effectors appear to have only a sympathetic nerve supply. Parasympathetic outflow from the central nervous system is via cranial nerves III, VII, IX, and X for the mediation of such functions as pupillary constriction, taste, and heart-rate deceleration. Spinal outflow is through sacral segments 2 through 4 for functions such as bowel and bladder control. Sympathetic outflow is from the first thoracic spinal segment to the second or third lumbar level. The first four or five segments of the thoracic spinal cord are involved in pupillary dilation, cardiac acceleration, contraction of the upper eyelids, and thermal regulation of the face.

The autonomic nervous system has a vital cenesthetic sensory component. Visceral sensory input arising from the internal organs of the body differs from sensory input from the surface and musculoskeletal structure of the body. Visceral sensations are poorly localized, nonspecific, extreme in intensity, and associated with generalized reactions, such as faintness, blanching, apnea, and vomiting. These sensory impulses are transmitted via sympathetic and parasympathetic pathways to the brain stem and the reticular formation. They comprise the stimuli from the internal world that form the continuous background sensory stream of the state regulating system with its foreground pleasurable or distressing emotional states.

THE RETICULAR ACTIVATING SYSTEM

The reticular activating system controls the overall degree of central nervous system activity, including wakefulness and sleep. Its functions include determination of operational modes, filtering of all sensory input, participation at all levels of cortical function, modulation of motor output, multilevel control over most visceral functions, and production of a spectrum of states of consciousness from deep coma to maximum vigilance. It is a core of neurons shielded from direct contact with the environment, on the one hand, and from the cortical centers, on the other—yet continually washed by reflections of excitation patterns flowing from both. These samples of ongoing activity are then integrated within the elements of the mosaic. The resultant output, expressed as an intensity continuum, is discharged widely upon centers upstream and downstream and throughout the reticular activating system itself.

The reticular activating system's anatomical base is the reticular formation, a patchy collection of neurons that extends from the medulla through the core of the brain stem to the thalamus, where thalamic nuclei serve as relays for widespread cortical excitation. The reticular formation is richly connected by afferent and efferent pathways to neural structures in the cerebral cortex and in the spinal cord (see Figure 9-12). The brainstem portion is basically responsible for wakefulness. The locus ceruleus, sometimes considered to be a special derivative of the reticular formation, is a tiny cluster of catecholaminergic cells in the pons; its axons, with very large numbers of collaterals, project to many parts of the brain stem and basal ganglia and to the entire cerebellar and cerebral cortices. Pain fibers reaching the midbrain reticular for-

EFFECTOR ORGANS	CHOLINERGIC RESPONSE	ADRENERGIC RESPONSES
Eye		
Radial muscle of iris		Contraction (mydriasis)
Sphincter muscle of iris	Contraction (miosis)	
Ciliary Muscle	Contraction for near vision	Relaxation for far vision
Heart		
SA node	Decrease in heart rate; vagal arrest	Increase in heart rate
Atria	Decrease in contractility, and (usually) increase in conduction velocity	Increase in contractility and conduction velocity
AV node and conduction system	Decrease in conduction velocity; AV block	Increase in conduction velocity
Ventricles		Increase in contractility, conduction velocity, automaticity, and rate of idiopathic pacemakers
Blood vessels		
Coronary		Constriction (α receptors)* Dilation (β receptors)*
Skin and mucosa		Constriction
Skeletal muscle	Dilation	Constriction (α receptors) Dilation (β receptors)
Cerebral		Constriction (slight)
Pulmonary		Constriction
Abdominal viscera		Constriction (α receptors) Dilation (β receptors)
Renal		Constriction
Salivary glands	Dilation	Constriction
Lung		
Bronchial muscle	Contraction	Relaxation
Bronchial glands	Stimulation	Inhibition (?)
Stomach and Intestines		
Motility and tone	Increase	Decrease (usually)
Sphincters	Relaxation (usually)	Contraction (usually)
Secretion	Stimulation	Inhibition (?)
Gallbladder and ducts	Contraction	Relaxation
Urinary bladder		
Detrusor	Contraction	Relaxation (usually)
Trigone and sphincter	Relaxation	Contraction

Ureter Motility and tone	Increase (?)	Increase (usually)
Uterus	Variable	Variable
Male sex organs	Erection	Ejaculation
Skin Pilomotor muscles Sweat glands	Generalized secretion	Contraction Localized secretion of palms
Spleen capsule		Contraction
Adrenal medulla	Secretion of epinephrine and norepinephrine	
Liver		Glycogenolysis
Pancreas Acini	Secretion	
Islets	Insulin secretion	Inhibition of insulin secretion (α receptors) Insulin secretion (β receptors)
Salivary glands	Profuse, watery secretion	Thick, viscous secretion
Lacrimal glands	Secretion	
Nasopharyngeal glands	Secretion	
Adipose tissue		Lipolysis
Kidney		Renin secretion

* α receptors respond only to norepinephrine and β receptors to epinephrine.

Figure 9-11. Responses of organs to autonomic nerve impulses and circulating catecholamines. (Modified from L. S. Goodman and A. Gilman, *The Pharmacological Basis of Therapeutics,* 5th ed., copyright 1975 by Macmillan Publishing Co., New York.)

mation are expecially numerous, providing a structural basis for arousal through nox-ious stimulation. The thalamic portion plays an important role in directing atten-tion and controlling the overall intensity of cortical activity (Guyton, 1977).

THE LIMBIC SYSTEM

The limbic system is another core infor-mation processing system interposed be-tween sensory input and motor output. The highest order of sensory inputs from the cerebral cortex together with emotional associations from the amygdala are pre-sented to the hippocampus for processing by the rest of the limbic system. The system does not directly affect motor actions but influences choices of them. It is the gateway for learning based upon knowledge.

The limbic system is especially con-cerned with emotional experience, laying down memories, and olfaction, in addition to survival-related behavior, such as fight-ing and fleeing. Different parts of each lim-bic system structure exert facilitatory and inhibitory influences upon the systems con-nected with it. These systems energize and regulate organized patterns of behavior and thought (Isaacson, 1975).

The limbic system contains three major circuits. The first centers in the amygdala and involves emotions concerned with self-preservation, such as aggression and fear. The second system centers in the septal area and involves motivations concerned with preservation of the species, such as sociability and sexuality. Both of these systems are present in lower animals and receive much input from the olfactory apparatus. The third system reaches its greatest size in humans and includes the mammillothalamic tract and fibers continuing to the cingulate gyrus. It also may serve social and sexual functions like the septal circuit, shifting them from the olfactory to the visual and auditory regulation of behavior (MacLean, 1970).

The anatomic components of the limbic system include an outer ring, the cingulum, that encircles the hilum of the hemispheres like a hem (see Figure 9-13). This outer ring is closely connected with the frontal cortex and the thalamus and contains an analyzer of sensory information through these connections. The prinicipal path from the limbic system to the cerebral cortex is via the medial-dorsal thalamus to the orbital surface of the prefrontal cortex.

The inner ring of the limbic system consists of ancient cortical components (the olfactory system, hippocampus, fornix, and temporal lobe hippocampal gyrus), and noncortical components (the midline septum raphae nuclei and the amygdalae). Activities in this complex are transmitted to the posterior hypothalamus.

The medial temporal lobe structures, particularly the hippocampus, are involved in the acquisition of long-term memories. The hippocampus itself, however, is not the site of the structural changes of long-term memory, which primarily involves the cerebral cortex (Milner, 1972). The hippocampus plays a role in determining the

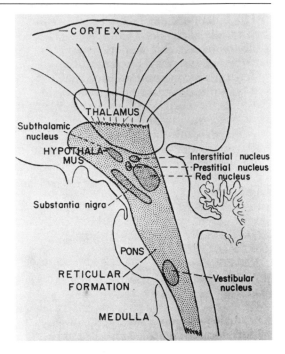

Figure 9-12. The reticular formation and associated nuclei. (From A. C. Guyton, *Textbook of Medical Physiology,* 6th ed., copyright 1981 by W. B. Saunders, Philadelphia PA. Reproduced with permission.)

focus of attention by channeling incoming sensory signals to the limbic system, thus associating emotional characteristics with sensory signals and transmitting information to the pleasure or distress areas of the limbic system.

The hippocampus prevents the registration of fortuitous signals and helps organize information for long-term storage through two interconnected circuits (Vinogradova, 1975). The first is the hippocampal-reticular "regulatory circuit" that mediates alerting, searching, and sampling behaviors. It is linked with the affective system and evaluates the novelty, but not the specific qualities, of information signals. It facilitates attentional processes by decreasing the general hippocampal inhibitory

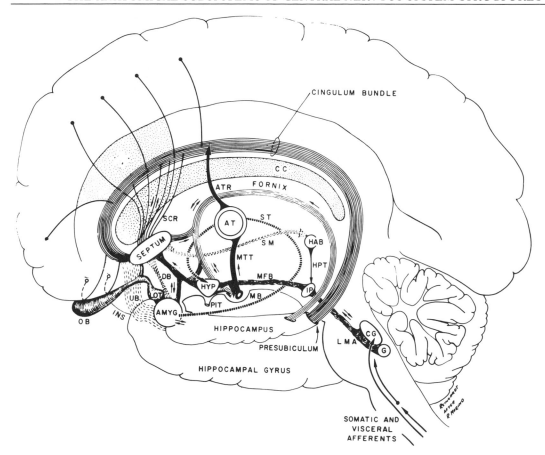

Figure 9-13. Schematic drawing of the limbic system. OB, olfactory bulb; LOT, lateral, olfactory striae; INS, insula; UB, uncinate bundle; DB, diagonal band of Broca; AMYG, amygdala; SCR, subcallosal radiations; HYP, hypothalamus; AT, anterior thalamus; MB, mammillary body; MTT, mammillothalamic tract; ATR, anterior thalamic bundle; SM, stria medullaris; HPT, habenulointerpeduncular tract; IP, interpeduncular nucleus; LMA, limbic midbrain area of Nauta; G, nucleus of Gudden; CG, central gray; CC, corpus callosum. (From H. T. Ballantine, W. L. Cassidy, N. B. Flanagan, and R. Marino, "Stereotaxic Anterior Cingulotomy of Neuropsychiatric Illness and Intractable Pain," *Journal of Neurosurgery, 26,* 1967, 488–495. Copyright 1967 by the American Association of Neurological Surgeons, Chicago IL. Reproduced with permission.)

output to the reticular formation with a resulting increase in the activity of the ascending reticular formation and consequent general increase in brain arousal. The second circuit is the hippocampus-mamillary body-anterior thalamic nuclei-cingulate cortex "information circuit" that mediates registration in awareness and memory of the quality of information that has passed through the "regulatory circuit."

Bilateral removal of the hippocampus makes it difficult to store new memories, especially verbal information, by reducing the capacity to hold information in the face of competing sensory input that distracts

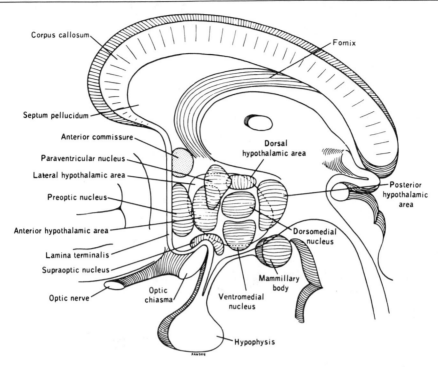

Figure 9-14. A three-dimensional schematic drawing of the hypothalamic nuclei. (From E. L. House, B. Pansky, and A. Siegel, *A Systematic Approach to Neuroscience,* copyright 1979 by McGraw-Hill Book Company, New York. Reproduced with permission.)

attention. Under conditions of environmental uncertainty, increased arousal is normally suppressed by the hippocampus. Failing such suppression because of surgical or accidental damage to the hippocampus, the responses to environmental uncertainty are exaggerated. The hippocampus also suppresses neural systems responsible for the patterns of on-going behaviors and established ways of responding. With hippocampal damage in experimental animals, the lack of this suppression causes perseverative activities based on old established patterns of behavior with impaired retrieval of newly stored information. This interference makes the animal less able to cope with the environment.

Each amygdala serves as a sentinel that transmits signals to the hypothalamus. The hypothalamic nuclei are ready at all times, but are kept in low key by the inhibitory regulation of the amygdalae, which function as biasers. The usual function of the amygdalae is to help control the overall pattern of behavior demanded by an occasion. Stimulation of portions of the amygdala can cause sexual activities, such as genital erection, copulatory movements, ejaculation, ovulation, uterine activity, and premature labor. The bilateral removal of a monkey's amygdalae impairs its ability to assess and relate visual input to stored memories (Watts, 1975).

The various structures of the limbic system regulate regions of the posterior hypothalamus, which itself is facilitory and inhibitory (see Figure 9-14). The lateral portion of the hypothalamus is considered to be responsible for the activation and maintenance of behavior sequences and the medial portion for causing the cessation of behavior. All structures of the limbic system act to regulate the lateral and medial portions of the hypothalamus, but each structure probably is especially tuned to certain types of events of the external or internal worlds. For example, the amygdala, may be responsive to changing conditions of hunger, sex, and aggression; the septal area to thirst and some emotional reactions; and the hippocampus to the relationship of present circumstances to what is expected.

Reverberating circuits within the limbic system flow back and forth to the neocortex, the hypothalamus, and its endocrine satellites, and the reticular formation. They provide an anatomic substrate for the state regulating system.

The nucleus accumbens located within the head of the caudate nucleus of the corpus striatum has well-established functional connections with the limbic system. It receives input from the amygdala, the septum, and the hippocampus, and presumably is the portal of entry for the neurotransmitter dopamine to the limbic system.

The limbic system determines whether stimuli are experienced as pleasurable or distressing. The major pleasure centers are located in the septum along the course of the medial forebrain bundle and in the ventromedial nuclei of the hypothalamus. The principal centers for distress and escape tendencies are in the central gray area surrounding the aqueduct of Sylvius in the midbrain and in the periventricular and perifornical structures of the hypothalamus and thalamus (Guyton, 1977). Human emotions also are dependent on neuronal pathways linking the limbic system with parietal and frontal areas of the right hemisphere under the surveillance and control of the left frontal cortex, so that the left hemisphere can inhibit the emotionally toned activities of the right hemisphere (Flor-Henry, 1976). The central nervous system thereby is wired for reason to prevail over emotion.

THE NEUROENDOCRINE SYSTEM

The hypothalamus is the common meeting place for the central nervous and neuroendocrine systems. It contains neurosecretory cells that have the characteristics of both nerve and endocrine cells. They receive information, as does any neuron, through neurotransmitter mechanisms, but they also manufacture and respond to hormones.

The cerebral hemispheres influence the hypothalamus through the limbic system. The hypothalamus is the most important output pathway through which the limbic system controls the involuntary, vegetative functions necessary for life, such as the regulation of heart rate and arterial pressure, body temperature, body fluid osmolarity, food intake, and secretion of pituitary hormones (see Figure 9-15). The posterior hypothalamus is the site of mechanisms for self-preservation that are inhibited by the ventromedial nucleus.

As a target organ of the limbic system, the hypothalamus is the ultimate elaborator of autonomic and neuroendocrine responses through feedback loops of reciprocal interactions among hypothalamic, pituitary, thyroid, adrenal, and gonadal hormones (see Figure 9-16). Neurons of the reticular formation take over from the hypothalamus. The descending pathways to autonomic motor neurons typically are interrupted at numerous levels so that no single excitation can affect the innervation of the viscera upon which life depends.

Because of its relevance to stress and learning, the neuroendocrine system is described in greater detail in Chapter 12.

FUNCTION	AFFERENTS FROM	INTEGRATING AREAS
Temperature regulation	Cutaneous cold receptors; temperature-sensitive cells in hypothalamus	Anterior hypothalamus, response to heat; posterior hypothalamus, response to cold
Neuroendocrine conrol of: Catecholamines	Emotional stimuli, probably via limbic system	Dorsomedial and posterior hypothalamus
Vasopressin	Osmoreceptors, "volume receptors," others	Supraoptic and paraventricular nuclei
Oxytocin	Touch receptors in breast, uterus, genitalia	Supraoptic and paraventricular nuclei
Thyroid-stimulating hormone (thyrotropin, TSH)	Temperature receptors, perhaps others (?)	Anterior hypothalamus, dorsomedial nuclei
Adrenocorticotropin hormone (ACTH) and β -lipotropin (β -LPH)	Limbic system (emotional stimuli); reticular formation ("systemic" stimuli); hypothalamic or anterior pituitary cells sensitive to circulating blood cortisol level; others (?)	Paraventricular nuclei
Follicle-stimulating hormone (FSH) and luteinizing hormone (LH)	Hypothalamic cells sensitive to estrogens; eyes, touch receptors in skin and genitalia or reflex ovulating species	Anterior hypothalamus, other areas
Prolactin	Touch receptors in breasts, other unknown receptors	Arcuate nucleus, other areas (hypothalamus inhibits secretion)
Growth hormone	Unknown receptors	Anterior hypothalamus, other areas
"Appetitive" behavior Thirst	Osmoreceptors, subfornical organ	Lateral superior hypothalamus
Hunger	"Glucostat" cells sensitive to rate of glucose utilization	Ventromedial satiety center, lateral hunger center, also limbic components
Sexual behavior	Cells sensitive to circulating estrogen and androgen, others	Anterior ventral hypothalamus, plus, in the male, piriform cortex
Defensive reactions Fear, rage	Sense organs and neocortex, paths unknown	Diffuse, in limbic system and hypothalamus
Control of various endocrine and activity rhythms	Retina via retinohypothalamic fibers	Suprachiasmatic nuclei

Figure 9-15. Summary of hypothalamic regulatory mechanisms. (From W. F. Ganong, *Review of Medical Physiology,* 12th ed. Copyright 1985 by Lange Medical Publications, Los Altos CA. Reproduced with permission.)

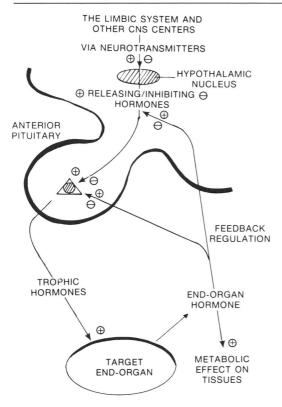

Figure 9-16. Feedback loops between hypothalamic, pituitary, thyroid, adrenal, and gonadal hormones. Pituitary hormone secretion is modulated by the concentration of each end organ hormone in either a negative (−) or a positive (+) direction. (Reprinted by permission of Elsevier Science Publishing Co., Inc., from L. J. Kryston, *Endocrine Disorders.* Copyright 1981 by Medical Examination Publishing Co., Inc.)

THE THALAMUS

The thalamus is the principal clearinghouse for all sensations, except smell, and is centrally involved in conscious awareness.

Three kinds of messages come to the thalamus (Cotman & Mc Gaugh, 1980). The first are discriminative sensory messages from the body that pass through its posterior aspect. Auditory signals pass through the medial geniculate nucleus, visual signals through the lateral geniculate nucleus, and somesthetic signals through the somesthetic nuclear complex of the thalamus. The second kind are the affective system's pleasurable or distressing contributions. The third kind is nonsensory information from the cerebellum, basal ganglia, and limbic system; these centers exploit the central location and integrative circuitry of the thalamus passing through its forward half. These forward connections implicate the thalamus as a key communication link for many forebrain mechanisms of motor control and emotion in addition to its sensory linkages. Consequently, lesions of the front half of the thalamus may produce the types of tremors and movement disorders seen in cerebellar or basal ganglia lesions and the emotional symptoms and deficits in learning, memory, and planning that follow damage to limbic pathways.

The thalamus does more than filter and sift out messages. It passes abstract and detailed reports up to the cortex for further review. It is an immensely important structure, if not the dominant one, in maintaining consciousness, alertness, and attention. In these elusive functions, it works with the cerebral cortex and the reticular formation through diffuse reticular pathways that connect with a thalamocortical activating system. In this way the brainstem, of which the reticular formation and thalamus are parts, turns on the cortex, as one would turn on a television set. "Pictures" of specific perceptions and images thereby are displayed with background activation from the auditory, visual, and somesthetic areas of the cortex.

The thalamus illustrates particularly well the fact that no part of the brain works alone. There is no place, therefore, that is the site of a particular brain function, any more than a city is the site of government functions. Thus the thalamus is a partner with many other brain structures in many functions, but it is not where those functions take place. The mystery of generalized brain activity was highlighted by Penfield (1975), who said, "There is no room or place where consciousness dwells."

THE CORTICAL RECEPTIVE ZONES

The primary sensory receptive areas of the brain are the calcarine cortex of the occipital lobe for vision, the postcentral gyrus of the parietal lobe for somesthesia, and the anterior transverse gyrus of the temporal lobe for hearing. The primary cortical sensory zones are independent of attitude, interest, and emotions and relatively objectively reflect the external world.

The primary cortical areas are in two-way communication with the thalamus. The functional state of the cortex thereby influences the manner in which the sensory way stations of the thalamus screen and transmit the cortically directed flow of information. This active receptive process of selection and synthesis of the elicited associations to a stimulus occurs through the thalamocortical projections: the visual cortex projects back to the thalamic lateral geniculate body from which it receives its input, the somatic sensory cortex projects back to the thalamic ventral nucleus, and the auditory cortex projects back to the medial geniculate body of the thalamus.

The primary visual, somatic, and auditory cortical areas embody the first cortical step in sensory processing and together account for about a fourth of the cerebral mass. The primary cortical zones are highly specialized and capable of minute differentiation of stimuli. In each of these primary cortical areas, distinctive patterns of reception occur. For example, the parts of the body are represented in order along the postcentral parietal gyrus, with the legs at the top and the head at the bottom of this gyrus. This arrangement is shown in the sensory homunculus pictured in Figure 9-17. Those areas of the human body that have the greatest sensitivity have the largest representation in the cortex.

From these primary sensory zones, fibers pass to adjoining secondary, tertiary, and quarternary association areas, which constitute the largest part of the cerebral cortex (Popper & Eccles, 1977). More advanced stages of processing take place in the association areas, in which there is a spreading and mixing of input from the sensory organs (see Figure 9-18).

The secondary association areas enable the reflection of complex groups of stimuli and relationships between the components of the perceived objects within a particular sensory modality. Neural processing from the primary cortical areas to other parts of the cortex typically involves a sequence of these association areas with the destination of the hippocampus or the amygdala, or both, in the limbic system. The limbic system, in turn, projects back to the cortex, particularly to the frontal lobe. These connections relate emotional context to sensory perceptions. The auditory cortex is a small region of the temporal lobe that can be covered by a 50-cent piece. It lies on the lower bank of the Sylvian fissure, toward the rear of the temporal lobe. It adjoins a secondary association region, where the movements and positions of the head signaled by the inner ear are registered. Secondary associational areas of the parietal somesthetic cortex analyze and combine sensations from the skin and deeper regions of the body, including its joints, where angles indicate position and movement.

The tertiary association areas deal with the most complex forms of spatial and temporal relationships between groups of stimuli and responses to the outside world. In them interaction between the different

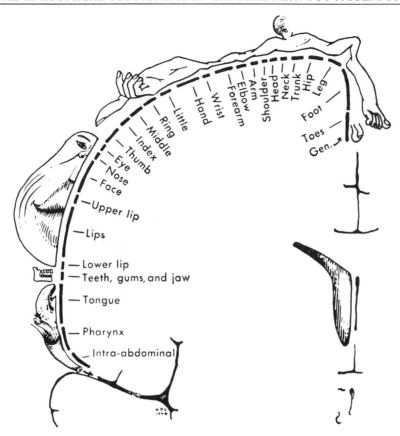

Figure 9-17. The proportional sensory representation of the body in the postcentral gyrus of the parietal lobe. (Reprinted with permission of Macmillan Publishing Co. from *The Cerebral Cortex of Man* by W. Penfield and T. Rasmussen. Copyright 1950 by Macmillan Publishing Co.; copyright renewed © 1978 Theodore Rasmussen.)

sensory modalities takes place. Three specialized tertiary areas can be distinguished: the superior parietal region, the inferior parietal region, and the temporo-parietal-occipital region. The superior parietal region is important for the integration of movements of the whole body with visual reception and the body image. The result is a larger, more meaningful picture in which one's self-image contrasts with its environment (Cotman & McGaugh, 1980). The inferior parietal region integrates generalized and discrete discrimination between objects with the act of speech under visual orientation toward the external en-

vironment. The temporo-parietal-occipital region of the angular gyrus integrates auditory and visual reception, particularly with regard to the semantics of spoken and written language (Luria, 1980). Forms of perception with spatial imagery, such as reading and writing, also involve this area (Gaddes, 1980).

Such a weave of sensory impressions is necessary if we are to know what sights, sounds, and other sensations mean. For example, a metallic click takes on added significance if we see someone pointing a camera at us. From such combinations we arrive, moment by moment, at knowledge

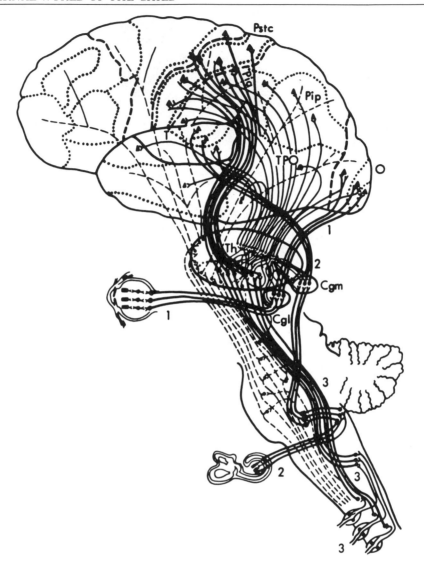

Figure 9-18. Scheme of the cortical-subcortical relationships of the primary, secondary and tertiary zones. (1) visual system; (2) auditory system; (3) cutaneokinesthetic system; (t) temporal region; (O) occipital region; (Pip) area 39; (Pia) area 40; (Pstc) postcentral region; (TPO) temporoparietal-occipital subregion; (Th) thalamus; (Cgm) medial geniculate body; (Cgl) lateral geniculate body. (From *Higher Cortical Functions in Man* by Aleksandr Romanovich Luria. Copyright © 1966, 1980 by Consultants Bureau Enterprises, Inc., and Basic Books, Inc., Publishers. Reprinted by permission of Basic Books, Inc., Publishers.)

of what is going on around us. Damage to the parietal lobe results in losses in knowledge of the significance of things called agnosias ("not knowings"). There may be an inability to localize sensations or recognize the meaning of palpated objects. There also may be loss or failure to heed the meaning of visual and auditory cues, even though sight and hearing remain intact ("psychic blindness and deafness").

The temporal lobe is an extension of the ancient limbic system, which in lower animals is concerned with smell and in humans with emotions. It is the center for the integration of experience. The perception, recording, and retrieval of events involve this large, anatomically diversified lobe of the brain. Here sensory imagery and emotions are synthesized into three-dimensional reality bounded in space and time. Our own sense of personal cohesion and familiarity with our surroundings are dependent on the smooth functioning of the temporal lobe (Cotman & McGaugh, 1980).

Stimulation of the temporal lobe during brain surgery calls forth psychical phenomena of a high order. Such responses are not evoked from other parts of the cortex, from which only fragments of functions may be obtained. Hallucinations and illusions unfold from stimulation of the temporal lobe in a progressive and dramatic manner, like a motion picture with sound and color. The illusions may be accompanied by a sense of déjà vu, as experiences that happened before. They are based on the person's memories and dreams. Apparently memories of all types—pictures, sounds, melodies, incidents—are accessible to retrieval from here.

Thus parts of the temporal lobe seem to be involved in the process of recording and storing events, along with their evaluation as agreeable or disagreeable. The "replay" circuits for experiences already "on tape" may survive damage to other components of the recording machinery, but with larger or more generalized types

of brain damage long-term memory loss is an inevitable, well-known consequence. Information storage probably does not take place in the temporal lobe alone, even though auditory and olfactory memories appear to draw heavily upon its neurons and connections. Storage apparently is the responsibility of the whole brain, particularly the thalamus and the cortical regions it ties together.

With the concerted activity of the prefrontal areas, the temporo-occipital-parietal quaternary association areas are the sites of the highest processes of abstraction where perceptions, images, nonverbal symbols, and verbal symbols are elaborated into concepts and hypotheses.

THE FRONTAL LOBE SYSTEMS

The great size and enormous number of direct connections of the frontal lobes with other parts of the brain are the most uniquely human of all aspects of the central nervous system. In certain species, however, such as the chimpanzee, gorilla, whale, and elephant, the frontal lobes are large and well fissurated. The brains of these animals are now receiving long overdue attention.

The human frontal lobes are extraordinarily well informed on the encyclopedic range of events transpiring in other regions of the nervous system; and they exercise a powerful, highly selective influence over many of these occurrences. The frontal lobe has three major areas: the smallest is the precentral motor cortex, the next is the extrapyramidal area, and the largest is the prefrontal cortex. The precentral gyrus of the frontal lobe directs the motor activity of the voluntary musculature. The body parts are represented as indicated in Figure 9-7. The extrapyramidal area is involved in stereotyped coordinated body movements.

The prefrontal area has four major functions. The first is to maintain a steadfastness of purpose, or focused attention, against distracting stimuli from the environment by suppressing less relevant stimuli and delaying responses to them. In concert with other systems, the frontal lobes play an essential part in the higher forms of regulating states of activity and awareness. They help accomplish registration and reinforcement of messages. An electrical pattern originates in the supplementary motor area in the frontal lobes whenever an organism is preparing to perform an activity. Perhaps this is a signal that the brain is busy and inhibits irrelevant input (Pribram & Luria, 1973). A second function is to anticipate the future by the organization of strategies and the execution of intentional and purposeful behavior. A third function is to plan sequential functions through the organization of skilled acts or thoughts into an orderly series. The frontal lobes are especially concerned in structuring context-dependent behavior both temporarily and spatially. A fourth function is to make choices, initiate the transformation of them into motor action, and match the effect of the action to the original intention (Arieti, 1976).

THE CEREBRAL HEMISPHERES

Each person shows some evidence of the brain's asymmetry. Most people prefer to use their right hand for writing, their right foot for kicking, and their right eye for sighting. Conversely, the majority prefer their left hand for identifying objects by touch, their left ear for listening to music, and their left visual field for identifying faces. These preferences reflect a clear division of labor between the left and right hemispheres.

The notion that information originating from the right side of space is largely mediated by the left cerebral hemisphere, and vice versa, has been generally accepted for years. The right cerebral hemisphere was considered to be the "minor" hemisphere that did little more than control contralateral body movements. Conversely, the left hemisphere was considered to be the "dominant" hemisphere, responsible for the many processes subsumed by language and other higher cognitive functions. Through the application of modern behavioral and electrophysiological techniques, however, many functions have been demonstrated to be primarily mediated by either the left or the right cerebral hemisphere (Benson & Zaidel, 1985).

In fact there are significant structural differences between the two cerebral hemispheres (Bryden, 1982; Corballis, 1983). Each hemisphere of the brain, while similar in neuronal structure, differs in total mass and weight, as well as in significant integrated functions. For example, the size of the planum temporale containing Wernicke's area is one-third larger on the left than on the right in 65 percent of both adults and infants (as shown in Figure 9-19), larger on the right in 11 percent, and equal in 24 percent (Galaburda & Kemper, 1979). Left-handed persons tend to have smaller or reversed asymmetries as compared with right-handed persons; they also tend to have larger corpus callosi (Witelson, 1985). In addition, in both left- and right-handed persons, more complex branching patterns are seen in the frontal lobe speech centers of the hemisphere dominant for speech (Marz, 1983).

Although receiving the same sensory information, each hemisphere processes it differently because of the interplay of genetic and learned factors (Fadely & Hosler, 1979). The differential capacities of each hemisphere provide the basis for a seeming duality of being and awareness in each of us, which is usually synthesized into a single consciousness of a unified being (see Figure 9-20). This dual system increases the

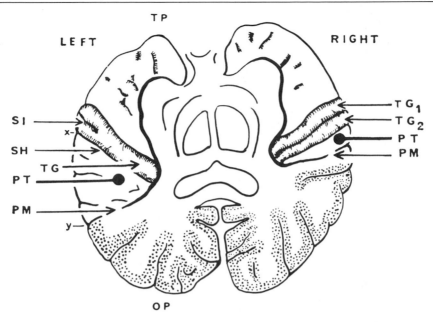

Figure 9-19. Horizontal section through cerebral hemispheres showing asymmetric (left larger than right) planum temporale (PT). The posterior margin (PM) of the planum temporale slopes backward more sharply, and the anterior margin formed by the sulcus of Heschl slopes forward more sharply on the left than on the right. In this brain there is a single transverse gyrus of Heschl (TG) on the left but two on the right (TG₁, TG₂). (From N. Geschwind and W. Levitsky, "Human Brain: Left-right Asymmetries in Temporal Speech Region," *Science, 161,* 1968, 186–87. Copyright 1968 by the American Association for the Advancement of Science. Reproduced with permission.)

chances of finding innovative solutions to novel problems, but also has the inherent potential for internal conflict. It is presumably to deal with this conflict that one hemisphere comes to patterns of dominating the other. When the hemispheres are surgically disconnected by commisurotomy, which severs the corpus collosum but not subcortical connections, the same individual can be observed to use one or the other of two distinct forms of mental approach and strategy, much like two different people, depending upon whether the left or right hemisphere is in use (Sperry, 1982).

There is no doubt that hemispheric specializations are important properties of the brain (see Figure 9-21). However, it is the collaboration and balance of the various neural components working together as an integrated whole that is the most important hallmark of human functioning. Optimally the two halves of the brain work closely together as a unit with the leading control being in one or the other. Thus each hemisphere has specialized functions in which the other participates so that each hemisphere is capable of low-level performance on tasks for which it is not specialized (Wexler, 1980).

The Wada technique is used to determine hemispheric lateralization through the introduction of sodium amytal into a carotid artery, anesthesizing one of the hemispheres. When this is done, 98 per-

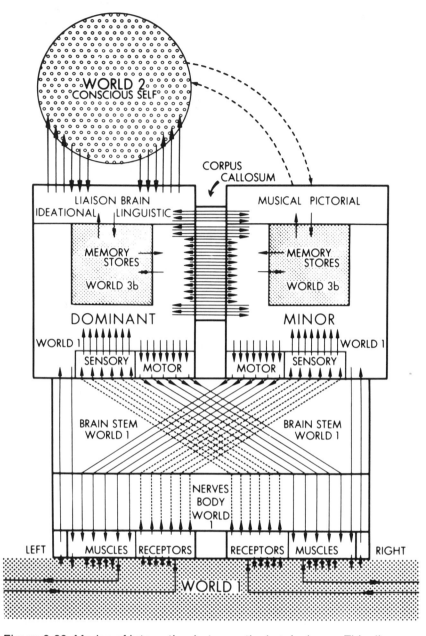

Figure 9-20. Modes of interaction between the hemispheres. This diagram
shows the principal lines of communication from peripheral receptors
to the sensory cortices in the cerebral hemipheres via the motor cortex
to muscles. Both of these systems are largely crossed as illustrated, but
minor uncrossed pathways are also shown by the vertical lines in the
brainstem. The dominant left hemisphere and minor right hemisphere
are labeled, together with some of their properties. The corpus callosum is shown as cross-linking the two hemispheres. In addition, the
diagram displays the modes of interaction between Worlds 1, 2, and 3,
as described in Chapter 16. (From K. R. Popper and J. C. Eccles, *The
Self and Its Brain,* copyright 1977 by Springer-Verlag, Heidelberg, West
Germany. Reproduced with permission.)

FUNCTIONAL UNIT	LEFT HEMISPHERE	RIGHT HEMISPHERE
State Regulating Orientation to environment	Active, time-oriented	Receptive, timeless
Consciousness	More conscious	More unconscious
Emotional expression	Evaluative emotion	Intuitive emotion
Information Processing Mode	Sequential, temporal	Simultaneous, direction oriented
Visual	Recognition of meaning of letters and words	Letter and word form recognition, whole, depth, face, geometric perception
Auditory	Sound meaning recognition, synthetic numerical abilities	Non-speech sound recognition, melodies
Memory	Verbal-auditory	Visual
Symbols	Conceptual: verbal-words	Perceptual: visual and haptic images, dreams, fantasies
Programming Mode	Secondary process, analysis, orderly	Primary process, synthesis, spontaneous
Motor	Active, skilled movements	Receptive gestures, emotional expressions
Thinking	Logical, convergent, abstract	Creative, divergent, concrete
Values	Socialized, learned through language, materialistic	Aesthetic, compassionate
Language	What is said, syntax, advanced reading	How it is said, spelling, beginning reading
Academic Interests	Mathematics Science Technology	Painting Sculpture Music Mysticism

Figure 9-21. Examples of hemispheric specialization when the left hemisphere is dominant.

cent of right-handed individuals have language represented in the left hemisphere; the remainder have language in the right hemisphere or bilaterally. Thus the generalizations that follow regarding right and left hemisphere functions have exceptions. In fact, speaking of right and left brain functions really is a metaphor since in some persons right brain functions reside in the left hemisphere, and vice versa.

In 1874 Hughlings Jackson noted an association between the right hemisphere and imagery, which has been confirmed by subsequent research. The left and right hemispheres have been described as word and picture processors respectively. Verbal information tends to be discrete and sequential whereas pictorial information tends to be organized in simultaneous and spatially parallel form. The information-processing style of the left hemisphere is verbal, linguistic, and, in propositional memory, most appropriate for abstract thought. The style of the right hemisphere is imaginal and most conducive to processing concrete information in associational memory (Ley, 1983). This is supported by differential changes in electroencephalographic patterns between the two hemispheres in the visual and verbal imagery involved in spatial and verbal arithmetic tasks (John & Schwartz, 1978; Ornstein & Galin, 1977).

The left hemisphere analyzes and breaks down information into temporal sequences and is concerned with skilled movements and actively manipulating the environment. The left hemisphere is verbal-analytic and is the site of language functions, time awareness, logic, organization, values learned through language, verbal memory, and socialization capabilities. The left temporal lobe anterior to the speech zone is essential for verbal memory and word recognition. The left frontal lobe is necessary for word fluency. Verbal tasks cause a greater increase in blood flow to the left hemisphere and spatial tasks to the right hemisphere (Gur et al, 1982). There is even some evidence that the left hemisphere is involved in the mediation of pleasurable emotions and the right in distress emotions (Ahearn & Schwartz, 1979; Harman & Ray, 1977).

The right hemisphere is concerned with monitoring and perceiving events in the world as they happen rather than subjecting them to purposeful analysis. It specializes in synthesizing fragments of sensory information into whole percepts and uses simultaneous perceptual processing. The right hemisphere cannot speak, but it can match names of objects and sounds of objects. When words are presented exclusively to the nonlanguage hemisphere, subjects are able to spell and recognize simple words but are unable to comprehend sentences, to speak, or to perform other, more complicated linguistic tasks. The left hemisphere is responsible for what we say and the right for how we say it. Thus the right hemisphere handles the emotional components of language: the prosody (melody, pitch, rhythm, and stress of speech), spontaneous displays of emotion, gestures during conversation, and emotional variation in speech (Ross, 1982).

The right hemisphere carries out a range of integrative functions, including holistic, spatial, directional, and visual perception. Examples are fitting designs into matrices, judging whole circle size from a small arc, discriminating and recalling nondescript musical chords, sorting block sizes and shapes into categories, and perceiving wholes from a collection of parts, as well as the intuitive perception and apprehension of geometric principles, two-dimensional point localization, dot and form enumeration, Braille recognition, and stereoscopic depth perception.

The right temporal lobe is essential for face recognition and maze learning and other spatial tasks. The right occipito-temporal region recognizes familiar faces, and the right hippocampal and parietal areas learn new faces (Benowitz, 1980). The right hemisphere interprets the emotional significance of facial expression, mannerisms, and gestures, as illustrated in Figure 9-22 (Heilman & Satz, 1983). It also is used to empathize with another's feeling and to respond to tenderness. When we watch the happiness of young children and the cautious glances between a couple in a park, consciousness is distinctly different than when we think in words or listen to someone else.

There appears to be a dissociation between emotional and cognitive transmission between the hemispheres; emotional transmission is probably through brainstem pathways and the anterior commisure

Figure 9-22. Stare at the nose of each. Which face is happier? The bottom face looks happier to right-handed persons who judge the face with their right hemispheres. (From *The Origin of Consciousness in the Breakdown of the Bicameral Mind* by Julian Jaynes. Copyright © 1976 by Julian Jaynes. Reprinted by permission of Houghton Mifflin Co., Boston.)

and cognitive through the corpus callosum. Emotional responses to words can be transferred between the hemispheres in the absence of the transfer of recognition of the words. For example, the right hemisphere is capable of emotional responses to visual stimuli, as illustrated by the exposure of an innocuous picture to a subject's left hemisphere and a pornographic picture to the right hemisphere. In this situation a subject names the innocuous picture and simultaneously blushes.

Lesions in the right hemisphere may give rise to inappropriate emotional responses to the patient's own condition, such as indifference, called anosognosia, and also may impair recognition of emotions in others. Furthermore, a person with a disorder of the right hemisphere usually understands the meaning of what is said through the left hemisphere, but may show aprosody and fail to recognize the angry or humorous intonations of speech (Geschwind, 1979b). A patient with damage on the left side may not be able to comprehend a statement but still can recognize the emotional tone with which it is spoken through the intact right hemisphere. Left-hemisphere damage may cause aphasia, alexia, agraphia, acalculia, and right–left disorientation. It also may cause an ideomotor apraxia, which is the loss of the ability to perform a purposeful motor action, such as lighting a match.

Beginning readers rely upon the right hemisphere and advanced readers on the left. Inadequacy of right–brain function may result in difficulty in letter recognition and recall. Left–side immaturity may be associated with delayed language development, poor sequencing, and problems with auditory memory and verbal recall.

Musical disturbances are not independent of speech disturbances, as disturbances of drawing seem to be, but neither are they closely intertwined with them, as literary deficits seem to be. In most persons musical capacities cannot be consigned to a single hemisphere. There appears to be a strong right-hemisphere bias, however, for the melodic component of music (Gardner, 1976).

Right-hemisphere thinking is similar to the visual, surreal, and emotional aspects of a dream. The right hemisphere is most active during REM sleep when most visual dreaming takes place. Seizures from the right temporal lobe tend to produce dreamlike experiences, and right-hemisphere injury tends to disrupt dreaming (Bakan, 1978). Albert Einstein was a right-brain thinker in visual spatial imagery and apparently could not think verbally. Helen Keller, on the other hand, apparently was a left-brain thinker and could only think after she developed the capacity for language.

Because the relationship between cerebral dominance of a variety of functions and peripheral manifestations of lateralization are complex, much remains to be learned. If appears, however, that our technologically oriented Western culture has selectively favored the dominant "Aristotelian" left hemisphere with its analytic, rational, sequential processes. Largely ignored in our culture has been the nondominant "Platonic" hemisphere with its nonverbal, synthetic, intuitive functions.

SUMMARY

The anatomical subsystems of the structures of the central nervous system are accessible to the techniques of gross and microscopic anatomy. Still, so much redundancy prevails in these subsystems that only general conclusions can be drawn regarding their significance.

The special sensory systems process information from the external world through the odor-detecting olfactory neurons, the sharp to diffuse pain and temperature nerve fibers, the sensitive touch and pressure nerve endings, the movement-sensing fibers of proprioception, the integration of touch and proprioception in the haptic sense, the light sensitivity of the continuously moving retina, the tympanic membrane's vibration to moving air, and the movement of particles and fluid in the vestibular vesicles with shifts in head position. Our sensory systems present stimuli to the brain. There they are analyzed, first singly and then in combination, in relation to our present situation and past history.

Much sensory processing occurs at the receptors in the coding of stimuli. These coded signals are then passed to the brain or spinal cord in an organized, well-defined, topographical manner. The cochlea is represented in a tone map in the medial geniculate and again in the auditory cortex. The retina is laid out in a spatial map in the lateral geniculate and again in the visual cortex. Receptive areas of the skin form a spatial map in the somatosensory thalamus and again in the primary somesthetic cortex where patterns are coded for other brain systems to read.

The visual system involves the sensory components of sight and the motor components of focusing and fixing the eyes. The importance of vision is indicated by the facts that the optic nerve connects directly with the thalamus and that as much of the motor cortex is devoted to vision as the rest of the body. On the other hand, the auditory system has many side paths through which to trigger motor reflexes.

The motor system consists of an automatic extrapyramidal aspect extending from the midbrain to the premotor frontal cortex and concerned with the generalized tonus of the body and with rhythmic and repetitive body movements. Body parts are spatially represented in the upper extrapyramidal system. The voluntary motor system originates in the pyramidal neurons of the frontal motor cortex and is concerned with intentional movements of the opposite side of the body. The parts of the body are represented in the motor cortex proportionate in size to the precision with which a part is used in voluntary movements.

The cerebellum controls basic ascending sensory and descending motor circuits of the central nervous system by monitoring and coordinating intentional actions. The mapping of the cerebellar cortex permits inner representations of spatial relationships with the environment.

The body's internal state is monitored and regulated by the autonomic nervous system, which attends to adjusting heart rate, maintaining body temperature, and providing a burst of energy when necessary. Under the control of the hypothalamus, the autonomic nervous system is the primary vehicle for the survival instincts through its parasympathetic division, which is concerned with appetitive life-maintenance processes, such as digestion, respiration, and elimination, and through its sympathetic division, which mediates affective fight-or-flight mechanisms. It also is the source of cenesthetic inflow to the brain from the internal visceral world.

The reticular activating system extends from the medulla to the thalamus and controls the overall degree of CNS arousal. It processes energy from the internal and external worlds as well as generating its own.

The limbic system attends to emotions and awareness. It consists of two rings of structures originally derived from the organs of smell. The outer ring is the cingulum, which is closely connected to the frontal cortex and the thalamus. The inner ring connects to the hypothalamus and consists of the olfactory nerve, hippocampus, fornix, temporal hippocampal gyrus, septum, raphae nuclei, and paired amygdalae. The hippocampus is the central structure of the limbic system and is concerned with forming memories. It recognizes novelty and tells us where we have been and where we are going.

As the target organ of the limbic system, the hypothalamus is the ultimate elaborator of autonomic and neuroendocrine responses through which involuntary, vegetative life functions are regulated. It sends hormones into the bloodstream to adjust the internal milieu of the body and control reproduction and maturation.

The thalamus is a major integrating center of the brain. It maintains alertness and consciousness through a diffuse thalamocortical activating system. It brings information to the attention of the cortex. The visual, auditory, and somatosensory cortices form perceptions of the external world. The motor cortex orchestrates the neuronal patterns that drive spinal motor neurons to move muscles. The basal ganglia ensure smooth background sensory and motor activity. The parietal cortex matches the body image with immediate surroundings. The temporal lobe works in collaboration with other lobes in the emotional coloration of experience and the recording, storing, and retrieval of memories.

The primary sensory receptive areas of the brain for vision, hearing, and somesthetic impulses are connected by a series of asssociation areas. The secondary association areas enable reflection upon relationships between the components of perceived objects and groups of stimuli. The tertiary association areas deal with complex forms of spatial and temporal relationships between groups and stimuli. The temporo-parieto-occipital association areas are the sites of the highest processes of abstraction.

The frontal lobes play an essential role in regulating states of awareness and activity. The prefrontal cortex focuses attention, anticipates the future, plans sequential acts, and transforms decisions into actions. The extrapyramidal cortex coordinates background muscular tonus and automatic movements. The precentral motor cortex is the site of discharge for voluntary motor activity.

Each hemisphere of the brain processes

the same information through somewhat different structures. The two halves of the brain work closely together with the leading control of specific functions ordinarily lodged with one or the other. The left hemisphere analyzes and breaks down information into temporal sequences and is concerned with actively manipulating the environment through skilled movements. The right hemisphere is concerned with monitoring events as they happen rather than subjecting them to purposeful analysis. It is concerned with the big picture and intuition. It specializes in spatial and general feature recognition. The two hemispheres work in harmony as an effective team. The left hemisphere is responsible for what we say and the right for how we say it.

Knowledge of the anatomical subsystems of the central nervous system structures impressively brings out the degree to which the neural sciences are approaching explanations of behavior. At the same time, the enormous complexity of the brain, and how much we do not know, is evident.

CHAPTER

10

The Development of the Central Nervous System

Evolution does not produce novelties from scratch. It works on what already exists, either transforming a system to give it new functions or combining several systems to produce a more elaborate one.

Francois Jacob, 1960

The brain is not a perfectly designed instrument. It is a conglomerate of several different earlier brains, each built on top of the other, like an old house with succeeding additions. The original structures remain intact but original functions have been shifted elsewhere, much as when a new kitchen is built the old one remains as a pantry. Thus we carry the evolution of the brain within the different parts of our brains, each formed in different eras (Ornstein & Thompson, 1984).

The human central nervous system (CNS) can be seen as an outgrowth of three previous systems (MacLean, 1980): the reptilian, paleomammalian, and neomammalian brains (see Figure 10-1). The reptilian brain includes the basal ganglia, diencephalon, midbrain, brainstem, and cerebellum. Upon this fundamental core, the limbic system of the paleomammalian brain was imposed. Last, the neocortical mantle of the neomammalian brain emerged.

In a sense the last two levels are luxu-

ries. Animals with at least reptilian brains eat, sleep, mate, fight, and flee. They learn quickly and remember important things indefinitely. They are well suited for the formation of habits that relate them to a relatively constant environment. The species changes and survives as a result of changes in the gene pool, but the individual does not. If individuals of a species are to cope with changing environments, they must be able to terminate established behaviors and form new ones, as permitted by the paleomammalian and neomammalian brains (Isaacson, 1975).

The evolution of the human CNS has been responsive to ever greater functional requirements and has given rise to new unfathomed capacities (Eccles, 1989). The basic structures that evolved in reptiles and mammals were maintained and enlarged with canalized anatomical bases for the behaviors they mediate (see Figure 10-2). Human neural pathways were built upon, and still operate through, these primitive areas, which must be inhibited to keep them from interfering with the newer systems.

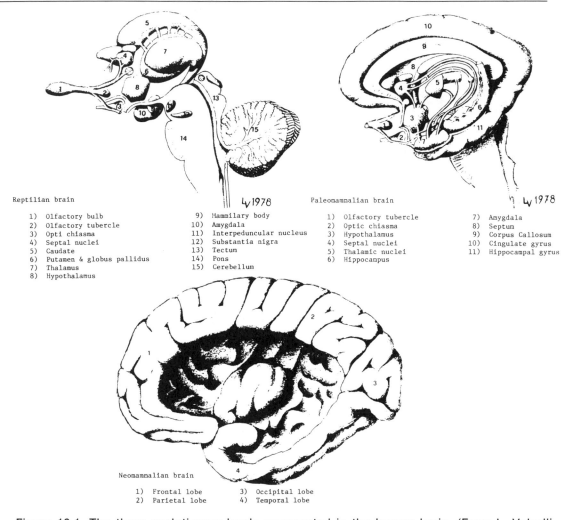

Reptilian brain   Lv 1978   Paleomammalian brain   Lv 1978

1) Olfactory bulb   9) Mammilary body   1) Olfactory tubercle   7) Amygdala
2) Olfactory tubercle   10) Amygdala   2) Optic chiasma   8) Septum
3) Opti chiasma   11) Interpeduncular nucleus   3) Hypothalamus   9) Corpus Callosum
4) Septal nuclei   12) Substantia nigra   4) Septal nuclei   10) Cingulate gyrus
5) Caudate   13) Tectum   5) Thalamic nuclei   11) Hippocampal gyrus
6) Putamen & globus pallidus 14) Pons   6) Hippocampus
7) Thalamus   15) Cerebellum
8) Hypothalamus

Neomammalian brain

1) Frontal lobe   3) Occipital lobe
2) Parietal lobe   4) Temporal lobe

Figure 10-1. The three evolutionary levels represented in the human brain. (From L. Valzelli, *Psychobiology of Aggression and Violence,* copyright 1981 by Raven Press, New York. Reproduced with permission.)

The reptilian brain probably operates like a map so that the inner picture for a frog is a direct, although radically diminished, representation of what its eyes convey inward. This maplike mind seems to be an early statement of a capacity that generally becomes elaborated in the right hemisphere of the human brain. Whereas most animals seem to live in a world of space, humans live in a world of both space and time. This appears to be the result of the left hemisphere's development of a sense of time (Loye, 1983).

The evolution of homo sapiens beyond the apes can be appreciated by comparing the 4.3 billion neurons of a chimpanzee with the ten billion of a human. The number of neurons related to basic functions of the body are essentially the same in humans and chimpanzees, however, homo

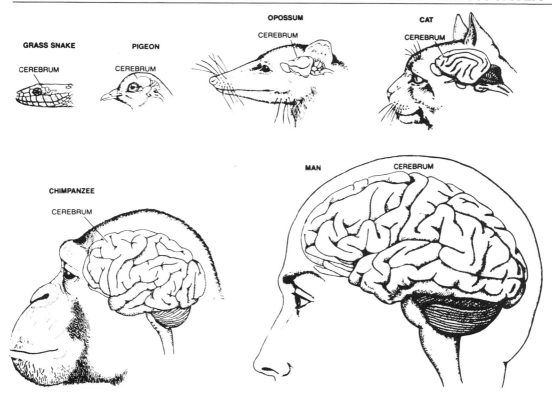

Figure 10-2. The cerebrum enlarges progressively in a series of vertebrates drawn to the same scale. The small brains of lower vertebrates are smooth and tubular, but the larger cerebral hemispheres of higher species acquire many folds. (From D. H. Hubel, "The Brain," *Scientific American, 241,* 1979, 45–53. Copyright 1953 by Scientific American, Inc. All rights reserved.)

sapiens has 8.5 billion cerebral cortex neurons compared with 3.4 billion for chimpanzees.

Remarkably, the evolution of the brain occurred in such a way that its capacity has exceeded its actual functioning levels. Thus the primate brain has the ability to perform beyond its current level of functioning, and by inference humans have even more spectacular unrealized potentials. For example, an orangutan was taught to make and use a stone tool to cut a cord in order to release the lid of a box and gain access to food (Wright, 1972). Moreover, chimpanzees have been taught the rudiments of human language through the visual modality (Gardner & Gardner, 1969; Premack & Premack, 1972). However, they are unable to employ language in both visual and auditory modalities as do humans (Fishbein, 1976).

From A. Africanus over a million years ago to the appearance of homo sapiens some 200,000 years ago, the neocortex enlarged markedly, with a great increase in neurons mediating information-processing capacities. The growth of the neocortex was greatest in the temporal, parietal, and frontal lobes, which are the areas of the brain underlying language, imagery, spatial understanding, complex memory, skilled movements, and planning abilities.

EMBRYOLOGY OF THE HUMAN BRAIN

At birth the human brain comprises 33 percent of body weight as compared with 2 percent in adulthood. By the age of five, it has virtually achieved its adult size (see Figure 10-3). The gross changes that take place during the embryonic and fetal development of the brain have been known for almost a century, but comparatively little is known about the underlying cellular events that give rise to the particular parts of the brain and their interconnections.

The CNS originates from ectoderm as a flat sheet of cells called the neural plate on the dorsal surface of the developing embryo during the third week of gestation (see Figure 10-4). Folds subsequently develop along the lateral margins of the neural groove. Deepening of the groove and fusion of the folds that border the neural plate result in the formation of the neural tube. The midportion of the neural tube is formed first, then its ends. The anterior end closes on about the 23rd day of gestation and the posterior end some two days later (Cowan, 1979).

The anterior portion of the neural tube is destined to become the brain, giving rise to the forebrain, midbrain, and hindbrain. The forebrain develops two lateral bulges from which the cerebral hemispheres are derived. From the hindbrain originate the pons, medulla, and cerebellum. Continued growth of the fetal cerebral hemispheres causes folding of the brain tissue and the formation of gyri, especially striking during the last third of gestation.

The tissue of the brain relates to the same sources as the body tissue it represents. Thus the cerebral cortex is organized according to the three primitive embryological layers: ectoderm spawns the skin and relates to the posterior parts of the cerebral cortex that deal with the external world, mesoderm gives rise to muscle and relates

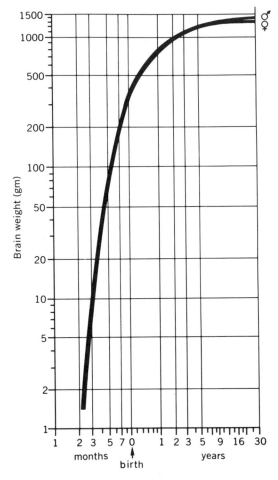

Figure 10-3. Growth curve of the human brain. (From R. J. Lemire, J. D. Loeser, R. W. Leech, and E. C. Alvord, *Normal and Abnormal Development of the Human Nervous System,* copyright 1975 by Harper and Row, New York. Reproduced with permission.)

to the parts of the brain with control over muscle, and endoderm gives rise to the body's internal organs and relates to the lower parts of the brain with visceral functions (Pribram & Luria, 1973).

The progressive covering of nerve fibers with myelin makes possible orderly and efficient transmission of nerve impulses so that fiber tracts begin to function

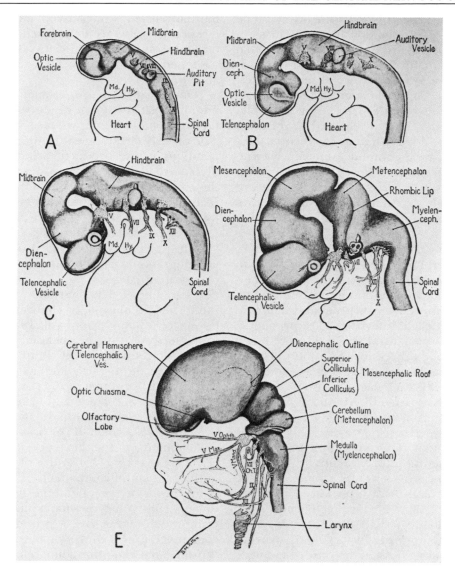

Figure 10-4. Five stages in early development of the brain and cranial nerves. (From B. M. Patten, *Human Embryology,* 2nd ed., Blakiston Co. Copyright 1953 by McGraw-Hill Book Co., New York. Reproduced with permission.)

when they are covered with myelin. The process of myelination proceeds in a sequential fashion and begins in the spinal cord by the third month of gestation, which accounts for the existence of fetal reflexes. The onset of myelination in the brain occurs three months later. For example, acoustic fibers are myelinated by the third trimester of gestation, whereas cortical association areas continue to myelineate into the third decade of life (Minkowski, 1967). At birth only a few areas and tracts are completely myelinated. Among these are brainstem centers that control the act of sucking, a behavior present at birth.

During early growth of the brain, there is an overabundance of neurons and synapses. Between the twentieth week of gestation and the end of the first year of life, millions of neurons migrate and interconnect with each other. They are pruned by a process of natural selection caused by a variety of both genetic factors and environmental factors in the uterus and external world, such as hormones, dietary chemicals, toxins, infections, and sensory events.

The mechanisms responsible for the proliferation, migration, and differentiation of neural cells, although as yet largely unknown, are subjects of current interest. Because neurons are produced in larger quantities than are actually needed, the potential integrity of the nervous system seems guaranteed. In fact many neurons expire early, possibly because they made inappropriate movements or connections. The development of most regions of the vertebrate nervous system includes a distinct phase of neuronal degeneration that adjusts the neuronal population to functional needs (Cowan et al, 1984).

How neurons "know" where to move is, as yet, veiled in secrecy. The mechanisms that guide the migration of cells may work independently within different structures of the brain. Migration is time linked so that neurons "know" their final destination only for a limited period of time. The mechanisms by which axons locate their terminations also are time linked. An axon originates as a thread of cytoplasm that is "pumped" out of the cell body (Rourke et al, 1983).

Once formed, neurons sometimes must migrate relatively great distances to reach their genetically programmed positions. The orderly development of the brain depends upon the production and location of a specified number of neurons and upon the elimination of a variable proportion of neurons after the circuitry has been established. Thus neuronal death is a prominent feature of development.

The processes of neuronal proliferation and migration usually occupy the first half of gestation. Beyond the 20th week, the development of dendrites and axons and the formation of synaptic connections predominate (Menolascino et al, 1983). With the exception of the cerebellum, the brain probably acquires its full complement of neurons prior to birth and, perhaps, as early as the beginning of the last trimester of gestation. Subsequent growth is in interneuronal connections (see Figure 10-5).

The development of the brain, like the development of other biological structures, is subject to error. One source of variation in the anatomical components of the brain is the result of the migration of neurons during embryonic development. Considering the distances over which many neurons move in the course of development, it is not surprising that some cells are misdirected to abnormal positions. Such neuronal misplacements have been recognized by pathologists in disordered brain development, but even during normal development, a proportion of migrating cells may respond inappropriately to directional cues and end up in aberrant locations. In one population of neurons studied from this point of view, about 3 percent of the cells were found to migrate to abnormal locations; most of these misplaced neurons degenerated later, however (Cowan, 1979).

Chemical factors influence neuronal

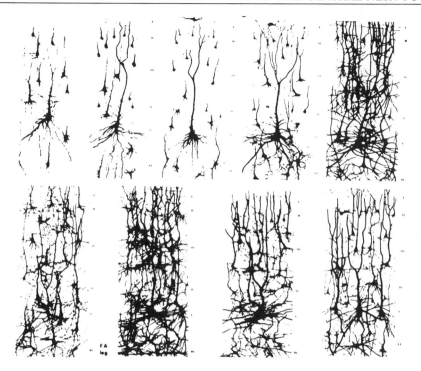

Figure 10-5. The appearance of neurons in the motor cortex. Upper row, left to right: at 8 months premature, newborn at term, 1 month, 3 months, and 6 months. Lower row, left to right: 15 months, 2 years, 4 years, and 6 years. (From R. D. Adams and M. Victor, *Principles of Neurology,* copyright 1977 by McGraw-Hill Book Co., New York. Reproduced with permission.)

migration. For example, nerve growth factor (NGF) is a protein that is necessary for the growth and maintenance of sympathetic and certain sensory neurons (Mobley et al, 1977). It acts to maintain the viability and to accelerate the maturation of neurons in the fetus. It appears also to attract neurons and to influence the maintenance of mature sensory cells.

The information required for a neuron to generate its distinctive dendrite branching is genetically determined. During the normal development of the brain, a second source of error occurs, however, when neurons are subject to a variety of local mechanical influences that modify their forms. A striking example of this is seen in the cerebellum. The Purkinje cells normally have a characteristic planar arrangement that is oriented at right angles to the axons of the granule cells that constitute their principal input; if for any reason the usual arrangement of the granule cell axons is disrupted, the planar distribution of the dendrites of the Purkinje cells is correspondingly altered (Cowan, 1979).

A third source of variation occurs, because the sensory input growing neurons receive affects their final form. It is possible to alter markedly the final appearance of a neuron's structure and its connections by intefering with its function during critical periods in its development. For example, visual deprivation after birth in a macaque monkey produces structural changes, perhaps by placing cells that are connected with the deprived eye at a disadvantage in competing for synaptic sites on the target cells in the visual cortex. Another example is the failure of specific cells in the sensory cortex to develop when mouse whiskers are removed. As little as six hours of normal visual experience at about 42 days of age, however, can reverse the loss of specificity and produce an almost normal distribution of visual cortex cells in visually deprived cats, providing evidence of the great plasticity of these cortical cells at the height of a critical period (Cooper & Imbert, 1981).

Fourth, errors can be made during the formation of neural connections. It appears, however, as if most misdirected axons and whatever inappropriate connections they form are eliminated at later stages in development. How they are recognized as being erroneous, and how they are subsequently removed, remains a puzzle. In many regions of the brain, the number of neurons originally generated greatly exceeds the number of neurons that survive beyond the developmental period. Cortical synaptic density appears to increase during infancy, reaching a maximum of about 50 percent above the adult mean at age one to two and thereafter declining until about age 16. The number of neurons thus is adjusted by selective cell death that involves from 15 to 85 percent of an initial neuronal population. It is assumed that the limiting factor determining the final number of cells is the number of functional contacts available to the axons of the developing neurons.

Neurobiologists are only beginning to learn about these aspects of neuronal development, and it is becoming clear that neurons are considerably more adaptable than had been imagined. For example, it has recently been shown that some neurons can switch their neurotransmitter from norepinephrine to acetylcholine under the influence of certain environmental factors, whereas others can change their principal ion, such as calcium to sodium, at different developmental stages. Although forebrain neurons have been found to turn over constantly in birds, all primate, and by impli-

cation human, neurons are generated during prenatal and early postnatal life and endure thereafter (Rakic, 1985).

Considering the complexity of the developmental mechanisms involved, it is hardly surprising that errors are found. What is impressive is that they appear infrequently and that they often are effectively eliminated (Cowan, 1979). The ability of the brain to reorganize itself in response to external influences or to localized injury currently is one of the most active areas in neurobiological research, not only because of its bearing on the capacity of the brain to recover after injury, but also because of what it reveals about normal brain development.

Clinical evidence suggests that the right and left hemispheres have primary and secondary programming possibilities so that the left hemisphere is the primary site of language and the secondary site of visual-spatial functions, with the converse applying to the right hemisphere. As the corpus callosum develops, each hemisphere inhibits the secondary programming of the other, which enhances each one's primary functions. For this reason, early in the myelination of the corpus callosum, before the age of five, the primary function of a damaged hemisphere may be picked up by the other hemisphere, albeit less competently. The fact that children whose corpus callosum fails to develop show language and visual-spatial functioning of each isolated hemisphere supports this possibility.

All of these phenomena help to explain the plasticity of immature central nervous systems, which may recover more completely from injury than when fully mature. Before the age of eight or nine, a child can develop normally neurologically, even after severe brain damage. But by the age of ten or twelve, the prognosis is similar to that for adults. The degree to which significant behavioral adaptation following brain impairment occurs depends on a number of factors. The main factors are the age at onset of a lesion and the extent of compensatory environmental stimulation (Rourke et al, 1983).

There appear to be qualitative differences between prenatal lesions and those occurring in childhood and adulthood (Geschwind, 1985b). For example, delimited damage in the fetus may result in lowered function in one area and superior function in others. After birth there may be recovery of function of a damaged area, but at the expense of other abilities. In adults lesions appear to diminish functions of the damaged areas without affecting those of other areas.

The developmental status of a function and the maturation of its neural substrate are other factors that influence recovery. The damage of immature nerve tissue may have no immediate behavioral consequences at all. However, functional deficits may show up later in life when more sophisticated functioning depends upon the damaged brain region. The substitute mechanisms that lead to recovery of function may be physiological or environmental in nature, or both. Brain damage in one area leaves the remaining tissue intact. Physiological restorative mechanisms, such as regenerative and collateral sprouting in neuronal processes, may bridge the damaged tissue. Other recovery models suggest that healthy tissue rearranges its functions to compensate for damaged regions. The intact parts of a damaged brain also may form new interregional connections to subserve fresh behavioral strategies that enable the brain to solve old problems in new ways. The possibility that new strategies can be taught is of great clinical importance (Rourke et al, 1983).

The immature CNS, therefore, is quite different from the mature one. Each of the developmental stages has its own more or less specific pattern of reaction to damaging factors. For some, such as anoxia, the vulnerability increases with increasing maturation. For others, such as viruses, toxic drugs, and x rays, the opposite is true. As long as maturation is not complete, the developmental strategies can be changed as a reaction to damage, especially by compensation for loss of neurons through such mechanisms as increased proliferation of supportive cells, reduced spontaneous cell death, continued growth of neuronal processes, and the formation of additional synapses. These compensatory mechanisms make the brain an extremely plastic organ (Ebels, 1981).

Brain Malformations

Genetic errors, as well as traumas, toxic agents, and diseases, may induce a variety of developmental malformations. The defective closure of the neural tube may affect the whole tube or parts of it. Cranioschisis results from defective closure at the brain region of the tube and myeloschisis at the spinal region. Neural tissue may protrude in each condition or largely be absent as in anencephaly, in which the telencephalon and part of the diencephalon may be missing (Rourke et al, 1983).

Spina bifida is a developmental abnormality from a minor failure of the neural tube to close. Protrusion of spinal tissue and fluid often is visible as a bulging sac in infants with a meningomyelocele. They frequently develop hydrocephalus, a condition in which part of the ventricular system is enlarged due to increased pressure caused by obstruction of the flow of cerebrospinal fluid.

Microcephaly usually results from brain damage, which, among other factors, may be caused by environmental agents, such as rubella virus and x-radiation. The development of a small skull occurs secondarily and mental retardation often results. While cranio- and myeloschisis are related to the failure of the neural tube to close, holoprosencephaly, a single nondifferentiated hemisphere, is produced by the failure of the prosencephalic vesicles to evaginate.

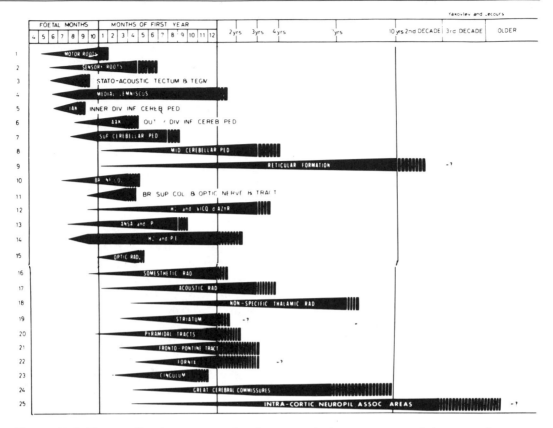

Figure 10-6. The myelination progression in anatomical components of the central nervous system. The vertical stripes at the end of graphs indicate approximate age-range of termination of myelination. (From A. Minkowski, ed., "The Myelogenetic Cycles of Regional Maturation of the Brain," *Regional Development of the Brain in Early Life.* Copyright 1967 by F. A. Davis Co., Philadelphia PA. Reproduced with permission.)

BRAIN MATURATION AND BEHAVIOR

The various anatomical and neuroregulator subsystems of CNS structures mature at different rates so that their interconnections are completed at different times (see Figure 10-6). Education plays a key role in CNS development as well (Chall & Mirsky, 1978).

Hemispheric asymmetry of function and its anatomical correlates show a developmental pattern (Schacter & Galaburda, 1986). Indeed, it may be that functions in some individuals are equally mediated by both hemispheres at the onset of life and then lateralize as the brain matures. Unique responses in the two hemispheres, however, can be seen as early as two weeks after birth. The language area of the temporal lobe usually is larger than the right at birth. When infants hear sounds that contain phonetic structure, the left hemisphere of the brain is activated, while the right appears to be at rest. Conversely, with nonlanguage sounds the right hemisphere becomes active, while the left remains inactive (Diamond, 1971).

The left hemisphere tends to mature

more slowly than the right but eventually is larger. The visual cortex matures earlier than the auditory cortex. Myelination of the corpus callosum is evident at nine months and is substantially advanced by age four, however, it is not fully myelinated until age ten and beyond (Galin et al, 1979). Thus the emergence of cerebral lateralization functions continue at least until puberty (Salamy, 1978). Consequently there is a sequential development and stabilization of motor laterality, sensory laterality, lateral orientation, and language lateralization from birth to about 13 years (Wexler, 1980).

A child's earliest awareness of being comes from the naturalistic mode of thinking of the right hemisphere, which responds largely to pain and pleasure, love and tenderness, and threat or security. A child is not aware of social conceptions of "right" or "wrong" until values are learned through language. The young child learns language and, thereby, socially acceptable behavior through the left hemisphere. Conflicts, therefore, may develop between right hemispheric tendencies and left hemisphere language based social values, which usually dominate and lead to the logical time-oriented behavior required by social roles.

The natural inability of adults to recall memories of eary childhood is called infantile amnesia. It probably is due to the incomplete storage of memories during early life because of the later maturation of the hippocampus; the loss of stored memories during the course of development; the inability to retrieve stored memories, because the contextual clues that guide retrieval change radically between infancy and childhood; and the psychological defense mechanism of repression (Kail, 1984). It also may not be as extensive as previously thought when appropriate recognition cues are available (Daehler & Greco, 1985).

The angular and supramarginal gyri, which are critical for reading, are not found in subprimate species and appear only in rudimentary form in the higher apes. In keeping with its late phylogoenetic development, the angular gyrus matures in late childhood and is one of the last cortical areas in which dendrites appear. The region receives very few thalamic nerve fibers so that its connections are predominantly from other cortical regions. It is a tertiary association area and is not adjacent to the primary projection areas for vision, hearing, and somesthetic sensibility, but rather at the point of junction of these areas.

Studies of intersensory development, which reflects the maturation of the angular gyri, indicate that the integration of the kinesthetic modality with visual and haptic modalities does not take place until the age of seven or eight. This also applies to auditory-visual integration of temporal and spatial patterns. Prefrontal lobe mediated problem solving strategies in addition to the capacities to attend selectively to relevant stimuli, suppress inappropriate responses, and shift cognitive set appear to reach adult levels of maturity by the age of ten years (Chelune & Baer, 1986).

Myelination of the brain continues to take place through adolescence and into adulthood (Yakovlev & LeCours, 1967). Myelination tends to occur in functional units rather than in geographical areas. Thus the reticular formation, which is concerned with attention and arousal, continues to myelinate through puberty, and possibly beyond. The frontal lobes are the last to mature and presumably are the last to be integrally involved in human mental life. They assume critical importance for those aspects of thought that emerge in adolescence.

The neuroregulator systems apparently develop at different rates. For example, the dopamine and serotonin systems gradually mature throughout childhood, whereas the acetylcholine and norepinephrine systems do so during early childhood.

Electroencephalographic patterns also

show a developmental progression. Definite shifts in patterns occur at ages during which key cognitive shifts take place: at about three months of age, between six and 12 months, at about two years, and between four and six years. Significant changes in the electroencephalogram between the ages of nine and 11 correspond to the onset of the capacity for formal operations (Eeg-Olafsson, 1970). An individual's characteristic adult electroencephalographic pattern becomes established at about 15 to 16 years of age with stabilization at about 18 (Lewis, 1982; Thatcher et al, 1987).

The available data suggest that the curves for cerebral metabolic rate, amplitude and duration of stage 4 sleep electroencephalographic waves, and cortical synaptic density rise steeply after birth to a maximum of about twice the adult level from 2 to 5 years, maintaining high levels and then declining to the adult level at the end of the second decade, with the steepest falloffs between the ages of 10 and 15 (Feinberg, 1987). Thus, intense changes in brain physiology and structure accompany the biopsychosocial changes of adolescence.

SUMMARY

The human central nervous system is built upon the reptilian, paleomammalian, and neomammalian brains of our animal ancestors. A child's brain recapitulates this phylogenetic sequence in its maturation and possesses enormous unrealized capacities. The maturation of the human brain continues into the third decade of life.

In the course of development, neurons migrate and are affected by surrounding mechanical and chemical influences in addition to sensory stimulation. Consequently errors and aberrations in neuronal structures and connections commonly occur but are usually corrected by cell death. Lasting effects may persist, however, in both obvious and subtle malformations of brain tissue.

The CNS is remarkably plastic in its development so that, prior to the age of eight or nine, substantial brain damage can occur without evident functional repercussions. The CNS can compensate for injuries by shifting its maturational strategies in response to environmental stimulation and the growth of neuronal processes and supportive cells.

In spite of the anatomical boundaries between parts of the brain, there is no reason to assume that the contribution of any one part does not change over the course of a lifetime. In fact, it is likely that the activity of the central nervous systems of children are constantly in flux with cells dying, new synapses being formed, and neuroregulator levels changing.

The progressive development of mental and behavioral capacities in children can be related to maturational events in their brains at the various stages of childhood. The development of the brain is reflected in a child's growing capacities to work in school.

11

An Integrated Model of the Central Nervous System

The human mind is a stream running after some half-sensed
goal, yet capable of attention, forming objects like an artist
and concepts like a geometrician, while the whole organism,
acting like a sounding-board, generates the emotions that
reason is meant to serve.

Jacques Barzun, 1983

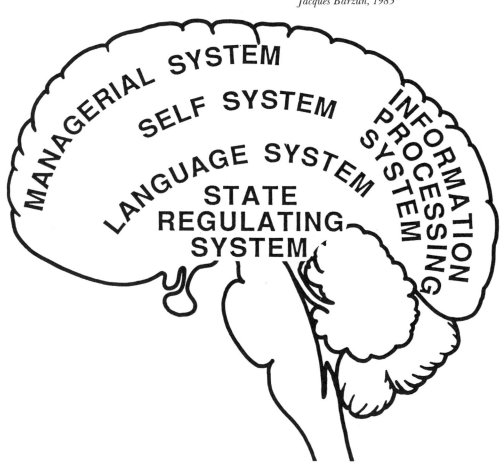

The relation between the brain and the mind was apparent to ancient Greek philosophers. Hippocratess knew that joy as well as pain arose from the brain. In the 17th century, however, Descartes strongly influenced later thought by separating the mind from the body—and, by implication, from the brain. This Cartesian dichotomy remains with us today as we pursue the elusive soul; however, we now can understand most mentation as not just a product but as a phase of neuronal activity (Bohm, 1980; Churchland, 1986; Langer, 1967; Kandel, 1979).

Over the years studies of the brain have been devoted to the functions of its parts and its entirety. The historic revelations of Broca and Wernicke in Germany in the 1860s on the nature of aphasias first stimulated interest in localizing brain functions. Later in England, however, Hughlings Jackson believed that all parts of the brain participated in every cognitive activity. More recently both localizing and holistic approaches have placed the neural sciences on the threshold of solving many of the brain's mysteries.

The most dramatic evidence of the localization of mental activity in the brain was provided by Wilder Penfield's demonstration of the existence of the "stream of consciousness" proposed earlier by William James. Before performing surgery to remove seizure-producing scar tissue, Penfield applied a gentle electric current to a series of sites on the exposed surface of the brain. This procedure made it possible to map out the motor and sensory areas of the cortex (Figure 11-1).

Penfield's electrical stimulation of the auditory areas of the temporal cortex caused patients to experience only a particular sound. Stimulation of the nonauditory aspects of the temporal cortex, however, produced illusions of the present or flashbacks to past events, including auditory, visual, somatic, and labyrinthine sensations, as well as emotions. These areas probably do not contain the brain's record of auditory and visual memories but rather distill amalgamations of them that were reported by those patients (Jaynes, 1976).

Penfield described what seemed to be happening by a parable (Penfield, 1956):

> Among the millions of nerves cells that clothe certain parts of the temporal lobe, on each side there is a thread of time that has run through each succeeding, wakeful hour of the individual's past life. It is like a pathway through an unending sequence of nerve cells, fibers, and synapses. When, by chance, the neurosurgeon's electrode activates some portion of the thread, there is a response as though that thread were a strip of movie film on which are registered all of those things of which the individual was once aware.

From this evidence it appears that the "stream of consciousness" is available in some way for the comparison and interpretation of new experiences throughout life.

The mental correlates of brain activity also have been profitably explored through other routes. For example, a difference in evoked brain waves has been reported between the correct and incorrect perception of visual forms. Furthermore, differences in brain waves occur between perceptions that are made tentatively and with certainty (Radilova & Radil-Weiss, 1983).

The classical localization of psychological functions within specific parts of the brain and the holistic view ultimately were united by the identification of functional brain systems (Gardner, 1976; Orbach, 1982). These systems are composed of centers and networks. According to this view, each mode of psychological activity is a functional system based upon the interaction of parts of the brain (Pribram & Luria, 1973). Most basic brain functions, such as movement and sight, have localized ele-

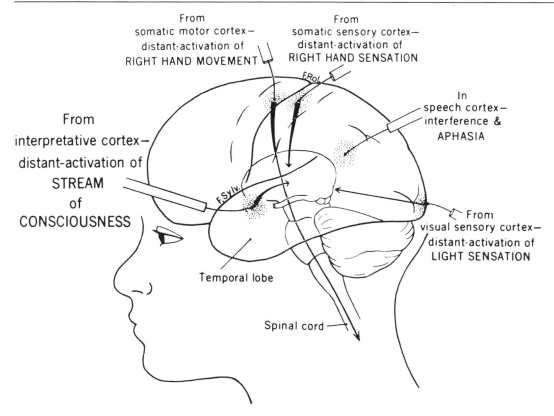

Figure 11-1. Activation of the brain causes different responses depending on the area. (From Wilder Penfield, *The Mystery of the Mind: A Critical Study of Consciousness and the Human Brain,* with discussions by William Feindel, Charles Hendel, and Charles Symonds. Copyright © 1975 by Princeton University Press. Reprinted with permission of the Literary Executors of the Penfield Papers and Princeton University Press.)

ments, while symbolic activities, such as thought and the exercise of will, do not (see Figure 11-2). The exercise of will thus probably involves the whole brain and the resulting action emanates from specific areas. Complex mental tasks—such as speaking, silent and oral reading, and counting—call for the interaction of a number of parts of the brain, as illustrated in Figure 11-3. These interactions are analogous to computer programs in which different routines are brought into play depending on the problem to be solved.

Central nervous system (CNS) functions then are the complex adaptive activities of individuals who are responding to their environments in time and space. They are not fixed functions of one particular part of the brain but of schemes in neural networks that guide the individual toward a goal. For example, walking is not performed by a fixed series of innervations but involves a complex and changing functional system, the links of which constantly vary as the course of the movement evolves in response to the terrain and obstacles (Finger & Stein, 1982).

The CNS is continuously in a state of excitation, never inactive. Any stimuli introduced into it thus have a figure and

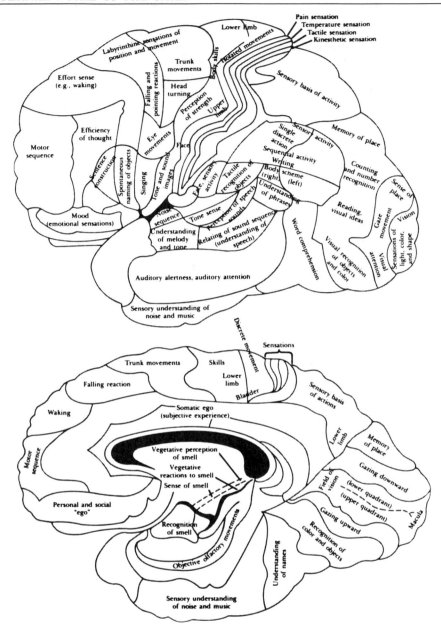

Figure 11-2. A functional map of the adult human brain. The upper map shows the left lateral surface and the lower map shows the medial surface. (From T. G. R. Bower, *Human Development*. W. H. Freeman and Company, copyright 1979.)

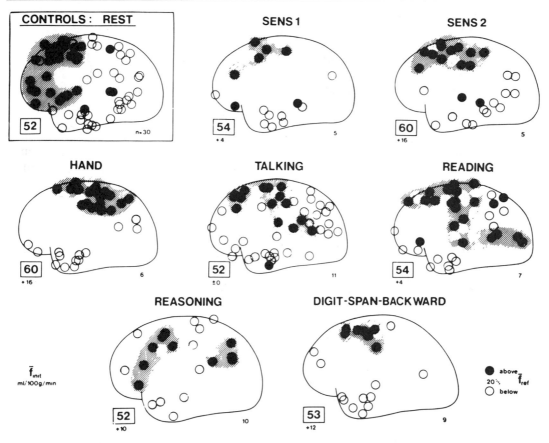

Figure 11-3. Cerebral blood flow patterns recorded during seven types of cerebral activity. SENS 1 is with low-intensity electrical stimulation of the skin of the contralateral hand, and SENS 2 is the same with high-intensity stimulation experienced as slight pain. HAND is during voluntary hand movements. Talking and reading produced a Z-like increase involving premotor, rolandic, and posterior sylvian regions. Reading produced increased occipital blood flow. Reasoning activated prefrontal and parietal areas. Digit-span-backward activated frontal lobe areas. (From D. H. Ingvar, "Functional Landscapes of the Dominant Hemisphere," *Brain Research, 107,* 1976, 181–197. Copyright 1976 by Elsevier Scientific Publishing Co., Amsterdam, The Netherlands. Reproduced with permission.)

background character. We usually ignore the background and pay attention only to the figure. Neither, however, can be properly evaluated without the other (Goldstein, 1963). The CNS also determines what it perceives, how it recognizes those perceptions, and what it does with them.

In contrast with other organ systems, the CNS has enormous plasticity and unrealized capabilities. Chimpanzees can be trained to do things unknown in their natural state. Human beings also use only a fraction of their potential. This is the result of the extensive redundancy in brain structures, the opening of new horizons as each new function was acquired in evolution, and the brain's capacity to mold itself.

A physics-based theory of the CNS has been advanced that relies on the principles of holography (Pribram et al, 1974; Pribram, 1980). Holography is a process in which a three-dimensional image is encoded on a two-dimensional plate. Each portion of a holographic plate contains all the information necessary for reconstituting a realistic image of the whole. The characteristics of the CNS that correspond to holography are the interpretation of frequencies and phases of stimuli, the widespread distribution of information so that a brain lesion fails to eradicate specific memory traces, the enormous storage capacity and the ease with which information can be retrieved, the capacity for associative recall, and the capacity for powerful correlations that are accomplished almost instantaneously.

Still the CNS is far more complex than the most elaborate product of human technology. It operates both digitally and analogically as an elaborate feedback system that registers discrepancies between the environment and an internal state and sets in motion behavior to correct those discrepancies (von Neumann, 1958). Lowen constructed a model of the CNS using the languages of mathematics, computers, and psychology (Lowen, 1982). The model assumes a dichotomous organization of CNS processes, so that each is in dialectic opposition to another as in excitation and inhibition, the sympathetic and parasympathetic nervous systems, and the pleasure and distress systems. Each opposing characteristic works both together with and against the other. Intriguingly, this interplay of opposites is represented in the yin-yang symbol in which the dark half stands for yang, the active principle, and the light half stands for yin, the passive principle (Figure 11-4). Each half of the symbol contains the germ of its antithesis as well.

Lowen's model also assumes fundamental dichotomies in the focus of attention on the world of people versus the world of things, in processing information in concrete versus abstract ways, in processing information in wholes by context versus

Figure 11-4. The dark half represents the Yang (the active principle) and the light half represents the Yin (the passive principle). Each half contains within it the germ of its antithesis.

sequentially arranged detailed steps, and in the general orientation of persons toward the external world versus toward the internal world (Lowen, 1982).

The powerful role of the interplay of opposites is inherent in the human CNS, which is a self-regulating system through opposition. The simplest example is a pair of hands. The two hands not only are mirror opposites of each other but are opposite in their functions when they work together. One tends to holding and the other to manipulating. The function of each hand is specialized and differentiated. Each acts in contrary fashion, yet each needs the other. As a pair they can cooperate effectively, because they are diametrically different, and a greater unity grows out of their opposition. Furthermore, it is characteristic of a pair of opposites that only one is dominant.

Lowen's model, also, takes into account a developmental course from prelingual to lingual capacities; energy dispositions that determine character types; the differential impact of hearing, vision and the contact senses; and the outflow of behavior through the hands, mouth, the rest of the body, and intellect. Lowen concludes that the brain's control of behavior grows out of tension between hierarchically organized dichotomous systems.

A number of theoretical conceptions support this hierarchical view of the CNS (Bronson, 1965; Flor-Henry, 1976; Powell,

1979; Yakovlev, 1948). The lower centers of the brain comprise systems that regulate basic life processes, the general level of alertness and responsiveness, and the postural muscle tone. These systems seek pleasure and the avoidance of distress. They press for immediate satisfaction. They are the sources of patterns of behavior that reflect the appetitive and adaptive instincts, with the cravings and emotions that accompany them.

An intermediate set of systems mediate cognitive and language functions. These systems provide the basic equipment for relating to the material and interpersonal environment through perception, comprehension, and communication.

The highest level of functioning is mediated by systems for specific focusing of attention and for voluntary goal-directed behavior. These systems mediate the passions of lower systems and the constraints and exigencies of the external world.

Hughlings Jackson's postulate that higher levels of the nervous system represent and re-represent all lower centers has been verified. Thus the functions of lower systems are controlled by, but are not replaced by, phylogenetically newer structures (Jackson, 1958). The lower centers thereby continue to play roles in the functioning of the higher centers (Bernston & Micco, 1976). Still, the capacities of the highest centers far exceed the aggregate of lower centers.

A clinically useful view of the CNS that brings together all of these ideas was delineated by Luria, who described different functional levels, each making its own contribution to mental activity (Luria, 1973).

He distinguished three principal functional systems of the brain: one for regulating the waking state through which attention, motivation, and emotion determine how an individual relates to the environment; a second for obtaining, processing, and storing information through which the environment is perceived and recognized; and a third system for programming, regulating, and verifying mental activity through which a person thinks, judges, decides, acts, and verifies those actions. Each of these basic systems consists of overlapping hierarchical brain centers built one upon the other. Recent evidence suggests the validity of adding the fourth and fifth functional systems of language and the self.

Luria's conceptualization of brain functioning was anticipated before the turn of the century by Sigmund Freud (Pribram & Gill, 1976). Freud then recognized that electric currents were present in the brain in two basic forms: as neuronal discharge and as graded potential differences within a neuron. This conception provided a model of the brain with both the capacity for instant action through the former and for the storage of information through the latter.* Freud further proposed that there were three basic systems of neurons: (1) permeable phi neurons with long fibers and few synapses primarily responsible for external sensory reception and motor discharge (resembling Luria's processing and storage system); (2) relatively impermeable psi neurons of shorter length with more synapses primarily responsive to internal excitation and storing excitation for memory and motive (resembling Luria's state

---

*In Freud's view the ego is a network of phi and omega neurons in associational areas of the cortex that excite each other by inhibiting the memory-motive structures of the primary process. The ego may allow discharge of the phi system excitation; however, the ego institutes psi cathexis as a defense against the phi discharge. In neurophysiological terms the ego operates primarily through inhibition of facilitory structures by feedback processes, making possible willed actions specific to the exigencies of the internal and external environment. The stimulus barrier of the ego scales down the intensity of external stimuli to manageable proportions, thereby reducing the need to withdraw from external stimuli through denial or flight and permitting time for thinking (Pribram & Gill, 1976).

regulating system); and (3) omega neurons (resembling Luria's programming system) responsive to the periodicity of the excitation of the phi neurons and furnishing excitation to the psi system.

Because of its multiple determinants, human behavior is not well suited to scientific examination. Yet current theories and research can be usefully related to each other with the anticipation that what is accepted today will be modified later. Figure 11-5 represents my synthesis of the foregoing theoretical conceptions of the CNS as a framework for assembling clinical and experimental knowledge. It employs general systems theory as a setting for Luria's functional units of the brain, psychoanalytic conceptions of character, and the links between behavior and social context. Although the psychoanalytic terms id, ego, and superego have not been employed, their relevance throughout the model is evident. They usefully emphasize the way in which the mind is divided against itself.

This model of the CNS contains inevitable flaws; however, the time is ripe for integrating efforts of this kind (Mayr, 1982; Shapiro & Weber, 1981).

THE STATE REGULATING SYSTEM

All living systems require transitional zones that filter and modulate the constant flow of external and internal stimuli in order to maintain homeostasis of the body (Silbermann, 1979). The state regulating system based in the hindbrain and forebrain performs these functions and maintains cortical tone essential for the organized course of mental activity. The states of hunger, sleep, alertness, and quiescence can be understood as dynamic, rhythmic activities related to neuroregulator and neuroendocrine activities in the state regulating system (Anders, 1978).

The state regulating system is made up of an intricate set of interacting positive and negative feedback processes that act upon the sensory inflow to the brain and exercise facilitating and inhibitory influences on the somatic and visceral musculature in order to maintain a steady state within the organism as it interacts with the environment. The major components of the state regulating system are the limbic system, the extrapyramidal system, the reticular activating system, the autonomic nervous system, and the neuroendocrine system (see Figure 11-6). These systems are the determinants of the characteristics of temperament as reflected in arousal, consciousness, and the appetitive and adaptive instincts. As indicated in Figure 11-5, the state regulating system involves all of the structures of the CNS except the input transducer.

Arousal

The means by which the central nervous system maintains its ability to attend selectively to stimuli is a highly complex matter. Informational input to the brain is into a system that already is actively excited. Behavior thus results from interaction of this background of excitation with foreground sensory input, as eloquently described by Lashley (1951):

> Far from merely resounding to the tunes played on its sensory organs, the brain orchestrates its own intake through pathways that are capable of controlling the sensitivity of the receptors themselves and the amplitude of the impulses transmitted along them. Although responsive to the stimuli impinging upon the organism, the central excitatory state in itself determines from moment to moment whether, how, and in what pattern incoming messages are registered. Arousal is maintained through the interaction and mutual stimulation of the reticular activating system, cerebral cortex and spinal cord.

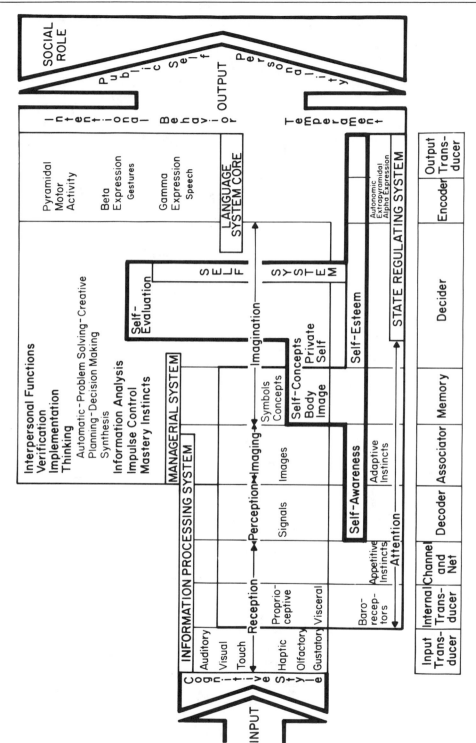

Figure 11-5. An integrated model of the central nervous system.

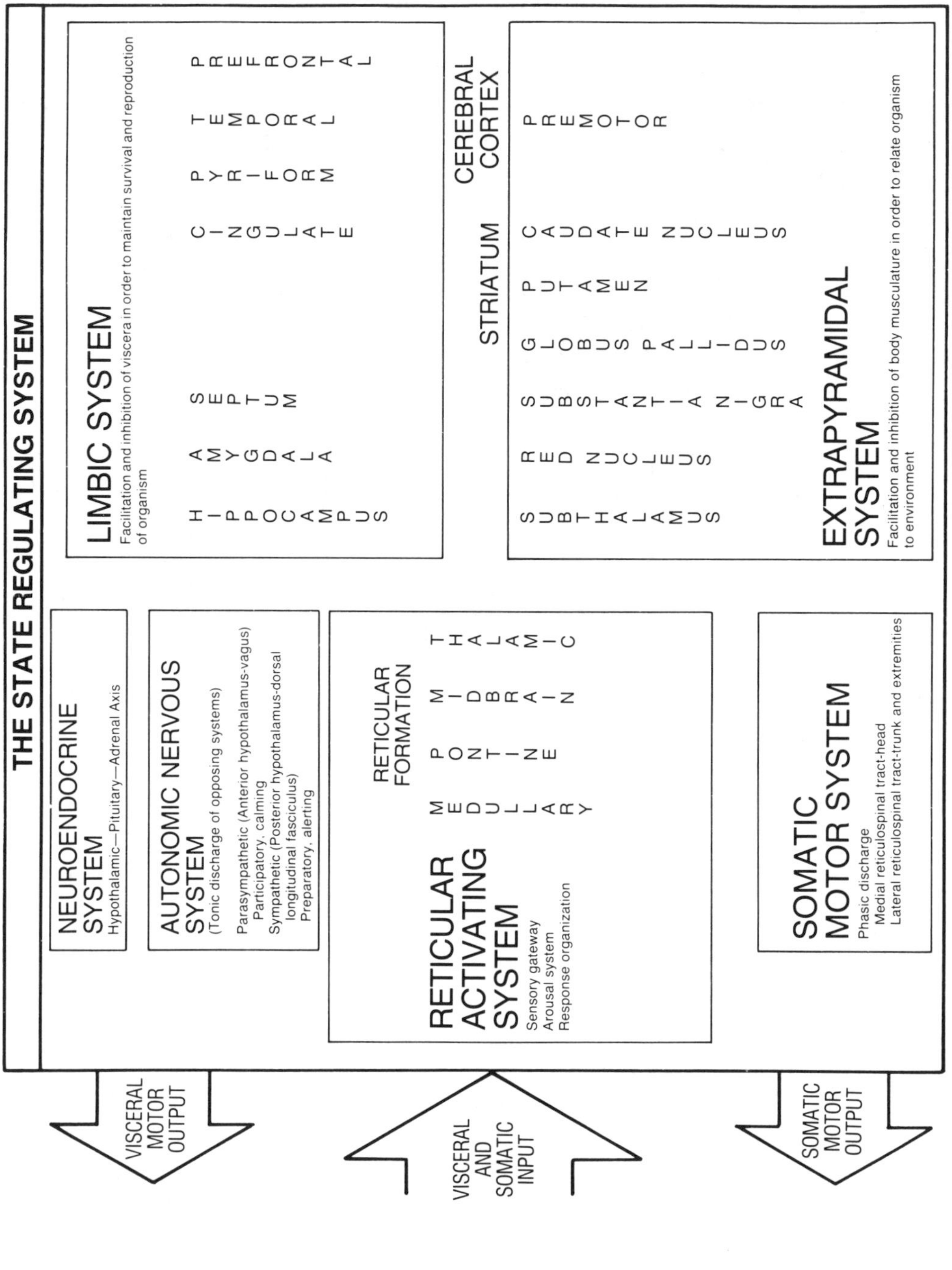

THE STATE REGULATING SYSTEM

NEUROENDOCRINE SYSTEM
Hypothalamic—Pituitary—Adrenal Axis

AUTONOMIC NERVOUS SYSTEM
(Tonic discharge of opposing systems)

Parasympathetic (Anterior hypothalamus-vagus)
Participatory, calming
Sympathetic (Posterior hypothalamus-dorsal longitudinal fasciculus)
Preparatory, alerting

RETICULAR FORMATION

MEDULLA   PONS   MIDBRAIN   THALAMIC

RETICULAR ACTIVATING SYSTEM
Sensory gateway
Arousal system
Response organization

LIMBIC SYSTEM
Facilitation and inhibition of viscera in order to maintain survival and reproduction of organism

HIPPOCAMPUS   AMYGDALA   SEPTUM   CINGULATE   PYRIFORM   PREFRONTAL CORTEX

STRIATUM

SUBTHALAMUS   RED NUCLEUS   SUBSTANTIA NIGRA   GLOBUS PALLIDUS   PUTAMEN   CAUDATE NUCLEUS

CEREBRAL CORTEX

PREMOTOR

EXTRAPYRAMIDAL SYSTEM
Facilitation and inhibition of body musculature in order to relate organism to environment

SOMATIC MOTOR SYSTEM
Phasic discharge
Medial reticulospinal tract-head
Lateral reticulospinal tract-trunk and extremities

VISCERAL MOTOR OUTPUT

VISCERAL AND SOMATIC INPUT

SOMATIC MOTOR OUTPUT

Figure 11-6.

The reticular activating system is the background source of arousal for the CNS. The limbic system is a second foreground arousal system and is the source of the judgments of pleasure and distress. The two arousal systems function in an integrated fashion; each suppresses the activity of the other. This reciprocal inhibition places the two systems in a state of dynamic equilibrium.

Input to both arousal systems is from collaterals of the direct sensory pathways from the sensory receptors to the neocortex. At low or intermediate levels of sensory input, the limbic system predominates over the reticular activating system, since the suppressing effect of the hippocampus tends to diminish positive feedback from the reticular activating system to the neocortex. At high levels of sensory activation, the reticular activating system predominates over hippocampal suppression. The frontal cortex also reciprocally exercises arousal and inhibitory effects on the reticular activating system, so that the cortex is able to regulate its own arousal (Routtenberg, 1968).

The reticular activating system is charged by three principal sources of stimuli. The first are the internal metabolic processes of the body. The second are the stimuli from the outside world that activate the orienting reflex. The third are the internal intentions, plans, and forecasts of the managerial system that focus attention and maintain concentration. The most important initiator of reticular activity is not the external sensory system but the neocortex, which initiates and sustains reticular excitation for specific purposes. This cortical input constitutes a booster that is essential for efficient attention and learning. The reticular activating system also may protect the cortex from repetitive, monotonous stimulation through the process of stimulus modulation, as reflected in habituation.

The complexity of sensory stimulus modulation is illustrated in Figure 11-7, in which three levels are proposed (Ornitz, 1983). The first level involves the interaction of vestibular and brainstem reticular formation centers. They center around the midbrain, pontine, and medullary reticular formation (RF). The second level involves the convergence of somatosensory, visual, vestibular, and other sensory inputs upon the medial thalamus. This level centers around the centro-median-parafascicular complex (CM-Pf) and brings in the neostriatum, globus pallidus, and substantia nigra. The third level involves the reticular nucleus of the thalamus and the mesencephalic reticular formation. This level centers around the thalamic reticular nucleus (ThRN) and modulates interaction between specific thalamic nuclei and the cerebral cortex under the control of the brain-stem reticular formation, the CM-Pf, and other specific thalamic nuclei.

Neurotransmitters play an important role in attention. Vigilant attention is maintained by the norepinephrine generated in cells in the locus ceruleus and transmitted to the limbic region and the entire neocortex for the maintenance of arousal. Serotonin facilitates flexible levels of arousal by dampening large and magnifying small inputs and is generated in the pontine raphe nuclei and transmitted to the hypothalamus, the basal ganglia, and the neocortex (Betz, 1979). Dopamine is involved in the mesolimbic system's emotional modulation and the striatonigral system's regulation of movement, including that involved in attention.

Consciousness

Consciousness is a state of attention with multidimensional perceptual representation of an organism and its environment (Schwartz & Schiller, 1970; John, 1976). It is a pattern of arousal that is continuously evolving and changing (McClelland, 1985). At any one time, it reflects both the content

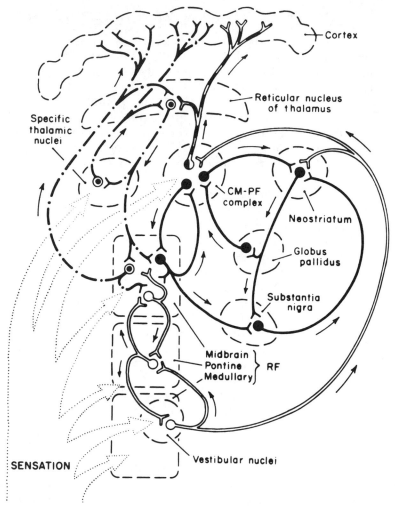

Figure 11-7. Schematic representation of the modulation of sensory input impinging on several levels of the reticular formation (RF), the nonspecific thalamic nuclei (represented by the centro-median-parafascicularis (CM-Pf) complex) and the specific thalamic nuclei. Sensation is modulation by those neuronal loops which impinge on each other in the midbrain RF, the CM-Pf complex, and the reticular nucleus of the thalamus (ThRN). The vestibulo-midbrain RF loop (open lines) transmits modulated sensory input to a neuronal loop comprised of midbrain RF and ThRN (dot-and-dash lines) which modulates sensory transmission through the specific thalamic nuclei, and to a complex neuronal loop (solid lines) composed of midbrain RF, substantia nigra, CM-Pf, and neostriatum. The vestibulo-midbrain RF loop impinges on the former loop at the midbrain RF, and through vestibular projections to the specific thalamic nuclei. The vestibulo-midbrain RF loop impinges on the later loop at the midbrain RF, and at the CM-Pf and neostriatum. The three loops interact in such a way that all effects summate on neurons on the ThRN, the axons of which project back upon thalamus and midbrain to provide final modulation of sensory information flowing rostrally toward the cortex. (From E. M. Ornitz, "The Functional Neuroanatomy of Infantile Autism," *International Journal of Neurosciences, 19,* 1983, 85–124. Reprinted by permission of E. M. Ornitz and publishers. Copyright © Gordon and Breach Science Publishers Inc.)

of recent inputs to the memory system and the context in which the input occurs.

In humans the "stream of consciousness" flows with great efficacy in day-to-day affairs influencing information processing, thoughts, feelings, and behavior, which themselves regulate the flow of consciousness. There are striking differences in the extent to which individuals consistently attend to their streams of consciousness (Pope & Singer, 1978). For example, one's awareness of the passage of time reflects one's view of the meaning of life itself. Is time a purposeless, endless stream or is it the expression of a cosmic drama? How this is answered influences whether the passage of time is viewed as an enemy or a friend.

There is a difference between attention that does and does not involve conscious awareness. Penfield (1975) distinguished between them by describing the automatic sensorimotor mechanism and the centrencephalic mechanism (see Figure 13-2). The automatic sensorimotor mechanism coordinates previously programmed activity and handles most of our ongoing activities without consciousness by carrying out such actions as reading, writing, and speaking more skillfully than could be done by conscious direction. We reserve consciousness for particularly demanding tasks, or leave it as a free space for scanning attention, for thought and decision making, or for reverie (Goleman, 1985). Attention with conscious awareness appears to be activated by the centrencephalic mechanism in the diencephalon. When epileptic discharges occur in this area, absence seizures with loss of conscious awareness occur, with later amnesia. In psychomotor seizures, the person becomes a mindless automaton, operating only through the automatic sensorimotor mechanism and capable only of automatic behavior without conscious awareness. Inactivation of the centrencephalic mechanism also occurs normally in sleep and pathologically with brain lesions.

The cerebral cortex, then, is not the site of consciousness; the centrencephalic mechanism is. We do not know whether the stream of consciousness is recreated each time the centrencephalic mechanism goes into action or whether the centrencephalic mechanism switches awareness off and on of a continuing stream. The latter possibility is favored by the fact that alert vigilance can be reliably detected in the electroencephalogram when conscious awareness does not exist (Davidson et al, 1983).

Consciousness appears to be an energy field that operates above and beyond measurable electrical activity (Penfield, 1975). If the corpus callosum is intact, a flow of information can occur between the two hemispheres, and the bioenergy field of consciousness can utilize this integrated information simultaneously. When the corpus callosum is severed, apparently the energy field of consciousness still moves from one hemisphere to the other, but it is unable to integrate information simultaneously from both. Severing the connections between the two hemispheres apparently affects the efficiency of the energy field, but not the field itself (Popper & Eccles, 1977).

Conscious attention to stimuli seems to facilitate the subsequent passage of potentials along a given neuronal connection in the same pattern and thus to facilitate learning. The hippocampus appears to hold the keys of access to the record of the stream of consciousness (Penfield, 1975).

Alerted consciousness requires a sufficient duration of stimulus buildup and does not occur as soon as impulses arrive in the primary sensory cortex. The initial evoked response is followed by a change in the background frequency of numerous neurons firing in the area at which time consciousness occurs (Popper & Eccles, 1977). Moreover, the onset of cerebral activity precedes by at least several hundred milliseconds the subjectively reported time of a conscious intention to act (Libet et al, 1983). Also, a cortical stimulus begun prior to a skin stimulus may be consciously experienced as if it occurred after the skin stimulus. Antedating mechanisms of some kind may explain why sometimes one can act before awareness of the intention to act, as in athletic performances and conversational repartee (Cotman & McGaugh, 1980).

At the present time, the relationships between consciousness and the brain are unresolved. At best subjective experiences are difficult to handle with existing scientific methodology. It is inappropriate to insist that consciousness must derive from existing principles, as it is obvious that not all principles are known. Not long ago we were unprepared to deal with acupuncture. There could be currently unrecognized forms of energy that operate in the brain and produce consciousness.

Instinctual Programs

The two fundamental purposes of self and species preservation are subserved respectively by the appetitive and adaptive instincts through limbic structures that act as bridges that link cortical systems with the hypothalamic and striatal instinctual centers.

The limbic system is the vehicle for motivation for self-preservation based upon appetites and affects and the dispositions to approach and withdraw. It provides for the tonic and phasic arousal of conscious behavior, the experiences of pleasure and distress, and, together with the extrapyramidal system, the general tonus of the musculature and the nuances of postural and rhythmic movements (see Figure 11-6). Self-preservative behavior also is regulated by the amygdala nuclei of the limbic system through the release of inhibition of the defensive behaviors of fight and flight (Heilbrunn, 1979). The medial amygdala mediates rage and the anterior cingulate cortical gyrus mediates fear; the mesencephalic central gray matter mediates fear and rage. The prefrontal cortex handles the weighing of emotional priorities and initiating motor strategies to maximize drive satisfaction.

The limbic septum mediates species preservative behaviors, such as approach, social and genital contact, food procurement, and nurturance of the young. Hypothalamic nuclei initiate and terminate drive behaviors, such as aggression and sexual responses. The corpus striatum mediates instinctually based social behavior, such as mating, homing, and forming social hierarchies.

There are two major routes for the social communication of emotions (Betz, 1979). The first consists of the frontal motor cortex and the pyramidal tracts through which voluntary expressions of emotions occur. The second consists of the descending extrapyramidal fibers from subcortical regions to the visceral motor outflow from the spinal cord. The resulting behavior from the latter is involuntary, making it difficult for one to disguise private emotions from public recognition. The higher centers of the extrapyramidal system are the sources of patterned inistinctual forms of motor expressions of emotions, such as laughter and facial expressions. In the middle extrapyramidal centers are provisions for postural righting reflexes involving diffuse and repetitive flexion and extension movements. In the lower extrapyramidal centers, rhythmic movements of head muscles are coordinated, such as those involving phonation and eye movements, in addition to those involved in breathing.

Thus inner motivational and emotional events are outwardly expressed voluntarily and involuntarily through bodily actions. Individuals reveal themselves and are known to others by their characteristic modes of behavior. Subjectively generated and experienced emotions are simultaneously expressed at the body periphery in the form of facial expression, tempo and direction of movement, body attitude, gesture, and vocalizations (Yakovlev, 1972).

THE INFORMATION PROCESSING AND STORING SYSTEM

The information processing and storing system receives, analyzes, and stores information. It draws upon the lateral and posterior regions of the cerebral hemispheres. This system receives stimuli from the external visual, vestibular, auditory, tactile, proprioceptive, gustatory, and olfactory sensory receptors in addition to the internal visceral receptors. As indicated in Figure 11-5 the information processing system involves the input transducer, the internal transducer, the channel and net, the decoder, the associator, the memory, and the decider structures of the central nervous system (Miller, 1978).

As will become evident later, there is a critical distinction between information and meaning (Dretske, 1981). Information is the raw material from which meaning is derived. The higher-level attributes of intelligence in the form of interpreting signals, holding beliefs, and acquiring knowledge are the result of progressively more efficient ways of extracting meaning from information.

The Input Transducer Subsystem

The subsystems that process information from the outside world begin with the sensory organs, which are input transducers. They bring external markers bearing information into each sensory system and change them into other energy forms suitable for transmission within a particular sensory system. The eyes, the vestibular and auditory components of the ears, the

chemoreceptors in the nose and tongue, and a diverse group of differently adapted receptors in the skin and tissues form this subsystem.

As an illustration, the retina is the input transducer for the visual system. The extraocular muscles direct the line of vision of the eyeball, the ciliary muscles of the lens of the eye focus light, and the retina transforms light into transmittable energy.

Sources in the eyeball itself, such as floaters, retinal blood vessels, and the optic nerve, not only can be perceived directly but may stimulate complex dream and illusion imagery (Horowitz, 1983a).

The Internal Transducer Subsystem

The internal transducer subsystem sends reports of the states of components of the CNS into the channel and net for transmission to central components. It includes the endings of postsynaptic neurons that synapse with the presynaptic neurons of pain, pressure, fullness, or other states of organs; enteroceptors such as sensors in the brain and blood vessels; and pressure transducers in muscles. Input from the body originates from the hypothalamic receptor cells that control hunger, thirst, body temperature, and the osmotic pressure of the blood. It also originates from the brainstem centers that control carbon dioxide content and acidity of the blood.

The internal transducer does not receive input from the environment through the input transducers. The internal states of sensory organs like the eye, however, are reported by internal transducer components. The impulses resulting from increased intraocular pressure are processed by the internal transducer subsystem.

The Channel and Net Subsystem

The channel and net subsystem has afferent and efferent neural, vascular, and endocrine components that carry neurotransmitter and hormonal information inputs from the environment to all parts of the central nervous system. These intermingle with internal sensory stimuli arising from appetitive and affective instinctual centers and visceral organs. Interaction of information from these manifold sources is ensured by the great number of interconnections that form the bases for the sensorimotor reflexes. In general the nerves and tracts that connect brain centers and nuclei with each other and with peripheral nerves belong to the channel and net subsystem.

The channel and net subsystem both conveys sensory stimuli to cerebral cortical centers and connects them to the neuroendocrine and autonomic nervous systems by way of the hypothalamus, thereby influencing the state regulating system. Hypothalamic centers relay signals to the anterior pituitary gland, which affects other endocrine glands, such as the thyroid, adrenal cortex, ovary, and testis, as well as tissues throughout the body.

The Decoder Subsystem

The decoder subsystem personalizes information by converting the coded information input received from the input transducer through the channel and net subsystem by the sensory projection areas of the cerebral cortex into spatio-temporal patterns that become perceptions as they are interpreted in the context of stored information about previous experiences.

For the visual system, the decoder includes the lateral geniculate body, where decoding and systematic modification of signals begin. The geniculate ganglion cells respond more differentially than the retinal ganglion cells to spatial differences in illumination as opposed to diffuse illumination. The cerebellum contributes to decoding by sequencing sensory input through selective inhibition and facilitation of transmission rates (Levinson, 1980). The simple cells of the primary visual cortex respond to linear form in one position and spatial orientation with specialization for slits, dark bars, and edges. The complex cells of the primary visual cortex are movement and changing contrast detectors.

The Associator Subsystem

The associator subsystem involves wide cortical associational, subcortical, and spinal areas. Particularly involved are the temporal and frontal lobs, the hippocampus, the thalamic nuclei, the limbic system, and the corpus callosum. The vestibulocerebellar system is involved at the associator level, and its integrating functions operate at the decider level as well (Frick, 1982). The tertiary parietal association areas correlate signals from external and internal sensory sources and direct signals to higher levels of the brain.

The meaning of perceptions is provided at this stage by linking information input with existing knowledge and experience. Since learning essentially is the long-term survival and availability of experience (Rapaport, 1951), the associator subsystem carries out the first stage of the learning process in forming associations among items of information in the system. For example, this is the stage at which graphemes are automatically translated into phonemes in facile reading. Defense mechanisms operate at this level when anxiety is triggered by perceptions. Internal images also may distort and interfere with external perceptions at this level.

The Memory Subsystem

The memory subsystem enables learning by maintaining and retrieving information in storage. Information is screened for salience by memory at every stage of its processing. Memory registers sequences of events for conceptual organization and permits the analysis of stimuli. At the same time, information in storage is subject to alteration and loss through simplification and decay.

Memories are stored over large regions of the brain by small but coherent modifications of large numbers of synaptic junctions that alter the relation between presynaptic and postsynaptic electrical potentials; neuroglial cells also are involved (Cooper & Imbert, 1981). Ribonucleic acid (RNA) and deoxyribonucleic acid (DNA) are the molecular carriers of genetic information. The memory subsystem particularly involves the superior levels of the reticular formation, hippocampus, fornix, mamillary bodies, thalamus, amygdala, frontal lobes, and corpus callosum. The hippocampus plays a crucial role in selecting memories for storage.

Recent developments in theories of human memory have rendered the concept of a discrete memory trace obsolete. Information is stored in memory according to various forms of coding, each incorporating different features of the material to be retained in electrochemical circuits (Hintzman, 1978). The holographic model may represent the mechanism of memory.

THE LANGUAGE SYSTEM

Because of its discretely canalized neuroanatomical basis, the language system warrants separation from the information-processing system (see Figure 11-8). Its central role in human functioning is illustrated by the fact that it is the only system that extends from the input transducer to the output transducer levels (see Figure 11-5).

The first steps were taken toward an understanding of the cerebral organization of speech in 1861, when Broca localized motor speech, and in 1873, when Wernicke identified the sensory site of speech. The language area of the brain surrounds the Sylvian fissure from Broca's area in the posterior left frontal gyrus through the parietal angular gyrus to Wernicke's area in the posterior third of the superior temporal gyrus, which is connected to the frontal lobe by the arcuate fasciculus. The ventral lateral area of the thalamus is involved, as well. There are significant individual differences in the size of the language areas (Ojemann & Mateer, 1979b).

Evidence for the localization of language functions comes from studies of cerebral blood flow (Ingvar & Schwartz, 1974). Both speech and oral reading cause a Z-like change in the resting blood flow pattern in the left upper speech cortex and hand–arm–face–tongue area of the frontal and parietal sensorimotor regions, as well as Broca's anterior speech cortex, the mid-Sylvian region, and Wernicke's posterior speech cortex (see Figure 11-3). This pattern confirms Sigmund Freud's early hypothesis that all of these areas were involved in language production and corresponds to Penfield and Robert's observations of the interference with language produced by electrical stimulation of them. This pattern also is consistent with the three functional divisions of the human perisylvian language cortex derived from electrical stimulation mapping of them. One surrounds the final motor pathway for speech and constitutes a common system for language production and understanding. The second is for short-term verbal memory, and the third is related exclusively to syntax (Ojemann & Mateer, 1979a).

The thalamus integrates language with associated functions, such as verbal alerting responses, short-term memory, and respiratory control (Ojemann & Mateer, 1979b). In most persons the lateral posterior nucleus of the thalamus with connections to the asymmetrical inferior parietal lobe

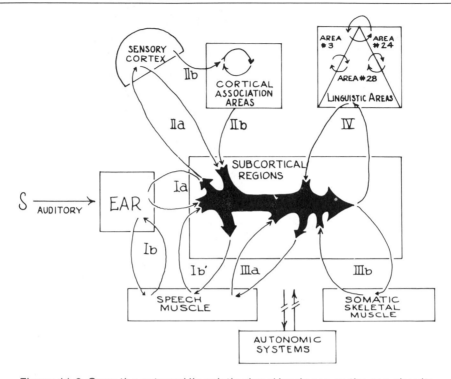

Figure 11-8. Once the external linguistic signal impinges on the ear, circuits of the class Ia and Ib are simultaneously activated. Circuit class Ib directly functions with the speech musculature, while in circuit Ia information enters the subcortical regions of the brain, whereupon the ear receptor is modulated by feedback. Next the information is processed between the speech musculature and the subcortical regions (circuit class Ib). The incoming information is directed to the sensory cortex for integration from the two separate receptors by circuit class IIa. Cortical-subcortical circuits also are activated through the cortical association areas through circuit class IIb. Following this initial processing, cerebral to skeletal muscle circuits are activated (IIIa) for the speech musculature and (IIIb) for the nonoral skeletal muscle; the function of circuit class III is in the generation and transmission of verbal coding for lexical-semantic processing in conjunction with the three major linguistic regions of the brain through circuit class IV. (From F. J. McGuigan, *Cognitive Psychophysiology*, 1978, Lawrence Erlbaum, Hillsdale, NJ. Copyright 1978 by F. J. McGuigan. Reproduced with permission.)

shows a significant left-sided bias, reflecting the apparent language specialization of the dominant thalamus (Eidelberg & Galaburda, 1982).

The inferior parietal lobe, which includes the angular and supramarginal gyri, appeared phylogenetically in homo sapiens and freed humans from the emotional domination of the limbic system through the capacity for language. In monkeys there is a forerunner of this area, however, they are only able to establish associations between nonlimbic, that is, visual, tactile or auditory, and limbic stimuli. Only humans can readily form associations between two nonlimbic stimuli. The acquisition of speech depended upon the ability to form associations between the somesthetic, visual, and auditory modalities. This ability enabled learning the names of objects. In addition the ability of the angular gyrus to function as a visual memory center for words by forming and storing associations between visual symbols and sounds permitted reading (Geschwind, 1965).

THE MANAGERIAL SYSTEM

Luria's system for programming, regulating, and verifying actions meets the needs of the individual in the surrounding world. Ornstein refers to it as the mental operating system (Ornstein, 1986). For convenience I call it the managerial system. As indicated in Figure 11-5, it involves the associator, memory, decider, encoder, and output transducer structures of the CNS.

The highest components of the managerial system are located in the frontal lobes and occupy about one quarter of the total brain mass. The prefrontal cortex has rich redundant connections with lower levels of the brain and virtually all other parts of the cerebral cortex. Thus the managerial system's echelon includes the frontal lobes, the sensory associational cortices, the diencephalon, the reticular activating system, the cerebellum, and the spinal-cord motor neurons. All of this is closely integrated with the state regulating and information processing systems. These connections are two way in character so that the prefrontal cortex is in a particularly favorable position for acting upon the reception and synthesis of the complex flow of impulses between all parts of the brain.

The following functions have been ascribed to the prefrontal cortex (Harris, 1986). The dominant prefrontal cortex devises action plans, while the nondominant prefrontal cortex assesses their progress. The dominant prefrontal cortex is

field independent and regulates the internal world through its ability to integrate sequences of information. It experiences consciousness of time, planning, and goal formation. The nondominant prefrontal cortex is field dependent, assesses the external world, and forms images through processing configurations of information. It directs the concentration necessary for feature detection in the environment, accords percepts meaning from long-term memory, and affirms or disaffirms that attributes of things exist in reality.

The managerial system is intimately associated with sensorimotor schemes. The execution of the simplest intentional act requires a highly complex series of afferent and efferent exchanges at the many hierarchical levels that control voluntary movement (Eccles, 1973). At the lowest level, there is the motor neuron in the spinal cord and the nerve fibers from it to 100 or so muscle fibers that each enervates. At the highest level is the supplementary motor area of the frontal cortex, which initiates discharge in the frontal motor cortex, where there is a strip display of the body from toes to tongue similar to the sensory strip in the parietal lobe (Eccles & Robinson, 1984). The axons of the pyramidal cells of the motor cortex connect directly or indirectly to the motor neurons of muscles.

The initial component of voluntary action is the intention to act, which is not a direct response to an external stimulus but results from inhibiting all except the selected response from a blueprint of possible behavior that must be formed in order to achieve a person's intention (Figure 11-9). All of this takes place in 150 milliseconds (Libet, 1989). This blueprint demands constant, invariant results for successful completion. Movements thus are programmed by the brain in the supplementary area of the frontal lobe before they begin (Goldberg, 1985). For instance, the fulfillment of the simple motor task of

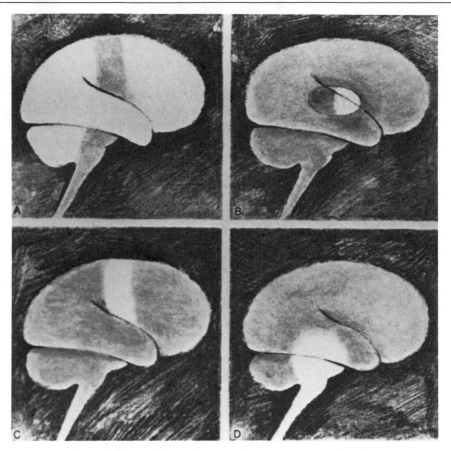

Figure 11-9. As a willed movement is about to happen, the cerebral cortex, basal ganglia, and cerebellum are activated in preparation for activity (A); the motor homunculus, however, is quiet. Next (B) only the thalamus is active, collecting reports from the cerebellum and the basal ganglia. Then (C) the motor homunculus is activated as commands are being sent to motor neurons. Finally (D) the brainstem and spinal cord motor neurons are firing, and intense supportive activity by local interneurons is in progress. (From C. W. Cotman and J. L. McGaugh, *Behavioral Neuroscience,* Academic Press, New York, copyright 1980. Reproduced with permission.)

picking up a cup requires the constant, invariant result by which that action is completed. Because of the infinite degree of freedom to move and the constantly changing tone of the muscles, afferent feedback of the changing state of the muscular system is necessary at each moment. In addition there must be an automatic analysis of the visual and spatial coordinates in which the movement takes place through a system of kinesthetic signals indicating the position of the body. A constant supply of afferent information, therefore, is essential for the successful performance of the final component of every voluntary movement in order to check on its course and correct mistakes. This is done through the continuous comparison of an action performed with the blueprint of the original intention. During such an act, cerebral blood flow increases in the sensory and motor strips of the parietal and frontal cortices, as well as prefrontal areas (Ingvar & Swartz, 1974).

In living system terms, the primary central nervous system structures of the managerial system are the decider, encoder, and output transducer.

The Decider Subsystem

The decider subsystem handles executive functions. It analyzes, assimilates, and synthesizes information from all of the other subsystems, reasons, and makes decisions. It devises blueprints of actions, implements them by transmitting information to the entire organism, and verifies their efficacy. The decider establishes purposes and goals on the basis of motivation from drives, emotions, and aspirations.

Because both rational and irrational factors are involved in the functions of the decider, an understanding of its modus operandi is enhanced by the psychoanalytic concepts of primary and secondary processes (Gedo & Goldberg, 1973; Noy, 1979). In general systems terms, the primary process tends to increase entropy through emotional and intuitive responses, and the secondary process draws information into the system through logical reasoning and tends to decrease entropy. The tension and cooperation between the two processes ensure the synthesis of self-interests and environmental considerations necessary for optimal adaptation.

The primary and secondary processes involve two different energy-discharge patterns. The sites of primary and secondary process activity in the brain are suggested by neurosurgical evidence. Primary process motor discharge involves muscle movements that are not disturbed by surgical resections of the precentral motor cortex of the brain. Such resections, however, do impair secondary processes actions, because images involved in such actions are disrupted. In addition, secondary process problem-solving thinking during psychological testing causes a more intense pattern of cerebral blood flow in the prefrontal and postcentral association cortex than does primary process reflection (Ingvar & Schwartz, 1974). Furthermore, a state of relaxed, nonfocused primary process receptivity correlates with the presence of alpha waves in the electroenecephalogram, which disappear with secondary process problem-solving thinking (Dixon, 1981). Thus the secondary process appears to reflect prefrontal lobe functioning.

The primary process operates according to self-interests so that external perceptions are interpreted in terms of whether they satisfy, frustrate, or threaten the individual. This enables distinguishing between what is personally pleasurable and what is distressing, thereby ensuring the satisfaction of personal needs and the avoidance of dangers. The primary process, under the domination of seeking pleasure and avoiding distress unburdens the mental apparatus of excitation by discharge into the body leading to emotional expressions.

In the primary process, images organized around drives hold sway. Images readily merge with each other and with percepts in what is called condensation. There is merging of motor and emotional elements with a lack of separation of internal imagery from perception, emotion, and motor action. This merging has been called syncretism (Werner, 1948). These inner images possess a vivacity equal to that of a true percept. For example, the eidetic images of children are regarded as real by them. As a result a child's wishes can be given magical omnipotent, omniscient powers.

The primary process expressed in dreams, parapraxes, and free associations is not a disorganized, seething cauldron. It can be regarded as the enduring equivalent of Piaget's preoperational phase of mental activity. Were the primary process truly chaotic, we would not be able to understand dreams, neurotic symptoms, or the errors of everyday life (Basch, 1977).

The semiautonomous feedback loops of the primary process rise and fall within the frontal area, limbic system, and brainstem in the form of profound unsatisfied oral needs, unresolved narcissistic wounds, grandiose overevaluation of the self, and unrelenting sadistic and masochistic yearnings. Everything that happens in learning, perception, imagination, thought, motivation, and judgment is influenced by these powerful entities. These pulsing continuing presences operate outside of conscious awareness during the waking state and are thrust at regular intervals during sleep into dreams (Noshpitz, 1982).

The primary process enters conscious awareness in the dream, which is a mental experience occurring in sleep that is accompanied by hallucinated imagery, bizarre elements, temporary acceptance of these phenomena as real, strong emotion, and poor subsequent recall (Hobson & McCarley, 1977; Noshpitz, 1982). The pontine giant cells of the reticular formation show peak activity during dreaming. As much as five minutes before dreaming sleep is evident, these giant cells begin to fire. They are followed in about ten seconds by the discharge of cortical neurons. Rapid eye movements (REM) follow the pontine giant cell discharge, but precede the cortical discharges, by several milliseconds. Hence the eye-movement system may give rise to the dream experience rather than cortical activity generating images that are then scanned by the eyes. The congenitally blind do have REMs even though they do not dream in visual images (Horowitz, 1983a).

Actual dream construction may be a product of the synthetic action of the frontal lobes upon the inchoate sensory data sent forward by the giant pontine cells. The frontal lobes may engage in a search of stored memories, striving to cull out images and make sense out of the available potpourri of impressions. Since dreaming occurs predominantly in the REM phase of the sleep cycle, experiments in REM sleep deprivation suggest that dreaming plays an essential role in the integration and the maintenance of normal mental functioning (Freedman et al, 1986).

In contrast with the primary process, the secondary process permits successful adjustment to and modification of the environment to suit an individual's needs. It can disconnect its functioning from immediate internal needs. The secondary process discharges energy in a goal-directed, orderly manner and draws heavily upon conscious awareness (Dixon, 1981). At brainstem and cerebral cortical levels, the vestibulo-cerebellar system also plays an important role in the secondary process through sensorimotor coordination (Frick, 1982).

The secondary process integrates the various cognitive processes and deploys the logical knowledge available to the individual. The nature of the secondary process is expressed in progressively more sophisticated ways at each stage of development. Most broadly stated, the hypothesis theory of learning corresponds to the operation of the secondary process, because it posits that a child has a repertoire of hypotheses that are tested in an attempt to attain the solution of a task. The hypotheses are tried and rejected until one is found that consistently results in the correct response (Gholson, 1980).

The Encoder Subsystem

The encoder subsystem alters the internal code of information from a private code to a public code, which can be interpreted by other organisms.

Alpha encoding influences glands that emit chemical signals that stimulate other persons' smell or taste. Beta encoding is of external organs that emit sounds and movements evident to others. Gamma encoding is of symbolic language and includes conversion of an idea into a grammatical sentence by synactical rules and then conversion of the morphemes of sentences into orderly sequences of phonemes in speech.

The encoder subsystem involves all of the cerebral cortex, but particularly the temporo-parietal region of the dominant hemisphere. It is the site of difficulty, for example, for persons who can read but make spelling errors in their writing.

The Output Transducer Subsystem

The output transducer subsystem changes encoded information into other matter–energy forms that can be transmitted to the environment.

Alpha-coded information is expressed through secretions of the exocrine glands. Beta-coded information is expressed through behavior involving the voluntary nervous system and may have accompanying autonomic nervous system effects, such as through the skin in blushing. This is the mode of nonverbal communication that conveys unconscious and conscious messages to others. Gamma-coded information is expressed through spoken language mediated by Broca's area of the frontal lobe and the organs of articulation. This stage is impaired in persons who have difficulty in writing legibly.

THE SELF SYSTEM

As subjective experience extends through time, memories accumulate and constitute the basis of the self system, as depicted in Figure 11-10 (John, 1976).

The self system draws upon the structures of the other four functional systems of the brain. The frontal lobes, however, play a crucial role as the integrating station for information from the posterior regions of the brain involved in the processing of all sensory information and the limbic system in which motivational and emotional processes are centered (Penfield, 1975; Gardner, 1976). Because the self system contains a strong language component, the left hemisphere may be predominantly involved.

The components of the self system may be as follows (Harris, 1986). The medial aspects of both prefrontal lobes integrate imagery of bodily sensations while the lateral aspects of both prefrontal lobes integrate imagery of the body as a tool. The medial aspects of the dominant prefrontal lobe mediate the self system experienced as "I want" by integrating appetitive and adaptive instinctual drives and initiating fulfillment of cravings and the expression of emotion. Its lateral aspects mediate the self system experienced as "I will." They integrate verbally generated conscious purposes and control intentional actions of the body. The medial aspects of the nondominant prefrontal lobe mediate the self system experienced as "me" in the sense of "my feelings" by integrating the cenesthetic sensations that comprise self-esteem and the somesthetic feelings of emotions, as both reflect the progress of intentional actions in the external world. Its lateral aspects mediate the self system experienced as "me" in the sense of "my body" in the external world. They integrate perceptions of the external world and self-images and self-concepts.

The self system has a relationship to neural events but may not be identical with them. The electrical activity resulting from willed action originating in the supplementary motor area of the frontal lobes, presumably reflecting the self, leads to a wide-ranging negative potential over the surface

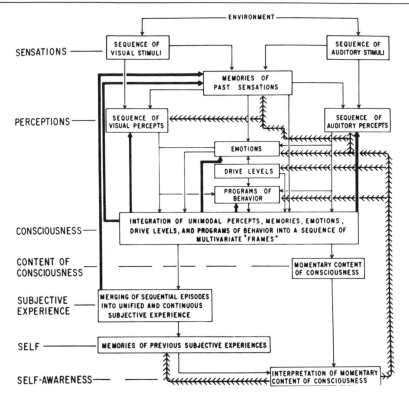

Figure 11-10. Levels of the self-system. (From E. R. John, "A Model of Consciousness," in G. E. Schwartz and D. Shapiro, eds., *Consciousness and Self-Regulation, Volume 1,* copyright 1976 by Plenum Press, New York. Reproduced with permission.)

of the brain that concentrates on the pyramidal cells appropriate for a specific action (Popper & Eccles, 1979; Eccles & Robinson, 1984). When the self system decides to turn attention to a certain matter, it activates the centrencephalic mechanism, which causes the sensorimotor mechanism to inhibit the inflow of information that is unrelated to the self system's new interest. At the same time, it allows relevant information to pass through into the stream of consciousness.

Evidence for a separation between the self system and specific neural events is found in the work of Penfield (1975). When he stimulated the brain areas of the stream of consciousness, the patients considered their situation in an aloof and critical manner as if the content of their consciousness depended on specific neuronal activity but self-awareness did not. There was a distinct difference between consciousness and self-awareness, as though they were separate functions.

For example, a patient lying on the operating table exclaimed that it was astonishing to realize that he was laughing with his cousins on a farm while he also was fully conscious of being in the operating room and being electrically stimulated. He assumed the surgeon was responsible for the phenomenon, not himself, but recognized the "flashback" as his own personal experience. He remained aloof and passed judgement on it all.

Thus Penfield's operative patients were aware of lying on the operating table and could talk about the evoked experiences. They alluded to the dreamlike, but vivid, quality of the experiences they were witnessing, but in which they were not participants at that moment (Gardner, 1976).

Furthermore, the stream of consciousness is not recovered as simple reruns of memories. When Penfield's subjects saw themselves in the visual images they reported, the electrical stimulation of the temporal lobe did not directly activate memory traces. Instead it induced a state of consciousness in which the content of the memories was formed by a process resembling dream construction with displacement, distortion, and condensation (Horowitz, 1983).

The self system appears to be an entity that reads out and integrates selections from the multiple modules of the dominant cerebral hemisphere so as to give the unity of conscious experience from moment to moment (Popper & Eccles, 1979). In addition, the self system exercises a superior and controlling role upon brain centers. It probably is an epiphenomenon of the brain (Brown, 1977).

INTERPERSONAL RELATIONSHIPS

A person relates to others through social roles in which people hold expectations of each other. These role relationships take place in the face-to-face groups of families, school classrooms, peer groups, and other interpersonal encounters. For most children these transactions occur in the ecological and social contexts of homes, schools, and community gathering places.

Attempts to integrate sociological and psychological concepts have been frustrating because the language of sociology describes how people behave with one another when they are working toward mutually shared goals. In contrast the language of psychology describes internal dispositions only vaguely related to the outside world. We need linking concepts that have meaning for both social interaction and individual personality. The work of Talcott Parsons offers them. Although in its early stages, research in cross-level abstract systems is promising (Miller, 1986).

Every human being simultaneously is a behaving organism, has a personality, is a member of a social system, and is a participant in a cultural system. Parson's general theory of action contains these four basic interpenetrating systems in his behavioral, personality, social, and cultural systems (Parsons, 1977). This theory bridges the individual and society by focusing on the actor in a situation. The output of the central nervous system occurs through a *behavioral system* in which the acting individual deals with the environment and a *personality system* concerned with motivational predispositions (Lidz & Lidz, 1976; Loubser, 1976; Parsons, 1978). The behavioral system corresponds to the information processing and managerial systems, which mediate relations between the inidividual and the ecological world of things. The personality system corresponds to the external aspects of the self and interdigitates with multiple social roles in order to serve motivational and goal attainment purposes.

The *social system* integrates individuals and culture through roles based upon influence, authority, economic, community, political, and educational factors. Social codes incorporate values into rules for the use, transformation, and combination of symbols that serve as messages, such as money, titles, and commitments. The *cultural system* is devoted to maintaining the social system over time through the definition of situations by values, customs, and the institutionalization of new patterns. In contrast with a cultural system, which is concerned with symbols that develop, communicate, and perpetuate attitudes toward life, a social system organizes human actions to deal with the day-to-day circumstances of living.

The general theory of action takes both the actor and the situation of action into account. The actor is seen as in constant tension with a situation that is fraught with seven contingencies (Loubser, 1976). First is the contingency of actors having different symbolic representations of objects, which introduces problems of communication. Second is the contingency of all actors acting at the same time; hence there is a problem of temporal order. Third is the contingency of actors assigning unique or conflicting meanings to symbolic representations of objects; hence there is a problem of meaning. Fourth is the contingency that all actors would make claims on the same aspects of the situation for the attainment of their goals; hence there is the problem of scarcity of resources. Fifth is the contingency of the action of each actor interfering with the attainment of the goal state of other actors; hence there is the problem of control over the action of others or of political order. Sixth is the contingency of conflicting or otherwise incompatible values between actors; hence there is a problem of value conflict. Seventh is the contingency that the motivational needs of the actors may be incompatible, conflicting, or mutually exclusive; hence there is a problem of differing motivations. The general theory of action attempts to account for the ways in which actors attain their goals, at least some of the time, in spite of all these contingencies and problems.

A useful distinction can be made between personality and character traits. This makes it possible to conceptualize the external behavioral manifestations of personality traits as the result of the internal operations of character. The word "character" derives from roots for engraved essential qualities whereas the term "personality" derives from the exterior presentation of a person, as in the persona, or mask, of an actor. Internal character traits thus include temperamental style, cognitive style, impulse control, thinking style, and values. Examples of externally observable personality traits are aggressiveness, forgetfulness, stubbornness, and shyness.

In this definition character traits are identified with central nervous system functions. Thus, as the essential qualities of one's character, CNS functions are influenced by genes, parental attachments, conflicts between drives and the external world, and cultural values. Through families the social order reproduces itself in the character traits of children. In this sense one's character is the crystallization of the cultural and social processes of a given epoch. The nuances of character are reflected in personality traits that change with the times.

Figure 11-11 illustrates the application of role and self theory in the case of a boy who shows different sides of himself with different people in specific places at specific times (Westman et al, 1966). In this case a boy's teacher in school sees him as helpless and inept, although potentially bright. Beneath the "pseudostupid" public self, or personality, is a subjective private self pervaded by the child's view that he is "stupid."

This same child shows other aspects of his personality in his relationships in school, as well as at home. In his relationship with his teacher when she is an authority figure and he is a helper, he is objectively seen by the teacher as a "charmer" but subjectively sees himself as "helpless." With a peer in the role relationship of classmate, he objectively appears to be a "clown" to others but sees himself as "friendless." Underly-

INTERPERSONAL RELATIONSHIP IN SETTING

Child in Specific Setting

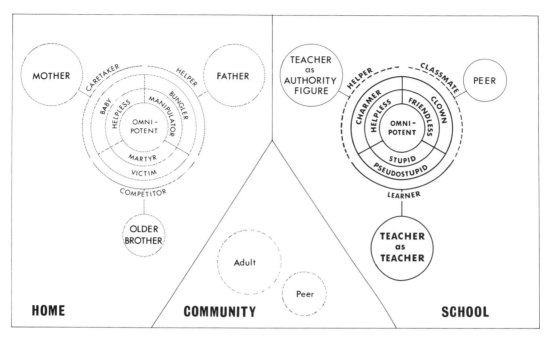

Figure 11-11. An illustration of the variety of personality facets a child shows in different role relationships and places. The underlying self-concepts are also depicted.

ing all three of these public and private selves elicited by different role relationships is one core aspect of his self—his omnipotence.

If we examine the same child's relationship in the home sector of his life with his mother, father, and an older brother, we can similarly describe his behavior objectively as seen in each role relationship, his subjective impression of himself in that role relationship, and the underlying core aspect of his self. In the role relationship of his father's helper, his public self is seen as a "bungler," but privately he sees himself as a "manipulator," provoking his father through his ineptness. In a caretaking role relationship with his mother, he is seen by her as "baby." His view of that relationship is as being "helpless." In a competitive relationship with his older brother, he displays the public self of a downtrodden "victim." His own view of that relationship is as an ultimately victorious "martyr."

This child's character is reflected in his cognitive and temperamental styles. His cognitive style is expressed in his tendency only partially to perceive environmental stimuli, his subjective confusion, his difficulty in handling abstract symbols, and his forgetfulness. His temperamental style is manifested in his slouching posture, low frustration tolerance, immature mannerisms, nonchalance, and maddeningly persistent ineptitude.

This analysis illustrates the way in which the sociological concept of role can be articulated with the psychological concept of personality as an expression of cognitive and temperamental character traits.

SUMMARY

The distinction between mind and body is no longer tenable. With the possible exception of the elusive self, the mind is a phase of the brain's activity. As such an understanding of the way in which the enormously complex brain works requires models for relating the components, structures, processes, functions, and output of the central nervous system.

Past models of brain functioning have either emphasized localizing of holistic approaches. The truths in each view have led to our current understanding, in which the brain is seen as acting as a whole through definable functional systems. An integration of Luria's conceptions of functional brain systems with the general theory of living systems is a useful way of conceptualizing present knowledge.

The general theory of living systems identifies structures of the CNS that warrant attention in understanding the process of learning. Information-processing structures can be conceptualized as the input transducer, internal transducer, channel and net, and decoder. Emotions are subsumed by the associator and memory structures. Thinking is largely in the province of the decider. Observable behavior can result at several levels from the encoder and output transducer subsystems, from the autonomic discharge of the channel and net subsystem, and from the automatic and voluntary actions of the decider subsystem.

The CNS can be profitably viewed as consisting of five functional subsystems. The state regulating system determines how a person relates to the environment through its role as a transitional zone in which arousal, consciousness, and emotional expressions take place. The information processing system handles stimuli from the external and internal environments though perception, recognition, and memory. The language system enables interpersonal communication and the acquisition of symbolic and conceptual knowledge. The managerial system meets the needs of the individual in the surrounding world. The self system endows human beings with unique qualities so that the present, past, and future can be brought together in purposefully expressing, monitoring, and achieving objectives in social and environmental contexts. Interpersonal relationships can be understood in the context of the interaction between social roles and the public aspects of the self as manifested in one's personality and behavior.

CHAPTER

12

Temperament

We are naturally endowed with a sense of compassion which
is the germ of our humanity; our sense of shame is the germ
of dutifulness; our sense of courtesy, of modesty; our sense
of right and wrong, of wisdom. These four senses are as
much a part of the person as are his four limbs.

Mencius (371–289 B.C.)

The word temperament is derived from the Latin root that means to regulate and blend qualities. It, therefore, is an appropriate generic designation for the output of the state regulating system, which sets the tone for information processing and action. As such temperament can be defined as an individual's disposition to interact with the environment expressed through the state regulating system functions of attention, movement level, and motivation. Individual differences in temperament are related to the genetically mediated intensities of instinctual drives (Mangan, 1982). More restricted definitions of temperament overlook these instinctual motivational roots.

At the objective level, temperament is manifested through attention behaviors, autonomic nervous system expressions, and bodily movements. Subjectively, temperament is experienced as the level of consciousness and the visceral sensations of cravings and emotions. This chapter lays the foundation for dealing later with the clinical and educational impacts of temperament by examining current ideas about

its attentional and motivational ingredients (Figure 12-1). Movement levels will be discussed in Chapter 21.

ATTENTION

Attention has two fundamental dimensions. The first is the level to which attention is involuntarily or voluntarily directed and the second is its degree of specificity. Within these two dimensions, six different attentional processes can be distinguished.

Involuntary Attentional Processes

The involuntary processes of attention are vigilance, which permits the routine reception of stimuli; the orienting and startle responses, which are reflexive reactions to stimuli; and stimulus regulation, which filters stimuli for processing.

Vigilance

Vigilance is automatic attentiveness to the general perceptual field, so that the ap-

I. *Attentional System*
   A) Involuntary Processes
      1) Vigilant Arousal
      2) Orienting, Startle and Defensive Responses
      3) Stimulus Modulation
   B) Voluntary Processes
      1) Scanning Attention
      2) Focal Attention
      3) Concentration
II. *Motivational Systems*
   A) Appetitive Instinctual Systems
      1) Rest
      2) Alimentary
      3) Elimination
      4) Sexual
      5) Defensive
      6) Motor Activity
   B) Adaptive Instinctual Systems
      1) Affiliative
      2) Aggressive
      3) Mastery
      4) Self-esteem Regulation
      5) Defensive
   C) The Affective System
      1) Functions of the Affective System
         a) Mediating Drive Motivations
         b) Automatic Judgments
         c) External Signaling
         d) Internal Signaling
      2) The Processes of the Affective System
         a) The Pleasure System
         b) The Distress System
           i) Pain
           ii) Anxiety
           iii) Depression
         c) Role of Affective System in Information Processing
           i) Autonomic Defensive Stress Response
           ii) Autonomic-Adrenal Medullary Stress Response
           iii) Neuroendocrine Stress Response

Figure 12-1. Components of the state regulating system whose output is expressed in temperament.

pearance of stimuli can activate the involuntary orienting and startle responses and voluntary attention (Parrill-Burnstein, 1981). Vigilance is dampened by the rest instinct, but even when consciousness is dormant during sleep, a degree of vigilance continues, permitting responsiveness to especially significant stimuli.

Vigilance results from arousal functions of the reticular activating system, the limbic system, and the frontal lobes. The arousal system also includes the amygdala, which coordinates autonomic responses; the corpus striatum, which maintains the readiness of postural, motor, and attention response sets; and the hippocampus, which coordinates arousal and the readiness to respond (Pribram, 1981).

Orienting, Startle, and Defensive Responses

The most elementary forms of involuntarily directed attention are the automatic orienting, startle, and defensive responses (Kimmel et al, 1979; Westman & Walters, 1981). These responses are intimately linked with the autonomic nervous system, as seen in cardiovascular, respiratory, and pupillary changes, which can be measured by electrophysiological techniques, such as pupillography, the psychogalvanic reflex, and the electroencephalogram.

The orienting response occurs when novel or unexpected stimuli appear in the sensory field, and it facilitates their reception. It inhibits the automatic behaviors of the basal ganglia when triggered by a mismatch between sensory input and sensorimotor schemes (Pribram, 1979). The corpus striatum appears to control changes in the direction of attention (McKenzie et al, 1984). Because postural and perceptual sets are continuously operating in the basal ganglia on the basis of prior experience, most behavior can procede relatively automatically. But when the unexpected occurs, the orienting mechanism computes the consequences of maintaining ongoing behavior in the face of distraction or of allowing the distraction to control behavior.

Startle is an extreme reflexive brainstem response that functions without participation of the cerebral cortex. The defensive response is an emotional reaction when stimuli are perceived as painful or threatening and is described in more detail later in this chapter. In contrast with the startle and defensive responses, the ori-

enting response generally enhances stimulus input (Graham, 1979).

Individual variations in the orienting, startle, and defensive responses are evident during infancy. Most infants startle at a sudden loud noise and quickly achieve equilibrium. Some children are parasympathotonic, so that their heartbeat tends to remain slow, blood pressure low, and digestion inhibited with orienting and startle responses. In contrast, sympathotonic children tend to show facial pallor, acceleration of heartbeat, and increase in blood pressure with the orienting and startle responses (Mosse, 1982). The startle response restores equilibrium slowly, and its physiological concomitants subjectively are experienced as fear.

Stimulus Modulation

The efficient functioning of the brain requires automatic mechanisms for modulating the flow of external and internal sensory stimuli. Without them, even routine sensory input would be overwhelming. In addition to the limited capacities of the sensory channels, therefore, the reticular activating system, limbic system, thalamus, and cerebral cortex operate in concert to protect the brain through thresholds of responsiveness. These mechanisms are referred to collectively as the stimulus barrier in the psychoanalytic literature.

Stimulus modulation is a complex function that involves (1) perceptual thresholds in the sensory modalities; (2) active integration of stimuli, so as to make them more tolerable; (3) changes in state of consciousness, as in drowsiness or sleep; and (4) directed motor actions to contain motor responses to stimuli or to withdraw from them (Gedimen, 1971).

Thresholds of responsiveness are measurable evidence of stimulus modulation and can be conceptualized as demarking a range of activation that has as its lower

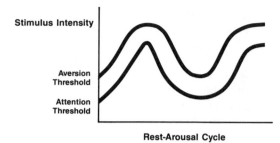

Figure 12-2. Threshold of responsiveness model. Between the attention and aversion thresholds is the range of stimulation to which an infant responds attentively and with pleasure. (Adapted from T. Field, "Affective Displays of High-Risk Infants during Early Interactions," in T. Field and A. Fogel, eds., *Emotion and Early Interaction,* Lawrence Erlbaum, Hillsdale, NJ, 1982.)

limit an attention threshold and as its upper limit an aversion threshold as depicted in Figure 12-2. The upper and lower thresholds of this activation range may shift and the range width may vary as a function of an individual's rest–arousal cycles, particularly during infancy (Field, 1982).

In infancy positive emotions tend to arise when sensory stimulation falls within the activation range between the attention and averting thresholds. When the upper limit of the activation band is approached, however, an infant manifests an averting response, such as gaze aversion. If that threshold is exceeded, a distressful emotion, such as fussing or crying, occurs.

More specifically, electrophysiological evidence exists for stimulus modulation. For example, the amplitude of sensory evoked responses on an electroencephalogram tends to increase with stimulus intensity to a certain point. Further increases in intensity do not cause corresponding increases in amplitude, however, and may result in decreases. As specific examples, noise tolerance has been correlated with a tendency to reduce auditory evoked re-

sponses with increasing stimulus intensity, and pain tolerance correlates with reduced somatic evoked responses with increased stimulus intensity (Buchsbaum, 1976). Individual differences in stimulus modulation take place so that in some individuals the evoked brain-wave amplitude is augmented and in others it is reduced by the same sensory stimuli.

From birth babies seek out and respond to those stimuli which they can assimilate and to which they can accommodate, achieving ever-higher levels of integration and control as they mature. The stimulus-modulating mechanism of infants admits those stimuli most consonant with adaptive needs and excludes those that overtax adaptive capacities, but their stimulus-modulating mechanism is easily overwhelmed (Fogel, 1982). This state is represented by the upper right portion of Figure 12-3. From this neonatal state, an infant may take one of three possible developmental paths. Most infants progress along the diagonal and develop stimulus modulation, so that they can transform an experience of overwhelming excitement to one of contentment or an experience of overwhelming distress to one of security. Significant individual differences occur in stimulus modulation, however, so that some infants are able to tolerate high levels of arousal (see upper left corner of Figure 12-3). Other infants fail to develop adequate stimulus-modulating capacities and remain on the right-hand side of Figure 12-3, showing continued withdrawal from stimuli and distress even during moderate states of arousal.

The role of the stimulus-modulating system in the development of attachment bonds is evident (Esman, 1983). Although during early life a parent supplements an infant's stimulus-modulation mechanisms, the successful interaction of the infant's innate stimulus-modulating capacities and the parent's sensitivity to that infant's need for comforting play key roles in facilitating

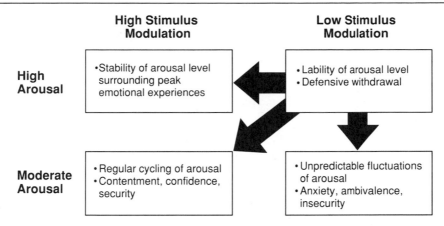

High Stimulus Modulation   **Low Stimulus Modulation**

High Arousal
- •Stability of arousal level surrounding peak emotional experiences
- • Lability of arousal level
- • Defensive withdrawal

Moderate Arousal
- • Regular cycling of arousal
- • Contentment, confidence, security
- •Unpredictable fluctuations of arousal
- • Anxiety, ambivalence, insecurity

Figure 12-3. The relationship between stimulus modulation and arousal levels. Infants are presumed to move from a state of high arousal and low stimulus modulation to one of the other states during the course of development. (Adapted from A. Fogel, "Affect Dynamics in Early Infancy: Affective Tolerance," in T. Field and A. Fogel, eds., *Emotion and Early Interaction,* Lawrence Erlbaum, Hillsdale, NJ, 1982.)

bonding between infant and parent (Fogel, 1982). Furthermore, an infant's stimulus-seeking behavior is in the service of attachment to others, whereas stimulus avoiding is a precursor of psychological defenses.

In addition to individual patterns of stimulus modulation, shifts in specific thresholds of responsiveness occur regularly throughout life through conditioning, as evidenced by the phenomenon of habituation in which an individual becomes unresponsive to repeated irrelevant stimuli. This permits automatic activities, such as immersion in the content of a story without awareness of the act of reading.

Voluntary Processes

Acts of voluntary attention are quite different. On the one hand, there is scanning attention of a large stream of incoming stimuli, such as might be given by a music critic while listening to an orchestra, or by a psychotherapist searching for a meaningful thread in the free associations of a patient. Next there is the instant shift from vigilance to precise focused visual attentiveness, when an otherwise preoccupied person suddenly catches a ball thrown by a playing child. At the other extreme is the sustained focus of attention upon a tissue viewed through a microscope. Thus voluntary attention involves conscious searching of the perceptual field through scanning, focusing upon relevant stimuli, and concentration.

Scanning Attention

Scanning attention is searching for patterns in a stimulus field through the random shifting of sensory systems around an inidividual's spatial field (Plutchik, 1977). It largely is a function of the associative cortex that directs the reticular activating system and coordinates motor activity and sensory intake.

Scanning attention appears to consist of a dimension of passive versus active scanning and a dimension of narrow versus broad scanning. At the developmentally immature end of the spectrum is the infant, who directs attention passively and narrowly limits attention to a small segment of a stimulus field. At the developmentally mature end is an older child who scans actively and broadly (Santostefano, 1978).

Focused Attention

Focused attention involves consciously selecting, excluding, reducing, and facilitating stimuli. Information processing at all stages depends upon focused attention under the influence of the prefrontal cortex as a crucial determinant of memory storage. Conversely stored memories influence focused attention.

Focused attention also has been described as field articulation. It is the selective deployment of attention by withholding attention from irrelevant information and directing it to relevant information. At the developmentally immature end is the young child who devotes attention to both relevant and irrelevant information and is easily distracted. At the developmentally mature end is an older child who withholds attention from irrelevant, while simultaneously sustaining attention to relevant, information (Santostefano, 1978).

Concentration

Concentration is the extension of focused attention into the sustained processing of stimuli and can be measured by its intensity and span. It is a more useful concept than attention span because it implies active processing of stimuli in a task whereas attention span could refer to passively staring at stimuli, such as words, without processing them (Levy & Hobbes, 1981). Concentration usually is accompanied by the loss of conscious awareness of an activity. During concentration the serotonin system is involved in inhibiting the general flow of neuronal impulses from the external and internal worlds.

An optimal level of arousal is necessary for concentration and effective task per-

formance. The Yerkes-Dodson law states that a curvilinear relationship exists between stimulus intensity and task-performance efficiency (Powell, 1979). The attractiveness of a stimulus tends to be neutral when it produces low arousal, increases to a maximum for intermediate degrees of arousal, and then decreases to aversive levels as arousal increases further (Berlyne, 1974). Thus the level of arousal produced by a stimulus is a function of the nature of the stimulus, the existing arousal state, and the motivation of the individual. Figure 12-4 illustrates the relationship between overall level of arousal and concentration on the performance of tasks.

Concentration involves the loss of conscious awareness of the passage of time. It, therefore, is enhanced by pleasurable relaxation, which removes awareness of the passage of time. In contrast, conscious awareness of the passage of time tends to be experienced as distressing. More to the point, distress evokes consciousness of the passage of time and interferes with concentration.

MOTIVATION

Theoretical models of human behavior have been notoriously unable to deal with the question of motivation. Recent thought, however, casts motivation in an electrical model, anticipated by Sigmund Freud in his *Project for Scientific Psychology* in 1895.

Our current knowledge of neurophysiology indicates that the brain's energy is derived from sensory input from the external world and the organ systems of the body, in addition to the reticular activating system itself (Pribram & Gill, 1976). In this conception of motivation, minute amounts of the brain's energy originating in sensorimotor schemes are transmitted throughout the CNS and excite, inhibit, and regulate the discharge of comparatively massive

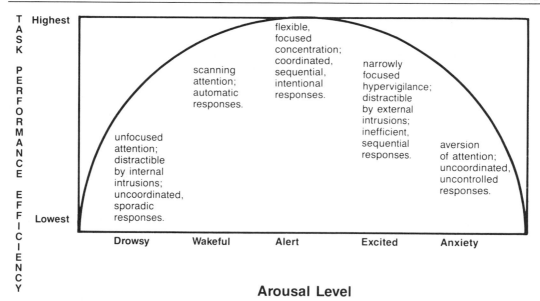

Figure 12-4. Efficiency of performance curve related to level of arousal. (Adapted from T. Cox, *Stress,* University Park Press, Baltimore MD, 1978.)

amounts of energy in the somatic and visceral musculature (Basch, 1976a).

Subjectively motivation is experienced as bodily sensations in the form of appetites and emotions. Appetites ensure maintaining the integrity of the body in the form of hunger, thirst, and lust, which motivate corresponding behavioral patterns of feeding, drinking, and reproduction. Emotions amplify these appetites, facilitate automatic judgments, and signal one's internal state to oneself and others.

Inquiry into the sources of appetites and emotions inevitably leads to the question of instincts. Until recently the application of the term *instinct* to humans was in disfavor, because it was construed to be a simple, rigid pattern of behavior characteristic of other animals. The less specific terms of drive and need were preferred for describing complex human behavior. As a result the genetic roots of human behavior were deemphasized.

The work of Piaget and ethologists with their emphasis on innate mental structures,

however, has revived interest in the genetic determinants of human behavior, and specifically in Jung's theory of archetypes. For Jung life was motivated by an attempt to bring innate archetypal programs into their fullest possible expression in an individual (Stevens, 1982). Intriguingly, modern knowledge of the structure of the brain verifies the existence of universal human instinctual programs, although they are less completely formed and more dependent upon environmental releasers than in other animals (Compton, 1983). Sensorimotor schemes are rooted in these instinctual programs.

The instinctual side of our lives has been overlooked in psychological research because of the acessibility of our bright, but shallow, conscious sensory impressions. The subtle, but far more influential, background brain activity that decisively influences behavior is less accessible to study. This unconscious substrate provides subliminal awareness of our continuity in time and space. Although poorly localized and vague, the instinctual mode of experience is inherent in our relations with the surrounding world, including temperature and gravitational and interpersonal influences. Moreover, it is the source of the haunting irrational forces that interplay with rational processes (Lewis, 1965; Lowe, 1962).

Human instincts are genetically determined cyclic behavioral tendencies that serve self and species preservation through sensitization to specific types of stimuli and stereotyped behavioral patterns. They are general blueprints for behavior influenced by environmental experiences and mediated through innate, canalized sensorimotor schemes (Gould & Gould, 1981).

Instincts explain unlearned behavior shown by all members of a species under the same circumstances and in individuals even when circumstances change. The latter criterion is crucial because common environmental influences can produce common forms of human behavior (Montagu, 1980). Instincts depend upon environmental releasing stimuli and are elaborated by learning but do not need to be learned in their fundamental forms. For example, one does not need to learn how to be happy, sad, or curious.

In humans instincts are highly influenced by learning. In fact the cerebral cortex developed as a protective mechanism to shield the forebrain from the total mobilization that can be triggered by instinctual patterns. The destruction of cortical tissue may obliterate suppressor pathways so that lower centers fire without cortical evaluation, and instinctual behavior emerges. More specifically, the associational cortex delays the activation of behavior until stimuli can be evaluated as to their significance. Furthermore, the inhibitory activity of the prefrontal cortex provides the human being with more freedom and flexibility in living out insinctual programs than any other animal.

Thus human beings have a high degree of control over the expression of instinctual programming of the brain. Most human instinctual imperatives are not absolute, because they are incomplete. Consequently, life experience transforms instinctual programs into modes compatible with the life circumstances of the individual. For example, instinctual programming of the first two years of life requires reciprocal interactions between infants and parents in order to develop the components of character. When human interaction during critical periods of early life is lacking, character development may be permanently affected, as illustrated by extremely neglected and feral children.

All of this means that the social environment largely determines how genes express themselves in humans (Bower, 1979). From the most loving to the most murderous, human beings are potentially capable of any form of behavior, depending upon their socialization. Environmental experience interacts with genetic potential, or the *genotype*, and the resulting behavior, or the *phenotype*, is the expression of that interaction. Human beings become what they are as social beings largely as a consequence of the organizing or disorganizing influences of the environment acting upon an individual's unique potentials. The genetic determinants of behavior set limits and define directions—but they are genetic tendencies only. Human inheritance is expressed in our ability to shape ourselves, not as the creatures but as the creators of our destinies (Montagu, 1976).

For descriptive purposes, instinctual systems can be regarded as having component, structural, process, function, and output characteristics. The components are bodily organ system *sources* that include neural circuit structures originating in the lower centers of the brain, particularly the hypothalamus and basal ganglia. A process is a *drive* that is experienced as an appetite or a pleasurable emotion. A function is a *wish,* which is the imagery of the drive that

Appetitive Instinctual Systems	Adaptive Instinctual Systems			
	Systems	Affective System		
		Motivations	Emotions	
			Feelings	Expression
Rest Fatigue–Sleep	**Affiliative**	Pleasure Approach–Facilitate Parasympathetic tonus	Love Empathy Humility	Affection Sympathy Submission
		Distress Withdrawal–Grief Parasympathetic Discharge–Crying	Loneliness	Grief
Alimentation Hunger–Satiation	**Aggressive**	Pleasure Approach–Facilitate Sympathetic Discharge–Fight	Thrill Greed Ambition	Excitement Acquisitiveness
Elimination Excretory Urges–Relief		Distress Withdrawal–Fight Sympathetic Discharge–Anxiety	Anxiety Disgust Anger	Fear Contempt Rage
Motor Activity Liveliness–Exhileration	**Mastery**	Pleasure Approach—Facilitate Autonomic equilibrium	Interest–Awe Enjoyment Surprise, Pride	Curiosity Joy–Smile Surprise, Dignity
Sexual Lust–Ecstasy		Distress Withdrawal–Depression Interrupt ongoing responses Inhibition of autonomic tonus absence of crying, loss of appetite, constipation, sexual dysfunction	Boredom Humiliation Pain, Guilt Confusion Depression Helplessness Hopelessness	Impatience Shame, Anguish Bewilderment Frustration Discouragement Despair Sadness
Defensive Vigor (Fight)– Panic (Flight)	**Self-Esteem Regulation**	Pleasure Approach–Facilitate Autonomic equilibrium	Euphoria Amusement	Contentment Laughter

Figure 12-5. Appetitive and adaptive instinctual systems.

is induced when immediate gratification does not take place. A wish results, therefore, when there is a discrepancy between perception and drive programs (Holt, 1976). An output is an *aim*, which is the action that expresses a drive modulated by the affective system. Each instinct also has an *object*, which is an aim's environmental target that pleasurably satisfies an instinctual program.

Our brains daily follow instinctual blueprints that can be classified as appetitive or adaptive (see Figure 12-5). In the terminology of the general theory of living systems, instinctual programs are the processes that underlie motivational functions. The informational output of the CNS involves the adaptive instinctual systems and takes place through the publicly manifest aspects of the self evoked by social roles in the form of personality and intentional behavior. The CNS also governs matter–energy outputs of the appetitive instinctual systems, as through heat exchange, respiration, and excretion.

The Appetitive Instinctual Systems

The most basic instincts are appetitive in nature. The appetitive instinctual systems primarily are concerned with the transfer of matter–energy in and out of the body, so that an organism can remain viable and reproduce (Tomkins, 1968). Receptors in the core of the forebrain register stimuli from the internal organs as appetitive drives, such as hunger, thirst, sleepiness, and lust. These drives, or cravings, ensure individual survival through corresponding activities, such as eating, drinking, eliminating wastes, breathing, body movement, and regulating body temperature, in addition to species survival through the aims of sexual behavior. Fulfillment of these cravings provides relief and lack of fulfillment leads to discomfort in an organ system.

Rest–Sleep Instinct

The first instinct essential for individual survival furnishes the bodily climate needed for recharging metabolic systems. Inclinations to rest and sleep arise from the hypothalamus and chemical changes in the somatic musculature and are expressed through the drive to sleep, the aim to achieve a resting state, and the object of a recumbent situation that minimizes external stimuli. This instinct leads to withdrawal, loss of conscious awareness through dampening sensory and motor systems, and sleep.

The rest–sleep instinct operates continuously and influences attention and thresholds of responsiveness. The rest instinct constitutes a persistent tug toward withdrawal from the external world. The lack of personal relevance of external stimuli promotes disengagement and self-immersion, so that this waxing and waning tendency toward inactivity and sleep poses an important obstacle to schoolwork, for example. The pleasures of meditation and solitude also are partial expressions of this instinct.

Alimentary Instinct

The alimentary instinct ensures the obtaining of energy sources for physical and mental activity. It arises from the gastrointestinal tract and the anterior hypothalamus as the drives of oral cravings that motivate the aim of acquiring the object of food (Rolls, 1981).

The olfactory and gustatory sensory systems are intimately involved in alimentation. Smell plays a greater role in human behavior than is generally recognized. In addition to its obvious role in relation to eating, smell plays a key part in attachment behavior in infants and in sexual and aggressive behavior in later life (Ebling, 1981).

The alimentary instinct constitutes the primordial prototype of motivation for acquiring possessions and knowledge. The process of learning itself is an analog of eating, involving the ingestion of information rather than food. The literal oral appetite for learning is seen in young children, who greet enticing experiences with open mouth and salivation. The deepest sources of motivation for learning thus may lie in the pleasures of oral gratification.

Elimination Instincts

The third complex consists of elimination instincts that ensure the removal of bodily wastes through perspiration and the drives of urination and defecation, which lead to behaviors whose aims are objects that provide relief.

The elimination instincts may be the prototypes of literal and symbolic wishes to produce things. Learned attitudes and emotions associated with the management of bodily products have a bearing upon self-esteem and pleasure in making things. Conversely, internal conflicts based upon these bodily functions may cause inhibitions in pleasurable productivity.

Sexual Instincts

The fourth group of instincts governs sexual behavior. It differs from the others in that it is not necessary for individual survival but is essential for species survival. The sources of sexual instincts are in hypothalamic and hormonal mechanisms.

Their drives are experienced as lust, and their aims are behaviors that lead to discharge through bodily manipulations.

The male testes and the female ovaries produce sex hormones, even in the fetus, that control the development of internal and external reproductive structures; these, in turn, control reproductive cycles and motivate sexual behavior in later life. In humans learning plays a preponderant role in shaping sexual behavior, attitudes, and emotions.

Defensive Instincts

Although not strictly appetitive in nature, the fifth instinctual complex is devoted to automatic defenses against danger in the form of fight-or-flight responses, which produce emergency motor reactions to protect an individual from external threats. The perception of danger from internal images also can evoke these responses with or without conscious awareness and motor discharge.

The sources of the defensive instincts may lie in the amygdala, stria terminalis, ventromedial hypothalamus, and midbrain central gray matter (Gray, 1971). Stimulation of the posterior and ventrommedial amygdala, hippocampus, and hypothalamus produces rage and fear. The septal area appears to be an important center for suppressing rage (Moyer, 1976; Tarpy, 1977).

The defensive drives are fright or combativeness; the aims are avoidance or attack; and the objects are achieving escape from, or destruction of, the perceived threat. The phenomenon of stranger anxiety is a reflection of this instinctual complex; its purpose is to alert the infant to possible danger from others who are unfamiliar.

Motor Activity

The appetite for motor activity varies widely among individuals and follows a maturational progression from the diffuse actions of an infant, through crawling and walking, to the more sophisticated urges to be physically active, as ultimately expressed in manual labor or recreational activities.

The sources of this instinct lie in the somatic musculature and the corpus striatum, which is the stronghold of instinctual, stereotyped motor activity related to posture, vocalizations, and the expressions of emotions. The drive is the urge for movement; the aim is to be physically active; and the object is a vocational or recreational activity.

The Adaptive Instinctual Systems

A second class of instincts evolved in order to ensure individual and species survival in a complex social world. Most animals act simply to fulfill individual- and species-preserving appetitive instincts. Animals that live in groups, however, developed the more sophisticated ability to become attached to and communicate with each other. Thus adaptive instinctual systems evolved phylogenetically in the basal ganglia and through expansion of the limbic system around the diencephalon in order to serve individual and species survival more efficiently. They are heavily involved in the exchange of information with the environment. Whereas appetitive instinctual behavior is relatively simple and related to a particular instinct, adaptive instinctual behavior is complex and serves all of the appetitive instincts (see Figure 12-5).

The adaptive instincts can be classified as belonging to affliative, aggressive, mastery, and self-esteem regulation systems.

The Affiliative Instincts

Humans are programmed for living in groups and have the innate potential for acting in the interest of mutual aid through social codes that promote group survival. The affiliative instincts are expressed through drives for gregariousness, verbal communication, and reciprocal obligations to others. These basic motivations underlie the social evolution of homo sapiens and arise in the context of affiliative attachment to parenting adults (Emde & Harmon, 1982; Pugh, 1977; Williams, 1977).

The affiliative instincts initially ensure individual survival and ultimately survival of the species through motivation for social relationships (Alloway et al, 1977). They promote affectional infant–parent attachment bonds and are expressed through both nonverbal and verbal communication. The instinctual nature of attachment and the capacity for empathy is illustrated by such behaviors as an infant's orientation toward the human face, which is based upon a canalized occipitotemporal area of the cerebral cortex (Brothers, 1989). Sucking, clinging, visual following, crying, and smiling are additional examples (Bowlby, 1958). The genital appetitive contribution to these instincts undergoes progressive changes with maturation. The reciprocal give and take of peer relationships during childhood expand attachment bonds to general affiliative capacities (Bemporad, 1984).

Five distinct affiliative subsystems in primate development have been described (Harlow, 1974): the mother–infant, infant–mother, peer, heterosexual, and paternal systems. A similar differentiation in humans is expressed in Jung's theory of corresponding archetypes (Stevens, 1982).

In social mammals fear is a potent force for keeping rearing groups intact and social orders stable. Fear of strangers particularly serves the immediate purpose of binding infants to their parents. Through propelling infants to comforting by their parents, fear enhances attachment and an infant's sense of security. From this secure base, a child can explore the world (Suomi & Harlow, 1976).

The Aggressive Instincts

The aggressive instincts motivate acting upon the environment in order to ensure the survival of the individual. Their purpose is to deal adaptively with a frustrating external world (Rothstein, 1983). To put it in primitive terms, we must eat and avoid being eaten. The muscles of the body also simply crave activity.

The term aggression has a variety of meanings. In general, aggressive behavior can be seen as ranging on a continuum from assertiveness, which may be perceived as hostile by others if unwittingly intrusive, through attacking a problem, to murder, which may not be intended as hostile if in self-defense. Thus the coloration of aggression depends upon the emotional state of the actor and the perspectives of those who are acted upon in addition to observers. The shift from assertiveness to hostility seems to take place when the intent to demean or otherwise hurt another person becomes involved. The emotion of anger lowers one's threshold for hostile aggression and may be experienced as either pleasurable or distressing.

From the instinctual standpoint, aggressive behavior may be predatory, status based, fear induced, frustration induced, maternal, or sexual (Moyer, 1976; Wilson, 1980). These forms of aggressive behavior are elicited by different situations.

Predatory aggression is elicited by objects of predation. It involves directed exploring, stalking, and attack, and may involve alimentary and fighting appetites. The expression is quiet and efficient, with very little emotional display. It is not dependent upon, but is enhanced by, hunger, and it is inhibited by fear.

Status-related aggression is ritualized and involves relatively harmless attacks related to territorial and dominance issues. In subhuman animals specific postures of a defeated animal inhibit further attack by the victor. Learning plays an important role in dominance patterns established through this form of aggression, which is inhibited by fear. Androgens appear to play a more limited role in sex differences in aggressive status behavior in humans than in lower animals (Meyer-Bahlburg, 1981).

Fear-induced aggression is seen when an animal is unsuccessful in its attempts to escape. It involves defensive instinctual responses (Moyer, 1976).

Frustration-induced aggression can be differentiated from the other types by the diversity of eliciting stimuli. It is an expression of anger caused by frustration, deprivation, pain, or a variety of physiological dysfunctions. This form of aggression may result from competition with others for attention or resources. Hypoglycemia also contributes to this type of aggressive behavior.

Maternal aggression appears to be hormonally based and is related to pregnancy, parturition, and lactation; it is responsive to the behavior of the young, particularly their distress vocalizations (Lewis, 1982).

Sex-related aggression is elicited by the same stimuli that elicit sexual behavior. In some animals it is difficult to distinguish mating behavior from intense aggression. It plays a significant role in human sexual behavior, as well (Moyer, 1976; Stanley-Jones, 1970). In humans gonadal hormones fuel aggression, directly in males in the form of high androgen levels and indirectly in females through the fall in progesterone levels during the premenstrual period (Valzelli, 1981).

There is little disagreement among comparative biologists that the capacity for aggression is a part of the biological heritage of primates (Harlow, 1974; Moyer, 1976; Valzelli, 1981). How it is expressed, however, is a function of socialization (Montagu, 1976; Zillmann, 1979). Innate aggressive tendencies emerge through developmental progression at different ages, depending upon species, sex, and individ-

ual differences (Harlow, 1974). Aggressive responses can be elicited from children by imposing frustrations and interfering with goal-directed activities.

Rage is the initial response of infants to frustration when expectancies are not fulfilled. It also is involved in the first stage of the protest–despair–detachment sequence of the childhood response to separation. Thus rage is associated with both the basic defensive instinct to fight and the more specific aggressive adaptive instincts. As such it performs both a priming function for attack and a signaling function of possible attack to others.

Between the ages of two and three, children exhibit aggressive temper outbursts as a result of conflicts with parents during impulse-control training. The emotion of rage is tapped and, unlike during infancy, can achieve motor discharge in ways directed toward other persons. The impulse to attack, therefore, apparently is part of a child's innate equipment.

Aggressive behavior in later life is conditioned through modeling and social reinforcement. Aggressive children, for example, are likely to have been reared by emotionally distant parents who used excessive physical punishment (Shaffer et al, 1981). Insufficient pleasurable bodily stimulation in early life also may contribute to human and primate violent behavior (Mitchell, 1975; Prescott, 1975).

Aggression, then, is behavior that satisfies vital needs and removes or overcomes threats to individual and species preservation. Except for predatory activity, for subhuman animals aggressive behavior does not involve destruction of the opponent. Destructive violence toward other members of the same species is a uniquely primate expression of aggressiveness (Valzelli, 1981).

The Mastery Instincts

The mastery instincts evolved to ensure survival of both the individual and the species. They include a wish to explore as well as a need for mastery. At the simplest level, the lack of sufficient correspondence between a perceptual set aroused by an appetitive drive and the perceptual pattern of the surroundings initiates searching behavior until correspondence and closure of a behavioral pattern occur (Lewin, 1951; Zeigarnik, 1965). This motivation for sensorimotor closure lies beneath urges to master the internal and external world, with resulting personal competence. The tendency toward repetitive and exploratory activity, therefore, may be regarded as a biological property of a child. Mastery motivation can be measured empirically in terms of persistence at age-appropriate tasks (Morgan & Harmon, 1984).

The mastery instincts are derived from pleasure that flows from the interrelated physical and mental actions that fulfill appetitive, affiliative, and aggressive instincts. As a child matures, pleasure results from simply fulfilling a desire, as illustrated by the prototypical exhileration of a toddler on first walking and a two-year-old's smile when a challenge is mastered (Kagan, 1971; Zelazo, 1972). When mastery is exciting for both child and parents, a solid foundation for later learning develops. Pleasure in achievement also provides a foundation for a sense of responsibility for one's actions and for self-actualization.

An important drive in the mastery system is curiosity, which leads to reaching toward the widening world and is the wellspring of learning. During the course of development, a child moves from a world that is the direct outcome of personal interpretation into one with a culturally determined language and systems of meaning. Thus the pleasures of discovery, enlightenment, and insight shift from oneself to sharing concepts with others. The optimal result of curiosity is the gaining of knowledge (Cobb, 1977).

When curiosity is not followed predominantly by discovery and mastery, a child becomes wary of learning. If a child also finds that certain topics give rise to parental disapproval, direct or sensed, curiosity in those areas is inhibited. For example, parental reactions to exploration of their bodies and their bodily products influence young children's comfort with and knowledge about their bodies. To the extent that mysteries remain regarding their own bodies, children are burdened with unrequited curiosity, and illusions about themselves are unchallenged by reality.

Self-Esteem Regulation

Self-esteem regulation is an adaptive instinct that depends upon interpersonal experience. It appeared during the course of human evolution as a monitoring system sensitive to the functioning of the managerial system. It blends components of the affiliative and mastery instinctual systems. As the subjective experience of the tonus of the pleasure system, it is a state of visceral well-being responsive to efficient personal functioning in relation to one's internal and external worlds. It affords the basic pleasurable emotional tone of euphoria beyond the pleasures that arise from satisfaction of the appetitive instincts, and thereby ensures a sense of well-being that promotes engagement with the tasks and challenges of life. It provides a cushion to help one absorb failures and disapproval by others.

In contrast with other emotions that arise from internal sources, self-esteem also depends upon external factors, particularly during early life. Self-esteem is the basis for fulfilling the human species' commitment to reciprocal obligations because of its sensitivity to the expectations of others, in both the positive form of pride and the negative form of shame. It provides an orientation toward learning from others through identification with them, thus facilitating development of the managerial system's skills needed for group living.

Self-esteem permits an individual to derive pleasure from achievements that promote confidence in one's ability to deal with reality. This invites the admiration of others and, in turn, awareness of one's own value. Thus self-confidence results from being valued by others, fosters self-esteem, and increases one's value to others (Branden, 1969).

A similar instinctual system is seen in other species and is a noteworthy characteristic of the canine genus.

The Affective System

The *affective system* mediates pleasure, distress, and emotions associated with the appetitive and adaptive drives. The appetitive drives are experienced as bodily cravings, which cause distress when unsatisfied and pleasure when satiated. The adaptive drives are experienced as generalized pleasure or distress and as specific emotional states of increasing sophistication.

The affective system permits the instantaneous assessment of situations through judgments reflected by the emotional state a stimulus pattern evokes. The system is activated by the contact of perceptions and images with the sensorimotor schemes of the drives. Negative emotions block the tendency to accommodate to stimuli and thereby protect the organism from threats. Positive emotions foster accommodations by encouraging exploration of and learning about the environment.

Initially in evolution emotions were directly related to survival (Hamburg et al, 1975; Zillmann, 1979). The capacity to respond to dangerous circumstances with a sudden burst of energy made escape or attack possible and enhanced individual survival. Failure to fight or flee meant losing food or dying. As life became more secure and complex, less intense emotions developed as signals both to the person and to others. Thus emotions guide reactions to events and to other individuals in addition to eliciting responses from others (Hart, 1975).

Distressing experiences have a signal function, which warns the individual and others that attention must be paid to something that is wrong so that resources can be mobilized to correct the situation. The resulting attentiveness and vigorous motor behavior have adaptive value when an organism's well-being is threatened, or when the attainment of food, mate, or shelter is placed in jeopardy. Consequently, natural selection favors those populations whose affiliative emotions impel individuals to do what the species needs for survival.

Emotional responses that facilitate the survival of human populations, however, may be maladaptive for the individual. Since societal change has moved much more rapidly than genetic change, human emotional responses that were suited to past environments may be less suitable for the present environment. Life in contemporary societies has become an extremely complex affair, but our emotional responses have not changed correspondingly. In contemporary society we react to the unavoidable threats to our well-being with inclinations toward vigorous motor actions, which are not possible because of social prohibition of such actions. People thus become excited about countless matters, whether or not physical actions can be utilized to cope with them. In another vein, pleasurable emotions can be maladaptive, as when unprotected copulation leads to population excesses.

Fortunately, in modern society, it is possible to control one's emotional behavior through the appraisal of the appropriateness of emotional feelings. Thus the reflection upon emotional imagery can be viewed as an evolutionary refinement that permits decision making regarding different options for action (Plutchik, 1980; Zillman, 1979).

Functions of the Affective System

The term *affect* tends to be used in the psychiatric literature and *emotion* in the psychological literature, but they frequently are used synonomously. Affect often is used to refer to autonomic and motor bodily events whereas emotion is limited to subjective awareness of them (Basch, 1976b). Parsimony argues against these distinctions, however, since the literature deals with the motor, autonomic, and subjective experience of emotions. For this reason I will use emotion instead of affect to denote transient states of the *affective system,* the term generally used to describe the structures and processes that produce emotions. This leaves open the use of affect to describe sustained states of the affective system, often referred to as moods. Terminology in this area has been unclear, but the commonly used term emotion can facilitate understanding—until it can be replaced by something more precise (Karli, 1981).

Darwin's early view of emotions as internal primers for action and external communication signals remains useful today (Buck, 1984; Engel, 1963; Knapp, 1963; Tomkins, 1962, 1980). Since his time a number of theories have been advanced about the nature of emotions. James emphasized the role of the autonomic nervous system and motor events, Cannon and Bard emphasized the diencephalon, Papez the limbic system, and Schachter the interaction between central cognitive and peripheral events in emotions (Cox, 1978). Parsons placed emotions at the center of social systems because of their importance in attachments to other persons and groups, thereby enabling the formation of moral codes (Parsons, 1977).

Because theories and empirical research usually deal only with aspects of emotions, precise definitions are needed to ensure that people are referring to the same things. The word emotion derives from the Latin root "to move away from."

Contemporary usage defines an emotion as a more or less genetically programmed CNS response expressed through muscular movements, autonomic nervous system manifestations, and subjectively experienced imagery (Candland, 1977; Clynes, 1977; Ekman, 1980).

Emotions are neurochemical events elicited through internal visceral and external pain and temperature pathways (Pribram, 1981). They can be seen as a kind of running progress report or "readout" of the state regulating system (Buck, 1984). Emotional elicitors are both external and internal stimulus patterns that trigger emotional receptors (Lewis & Michalson, 1983). Emotional structures are relatively specific sensorimotor schemes that mediate changes in the physiological and cognitive state of the organism. For example, greater left frontal cortex activation is elicited in an infant confronted with a happy, as compared with a sad, face (Davidson & Fox, 1982). Once evoked, an emotion has a characteristic inertia and persists for a period of time.

Emotions can be evoked by both the absolute level of stimulation and increases or decreases in stimulation (Tomkins, 1962, 1981). The various emotions, therefore, are related to stimulus intensity and gradients over time so that a sudden increase in stimulus intensity may be frightening whereas a gradual increase in the same stimulus may be exciting, as in the tactile stimulation of caressing. In this view there are three basic kinds of emotional processes: those for which the density of neural stimulation is increasing (interest, excitement, fear), those for which the density is decreasing (pleasure), and those for which the density of neural stimulation remains constant (distress).

Tomkins proposes three principles that apply to competition between these three types of emotions:

1. Constant density emotions prevail over decreasing density emotions so that

enjoyment is vulnerable to exclusion by distress.

2. When there is competition between increasing density emotions and constant density emotions, the former prevail for short periods, but the latter prevail over longer periods of time. Thus excitement may prevail over distress, such as resulting from hunger and fatigue, but as soon as the source of excitement fades, distress returns.

3. Continuing novelty favors increasing or decreasing over constant density emotions.

This conception in which emotions interact with each other is useful because emotional states are complex. One emotion can bring forth another emotion that amplifies, inhibits, or interacts with the original emotional experience (Izard, 1972). Some emotional states, therefore, are mixtures of pleasurable and distressing feelings.

The varieties of emotions and their combinations have been described repeatedly (Izard, 1972). They can be usefully categorized as primary, secondary, and tertiary, according to the degree to which they involve lower and higher brain centers. Primary emotions are the most primitive and have (1) a specific, innately determined neural substrate; (2) a stereotyped neuromuscular and autonomic expressive pattern; and (3) distinct subjective feeling imagery. Each of the primary emotions has unique adaptive motivational functions. The primary emotional states are pleasure with the specific emotions of euphoria, interest, and surprise leading to laughter, and distress, with the specific emotions of pain, fear, and panic leading to crying. The appearance of these emotions early in human development in addition to their general presence in other species, with the equivocal exception of crying and laughter, supports their primary nature. Specific characteristics of these emotions are illustrated in Figure 12-6.

Secondary emotions lack discrete representation in lower brain centers and emerge later phylogenetically and ontogenetically as elaborations of the primary emotions. Like the primary emotions, however, the secondary emotions show cross-cultural universality in humans and have externally visible manifestations. They involve higher brain levels and are subject to learning and degrees of voluntary control. They include joy, affection, disappointment, loneliness, grief, amusement, hate, disgust, sadness, thrill, curiosity, confusion, and shame (Ekman, 1980).

A third group of emotions are not externally visible as such and are learned derivatives and mixtures of the more basic emotions (Neubauer, 1982). This tertiary group consists of emotions such as sympathy, empathy, hope, humility, ambition, greed, envy, jealousy, awe, pride, boredom, impatience, guilt, helplessness, and hopelessness.

The compound emotions of anxiety and depression have both acute and chronic manifestations and are expressed thrugh a variety of somatic and psychophysiological manifestations. Anxiety appears to be a mixture of sustained hyperarousal and fear with generalized autonomic hyperfunctioning weighted toward the sympathetic nervous system. Depression appears to be related to the sustained ineffective mobilization of the fight-or-flight autonomic-adrenal medullary stress response. It also appears to reflect the chronic bodily manifestations of helpless sadness and crying, as seen with the loss of affectional support. Because of their complexity, anxiety and depression will be discussed later in greater detail.

The multifaceted nature of emotions can be illustrated by examining their functional manifestations in mediating drive motivations, automatic judgments, communicating one's internal state to others, and signaling one's internal state to oneself.

Mediating Drive Motivations. First we will consider the priming functions of emotions

	Euphoria	Pain	Fear–Anxiety	Rage	Panic	Depression
Arousal	Moderate or Decreasing	Increasing	Hyperarousal	Increasing	Increasing	Increased
Subjective State Imagery	Visceral and somatic placidity		Impending calamity Muscle tension and tremor Dread, worry Guilt, mouth dryness Sweating, palpitations	Anger Thrill	Loneliness	Past calamity Despair, sadness Discouragement Self-devaluation Visceral distress Hopelessness, helplessness
Neuroanatomical Sites	Prefrontal Cortex Limbic System Lateral Hypothalamus Brainstem Cerebellar fastigial and dentate nuclei	Peripheral receptors Midbrain reticular formation Limbic system Prefrontal lobes	Anterior-medial hypothalamus Midbrain reticular formation Hippocampus Cingulate gyrus	Temporal cortex Amygdala Lateral hypothalamus Autonomic defensive response Sympathetic-adrenal medullary response	Anterior lateral hypothalamus	Limbic-Hypothalamus Adrenal-Cortical Neuroendocrine ↓ resting synaptic membrane potential
Neurochemical Mediators	↑ GABA ↑ Endorphines Parasympathetic	Endorphins and Enkephalins mediate Sympathetic	↓ GABA ↓ Endorphins ↑ Calcium in neurons ↑ Sympathetic discharge ↑ Peripheral epinephrine ↑ Central norepinephrine (locus ceruleus) ↓ Parasympathetic discharge	↑ Peripheral epinephrine ↑ Norepinephrine ↑ Testosterone	Analog narcotic withdrawal Massive sympathetic discharge	↓ Biogenic amines ↓ MHPG ↑ Sodium in neurons ↑ Cortisol ↑ ACTH ↓ Testosterone
Elicitors	Assimilable stimulus patterns to sensorimotor schemes Efficient CNS functioning- Self-esteem	Stressors Threat to tissue	Stressors Fear—overt threat to body surface Anxiety—fear of lack of gratification, future calamity, uncertainty (input overload—inefficient CNS functioning)	Manageable danger Frustration of expectancies Inability to gratify	Loss of support	Loss real, symbolic, or past fantasized
Behavior	Approach Exploration Investigation Expectancy	Avoidance Withdraw	Avoidance Withdrawal Impaired concentration	Vigorous attempts to secure Attack	Distress vocalization Crying	Psychomotor agitation or retardation

Figure 12-6. Characteristics of key emotions.

208

in mediating the appetitive and adaptive drives.

Emotional patterns tend to cluster around the adaptive group of instincts, just as cravings express appetitive instincts. They generally act as analog amplifiers and lead to motivations to approach or withdraw (see Figure 12-5). The more specific motivations are to escape, attack, cooperate, mate, cry for help, affiliate, groom, reject, and explore. Emotions also can produce disruption of ongoing behavior by paralysis of action, confusion, and disorientation.

The pleasurable emotions clustering around the affiliative drives may be consciously experienced as affection, sympathy, and empathy. When affiliative strivings are frustrated, the emotions of sadness, loneliness, and grief may be experienced. Pleasurable aggressive emotions may be consciously experienced as excitement, ambition, and thrill. When aggressive strivings are frustrated, distress may extend to the emotions of anxiety, disgust, and anger. When pleasurable mastery strivings are frustrated, the emotions of impatience, boredom, shame, guilt, disappointment, discouragement, and hopelessness may be experienced. Self-esteem is experienced as variations in euphoria.

Emotional discharge in itself is an avenue for the expression of frustrated drives. For example, crying, laughing, and angry outbursts can lead to a state of relaxation and normalization, as can trembling and yawning (Jackins, 1978). As a limbic-based response, crying is expressed through parasympathetic discharge and extrapyramidal rhythmic movements, so that lacrimation is accompanied by sobbing, loss of muscle tone, prone posturing, and vocalization (Lipe, 1980).

Emotions color a wide variety of stimuli, such as other emotions, imagery, and perceptions. They are modulators of arousal, and thus high arousal states are associated with such emotions as anger, disgust, anxiety, and ecstasy (Field, 1982; Lader, 1975). Emotions also become linked to concepts that influence emotional experience, so that political ideology in itself can be fraught with emotion (Leventhal, 1979).

Automatic Judgments. Emotional responses provide instant judgments about stimulus patterns on the basis of instinctual and learned sensorimotor schemes. They automatically block accommodation until further assessment of the situation can take place.

Emotions are phylogenetically sophisticated mechanisms not available to lower animals, which are obliged to respond to externally induced direct organ satisfaction as a signal of "good" and pain as the signal of "bad." As animals ascended the evolutionary ladder, they acquired internal reward and punishment systems for making judgments in the form of generalized pleasure and distress (Valzelli, 1981). As a result, emotions greatly enlarged the range of an organism's ability to appraise the desirability of movement toward or away from a situation. For example, fear makes an animal cautious; anger motivates the removal of obstacles; friendliness promotes socialization; rage impels vigorous attempts to secure drive satisfaction; and panic subserves social cohesion by signaling distress and motivating closeness to support figures (Panksepp, 1981).

Emotions thereby serve the purpose of automatically guiding responses to events as good or bad in the light of the appetitive and adaptive drives, and in prioritizing drives themselves. They thus reflect the biases of instinctual programs and enduring memories of significant aspects of past situations.

The *defensive response* is an automatic judgmental reaction of the autonomic nervous system to novel stimulus patterns (Davis et al, 1955). As an extension of the orienting and startle responses, the autonomic defensive response flags a situation as demanding urgent attention by preparing the body for immediate action. It appears first in the form of skeletal muscle tension that quickly reaches its peak and decays within a few seconds. Next there is a decrease in skin electrogalvanic resistance, which changes more gradually than the skeletal muscle tension. Pupillary dilation occurs as well. A variety of circulatory responses follow. First there are an acceleration of pulse rate and a decrease in pulse pressure, then a constriction of the finger and dilation of facial blood vessels, as in blushing, followed by a slowing of pulse rate and an increase in pulse pressure. Finally there is a shift to slower, deeper breathing. The defensive response also includes a reduction in salivary and gastric secretions and slowing of digestive processes. When the face turns red, as in anger, or pales, as in fear, so does the stomach lining (Wolf, 1965).

Although the defensive respnse largely involves the sympathetic nervous system, it has some parasympathetic aspects. The autonomic activation is immediate and of limited duration because of the inability of sympathetic nerves to continue releasing neurotransmitters under sustained high stimulation. It occurs with a variety of emotional feeling imagery. It does not completely habituate, although under laboratory experimental conditions, substantial apparent physiological habituation has been reported (Everly & Rosenfeld, 1981).

In general the autonomic nervous system participates in the elaboration of emotions by providing multiple pathways and many levels of integration, which facilitate functional responses when the organism is thrown off balance (Sigg, 1975). Emotions involve the same bodily mechanisms that maintain body temperature through the control of heart rate, blood pressure, vasomotor tone, and sweating. Defense against cold is mediated by the sympathetic nervous system, which also is a neural mechanism in rage. Defense against heat is mediated by the parasympathetic nervous system, which also is a neural mechanism in lust. Human emotions, therefore, appear to be an evolutionary outgrowth of mammalian defenses against heat and cold (Stanley-Jones, 1970).

The autonomic manifestations of emotions can be measured by changes in body temperature, electrical resistance of the skin, muscle tone, and visceral activity. Emotional displays are seen in animals even after nerves to the viscera are severed, however, indicating that the autonomic component is not essential to them (Cannon, 1927). The sympathetic and parasympathetic manifestations in the various organ systems are described in Chapter 9. The psychophysiological concomitants lack a strict one-to-one correspondence to specific emotions. For example, one person may become pale when angry and another flushed.

Even within the same person, the autonomic concomitants of an emotional state vary at different times (Clynes, 1973). According to the *law of initial values*, the magnitude and direction of autonomic response to stimulation are functions of the prestimulus level. The higher the prestimulus level of autonomic functioning, the smaller is the response to a function-increasing stimulus. At more extreme prestimulus levels, there is a tendency for there to be no response to stimulation, and even for paradoxical responses, which reverse the typical direction of responses (Wilder, 1957). Thus the automatic judgments provided by emotions may be inconsistent and unrealistic.

External Signaling. Primary and secondary emotions are visible through the involuntary bodily expressions of extrapyramidal, autonomic, and hormonal activity. They convey externally evident voluntary signals and involuntary embellishments by autonomic discharge, such as blushing, and the coloration of behavior, as in the tone of voice and gestures (Buck, 1984).

The most important route of emotional

expression is through the face. The facial expressions of babies are instinctually canalized and are the same as seen in other primates for such emotions as interest, excitement, enjoyment-joy, distress-anguish, fear-terror, shame-humiliation, anger, contempt, surprise, and sadness (Tomkins, 1962, 1970, 1981; Demos, 1982a). These emotional displays by infants and young children are vital signals to caregivers. The most important interactions between young child and caregiver are through the affective system (Demos, 1984).

Facial expressions are perceived as social appeals and responses in human interchange. Emotional responses tend to be elicited specifically, and so we smile with joy at the smile of another, exhibit fear when threatened, are excited by new information, and show shame when others disapprove (Tomkins, 1962). Facial expressions also can test the response of others to one's attitudes before one is committed to action and so make a total behavioral reaction unnecessary (Izard, 1982).

The nature of an emotion, therefore, includes expression by an output modality, such as tone of voice or gesture. The expression usually follows a sequence of degrees, so that euphoria extends to smiling and joy to laughter (Gruner, 1978). The experience of satisfaction that takes place depends upon how precisely the output form represents the inner state. The vicissitudes of socialization, however, progressively inhibit the full expression of emotions (Clynes, 1973; 1977). The surface manifestations of emotions and associated feeling imagery come to diverge upon the learning of cultural, gender, and personal rules for displaying them. Except for their involuntary manifestations, emotions can be concealed from others. Social values and personal circumstances, therefore, govern the degree and manner of concealment of emotions (Malatesta, 1982).

Internal Signaling. Another function of emotions is to signal automatic judgments about the nature of situations to oneself through conscious awareness of the perceptions and imagery arising from the autonomic and somatic musculature of the body. Specific bodily reactions and emotional imagery are determined by a person's automatic evaluation of a stimulus pattern of actual or impending events in the light of contextual clues, past experience, and individual differences (Schachter, 1971; Lewis & Michalson, 1983).

The James–Lange theory of emotions holds that the autonomic and somatic aspects of emotions are perceived as feelings. Thus we do not feel grief and then weep, nor are we seized by fear and then run—but the reverse (Barzun, 1983; Lange & James, 1967). Although regarded as an oversimplification for many years, the accumulating evidence supports the intimate relationship of sensory input from the body and the imagery of feelings (Lader & Tyrer, 1975). For example, simply contracting the facial muscles into the basic emotional expressions can bring forth autonomic activity, underscoring the centrality of the face itself in emotional experience (Ekman et al, 1983). The facial musculature may play a role in regulating cerebral blood flow and thence the activity of neurotransmitters (Zajonc, 1985). Conversely, even when facial expression is unrevealing, imagining a happy, sad, or angry situation produces specific patterns of electrical signals in the muscles of the face (Schwartz et al, 1980).

The imagery of emotions tends to be specific; however, the associated physiological responses may vary according to how much and what type of autonomic body functions are included in a particular emotional state. Different emotions are perceived as imagery involving various regions of the body in the same way that visual images arise within the space of the body. The imagery of emotional feelings usually is from internal sensory stimuli from bodily parts, but it may be visual or auditory as well. The images appear to be more complex than visceral perceptions, which result from the psychophysiological manifestations of emotions. For example, anger may have the imagery of waves engulfing the body, joy a lightness in the body, and affection a flow from within the body outward (Clynes, 1973).

Imagery from a variety of sources can arouse pleasure and distress through the anticipation of reward or punishment (Koestler, 1978; Singer, 1976). Verbal expressions and motor acts, such as through role-playing scripts and intellectual discussions, can elicit intense emotions (Lang, 1979; Young, 1978). Conversely, acts of imagination can cause physiological responses in visceral and glandular processes, such as when imagery of a gourmet meal activates the flow of gastric juices.

The specific imagery of an emotion results from a person's past experience and knowledge about a particular event (Gray, 1971). Feeling imagery also is colored by socially and culturally learned words (Leventhal, 1979). For example, the parallel between the effects of punishment and the omission of anticipated reward has given rise to the hypothesis that fear is functionally and physiologically identical with frustration (Gray, 1971). The labeling of one's emotional state as fear or frustration may be a result of knowledge of the events leading up to the same physiological state, so that the feeling upon the sight of a snake is called fear and the feeling resulting from a broken date is called frustration. These reactions may differ only in intensity, so that frustrating nonreward may be a less intense form of fear. In rats high susceptibility to fear is accompanied by high susceptibility to frustration. At the least, the covariance of fear and frustration deserves close study. They both constitute distress with apparently similar outcomes.

The situation becomes even more complicated when feeling imagery does not correspond to the emotional state from which it is derived because unconscious defense mechanisms intervene. Conscious reporting of emotions thus may be unreliable because of defensive repression or modification of them (Brenner, 1982). For example, one may show the autonomic and somatic manifestations of the emotion of anger and not be consciously aware of feeling angry. In addition, anger may be attenuated to become irritation and annoyance. Indirect expressions of anger may be evidenced as a result of one person's disappointment in others, as when a martyr evokes guilt in others as a means of hurting them. Anger may be disguised by feelings of hopelessness and futility, and somatic symptoms may result from the chronic autonomic manifestations of anger (Madow, 1972).

The physiological manifestations of emotion can occur without imagery in persons with brain lesions. For example, a patient with a stroke presumably affecting the limbic structures was subject to frequent, unaccountable crying episodes that occurred without feeling sad (Churchland, 1986).

Processes of the Affective System

The basic process of the affective system is the *pleasure–distress system*, which has fairly well-defined anatomical substrates in the brain, as illustrated in Figure 12-7 (Valzelli, 1981). It has been described as an internal reward–punishment system (Weil, 1974). The positive experience of emotions stems from the pleasure system and the negative experience of emotions from the distress system (Amosov, 1967). Pleasure fosters approach behaviors, such as exploration, orienting, eating, predatory attack, and mating. Distress elicits protective behaviors, such as defensive attack, retreat, and crying for help.

The pleasure–distress system can be seen as an analog amplifier of appetitive and adaptive drive states and sensory stim-

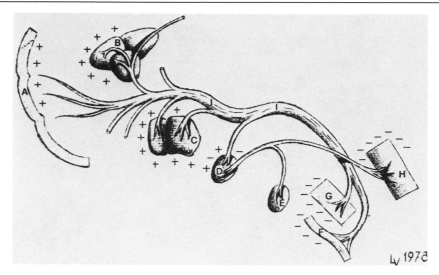

Figure 12-7. Human pleasure (+) and distress (−) system. (A) frontal cortex, (B) septal nuclei, (C) hypothalamus, (D) mammillary body, (E) interpeduncular nucleus, (F) ventral tegmentum, (G) lateral tegmentum, (H) periaqueductal gray matter, and (I) medial forebrain bundle. (Adapted from L. Valzelli, *Psychobiology of Aggression and Violence,* copyright 1981 by Raven Press, New York. Used with permission.)

uli. For example, an infant's hunger produces an increase in the level of neural stimulation to a level of distress that triggers crying, as an amplification of the underlying hunger and a signal to the external world of the infant's need to be fed. The emotion of crying persists until the infant is fed, with resulting pleasure, or becomes exhausted and falls asleep (Tomkins, 1981). Sensory input also may be amplified with pleasurable and distressful qualities, especially from the erogenous zones (Stanley-Jones, 1970). The same stimulus pattern may be experienced as pleasurable or distressful, as with pain that is pleasurable in a sexual context.

Pleasure results from the gratification of internal needs in the form of relief and tranquility and from the satisfaction of external mastery in the form of delight and exhilaration (Pribram, 1981). Distress results from the failure to achieve either internal or external mastery. Thus a person may be gratified and calm but still dissatisfied and apathetic.

As can be seen in Figure 12-8, the brain centers that tend to trigger pleasure tend to suppress distress, and vice versa, so that the two systems operate in a counterbalancing way. The core of the pleasure system is in the hypothalamus and the autonomic nervous system. The anterior hypothalamus is devoted to anabolic visceral activity via the parasympathetic nervous system and the lateral hypothalamus to approach behaviors. Cravings mediated by the anterior hypothalamus are appetites for food and sexual gratification. The distress system is less well defined in the hypothalamus but probably lies in its connections with the amygdala, dorsomedial thalamus, and tegmentum (Panksepp, 1981).

A balance between pleasure and distress facilitates adaptation, and an imbalance can be maladaptive. For example,

Emotions	Stimulation of Brain Components	
	Triggers	Suppresses
Pleasure (Euphoria-Joy)	Prefrontal Cortex Subcallosal Cingulate Gyrus Septal Nuclei Olfactory Tubercles Preoptic Nuclei Head of Caudate Nucleus Medial Geniculate Body Medial Hippocampus Medial Amygdala Ventromedial Hypothalamus Medial Forebrain Bundle Supramamillary area Subfornical area Substantia Nigra Raphe Nuclei Locus Ceruleus Cerebellar Fastigal & Dentate Nuclei Peripheral Tactile Receptors	Periadqueductal Gray Matter Nauta's Limbic Area Mesencephalic Tegmentum Cingulate Gyrus
Fear-Anxiety	Cingulate Gyrus Hippocampus Mesencephalic Tegmentum Periaqueductal Gray Matter Nauta's Limbic Area	See Pleasure Triggers
Rage	Lateral Hypothalamus Dorsomedial Hypothalamus Centromedial Amygdala Temporal Lobes	Septal Nuclei Medial Amygdala Head of Caudate Nucleus

Figure 12-8. Emotions evoked by the stimulation of brain components. (Adapted from L. Valzelli, *Psychobiology of Aggression and Violence,* copyright 1981 by Raven Press, New York. Used with permission.)

when experimental animals could stimulate their own pleasure centers electrically, they did so incessantly and became exhausted and died (Valzelli, 1981). In contrast, counterbalancing can be seen when continuation of pleasurable responses becomes distressing (Sem-Jacobson & Styri, 1975). The crucial element in the balance of the pleasure and distress systems is the balance between the parasympathetic and sympathetic systems, even though individual differences in autonomic reactivity typically lead one system to predominate somewhat over the other (Lester, 1974).

For example, individuals with dominant parasympathetic systems tend to have excessive salivation, dry palms, a slow heart rate, and high intestinal motility. Individuals with a dominant sympathetic system tend to have dry mouths, moist palms, and rapid resting heart rate.

The counterbalancing posture of the pleasure and distress subsystems sets the stage for conflict between, and the distortion of, specific emotional states that tend to be experienced as either pleasurable or distressful, but also can reverse their valence. Tears may flow in response to sadness or to joy. Rage may be distressing or zestful. The source of much maladaptive behavior may lie in painful emotions that have been endowed with pleasure as well. For example, electrical stimulation of the same areas of the anterior cerebral cortex can produce sudden emotional outbursts in a positive or negative direction (Olds & Olds, 1964). Ambivalence also is seen, in that a specific stimulation may be pleasurable on one occasion and distressful on another.

The Pleasure System. The pleasure system reinforces ongoing responses to stimuli. It may be conceptualized as the command system for exploration– investigation–approach behaviors (Panksepp, 1981). The pleasure system, therefore, is a positive feedback mechanism that reinforces behavior by heightening motivation and discharges energy into the environment through motor activity. In this sense it is an expression of the second law of thermodynamics, which mandates the expenditure of energy in the direction of entropy (Holt, 1976).

Pleasure is experienced as a generalized state ranging from contentment to ecstasy. In its nonspecific form, pleasure is the perception of self-esteem as euphoria resulting from the efficient functioning of the central nervous system. In more specific forms, it corresponds to the psychoanalytic concept of libido and positively colors the range of emotions, cravings, and bodily sensations.

Electrical stimulation of anterior aspects of the brain produces three degrees of pleasure: (1) a relaxed feeling of contentment, (2) relaxed enjoyment and smiling, and (3) enthusiastic enjoyment and laughter (Sem-Jacobson & Styri, 1975). The widespread sites in the brain ranging from the prefrontal cortex to the peripheral nerves that produce pleasure highlight the role of the emotional rewards in drive gratification (Figure 12-5). Pleasurable experience is usually anabolic and parasym-

pathetically mediated. Parasympathetic activity lacks the unitary and focused character of sympathetic activity and occurs during rest and tranquility with slowing of the heart and enhancement of the bodily functions of digestion, growth, and repair.

Examples of stimulus conditions that regularly elicit states of pleasure are (1) erogeneous stimulation, (2) sweet gustatory stimulation, (3) a moderate level of arousal, (4) the interruption of distressful stimulus conditions, and (5) release from muscular restriction (Weil, 1974).

The Distress System. The terms of unpleasure, displeasure, and distress are used synonymously; however, distress is used here because it connotes a general, pervasive, and nonspecific negative emotional state. Distress captures the manifestations of aversive states in early life before the appearance of more specific emotions. It also equates negative emotional experience with stress and stressors. The subjective experience of distress ranges from hyperarousal to fear and rage, as expressed in the fight-or-flight response. Its prototype is the nonspecific crying of infants (Compton, 1980).

The first law of thermodynamics mandates the conservation of energy so that a change in energy level elicits an equal and opposite reaction. In living organisms this is seen in negative feedback mechanisms through which a mismatch between two output settings produces an error signal, which controls the operation of the system until equilibrium is reestablished. Distress signals dissonance between actual and expected perceptions. Distress, therefore, can be seen as a signal that triggers negative feedback and inhibits responses to ongoing stimuli (Holt, 1976). It blocks accommodation to a situation and may precede avoidance, attack, or escape behaviors. In response to external surface receptors, distress evokes avoidance behaviors through activation. In response to visceral receptors, distress evokes aversion and inhibition of drives. It blocks experiencing pleasurable bodily sensations.

The brain sites producing distress are more limited in scope and specific than those producing pleasure (see Figure 12-8), perhaps reflecting the more direct relationship of distress to events in contrast with pleasure, which reflects more generalized bodily states. Electrical stimulation of anterior aspects of the brain produces three degrees of distress: (1) restless tension, (2) irritable sadness, and (3) anger, fear, depression, or crying (Sem-Jacobsen & Styri, 1975). Stimulation of the periventricular nuclei of the hypothalamus produces visceral discomfort, and stimulation of the midbrain reticular formation produces fear, rage, and pain (Weil, 1974). Fear appears to be more related to the midbrain, hippocampus, and cingulate gyrus, and rage more to the lateral hypothalamus, amygdala, and temporal lobes. Panic may be related to the anterior lateral hypothalamus (Panksepp, 1981).

Distress largely is catabolic and is mediated by the sympathetic nervous system. Sympathetic emotions are activated under emergency conditions and mobilize resources to permit the greatest gain for a brief period, even though at an extremely uneconomical cost, especially with panic and rage (Amosov, 1976).

Examples of stimulus conditions that regularly elicit distressful states are (1) pain, (2) bitter gustatory stimuli, (3) excessive sensory stimulation, (4) deficient sensory stimulation, (5) interruption in conditions charging the pleasure system, and (6) behavioral restriction (Weil, 1974).

Three emotional states associated with the distress system merit special consideration because of their significant influence on learning. They are pain, anxiety, and depression.

PAIN. Physical pain is the most primitive form of distress. It alerts the organism to danger to body tissue and provides specific information as to where the problem is lo-

cated. Pain results from the intensity of stimuli (Pribram, 1981).

Pain is a sense like seeing or hearing; it has its own specialized nerve endings and pathways. Pain receptors synapse in the substantia gelatinosa of the spinal cord. Pain messages then travel to the brain via the ascending spinothalamic and reticular tracts and terminate primarily in the periaqueductal gray and midbrain areas. From the ascending reticular formation, pain input evokes the septal-hippocampus control system and the frontal cortex. The endorphins and enkephalins appear to be naturally occurring mediators of pain.

There are at least four components in the experience of pain. First is a discriminative component, which analyzes sensory input for location, rate of onset, and intensity of the painful stimulus pattern. Pain usually is experienced in the body part directly affected; however, sensations due to visceral malfunctions are transferred to the skin as referred pain. The actual locus of the pain experience is in the brain, as evidenced by phantom limb pain, in which the ghostly sensation of a lost arm or leg is felt (Cotman & McCaugh, 1980).

Second, there is a motivational component of pain that drives the organism to take action. Traumatic pain has autonomic emotional accompaniments, whereas pain from lesions is a locally evoked sensation (Stanley-Jones, 1970).

Third, there is a cognitive-evaluative component of pain that allows comparison of present input with past experience (Mayer & Price, 1982). Lesions of the frontal lobes render patients indifferent to pain. The perception of pain, therefore, depends on one's cultural attitudes, past experience, meaning attached to a situation, arousal, and anxiety level.

Fourth, the external manifestations of pain communicate distress to others. This is particularly significant for infants and young children.

Chronic nonprogressive pain may be

primarily a disturbance in the central integrative subsystem of pain. Acute pain has been compared to chronic pain as fear is to anxiety and grief to depression (Swanson, 1984).

The relation between physical pain and the development of emotions in childhood deserves attention (Brenner, 1982). Physical pain resulting from injury or illness is often intense, and in some cases is chronic or recurrent. The imagery of childhood illnesses and injuries is woven into the fabric of instinctual life. Consequently, illness or injury may be experienced as evidence of a parent's malice or faithlessness or may be regarded as consequences of incestuous or castration fantasies.

When children experience physical pain in a dentist's chair or in a doctor's office as unbearably discomforting, the drilling or injection may unconsciously symbolize for the child internal conflicts associated with guilt or anxiety. Even in adult life, physical pain is greatly influenced by unconscious psychological factors and stress responses, which magnify or minimize pain. The latter is seen in athletes and soldiers in the excitement of competition and battle, when injuries that would otherwise be painful go unnoticed (Brenner, 1982).

ANXIETY. Under circumstances of ill-defined danger from the internal world and incapability of action, distress becomes anxiety. The unpleasant subjective experience of anxiety is viewed in living systems theory as a signal that the adjustment processes of one or more subsystems of the central nervous system are failing.

Anxiety and physical pain can be differentiated by the sources of stimuli producing them but not by their higher neural mechanisms. Physical pain results from input to the reticular formation from receptors in the body. Anxiety arises from the limbic–hypothalamic–reticular circuits themselves. Thereafter, pain and anxiety are mediated by the same neural substrates, including the septohippocampal system and its monoaminergic inputs from the brain stem, especially the dorsal ascending noradrenergic bundle (Gray, 1982). For this reason anxiety can be regarded as psychic pain.

The term anxiety is ambiguous, and is described as either a primary emotion (Kandel, 1983) or a compound mixture of emotions (Izard, 1972). In fact it may be generalized heightened synaptic transmission, which is the final common pathway of a variety of causes. A close look at the clinical and research evidence regarding the phenomenology of anxiety, therefore, is warranted in arriving at a definition.

First of all, anxiety can be described in terms of its subjective and objective manifestations. The subjective aspects of anxiety are experienced as psychic or somatic symptoms. Psychic anxiety is comprised of worry, dread, increased vigilance, apprehension, difficulty concentrating, restlessness, impairment of memory, and insomnia (Cattell, 1972). Somatic anxiety is manifested as chest constriction, nausea, throat tightness, labored breathing, muscle tension and aching, and leg weakness. Visceral symptoms are mouth dryness, sweating, tremor, increased respiratory rate, palpitation, giddiness, urinary frequency, paresthesias, and abdominal discomfort. Both psychic and somatic anxiety are associated with high autonomic arousal; psychic anxiety, however, tends to occur with high cortical arousal in introvert-intellectualizing individuals and somatic anxiety with low cortical arousal in extrovert-impulsive individuals (Schalling et al, 1975).

The objective behavioral manifestations of anxiety include heightened alertness, restlessness, attempts to avoid situations, impaired motor coordination, inhibition of ongoing behavior, and performance deficits on complex cognitive tasks. The objective physiological signs of anxiety are increased muscle tension, increased heart rate and blood pressure, rapid respiration, drop in resistance in galvanic skin response, pallor in the extremities, diarrhea, and frequent urination (Bootzin & Max, 1980).

Autonomic measures, somatic measures, the electroencephalogram, and endocrine indices point to heightened arousal with anxiety (Lader, 1980). For anxious persons the electroencephalographic evidence of mental activity continues in the resting state (Livanov, 1977). This may be related to the fading of gamma aminobutyric acid (GABA) inhibition of neurotransmission (Nesteros, 1981). Indeed, a benzodiazepine-receptor-mediated model of anxiety has been proposed in which an antagonist causes anxiety relieved by a benzodiazepine, which potentiates the inhibitory action of GABA (Insel et al, 1984). Anxiety also reflects overfunctioning of the autonomic nervous system, particularly the sympathetic branch, with increased acetylcholine, adrenocorticotropic hormone, and ketosteroid output.

A good deal of the confusion surrounding the concept of anxiety, therefore, stems from the failure to differentiate it from heightened arousal. Arousal includes reactivity to all sources of inner and outer stimulation, and in itself is not unpleasant. Heightened arousal, however, is experienced as distress manifested by tension, an inability to concentrate, and restlessness; it also is characterized by low parasympathetic tonus, fast reaction time, rapid ideomotor performance, and an increase in blood glucose and pulse rate (Cattel, 1972). In humans continuous infusions of epinephrine produce the objective manifestations of anxiety with sweating, tachycardia, hypertension, and cutaneous pallor (Selye, 1976b). This has been regarded, however, as representing hyperarousal that may be interpreted as anxiety, depending upon a person's set and setting (Schachter, 1964). In states of high arousal in which a person is able to be active, there are high levels of both epinephrine and norepinephrine. In states of high arousal in which a person

cannot be active or is helpless, there are high levels of epinephrine only (Gray, 1971). In an experimental situation, increasing a subject's control over punishment decreased the rise in epinephrine but not norepinephrine (Selye, 1976b).

Thus the continuous or intermittent secretion of epinephrine during times of high arousal and muscular inaction appears to cause the subjective and objective symptoms of anxiety (Stanley-Jones, 1970). This suggests the paradigm that, when external constraints give rise to rage and aggression, they present physical obstructions against which muscles can be exerted; the circulating epinephrine then is "used up" and does not remain to cause the symptoms of anxiety. If action is blocked by an internal inhibition, however, epinephrine is not taken up by the muscles and remains in circulation. This may cause the posterior hypothalamus further to stimulate the adrenal medulla with the risk of positive feedback runaway production of more epinephrine. In this paradigm, then, anxiety could be a warning of positive feedback runaway and a signal that CNS mechanisms are not operating efficiently. In this sense it would be the antithesis of euphoria.

It appears that central norepinephrine also can produce anxiety, perhaps through the activity of the locus ceruleus (Goldberg, 1982). This is supported by evidence that high levels of endogenous monamine oxidase inhibitors are associated with anxiety (Sandler, 1983). The locus ceruleus is a regulatory center for arousal activity and contains inhibitory neurons that are responsive to GABA. Hypoglycemia and metabolic alkalosis resulting from hyperventilation also produce the subjective and objective manifestations of anxiety (Lader & Tyrer, 1975).

Neurophysiologically, then, anxiety involves generally heightened neurotransmitter release, autonomic discharge, and neuroendocrine activity in a state of physical inactivity (Lewis, 1980). The experience of anxiety, therefore, is the final common pathway for a variety of physiological mechanism. The ultimate neurochemical basis of anxiety may be increased synaptic transmission through enhancement of neurotransmitter release by depressing a potassium channel, thereby increasing the influx of calcium to neurons (Kandel, 1983).

The relationship between fear and anxiety has been confusing. As an acute manifestation of distress, fear usually is defined as a sudden, brief expectation of being unable to cope with a situation; it is experienced as trepidation, apprehension, fright, dread, or terror. The external and internal elicitors of human anxiety are less objective than those of fear, so that internal imagery dominates in anxiety (McReynolds, 1976). In early childhood both external and internal dangers cause fear, because the syncretic merging of perception, emotions, and internal imagery renders internal imagery just as fearsome as external perceptions. As external perceptions and internal imagery are more clearly differentiated, the fear of internal images is not susceptible to resolving action and is experienced as anxiety, which then can be seen as fear with its physiological concomitants but without discharge through action. In this way anxiety can become chronic when based upon unconscious dangers because of its inaccessibility to definitive action. There is evidence that fear, as is anxiety, is more dependent upon epinephrine, and anger upon norepinephrine, secretion of the adrenal medulla. Both fear and anxiety are multilevel response patterns to aversive stimuli, having both external perceptual and internal imagery elicitors.

Psychologically, then, anxiety can be seen as the degenerate product of heightened arousal, distress, and the inability to act effectively as illustrated in Figure 12-9 (Cattel, 1972). In a prolonged setting of uncertainty, inactivity, and high arousal, fear becomes anxiety (Lewis, 1980). In it-

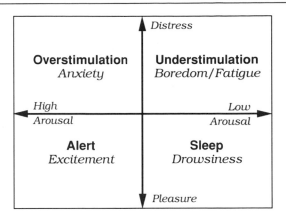

Figure 12-9. Anxiety in an orthogonal model of arousal and distress. (Adapted from T. Cox, *Stress,* University Park Press, Baltimore MD. Used with permission.)

self anxiety is impotent fear of future danger, of the lack of drive satisfaction, or of the loss of control of internal and external phenomena (Cattell, 1980). In living system terms, anxiety results from the impending future failure of homeostatic mechanisms that maintain arousal, affective, and psychomotor systems in negative feedback. Parenthetically, in contrast, depression results from the present and past failures of these mechanisms and present and past frustrations.

Unlike the causes of physical pain and fear, the stimuli that elicit anxiety arise from internal imagery from consciously unknown sources. Psychologically, therefore, the nature of the dangers cannot be realistically evaluated, and action cannot be taken to avoid them. Physiologically the resulting heightened arousal and distress progress to the flight reaction of the autonomic–adrenal medullary response, which cannot be discharged through motor action.

The current evidence points to signal anxiety as a final psychological common pathway that is fed from multiple sources. Anxiety has signaling functions, as do physical pain and fear. From clinical observations, Sigmund Freud developed an extensive and compelling theory of anxiety as an adaptive signal of danger that a traumatic helpless state will ensue (Fischer, 1982). In this view anxiety is stimulated by the danger that instinctual desires, which in the past actually did, or potentially could, overwhelm the individual, will call forth retribution or retaliation from others or create shame or guilt based upon internalized values. Because the future dangers signaled by anxiety are forecast by current fantasies of past events, these dangers are relatively inaccessible to accurate analysis of their true nature and to ameliorative actions. Anxiety, therefore, is maladaptive when the danger is based upon unconscious neurotic conflicts.

Signal anxiety can be subdivided into three forms on the basis of clinical characteristics and response to psychopharmacological agents. These forms are panic attacks, anticipatory anxiety, and chronic anxiety (Kandel, 1983).

Whereas fear evolved as a protection against threats to the body, panic appears to be a reaction to actual or fantasied loss of interpersonal support and, therefore, subserves a social cohesion function (Panksepp, 1981). Panic attacks usually are brief, spontaneous episodes of terror without clearly identifiable precipitating causes. The attacks are characterized by a sense of impeding disaster accompanied by massive sympathetic nervous system discharge. This kind of anxiety may result from a lowered threshold for separation anxiety, so that panic as a response to separation misfires without appropriate environmental triggers; this form of anxiety may be prevented by antidepressants (Cooper, 1985). There also is a striking similarity between the signs and symptoms of opiate-withdrawal reactions and panic attacks. The drug clonidine inhibits the locus ceruleus, the major brain center controlling norepinephrine activity, and alleviates the symptoms of opiate withdrawal and panic anxiety. This suggests that the norepinephrine system interacting with brain endorphin systems plays a role in panic states (Panksepp, 1981; Sweeney et al, 1980).

Anticipatory anxiety also is typically brief. Unlike panic attacks, however, anticipatory anxiety is triggered by an identifiable signal, real or imagined, that has come to be associated with danger. Because time is not defined in the unconscious, anxiety as an anticipatory state can apply to past dangers, which are perceived as immediate or forthcoming (Compton, 1980).

Anticipatory anxiety follows a complex developmental course (Yorke & Wiseberg, 1976). The poorly organized motoric distress, devoid of psychic content, in response to noxious and ungratified appetitive stimuli of infancy probably is the antecedent of anticipatory anxiety. As development progresses, a psychic experience of distress appears. With further development, emotional differentiation occurs so that anxiety rather than simple extreme distress can be discerned. Characteristic forms of anxiety emerge sequentially related to fears of abandonment, loss of body boundaries, loss of love, and punitive body mutilation. Ultimately, fear of one's own impulses in the form of guilt becomes an important source of anxiety (Compton, 1980). Guilt proneness, low self-evaluation, and uncertainty of internal control are highly correlated with clinical anxiety (Cattell, 1972).

Anticipatory anxiety thus signals the impending or actual collapse of control over internal urges (Averill, 1976). When the sum of externally generated task-relevant information and internally generated task-irrelevant information exceeds the total processing capacity of the information processing system, anxiety results from information input overload (Hamilton, 1983). When drives are not sublimated into realistically attainable aims, the pressure for their discharge creates distress, which may be experienced as impatience or boredom.

With children, this interferes with the performance of schoolwork. One result is daydreaming, which provides fulfillment of a drive through imagery. The child's attention, then, is deflected from engaging with the present to wish fulfillment in the future. When a child is highly aroused and unable to be physically active, the subjective and objective manifestations of anxiety appear.

In other words, anticipatory anxiety signals one's inability to organize, comprehend, and respond appropriately to a complex stimulus world, as seen in relatively pure form in Goldstein's catastrophic reaction and in experimentally produced cognitive dissonance (Korchin et al, 1958). Anxiety also may result from the overwhelming of cerebellar functioning and sensory-motor dyscoordination, as in the primitive fear of falling, adding the possible role of vestibulo-cerebellar dysfunction in phobias and other neurotic symptoms (Levinson, 1980).

Chronic anxiety occurs when danger is associated with a wide range of phobic environmental cues through the defenses of projection and displacement or when the danger of the breakthrough of repressed internal imagery is always present. There also is overly active arousal related to a failure of GABA inhibitory activity; this form of anxiety is responsive to benzodiazepines, which potentiate GABA activity (Cooper, 1985). The psychological defenses involved are the internal counterpart of the fight-or-flight responses. Rather than directed toward external sources of danger, they ward off internal dangers triggered by signal anxiety. Although uncomfortable, chronic anxiety is more tolerable than the panic associated with the unconscious imagery.

DEPRESSION. Both anxiety and depression are associated with images of calamity. With anxiety, however, calamity is impending, while with depression calamity already has taken place (Brenner, 1982). Depression thus is an outgrowth of distress associated with the loss of relationships, health, self-esteem, security, things of symbolic value, and discrepancies between desired and actual self-concepts. The losses may be of real, symbolic, or fantasied importance (White et al, 1977). In an overly simplified sense, anxiety is fear, and depression anger, that cannot be resolved through action.

Actually, depression is a compound emotion derived from varying degrees and durations of anxiety, panic, grief, fear, and anger. The feeling state of depression is the sadness of helplessness and hopelessness. Depression, therefore, is a mood state that results from the final common neuroendocrine pathway of multiple emotions resulting from adaptive failure and related to genetic predisposition, development predisposition, and psychosocial and physiological stressors (Akiskal & McKinney, 1975; Akiskal, 1979; Whybrow et al, 1984).

According to this integrated model of depression (Figure 12-10), depressive and manic behaviors result from a failure in the homeostatic mechanisms that maintain the arousal, affective, and psychomotor systems in balanced negative feedback. The resulting perception of oneself as losing control serves as an additional stressor, producing increments in arousal and additional decrements in coping abilities. Thus, unchecked by negative feedback, a vicious circle occurs of more arousal, more hopelessness, and more evidence of purposeless psychomotor activity (Akiskal & McKinney, 1975). The central nervous system shifts from an open, transactional state toward a closed, reactive state (Basch, 1975).

Studies of patients with affective disorders, including those with severe psychomotor retardation, indicate that hyperarousal is a prominent characteristic of both depressive and manic states. This may result from intraneuronal sodium accumulation with consequent lowering of

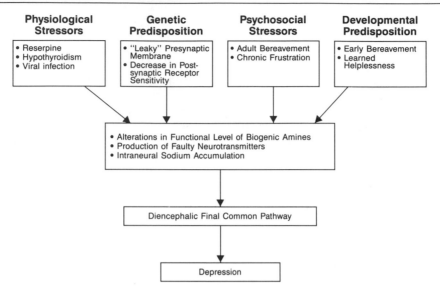

Figure 12-10. Depression as a final common pathway. (From H. S. Akiskal and W. T. McKinney, "Overview of Recent Research in Depression," *Archives of General Psychiatry, 32,* 1975, 285–305. Copyright 1975, American Medical Association. Reproduced with permission.)

the resting membrane potential and lowered thresholds of arousal (Akiskal & McKinney, 1975). A decrease in synaptic biogenic amine neurotransmitter release may give rise to the symptoms of depression and an increase to manic states (Barchas et al, 1977b; Whybrow et al, 1984). An imbalance between cholinergic and norepinephrine systems has been proposed so that increased cholinergic activity is associated with depression and increased norepinephrine activity with mania (Nadi et al, 1984).

Rather than being attributable to simple increases and decreases in neurotransmitter levels, the vulnerability to affective disorders probably lies in the inefficient regulation of their levels (Siever & Davis, 1985). In the same way, antidepressants perturb and engage central nervous system regulatory mechanisms. For example, imipramine appears directly and indirectly to affect norepinephrine neurons, and tricyclic antidepressants appear to affect serotonin neurons (Whybrow et al, 1984).

The neuroendocrine system apparently is involved in the rhythmic phenomenology of depression. The hypothalamic–pituitary–endocrine system operates as an open-loop control of pituitary function, so that pituitary hormone secretions are driven by the brain in bursts, alternating with periods of decreased secretion. This gives rise to both circadian rhythms of secretion and the possibility of sustained periods of hormonal excesses or deficiencies, as seen in clinical depression (Rubin & Kendler, 1977). Elevated levels of the principal hormone of the adrenal cortex, cortisol, are often observed in chronic stress and clinical depression. Since adrenocortical steroids and their metabolites affect brain function and behavior, an inborn error of metabolism in a steroid pathway might have a bearing upon stress responses. The responsivity to stressors is under genetic control in lower animals and, by implication, also in humans. At the same time, early life experience, as shown by the effects of human handling on rats, plays a critical role as well. In humans high responsivity to stressors has been correlated with reactive depressions (Gray, 1971).

The relationships between *depression* and *bereavement* are important. Bereavement refers to the real or symbolic loss of significant attachment objects and typically results in a complex series of responses, of which two aspects may be distinguished: *grief* and *mourning* (Averill, 1976). Grief, the opposite of joy, is a set of stereotyped physiological and psychological reactions; mourning is a conventional behavioral pattern dictated by the mores and customs of culture. Mourning may be exhibited for social reasons with little or no emotional grief. And conversely, grief may be experienced under conditions for which no mourning practices are prescribed. But grief and mourning often are experienced together.

Grief is a naturally occurring form of depression seen in animals and all human cultures in response to the loss of an attachment object (Averill, 1976; Bowlby, 1980). Distinct in depth and duration from the simple excitation of the distress system in transitory emotional states, it is connected with basic attachment programs whose interruption leaves an enduring vacuum (Amosov, 1967). Grief reactions in rhesus monkeys are ameliorated by the antidepressant imipramine (Suomi et al, 1978). Grief typically evolves in three overlapping stages:

Stage 1: Protest and yearning. The first stage of grief consists of panicky protest over the fact of bereavement and an intense yearning to recover the lost object, and may be accompanied by considerable psychological distress and heightened physiological arousal. Typical of this period are motor hyperactivity; preoccupation with memories of the lost person; imagining the presence of the lost person; focusing attention on those parts of the environment that are associated with the person; calling out for

the lost person, either symbolically or actually; and an urge to search for the lost person.

Stage 2: Disorganization and despair. Eventually the fact of the loss is accepted and attempts to recover the lost object abandoned. This is generally a slow and painful process. Typical symptoms during this stage of grief are apathy and withdrawal or, occasionally, compulsive overactivity. A loss of sexual desire is common, as is an inability to concentrate on routine tasks or to initiate new activities. A variety of somatic complaints also may arise, including anorexia and other gastrointestinal disorders, loss of weight, and sleep disturbances.

Stage 3: Detachment and reorganization. The symptoms of the preceding stage are ultimately relieved when the person becomes detached from the lost object and establishes new relations. This involves a complex process, and its successful completion requires the establishment of new ways of perceiving and thinking about the world and one's place within it. Following such reorganization detachment may be so complete that return of the lost object may be greeted with indifference, or even rejection.

The correct blend of intelligence and emotional bonding in animals is needed to produce a state of grief obvious to an observer. The amygdala appears to play a crucial role in attachment behavior by initiating the fight-or-flight responses when the loss of valued objects is threatened. Amygdalar discharge decreases during relaxed grooming periods, which are expressions of attachment in monkeys (Henry & Ely, 1980).

Furthermore, during the course of evolution, a new reaction was grafted upon the fight-or-flight response in the form of submission to the demands of a dominant animal by inhibiting behavior via depression. In the submissive response, hostile protest is converted into withdrawal, which includes depression. The hippocampus is involved in turning off the fight-or-flight response patterns under circumstances of helplessness when each individual knows one's place in a status hierarchy (Henry & Ely, 1980). The observation that acetylcholine stimulation of the hippocampus produces rage–fear and sometimes depression (Heath, 1964), supports the clinically evident relationship of depression to hostility. Furthermore, depression tends to follow angry responses that have not elicited a rewarding outcome and have a low probability of effective action.

As in the case of anger, depressive responses can be adaptive in a medium range of intensity. Feelings of sadness and discouragement may lead one to consider ways of changing one's situation. More sustained depressive responses are seen when monkeys compete in social situations, and corticosteroid levels remain high in the defeated monkey whereas they decline in the victor. This response appears to have adaptive value, as the chronic stress reaction of the defeated animals leads to withdrawal (Leshner, 1978). Although the pituitary–adrenal cortical response builds up, the depressed animal no longer competes but accepts frustration and loss of control. While depressed, the animal learns submissive behavior rapidly to avoid the lethal consequences of defying dominant members of the same species. By submitting, the animal can remain with the group and gain access to desired means of survival.

Moreover, the state of sadness may elicit heightened interest and sympathy from significant others. For example, a child's depression may alert a parent that the child is in potential danger. Even the state of depression in adults is akin to the helpless crying of infancy (Gaylin, 1968). The loss of external support or the attainability of desired self-concepts produces depression analagous to crying, which originally served as an appeal for help from caregivers.

Depression, therefore, may be a response of survival value to social animals with a high learning capacity. Attachment and yielding behavior have evolutionary adaptive value, because they reduce social conflict and tend to stabilize the control of social hierarchies (Henry & Ely, 1980). For both anger and depression, there appears to be a curvilinear relation between intensity of the emotional response and the effectiveness of behavior in adaptation. At low and moderate intensities, survival probabilities are increased, but at high intensities they are lowered. Still, these long-range purposes underlie the evolutionary process.

Animal and human experiments suggest that learned helplessness from experience with uncontrollable events reduces motivation to respond in new situations even when outcomes are controllable, and impairs the ability to learn in new situations. There are close parallels between the behavioral signs of learned helplessness and the symptoms of depression (Garber et al, 1979). The self-castigation, the unwarranted negative conclusions, and the notions that the future cannot be different all militate against the person's exploration of adaptive problem-solving strategies and the appropriate use of oneself and others as resources. Passivity, reduced motivation, and despair then follow. These negative attitudes not only are related to the onset of the depressive syndrome but play a significant role in its maintenance by casting the depression in negative terms and thereby intensifying the depressive symptoms.

THE ROLE OF THE AFFECTIVE SYSTEM IN INFORMATION PROCESSING. Quoting Selye:

> I cannot, and should not, be cured of my stress but merely taught to enjoy it. (Hans Selye, 1950)

Generating emotional reactions depends upon the relevance of a stimulus pattern and the cues it evokes to the sensorimotor schemes of drives. The immediate assessment of this relevance is performed by the affective system in the form of an emotional response. Negative emotions signify that something is wrong and serve self-preservation. On the other hand, positive emotions signify that ongoing processes are in harmony with one's interests (Simonov, 1975).

The affective system is intimately involved with information processing and has a reciprocal relationship with the neuroendocrine system, which can prime the affective system and extend emotional states through hormonal influences (Leshner, 1977). Research points to the role of cortical, limbic, and reticular systems in the generation of emotions (Powell, 1979). The temporal cortex is associated with aggression control, and the orbital frontal cortex and cingulate gyrus play roles in mood states. Lesions in the limbic system dampen the intensity of behavior and inhibit negative emotional experience.

Selye's classic work on stress provides a framework for understanding the operations of the affective system (1976a). His terms *stressor* and *stress* are comparable to stress and strain in physics. When the balance of internal homeostasis is tipped by a stressor, stress responses of the body are evoked to reestablish homeostasis (Selye, 1980). In Piaget's terminology a stressor calls for the accommodation of sensorimotor schemes. Stress is inherent in living and can be pleasant (eustress) or unpleasant (distress). Although from an individual's standpoint stress is internal and a stressor is external, the situation is not simply one of stressor and respondent. Stressor and stress are parts of a feedback loop in which the individual makes attempts to shape the environment as well as being influenced by it. Individual differences also are critical, so that one person's distress may be another person's eustress (Kutash, 1980).

The inaccurate use of Selye's terminology has led to confusion when stress is used instead of the more precise term, stressor, to describe a stimulus that produces stress responses in the body. It also is important to distinguish between two forms of stress responses: *eustress* and *distress*. The eustress response can be seen as an expression of the pleasure system. The distress responses prepare an organism to face increased demands through a system of regulatory measures that mobilize energy sources and decrease sensitivity to pain via a network of nervous, endocrine, circulatory, and metabolic processes. Distress is a response to the cognitive appraisal of a situation as potentially threatening. The distress responses have evolved for species survival but are not necessarily advantageous for the individual when prolonged (Vigas, 1980). How long they last and their intensity are functions of individual coping skills, self-confidence, adventurousness, an individual's perception, and knowledge of situations and the stressors themselves (Cattell, 1972; Powell, 1979).

In Selye's view stressors produce two types of stress syndromes in the body (Selye, 1976a). The first are nonspecific changes in an organ system called the local adaptation syndrome. A repeated occurrence in normal living, the local adaptation syndrome generates a range of pleasurable and distressing emotions. For example, competitive running may be preceded by anxiety, be fired by aggressiveness, and produce muscular and cardiovascular exhaustion, which is reversible by rest and is followed by euphoria. The second kind of stress reaction is the general adaptation syndrome, which has pathological consequences and will be described later.

To illustrate the complex processes of the affective system, Figure 12-11 was constructed from the ideas of a number of authors (Candland, 1977; Cattell, 1972; Cox, 1978; Gray, 1982; Henry, 1980; Lader & Tyrer, 1975; Leshner, 1977; Mandler, 1975; Plutchik, 1977; Reiser, 1984; &

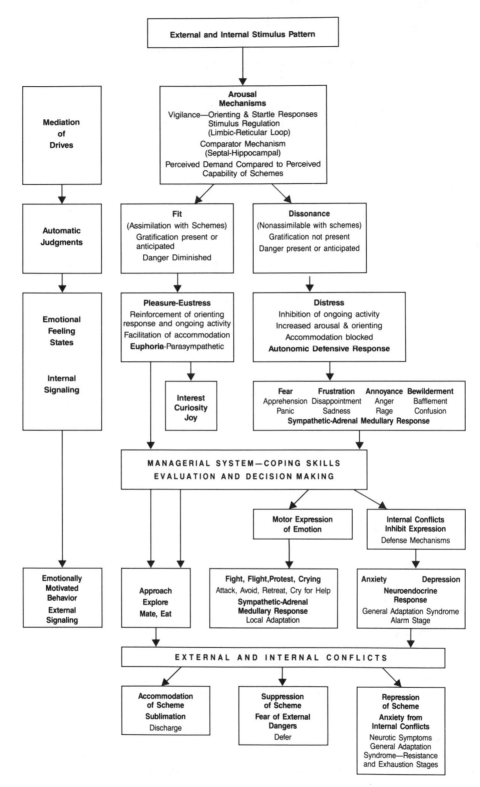

Figure 12-11. Operation of the affective system in the cognition of drive-related stimulus patterns.

Routtenberg, 1968). This model shows the interplay of the information processing and state regulating systems in emotional experience. In this figure a stimulus pattern evokes the affective system because it has relevance to drive sensorimotor schemes. Sudden, intense stimuli cause the startle reflex at the brainstem level. Less intense incoming sensory impulses diverge from the main ascending pathways to the neocortex to innervate the reticular formation via the limbic-reticular arousal loop, which excites and inhibits the cerebral cortex. In general, excitation has a lasting effect whereas inhibition quickly dissipates.

Gray (1982) postulates a comparator mechanism that compares stimulus patterns with expected patterns and determines fit or dissonance. The comparator appears to be in the septal-hippocampal components of the limbic system. If a perceptual pattern matches an expected pattern and can be assimilated by an existing scheme, the comparator continues to function in a monitoring mode, and the process of assimilation takes place. When a perceptual pattern does not match the expectations of a scheme, assimilation cannot take place. As a consequence the comparator shifts into a controlling mode and inhibits ongoing behavior, increases arousal level, and heightens the orienting response to the stimulus source (Eckblad, 1981; Sokolov & Vinogradova, 1975). The orienting response is particularly sensitive to significant details, as in nonverbal communication (Graham, 1979; Lewis, 1972); however, it fades rapidly with repetition of the stimulus pattern. The habituation of the orienting response results when a scheme accommodates to the properties of the stimulus that evokes the orienting reflex, so that the properties of the incoming stimulus are identical to those of the scheme (Pribram, 1979).

The orienting response is influenced by internal stimuli. An external pattern that ordinarily might be ignored elicits the orienting response under certain internal conditions that act as biasers of attention. For example, cenesthetic input from the concentration of glucose influences hunger; of salt, thirst; of serotonin and norepinephrine, sleep; of dopamine, elation and depression; of endorphins, novelty and pain; and of enkephalins, effort and comfort (Pribram, 1981).

In higher animals the control of the comparator system appears to have passed to the orbital frontal cortex, which carries out complex interpretative analyses that are fed back into the limbic system (Gray, 1971). The initial meaning of a stimulus pattern may be analyzed by the hippocampus and the assessment of threat carried out by the amygdala, whose outputs are transmitted along the fornix, the stria terminalis, and the medial forebrain bundle to the medial hypothalamus to call forth either approach or avoidance behaviors. The pleasure–distress system can be seen as operating with the comparator as a first-line mechanism for assigning valences to perceptual patterns; pleasure facilitates ongoing behavior in the monitoring mode, and distress inhibits behavior in the controlling mode.

When the comparator mechanism renders a judgment that a stimulus pattern is familiar and satisfies subjective requirements, pleasure results. In contrast, its judgments of dissonance in the form of novelty and error produce distress (Harris, 1986). Novelty is dissonance between external stimulus patterns and internal schemes. Error is dissonance between motor actions and sensorimotor schemes. On an inverted U-shaped curve of stimulus pattern novelty, pleasure tends to be experienced in the vicinity of the middle-range limit and distress at either extreme (Eckblad, 1981). Distress blocks accommodation until further evaluation of the situation from long-term memory can occur.

Novelty distress may become agorapho-

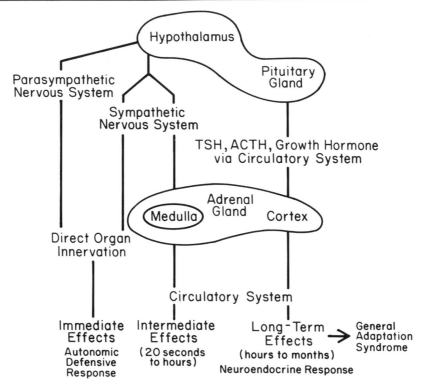

Figure 12-12. The three distress response axes. (Modified from G. S. Everly and R. Rosenfeld, *The Nature and Treatment of the Stress Response,* Plenum Press, New York, 1981.)

bic panic anxiety mediated by the norepinephrine system. When fight-or-flight responses are ineffective or impossible, kindling may occur in which the amygdala and septal nuclei drive the hippocampus to form long-term memories of the traumatic experience. Error distress causes the musculature to oppose actions and may be experienced as varying degrees of claustrophobic muscular tension, perhaps because of insufficient GABA inhibition of dopamine-mediated instinctual strivings (Harris, 1986).

In summary, perception brings the environment into the person in the form of internal representations of the environment. Conversely, actions project a person on to the environment through attempts

to fulfill cravings. To the extent that an attempt appears to be feasible, action follows. To the extent that an attempt appears to be infeasible, the person experiences distress and turns to self-regulatory mechanisms, as a reaction to the uncontrollable or to prepare for another attempt (Pribram, 1977).

Distress is experienced when drive gratification is frustrated or danger perceived. Thus distress results from both the cognitive interpretation of stimuli and emotional arousal. Distress can progress into three major response axes: the autonomic defensive, the sympathetic-adrenal medullary, and the neuroendocrine (see Figure 12-12).

In essence human beings are quite capable of dreaming up dangerous situations and falling short of unrealistic goals. We also can believe ourselves to be unworthy and unloved when there is little objective evidence to support such notions. Our physiological responses to these symbolic situations, however, are no different than when there are objective reasons for fighting or fleeing or when there has been actual loss of an essential nurturing parent (Whybrow et al, 1984).

AUTONOMIC DEFENSIVE RESPONSE. The first distress response has been called the defensive response and involves the sympathetic and parasympathetic branches of the autonomic nervous system. It is the immediate stage of the human fight-or-flight response. Following the complex cortical and limbic integrations that interpret a stimulus pattern as threatening, neural impulses descend to the posterior hypothalamus, where sympathetic activation takes place, and to the anterior hypothalamus, which governs parasympathetic activity. Sympathetic pathways generally excite end organs whereas parasympathetic pathways inhibit them.

There are marked individual differences in responses to perceived dissonance between expectations and a stimulus pattern, so that the same stimulus pattern may evoke an orienting response in one person and the autonomic defensive response in another (Haskins, 1981). The sensory images of the autonomic defensive response in itself are distressing, and these feelings act as signals to one's own decision making apparatus. If the autonomic and motor reactions reflect the tendency to act on the annoying condition so as to reduce or terminate the distress, the individual experiences anger, which indicates that one's interests are threatened and prepares one for action to correct the situation. If the autonomic and motor reactions reflect a tendency to avoid the annoying condition, the individual experiences fear, which in-

hibits approach behaviors in dangerous situations. If the feelings and courses of action are deemed appropriate, the person continues to respond angrily or fearfully. If they are deemed inappropriate, the individual inhibits the motor reactions in question and experiences a reduction of feeling imagery.

Emotional signals also are transmitted to others, who then may respond to the situation. At a medium range of intensity, anger and associated aggressive actions are likely to bring about a result that is desirable to the person and acceptable to others. At high intensity the risk of injury becomes great for the initiator, as well as for others, so that extreme behavior readily can become maladaptive (Hamburg et al, 1975).

SYMPATHETIC–ADRENAL MEDULLARY RESPONSE. In order to maintain high levels of responses to stressors for a longer time, the second major distress axis involves the sympathetic nervous system and adrenal glands in the second stage of the fight-or-flight response, which prepares the body for motor activity in response to a perceived threat (Everly & Rosenfeld, 1981). The net effect of the sympathetic–adrenal medullary response is to mobilize nutrients to skeletal muscles and to increase coagulability of the blood (Henry, 1980; Selye, 1976b).

The dorsomedial amygdala appears to represent the highest point of origin for the fight-or-flight response. From there, impulses pass to the lateral and posterior hypothalamic regions. Neural impulses continue to descend through the sympathetic nervous system via the the thoracic spinal cord, converging at the celiac ganglion, and then innervating acetylcholine-mediated nerve endings in the adrenal medulla, which in turn release both epinephrine and norepinephrine into the blood stream. Whereas epinephrine largely is associated with arousal and fear, nor-epinephrine is associated with active goal-directed behavior and the fight aspect of the fight–flight response (Henry, 1980).

The sympathetic–adrenal medullary effects are functionally identical to the initial autonomic defensive response, except that its activation takes 20–30 seconds and the duration of effect is tenfold longer. Residues of this slowly decaying activation influence subsequent experiential states so that annoyance, for example, may continue from prior situations.

Conflicts that produce distress arise from a variety of internal and external sources (Epstein, 1982). When these conflicts cause fear and one is unable to act, anxiety is experienced. Internal conflicts occur between primary process urges for immediate gratification and secondary-process-based delay, excitatory and inhibitory influences of pleasure and distress, simultaneously experienced drives, competing emotions of differing valences, internal and externally based images, active and passive motor tendencies, and desired and actual self-concepts. Conflicts between external and internal sources arise from environmental dangers, loss of attachment figures, lack of gratification resources, choices between different approach tendencies, choices between different avoidance tendencies, and choices between approach and avoidance.

Fear that leads to action does not result in anxiety. Anxiety is the reflection of the mobilization of the organism for fight or flight without adaptive action. This mobilization activates the neuroendocrine axes with ineffective discharge into the viscera, in contrast with the adaptive discharge of drive satisfaction through the musculature.

NEUROENDOCRINE RESPONSE. Although the effects of the adrenal–medullary catecholamines outlast the effects of the autonomic defensive response, an even more extended distress response is mediated by the neuroendocrine system comprised of the adrenal cortical axis, the somatotropic axis, and the thyroid axis (Everly & Rosenfeld,

1981). This phase assures energy availability during prolonged stressful situations that are not being effectively mastered through action (see Figure 12-13).

The limbic response to a stressor is among the most potent and prevalent sources of increased pituitary secretion so that the neuroendocrine distress response is determined by emotionally based judgments of the significance of stressors (Henry, 1980). The hippocampus, which is the highest point of origin of the pituitary–adrenal–cortical axis, and the amygdala play complementary roles in the neuroendocrine distress response (Henry, 1980). From the septal–hippocampal complex, neural impulses descend to the median eminence of the hypothalamus. The neurosecretory cells there release corticotropin-releasing factor, which descends to the anterior pituitary gland, which releases adrenocorticotropic hormone, which, in turn, stimulates the adrenal cortex to secrete the corticosteroid hormones cortisol and corticosterone, into the bloodstream—doubling their blood levels in 15 minutes and tripling them in one hour. The adrenocorticoid hormones increase glucose production and relase fatty acids into the bloodstream. Thus the adrenal–cortical axis can rapidly supplement adrenal–medullary catecholamine release with corticosteroid hormones. The response of peripheral cells in the body to corticosteroids, however, may take from several hours to a day or so.

The somatotropic axis appears to share the same basic mechanisms as the adrenal–cortical axis from the septal–hippocampal complex to the anterior pituitary, except that the somatotropin-releasing factor passes from the hypothalamus to stimulate the anterior pituitary to release growth hormone, which in turn causes the adrenal cortex to release mineralocorticoids, which also increase the levels of glucose and fatty acids in the blood (Everly & Rosenfeld, 1981).

The thyroid axis also shares the sep-

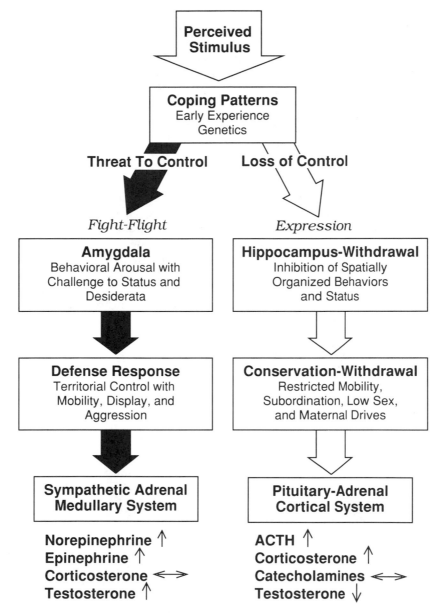

Figure 12-13. Depending on an individual's coping abilities, a stimulus is perceived either as a threat to control with ensuing arousal of the fight-flight defense response or as loss of control with conservation, withdrawal, and depression. The ensuing hormonal patterns emphasize the catecholamines in the fight-flight state and the corticoids in the helpless-depressed state. (Reprinted by permission of the publisher from "Present Concept of Stress Theory," by J. P. Henry in *Catecholamine and Stress,* edited by E. Usdin, R. Kvetnansky, and I. J. Kopin. Copyright 1980 by Elsevier Science Publishing Co., Inc.)

tal–hippocampal complex and median eminence of the hypothalamus, however, thyrotropin-releasing factor is sent to the anterior pituitary, where it stimulates the release of thyroid stimulating hormone, which in turn causes the thyroid to release thyroxine. This increases the general metabolic rate, heart rate, blood pressure, and sensitivity of tissues to catcholamines.

The general adaptation syndrome appears to be an extension of the neuroendocrine axis response. It is activated by persistent stressors and produces a specific effect on the adrenal glands, thymus, and stomach. The fully developed general adaptation syndrome consists of three stages: an alarm reaction, a stage of resistance, and an ultimate stage of exhaustion.

During the alarm phase of the syndrome, the three endocrine axes are activated. If a frustrating barrier results in anger without action and consequent helplessness, the physiological changes follow the neuroendocrine response pattern with behavioral withdrawal and decreased motor activity, and the stage is set for depression. This withdrawal is accompanied by increased cortisol output, decreased brain biogenic amine levels, and depressive symptoms.

The next phase is the stage of resistance, during which there is a dramatic reduction in most alarm-phase processes as the body attempts to maintain homeostasis. Anxiety based upon the tenuous ability to control the internal situation is repressed. The subsequent anxiety state may be handled through defenses, or repression with the formation of neurotic symptoms, which in turn produce another level of problems, such as conversion symptoms, psychophysiological reactions, and depression (Cattell, 1972).

Most stressors act for a limited time and produce changes corresponding to the first and second stages of Selye's syndrome. Under prolonged stress, however, there is a third stage of exhaustion with a massive shutdown of bodily activities directed toward growth, reproduction, and resistance to infection in favor of the return of alarm mechanisms, which promote readiness for high-energy action and paradoxically undermine health. The sustained effects of elevated cortisol levels may be gastric ulceration, inhibition of immune responses, hypertension, atherosclerosis, sterility, and personality changes. At this stage the survival of the organism is imperiled (Everly & Rosenfeld, 1981).

In more general terms the development, onset, and course of a range of illnesses may be affected by central nervous system and neuroendocrine modulation of the immune system in response to stressors (Stein & Schleifer, 1985). Thus the brain's regulation of the immune system plays a key role in the onset and course of disease.

Development of the Affective System

All of the adult emotions emerge from the generalized pleasure and distress states of infancy as they are modified by maturation of the brain and learning (Engel, 1963). There is a developmental line for the differentiation of emotions, as outlined in Figure 12-14, as an important dimension of character development (Brenner, 1982).

The initial level of emotional expression in infancy is through either contentment or panicky crying with an intermediate distress state. These expressions support homeostasis of the body during early life. Pleasurable contentment reflects a homeostatic internal state, and the distress of crying indicates impending or actual disruption of homeostasis. The two basic modes of waking infantile behavior are the feeding cycle and the frustration reaction (Stanley-Jones, 1970). The feeding cycle is a rhythm of about four hours mediated by the parasympathetic system, which mobilizes the gastrointestinal tract and is com-

AGE	PLEASURABLE (Positive Feedback)	DISTRESSING (Negative Feedback)
Neonatal	Contentment	Distresss, crying (panic)
3 months	Smiling, euphoria, interest, surprise, delight	Anger, pain, crying (hunger, anger, pain, attention, panic, weeping)
8 months	Amusement, joy, laughter	Stranger fearfulness
12 months	Affection, elation	Loneliness, separation anxiety, disappointment
24 months	Thrill, curiosity	Grief, disgust, shyness, helplessness, sadness, mortification
4 years	Lust, greed, sympathy, joy	Envy, jealousy, hate, guilt
6 years	Awe, pride, hope	Boredom, despair, discouragement, hopelessness, rivalry, contempt
11 years	Ambition, humility, empathy, tenderness	Confusion, misery

Figure 12-14. The developmental line of emotions.

pleted by oral sucking. The frustration reaction to unfulfilled expectanies is a sympathetic discharge.

The first level of distress emotions can be seen in the various forms of crying in infancy. During the stage in which there is little differentiation between one's body and other objects, the experience of distress can be described as undifferentiated pain-anxiety. During the middle of the first year, as the infant distinguishes between the infant's own body and a parent, the primitive pain-anxiety becomes differentiated into pain in relation to one's body and anxiety in relation to other persons (Szasz, 1957). Still pain or anxiety express an accusation directed toward a significant person as a demand for help. Thus both pain and anxiety in early life are appeals for intervention and serve an interpersonal communicative purpose. Distinctive pat-

terns of crying take place as expressions of hunger, rage, pain, attention seeking, and panic occasioned by disappearance of attachment figures (Wolff, 1969). They all reflect degrees of a general state of irritability and breakdown in homeostasis. As an external signal, crying invites the parent to respond to the rhythmic needs of the infant and restore homeostasis. Tearing itself may be a concomitant of crying originally designed to moisten the mucous membranes, which are likely to dry out during crying, and to provide antimicrobial lysozyme.

A second level of emotional expression is added to the crying–contentment continuum in the form of smiling. Early internally generated smiling occurs reflexly and apparently is a manifestation of rhythms during the REM state. Smiling undergoes a major shift between two and three months of age, from a solely internally to an externally generated response reflecting exploratory tendencies. Smiling then takes place in response to stimuli, such as the human face, and assumes a social character related to emotional state (Emde et al, 1976). Smiling thus signifies an infant's active tuning in to the parent.

The anlage for pleasurable responses can be seen in the various forms of smiling in infancy. The basic emotions of euphoria and joy are associated with smiling states and signify the efficient functioning of the central nervous system. Later they are expressed in laughter related to personal and social actions (Freedman et al, 1967).

The earliest and simplest type of pleasure results from the satisfaction of a drive. The next level is reached in the process of development, when a link is established between drive satisfaction and human relationships. The ambiguous word love is used to describe this type of pleasure. The next level is when materials that fulfill drives and love are endowed with pleasure. Thus additions to our bodies or selves are experienced as pleasurable. The most advanced level of pleasure is an expression of satisfying human relationships. Whereas pain is a command for action, pleasure in the form of contentment or happiness calls for no action and, in fact, is a wish for no change in an existing situation (Szasz, 1957).

Initially limited to primary expressions, emotions are refined in the course of development. The nonspecific, undirected total emotional responses of early infancy become progressively integrated with facial and behavioral expressions, which serve to communicate pleasure or distress to the outside world and ultimately are experienced as identifiable feeling states (Spitz, 1963). As young as three months, infants show evidence of interest, joy, surprise, sadness, anger, distress, panic, and pain (Malatesta, 1982).

A third level of emotional development is the appearance of stranger fearfulness, marking the development of a fear system between seven and nine months of age. Before this time distress is associated with physical discomfort such as pain, changes in body temperature, uncomfortable positions, and hunger. Now distress occurs in response to specific patterned environmental stimuli. In experimental animals this seems to be a fear of threats to the integrity of the body surface (Panksepp, 1981). It appears in infants as the body image forms and has two prominent phases. The first response is looking for several seconds; the second phase is overt distress expressed in a facial expression of fear. There also is anticipatory cardiac acceleration as a manifestation of a major organismic shift toward a full-scale emotion with internal and external meaning. Stranger fearfulness portends action by the infant in the form of withdrawal or avoidance (Emde et al, 1976). At this stage the attachment bond of the infant is specific, so that both infant and parent are tuned in to each other.

Once speech is established, emotions no longer are the only means of communicating needs, as verbal communication adds a more refined mode (Shapiro, 1965). Children learn to interpret and evaluate their emotional imagery through verbal labels provided by caregivers and through the nonverbal behaviors of others (Lewis & Michalson, 1983). The subjective experience of emotions progresses from an infant's preverbal awareness of bodily sensations and movements to verbalized individual emotions and lastly to blends of emotions (Lane & Swartz, 1987). Unlike the language used to describe events in the external world, the language of emotions is tied to bodily processes, which are subtle and elusive, and so are seldom verbalized, except under special circumstances. Children are able to talk of these images, but there may be little encouragement from adults for them to do so (Lewis et al, 1971).

Just as genetically determined responsivity to stressors influences a child's reaction to stressful situations, there is evidence from animal research that early life experience can have an enduring effect on the nature of distress responses. Furthermore, variations in early life of steroid hormones can have lasting effects upon behavior (Hamburg et al, 1975). Infants whose distress responses are in either a fight or flight mode with increased cortisol excretion may be predisposed to anxiety; those who respond in a drowsy, withdrawal mode with decreased cortisol excretion may be predisposed to depression (Emde et al, 1986).

SUMMARY

As the output of the state regulating system and a determinant of character, temperament refers to one's disposition to interact with the environment. The dimensions of one's temperament are reflected in attention, movement levels, and instinctually motivated behavior.

The involuntary attentional processes are vigilance; the orienting, defensive and startle responses; and stimulus regulation. Voluntary attention occurs in the form of scanning, focusing, and concentration.

The deployment of attention depends upon motivation, which can be understood in terms of electrochemical energy derived from the external world, the internal organ systems, and the reticular activating system. Motivation arises from appetitive and adaptive instinctual structures modulated by the processes of the affective system.

Current evidence permits the delineation of instinctually programmed appetites and emotions with greater precision than has been possible in the past. Our understanding of instinctual sensorimotor schemes, the hypothalamic–neuroendocrine axis, and the limbic system provides a neuroanatomical basis, and our knowledge of specific neurotransmitters provides a neurophysiological basis, for conceptualizing these phenomena.

Human instincts are genetically determined cyclic tendencies toward behavior that serve individual and species preservation purposes. They are incompletely formed and generally require environmental releasers and are shaped by learning. Their sources lie in organ systems of the body, their energy is channeled through drives reflected in wishful imagery, their expression is through the goal-directed action patterns of aims, and their satisfaction lies in environmental targets.

The appetitive instinctual systems arise from stimuli from internal organs, which activate receptors in the hypothalamic–autonomic–endocrine axis and are consciously experienced as bodily cravings. The appetitive instincts are rest, alimentation, elimination, sexuality, motor activity, and fight–flight.

The adaptive instinctual systems are based in the limbic and extrapyramidal systems and interplay with the appetitive instincts so as to facilitate self and species survival in group living. The adaptive instinctual systems are affiliative, aggressive, mastery, and self-esteem regulation.

In addition to reflecting internal states of excitation, the affective system primes the individual for action through mediating drive motivations, making automatic value judgments, signaling one's internal state to oneself, and communicating it to others. Emotions consist of neural programs of patterns of motor and autonomic discharges, consciously experienced imagery, and motivations.

As the general responsive apparatus of the affective system, the pleasure–distress system operates as an analog amplifier of appetitive and adaptive drives and endows sensory input with positive and negative valences in the service of defense and adaptation. Pain, anxiety, and depression are prominent forms of distress beyond the level of aversive hyperarousal.

Emotions are generated by the qualities of stimulus patterns and evoked cues that relate them to the sensorimotor schemes of drives. The pleasurable emotions lead to approach behaviors, and distress leads to defensive behaviors, which are mediated through the autonomic defensive, the sympathetic–adrenal medullary, and the neuroendocrine responses. Stressful situations may be mastered through the local adaptation syndrome or pose chronic problems through the general adaptation syndrome.

The sensorimotor schemes of instincts impose a primitive organization on an infant's experience and discharge of drive tensions. The affective system follows a developmental progression from primitive diffuse pleasure and distress to increasingly sophisticated emotional states. Emotional development is an important dimension in the formation of character.

During the course of development, arousal, appetitive, adaptive, and affective patterns uniquely characterize an individual's temperament as reflected in attention, movement level, and motivation. Without the capacity for concentration, and without motivation derived from cravings and emotions, children cannot learn in school.

CHAPTER

13

Cognition

Like ourselves . . . they see only their own shadows, or the
shadows of another, which the fire throws on the opposite
wall of the cave.

Plato, The Republic

Although appearing precise, cognition really is an ambiguous term. Its definitions range from sensory perception to thinking and view it as both information processing and a skill.

The word cognition is derived from the Greek root "to know." For Piaget it was "knowing." Modern philosophy regards cognition as the ability to provide the right answers to questions rather than as an entity in itself (White, 1982). The model of the central nervous system described in Chapter 11 helps to clarify the meaning of cognition. As the output of the information-processing system, cognition is "knowing" something and is a major function of the central nervous system (CNS). Cognition, then, can be seen as "knowing," and the use of what one knows can be seen as a function of the managerial system.

From the point of view of evolution, cognition developed as a means of predicting events by making internal models of the environment. To adapt to a dangerous environment successfully, an organism had to be able to recognize things and communications; to store some of this information in memory; to retrieve stored

information when necessary; and to use the retrieved information as a basis for actions (Plutchik, 1977). In humans the evolution of memory and symbol formation led to the capacity to name objects. The appearance of the ability to construct abstract concepts meant escape from living solely in the present, especially when organized around language, which can succinctly embody information and its meanings (Hamilton, 1983).

The work of psychologists on cognition has followed experimental, developmental, social, psychological, and anthropological lines. The experimental tradition has focused on such phenomena as memory, concept formation, and cognitive styles (Santostefano, 1978). The developmental perspective has studied the unfolding of children's successive views of the world from frameworks such as Piaget's developmental stages. Social, psychological, and cross-cultural studies have focused on attitudes (Glick, 1975; Scott et al, 1979). Currently information-processing theories and computer models of cognition are receiving special attention (Guilford, 1982; Norman, 1981).

Cognition is the output of the information processing and storage system within which sensory inflow from the external and internal worlds goes through many stages of selection, appraisal, and interpretation before influencing behavior. All but the most preliminary of these stages require that, in order to be assimilated, sensory inflow must be related to information already stored in long-term memory. Thus, the preparatory set of the brain determines the selection of incoming information (Evarts et al, 1984). Unlike a computer, the brain does not store information in a neutral fashion (de Bono, 1968). Instead schemes form and use patterns of information. These patterns of information determine the types of new information that can enter the brain so that there is no such thing as neutral, objective information in the mind. For example, the word "textile" spoken to a group means a shirt, dress, factory, or international competition to different people. Abstracting a relatively neutral concept of "textile" requires deliberate effort, and it is never completely objective.

The highly varied ways in which individuals respond to the same stimuli is reflected in their responses to the ambiguous Rorschach and Thematic Apperception tests. Yet each of us believes that we sense objects and events in the world precisely. Even more deceptively, we perceive an everyday world of color, hardness, and "reality" rather than the underworld of atoms and quantum mechanics. Thus our brains construct knowledge of the world that is useful for personal survival purposes but really is at variance with the realities of physics (Gregory, 1981).

Our sensory nerves are uniquely adapted to sample the energy states of the world about us. Heat, light, force, and chemical stimuli are transduced at the peripheral nerve endings, and coded replicas of them are dispatched to the grey mantle of the cerebral cortex. These sensory nerves are not high-fidelity recorders, however, for they accentuate certain stimulus features and neglect others. We perceive what we are set to perceive. The transmission of information is not direct but via synaptic relays, which act to modify messages so that the brain receives adjusted images of peripheral stimuli. Even the simplest stimulus, such as a flash of light or a tap on the skin, is signaled to the primary receiving areas of the cerebral cortex in the form of coded nerve impulses in various temporal sequences transmitted by many parallel fibers. The neurons are never completely trustworthy, however, because they allow distortions of relations between the external and internal world.

Sensory information is used to form personally significant maps of the external world and of our place within them (Mountcastle, 1975). Fortunately, human sensory perceptions are similar enough that they can be communicated between persons by verbal descriptions. Beyond that, however, each perception is influenced by internal information that makes each of us uniquely private. Stimuli that evoke emotional responses and imagery are particularly susceptible to personalized and distorted interpretation. Each of us constructs from within a highly personal view of the external world.

There appear to be three basic processes in the information processing system. The first is encoding information through the process of assimilation in the anatomical sensory systems themselves, including the sense organs and their internal connections. The second level is figurative accommodation from the primary sensory cortical areas, the associational cortical areas, and the limbic system to the diencephalic seat of conscious perception and imagery. The third level is between the hippocampus and the medial cortical areas, in which operative accommodation to information takes place as a function of sensorimotor schemes that are the repositories of knowledge. Assimilation, figurative accommodation, and operative accommodation are key processes that will be described more fully in Chapter 17.

The human mind is a large repository for storing everything a person "knows," such as experiences, facts, beliefs, skills, feelings, and concepts, coupled with a limited-capacity "working space," which allows the person to reflect upon a few things at a time. The core structures that enable cognition, then, are short-term memory, which determines what we can operate upon at any given point in time, and long-term memory, in which lie the mechanisms for storing, organizing, transforming, and retrieving information (Calfee, 1983).

Memory is not an anatomically discrete subsystem in itself. It involves several stages of information storage: precategorical, short term, intermediate, and long term. Influencing the type and amount of material that is processed at each stage of memory is the degree to which attention is deployed to one aspect or another of a given array of stimuli. While stimulus features are synthesized into an initial literal copy, or icon, without it, focused attention determines the fate of the sensory image in short-term as well as long-term memory. Reciprocally, short-term and long-term memory influence focused attention. Thus the conscious mind plays a key, but not indispensable, role in memory.

Long-term memory is the ability to so understand and encode information that it can be brought out later under conditions quite different from those in which it was originally introduced (Gardner, 1976). Piaget viewed long-term memory as conservation of a scheme, and, therefore, as part of the operations of schemes. The evidence suggests that memories are patterns of electrical activity embedded in schemes throughout the brain (Bennett, 1977). Patterns of activation come and go, but they leave behind changes in the strengths of interconnections among the basic processing elements rather than copies of the patterns (McClelland, 1985). Learning amounts

to making changes in the strengths of these interconnections. The retrieval of a memory trace amounts to reinstatement of a prior activation pattern of interconnections. Recognition is reinstatement of the context of an ongoing activation pattern.

The search for evidence that memory takes place through permanent modification in neural tissue has been troublesome. Elsewhere in the body, when a structure changes, there is growth of tissue. But in the brain the evidence is that the number of neurons does not increase after an initial period subsequent to birth. Thus learning apparently occurs in the absence of increases in neuron population. Although the neuroglia, the supporting elements of neural tissue, can increase in number over the lifetime of an individual, the most plausible explanation of memory is through modification in chemical processes and nerve fiber growth. We know that experientially initiated and guided growth of new nerve fibers alters the spatial patterns of junctional relationships among neurons. Long-term memory, therefore, probably is a function of junctional structures (Pribram, 1977). The growing evidence is that synaptic molecular mechanisms are involved in memory, such as a calcium proteinase-receptor process (Lynch & Baudry, 1984) and encoding of neurotransmitters (Black et al, 1987).

Fortunately progress has been made in developing a general systems model of information processing that breaks information processing down into manageable stages (Guilford, 1982; Johnson & Mykelbust, 1967; Killen, 1975). This model is illustrated in Figure 13-1, in which cognition is defined as the output of the information processing and storage system, which has the following components: (1) reception, (2) perception, (3) imaging, (4) imagination, and (5) knowledge. In this model the output of the information processing system is cognition in the form of recognition, comprehension, and knowledge. The

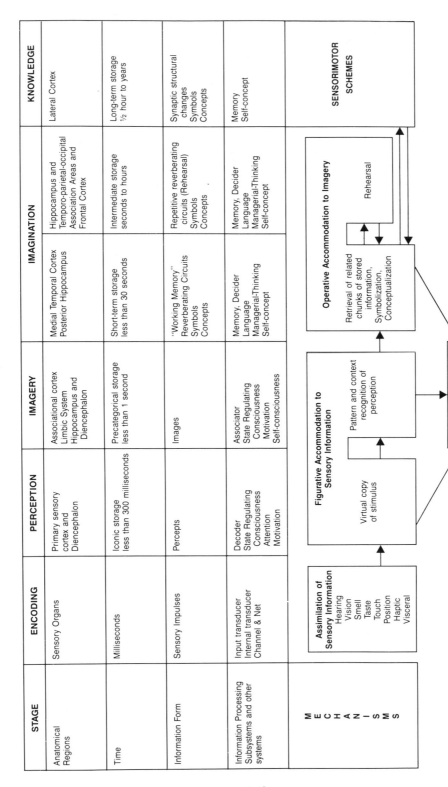

STAGE	ENCODING	PERCEPTION	IMAGERY	IMAGINATION		KNOWLEDGE
Anatomical Regions	Sensory Organs	Primary sensory cortex and Diencephalon	Associational cortex Limbic System Hippocampus and Diencephalon	Medial Temporal Cortex Posterior Hippocampus	Hippocampus and Temporo-parietal-occipital Association Areas and Frontal Cortex	Lateral Cortex
Time	Milliseconds	Iconic storage less than 300 milliseconds	Precategorical storage less than 1 second	Short-term storage less than 30 seconds	Intermediate storage seconds to hours	Long-term storage ½ hour to years
Information Form	Sensory Impulses	Percepts	Images	"Working Memory" Reverberating Circuits Symbols Concepts	Repetitive reverberating circuits (Rehearsal) Symbols Concepts	Synaptic structural changes Symbols Concepts
Information Processing Subsystems and other systems	Input transducer Internal transducer Channel & Net	Decoder State Regulating Consciousness Attention Motivation	Associator State Regulating Consciousness Motivation Self-consciousness	Memory, Decider Language Managerial-Thinking Self-concept	Memory, Decider Language Managerial-Thinking Self-concept	Memory Self-concept

MECHANISMS

Assimilation of Sensory Information
Hearing
Vision
Smell
Taste
Touch
Position
Haptic
Visceral

Figurative Accommodation to Sensory Information
Virtual copy of stimulus
Pattern and context recognition of perception

Operative Accommodation to Imagery
Retrieval of related chunks of stored information, Symbolization, Conceptualization
Rehearsal

SENSORIMOTOR SCHEMES

LOST

Figure 13-1. Model of cognition of drive-unrelated stimulus patterns.

240

chapter concludes with several examples of extensively described cognitive styles, which contribute to the output of the CNS in the form of personality traits.

RECEPTION

Reception is the component of the information processing system that translates sensory information received by the organ input transducers of vision, hearing, touch, smell, taste, position sense, and visceral sensations into signals that can be processed within the CNS. The receptive encoding of the sensory organ systems extends through the input transducer and channel and net structures. Receptive encoding is an aspect of Piaget's process of assimilation in which sensory input is transformed into forms that correspond to existing schemes.

The actual transmission of impulses occurs through chunking bits of information into one. When the frontal cortical system becomes involved in the orienting reaction, information being simultaneously processed is chunked into discrete units. Then as the posterior cortex becomes involved in the attentional process, bits of information in chunks are separated from each other, enhancing the ability to make discriminations between forms of sensory input (Pribram, 1977).

PERCEPTION

The second component of the information processing system is perception at the decoder level. A percept is the immediate momentary sensory registration of an external or internal stimulus. Perception is a form of memory. As an outwardly directed process that induces change in the CNS,

perception is an aspect of figurative accommodation in Piaget's terminology. To become conscious, a percept probably is mirrored by a centrencephalic feedback mechanism that produces conscious awareness of it (Tomkins, 1962; Penfield, 1975).

Iconic storage is a function of the decoder system that facilitates retention of a percept for about 300 milliseconds. This is the range of perception involved in fluent reading in which the life of word percepts is estimated to be approximately 250 milliseconds, the average duration of fixations between saccadic eye movements. We do not see an entire visual field in a single glance. An integrated perception of a continuous world must be constructed out of many glances. All that we know about the visual world around us is constructed in icons of about ¼ second in duration (Haber, 1971).

Iconic storage is a hypothetical preconscious capacity that detects, registers, and transiently holds very large amounts of information as literal copies of the sensory stimuli. Thus all or most of the properties of the stimulus remain available briefly in iconic storage even though the stimulus itself is not physically present. Brain-stem reflexes to sensory stimuli, such as the eye-blink response, occur during this stage (Anthony & Graham, 1983). Information not transferred further in perception before the icon decompensates is lost (Saccuzo & Braff, 1981).

The familiar patterns stored in memory serve as templates so that signals that fit them are facilitated whereas those that do not are regarded as noise and inhibited. For example, after the surgical removal of lens cataracts, congenitally blind persons require the sense of touch to confirm their unfamiliar visual perceptions (Horowitz, 1983).

Although based upon reflexes at subcortical levels, the ability to localize tactile stimuli as in two-point discrimination and to identify designs drawn on the skin depends upon tactile discriminatory sensation at the cortical level. Both tactile and proprioceptive sensations must be analyzed at the cortical level in order to recognize objects by touch without vision; this integrative capacity is referred too as the haptic sense.

Imitation, perception, and imagery are three different instruments of Piaget's figurative accommodation. Imitation is the figurative mimicry of an ongoing external event in motor activity. A perception is the figurative mimicry of an ongoing external event in sensory activity. An image is an internal mental representation of a past external or internal event. In contrast, operative accommodation uses percepts to create personalized knowledge and involves later levels of information processing. In reading, figurative accommodation is perception of the pages of the book. Operative accommodation is deriving the meanings of the words on a page (Furth, 1981).

The perceptual apparatus abstracts color, size, and position from images, in addition to determining the shapes perceived. For example, color is perceived as a property of matter and not of the light that illuminates it. Similar manipulations enable maintaining the apparent size of approaching or receding objects. A tennis ball, for example, creates an objectively larger retinal image from a distance of two than from six feet. As the ball draws nearer, focusing both eyes on it entails an increase in the curvature of the lenses and a convergence of the two eyes' axes. Informed by those muscle responses that the tennis ball is moving, the brain manufactures a phantom copy which shrinks in proportion to the proximity of the actual ball to maintain the constant size of the ball. We perceive a mental synthesis not the myriad bits of sensory data absorbed by individual sensory receptors, as further illustrated by the perception of a tree from a simple sketch.

IMAGING

The significance of imagery in processing information, learning, thinking, motivation, emotion, and human behavior has been well established (Jacobson, 1967; Sheikh, 1983).

Imaging is not a single ability but a complex component of information processing. Images depict information, and images of objects can be mentally manipulated, much like the corresponding actual objects. Images share some of the brain mechanisms used in perceiving in the same modality, and hence can interfere with perception. Images occur on a "mental screen" that has a grain that obscures details if they are too small and also has a limited size capacity. Images can be used in a number of ways—from improving one's memory to reasoning (Kosslyn, 1985).

Imagery is the neural pattern that represents sensory experience in the absence of the stimulus. It has properties of a hologram and takes place at the interface between perception and memory through the interaction of cortical sensory units (Pribram, 1977). Conscious imagery is experienced when the neural imagery pattern plays upon the centrencephalic mechanism of consciousness. Images are vehicles for operative accommodation through which schemes change by forming symbols and concepts. Piaget proposed that memory consists of schemes and that images are tools that schemes employ to aid thinking. He held that children imitate aspects of the environment or anticipate the consequences of their actions by utilizing images (Piaget & Inhelder, 1973).

Contemporary research indicates that there is a general capacity to image in all sensory modalities with individual differences in vividness and modality preference (Sheehan et al, 1983). Some people appear to have little vivid imagery. However, some

4 percent of the adult population have exceedingly vivid imagery so that they fully experience their imagery in seeing, hearing, smelling, and touching. They also are easily hypnotized (Wilson & Barber, 1983).

The Mechanisms of Imaging

The verb imaging more appropriately describes the formation of images than does the noun imagery (Bugelski, 1971). The mechanisms of imaging are unclear and probably manifold with conscious, preconscious, and unconscious elements (Block, 1981; Corballis, 1982). We can say that imaging occurs in the associator and memory structures of the CNS and that the retrieval of memories results in images, such as through revisualizing or reauditorizing images of past perceptions. An example is the sensory experience evoked by thinking of one's home with its sights, sounds, and smells. Thinking in words is an example of verbal imaging. Sensory imagery also can be evoked by electrical stimulation of the brain.

Imaging occurs in immediate or precategorical memory between iconic and short-term storage (Vellutino, 1979). Precategorical storage is believed to take place in less than one second and can be reflected in conscious images so that one may be able to repeat a telephone number or reproduce a novel design without more lasting memories of them. In Piaget's terminology imaging corresponds to figurative accommodation during precategorical storage.

Pattern and context recognition take place when precategorical images are compared with stored memories. If a pattern is unique, it may be stored. If it duplicates previous experience, the stored data may be intensified. Precategorical storage also is the stage in which automatized thinking is triggered, such as in driving a car or facile reading. Words even may be processed

at this level without meaning, as in hyperlexia. Precategorical memory is thought to be a function of the hippocampus of the limbic system as it processes information from the sensory cortical association areas.

Imagery is regarded commonly as subjective and perception as objective. Early in this century, however, Hughlings Jackson held that both imagery and perception really were two degrees of objectivity involving the same cerebral centers (Evarts, 1962; Segal, 1971; Taylor, 1932). The most recent evidence portrays imagery and perception as complementary, reflecting the activity of overlapping neuronal networks (Marks, 1983). For example, imagery is associated with the same sensory and motor responses as the perception of stimuli (Davidson et al, 1983). Thus images are mental representations with the sensory qualities of seeing, hearing, smell, taste, touch, and movement. Moreover, they are constructions of both perceptions and memories (Horowitz, 1983).

There are four basic differences between percepts and images. First is the vividness of percepts and the faintness of images. In perception there is strong cerebral activity, whereas in imagery cerebral activity is slight. As conscious vividness of an image increases, the electroencephalogram shows greater activation (Horowitz, 1983). For example, when one sees a brick, the image of a square, red thing is part of one's consciousness. In thinking of a brick, there is a fainter but still similar conscious image of a brick as perceived visually. Second, perceptions are experienced as taking place in the particular sensory organ involved, whereas, unless intense, images tend to be experienced as taking place in the head. Third, perception is activated only by external or internal sensory stimuli, whereas imagery may be activated by sensory percepts, the memory system, or both. Fourth, imagery is derived from a continuous stream of formerly acquired memo-

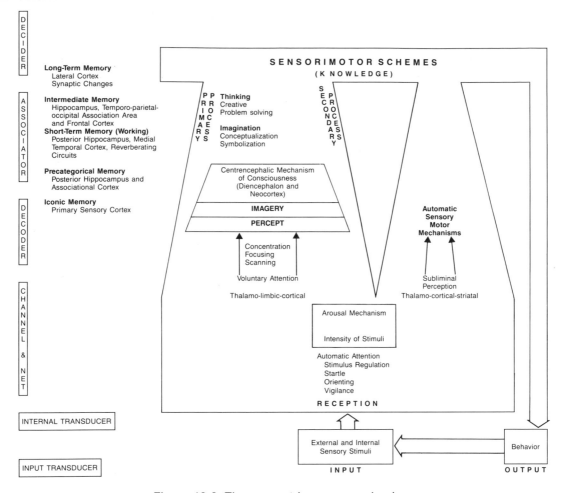

Figure 13-2. The percept-imagery mechanism.

ries, whereas percepts are restricted to episodes of current stimulation (Richardson, 1983; Taylor, 1932).

The mechanisms of imaging involve the integration of attentional, information processing, consciousness, and memory functions. Thus imaging reflects the interaction of the state regulating and information processing systems. The evidence suggests that conscious imagery is the result of the excitation of an apparatus of consciousness by ongoing neural events rather than of a searching scanner that illuminates conscious awareness of neural discharges. This apparatus of conscious imagery appears to involve the midbrain reticular activating system and the thalamus.

Drawing upon the work of Horowitz (1983), I developed a model of the percept-imagery mechanisms as illustrated in Figure 13-2. In this model sensory stimuli from external and internal sources enter the process of reception under the influence of conscious attention in the form of the automatic mechanisms of vigilance, the orienting response, the startle response, and stimulus regulation. Then depending upon the intensity of the stimuli and the level of arousal of the reticular activating system, perception may proceed to conscious awareness of a percept through cortico-limbo-thalamic circuits or proceed directly to automatic action without conscious awareness through thalmo-cortico-striatal circuits (Mishkin et al, 1984).

The act of becoming conscious of perceptions and images transforms impulses into another form at the interface of the information processing system and the state regulating system. This process of conscious awareness seems to facilitate entry into long-term storage (Penfield, 1975). Conscious awareness thus has multiple determinants related to the success or failure of intentional behavior and motivational factors. It is invoked particularly when automatic mechanisms operating outside of conscious awareness are ineffective (Piaget, 1976).

Conscious awareness takes place through the attention mechanisms of scanning, focusing, and concentration. When these occur during the stage of iconic memory, a copy of the stimulus is consciously experienced as a percept. When the stimulus has left the field or attention is diverted or excluded from it, imagery may be experienced automatically as an afterimage, involuntarily as in a daydream, or voluntarily as in the deliberate use of one's imagination. Imaging thus is influenced by perception and sensorimotor schemes through imagination, which takes place in both primary and secondary process modalities.

From the point of view of the temporal sequences of brain events, percepts are a function of iconic memory of less than 300 milliseconds, imaging of precategorical storage of less than one second, imagination of short-term and intermediate storage of from seconds to hours, and thinking of short-term to long-term storage of seconds to indefinite periods.

The evidence suggests that the mechanism of consciousness is a percept-im-agery system, which in the model depicted in Figure 13-2 is a series of matrices upon which percepts and images are displayed. Unless these matrices are activated, no percept or image appears in conscious experience. In this model, then, there are no percepts or images outside of consciousness, only the reverberating electrochemical circuits of schemes. Furthermore, the most vivid representation is a percept that occurs in the presence of the stimulus during iconic storage. The least vivid representation is the faintest image of an internal reverberating circuit. These matrices may be dominated by internal imagery when external sensory percepts are minimal or when the intensity of scheme activity is high. Under situations of high sensory stimulus input or low stimulus input regulation, the matrices may be dominated by sensory percepts to the exclusion of imagery.

In this model the central percept-image apparatus shows varying preferential receptivity to perception or to internal image formation. Both external and internal sources provide contents to this apparatus. Percepts thus influence image formation, and internal images influence percepts. When one is faint, the other tends to dominate. As a person becomes less wakeful or is not engaged in a task, images occur more frequently, attain greater vividness, and escape the limitations of internal censorship. The contents of images then tend to be derived more from inner sources and less from external sensory stimuli. Consequently they follow progressively more primitive styles and tend to be controlled by wishes or emotions more than by external reality (Horowitz, 1983). Developmentally, imagery is an earlier organizer of meaning than is language, which builds on a substrate of imagery (Paivio, 1971). For example, the abstract noun nation has no perceptual grounding but evokes imagery.

This distinction between percepts and images provides a theoretical basis for un-

Image Vividness
1. Hallucinations
2. Pseudohallucinations
3. Imagination images

Image Context
1. Hypnagogic or hypnopompic images
2. Dream images
3. Psychedelic images
4. Flashbacks
5. Flickering images

Image Interaction with External Percept
1. Illusions
2. Perceptual distortions
3. Deja vu
4. Derealization and depersonalization
5. Negative hallucinations
6. Afterimages
7. Phantom Limb

Sensory Modality Images
1. Visual
2. Spatial
3. Verbal
4. Motor

Images from Internal Sources
1. Entotopic images
2. Eidetic images
3. Imagination images

Figure 13-3. Classification of images. (Adapted from M. J. Horowitz, *Image Formation and Psychotherapy,* copyright 1983 by Jason Aronson Inc., New York. Used with permission.)

derstanding the learning problems children experience when imagery of their internal worlds interferes with percepts of their external worlds.

The Phenomenology of Images

The phenomenology of images can be described according to vividness, context, interaction with external perception, sensory modality, and internal origins (see Figure 13-3).

Image Vividness

The vividness of an image is proportional to the degree of its prominence in consciousness. The most vivid images are hallucinations in which an image of internal origin assumes the clarity of a percept. Pseudohallucinations are vivid images like hallucinations, without the conviction of reality. In another vein, the imagery of imagination ranges from faint to moderately vivid.

Image Context

Images can be classified by the context in which they occur. Hypnogogic images commonly occur in the twilight state between wakefulness and sleep; hypnopompic images probably occur in one of five persons during the transition from sleep to wakefulness (McKellar, 1957). Night dreams are largely visual experiences. Psychedelic images produced by hallucinogenic drugs and deliria are extraordinary and often accompanied by an uncanny sense of omnipotence and omniscience. Flashbacks are images that may be chemically induced and repeat past percepts. Flickering images consist of a rapid succession of scintillating images that occur in states of fatigue and probably result from decreased cerebral blood flow.

Images and External Percepts

A third dimension is the interaction of imagery with percepts. The most extreme is the illusion in which a perceiver distorts percepts of stimuli with a conviction of reality. Percepts also can be distorted without a sense of reality so that they are recognized as aberrations. Déjà vu experiences are illusions of familiarity with a situation. Derealization occurs when the perception of current external experience does not seem real. In depersonalization one's body may be perceived as foreign and dislocated

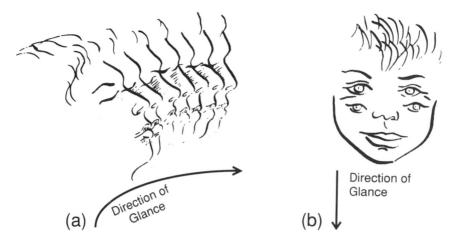

Figure 13-4. An example of paliopsia. After taking hashish, the subject noted this type of after-image. (a) When he shifted his gaze across the features of his companion, he noted a chain of images. (b) When he moved his gaze downward, the eyes were duplicated. (From M. J. Horowitz, *Image Formation and Psychotherapy,* copyright 1983 by Jason Aronson Inc., New York. Reproduced with permission.)

from one's self-image. More extreme than selective inattention, negative hallucinations are exclusions of perceived stimuli from conscious awareness.

Afterimages may be positive residues of a stimulus, such as the visual sensation of light in the darkness that follows exposure to a lightning flash, or negative residues, such as the appearance of a dark area when the eyes are closed after looking at a bright window. Paliopsia is a rare afterimage following a shift in gaze, such as moving one's eyes from a person to a lampshade and seeing an eye on the lampshade; it is noted in certain brain lesions and under the influence of hallucinogenic drugs (see Figure 13-4). A phantom limb is the more complicated persistence of sensation from an abruptly lost body part.

Sensory Modality Images

Although imagery can take place in any sensory modality, four prominent forms of imagery merit particular consideration: visual, spatial, verbal, and motor. Synesthesias are blends of more than one sensory modality, such as color sound or sound visuals. An example of synesthetic sound–visual correspondence is seen in Figure 13-5 in which the sound of "maluma" evokes round and "takete" sharp visual imagery.

Visual Imagery. Visual imagery may be present in all persons, except those born blind, so that visualizing scenes or events occurs commonly. Modern education plays a role in superimposing verbal on visual imagery (Jacobson, 1967).

The place where a visual image appears in relation to one's brain varies from an indefinable location in front of the eye to a distance corresponding to reality. Some persons can visualize objects as if they were partially transparent, such as perceiving all of the rooms of an imaginary house at a single mental glance. Others can visualize themselves as actors on a mental stage.

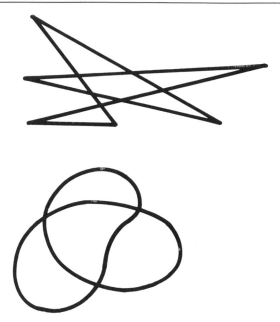

Figure 13-5. An example of synesthesia: Which figure looks like the sounds "maluma" and which like "takete"?

The encoding of visual imagery occurs on different levels—first as a neural network of features from which conscious images may be formed and second at a higher unconscious level of abstract conceptual representations that control the activity of the lower levels (Marks, 1983). Visual imagery has been associated with movement of the extraocular muscles (Jacobson, 1967).

Visual imagery offers a vehicle for thinking that may transcend verbalization. Verbal thinking involves an internal voice that is limited in speed and scope. Visual thinking, unfettered by verbalization, is faster and often more creative than thinking in words.

Spatial Imagery. Although closely related to visual imagery, the evidence points to the existence of at least three distinct spatial abilities: spatial visualization, spatial orientation, and spatial manipulation (Hunt, 1983).

Spatial visualization is the ability mentally to manipulate, rotate, twist, or invert pictorially presented visual stimuli (see Figure 13-6). The underlying ability seems to involve a process of recognition, retention, and recall of a configuration in which there is movement along its three-dimensional parts (McGee, 1979). The ability to imagine objects and environments from unfamiliar points of observation probably is through constructing spatial images and then operating on them (Olson & Bialystok, 1983). An adult capacity for spatial visualization is achieved between the ages of nine and 13, although there are adult individual differences in this capacity (Carter et al, 1983).

Spatial orientation is the aptitude for remaining unconfused by the changing orientation in which a configuration may be presented and to determine spatial relations to one's body orientation.

Beyond spatial visualization and orientation is the more abstract imagery involved in *spatial manipulation.* For example, the imagination of chess champions is not a static, picturelike memory but a very complex, interactive abstract spatial imagery. The need for abstract mental imagery in order to carry out higher-level spatial thought processes may relate to Sir Francis Galton's unexpected finding that some of his scientifically accomplished friends were deficient in picturelike imagery. They engaged in higher-level abstract spatial imagery that could be reproduced in visual and motor forms (Dixon, 1983).

Verbal Imagery. In contrast with the other forms, verbal imagery is of symbols, not of concrete sensory percepts. Verbal imagery is a derivative of speaking to oneself, as seen in the way young children describe their actions aloud. Furthermore, in performing addition mentally, the names of numbers may be mentally verbalized without imagery of the numbers themselves.

When speaking to oneself silently, there may be a slight discharge in the left cerebral motor area related to movements of the muscles of speech with an associated

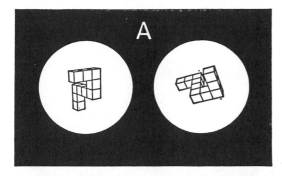

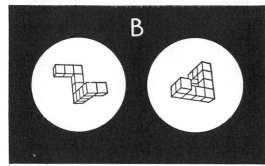

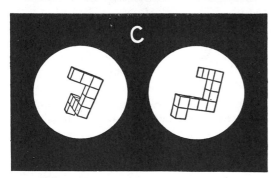

Figure 13-6. The subject is asked to identify the two identical pairs. The pairs in A and B are the same except for being rotated to a different position in three-dimensional space. The pair of structures in C are not the same. (From R. Shepard and J. Metzler, "Mental Rotation of Three-Dimensional Objects," *Science, 171,* 1971, 701–703. Copyright 1971 by the American Association for the Advancement of Science. Reproduced with permission.)

faint image (Ley, 1983). In silent verbal imagery, the discharge is so small that lower centers are not engaged, and no speech movements are produced. This left-hemisphere activation detected with subvocal speech probably should be regarded as the verbal linguistic activity of the left hemisphere, rather than as reflecting auditory imagery, which may be a right-hemisphere function. In speaking aloud there is a strong discharge of the same cerebral centers, when lower motor centers and the articulatory muscles are engaged.

The greater intensity of brain activity in visual than in verbal imagery is suggested by the finding that persons inclined toward visual imagery block alpha rhythm while forming images to a greater degree than persons who are inclined toward verbal imagery (Horowitz, 1983a).

Motor Imagery. In the imagery of pantomime, as when a deaf-mute person communicates in sign language, there are strong discharges of cerebral motor centers with accompanying vivid psychical states. When a deaf-mute person thinks, there may be slight discharges of cerebral motor centers with accompanying faint images of movements. Thus symbolic movements have images as does speech. The covert movements of signing even may be evident while a deaf person is thinking (Taylor, 1932; McGuigan, 1978).

Motor imagery can be emphasized in the blind deaf-mute person or selectively lost as in agraphia. An adult with agraphia resulting from a stroke loses the ability to move the hand according to the internal pattern of motor movement of writing. On the other hand, a stroke victim with alexia can trace letters with a finger and so recognize the motor patterns of a letter image that cannot be recognized visually alone. That patient reads by writing.

Some sort of motor imagery may allow the generation of motor actions from a model of what is to achieved. This image, however, is more akin to a computation of frequencies than to a photograph (Pribram, 1979).

Images from Internal Sources

Four types of imagery from internal sources can be distinguished: entotopic, eidetic, imagination, and daydreaming.

Entotopic images are initially meaningless forms evoked by stimuli arising from the internal structure of the eye, such as floaters in the vitreous humor, retinal blood vessels, and blood cells. They may become endowed with symbolic meaning. For example, one patient interpreted the visual imagery resulting from progressive retinal detachment as a religious experience.

Eidetic images are extremely vivid images of events and objects with percept-like qualities but of internal origin. They are more common in children, in whom they often occur as imaginary companions, than adults, as this capacity diminishes with age. Currently the term eidetic imagery also is used to describe vivid imagery experiences voluntarily created with the intention of intensifying their vividness in imagery therapy.

Imagination imagery varies in vividness and controllability and occurs in the form of hazy etchings in any sensory modality. It lacks the compelling crispness of eidetic imagery and takes place both spontaneously and voluntarily (Richardson, 1983). The visualization of one's body from an external point is called an autoscopic phenomenon. Mystical supernatural hallucinatory or pseudohallucinatory experiences also occur. Number and diagram images are used by some visualizing people for arithmetical calculations, such as by visualizing numbers as a ladder (Horowitz, 1983a).

Dreaming imagery is spontaneous imagination imagery that emerges when attention is withdrawn from the external world and is focused upon events in the inner world in sleep or in daydreaming. The primary process takes over in conscious night dreaming or daydreaming, which also may serve as a vehicle for creative insight (Richardson, 1983).

Pattern and Context Recognition

Recognition depends upon matching perceptions with images or memory patterns that are stored according to various codes. Some of these codes are there because of genetically determined schemes. For example, for a young bird, a shadow across a visual field signifies danger; for a stickleback fish, a red belly signifies male. Other codes are present because of learning prior maps of an environment. A novel stimulus is compared in some manner with a preexisting code or map, as described in the model of the processes of the affective system in Chapter 12. If the comparison indicates that the sensory event is not significant—for example, that a shadow is a cloud or a movement simply a bush waving in the wind—then the event is not registered in short-term memory, but most likely is lost. However, if the comparison suggests that the sensory event is important, such as food, a mate, or predator, then the information goes into short-term storage and activates the retrieval of memories related to the personal significance of the stimuli (Hintzman, 1978; Plutchik, 1977). The managerial analytic function in thinking goes beyond personal relevance to assessing the meaning of information as a basis for problem-solving and creative thinking.

Continual interaction between the conscious mind and the rest of the brain is just as necessary in recognition as in voluntary action (Popper & Eccles, 1977). The images triggered by a stimulus pattern are checked against the expected result by the conscious mind. Recognition occurs when an image or memory pattern of a previously encountered event is recovered. The conscious mind may discover that the retrieval is erroneous and institute a further search through the memory banks and attempt to secure an image that is recognized as being correct.

Computer memories are location addressable so that information is assigned to a particular place in the machine independent of the character of the neighboring information. In contrast human memories are content addressable and stored with similar experiences in an associative network that at any given time can deliver information concerning related events or items. Simple recognition memory apparently does not vary much between individuals whereas associative memory does so widely (Campione et al, 1985). Human memory actually does not statically store anything but changes as a function of experience. Thus human memories are less correct, but richer, than computer memories (Calfee, 1983). Furthermore, the retrieval processes aroused are accompanied by emotional reactions and may not be orderly or systematic. Parenthetically, the logical seriation that occurs in remembering events apparently is in the reporting, not necessarily the recall, of memories (Bugelski, 1983).

Tip-of-the-tongue phenomena demonstrate that a target memory, such as a name, may be inaccessible for immediate retrieval, but is nonetheless in storage. Memories, therefore, are collections of independent attributes that can be forgotten or retrieved at different rates. When cues similar to these memory attributes are encountered, the memory attributes presumably are aroused and become accessible for retrieval. Because attributes that have been aroused, in turn, activate others that constitute the same memory, the probability that the target attribute will be retrieved improves over time. The tip-of-the-tongue phenomenon may be a protracted instance of the regular retrieval process that occurs when insufficient memory attributes are

initially aroused. This suggests that retrieval is a continuous rather than discontinuous process, as seen when a memory suddenly appears long after efforts to recover it began (Fagen & Rovee-Collier, 1983).

IMAGINATION

Comprehension does not result from the simple passage of information through a series of steps. Piaget's voluminous writings are testimony to the elaborate ways in which children construct knowledge through operative accommodation. Now computer simulations are beginning to suggest the nature of higher-level information processing (Anderson, 1983b).

Knowledge can be acquired without thinking, and one can think without acquiring knowledge. A term other than thinking, therefore, is needed to describe how information is understood and transformed into knowledge. Imagination serves this purpose very well. Although popularly connoting fanciful thinking, the word imagination also means the acts of forming images of what is not actually present, creating new images of what has not been actually experienced, and creating images by combining memories of previous experiences. Thus imagination can be defined as the system in which symbolic and conceptual images of percepts from the external and internal worlds are formed and comprehended (Cooper & Shepard, 1984).

Whereas imaging occurs during precategorical storage, imagination takes place in short-term and intermediate memory and is an unconscious process that surfaces in conscious imagery. Metaphorically an image is a perching in the continuous flight of imagination (Begg, 1983). It is a quasi-perceptual experience, which should be clearly distinguished from the process that underlies it (Richardson, 1983). Therefore, I use imaging to denote a potentially conscious experiential phenomenon and imagination to denote the system that employs imaging in symbol and concept formation. Imagination is the workplace and playground of thinking; however, symbol and concept formation can take place without thinking so that imagination and thinking deserve separate consideration. Imagination corresponds to Piaget's semiotic operations of schemes through which information and actions on that information are transformed into symbols and concepts (Furth, 1981).

Imagination is the capacity for mental representation through which a young child can realize desires that cannot be immediately gratified. A young child's play is imagination in action, and imagination in older children and adolescents is play without action (Vygotsky, 1978). The conceptual abilities of children are stretched through play and the use of their imaginations in play. Developmentally, as the cerebral hemispheres lateralize, imagination improves through the growing imaging capacities of the right hemisphere. The imaging and language systems develop somewhat independently of each other and become well integrated around the age of seven years, corresponding to the consolidation of concrete operational thinking (Tower, 1983). This permits a child to experience images as autonomous from actions and immediate percepts. The child then becomes free to think about internal images.

Although studies of blind and deaf children show impoverishment of imagery in the modality of deficit, they show little deficiency in imagery itself. So imagination is not strictly dependent on perception but on the level of sophistication of brain processes (Tower, 1983).

Actually, imagination can be seen as the short-term and intermediate memory systems. Short-term "working" memory is of limited capacity and under 30 seconds' duration. The number of chunks of information that can be stored in short-term memory is estimated to be four to seven for children five to ten years old and five to nine for most adults. Information is retained in short-term memory and prepared for permanent storage through voluntary attentional recoding and rehearsal processes. Deficiencies at this stage of information processing have been cited as the basis for many of the differences observed between problem and facile readers (Vellutino, 1979).

Short-term memory is thought to be a function of reverberating neural circuits that center in the medial region of the temporal cortex, which receives impulses from the precategorical circuits of the limbic system (Zola-Morgan et al, 1982; Watts, 1975). For example, a patient with destruction of the inner surface of the temporal lobes, including the hippocampus, was unable to transfer information from short-term to long-term storage (Geschwind, 1979). Loss of recent memory also occurs during sleep, anesthesia, seizures, senility, extreme anger, and brain concussion.

The posterior hippocampus may play a key role in the initial stages of imagination. It appears to be involved in short-term working memory in comprehension by relating present situations to previous ones by holding an image of a percept, retrieving similar schemes, and comparing and modifying the external and internal images until a match occurs. Then the current situation is deciphered according to relevance and similarity to existing schemes. When the percept-image apparatus is in perceptual use, internal images are inhibited. The hippocampus, therefore, may exert inhibitory control over incoming information to permit flexible shifting between percepts and imagery without confusion between the two or excessive centering on one or the other (Horowitz, 1983).

Short-term memory provides a selective window for long-term storage by reducing the amount of relevant information to manageable proportions. It builds up and maintains an internal model of the immediate environment and what has happening in the world over the past minute or two. It also provides a working space for central processing, allowing the temporary storage and manipulation of information (Ohrman, 1979).

Intermediate memory is the zone of most schoolwork and bridges seconds to hours, probably through the repetitive hippocampal circuitry of short-term memory and the activity of medial cortical regions. Symbolization and conceptualization take place during this stage through the activity of the temporo-occipital-parietal association areas under the influence of the frontal lobes.

Symbolization

The word symbol derives from the notion of a strange thing thrown together with something familiar to connect the unknown with the known. Unfamiliar percepts can be endowed with familiar meaning by symbols that also provide a shorthand for describing them. Images in themselves may be symbols.

Symbol formation is a means of creating order and connectedness between the internal and external worlds (Deri, 1984). Symbolization enables the representation of an object by abstract images, such as figures and words, and is expressed in speech, writing, and drawing. It entails both selectively excluding and articulating features of the original raw materials. Except for the congenitally deaf, symbolization takes place largely through verbal imagery. Chimpanzees can connect symbols with objects and word symbols with words in sentences (Deich & Hodges, 1979).

Developmentally the use of symbols begins and continues in nonverbal ways. At first one object stands for another similar object. Then a part of the body represents an object or an idea. Next the entire body represents something else, such as a lion. Finally the whole child may represent someone else in role-taking play (Tower, 1983).

The naming of objects in acquiring language is an obvious use of verbal symbols (MacNamara, 1982). At first the name is regarded by a child as an inherent property of a thing; the name is the thing. Gradually the name becomes a picture of the thing, then a diagram, and ultimately an abstract symbol. Thus symbolization progresses from being a part of an object to becoming detached from it. Whereas a child is conscious of the symbolic value of words between the first and second year, the symbolic character of a drawn figure may not be understood until the third year (Werner, 1948).

Images of things play a key role in the comprehension of language and in the storage of information gleaned through language. To the extent that words and the images of things are connected, communication and memory are facilitated (Begg, 1983). A child quickly discovers that verbal symbols offer efficient means of communicating images of experiences.

Conceptualization

The world of sensory experience is composed of an enormous array of different objects, events, and people. No two people have identical appearances, and even objects change from moment to moment with alterations in light or in position of the viewer. If we fully used our capacity for registering differences and responded to each one as unique, we would be overwhelmed by the complexity of our environment. Accordingly we have the ability to override this diversity by organizing it into categories in the form of concepts that identify the similarities between stimuli and thereby reduce the complexity of experience (Bruner et al, 1956).

As the highest level of cognition, concepts are personalized information about the properties of percepts, images, and symbols. To know something is to have concepts of it. Long-term memories are largely in the form of concepts, which in Piaget's terms are the result of operational accommodation. Although concepts may be formed with nonverbal symbols, verbal symbolic imagery is more efficient. Examples of concepts are descriptions of one's home and patriotism.

A concept is formed when one perceives that two qualities can be placed in the same class. It is any describable regularity of real or imagined events or objects. The ability to classify common features of things, persons, and other concepts allows one to cope with an otherwise overwhelming mass of details. Concepts are hierarchically related to each other from deep core to superficial levels (Bourne, 1982). In its earliest form, a concept is simply an awareness of similarities between immediate perceptions. For example, a child recognizes black objects as different from red objects and becomes aware of the passage of time through the sequence of one's own movements. Next categorical concepts occur at the concrete level so that round objects are recognized as balls, and there is awareness that waiting is involved before an event will take place. Then abstract categories are formed at hierarchical levels so that words are used for black balls, and hours and minutes are used to designate time periods.

In forming a concept, one must first discriminate between the relevant and irrelevant features of data. Second, one must generalize by identifying the features that belong to a particular category (Perkins, 1974). Thus concepts are abstractions of things, events, and qualities. They are shorthand notes taken on reality and, like notes, may be misleading even when perfectly definite in themselves (Bourne, 1982).

Conceptual abstractions form a ladder that takes the climber into the clouds where differences between things disappear. For example, take a small, round red object that you see, touch, and smell and call it a MacIntosh apple. By naming it a MacIntosh, it is merged with many similar items, each in some way different from the one in your hand. If you use only the word apple, the concept now includes yellow and green colors, and possibly elongated forms of unlike size and taste. Your apple has twice been lost sight of. If you go on to speak of a fruit, the term lacks all power to compel a correct image of what is in your hand. By the time foodstuff is invoked, only the most general idea of function remains. Then comes organic matter, and the next step is bare object, at which point all things become the same (Barzun, 1983).

Still concepts, no matter how often misused, mistaken, and revised, are as real as percepts. Abstractions command as much feeling and action as do the concretes with which they deal. That is why they are so dangerous and must be used carefully to avoid misunderstanding (Barzun, 1983).

Conceptualization can be simply an act of cognition or extend into thinking by analysis of percepts and erecting and testing hypotheses about common elements. In thinking conceptualization can be carried out by deduction from laws, premises, or other generalizations or by induction through which specific instances are combined. Both deduction and induction are most effectively used together, with conclusions based upon one method verified by the other (Perkins, 1974).

Becoming conscious of one's own action may transform it into a self-concept. One may examine one's own actions and construct a concept to account for them as if they were of another person. Such a proc-

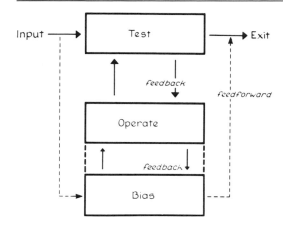

Figure 13-7. The TOTE servomechanism modified to include feedforward. Note the parallel processing feature of the TOTE. (From K. H. Pribram, "Self-Consciousness and Intentionality," in G. E. Schwartz and D. Shapiro, eds., *Consciousness and Self-Regulation, Volume 1.* Copyright 1976 by Plenum Press, New York. Reproduced with permission.)

ess may be as laborious and present the same risks of omissions and distortions as if it were of a stranger (Piaget, 1976).

TOTE is an acronym for test, operate, test, and exit. It was developed as a more suitable model for analyzing concept formation than the traditional stimulus –response unit (Hunt, 1962; Pribram, 1976). The TOTE model specifies four stages in learning concepts: a test to determine differences between the present and desired state of affairs, an operation to reduce these differences, a second test, and finally an exit when no differences exist (see Figure 13-7). The bias produces conscious voluntary control as a feed-forward, open-loop mechanism superimposed upon an error-processing, feedback, closed-loop system.

In concept learning the TOTE test phase corresponds to a check of a hypothesis against known data. If the first test reveals that the current hypothesis is not compatible with known data, the operating phase, or hypothesis-computing function, is activated. Its inputs are the current hypothesis and the information that this hypothesis led to a certainty of error. A new hypothesis is generated by the operating phase and tested in the second test phase.

In sum concepts are formed in a hierarchy of levels, ranging from simply knowing that a four-footed animal is a dog, in which the concept is one step from the percept, to the principle of entropy, which is a concept built upon concepts. An important distinction exists between knowing a concept and understanding its application. For this reason teaching both the abstract meaning of a concept and its application is important. For example, entropy can be first taught as a principle in physics and then comprehended by applying it to one's own life and death.

KNOWLEDGE

The knowledge system is long-term memory that employs operative accommodation to form abstractions from things and states (Hamilton, 1983). In contrast the imagination system is short-term and intermediate memory and transforms information into comprehensible symbol and concept outputs. As long-term memory, the knowledge system includes sensorimotor skill programs; symbols and concepts; figurative, spatial, and semantic networks; hierarchies of expectancies and probability indices of the recurrence of past events.

Long-term memory takes place in sensorimotor, symbolic, and conceptual schemes that use data available in a common pool and perform computations upon these data. These schemes then both send new results back into the common pool or to other schemes and request specific information from other schemes. A conceptual scheme thus consists of a framework for tying together information about a core concept (Norman & Bobrow, 1976).

Knowledge, or long-term memory, is thought to be an unlimited capacity system that holds information indefinitely in lateral cortical areas (Watts, 1975). Long-term memory contains one's fund of knowledge that is categorized and integrated as a network of associations among concepts (Anderson, 1983a). It influences all other memory processes and is, in turn, influenced by them.

For percepts to be stored for recall, their images must be transmitted through the temporal interpretive cortex to the hippocampus, amygdala, and thalamus. This demonstrates the importance of the limbic system in learning (Mishkin & Petri, 1984). The neurotransmitter dopamine plays an essential role in this process.

About 30 minutes to three hours seem to be required for long-term memory to begin through metabolically induced synaptic changes involving an increase in brain metabolism, with the manufacture of proteins and other macromolecules required for increasing membrane chemical transmission mechanisms. It is based on modified synaptic connections in neural networks either by growth of axon branches and dendrites or by changes of synaptic efficacy through the transport of proteins from the cell body along axons and dendrites. Thus memory storage can be affected not only by the inhibition of the synthesis of proteins but by prevention of their transport to synaptic sites (Sinz & Rosenzweig, 1983).

Long-term memories probably are stored in three basic forms. One is episodic figurative memory of events in the context of a particular time and place. This record probably is stored in the temporal lobe in the stream of consciousness. The second form is spatial memory of directions and places, and probably is stored in the nondominant hippocampus, corpus striatum, and cerebellum. The study of patients hav-

ing resections of brain tissue suggests that the dominant hippocampus is a semantic map concerned with the laying down or consolidation of verbal and word memories, and the nondominant hippocampus is a cognitive map of temporal, pictorial, and spatial memories (O'Keefe & Nadel, 1973). The third form is semantic memory, which consists of symbols and concepts, probably stored as knowledge in the reverberating circuitry of sensorimotor schemes of diencephalic, limbic, and lateral cortical areas.

Episodic and spatial memories can be recovered as sensory-related images that are likenesses of the remembered events or things. This record of spatial objects and temporal events encountered in one's experience allows recognition and commerce with things and people unique to those experiences. Semantic memories can be recovered as symbols that stand for events or things. Knowledge in the form of concepts can be recovered as language symbols or abstract sensory images that allow understanding and communication of spoken and printed language.

Since it is the primary anatomical substrate for the coordination of body position and movement, the vestibulocerebellar system may be the foundation upon which experience and ultimately the entire personality are organized through its role in forming cognitive maps of spatial relationships in the environment (Parrill-Burnstein, 1981). For example, cognitive mapping is involved in the development of motor proficiency that enables movement through space with ease, of revisualization so that visual stimuli received from the visual fields can be mentally represented, of mental rotations so that the movement of objects can be imagined, and of perspective taking so that a corresponding view can be taken of an object moved to another position (Parrill-Burnstein, 1981).

Mapping skills are part of a child's general cognitive development (Parill-Burnstein, 1981). Such skills as visual closure and object permanence are learned prior to the age of three. At the age of three, children are able to infer that others see some objects that they do not see. By age five a child can infer another's visual perspective for one object. By seven a child can mentally rotate objects. By nine relationships between objects can be ascertained and problems requiring perspective taking can be solved.

Permanent memory actually may not be possible because of the phenomenon of forgetting, which occurs as a result of proactive interference from similar material learned previously, retroactive interference by similar or irrelevant stimuli, and disuse decay (Hintzman, 1978). Furthermore, the psychological defense mechanism of repression plays an important role in conscious forgetting. Another variable in long-term memory storage is the level of complexity of a concept. Some persons have difficulty with semantic-concept, but not sensorimotor-concept, memory (Wickelgren, 1975).

COGNITIVE STYLES

Cognitive styles describe the ways in which individuals process information and conceptually organize their environments (Guilford, 1980; Kogan, 1976). Cognitive styles are intimately interwoven with temperamental, language, managerial, and self structures as part of one's total character structure. As such they are manifestations of central nervous system output.

Cognitive style is one of the determinants of adaptive behavior, defense mechanisms, and pathological symptoms. It differs from intellectual ability in a number of ways. Cognitive style is qualitative and bears on how knowledge is acquired whereas intellectual ability reflects the contents of cognition and is measured by quantitative

levels of competency. Having more of an intellectual ability is consistently better than having less. In contrast, neither pole of a cognitive style has more adaptive value than the other in itself, although each may have greater value under different circumstances (Messick, 1976, 1984).

Cognitive styles develop slowly, are shaped by experience and are not easily modified by training. They are relatively stable over time in similar situations; however, people may not show the same cognitive style in different situations (Goldstein & Blackman, 1978).

A variety of cognitive styles have been described depending upon the orientation and experimental methods of investigators. The time is ripe for a reorientation of research on them. There is more to the study of cognitive styles than of traditional individual differences between persons. Indeed, in its original meaning, cognitive style referred to the patterning of cognitive dimensions within a person (Kogan, 1976). Consistent with a multilinear model of development, therefore, the balance and patterning of cognitive styles within individuals merit study.

At this time four cognitive styles show reasonable consistency in the literature. They correspond to commonly observed behavioral tendencies. Further research undoubtedly will identify more useful patterns.

Cognitive Rigidity Versus Flexibility

The first pattern combines characteristics referred to as rigid–flexible and concrete–abstract (Goldstein & Blackman, 1978; Kogan, 1976; Santostefano, 1978). Cognitive rigidity refers to fusing images of present and past information so that a few narrow categories are imposed upon new information with reliance upon concepts that are concrete and bound to the physical properties of stimuli. As a result behavior

Figure 13-8. Classical Gestalt figure with configurations of either two faces or a vase.

tends to continue in previous dispositions and not be efficiently adapted to changes in situations. These persons tend to impose templates excessively upon their sensory input and accordingly selectively attend to their experience. They tend to be intolerant of ambiguity and have limited synthetic powers.

Cognitive flexibility refers to differentiating present from past information and employing broad abstract categories related to the functional properties of stimuli and resulting in behavior that is adaptive to changing circumstances. Cognitively flexible children tend to have strong synthetic capacities and are versatile learners who can vary their strategies according to the demands of a task and handle diversity and inconsistency.

Cognitive flexibility is reflected in such specific ways as the way in which one can recognize embedded figures. For example, the two faces in Figure 13-8 can also be

seen as a vase. Cognitively flexible people can easily switch from the faces to the vase.

Cognitive rigidity as a defense is illustrated by the following case:

Jim protected himself from the pain of humiliation by errors in spelling and spatial orientation through denial in fantasy, which produced cognitive rigidity. Whenever Jim felt threatened by a mistake, he dug into a stance of omniscience in which he felt he could not be wrong. He then regarded teachers and parents who tried to confront him with his errors as mistreating him. He tuned them out as he immersed himself in his omnipotent fantasy life. The result was extreme stubbornness and failure in schoolwork.

Automatization

Cognitive automatization refers to the capacity to process automatically information in complex forms (Hopkins, 1979). This permits the unconscious, rapid assignment of meaning to percepts as is found in facile reading. Weakness in automatization makes it necessary to deal with perceptions as though they were unfamiliar. Strength in this capacity facilitates efficient recognition of familiar percepts.

Field Dependence Versus Independence

The most discussed cognitive style in recent years has been field dependence versus independence. This quality refers to an individual's need for feedback from external referents, both in the form of interpersonal interaction and of stimuli from things. The field dependence –independence cognitive style also has been described as a global-articulate cognitive style. It defines the degree of differentiation a person imposes on a display of information. At one end are individuals who consistently experience and organize information in global and diffuse terms and who are field dependent. At the other extreme are individuals who consistently experience and organize information in delineated, structured terms so that parts of the field of information are differentiated from the background context, and their discreteness is maintained (Santostefano, 1978).

The rod and frame test was used in early research on field dependence–independence. In this test a subject seated in complete darkness views a luminous rod suspended with a luminous frame. Both the rod and the frame can be rotated independently. Initially the rod and frame are both rotated, and the subject is told to direct the examiner to adjust the rod to a position that the subject believes is vertical. Some subjects are accurate in this task when the frame deviates from a vertical orientation and are termed field independent. Others orient the rod in relation to the tilted frame only and are termed field dependent, because their perception tends to be dependent upon the surrounding environment (Goldstein & Blackman, 1978).

Field dependent people tend to be tactful, warm, accommodating, and accepting of others. They tend to rely on external referents and to take things at face value. Their judgments are influenced by attributes other than those defined as relevant to the task. In extreme they tend to be passive and have poor impulse control, low self-esteem, and an undifferentiated body image.

Field independent people tend to be self-reliant, and their cognition is colored by their attitudes and needs. They tend to be insensitive in social situations and in extreme are rude, inconsiderate, manipulative, and cold (Witkin & Goodenough, 1981). They tend to be differentiated persons who perceive the world as discrete and structured. They have definite senses of body boundaries, their individuality, inter-

nalized standards, and, in extreme, are likely to use primitive defenses, such as denial and projection.

People who show the characteristics of a field dependent or field independent style with a high degree of regularity are designated as "fixed." Those who show both styles are "mobile." Adult males tend to be more field independent than females. Males with pronounced masculine physical characteristics and early puberty tend to be even more field independent (Witkin & Goodenough, 1981). Evidence of continuity between field independence–dependence from the preschool to later school years has been found (Kogan, 1976).

Cultures that are tight in social organization and stress conformity tend to produce field dependent members. Nomadic, mobile cultures, for example, tend to be more field independent than stable, agricultural cultures. The usual development from child to adult proceeds from relative field dependence to independence, whereas the development of cultures appear to follow the opposite course. Family environments that encourage separate functioning in children are likely to produce children who develop in the direction of field independence (Witkin & Goodenough, 1981).

It is evident that years of research on field independence–dependence have not provided a thorough understanding of the idea. At the same time, the fact that research on field independence shows no signs of waning after a quarter of a century testifies to its fertility.

Locus of Control

Locus of control characterizes an individual's perceptions of causality as either internal or external to the self. Individuals with an internal locus of control think of themselves as responsible for their own behavior, deserving praise for successes and blame for failures. Individuals with an external locus of control see outer forces, circumstances beyond their control, luck, or other people as responsible for what happens (Lindal & Venables, 1983). There is evidence that a greater sense of internal control can be learned; it is a highly desirable trait in school (Maccoby, 1980; Rotter, 1966).

In extreme a sense of being controlled by external forces produces a paranoid outlook. On the other hand, an exaggerated internal sense of control over the external world may endow a person with magical thinking. In most persons there is a realistic and flexible balance between a sense of internal and external control (DeCharms, 1968).

SUMMARY

Cognition is our recognition, comprehension, and personalized knowledge of our external and internal worlds. Many factors influence cognition so that each of us places unique interpretations upon the same sensory information as we process it. Cognition is the output of the information-processing system, which includes the following component systems: reception, perception, imaging, imagination, and knowledge.

Reception involves the encoding of information from the external and internal worlds by the sensory systems into forms that can be processed by the central nervous system.

Perception is the unconscious, preconscious, and conscious immediate registration of information by the primary cortical areas as percepts that are virtual copies of sensory stimuli in iconic storage for up to 300 milliseconds.

During the stage of sensory modality-centered imaging, precategorical storage of up to one second permits dealing with sensory information after stimulus reception has ceased. Sensory information is synthesized and compared with previous experience through reverberating circuitry activity of the sensory associational cortices and the hippocampus. Recognition through the retrieval of information from memory storage requires optimal cortical tone and depends upon cues that evoke activity in the memory banks.

Imagination employs the short-term storage of working memory of up to 30 seconds and involves the processes of symbolization and conceptualization. Symbolization enables the mental representation of percepts and images by convenient shorthand devices. Conceptualization is acquiring knowledge by storing personalized information about the properties of percepts, images, and symbols. Short-term memory is thought to be a function centering in reverberating neural circuits of the medial region of the temporal cortex.

Intermediate memory is the zone of schoolwork and extends imagination from seconds to hours, permitting higher levels of symbolization, conceptualization, and the imagery of thinking to take place. These activities involve the tertiary cortical associational areas under the influence of the frontal lobes and probably draw upon reverberating hippocampal circuitry.

Long-term memory is an unlimited capacity system that holds information in the form of symbols and concepts indefinitely. It is the seat of knowledge and reciprocally influences earlier levels of cognition. Long-term storage probably involves metabolically induced synaptic changes in the lateral neocortical areas.

Thus information from the external and internal worlds must be acted upon to make it usable before the brain can act upon it. The process of assimilation translates sensory information into forms that can be processed by the central nervous system. The brain figuratively accommodates to this information by first making virtual copies of it in the primary sensory cortical areas and then by personalizing it in the form of images, symbols, and concepts through operative accommodation.

Four varieties of cognitive styles are mentioned. They are cognitive rigidity versus flexibility, degree of automatization, field dependency versus independence, and locus of control.

The core of education is acquiring knowledge and skills through understanding and employing information. As this discussion of cognition reveals, it is not a simple matter.

C H A P T E R

14

The Language System

The true use of speech is not so much to express our
wants as to conceal them.

Oliver Goldsmith (1728–1774)

anguage is both an integral dimension of character development and a reflection of that
development (Lewis, 1977). It enables human beings to delve into the essence of things, transcend the limits of their
perceptions, organize their behavior, and
transmit information to succeeding generations (Luria & Wertsch, 1982). It also
is a lubricant for social relationships with
verbal and nonverbal aspects.

Innate in homo sapiens, spoken language is based upon the specialization of
brain centers that make up the language
system (Lenneberg, 1964; Ojemann & Mateer, 1979b). The evolution of language
progressed from gestural sound and movement signals to symbols, then to spoken
words, and finally to written words some
5,000 years ago. Speech probably emerged
about one million years ago with the appearance of *homo erectus*. The contemporary form of spoken language became
widespread about 40,000 years ago. Written symbols with magical or religious significance date from the cave paintings of
the paleolithic period.

From the evolutionary point of view,
the language areas of the brain still are not
fully stabilized. It is possible that the an-

gular gyrus of the parietal lobe may be canalized for the recognition of visual symbols
but not for words, since the ability to read
is a comparatively recent human acquisition. Therefore, there is great individual
variability in rates of maturation and in
forms of language system components
(Joynt, 1974; Geschwind, 1982).

Parenthetically it is likely that music
evolved with language as a social communication tool because it contributed to
group cohesion (Sloboda, 1985). Music, as
does language, involves the grouping of
sounds on the basis of similarity, proximity,
and continuity as melodies rather than
words.

LANGUAGE SYSTEM PROCESSES

The processes of language include *receptive
language*, which is the comprehension of
the meaning of words; *expressive language*,
which includes encoding and articulating
speech and gestures; and *inner language*,
which includes the lexical fund of knowledge and the syntactic ability to organize

262

words into coherent sentences. Language involves the state regulating system in its nonverbal form, the information processing system in its receptive and inner aspects, and the managerial system in its inner and expressive aspects (see Figure 14-1).

The comprehension function of receptive language occurs before the production of words, as a child learns to recognize and make fine discriminations between sounds. The understanding of words unites a child with the experiences shared with other persons. Symbolic language is a fundamental tool in achieving mastery of one's external and internal worlds, as naming things brings them into a child's personal domain. Most important, a word becomes "mine" and stands for something between "me" and others, just as a transitional object is a personal possession that can take the place of a parent. Words also identify and facilitate mastery of inner states. As words are used for communication, they serve both to fulfill inner needs, as when children speak to themselves in play, and to enhance mastery of the external world through speaking with others. Intriguingly, the capacity to write precedes the ability to read words (Montessori, 1974).

Although we usually think of expressive language as spoken words, its origins and current expression involve vital nonverbal elements. For the deaf language is manual, not spoken. Therefore, it is useful to distinguish nonverbal signals, which are objective, from symbols, which are subjective (Pribram, 1977). The most primitive signals have been described as alpha and beta coded. In this terminology spoken language is referred to as gamma coded.

Alpha-coded signals are from glandular secretions, which contain chemical signals reflecting basic emotional states detected by smell or taste.

Beta-coded signals consist of sounds or movements of the skeletal muscles produced by emotions and accompanying

autonomic nervous system effects, such as through the skin in blushing. They directly express one's wishes and emotions in order to influence the external world both consciously and unconsciously (Furth, 1981). Animals regularly employ signals of increasing phylogenetic complexity. Vervet monkeys, for example, are adept at identifying group members by voice and appear to have vocalizations that reflect a complex classification of other group members according to kinship and dominance relationships. Their alarm calls also appear to function in a semantic fashion by signaling the presence of specific predators (Snowden et al, 1983). Chimpanzees can use signals, such as beckoning, to signify "come-give me." They also can communicate their wishes in American sign language (Rosenthal, 1977).

Human language evolved from pointing, a "give me that" and "don't touch this" affair consisting of signals (Korzybski, 1933). This nonverbal basis of language has been obscured by the customary emphasis upon spoken words. Recent sound-film microanalysis has revealed that speech and body motion are synchronized. Therefore, when a person speaks, words and gestures are integrated at the same time. The body of an intent listener also moves in synchrony with a speaker's speech (Condon, 1985).

The leader of the structuralist movement in anthropology, Levi-Strauss, pointed out that unspoken messages were the key to understanding intangible culturally determined interpersonal relationships (Leach, 1970). These nonverbal messages are so complex that speech can only approximate them, and then in such a laborious fashion that only sophisticated adults can understand them. Yet they are grasped instantaneously in all their complexity by young children.

Nonverbal body messages signal our attitudes, wishes, desires, and fears, while the accompanying speech both conveys

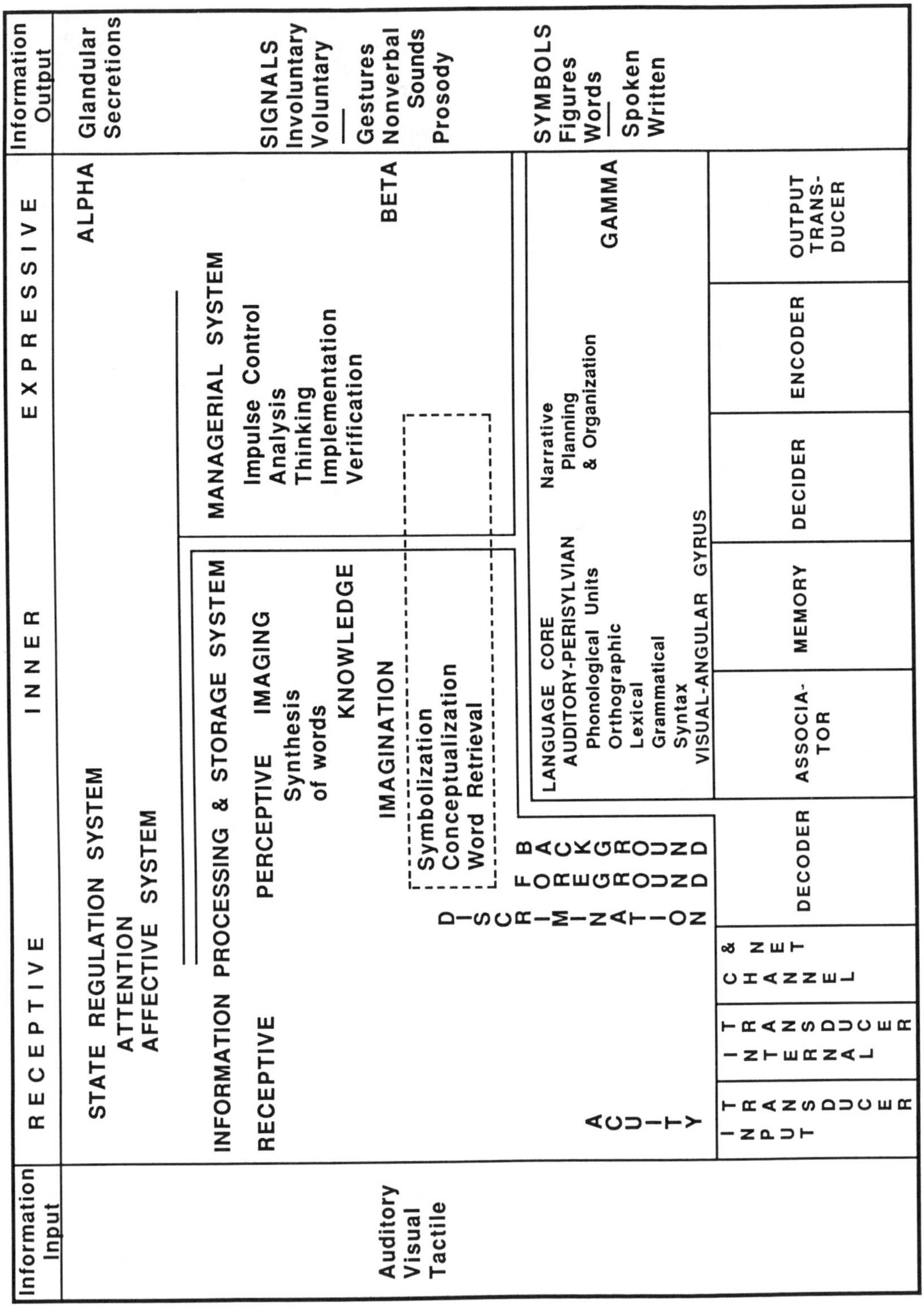

Figure 14-1. The language system.

and conceals meaning (Birdwhistell, 1970). Verbal language cannot describe a total experience as it occurs but must take apart and laboriously list sequentially interactions that occur simultaneously. The attempt to verbalize one's experience itself, however, may permit its meaning to be consciously understood and accessible to change, as in psychotherapy.

Gamma-coded information is expressed through symbolic language, which in spoken form consists of an idea converted into a grammatical sentence by synactic rules and then into morphemes, which are converted into orderly sequences of phonemes. A symbol is something that stands for another thing. Figures, words, and manual signs are used as symbols to express one's interests. Symbols are learned from past experience and derive meaning from the context in which they appear. Chimpanzees can use figure symbols, such as a square, to signify a banana.

The young child uses speech to speak to oneself. Vygotsky suggested that this egocentric speech goes underground developmentally to become inner speech. Egocentric speech and its derivative inner speech help a child to think more precisely and to develop control over their motor actions (Luria & Yudovich, 1959). The system for inner speech expresses emotional states through vocalizations, which become more frequent and differentiated during development, enabling a child to express a variety of feelings. In subsequent years inner states are verbalized as declarative statements, such as commands and threats.

Inner speech subserves a child's drives and feelings about the environment. It has an initially active short and a later developing long sensorimotor circuit. The highest correlating center of the short circuit appears to be the hypothalamus. The long circuit of the system links the hypothalamus with the limbic area, the temporo-occipito-parietal associational zone, and the motor-speech centers in the frontal lobe. The short and long circuits show a matur-ational pattern. The short circuit becomes active first; the long circuit stabilizes at some point between five and ten years of age (Rourke et al, 1983).

THE DEVELOPMENT OF LANGUAGE

The linkage of the maturation of specific neural centers with the sequential acquisition of speech has yet to be definitely made. The development of intentional communicative language is closely linked to the establishment of the temporo-occipito-parietal associational area and its connections with the thalamus. The outer sections of the temporo-occipito-parietal area begin to function between five and 12 years of age, followed by its more central parts (Rourke et al, 1983). However, there are a number of innate capacities upon which spoken language builds, such as a baby's recognition of the mother's voice before sighting her and predispositions to syntax and grammar (Lasky, 1985). A child does not just soak up the mother tongue, but also actively constructs language.

Speech is the means by which one expresses one's internal world, so that words organize and symbolize inchoate sensations arising from within a child's body. In addition the parent participates in an exchange that helps to develop a child's capacity for empathy from hearing the voice and thoughts of another person. For example, babbling begins at about the same age in deaf and hearing children, but its progression to speech depends upon hearing and social interactions (Lasky, 1985). Verbal communication also facilitates understanding others and affection for them.

During the first year, the language system gradually becomes intentionally communicative by mediating behaviors, such as turning the head toward someone's voice, responding differentially to angry and friendly talking, and repeating simple words spoken by a parent. During the second year, the vocabulary increases; there is practicing to comprehend speech and to use language to communicate. In the subsequent years, verbalization increases markedly, and during adolescence speech becomes an effective means for communicating ideas to others (Rourke et al, 1983). There is a remarkably powerful instinctually based necessity for interaction with like members of the same species. Learning language thus proceeds most rapidly when it is absolutely necessary for communication with peers (Geschwind, 1985a).

A maturing child progresses from using signals to using symbols that are influenced by the child's cognitive organization of the world and the surrounding social communication system. Consequently, in addition to genetic factors, there is great variability in early language development deriving from individual social experiences (Nelson, 1977b). All symbols can be interpreted differently, because each one holds a different meaning for each interpreter of it. No two persons inhabit precisely the same semantic universe (Eco, 1983). Ambiguity, therefore, is inherent in life.

Vygotsky claimed that language and thinking develop independently until two years of age and that children learn to think in words thereafter. Evidence that between the ages of two and four is a critical period for language development comes from the observation of children with sensory disabilities (Rourke et al, 1983). For example, recurrent ear infections during that period affect language development. Another example is that the language training of deaf children is said to be more effective if started before the age of two and less so after the age of four.

As a child matures, inner speech progressively condenses into single words or fragments of words, which accomplish in thought what sentences and phrases accomplished earlier. A child whose inner speech is well developed should be able to process information more rapidly and react more quickly than a child who is slow in this development. Inner speech may be an important mechanism for regulating inhibition and arousal. This suggests that encouraging a child to talk to oneself may be useful in strengthening self-control (Dykman et al, 1970; Luria, 1961).

Through speech children free themselves from the immediate constraints of their environments. They prepare themselves for future activity. They plan, order, and control their own behavior, as well as that of others. Once inner speech becomes a pervasive part of the higher psychological processes, speech acts to organize, unify, and integrate many disparate aspects of children's behavior (Vygotsky, 1962). A further step for children is learning how to engage in conversations with adults and in school (Wells, 1983).

Language plays a central role in emotional development. It is through words that emotions eventually become firmly linked to mental images. Our self concepts are stored in the form of emotionally impregnated words gathered throughout our lifetimee—first our parents' words, rich in emotions of admonition or encouragement, and later the words of other adults and peers. Without words for emotions we could not think about what we feel.

Words are the most effective means of communicating meaning to others, but they also are commonly used to conceal intent and to manipulate others. Furthermore, they are used to affect and produce responses from others, like cries and gestures (McDougall, 1985). Children learn early in life to fear words that humiliate or threaten abandonment. They also learn to use words as weapons and to protect themselves against the hurtful words of others, as illustrated by the phrase:

Sticks and stones may break my bones but words will never hurt me!

WRITTEN LANGUAGE

Reading is a remarkable achievement. It is not an innate central nervous system function but a highly contrived process that must be learned. How reading came to be an essential human function is an intriguing question.

At first the key to rapid, successful human evolution was communication made possible by gestures and spoken symbols (Hardy, 1978). The time segment of evolution encompassing written language is miniscule, however, and the time segment of widespread literacy is even more minute. The earliest written symbols were pictographic scripts that represented parts of a story (Ogg, 1948). Their appearance marked the beginning of civilization as we now know it. Pictographs gave way to ideographic writing over 8000 years ago in Babylon, when a written symbol began to stand for an idea rather than a thing. At least 7000 years ago Egyptians made the transition from ideographs to a phonetic alphabet in which written symbols denoted the sounds of spoken language. With a phonetic alphabet, orderly, directional writing became possible.

The development of writing thus followed from gestures, to pictures, to alphabets that expressed spoken language (Huey, 1908). With the written word came enormous opportunities. Knowledge could be accumulated; laws could be codified; business transactions could be stored; and myths, histories, and poems to answer great questions and stir peoples' hearts could be recorded.

It is likely that reading out loud and the production of an unvoiced auditory image involve a specific neural circuit in which the stimuli travel from the visual cortices of both hemispheres to the angular gyrus of the language-dominant hemisphere. The stimuli received by the right-hemisphere visual cortex must traverse the posterior part of the corpus callosum to reach the left angular gyrus.

The angular gyrus of the parietal lobe is of fundamental importance in reading and is located at a point equidistant from three important parts of the brain: the occipital visual projection area, the auditory projection area in the temporal lobe, and the tactile area of the parietal lobe. It is of interest that blind persons appear to have the primary sensory area for reading braille in the postcentral parietal convolution in contrast with the angular gyrus in visual reading persons (Critchley, 1970). Reading also involves the integration of right-hemisphere visual form perception with left-hemisphere speech.

From the angular gyrus, additional neural processing is necessary for word selection and comprehension. The stimulus also is forwarded to the anterior language area where the relational value of the written words is interpreted and, if the material is to be recited, the entire collection of stimuli is put into verbal motor patterns. The production of phonemes from written material appears to involve the posterior aspects of both hemispheres and most of the language areas of the left hemisphere (Benson, 1984).

Additional portions of the right hemisphere also appear to be involved. Written words—at least those that are imageable —appear to stimulate other portions of the right hemisphere, from which visual images appear, somewhat analogous to the auditory images formed by the left hemisphere. Normal reading thus appears to activate both hemispheres. The functions of the two sides of the brain appear quite different, however. If one introspectively observes the reading of novels and romances and compares this with the reading of technical or philosophic works, a considerable difference can be noted in the ease with which they are accomplished. One obvious qualitative difference between the two is the relatively large number of imageable words in the former and the relative infrequency of imageable words in the latter. For almost everyone the reading of an imageable text is easier and pleasanter. The reading performed by the right hemisphere helps make this difference (Benson, 1984).

Oral reading involves an additional stage in the process of reading via the arcuate fasciculus to the motor speech area. Appropriate patterns of neural activity in the speech area pass to the left frontal lobe motor strip areas for vocalization, causing the coordinated contractions of the muscles that produce speech. There are significant individual variations in this encoding and motor discharge.

SUMMARY

Spoken language has been a human function long enough to become an innate capacity. It is possible that this extends to visual symbols, but not to words, since reading is such a recent evolutionary acquisition.

The language system consists of receptive, inner, and expressive processes based upon core structures within the frontal and temporal lobes surrounding the Sylvian fissure. The language system involves the state-regulating attentional and affective systems in nonverbal expressions, the information processing system in its receptive and inner aspects, and the managerial system in its inner and expressive aspects.

Nonverbal language consists of bodily signals that directly express wishes and emotions in order to influence the external world. Symbolic language consists of figures, words, and manual signs that indirectly express one's interests to other persons. Comprehension precedes the production of words in developing children.

Written language adds the occipital and parietal lobes to the language areas of the brain. The angular gyrus of the parietal lobe is of particular importance in reading.

Language is both an integral part of character development and a reflection of that development. For academic learning there must be sufficient competency in language to permit understanding instructions and communicating to others one's subjective experience. It also is important for teachers to be aware of both the nonverbal signal and the verbal symbolic forms of language. It also is important to recognize reading as a language function.

15

The Managerial System

The power to reflect is what makes us able to plan our future
in such a way as to avoid what seems inevitable.

Richard Leakey, 1965

The adaptive instincts underlying motivation largely involve holistic cognition and spontaneous communication by emotions, both of which are associated with the right cerebral hemisphere. In contrast the managerial system is concerned with making sense out of the external and internal worlds and involves information analysis and verbal communication, both of which are associated with the left cerebral hemisphere.

As an elaboration of the mastery drives, the managerial system fulfills an individual's needs in the risky world of people, things, and places. In carrying out the purposes of the self, the managerial system draws upon the knowledge of the information processing system within the prevailing arousal and emotional tone of the state regulating system and employs the language system in thought and expression. The managerial functions, also, are employed to deal with drive derivatives and self-evaluations that cause distress.

Although emerging from inborn sensorimotor schemes, each component of the managerial system is shaped by learning and, in turn, becomes a tool of learning as children assume increasing responsibility for themselves. The managerial system can be studied through both observable behavior and reported subjective experience. It contains adaptive subsystems and mediates interpersonal instinctual systems (see Figure 15-1.

ADAPTIVE COMPONENT SYSTEMS

The adaptive subsystems of the managerial system enable us to model the world in our minds, experiment with it, and act upon what we have imagined (Hunt, 1982). They mobilize knowledge, skills, and instinctual resources to meet personal needs in dealing with the environment (King, 1973). By the restraint and modulation of the drives, they relate inner forces to the external world through intelligent actions. They enable individuals to (1) reflect upon what is happening (impulse control), (2) know what is happening (information analysis), (3) decide what to do (thinking), (4) carry out actions (implementation), and 5) verify their actions (verification).

I. *ADAPTIVE MANAGERIAL COMPONENTS*
A. Impulse Control
   1) Drive Gratification Delay
   2) Flexibility
   3) Toleration of Distress
   4) Modulation of Emotions
   5) Selective Drive Regression
B. Information Analysis
   1) Distinguishing External and Internal Stimuli
   2) Determining Relevance of Perceptions
C. Thinking
   1) Synthesis
   2) Decision Making
   3) Planning
   4) Thinking Styles
      a) Automatic
      b) Problem Solving
      c) Creative
D. Implementing Actions
E. Verifying Actions
II. *INTERPERSONAL RELATIONSHIPS*
A. Affiliative Capacities
   1) Affectionate Bonding
   2) Empathy
   3) Receptive and Expressive Communication
   4) Fidelity
   5) Intimacy
B. Aggressive Capacities
   1) Basic Trust
   2) Autonomous Self-Control
   3) Initiative
   4) Negotiating Skills

Figure 15-1. The managerial system.

Impulse Control

Throughout life our primitive natures require restraint (Long, 1974). The impulse control system does this by inhibiting internal phenomena. The system's processes include postponing drive gratification, overcoming resistance to change, tolerating distress, modulating and refining emotions, and selectively regressing in drive expression. These processes can be seen as elaborations of the state regulating system's process of stimulus regulation. They are mediated by higher levels of the limbic system and the prefrontal cortex.

An inborn basis for impulse control is suggested by its value for species and individual survival. Jung held that the capacity to be responsible to others was an intrinsic component of the parental archetype, because a society could not survive without it (Stevens, 1982). Furthermore, the foundation for a later life of greater comfort is laid when a child learns the limits of personal influence and impulse control early. Not only does the child who lacks impulse control provoke continued limit setting in school and the community in later life, but the child clings to earlier fantasies of omnipotence and experiences the world as frustrating and unfair.

Children need firm and fair limits from adults, who model coping with frustrating situations and accepting limits themselves. A living relationship between children and adults around control issues gives the elbow room necessary for growth. Social support of the value of impulse control also is needed. Since self-indulgence is frequently modeled and implicitly encouraged by public influences, however, adults significant to a child may be the only dependable sources of modeling impulse control (Westman, 1979a).

Drive Gratification Delay

The ability to delay the gratification of drives permits reflection upon cravings and emotions before acting upon them. Beyond the stimulus regulation threshold for internal stimuli is the capacity to restrain drive pressures so that their imagery can be analyzed and brought into thinking. Without this capacity for delay, a person is at the mercy of urges for immediate drive gratification that actually may interfere with realistically fulfilling the drives (Zelnicker & Jeffrey, 1976).

Flexibility under Changing Circumstances

Successful adaptation depends upon flexibility handling changing circumstances. Adjusting to change poses frustration for everyone throughout life. However, changing an idea is much more difficult than affirming it, so that frustration is experienced when circumstances are not in accordance with one's expectations. The impulsive response to changing circumstances is to maintain the status quo. Inhibiting this tendency is essential to permitting the emergence of new responses (Piaget, 1974).

Tolerating Distress

Daily living results in frustrations that must be tolerated, so that one is not carried away by emotions that impede the higher functions of analysis and thought. The buffering effects of self-esteem play a role in one's ability to tolerate distressing emotions, which are felt more keenly when self-esteem is low. Thus self-esteem underlies the ability of the managerial system to tolerate a range of distressing emotions.

Modulating Emotions

Wide variations occur in the intensity of appetitive and affective drives. The ability to modulate their intensity plays a key role in analyzing and thinking about them. The modulation of emotions takes place through the capacity to sublimate them from raw to more refined forms. For example, aggressive drives can become assertiveness in acquiring knowledge and excitement in the challenge of problem solving.

Selective Drive Regression

Because of the constraints of social living, the drives generally are under varying degrees of inhibition. Opportunities for spontaneous, uninhibited drive gratification, therefore, are needed in order fully to exercise our instinctual equipment. Judging when inhibitions can be released is important. Play and recreation offer appropriate and socially sanctioned opportunities for regression into primitive forms of behavior. For example, through play one can vent aggression toward one's opponent.

Information Analysis

The information processing system's output provides data for the managerial system. The analytic function of the managerial system carries cognitive knowing further by distinguishing between stimuli that arise from the internal and external environments and by determining the significance of recognized percepts. The parietal lobe association areas play a central role in the information analytic system.

Distinguishing External Percepts and Internal Images

The term reality testing has been used to define the ability to discern between objective and subjective phenomena and is synonymous with the process of information analysis. Reality sense refers to the pleasure of competence derived from the mastery drives when reality is correctly perceived.

William James approached the question of reality not by asking what reality is but by asking, "Under what circumstances do we think things are real?" Through this question, he called attention to the fact that consensus determines what people conclude to be "real." There actually are many experiences of reality, such as moving from sleep to wakefulness, conversing in a theater before the curtain rises for a play, and leaving a psychotherapy session to confront the everyday world. Each of these discrete experiences has been defined as a frame within which various levels of action can be described (Goffman, 1974). Thus a frame is a generally agreed upon basic set of elements or principles that define a specific social event and distinguish it from other events (Spruiell, 1983). Reality, then, is defined by consensus within a specific frame and has both perceptual and social determinants.

An important distinction can be made between objective reality, which is based upon consensual perceptual validation, and social reality, which is based upon accepting another person's symbols and concepts. For example, objective reality may conflict with social reality when a child must accept erroneous adult subjective views of reality, which the child correctly perceives in another way (Abend, 1982).

The psychological terms *leveling* versus *sharpening* refer to the information analytic function. Leveling is the tendency to blend external perceptions with internal imagery, and sharpening refers to the tendency to distinguish between them (Messick, 1976). The percept-image model described in Chapter 13 suggests a mechanism for internal and external worlds of experience by inhibiting internal imagery during external perception, and vice versa (Horowitz, 1983; Noshpitz, 1982). Under certain circumstances, however, internal images may continue to "project on the screen" and color or dominate external perceptions. As an illustration, under boring circumstances, daydreams can become almost hallucinatory, so that a child becomes lost in internal imagery and fails to heed a teacher.

Determining the Meaning of Perceptions

Piaget held that a child does not take in preexisting reality but rather constructs and reconstructs a personal reality out of each experience. Thus concepts of the meaning of things are continuously modified as new data are received. From the developmental point of view, all of the

knowledge acquired in early life must undergo revision as a child's powers of analysis increase. The information analysis system updates this knowledge and applies it to current situations. The extent to which this does not take place causes childhood distortions that persist into later life.

A child and an adult may perceive different meanings from similar percepts without distorting them; the child's reality just may be different. For example, for a young child the meaning of a white uniform may be that the child is to receive an injection whereas for a parent the uniform means expertise. Thus a child's reality is related to one's age level and personal experience (Elkind, 1982).

Thinking

> The disciplined, or logically trained mind . . . is the one that best grasps the degree of observation, forming of ideas, reasoning and experimental testing required in any special case, and that profits the most, in future thinking, by mistakes made in the past.
>
> John Dewey, 1910

Because it is exceedingly difficult to conceptualize, thinking has eluded scientific study. Our knowledge of the central nervous system now permits definitions of thinking that bring it within the reach of scientific study. Although thinking traditionally has been regarded as a form of cognition, cognition can be limited profitably to the accumulation of knowledge in the information processing system, so that thinking can be seen as the manipulation of knowledge linked to action by the managerial system. Cognition is related to the vicinity of the occipital, temporal, and parietal lobes whereas thinking centers in the frontal lobes. In general systems terms, thinking is the activity of the decider system, which employs the information processing system's output but is not contained within it.

Although not easily observed, thinking is a constant fact of life. Thinking may be initiated consciously and reflected in conscious imagery; however, it operates outside of conscious awareness. It not only occupies most of waking and sleeping time but is reflected in muscle tonus and is colored and directed by cravings and emotions (McKim, 1980). As stated by Henrick, "Motility is the cradle of the mind."

Thinking makes the human being, and perhaps other animals, active forces upon, rather than passive recorders of, the surrounding world (Griffin, 1984). Still, wavering and diverse moods and changing views easily influence thinking, making the human being a specialist in misunderstanding. The cause is less one of passion overcoming reason and more that of the uncharted, unconscious primitive flooding of thought by the primary process (Barzun, 1983). Thinking is by no means synonymous with rationality.

Sigmund Freud described thinking as trial action, which occurs when direct satisfaction of a drive is not possible. It enables one to seek satisfaction through detours. This corresponds to Luria's conception that thinking occurs when a drive is not satisfied. Piaget also referred to thinking as action in a symbolic medium. Freud, Luria, and Piaget thus saw thinking as internal action. Even the neuroanatomical structures of thought and action are juxtapositioned in the frontal lobes. The motor concomitants of thought and dreams include the muscles of speech articulation, skeletal muscles that function in nonlinguistic communication, and smooth muscle controlled by the autonomic nervous system in emotional expression. Thus a variety of skeletal and smooth muscle responses occur when individuals silently engage in thinking (McGuigan, 1978). Thinking is intimately associated with action.

Piaget saw thinking as internal ordering of one's personal interaction with the world. For him the fundamental elements of thought were inborn sensorimotor schemes around which sensory input is organized. The symbol system of language expresses that internal organization. Reading provides content for thinking, and writing expresses thought, however, thinking is not dependent on words. On the contrary, Piaget held that language is dependent on thinking.

The consciously experienced vehicles for thinking may be visual, verbal, proprioceptive, or haptic. These forms are the imagery of thought, not thought itself. For those without sensory impairment, thinking does seem to be internal speech. Deceived by our own experience, we regard verbal symbols as the process rather than as the product of thinking. Thinking is not tied to any particular type of imagery, however (Amosov, 1967). The brain invents images and symbols that serve intelligence and communication so that the deaf create visual and haptic and the blind auditory and haptic symbols. The thinking processes of the deaf in particular can be explained without recourse to language (Furth, 1966; Meadow, 1975).

Although inextricably woven into the fabric of adult thinking, words were not the original form of thinking in human evolution. Locke (1959) eloquently expressed the origin of words:

> Man, though he have great variety of thoughts, and such from which others as well as himself might receive profit and delight, yet they are all within his own breast, invisible and hidden from others, nor can of themselves be made to appear . . . it was necessary that man should find out some external sensible signs, whereof those invisible ideas, which his thoughts are made up of, might be made known to others. For this purpose nothing was so fit, either for plenty of quickness,

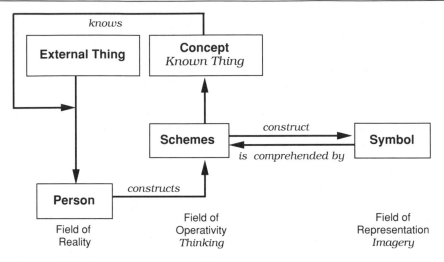

Figure 15-2. The three fields in Piaget's Theory of Knowledge. (Adapted from H. G. Furth, *Piaget and Knowledge: Theoretical Foundations,* 2nd ed., The University of Chicago Press, Chicago, 1981.)

as those articulate sounds, which with so much ease and variety he found himself able to make. Thus we may conceive how words . . . came to be made use of by men as the signs of their ideas; not by any natural connection . . . between particular articulate sounds and certain ideas, for then there would be but one language amongst all men, but by a voluntary imposition, whereby a word is made arbitrarily the mark of such an idea.

Language, cultural institutions, and the learning process interact and shape the content and the form of thinking, but not the process itself. The distinction between imagery and thinking itself was made by Piaget as illustrated in Figure 15-2. In the field of reality are the external thing and the person. In the field of operativity, schemes carry out the operations of assimilation and accomodation. The known thing or concept is related to the external thing not as a symbol that stands in the place of the thing but as attributes by which the thing is known. In contrast, a symbol is constructed by the scheme as an internal im-

age, which may be a tool of thinking and expressed behaviorally in symbolic play, gestures, or a written word (Furth, 1981).

Much of what is called thinking actually is using imagery in the exercise of imagination, as in the association of emotion and concept in "to think of changing schools is frightening," or as in retrieving a concept in "can you think of her address?" Moreover, the imagery of thinking may partially gratify wishes. It also may be the first expression in awareness of emergent and previously hidden ideas or feelings (Horowitz, 1983). Thus the imagery of thinking may give rise to pleasure itself.

Thinking takes place largely in the lateral aspects of the cerebral hemispheres. It involves the search and exploration functions of the frontal lobes, the perceptions and imagery of the sensory cortex, the study of relations of the associational cortex, the satisfactions of the pleasure and distress centers of the affective system, the center of self-awareness in the diencephalon, and the dorsomedial thalamic nuclei that mediate the limbic mood system (Young, 1978). The prefrontal areas have a special role in thinking concerned with logic and creativity (Watts, 1975).

Children think about their lives as do adults, but with less refined means. At around the age of six, the first true operational structures for thinking appear so that a child can develop classification systems beyond personal symbols. The developmental process of thinking is toward decreased dependence on one's own actions and a greater freedom from and control of symbolic signifiers (Furth, 1981). Thus the development of thinking moves from a stimulus–response and trial–error level, through a symbolic representational level, to conceptual thinking about concrete objects, and ultimately to conceptual thinking about thoughts themselves through formal operations.

Thinking can be further understood by examining its processes, which can be viewed as (1) synthesis, (2) decision making, (3) planning, and (4) specific modalities.

Synthesis

Thinking begins after impulsive responses are controlled and information is analyzed so that information synthesis can take place. Synthesis is the ability to combine elements identified by the information analytic system within a given time frame. The synthetic process abstracts, relates, distills, spatially rotates, and classifies attributes of perceptions, imagery, symbols, and concepts. It has roots in the affiliative and mastery instinctual systems. A prototype might be the fusion of male and female elements to form a new human being (Nunberg, 1955).

Persons may be ordered along a continuum from concrete to abstract, depending on their ability to analyze and synthesize information. A child who is limited in analyzing and synthesizing ability is said to be concrete; a child who is high in analyzing and synthesizing ability is said to be capable of abstractions. This continuum also has

been termed integrative or conceptual complexity and is an ingredient of the rigidity versus flexibility cognitive style dimension (Goldstein & Blackman, 1978). The ability to abstract permits flexible and sophisticated classification of knowledge so that a variety of alternative courses of action can be identified in a particular situation.

Decision Making

In order to make decisions, one must be able to evaluate the information produced by analysis and synthesis. The process of thinking involves choosing the alternatives most likely to succeed. Alternatives are evaluated by making judgments of the quality, quantity, and meaning of information by comparing it with drive aims, values, and the expectations of other persons.

Children cannot develop socially rewarding lives without values to guide decision making. Kohlberg (1977) postulated a series of stages in the development of values that follow a sequence from fear of authority and pleasure seeking, through interpersonal approval, law and order, moral reasoning, and ultimately universal ethical principles. Unless a child has progressed to the level of interpersonal approval, functioning in schools is difficult.

The processes of evaluating situations and deciding goals are at the center of developing social competence. Five general types of social goals for children have been found (Renshaw & Asher, 1982): positive outgoing goals that are highly friendly and assertive; positive accommodating goals that are highly friendly but less assertive and more focused on slowly building peer relationships; avoidance goals that reflect a sense of helplessness and a desire to avoid negative feelings in a situation; hostile goals that are focused upon revenge; and rule-oriented goals that are neither friendly nor hostile but are focused upon the rights and interests of children in a particular situation.

Unfortunately for children, our affluent, technological society is characterized by many attractive alternatives that create conflicts for them prematurely. The young particularly are vulnerable to attractive alternatives without values that can guide them in making choices (Lipowski, 1975).

Planning

Once decisions have been made, planning aims to achieve the most efficient and safe course toward a goal. It also requires suspension of action in accordance with an objective and the anticipation of the consequences of actions. Planning provides for sequential actions through knowing how to begin, order, and carry out activities. It involves devising tactics for putting the strategy into effect. It is based upon an awareness of and ability to live within time relationships.

Modes of Thinking

Thinking takes place in several modes related to the degree of conscious awareness, of involvement of the primary and secondary processes, and of novelty of a situation. The automatic, problem-solving, and creative modes deserve particular emphasis.

Three conditions promote effective thinking. The first is a challenge, so that one thinks best in a situation that one desires to change. The second is accurate information, so that thinking is impaired when information is incorrect, inadequate, or unavailable. The third is flexibility, so that one has easy access between conscious and unconscious levels, can solve freely from one mode of thinking to another, and can use several forms of thinking imagery interchangeably (McKim, 1980).

Automatic Thinking. Much vital thinking takes place beneath conscious awareness (Tanguay, 1984). For example, automatic thinking allows the driver of an automobile to carry on a conversation while navigating through traffic. The absence of conscious awareness of thought, then, is not an indicator of lack of complexity. On the contrary, conscious awareness of action indicates a lack of mastery that further learning can raise to the level of automatic thinking (Basch, 1975).

Great individual variability exists in the degree to which people can automatically sort out and organize experiences and knowledge by preconscious thought processes. Some can make use of these processes better in the absence of stress and others when under stress (Zeigarnick, 1965).

Problem-Solving Thinking. The sequence of brain activities in problem solving appears to be as follows (Loye, 1983). A problem calling for solution is detected at some level of awareness. To solve the problem, both the desired outcome and the conditions likely to prevail in the future must be forecast. Via the reticular network and many other channels, the frontal lobes call for information from the senses and memory and activate the motor centers, if the eyes, ears, or hands must gather data. The right brain produces a quick gestalt, linking the problem to a first-guess solution. The left brain produces an analysis of how the problem may be solved as a sequence of specific steps. The frontal lobes consolidate these analyses into a first forecast, which is relayed to other forebrain, midbrain and brainstem areas for evaluation. The forecast is then tested, either through imagining what it will mean when put into effect or through actual trial. Test results are then fed back with forecast revisions until the best forecast is made or until the action it guides is completed.

From different perspectives Freud, Piaget, and Luria arrived at similar views of problem solving (Luria, 1973; Pribram & Gill, 1976). All three stressed the importance of language in bringing images into conscious awareness so that relationships can be made between them. They also distinguished two basic ways of solving problems. I have defined the first type as the imagination system, which is linked to percepts and is of practical, observational, and judgmental nature, as in forming a block design. Imagination simply associates phenomena in their entirety as one train of images suggests another, and images in different modalities are synthesized. The second type is problem-solving thinking, which is linked to memories of past interactions with the world and involves abstract classification and logical deduction, as in solving an arithmetic problem. It is reasoning in which abstractions are taken as equivalent to the data from which they come so that generalizations can be made.

Problem-solving thinking includes stimulus analysis, through which the existence of a problem is recognized; selective attention, through which certain attributes of stimuli are attended to and others are ignored; categorization of stimuli; response generation, in which alternative hypotheses about solutions to the problem are raised through synthesis, decision making, and planning; and response execution, in which a hypothesis is tested through the implementation function and is modified by feedback about the feasibility or accuracy of the hypothesis through the verification function (Gagne, 1959; Parrill-Burnstein, 1981).

Problem-solving thinking may take place in the form of memory images of analogous solutions that are recalled. These images may occur in the verbal form of talking to oneself or in visualizing spatial images. This form of thought can be performed through the artificial intelligence of computers (McCorduck, 1979).

Problem-solving thinking also may employ inductive and deductive reasoning (Pelligrino, 1985). One of the most pervasive aspects of human thought is the capacity to form wholes from parts by generalizing from specific experiences and forming new, more abstract concepts through the process of inductive reasoning. Induction is the development of general rules or concepts from sets of specific instances. The development of a child and learning from instruction take place largely through inductive processes. By analyzing the similarities and differences between specific experiences, we extract the general characteristics of classes of objects, events, and situations. Through inductive reasoning new information is learned by making use of analogy to existing knowledge. Thus models are created and compared with other models for consistency. For example, a dog and a cat are both animals.

Deductive reasoning extracts parts from wholes. It involves the ability to understand premises and to imagine a state of affairs that corresponds to them, in addition to the ability to construct integrated mental models based upon verbal descriptions. Then it involves the ability to search for alternative models of premises and to discover what, if anything, they have in common. Finally, it involves the ability to express in words the state of affairs represented in the models. A simple example is (Johnson-Laird, 1985): John is taller than Eric. Eric is taller than Dan. Who is the tallest?

Thinking has been described on the dimension of convergence–divergence (Guilford, 1980). Convergent persons rely upon analytic, rational, problem-solving thinking (Hunt, 1982). They tend to relish technology, to be cautious about expressing feelings, to overcategorize and stereotype attitudes, and to gravitate toward mathematics and the physical sciences (Hudson, 1967).

Creativity. Sigmund Freud stated:

The constraint which intellect imposes upon imagination hinders the creative

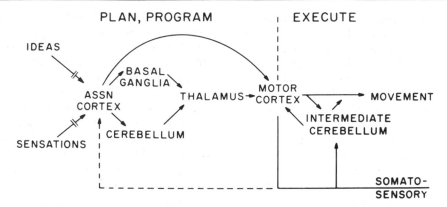

Figure 15-3. Scheme showing the general pathways in the execution of the control of movement. (From C. W. Cotman and J. L. McGaugh, *Behavioral Neuroscience,* copyright 1980 by Academic Press, New York. Reproduced with permission.)

work of the mind by examining too closely the ideas already pouring in, as it were, at the gates . . . In the case of a creative mind, it seems to me, the intellect has withdrawn its watchers from the gates, and the ideas rush in pell-mell, and only then does it review and inspect the multitude. The uncreative mind rejects too soon and discriminates too severely.

Sigmund Freud, 1938

In creative thinking imagery derives from unconscious sources, while the impulse control system temporarily suspends its censorship. Images pertaining to repressed motivations stay conscious in a vague way before the arduous work of elaboration provides them with the know-how that makes them communicable. Creativity is described in detail in Chapter 17.

On the dimension of convergence–divergence (Guilford, 1980), divergent persons tend to prefer intuitive creative thinking, to use wide conceptual categories, and to accept thematic, as opposed to analytic, links between concepts. They also are likely to be impulsive and emotionally uninhibited, and in later education

to tend toward artistic endeavors or the social sciences.

Implementing Actions

One's thoughts and instinctual drives are implemented through motor actions in the form of behavior, such as speaking, writing, and performing a task. Motor actions depend upon the ability to initiate and sequence internally generated impulses through the output transducers via the extrapyramidal and pyramidal tracts to the skeletal muscles.

In the course of walking, for example, the brain blends sensory perceptions, takes into account the present state of the body, consults past memories, and considers future goals. The model in Figure 15-3 illustrates the general nature of the transactions involved in intentional body movements. The association cortex is an important participant in the early phases of evolving movement by integrating information from various primary sensory cortical areas. Activity from the association cortex feeds directly to the motor cortex as well as to the thalamus via the cerebellum and basal ganglia. It appears that the cerebellum and basal ganglia provide internal models of actions in the external world. Sensory inputs, motivation, behavioral goals, and learned information all play roles in the programming of movements. Moreover, many corollary discharges are operating throughout the brain to supply the necessary information in order to assess options and maintain focused action. The cortical areas converse with each other indirectly or directly as part of the blend. The motor cortex then directs the muscles with the modulation and verification of the cerebellum.

For research purposes, seven important elements of a mental act can be analyzed. First is the content or subject matter. Next is the operation, which is internalized, organized, coordinated activity that elaborates upon information derived from external and internal sources. Third is the figurative, pictorial, numeric, symbolic, or verbal language in which the mental act is expressed. Fourth is the phase of the act itself, whether it be at the input, elaboration, or output stage. Fifth, the level of complexity is the quantity and quality of units of information necessary for the act. Sixth, the level of abstraction may involve operations on the objects themselves or varying degrees of abstraction upon them. And last, the level of efficiency is the rapidity and precision of the act (Feuerstein, 1980).

Verifying Actions

Verification is the comparison of feedback from the results of an action with its original purpose. Even performing a simple act, such as handwriting, requires an elaborate system in order to activate some and inhibit other muscle groups, coordinate the eyes and the hand, and ensure that the written letters and words correspond to intentions. The verification of more complex activities is illustrated by a student checking and correcting one's schoolwork. At an even more complicated level, it involves ascertaining the effect of one's behavior upon others through sensitivity to their actions and emotions.

One of the most distinctive features of the human intellect is the awareness of one's own thinking processes. Children gradually acquire this capacity to monitor and guide their own thought processes. Thus the mind can observe and correct itself. This occurs both automatically without conscious awareness and as a laborious process in self-analysis (Hunt, 1982).

INTERPERSONAL COMPONENT SYSTEMS

A major share of the output of the managerial system is relating to other persons. The study of interpersonal relationships has been fraught with formidable methodological problems. It is difficult enough to analyze the behavior of an individual, and the variables multiply when the field of study contains two or more people. Fortunately, the integration of role, self, and developmental theories provides a background for describing individuals in specific role relationships that draw out corresponding aspects of the self in the context of the stages of the life cycles (Parsons, 1964). Through Erickson's theoretical stages of the life cycle, one progressively develops in the context of optimal role relationships: basic trust, autonomy, initiative, industry, identity, intimacy, generativity, and integrity (Erikson, 1959).

Lorna Benjamin's Structural Analysis of Social Behavior offers a useful tool for research on interpersonal relationships (Benjamin, 1981, 1987). It is based upon a theoretical model that has demonstrated construct validity, content validity, and reliability. Furthermore, it draws upon subjectively reported and objectively observed data in developing a picture of how individuals view themselves and others, how they are viewed by others, and how their intrapsychic identifications are shaped.

The Structural Analysis of Social Behavior identifies four basic interpersonal styles based upon variations on the dimensions of approach or withdrawal and dependent or independent behaviors. Type I is characterized by an independent-approach tendency expressed through reflective autonomous and empathic behavior. Type II reflects independent-withdrawal tendencies expressed through reliance on internal imagery, caring for oneself, and going one's own way. Type III denotes dependent-withdrawal tendencies reflected in apathetic, sulking conformity, and wary fearfulness. Type IV refers to dependent-approach proclivities through deferential acceptance of others and submissive conformity.

The central nervous system outputs that interface as personality traits with other persons in role relationships can be described as the managerial system mediates the affiliative and aggressive instinctual systems.

Affiliative Capacities

Of all the qualities needed for successful living in society, the most important is the ability to relate to other people, as expressed in approach and withdrawal behaviors. In considering the significant elements in human relationships, it is essential to bear in mind that children are particularly changeable in different social contexts and ongoing role relationships. A child may appear to be one kind of person in one setting with a particular adult and an entirely different person at another time and place. The description of children's personality traits, therefore, must take into account specific circumstances.

A distinction should be made between simply relating exploitatively to people, the impairment of which is seen in the autistic child, and forming affectionate bonds with people, the impairment of which is seen in the socially adept but affectionately unattached narcissistic character. In contrast with affectionate bonds, the ability to relate exploitatively to other people does not in itself include feelings toward other people. Ordinarily, under optimal circumstances, the abilities to relate to and to care about others are not separated when children are raised by committed parents, who facilitate the expression of affiliative drives through mutual dependency, trust, and affection.

Another affiliative quality that facilitates relating to adults and forming peer relationships is the capacity to empathize with others. This outgoing quality is expressed through interest in receiving and providing positive feedback to others. Also inherent in relating to others is the ability to communicate both expressively through disclosing and receptively through listening. Self-esteem enhances relations with others, because basically positive experiences with significant others in the past provide a positive feeling tone for current interpersonal relations.

Developmentally the achievement of an awareness and confidence in the variegated components of one's self makes it possible for adolescents to devote their energies to relationships with others through the capacity for fidelity. To complete the stages of the life cycle, adults achieve the capacity for affiliation and affection through intimacy. As the individual matures, the capacity for generativity enables caring, nurturance, and productivity. In later life, a sense of personal integrity enables the renunciation of earlier physical powers with the elaboration of wisdom.

Aggressive Capacities

On the general dimension of independence and dependence, the most important capacity is oppenness to receive knowledge and to learn skills from those with greater expertise. This capacity flows in children from a sense of basic trust of authority figures and is accompanied by an optimistic attitude toward educational enterprises. Coexisting with this capacity to depend upon others appropriately is the ability autonomously to assume responsibility for self-control so that it is not necessary for others to control the child.

From the reservoir of motivation arising from the aggressive instincts, assertive strivings can facilitate taking the initiative and expressing oneself in school with teachers and peers so that it is not necessary to be motivated by others. This capacity provides an internal source of direction and purpose. Although susceptible to the intrusive exploitation of others, the disposition to be assertive is an important ingredient of success in school and in leadership roles with peers. A degree of constructive manipulation of others is necessary to preserve one's own integrity, as one appropriately submits to the influence of others. Diplomacy is the lubricant of human relations.

The achievement of the capacity for industrious work provides methods for relating to others in the performance of tasks. The ability to negotiate and balance personal needs with the expectations of others also minimizes conflict and promotes goodwill.

SUMMARY

As an elaboration of the mastery drives, the managerial system is devoted to fulfilling one's internal needs in the external world of people, places, and things. The adaptive managerial subsystems enable expression of the appetitive and adaptive instinctual systems through mastery of oneself and the external world. The managerial system also mediates the interpersonal affiliative and aggressive instinctual systems.

The adaptive managerial subsystems are impulse control, information analysis, thinking, implementing actions, and verifying actions. Impulse control is composed of the processes of delaying drive gratification, flexibly handling change, tolerating distress, modulating emotions, and selectively regressing in drive expression.

The information analytic system's analysis of cognition is an essential stage in providing data for the other managerial systems. It employs the processes of distinguishing between external and internal stimuli and determining the relevance of perceptions.

Whereas cognition is knowledge, thinking is the manipulation of knowledge. Thinking employs the imaging and imagination systems of the information processing system. It may be initiated by the conscious mind and reflected in imagery, however, it is a process underlying both and operates outside of conscious awareness. The basic processes of thinking are synthesis, decision making, and planning, all of which are employed in automatic, problem solving, and creative modalities.

The implementation of intentions takes place through encoding internally generated information into forms that can be expressed through the output transducers of the skeletal muscles.

Through internal and external sensory feedback, the effects of one's behavior are verified, so that adjustments can be made in expressive actions. The elaborate verification system operates at a variety of levels from the simplest motor task to ascertaining the effect of one's behavior upon others.

The output of the central nervous system occurs in the context of role relationships, situations, and specific people that draw out appropriate personality traits related to the stages of the life cycle. Particularly important for success in school on the affiliative dimension are the ability to appropriately trust others, autonomy in self-control, the capacity for empathy with and nurturance of others, the ability to communicate with others receptively and expressively, and a foundation of self-esteem that releases one from self-preoccupation.

On the dimension of aggressive motives, the capacities for assertiveness in the form of taking the initiative on tasks and for dependency in authority relationships are important. The ability to negotiate diplomatically and balance personal needs with the needs and expectations of others also is important for successful adult and peer relationships, with a particular emphasis upon fidelity during adolescence. The capacities for intimacy, generativity, and wisdom have their roots in childhood and achieve primacy as adult life progresses.

The managerial system straddles the state regulating and information processing systems, organizes itself around the language system, operates at the behest and for the benefit of the self, and also has a life of its own in the form of a vast reservoir of automatic mechanisms for negotiating the routines of life, so that human beings have the luxuries of contemplating their existences and of artistic and scientific creativity.

16

The Self System

As soon as we let ourselves contemplate our own place in the picture, we seem to be stepping outside of the boundaries of natural science.

Lord Adrian, 1966

We live in three worlds: the external world I of physical objects; the internal world II of subjective experience; and the world III of culture, which combines the external and internal worlds (Popper & Eccles, 1977; Eccles & Robinson, 1984). World I consists of things and living organisms, including our own bodies. World II consists of consciousness of oneself and death. World III consists of theories about oneself and death, works of art, and science (Figure 16-1). The self is the center of human experience of these three worlds (Lichtenstein, 1977). In this model, worlds II and III constitute the self in the field of human actions (Parsons, 1977, 1978).

Even in prehistoric times when human beings were preoccupied with physical survival, a need existed for world III (Eccles, 1989). As a result, cultural traditions that passed knowledge from one generation to the next emerged to provide personal meaning in life through the continuity of group membership.

The instinctual bases for achieving meaning in life lie in the affiliative and mastery drives. The affiliative drives offer pleasure from interpersonal relationships, which give one significance to others. The mastery drives provide satisfaction from the efficient fulfillment of internally generated needs. As a means of reinforcing the mastery drives, an internal monitoring system evolved in the form of self-esteem, which is experienced as euphoria, when the managerial system is functioning efficiently; of self-respect, when actual self-concepts are in harmony with desired self-concepts; and of pride arising from positive self-evaluations. From these components, the self arose during the course of evolution.

Just as the musculature seeks action and pleasurably responds to optimal physical conditioning, the brain seeks activity and pleasurably responds to efficient functioning. The self is the mechanism for achieving this by linking the individual to the purposes of group living and the meaning of culture, so that disparate parts of life are experienced as parts of a larger order. The pleasurable emotions available to the self further survival of the species by motivating individuals to promote group interests. Distress, also, constitutes a source of mo-

WORLD I — *Physical Objects*
    Things and Living Organisms
    One's Body

WORLD II — *Subjective Experience*
    Conscious awareness of oneself
    and death (State Regulating
    System)
    Self-awareness — the "I"
    Self-esteem

WORLD III — *Created by the Human Mind*
    Thinking — Theories about oneself,
    death, art and science
    Self-concept (Information
    Processing System)
    Self-evaluation (Managerial
    System)

Figure 16-1.

tivation, when the self is experienced as lonely and without the sense of belonging to larger entities.

The self eludes precise definition. We cannot study or describe the self per se. Only its introspectively and empathically perceived manifestations can be apprehended (Kohut, 1977). Like all reality the self is not knowable in its essence. It, also, is not possible to think of the self without including the self consciously experiencing itself. Accordingly, the self has meaning to oneself but not to an observer. For example, in psychoanalysis what the analysand calls the self, the analyst calls the ego. For this reason the scientific value of the conceptualization of the self as a psychic structure has been questioned. Sigmund Freud's conception of *das Ich*, however, included both the internally experienced self and the externally described ego; the latter has received more attention in subsequent psychoanalytic writings (Sprueill, 1981). For our purposes the self is a useful conception that facilitates the description of one's inner experience and its developmental course.

From a systems point of view, the *person*

is a sociological term; persons can be touched and heard, their emotions can be registered, and their thoughts can be recorded. The *self* is a psychological term and is an abstract, almost mystical, conception of mental functions and subjective experiences. The *individual* is a biological term; individuals can yield blood samples and activate electrical tracings (Beres, 1981).

Most important, the self is the seat of one's continuity in time and space and is based upon the sum total of past experience (Bronowski, 1972). A record of this experience is neurally encoded in Penfield's stream of consciousness, which separates each person from all others by conferring a sense of temporal continuity and spatial cohesion upon disparate experiences throughout life (Penfield, 1975).

In essence the self is personal invariance within the process of transformation inherent in life (Lichtenstein, 1977). Like a hologram the self is at once a coherent whole and an aggregate of discrete parts. The self links inner experience to the external world and maintains an inner congruence with the ideals and aspirations of social groups. The conscious experience of having a self is based upon knowledge both of one's existence and that others recognize one's existence. When it is smoothly functioning, there is little conscious awareness of the self. Under pathological circumstances, however, the consequences of fragmentation of the self and disparities between its parts are painfully evident, as will be described in Chapter 26.

Winnicott's *potential space* lies between the individual and the environment and corresponds to the self. It is the area of all experience through which one can reach intense sensations, and thus awareness of being alive. The potential space is neither inside in the world of dreams nor outside in the world of shared reality. It is the paradoxical third place that partakes of both the internal and external worlds at once. Any activity can come within the potential space insofar as it involves an individual's creativity and sense of being personally present. Communication through the mutuality of experience, and thus teaching and learning, takes place in the potential space of the self (Davis & Wallbridge, 1981).

The inner and outer faces of the self were described by Erik Erikson as one's inner self-identity, which is the subjectively experienced self. The outer self-identity, or external face of the self, was made up of the observable characteristics of one's personality (Erikson, 1959). A more parsimonious terminology is to refer to one's subjective aspect as the self and to one's externally observable aspect as one's personality. The self thereby bridges the intrapsychic and sociocultural environments and is expressed through aspects of one's personality that are evoked whenever a person enters another's presence in role relationships. The dramatic performance of the self arises from a particular scene and is influenced by whether its manifestations in personality are credited or discredited by its audience (Goffman, 1959).

The origins of the self lie in the innate sensorimotor schemes of early life, which remain indelibly stamped reference points for later experiences (Basch, 1979). Three fundamental dimensions of the self can be distinguished as they emerge during the course of development: (1) the self-as-agent (the "I will"); (2) the self-as-locus of experience (the "I want"); and (3) the self-as-object (the "me") (Schafer, 1968). There is suggestive evidence that the "I" and "me" experiences are mediated by the prefrontal lobes (Harris, 1986). The "I will" may be by the lateral and the "I want" by the medial aspects of the dominant prefrontal cortex. The concepts of "me" may be mediated by the lateral and the feelings of "me" by the medial aspects of the nondominant prefrontal cortex.

In the course of development, the first to emerge is the self-as-agent, or as a doer and knower. By the end of the first month of life, a baby can be observed to take the initiative as a doer by exploring stimuli and by showing expectancies of environmental events. By four months, an infant is both a knower and doer, as is evident in goal-oriented behavior. The second phase of the self-as-locus emerges later in the first year as the child appears to experience pleasure from being an effective doer. During the second year, there is evidence of monitoring oneself as an object in the form of observing how others react to oneself and then proceeding to integrate those cues with one's own acts through imitation. This extends into internalizing parental prohibitions as one's own and further treating oneself as an object. Finally, the clear differentiation of one's will from other's wills is seen in oppositional behavior through which a child asserts oneself by saying "I won't do it" (Stechler & Kaplan, 1980).

Children become aware of their selves through "I" and "we" discriminations in early life and later by assuming roles and playing the parts of others. Playing the role of one person and then of another is the medium through which the self becomes aware of its own nature, as distinguished from those other selves whose roles it takes (Mead, 1936). Through play a child also develops the empathy needed for cooperative effort toward socially desirable ends (Davis & Wallbridge, 1981).

Extensive research has been carried out on the self under descriptive terms, such as self-concept, self-esteem, self-regard, self-acceptance, and self-ideal. An analysis of this research points to the need for greater precision in definitions and a coherent theoretical model in order to permit scientific dialogue and to ensure that pertinent variables are taken into account (Guntrip, 1973; Wylie, 1979).

A model of the self in accord with current knowledge of the central nervous system is depicted in Figure 16-2. In this model the self straddles the four other component systems of the brain and can be viewed as a fifth component. The state regulating system is the site of self-con-

	Self-Awareness	Self-Esteem	Self-Concept	Self-Evaluation
Function	Awareness of internal and external worlds	Group living with reciprocal obligations	Action as a person in continuity of time and coherence of space	Enables adaptation by adjusting self-concept to reality
CNS Functional System	State regulating system	State regulating system Managerial system	Information Processing system Language System	Managerial system State regulating system
Development	Individuation from parent	Pleasure in body and its products and attachment to parents	Body Image Self-Image and percept Concept formation	Evaluation of parents
Subjective Experience	"I"	Emotions of well being pleasure–distress–shame Feelings of one's self "We"	Knowledge of properties of self	Emotions of anger and love toward self—guilt feelings about one's self-concept
Mode	Personal Figure-ground discrimination	Competent, reliable functioning of managerial system	Desired and actual concepts	Treating self as object by comparing actual with ideal concepts
Behavior	Relating person	Resiliency in meeting challenges of living	Seeking goal attainment acknowledging strengths and weaknesses	Correcting personal characteristics

Figure 16-2. The self system components.

sciousness and self-esteem, and the source of emotions funding self-evaluation. The information processing system and the language system are the bases of the self-concept, which includes knowledge of one's personal qualities, particularly of self-boundaries in space and time, gender, talents, and skills. The managerial system supplies the value-laden judgments of self-evaluation.

SELF-AWARENESS

The experience of what has happened is called being conscious, really not of now but of then. For the present moment cannot be grasped.

William James

In the evolution of animals, four levels of consciousness can be distinguished: (1) reptilian (subcortical), as in sleep, wakefulness, and drive-related states; (2) paleomammalian (limbic), as in a dream; (3) neomammalian (neocortical), as in sentient consciousness of one's activity; and (4) human (asymmetrical neocortical), as in conscious awareness of the self as a subject and object (Brown, 1977).

All animals with central nervous systems discriminate signals into figure–background patterns that distinguish their own bodies from the environment. Chimpanzees can even recognize their own faces in a mirror (Maccoby, 1980). Human infants develop this capacity for consciously perceiving their bodies as represented in the body image of the parietal sensory strip. Unlike chimpanzees, children further achieve a symbolic capacity in which their selves can be experienced through the use of personal pronouns (Popper & Eccles, 1977). The subjective "I" is the consciously observing "eye" of the self and the initiator of thinking and motor activities. The neuroanatomical specificity of the "I," or self-aware aspect of the self, is suggested by an adult brain injury case in which it was the only intact brain function remaining (Luria, 1980). It appears to be a function of the dominant prefrontal lobe (Harris, 1986).

The experience of Helen Keller (1908), who was deprived of visual, auditory, and language modalities, dramatically illustrates the impact of discovering self-awareness:

I can recollect no process which I should now dignify with the term thought . . . because before I was taught, I lived in a sort of perpetual dream . . . An idea—that which gives identity and continuity to experience—came into my sleeping and waking existence at the same moment with the awakening of self-consciousness. Before that moment my mind was in a state of anarchy in which meaningless sensations rioted, and if thought existed, it was so vague and inconsequent, it cannot be made a part of discourse.

Thus self-awareness is an exquisitely evolved personal construction that permits separation of oneself from other persons and enables the achievement of a relatively stable, yet expanding, personal world. It is the self-as-agent that can perceive and act upon other aspects of the self-as-object. It is the part of the self experienced as "I want" and "I will."

Self-awareness took over the direction of human evolution as homo sapiens was transformed into a cultural animal sensitive to knowledge, beauty, and morality (Laszlo, 1972). Self-awareness emancipated human beings from the confines of their sensory realities and placed them into worlds they themselves created. Through thinking they could surround themselves with ideas, modes of feeling, and beliefs, which were only indirectly related to the experienced world around them. At the same time, self-awareness is open to expansion, as illustrated by meditation techniques that stimulate awareness of ever-growing aspects of the self (Ornstein, 1972).

Through self-awareness, we perceive images that no one else knows about. We also are aware that we laugh, cry, converse, and aggress—all of which can be observed by others. We become aware of ourselves, as well, by discovering that others view the world differently than we do. Infants do not know that others have a different perspective, but older children do. The awareness of others' perspectives—part of the waning of self-centeredness that occurs throughout childhood—sharpens the distinction between oneself and others. If each person has a particular perspective, one's own perspective makes one unique. This accentuation of uniqueness heightens one's sense of self.

We usually are aware of the distinction between inner private feelings and outer public behavior. Our senses are directed toward the environment that surrounds us, and we spend most of our waking hours perceiving this environment. But when we do attend to ourselves, we can perceive private and public aspects. The private aspects are so named because they can be observed only by the experiencing person. Private images are difficult to study scientifically, but it can be done through dreams and daytime imagery (Buss, 1980). Only oneself can perceive a toothache, the taste of an apple, a fleeting image of a childhood memory, a momentary urge to kill, or a flicker of fear. Others can infer one's inner imagery but obviously only oneself can perceive it directly. In contrast to the covertness of the private aspects of the self, the public aspects are overt. Other people can notice one's hair, posture, facial expression, gestures, manners, or the way one speaks. These same things can be observed from one's own perspective. Public self-awareness, then, consists of attending to the same aspects of one's appearance and behavior that others can observe. It is a focus on oneself as a social object.

Self-awareness is more appropriately viewed as a system rather than as a thing, a repository, or a function (Jaynes, 1976). It operates by way of analogy with an analog "I" that can observe itself in space. It thus can be seen as an inner spatial analog of the world. There may be little in consciousness that is not an analog of something that was in behavior first.

Jaynes asks us to consider what it is like to understand persons speaking to us (Jaynes, 1976). In a sense, we let them become parts of us for a moment. We suspend awareness of ourselves, after which we again become aware of ourselves and accept or reject what they have said. But that brief moment of suspended self-awareness is the essence of understanding language; therefore, to hear is actually a kind of obedience to the speaker.

The explanation of self-aware human volition is a profound problem that has not been solved. The earliest Greek writing suggests a different mentality from our own by its lack of self-awareness. Since we know that Greek culture quickly became a literature of self-awareness, Jaynes regards the *Iliad* as standing at a turning of the times, and as a window into those unsubjective times when every kingdom was in essence a theocracy and every person the slave of internalized voices of leaders heard whenever novel situations occurred.

Jaynes offers the intriguing theory that language preceded self-awareness as we experience it today. He proposes that the volitional "I" evolved in homo sapiens in a laborious manner, much as it does in the developing child. In his view there was a time in which gods replaced venerated leaders and religions functioned to maintain the coherence and discipline of group living. Through the upheavals of civilizations and the observation of different motives in others, humans gradually became aware of their own selves as discrete, motivated beings. Therefore, the observation of differences in others may be the origin of self-awareness. It is possible that before self-awareness people posited self-awareness in others, particularly contradictory strangers, as the thing that caused their different and bewildering behavior. By first supposing the self-awareness of others, they may have inferred their own.

Jaynes proposes that several factors may have been at work in the evolution of self-awareness: (1) the weakening of reliance on speech by the advent of writing; (2) the unworkableness of the internalized voices of leaders in the forms of gods in the chaos of historical upheavals; (3) the positing of internal causes of behavior in the observation of differences in others; (4) the survival value of concealing one's thoughts; and (5) a modicum of natural selection. Whether or not it took place in this way, there is little doubt that self-awareness is a recent acquisition in human evolution.

SELF-ESTEEM

Confusion about self-esteem exists in the literature because it tends to be personified as something that can be injured and that exercises judgment (Mack & Ablon, 1983). The word esteem itself is ambiguous because it implies both judging and feeling. Current knowledge of the brain's functional systems can help to formulate a more precise definition of the term.

A self-esteem regulating system can be seen as a feedback system in the state regulating system that registers the efficiency of the operations of the central nervous system. It may be mediated by the non-dominant medial frontal lobe (Harris, 1986). In this view self-esteem is not a judgment but the pleasurable experience of "me." Moreover, the self-esteem regulating system's innate and developmentally conditioned sensitivity to the emotional states of others is a key mechanism for linking the individual to other persons and society.

Although a facilitating rather than an evaluating system, self-esteem does have the quality of goodness, when it pleasurably registers efficient central nervous system functioning, and badness, when it is replaced by the distress of inefficient central nervous system functioning. It does not, however, actually make judgments about oneself. Self-evaluation can be seen more parsimoniously as a judgment making system employing the managerial system. Another important distinction can be made between self-esteem as an emotional state and self-concept as knowledge about oneself in the form of concepts, which reside in the information processing system.

As the emotional state of experiencing oneself, self-esteem thus continuously reflects the functioning of the central nervous system (Spruiell, 1975). Self-esteem is not a feeling *about* oneself but is a feeling *of* oneself when the central nervous system is functioning well and when the approval of others exists. It is an indicator of competence in managing one's internal and external worlds. When the central nervous system functions well, self-esteem is positive feedback experienced as euphoria. In fact the word euphoria derives from the Greek root of "bearing well." An optimal level of self-esteem is experienced as a cenesthetic feeling of being at home in one's body, a sense of self-confidence, and an assuredness of recognition and acceptance by those who count in one's life (Briggs, 1975).

The skin, the musculature, the mouth, the gastrointestinal tract, the urinary tract, and the genitalia provide the massive flow of tactile, proprioceptive, and visceral stimuli that is perceived pleasurably as self-esteem and distressingly as visceral pain, anxiety, and depression. The limbic system modulates, refines, enhances, and blends this internal sensory flow, which operates under the influence of the neuroendocrine system. All of this provides the basis for a sense of well-being and highlights the importance of satisfying bodily needs in self-esteem regulation.

High and low self-esteem most precisely refer to a continuum of high to low levels of euphoria. The loss of self-esteem, then, refers to the loss of the buffering pleasurable feeling of euphoria when distressful emotions intrude. When the central nervous system is not functioning well, self-esteem is interrupted and distress appears. A sudden interruption of self-esteem is experienced as helplessness in the form of the emotions of shame and humiliation. Intrapsychic conflict created by the lack of drive satisfaction, inadequate mastery, and the negative evaluation of bodily functions contributes to the loss of self-esteem. When self-esteem is persistently interrupted because of anxiety stimulated by forbidden internal wishes or by separation from valued persons, feelings of depression may result.

A person without self-esteem is anxious to escape the terror of life. Not creativity, but safety, is the ruling desire. The primary motive, then, is not to afford oneself the enjoyment of existence but to defend oneself against painful feelings of inadequacy. Without self-esteem life is a chronic emergency. The anxious person feels a profound sense of helplessness, of impotence, and of shapeless, and impending, disaster. When one suffers from this kind of dread, the cause does not lie in the external world; it lies within oneself. Anxiety is an alarm signal, warning that one is in an improper psychological condition; it is the mind's signal of inefficiency and loss of control (Branden, 1969).

Self-esteem regulation begins in the emotional transactions between parent and infant and later is influenced by emotions experienced with parents and other significant adults, siblings, and peers. Self-esteem thus reflects the ways significant family members felt, thought, and acted toward a child. When a child is loved and respected as a unique human being, rather than for the gratification of parental needs, that child acquires growth facilitating self-esteem (Dai, 1952). Thus, parental warmth, acceptance, respect, and clearly defined limit setting are correlates of self-esteem (Coopersmith, 1967).

A person's self-esteem to a degree remains responsive to parental emotions throughout life. That responsiveness to parents is transferred to peer groups, teams, one's nation, religious groups, and professional organizations so that later in childhood and adult life one's self-esteem is influenced by salient persons and groups. The temporary loss of self-esteem in some adults whose athletic team has lost is an illustration of this influence. Self-esteem connects the individual's emotional state with others. Still, self-esteem can prevail to weather onslaughts from others and, when solidly established, permits relative freedom from the need for approval from others in addition to an inner source of strength to oppose others, if necessary (Spruiell, 1975).

Self-esteem is enhanced developmentally when a child's locus of control is internal. It tends to be interrupted more readily when a child's locus of control is external, and the child feels under the influence of others. Gradations in terms of locus of control thus influence self-esteem. Self-esteem is optimal when a child feels competent; when there are stable, enduring, dependable interpersonal relations; when one is accepted by larger groups; and

when one's drives are channeled in socially acceptable forms.

SELF-CONCEPT

Self-concepts are knowledge about one's attributes and require the developmental capacity simultaneously to be both subject and object. For example, when a girl says, "I have brown hair," she is a subject responding to herself as an object. This capacity makes it possible for human beings to have actual and desired conceptions of themselves (Rosenberg, 1979).

Our actual self-concepts are based upon more or less accurate knowledge of what we are. Our desired self-concepts are what we wish to be. Discrepancies between actual and desired self-concepts can be potent sources of motivation to learn in school (Perkins, 1974).

Self-concepts are based upon knowledge of one's qualities in space and time. They include knowledge of one's physical characteristics; personal dispositions, such as attitudes, skills, values, character, talents, habits, and interests; social labels, such as gender, family, race, and age; and characterizations of one's behavior, such as being learning disabled, a "jock," or a "freak" (Rosenberg, 1979).

Underlying self-concepts, which can be summoned at will, are *self-images* that endure in time and space, the most fundamental of which is the body image. A stable self-image, or experiencing of oneself, is needed for functioning in a variety of situations. We must always be the same person and yet be able to operate effectively in different roles that require different faculties. Thus the self-image can be conceived of as a field consisting of many functional units. An activated unit of the self-image becomes the foreground figure of self-awareness and the organizing unit of one's personality and behavior at a particular time and place. The remaining unit of the self-image, then, is the background that imparts continuity to self-awareness (Eisnitz, 1980).

The components of the self-image vary in stability, clarity, accuracy, and verifiability, because they are based upon a combination of primary and secondary process modes. In the primary process mode, self-images are a collage of sensations, wishes, and experiences. In the secondary process mode, persons perceive themselves more or less accurately as an aggregate of physical and mental capacities (Noy, 1979). Basic self-images are formed from the incorporation of the images of other persons through the process of identification.

A mature self-image is characterized by a sense of being a willful actor in space and of having historical continuity in time. Conversely, without an integrated self-image, space and time are disconnected and events seem to happen to one. A self-image in space gradually emerges from an infant's vague *body image* that reflects the sensory importance of body parts rather than their actual configuration. The sensations of gravity and movement are intermingled with muscle, joint, and skin information to complete the body image. Vestibular information orients the body image to surrounding space and is especially important in navigating movements of the entire body. Knowledge of oneself in space also depends upon external differentiation of one's body and will from those of parents (Santostefano, 1980). The spatial boundaries of the sensorimotor body image are based upon the enduring homunculus in the sensory strip of the parietal lobe, which is intimately connected to the homunculus of the motor strip of the frontal lobe (see Chapter 9).

The body image operates at four levels. The first is the level of sensorimotor schemes of the cerebral, corpus striatum, and cerebellar homunculi that localize stimuli on the body surface and orient body parts in relation to each other and the tempos of body actions (Buss, 1980). When one tickles the sole of one's own foot, double stimulation is perceived of sensations from the fingers touching the foot and sensations from the foot being touched. Such a combination of both active and passive stimulation arises only in self-directed perception. Being stimulated by someone else induces different sensory events; thus tickling by another person produce a stronger sensation than self-tickling. Consequently self-induced sensory events are different from sensory events induced by others. This distinction provides a basis for inferring a self. A well-organized body image is a map of every body part and relationships among parts and their movements. It enables one to feel what one's body is doing without looking at or touching it (Ayres, 1979).

The second level of the spatial body image consists of awareness of the body boundaries that define where the body ends and the not-body begins. These boundaries differentiate experiences that happen to oneself from those that do not and orient body sensations up and down and front and behind in space. Events inside the body can be distinguished from events occurring outside of it, a discrimination learned very early in life between "me" and "not me."

The third level involves recognition of one's body based upon images of the body's appearance stored in posterior cortical areas (Pribram, 1981). The limitation of external sensory receptors restricts perceptions of one's own body to its front, back, and side aspects (van der Velde, 1985). The notion of one's body as an entity, therefore, results from a composite of innumerable body images, perhaps through a holographic process. The recognition of one's image in a mirror appears to be limited to humans and a few higher primates, including chimpanzees. Monkeys and lower animals are not capable of mirror-image recognition.

The last level is the body concept, which consists of formal knowledge of the body, as can be expressed through words (Santostefano, 1978; Shontz, 1969). This includes concepts of one's physical characteristics, such as age, race, and gender. These attributes transit into more abstract attributes of the self experienced as self-concepts. The lateral aspects of the nondominant prefrontal cortex appear to integrate these functions (Harris, 1986).

In addition to orienting us in space, our self-image provides a sense of continuity in time. The self-image in time is based upon the internal rhythmicity imposed upon daily life by the appetitive instincts, particularly sleep, alimentation, and elimination. A child's orientation in time comes to include concepts of time based upon words with temporal significance, an understanding of the scales used to measure time's passage, a knowledge of growing older, and the ability to coordinate activities in sequence and fit them into a larger time frame (Kronick, 1981).

An important external source of time awareness that conflicts with these internally generated rhythms lies in the demands of the Western industrialized world necessitated by schedules for carrying out and completing work. This culturally based time frame is structured for children by parents at home and by teachers in school. Cultural values regarding time shape these external sources, so that attitudes toward the passage of time vary widely between cultures. Cultures differ in emphasis upon planning for the future or hoping that the future will be better than the present or the past (Spiegel, 1971). This has a direct bearing on the formation of desired self-concepts whose fulfillment depends upon achievements and the passage of time.

It is apparent that actual and desired self-concepts acquired in the family are the most basic. Desired self-concepts have their origins in infantile narcissism and are initially grandiose. Under optimal circumstances, parental limit setting and positive responses to a child's realistic abilities encourage the emergence of realistic actual self-concepts. Parents stimulate the development of young children's self-concepts through reinforcing their realistic qualities and also through failing to meet their children's needs all of the time, thereby stimulating them to discover concepts of their abilities independently (Davis & Wallbridge, 1981).

Thus self-concepts are influenced by the internalized views of significant others. With the development of the capacity for conceptualization, a child shifts from definitions of self-concepts based upon external visible characteristics to internal personal qualities. Facts about oneself shift from the province of an all-knowing external authority to one's own knowledge about oneself. In this way children gradually achieve a sense of being independent persons who are continuous in time and can relate to the past and anticipate the future.

SELF-EVALUATION

I maintain that one must be cautious about valuing oneself, and likewise conscientious about giving a true account, high or low . . . To claim for oneself less than there is warrant for is silliness, not modesty . . . and to claim more is not always presumptuous, it may also be silliness.

Montaigne, 1580

Self-evaluation is an internal feedback system that enables an individual to make judgments about the self in order to reinforce or change personal qualities, and thereby modify self-concepts. It appears developmentally as a means of preserving a sense of the presence of parents. Without an effective capacity for self-evaluation, an individual is dependent upon others for guidance and control. The self-evaluation system, or the conscience, directs emotions toward the self so that pleasure and displeasure with oneself take place when attributes of the self are judged to be good or bad. Thus, self-evaluation produces the feelings one has about oneself, whereas self-esteem is the feeling tone of oneself. When the aggregate of self-evaluation is positive, the result is self-respect.

Self-evaluations are judgments about self-images and self-concepts that in turn become parts of them. Self-evaluation is complex and employs comparisons of actual and desired self-concepts based on an individual's values and how one assumes that others view oneself.

Mature self-evaluation occurs when a self with a sense of accountability for past, present, and future actions has at its disposal a managerial system capable of impulse control, accurate analysis, and problem-solving thinking. If a child has not progressed developmentally to a level of accepting accountability for one's actions, there is little basis for assuming responsibility for and having feelings toward one's attributes. Moreover, if impulse control is weak or inflexible, unacceptable internal imagery may emerge and, if the information analytic system is weak as well, the resulting inability to separate internal imagery from external action may produce irrational guilt; one feels guilty because of unacceptable imagery even though it is not acted upon. Reasonable self-evaluations, therefore, depend upon mature managerial functions. In turn, developmental lags in managerial functions can produce unreasonable and potentially devastating self-evaluations.

Self-evaluations vary in priority, stability, clarity, accuracy, and verifiability. They can be studied through questionnaires and interviews (Miskimins, 1972). Some elements rank high in one's hierarchy of values whereas others are relegated to the periphery. Being a student may be highly valued for one child and being an athlete for another. One element may become inordinately prominent, such as academic success for a student obsessed with grades. Inconsistency may exist between the components of self-evaluation, so that one may highly value attractiveness but place a low value on intelligence. In the course of development recognition by oneself of a newly acquired skill may evoke not only a pleasurable self-evaluation but also a mild, transient depersonalization until the skill is integrated into the self-concept. This is reflected in such exclamations as "was that me?" and "I could not believe I was able to do that" (Horowitz & Zilberg, 1983).

When desired self-concepts are realistic, the self-evaluation function has an easier task in assessing the degree to which one's capacities match them. When desired self-concepts are unattainable, the self-evaluation function may conclude hopelessness. When self-evaluation is based upon unrealistic, inflated self-concepts of being omnipotent and omniscient, hubris results.

The adoption of parental standards forms a crucial basis for self-evaluation. On the way to developing realistic self-concepts, children delegate their omnipotence and magical powers to this parents, who are then suposed to use those powers for their benefit. When they discover that their own parents' actual powers are limited, children are forced to give up or repress this highly satisfying picture of themselves. As early adolescents they become acutely aware of what others think of them and uncertain about their self-concepts. As later adolescents they establish a new modus vivendi and never again attain the unreflective and confident self-evaluation of early childhood (Rosenberg, 1979). Still, even in adulthood a dream of omnipotence presses ever forward. We never completely rid ourselves of all traces of infantile megalomania. Fortunately, in play we can appropriately realize these grandiose aspects of our self-concept (English, 1963; Chassequet-Smirgel, 1976).

To be successful in school, a child must have desired self-concepts within realistic grasp. Some underachieving children of average ability with inflated desired self-concepts are not content to be average students. They entertain the fantasy that if they tried, they would be superior students. Since they do not try, their true ability level is not revealed and their secret omniscience is not challenged. The ability to function as a student depends upon accepting one's lack of knowledge and the desire to achieve a more learned state. Learning in school thus is blocked by the extremes of omniscience or helplessness. In between is the vital zone of teachability based upon an accurate capacity for self-evaluation.

STAGES OF DEVELOPMENT OF THE SELF

The stages of self development denote the level at which a child has created a unique self. For convenience these levels can be designated as the *sensorimotor self*, the *symbolic self*, the *conceptual self*, the *evaluative self*, the *integrative self*, and the *interdependent self*. Kegan (1982) reviewed the work of others and offered a model in which the evolving self moves through a series of temporary solutions to a lifelong tension between yearnings for inclusion with and distinctness from others (Figure 16-3).

In Kegan's model each developmental stage hinges on the fundamental issue of how differentiated the self is from its surroundings. Each stage involves a continual moving back and forth between resolving the tension between inclusion and distinctness slightly in favor of autonomy at one stage and in favor of inclusion at the next. A child moves from the internal imagery-embedded impulsive balance to the self-sufficiency of the imperial balance; from the overdifferentiated imperial balance to overinclusive interpersonalism; from interpersonalism to an autonomous, self-regulating institutional balance; and from the institutional stage to a new form of openness in the interindividual stage.

Kegan's helix makes it clear that children move back and forth in their struggle with tension between differentiation and integration and that their balances always are slightly imbalanced. In fact, because each of these balances is imbalanced, each is temporary. The model suggests a way of understanding the nature of vulnerability to growth at each level. It enhances developmental frameworks that define development solely in terms of increasing autonomy and lose sight of the fact that adaptation involves both differentiation and integration.

The components of the self ripen predominantly during these developmental stages as follows: self-esteem during the sensorimotor stage, self-awareness during the symbolic stage, self-concepts during the concrete operations-play stage, and self-evaluation during the concrete operations-work stage.

The *sensorimotor self* is reflected in the creation of a body image from interaction with a child's own body and surroundings during the first 18 months of life. If the development of the self does not proceed consistently beyond this level, the child is severely disabled at the psychotic level.

Infants apparently are innately aware of self-organizing processes and selectively responsive to external interpersonal events (Stern, 1985). The earliest body images are those of internalized parts of attachment figures. The infant forms internal images of the physical features of the mother for which innate templates exist, such as facial recognition. These images are associated

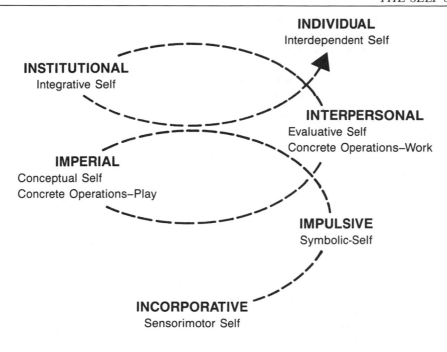

INDIVIDUAL
Interdependent Self

INSTITUTIONAL
Integrative Self

INTERPERSONAL
Evaluative Self
Concrete Operations–Work

IMPERIAL
Conceptual Self
Concrete Operations–Play

IMPULSIVE
Symbolic-Self

INCORPORATIVE
Sensorimotor Self

INDEPENDENCE   **INCLUSION**

Figure 16-3. The stages of self-development. (Adapted from R. Kegan, *The Evolving Self,* Harvard Press, Cambridge MA, 1982. Used with permission.)

with pleasure and distress, so that internal sensations and parental images are reciprocally connected. These images of the bodies of others are the building blocks upon which a child constructs identifications with others. Thus the formation of body images of others is intertwined with the formation of images of one's own body. They both take place through the same external sensory receptors (van der Velde, 1985).

The *symbolic self* emerges with the capacity to use language in the form of personal pronouns to represent wishes and needs. Self-awareness develops, and the self is experienced as having good and bad poles between 18 months and 3½ years of age. Then the self is embedded in imagery related to a child's drives. The frustration of a child's impulsive wishes and needs is tantamount to the temporary loss of the self-image, as exemplified by the catastrophic reaction of the temper tantrum. Shame may be a reflection of the wish that the self-image would disappear under humiliating interpersonal circumstances at this stage.

The *conceptual self* appears between 3½ and six years of age as a child begins to be aware of attributes and acts in basic social roles. At this stage the self is compartmentalized according to these roles. The importance of defining one's and others' power contributes to the tendency to feel manipulated by others and to control others. This meaning is aptly captured by designating this as the imperial stage (Kegan, 1982). The beginning self-evaluation function introduces guilt as a reflection of adverse judgments made of the self, in part reflecting the incorporation of the judgments of others.

The *evaluative self* is a product of the growing capacity of a child to conceptualize and to be sensitive to the evaluations of others based upon strong affiliative strivings between the ages of six and 11. The capacities to make judgments about oneself and to control impulses permit more efficient mediation of a child's needs and those of others. The self becomes more distinctly defined through self-evaluation based upon comparisons with the attributes of others. Children tend toward conformity and are sensitive to embarrassment during this stage.

The *integrative self* draws upon the capacity to engage in formal operations between the ages of 11 and 18. This ability to theorize about oneself permits self-observation and the conceptualization of one's self as a discrete, autonomous entity composed of many parts. The young person tailors self-evaluation to the values of the culture so that in the Western world an achievement orientation colors one's self-evaluation. This is expressed through the tendency of the young person to create an imaginary audience before which one continually performs (Elkind, 1982). At the same time, the trend toward autonomy places the young person in the position of defining self-concepts by contrasting them with prevailing adult expectations.

The *interdependent self* emerges during early adulthood as the individual fits a diverse range of self-concepts into an expanding number of social roles. During this time desired self-concepts are tested in relation to actual self-concepts. At this stage the self has achieved sufficient autonomy to permit intimacy with others and the capacity for interdependence from a position of strength. The self can treat the self both as independent and as part of a community.

SUMMARY

The self is the center of the human experience of the worlds of objects and living things; of awareness of oneself and death; and of theories of oneself, death, works of art, and science. As the interface between the individual and society, the self provides a person's sense of continuity in time and coherence in space. The subsystem outputs of the self can be described subjectively and are manifested in personality traits as seen by observers.

Self-awareness is reflected in consciousness as the perceiving and initiating component of the self. As an emotional component of the self, self-esteem monitors the functioning of the managerial system and is pleasurably experienced as euphoria with roots in early levels of body functioning and emotional transactions with parents. The self-concept is comprised of the knowledge of one's attributes, ranging from the body image to desired and actual self-concepts. Self-evaluation makes emotionally colored judgments about actual as compared with desired self-concepts.

The stages of self development can be defined as the incorporative sensorimotor self during the first 18 months, the impulsive symbolic self between 18 months and 3½ years, the imperial conceptual self from 3½ to six years, the interpersonal evaluative self from six to 11 years, the institutional integrative self from 11 to 18 years, and the individual interdependent self of adulthood.

The neurophysiological evidence supports the existence of a self which springs from the human capacity to represent oneself in symbols and concepts, monitors how successfully we are living the present, holds our hopes for the future and remarkably uses the tools of the scientist and the riddles of the philosopher to make sure it is really there (Gardner, 1981).

IV

Working in School

The whole aim of good teaching is to turn the young learner, by nature a little copycat, into an independent, self-propelling creature, who cannot merely learn but study . . . This is to turn pupils into students . . .

Jacques Barzun

THIS SECTION is of particular relevance to educators. However, the relationships between the stages of child development and later learning capacities have implications for clinicians as well.

Learning is simply a living organism's capacity to use experience to maintain itself. As such human learning is tantamount to surviving and is a fundamental process of the central nervous system. Learning takes place through the accommodation of schemes as an inner model of the external world is learned in the form of knowledge and skills. It occurs automatically in two innate forms: conditioned and instrumental learning.

Learning also can occur through creativity in which one's internal world reciprocally modifies the external world. Developmentally, creative learning evolves from play into schoolwork.

Didactic learning is a special form of learning characteristic of schoolwork but lacking a direct connection to drive motivation. The aim of instruction in reading, writing, and arithmetic is to shift these skills to the level of conditioned automaticity so that they become the vehicles for literacy and social functioning rather than ends in themselves.

Writing is one of the most complicated of human abilities because it involves cognition, language, and motor action. In itself it is a form of creativity. Because it is less critical in society, learning arithmetic has received less attention than learning to read as a source of difficulty for children.

The successful performance of schoolwork depends upon the gradual development of a series of competencies during childhood. These competencies are products of central nervous system functions that develop through maturation of the brain, transactions with the environment, and the creations of a particular child.

Children with learning problems in school frequently show immaturities in the developmental progression of essential personal competencies. These basic competencies are individuation as a person, the tolerance of frustration, a realistic view of one's personal power, age-appropriate cognitive and language skills, temperamental qualities conducive to cooperation with adults, the urge to satisfy one's curiosity, a mature managerial system, self-esteem, and internalized values supporting the purposes of education.

17

The Nature of Learning

The order of teaching must follow the order of
learning . . . the way of discovery is the primary way of the
mind to truth, and instruction merely imitates nature in
imitating discovery.

Mortimer Adler, 1977

In essence, learning is the capacity of living systems to use experience in maintaining their existences (Brown, 1976; Fishbein, 1976). It is a basic process of the central nervous system. Human beings have prospered because of their capacity to learn to use fire, make tools, speak, domesticate animals, cultivate crops, and alter the face of the earth.

Human learning is not just reacting to environmental experience by recording stimuli as does a camera. Rather, it is acting upon the perceived environment based upon experience (Siegler, 1983). Learning is not simply changing behavior but changing the meaning of experience (Novak & Gowin, 1984). We learn by correcting our mistakes, that is, by first identifying them and then trying to improve on them (Berkson & Wettersten, 1984). For this reason learning is influenced by many personal factors. Ample evidence exists that the way one learns to encode information also changes within one's lifetime. For example, at first innovative music may be experienced as cacophonous; later the same music may be heard as eminently harmonious.

Learning takes place with varying de-

grees of durability, access to conscious awareness, complexity, and intention. Thus learning can range from becoming accustomed to monotonous stimulation to creative discovery. In the course of human development, learning also progresses from the simplest to the most complex levels because of as yet incompletely understood changes in the anatomical and physiological components of the brain. Furthermore, during the course of development, children learn how to learn intentionally.

In addressing the nature of learning, I will touch upon the development of learning capacities; learning as a process of the central nervous system; an epigenetic model of learning; and the conditioned, instrumental, didactic, and creative modalities of learning.

THE DEVELOPMENT OF LEARNING CAPACITIES

Learning begins before birth as illustrated by the influence of prenatal sounds on a newborn's auditory preferences (DeCasper & Fifer, 1980). As babies learn how to control their hands, they painstakingly build pictures of their own bodies and the bodies of adults. In the process the repeated clashes between an infant's wants and reality lead to the ability to distinguish inner and external perceptions and imagery. Later a growing fund of knowledge of the existence of animate and inanimate things is accumulated through a child's ability to manipulate them (Westman, 1979a).

A child's curiosity leads to contact with the widening world and is the wellspring of learning. Basically open to exploring all aspects of the world, a child finds that certain areas give rise to distress in the form of parental disapproval, and curiosity in those areas is inhibited. For example, parental reactions to young children's exploration of their own bodies and bodily products influences the children's degree of comfort with and knowledge about their bodies. To the extent that mysteries remain regarding their own bodies, children are burdened with unrequited curiosity and illusions about themselves. The optimal outcome of curiosity is the sensation of mastery through gaining knowledge and resolving ambiguities. The result is a satisfying sense of competence, as illustrated by the prototypical exhilaration of a toddler on first taking steps alone. When this kind of learning is exciting for both a child and a parent, a solid foundation for later learning develops. When curiosity is not predominantly followed by mastery, a child becomes wary of learning.

All learning builds upon existing knowledge and abilities. It is not putting information into an empty receptacle. The learning process is the vehicle for a child's gradual modification of existing imagery and concepts about the self, others, and the world in the light of reality. Depending upon a child's age, the perception of reality is more or less accurate and always influenced by existing mental set.

Play is a child's means of learning about the world. In fact, a child's play is a cue to the level at which useful learning can take place. Children first learn about the nature of things they can personally manipulate. Later cooperative play permits children to learn about life situations through pretending. Through play a child discovers facts about the steadily enlarging world of things and people.

From a baby's rattle, through a toddler's teddy bear, to a young child's tricycle, the methods and objects employed in fostering learning should be appropriate to the child's motor, cognitive, and social levels of development. Thus learning progresses from deeply ingrained conditioning to problem solving through the delay of action permitted by imagery, the symbols of language, and concepts. All of these learning modalities remain available throughout life.

Of createst importance is a child's interest and curiosity as a guide to education during the early years. One can impose adult learning methods; however, they are not useful to a child if they do not draw upon the child's curiosity. The danger of imposing adult learning patterns on young children is that the motivation for learning—curiosity—and the means of learning—play—may be sidetracked or squelched. This deprives a child of progression through the necessary developmental sequences that precede academic learning. A child then may prematurely adopt adult rationality, leaving a core of unmodified infantile images covered by a pseudoadult facade.

The premature imposition of adult expectations, such as learning to read, without an expression of interest may not engage children's imagery. The learning task then may become an unintegrated skill, which is seen by children as an accommodation to the adult world but not as a part of themselves. Resistance to that foreign part of oneself may be expressed through blocks to later academic learning. Conversely, when a child's interest is captured and the cognitive and language capacities are present, academic learning, such as learning to read, takes place with ease.

LEARNING AS A PROCESS OF THE CENTRAL NERVOUS SYSTEM

In the 1960s animal research disclosed that variations in the social and sensory qualities of the environment could affect the cellular components of the central nervous system (Cotman & McGaugh, 1980; Valzelli, 1981; Pardes, 1986). For example, rats raised in an enriched environment were found to have developed thicker cerebral cortices than rats raised in standard laboratory cages. Moreover, rats reared in even more stimulating outdoor environments showed greater brain growth than those in the enriched laboratory situation (Rosenzweig et al, 1972).

Despite the evidence that environmental stimulation at any age increases brain weight, no direct correlation between neural growth and learning has been established as yet (Diamond, 1988). The most likely factors involved are changes in synaptic membrane permeability, neuronal threshold levels, glial cells, chemical sensitization of neurons, and sensitization to specific activation patterns (Brown, 1976; Pardes, 1986). Knowledge of the biochemical and neurophysiological basis of learning is expanding rapidly. For example, the enzyme pyruvate dehydrogenase in the mitochondria of neural cells has been found to enhance the activity of neurotransmitters (Menolascino et al, 1983).

Neuroregulators and hormones influence learning. For example, drive-motivated learning may be mediated by dopamine neurons and opioid peptides; pleasurable problem solving may be mediated by norepinephrine neurons. The positive reinforcing hormonal influence on memory, particularly with stressful events, may take place through increased blood glucose levels caused by heightened adrenal epinephrine (Gold, 1987). However, the steroid hormones involved in sustained distress also may interfere with the activities of the hippocampus, which plays a key role in learning.

Learning probably involves a sequence of physiological events: neuronal activation causes an influx of calcium into the axon terminal, which, in turn, causes the synaptic disc to become more curved and the dendritic spine to grow thicker. This is followed by an increase in the overall size of the synapse and, finally, by the growth of new synapses and dendritic spines. If learning does follow this sequence, it follows that the mental potential of an individual should vary with the ability of neurons to sprout new synapses. In Down Syndrome the lack of this plasticity is evident in a lesser degree of neuronal change around the time of birth and the existence of smaller synapses throughout life. It also appears that Down Syndrome neurons are deficient in their ability to absorb and process calcium (Petit et al, 1987).

There appears to be a major difference between learning factual knowledge that is specific to a particular context and learning sensorimotor skills that become automatic (Pribram, 1979). Computer simulations, also, suggest a distinction between what are called declarative and production memory systems (Anderson, 1983b). The observation that adult patients with severe memory impairment could still learn led to the hypothesis that two separate retention systems in the brain store the effects of experience in fundamentally different ways (Mishkin et al, 1984). In this model experiences can be construed as stored through both an *imaging system* responsive to incentive and a *conditioning system* responsive to reinforcement. The former is reflected in conscious memory for a particular event at a particular time and place; it also is referred to as fact or declarative memory storage. The latter is observed by noting the effects of past experience on subsequent behavior; it also is called skill, procedural, or production memory storage. Developmentally, conditioning precedes imaging memory (Moscovitch, 1985).

The imaging system subsumes both recognition memory and associative recall and utilizes circuits within the limbic and diencephalic regions of the brain together with closely associated medial-temporal and prefrontal cortical areas. It can store knowledge in as little as one trial. The limbic system appears to participate in this memory process in at least two different ways. First, the amygdala contributes with the hippocampus to the cortical storage of the stimulus image, thereby allowing for stimulus recognition. And second, the amygdala contributes to the attachment of emotional value to the recognized image. Thus the affective system plays a key role in reinforcing memory retention. In the absence of the hippocampus, there is little impairment in either of these processes, since the amygdala alone can mediate both of them effectively. In the absence of the amygdala, there is an impairment only in appreciating the emotional significance of a perception, as the hippocampus can support perception recognition. But in the absence of both the hippocampus and the amygdala, there is a profound impairment in recognizing a perception and in acquiring mnemonic associations with it (Mishkin et al, 1984). This memory system is impaired in adult amnesias.

The complex functions of assimilating new information, associating it with memories of past experience, and formulating a plan to govern new behavior adaptively during imagery learning required a very large prefrontal cortex in early mammals.

Rather than continuing to add on prefrontal cortex as the sole means of this form of learning, the brain may have evolved, in computer terms, off-line processing so that the brain could continue imagery learning in REM sleep (Winston, 1985). In this view, dreams are a window on the neural process in which strategies for behavior are being set down, modified, and consulted.

The more primitive conditioning system, which is presumed to mediate the learning ability that remains despite amnesia, also stores experiences but in an entirely different manner. This second system probably involves connections of the cerebral cortex with the corpus striatum and associated structures within the extrapyramidal system and cerebellum. Classical conditioned response learning reflects the capacity to make new responses to old, repeated stimuli, whereas operant or instrumental conditioning makes old responses to new stimuli (Plutchik, 1977).

Unlike the imaging system, the conditioning system requires more than a single trial for the mastery of a task, with each successful trial strengthening a habit incrementally. It involves the gradual development of a connection between an unconditioned stimulus, such as a bell, and an instinctually based response, such as the salivation of dogs in Pavlov's classic experiments. The unconditioned stimulus is automatically reinforced by a stimulus associated with a drive's aim and object, such as salivating with hunger for food. Conditioned learning does not involve recognition and associative memory. What is stored in the conditioning system is not the neural representations of such items as objects, places, acts, emotions, and the learned connections between them, but simply the probability that a given stimulus will evoke a specific reponse due to the reinforcement contingencies operating at that time (Mishkin & Petri, 1984).

An important form of conditioned learning is habituation, which is learning not to respond to a stimulus, which by meaningless repetition loses significance to the organism. Distractibility may be a manifestation of inefficient habituation (Mosse, 1982).

The corpus striatum antedates both the cerebral cortex and the limbic system in phylogenesis and ontogenesis. Whereas infants can readily acquire conditioned habits, they are seriously deficient in forming memories, presumably because the cortico-limbo-thalamic circuit, which constitutes the imaging system, has yet to develop. An infant learns primarily through conditioning. Even the reflexes present at birth in humans, however, involve cortical and subcortical feedback loops. Most learning after infancy probably involves both the imaging and the conditioning systems. The imaging system satisfied motives, which can range from hunger to intellectual curiosity (Mishkin & Petri, 1984).

In this dual-system model of retention, the ingredients of an experience can enter into the learning process in two ways: as knowledge stored in a cortico-limbic system and as habits stored in a cortico-striatal system. The imaging system offers short-term flexibility, and the conditioning system offers long-term reliability. Although the imaging and conditioning systems usually are synergistic, they also can operate independently and sometimes conflict.

AN EPIGENETIC MODEL OF LEARNING

Throughout the ages controversy has raged over the role of nature and nurture in human learning. On the nature side, Plato held that knowledge is built upon innate pure ideas. On the nurture side, Aristotle held that knowledge is obtained through one's senses. These polarized views still dominate popular thoughts about learning.

Freud, Piaget, and Erikson found themselves in the nature versus nurture debate, but their observations did not support this dichotomy. Since neither hereditary nor environmental factors are sufficient in themselves to explain the learning process, only a model that reflects the interaction of both and adds a child's unique contribution to the process is accurate. Such a model is provided by the concept of epigenesis, in which each stage of development builds anew upon the internal structures of the preceding ones.

Freud, Piaget, and Erikson postulated an epigenetic unfolding of innate and acquired mental structures in predictable stages in transaction with environmental experiences. They developed complementary theories of character and intellectual development. Freud evolved a broad-gauged theory stressing both the internal world of drives, emotions, and imagery and the external world of human relationships. Piaget restricted his focus to the mental structures that underlie the images, symbols, and concepts children develop of their inanimate environments. Erikson placed the individual in a social context.

Because of his emphasis upon learning, we will consider Piaget's theories in particular. As a philosophical structuralist, along with Levi-Strauss and Chomsky, Piaget cast knowledge and intelligence in biological, environmental, and transactional terms, extending them from the realm of philosophy (Gardner, 1981; Rossi, 1983). He held that everything a child knows is a construction of the child's brain, which does not merely take in stimuli from the external world but builds its own view of the world in accordance with its capacities and purposes. What are constructed are not copies of things and events but models of them, which enable a child to make sense of experience. Each child, therefore, experiences life in a unique way (Furth, 1981). Piaget acknowledged that emotions play a critical role in determining when something is learned or whether something is learned but not how it is learned (Tenzer, 1983). Reading Piaget provides access to a rich store of psychological insights and theoretical speculations in addition to a profusion of intriguing empirical observations. In so doing, however, it is well to recognize the vagueness and internal contradictions of his writings (Boden, 1979).

In Piaget's terms learning takes place in the context of *equilibration* through the processes of *assimilation* and *accommodation* in superficial figurative and deeper operative modalities. The application of computational theories and methods in the construction of artificial intelligence is shedding light on this process (Boden, 1981).

Equilibration

Piaget's *equilibration* is self-regulation that creates a dynamic balance between the individual and the environment through the operations of schemes at various stages of development.

Schemes

Sensorimotor *schemes* are stable, slowly changing central nervous system structures, resembling computer programs, that result from transactions between the individual and the internal and external worlds (Eckblad, 1981). A scheme is an internal design for action and the operation of a scheme is an internal action. An example of the behavioral manifestation of a simple sensorimotor scheme is the programmed sequence of using silverware in dining. Sensorimotor schemes are the repositories of long-term memory storage of symbols and concepts. They require nutrients in the form of sensory stimuli and atrophy without them, as does the body without food. This need of the central nervous system for stimulation has been described as stimulus hunger (Fenichel, 1945), the mastery

drive (Hendrick, 1943), and as the need for competence (White, 1959).

Schemes can be regarded as self-organizing neural circuitry that account for recognition, associations, learning, and memory (Edelman & Finkel, 1984). They underlie adaptive behavior and grow out of the coordination of sensorimotor activity (Hebb, 1949; Buchtel, 1982). Schemes are private inarticulated theories about the nature of events, objects, or situations. Thus one's total set of schemes constitutes one's private theory of the nature of reality (Rumelhart, 1978).

The central nervous system is organized in millions upon millions of schemes having billions of interconnections. All schemes are richly linked with others and tightly linked with closely related schemes (Hart, 1975). Different areas of the cerebral cortex specialize in handling different sensory inputs so that at least major schemes are not localized, but instead are networks reaching into many regions of the cortex and for sensorimotor schemes into subcortical areas. Unlike the digital computer, which cannot handle many simultaneous inputs, the central nervous system tolerates hundreds of thousands and can carry on a host of simultaneous operations. During most of our waking hours, we execute intricate programs without giving thought to them. We become consciously aware of them only when hitches occur.

Piaget demonstrated that each child experiences the world differently from the beginning. Initially an infant is bathed in undifferentiated unknown stimuli. The central nervous system organizes these stimuli within its innate components into schemes, which later may be consciously perceived as images. This mental distillate of knowledge grows into a rich capacity to process and utilize information as the process of learning accelerates.

Kant was convinced that the prime function of the intellect was to conceptualize the data of the senses. He generally

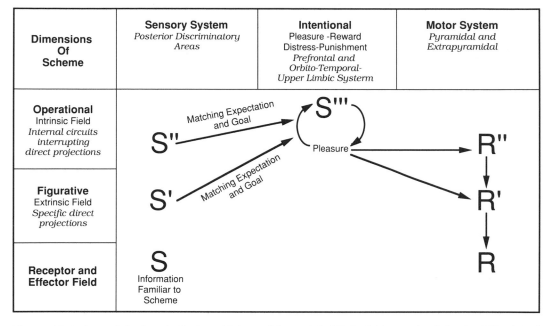

ASSIMILATION
Perception + Expectation + Goals → Response

Dimensions Of Scheme	Sensory System *Posterior Discriminatory Areas*	Intentional Pleasure -Reward Distress-Punishment *Prefrontal and Orbito-Temporal-* Upper Limbic Systerm	Motor System *Pyramidal and Extrapyramidal*
Operational Intrinsic Field *Internal circuits interrupting direct projections*			
Figurative Extrinsic Field *Specific direct projections*			
Receptor and Effector Field	Information Familiar to Scheme		

Figure 17-1. A model of assimilation. (Adapted from J. L. Weil, *A Neurophysiological Model of Emotional and Intentional Behavior,* 1974. Courtesy of Charles C. Thomas, Publisher, Springfield IL.)

referred to schemata as the means whereby abstract categories were brought into concrete use (Kant, 1979). Bartlett (1932) described a scheme as a dynamically flexible organization of past events, their characteristics, contexts, and implications, with a large capacity for further modification by new events. Despite difficulties in defining it precisely, the scheme has acquired new relevance and importance in the paradigms of artificial intelligence methodology (Hamilton, 1983).

Operations

In the course of development, a child acts upon and analyzes parts of the world that evoke interest and gains knowledge through the *operations* of schemes. Knowledge itself lies in the operation of schemes. The intense operation of a scheme can be seen in a state of work or play in which a person becomes one with a task and is unaware of anything else. In this state one system of schemes enters a loop of repeated activation and inhibits other processes, absorbing nearly all self-awareness in its activity (Eckblad, 1981).

The operations of schemes take place through the interplay between *conservative* and *innovative* tendencies (Piaget, 1950). In Piaget's epigenetic model, the two poles of learning are conserving the patterns of schemes, on the one hand, and modifying them, on the other, thus combining continuity and novelty through conservation and innovation.

The conservative tendency is expressed through the process of *assimilation*, which limits the acceptance of information to that which can be handled by the schemes (Figure 17-1). Information that does not match

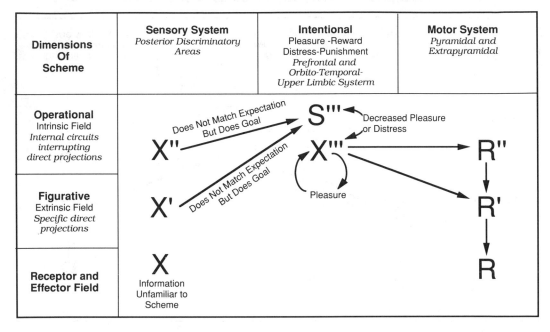

Figure 17-2. A model of learning. (Adapted from J. L. Weil, *A Neurophysiological Model of Emotional and Intentional Behavior,* 1974. Courtesy of Charles C. Thomas, Publisher, Springfield IL.)

with existing schemes cannot be assimilated. The innovative mechanism is *accommodation*, which alters schemes to correspond to information that cannot be assimilated (Figure 17-2). A child's interest in the external world causes accommodation, which changes schemes to allow for the assimilation of novel information (Tower, 1983).

Assimilation is knowing what an object is and what an object is not. Assimilation may omit information contrary to a current belief by not noticing it or incompletely noticing it. Accommodation comes into play when assimilation does not suffice to bring about an intended result. Accommodation then changes a belief to correspond to new information, which thereby becomes assimilable.

The process of assimilation may be based in frontolimbic systems that tend to maintain stability by recourse to existing knowledge. It involves context-sensitive, controlled interactions with the external environment by selectively structuring relevant and screening out irrelevant stimulus patterns. The process of accommodation may be based in posterior cortical systems that modify existing schemes through processing external stimulus patterns relatively free of context (Pribram, 1981).

Equilibration, then, is the inborn tendency of schemes to assimilate and impose internal organization on experience, when it is possible, and to accommodate by reorganization of schemes, when experience is unfamiliar but relevant to them. Because accommodation is the adjustment of a scheme to changing information, it constitutes learning, which Piaget described as either *figurative* or *operative*. Accommodation takes place in both the limbic imaging and extrapyramidal conditioning forms of learning.

Figurative learning, or accommodation, occurs when acquired information must be used repeatedly in order to be retained in memory, because it is a replica of external stimuli in symbolic or conceptual schemes, which are not integrated into sensorimotor schemes. It is the mechanism for didactic learning. Examples are learning lock combinations and memorizing dates for a history examination.

In *operative* learning, or accommodation, knowledge is incorporated into existing sensorimotor schemes and is not lost even if infrequently used. Operative learning brings emotions and internal imagery into play upon information in the construction of images through evocative memory (Fraiberg, 1969). It enables a child to grow in knowledge through interrelating and hierarchically integrating schemes into overall intelligence. It is called instrumental learning later in this chapter.

An example of operative accommodation is seen in a boy who learned that dogs are friendly. Upon seeing a strange dog, he approached it because of his assimilation of the perception of the dog into the category of friendly. The dog bit him and produced an operational accommodation of his dog category. Thereafter, he perceived dogs as being both friendly and potentially dangerous.

Kindling is an as yet incompletely understood mechanism in operative learning (Harris, 1986). It refers to the limbic response to repeated stimulation that ultimately drives the hippocampus to take in new experience and to form long-term memories. It was discovered when periodic subliminal electrical stimulation of the amygdala or hippocampus resulted in the progressive development of seizures through a number of stages.

A distinction should be made between learning about the external inanimate world, studied by Piaget, and the external emotionally colored human relationships, studied by Freud. Piaget focused on age-appropriate actions persons perform on inanimate objects. Freud focused on the unconscious and conscious emotion-laden stimuli involved in interpersonal relationships. In so doing Freud described identification as a special form of learning from other people. Identification is operative accommodation of sensorimotor schemes to emotion-laden interpersonal relationships. Through identification children take on abstract principles from the behaviors of those adults to whom they are emotionally attached, rather than literally imitating them (Elkind, 1982).

Stages

Piaget demonstrated that the brain has a developmental timetable in which more elaborate schemes evolve by small steps from previous simpler schemes and reorganize so that the final outcome is quite dissimilar from the original. Although building upon existing schemes, each stage reflects a new level of brain functioning. An example is the ability to classify objects acquired by a school-age child during the stage of concrete operations. Later, during adolescence, the same person learns how to solve an algebra problem, which reflects even more complex schemes at the level of formal operations.

The earliest schemes are sensorimotor and result from attachment bonds with a parent, recognizing parts of one's own body, and managing internal stimuli. An infant who has difficulty in processing and retaining visual-spatial and auditory stimuli and in predicting temporal events may become inefficient later in the analysis, synthesis, and memory of events and may have difficulty comprehending the boundaries and nuances of human forms, sounds, and smells. Such an infant may fail to respond adequately to a parent, who consequently may become perplexed by and insecure with the child. As a result the bonding process may be impeded. Conversely, a parent who does not notice visual-spatial details may not respond adequately to an infant's nonverbal language. The way in which infants' sensorimotor schemes are organized toward their parents affects the way in which they relate to other aspects of the animate environment (Kronick, 1981).

Operative accommodation applies to internal, as well as external, stimuli. It modifies emotion-laden internal states of craving into states of wishing. These become further modified into states of expecting, permitting the analysis of reality (Pribram & Gill, 1976). The accomodative modification of schemes takes place through both the developmental acceleration of each stage and conflicts. Although each stage builds upon preceding stages, the appearance of new capacities creates opportunities for new thrusts and compensations, such as with the acquisition of formal operations.

Although their sequence is predictable, a variety of factors influence the rate at which developmental stages unfold. The rate of maturation of the brain is an obvious determinant that limits the effect of training introduced before a child has achieved the required structural maturity. Another element is intelligence determined by genetic potential in a particular area. Yet another factor is experience as revealed in economically disadvantaged children, who have limited language, problem solving, and conceptual skills because of the lack of opportunity to develop them. The factors of age, intelligence, and social background thus influence the expression of these developmental stages.

Internal and external conflicts can cause distress and momentary regressions, and, can lead to the accommodative modification of schemes. On the other hand, anxiety can cause schemes to become inaccessible to accommodation and so remain fixed at an early stage of development. In this way intellectual functioning can be affected by internal conflicts that prevent the accommodation of unconscious sensorimotor schemes, such as cravings, to become conscious realistic motivations. When that repression is lifted through psychotherapy, the access of unconscious cravings to external stimuli permits accommodation to reality to occur. Thus intellectual functioning can be enhanced through the resolution of unconscious conflicts.

Learning Modalities

In the light of the preceding, four basic learning modalities can be identified: conditioned, instrumental, didactic and creative (Figure 17-3).

Conditioned learning is the simplest form and automatically produces a response to an appropriate stimulus. *Instrumental* learning is the intentional learning of skills and knowledge that fulfill drive aims and advance coping skills through the operative accommodation of sensorimotor schemes. It involves the imaging retention system with affective system reinforcement. It often occurs effortlessly; for example, one quickly learns the location of shops in a new city.

In contrast, *didactic* learning does not provide drive fulfillment but presumably has long-range benefits for the individual. It largely involves figurative accommodation of symbolic and conceptual schemes without reinforcement by the affective system. It is the centerpiece of formal education.

Creative learning involves the action of sensorimotor schemes upon external information. It thereby places a personalized stamp upon knowledge, which becomes integrated into sensorimotor schemes. The

Neural Networks	Mediating Areas	Learning Modalities
Reflexes	Brain stem	——
Instincts		Conditioning
	Striatum	
Sensorimotor schemes	Limbic system	Instrumental
		Operational
		Accommodation
		Creative
Sybolic schemes	Cortical	Didactic
	Association	Figurative
Conceptual schemes	Zones	Accommodation

Figure 17-3. Relationship among learning modalities, neural networks, and anatomical subsystems.

operative accommodation of sensorimotor schemes through the creative process results in the reward of personal mastery.

Conditioned Learning

It is likely that each new neural pathway, neurotransmitter, hormone, and metabolic process that serves learning has been elaborated upon in the evolution of animal brains so that primitive processes are embedded in even the most sophisticated forms of learning.

The first step toward a true nervous system occurred in the flatworm, which gained fame in experimental psychology. The flatworm shows the beginnings of a synaptic type of nervous system and demonstrates habituation, a form of conditioned learning in which the organism responds to repeated irrelevant stimuli by eventually disregarding them. It apparently results from the lack of assimilation by schemes (Cotman & McGaugh, 1980). Furthermore, conditioned behavior has been transferred biologically between animals. For example, rats who were injected

with RNA from other rats trained to approach food upon a certain stimulus learned that particular conditioned response more rapidly than did rats who were not so treated (Guyton, 1977).

Conditioned learning probably takes place through cortical-striatal centers. It occurs through trial and error with little awareness of the underlying process of acquisition. The simplest form is coexcitation in which two simultaneous excitations tend to form a weak association. Operant conditioning is the reinforcement by a stimulus of a response that leads to drive satisfaction. Classical conditioning is a combination of coexcitation and operant conditioning (Cattell, 1980).

Brain wave recordings show that novel sensory stimuli excite the cerebral cortex. But repetition of a stimulus leads to almost complete extinction of the electroencephalographic response. If a stimulus causes either pleasure or distress, however, the electroencephalographic cortical response becomes progressively more intense. Thus an animal builds up strong memory traces for stimuli that are either pleasurable or distressing but habituates to indifferent sensory stimuli (Guyton, 1977).

Instrumental Learning

As operative accommodation, the capacity for utilitarian instrumental learning is innate because of the canalization of sensorimotor schemes (Fishbein, 1976). Through instrumental learning symbols and concepts are built into sensorimotor schemes. Accordingly, instrumental learning keyed to maturation of the brain is the engine of the developmental process through which each child recapitulates the evolution of the species as the brain matures. It ensures that the individual will profit from experience with survival value.

The motivation for instrumental learning arises from the drives and depends upon all of the functional units of the brain for the analysis of stimuli and to carry out actions. It is influenced by motivation, character, society, and culture (Hillner, 1978). Instrumental learning takes place when two drive aims conflict, and a third confluent kind of action that satisfies both or inhibits one occurs. It also takes place when the aims and objects of drives are altered or replaced (Cattel, 1980).

An illustration of the complexity of instrumental learning is seen in an example of a six-year-old girl learning to ride a bicycle (Ross, 1977):

> After many efforts that ended in failure, one night she had a dream in which she was riding her bike by herself. The next morning she got on her bike and rode triumphantly down the street. She had continued to learn to ride her bicycle while sleeping.

Didactic Learning

Children do not need to learn how to engage in conditioned or instrumental learning as they do for didactic learning. Because it is a special form of learning defined by the educational setting and the roles of teacher and student, didactic learning deserves special attention. It differs from other forms of learning, such as through tutoring, coaching, or apprenticeship, because it is designed for groups and is necessarily distant from practical application. It is regarded generally as the most cost efficient means of conveying vast bodies of knowledge in limited periods of time to large numbers of students.

In the typical setting of didactic learning, a child must accept the authority of teachers and be motivated to pay attention to, and then concentrate on, a task. The child must be able to see, hear, and interpret stimuli as the teacher does. Most important, the child must be able to understand the purpose of the task; know how to begin, carry it out step by step, and finish it; coordinate and communicate ideas about the task verbally and in writing; and recognize when errors are made and want to correct them. All of this must be remembered and carried ahead to the next day, when something new and unfamiliar is added.

Computers offer promise as aids in understanding didactic learning processes that rely upon precision and predictability, because a computer program must be expressed clearly as a set of instructions. Because clarity is essential, work on artificial intelligence provides a rich source of clear distinctions between many types of symbolic representations and interpretive processes (Boden, 1977). HACKER is an artificial intelligence program with features comparable to aspects of didactic learning. However, it cannot replicate human intuition (Dreyfus & Dreyfus, 1986). It can learn how to plan the assembly of stacks of bricks, because it can profit from its mistakes. Its mistakes are not simply wrong, but are inadequate first attempts at mastery of its problems and guide appropriate adjustments in order to reach goals (Sussman, 1975). Ironically the inherent errors of these machines are more readily accepted than those of children.

Didactic learning is figurative accommodative learning in Piaget's sense. As such it does not engage the affective system and is at risk for having little enduring value. It depends heavily upon the degree to which teacher and student function effectively in their respective roles. How a teacher and student embrace their roles is a function of the set of each. For this reason a brief discussion of *cognitive set* is in order.

A person's cognitive set is the person's disposition to perceive, approach, and respond to a given situation and is influenced by cognitive style, attitude, level of arousal, distracting internal imagery, and motivational state (Siegler, 1983). When information is perceived as incompatible with one's set, cognitive dissonance occurs. When this happens one can reduce the dissonance by adjusting one's set or distorting or rejecting the information (Festinger, 1962). The inherent disparity between teacher and student expectations makes their sets vulnerable to dissonance and rejection of information on either side.

In particular, a child's set determines how accurately the child perceives information. Young children, for example, often extend their understanding of general rules for forming plural and past tenses beyond the nouns and verbs to which they apply. They may say "comed," "goed," "runned," and "breaked," even though they have not heard these said by other people. Similar distortions are frequently evident in the errors that children make in school. Prior to acquiring the ability to think in formal operational terms and to appreciate the purpose of education, children's sets in school are influenced by motives related to affection, fear, rivalry, and pride.

Didactic learning can be enhanced by helping a child grasp underlying principles that give personal meaning to the subject being studied, thereby converting didactic to instrumental learning—which enables students to learn concepts operatively in-

stead of figuratively (Perkins, 1974). When children gain pleasure from mastering academic tasks, instrumental learning is taking place. Didactic learning also can be converted to conditioned learning through repetition, as in the learning of multiplication tables. When didactic instruction fails, teachers might examine whether a child is accurately receiving the essential information in a given problem. Like adults, children often fail to understand all of the dimensions of new material. The teacher's instructions should alert the child to what to expect. Unfamiliar material, for example, can be learned more easily if it is organized under more general, inclusive, higher order concepts. When children do not fully understand a task, they obviously cannot succeed (Siegler, 1983).

Creative Learning

Adults often regard children as vessels into which knowledge is poured through didactic learning. In this view the purpose of education is simply to expose children to information. For self-motivated children who possess basic academic skills, this may work. For many children, however, it is not enough (Rawson, 1982). Their interest must be ignited. A useful means of doing so is through bringing a child's creativity into academic learning. The challenge is to tap the wellspring of a child's urge to be creative.

Experiments concerning didactic methods of teaching raise the question of whether or not a child who passively receives information from adults without the creative struggle of modifying schemes will learn anything later without such help (Inhelder et al, 1974). As didactic learning may cause changes in schemes through an external influence, creativity causes changes in schemes from an internal influence. Creative learning is discovery and expansion of one's own knowledge and abilities. Productivity in adult occupations and children's schoolwork is enhanced by the creative process in which a person produces something that has not existed before for that person. Creativity, therefore, is personalized learning resulting from actions based upon internal imagery adapted to the external world. The vexing problem is how to link externally prescribed didactic learning to a child's internal motivation to create. A consideration of children's play and creativity in adults may help to deal with this dilemma.

Play

The dichotomy between play as a child's activity and work as an adult activity came out of the 19th century and was accentuated in the 20th century by reactions to the abuses of child labor. This separation of play and work has made it difficult to envision play as a form of children's work or as having an important role in adulthood (Plant, 1979).

Empirical research confirms a developmental progression in creativity beginning with a child's expression of curiosity through play (Tower, 1983). A rich imagination appears to enhance the adaptation of young children so that those who show more joy in their play tend to be happier and more cooperative than those who do not (Singer, 1976).

Simply by growing up, a child is involved in creativity—the infant's discovery of a foot, the toddler walking unaided for the first time, and the young child who recognizes the meaning of a word. The apparent difference from adult creativity is that for the infant or young child the creative event seems to be effortless in contrast with the creative adult's tedious effort. Overlooked, however, is the extended experimentation and effort that preceded the infant's discoveries and the young child's achievement of literacy. Indeed, both the

young and the older labor in their creative acts.

The emergence of play depends in part upon a young child's experience of play with adults. Although subject to individual differences, infants raised with exposure only to purposeful behavior by adults may not fully learn to play (Garvey, 1977). Because they project themselves into adult activities and rehearse their future roles and values in play, children acquire social motivations, skills, and attitudes more effectively through imitation in play than through training.

Initially children's play consists of recollections and reenactments of real situations. Through their recognition of implicit rules governing their games, children also achieve an elementary mastery of abstract concepts (Vygotsky, 1978). Exercise of their imagination fosters the development of concentration, memory skills, thinking, language development, self-awareness, self-regulation, social sensitivity, and interpersonal skills (Tower, 1983). Thus the development of imagination through play is a central aspect of overall character development.

Play helps a child master important skills as well as to learn facts and about relationships. In play children set up and solve problems without dependence upon adult approval. They find pleasure in completing tasks themselves. They learn to think things through and to plan ahead (Marzollo & Lloyd, 1976; Bjorklund, 1978). One of the social realities children discover during their play is how other children react to them.

Children gradually season infantile notions with facts through the adaptation of internal imagery to reality in play. Curiosity is the motive for adjusting inner beliefs to the realities of the external world. Play is stepping into a temporary sphere in which pretending is less than, and yet far more than, the real world it approximates. Children then gradually relinquish play as the modality for learning to adopt more realistic games and, ultimately, schoolwork. As the young child's work, play needs to flower as a precondition for later academic learning (Omwake, 1963).

A child who is able to enjoy playing, both alone and with other children, and who employs a rich imagination in games that depend upon an exact perception of reality is capable of becoming a person welcomed by the world at large (Piaget & Inhelder, 1969; Davis & Wallbridge, 1981). Conversely, a child who is unable to abide by the ethical values of fairness and rules involved in games is likely to have later difficulties in social relationships (Huizinga, 1944). Freud's formulation of psychological health as the capacity to love and to work could include the capacity to play, as well.

The play of children forms the basis for work in the adult sense. The consecutive forms of play with parents, with things, with filling and emptying, with toys, with role playing, and with games and hobbies are motivated by attachments to people, the pleasures of intake and elimination, constructive and destructive tendencies, and erotic urges. An investigative spirit, imagination, and skills develop from curiosity when there are opportunities for exploration as well as models for identification. Finally, when a child outgrows the need for immediate pleasure, play merges into work (Freud, 1981b).

Play provides the opportunity for children to learn, develop, and perfect new skills that build competence. It is a child's natural mode for mastering distress evoked by the overwhelming experiences of everyday life and builds the capacity to cope with internal and external stress. It enhances the capacity to analyze and mediate between internal and external stress. It enhances the capacity to analyze and mediate between internal and external perceptions

and images. It repeats and confirms gratifying experiences that fuel a child's investment in life (Cotton, 1984).

The play of children offers a route to understanding the potential relationship of creativity to schoolwork through the play–competence spiral: learning leads to more sophisticated play, and play provides an experience of mastery that leads to more learning (Chance, 1979). Play is not an interlude or an indulgence, but is a vitally important activity that exists in primates and in all human societies as an essential feature of the development of the young (Norbeck, 1978; Rosenblatt, 1981).

Creativity

The desire to do things with one's hands and to be creative may derive from atavistic survival capacities for digging and cutting, fashioning flints and pots, spinning yarn, and weaving cloth. At the same time, the absorption of hand, eye, mind, and spirit in an artistic task provides an oasis of peace, refreshment, and tranquility possible in few areas of modern life (Mendelowitz, 1963).

Creativity is a transformation of internal motivations and imagery through self-disciplined effort into actions and products that are satisfying to the individual, and possibly to others. Creativity thus is not a single intuitive act, but a consistent and sustained activity. The creative process has been described as the obverse of dreaming in that the creator tries consciously to reverse unconscious censorship and to use dream mechanisms for the purposes of concretizing and abstracting. In this sense the creative process is the realization of a dream (Rothenberg, 1979).

Creativity may be seen as the interaction between the holistic, primary process of the right cerebral hemisphere and the analytic, secondary process of the left hemisphere. Spatial imagery is one of the main functions of the right hemisphere and so bears an important relationship to the creative process (Forisha, 1983).

Creative learning starts with the self-conscious process of problem-solving thinking (Anderson, 1983b; Calfee, 1983). It is facilitated by focusing upon the whole task, analyzing its parts, and reconstructing the whole as the individual confers form, configuration, and meaning upon perceptions. Creative breakthroughs usually are preceded by secondary-process logical, linear thinking, as an individual defines and redefines a problem. Then there comes a moment of insight when an answer presents itself, and finally the mind tackles the difficult job of evaluating the insight and putting it into a form in which it can be communicated and applied to a problem. For example,:

> The chemist Kokule came upon one of the most important discoveries of organic chemistry, the structure of the benzene ring, in a dream. Having pondered the problem for some time, he had a dream in which a snake seized hold of its own tail and whirled mockingly before his eyes. He suddenly awoke and realized that organic compounds, such as benzene, were not open structures but closed rings (McKim, 1980).

Creative learning is not merely the associative repetition of reasons that are already known. One may be puzzled by things that do not fit together until suddenly there is a flash of understanding, and one sees how all of the pieces make up one whole (Bohm, 1980).

Creativity can be seen as resulting from four conditions (Ghiselin, 1952). First, there is original imagery and a conscious impulse to act. Second, that imagery is developed through a period of gestation during which there usually is a conscious struggle to lay out the essential structure of the work. Third, there is a period of spontaneous

outpouring from unconscious depths. The last step is the conscious reshaping, pruning, and refining of the final work. The capacity to originate occurs more commonly than the capacity to develop and execute imagery. Darwin, for example, was not the first to conceive of evolution. His achievement was to provide such massive evidence that the idea was then seriously entertained (Pickering, 1976).

In creative activity the person is inspired. Imagery flows and new things appear that were never before known. Concentration and labor follow. The creative person works through ambiguity in a state of immersion in the process. During the course of creating, a person may experience depression, anxiety, or feelings of inadequacy. The passionate interest of the creator, however, leads to the exhilaration of the moments of discovery, which are akin to sublime bliss. There is a feeling of satisfaction on completing the created work (Stein, 1975).

Humor provides a back-door entry to the domain of creativity, because it is the only example of a complex intellectual stimulus that releases a simple bodily response—the laughter reflex (Koestler, 1978). The emotion involved in humor is mediated through the sympathetic branch of the autonomic nervous system and has a stronger momentum than the subtle processes of secondary-process reasoning and is discharged in laughter. But this reflex could only arise in a person whose reasoning has gained a degree of independence from biological drives, enabling the perception of the emotions as redundant—to realize that one has been fooled (Koestler, 1978).

Humor is perceiving a situation or event in two mutually exclusive contexts. The result is an abrupt transfer of consciousness to a different track governed by a different logic. This intellectual jolt deflates one's expectations. The suddenly aroused emotions are flushed out in laughter. The sudden clash between two mutually exclusive contexts produces the comic effect. It compels perceiving a situation in two incompatible frames of reference at the same time.

In a similar vein, in Janusian thinking, a characteristic of highly creative people, opposites are conceived simultaneously. A creative thinker goes beyond ordinary logic into realms of the unexpected and the unknown and discovers affirmation of the opposite to traditional belief. For example, Einstein's happiest thought was the sudden recognition that a man falling from the roof of a house is simultaneously in motion in relation to the house and at rest in relation to a hammer he was holding (Rothenberg, 1983). In contrast to creative Janusian thinking, a schizophrenic person seems to be unaware of logical contradictions in opposite thoughts.

Creativity is expressed in a variety of ways. The arts are directed toward the senses. A writer appeals to all of the senses through the images of words created by the reader. A painter creates visually stimulating objects. A dancer creates body movements that are visually stimulating to others and proprioceptively satisfying to the dancer. A composer creates symbols that become music when performed by musicians, who create sounds.

Acquiring the skill of reading can be a creative process, as seen in the satisfaction shown by a young child who triumphantly reads a word or sentence, paralleling the pleasure of an author in creating new ideas. Conversely, the frustrations of children struggling with words compares to the frustrations of writers grappling with expressing emerging insights.

Just as an artist masters painting skills in order to express ideas, a reading child masters the alphabet, syllables, words, syntax, and grammar so that imagery can flow from the symbolism of printed words. As the artist must gain freedom from self-consciousness of the act of painting, a child must gain freedom from awareness of the act of reading in order to absorb meaning from words. Both painting and reading depend upon suspending self-consciousness that may interfere with the creative process.

Our understanding of creativity has been derived from the analysis of the creative process in adults, especially those with the talents of genius. The following characteristics have been described in these creative adults. They have a tolerance for ambiguity, conflict, and the unknown. They are capable of controlled regression, are inner-directed and imaginative, and obtain pleasure from observation of their internal and external worlds. They may be right hemisphere oriented in their nonlinear, holistic, intuitive approach to life.

Although creative people tend to be flexible and inventive in their own fields of endeavor, they may have difficulty adjusting to the demands of daily life. They may show evidence of compensation for insecurity and frustrated power motives (MacKinnon, 1965). Freud held that a character analysis of highly gifted individuals might reveal a mixture of efficiency, perversion, and neurosis (Freud, 1932).

Impediments to Creativity

Social and environmental forces play crucial roles in creative performances (Amabile, 1983). Most young children participate eagerly in artistic expression and have freely creative imaginations. They sing, dance, draw, paint, model, build, and write naturally and without self-consciousness. Their creative expression flows in their play. However, many forces in early life operate to suppress their creative imaginations so that the primordial originality of infancy is lost in the process of socialization (Arieti, 1976).

The conspiracy of silence that surrounds a child's struggle over lustful and destructive impulses and curiosity about forbidden things about the body and its functions is part of the inhibiting socializing process. Also, when children believe that their productions will be evaluated by adults, they are less creative than at play (Amabile, 1983). When play is restricted in young children, they may fail in academic learning later (Omwake, 1963). In advertisements, movies, television, and comic books, society also assails children with a wide variety of images that shape superficial and cynical attitudes toward sexuality and aggression (Mendelowitz, 1963).

Of greatest significance is the relative absence of creativity in the academic pursuits of school-age children. Although the glint of creativity can be seen during the early school years, it is seen less as the process of schooling enfolds older children (Gould, 1972).

Apparent creative abilities develop rapidly from kindergarten through the third grade (Torrance, 1963). A sharp decrement occurs between the third and fourth grades. Gains occur in the fifth and sixth grades but creativity again drops in the seventh. The eighth, ninth, tenth and 11th grades show a gradual recovery of creativity. Common educational hindrances to creative thinking are premature attempts to discourage imagery; restrictions on curiosity; overemphasis on preventing injury and avoiding risks; misplaced emphasis on verbal skills; destructive criticism; and coercive pressure from peers. The following case example illustrates the complicated interaction of a child's personality, family, and school in the perversion of creativity:

Twenty-four-year-old David was first seen by the Learning Disabilities Service at his request to determine whether or not he had learning disabilities. He graduated from high school as one of the lowest in his class, although his intelligence test scores were in the superior range, and he had a flair for designing computers. After two years, he dropped out of college because of failing grades and worked as a janitor.

David had been seen by numerous physicians, mental health professionals and learning disability specialists. His general impression of their opinions was that he had an auditory memory deficit that interfered with listening in class work and with following instructions, in addition to chronic anxiety manifested by a variety of psychophysiological symptoms.

David's prenatal and perinatal history was not unusual. He was an easy infant to parent and an energetic toddler, who charmed adults. His father was a busy professional, who saw issues in black and white terms and was uncomfortable in showing affection to his children. His mother enjoyed David's popularity with adults and tried to use tactful persuasion as a disciplinary technique.

Prior to the fourth grade in school, David was regarded by his parents as an exuberant, happy child. They saw him as a "born leader," although the directions in which he led other children often were impulsive and based upon his own egocentric perspective.

David was painfully frustrated in two areas. First, he found himself continually corrected by adults for his misbehavior, which he did not recognize as such until someone forcefully intruded upon him. For example, his mother recalled that David did not seem to hear or understand instructions until she held him by his shoulders and forced him to look at her. The second area of frustration was in schoolwork, where he found that no matter how hard he tried, he could not get the answers expected by his teachers. David learned to read and cipher easily; however, as schoolwork involved more complicated questions, he found that his answers were "wrong by someone else so that I never came up with the right answers." Still he stubbornly held to the conviction that he was right, and the others were wrong, as a defense against experiencing criticism as a painful, devastating attack. In retrospect his father recalled that David brought him social studies papers with answers marked wrong, but when given a chance could show that his answer was the logical result of alternative reasoning.

At first David was crushed by his poor grades, because he wanted to please his parents, who set high academic standards for their children. From the fourth grade onward, however, David became convinced that he was "bad," because he thought he could not behave or achieve academically as a "good" boy. To avoid the painful mortification of feeling "bad," he turned inward into his "shell." He increasingly experienced criticism as a devastating attack from which he had to protect himself. He felt discouraged, angry at himself, depressed and resentful of teachers, who "never gave me a graceful way to accept their answers. They just told me I was wrong." His mother recalled that David became a "tense, angry boy."

David became forgetful and could not remember to do homework or to follow instructions given by his parents. In retrospect he discovered that forgetting assignments was a "handy way of avoiding the embarrassment of having the wrong answers." More devastatingly, however, in spite of his worry about them, David's behavior persisted in creating situations of embarrassment and distress through inefficiency in his schoolwork. When he tried to listen to his teachers, a fog came over his brain. His mother recalled adjusting to David's forgetfulness by not expecting as much of him as of her other children. School personnel thought that he would try harder if she cracked down on him. This did not make sense to her, because she saw David working hard, al-

though inefficiently, on his schoolwork. As he looked back in psychotherapy, David reconstructed a pattern in which he progressively "destroyed myself" in school by his expectation of failure, which interfered with his ability to recall material learned in class on tests or recitation. He could not remember facts when he tried to produce them because of the repression of information that would lead to his success in school.

Although David was marginally aware of resentment toward his parents during his school years, he was more aware of anger at himself and a diffuse pattern of resisting an "authority ghost." During his college years, this also appeared in the form of resenting and resisting any form of housekeeping.

In individual psychotherapy David first became aware of a panicky feeling that if his parents were involved in family therapy, they would be dragged into his agony and hurt. In the transference he then became aware of irrationally feeling attacked by the therapist. Rather than withdrawing into his embattled shell, he counterattacked and became aware of his destructive rage at the therapist and then at his parents. In family therapy he discovered that his parents were able to handle his anger and their own guilt. They also verified his weaknesses and called attention to his many strengths.

At the core of David's interactions with authority figures lay a sensitive, intuitive apprehension of reality and an exquisite sensitivity to criticism accompanied by a grandiose conviction of his own innate perfection. As his school failures mounted, rather than tempering his points of view through dialogue, David clung to his egocentricity and became increasingly enraged at himself for his flawed perfection, and because he could not convert adults to his views. He could not bear the primitive intensity of his rage at adults because of his dependency upon them. He sabotaged them, however, by failing academically and toppling the "family tower of academic excellence." David's creativity had been stifled, and because of his narcissism was converted into a chronic struggle with authority figures.

The degree of effort required to learn is a measure of intrapsychic interferences within the person (Kubie, 1962). Interference can be generated by a myriad of factors, ranging from limitations of a child's inbuilt equipment to life experiences. For example, individual variations in the ability to deal with spoken words can range from word deafness to a tape-recorder auditory memory. The ability to deal with written words can range from word blindness to a photographic memory. Moreover, the separation of the secondary and the primary processes, which is forced on a child by psychological defenses and reinforced by the demands of education and society, may lead to progressive alienation from one's inner resources and blocking of creativity. The defense mechanism of isolation creates an asymmetrical situation in which secondary-process modes of imagery are conscious and open to reflective scrutiny while primary-process imagery is repressed, thus preventing an integration of the two modes (Noy, 1979).

Enhancing Creativity

Neurosis and creativity can be seen as contrasting attempts to solve the same underlying conflicts. Neurosis is an attempt to restore inner order by preventing the free expression of dangerous wishes and by splitting identification systems with opposite valences apart. Thus neurosis is characterized by the tendency to resist change, whereas creativity is a search for new solutions to old problems. Neurosis is a regression to past infantile patterns of adaptation, whereas creativity is a progressive attempt to create new and daring adaptations that have never been tried before

(Noy, 1979). At the same time, neurotic conflicts can be sublimated in creative activities that serve as an outlet for potentially destructive impulses (Mendelowitz, 1963). For whatever reasons, learning becomes more pleasurable and efficient when creativity can be tapped in school.

One of the first principles in enhancing creativity is to increase the amount and diversity of information and experience that one has available. This can be done by exposing oneself nonjudgmentally to a new body of knowledge without trying to evaluate it. Another technique is Janusian thinking, in which wo contradictory images are held at the same time until a new image emerges (Rothenberg, 1979). Brainstorming in a free-wheeling manner without the need to criticize is one of the best-known techniques for stimulating creativity. Problem redefinition also is helpful. Getting distance from a problem is desirable, as in using metaphors and analogies (Stein, 1975). Achieving vivid internally generated imagery through meditation techniques also enhances creativity (Ostrander & Schroeder, 1979).

To develop creativity a child needs time away from external demands and space that is free from the interference of others. Perhaps this simple need for privacy and the tacit approval of idiosyncratic play explains why children from large families are less likely to be creative and why partitioned space facilitates imaginative play (Field, 1980; Freyberg, 1973). A setting that provides clear guidelines for acceptable behavior and a few rules is optimal in fostering creativity, whereas one that is totally adult directed leaves little room for it, and a laissez-faire setting lacks inspiration for it (Tower, 1983). Still, working environments conducive to creativity vary with individuals; for example, Shelly and Rousseau liked to be bareheaded in the sun while they worked.

Young children learn most easily tactually and kinesthetically. Visual modality strength develops next, followed by the auditory modality, which may not mature until the age of ten or 11 (Price et al, 1980). Awareness of these development emphases can facilitate teaching at these levels.

SUMMARY

Learning is the capacity of a living system to use experience to maintain itself. The developmental process is a combination of maturation of the brain and learning reflected in the growth of the cellular and chemical components of the central nervous system. The cortical-striatal system may be the locus of the conditioned learning of habits and the cortical-limbic system the locus of acquiring knowledge.

A child's curiosity leads to contact with the widening world and is the wellspring of learning. The learning process is the vehicle for a child's gradual modification of concepts about the self and external world in the light of reality. The result of successful learning is a sense of competence.

An epigenetic model of learning, arising from the work of Freud, Erikson, and Piaget, postulates mental schemes that have innate cellular and acquired chemical components in the central nervous system. Schemes follow a developmental sequence in which each stage builds upon the preceding one, as it also results in a new qualitative level of capacity. The two poles of learning are the conservation of existing schemes, on the one hand, and their modification, on the other. Schemes thus assimilate congenial information from the external and internal worlds and accommodate by changing to assimilate new information.

Through their operations schemes are related to each other hierarchically and are integrated with drives, emotions, images, symbols, and concepts. This may occur through reflective abstraction of principles from one's action upon things and from persons of emotional significance. The boundaries between images of the external inanimate world and the internal images of emotionally colored human relationships and the drives, emotions, and self-concepts optimally are permeable. When they are rigid and impermeable, split-off segments are formed, with resulting persistent immaturity and impairment of mental functioning.

Conditioned and instrumental learning that directly fulfill drives through advancing coping skills are an essential aspect of living. Didactic learning in school, however, is without immediate benefit except as one is motivated by pleasing teachers or parents, competing with peers, or enhancing one's status. In solving a problem, one can form symbolic and conceptual schemes through didactic learning. The greatest retention follows, however, by actually using the solution of the problem in a practical life situation, so that symbols and concepts become integrated with sensorimotor schemes.

Creativity is a means of personalizing learning by articulating one's resources with the environment. The play of children is a creative process, as is the early mastery of complex skills, such as learning to read. In the play–competence spiral, learning leads to more sophisticated play, and play provides an exciting creative experience of mastery that leads to more learning. As the work of young children, play lays the foundation for later schoolwork.

Creativity is a self-disciplined effort that transforms internal motivations and images into actions and products that are satisfying to the individual, and possibly others. Creativity can be impeded by premature demands for rational, adult thought and behavior and by internal defenses against drives, emotions, and images. Although the glint of creativity is seen during early childhood, the process of schooling gradually diminishes it. To the extent that creativity and instrumental learning can be tapped in education, schoolwork can be pleasurable and have an enduring impact.

Children have an inherent urge to acquire the knowledge necessary for survival and personal satisfaction. An inner model of the outside world is created through learning so that a child can cope with both inner and outer worlds efficiently. For some children this model is too rudimentary to enable successful work in school. For others it is heavily involved in defensive processes that vitiate efforts at scholarship. For most children learning becomes integrated with aggressive and affiliative strivings that are sublimated in successful schoolwork.

Learning is the vehicle through which children develop knowledge and skills by the gradual modification of sensorimotor, symbolic, and conceptual schemes. The lasting reward is satisfaction through competence.

18

Learning Academic Skills

Reading is a hybrid of consciousness, half meaningful and half imaginative.

Jean Paul Sartre, 1950

This chapter is devoted to current knowledge about the ingredients of learning the basic academic skills of reading, writing, and arithmetic. Reading receives the most attention because of its central role in all academic learning.

READING

Early writing was regarded as magic. It conferred enormous powers on those privy to its secrets. Because it then was a prerogative of a privileged class, literacy was guarded jealously as the source of authority and not shared with the masses (Eisenberg, 1979). Eventually literacy came to be a necessity rather than a luxury with the invention of the printing press 500 years ago. Present-day children are expected to read.

We are now in the second literacy revolution in the United states. The first took place early in this century, when the goal was to bring citizens to a fourth-grade level of functional literacy, a level now achieved by mildly mentally retarded adults. Now we seek a general level of literacy expected of high-school graduates. The simplest army manual is written on an eighth-grade reading level, and most naval technical manuals require an 11th- or 12th-grade level (Chall, 1979). Figure 18-1 summarizes typical educational achievement expectations for the elementary grades. The actual literacy level in the United States, however, falls short of these levels. In 1975 the U.S. Office of Education-sponsored Adult Performance Level Study disclosed that 22 percent of adults between 18 and 65, or 23 million people, could not read at a fourth-grade level (Flesch, 1981). That situation apparently has not improved.

In a world overloaded with information, the advantage will go to those who can sort important information from the trivial. A society in which reading skills are not sufficiently cultivated has much to fear. Functional literacy is needed for an individual to perform productively in modern society as a family member, consumer, and worker. This becomes increasingly evident with the transition of our society into the Information Age. Literacy in itself, however, does not produce skills in memory, classification, and logical inference, so that learning to read is not sufficient as an early

GRADE	READING	SPELLING	WRITING	MATHEMATICS
Kindergarten	Recognize letters and own name Left-right progression	First and last name aloud	Print own name and numbers to 9	Count to 10 Size and shape recognition Concept of ½ Identify clock and coins
First Grade	Recognize consonants, vowels Comprehend story titles and pictures Read 250–350 words	Spell simple words	Print all upper and lowercase letters	Count to 20 Simple addition and subtraction Concept of ⅓ and ¼ Tell time by hour and value of coins
Second Grade	Recognize consonant and vowel blends Comprehend main ideas and sequence of events Read 950–1,700 words	Formal instruction in spelling begins Use picture dictionary	Create representation of a scene, object, or character	Count to 100 and by 2's Column addition and subtraction; place value Concepts of point, line, and line segment Concept of ⅔, ⅜ Use calendar and tell time by ½ hour Know directions on globe
Third Grade	Recognize "R" controlled vowels Read 1,900–3,300 words	Spelling and phonic rules Use of dictionary Diphthongs Digraphs	Cursive writing begins	Count by 5's, 10's; 3 and 4 digit numbers Complex subtraction and addition Simple multiplication Angles, bisecting and segmenting lines Lowest common denominator Add money and make change Know days, weeks, months, and years
Fourth Grade	Recognize prefixes, suffixes, roots, and multisyllabic words Comprehend comparisons, predictions, conclusions, character descriptions Emphasis on silent reading begins Read 2,800–3,500 words	Spelling of 2,000 words mastered Alphabetize Use telephone book	Create representation by applying theme from literature to own experience	Roman numerals and decimals Simple division; 2 digit multiplication Work with ruler and compass; diameter and circumferences Fractions and mixed numbers Linear and liquid measurements
Fifth Grade	Enhancement of reading rate, vocabulary, and automatization Emphasis on study skills of outlining, summarizing, and notetaking Read 4,500–6,000 words	Combine parts into new words Use pronunciation key in dictionary	Book reports, essays	Round off numbers; measure areas More complex fractions Use scales on maps and latitude and longitude on globe Equivalents and conversions Division with 1 digit Know Celcius and Fahrenheit
Sixth Grade	Continued enhancement of silent reading skills Emphasis on skimming and detailed reading styles Read 6,000–8,500 words	Over 3,000 words mastered Know word roots Use card catalogue	Write short stories, poems Create new point of view	Division with 2–3 digit divisors Measure angles and complex areas, construct shapes, use compass Expand money concepts Calculate averages Use computer language and write simple programs

Figure 18-1. Timetable for acquiring academic skills.

educational goal (Scribner & Cole, 1981). Learning how to think is more important.

Reading is an essential building block for academic learning and later life. Through the material they read, children acquire ways of thinking, feeling, and knowing that bring them closer to the world in which they live. Some children learn to read naturally and effortlessly at home. Most children, however, learn to read in school, and for some that task is difficult. Learning to read is at the core of a complex encounter between a young child and society that takes place in school.

A broad view of learning reading can be gained from surveying five factors: locale, language development, the act of reading, automatic reading, and instruction in reading.

Locale of Instruction

Learning to read requires a setting that provides comfortable adult authority relations, supportive peer relations, conducive physical arrangements, and effective teaching methods. Learning to read also depends upon a child joining the schooling process rather than opposing or being overwhelmed by it.

Many children learn how to read prior to entering school. An increasing number of youngsters pick up reading without being specifically taught, in part as a result of television programming. Nursery schools and Operation Headstart also lay the foundation for learning to read by stimulating the development of basic reading skills. Programs for young, disadvantaged children especially can be designed to prepare them for a literate society by expanding their spoken vocabularies (Pflaum, 1974).

Reading difficulty is associated with various attributes of the individual, such as being a boy, being poorly prepared for school, being comparatively slow in language development, and being dyslexic.

None of these characteristics are insurmountable barriers to literacy, however. Those who fail are responding largely to their learning environments, which include both the school and home (Calfee, 1983). Reading competence in children is particularly related to family background factors, such as parents' level of education, socioeconomic status, and the presence of reading materials in the home (Gibson & Levin, 1975).

Language Development

Reading is a language skill that involves high-level perceptual processing. Although they both are part of learning language, learning to speak and learning to read are very different (Kinsbourne & Caplan, 1979). The language system for speech is inborn, whereas it must be constructed for reading. Also, children are bathed in spoken language from birth. Moreover, sounds of speech are heard sequentially, because the auditory system is linked to time, but printed words occur in the context of competing visual stimuli in a given space. The beginning reader must first perceive the meaning of spoken messages, then acquire the same ability with written messages (Ausubel, 1969).

Most children learn to read their native language by reconstructing written into spoken symbols. Spoken language thus aids in deciphering the meaning of words, because reading is a direct transition from letters and words to speech (Brown, 1980). Written language often deviates from spoken sounds, however, and has its own rules and is not aided by the melody, emphases, pauses, and prosody of speech.

Beginning readers may approach reading instruction in a state of confusion about the purpose and technical features of the written word. This confusion is an important factor in the success or failure of learning to read (Downing, 1979). Children need to know that letters and words can be transformed into their familiar spoken language. They need to know that the written word is not a completely new symbol but actually the written equivalent of familiar spoken words whose meaning and syntax are known to them (Ausubel, 1969). Learning to read is simply discovering a new way to express words they already know. Children work themselves out of their initial confused state about the functions and features of written language, but confusion recurs at later stages as new subskills are added.

The reading process depends on a continuous interaction between the visual features of letters and words (Haber & Haber, 1981). Children who learn to read by themselves appear to have grasped this insight whereas children who need to be taught to read have not (Torrey, 1979). Beginning readers must understand that letters are two-dimensional abstract forms that bear no immediate relationship to objects or feelings, but whose only meaning is in their sounds. For this reason learning the names of letters before learning their sounds confuses many children. Furthermore, they must learn that letters represent speech sounds that are part of every word. An explanation of these connections is indispensable, because not all children can deduce this on their own. It is confusing to tell children that a group of letters means a house when those letters really stand for the spoken word "house," not for the house they see; pictures do that, but not alphabetical words (Mosse, 1982).

Knowledge of the native language being read is at the heart of reading, and without that knowledge facile reading cannot take place (Gough, 1974; Strong, 1973). For this reason the profoundly deaf child does not learn to read as well as the nondeaf. One can learn to read a second language without first learning to speak it; however, this usually is done by converting foreign-language written words and phrases into their spoken form, and so involves learning the foreign tongue as well.

Research has shown that learning to read first in one's native language facilitates the learning of a second language when such an approach is valued by families and the community (Downing, 1979). Research has not supported the idea, however, that dialects should be used in teaching children to read, which then entails a second step of learning the common pronunciation. It is more useful for children to learn to read a language in its most used form (Chinn, 1984; Pflaum, 1974).

Learning to read depends upon the smoothness of visual and phonetic interaction between the hemispheres. The beginning reader relies on right-hemispheric strategies to connect novel visual shapes with a spoken word. A shift to left-hemisphere activity takes place as children advance from single-word to fluent reading (Bakker, 1983). Children with speech mediated by the left hemisphere are favored at that stage (Bakker, 1979). For spatially oriented children, who have difficulty with language and whose minds wander into the broad meaning of life, reading must be tied to their interests (Dixon, 1983).

Learning to read involves applying the basic rules of language (Gibson, 1971). These characteristics of written symbols will be treated under the following headings: phonological rules, semantic rules, and syntactic rules.

Phonological Rules

As do other alphabetical languages, English consists of graphemes, the letters of the alphabet, and morphemes, the smallest combinations of letters that symbolize meaning in the form of syllables, prefixes, suffixes, and inflexional endings. Neither morphemes nor graphemes consistently correspond to the same spoken sounds. The smallest unit that consistently represents a sound is a phoneme that consists of a single or cluster of graphemes, which have a prescribed pronunciation in a given context according to the phonological rules of English (Gibson, 1966).

Words are composed of strings of phonemes. English is organized around 46 phonemes rather than the more than 1000 morphemes available. Phonemes react with other phonemes in their immediate environment, the nature of the word in which they occur, and even the sentence in which a word appears. What we hear is not the visual segments of which a word is constituted but the sounds that result from the application of phonological rules to those segments. The sounds of a word constitute a filing system in that a sound serves as an address where an item can be located. There are two sides to each word. Its inner side is an abstract image of a string of phonemes. Its outer side is a spoken expression derived from that abstract form by means of phonological rules. Thus written words connect visual characters with sound images.

When a correspondence is established between visual symbols and phonemes so that a visual image is mapped upon an auditory one, a child builds a fund of words, or lexicon. The disadvantage of the English phonemic system is that a particular visual symbol does not always go with the same phoneme. The phonological rules of English, however, provide a means by which beginning readers can directly read words they have never seen written before by sounding them out. The lack of surface correspondence between sound and visual symbol also can be compensated for by unconscious relationships between grammatical context and meaning (Chomsky, 1968, 1970).

Reading can be dissociated from sounds, as illustrated by the fact that deaf-mutes can learn to read. Generally, however, reading is a sound–symbol association process (Bateman, 1969). This is reflected in the way that children move their lips in sounding out words as they learn to read. The fluent reader automatically converts printed forms into phonological ones in a shift from subvocalized reading to reading that transcends the vocal apparatus and becomes an automatic process, as acquired in speed reading.

Semantic Rules

An adult vocabulary includes around 100,000 words. In an alphabetical language, there is no way to determine meaning from the simple perception of a word's form. The connection between form and meaning is almost totally arbitrary and varies with context. Thus to understand a word, readers, or listeners, have no choice but to consult their mental dictionaries. For example, evoked brain potentials differ when a person is presented with the word "rock," depending upon whether that word is used to mean stone, a type of music, or a rocking chair. The brain codes and classifies not on the basis of rock as a vocal sound but on the basis of the meaning conveyed.

It is not the sound of a word that creates the meaning, but the meaning that organizes the sound (Huey, 1908). One must know a language to know what clumps of sounds are words. One also must know what a word means to recognize it correctly. Persons with auditory-linguistic dyslexias in particular have difficulty recognizing abstract words without concrete meaning, such as "the," because they require concrete meaning for words in order to recognize them easily.

Syntactical Rules

The mind is assailed as it were by every word in the paragraph. It must select, repress, soften, emphasize, correlate and organize, all under the influence of the right mental set or purpose or demand (Thorndike, 1917).

One of the most remarkable feats of the human intellect is the ability to understand sentences quickly and effortlessly (Gough, 1974). The comprehension of sentences is fundamentally different from the comprehension of words. The meaning of words is found by looking them up in our mental dictionaries. Sentences, however, are virtually new on each encounter. The meanings of sentences are not found in our memories but must be computed on the basis of the meanings of their constituent words and the syntactic rules of language.

The meaning of a sentence is determined by more than the surface structure of the meaning of its words, their order, and their grouping. Sentences have a deep structure, a level at which the crucial grammatical relations are defined based upon an innate rule system. The means by which a reader arrives at an understanding of meaning through the deep structure is not known, but probably employs inductive leaps, or thinking. The process of reading information from sentences carries one beyond words and gives significance to the text itself. For example, a boy reading about a bicycle may trail off into visual imagery of riding a bicycle himself.

The Act of Reading

The ability to read is not directly measurable and must be inferred from a child's observable behavior. With cooperative children it is possible to measure reading ability through testing. Reading is an exceedingly complex process, however, and all of its components enter into an accurate assessment of a child's reading ability. Kenneth Goodman (1982) aptly described reading as a psycholinguistic guessing game.

Jeanne Chall proposed five stages in reading development, beginning with an initial decoding stage in grades 1 and 2; a second confirmation and fluency stage in grades 2 and 3; a reading for learning stage corresponding to the introduction of the social and physical sciences in grade 4; a reading for multiple viewpoints stage in high school, and finally a constructing knowledge for oneself stage at the college level (Chall, 1983).

The ability to read and to write require a broader range of skills than any other human endeavor (Figure 18-2). These skills depend upon the progressive myelinization of the cranial nerves, permitting hearing and seeing; myelinization of the spinothalamic and corticospinal tracts, permitting touching and moving objects; and myelinization of cortical associational pathways, permitting symbolizing and thinking. All of these capacities depend upon environmental stimulation by things and persons.

The complexity of reading defies existing model-building capacities (Gibson & Levin, 1975; Rourke, 1978). For practical purposes, however, the following aspects of reading merit attention: visual and auditory attention, vision, eye movements, word recognition, comprehension of text content, and oral and silent reading.

Visual and Auditory Attention

To recognize written letters and spoken words, children need to be reasonably mature lookers and listeners (Kinsbourne & Caplan, 1979).

Adults can scan with shallow attention over a wide expanse or focus their attention sharply to take in an inconspicuous detail. They can pick out nuances of location, relation, and texture, while ignoring eye-catching stimuli. These focusing abilities are necessary for concentration when there are distracting stimuli.

Young children cannot focus their attention in such an expert fashion. Their attention is trapped by visual attributes in a perceptual developmental hierarchy (Kinsbourne & Caplan, 1979). For vision

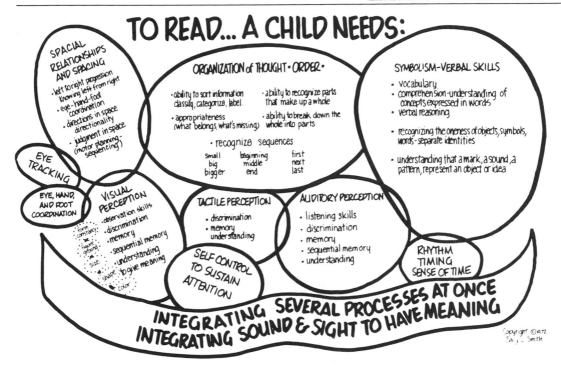

TO READ... A CHILD NEEDS:

SPACIAL RELATIONSHIPS AND SPACING
- left to right progression knowing left from right
- eye-hand-foot coordination
- directions in space directionality
- judgment in space (motor planning, sequencing)

EYE TRACKING

EYE, HAND, AND FOOT COORDINATION

VISUAL PERCEPTION
- observation skills
- discrimination
- memory
- sequential memory
- understanding to give meaning

(form constancy) (figure ground) size shape color

ORGANIZATION of THOUGHT • ORDER •
- ability to sort information classify, categorize, label.
- appropriateness (what belongs, what's missing)
- ability to recognize parts that make up a whole
- ability to break down the whole into parts
- recognize sequences

small	beginning	first
big	middle	next
bigger	end	last

SYMBOLISM-VERBAL SKILLS
- vocabulary
- comprehension-understanding of concepts expressed in words
- verbal reasoning
- recognizing the oneness of objects, symbols, words-separate identities
- understanding that a mark, a sound, a pattern, represent an object or idea

TACTILE PERCEPTION
- discrimination
- memory
- understanding

AUDITORY PERCEPTION
- listening skills
- discrimination
- memory
- sequential memory
- understanding

SELF-CONTROL TO SUSTAIN ATTENTION

RHYTHM TIMING SENSE OF TIME

INTEGRATING SEVERAL PROCESSES AT ONCE
INTEGRATING SOUND & SIGHT TO HAVE MEANING

Copyright © 1972 Sally L. Smith

Figure 18-2. The brain functions involved in reading. (From Smith, Sally L. (The Lab School of Washington), 1980, *No Easy Answers: The Learning Disabled Child at Home and at School,* New York: Bantam Books. Reproduced with permission.)

the dimensions of shape and color are first on this hierarchy. Size, location, orientation, sequence, and texture are relatively less significant and are likely to be overlooked by young children, who remain engrossed in the forms and colors that confront them. Young children also inspect things incompletely: their focus is arrested by eye-catching features, and they ignore other parts. Their focus is redundant, so that certain features may be inspected repeatedly even though recognized at first glance. Their focus also is unsystematic, so that their attention flits between salient features without consistent direction or organization.

Thus a child's attention focusing and span of concentration develop according to hierarchical principles, just as does the perceptual apparatus. This means that the way perceptions are registered depends upon how precisely a child's attention is focused. For this reason young children notice only some words on a page, some letters in a word, or a part of a letter, thereby making mistakes in reading.

When learning a word, it is helpful to remember the context in which it was first heard or read. As the experience is repeated, the importance of the context disappears. A child with immature inspection strategies notices different things about a word each time it appears. For example, a teacher may show a young child the word car five times. The child may notice the "a" one time, the "c" another time, the "r" another, the "ca" another, and the "ar" yet another. That child needs help in focusing on distinctive attributes that differentiate the word from other comparable forms by drawing attention to individual phonemes and building up syllables (Kinsbourne & Caplan, 1979).

Initially children try to break a word into its constituent speech sounds incompletely, redundantly, and unsystematically. It is easier to hear and reproduce a whole word than to identify its constituent speech sounds. Breaking up words calls for an analytic listening attitude and requires deliberate effort. What are regarded as auditory discrimination deficits may actually be related to the fact that the child is not paying attention to the whole word sound.

For the young child, learning is based upon drives and emotions at the level of preoperational or magical thinking. The muscular movements involved in forming the sounds of letters may evoke primitive sensual imagery and associated emotions. This quality may distort the meaning of written symbols. At the same time, reference to the body and its functions in early reading instruction may tap children's curiosity about their bodies (Duplaix, 1950).

The dominance of primary process urges and emotions may interfere with learning the alphabet, when omnipotent grandiosity clashes with teaching efforts that are perceived as coercive by a child. Learning to read involves relinquishing an all-knowing omniscience and depends upon a willingness to engage with the unfamiliar. Moreover, when internal imagery predominates, there is little motivation for paying attention, concentrating, and carrying out the work of learning to read (Fenichel, 1945).

Vision

Unlike spoken language, reading is such a recent human acquisition that neither the brain nor the eyes have accommodated to it through evolution. The eyes are not designed for prolonged fixed near-vision. The prevalence of myopia in the developed countries is mute testimony to the visually unnatural character of reading.

The perception of words obviously depends upon the presence of intact vision. The development of 20/20 vision and the coordination of the eyes to allow depth perception is not established until about the age of six. The functional efficiency of the eyes can affect a child's ability to concentrate and sustain effort, as well as the attitude toward reading. Headaches and dizziness can result from eye strain. Visual handicaps that interfere with learning to read are relatively common, necessitating ruling out problems in visual acuity, such as myopia or hyperopia, and rarely in fusing images, such as with aniseikonia.

Malfunctioning of the autonomic and glandular systems of the body also can affect the efficiency of ocular functioning (Taylor, 1966). Psychophysiological immaturity may impair a child's ability to carry out efficient reading as a coordinated physiological activity.

Because reading takes place in the brain and not the eyes, one can learn to read without vision, as through braille. For the blind touch is the critical sensory system. Skill in touch reading is a highly individual matter related to the touch sensitivity of the reading fingers as well as to the size of the braille characters, clearness of embossing, and even the paper (Merry, 1932).

Eye Movements

In reading the brain seeks information from printed symbols and directs the eyes across the lines of print in a series of saccadic fixations. In the process there is a simultaneous rapid flicking rotation of the eyes around their vertical axes while reading horizontal lines (Rayner, 1983).

Learning to read involves converting a child's short, irregular, regressive saccadic eye movements and long pauses into the refined habits of the advanced reader in which the eyes move across the page from left to right in series of broad, rhythmical movements, pausing for a fraction of a second at regular points along the line in order to gather up as many words as possible, proceeding to the end of the line with minimal regressive movements, and returning to the beginning of the next line with an accurate return sweep. The left-to-right procedure of reading is unnatural in the sense that it is not required in a child's other perceptual activities. For this reason children must learn a left-to-right reading habit (Taylor, 1966).

Eye movements usually become stable by the age of nine. Beginning readers visually fixate many times on a line and on a single word. Since habitual eye movements of left to right and the return sweep from the end of one line to the beginning of the next have not been established, young children often lose their place on a page. Skilled readers, however, fixate only two or three times on a line and spend about 6 percent of the time in eye movements and 94 percent in fixation (Gibson & Levin, 1975).

In saccadic movements the point of fixation of the eye moves from one object with a quick jump to a new target on the peripheral retina. In horizontal saccades abduction controlled by the abducens cranial nerve begins to move shortly before the adducting eye controlled by the oculomotor nerve. The abducting eye has a tendency to move gradually on the new target whereas the adducting eye has a tendency to overshoot (Miyoshi et al, 1981). These coordinated eye movements are thought to be controlled by a feed-forward system through the cerebellum. It is possible that inefficiencies in this sequence of events could contribute to reading problems.

In the touch reading of braille, the dots of a character are not felt separately but as a shape (Merry, 1932). Slight finger movements, like eye movements, are necessary to recognize the shape formed by the dots. These movements are at first voluntary and become automatic through practice. Generally the blind use both index fingers for reading. The rapidly moving right finger takes care of synthesis and the more slowly moving left finger works analytically. With practice the synthesis and analysis of both fingers become simultaneous.

Word Recognition

Light reflected from marks on paper is projected from the retina to the primary visual cortex of the brain in the encoded form of impulse frequencies (Popper & Eccles, 1977).

Perception of depth at an edge is a primitive capacity both phylogenetically and ontogenetically (Gibson, 1970). Solid objects that possess depth at their edges are discriminated earlier than two-dimensional pictures or line drawings. Three-dimensional forms, therefore, are distinguished more readily than two-dimensional forms. Accordingly the visual system is not especially well suited to discriminating two-dimensional letters (Turvey, 1974).

The next stage is the transmission of the encoded visual information in the primary cortex to the visual association areas, where there is a further stage of reconstitution of a visual image. Although there are cells in the visual cortex that respond to certain invariant features of stimuli, such as curvature and orientation of edges, Gestalt research has shown that the recognition of similarities and differences between the shapes of letters and words is a function of higher mental organizations, not just the physical properties of the stimulus pattern (Goldmeier, 1972). Similarities in configurations are based upon the relationship of parts to each other. For example, a triangle contains three lines and three angles, but it is the way they fit together that affords a recognizable triangle.

The beginning reader must learn to identify and distinguish two types of graphic shapes in the form of alphabet and non-alphabet symbols. The English alphabet consists of 26 letters, each with an upper- and lowercase form that can be printed in typographic, manuscript, or cursive style. There thus are at least six possible graphic forms for each letter. The nonalphabet symbols are abbreviations, punctuation marks, numerals, and mathematical signs. The beginning reader must learn that some aspects of letters are not relevant, such as size and color.

Children between the ages of three and five reverse shapes and letters not because they see letters in a different way than do adults, but because they do not know that it matters as to which way a configuration is turned. Form constancy is learned in infancy so that from whatever angle a baby sees a bottle, it is still a bottle. Recognizing the shape of a thing, however, is different from its spatial orientation, so that even an adult may recall the shape of a cup but not which way it was turned (Money, 1966).

Reading requires both form and directional constancy, which mean that significance changes according to certain changes in external appearances (Money, 1966). Directional constancy means that to retain its name, an alphabetical character must always be directionally oriented the same way. Form constancy, however, does not hold with letters, so the beginning reader is ensnared at the outset by differentiating capitals from lowercase and by equating print and cursive script. Minor differences, such as the orientation of a letter or the relative positions of two letters in sequence, also have completely different significance, for example, b, d and on, no (Kinsbourne & Caplan, 1979). Thus the problem in confusing b and d may be due to lack of attention to the significance of direction, not in misperceiving them.

Until beginning readers have developed directional and form constancy, they make errors based upon rotation, form, and serial sequence of letters. Right–left mirror rotations are the most common because mirroring takes place when one touches different parts of one's own body, notably the face, with one's hands. When the left and right hands replicate each other, such as when reaching for some-

thing, they automatically mirror each other. Successful reading occurs in spite of distortions of printed words, so that the distinctive spatial features of letters are only a part of the recognition process.

When perceptions are registered in the form of images, precategorical memory permits the retention of an image so that associations can be linked with it. The word image thus becomes associated with stored images, and the word gains meaning through its connection with other symbols and concepts. Word perception, instant recognition, and phonetic and structural analysis provide a word with meaning. From perceptual data alone, one cannot pronounce unfamiliar written words and recognize their meaning. It is necessary to form associations between the correctly analyzed visual and auditory images, pairing them so that the way a word looks corresponds to the way it sounds (Kinsbourne & Caplan, 1979). At the next stage, the information relayed from the visual association neurons to other parts of the brain is converted into word images, which, in turn, are interpreted as meaningful sentences in the process of conscious recognition (Popper & Eccles, 1977).

Words also have personal meanings that reflect previous experience as well as their commonly accepted definitions (Shapiro, 1979). Three attributes of words illustrate this fact: (1) the denotative, (2) the connotative, and (3) the communicative. The denotative function is the personal meaning of a word to an individual. A person's thoughts and feelings with regard to personal meaning determine the connotation of a word. The commonly accepted definition of a word is its communicative function (Hardy, 1978). Thus each word is encoded on personal, denotative, and connotative in addition to public communicative definitional dimensions. It is only after the entries are made on all the pertinent dimensions that the complete meaning of a word is achieved.

Each encoding process of a word takes a small but finite amount of time and is not done simultaneously for all aspects of that word. If a word is withdrawn from perception before it is completely encoded, the meaning that occurs for the word is but a fragment of the total meaning (Wickens, 1970b). This highlights the importance of attention and forming multiple associations in learning new words. Furthermore, the less similar these dimensions, the more they interfere with each other in short-term and long-term memory (Wickens, 1970a). The connotation of pleasure or distress influences positively or negatively the access to a word's meaning. The perseveration of one dimension can interfere with the involvement of another. The fluid exchange of information from short-term to long-term memory is necessary for shifting the focus of attention from one word to another (Vellutino, 1979). Therefore, there are a variety of points at which the recognition of a word can be impeded.

The preexisting images and emotions evoked by words include stimuli from the reading context in addition to the denotative, connotative, and communicative dimensions of words. There are many stimuli that come within a child's range of perception during reading in school from a page of a book, the whole book, the desk, peers, the classroom, and the teacher. If an aspect of the perceptual field triggers anxiety, the reading process is blocked. Pleasure or distress can be evoked by the transactional context and affect learning to read.

Comprehension of Text Content

Using knowledge of context enables reading under unfavorable conditions, such as illegible handwriting, by guessing a word by syntax, or knowledge of the writer's intention. Not every word comes into visual perception form in facile reading. Remarkably, tachistoscopic experiments have shown that, in efficient reading, words are not actually consciously perceived, but their meanings are. Grasping meaning acquires a degree of independence from actual visual perception (Namnum & Prelinger, 1961).

The comprehension of a written message includes the literal meaning and the implied meaning. At the literal level is understanding facts; securing the main idea; following directions; recognizing sequence of time, place, events, or steps; and identifying stated conclusions. At the implied level are drawing inferences; determining characterization and setting; sensing relationships among events and characters; anticipating outcomes; determining the author's purpose by identifying the tone, mood, and intent of the passage; making comparisons and contrasts and drawing conclusions; and making generalizations.

Intellectual judgment and emotional responses are the foundations for literary appreciation. The information gained from reading may lead to revised concepts, expanded understandings, changed attitudes, and new insights and ideas.

Oral and Silent Reading

A host of contextual factors also are brought into play by the act of performing in the presence of a teacher and peer group, when oral reading occurs in the classroom. Oral reading of words may take place without comprehension as well.

On the other hand, silent reading is a solitary act. When people engage in reading, they may desire privacy and silence and resent interference. The world of the reader is like that of the dreamer, drawing upon right-hemisphere imagery. Silent reading ability also may exceed or be less than oral reading ability.

Automatic Reading

Once facility in reading is acquired, spoken language no longer plays a mediating role in the perception of meaning from written messages. The automaticity of the various processing levels distinguishes the skilled from the unskilled reader. The fluent reader perceives directly both the communicative meaning of words and their syntactic connections without prior need for reconstructing words or phrases into their spoken counterparts. Automatic reading, therefore, requires much less effort than reading that involves subvocalizing and determining the meaning of words (Pflaum, 1974).

Flexibility in reading rates is characteristic of automatic readers. They can scan for details by glancing rapidly over a page and skim quickly to derive an overall view of the material (Downing, 1979). The fluent reader can adapt rapid and slow strategies to the comprehension demands of a reading task (Robinson, 1966).

Fluent readers build up expectations for the reading material, which reduces the need to read every word. They resort to word or letter identification only when more general hypotheses about syntax or semantics have failed. These general hypotheses or expectancies rely upon context (Haber & Haber, 1981).

A well-organized and relevant background of knowledge facilitates reading comprehension and recall. A person with knowledge and organizing ability can enhance comprehension of a text, even when it is poorly organized, by recognizing relations between the text and the reader's relevant knowledge (Wittrock, 1981). Thus the content of the text influences reading comprehension so that fluent readers grasp the author's meaning as well.

Fluent readers also correct their own errors and thereby improve their performance. The act of reading itself becomes endowed with pleasure. A skilled reader absorbed in a book is lost in the content of the material. Awareness of reading as a distinct process in itself is lost as the printed word blends into internal imagery. Skilled reading is a tool for developing imagination, personal attitudes, and thinking.

Instruction Methods

Most young children come to school with an interest in learning to read. They are captivated easily by wondrous folk and fairy tales and the great children's literature. They need to touch and feel to learn. Yet beginning reading programs often continue to demand that children sit quietly (they need mobility) in hard chairs (they prefer informality) and listen carefully (they are not auditorily facile) to phonic rules (they are not analytic) (Carbo, 1982). It is no wonder, then, that when some children experience reading as a school task too early, they try to escape by talking, doodling, teasing, daydreaming, and disrupting (Staats & Staats, 1962).

The useful concept of reading readiness developed originally from an untenable comparison of learning to read to learning to walk and speak, both of which are innate functions. Reading has not attained this evolutionary status, and the range of individual differences in readiness to read are much more marked than in learning to walk or speak (Coltheart, 1979). Readiness to read also is dependent upon instructional methods. Decades of study and experimentation have revealed that some children can be taught to read at the age of three or four and enter school reading, but others do not make smooth progress until the age of nine. Early readers could be children with inherited traits that make reading especially easy for them. The ability to read also may be distinct from general intelligence and other verbal abilities.

The evidence is that children attain reading readiness between four and nine years of age. The school systems of different countries have averaged this by beginning reading instruction between the ages of five and seven. The importance of avoiding an initial unfavorable experience with reading is recognized in Sweden and Denmark, where reading instruction usually begins at the age of seven and is surrounded by supportive services for those who are not ready (Gibson & Levin, 1975).

With effort children can be taught to read before they are maturationally ready; however, they may actively reject reading because of their frustration. On the other hand, they may try to please adults, but reading becomes associated with pain, which may lead to later avoidance of it. In time they may learn to read, but their spelling and vocabulary remain poor. Withdrawal from academic work may result, with attendant unhappiness and insecurity (Marcus, 1967).

Children who are not ready to read as they start school usually are not thought of as normal variants but are regarded as having developmental lags or deficits. Thus beginning reading instruction at an arbitrarily selected age does injustice to them and unduly holds up those who are ready early (Kinsbourne & Caplan, 1979).

A disadvantage of beginning reading instruction at too young an age is that children can be subjected to unnecessary failure. Provision must then be made for remedial instruction; however, in the long run, this can undermine their motivation to achieve. These children find that they cannot learn to read within the first few years of school. They erroneously feel that they are poor readers, that reading is not enjoyable, and that they will never be successful in reading. Emerging evidence now indicates that some classrooms provide little chance for any student to learn to read and that many provide little chance for some children. The reading success of children, therefore, is strongly influenced by the schools they attend and their teachers (Calfee, 1983).

Another problem is that children who learn material at a time when they are maturationally unready may not be learning it in the same generalizable way they would if they were taught later. They may be learning to read in a way that ultimately is not a useful strategy. For example, children may learn words by rote but not know the underlying linguistic principles. This problem has been encountered in a broader sense with older children who have been taught to read by the look-say method (Kinsbourne & Caplan, 1979).

The beginner's fear of failing in reading is obvious and necessitates gentle teaching. But risks and fears exist at all stages of reading development. Each reading act requires new integration and new understanding. Therefore, it is important for readers at all stages to feel free to try, to make mistakes, and to know that help is available. Students at the higher stages of reading need supportive teachers, just as do those reading their first primers (Chall, 1983b).

In every language two emphases for teaching reading exist: the *phonic* or *code emphasis* and *look-say* or *meaning* methods. The phonic or code emphasis method refers to teaching decoding skills at the beginning of reading instruction as a route to word recognition and comprehension by giving early attention to letters and sounds (Chall, 1983a). The look-say or meaning method stresses directly learning the meaning of words. In itself each leaves out a child's need to understand why people read and write in the first place (Downing, 1979).

Between 1890 and 1920, elaborate synthetic, phonic systems were used in teaching reading. In 1908 Huey described the teaching of reading as "an old curiosity shop of absurd practices." Between 1920 and 1935, the emphasis was placed upon reading silently for the meaning of words, and phonics was looked upon as outmoded. From 1935 to 1955, phonics gradually began to return, supplemented by visual and contextual clues (Chall, 1983a).

Early in this century, experimental psychology abandoned reading to educational researchers on the grounds that it was too complex to be amenable to learning theory paradigms. The educational researchers, in turn, engaged in a seemingly endless round of doubtful methodological comparison studies on whether the phonics or whole-word methods were better ways to teach reading, culminating in the monumental U.S. Office of Education first grade reading studies of the mid-1960s, which generally concluded that the teacher variable was the most significant in successful reading programs (Brown, 1980). In 1975 the teaching of reading still could be depicted as faddish, with each new method "widely trumpted, vociferously defended and then abandoned except by a few faithful acolytes" (Gibson & Levin, 1975). The controversy between phonic and look–say advocates was vividly described by Flesch (1981).

In pure form neither the phonic nor the meaning method inherently is based upon awareness that learning to read is thinking. Advanced automatic reading obviously is a tool of thinking. However, learning to read also is thinking, because it requires focused attention, concentration, perception, association with memories, concept formation, and symbolization in addition to the adaptive managerial functions of impulse control, analysis, synthesis, decision making, planning, problem solving, and implementing and verifying actions (Critchley, 1970; Money, 1966).

Learning to read involves learning the nature and purpose of spoken language in written form. A visual code for speech must be acquired with an understanding of the principles and strategies underlying it. Learning to read is developing a new attitude toward language, whereby conscious attention to the structure of words and sentences takes place alongside attention to meaning so that a text is seen as a source of information (Donaldson & Reid, 1982).

The Phonic Method

Children come to school with a rich speaking vocabulary. As soon as they are able to recognize their written forms, known words become their reading and spelling vocabulary. If a written word is new to a child, that word is added to the speaking vocabulary (Flesch, 1981).

Children are familiar with spoken language because the linguistic analysis of spoken language into phonology, semantics, syntax, and discourse comes naturally with the acquisition of speech. Thus by linking reading to these parts of spoken language, a unifying thread can be shared between both domains (Calfee, 1983).

Since reading initially involves turning printed symbols into sounds, the phonic method logically helps children reach the eventual goal of comprehending what they read by first mastering the process of word-to-sound conversion by discriminating the essential written symbols, discriminating sounds, and applying sounds to letters (Pflaum, 1974).

For some young children, however, the way in which beginning reading instruction in English takes place requires them to reflect on phonemes in a way that is simply beyond their capacity (Sheridan, 1983). Therefore, they attempt to go directly to meaning, guess frequently at words from context, and try to read words as wholes. They may then construe reading as a matter of guessing from shape and context (Liberman, 1983).

The phonic method stresses from the start how visual symbols represent sounds. There are two ways of teaching phonic analysis. The letters-in-isolation approach involves teaching letter sounds in isolation and then blending them into whole words. The second is to break words down into letter sounds. Both approaches teach the alphabetic basis of written words as a more or less lawful relationship between combinations of spoken phonemes and analogous combinations of written graphemes. The phonic method teaches how to convert graphemes and combinations of graphenes into their phonemic equivalents and then how to blend several graphemic combinations and construct them into spoken words. Beginning readers are unable to apprehend directly the syntactic functions of words in sentences. To perceive a word's meaning, therefore, they are taught to reconstruct it into a spoken message and rely on their intuitive knowledge of the syntax of the spoken language.

The phonic approach gives a child a lawful code with which to reconstruct written words into their already meaningful spoken equivalents. Word recognition thus becomes more a matter of rational problem solving than of random guessing. Once words are learned, their sounds fade away, and their meaning is recognized by sight. Computer studies show that only 2.5 percent of all English words are not spelled according to phonic rules; however, there are some 180 phonetic rules (Flesch, 1981).

The most important argument for the phonic method is that one can learn to read by memorizing sight words, but it is extremely difficult to become an independent reader without the ability for phonic analysis (May, 1973). Phonic instructional programs also provide an easily structured, teachable curriculum of limited duration. Theoretically in two years, a child can be taught all of the letter–sound correspondences necessary for oral reading.

Unfortunately, not all children respond well to this regimen. The rules and regularities of pattern drills may be too abstract and intrinsically uninteresting for them. For these children microcomputers can be used to make reading more stimulating. Microcomputers allow children to have a more active involvement with a text by constructing stories using prewritten parts. The computer sets a goal for the student and evaluates the finished story based on how well a goal is met. A brief computer-animated cartoon can reinforce the meaning of a simple sentence. Computers that speak aid these children in finding words with the same sound on the computer screen.

The Meaning Method

Look–say, also called whole-word or meaning, methods of teaching reading have been associated with progressive education and phonic methods with the drill of traditional schooling (Chall, 1983a). Indeed Horace Mann praised the sight over the phonic method by describing it as an "excursion to the fields of elysium compared to the old method of plunging children, day by day . . . in the cold waters of oblivion . . .". Meaning-emphasis reading instruction refers to giving meaning to print from the outset by using words, phrases, and sentences through contextual and visual clues.

The meaning approach begins with a look–say emphasis, bringing in phonics when a child wants to learn a new word. Then the word is attacked and broken down into sounds to connect it with the spoken vocabulary. This approach stresses acquiring meaning through learning whole words on sight, the development of a vocabulary of common words, the gradual introduction of the alphabet and phonics, and emphasis upon story content. The stress is on reading comprehension rather than the precise teaching of reading skills.

Children who learn to read by the look–say method tend to develop spontaneous impressions about grapheme-phoneme correspondence and to use these impressions in deciphering unfamiliar words. But this haphazard and unguided discovery of grapheme–phoneme correspondences is less efficient than a systematic, programmed, guided approach for many children. The look–say method has been disastrous for dyslexic children, who need systematic instruction in decoding skills (Brown, E.R., 1980). Children with reading difficulty may memorize words by their position on the page. They also may attempt to cover up their difficulty by guessing words they know to be related to a theme. Thus teaching methods that do not involve accurate word reading may conceal difficulty in learning to read (Mosse, 1982).

Research on reading instruction over the past 60 years supports the phonic, code-emphasis approach; however, the look–say, meaning-emphasis approach has endured because published materials for teachers have tended to be based on this method (Bateman, 1969; Kaluger & Kolson, 1969). A programmatic test of phonic and look–say approaches was made in Project Follow-Through, which began in 1967 with the aim of continuing through the third grade the gains that children had made in Head Start programs. This study found that the DISTAR program (Direct Instruction for Teaching and Remediation) with a structured phonics curriculum was superior to less-structured meaning curricula (Rhine, 1981; Becker et al, 1982).

The evidence supports beginning reading programs that are phonic oriented. Furthermore, direct phonic teaching of letter sounds, separating letter sounds from words, and blending sounds are more effective than indirect phonic teaching that infer sounds from known sight words. Current basal readers include more phonic techniques in the primary grades than prior to the 1970s and involve a combination of phonic and meaning approaches. Following a grounding in phonics, a meaning emphasis in the third grade appears to be generally advantageous (Chall, 1983a).

The phonic and meaning approaches, therefore, are not mutually exclusive; children can respond to the memory of a word shape, figure out words in some kind of sound–symbol correspondence, find small words within larger ones, and make use of context to recognize words. The picture alphabet of the *New England Primer* of 1690 combined letters with pictures and with the sounds of familiar words—a multiassociational method (Huey, 1908). Advocates of the phonic method often teach whole-word recognition of common words as a means of making possible earlier reading of a simple text and enhancing the beginning reader's interest, self-confidence, and motivation. Look–say advocates typically introduce varying degrees of phonic analysis after their pupils acquire some reading fluency. The central role of pronunciation skills in learning to read suggests that reading teaching that emphasizes these skills should be particularly effective. The active use of the body in pronunciation and gestures reinforces reading instruction. New words also can be introduced in an informative context with pictures and diagrams (Mitchell, 1982).

The differences between the phonic and meaning schools of thought today are theoretical rather than dominant in practice so that the controversy over the role of each in reading instruction is less as to whether it should be used, but how. Knowledge of these approaches in addition to the initial teaching alphabet provides a variety of techniques that can be adapted to the particular needs of children who have difficulty learning to read.

The Initial Teaching Alphabet

The fact that a child can begin very early to perceive correspondences between printed and spoken patterns and transfer them to reading of unfamiliar items as units has suggested that a more easily recognized alphabet, such as the Initial Teaching Alphabet (ITA), might facilitate learning to read.

Special phonetic alphabets were introduced by Leigh in the 1870s and the Funk and Wagnall's Scientific Alphabet and the Shearer System in 1894 (Huey, 1908). The Initial Teaching Alphabet was devised to simplify spelling. Extensive experimentation in Great Britain demonstrated its sustained superiority to traditional methods of teaching reading. In essence it reduced the cognitive confusion of the learner and accelerated the achievement of cognitive clarity (Downing, 1979).

These early reading programs designed to ease the pain of phonic analysis by introducing symbols that supplement the alphabet have not proved to be advantageous for the average student. Use of a mysterious, intriguing alphabet, however, might stimulate some children (May, 1973).

WRITING

Writing is the act of committing thoughts to written form. It encompasses language as well as visual, auditory, haptic, and manual abilities. As a product of one's internal organization, it is a form of creativity (Chalfant & Scheffelin, 1969). Intriguingly, the ability to write precedes the ability to read in the typical development of children (Montessori, 1974). This has been exploited successfully in "writing to read" programs that employ a computerized multisensory approach to teaching reading at the kindergarten level (Martin & Friedberg, 1986). Spelling is the developmental link between writing and reading (Read, 1986).

A complex chain of decoding and encoding in the brain is involved in the visual–motor act of writing. The hands are represented in the contralateral hemispheres, though with subsidiary cross-connections. The sensory aspect is in the parietal lobe and the motor aspect in the frontal lobe. Each eye is related to both cerebral hemispheres, the right half of the visual field to the left hemisphere and vice versa to the right hemisphere. Each macular area has similar bilateral hemispheric representation. The complex cerebral interrelationship between these different

schemes of cerebral localization provides numerous opportunities for individual variations (Money, 1966).

As the usual medium for schoolwork, writing involves the following elements: intention to communicate in graphic form; formulation of a message by sequencing the general content of the message and retrieving the appropriate auditory-language symbols that express the intent of the communication; retrieval of the graphic-language symbols that correspond to the selected language symbols; and organizing and executing the graphic-motor sequence with correct spelling and form of written symbols.

Casual approaches to teaching writing are apt to create writing and reading problems in themselves. It is important to learn letter forms and sounds simultaneously so that a fixed association can develop between them. This can be done by teaching reading and writing with the help of sound–letter combinations beginning with precisely formed lowercase printed letters with the directional help of the clock face (Spalding & Spalding, 1969).

Cursive writing has been the traditionally taught form, but there is no justification for adding cursive writing to printing as a burden for children who have difficulty writing.

ARITHMETIC

Mathematics is the science that deals with space configurations, such as quantities, magnitudes, and forms, through the use of numbers and other symbols. Arithmetic is the branch of mathematics that deals with numbers and their computation through addition, subtraction, multiplication, and division. Unlike letters, arithmetical numbers represent concrete entities. In contrast, other forms of mathematical expressions are abstractions that depend upon the appreciation of Gestalt forms.

Just as does the written word, basic mathematical skills open the door to vast realms of knowledge. And just as they vary in reading aptitude, children differ in mathematical aptitude. Even sophisticated mathemeticians can be described as "algebraic" or "geometric" thinkers who avoid mathematical areas in which they are weak (McGuinness, 1985). Consequently, there are considerable individual variations in facility in learning the various aspects of mathematics (Mayer, 1985). The cerebral arithmetic apparatus apparently is organized in the left hemisphere of right-handed people, just as are the reading and speech apparatuses. However, the right hemisphere in both left- and right-handers may be of special importance for abstract mathematics, as it is more efficient in spatial faculties.

Because it is the essential component of mathematics for social functioning, I will focus on arithmetic. The language of arithmetic is nonverbal. It concerns the properties and relationships of quantities and magnitudes in our spatial world. Knowing the spoken words of verbal language is to reading as knowing quantity, size, shape, and location is to arithmetic. As for verbal language, there also is a vocabulary, such as numbers, and a grammar, such as equations (Rosner, 1979).

A number of different cognitive abilities are involved in comprehending the structure of numbers, performing arithmetical operations, and developing quantitative concepts. They follow an orderly succession as a basis for arithmetic skills.

Forming Sets

The ability to group things into sets presupposes the ability to attend selectively to one item at a time and to match and group items with each other according to a common feature (Kinsbourne & Caplan, 1979). This requires the ability to discriminate among different sizes, shapes, and quantities, and an understanding of one-to-one correspondence between similar things.

Comparing Sets

The next step is to compare sets, such as matching pictures according to the number of objects they contain (Wallace & Kauffman, 1973). This depends upon the ability to discriminate smaller–bigger, longer–shorter, and heavier–lighter. Number concepts start with manipulating objects arranged in space. A child then assigns a different numeral to each item in a set. This leads to counting and the ability to order numbers and sets.

Number Conventions

Next children learn denominations of currency; relative ages of family members; units of length, weight, and time; and parts containing the same number of elements. In this way the generality of number concepts and the conventions that govern their use become familiar.

Part–Whole Relations

Next part–whole relationships become subject to manipulation. Given two parts one may infer the whole. Given the whole and one part, one may infer the missing part.

Problem Solving

Having mastered these concepts, first in concrete instances and then in their generality, a child is ready to operate on sets symbolically and in a position to learn the vocabulary of arithmetic, the definitions and varieties of sets, the concepts of cardinal and ordinal numbers, and the basic operations performed on numbers (Kinsbourne & Caplan, 1979). A child thus acquires a number-fact vocabulary that permits solving unfamiliar problems through an understanding of the relationships that exist among all number facts (Rosner, 1979). Problem solving is at the core of arithmetic and mathematical operations. With increasing age problem solving becomes more systematic, solutions tend to be less stereotyped, the frequency of trial-and-error approaches to problem solving declines, and hypothetical approaches and insightful solutions become more common (Luria, 1980).

The basic arithmetical acts are (1) saying, reading, and writing the words for numbers; (2) writing and reading the figures for numbers; (3) counting; (4) understanding the relative value of a number compared with other numbers; (5) reading, writing, and understanding the arithmetical signs; (6) recognizing the arrangement of numbers to do addition, subtaction, multiplication, and division; (7) understanding the calculation and placement significance of 0; (8) understanding the placement value of all numbers; (9) doing arithmetic mentally without the use of concrete objects or written material; and (10) developing the necessary conditioned responses so that basic arithmetic acts become automatic (Mosse, 1982).

SUMMARY

The basic academic skills are reading, writing, and arithmetic. Without reading ability one cannot achieve the fullness of human experience. Reading is essential to an appreciation of one's cultural heritage, thoughts about human nature, and occupation. Although a required skill in modern society, reading has not been necessary to survival for long enough to gain assured genetic expression as has speech.

As an infant matures, walking becomes automatized so that children can forget that they are walking and discover what they can do while walking. In a somewhat less but still automatized fashion, children use speech to express ideas without attention to the act of speaking. Reading, however, is not based upon the maturation of innate structures so that its acquisition depends entirely upon learning. For many children this seems to occur easily. It is a laborious process, however, for children who are economically disadvantaged, of low intelligence, from problem families, maturationally immature, or vulnerable because of difficulties with various aspects of the reading process.

As a derivative of spoken language, reading is based upon the fundamental rules of phonology, semantics, and syntax. These principles underlie the conversion of speech to written words as a child discovers that written words stand for spoken words. In addition, necessary prereading competencies are the ability to concentrate on the task at hand, the mental capacity to deal with abstractions, and the ability to remember forms and principles.

The act of reading itself involves visual and auditory attention in addition to visual and eye-movement efficiency. The recognition of words is based upon form and directional constancy in addition to their denotative, connotative, and communicative meanings. The comprehension of written passages involves progressively less emphasis upon the precise perception of words and more on their meaning, which is strongly influenced by sentence content and structure. Oral reading involves the additional steps of encoding and transducing language in particular social settings influenced by the presence of teachers and peers. The aim of reading is to achieve an automatic skill in which one loses conscious awareness of the act of reading and can become immersed in the meaning of a written passage.

Because it is at the heart of elementary education, instruction in reading is crucial. The teaching of reading has fluctuated between the phonic and look–say methods; the former emphasizes learning the sound–visual code and the latter the meaning of whole words. The predominant use of the look–say method has posed problems for many dyslexic children. Educational research has disclosed the overall superiority of the phonic method, so that in actual practice reading today usually is taught by some mixture of the phonic and look–say methods. Still neither method is sufficient, if learning to read is not recognized as thinking, and if children do not understand why and how they should learn to read.

Writing is the most complicated action of the central nervous system and is a form of creativity in itself. In addition to reading, it involves thinking, retrieving auditory language, encoding graphic language symbols, and transducing them in coordinated visual-motor form. It is the medium through which schoolwork usually is evaluated and is the crucial arena of spelling.

Mathematics is the abstract science of space and numbers. Arithmetic is the branch of mathematics that deals with the computation of numbers through addition, subtraction, multiplication, and division. Arithmetic requires the basic abilities to group things into sets, compare sets, know conventions of number use, understand part–whole relations, and engage in problem solving.

After the early grades, teachers teach a discipline and not reading. This shortsightedly fails children who have difficulty understanding a subject because they cannot read well enough. Reading accordingly should be within the purview of general teaching responsibilities.

Learning to read and write, however, does not bring knowledge. What matters most is the use that people make of their literacy. Reading programs in themselves cannot produce people who are logical in their thinking, are informed voters, or are responsible citizens. Until people find a good reason to participate in literate culture, literacy will make a cultural difference only for a few.

CHAPTER

19

The Development of Competencies for Schoolwork

The object which the numerous inpouring currents of the baby bring to his consciousness is one big blooming, buzzing confusion. That confusion is the baby's universe; and the universe of all of us is still to a great extent such a confusion, potentially resolvable, and demanding to be resolved, but not yet actually resolved into parts . . . Here the young child meets and greets his world; and the miracle of knowledge bursts forth.

William James, 1892

Until recently a newborn's world was believed to be a place of "booming, buzzing confusion," as James wrote at the turn of the century. We now know that babies come into the world with a variety of capacities and that learning begins before birth. Still human beings are born prematurely because of the evolutionary discrepancy between fetal head size and the maternal pelvic cavity. Relative to other mammals, the expected period of human gestation would be about 18 months (Gould, 1976). Thus human newborns really are embryos, and remain that for much of the first year of life.

At birth the cognitive capacities of a baby enable reaching out to parents (Thomas, 1981; Stratton, 1982). Because the newborn is incapable of self-regulation, a baby seeks to form a dyadic unit in which the mother regulates the life of the baby. After attachment to caregivers, a child gradually becomes a differentiated individual from them.

Vygotsky's maxim was that all development occurs twice: once on the interpersonal plane and again on the intrapsychic. Regulation by the parent becomes self-regulation as a child acquires functions that the parent reliquishes. Between what an infant can do on the infant's own and with another's help is a zone that exists as a potential space for activity between child and parent (Vygotsky, 1978; Davis & Wallbridge, 1981). This zone, the foundation of the self, is the margin for growth available to a child to acquire knowledge from a more knowledgeable person. It is an innate mechanism for facilitating the transmission of culture. To the extent that the zone is active, a child grows further. To the extent that it is inactive, a child's potential is not realized. This is a paradigm for child–teacher relationships as well. Throughout life the spark between teacher and learner remains a vital factor in learning.

Psychoanalytic theories of child development stress a child's identification with significant adults, so that a child's character is formed from an amalgamation of introjects of significant others. Piaget added to this formultion the factors within a child that work upon life experiences and parental influences. A child, therefore, is much more than a synthesis of internalized images, values, and action tendencies from parents.

Piaget recognized the role of maturation of the brain in development but did not believe that it is sufficient in itself to produce the various stages of development. He highlighted the facilitative nature of the child's interaction with people, objects, and events in the environment. Consequently, he expected great individual differences in the rate of development, even from culture to culture, although the sequence of the stages would not vary. Vygotsky further emphasized the interaction between changing social conditions and a child's biological substrate of behavior. Thus children actively create their own knowledge of their external and internal worlds. Their cultures form templates for their underlying conceptions of themselves, their societies, and human nature (Shweder & Levine, 1984).

In general, the development of a child progresses from an intitial diffuse state to differentiation of parts, which are then synthesized into a whole. Development essentially revolves around how embedded and how differentiated children are from their surroundings. Each evolutionary stage is a temporary solution to the lifelong tension beween yearnings for both dependency and differentiation (Kegan, 1982).

There are epigenetic developmental stages that depend upon a child's maturation in a specific environmental context (Shafii & Shafii, 1982). Social interactions influence the process of development so that both continuity and change occur over time. The complexities of the developmental process, therefore, make linear prediction over time unrealistic. The brain is continually maturing so that it is a new structure at each developmental stage. Each new level introduces capacities quite different from those that existed previously (Kagan, 1979). Short-term-memory storage space increases with age, thereby facilitating progressively more complex levels of problem solving (Case, 1985). In a sense at each stage of optimal development, a new person emerges.

The developmental abilities of deaf and blind children are dramatic tributes to the plasticity of the human brain. This plasticity makes possible a host of alternative developmental pathways, depending upon the characteristics of a child and the nature of the environment. The key is the fit between a child and environment (Thomas, 1981; Thomas & Chess, 1984). When synchrony between child and environment is present, optimal development in a progressive direction is possible. Conversely, dissonance between environmental opportunities and expectations and the capacities of a child distort development, and maladaptive functioning may occur unless the child has overriding talents. Figure 19-1 depicts this relationship between a child's capacities, environment, and developmental outcome.

The general goal of human development is task mastery so that an individual can contribute to personal and species survival. The vital role of group living in achieving these goals adds competence in becoming a member of one's culture as well (Thomas & Chess, 1980). Children vary widely in the rates at which they progress toward these goals (Thomas et al, 1963). More critically, distortions, arrests, or delays in the development of all, some, or one of the critical brain functions can alter aspects of the developmental course.

Most children's learning problems can be related to individual differences in developmental rates and brain structures that

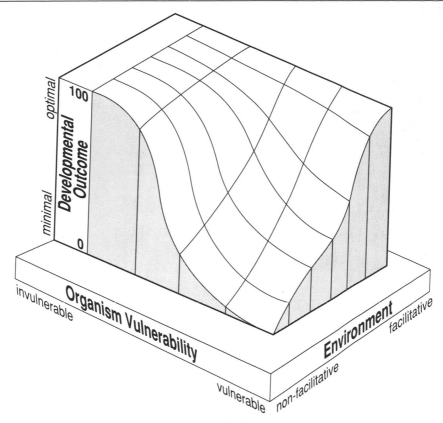

Figure 19-1. A three-dimensional model of organism-environment relationships and developmental outcome. (Adapted from F. D. Horowitz, "Toward a Model of Early Infant Development," in C. C. Brown, ed., *Infants at Risk, Pediatric Roundtable No. 5.* Johnson and Johnson Baby Products, Piscataway NJ. Used with permission.)

influence temperamental, cognitive, language, managerial, and self levels of functioning when compared with expectations for that child at a particular age. In most instances, immaturity, variance, and interference with socialization lie beneath a child's difficulties with schoolwork. This viewpoint encourages a hopeful rather than a despairing attitude toward children who differ from their age mates.

For all of these reasons, an understanding of both the developmental stages and the unfolding of specific central nervous system (CNS) functions in the socialization process is essential in understanding the behavior of a particular child (Greenspan

& Lourie, 1981). We will examine at each level the state of development of temperament, cognition, language, the managerial system, and the self, as summarized in Figure 19-2.

THE CONCEPT OF DEVELOPMENTAL STAGES

A variety of models for the developmental stages of childhood have been formulated. Of them all, Greenspan's integration of psychoanalytic and Piagetian theories pro-

Stage	TEMPERAMENT		COGNITION	LANGUAGE	Interpersonal Relations	MANAGERIAL SYSTEM			SELF
	External Attention	Internal Motivation				Adaptive Functions	Thinking	Values	
SENSORIMOTOR SOMATIC 0–3 months	Orienting and startle responses; Attend to one stimulus at a time	Wide variations in energy levels; Alimentary and sleep drives dominate	Imprinting; Orients to face	Smile and coo at 3 months	Receptive and dependent; Infant-mother gaze; Multisensory attachment	Shift in body rhythms: sleep, feeding, avoidance; External regulation of body functions		Pleasure and distress	Sentience
SENSORIMOTOR IMAGERY 3–18 months	Responds to need satisfying sources	Impulsive; Curious; Alimentary and acquiring drives dominant	Seeks sensory stimulation; Syncretic imagery; Omniscient; object permanence	Babbling; Mimicry; 30–50 words	Receptive and dependent; Omnipotent; Symbiosis-individuation; Reciprocity with caregiver; Practicing phase	Operant conditioning; Denial; Splitting of good and bad; Weaning	Syncretic imagery	Good or bad world	THE SENSORIMOTOR SELF; Differentiating body and wishes of self and non-self; I am center of universe; Body image
SYMBOLIC 18 months–3½ years	Attends to narrow segment of field-focusing and brief concentration	Curiosity; Assertive anal drives dominant	Symbolic imagery; Animism; Dreams real	24 months—two-word phrases; 36 months 1,000 words	Exploitative; Wary; Shame; Rapprochement phase; Parallel play; Object constancy	Synthesis; Analysis; Fragile impulse control; Projection—externalizes blame	Ideas linked to emotions; Syncretic magical thinking	Incorporates good and bad values	THE SYMBOLIC SELF; Self awareness of I—recognition in mirror; I am active in world; I am a person; Self-esteem/shame; Self-concept developing and dependent on others
CONCEPTUAL PLAY 3½–6 years	Concentration on drive based activity	Stabilization of mood; Curiosity; Genital affectional drives dominant; Threshold of responsiveness increasing	Concepts; Distinguish size and magnitude; Distinguish internal and external imagery	Words used to describe experiences and concepts; Conservation of information	Manipulative; Deals with relations between self and others; Cooperative play	Tolerates frustration; Delays gratification; Creative acts; Repression; Denial in fantasy; Instrumental learning; Mastery drive	Creative intuitive thinking; Organization and differentiation of imagery	Incorporates parental values	THE CONCEPTUAL SELF; I am continuous; I am a boy or girl; Self concept stable; Guilt
CONCEPTUAL WORK 6–11 years	Concentration on academic tasks; Looking and listening skills	Pleasure in motor activity; Boredom	Concepts of space and time; Distinguish own thoughts from others; Concepts of weight and quantity	Facile; 4–26 thousand words	Conforming; Belongs to group	Didactic learning; Organize activities; Planning; Decision-making; Flexibility; Controlled regression; Skill building; Competence drive	Rational creative problem solving; Automatic thinking	Developing own sense of morality	THE EVALUATIVE SELF; Self-evaluation; Aware of social acceptability; Desired and actual self-concepts
THEORETICAL 11–18 years	Independent concentration	Refinement of all drives	Conservation of volume; Conceptual complexity; Distinguish real and potential	Facile	Peer-oriented for self differentiation	Flexible; Cope with inner conflicts	Logical debate; Hypothetical and deductive reasoning	Forming independent values	THE INTEGRATIVE SELF; Individual self-identity; Self-respect; Conscious of self apart from group; Objective self-evaluation

Figure 19-2. Stages of development.

vides a useful framework for understanding the development of competencies necessary for schoolwork (Greenspan, 1979a). Because of our particular interest in how children gain knowledge, I have adapted Greenspan's terminology to emphasize the development of thought in light of the maturation of the brain and Erikson's conceptions of the life cycle.

The CNS is continuously changing throughout development; however, it is likely that key neuronal connections produce surges in the appearance of new capacities that underlie the stage transitions (Epstein, 1978; 1980). Spurts in brain growth are found during the periods of three to ten months, two to four, six to eight, ten to 12, and 14 to 16 years of age, with growth plateaus in between. A sex effect is reported between ten and 12 years and 14 to 16 years; girls are ahead during the former and boys during the latter of these periods. The increment of brain growth during the ages two to four is of particular importance because of the establishment of binocular vision, speech, and the fusion of language and thought during that period. The mechanisms that underlie these developmental stages are only beginning to be understood (Sternberg, 1984).

Each developmental stage demarcates the prominence of a new level of functioning that holds sway over the next stage. Forerunners of each stage also exist in preceding stages. Thus earlier modes are not replaced but persist and shape later modes so that degrees of fixation persist and regression to earlier stages occurs (Santostefano, 1980).

The first developmental stage is the sensorimotor stage, which can be subdivided into a somatic phase from birth to three months and an imagery phase from three to 18 months. The second is the symbolic stage, from 18 months to three and a half years. The third is the conceptual stage, subdivided into an intuitive-play phase from three and a half to six years and a conceptual-work phase from six to 11 years. The last is the theoretical stage, from 11 to 18 years.

SENSORIMOTOR STAGE

The sensorimotor stage is the human ontogenetical expression of the reptilian subcortical and paleomammalian limbic phylogenetic stages in which sensory impressions of the world elicit actions upon it. There are no symbols or concepts. During the somatic phase, there apparently are no mental images, which appear later during the imagery phase.

Somatic Phase

The somatic sensorimotor level of functioning largely reflects the activity of the reptilian subcortical centers of the brain, such as the reticular formation, midbrain, basal ganglia, and hypothalamus. The developmental achievement of this stage is a sense of basic trust in the environment. In so doing a baby progresses from reflexive responses and behavior determined by instincts to self-regulation and purposeful action through forming attachments.

Newborns have far more capabilities than previously thought (Bruner, 1980). During the first three months, inborn reflexes propel infants to learn how to move themselves and external objects as they become aware of themselves and the world around them. There is no distance between a perception and action; both have an immediate, automatic, and labile quality. The baby responds to a sensory stimulus with a motor reaction so that operant conditioning is the learning modality (Brown, 1977). Still, neonates have far more capabilities than previously thought.

The role of imprinting, a primitive

form of learning, has relevance during this phase. In animals imprinting is elicited by an experience that takes place at a critical period in early life and is enhanced by discomfort (Rauschecker & Marier, 1987). Later instrumental learning does not depend upon experience at critical periods and avoids discomfort. In the absence of an appropriate experience at a critical period, functions relying upon imprinting may be left with an enduring deficit (Bateson, 1974; Hess, 1964, 1973). We know that human perception is affected by early sensory stimulation, but it is unlikely that absolute critical stages exist in humans for more complex functions. Furthermore, critical periods probably occur in the maturation of specific systems, not the brain as a whole (Rodier, 1980). The critical period concept, however, remains worthy of study in humans.

Temperament

Activity Level. Newborns vary immensely in spontaneous motor activity levels. The most active are almost 300 times more active than the quietest (Irwin, 1932). Very active babies tend to be less cuddly and more resistant to holding than the less active.

The rhythms and depth of sleep change rapidly from seven or so short naps during the first month to between two and four longer periods of sleep by six weeks as a baby adapts to day and night rhythms.

Attention. Newborns scan the environment and are attracted to the physical properties of stimuli; however, focusing of attention is transient and limited to a small number of situations. Considerable individual variations exist in their stimulus regulation thresholds. Movement and contour edges and intermittant and intense sounds especially attract their attention (Taylor, 1981).

Emotions. The young baby largely expresses manifestations of pleasure in the form of contentment and distress in the form of crying, when needs are not satisfied. Hunger, sleep, and sexual drives as instincts, as advances over reflexes, are prominent at this stage (Brown, 1977).

In neonates evidence for the early discrimination and imitation in others of happiness, sadness, and surprise has been reported (Field et al, 1982).

Cognition

The auditory system is more developed than the visual system at birth. A baby may recognize the voice of the mother at less than one week of age and differentiate pure tones from noise. A large area on the underside of each occipital lobe, extending to the inner surface of the temporal lobes, is canalized for the recognition of human faces (Dixon, 1981; Geschwind, 1979a). The one- to two-month-old baby smiles in response to faces and to a piece of white cardboard with black ovals on it (Walk, 1981). By three months babies recognize and prefer the human face over other visual stimuli.

The cerebral processes associated with learning in early life are fundamentally different from those that take place with later maturation of the nervous system. For example, the perception of objects by sight depends upon the gradual development of a myriad of visual programs. This is strikingly demonstrated in children who are born blind and gain sight after surgery. They are able to recognize only the objects they already know by touch. Everything else apparently is seen only as a swirling mass that may be disturbing, so that they quickly shut their eyes again. With patience they learn programs for seeing, but it is a slow and distressing process, unlike the gradual acquisition of programs for seeing at the appropriate time of the developmental sequence for sighted children (Young, 1978).

Babies born blind because of corneal

opacities do not develop accurate vision unless the defect is repaired by corneal transplant early in life, suggesting a critical role for imprinting in this function in humans. In a similar vein, the dreams of older children born blind may not contain visual, or the congenitally deaf auditory, images because the patterns of cerebral visual and auditory organization fail to evolve without early perceptual experience (Kolb, 1973).

Language

A baby is innately capable of reciprocal communication in the form of imitating facial expressions of a caregiver in the early weeks of life (Field et al, 1982). Language development is enhanced in this interpersonal context as a core of empathy develops from resonant emotional responses between baby and caregiver (Stern, 1980). By three months a baby can smile and coo in response to speech.

Managerial System

At birth a newborn and mother shift their interdependence of rhythms from the uterine to the external environment (Brazelton et al, 1980). The process of bonding takes on an interpersonal dimension as the infant organizes alert, sleeping, and feeding patterns within the context of learning conditioned by caregiving (Davis & Wallbridge, 1981; Shafii & Shafii, 1982). Extra uterine attachment begins in a multisensory, emotional field epitomized by the enraptured gaze between baby and mother. This adds vision and more refined hearing to the tactile and proprioceptive interaction between fetus and mother in utero. The visual gaze resembles a hypnotic state and may set the stage for later learning from charismatic figures.

Shifts in bodily rhythms constitute a baby's defenses, as through sleep that tunes out offensive stimuli. A baby possesses stimulus regulation as a buffer against excessive stimulation and can use avoidance, as when turning away from noxious stimuli. A baby also can turn to the calming effect of feeding when stimuli are overwhelming. There is a reciprocal interaction in which babies and parents influence and respond to each other. By three months infants can differentiate their primary caregivers from others (Dixon et al, 1981).

Operant conditioning learning can be seen when a baby stumbles upon a new experience as a consequence of an act and tries to recapture the experience by reenacting the original movements in a rhythmic cycle (Flavell, 1963).

Self

An early kinesthetic awareness of the self appears to be present at birth, akin to animal sentience (Amsterdam & Levitt, 1980). Three-month-old infants have been reported to respond with greater excitement to other babies than to mirror images, suggesting an early awareness of differences between one's body and that of another infant (Field, 1979).

A baby's self-esteem begins with the mother's pregnancy and her ability to place the baby in the center of her world. Under optimal circumstances her baby is bathed in attention and affection at birth. The baby feeds on the pleasure of being loved and respected as a foundation for loving and respecting oneself (Rado, 1956).

Imagery Phase

This phase from three to 18 months represents ontogenetic progress to the phylogenetic paleomammalian level, which operates from structures centering around the limbic system. The developmental achievement of this stage is to construct a body image differentiated from others. Passively registered mental representations in the form of imagery begin to reflect memories that accumulate from perceptions over time and permit the stringing together of units of experience (Kagan, 1979). The infant now can initiate and respond to purposeful communication. Instrumental learning from the consequences of an infant's actions also can take place, based upon feedback in subtle signaling between infant and parent imitating each other.

The principal characteristics of this phase are an infant's interest in bodily functions as well as in an expanding world of people and things.

Temperament

Activity Level. Wide individual variations in activity levels are seen in infants, ranging from the energetic and robust, who actively seek contact with the world, to the quiescent and passive, who require stimulation to engage their interest. These activity patterns tend to persist in later life (Korner et al, 1985). This quality relates to the establishment of sleep-waking cycles of varying duration and frequency. By four months most infants sleep through the night.

Triumph over gravity gradually takes place with sitting, crawling, and walking that permit negotiation with the spatial world.

Attention. The capacity of infants to manage excitation results from the development of inhibitory mechanisms. The threshold, latency, tempo, spread, rate of recovery, and habituation readiness of their responses to stimulation can be measured.

By the age of three months, the previous experience of an infant begins to play a role in behavior, so that the novelty of stimuli evokes attention. Habituation occurs as attention wanes when stimuli are repeated. Alpha rhythm in the electroencephalogram and the physiological components of the orienting reflex appear (Taylor, 1981).

The development of voluntary attention has a long interpersonal history in chil-

dren so that acquiring efficient and stable, socially organized attention does not occur until about the age of five. An infant cannot follow a simple verbal instruction directing attention to a certain object. Even during the second year of life, the orienting response to a distracting stimulus easily overrides voluntary attention, which has only begun to appear so that a spoken instruction cannot overcome stimuli competing for involuntary attention.

Vygotsky held that initially the complex function of attention is shared between two persons. The orientation reflex initially focuses an infant's attention on things. The mutuality of gaze between infant and parent maintains attention and evokes automomic responss from each partner, forming the prototype for the concentration of attention. The mutuality of gaze facilitates the infant's attentional state, leads to accelerated motor activity, to deceleration toward sleep, or to repetition of the cycle (Brazelton, 1980). This cycle is the prototype for a person's habitual response to stimuli from the external world.

A parent attracts an infant's attention and triggers psychological processes by naming an object perceived by the infant. Then, as a child learns to speak, attention can be focused to name an object as distinguished from the rest of the environment. The function that hitherto was shared between two people becomes an internal organization of the child. A child's voluntary attention thus is shaped by interpersonally induced attention and becomes an internal process.

Infants take in sensory stimulation as they do food. Accordingly, there are individual variations in the need for and the tolerable ranges of stimulation (Thomas & Chess, 1980). Some "slow to warm up" infants are hypersensitive, inward turning, immobile, underactive, and lacking in curiosity. Other infants with "difficult temperaments" need to be comforted by kinesthetic, auditory, and visual stimulation through light body massage, singing, and talking. With this stimulation these infants enjoy and look forward to playing and singing, and their sleeping and eating schedules begin to regulate (Berlin, 1981).

Emotions. Emotions communicate the internal state of an infant, initially diffusely and later more specifically. Infants have outbursts of temper that are seldom focused and sustained (Maccoby, 1980). The parent's gradients of emotion fine tune an infant's responses. For example, the pitch of a caregiver's voice means more to an infant than the actual words used. The difference between what is expected by the infant and what acutally happens influences the intensity of the baby's emotional responses (Stern, 1980). Small differences are soothing; great differences are disrupting. Deaf children may have difficulty modulating emotions because the auditory channel, which is important in gradient perception, is not available.

Another consideration is whether the emotional signals match the behavior of a caregiver. For example, a caregiver may deceptively express mock surprise or a forced smile. This discrepancy is sensed by an infant and induces tension because of the infant's subtle perception of conflict between the caregiver's behavioral expression and emotional tone. When this discrepancy is of mild degree and frequency, it models a capacity that facilitates social transactions that transcend their particular immediate emotional state (Stern, 1980). When the discrepancies are great and persistent, however, an infant may be confused and deprived of needed authentic emotional interchanges.

At three months infants show pleasure in the form of interest, surprise, and smiling. Their distress is evident in fussing and crying based upon hunger, anger, pain, and impatient attention seeking.

By eight months pleasure is manifest in amusement, joy, and laughter. At this time many children show fearfulness in the presence of strangers. Separation anxiety also appears during the second year when apart from attachment figures, reflecting fear of abandonment.

By 12 months affection, curiosity, and thrill are evident as pleasurable emotions. Distress is seen in the form of loneliness, disappointment, grief, helplessness, and shyness.

Cognition

During this phase cognition begins to include the formation of an image that interposes delay between a stimulus and a response. The development of imagination liberates a child from immediate reactiveness to the environment. Imagination enables the pursuit of aims beyond the present environment and permits deliberate, conscious action, as in searching for vanished objects, a capacity referred to as object permanence. Piaget regarded the transformation of perceptions into images as conservation because the formation of images permits information storage. These images, however, are merged with internal stimuli so that perceptual awareness at this stage probably is similar to dreaming.

Images can be seen as drive-energized memory traces whereas emotions are drive-energized discharges into the motor and autonomic systems. Images and emotions both arise when a drive-satisfying object is absent, and neither can discharge more than a portion of the drive tension. In Freud's view initial imagery is a hallucinated wish fulfillment of a percept previously associated with satisfaction (Rapaport, 1951).

Thus infants construct their personalized images of things. For example, as they look at, touch, drop, push, and grab a cup, they begin to form an image of it. Their images are based upon their actions upon the cup and their active exploration of it, not passive looking and abstracting.

An infant undergoes an ever-widening

expansion of spatial awareness from bodily space through locomotor space and through perceptual space to images of space. In other words, the newborn lacks spatial awareness and gains it through bodily discovery. Later, space is the area in which the infant moves. Then space is used as a defining perceptual attribute of things, such as object arrangements or figural relationships. Later in life, space may be recognized as an attribute that all material objects possess and can exist as a ground for a figure, which, in turn, is a ground for another figure (Eliot, 1975).

Object permanence procedes allowing one object to stand for another and then an image to stand for an object and next an experience. As imagery becomes more elaborate, sensorimotor schemes flourish. Sensorimotor images evident at 18 months of age are based on schemes upon which future understanding is built, expectations established, and new perceptions matched. Initially imagery of the external world is a direct sensory representation of concrete experience, but the process of accommodation creates new images when perceptions do not match existing images. As an image is replayed and associated with other images, it becomes familiar, and this recognition of the familiar results in joy. Thus, on the one hand, interest fuels differentiation, and, on the other hand, joy motivates integration. A securely attached child can engage in age-appropriate imagery when free to show curiosity if new information does not match the templates of existing images, and to show joy when the unknown is reduced through a match between a perception and an internal image (Tower, 1983).

Language

Language is the basis for social learning in humans. It is a mechanism by which a child directs onself and symbolically internalizes and organizes experience. A child depends heavily on language for relating to others (Lenneberg, 1967).

Language initially communicates emotion rather than meaning. The spoken aspect of language never loses this close emotional connection. Spoken language gradually emerges from babbling, which is a necessary preliminary to gaining articulatory control of the speech organs. Babbling is a vehicle for both social interaction and the expression of an infant's pleasure. Imitation and play with sounds are involved in vocabulary building. Through interaction with a caregiver, a child builds internal language.

There are no true organs of speech. The mouth, tongue, and pharynx have other primary functions, as do the neural substrates in the motor speech area in the frontal cortex, which is derived from the areas representing the hand and mouth. The utterance of sound has an autoerotic component involving the diaphragm, lungs, larynx, palate, tongue, lips, teeth, and mouth, in addition to the anus in boys and the anus and vulva in girls, as is evident in observations of infant babbling (Walsh, 1968). As babbling merges into verbal language, the activities of both ends of the alimentary tract and the respiratory tract are employed.

Even though different languages have no historical connection between them, each language is based on the same principles of phonology, semantics, and syntax. From the beginning of a child's language development, the canalized form of semantics and syntax are manifest. The young child has semantic awareness in the sense that actions have actors, are on objects, are experiences, have instruments, and have a locus. Syntax is evident in the appropriate use of nouns and verbs in sentences.

Even in the presence of developmental retardation, the order of the language developmental milestones follows a programmed sequence. The timetable of language development is as follows (Bruner, 1980; Lenneberg, 1964, 1967; Wigg & Semel, 1980):

16 weeks—turns head in response to human sounds
20 weeks—vowel-like and consonant-like cooing sounds
6 months—cooing changes to babbling resembling syllable sounds
8 months—babbles with inflections of speech and repetition of syllables
10 months—distinguishes between words; waves bye-bye
12 months—understands some words; says mama, dada, imitates word sounds
18 months—repertoire of between 30 and 50 spoken words

The treatment of Genie, a 13-year-old girl who had been restrained, abused, and confined in a small room since the age of two, supports the existence of a critical period for the development of language. She did develop language and socialized behavior to a degree, thus permitting some education, but never completely. Of interest also are the observations that she resisted work, masked her capabilities, and had tantrums when pressed into learning tasks (Curtiss, 1977).

Managerial System

The inevitable clashes between an infant's wants and reality lead to the ability to distinguish inner wishes from external reality. The achievement of object permanence also permits awareness of immediately absent things and actions. These factors set the foundation for the analysis of reality. Infants also show the capacity for an early form of abstraction by recognizing objects across sensory modalities. The boundaries between internal and external stimuli are relatively undifferentiated, however, and an infant has a long way to go before reality generally is perceived accurately.

All of an infant's senses are integrated in the hear, see, touch, mouth sequence. As an early form of sythesizing activity, this sequence is the foundation for knowing how to begin, order, and carry out activities. It is the paradigm of a sensorimotor scheme. The underlying mechanism is ingesting, incorporating, and fusing with objects based upon the process of feeding. Through this growing physical exploration ending in the mouth, a fund of knowledge is accumulated—first of the existence of things, both animate and inanimate, and then of the ability to manipulate them. In this way an infant learns to sort out those things that can be managed from those that cannot and that warrant defensive maneuvers. An infant can distinguish beginning cause and effect by anticipating the effects of a physical execution prior to an act. Thus an infant begins to anticipate consequences and to make choices. The infant can make deliberate efforts to influence the external world by swinging, rubbing, striking, and shaking objects, with the intense interest in the sights and sounds that these actions elicit.

Interaction with a caregiver strongly influences a child's growing capacity to learn about the animate and inanimate world by organizing internal structures of the managerial system. Vygotsky introduced the idea that the source of organized voluntary action lies not within a child, or in the direct influence of past experience, but in a child's interpersonal history when functions were shared between two people. When a parent gives the child the spoken instruction to "take a cup," the child obeys the instruction. In the next stage of development, children, who had previously followed an adult's instruction, learn to speak and subordinate their behavior to their own spoken instructions. In this view functions previously shared between two persons become methods of organization of a child's intentional behavior.

At first an infant's social interaction varies according to the responses of other people, although infants also vary in their receptivity to physical contact in the form of cuddling. Over time, however, selectivity in relationships develops and is no longer dependent upon an adult's responses of the moment. Infants then seek their parents and tend to avoid strangers.

The capacity to form mental images in sensorimotor schemes is the key to understanding the attachment process. An infant's initial sensory experience is of parts of the body and environment before they are integrated into a whole body image separate from the external environment. Thus sensory perceptions of parents are incorporated in sensorimotor schemes of the self-system as an infant forms whole body images. Furthermore, these schemes are endowed with positive or negative valences by the pleasure–distress system. For example, when an infant experiences hunger and a mother provides food and cuddling, both internal and external stimuli are included in forming sensorimotor schemes of the feeding, nuturing child–parent relationship. Under usual developmental circumstances, the pleasure associated with the external sensory perceptions of the nuturing parent simultaneously reinforces the pleasure of internal oral gratification. Consequently, parenting can enhance an infant's pleasurable experience of bodily sensations so that the body images that make up the foundation of the self are experienced as pleasurable. Because it expands an infant's self-awareness, interaction with a parent also reinforces the infant's growing organization of the self system. Thus sensory input from the parent is incorporated in an infant's sensorimotor schemes of the self, thereby "attaching" the infant to the parent.

Behaviors reflecting attachment include differential smiling, greeting responses, following, separation protest, and flight to the attachment figure as a haven of safety. The effects of distress sharply differentiate attachment from other forms of social interaction; whereas social play is inhibited by distress, attachment is intensified. The presence of an attachment object provides a secure base and reduces distress while promoting exploration and other adaptive responses. By the age of 18 months, children may show multiple attachments; however, each attachment is specific and not interchangeable (Rutter, 1981a). Attachment figures inevitably are periodically absent. This intensifies images of them. Such images constitute major organizations within the developing memory store as identifications.

Mahler described the psychological unfolding of the individual child as a separation–individuation process (Lax et al, 1980). During the first hatching phase of differentiation at five to six months, infants can push themselves away from their parents, and through their burgeoning locomotion, see and grasp an enlarging world in which parent and stranger are increasingly contrasted. During the third quarter of the first year, many infants show wariness with strangers as a response to the unfamiliar.

With the onset of crawling, the practicing phase begins at about seven to ten months and lasts until 15 or 16 months, undergoing a spurt with the onset of walking. A toddler begins to explore the world using the attachment figure as a home base for refueling through physical contact. During this time the weaning process contributes to individuation. Separation anxiety tends to peak at 18 months, and diminishes thereafter.

Infants need consistency of format with the fine tuning of a parent in an emotionally warm ambience of playfulness (Bruner, 1980). They need environments that allow extended play in the buffering presence of a caregiver. The interplay between an infant's innate competencies and adult assistance provides the potential space within which socialization takes place.

The defenses emerging during this phase are denial, avoidance, displacement, condensation, and splitting between the good and bad parts of the emerging self. A child's attachment to parents is a powerful motivator of learning. Feral children illustrate the profound consequences of the lack of attachment figures on the development of the managerial system.

Peer interaction between year-old infants is based on both attraction and struggles usually centered around objects such as toys. In these interactions infants differ on a continuum of initiating pleasurable interaction.

Self

As babies emerge from their egocentric shells, they make contact with parts of their own and their parents' bodies, both perceived as parts of the same external milieu. The infant is presumed to enter a state of symbiotic union with attachment figures. Through discovering that they can control their own hands, slowly and painstakingly, infants build pictures of their own bodies, and the bodies of other persons as separate entities. There is an integration of sensory experiences in the formation of a body image that becomes differentiated from the caregiver. Interwoven with growing awareness of an infant's own body is awareness of animate and inanimate objects in the world as well.

An infant slowly emerges from a symbiotic state in which parent and child respond to each other as if they were physical and psychological extensions of each other. This form of relatedness constitutes a mutually affirmative response to each other's being (Lichtenstein, 1977). Erik Erikson suggested that a sense of an "I" literally begins with the meeting of a parent's and infant's eyes.

Self-awareness may be present during this phase in the belief that "I am the center of the world." It also is manifested at about eight months in many children in the form of stranger fearfulness, which signals awareness that there are adults who are not connected with the child. Between nine and 18 months, children can recognize their own faces in a mirror (Lewis & Brooks, 1975; Maccoby, 1980; Muller, 1983).

Self-esteem exists first in the regulation of emotional states between parent and infant and later in connecting inner homeostatic with social states. Self-esteem arises from pleasure from one's body and bodily products. The foundation for self-esteem thus is laid in an infant's experience of bodily functions. When they are rhythmic and comfortable, bodily sensations arising from hunger, sleeping, elimination, and movement provide a somatic basis for pleasurable feelings about the self.

As motor maturation allows greater individuation, parental admiration becomes internalized in the form of self-esteem. The craving of a toddler for attention and adulation reflects the child's dependency upon parental esteem. At this stage suspension of parental approval is experienced as a catastrophic interruption in the child's developing self-esteem. The continued background of parental adulation and foreground of parental separating from and disapproving of the child's actions creates an ambience in which a child gradually develops self-esteem in the face of the temporary loss of parental approval. The acceptance of the limit-setting parent confirms a child's worth to the parent, and thence to the self.

Thus the developmental line for self-esteem regulation begins with an infant's feelings of well-being resulting from empathic caregiving, from the infant's experience of being able to affect the environment, from the incorporation of positive parental qualities, and from comfort with internal sensations. A child's need for parental adulation matures into the child's capacity to soothe oneself through self-esteem. Infantile narcissism with its grandiosity, omnipotence, and omniscience mellows to become more realistic and mature forms of self-confidence and pride.

Loving parents create a climate in which

children become familiar with and master their own body functions, intellect, and emotions. However, love is not enough. Just as important is a parent's respect for a child's need to achieve autonomy through mastery of one's own body. Respect for the uniqueness of a child permits the child to develop self-knowledge of the child's own abilities as a foundation for self-concepts. The discovery that "I can do it" is the key. The pleasure of parents in a child's mastery fosters positive self-evaluation. Of particular importance is mastery of one's own imagery, emotions, and internal organization. All of this fosters self-confidence.

SYMBOLIC STAGE

From about 18 months to three and a half years, Greenspan identifies a representational-symbolic stage corresponding to Piaget's preoperational phase. In this developmental sense, symbols are abstract images that serve the purpose of communication. This is a period of rapid speech development as a toddler learns to understand and to express wishes through spoken words. The developmental task for the toddler is to achieve autonomy as person.

This stage corresponds to neomammalian phylogeny and reflects the growth of the frontal and temporo-parietal integration cortical areas of the brain. Cerebral lateralization, also becomes possible through myelinization of the corpus callosum (Brown, 1977).

Temperament

Activity Level

At no time in life is the activity level higher than during this stage when the speed at which the body burns its fuel, the basal metabolism rate, is at its highest. Throughout childhood boys have a higher basal metabolism rate than girls (Eichorn, 1970). Optimally children of this age alternate volitional activity with passive receptivity, both of which are experienced as pleasurable.

Attention

An infant scans narrow segments of an informational field slowly and passively. The toddler can scan increasingly larger segments of a field of information and focus attention more precisely (Santostefano, 1980). The span of attention also lengthens as powers of concentration develop. Not until four or five years of age, however, is the ability to follow a spoken instruction strong enough to override the influence of significant distracting stimuli.

Emotions

More refined emotional states now progressively emerge. Most toddlers' actions are colored by emotions, as is evident in their exuberance and sharply defined pleasure and distress (Brown, 1977). Signal anxiety in the forms of awareness of danger and the loss of parental approval appears at around the age of two. By the age of three, unmistakably aggressive behavior appears in the form of threat gestures and attacking targets, primarily during struggles over play materials and the control of space. As a child approaches four, more stable moods are seen because of increasing analysis and synthesis of symbolic imagery and emotions (Maccoby, 1980).

Dramas between children emerge in play in the form of exploration, protest, aggression, separation, and rejection. A child also begins to develop a connection between loving and hating. Children who do not learn to express them appropriately persist in separating love and hate and may live in two separate worlds, that which is loved and that which is hated.

Cognition

A toddler's perceptions are strongly influenced by existing mental set, waking state, and internal imagery. Prior to this stage, perceptions were limited largely to those that served sensorimotor schemes. In that form perceptions became figures in the background configurations of sensorimotor schemes. During this stage the CNS becomes able to handle perceptions that stand for concrete objects and their semiotic images in the form of signs and symbols.

This capacity to form symbolic schemes abstracted from the totality of an original pattern is like drawing a cartoon in which the details are eliminated and essential relationships are parsimoniously retained (Basch, 1976). During the middle of the second year children may show evidence of an early form of logic when they group and regroup small sets of playthings, seemingly taking into account their forms and functions without using language symbols (Langer, 1986).

Through learning to use symbols, such as words, drawings, and gestures, a child can relate to a variety of physical and social objects. Awareness of magnitude seems to emerge quite early in cognitive development. "Littlest," "middle," "many," and "more" are understood between the ages of one and two and a half years. "Bigger" and "smaller" are usually comprehended by three and four-year-olds. As an understanding of time unfolds, the word "today" appears at about two years, "tomorrow" at two and a half, and "yesterday" at three. Morning and afternoon can be distinguished by four years of age.

A three-year-old can remember three digit numbers and a four-year-old four digits (Luria, 1980). Between two and four, a child discovers that marks on a page are related to hand movements and attempts to control the directions of the scribbled lines. When scribbling becomes controlled, it represents imaginative play activity (Mendelowitz, 1963). At the age of three, most children can copy a circle. Three-year-olds also can be taught to write words (Montessori, 1974).

During this stage a toddler is able to recognize objects separate from oneself, but those objects are subject to the child's perception of them. If a child's perception of an object changes, the object itself changes. For example, the child is unable to hold a perception of the liquid in one container with a perception of the same quantity of liquid in a taller, thinner container. Similarly, the child's inability to hold two perceptions at the same time is paralleled by the inability to hold two feelings about a single thing together—either the same feelings about a thing over time or competing feelings at the same time. If an urge cannot be gratified, the entire being of the child is threatened. This explains why the toddler lacks the capacity for ambivalence, so that a tantrum is an example of a system overwhelmed, because there is no self yet that can serve as a context upon which competing impulses can play themslves out; the impulses are the self (Kegan, 1982).

Symbols also can be used to stand for wishes and things as expressed in the imagery of fantasy. The syncretic merging of the breast, penis, baby, feces, and urine equates body parts and products in fantasies.

The frustrating separation– individuation process stimulates the capacity for imagery of a child's parents in particular. Symbolic wish fulfillment takes place in the form of magical thinking in response to frustration. On the other hand, symbolic imagery also makes possible new internal dangers expressed through fears and phobias, such as night fears. Moreover, dreams are regarded as realities potentially visible to others, and anything that moves is endowed with life.

Language

The ability to learn language is so deeply rooted in children that they learn it even in the face of dramatic handicaps. Congenital blindness, for example, does not prevent word acquisition by touch.

By the latter half of the second year, language shifts from using words mainly to identify things and people to asking for, and talking about, objects that are not present. This progression from concrete to symbolic labeling permits a child to discriminate between sounds and to attach meanings to them in the form of words:

> *24 months*—repertoire of more than 50 words; two-word phrases; prepositions, adjectives and adverbs appear; repetition of words and phrases in solitary dialogue
> *30 months*—dramatic increase in spoken vocabulary; many phrases containing three to five words; conjunctions appear
> *3 years*—vocabulary of about 1000 words; pronunciation clear
> *4 years*—language well established

The use of words must be distinguished from knowledge of their meaning. For example, a nine-month-old can say "mama," but not know what mother means; a two-year-old can learn the meaning of I, but not we; and a three-year-old can learn to say the word "adoption," but not comprehend its meaning.

The understanding of spoken language precedes the ability to use speech expressively. Receptive language is the perception of expressive speech from another source and involves decoding of the perceived spoken expression, identification of its significant elements, reduction of these elements to the same internal speech of expressive language, and, finally, detection of the motive lying behind the words. Expressive language begins with an image of an internal language scheme that is encoded into spoken form. Language then is both a method of analyzing and generalizing incoming information and a method of formulating and expressing thoughts.

Whorf grasped how a culture's language influences the content of thoughts and highlighted the way in which the structure of a person's language influences one's knowledge of the environment (Carroll, 1956). Thus one's picture of the universe is influenced by the language of each culture. Speakers of different languages see and evaluate the world differently. At the same time, Piaget held that language development reflects a child's cognitive capacity rather than determines it.

Freud believed that words play a vital role in thinking, because speech brings imagery to consciousness (Pribram & Gill, 1976). He viewed speech in psychotherapy as essential to permit the unconscious sources of imagery to become images at the same conscious level with perceptual processes so as to lend them reality through the act of speech. He, therefore, viewed speech as the essential tool of psychotherapy. This highlights the importance of learning words to express feelings in early life.

Managerial System

The relatively accurate analysis of reality is gained slowly and sometimes painfully, because symbolic images are initially closely linked to emotions. Just as dreams and nightmares are regarded as real, toddlers are strongly emotionally invested in their symbolic imagery, simply because the images are theirs. Through the corrective experience of analyzing reality, symbolic images are gradually separated from the primitive emotions of lust and aggression so that they are no longer tenaciously held simply because they are "mine." This may explain why immature school-age children stubbornly adhere to their own knowledge and ideas in the face of reality. They resist instruction and enter into conflict with teachers because they believe they are right. This has been referred to as cognitive conceit (Elkind, 1981).

Pleasures derived from the control of the body and inherent in walking and in control of the anal and urethral sphincters constitute the basis for a growing sense of mastery. The achievement of sphincter control in particular provides toddlers with the mastery of internal substances that are both within and separate, that can be put out or withheld, and that are under their own control. The delight from general muscular control through grabbing, tearing, destroying, and smearing infuses opposing others with a sense of personal mastery through saying "no."

The synthetic function of the managerial system can be seen operating by the age of three, not only in mediation between the inner and outer world, but in the union and modulation of drives and cognition. The ability to manipulate and categorize images of the internal and external world constitutes the essence of thinking. Thinking serves the drives, including the mastery drive itself, and can be seen as experimental action serving drive gratification. Thinking is reflected in the imagery of the sensory world arising from within the body and arriving from the outside world via the special senses. It has an unconscious effortless component following the principles of the primary process. It also has a goal-directed effortful component under the aegis of the secondary process and experienced in its conscious, preconscious, and unconscious aspects. Thinking develops an autonomy of its own through binding drive energy. This autonomy is relative, however, so knowledge at this stage remains linked to drives and is not infallible (Shapiro, 1979).

During the symbolic stage, a child's reasoning is neither deductive nor inductive but is transductive, that is, from particular to particular. If two things have a common property, they are the same. On the other hand, if a part changes, the whole is different. For example, on a walk through the woods, a toddler does not know whether a series of flowers is seen or the same flower time after time. At least the child can identify flowers.

A young child's inability to make logical inferences results in part because of a limited short-term memory capacity, which results in losing information. A young child and an adult both look at the same region of space but see quite different things and reflect upon what they see with different powers of memory and experiential backgrounds. Another factor may be the lack of a hypothetical attitude so that a young child does not understand that problems exist. To solve a formal problem, a child must adopt a hypothetical attitude toward it by accepting that such a state of affairs might exist, setting it up mentally, and then working on it. Thus the issue is not one of illogicality, but of lacking the memory-based integrating capacities of imagination, conceptualization, and problem solving.

Mahler described a rapprochement subphase of separation–individuation between 15 and 24 months (Mahler et al, 1975). The previous interest in foraging out from a home base of the practicing phase is replaced by a seemingly constant wish for the caretaker to share every new acquisition, skill, and experience. The toddler enjoys bringing objects to caregivers. The toddler is discovering that the world is frustrating, and an older person's help is needed in order to cope with it. The wooing behavior of toddlers toward their caregivers also may take on coercive tones in an effort to get them to participate in maintaining the child's infantile omnipotence. Still the child must gradually give up delusions of grandeur, at times leading to dramatic fights with parents. The parents' continued availability, sharing of the toddler's exploits, and playful reciprocity permit verbal communication to help resolve conflicts.

After about 18 months, the maturational capacity to distinguish between interpersonal relationships enables a child to experience "primal scene" traumata, which are any exclusive engagements between parents in which they are impervious to their child's wishes and expectations. These encounters often enhance a child's grasp of reality by challenging infantile omnipotence (Harris, 1986).

By the beginning of the third year, the predictable emotional participation of a parent seems to facilitate the rich unfolding that is taking place in the toddler's thought processes, analysis of reality, and coping behavior. The essence of the rapprochement phase is an effort to use the parent as a means of maintaining infantile omnipotence, but through parental limitation of that effort also results in the discovery of the child's own realistic capacities (Lax, 1980). Thus in its most fundamental sense, adherence to reality is the result of successful individuation fostered by parental limit setting (Wood, 1981).

At about the middle of the second year, imagery is expressed in make-believe play as children turn to symbolic games about the nature of things they can personally manipulate. After about 20 months, children imitate peers and begin to share toys and activities. Dyadic play interactions emerge, such as that of giver and receiver. Rates of aggression between children increase from two to four years, but then decline; hostile activity usually is less common than positive, however, so that positive social interaction blooms (Rosenblatt, 1981).

Self

Upright posture and walking give a toddler the ability to reach out and hold on, to throw and push away, to take things, and to keep them at a distance. This sense of power contributes to self-consciousness and the basis for self-concepts. As children literally stand more firmly on their own feet, they delineate their worlds as "I" and "you" and "me" and "mine" (Amsterdam & Levitt, 1980).

The development of self-awareness is seen between 18 and 24 months in the form of a child's ability to identify one's own image in a mirror. Self-awareness also is indicated by the shyness of toddlers. The awareness of the self as an object proceeds to awareness of the self as a subject, as personal pronouns appear between 21 and 24 months and precede the use of pronouns for others, such as "you" (Lowe, 1975). Verbs also are applied to a child's own actions before those of others. Thus a child first appears to be a solipsist with an explicit notion of oneself, but not of others (Huttenlocher, 1983).

A child's capacity to transform impulses and perceptions into symbols brings into being a new subject–object relation, which creates an enduring self. The self does its own praising, so to speak, but needs the information that it is correct as a confirmation. It can store memories, feelings, and perceptions, rather than be them (Kegan, 1982).

Just as a child's mastery and consciousness of the material environment are extended by the newly acquired ability to speak, so also is awareness of self. The ability to use the personal pronoun "I" conveys a sense of being an active, continuous force in the world. When children become conscious of their names, when they learn to name the various parts of their bodies and when they learn to use personal pronouns, the words themselves become important determinants of their self-concepts.

Toward the end of the first year, as the child becomes capable of object permanence and of differentiating strangers from caregivers, the first discernible stage of object constancy, which is achieved at the end of this stage, is entered. In association with walking and talking during the second and third year, the child develops the capacity to retain the full image of, and emotional tie to, parents so that the child can feel their nurturing, guiding presence even when they are a source of frustration or disappointment or are absent. Children, then, are developing integrated self-concepts, so that they know their parents are separate from themselves and that both themselves and their parents are continuous over time (Solnit & Neubauer, 1986).

Winnicott called attention to the ambivalence involved in establishing oneself developmentally. The most aggressive and, therefore, the most dangerous words are to be found in the assertion "I am." For a young child, these words create a sensation of infinite exposure, when the "not me" is felt as separate and rejecting. For this reason the risk of the "I am" moment is minimized when a child is securely accepted and reassured by a parent (Davis & Wallbridge, 1981).

The acquisition of speech plays an enormous role in the development of the self. One learns not only to perceive and interpret one's perceptions through language but also to be a person. The autistic situation of Helen Keller prior to her breakthrough by learning a word dramatically illustrates this point. It was only when Ann Sullivan held Keller's hand under the spout of a pump that she connected the word "water," a word apparently recollected from her preillness period before 19 months, with the cool, tactually experienced stream. She realized once again that things had names and that the manual alphabet was the key to them all:

> Suddenly, there was a strange stir within me—a misty consciousness, a sense of something remembered. It was as if I had come back to life after being dead . . . I understood that it was possible for me to communicate with other people by these signs. Thoughts that ran forward and backward came to me quickly—thoughts that seemed to start in my brain and spread all over me. I think it was in the nature of a revelation . . . I felt joyous, strong, equal to my limitations. Delicious sensations sizzled through me, and sweet strange things that were locked in my heart began to sing (Brooks, 1956).

At the beginning of the second year of life, two key events occur that may lead to a negative evaluation of a child's concept of one's body. These are locomotion and the intentional reaching for and stimulation of one's own genitalia. Being too active for adult tastes in these endeavors can lead to punishment and to a child's negative evaluation of body movements. The most frequent negative reaction is by a parent, who punishes a child for genital exploration. Thus whether it is too active or the source of forbidden pleasures, the body may be regarded as a shameful object and negatively evaluated by the child (Amsterdam & Levitt, 1980).

On the other hand, parental acceptance of a child's body and its functions sets the stage for positive self-evaluation. If children are permitted to make decisions that are appropriate for them, such as when they need to use the toilet, they develop a sense of being able to take responsibility and make decisions for themselves. Whether a child acquires a healthy sense of autonomy, or is burdened with excessive feelings of shame and doubt, depends upon the skill with which a parent matches expectations to a child's abilities (Elkind, 1981). The foundations for a moral evaluation of aggression and self-awareness appear to be universal achievements of the second year of life (Kagan, 1982; Kohlberg et al, 1983).

Self-esteem regulation is influenced positively by parental acceptance of a child's negativism in the context of limit setting, elation over developing motor skills, the differentiation of oneself from others, experiencing "I," and identification with a competent, loving parent.

CONCEPTUAL STAGE

From the ages of three and a half to ten, Greenspan postulates a representational–structural stage corresponding to Piaget's last conception of concrete operations (Furth, 1981). During this stage concept formation occurs in the form of knowledge about the properties of perceptions, images, and symbols. The cognitive task of this stage is to construct concepts of objects, events, and values as abstractions separate from one's immediate perception of them and to coordinate different perspectives.

The conceptual stage can be divided into two phases: the intuitive-play phase (three and a half to six) and the schoolwork phase (six to 11).

Intuitive-Play Phase

The appearance of new zones of cellular differentiation in the frontal and temporo-parietal cortex, in addition to increasing asymmetrical cerebral dominance, permits the emergence of the ability to gain knowledge about things in the form of concepts (Brown, 1977). The overall developmental task of this phase is achieving the capacity for personal initiative through a child's intuitive knowledge of the world.

Temperament

Activity Levels. The sheer physical pleasure from movement leads children of this age to thrive on high levels of motor activity interspersed with increasing intervals of purposeful play.

Attention. From a baby's rattle through a toddler's teddy bear to a young child's tricycle, the objects employed to engage a child's attention reflect the child's motor, cognitive, and social levels of development. By the age of four, the major determinant of attention is no longer novelty, which gives way to active, purposeful searching based upon interest and curiosity. By five more efficient, stable, socially organized attention is possible for limited periods of time. At this age children can override distracting stimuli and follow instructions when motivated to do so.

Emotions. During this phase, children are capable of experiencing more complex emotions. By the age of four, lust, greed, sympathy, envy, jealousy, hate, and guilt may be evident. By the age of six, awe, pride, hope, hopelessness, despair, discouragement, disgust, contempt, and rivalry appear. Boredom also is evident as children enter more structured environments in which their interest is not maintained.

Children of this age are curious about and eager to explore their worlds and ask endless "why" questions. When their initiative is encouraged, they expand their interest in the world. If children's questions are ignored or answered cursorily, or a child's explorations result in punishment, a sense of guilt over curiosity may result (Elkind, 1981).

Curiosity that does not have an aggressive element is a nonproductive response of wonder, surprise, or awe. This is the primitive form of curiosity in infancy and early childhood. The motivating force for problem-solving learning is derived from an impulse to attack aggressively the elements of a problem. Problem solving is enhanced developmentally when an element of aggression is blended with curiosity in the form of assertive eye–hand coordination and locomotion in ever-widening exploration (Gardner, G.E., 1971).

During this phase children experience fear based upon internal and external danger with a limited ability to distinguish and place the sources in perspective. They are concerned about bodily injury to themselves, their parents, or other people significant in their lives. These concerns may be mixed with feelings of guilt generated by the notions that they themselves, through their own naughtiness, or through their own felt or voiced resentments, bring about such disasters.

Many young children live amid scores of warnings of dangers from adults, who wish to protect them from harm. The possible dangers associated with fire, electricity, dogs, poisons, falling from high places, automobiles, lightning, and strangers are emphasized. Their relative physical smallness and lack of strength make children feel all the more vulnerable to danger. Thus children usually are told of all the possibilities of harm without the perspective of the probabilities that it will occur with them and the ways they can handle dangers.

With this background many young children approach the unfamiliar and unknown with trepidations that influence their attitudes toward schoolwork. When curiosity evokes feelings of helplessness in addition to expectations of frustration, failure, or punishment, the resulting fear blocks interest in learning. In the same way, if the aggressive component of attacking a challenge evokes fear of one's own urges, the ability to perform schoolwork is impeded. The tension evoked by the new and unfamiliar can spawn excitement for learning, but, if it triggers fear related to curiosity or aggression, a learning endeavor can be blocked.

Cognition

In this phase the operations of sensorimotor schemes permit the formation of concepts so that the young child can recognize the properties of objects in the world intuitively without the simultaneous use of sensorimotor functions, such as touching, turning, pulling, or mouthing. A child can form images of the surrounding world, which are distinguished from the things they represent. Furthermore, learning can take place by modifying existing knowledge. For example, reading letters can be built upon verbal language.

The ability to retrieve memories of related past events takes place around the age of four or five, as a child is able to associate similar events. For example, one child recognized that a party dress also could be worn to a wedding. Moreover, this is the time in which a child develops the ability to retrieve memories in the absence of external cues. Thus memory development proceeds from single novel experiences to fused representations to differentiated representations that are capable of being recalled and shared in the absence of external cues. The lack of memories of early life, or infantile amnesia, therefore, probably is a function of developmental incapacity in addition to repression and dependency upon recognition cues (Nelson & Ross, 1980; Daehler & Greco, 1985).

Children younger than five usually are unable clearly to separate the fictional world of a story from reality (Reyna, 1985). They are likely to make a magical interpretation when experiencing difficulty in understanding a metaphor. This probably is because the ability to engage in symbolic, fantasy play, such as pretending to feed a doll, precedes using metaphors, such as calling a piece of string "my tail." In fantasy a child overrides the rules of reality; in a metaphor only words are exchanged.

Between four and six, a child begins translating experience and concepts into pictorial symbols. The capacity for discriminating two-dimensional figures appears. At the age of four, most children can copy a cross, at five a triangle and at six a diamond. People are the subjects most frequently represented in drawings. At first a large circle head with arms and legs serves as a standard human symbol. Then, between five and six, hands, feet, facial features, and other body parts are added, although spatial relationships may not be accurate (Mendelowitz, 1963). Time relationships begin to be made, so that at the age of five most children know how old they will be on their next birthday (Luria, 1980).

The oedipal triangulation may facilitate abstract concept formation, because a child is able to sample parent-responding-to-a-child, parent-responding-to-other-parent, and child-responding-to-both. These opportunities provide the roots for multiple perspectives and the relative nature of knowledge (Edelheit, 1972).

Language

The rapid development of language takes place between two and five years. By five or six, children are pronouncing simple words correctly and completely. How a child receives, organizes, and makes use of the conglomerate of auditory stimulation directly influences the level of language that can be attained.

The ambivalence of oedipal strivings during this stage causes preoccupation with emotion-laden internal events. Language can be a helpful tool in expressing these feelings and in conceptualizing parent–child relationships (Lewis, 1977). Language permits the use of symbols for describing and organizing a child's experience.

Cultural factors influence the form of language and thinking and one's capacity for verbal planning. Disadvantaged children may show a relatively limited capacity for verbal planning and delaying action (Miller & Swanson, 1960).

Managerial System

This is the phase of intuitive thought. The young child is dominated by egocentric interpretations rather than logical reasoning. Difficulty distinguishing between internal and external imagery makes the analysis of reality tenuous. The child also tends to emphasize parts rather than wholes in perceptions. Still the discovery of accurate knowledge provides a sense of power as a child becomes aware of how one comes to know things. "I can do it" is a reflection of this pleasure from the mastery drives.

Children threatened with corporal punishment or coaxed by external rewards develop neither courage nor self-control. When an activity itself is initiated by a child, however, a sense of personal achievement follows. Curiosity impels children to discover facts about their enlarging world. Otherwise a child only learns to fear an unpleasant consequence that by cleverness might be avoided. Thus punishment increases deception, not morality. Unfortunately, adults may recognize the undesirability of corporal punishment in their own lives but continue to use it with their children (Key, 1909). A middle course between gratification and frustration, between strictness and indulgence, and between physical force and moral guidance is more useful (Freud, A., 1981a). Children on the early side of five to seven need rewards that are fairly immediate, sensual, and praising, because they experience mistakes as catastrophic. Children on the older side may feel more rewarded by knowing that they are correct (Kegan, 1982).

Object constancy has been achieved in Mahler's sense of the fusion of good and bad parent images at the beginning of this phase. This is extended from dyadic relationships to the oedipal triangular relationships with family members. These triangles involving parents and siblings evoke contradictions of love, hate, and rivalry. The ability to manage these conflicts is influenced by the openness and comfort of communication between family members and the security of parental attachments.

Play is a child's means of taking the initiative in learning about and mastering the world. As the voluntary work of childhood, play is intricately related to a child's integration and mastery of experiences (Garvey, 1977). Cooperative play permits children to digest life situations through pretending. Children raised with exposure only to adult expectations may not fully learn to play. Play with language is important in developing not only vocabulary but symbolic imagery. It is to a child's advantage to expose egocentric beliefs to reality through play and gradually season infantile notions with facts. Children then can relinquish play as the modality for learning and adopt more realistic games, and ultimately academic work. Satisfaction from a play activity itself gives way increasingly to pleasure in the product of an activity (Freud, A., 1976). As the work of the young child, play is a precondition for later academic learning in school (Omwake, 1963).

Self

With a growing awareness of time, a sense of being a continuous self in the world emerges, as well as awareness that other persons have their own existences.

Young children do not realize that people can hide their inner imagery and feelings. They believe that their actions betray their imagery. The ability to reflect on one's own imagery and actions makes it possible for a child to conceal inner feelings in order to avoid embarrassment or ridicule (Selman, 1981). The first successful "lie" thus serves a developmental purpose by demonstrating to the child that one's imagery is one's own and inaccessible to others.

A distinguishing feature of this stage is that the child has a self-containment that was not there before; the child no longer lives with the sense that an adult can read the child's private feelings. The child now has a private world with a more or less consistent notion of "what I am" as contrasted with the earlier sense "that I am" and the later sense of "who I am."

With the capacity to have urges rather than to be them comes a new sense of freedom, power, and independence. Things no longer just happen in the world; the child now has something to do with what happens. This liberation carries new risks and vulnerabilities that accompany a sense of responsibility. If I now have something to do with what happens in the world, then whether things go badly or well for me is a question of what I do. Looming over this newly won stability, control, and freedom is the threat of the old lability, loss of control, and subjugation from outside.

The oedipal theory explains how a child learns to focus erotic drives, adopt a gender role, and form moral values (Fisher & Greenberg, 1977). It holds that a child identifies more with the same- than the opposite-sex parent through a process of coping with erotic feelings toward the opposite-sex parent and hostility toward the same-sex parent. Innate castration anxiety in boys contributes to the expectation that experiencing erotic impulses will lead to being attacked and hurt. The male begins with his attachment to his mother, develops rivalry with his father and fantasies of sexual closeness with his mother, and ultimately identifies with his father and gender role. The usual motivation for a boy to identify with his father is less fear and more love in response to his father's nurturant friendliness. In the female version of the oedipal theory, or the Electra complex, the girl's fantasy is that she is her father's preferred love and that she could displace her mother as the woman of the house. Since she is dependent upon her mother, her rivalry with her mother threatens loss of her mother's love. She resolves this dilemma through identification with her mother.

Just as the primal scene shatters infantile omnipotence at the end of the sensorimotor period, so the oedipal fantasy of possessing the parent of the opposite sex and rivalry with the parent of the same sex crumbles under the weight of reality.

Gender identity usually is established by the age of three. For boys individuation from the mother is necessary for establishing a masculine gender identity. For girls femininity does not depend upon individuation but upon continued attachment. Thus male gender identity may be threatened by intimacy with a mother, while female gender identity is threatened by separation from her (Gilligan, 1982).

Ultimately the self is an amalgam of

identifications with parents as reflected in ideal self-concepts and both positive and negative self-evaluations. The development of a conscience is liberating. The internalization of others' voices in one's conscience releases a child from feeling controlled or manipulated by others and forms the foundation for self-control. Moreover, self-esteem is influenced by the organization of a child's inner world through incorporating parental values, the personal mastery of skills, and acceptance by peers. Thus the self arises from the selective identification with significant others to form a new configuration, which in turn is dependent on the process by which society identifies and recognizes young persons. All through childhood tentative crystallizations of the self take place, which make individuals feel and believe they know who they are, only to find that such self-certainty falls prey again and again to the discontinuities of development itself (Erikson, 1968).

Conceptual-Work Phase

Between the ages of six and 11, the further maturation of the prefrontal and associational cortex and the reticular activating system brings the capacity for organizing oneself to deal with the requirements of schooling. The overall developmental task is achieving the capacity for industrious work.

Temperament

Activity Level. During this stage there is a progressive increase in aptitude for motor skills as reflected in reaction time, sequencing of component muscular systems, and the timing of movements. These functions permit more consistent and rapid execution of purposeful actions. A child can gauge activity with increasing precision to task and social context.

Attention. Up to the age of five, extra-neous stimuli readily interfere with learning. Beyond this age, however, complementary stimuli can be used to present material in novel and interesting ways. Increasing powers of concentration become evident. Children also become progressively more able to divide their attention, so that by the age of eight a child can listen to a teacher and take notes on what is being said at the same time (Taylor, 1981).

Emotions. Instinctual drive tension can be managed through repression; however, it also can be more usefully sublimated into motivation for schoolwork. Thus the drive organization of images yields to conceptual organization through intellectualization and rationalization.

Cognitive dissonance is a common school-based source of anxiety for children. When a child does not have the cognitive equipment to understand and resolve events and perceptions, dissonance between a child's cognitive organization and the complexity of information creates distress. This is counterbalanced by "cognitive conceit" through which children feel that if they know some things that adults do not know, then they must know everything (Elkind, 1981).

Cognition

A child gradually comes to rely more heavily upon knowledge than action as conceptualization catches up with and outstrips action at about 11 to 12 years of age (Piaget, 1978).

It is critical to the aims of academic learning that internal imagery be distinguished from perceptions and images from the external world. A shift to clear awareness that symbols are only symbols and that dreams are only dreams is necessary to ensure that a child can deal with words and stories as being only that. The stage of concrete operations makes that possible so that a child can deal with symbols simply as images. The properties and qualities of objects also can be considered apart from objects themselves as the capacity to conceptualize appears. The world then can be seen in terms of part and whole, and past and present, relationships. Initially concepts are formed of the spatial characteristics of things. Between six and nine, concepts can be formed of similar properties of things. After nine concepts can be formed by forming classes of things (Parrill-Burnstein, 1981).

Developmental progression takes place in a child's sense of space. Space originally is one aspect of a child's consciousness of one's body and lacks a relationship to the external world. Although left and right may not be experienced as specific objective qualities attached to spatial forms, they may be known as early as three as qualities of action. Most children know right and left on their own body by the age of six. At eight a child can distinguish right and left on other persons. Nine-year-olds can correctly imitate movements of the left and right hands of persons facing them (Werner, 1948). During the early school years, a child can appreciate the concept of conservation of quantity by the age of seven, weight by the age of nine, and volume by the age of 11 (Luria, 1980).

A child's sense of time also follows a developmental course. For a child the conception of time begins as a sort of substance brought together as discontinuous pieces. For example, events divide time, such as breakfast, midday, nap, and supper. Each year is divided by birthday, Easter, and Christmas. Even six-year-olds still use personalized concrete situations to designate time. For example, the time of getting up in the morning is "when my mother calls me" (Werner, 1948). A six-year-old can tell what time it is when the hands show the hour, but finer divisions of time are difficult to grasp. Seven-year-olds know the time of day, the month, the season, and how many minutes are in a half hour. Eight-year-olds know the day of the month

and the months of the year (Luria, 1980). Awareness of the finality and inevitability of death usually occurs at nine or ten.

Between six and nine, children tend to show similar simple drawings of the human figure, use baselines to indicate space relationships between ground and sky, and depict interactions between children and things (Mendelowitz, 1963). Between nine and 12, figures become more accurate anatomically, are clothed, and the first signs of space perspective appear. Depending upon acculturation, boys tend to draw scenes of conflict, vehicles, sports activities, and feats of adventure, while girls tend to draw houses, clothes, flowers, and animals with their young.

At seven or eight, a child is as capable as an adult of processing and remembering sensory information. The categorizing of information, involving translation across sense modalities or systems of symbols, however, develops more slowly and continues to improve through the adolescent years (Gardner, 1976).

Children now have the capacity to learn and operate according to rules that make it possible to learn the principles of reading and arithmetic. They also are able to play complex games and enter the culture of childhood, which is a body of rules that have been handed down by oral tradition over the centuries. The sayings, superstitions, jokes, and riddles of childhood are the initial stage of social interaction among peers, who share common ways of dealing with the world. Some children, who are adult socialized too early, are deprived of this rich cultural heritage and the opportunity to interact with peers on a level that is unique to childhood (Elkind, 1981).

Language

There are five kinds of vocabularies: an understanding, a speaking, a reading, a writing, and an emerging vocabulary. The last is comprised of words that have been encountered but not yet entered into the preceding four categories through learning. Estimates of vocabularies of beginning school children range from 4000 to 26,000. Even for adults, however, approximately 400 words comprise 80 percent of everyday conversation (Kaluger & Kolson, 1969).

A child learns the language of the culture as a byproduct of striving to meet evolving personal needs and to solve developmental tasks (Halliday, 1975). At the age of six, children do not attempt to place themselves in the point of view of the hearer; they assume that they are understood (Piaget, 1959). During the school years, children become increasingly able to tailor their language to the perspectives of others.

Managerial System

By this phase most children have acquired sufficient impulse control to sit quietly in class. They are able to relate to and identify with their teachers, to delay gratification, to pay attention, to persist in activities, and to enjoy mastery experiences (Weil, 1977). They are increasingly capable of rational, logical thinking about what has been observed.

An example of this progression in mental capacity is a five-year-old boy who could make one puppet bite another in play. At six the child could say that he felt angry, because he could not have his way. At seven he could understand that he was angry, because he could not have his way all of the time. At eight he could recall that he was angry at his father because of the latter's past behavior. In this progression intellectual insight that permitted relating the present to the past was not possible until the age of eight.

Between five and seven, children can recognize that others can have different thoughts and can discriminate intended from accidental actions. They are aware of family relationships. People are character-ized by appearance and possessions and with simple evaluative traits, such as nice and mean. At seven and eight, peer relations have a cost–reward character marked by an emphasis on common activities, close social contact, and similarity in outlook. From eight to 11, children are able to view simple social episodes from another person's perspective. They then can infer the feelings of others (Shantz, 1975). At nine and ten, friendships begin to be based upon shared values, rules, and sanctions.

Halfway between play and work are hobbies, which have certain aspects in common with both activities. Hobbies involve a preconceived plan undertaken in a realistic way and carried on over a period of time. They also provide experience in mastering frustration (Freud, A., 1976).

Self

In Erikson's view the self develops gradually out of the many identifications of childhood blended with innate and acquired personal qualities. The self, however, is more than the sum of successive identifications of the earlier years and is a continuously changing, synthesized whole experienced as differentiated from other persons. The development of one's self-concept thus is a bootstrap operation drawn from the individual's total interaction with the world (Gardner, 1976).

With the emergence from an embeddedness in one's own needs, a child's viewpoint becomes "I no longer am" my needs rather "I have them." By having needs a child can now coordinate one need system with another, and, in so doing, become empathic and oriented to reciprocal obligations. The intrapsychic consequence is that a child is able to coordinate points of view within the self, leading to the experience of subjective inner states and the ability to talk about feelings.

Still a child early in this phase is not facile with anger, and may, in fact, not even be angry in situations that might be expected to make a person angry. Anger owned and expressed is a risk to the interpersonal fabric. Children of this age undergo experiences, such as being exploited or victimized, that do not make them angry, because they cannot know themselves as separate from the interpersonal context; instead they are more likely to feel sad, wounded, or incomplete. A child's interpersonal balance during this phase cannot bring onto itself the obligations, expectations, satisfactions, purposes, or influences of interpersonal relationships (Kegan, 1982).

By the age of six, children recognize that they are distinct individuals in terms of their physical appearance, gender, and behavioral capacities. By eight and nine, they also recognize covert and personalized differences in feelings and attitudes (Guardo & Bohan, 1971). Children can then evaluate themselves as they form a self-concept that represents their effort to make sense of their experience and to keep a record of it (Gardner, 1976).

The self is now aware of the self as subject and the self as object and as an active manipulator of one's inner life and outer actions (Selman, 1981). The child can take into account the point of view of another person, for example, through playing by rules. The awareness of the importance of other selves is evident from the meaningful use of plural pronouns.

The school years bring self-evaluation into play as a selective filter for self-esteem regulation so that children can shift from meeting the standards of others to meeting their own internal standards. The mastery of skills and the availability of the defenses of repression, sublimation, rationalization, and intellectualization enhance self-esteem. At the same time, failure, and rejection by others deplete self-esteem.

During this phase children establish a sense of industry when they feel they can succeed in schoolwork. When they cannot, an abiding sense that whatever they undertake will end up badly and a sense of inferiority may result (Elkind, 1981).

THEORETICAL STAGE

The human being flowers during adolescence with the ability to think about thoughts. In so doing the pleasures and pain of life are the sharpest when first perceived. Although additional refinement extends into the third decade, the central nervous system virtually matures by the age of 18. Prior to that age, the sequence of adult functions unfolds after the age of 11, each one attended by the excitement of pristine experience ranging from the discovery of sunsets to the flaws of society. The appearance of diaries, poetry, and theories signals the readiness of teenagers to delve into the mysteries of life.

All of this results from the appearance of Piaget's formal operations based upon maturation of the prefrontal cortex and the activity of the neuroendocrine system. With the onset of puberty, physical maturation climaxes in every organ system as the body assumes its adult form. The age of onset of puberty varies widely between individuals and the sexes. Figure 19-3 depicts variations in height that generally reflect the great individual range in pubertal development. Girls mature physically about two years earlier than boys, with the onset of the menarche spread between ten and 16 and of seminal emissions between 13 and 17. Consequently some girls and boys have completed pubertal maturation before others of the same age have begun theirs (Lewis, 1982).

Adolescence is the psychosocial response to puberty and is dependent upon culture. Early adolescents are preoccupied with their bodily changes as they explore peer relationships within the context of dependency upon their families. Middle

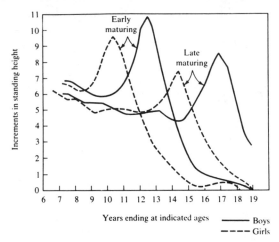

Figure 19-3. Velocity of increase in height of early-maturing and late-maturing boys and girls. (From *Human Development and Learning*, 2nd ed., by Hugh V. Perkins, © 1974 by Wadsworth Publishing Co., Inc. Used with permission of the publisher.)

adolescents are preoccupied with peer relationships, developing athletic and recreational skills, and coping with the rigors of schooling, while they seek certainty in their lives. Late adolescents are preoccupied with commitments to other people, work, and careers, as they struggle with assuming unique, independent life-styles in the face of growing awareness of the uncertainties of life.

The developmental tasks of adolescence in Western societies are to achieve independence from one's family; develop love relationships outside of one's family; achieve mastery of impulses, thoughts, and interpersonal relationships; and solidify the self. In our complex society, attaining these objectives extends into the adult years and involves considerable experimentation.

Temperament

Activity Level

The surge of hormones adds to the young person's energy level together with pro-

gressively increasing endurance. Although there are individual variations, most teenagers require far more physical activity than is programmed for them (President's Council on Physical Fitness and Sports, 1980). Particularly for the early adolescent, the requirement of passivity imposed by schooling creates sometimes unbearable physical tension.

Attention

As puberty progresses the pressures of internal sensations and imagery assume increasing importance. The younger child was distressed by external stimuli that now can be managed more efficiently. Internal stimuli, however, pose distractions that vary with the content and methods of education. This heightens the significance of personal motivation so that attention in the classroom requires inspired teaching, and concentration on homework requires self-discipline. In later adolescence the modulation of hormonal influences and the further maturation of the state regulation system bring heightened powers of concentration.

Emotions

Adolescents swing between the extremes of emotions and moods under the pleasures and frustrations hormones produce. Most significantly, the capacity for refined emotions emerges so that experiences such as awe, tenderness, empathy, assertiveness, and intellectual excitement become available as sublimated expressions of more primitive emotions. Still raw emotions break through and pose problems for the individual and other affected persons. This results in transient passions of love, hate, and misery. For most adolescents, however, these confusing upheavals are not unmanageable and stimulate further progress toward maturity and coping with uncertainty.

Cognition

The cognitive processes of adolescents have progressed to the point that symbol and concept formation occur as a matter of course. In many respects their cognitive abilities surpass those of adults who have become jaded by the continual exercise of their intellects. Adolescents accordingly excel at games involving visual-motor coordination and understanding sophisticated rules.

Language

During adolescence all of the capacities for learning and utilizing language exist. The refinement of language depends upon educational opportunities, the expectations of adults, and motivation, which reflects both personal and cultural factors.

Managerial System

The adolescent's capacity for analyzing external stimuli progressively sharpens, so that distinguishing between internal and external stimuli occurs with ease. This permits differentiating between that which is possible and that which exists. The capacity to think about thoughts, Piaget's formal operations, emerges at about the age of 11. This brings the ability to view one's internal world in a hypothetical sense, as reflected in the realization that internal experiences unavailable to conscious awareness influence behavior. The adolescent can conclude that "something made me do that" and recognize that it did not arise from external events (Selman, 1981).

The capacity for the synthesis of environmental and internal experience permits the integration of personal knowledge, so that shifts in personality may occur. Intellectualization and rationalization enable the adolescent to reconcile conflicts between impulses and reality.

The adolescent develops the ability to engage in hypothetical-deductive reasoning so that "if-so-then-so" and "either–or" types of thinking become possible. Axiomatic systems can be set up, and inferences and deductions can be made enabling logical debate (Selman, 1981). Still adolescents dream of bringing the world into line with their points of view. One factor in the distress of adolescents is the sudden decentering of their views of the world resulting from awareness that there are other viewpoints than their own. Part of the rebelliousness of adolescents is based upon their residual egocentric view that their opinions are the only valid ones (Anthony, 1982).

Alongside the adolescent's need to admire and idealize is an equally pressing need to achieve independence by challenging adult authority. Partly because they are becoming intellectually mature and partly because their insecurity demands the approval of peers, teachers, and parents, their schoolwork is extremely important to them. Consequently, they are sensitive to criticism, and their attitudes toward their work fluctuate between elation and disparagement. An often unrealized socially acceptable channel for expressing rebellion against elders and the conventions of society is through the arts, which are natural outlets for the sublimation of emotional conflicts and sexual urges. The arts provide a means for extending adolescent experience beyond the boundaries of self, family, and society by assuming adult roles that distinguish them from children (Mendelowitz, 1963).

Peer relationships are crucial to adolescents. Many teenagers live by the rule of the pack. They band together against, or at least apart from, the adult world. By separating themselves into their own subculture, they integrate their childhoods with the present and prepare to deal with the future. In the process their communications may be incomprehensible to adults.

Self

Formal operations make possible the construction of theories about oneself. This may lead to elaborate constructions of desired self-concepts. Opportunities to compare actual and desired self-concepts require consistent experiences of the self in the form of gender, student, work, personal skill, and social roles. At the same time, the rapid changes in body configuration require adjustments in body image and may cause transient preoccupation and discomfort with body features.

In separating itself from the context of the interpersonalism of the schoolwork stage, the adolescent self maintains a coherence across a shared psychological space and so achieves a sense of self-dependence and self-ownership (Kegan, 1982). In moving from "I am my relationships" to "I have relationships," there is now an "I" who is doing this having and who in coordinating or reflecting upon mutuality brings into being a separate self. A strength is the young person's new capacity for owning oneself as a teenager among peers, rather than having all the pieces of oneself owned by various roles with parents and teachers. In this strength lies a limitation, however. The self's meanings largely are derived out of the peer organization.

During adolescence the "personal fable" is a belief in one's own invulnerability. This is reflected in the belief that others grow old and die, but not me. There also remains an egocentric assumption that others share one's feelings and thoughts about oneself reflected in an "imaginary audience." Thus adolescents assume that others are as concerned as they are about their personal appearance, giving rise to world-shaking consequences. There is a tendency to assume that one's evaluations of oneself are those of others (Elkind, 1981).

The determinants of self-esteem regulation are radically transformed by the dramatic physical and cognitive changes of puberty. The approval of others shifts from significant adults to peers. The focusing of attention on one's body is associated with assessment of whether one is sufficiently attractive or strong, or masculine or feminine. Formal operations enable a new basis for self-evaluation on abstract qualities, such as comparisons with past, present, and future possibilities and evaluation of the internal world of private invisible emotions, attitudes, wishes, and secrets. The desired self-concepts lead to setting goals for oneself and guide self-evaluation. The development of a personal, attainable ethical system, reliable defenses, adaptive skills, and impulse control further enhances self-esteem (Cotton, 1983).

Supplanting adolescent egocentricity is the developing capacity for empathy. During early adolescence empathy emerges in sharing disclosures and interests with peers. Increased coordination of social interaction occurs, and peers become the source of feedback enhancing self-evaluation and self-concept (Hartrup, 1981). Through empathy an adolescent can consider the self, the other person, the inner experience of each, and the relation between the self and the other person as a third-party observer might understand it. This also results in a tendency to try to explain the thoughts, feelings, and intentions of other people (Shantz, 1975). Consciousness of the discrepancy between one's actual self-concepts and one's desired self-concepts emerges with the adolescent's ability to adopt the perspective of others (Kronick, 1981). The process of forming a coherent self is punctuated by uncertainty and confusion, as the adolescent defines and evaluates self-concepts.

Self-development is by no means completed during adolescence but continues throughout life, as outlined in Erikson's stages of the life cycle. The optimal adult level of self-development is as individuals who are known in relation to their actual or potential recognition of themselves and others as value-originating, action-generating, history-making people (Kegan, 1982). One's self is no longer limited to the mediation and control of others but expands to mediate one's own and others' needs. One has a career; one no longer is a career. The self becomes less vulnerable to the kind of ultimate humiliation, which the threat of performance failure holds out at earlier ages, for performance is no longer the ultimate. Thus a mature adult seeks information that might cause the self to alter its behavior as a part of a wider transformation made possible by accommodation to others.

SUMMARY

Children build upon developmental stages that evolve sequentially through both continuities and discontinuities from the progressive maturation of their brains. The successive sensorimotor, imagery, symbolic, conceptual, and theoretical developmental stages become interwoven to form new functional systems. During each stage a new person emerges. Thus from an initially labile state, children become increasingly stable as they learn to become more articulate, definite, and precise.

Development is a series of cognitive transformations that liberate the growing child from embeddedness in the environment. At first the infant experiences the world as an extension of the self, an extreme form of egocentricity. With progressive decentration things and persons are perceived as independent of the child's actions upon then, and knowledge is constructed about them. Ultimately the capacity for formal operations frees the child from embeddedness in the perceptual world. The realm of the possible and hypothetical is opened up so that one can appreciate one's position among the other things and people.

A child's temperament progressively becomes adaptively regulated, permitting concentration in play and work. Cognitive skills progress from simple stimulus registration to complex concept formation. Language provides the symbolic foundation for communication and knowledge acquisition. The managerial system becomes increasingly differentiated, integrated, hierarchically organized, and capable of problem-solving and automatic creative thinking. The self progresses from fragments embedded in parent and teacher relationships to a differentiated, integrated self capable of objective self-evaluation.

A metaphorical caricature of the behavioral modes that lie within us and are elaborated upon through the stages of development is to imagine that each of us contains the capacities of a frog sitting on a lily pad (somatic sensorimotor stage); a predatory wolf (imagery sensorimotor stage); a tool-making hunter and gatherer (conceptual stage); and an idealistic poet (theoretical stage). The central nervous system structures underlying these stages are available to the adolescent and await the tempering of adulthood.

In the first three years of life, the formation of images and symbolic representations of the external world are dominant issues. By the fourth and fifth years, discovery of one's internal world becomes central. Then the balance shifts again to emphasis on learning about the outer world in school. With the advent of puberty, the capacity to think about thoughts results in new intellectual achievements, but once again the internal world demands attention. Finally, with adulthood, equilibrium is established between the external and internal worlds.

The successful negotiation of the developmental stages for each child depends upon a combination of internal and external circumstances. For cognitive development and mastery of the inner and outer worlds, the indispensable elements include the intactness of sensory equipment and environmental stimulation at appropriate periods. For emotional development the progression from pleasure in bodily functions to pleasure in knowledge and skill is important. Dissonance between environmental opportunities and expectations and the capacities of a child distort development, and maladaption may occur unless a child has overriding talents. Overchallenging children prior to their developmental readiness can cause frustration and discouragement.

Parental values supporting the value of education are important. It is possible for youngsters to learn even when their parents are indifferent to academic learning, but such children possess unusual qualities. On the other hand, the manifold factors that contribute to developmental arrests can lead to school failure in spite of optimal parental support.

The development of the capacity to do schoolwork depends upon: (1) personal individuation through identification with parents; (2) developing a tolerance of frustration and a realistic view of personal power; (3) the availability of critical cognitive and language skills with temperamental qualities conducive to cooperation with adults; (4) the reasonable presentation of information that satisfies curiosity and fosters realistic knowledge; (5) the development of an effective managerial system; (6) self-esteem based upon personal achievements and mastery; and (7) the acquisition of values supporting schooling.

Our current knowledge of child development is far from complete and raises many questions about the relationship of early developmental variations to academic learning problems. A wealth of implications await investigation. Still awareness of child development is an essential foundation for understanding children's learning problems that frequently bear imprints of the vicissitudes of earlier stages of development.

The Clinical Approach to Functional Disabilities

If we treat people as if they were what they ought to be, we
help them to become what they are capable of becoming.

Johann Wolfgang Goethe, 1805

THE MOST important professional barriers to helping children with learning problems in school are the fragmentation and lack of continuity of services for them. There also is a disruptive separation of diagnostic and treatment efforts. The clinical process offers a means of surmounting these obstacles by building treatment outward from a child's understanding of one's own strengths and weaknesses to involve other systems important to that child.

The clinical process is based upon the problem-solving premise that the needs of an individual child will be understood, that services will be provided to meet them, and that services will continue until the problems are remedied. The clinical process is carried out through the formation of a team that includes the child and parents. Because particular professionals may not be able to continue as members of the team throughout the time required to resolve a child's problems, the aim is to place the child's parents in the position of understanding and advocating their child's needs with or without continuing professional support.

20

The Clinical Process

> . . . each child presents an individual problem, not only because of the diverse influence of a considerable number of environmental conditions, but also because of the relative part played by each of the three major functions—vision, audition, and kinaesthesis—varies markedly in different children as does the child's emotional reaction to his difficulty.

Samuel Torrey Orton, 1937

Because of the variety of factors that contribute to a child's academic learning problems, diagnostic evaluations should include emotional, character, family, educational, and social factors.

Children with learning problems find schoolwork frustrating, and most feel inferior and stupid. Many have symptoms, such as phobias, mood variations, temper outbursts, restlessness, insomnia, enuresis, and somatic complaints. Some even deny their school difficulties and confabulate stories of academic success (Levinson, 1980).

When children with learning difficulties improve as a result of a particular treatment, there is a tendency to use this as evidence of a particular primary cause. In fact it usually is not possible to assign primary or secondary significance to factors that contribute to children's learning problems.

The evidence upon which this book is based makes it unnecessary—in fact impossible—to think in terms of causes in either biological or psychological or primary or secondary terms. Modern scientific thinking recognizes the transactional nature of brain structures, intrapsychic conflicts, and environmental interactions. Therefore, a clear-cut distinction between biological and psychological phenomena is not scientifically possible (Kandel, 1979).

An exclusive diagnostic emphasis on a child also is inappropriate, because it implies that the causes of a child's problem lie solely within the child. Furthermore, it implies that it is necessary to locate a cause in a child in order to proceed with treatment (Lidz, 1981). Both of these assumptions ignore the fact that much can be done at different system levels to help a child who is foundering in school.

A child's academic learning problems are most realistically viewed in the context of that child's personal qualities and life experiences. This means that an understanding of them involves a series of hierarchical levels: the society, the school, the classroom, the peer group, the family, and the individual (Becvar & Becvar, 1982). Because learning problems usually are identified by adults, not the children, our attention naturally is drawn to the social and interpersonal contexts in which a child is having difficulty. It therefore makes a difference whether a particular boy is identified as having a problem because he is failing in school and lives in an unstable home, because he is disruptive in his classroom, because his parents are dissatisfied with his school grades, or because he asks for help with schoolwork. The difficulty at one system level may be largely related to a higher or lower system level. Thus a family's difficulty may result from social conditions, a child's frustrations from family interactions, and a child's difficulty with schoolwork from inefficient brain functioning.

Rather than searching for an elusive single learning disability in these children, a more theoretically sound and practical approach is to help children discover their weaknesses and strengths in schoolwork with the assistance of parents, teachers, siblings, and clinicians. In so doing the clinical process can be used to apply scientific knowledge to the problems of each of these children. The clinical process is a method originally developed in the health-care system in order to understand and resolve complicated human problems. As science advances knowledge, the clinical process also permits appropriate adjustments in practices.

Before proceeding to a description of the clinical process, the role of a clinical system deserves special attention. If systems surrounding a child were functioning efficiently, a clinician would not be needed. Thus the clinical system is called upon to alter aspects of other systems and, necessarily, is a foreign body to them. The clinician's role, therefore, is to become a temporary part of systems pertinent to a child's problems. For this reason the success of clinical interventions depends upon the extent to which the clinical system merges around a problem area with the systems to be assisted. Without a merging of systems, clinicians may be perceived as inimical to the system needing help. That merging must be partial and temporary, however, or else the systems to be helped may become dependent upon the clinical system.

This chapter describes a comprehensive clinical evaluation with recognition that all of the details are seldom applicable to a particular case. In the clinical process, a complete developmental, medical, and family history is obtained, supplemented by health and school data, including examinations of vision and hearing, psychological testing, developmental assessments, educational achievement tests, teachers' observations, clinical interviews, and other appropriate diagnostic procedures (Mosse, 1982). The details of a child's school successes, failures, and reactions in each subject in each grade help to gauge the extent of a child's difficulty with schoolwork.

Each clinician develops a style and procedure, which permit an assessment of the different responses that children show to that structure. The role of the clinician is less carrying out tests that reveal answers and more integrating and synthesizing information obtained from a variety of sources (Barkley, 1981; Lidz, 1981; Weil, 1977).

The clinical process can be divided into an interviewing stage with history-taking and examination components; an investigative stage consisting of educational assessment, psychological assessment, general medical evaluation, vision assessment, neurological evaluation, medical laboratory procedures, and genetic evaluation; and, finally, a treatment-planning stage.

THE CLINICAL INTERVIEW WITH CHILD AND FAMILY

Interviewing is both an art and a science. It is an art when an interviewer can put people at ease and sense their hidden concerns. It is a science when an interviewer employs techniques, such as encouraging free expression without influencing it.

The actual conduct of an interview depends upon whether or not one is using a playroom, an office with play facilities, or a place without children's materials, where paper and pencil may be the best one can offer. Optimally the interviewing environment should be comfortable for all ages. An office with the atmosphere of a living room stocked with play materials offers the most flexible enviroment for achieving rapport with persons of all ages.

The interview should have structured and unstructured phases over a period of several continuous hours. Most of the interviewing is largely unintrusive and sensitive to nonverbal communication and underlying attitudes. This enhances the expression of ideas and feelings that accurately reflect the persons' concerns rather than what they perceive the interviewer wants or does not want to hear.

The clinical interview has both diagnostic and therapeutic elements that run throughout the interviewing process. The aim is the enlightenment of the clinician and parents, but most importantly the child. Bearing these themes in mind is helpful since even inquiry about the presenting problems contains therapeutic elements, as parents are encouraged to formulate their concerns in the presence of their children. The experience of giving a history in itself helps parents develop a perspective on their child's problems. Throughout the interviewing process, then, there is a useful reframing of problems and relationships that gradually shifts the emphasis from the search for a professional who will cure a child to a collaborative team effort involving child, parents, and professionals. More specifically, the individual interview with the child may well be the first time that child has ever openly expressed feelings and in itself promotes a new level

of self-awareness. The interviewing process can be a rich experience for all.

The Family Interview

Since a child is the dependent part of at least a child–parent unit, a complete evaluation depends upon knowledge of a child's family. The evaluation of the family includes interactions with the entire family, subsystems within the family, and individuals alone. This can be accomplished by initially assembling the family and proceeding through various combinations with emphasis on the individual interview with the child, and closing by reconvening the family for gathering additional information and sharing impressions.

In some instances, particularly with teenagers, rapport may be facilitated by seeing the young person first after the initial family discussion and before talking with the parents. This is especially helpful when it is evident that the young person feels scapegoated and, therefore, might feel accepted and understood by being the first one to speak privately with the clinician. Depending upon circumstances siblings also can be seen individually or as a group.

Much valuable information about parent and sibling influences is missed if the entire family is not included in aspects of the interviewing process. Seeing the family together initially while defining the presenting problems helps convey the message that a child's problems can be discussed openly. This is a particularly important first step in reducing the embarrassment, shame, and guilt often experienced by children and their parents.

During the initial phase of the interview, the clinician should ascertain the names the children prefer to be called, explain the procedure, and invite family members to describe their views of the problems they would like to work on. The wording of this initial inquiry is useful in shifting the family's expectations from those of receiving a cure from the clinician to collaborating in a joint effort to resolve the problems. The complaints elicited from each family member usually center around the referred child and may vary considerably in emphasis. As one father put it, "I want a button to press that will cure my child." For this reason asking the family what they would like "to work on" sets the tone for later treatment plans.

When pictures of each family member's perspective and expectations are obtained, the clinician can draw from them and clarify the reasons for the evaluation. It is important to describe the problems in terms that the child can understand. The presenting problems should be recorded in the words of the child and other family members and characterized as to onset, frequency, intensity, precipitating circumstances, associated problems, and response to prior treatment. During this phase of the interview, rapport can be established with each family member in order to facilitate their cooperation in discussing personal matters.

Valuable information can be obtained from the ways family members accommodate to the surroundings, seat themselves, and respond to each other. As the interview progresses, observation of all of the family members together reveals verbal and nonverbal interaction patterns. Observations can be made on the interactions of family members and on the child's alertness, attentiveness, perceptiveness, emotional states, and responses to limits. An orderly approach is justified in order to ensure coverage of important topics and to provide a reasonably standard interviewing process that facilitates comparison with other children and families.

Depending upon how rapport with family members develops, parts of the family can be seen next. Most preadolescent children respond with relief to leaving the office, while the parents are seen to obtain developmental, family, and marital histories. While waiting children can do such things as Draw-A-Person and Draw-A-Family, and parents can respond to questionnaires such as the Lewis Parental Relationship Questionnaire (Lewis, 1979). A brief autobiography written by a parent provides information and a handwriting sample.

The history taking is facilitated by reviewing previous records and reports in addition to a previously completed parent questionnaire devoted to behavioral, demographic, family history, developmental, and school performance matters. The use of a baby book is helpful in verifying developmental landmarks and providing clues as to the emotional and social climate of the family during the child's early life. The details of the early history of pregnancy, labor, birth, and development may reveal both significant data and that inordinate weight has been given to events, such as a mother's fall during pregnancy, and thereby identify smoldering parental guilt.

The history should include significant illnesses; accidents, particularly head traumas; hospitalizations, including age, duration, and the child's response to them; medications; allergies and diet, with particular attention to associations between specific items, such as refined sugars and behavior. The family history is especially important in identifying possible genetic factors in a child's problems. When it appears to be implicated, time should be set aside to detail the family pedigree. The school histories of parents and relatives are particularly important. The background of each parent should be elicited and the history of the marriage outlined with particular sensitivity to marital problems, environmental stresses, and changes in residence, as they relate to the development of the child. The parents' aspirations for, and views of, their child should be explored in addition to sibling relationships.

Obtaining a personality profile of the

child can be done by inquiring about hobbies, athletic interests, recreational preferences, and peer relation patterns. Evidence of personality change should be sought. A description of a typical day in the child's life can be revealing, even in its sparsity. This should include a picture of the child's living arrangements at home and the amount of time spent with parents. It also should explicate the child's life in school, particularly special education components and the child's reaction to them.

The child's school history should be taken as the cumulative school records are reviewed. Particular note should be made of trends in academic achivement, behavioral observations, the impact of specific teachers, and the child's attitude toward school. Attention should be devoted to the observations of previous teachers to elicit evidence of both the child's weaknesses and strengths. Previous efforts to help the child and the results should be noted.

A review of body systems screens for problems that may not seem directly relevant to the presenting complaints. Specific inquiry should be made about headaches, sleep disturbances, weight loss or gain, enuresis, encopresis, seizures, clumsiness, hearing and visual difficulties, phobias, depression, anxiety, and hyperkinesis. Optimally this should be done with both the parents and the child.

In evaluating families care must be taken to consider the cultural and socioeconomic context in which the family lives. Each family should be viewed against the cultural realities rather than romanticized images of families. Healthy families strike a balance between antagonism and love in their intimate relationships.

Degrees of success or failure in the paired family roles of husband and wife, father and mother, parent and child, and child and sibling bear directly on the adaptation of family members. Despite distortions of their individual personalities, parents may interact in such a way that their children are not especially affected. At the same time, relatively healthy parents may interact pathologically and adversely affect their children.

The major areas of emphasis in assessing a family are control, communication, individuation, coping patterns, and the progress of both the family in its development cycle and of each individual's personal development (Westman, 1984):

1. *Control.* The most important issue in a family is the overt and covert distribution of power. In most families power over its members largely resides within the family unit, although disorganized families lack internal controls and find themselves brought under external sources of control, such as courts and social agencies. In healthy families the power usually is shared by the parents, who cooperate in maintaining the stability and goal directedness of the family. In assessing this dimension, the role of each family member in the power structure should be determined. Measures of the family control system are the intensity of overt conflicts and the presence of covert, manipulative maneuvers.

2. *Communication patterns.* Because communication depends upon both the sender and the receiver of messages, the amount of talking in a family is less important than its expressive tone, which may be critical, complaining, or sarcastic and strongly influences how verbal messages are received. Nonverbal communications are the most important indicators of underlying attitudes, power patterns, feelings and perceptions.

A particular form of communication prominent in a variety of troubled families is the "double bind." This relational pattern consists of conflicting verbal and nonverbal messages, which cannot be acknowledged or resolved, occurring in a situation from which the receiver cannot escape.

3. *Individuation of family members.* As a

child-rearing and personal support system, the family can both meet dependency needs and foster the autonomy of its individual members. The maturity of each family member influences the degree to which that person contributes to, or impedes, the individuation of other family members. Under optimal circumstances mutual validation of each family member as a lovable and valued person is achieved.

The quantitative closeness of family members in shared activities can be readily assessed by inquiring about them. The more critical quality of family relationships is reflected in the degree of intimacy shared among family members. Particular care should be devoted to assessing whether a family's "togetherness" squelches or promotes individuation. Under circumstances in which all or certain kinds of emotions cannot be expressed, family members cannot learn how to identify, accept, and manage their feelings. Brothers and sisters and parents and children are mutually dependent but also are in opposition to, or in competition with, one another.

4. *Coping ability.* The coping abilities of a family depend most heavily upon the adult members. The most obvious forms of coping are with the practical economic and social problems of life in modern society. Each family casts an image of relative competency in the neighborhood and community. Although often related, coping ability in the affairs of the world may not reflect coping ability within the family. The ability to manage stress in the form of change or loss further reflects a family's coping ability. Disruption of a marriage imposes the the stress of divorce and living rearrangements on many families. Job and neighborhood changes also can be stressors.

A family's ability to resolve its internal problems is reflected in family decision making, such as in child rearing and the ability to recognize and address sources of tension and dissatisfaction in family members. The family's excessive use of defense mechanisms, such as denial, projection and displacement, obfuscates open, intelligible communication and results in faulty decision making.

The values held by a family also influence its coping ability. A family low in aspirations does not place a high value upon achievement by either the adults or children. Another factor is whether a family's values are compatible with dominant social values. Contemporary families tend to be characterized by a lack, rather than an excess, of values.

5. *Developmental state of the family.* All of the foregoing factors influence how a family progresses through its life cycle and meets its developmental tasks. The initial developmental task of a marriage is to manage disengagement successfully from each family of origin and reorder commitments to old friends, social activities, and career involvements. A second developmental task is to create an affectionate, empathic marital relationship in which ensuing children can prosper. During the adolescence and young adulthood of the children, the developmental task is to sustain integrated family life in the face of intergenerational value, communication, and dependency conflicts.

The Interview with the Child

The clinician's first responsibility is to establish rapport with the child. This begins at the initial point of contact, when a specific greeting to the child is important. Whatever interviewing structure is employed, a child responds to the place and behavior of the examiner in addition to the imagined or perceived reactions of parents and siblings.

Children should be informed about the purpose of the interview. They are less anxious when they feel like partners with the clinician in the attempt to solve their problems. Children are sensitive to non-verbal communication—to a smile, a touch on the shoulder, or a soft tone of voice. The conveyance of empathy to a child is essential in establishing rapport. These children have experienced many frustrating and disappointing failures that have eroded their self-evaluations. Accordingly, warmth and acceptance from the examiner during the initial phase of the interview are important; however, overly friendly behavior may obscure the manner in which the child forms new relationships.

The interview initially should be conducted in a spirit of easiness and enthusiasm in order to establish a dialogue with the child in a process of mutual discovery (Werkman, 1965). By making it absorbing and pleasant, the clinician can help the child to see the interview as an important experience.

The interview offers unique access to the personal worlds of children (Greenspan, 1981). Once their modes of communication are understood, children usually are straightforward in sharing their thoughts and feelings. They communicate by the way in which they look at—or avoid looking at—the clinician, the style and depth of their personal relatedness, their moods, the variety and types of their emotions, the way they negotiate space, and the themes they develop in talk and play.

The challenge for the clinician is to know when to step in and help a child communicate and when to stay out of the child's way. Thus the clinician must see, hear, and sense the data a child provides. These observations range from initial informal interactions in the hallway to formal interviewing procedures.

The aim of the evaluation is to determine how a child experiences the world at the current stage of development. In so doing it is important not only to assess the problem that precipitated the evaluation, but also how the child functions generally, the level of character development the

child has achieved, and how that level compares with age expectations.

Greenspan (1981) suggested a framework for the systematic observation of a child applicable in any setting, whether at home, in school, or in a clinic (see Figure 20-1). The first category is related to the coping abilities of the child. The second category concerns how the child relates to the examiner and other persons during the evaluation. The third category is the emotional tone of the child during the evaluation. The fourth concerns the specific anxieties that are elaborated during the clinical interview. The fifth category includes the themes that appear to underlie the child's behavior. Simmons (1981) provides a detailed description of a variety of methods for interviewing difficult and young children.

Unstructured Interview

The individual interview with the child can be initiated after the parent interview by having the child show the clinician the drawings made while the child was waiting during the parent interview. Then a period of unstructured play provides an informal view of the child. Since the child already has some familiarity with the office, the child can be invited to explore the play materials further. The unstructured play can be observed with particular note of its characteristics, such as persistence, repetitiveness, ingenuity, age and sex appropriateness, competitiveness, orderliness, themes, and intensity (Greenspan, 1979a).

When a separate playroom is used for interviewing, an explanation of the rules of the playroom after observing the child's initial reaction may be important: for example, that the child is free to play, speak and do as the child wishes, with the addition for some children that this does not include hurting the playroom, the examiner, or oneself. It is important to ensure that the playroom is well stocked with age-

Age	Coping Anxieties	Interpersonal Relationships	Emotional Tone	Core Anxieties	Thematic Level of Fantasies
1	Motor and speech milestones	Symbiotic	Pleasure-distress Variable	Global annihilation	Chaotic Pleasure-exploration Protest
2	Walking Talking	Individuation	Some mood stability	Loss of love of parent	Polarities of love and hate, good and bad, passivity and activity
3	Symbolic play Personal pronouns Internal parent images	Power struggles—shifting between autonomy and dependence	More differentiated love, sadness, and envy under sway of hunger, tiredness	Loss of love and loss of acceptance and approval	Fragmented themes repeat experiences Joy in mastery, power, and exploration
4	Self-regulation and brief concentration possible Self-concept building	Triangular relationships with parents and siblings Peer relations beginning	Moods stabilizing Emerging empathy Pride, shame, and humiliation	Loss of approval and fear of bodily injury	Symbolic themes in play Make believe distinct from but can dominate reality Power, control, security Curiosity, admiration Magic, Monsters
5 6	Drawing pictures Reading beginning Self-image clearly differs from others	Complex triangles in family Relates to peers and teachers Has capacity for separation	Moods stable Empathy and love; however, jealousy and hurt easily aroused Mortification	Loss of respect and approval Fear of bodily injury Self-evaluation produces guilt Mortification because of mistakes or peer reactions	Rich, complex, organized symbolic themes Can be swept away by fantasy, particularly at night Triangular themes of being left out, getting rid of parents Curiosity about bodies, secrets
7 8	Reading and writing Logical ideas Orderly sense of world Concentration	Peer relations expanding Best friend Games and rules	Stable moods Empathy Pleasure in mastery Discouragement with failure, but can persevere	Signal anxiety can be disruptive and lead to reaction formations Sensitive to peer disapproval Self-evaluation, self-respect and guilt	Shift of themes from extremes of control to balance to morality Organized cultural themes
9 10	Writing of ideas Athletic skills Logic dominates fantasy Self-control Follow instructions	Identifying with role models of same gender Best friends	Moodiness emerging Excitement and shyness in gender roles Capacity for sadness and loss of self-respect	Signal anxiety generally not disruptive and handled by sublimation and rationalization Sensitive to self and peer evaluations	Well-organized stories with social roles What I will be; aspirations Jokes Getting around rules Smugness of cognitive conceit Dominance-submission Sadism-masochism

Figure 20-1. Assessment framework for clinical interview of a child. (Adapted from S. I. Greenspan, *The Clinical Interview of the Child*, McGraw-Hill Book Co., New York. Used with permission.)

appropriate materials and not in disarray. For some preadolescents and most adolescents, the unstructured segment of the interview can be devoted to a discussion of interests and activities.

The development of themes takes place in verbal and nonverbal ways through drawing, playing, and other activities. Themes reveal the child's characterological structure as well as specific conflictual areas and provide clues regarding treatment. Note should be made of a theme's organization, richness, sequence, and relevance.

The organization of a theme is reflected in the logical links or lack of them between thematic elements. A theme's richness and depth are expressed in the degree to which a child can develop a story before encountering blocks that impede the unfolding of the story. The thematic sequence contains clues to a child's concerns and core issues as well as to the kinds of defenses the child uses against those concerns. A theme's age-appropriate relevance signals both the age level from which the child's conflicts may derive and how maturely the child handles those conflicts. Observations regarding these thematic elements in the context of the child's age allow developing hypotheses about a child's characterological structure and central conflicts, as illustrated in Figure 20-1 (Greenspan, 1981).

The mental status examination consists of observations combined with inquiry to assess a child's appearance, behavior, emotional state, manner and content of speech, orientation in time and space, memory, attention, insight, judgment, abstracting ability, and intelligence (Sonis & Costello, 1981).

A child's posture, gait, balance, tone of voice, flow of speech, level of voluntary and involuntary body movements, speech articulation, pencil grasp, drawing ability, and evidence of weakness of a body part can be observed. Particular note should be made of unusual mannerisms and speech patterns, such as echolalia or avoidance of personal pronouns. The intensity, speed, persistence, and adaptability of a child's reactions are important. A child's approach–withdrawal tendencies, threshold of responsiveness to stimuli, attention span, and distractibility also can be noted.

The use of the environment—first the waiting room and then the office or playroom—reveals how children integrate different elements in their lives. For example, some children take in all of the space from the beginning, then move around to a few different areas and ultimately synthesize them by creating a little world for themselves. Other children stay in a corner for the entire interview. Others impulsively touch many things in the room, but never relate to any one thing.

An assessment of how a child relates to other persons involves observing how the child treats the clinician as a person, how the relationship develops, and how differentiated it is. This begins from the first moment of contact and includes noting differences in the child's behavior when with the family and when alone. The child's eye contact and reactions to others as compared with play materials are important.

It is useful to distinguish between the clinician's objective and subjective evaluation of a child's mood, or sustained, pervasive feeling tone. The objective manifestations can be observed in the child's behavior and speech while engaging in unstructured play; the subjective are the feelings induced in the clinician. Examples of moods are irritable, depressed, and hypomanic, which may be objectively displayed through grouchy, morose, and flighty external appearances. Any discrepancy between what is observed and the clinician's subjective response suggests that the child's mood is more complicated than might be apparent.

The appropriateness of emotional displays is less easily determined in children than in adults (Goodman & Sours, 1967).

Many children smile in response to fear and tension. There is a type of smile, however, that lingers on a child's face and is accompanied by an averted gaze. This so-called "inner smile" may be a harbinger of serious internal distortions. The flexibility and appropriateness of the child's emotional display with play material should be noted in addition to the child's expressions of fearfulness, listlessness, sadness, enthusiasm, or anger.

Assessing the degree of anxiety in children is a special matter. Anxious children are apt to be irritable, restless, clowning, or disruptive. A child's anxiety may be expressed through motor activity as well as apathy, and anger may be expressed by withdrawal and inappropriate smiling or joke making. A youngster with a "slow to warm up" temperament may appear to be apprehensive. Anxiety may cause disruption of an ongoing style of relating or in the development of a theme. The disruption of a theme may suggest where the child's anxiety lies and how the child copes with it, such as by becoming disorganized or quickly changing the subject.

The Structured Interview

Structured interviewing is designed to obtain information regarding a child's subjective emotional state, somatic symptoms, sleep, eating and elimination patterns, worries, day and night dreams, depersonalization, thinking patterns, accuracy of the analysis of reality, and self-evaluation. At the same time, it is an opportunity to help a child understand why the evaluation is taking place and to build rapport as a basis for later interventions.

The purpose of the structured interview is to find out how the child experiences oneself and the world. The emphasis is upon the child's revelation of personal characteristics, inner thoughts, and feelings. This means that both clinician and child venture into the ill defined.

Useful topics to cover are the reasons for the evaluation, recreational and hobby interests, the child's neighborhood, the social and cultural background, peer relationships, family relationships, plans for the future, general health, fantasies and fears, social awareness, and schoolwork.

The clinician can facilitate a child's expressiveness with encouraging, repeating, and clarifying comments. Since children often need help in finding words for expressing their feelings and thoughts, offering a selection of words from which the child can choose is helpful. The clinician can support the elaboration of a child's communications.

In general it is desirable to obtain as much information as possible without asking "What?" or "Why?," both of which evoke associations with pedagogy and interrogation. The answer "I don't know" can be anticipated, particularly with "why's." The admonition in the *Little Prince* put it well:

> Grownups never understand anything by themselves, and it is tiresome for children to be always and forever explaining things to them (de Saint-Exupery, 1943).

Unlike adults, children often need license to express their feelings and attitudes, particularly those they regard as embarrassing or shameful. They may need comments as, "Older brothers can be a real nuisance; how is yours?" Using the third person also may be helpful: "Sometimes a girl might feel sad about that." Younger children may speak more easily by describing animals they wish they were or through puppets.

Specific inquiry should be made about a child's ideas of problem areas and why professional help is being sought. Their expectations should be brought out. In so doing an explanation of the clinician's role can be given, along with the perspective that many other children are seen for similar reasons. Using an example known to the child also is helpful in verifying that other children have similar difficulties.

A child's self-evaluation can be elicited through inquiry about what, if anything, the child would like to change about oneself. Children's fantasies about the causes of their learning problems range from feeling they are stupid to being punished for sins and even of being possessed by the devil. It is important to bring out these fantasies so that an appropriate explanation of the child's difficulties can be made. Some children also profit from an explanation of the different parts of the brain and how brain functions develop at different rates and to different degrees. Viewing these as individual variations can help the child shift from feeling bad, defective, or stupid. The child needs to know that causes are often unclear, just as one has difficulty explaining why some children can run faster or sing better than others. But as with running and singing, knowing a cause is less important than realizing that the child can improve.

Questions about favorite people, relationships with peers and teachers, and places the child would like to see shed light on the child's desired self-concept. Inquiry about body functions calls forth information about body image.

In exploring a child's thinking processes, inquiry about hopes, fears, suspicions, worries, hallucinations, delusions, ideas that other's are referring to them, and that they or others can tamper with the thoughts of other people is useful, with particular note of emotional reactions to responses. The assessment of thinking includes information about where the child falls on a continuum of rational–sequential versus intuitive–holistic thinking styles. Some children take rational, orderly, language–oriented, time-related approaches to their schoolwork. At the other extreme are children who appear to be less organized and verbal but more intuitive and

unconcerned about time. Children also differ in their use of auditory, verbal, and visual-spatial imagery in their fantasies.

The fantasies and dreams of children tend to be less distorted than those of adults. Some children who are unable to relate dreams can draw a picture of a dream and tell a story about it. Fantasy can be explored by asking a child to describe daydreams with inquiry as to whether they involve pretending.

Particular attention should be devoted to eliciting dominant fantasies that express immature preoccupations and serve defensive purposes. For example, some children harbor notions of omnipotence and omniscience by imagining that they are magical young children who never had to grow up, as was Peter Pan. Others achieve similar satisfaction from leaping into powerful adult roles, such as superman or superwoman. To learn about these fantasies, children can be asked if they like to pretend they are younger or are superheroes.

Orientation can be ascertained from a child's age-appropriate knowledge of self in time, place, and circumstances. Immediate precategorical memory can be tested by the repetition of digits, short-term memory by recall of neutral items mentioned earlier in the interview, and long-term memory by a child's ability to remember details of a recent birthday or summer vacation. Concentration can be evaluated by counting backward from 100 by sevens or threes or reciting the alphabet in reverse order. It also can be generally noted throughout the interview.

A child's level of insight can be estimated from awareness of the reasons for the evaluation. Judgment can be assessed by answers to questions such as, "What would you do if you smelled smoke in a movie theater?" It also is reflected in a child's descriptions of life events. Abstracting ability can be tested by the age-appropriate interpretation of proverbs and similarities between objects. An assessment

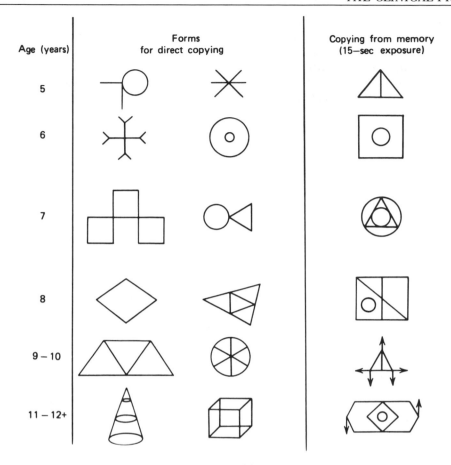

Figure 20-2. To assess visual-spatial-motor function, a child is asked to copy these forms using a pencil and unlined paper. The child should be asked to work carefully and repeat an inaccurate drawing in order to evaluate practice and effort factors. (From M. D. Levine, R. Brooks, and J. P. Shonkoff, *A Pediatric Approach to Learning Disorders,* copyright 1980 by John Wiley and Sons, New York. Reproduced with permission.)

of conceptualizing ability in addition to word finding ability can be made by asking a child to name other objects that fit into a category of things that are good to eat, such as bread and meat.

Intelligence can be estimated through conversation that explores a child's vocabulary, depth of knowledge, and problem-solving ability. Academic skill level can be estimated by engaging in reading and arithmetical tasks, with particular emphasis

on the child's subjective responses to unfamiliar material and errors. Draw-A-Person, Draw-A-Family, and writing sentences to dictation, spontaneously, and by copying them, can give thematic, cognitive, and language information. Copying designs can give an impression of visual-motor ability (see Figure 20-2).

As a part of the initial interview, a sensory and motor neurological screening examination should include the imitation of finger movements as a means of assessing the child's ability to orient motor actions to another person. This also reveals mirror movements, dyskinesias, and poor finger localization. Graphesthesia can be tested by a child's capacity to interpret sensory configurations on the skin, such as numbers on the tips of the fingers. Stereognosis can be assessed by the ability to recognize a shape without seeing it in one's hand and visual tracking by the ability of the eyes to pursue a moving target.

Gross motor abilities include a child's facility in moving through space, the capacity to enact motor tasks, and the capacity to sustain body position and interpret ongoing feedback during a motor act. This is assessed through heel and toe walking, standing on one foot, and rapid alternating movements.

Motor stance is a child's capacity to sustain a total body posture for a period of time through selective inhibition, task persistence, body position, and motor stamina. To assess this a child is asked to stand with feet together and hands stretched out with fingers spread widely apart, eyes closed, and tongue stuck out for ten seconds. This also reveals choreiform twitches of the outstretched fingers and tongue. The presence of a primitive vestibular postural reflex can be tested by turning the child's head to each side and noting whether or not the rest of the body follows. Cerebellar functioning can be assessed by the child's ability to touch, with eyes closed, the tip of the forefinger to the tip of the nose.

The acts of catching and throwing a ball entail the ability to judge visual-spatial relationships and to program a motor response based upon them. Visual-fine motor function can be assessed through copying figures with a pencil (see Figure 20-2). Associated movements, awkward pencil grip, motor dyspraxia in which the child has difficulty directing the pencil, finger agnosia, and poor eye-hand coordination thereby are revealed.

Terminating the Interview with the Child

At the end of the interview, it is important for the clinician to summarize and comment upon the findings in order to help the child consolidate the interview as a therapeutic experience, particularly if it had painful aspects. This sets the stage for subsequent contacts with the child. Observing how a child prepares for and deals with the ending of the interview is helpful, particularly with regard to putting away play materials and leaving the room. A child's comments, eagerness, or reluctance to leave and parting gestures, or lack of them, can reveal underlying attitudes previously unexpressed.

The clinician's feelings and fantasies during the interview can be helpful. From the clinician's point of view, a seductive child may invigorate, a sad child may leave one drained, an anxious child may make one tense or bored, an angry child may evoke anger, and a controlling child may be frustrating. The fleeting thoughts and subjective reactions of the clinician during the interview are significant, because they probably have been evoked by covert aspects of the child.

Interpretation of Findings

At the conclusion of the interview with the child, a useful technique is to ask the child to help the clinician explain what has been discovered to the parents. The child usually is reluctant to do so but agrees when it is made clear that the clinician will help. The child's responses assist the clinician in assessing the child's insight and motivation to change. The clinician can assist the child and then elaborate upon the points brought out, checking with the child for verification.

It is helpful in setting the stage for treatment that the clinician draw upon the immediate experience of the child and family during the interview to illustrate problem areas, so that the clinical formulations begin with the family's level of understanding rather than abstractions that have no immediate meaning to the family members. This approach also reinforces the theme that the clinician is not the source of change for the child but can form an alliance with the child and family in their pursuit of change.

It is essential that enough time be set aside for interpreting the clinical findings to the parents and child in order to satisfy their immediate questions. Three steps are helpful in achieving this. The first is devoted to highlighting the findings immediately following the clinical interview. Second, another meeting described later in this chapter is held to review the results of the evaluation in detail with the parents and child. Third, a follow-up meeting is held to review the findings and establish a definitive treatment plan with the parents and representatives of the child's school. This process permits the family to react to and digest the findings, and also helps the clinician assess the degree to which counseling or intensive family therapy will be needed in the treatment program.

The following case is an illustration of the initial interviewing process:

The Smith family was seen because their ten-year-old son Tom was severely underachieving in school. The family consisted of an accountant father; a homemaking mother; a 14-year-old daughter, Susan; the ten-year-old identified patient; an eight-year-old daughter, Jane; and a four-year-old son, Billy.

The family arrived late for the initial appointment because of Tom's procrastination. When seen together the mother and Tom sat close to each other on the sofa. The father sat opposite, apart from Susan and Billy. The clinician explained the evaluation process and asked what the family would like to work on. The mother

did the talking while the others sat glumly. As the interview progressed, Billy took up a dart gun and was admonished by both the mother and father not to point it at people. Although the mother spoke the most, the content of her complaints suggested that the father wielded the power in the family.

When seen together without the children, the parents divulged their belief that birth trauma had produced brain damage in Tom so that he had lagged behind since entering school. They described their marriage as satisfactory.

When seen alone Tom revealed his depressed, hopeless feelings, although he initially denied having difficulty with schoolwork and felt that the other kids were against him. Tom's family drawing placed him in a remote corner and his drawing of his father had numerous erasures. His draw-a-person was a vaguely identified girl. His reading level was two grades below the expected level for his age and intelligence. When he discovered that his brain was playing tricks on him by not recognizing words that he knew, he became curious about why and revealed the panic that he experienced when he made reading mistakes.

When Susan, Jane, and Billy were seen together, they rapidly engaged with the play materials appropriate to their ages. They agreed that Tom was lazy and did not try to do his schoolwork. Susan pointed out that he had no friends because he always had to have his own way. Billy blurted out that his daddy didn't love his mommy. They all agreed that they were afraid their parents would get a divorce.

When seen alone the mother acknowledged frustration with her husband's coldness and explosive temper. When seen alone the father revealed his frustration with work pressures and acknowledged that he had lost sexual interest in his wife long ago.

At the conclusion of the interview, Tom told his parents that his brain played tricks on him, and the clinician shared his impression that Tom's school difficulties resulted from the interplay of cognitive, intrapsychic, family, educational and peer-based factors. Mrs. Smith embraced the suggestion of family therapy as a means of sorting out these factors; however, Mr. Smith did not comment. Both parents did agree, however, to return for further discussion of treatment possibilities.

THE INVESTIGATIVE STAGE

The stage of formal investigation can follow or be integrated with the clinical interviewing stage. In some settings the clinical interviews are followed by referrals to other clinical disciplines. In other settings an interdisciplinary team is organized to carry out coordinated assessment batteries, with referral to other disciplines when indicated. The complicated nature of these cases favors an interdisciplinary approach, since it often is not possible initially to predict the relevance of a particular discipline to a specific child.

Although the terms evaluation and assessment are often used interchangeably, a useful distinction can be made between them (Lidz, 1981). Evaluation refers to clinical judgments about a child, including information obtained through the history, present observations, clinical interviews, laboratory procedures, and assessment procedures. Assessment refers to gathering specific data, usually from tests, to which a comparative value can be assigned, as for the purpose of determining eligibility for categorical school programs.

In all testing an important fact must be taken into account in addition to whether or not a child seems to be cooperative. When a child is tested, the tester assumes that the test given to the child is the task to which the child is responding. However, it is possible that the child has an entirely different view of the task. For example,

because of past failures, a child's task may be to get the excruciating experience over with as quickly as possible. or the child's task may not be seeing how well a test can be performed, but how badly it can be failed (Coles, 1983).

The ingredients of a comprehensive evaluation include developmental assessment, educational assessment, psychological assessment, medical evaluation, vision assessment, neurological evaluation, electrophysiological procedures, radiological techniques, and genetic evaluation. Each section is described to provide a general picture of the discipline's approach.

Developmental Assessment

There are three levels of developmental assessment for children. The first is screening. The second is diagnostic, of which the Pediatric Examination for Education Readiness is an example. The third is definitive evaluation in a multidisciplinary setting (Levine & Schneider, 1982). The clinical interview with the child usually is focused at the screening level.

Formal developmental assessment should be done by clinicians trained in child development and the administration of standardized testing batteries. The general limitations of testing apply, such as the child's degree of test-taking rapport and motivation, variations in performance from day to day, and the influence of anxiety in the testing setting. Most important, there are many reasons why a child may do poorly on a particular task. Consequently, each item on a developmental examination contains a differential diagnosis to account for performance on it. Impulsive children may perform carelessly on tests and should be asked to think and talk about a task before executing it. Conversely a child's success on a task may be misleading. For example, previous practice may account for the correct copying of a geometric form.

There are significant dangers in overreliance on developmental assessment for educational purposes because of socioeconomic and cultural factors. What constitutes educational readiness varies from one community to the next. Thus local norms are essential in evaluating the significance of findings (Levine & Schneider, 1982). A useful means of comparing children with their local peers is through observation of their behavior in groups. A rating scale for linguistic and peer play behavior has been devised for this purpose (Sherman et al, 1983).

General Developmental Assessment Instruments

Many behavioral and physiological measures are available for the assessment of early infant competence. Some are indicators of an infant's current status but poor predictors of later performance. Others show promise of greater predictive power. Most electrophysiological techniques assessing subtle differences in brain functioning are too new to have been used in longitudinal assessments. They can identify abnormalities during infancy, however, it is uncertain which abnormalities in young infants would be correlated with learning disabilities if the infants were followed longitudinally into childhood.

The Neonatal Behavioral Assessment Scale was created to evaluate a newborn's capacity to respond to the environment and to document state, autonomic, and affective changes that accompany responses to interpersonal stimuli (Brazelton, 1973). It assesses such behavior as habituation, attention preferences, and focusing attention. The behavior of infants also can be observed to assess their autonomic, motor, state, attention, regulatory, and adaptive functions (A1s, 1985).

The Pediatric Examination for Educational Readiness is designed for four- to six-year-old children; however, the areas it covers apply to older children with learning problems as well. It assesses developmental attainment, neurological maturation, selective attention and information-processing efficiency, the rapport and involvement of the child with the tests, task analysis, and physical status. The Pediatric Early Elementary Examination (PEEX) is a similar instrument adapted to children from seven to nine years of age (Levine, 1983). Other useful instruments for formal developmental assessment are listed in Figure 20-3.

Specific Information Processing Assessment

The efficiency with which children process visual and auditory information is particularly important in learning academic skills. The ingredients of these processes follow developmental courses and are subject to significant individual differences. Commonly used instruments for assessing perceptual and motor functions are listed in Figure 20-4.

Auditory Information Processing. When auditory acuity has been established as normal or appropriately corrected, a series of specific sound processing functions can be assessed (Johnson, 1967). Significant individual differences are found in these receptive and expressive auditory processing functions. Because auditory stimuli always are received sequentially, the assessment of any auditory function involves memory, unlike visual functions, which take place simultaneously.

Auditory attention is the ability to identify an auditory stimulus in competition with increasing intensities of distracting sounds and can be measured by the Goldman-Fristoe-Auditory Selective Attention Test. Particular attention should be given to a child's ability to distinguish voice sounds from background noise.

Auditory discrimination is the ability to distinguish sounds that signal a meaning change in language. The Wepman Test of Auditory Discrimination tests this function

DEVELOPMENTAL ASSESSMENT INSTRUMENTS		
Instrument	**Age Range and Time Required**	**Area of Emphasis**
Developmental Screening 1. Denver Developmental Screening Test LADOCA Publishing Foundation 4200 East Ninth Avenue Denver, Colorado 80262	2 weeks–6 years (20 minutes)	Perceptual, motor, language, social development
2. ANSER-Aggregate Neurobehavioral Student Health and Educational Review Educators Publishing Service 72 Moulton Street Cambridge, Massachussetts 02138	Form 1 — Ages 3–5 Form 2 — Ages 6–11 Form 3 — Ages 12 up Form 4 — Ages 9 up for students	Parent and school questionnaires for history and behavior
3. Pre-School Screening Instrument Stoelting Company 1350 S. Kostner Avenue Chicago, Illinois 60623	Ages 4–5 (20 minutes)	Motor, language, speech, behavior
Formal Developmental Assessment 1. Brazelton Neonatal Assessment Scale Heinemann Medical Books 23 Bedford Square London WC1B3HT, England	3 days to 4 weeks	Environmental, autonomic, emotional and attentional responses
2. Bayley Scales of Infant Development The Psychological Corporation 757 Third Avenue New York, New York 10017	Ages 8 weeks–2½ (45 minutes)	Perceptual, motor, memory, classification, language, social development. Best standardized of all
3. Pediatric Examination of Educational Readiness (Levine, M. D.) Educators Publishing Service 75 Moulton Street Cambridge, Massachusetts 02238	Ages 4–6	Neurological, physical developmental attainment, attention, information processing, adaption
4. Cattell Infant Intelligence Scale The Psychological Corporation See above	3–30 months (20–40 minutes)	Perceptual, motor. Motor deficit distorts score. Intended to be earlier extension of Stanford-Binet Intelligence Test
5. Gesell Developmental Schedules The Psychological Corporation See above	Ages 4 weeks – 6 years (20–40 minutes)	Motor, adaptive, language, social developmental

6. Pediatric Early Elementary Examination (Levine, M. D.) Educators Publishing Services See above	Ages 7–9 (40–50 minutes)	Fine motor, visual-motor visual processing, temporal-sequential organization, language, gross motor, selective attention, modality, specificity, adaptation, emotional state
Social Maturity Assessment 1. Vineland Adaptive Behavior Scales-Revised–1984 (Doll, E. A.) American Guidance Service Circle Pines, Minnesota 55014	Birth–Adult	Interview with caregiver on developmental skills and socialization
2. AAMD Adaptive Behavior Scale–1975 Revision (Nilira, K., Foster, R., Shellhaas, M., and Leland, H.) American Association on Mental Deficiency 5101 Wisconsin Avenue, N.W. Washington, D.C. 20016	Ages 3–Adult (variable time)	Observations by caregiver

Figure 20-3.

by asking a child to distinguish between subtle sounds, such as cap and cab.

Another function is auditory verbal comprehension. The child is given tasks that require the interpretation of verbal symbols but do not require a verbal answer, such as on the Peabody Picture Vocabulary Test in which the child is asked to point to objects. Children who have difficulty with auditory verbal comprehension may have serious problems adjusting to school when they tune out what the teacher is saying and become chronically inattentive.

Another function is auditory memory, as tested by repeating digits forward. Auditory memory difficulty is seen in children who cannot remember spoken instructions or explanations, such as received over the telephone. Another function is auditory retrieval. Persons with a dysphasic retrieval problem cannot remember words they want to say.

A child with a problem in auditory sequencing can remember words, but not the order of the sounds, for example, "Eskimos live in Salaka." It also can be tested by asking a child to repeat a hummed melody or to repeat a series of spoken words in precise order.

Another function is auditory analysis, which involves separating word sounds into syllables and segmentation of consonant blends as assessed by Rosner's Test of Auditory Analysis Skills. For example, when asked to say words slowly or to say a word syllable by syllable, a portion of the word is omitted.

Another function is auditory synthesis, which is the ability to blend syllables from sounds and sound combinations. Another function is syntax, which involves using sentence structures. Last, the intelligibility of speech is the function of articulation, which is the clarity and rate and pronunciation. A child's ability to attend to verbal detail, to unravel syntax, and to understand and respond to a question can be tested by asking the child several questions in one sentence.

Tests of the central auditory processing

PERCEPTUAL AND MOTOR ASSESSMENT TESTS

Instrument	Age Range	Emphasis
1. Bender Visual Motor Gestalt Test (Bender, L.) The American Orthopsychiatric Assn. 1775 Broadway New York, New York 10019	Ages 4–Adult (15 minutes)	Age level of visual-motor ability
2. Frostig Development Test of Visual Perception (Frostig, M., Lefever, W., and Wittlesey, J.) Consulting Psychologist Press 577 College Avenue Palo Alto, California 94306	Ages 3–8 (30 minutes)	Visual, motor and spatial relationships
3. Goldman, Fristoe-Woodcock Test of Auditory Discrimination (Goldman, R., Fristoe, M., and Woodcock, R. W.) American Guidance Service Publishers Building Circle Pines, Minnesota 55014	Ages 4–Adult (15 minutes)	Auditory attention including against noise background
4. Bruininks-Oseretsky Test of Motor Proficiency (Bruininks, R. H.) American Guidance Service, Inc. See above	Ages 4–16 (20–30 minutes)	Motor development age
5. Auditory Discrimination Test (Wepman, J. M.) Language Research Associates 2480 Durango Circle Palm Springs, California 92262	Ages 5–8 (10 minutes)	Auditory discrimination of subtle phonemic sounds
6. Peabody Picture Vocabulary Test—Revised American Guidance Service, Inc. See above	Ages 2½–Adult (30–40 minutes)	Auditory verbal comprehension
7. Test of Auditory Analysis Skills (TAAS) (Rosner, J.) Helping Children Overcome Learning Difficulties Walker and Company 729 Fifth Avenue New York, New York 10019	Ages 5–8 (15 minutes)	Separation of word sounds
8. Test of Visual Analysis Skills (TVAS) (Rosner, J.) Helping Children Overcome Learning Difficulties	Ages 4–8	Separation of pictures into parts
9. Audio-Visual Integration Test (Gardner, R.A.) Creative Therapeutics 155 County Road Creskill, New Jersey 07626	Ages 7–13 (15 minutes)	Association of tapping sounds with visual sequences of dots

Figure 20-4.

of verbal language are being explored (Willeford & Burleigh, 1985). They involve the discrimination and integration of verbal language presented to each ear by a dichotic apparatus. They can aid in identifying children who have difficulty understanding speech of less than optimal clarity and in noisy environments.

Visual Information Processing. A series of inquiries similar to those made into auditory functions can be made into visual functions. Visual discrimination can be assessed through a child's ability to distinguish similar designs. Visual comprehension can be tested by noting a child's response to simple pictorial stories. Visual memory can be tested by determining how efficiently a child remembers pictures or designs and by asking a child to reproduce a design that has been removed from view. Visual retrieval can be tested by determining whether a child can remember pictures of familiar objects.

Visual sequencing involves the correct placement of parts, such as lines, to form a pattern. It can be tested by finger–thumb opposition in which a child imitates the random sequence of opposing the thumb against each of the other fingers. Children with visual sequencing problems may have difficulty with word-analysis skills and spelling.

Visual analysis involves separating pictures into their parts. Rosner's Test of Visual Analysis Skills tests a child's ability to analyze a pattern into its separate parts, to read a map of dots, and to construct a map even after most of its landmarks have been removed. Visual synthesis means putting together designs to form recognizable pictures. Visual syntax involves putting together pictures in a meaningful series.

Intersensory Information Processing. Intersensory integration difficulties can be detected by such means as drawing a melody on a sheet of paper or asking a child to hum a tune represented by the line. Visual memory and auditory output can be assessed when the examiner traces a melody with a hand and asks the child to hum it (Shipley, 1980). Another method is Gardner's Audio-Visual Integration Test, which associates auditory tapping with visual sequences of dots (Gardner, 1979).

Reproducing a design with blocks reveals weaknesses in intersensory integration, motor planning, eye–hand coordination, and constructional praxis. Picture naming requires visual recognition skills and the vocabulary to name what is seen, word-finding capacity, and the ability to pronounce words properly.

Sequential directions require adherence to a particular time orientation and serial order of actions. They assess the ability to integrate a verbal input with a sequential motor output. An example is asking a child to pick up a penny, a pencil, and a key sequentially. Much schoolwork depends upon the sequential organization of information and carrying out tasks in a specific serial order. Children who have difficulty in this area may have problems with multiple-step directions, learning to spell, organizing their work, and mastering arithmetic.

Verbal spatial integration can be tested by asking a child to transform a verbal command into a specific action in space, such as putting a pencil above one's ear. To do this a child must understand verbal spatial concepts, hold them in memory long enough to enact them, and implement the motor plan of carrying them out.

Educational Assessment

A variety of instruments are available for the educational assessment of children. The clinical application of educational testing is found in the educational profiles of Orton and Kinsbourne.

Orton's educational profile included seven items: age, grade, mental age, reading, spelling, and handwriting speed. When a curve was plotted on each of these dimensions, he found three common profiles: (1) a fairly even profile, indicating adequate educational achievement; (2) a curve lower in mental age and arithmetic than in reading and spelling; and (3) a curve lower in the language subjects than in mental age and arithmetic typical of children with reading difficulties. In a similar vein, Kinsbourne (1977a) suggested a four-factor profile: skill achievement, error types, intelligence, and developmental readiness. Both of these profiles call attention to the importance of relating academic skill levels to intelligence and developmental level.

An assessment of a child's educational status includes formal testing of skills, behavioral observations of the child in school, and knowledge of the child's work performance in settings other than school (Swanson & Watson, 1982) The observation of a child at work can fine tune an understanding of the relationship between test findings and actual performance.

Individual Academic Skill Assessment

The key academic skills are reading, handwriting, spelling, and arithmetic. A number of tests are available for their assessment (see Figure 20-5).

Reading Skill Assessment. Gross criteria such as a two-year retardation in reading based on mental age often have been employed in defining a reading handicap without an analysis of the nature of a child's reading problem. That analysis is essential in order to detect educational disabilities before they result in handicaps. It is done most efficiently by working individually with a child in the task of reading. A method for teachers to assess reading levels individually at the beginning and during the middle of the school year as a basis for establishing performance objectives and for identifying cases for referral has been described (May, 1973).

Informal reading with children in a comfortable atmosphere free from tension, distraction, and time pressures is desirable. If the tone of inquiry is to help children discover the ways in which they read well and also to identify their troubles, the interaction can be one of adventure for them. The approach, therefore, should not be one of testing but that of a coach who works with a child to strengthen a child's reading skill.

A child's reactions to the examiner and to standardized reading paragraphs, such as the Spache Paragraphs, give clues as to how the child approaches reading (Spache, 1981b). Observation of children in the act of oral and silent reading reveals how they attack unfamiliar words; how rapidly they read; how they understand what is read; and how they respond to errors. Inquiry can be made about the subjective experience and feelings of the child while reading, particularly at points of difficulty. This helps the child to become aware of especially troublesome steps in the reading process.

Some children show a significant discrepancy between oral and silent reading behavior. Since this often is related to self-consciousness, establishing rapport with a child is essential for an accurate assessment of the child's skills through oral reading. A complete evaluation also should include evaluating the child's comprehension by answering questions about the content of silently read paragraphs (Spache, 1981a).

As a child reads, particular types of errors can be noted. It is useful to distinguish dysmetric, dysgnosic, dysphasic, and dyspraxic elements as described in Chapter 21 (see Figure 20-6). A particular child may have difficulty with one or more of these components of reading.

The ways in which words are misread provide useful clues (see Figure 21-3). A vestibulo-cerebellar dysmetria is revealed by visual gaze difficulties as reflected in the blurring of words and adjusting the distance of the page from one's eyes. Losing

READING AND ARITHMETIC SKILL TESTS		
Test	**Age Range and Administration**	**Emphasis**
1. Group Reading Test, Second Edition (Young, D.) Hodder and Stoughton Educational P.O. Box 702 Dunton Green Kent TN13 2YD, England	Ages 6–10 (20 minutes) Group	Easy, useful classroom reading screening
2. Diagnostic Screening Test: Reading (Gnagey, T. D.) Facilitation House Box 611-E Ottawa, Illinois 61350	Grades 2–12 (5–10 minutes) Individual	Quick screening of word attack skills and reading levels
3. Standardized Oral Reading Paragraphs (Gray, W. S.) Bobbs-Merrill 4300 West 62nd Street Indianapolis, Indiana 46206	Grades 1 to 8 (15 minutes) Individual	Assesses reading grade level
4. Reading Miscue Inventory (Goodman, Y. M., and Burke, C. L.) Macmillan Publishing Company 866 Third Avenue New York, New York 10022	Grades 1 to 8 (20–30 minutes) Individual	Identifies error pattern
5. Diagnostic Reading Scales, Revised Edition (Spache, G. D.) CTB/McGraw-Hill Del Monte Research Park Monterey, California 93940	Grades 1 to 8 (45 minutes) Individual	Assesses word recognition and reading comprehension by grade level
6. Gillingham Detached Syllables Educator's Publishing Service 72 Moulton Street Cambridge, Massachusetts 02139	Reading Age (15 minutes) Individual	Assesses understanding of phonograms and ability to sound out words
7. Key Math Diagnostic Arithmetic Test (Connolly, A. J., Nachtman, W., and Pritchett, D. M.) American Guidance Service Publishers Building Circle Pines, Minnesota 55014	Preschool through 6th grade (30 minutes) Individual	Useful in identifying specific mathematical difficulties

Figure 20-5.

Reading a book is difficult for me.

1) *Vestibulo-cerebellar dysmetria*

from
Re$_s$ding book is dif$_f$icult me.
at

2) *Visual-spatial dysgnosia*

Reabing a boot si diciffult for ne.

3) *Auditory-linguistic dysphasia*

Realing at books it dilled four me.

4) *Articulo-graphic dyspraxia*

Reating a buck is dicult for me for me.

Figure 20-6.

one's place and following a line with a finger also suggest a vestibulo-cerebellar dysmetria.

In oral reading the first step is determining whether or not a child has difficulty recognizing letters. If so, one should determine if the child recognizes the error on closer attention. The child may not be looking closely for spatial cues, such as directional orientation of the letters. Some children impulsively hurry through written material and do not attend carefully to the letters or words. One, also, should be alert for the distraction of attention by daydreaming or fantasies related to the words. For example, one boy's thoughts trailed off onto imagery of riding his bicycle when reading about a boy who was doing so. Other children focus attention so completely on letters and words that they do not grasp the meaning of sentences.

If letter sequence is altered, letters or words reversed, or words of similar sound configurations or meaning are misread, a visual-spatial dysgnosia is suggested. For example, a child may confuse b and d, p and g, or read form as from.

If errors are the result of poor rela-

tionships between the way words look and sound, such as in difficulty in blending the sounds of phonemes; grossly mutilating words by using only the first letters; adding extraneous letters; substituting a completely unrelated word; or confusing small, abstract words such as "the" and "at," an auditory-linguistic dysphasia is suggested. This also is suggested when a child knows a word and can match it with a picture but cannot sound it out. Grammatical errors, such as in tense, possessives, or pronoun use, may be part of this picture.

Particular attention should be devoted to the way a child attacks words. Lack of experience with words should be distinguished from difficulty in recognizing known words. If a child does not know the word and cannot sound it out, an auditory-linguistic dysphasia is suggested. If a word is not recognized but the child can break it down phonetically and blend its sounds and recognize its meaning, a visual-spatial dysgnosia is suggested. If both familiar and unfamiliar words are mispronounced or letters omitted, an articulo-graphic dyspraxia is suggested. Note also can be made of a child's use of clues to compensate for errors by anticipating the kinds of words likely to occur and by guessing about unfamiliar words from the context of a passage.

A child's responses to errors in particular should be noted. The presence of a phobic response to failure can be detected by asking how the child feels inside one's body by pointing to the head, neck, chest, and stomach when an error is made or a difficult word confronted. Some children readily acknowledge feeling sad, stupid, or embarrassed and are able to identify the somatic manifestations of anxiety in the form of "butterflies in my stomach," "heaviness on my chest," "lump in my throat," or "blow to my head."

Handwriting and Spelling Assessment. The development of handwriting usually occurs as follows (Levine et al., 1980):

Ages 4–5: Write name and some letters.
Ages 6–7: Write alphabet and some numbers.
Ages 8: Write sentences spontaneously.
Age 9: Describe a scene or picture in writing.
Age 10: Describe an event in writing.

The first step is analyzing a child's pencil grasp, including how efficiently it is tripod in nature, the tightness of grip, the application pressure, and the apparent comfort of hand position and eye distance from the page. A youngster with finger agnosia may rely excessively on visual feedback during writing and hold one's head close to the page. For example, such a child may have to see the pencil at the top of an "h" to know when to begin its descent. The constant need to monitor finger activity visually sharply decreases the speed of writing. Furthermore, an indicator of fine motor inefficiency is the presence of a variety of associated movements when a child writes, such as excessive mouthing, foot tapping, or mirror movements of the opposite hand.

Handwriting can be assessed from observation of a child under different circumstances, such as writing one's name, writing from dictation, copying for accuracy, and spontaneous expressive writing. The dygnosic child can write legibly spontaneously and to dictation, but makes copying errors. The dysphasic child can write accurately to dictation and in copying, but has difficulty writing spontaneously. The dyspraxic child has difficulty writing legibly to dictation and spontaneously but can copy words accurately.

Spelling errors parallel reading errors. Dysgnosic children misspell by altering letter sequences and by forming words phonetically, such as bog for dog and grate for great. Dysphasic children grossly mutilate words with little phonetic or visual resemblance in the spelling, such as ritt for right

and citizen for kitchen. Dyspraxic children omit or perseverate letters in words, such as bicle for bicycle and whell for wheel.

Mathematical Skills Assessment. Arithmetic handicaps are quite common but have received less attention than reading problems, because they are less salient to social and occupational functioning than reading. Moreover, children with arithmetic difficulties shift away from the subject as they progress through the school grades. This cannot be done as easily with reading. Problems with arithmetic are particularly prevalent among children with cerebral palsy and mental retardation (Levine et al, 1980).

The relatively concrete nature of arithmetic and the abstract nature of other forms of mathematics suggests that different cognitive abilities may be involved in each (Rosner, 1979). Children with arithmetic difficulty may have poor visual analysis skills, so that they have difficulty identifying key attributes of spatial patterns in the form of the properties and relationships of quantities and magnitudes. Children founder in mathematics if they have difficulty in handling the interrelations and abstractions of numbers.

Five clusters of arithmetical problems can be identified related to: (1) arithmetical language; (2) arithmetic readiness skills; (3) arithmetical concepts and computations; and (4) problem-solving thinking. The term dyscalculia can be applied to all categories except the first. A particular child may have difficulty in any or all of these areas (Wallace & Kauffman, 1973).

ARITHMETICAL LANGUAGE. Some children have difficulty recognizing numerical symbols just as they do letters and words. Visual-spatial dysgnosic children may reverse numbers (13 for 31, 6 for 9, 2 for 5), confuse script and symbol numbers (201 for twenty-one), and move from right to left in reading written numers. Auditory-linguistic dysphasic and articulo-graphic dyspraxic children may understand number concepts but be unable to write accurately while solving problems. All forms of dyslexic children obviously have difficulty with the aspects of mathematics that depend upon reading.

ARITHMETIC READINESS SKILLS. Prior to performing basic computations, a child must have several basic skills. First, a child must be able to discriminate between different sizes, shapes, and quantities. Some children have difficulty visualizing these spatial relationships. To test this a child can be asked to find the circular and the similar-size objects in a room.

Second, a child must understand one-to-one correspondence, such as recognizing that four place settings are needed for four people at a dinner table.

Third, a child must be able to count and recognize the significance of a number of things, such as by counting the number of objects in a room.

Fourth, a child must understand that groups of similar things form a set, such as by grouping coins of the same size and separating objects of different sizes into sets comprised of objects of the same size.

ARITHMETICAL CONCEPTS AND COMPUTATIONS. Basic computational and conceptual skills are fundamental to performing arithmetic problems.

First is an understanding of the place value of ones, tens, and hundreds and the concept of place by asking a child to write the number that is two tens and four ones. Some children have difficulty understanding greater and lesser values determined by the place of numbers and may try to subtract smaller numbers of higher value from larger numbers, for example, 25 from 7.

Depending upon age a child should know how to add, subtract, multiply, divide, and understand fractions. Some children rely upon finger counting for computations. Other children confuse the signs of addition, subtraction, multiplication, and division.

The ability to tell time involves number concepts and gradually develops from the hour to half and quarter hours to minute and second intervals and can be ascertained by asking a child to read a clock. An understanding of monetary values can be determined by making change both mentally and with coins.

Some children have been described as showing a developmental Gerstmann syndrome (Kinsbourne & Caplan, 1979). The full picture of the Gerstmann syndrome is finger agnosia, right–left disorientation, dysgraphia, and dyscalculia. In adults the underlying lesions have been reported to be in the angular gyrus of the parietal lobe and the second occipital convolution of the dominant hemisphere.

PROBLEM-SOLVING THINKING. Children with weaknesses in the managerial functions of impulse control, information analysis, and problem-solving thinking have difficulty with arithmetic, especially with story problems.

Some youngsters are unable to choose the correct process to solve a mathematics problem. They can perform well when they are told to add, substract, multiply, or divide, but they cannot make this decision themselves when given a word problem. These children also have difficulty shifting from one arithmetical computational modality to another. They persist in adding where subtraction is indicated, and they persist in subtracting where addition is indicated. They may be able to learn by rote but founder with abstract problem solving (Kinsbourne & Caplan, 1979).

Observation of a Child at Work

Another approach to assessment is directly to evaluate schoolwork, social behavior, and motivation through the observation of children at work and by inquiry into their subjective experiences. This can be done in a classroom, at home, and in diagnostic interviews. In each of these settings different dynamics obtain and differing reactions occur so that children may show dramatic variations in performance levels. They are responding to more than a specific academic task in each place.

In the classroom a child's performance is influenced by interaction with the teacher and the peer group. At home a child's relationship with parents and siblings and the presence of distracting activities play roles. Performance on a one-to-one basis may differ significantly from that in a classroom. In the individual interview, a child's achievement level, intelligence, cognitive style, and thinking style can be ascertained under the optimal influence of a supportive adult.

The advantage of direct observation is witnessing the context in which problem-solving behaviors occur and the interactional components of these behaviors. Because observation is time consuming, the clinician may rely upon teachers' and parents' descriptions, anecdotal reports, and rating scales (Lidz, 1981). Figure 20-7 outlines key points in forming a picture of a child's performance from the observation of behavior in school (Hewett, 1972).

Learning in school depends upon the overall efficiency with which a child follows instructions and develops a strategy for accomplishing a particular task. Many children with subtle learning problems may respond correctly, albeit slowly and with inefficient strategies, such as reflected in a prolonged latency of response between an instruction and beginning a task; prolonged time between initiation and completion of a task; and an excessive need to have instructions repeated (Levine & Melmed, 1982).

A variety of instruments have been developed for assessing child–environment interactions through ratings by observers, ratings by participants, interviews, or written reports, and the analysis of records (Adelman & Taylor, 1983). For example, instruments used for assessing hyperki-

netic behavior include individual tests, such as the Children's Embedded Figures Test of distractibility, the Children's Checking Task of sustained attention, and the Freedom from Distraction Factor of the WISC-R, in addition to behavioral scales, such as the Conners' Teacher Rating Scale and the Werry-Weiss-Peters Activity Scale (Goyette et al, 1978). A combination of these techniques is needed to yield valid results (Brown, 1982).

Diagnostically it is important to know whether a child breaks rules because they are not known or accepted, because they have not been learned, or because the child operates according to rules appropriate for a different social situation (Elkind, 1982). Children are not socialized by learning abstract social roles. They learn the rules, understandings, and expectancies in repetitive social situations, such as going to bed, eating out, and visiting neighbors, each of which has its own conventions.

Peer interactions can be analyzed in terms of social negotiation strategy levels (Stone & Selman, 1982). At the first *demand* level, a child does not distinguish between one's own and another's point of view in a situation. Relationships, therefore, are based on physical qualities or one's material needs and power. At the second *command* level, there is awareness of different perspectives in a given situations, but only one is considered at a time. Thus motivation comes from either one's own perspective or from an invoked external authority. At the third pragmatic *coordination* level, a child understands that oneself and others have differing perspectives in the context of interpersonal relations. At this level children can step outside a dyadic relationship and examine it from a third person's perspective. There also is an appreciation of the subtleties of group interaction.

Diagnostic teaching is an important individually applied tool for assessing a learning problem, because it permits experimentation with different approaches

1. Attention
   a. Does the child pay attention to the teacher?
   b. Does the child pay attention differently to visual, auditory, and tactual stimuli in learning tasks?
   c. Does the child retain directions and information?
   d. Does the child daydream?
   e. Is the child preoccupied with compulsive, ritualistic acts, such as excessive handwashing or pencil sharpening?

2. Motivation
   a. Does the child freely undertake assignments?
   b. Does the child display a broad range of interests in subject matter and activities in the classroom?
   c. Does the child fail to complete assignments?

3. Work Habits
   a. Does the child follow directions and start, follow through, and complete assignments?
   b. Is the child impulsive and uncritical in doing assignments?
   c. Does the child know how to locate sources of information?
   d. Can the child take notes?
   e. Can the child outline?
   f. Can the child use library tools?
   g. Does the child respect the rights of others?

4. Exploration
   a. Does the child have accurate knowledge about the environment and freely engage in exploration of it?
   b. Is the child overly dependent on the directions and choices of others in selecting interests and activities?
   c. Is there any evidence of motor, sensory or intellectual deficits that limit the child's capacity to freely and accurately explore the environment?

5. Social
   a. Does the child's behavior generally gain the approval of others and avoid their disapproval?
   b. Is the child overly dependent on obtaining attention and praise from others?
   c. Does the child withdraw from or antagonize peers?

6. Mastery
   a. Is the child pleased with the mastery of skills?

Figure 20-7. Outline for observation of a child in school. (From F. M. Hewett, "Educational Programs for Children," in H. C. Quay and J. S. Werry, eds., *Psychopathological Disorders in Childhood,* copyright 1972 by John Wiley and Sons, New York. Reproduced with permission.)

that can be tested on the spot. Diagnostic teaching is a test–teach–test instructional sequence of information and skills (Smith & Johnson, 1976). Evaluation through the use of instruction can incorporate children's knowledge and modes of learning and guide them toward new levels of learning. New information that builds upon what a child knows can be introduced and, when necessary, alternative forms of teaching can be used (Coles, 1983).

Psychological Testing

Psychological testing offers a systematic and comparatively objective means of assessing mental and personality functions (Goldman et al, 1984; Palmer, 1983; Sattler, 1982).

The basic properties of a useful psychological test are reliability, validity, and standardization:

> Reliability refers to the consistent measurement of qualities so that an individual tested on two different occasions will have relatively similar scores.
> Validity means that the instrument in fact measures what it is supposed to measure; for example, an intelligence test should primarily measure intelligence rather than personality traits or educational attainment.
> Standardization means that the test has been given to a variety of individuals representing different personal characteristics so that classification can be made in terms of norms.

Psychometric tests are designed to estimate intelligence, and projective tests are intended to reveal information about character and the internal world. Both psychometric and projective testing depend upon the professional administration of the tests on an individual basis and meet the criteria of reliability and validity more than do standardized tests based upon the completion of questionnaires.

Psychometric Assessment

Galton initiated the idea of measuring individual differences in mental abilities by purely objective methods. Binet invented the first practical test of intelligence and introduced the concept of mental age. Spearman found through factor analysis that all measurements of individual differences in complex mental performances are positively intercorrelated and substantiated Galton's conjecture that there is a general relationship among the various forms of mental ability—the "g" factor (Jensen, 1980).

The main faults with mental testing generally involve abuses and inadequacies in the use of tests rather than bias or other deficiencies in the tests themselves. In the terminology of genetics, test scores are measures of phenotypes, not of genotypes. They are merely correlates, predictors, and indicators of other social variables deemed important for achieving responsible and productive roles in society. In this sense psychometric testing reflects the value system of a society. Great care must be taken in inferring innate capabilities from psychometric data (Sattler, 1988).

The Concept of Intelligence. Intelligence tests have been developed pragmatically and measure abilities that make for success in academic subjects and that are influenced by environment, culture, innate ability, testing situation, and attitude of the subject. They do not tap artistic, musical, creative, or exploratory qualities. In one study children who measured the highest on intelligence tests did not measure highest on tests of creativity. Many important aspects of intelligence thus often go unmeasured when educational values stress information-processing types of learning rather than creativity (Getzels & Jackson, 1962).

Intelligence is not an entity in itself, but a theoretical construct (Gould, 1980; Jensen, 1980; Sternberg, 1982, 1985). It is a global concept that encompasses the functional competencies of an individual based upon cognitive style, temperamental style, language, managerial style, and self. It has an important developmental component so that success enhances and failure impedes the development of the factors that make up intelligence. Intelligence should not be treated as something a person simply "has" but as a fluid multifaceted resource that can be acquired and enhanced in the course of being used (Gardner, 1983; Lidz & Lidz, 1973). Intelligence is expressed in the ways individuals handle their internal and external worlds and the relations between them (Sternberg, 1985). Indeed the general pattern of living under home conditions that foster education and self-discipline fosters an increase in intelligence quotient through the school years (McCall et al, 1973). The term psychometric assessment is preferable to evaluation since the goal is not to isolate the cause of a problem, but to identify a child's strengths and weaknesses as they help or hinder academic learning.

At the neurophysiological level, individual differences in intelligence can be thought of as being a function of general factors of neural efficiency and adaptibility. Neural efficiency allows information to be processed quickly, preventing an overload of the limited capacity of working memory. Neural adaptibility conserves neural energy when an expected stimulus occurs and expends it more vigorously in response to unexpected stimuli (Vernon, 1985).

In the 1930s Vygotsky (1978) advanced the concept of the *zone of proximal development* as the distance between a child's actual developmental level as determined by problem solving by oneself and the level of potential problem solving possible under adult guidance or in collaboration with more capable peers. The growth of intel-

lectual processes, therefore, does not reach a terminal point; instead these processes continue to contain the potential for transcending their present stage.

Vygotsky conceived of mental ability as having two levels. At one a child can independently accomplish tasks and solve problems that required abilities possessed at a particular developmental stage. At the other level, the zone of proximal development is the ability to accomplish new tasks and problem solving through learning. Thus the level of accomplished learning can be extended to a level beyond it, which in turn provides the basis for further learning. With continued instruction the zone of proximal development then becomes the accomplished level of learning, and from this a new zone of proximal development forms. Therefore, to assess a person's mental abilities, both actual and potential ability levels should be tapped (Coles, 1983).

Vygotsky's view emphasizes a child's capacities for learning rather than what that child now knows and can do. Evaluating this potential is the most critical and least well-performed function of psychometric tests. Determining how children learn in test–teach–test formats is a promising approach to discovering their potentials for learning with instruction (Feuerstein, 1980).

A particular difficulty with populations of children with academic difficulties is that the validity of data on their intellectual functioning is questionable. Since children with learning problems in school often perform poorly on psychometric tests, there is an obligation to seek evidence that intellectual functioning may be higher than disclosed on test performance. For example, reports from professionals who have had contact with an individual may provide information suggesting a higher level of intellectual functioning (Adelman & Taylor, 1983).

Test-measured intelligence becomes more consistent with age. Developmental quotients under the age of one year bear virtually no relationship to later intelligence quotients. There is a degree of predictive reliability at age two; however, it is not until the age of six that statistically significant consistency is found (Sattler, 1988).

The prediction of achievement from intelligence quotients generally is affected by the phenomenon of *regression toward the mean*, so that children with lower intelligence quotients tend to show higher achievement closer to the mean and children with higher scores tend to show lower achievement closer to the mean (McLeod, 1979). Thus although individual intelligence tests do tend to predict academic success, the amount of variance in school achievement accounted for by measured intelligence may be no more than 30 percent (Kinsbourne, 1980). For these reasons the intelligence quotient plays a role in predicting success in school, but less so in the later enterprises of life.

Performance on psychometric tests reflects the speed and efficiency with which information is processed and retrieved (Eysenck, 1977). Poor test performance can reflect lack of experience in taking tests and the lack of a cultural achievement orientation in addition to personality factors that interfere with academic learning. Cultural concepts and values are significant factors in test performance and must be considered in selecting tests and interpreting results (Swanson & Watson, 1982). For these reasons modifications of testing procedures, especially those that are timed, are needed to determine whether or not a child truly lacks knowledge or a skill (Lidz, 1981). Research is being carried out on measuring intellectual functions by objective electrophysiological techniques (Giannitrapani, 1985).

Psychometric Tests. The battery approach to assessment contrasts with the use of individualized measures, tests, and procedures for each child who is examined. A battery places emphasis upon obtaining the same set of data from all subjects, regardless of the nature of their problems. This involves administering the same standardized procedures to all persons with the systematic application of interpretations. This is particularly well suited to neuropsychological testing, as illustrated in Figure 20-8 (Matthews, 1981; Rourke et al, 1983).

Several of the generally used individual psychometric tests are listed in Figure 20-9. A close look at the Wechsler Intelligence Scale for Children—Revised (WISC-R) will illustrate their contents (Bannatyne, 1974).

The WISC-R affords a comparison of verbal and performance intelligence quotients. A significant difference between verbal and performance quotient levels suggests a selective problem in either auditory-verbal or visual-spatial skills. For example, visual-spatial dysgnosic children show relatively lower abilities on the nonverbal items and auditory-linguistic dysphasic children on verbal items. Scatter among subtest scores suggests a child's weak and strong points (Stott, 1978).

Using the WISC-R in analyzing educational disabilities has two principal values. First, if reasonably uniform in subtest scores, it estimates a child's functional intelligence level. Many children of low average intelligence are inaccurately regarded as having specific educational disabilities by overly zealous adults who are unwilling to face that fact. However, the influence of test anxiety, interpersonal manipulation, and motivational factors must be carefully considered in each case.

Second, the subtests on the WISC-R shed light on four critical factors: acquired knowledge in the information, vocabulary, and arithmetic items; verbal conceptualization in the similarities, vocabulary, and comprehension items; spatial conceptualization in the picture completion, block design, and object assembly items; and sequencing abilities in the arithmetic, digit span, and coding items (Bannatyne, 1974).

For the reader who is not familiar with

**THE UNIVERSITY OF WISCONSIN
NEUROPSYCHOLOGICAL BATTERY**

Wechsler Intelligence Scale for Children — Revised

Seashore Rhythm Test — Auditory attention and concentration

Peabody Picture Vocabulary Test — Receptive Vocabulary

Speech Perception Test or Boston Speech Perception Test — Phonetic attention and concentration

Tactile Performance Test — Spatial problem solving, learning motor skills

Raven's Colored Progressive Matrices — Visual-spatial reasoning

Revised Knox Cube Test — Visual attention, concentration and memory

Verbal-Spatial Test — Visual attention, scanning, concentration, timed naming and memory

Motor Steadiness Battery — Fine motor control

Wide Range Achievement Test — Word recognition, spelling and arithmetic

Spache Diagnostic Reading Scales — Reading comprehension

Aphasia Screening Test — Language processing

Halstead Category Test — Concept formation, abstraction, reasoning and spatial abilities

Tactile Finger Recognition, Number Writing and Form Recognition — Agnosia, graphesthesia and stereognosis

Developmental Drawings — Copying geometric designs

Personality Inventory for Children — Parent completed information about child

---

Figure 20-8.

them, a review of the WISC-R subtests may be helpful. The verbal subtests include:

1. *Information.* Measures the ability to recall basic facts acquired from experience and education and relies upon auditory comprehension.

2. *Similarities.* Tests the recognition of likenesses between pairs of words ranging from the concrete to the abstract and requires conceptualization and flexibility in impulse control.

3. *Arithmetic.* Measures educationally influenced timed focusing of attention on the sequence of information in a question, short-term memory, and translation of words into mental numerical operations.

4. *Vocabulary.* Requires definition of words from concrete to abstract levels and measures word knowledge; correlates with general intelligence.

5. *Comprehension.* Experientially influenced measurement of analysis and synthesis of percepts, conceptual thinking,

common-sense reasoning, and judgment; less influenced by education.

6. *Digit span.* Recall of spoken numbers forward and backward; requires focused attention and immediate sequential memory that are relatively unaffected by experience but are by anxiety; correlates with general intelligence.

The performance subtests are:

1. *Picture completion.* Requires identification of missing elements in pictures and measures visual discrimination, visual memory, figure–ground discrimination, and attention. Measures awareness of and general orientation to one's environment.

2. *Picture arrangement.* Pictures must be arranged to make a story within a time limit; measures attention to visual details, visual analysis, synthesis of perceptions, and problem solving.

3. *Block design.* Through construction of a design from a picture within a time limit by arranging two colored blocks, it measures figure–ground analysis and synthesis of perceptions, problem solving, and motivation.

4. *Object assembly.* The timed construction of a familiar object from puzzle pieces involves part–whole analysis and synthesis of percepts, problem solving, attention, and visual-spatial closure.

5. *Coding.* The timed, rapid copying of symbols for appropriate numerals relies on attention, accuracy, speed of movement, shifting in visual-motor integration, visual sequential memory, visual discrimination, and cognitive flexibility.

6. *Mazes.* Mazes are run without lifting the pencil from the paper and require visual motor coordination, planning, and problem solving.

Even with adequate perceptual, psychomotor, verbal receptive, and verbal expressive capacities, a child can be enormously handicapped by deficiencies in the conceptualization and problem-solving realms. Such measures as the WISC arithmetic subtests are viewed as reflections of higher-order concept formation and problem-solving abilities. However, there are more thorough measures, such as Raven's Progressive Matrices, which taps concept formation, and the Halstead Category Test, which draws upon the capacity to benefit from positive and negative feedback regarding the correctness of one's performances.

The Porteus Mazes and the Tactual Performance Test are examples of tests that tap the ability to adapt one's behavior to fairly complex task demands through higher-order problem-solving strategies. The assessment of higher-order concept formation, problem-solving and hypothesis-testing skills can shed considerable light upon the nature and extent of a child's adaptive potential. Failing to tap this dimension adequately can lead to limited and distorted views of the neuropsychological status of a child.

Some of the variance on psychometric tests can be accounted for by individual differences in verbal and visual information processing (Hunt, 1983). Age is a factor because reading comprehension lags behind listening comprehension performances depend upon underlying modes of information processing. The relation between verbal and visual information processing and actual performance is analogous to the relation between muscle strength and athletic performance; performance requires the underlying strength, but strength does not guarantee performance. For example, performance on mentally rotating figures depends upon the underlying process of visualization. Performance in mental rotation can be assessed by displaying two shapes at different angles of orientation and asking an observer to decide whether the figures are identical or mirror images (Figure 20-10). This performance is related to marked individual

INDIVIDUAL PSYCHOMETRIC TESTS

Instrument	Age Range	Emphasis
1. Wechsler Preschool and Primary Scale of Intelligence The Psychological Corporation 757 Third Avenue New York, New York 10017	Ages 3 – 6½ (60 minutes)	Verbal, performance and full-scale I.Q.
2. Wechsler Intelligence Scale for Children-Revised (WISC-R) The Psychological Corporation See above	Ages 6 – 17 (60 minutes)	Verbal, performance and full-scale I.Q.
3. Stanford-Binet Intelligence Scale, Third Revision. (Terkman, C. M., and Merrill, M.) Riverside Publishing Company 8420 Bryn Mawr Avenue Chicago, Illinois 60631	Ages 2 – adult (60 minutes)	Largely verbal. Mental age and I.Q. score (may be higher than WISC-R)
4. McCarthy Scales of Children's Abilities (McCarthy, D.) The Psychological Corporation See above	Ages 2½ – 8 (40 – 60 minutes)	Verbal, perceptual, memory, motor, laterality; general cognitive index (I.Q. equivalent)
5. Peabody Picture Vocabulary Test (PPVT-R) American Guidance Service Publishers Building Circle Pines, Minnesota 55014	Ages 5 – 16 (30 – 40 minutes)	Picture-word associations for word recognition and meaning; verbal I.Q.
6. Halstead Category Test Reitan and Davison (1974) Clinical Neuropsychology Washington, D.C.: Winston and Sons	School age (40 – 60 minutes)	168 visual stimulus figures to be associated with underlying concepts of numbers, oddity, spatial position and relative magnitude
7. Raven Progressive Matrices The Psychological Corporation See above	Ages 4 – 10: Colored Progressive Matrices and Form Board; 6 – adult: Standard Progressive Matrices (30–60 minutes)	Measures conceptualization and reasoning by matching patterns with a matrix; expressive language. Relatively uninfluenced by culture.
8. Porteus Mazes (Porteus, S. D.) The Psychological Corporation See above	Ages 3 – adult	Measures higher order problem solving abilities, spatial visualization by performance on 28 mazes of graded difficulty. Nonverbal.

9. Reitan-Indiana Neuropsychological Test Battery for Children Neuropsychology Laboratory University of Arizona 1338 East Edison Street Tucson, Arizona 85719	Ages 5 – 8	Spatial conceptualization and memory; tactual performance, finger tapping, color form, ocular dominance, aphasia screening, form recognition
10. Halstead Neuropsychological Test Battery for Children Neuropsychology Laboratory University of Arizona See above	Ages 9 – 14	Tactual peformance, rhythm, speech sounds perception, finger tapping, form recognition, aphasia screening, grip, strength, lateralization
11. Culture Fair Intelligence Tests (CFIT) (Cattell, R., and Cattell, A.) Bobbs-Merrill 4300 West 62nd Street Indianapolis, IN 46206	Ages 4 – 8 Ages 8 – 14 Ages 9 – 16 (30 minutes)	Tests adaption to unfamiliar nonsense material. Presumably not culture or class biased.

Figure 20-9.

differences in the capacity for visualization. Strong visualization ability does not ensure efficient performance, however (Hunt, 1983).

The mosaic test consists of colored geometrical pieces that are arranged into a design in order to assess the use of internal and external information in planning and pattern execution (Mosse, 1982). Most children can form gestalts. Inefficient prefrontal lobe functioning is suggested when the shape of the design is determined by the first piece and the following pieces are put on each other's surfaces so that the whole pattern is not planned but is a response to the shape and color of the pieces. This reflects stimulus-bound excessive dependence upon immediate stimuli, or perseveration.

The intelligence quotient provides an idea of a child's general intellectual capacity and is a point of reference against which a child's achievement levels can be measured to ascertain underachievement. Even with classical mental retardation syndromes, however, underachievement often occurs, as pointed out long ago by Lewin (1951).

Mental retardation is a symptom complex, not a clinically sound diagnosis. The life experience and educational opportunities of the mildly retarded play a key role in their ultimate level of functioning. For example, through unbounded patience a child with Down syndrome, Nigel Hunt, was taught to read by the age of six (Hunt, 1967). His knowledge of words was astonishing and his powers of observation and memory of separate events acute. Actually he knew more than he evidenced and was wary of attempting anything before he was confident he could do it properly. His manner of thinking, however, was entirely concrete so that he could not appreciate the abstract idea of cardinal numbers used in addition and subtraction.

The diagnosis of mental retardation must be made cautiously because social, economic, and educational disadvantage in addition to character structure produce learning problems that result in the psychometric picture of mental retardation.

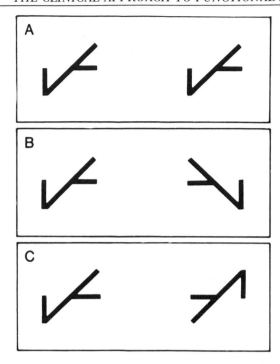

Figure 20-10. The mental rotation task. A subject must decide whether the two figures in (C) are identical (A) or mirror images (B). (From E. Hunt, "On the Nature of Intelligence," *Science, 219,* 1983, 141–146. Copyright 1983 by The American Association for the Advancement of Science, Washington DC. Reproduced with permission.)

Conversely some children with mild mental retardation may deceptively appear to have higher levels of intelligence than they actually do because they have been highly trained in verbal skills.

The concept of measurable intelligence, like the concept of health, strength, or beauty, is too global and nonspecific to be other than of heuristic value. It is unlikely that refinements in test construction will ever dramatically measure intelligence more effectively. Yet despite their limitations, intelligence tests are likely to continue to be used for practical reasons (Madge & Tizard, 1981).

Because of the limitations of psychometric testing, school psychologists are shifting from an assessment to an evaluation stance through engagement on a day-to-day basis with the whole process of education (Lidz, 1981). They rely less on test measures for classification purposes and more upon the evaluation of error patterns, coping strategies, strengths and weaknesses, and patterns of performance that suggest remedial strategies. More specifically, a test–teach–retest paradigm can be used to gauge more accurately a child's ability to learn.

Projective Psychological Assessment

Projective psychological tests reveal more about people than people realize they are disclosing. Thus the unlimited number of possible responses to ink blots or pictures bring out individual differences in cognitive styles, emotional patterns, imagery, intrapsychic conflicts, self-concepts, and self-evaluations (see Figure 20-11). All of this, however, makes the interpretation of projective tests difficult.

Figure drawings tap primitive levels that may not be accessible in verbal language. They provide information about one's body image, actual and desired self-concepts, self-evaluation, and attitudes toward people. Children tend to project their inner imagery into their drawings. When requested to Draw-A-Person and then asked about what the person is doing and fears, a child reveals literal or symbolic representations of one's own self-image. The Draw-A-Family can reveal significant information about a child's view of one's role in the family and attitudes toward and relationships among family members. In family drawings attention should be devoted to how figures are positioned in relation to each other and the omission of family members. Generally in figure drawings revealing points are the absolute and relative size of figures, detail included, placement

PROJECTIVE PSYCHOLOGICAL TESTS		
Instrument	**Age and Time**	**Emphasis**
Figure Drawing		
1) Draw-A-Person Test (DAPT) (Urban, W. H.) Western Psychological Services 12031 Wilshire Boulevard Los Angeles, California 90025	All Ages (10 minutes)	Self and body image
2) House-Tree-Person Test (HTP) (Buck, J. N.) Western Psychological Services 12031 Wilshire Boulevard Los Angeles, California 90025	All Ages (10 minutes)	Relation of self to human and physical environment
3) Draw-A-Family	All Ages (15 minutes)	Perception of roles in family
Personality 1) Rorschach Psychodiagnostics (Rorschach, H.) Grune and Stratton 111 Fifth Avenue New York, New York 10003	3–Adult (30 minutes)	Individual differences in personality structure, unconscious conflict, fantasies, and reality testing
2) Children's Apperception Test (CAT) (Bellak, L., and Bellak, S.) CPS, Inc. Box 83 Larchmont, New York 10538	3–10 years (45 minutes)	Cognitive and emotional styles, imagery, conflicts, and self-concept
3) Thematic Apperception Test (Murray, H.A.) Harvard University Press 79 Garden Street Cambridge, Massachusetts 02491	4–Adult	Adjustment patterns, fantasies
Parent Questionnaire Personality Inventory for Children (Wirt, R.D., Lachar, D., Klinedinst, J.K., and Seat, F.D.) Western Psychological Services 12031 Wilshire Boulevard Los Angeles, California 90025	3–16 years (2–3 hours) Completed by parent	Personality description on scales of achievement, intellectual screening, development, somatic concerns, depression, family relations, delinquency, withdrawal, anxiety, psychosis, hyperactivity, and social skills

Figure 20-11.

on the page, exaggeration of features, shading, and erasures.

The Children's Apperception Test for ages three to ten and the Thematic Apperception Test for ages six to adult consist of a series of ambiguous pictures and reveal information about cognitive style, conflicts, imagery, self-concept, and psychological defenses. A child's response to directions, logical organization of a story, richness of associations, and freedom of expressiveness reveal cognitive style characteristics, such as convergence and divergence. The degree of emotional display and the extent of involvement in a particular picture card reveal the access a child has to one's emotions. The stories themselves disclose troublesome feelings, conflicting attitudes, and underlying imagery about the self and others. The portrayal of characters in the stories tends to reveal children's concepts and evaluations of themselves and their interpersonal relationships. Children with school problems, for instance, often represent the main figure in their stories as stupid, troublemaking, and ostracized by family, teachers, and peers (Kinsbourne & Caplan, 1979).

The Rorschach Ink Blot Test has less structure than the Thematic Apperception tests and tends to elicit more primitive emotions and imagery. In interpreting responses to the amorphous ink blots, attention is paid to the content of the subject's responses; the sequence of responses; what parts of the card are used; and the relative attention devoted to the form, color, shading, and texture of the ink blots. The scoring of the test is related to both the content elicited and the nature of the determinants of the content in the five achromatic and five chromatic cards themselves. Theoretically the child projects unconscious wishes, imagery, and emotions on to the ink blots. The test, therefore, tends to bring out information about how a child analyzes reality and about internal imagery and conflicts.

General Medical Evaluation

An essential component of the clinical process is a general medical examination in order to rule out illness as a potential cause of school problems.

Under optimal circumstances developmental assessment is a part of a child's health care and takes place periodically at annual well-child visits. This permits the accumulation of perinatal and familial information in addition to developmental patterns throughout infancy and early childhood as a background for understanding later school problems (Accardo, 1980).

Two examples of medical problems that may be relevant to performance in school are recurrent ear infections and adenoidal hypertrophy. Children with recurrent otitis media in early childhood may be at risk for language-related learning handicaps (Leviton, 1980). Excessive adenoid tissue may produce respiratory obstruction and the sleep apnea syndrome, with daytime drowsiness alternating with hyperkinesis.

Impaired school performance also may be an early sign of a chronic illness, such as diabetes mellitus, kidney disease, or an immune disorder such as lupus erythematosis. Thyroid and pituitary disorders can be manifested in lack of motivation in school. Hyperthyroidism may cause inattentiveness and hyperkinesis. Hypothyroidism is an uncommon condition, which may produce functional impairment to the degree of mental retardation.

Assessment of Vision

All children with school problems should have a visual examination that includes assessment of visual acuity, accommodation and convergence efficiency, and eye movements (Schrier, 1979). Problems in any of these functions can produce symptoms of visual discomfort in performing school-work, especially reading.

When children have good visual acuity, poor binocular skills may be overlooked, resulting in subtle but significant visual stress that interferes with schoolwork. If a child has significant defects in acuity or binocularity, correction is essential for the performance of schoolwork. The Eyetech Vision Screening System is a useful screening device for visual acuity and eye-movement coordination (Schrier, 1979). It tests 12 different visual skills in under four minutes and can be used by nonprofessionals.

Color blindness affects 3 percent of boys and 0.2 percent of girls, and when undetected, can create difficulty in recognizing writing on green chalkboards in particular (Mosse, 1982). Accordingly a child's color discrimination should be assessed, as by the Ishihara Test Plates for Color Blindness.

Neurological Evaluation

The conventional neurological examination of the sensory and motor systems may contribute to the understanding of children's learning problems but seldom explains them (Touwen & Sporrel, 1979; Rapin, 1982). The techniques of the examination are related to the age of the child and are in an early state of refinement for newborns (Stratton, 1982a). The disciplines of occupational and physical therapy incorporate certain neurological assessments in their diagnostic procedures.

Neurological findings corroborate other indications of brain immaturity and lesions. Some indirectly influence learning through distracting manifestations, such as erratic body movements that produce restless behavior and finger agnosia that impedes handwriting. Other neurological conditions directly interfere with schoolwork, such as absence seizures and progressive diseases.

Neurological Examination

The neurological examination includes assessment of the cranial nerves, sensation, motor functions, coordination, and language (Gardner, 1979; Herskowitz & Rosman, 1982).

Cranial Nerves. Of the cranial nerves, the second, third, fourth, sixth, and eighth are relevant to schoolwork. The second optic cranial nerve is tested by assessing visual acuity and the visual fields through peripheral finger movements. Ophthalmoscopic scrutiny of the optic disks and retina is part of a complete examination.

Pupillary reactions to light and accommodation are subserved by the second and third cranial nerves. Extraocular movements reflect third, fourth, and sixth cranial nerve functions. Strabismus may be evidence of cranial nerve dysfunction or imbalance of eye muscles. With third nerve palsy, the eye on the affected side is turned down and outward with accompanying drooping eyelid and usually pupillary dilation. With sixth nerve paralysis, the affected eye is turned inward.

The eighth auditory and vestibulocochlear cranial nerve is involved in hearing, eye movements, and balance. Hearing tests for young children may be classified as formal and informal (Adler, 1983). The formal tests include pure tone audiometry, tuning forks, and speech audiometry, all of which require the child's active cooperation. The Brainstem Evoked Auditory Potential can be used to determine the reception of auditory stimuli in infants and uncooperative children. Informal tests include sound toys, sudden noises, and the voice. An easy, yet sensitive, test of hearing acuity in the voice range is to rub two fingers together next to each ear.

There are two types of hearing-loss patterns of particular clinical importance. One involves the conventional conductive and neurosensory patterns of complete loss that are the most important auditory causes of language retardation. The other is the "waterfall" pattern of loss, in which a child hears normally in the lower tones but not beyond approximately 1000 hertz. The waterfall pattern may escape attention because the child responds to many sounds, as do other children, but does not understand high-pitched voice sounds clearly because of hearing loss (Adler, 1983). For this reason audiometric testing is indicated for all children with attention problems (Freeman et al, 1981).

Nystagmus, or rapid extraocular movements, is related to the vestibular portion of the eighth nerve. The oculocephalic maneuver consists of turning the head rapidly from one side to the other or up and down; the eyes normally deviate opposite to the direction of the head turning. Caloric testing in which nystagmus is produced by irrigating the ear with hot and cold water is a more precise way of testing vestibular functioning.

The most common dizzy sensation associated with vestibular lesions is vertigo, an illusion of rotation, which may be accompanied by autonomic symptoms, such as nausea and vomiting and a variety of forms of nystagmus (Baloh & Honrubia, 1979).

Sensory-Spatial Functions. Higher cortical level sensory-spatial functions include stereognosis, graphesthesia, finger gnosis, and right–left orientation on oneself and others (Silver & Hagin, 1976). Stereognosis is tested by having a child identify a familiar object held in the hand with eyes closed. Graphesthesia is tested by the recognition, with eyes closed, of numbers or figures written upon the skin, particularly the fingertips.

Finger localization testing may involve naming and sequencing in addition to spatial awareness, depending upon how it is carried out. Consequently, finger gnosis is assessed by touching fingers while the child has closed eyes; then with eyes open, the

child is asked to point to the touched finger. A five-year-old can easily identify touch of fingers I and V singly. A six-year-old can identify bilateral simultaneous stimulation of I and V; a seven-year-old, bilateral simultaneous stimulation of fingers II and IV; and an eight-year-old, bilateral asymmetric stimulation, such as right finger IV and left finger III. Finger gnosis difficulty may persist in some children with reading difficulty into adulthood.

Right–left discrimination can be assessed by asking children to identify right and left on themselves and on the examiner. The average five-year-old can identify one's own right and left hand; a six-year-old can place the right hand on the right ear; a seven-year-old can place the right hand on the left ear; and an eight-year-old can accurately identify the right and left sides of another person.

Gross Motor Functions. Examination of the motor system includes both gross and fine motor skills and has been standardized in the tests listed in Figure 20-12. Difficulties in gross motor functioning may be reflected in a reluctance to participate in competitive physical activities; apprehension over physical education classes; difficulty in catching or throwing a ball, skipping, jumping, or balancing; delayed mastery of bicycle riding and clumsiness.

Examination of a child's gait is important. Rhythmicity and fluidity of natural walking should be noted along with associated arm movements, in addition to facility with special movements at the following ages (Levine et al, 1980):

Ages 4–5:   Skipping, hopping, walking on heels.

Ages 5–8:   Walking heel-to-toe forward and backward.

Ages 9–10:   Walking on sides of feet.

Lateralized motor disturbances may be brought out by asking children to walk on

TESTS OF MOTOR FUNCTIONING	
1) Gardner Steadiness Tester Creative Therapeutics 155 County Road Creskill, NJ 07262	Measures motor impersistence, tremors, choreiform movements, concentration, tension and anxiety.
2) Purdue Pegboard Test Lafayette Instrument Company P.O. Box 1279 Lafayette, IN 47902	Measures fine motor coordination.
3) Southern California Percepual-Motor Tests Western Psychological Services 12031 Wilshire Blvd. Los Angeles, CA 90025	Measures vestibulo-cerebellar functioning.
4) Bruininks-Oseretsky Test of Motor Proficiency American Guidance Service Circle Pines, MN 55014	Measures gross and fine motor skills on a developmental scale. For ages 4 through 14.
5) Body Schema — Tempo Regulation Test (Santostefanos, 1978)	Measures differentiation and regulation of tempos of fine and gross body movements in relation to body image.
6) Primitive Reflex and Postural Adjustment Scale (Friedlander et al 1982)	Measures persistence of postural and righting reflexes beyond expected levels in children.

Figure 20-12.

the outer sides of their feet as if they were bowlegged. When most children walk in this way, the posture of their arms is symmetrical, with both hands alongside the legs and fingers at ease. If lateralized motor dysfunction is present, the arm on the opposite side of the body is likely to be held outward or forward with the elbow bent and possibly the wrist flexed as the hand is closed. Most children lying flat on a solid surface show symmetrical positioning of their feet when completely relaxed. If one foot rotates outward, motor dysfunction of the opposite side of the brain is suggested (Brumback & Stanton, 1983).

Body position sense and regulation can be observed by having a child sustain balance while:

Ages 5–6:   Standing on one foot, eyes open (ten seconds).
Ages 7–9:   Standing heel-to-toe, eyes closed (15 seconds).
Ages 9–12: Standing on tiptoes, eyes closed (15 seconds).

The persistence of a primitive postural neck-righting reflex is suggested when the examiner rotates the child's head in each direction while the child stands with eyes closed and arms outstretched, and the entire body moves with the head as the arms drop or spread. This does not have particular significance up to the age of six (Gardner, 1979).

Fine Motor Functions. Difficulties in fine motor functions are suggested by a child's reluctance to trace, draw, cut with a scissors, or build models. Young children may use eating utensils awkwardly. Older children may have poor handwriting because of difficulty forming letters and an awkward pencil grasp. The Purdue Pegboard Test is a standardized instrument for measuring fine motor coordination (see Figure 20-12).

Fine motor functions may be impeded by the adventitious movements of extrapyramidal inefficiency and by sluggishness in execution. Adventitious movements during voluntary activity can be detected by asking the child to stand with eyes closed, arms outstretched, and fingers spread widely apart while keeping the fingers still. This also can be done for involuntary movements in a relaxed state by asking the child to sit back in a chair with eyes closed as if going to sleep and the palms of the hands placed on the thighs, while the examiner's hands cover the child's hands. In both of these states, jerking choreiform and writhing athetoid adventitious movements can be detected, together with movements used by the child to conceal them. Such adventitious movements provide a background of restless movement and contribute to hyperkinesis in some children. Another form of adventitious movements are mirror movements, or synkinesias, of contralateral digits or the lips and tongue during purposeful fine motor activity. This can be observed by looking for movements of the left side of the body while the child is asked to perform fine movements of the right hand.

Sluggishness in rapid movements, or dysdiadochokinesia, can be noted in finger tapping and alternating movements of palm and dorsum of one hand on the palm of the other. Praxis can be tested by asking a child to imitate finger movements while facing the examiner. A six-year-old can imitate thumb to the little finger and thumb to the index finger. A seven-year-old can imitate thumb to middle fingers. Children can be observed buttoning, which can be done by most five-year-olds, and tying shoelaces, which can be done by most six-year-olds.

Sensorimotor Coordination and Organization. Eye–arm coordination can be observed by having a child throw a ball at a target and catch a ball thrown by the examiner. Children under nine usually catch a ball with both hands; older children can do so with one hand. Some children with visual-motor integration problems may have particular difficulty with athletics that require considerable visual input and feedback, such as baseball and volleyball, but may perform well when coordination is proprioceptive or kinesthetic, as in swimming, skiing, and gymnastics. The selection of an area of competitive athletics is influenced by individual differences in these functions.

Complex motor organization involves planning, sequencing, and coordinating of output. It can be observed in a "Simon says" kind of game (Levine et al, 1980):

Ages 5–7: Imitate examiner's gestures: clap twice over head, twice behind back; clap three times in front of chest, twice behind back, once in front of chest; clap twice in front of chest, once behind back, once in front of chest, once behind back.

Ages 7–9: Hop twice on each foot in succession in place and repeat four times without stopping.

Ages 10–12: Jump and touch back of heels; jumb and clap hands three times before coming down.

Constructional praxis can be tested by asking the child to copy a complex design (see Figure 20-2).

The Body Schema-Tempo Regulation Test measures differentiation and regulation of tempos of fine and gross movements of the total and parts of the body and movements within the surrounding space of an office and on the confined space of a sheet of paper. In this test a child is asked to assume various body positions, perform sensorimotor tasks, describe body sensations, and make associations to them (Santostefano, 1978).

Language Functions. The assessment of speech begins with the quality of voice for such things as hoarseness, tremulousness, and high pitch. Rhythmicity of spontaneous speech should be noted. Repetition of phrases such as "hopping hippopotamus" elicits dysfluency. Palatal elevation and symmetry should be noted, as well as the gag reflex. Tongue movements can be assessed by having the child stick out the tongue, push it against the inside of a cheek, and lick an imaginary crumb off a lip. If a child can lick off a real but not an imaginary crumb lying on a lip, an oral apraxia that may accompany an expressive language disorder is suggested.

Nominal dysphasia can be detected by asking a child to name objects. Receptive dysphasia can be elicited by playing "hide and seek" with the named objects and asking the child to find these hidden objects sequentially. An expressive dysphasia is suggested by a child who is reluctant to speak and has difficulty finding words in spontaneous speech. The comprehension and writing of written language should be observed. Language assessment instruments are listed in Figure 20-13.

The Significance of Neurological Signs

Neurological signs commonly are classified as "hard" or "soft." Hard signs are indicators of specific central nervous system lesions regardless of age, whereas soft signs apparently do not have focal significance and occur developmentally in young children. Generally, then, a soft sign is a neurological manifestation that a child should have outgrown.

The overall trend of sensory development is toward finer, more exact differentiation of stimuli. The trend of motor development is toward increasingly precise

control over a repertoire of movement combinations. Early in development, however, overflow discharges, called synergisms, in muscle groups not directly involved in an act are seen. The neonate shows synergisms in the form of mass, overflow reflex responses to stimulation and in mirroring of the baby's own movements on the opposite side of the body. Undue persistence of these primitive synergisms constitute soft signs, for example, the tonic neck reflex and the involuntary clenching of one hand when gripping with the other. Examples of other soft signs and reflexes that disappear with growth are given in Figure 20-14. These signs may be significant when they are observed at an age when neural maturation usually causes them to be superseded; they follow maturational curves usually completed by the age of eight (Birch et al, 1970; Shapiro et al, 1978). On the other hand, hard neurological signs normally are not seen at earlier ages, such as asymmetrical deep tendon reflexes, strabismus, muscle tone asymmetries, and tremors.

Certain soft signs, such as astereognosis, finger dysgnosia, balance difficulty, and choreiform movements, can statistically discriminate groups of educationally disabled children from controls; however, they are of little significance in the evaluation of a particular child unless they pertain to schoolwork (Accardo, 1980; Hertzig, 1982; Kalverboer et al, 1978; Kinsbourne & Caplan, 1979). The NINCDS Collaborative Perinatal Project disclosed on an epidemiological scale the generally weak relationship between soft neurological signs and learning difficulties (10 percent) and hyperkinetic-impulsive behavior (13 percent) (Nichols & Chen, 1981).

A recently developed Primitive Reflex and Postural Adjustment Scale that measures the degree of occurrence of primitive reflexes, righting reactions, and postural adjustments has been reported to discriminate between normal and both neurolog-

LANGUAGE ASSESSMENT INSTRUMENTS		
Instrument	**Age Range**	**Emphasis**
Examining for Aphasia—Revised (Eisenson, J.) Psychological Corporation 757 Third Avenue New York, New York 10017	Ages 5 to Adult (60 minutes)	Evaluates expressive and receptive language and thought processes. Profile of strengths and weaknesses. Very useful but lacks norms.
Halstead Aphasia Test Industrial Relations Center University of Chicago 1225 East 60th Street Chicago, Illinois 60637	Ages 8 to Adult (15–20 minutes)	Tests for dysnomia, spelling dyspraxia, writing dyspraxia, writing dysgraphia, enunciation dysarthria, reading dyslexia, constructional dyspraxia, arithmetic dyscalculia, and auditory-verbal agnosia.
Illinois Test of Psycholinguistic Abilities—Revised (ITPA-Rev.) (Kirk, S. A., McCarthy, J. J., Kirk, W.) University of Illinois Press Box 5081, Station A Champaign, Illinois 61820	Ages 2½ to 10 (45–60 minutes)	Evaluates receptive, organizing, and expressive language in addition to aiditory-vocal and visual-motor forms. Yields age level. Depends upon cultural background. Useful for identifying areas for remediation.
The Basic Concept Inventory (Engelman, S. E.) Follett Publishing Co. 1010 West Washington Boulevard Chicago, Illinois 60607	Ages 3 to 10 (15 minutes)	Tests language comprehension and basic concepts

Figure 20-13.

ically handicapped and emotionally disturbed young children. The presence of primitive reflexes and poorly developed postural adjustments indicates developmental abnormality (Friedlander et al, 1982). All of these findings appear to relate to inadequate sensorimotor integration in the form of immature postural reactions, poor extraocular muscle control, poorly developed visual orientation in space, sound-processing difficulty, and limited ability to concentrate attention (Ayres, 1972).

More specifically, the articulo-graphic group of dyslexics tend to show difficulties in fine and gross motor coordination. The neurological organization of some children with reading difficulties may represent immaturity in spatial orientation and temporal sequencing because of incomplete hemisphere specialization, so that the triad of immaturity in right–left discrimination, praxis, and finger gnosis in children beginning school tends to predict learning difficulty (Silver, 1981a). This also is supported by the finding that auditory-linguistic dyslexic persons show a lack of hemispheric dominance for words on testing of each hemisphere's visual fields.

Thus clusters of "soft" signs of neurological immaturity have some predictive

AGE	MOTOR CONTROL	SENSORY DISCRIMINATION	SPATIAL ORIENTATION	IMMATURE SIGNS (PRIMITIVE REFLEXES)	COMPLEX SEQUENTIAL MOVEMENTS	VISUAL-MOTOR
5	Skips, hops, walks on heels	Identifies touch of a thumb or little finger	Identifies own right and left hand	Neck righting reflex covered by voluntary action	Can button	
6	Stands on one foot with eyes open for 10 seconds	Identifies bilateral simultaneous touching of thumb and little finger	Identifies right and left side of own body		Can tie shoes	
7	Can rapidly alternate pronation and supination movements of hands	Identifies simultaneous touching of middle fingers of same hand; also of face and hand	Touches right ear with left hand; contralateral awareness		Can imitate sequence of gestures; clap twice in front, once behind back, once in front and once in back; can tie shoes	Can move eyes independently of head
8	Can repeatedly oppose finger to thumb; heel-to-toe walking forward and backward; motor steadiness appears	Identifies bilateral asymmetrical touching of right fourth finger and left third finger	Identifies right and left on other	Finger spreading no longer associated with opening mouth and sticking out tongue (Touwen & Prechtl, 1970)		Reversals and mirror image errors disappear
9	Can stand heel-to-toe with eyes closed for 15 seconds		Consistent hand preference Identifies own and other contralaterally, your right hand to my left ear	Adventitious and synkinesias with rapid alternating movements, finger-thumb opposition and gripping disappears	Hop twice on each foot in place in succession, repeat 4 times with stopping; can catch ball with one hand	
10	Can walk on sides of feet; pincer grasp of pencil		Consistent eye and hand dominace			
11	Can stand on tiptoes with eyes closed for 15 seconds			Can walk on sides of feet without posturing of upper extremities	Can jump and touch backs of heels can jump and clap 3x before coming down	

Figure 20-14. Timetable for acquiring sensorimotor skills. (Adapted from R. A. Gardner, *The Objective Diagnosis of Minimal Brain Dysfunction, Creative Therapeutics,* Cresskill NJ, 1979; and M. D. Levine, R. Books, and J. P. Shonkoff, *A Pediatric Approach to Learning Disorder,* John Wiley and Sons, New York, 1980.)

417

value; however, they should be regarded only as associated factors in the context of an entire clinical picture. Only a few of these signs, such as those that contribute to visual tracking difficulty, clumsiness, language, and handwriting problems, are likely to have direct remedial implications (Levine & Melmed, 1982).

Neurological Syndromes

The neurological syndromes of childhood range fom benign self-limited episodes to relentlessly progressive degenerative disorders. They are suggested by the loss of previously gained skills and the delayed acquisition of, or the failure to acquire, new skills.

A syndrome of developmental apraxia and agnosia manifested in excessive clumsiness has been described. It is characterized by awkwardness in dressing, feeding, walking, writing, drawing, and copying (Walton et al, 1962).

A choreiform syndrome also has been described (Prechtl & Stemmer, 1962; Prechtl, 1978). This syndrome includes choreiform movements and problems with sequential organization, spelling, and mathematics.

Cerebral palsy refers to children with congenital brain injury resulting in pyramidal and extrapyramidal neurological signs. It occurs in about two of every 1000 persons in the United States. Males are affected slightly more than females. Of seven children born with cerebral palsy, one dies, three are incapacitated by neuromotor disabilities and mental retardation, two have disabilities responsive to treatment, and one has only mild deficits. Thus about one-half of the surviving children with cerebral palsy have normal intelligence, with little relationship between intelligence quotient and the severity of hemiparesis. But children with extrapyramidal cerebral palsy, who make up about 20 percent of the total group, have less intellectual impairment

than other groups. Even then their delay in developing language skills and their motor disabilities often result in underestimation of their intelligence.

Cerebral palsy represents one extreme on a continuum of congenital brain injury and poses the vexing question of *formes frustes* at the other end of the continuum, with varying degrees of sensorimotor and intellectual impairments that do not fall into definable syndromes.

Other neurological syndromes include storage disorders, demyelinating diseases, leukodystrophies, progressive viral disease, neurocutaneous disorders, brain tumors, metabolic disorders, hydrocephalies, and toxicities, such as from lead and drugs (Herskowitz & Rosman, 1982).

Microcephaly, as defined by head circumference of more than two standard deviations below the mean, is highly correlated with subnormal intelligence. Many microcephalic children function in the normal range of intelligence; however, the factor of head size cannot be disregarded.

Specific syndromes associated with mental retardation are neurofibromatosis and tuberous sclerosis. Another is Turner syndrome, which is a disorder in females in which there is a single X chromosome (XO karyotype). The clinical picture includes short stature, amenorrhea, sterility, and broadening of the neck folds. There also is impairment of spatial abilities and of right–left directional sense with a lower nonverbal WISC score.

Males with physical features similar to those of Turner syndrome manifest Klinefelter syndrome (XXY karyotype). They have small testes, gynecomastia, passive, immature personalities, poor peer relations, and school difficulties. The Turner and Klinefelter syndromes are responsive to hormonal treatment. In addition, inborn errors of metabolism can be associated with mental retardation, particularly phenylketonuria.

The fragile X syndrome has been found

to be a relatively common genetic form of mental retardation associated with behavior disorders ranging from autism to violent hyperkinesis (Hagerman & McBogg, 1983).

Adrenoleukodystrophy is a rare sex-linked genetically determined disorder that appears in boys between four and eight years of age with the initial symptoms of hyperkinesis, school failure, and later neurological and endocrine signs (Moser et al, 1981).

Dendritic spine dysgenesis is a possible etiological factor in Tay-Sachs disease of mental and motor retardation (Serban, 1978). The Kearns-Sayre syndrome is an example of another rare degenerative disease of unknown cause that affects the nervous and muscular systems. It is characterized by progressive external ophthalmoplegia, atypical pigmentary degeneration of the retina, and heart block. It may be associated with learning difficulties (Berenberg et al, 1977).

Electrophysiological Procedures

Although direct electrical stimulation of the brain can be carried out at the time of neurosurgery and through electrodes implanted for research purposes, the usual electrophysiological diagnostic approaches to the brain are indirect.

The Galvanic Skin Response (GSR)

The GSR reflects activity of the autonomic nervous system. It is obtained from two electrodes placed on the skin of the palm or surface of a finger as a weak constant current is passed through the circuit. The response to stimuli presented is directly influenced by sweat glands in the skin innervated by the sympathetic branch of the autonomic nervous system. Increases in arousal and changes in attention are reflected in changes in the conductivity tracing of the GSR.

The GSR is best known as a component of the lie detector. The technique has been used in studying attentional phenomena in adults and children with schizophrenia.

The Electroencephalogram (EEG)

Electrical activity first was recorded from the brains of animals by Caton in 1875 and in humans by Berger in 1924.

The EEG measures changes in voltage between two electrodes placed upon the scalp. In the monopolar recording technique, one electrode is placed over a relatively inactive site, such as the earlobe. In bipolar recordings each electrode is placed over a different brain area. What is recorded, therefore, is the difference between electrode sites and not the actual activity at one particular place. Tracings are made in the waking state as well as under special circumstances, such as during hyperventilation and sleep.

Although electroencephalography has been widely used with children with educational problems, its relevance is limited to two kinds of findings. One is the presence of spike discharges that indicate subclinical epilepsy even when no overt seizure activity is observed. In a few instances, when behavioral and learning difficulties are associated with paroxysmal spike activity in the EEG, anticonvulsants produce symptomatic improvement.

The other significant EEG finding is an excess of slow-wave activity for a child's age. The presence of a spike and slow-wave pattern is found in petit mal epilepsy. In addition, young children show a predominance of slow-wave activity in the delta (below four per second) and theta (four to seven per second) ranges. As the nervous system matures, the dominant frequencies are increasingly concentrated in the alpha (eight to 13 per second) range. Some children with learning difficulties have an excess of slow-wave activity; this presumably indicates either immaturity of brain development or failure of brain-stem centers to facilitate adequate cerebral cortical activity (Baird et al, 1980). The administration of stimulants to hyperactive children has been reported to shift dominant EEG frequencies from the theta to the alpha range. The reliability of this finding remains to be determined (Kinsbourne & Caplan, 1979).

Event-Related Potentials (ERP)

Event-related potentials in the EEG in response to somesthetic, visual, and auditory stimuli are used as a method for evaluation of central nervous system activities from peripheral receptors to the cerebral cortex.

Mild electric stimuli to the skin are used as somesthetic stimuli. A variety of stimuli have been used to generate visual evoked responses: light flashes, presentation of printed letters or other meaningful stimuli, or gridlike patterns. Auditory stimuli range from such sounds as clicks and noises to speech and to stimuli that differ solely in terms of prosodic contrast. Some types of auditory evoked responses, in particular auditory brain-stem responses, have been found to be useful in estimating hearing loss in otherwise untestable subjects. The ERP method also has been employed in studying the augmentation or reduction of sensory output by different persons.

Multivariate Statistical Electroencephalography

The conventional EEG is not sophisticated enough for making delicate judgments. A far superior technique is power-spectrum analysis, which is a method for quantitatively determining the relative distribution of different wave form frequencies within a given time frame (Kinsbourne & Caplan, 1979).

Even more complex procedures have been suggested for the analysis of EEG and ERP data through neurometrics and brain electrical activity mapping (BEAM).

Neurometrics is a method for recording EEG and evoked responses and analyzing the data. The EEG is recorded from monopolar and bipolar sites and broken into spectral bands. All of the data assembled are fed into a matrix of thousands of measurements on each subject upon which a discriminant analysis is carried out to determine if groups of persons can be distinguished from one another.

BEAM uses computers to produce a color contour map of the electrical activity at the brain's surface. The computers also can be used in ERP studies to average out the background noise that is present even when the brain is idling. BEAM uses many of the statistical methods of neurometrics but with a smaller data pool. The display can be made to move through successive EEG or evoked-response epochs in time to provide a moving picture of unfolding physiological processes.

Radiological Techniques

Methods for visualizing the brain were revolutionized during the early 1970s by the introduction of a series of brain-imaging techniques, which are relatively painless and harmless. Computerized tomography provides detailed pictures of the tissues of the human body by the use of computer-enhanced x rays. Positron emission tomography and magnetic resonance imaging offer promising tools for the study of brain activity in health and disease (Brownell et al, 1982).

Computerized Tomographic Scanning

The most widely used technique for brain imaging is computerized tomographic (CT) scanning. This technique involves sending an x-ray beam through a part of the body, such as the brain, to a set of detectors on the other side. Because the x-ray beam is diminished by the tissues it passes through, the information collected by the detectors can be used to construct a picture of different parts of the brain. The scanner reconstructs a computerized image of the brain by rotating around the body one degree at a time and collecting more information on the detectors. This process continues until the scanning process has been completed for a full 360 degrees. A modern CT scanner gives a vivid three-dimensional picture of the brain.

Positron Emission Tomographic Scanning

Positron emission tomography (PET) is a technique that gives good resolution like CT scanning and reveals brain structures in relatively fine detail. Further, it is a dynamic technique that permits the neuroscientist to watch the brain at work and to observe which parts of it become more active in response to various kinds of stimuli. It enables the functional neuroanatomical localization of markers, such as glucose, amino acids, and neuroleptics, by computerized imaging techniques.

Radioactive substances are introduced into the body and taken up in the brain, and their radiation is emitted from active parts of the brain. Information about the amount of radiation taken up is collected on a set of detectors that surround the brain in a 360-degree circle. As in CT scanning, the brain is broken down into relatively small grids and sectioned in slices that reflect in space and time the distribution of the positron-labeled substance and permit the analysis of physiological processes, such as blood flow, the utilization of metabolic substrates, and mapping neuroreceptor sties (Ter-Pogossian, 1980).

Magnetic Resonance Imagery (MRI)

Nuclear magnetic resonance is based upon radio-frequency signals emitted by atoms. These signals are used to evaluate the orientation of atom nuclei in a magnetic field. MRI does not employ potentially hazardous radiation and provides exquisitely detailed anatomic images and metabolic information. It can identify chemicals analytically and follow biological functions on a molecular level.

MRI scanning is accomplished by placing a person inside a large circular magnet. The electromagnetic forces produced by this magnet cause the hydrogen atoms in the body to move in response. When the force is then turned off, they move back to their original position, in the process producing an electromagnetic signal. Different tissues in the body produce different signals, depending on the mixture of elements they contain. As in the case of CT scanning, these signals can be fed into a computer, which then creates a picture of body tissues. While CT-scan sections tend to be fixed at relatively arbitrary points, the MRI scanner can produce many more different views of the three-dimensional structure of the brain.

Regional Cerebral Blood Flow

The technique of regional cerebral blood flow (RCBF) involves the use of radioactive tracers, which are taken up in brain tissue and can be used to visualize active parts of the brain. The labeled tracers emit photons, which can be measured either by mapping their flow on the surface of the brain or with a computer-assisted tomograph. The RCBF surface, or cortical, maps are accurate, but deep brain structures are not revealed.

Genetic Evaluation

Medical genetics is the application of the science of human genetics to medical problems (Reed, 1980). An estimated 20 percent of the population have known genetically influenced disorders themselves or in their families. Approximately 35 percent of all spontaneously aborted fetuses have chromosome abnormalities. At least 5 percent of all liveborn infants have a recognizable condition with a genetic implication.

In general, there are two groups of families for whom genetic services are indicated. The first group involves families at risk for the recurrence of birth defects, such as congenital heart disease, cleft palate, or visual and hearing impairment. It also includes families at risk for inherited diseases, such as muscular dystrophy, hemophilia, cystic fibrosis, mental retardation, and the dyslexias.

The second group of families are those at risk of first occurrence of a syndrome because of ethnic, age, or environmental exposure factors. Examples of disorders that are more frequent in ethnic groups are Tay-Sachs disease and Gaucher disease in Ashkenazi Jews, sickle cell anemia in blacks, and beta-thalassemia in populations of Mediterranean origin. Populations at risk because of age are older and younger pregnant women. Other risk-inducing factors are consanguinous marriages and exposure to environmental chemical mutagens and teratagens.

The following are examples of specific indications for referral for genetic counseling (Gabel & Erikson, 1980):

1. A history in a person or in family members of a genetic syndrome.
2. Dysmorphic physical findings of unknown cause, such as unusual facial appearance in a child or in other family members.
3. Mental retardation of unknown cause.
4. A family history of Down syndrome.
5. The presence of cleft lip or cleft palate.
6. A child with ambiguous genitalia.
7. A child with unexplained short stature.
8. A woman over 35 years of age who is, or who is considering becoming, pregnant, particularly if there is a known genetic risk.
9. A woman with multiple spontaneous abortions of unknown etiology.
10. An individual considering marrying a close relative.

The role of genetic counseling is to inform persons of current knowledge about these conditions and to assist them in planning and decision making.

TREATMENT PLANNING

The worth of a clinical evaluation depends upon its contribution to changing a child's life. Unfortunately many children have extensive school and clinical records that only document a child's continued failure and, in too many cases, ultimate extrusion from the educational mainstream. Over and over again, the fragmentation and lack of continuity of services lie behind the crumbling lives of these children. Moreover, the expectation that a particular professional approach would solve the problem often has deflected attention from the children and their parents as the sources of both understanding and constructive change.

The clinical process with its initial focus on children and their parents lays the foundation for building a coordinated program managed by a team comprised of professionals, parents, and the children themselves and designed to follow a child through the entire course of need. After the clinical interview, a vital next step is interpreting the clinical findings to the children and parents. Then a planning meeting can be held with the family and other professionals.

Interpretive Interviews with Children and Parents

The sharing of clinical information with children and parents should be done in both interpretive and educational contexts. Because they bring emotionally charged and naive attitudes to the clinical process, the challenge is to provide them with relevant information so as to ensure that it will be understood and used.

The child should be included in discussions of findings and treatment. Because parent and child are together, they can reinforce each other as questions arise. Children should hear about the areas in which they do well and about problem areas in a nonjudgmental way. These children often feel incompetent and perceive that others see them that way as well. They easily misinterpret comments about them as critical and accusatory. Sensitivity is needed to communicate honestly and in a way that a child perceives as supportive. Children should not be left with the impression that secrets are being kept from them. When adults have been secretive and accusatory about the school problem, open discussion is needed to defuse pathological interactions between child and parents.

The interpretive process should convey information to the child and parents at levels that can be heard and digested. Most families are frightened, ashamed, and hurt by the circumstances that led to the referral. Although the defenses of denial, projection, and displacement may conceal these emotions, they are there nonetheless.

Orton's words exemplify the need for an approach that addresses a child's guilt from being unable to learn and adults' guilt from being unable to teach:

> Children usually are interested in the story of how . . . their brains are not working just right for the particular subject in which they have met with trouble. An understanding of how the difficulty may have arisen often helps prevent a child from falling back on explanations based on emotional instability, nervousness, undue fears, or lack of self-confidence which in themselves often seem to operate as a vicious circle. An even more complete explanation to the parents and to the teachers of the specific nature of all of these difficulties is of prime impor-

tance in treatment of the child since the school failures have all too often been interpreted . . . with an implication of blame which may very easily foster an unwarranted feeling of guilt in the child or the parent or both (Orton, 1937).

Children who understand the clinical findings and the reasons for treatment recommendations can answer the taunts of peers and the criticism of adults with explanations of their school difficulties. At the least a child can say, "My doctor says I am not dumb."

In some instances parents are ready to hear specific diagnostic formulations; however, in most cases they need to understand the following points:

1. There are problems that justify their concern.
2. The causes of the problems are unclear but manifold in nature.
3. No one deliberately created these problems.
4. These problems commonly cause frustration, anger, guilt, and embarrassment for all concerned. Everyone tends to feel that they have failed.
5. They are not alone. These problems are encountered by many children and families.
6. The process of treatment is the route to answering their questions. In fact, when they no longer have questions, treatment will be finished. Discovering the important factors in the child's learning problems and what to do about them are the purposes of treatment.
7. What is likely to happen if nothing is done to reverse the present course should be made clear. Understandably children and parents wish that the problems would disappear or be outgrown. They need to know the realistic consequences of not dealing with the problems now.
8. Parents need to be relieved of the search for single causes and precipitating events

so that the focus can be shifted from blaming teachers, the child, and themselves to a definition and acceptance of the current state of affairs as a basis for constructive actions. In so doing the air may be cleared by encouraging expression of guilt and blame.

When informed of the results of intelligence testing, parents and child need an explanation of the overall significance of such testing and the factors it depends upon, including the child's motivation, educational background, and opportunities. The scores can be shared with them with an explanation of their significance. If psychometrics reveal reasonably valid estimates of potential ability, this should be interpreted to child and parent so that they have a realistic awareness of what optimal academic achievement might be. Unrealistically high expectations lie behind much parental disappointment in their children.

Review of achievement testing usually is more straightforward. Both child and parents generally are aware of limitations in achievement. They usually are not aware, however, of the important specifics. It is illuminating to know, for example, that a child may be able to read orally but not comprehend what is read. Or that two column numbers can be added easily but not three. Just as intelligence testing gives an idea of how much a child should be able to learn in school, achievement testing addresses what a child knows and which academic skills are lacking. It is particularly important to evaluate academic skill levels in the context of a particular child's cultural background and community correspondence to national norms. In some schools the grade-level score on standardized tests may be well below the average; in other schools it may be above.

The clinical findings related to a child's character and emotions are more difficult to interpret. Parents usually can see that motivational problems make it hard for a failing child to keep trying. It is more difficult for them to understand how neurotic conflicts can interfere with learning to read, even after children have outgrown their cognitive weaknesses. Parents may be responsive initially to outlining family dynamics, particularly as they relate to the child's manipulation of them and teachers.

The matter of prognosis is tricky. On the one hand, the outlook for most children is favorable if the child's problems are addressed successfully. On the other hand, the wishes to minimize the problem, to resolve the immediate crisis, and to hope that the child will outgrow the difficulties are so strong that adults are likely to hear a favorable prognosis and ignore treatment recommendations essential to achieving that result. For this reason it is important to highlight realistically the true functional incapacities of a child.

Most of these children are unable to function in the academic mainstream, which is equivalent to an adult's inability to hold a job. Most are social isolates, which means they are unable to function in their society, and also are unable to function comfortably in their families, which signifies impairment of close relationships. All of these characteristics would be regarded as serious functional impairments in adults; indeed as adults many of these children do become so handicapped. However, because of prevalent agism, which obscures the fact that children can suffer as adults do, the extent of their functional impairment and suffering tends to be minimized. For these reasons it is wise to validate the concern that led to clinical referral and realistically confirm the evident functional impairment and the likely outcome if intervention does not take place. The likelihood of a favorable outcome is related to the degree that a child's parents and school become seriously concerned about the child's welfare and commit themselves to the inevitably difficult steps involved in understanding and meeting the child's needs.

The responses of children and parents to clinical interpretations are helpful in assessing prognosis. To the extent that the interviewing process has been truly enlightening for them, they show the ability to grasp realistically a problem-solving approach. To the extent that they do not hear the formulations and persist in preconceived notions, additional time will need to be devoted to reframing their views and expectations so that a collaborative foundation for treatment can be created as discussed in Chapter 35.

The most effective treatment approach starts from within the child and progressively involves the child's family, school, and community. The first step is working with the child and parents so that the child understands the nature of one's learning problems and what can be done about them. Then parents are assisted in understanding the things that they can do to assist their child and interpret their child's needs to others. The aim is to make parents "the experts" for their child. To the extent that irrational forces are operating in a child and family, psychotherapeutic interventions are indicated at the individual and family levels. The overall aim is to remove irrational barriers to learning in the child and family so that rational remedial and compensatory techniques can be used effectively.

Family and Professional Team Planning

In formulating a treatment plan for a particular child, it is useful to draw upon the concept of child advocacy, which means assuming responsibility in varying degrees for promoting and protecting the developmental needs of both a child through individual advocacy and children in general through class advocacy (Westman, 1979).

The basic ingredients of child advocacy are system bridging, a developmental orientation, conflict resolution, fact finding, interdisciplinary teamwork, and the protection and promotion of the legal rights of children. At the level of primary care, the thrust of advocacy is through sensitizing adults to children's viewpoints, case-finding, developmental review, and system-bridging intervention. At the secondary-care level, the emphasis is on clinical evaluation, formulating a treatment plan, and ensuring coordination and continuity of care by the designation of a case manager. At the tertiary-care level, the emphasis is upon professional teamwork and stabilizing a child's life circumstances and parenting. The responsibility for substantially intervening in the lives of children falls within the legal system, and the understanding of the needs of children and formulating a plan for meeting them within the province of clinicians.

Bridging the family, clinical, and school systems is essential for establishing and maintaining rapport in carrying out the educational aspects of a child's treatment. The clinical process begins with access to information from the schools and collaborative planning with school personnel. Although there are confidential aspects of the clinical interviews that are not directly relevant to educational interests, the welfare of a child is served by including key representatives of that child's school in the planning process. A useful format is to include school personnel in a planning meeting after reporting to the child and parents. When parental motivation is a problem, school, and other community professionals may be helpful at earlier stages as well.

The clinical findings should be discussed with school personnel so that they can contribute their observations and knowledge of resources available to the child. Disagreements often arise between adults about a child's behavior, which differs from one setting to another and the interpretation of test performance. Each observer is seeing a different aspect of the child, and there is a subjective element in test interpretation. It is not a matter of one person being right and the other wrong. The challenge is to integrate and understand differing points of view so that disputation and polarization do not derail efforts to help the child in question. An explanation of the validity of differing points of view by the clinician at the outset of a planning conference can shift the focus away from previous positions, particularly when divergent views have existed between parents and school, so that both sides can give ground gracefully. Acknowledging the shared commitment of both parents and school to a child's welfare helps this process.

Planning for a child in school is influenced by the child's potential intellectual ability, academic skill levels, behavior problems, and emotional state (Adelman & Taylor, 1983). Chapter 30 is devoted to special education programs. In brief when intellectual functioning is not judged to be significantly below average for the referent group, but academic skill performance, particularly in reading, is below norms, regular classroom programs are appropriate with the addition of adjunctive services, such as personalized tutoring.

When behavior is judged as not uncontrollably disruptive or pathologically withdrawn but still is seen as significantly different from the referent group, regular programs are appropriate with setting modifications, such as transfer to a different teacher and classroom and the addition of adjunctive services, such as resource help for the classroom teacher and tutoring for the student.

Special class placement is indicated when a child's inadequate performance in school and in other critical activities is accompanied by academic skill levels significantly below average and behavior judged to be uncontrollable, dangerously aggressive, or severely withdrawn. In these instances, however, placement should not take place if it is likely that an outpatient treatment program will suffice to improve functioning in a regular classroom.

Available resources vary from one locale to another, but their use is influenced by whether a child actually wants help or is under external compulsion and whether there is parental approval (Adelman & Taylor, 1983). The accessibility of resources also depends upon private and public payment of fees and geographical factors. Finally, taking the steps necessary to become eligible for desired services necessitates knowledge of, and ability to comply with, administrative requirements. Although most families can handle these steps, some require professional advocacy to do so.

At the conclusion of the team planning meeting, it is useful to have both the school personnel and parents reiterate the next steps to be taken so that the plan to be followed is clearly articulated. The designation of who has assumed responsibility for the various components of the treatment plan should be clear. A coordinating person also should be identified to ensure monitoring of the treatment plan.

For many children parental advocacy is sufficient. A large number of children, however, depend upon professionals to play an advocacy role in their lives at the levels of identifying their need for help, understanding their special requirements, and ensuring that those requirements are met.

SUMMARY

A melange of barriers to understanding children with learning problems results from fragmented professional approaches to, and the lack of continuity of services for, a specific child. In particular, the separation of diagnosis from treatment and the isolation of each area of remediation limit the possibility of helping a child.

Depending upon the orientation of a professional discipline, children with learning problems in school are described as having such conditions as dyslexia, minimal brain dysfunction, right-brain dominance, family psychopathology, dietary deficiencies, and chemical intoxications. To make matters worse, each viewpoint attracts strong public support from those who seek a single cause for which there is a simple cure for a particular child's difficulty. Characteristic of the most popular approaches is a quest for something awry in a child's brain.

The clinical process brings the individually centered model of health care to bear upon children's learning problems. It places the child at the center of an evaluative process that builds outward to incorporate the critical systems impinging upon the child. The clinical process depends upon establishing rapport with a child and family in order to gather essential information about their past lives and current views of themselves and their life experiences. It further depends upon the integration of information gathered from other sources about the child and family, particularly the school, formal psychological and educational testing, appropriate health specialties, and medical investigative procedures.

The heart of the clinical process is interviewing the child and family. This provides access to the most important levels of understanding a child's needs and offers inherent therapeutic potential as the clinical process shifts the emphasis from doing something to a child to working out a team effort with the child.

The unstructured and structured aspects of the clinical interview include the family and a child with appropriate emphasis upon subsystems of the family, such as the parental, parent–child, and sibling subsystems. The flexible use of the interview permits eliciting the various views of a child's problems from family members; developmental, family, medical, and social histories; observations of interaction patterns; and a mental-status and developmental screening of the child.

Formal developmental assessment can be done by clinicians trained in child development and the administration of testing batteries adapted to the stages of development. Specific assessment of the processing of visual and auditory information is relevant to schoolwork.

The educational evaluation of a child brings together information from cumulative school reports, academic skill assessment with particular emphasis upon reading and arithmetical skills, and observations of the child at work in school. Educational test results should not be substitutes for careful and extensive study of a child's history and present functioning in various aspects of life. The emphasis should be upon a child's potential achievement levels. This requires moving from reliance on testing to teaching as a means of evaluation.

Psychometric testing can be helpful in estimating potential intelligence and identifying areas of weakness and strength. Projective psychological tests can be useful in elaborating character, emotional, and interpersonal dynamics.

A general medical evaluation is an essential first step for all children with learning problems to ensure that chronic or acute physical disease is not present. A complete visual assessment, including acuity and coordination of eye movements, also should be be carried out with each child.

The neurological evaluation is directed toward assessment of the integrity of sensory, motor, and higher level functions of the central nervous system, to detect both functional idiosyncracies that may contribute to learning problems and the presence of neurological findings that may reflect immaturity or *formes frustes* of clinical syndromes. Electroencephalographic and radiological techniques can be helpful in some cases but are not indicated as routine screening procedures. Genetic assessment and counseling may be indicated in certain instances.

From the point of view of helping a child, the interpretive stages of the clinical process are the most important. In general three steps are useful. The first is the general orientation of the child and family to the clinical findings as they emerge during the clinical interview. The second is the formal interpretation of clinical findings from all sources with the child and family. The third stage is developing a treatment plan

with other professionals, particularly from the child's school, with appropriate advocacy to ensure integration of the various treatment and educational elements and continuity of the program through monitoring and periodic review.

Through the clinical process, a child-centered treatment plan implemented by components involving each pertinent system level can be designed. The designation of a case manager, and professional advocates when needed, then can support parents' efforts to help their children. The goal is that parents become "the experts" for their children.

VI

The Diagnosis of Functional Disabilities

Endowment and chance determine a person's fate—rarely or never one of these powers alone.

Sigmund Freud, 1912

This section deals with the many ways in which central nervous system (CNS) functions can be ill suited for schoolwork. When the CNS operates efficiently, we are unaware of the role of the brain in our mental life and behavior. When it does not, however, we become acutely aware of the fact that the brain is the organ of the mind.

As defined in Chapter 2, the term disability is functioning of an organ system that falls outside of a given standard range and is susceptible to objective study. In applying this definition to the CNS, I refer to disabilities in concentration, vision, speech, impulse control, thinking, and self-concept in ways that may be unfamiliar to the reader. I do this to help overcome terminology barriers to recognizing that all of these problems really are disabilities of functions rooted in the tissues of the brain.

These functional disabilities of the CNS can give rise to educational disabilities and handicaps and may be responsive to treatment interventions in themselves. Although the terminology used in this book includes clinical diagnostic concepts, the CNS functional disabilities are described in terms familiar to all who work with children.

The most common temperamental functional disabilities seen in school children occur in the form of what are called attention deficits, hyperkinetic behavior, and affective disorders. A careful analysis of each child's situation, however, usually reveals that greater precision can be used in understanding a child's functional disabilities than these overly simplified concepts imply. In addition, when their basic needs are not met, children's motivation to pursue academic learning is compromised. Many children simply are preoccupied with meeting their basic emotional needs and taming their instincts, with resulting depletion of interest in school.

Cognitive disabilities range from deficits in the sensory organs themselves to obscure distortions and blocks resulting from psychological defense mechanisms. These disabilities involve visual and auditory reception; auditory, visual, and spatial perception; indermodal sensory integration; imagery and memory; symbolization; and conceptualization.

Specific language disabilities can take place at the levels of speech articulation and of variations in maturational rates in the development of receptive and expressive language. Of particular importance in school are written language disabilities in the form of developmental dyslexias, which are expressed in one or more of the stages in reading, spelling, and writing. The first are the dysmetrias, which result in faulty reception of information. The second are dysgnosias manifested in difficulties in recognizing percepts. The third are dysphasias, which interfere with the recall of meaning. The fourth are dyspraxias, which impair spelling and writing.

When the managerial system is not functioning efficiently, difficulties in beginning and effectively carrying out tasks appear. These problems are more readily detected by observing children in work situations than through testing. For this reason they are often overlooked. Their manifestations are in working abilities, thinking, and interpersonal relationships. Pervasive developmental disorders, the prefrontal lobe syndrome, and the impulsive personality involve disabling interferences in managerial functions.

Self-system problems can affect a child's capacity to do schoolwork and interpersonal relationships. Children may have excessive self-awareness that inhibits their performance or insufficient self-awareness that lowers the quality of their work. Low self-esteem produces a lack of self-confidence, and even depression. A fragmented self-concept leads to erratic and inconsistent behavior. Distorted self-evaluations lead to maladaptive attitudes, such as omniscience or helplessness. Manipulative interpersonal relationships are characteristic of the narcissistic, oppositional, passive–aggressive, and dependent personalities.

21

Temperamental Disabilities

Cultivate that power of concentration which grows with its
exercise, so that attention neither flags nor wavers, but settles
with bulldog tenacity on the subject before you.

Sir William Osler, 1903

hildren vary widely in their interests in intellectual, athletic, artistic, and musical activities. Consequently, successful teachers know the importance of engaging their students' interests by tapping their curiosity and their pleasure in self-assertiveness and mastery. Beyond interest, however, students also must be able to muster the energy required for concentrating on their schoolwork. Accordingly there is growing interest in individual differences in temperament as factors to be considered in education (Keogh, 1983).

Before invoking temperamental explanations, it is important to bear in mind that children may not perform well in school because they lack background knowledge and skills. When asked to perform tasks for which they are insufficiently prepared, they may appear unmotivated, inattentive, or restless. When what is asked of them is within their reach, the same children may be transformed into eager, intense workers (Wallach & Wallach, 1976).

With these considerations in mind, this chapter will outline significant difficulties related to observable manifestations of

temperament in the form of temperamental styles, attention problems, distracting movement levels, and affective disorders.

TEMPERAMENTAL DISPOSITIONS

Among the oldest conceptions of psychology are the four temperaments described by Hippocrates: the sanguine, the choleric, the melancholic, and the phlegmatic (see Figure 21-1). Intriguingly, modern research appears to validate these basic temperamental styles (Buss & Plomin, 1975; Gray, 1971).

These temperamental styles reflect the adaptibility of the affective system as expressed in an individual's susceptibility to emotional provocation and the intensity of emotion once aroused. Thus the sanguine and choleric types are both highly susceptible to emotional provocation; they differ in that the emotions of the sanguine person are mild and those of the choleric are strong. The melancholic and the phleg-

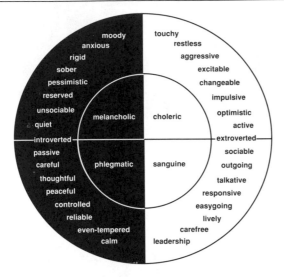

Figure 21-1. Eysenck's analysis of dimensions of temperament. The inner ring shows how the ancient "four temperaments" of Hippocrates and Galen may relate to the findings of modern experimental studies. (From J. A. Gray, *The Psychology of Fear and Stress,* copyright 1971 by McGraw-Hill Co., New York. Reproduced with permission.)

matic are similar in their resistance to the provocation of emotion; they differ in that the emotional intensity of the aroused melancholic is strong, and that of the phlegmatic is weak (McKellar, 1968).

The work of Thomas and Chess stands as a foundation for our modern conceptions of temperament in children (Chess & Thomas, 1986; Thomas & Chess, 1977). They describe the sanguine temperament as the "easy" child. Their "slow to warm up" child resembles the phlegmatic temperament, as does Kinsbourne's "overfocused" child (Kinsbourne & Caplan, 1979). Their "difficult" child resembles the choleric temperament, as does Kinsbourne's "underfocused" child. The manifestations of mild depression in children fit the melancholic temperament.

These comparisons are oversimplifications. Still the concordance between his-

torical and modern conceptions confirms the usefulness of temperament as a description of the behavioral manifestations of the state regulating system as expressed through motivation, attention states, movement levels, and mood.

The role of the instinctual systems in influencing temperamental style is indicated in Figure 21-2. The sanguine temperament is characterized by an outgoing, rhythmic expression of instinctual drives, whereas the choleric temperament is dysrhythmic, with conflict between the drives and their pleasurable and distressing expressions. The phlegmatic temperament results from the sluggish, but rhythmic, expression of drives, which are experienced as distressing in themselves. Within these temperamental styles, mood cycles in most persons follow monthly and seasonal rhythms (Eastwood et al, 1985).

ATTENTION PROBLEMS

The literature on children's attention problems has grown rapidly in recent years. Even when not formally taken into account in behavioral research in children, attention is a confounding variable that is most difficult to control and that contaminates many behavioral studies (Vellutino, 1979).

A child's attention is influenced by a host of internal and external factors. The context and nature of a task are critical. For example, a child may have difficulty listening without a simultaneous engaging visual stimulus (Palfrey et al, 1981). A child also may concentrate when receiving the undivided attention of an adult but not when in a group situation. That child's deficit is in the amount of attention received from others. Furthermore, there are a number of forms of attention, each of which can be affected by a variety of influences.

TEMPERAMENTAL DISABILITIES   433

TEMPERAMENTAL STYLES

TYPES	APPETITIVE INSTINCTS				
	Arousal-Rest	Alimentation-Elimination	Motor Activity	Sexual	Fight-Flight
SANGUINE—CHEERFUL Outgoing Rhythmic	+	+	+	+	
CHOLERIC—MOODY Irritable Dysrhythmic	±	±	±	±	+
PHLEGMATIC—CALM Inward Sluggish Rhythmic	+	+	−	−	−
MELANCHOLY—GLOOMY Inward Dysrhythmic	−	−	−	−	−

ADAPTIVE INSTINCTS

Affiliative		Aggressive		Mastery		Self-Esteem
Pleasure	Distress	Pleasure	Distress	Pleasure	Distress	Pleasure
+		+		+		+
+	+	+	+	+	+	−
+		−				±
	+		+		+	−

Figure 21-2. The relationship between temperamental styles and instinctual systems.

For these reasons I will describe the factors that interfere with the various aspects of attention in detail (see Figure 21-3). I will first deal with problems in involuntary attention that interfere with vigilance, orienting attention, and thresholds of responsiveness. Then I will consider difficulties in the voluntary attention functions of scanning, focusing, and concentration.

Involuntary Attention Problems

Interference with Vigilance

Interferences with vigilant wakefulness may be the result of nonspecific individual variations, seizure disorders, chemicals, sleep disorders, and physical illness.

Individual Variations. There is electroencephalographic (EEG) evidence of individual variations in states of wakefulness in children as reflected in the alpha-wave rhythm patterns in the posterior regions of the brain. In some children the alpha rhythm tends to be poorly organized and shows weaker responses to stimuli, suggesting sluggish vigilance. Stimulant medication may normalize the alpha activity in these children. More specifically, the EEG abnormalities of children with academic learning problems tend to normalize with stimulant medication (Accardo, 1980).

Seizure Disabilities. The incidence of epilepsy in the United States is estimated to be 0.5 percent of the general population. The various types of seizure disorders tend to appear in different age groups (see Figure 21-4).

Grand mal seizures occur at all ages and are characterized by an initial loss of consciousness accompanied by generalized tonic muscle stiffening and falling. Sometimes people have warning auras of the seizure, such as a "rising" sensation in the abdomen preceding loss of consciousness. A shrill cry may accompany the onset of the muscular convulsion. The tonic phase usually lasts for less than a minute, during which suspended breathing leads to darkening of skin color. Sustained muscular rigidity then merges into rapid, generalized, and synchronous muscle jerks accompanied by hyperventilation. Tongue biting, incontinence of urine and feces, and signs of autonomic hyperactivity, including hypertension, tachycardia, sweating, pupillary dilation, and heavy salivation, often occur. After the jerking phase, relaxation and deep sleep follow. Most grand mal seizures last two to five minutes, but attacks may go on for an hour or more. During the rigid phase of grand mal seizures, the EEG contains long runs of rapidly repeating spikes; during the convulsing phase, spikes and slow-wave discharges correspond with the motor jerking. After the convulsion, there is slowing of EEG activity, and focal abnormalities may emerge in persons with brain lesions. The EEG may be normal between epileptic attacks or contain spikes or sharp wave complexes. The immediate sequelae of grand mal attacks include fatigue, muscle weakness, headache, confusion, memory loss, irritability, and abnormal behavior (Solomon & Plum, 1976).

Petit mal seizures are seen in 6–12 percent of children with seizures. They follow a genetic pattern with an age of onset between four and 12 years, and they usually disappear during the second decade; however, 50 percent of these children may develop grand mal seizures. The typical petit mal seizure lasts from five to 30 seconds and is characterized by a sudden stare, sometimes accompanied by blinking of the eyelids and movement of the hands, upper extremities, and head. There is no warning of the attack, and normal activity is resumed afterward. The seizures may occur up to 50 times a day, particularly in the morning. The EEG characteristically shows a spike-and-wave pattern, sometimes only activated by hyperventilation (Solomon & Plum, 1976). Even with medication there is the possibility of interference with vigi-

	Involuntary Attention			Voluntary Attention		
	State Regulating System			Managerial System (Impulse Control, Analysis, Thinking)	State Regulating System	
	Vigilance (Wakefulness)	Orienting (Alertness)	Threshold of Responsiveness (Awareness)	Scanning (Sweeping)	Focusing (Detection of con-figuration, direction and sequence)	Concentration (Persistence, distractibility)

	Individual Variations
	
	Seizure Disorders
	
	Drugs—
	  Hypnotic
	  Stimulant
	
	Sleep Disorders
	
	Physical Illness
	  Fever
	  Diabetes
		Individual Variations	Individual Variations
			
			Immaturity
			
			Psychological Defenses
			  Selective Inattention
			
			Drugs—
			  Stimulants
			  Neuroleptics
			
			Parenting Styles
				Individual Variations
				
				Anxiety
				  Selective Inattention
					Individual Variations
					
					Immaturity
					  Figure-ground Discrimination
					
					Training
					
					Drugs
					  Stimulants
						Individual Variations
						
						Immaturity
						
						Training
						
						Anxiety, Depression, Fatigue, Confusion, Boredom, Somatic Symptoms

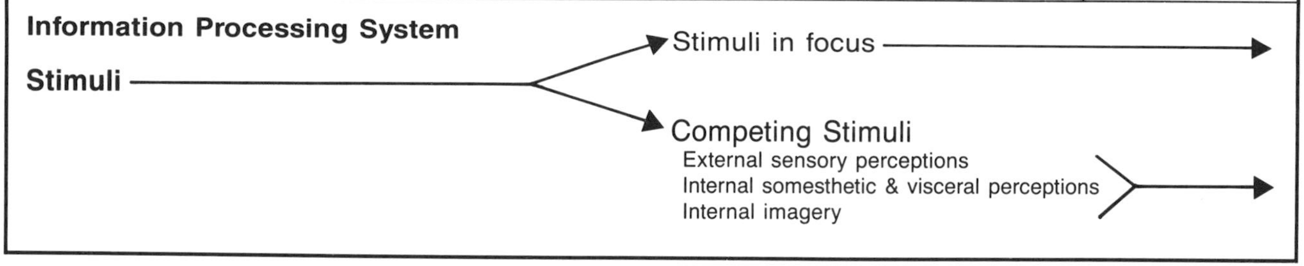

Information Processing System

Stimuli

Stimuli in focus

Competing Stimuli
External sensory perceptions
Internal somesthetic & visceral perceptions
Internal imagery

Figure 21-3.

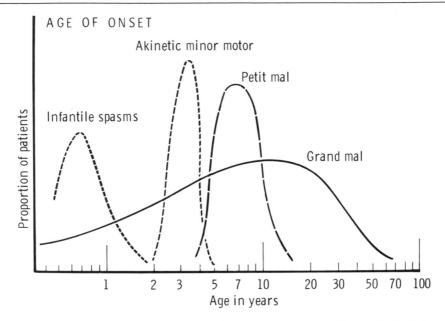

Figure 21-4. Age distribution of various seizure types. (From G. E. Solomon and F. Plum, *Clinical Management of Seizures,* copyright 1976 by W. B. Saunders Co., Philadelphia PA. Reproduced with permission.)

lance in the absence of overt evidence of seizures.

Psychomotor seizures are uncommon, may begin at any age, and last one to two minutes. They usually emanate from the temporal lobe and often are the result of a structural lesion. They vary widely in form but characteristically consist of automatic, steretyped movements, such as staring with lip smacking, chewing, and bizarre behavior. They often begin with bodily sensations, such as an unpleasant odor or a constricting sensation in the throat. They may be followed by confusion and aggressive behavior. During the waking state 40 percent, and during sleep 80 percent, show temporal lobe discharges in their EEG tracings. Environmental events and emotions play a role in the frequency of psychomotor seizures (Powell, 1981).

Minor motor seizures include myoclonic movements, which are sudden brief limb or trunk muscle contractions occurring singly or repetitively, and akinetic attacks, which are brief losses of postural muscle tone that cause the head or body to fall. Although occasional jerks of the body are seen in most persons, expecially when drifting off to sleep, repetitive myoclonic seizures are a more serious matter. Myoclonic attacks occasionally take place with grand mal epilepsy. More characteristically in children and adolescents, myoclonic attacks occur as a manifestation of a progressive degenerative neurological disease. Akinetic seizures or "drop attacks" usually emerge between the ages of two and five years, occur many times a day and are associated with mental retardation and progressive diseases of the brain. Thus myoclonic and akinetic seizures have a graver prognosis than petit mal epilepsy. Both are associated with spike and wave discharges of the EEG that differ from the consistent spike and wave pattern of petit mal by including polyspikes and waves.

Grand mal epilepsy does not in itself impair learning, except when behavior is affected by a brain lesion or when the self-concept related to the seizures affects the learning process. In contrast the frequent absence episodes of petit mal and psychomotor seizures interfere substantially with schoolwork (Gaddes, 1980). Myoclonic and akinetic seizures are rare but can be misunderstood and lead to problems in schoolwork and behavior. Pseudoseizures based upon conversion and dissociative defense mechanisms occasionally are seen in older adolescents and young adults (Gross, 1983).

Chemicals. Excessive dosage of anticonvulsive medication represents a readily reversible cause of learning disorders in children with seizure problems. Phenobarbital in particular may cause decreased vigilance, irritability, and restlessness. The most common cause of chemically altered vigilance in adolescents is self-administered psychoactive drugs, particularly marijuana.

Sleep Disabilities. Any interference with adequate rest may affect wakefulness during the day. When drowsiness, fatigue, or frank sleeping are seen in school, the various forms of insomnia should be explored as possible causes. Inquiries about a child's bedtime and relating that to actual sleep requirement, which varies with age and individuals, is the first step. An important ecological factor in urban areas that contributes to sleep disturbances is noise pollution (Mosse, 1982; Westman & Walters, 1981).

The insomnias are disorders regarding the initiating and maintaining of sleep; when transient, such a disorder may be related to stressful circumstances, and when persistent, to chronic anxiety or depression. Whereas situational stress and anxiety frequently inhibit the capacity to go to sleep, endogenous depression generally is manifested by early awakening.

The sleep apnea syndrome may be manifested by hyperkinesis, inattention, ir-

ritability, chronic fatigue, and daytime napping. These behaviors usually result from chronic sleep deprivation due to respiratory obstruction, such as from excessive adenoid tissue, and rarely from impairment of respiratory function on a diencephalic basis. The syndrome is suggested by fitful, restless sleep, snoring, and noisy breathing combined with daytime drowsiness alternating with hyperkinesis (Zales, 1982). In obese persons airway obstructive sleep apnea is called the Pickwickian syndrome.

Narcolepsy probably is a neurochemical disorder in the regulation of sleep characterized by intermittent attacks of irrepressible sleep, often accompanied by episodes of transient loss of muscular tone, called cataplexy (Roth, 1978). It affects less than 0.1 percent of the population. Narcolepsy may appear as early as three years of age; however, its onset usually is during adolescence. Narcoleptic sleep attacks last from 30 seconds to 15–20 minutes, and in most cases from two to five minutes; the affected person can be easily aroused and become completely alert. In addition to the sleep-inducing circumstances of passivity, attacks also can occur during monotonous or repetitive activities, such as riding a bicycle. Although narcolepsy tends to be lifelong and incurable, stimulant and antidepressant medications are useful in its treatment (Menkes, 1980). Cataplexy is a brief loss of muscular tone with falling but retention of consciousness during an emotional reaction such as laughter, anger, or surprise.

A rare case of daytime sleepiness is the Kleine-Levin syndrome of recurrent episodes of extreme somnolence and hunger encountered during adolescence (Menkes, 1980; Zales, 1982).

Illness. Drowsiness is a common early manifestation of physical disease. Febrile illnesses affect wakefulness and can lead to the extreme of coma. Metabolic diseases, such as diabetes, also insidiously can cause varying degrees of alterations in one's level of consciousness.

Orienting, Startle, and Defensive Response Problems

The same factors that decrease vigilance also retard the orienting ressponse. Sluggish arousal explains the slower reaction times, lesser physiological reactivity, and slower assimilation of information by some children who lack the capacity to process information at the same rate as other children. The cortical arousal of these children may be less efficient than others (Dykman et al, 1970).

In contrast the emotions of anger and fear heighten the orienting, startle, and defensive responses through automatic "fight-or-flight" mechanisms. Thus a child subjected to sarcasm or intimidation may enter an uncomfortable hyperalert state because of the resulting anger or fear. A parasympathetic "idling" tone is more conducive to learning in school than a sympathetic tonus, which heightens the orienting response to external stimuli.

Threshold of Responsiveness Problems

Exceeding the threshold of one's ability to process information because of information input overload is a problem for everyone in our increasingly complex society and can be handled by various adjustment processes, such as omitting, delaying, and queuing tasks; restricting information flow to a limited range of topics; filtering out less important pieces of information; and grouping input by oversimplifying (Miller, 1978). Underlying these deliberate ways of regulating information flow is the buffering of stimulus modulation in the various sensory modalities, of which the visual and auditory are the most relevant to children in school.

Inefficient stimulus modulation plays an important role in clinically significant distractibility. Pavlov noted differences in the "strengths" of the nervous systems of dogs. Later expansion upon this idea led to the description of human beings with "weak" nervous systems that lacked internal inhibition (Buchsbaum, 1976). In this view a "strong" nervous system has a high sensory threshold and augments responses with increasing sensory stimulation. A "weak" nervous system is more intensely excited by stimuli at lower thresholds and tends to exhibit reduced responses with increasing stimulus intensity. This description fits children who are easily distracted by stimuli and at the same time appear to be relatively unaffected by intense stimuli, such as pain.

What appears to be distractibility can result from excessive responsiveness to external stimuli, with ready shifting from one to another; it also can be the result of too little responsiveness so that a child is attracted to environmental stimuli of high personal interest and is oblivious to tasks of low interest.

The inefficient development of stimulus modulation may have repercussions in many areas of character development. An infant must be able to maintain alertness, inhibit crying and random movement, and sustain focused attention in order to attain an organized perceptual experience of the world. The increasing capacity to modulate stimuli may be seen in an infant's developing ability to tolerate fatigue and proprioceptive stimuli without showing overflow excitation. An inability to screen out irrelevant internal and external stimuli constitutes a serious functional disability (Fish, 1976).

Individual differences in thresholds of responsiveness can be seen in the way infants relate to their environments and establish rhythmic sleep–wake and feeding patterns (Greenspan, 1979). The character of early psychological structures, such as defenses, coping mechanisms, and cognitive styles, is influenced by these early patterns. For example, some infants have trouble habituating to stimuli, and so find it difficult to calm down after being stimulated. Children with low thresholds of responsiveness are prone to react to the most obvious and compelling stimuli around them, even when irrelevant. Moreover, thresholds of responses vary for different types of stimuli. For example, high-risk infants may be less sensitive to social interactions, for which they have a high arousal threshold, and more sensitive to noise, for which they have lower aversion thresholds than most babies (Field, 1982).

Thresholds of responsiveness also apply to internally generated stimuli and are reflected in the rhythmicity of bodily functions. The processing of such internal stimuli as hunger, thirst, elimination, sleep, and genital arousal may be erratic, blunted, or unbuffered in some children (Wilson & Calistro, 1977). When thresholds are low, there may be irregular sleep patterns, excessive movement during sleep, and body or head rocking. In general intense bodily urges do not fit readily into school schedules and can be distracting. Also, unbuffered conscious access to imagery derived from the drives may overwhelm a child with sexual, aggressive, and rivalrous emotions. The imagery of these internal experiences may be frightening for a child.

The primitive startle (Moro) reflex is the prototype of a reaction from which distress spreads when it is repeatedly evoked because of an inability to modulate responses to stimuli (Silver, 1977). Another reverberating source of primitive distress is autonomic lability, which may be detected in vasomotor responses—such as paroxysmal tachycardia; nocturnal sweating; pallor around the mouth; sluggish, unequal, eccentrically placed pupillary responses to light; and visceral responses, such as gastrointestinal symptoms.

Optimally awareness of the existence and functioning of the body remains just below the threshold of consciousness. This orientation toward one's body is illustrated by the way we wash and dress in the morning, knowing what we are doing, yet doing it without paying specific attention to these activities (Szasz, 1957). Some persons' attention, however, is excessively focused on their bodies, often with various degrees of apprehension. When children are attending to internal sensations from their bodies, their attention is distracted from activities around them. These distractions can be defensive imagery in the form of daydreaming or awareness of the sensations emerging from their bodies. Other persons seem to have little awareness of bodily sensations. In the extreme a schizophrenic person may perceive the body as detached from or foreign to the self. More commonly the stoic person does not complain about, or seem to notice, injuries and illnesses. At the other extreme, the seeking of dangerous situations involving possible bodily injury may represent a counterphobic attempt to master intense, unconscious dread of greater damage or mutilation (Szasz, 1957).

The development of thresholds of responsiveness is influenced by parenting. For example, two different parental reaction patterns can heighten hypersensitivity to stimulation in susceptible infants. One is the overprotecting and overcontrolling of an infant, leading the child to depend upon external stimulation. A second parental reaction is passivity and withdrawal, with shifting of attention away from a hypersensitive child, who then is left with excessive internal stimulation (Greenspan, 1979b). Neither of these extremes provides the middle ground of titrated soothing and stimulation needed to foster the development of internal stimulus-modulating mechanisms, such as selective inattention through which irrelevant external stimuli are simply omitted from further processing and repression that excludes irrelevant internal stimuli from conscious awareness.

Some children who have been exposed to chronic overstimulation, as in a household with frequently raving and ranting persons, paradoxically seek sensory stimulation in later life. They may be attempting to master past overstimulation by repetition of those circumstances, or they may be seeking less traumatic sources of stimulation (Gediman, 1971).

Premature infants tend to have lower and postterm infants higher thresholds to stimulation. The mother of a premature infant may need to provide less intense or variable stimulation to elicit her infant's attention whereas the mother of a postterm infant may need to provide more intense or variable stimulation to attract her child's attention. But both groups may have a narrow range of stimulation to which they respond with attentiveness and positive emotion. Thus the mothers of these infants tread a narrow line in gauging their stimulation so as not to exceed aversion thresholds (Field, 1982).

Low thresholds of responsiveness may lead to disorder, as in the sensory hypersensitivity noted in childhood schizophrenia, delirium tremens, and catastrophic stress reactions. Low thresholds of responsiveness in childhood have been related to schizophrenia in adults, and some adult schizophrenic persons have low stimulus thresholds that are aggravated by phenothiazines and improved with stimulants (Bellak, 1979; Wender et al, 1981). Moreover, some schizophrenic phenomenology may be due to compensations for low sensory thresholds in the form of omissions, errors, delaying responses, exclusion, approximation, and escapes instead of disengaging voluntary attention as do most persons (Holzman, 1978). Along this line, a screening program carried out by Venables on the island of Mauritius suggested that it may be possible to identify children at the age of three who have low thresholds of autonomic responsiveness and are at risk for difficulties in schoolwork, and perhaps later schizophrenia (Serban, 1978).

Voluntary Attention Problems

Classroom attention problems arise in at least three forms, which are often construed to indicate a child's interest in schoolwork (Keogh, 1977). These forms are scanning, focusing, and concentrating attention. All are necessary for success in school, but each may be independently deficient.

Scanning Attention Problems

For scanning the attentional apparatus must permit a free interplay of external stimuli and internal imagery. The scope of attention, therefore, can be altered by threatening internal imagery that evokes anxiety by differentially raising thresholds of responsiveness, causing selective inattention so that external stimuli are not consciously perceived. Selective inattention thus may result from blocking out external stimuli that arouse anxiety, guilt, and other distressing feelings and is synonymous with the psychological defense mechanism of denial (Mosse, 1982).

Many children must continue with life as usual while enduring ongoing threatening or anxiety-provoking situations at home. Because their hypervigilant attention is primed to focus on those threats, intrusive emotions and images can interfere with scanning attention in school (Horowitz, 1983b). This takes place in the form of pangs of emotion, rumination about stressful events, and unbidden thoughts irrelevant to the task at hand.

Some children who are not inclined to pay attention to adults have not completely individuated from their parents. They assume that others know and will meet their needs. Consequently, they pay little attention to their surroundings and feel unfairly treated when they must meet certain expectations.

Focal Attention Problems

Focused attention is an essential capacity that filters and channels stimuli relevant to a task at hand; consequently any interference with it impedes learning (Ross, 1977). In instructional situations focused attention depends on sensory systems, receptive language, and a child's understanding of what is expected.

Inhibition is the single most important function of the cerebral cortex. Inefficient inhibition leads to an inability to focus attention (Dykman et al, 1970; Holcomb et al, 1985). In attaining a mature level of inclusive and exclusive focal attention, a child passes through earlier stages of overexclusive and overinclusive attention (Kinsbourne & Caplan, 1979). The infant is overexclusive because of the ability to attend to only one stimulus at a time. This immature form of focused attention is reflected by a school-age child who attends to a fly on the wall instead of a letter on the chalkboard. Later young children are overinclusive and notice everything, resulting in distractability. Figure–ground discrimination may be difficult for some overinclusive children so they must devote special effort to focus attention in order to distinguish letters from their background; they need clearly printed materials of limited scope to minimize distractions. Ultimately children develop the capacity to distinguish readily figure and ground and to select salient aspects from masses of stimuli.

When learning to read, a child's focal attention upon the reading material itself is required. Information contained in printed words is processed sequentially and hierarchically so that attending to one set of features precludes attending to another. Effective reading then involves the flexible shifting of focus not only from one word part or word to the next, but also on cross-referencing one word feature to another. Poor readers have greater difficulty than facile readers in focusing attention upon the material they read (Vellutino, 1979).

One form of focusing difficulty in reading results when a child has not efficiently learned directional constancy in letter and word formation (Kinsbourne & Caplan, 1979). Directional orientation is lowest on the hierarchy of discriminating cues. Thus the ultimate stabilization of directional constancy depends upon a child learning the differences in printed letters that are identical except for directional orientation, such as b and d. The failure to acquire the basic linguistic skill of attending to the directional orientation of letters results in focusing inefficiency in reading. Another example is a child who recognizes configurational and directional information but not sequential cues, and so, sees the word loin but says lion.

Reading errors may be associated with impulsive, cursory response times, while better reading performance is associated with reflective slow response times (Kagen, 1965). Poor performances on perceptual tasks, such as the Bender-Gestalt test, also may result from impulsivity rather than actual impairment of perceptual skills. Such children do not carefully focus their attention on words in order to detect subtle visual configurational and sequential differences essential to the meaning of written symbols. They also may lose their place on a printed page.

Anxiety often interferes with focusing attention, as by dazed clouding of awareness (Horowitz, 1983b). The more anxiety evoked, the more an individual relies on evasive maneuvers to avoid the evoking stimuli, thus creating deficits in attention.

Hypnotic, anticonvulsant, and psychoactive drugs may influence focal attention. Sensory overload with complex and ambiguous stimuli also can flood the attention apparatus, so that focusing is impaired

(Rapaport, 1951). Weariness obviously interferes with focused attention, which is obliterated by sleep. On the other hand, television has more focusing attraction than either the printed word or the radio for children, because it stimulates both the visual and auditory modalities.

Concentration Problems

Concentration is the prefrontal-lobe-mediated, sustained focused attention of working memory that brings percepts into interaction with the imagery of memories and emotions. It requires a fixed, stable, attentive set focused on a task. It most clearly is experienced when one is reading a book or writing a paper and needs to keep firmly fixed on the sequence of mental activity. One must ward off distractions because it takes time to find the thread again once the attention set is lost. Gardner's continuous performance test is a sensitive measurement of concentration ability (Gardner, 1979).

Decreased prefrontal cortical arousal has been implicated in concentration problems (Mattes, 1980). The resulting lack of motivation is the most common reason for incomplete concentration; wandering thoughts lead to straying, although they also can lead to discovery (Levine & Melmed, 1982). Anxiety, depression, confusion, and somatic symptoms also interfere with concentration (Eysenck, 1977).

Some children cannot divide their attention even after they have learned how to concentrate upon a task. They only can give their full attention or none at all. Before they can listen to someone else, they must stop whatever they are doing and look at that person. They then have difficulty returning to the task (Mosse, 1982).

Narcissistic persons can concentrate intently on activities that flow from their personal interests and internal imagery. However, they cannot concentrate upon information or activities that originate from external sources, particularly those that involve accepting the influence or expertise of others.

Concentration draws upon motivation derived from drives. The intake of information through the eyes and ears parallels that of the ingestion of foodstuffs by the alimentary tract (Strachey, 1930). The open mouth and salivation associated with concentration in young children and chewing of pencils in older children illustrate the parallel between information and matter ingestion. Consequently the sublimation of alimentary drives is involved in the pleasurable ingestion of ideas. Conflict over oral drives, therefore, may deprive children of an "appetite" for learning. For example, repression may produce a "blank" mind when reading threatens to bring about the release of primitive devouring oral impulses instead of providing a sublimated outlet for them.

The sublimation of elimination drives is expressed through pleasure in producing a prized product and the pleasurable passage of thoughts. Repression of anal drives can be seen in obsessional thought with its preoccupation with details and compulsive orderliness, leading a child to miss the main point. The defense of reaction formation handles threatening imagery through the isolation of emotions from images so that irrelevant thoughts clutter the mind. The sublimation of urethral drives ordinarily permits sharp, incisive focus on educational materials. Their repression may cause a child to miss the point through an inability to concentrate on specific meanings. The following case illustrates the way repressed forbidden wishes can interfere with concentration on schoolwork:

> Thirteen-year-old Mark was unable to concentrate on his schoolwork because of repressed aggressive drives. His cool, "macho" facade conveyed indifference to his school failures. When he was con-

fronted with difficult schoolwork, yawning crept up from a burning sensation in his stomach, and he felt drowsy and slipped into fantasies in which he was a powerful hero. The stomach sensation ultimately proved to be "a boiling pot of evil rage" at his father and then powerful assertive strivings for himself. A dream from early childhood was recovered in which he became the "chicken man" after the brave part of himself left him and jumped into bed with his mother and father. As "chicken man" he then secretly wanted to dress in women's clothing and carry a purse.

Mark was unable to tolerate his own potent aggressive strivings and express them in productive schoolwork, because they symbolized unacceptable destructive and sexual wishes toward his parents. When confronted with challenges in school, his gastrointestinal reaction deflected his attention to diversionary omnipotent fantasies. His school failure fulfilled his masochistic wish to fail, and his "macho" behavior expressed his compensatory grandiose omnipotent fantasies.

The process of concentrating on academic tasks thus is based upon the expression of instinctual drives. Children with little capacity for sublimation are at the mercy of their primitive urges and have little motivation for the concentration required by schoolwork.

Concentration involves the loss of awareness of the passage of time. Comfortable cenesthesia from respiration and the tone of the visceral and somatic musculature underlies the pleasurable experience of relaxation in which awareness of the passage of time disappears. Conversely distressing internal sensations rivet attention upon the moment and interfere with concentration by evoking conscious awareness of the passage of time. Thus the inability to concentrate may reflect anxiety stimulated by forbidden imagery associated with tastes, smells, and visceral sensations associated with the respiratory, alimentary, and excretory tracts. One then may be unable to tolerate the anxiety triggered by these bodily sensations that emerge during states of relaxation, as described by a 16-year-old boy:

> I can't concentrate on anything. If I relax, I get tense. I worry about what is going to happen next and that I'm not going to get my work done. I want to blow off time and put off the work. Sometimes I have to hold on to the desk in order to keep myself from quitting studying. When I feel good inside about something, the same thing happens. It's as if I have to spoil good feelings. When I was younger, I used to feel like vomiting when I was excited. If I felt like somebody and as if I could do things, it made me scared. I guess I felt I shouldn't be big and strong.

For younger children, the loss of control of body functions and movements also may feared. A child who fears loss of sphincter control has difficulty comfortably experiencing related bodily sensations. Children with background adventitious muscular movements experience a continuous sense of unrest. Thus the inability to enjoy the visceral sensations of eating, urinating, and defecating, in addition to uncertainty regarding the ability to control these cravings and body movements, interfere with a child's ability to relax, relinquish awareness of the passage of time, and comfortably concentrate upon the flow of the stream of consciousness.

Distractibility also can result from internal conflicts that produce feelings of guilt, shame, and embarrassment, whether or not they are perceived as conscious worries. Daydreams and masturbatory urges also may deflect attention from schoolwork (English, 1963). Some children are preoccupied with worries about their parents and events at home (Silverman, 1985).

At each developmental stage, unresolved neurotic conflicts may exert a backward pull and cause regression to a lower stage. For example, when an unresolved alimentary drive expressed through preoccupation with dependent oral needs occurs during the oedipal stage, a child may be unable to perform the simple cognitive task of forming an age-appropriate independent relationship with a parent (Greenspan, 1979a). Early parent–child interactions thus play a role in determining a child's concentration powers. A parent's encouragement of a child's interests promotes the child's involvement in activities that foster persistence. When a parent largely imposes standards upon a child, that child may come to feel that personal involvement in activities is not valued and show distractibility and lack of persistence. Such children do not have the opportunity to assume personal responsibility for their actions and experience themselves as helpless. Give and take between parent and child may encourage a sense of competence, which parental direction hinders (Demos, 1982b).

A complex of factors influencing concentration come together around reading. A neurotic reading difficulty may result from the repression of instinctual drives because of anxiety stirred up by imaginary dangers. Errors in reading may serve as disguised ways of gratifying repressed impulses. Failure in reading also may represent a hidden antagonism toward adults expressed in passive resistance rather than in openly rebellious behavior (Blanchard, 1946; Silverman, 1985). A neurotic block of reading thus may be a disguised expression of repressed destructive wishes toward frustrating adults, and also relieve guilt stimulated by those wishes through atonement by self-punishment because of the reproof resulting from school failure.

Disinterest in learning to read may occur to avoid exposure of lesser talents so that some children give up on schoolwork as a way of evading competition in which they might appear inferior to siblings and peers. They feel helpless in the face of challenges and give up at the first sign of difficulty (Seligman, 1975).

Difficulties in studying at the college level offer a relevant model for concentration difficulties at earlier ages. Boredom and the inability to concentrate in college students may be related to adjustment reactions, such as homesickness, and developmental problems related to a search for cognitive understanding of the nature of the world and self-identity. Anxiety may relate to worry about one's family, love affairs, and financial problems. Depression may result from discrepancies between one's self-evaluation and ideals, as when the desired self as a uniquely gifted individual must be reconciled with the actual self as one of many students struggling in a competitive environment.

The "brain fag" syndrome described in African college students in England is relevant (Prince, 1960). Students with this condition had difficulty in studying, remembering, and concentrating. They reported, "The words don't go into my brain." There frequently was visual impairment: "I can't see the page; something comes down over my eyes." In addition, there were somatic complaints in the form of headaches, sensations over the scalp, dizziness, and easy fatiguability.

This syndrome corresponds to the impaired concentration, absentmindedness, and forgetfulness of anxious children. They worry about future events, such as tests, the possibility of injury or exclusion from peer group activities, or about meeting expectations, such as deadlines, keeping appointments, or performing chores. Their anxiety is typically expressed as concern about competence in a variety of areas with worry about what others think of their performance. They face each new learning task with the dread of failure. They may shun schoolwork to avoid the shame and embarrassment induced by the fear of imperfect performance (Kotkov, 1965).

The "brain fag" syndrome was interpreted as an unconscious rejection of the Western educational system. Those African students were in the process of abandoning the supports they had received from their traditional collectivistic societies and assuming the responsibilities and increased self-reliance of an individualistic society. In addition, they often were responsible to families that were supporting their educations and whose prestige and reputation rested upon their shoulders. In these cases there was much more at stake than for the European student (Minde, 1974). Similar factors may operate in children who experience significant dissonance between the values of their families, cultures, and schools.

Two other adult clinical situations may be relevant. The first is the generalized postconcussion syndrome characterized by headaches, lack of concentration, dizziness, and mild memory impairment often associated with irritability and anxiety. The second is the adult schizophrenic person who has difficulty in sustaining concentration and in dividing attention, suggesting difficulty in holding a train of thought in the proper channel (Baribeau-Braun et al, 1983).

Hypoglycemia should be considered when sporadic difficulty in concentration is encountered. It may occur suddenly about one-half hour after a meal or more gradually during the third or fourth hour. The symptoms of hypoglycemia are irritability, difficulty in concentrating, weakness, and perspiring. Dietary management through increased protein content can be helpful (Philpott & Kalita, 1980).

MOVEMENT PROBLEMS

A child's movements may signify the degree to which a child is, or is not, motivated to do schoolwork. In either instance children with comparatively high movement levels are predisposed to conflict with teachers and other children in classrooms in which quiet conformity is expected.

The noun motion captures the essence of this phenomenon more accurately than does activity. The word activity connotes purposeful action that may be pejoratively construed as naughty. The term hyperactive also is misleading, because children with excessive movements may not be more active than other children in all respects. If their running is measured by a pedometer, they may not run more than the average child of the same age. Nor do they always move about more from one place to another in a room. They do, however, wiggle, squirm, and sway their bodies while sitting or standing and fidget nervously or absently with objects. Restless children often cannot run as fast as other children, nor can they readily slow down their rates of movement, so that their movements actually tend to be disorganized in the light of the expectations of a given situation (Maccoby, 1980).

For these reasons the term hyperkinesis, which means excessive movement, is preferable to hyperactive, because it refers to generally increased body movement and more accurately describes children's restless, fidgety, purposeless motions that are age inappropriate and excessive for a specific task and social context. Moreover, hyperkinesis implies that a child is having difficulty controlling body movements and focuses on a problem the child is experiencing rather than the discomfort adults may experience in that child's presence. It includes movements of the body governed by the basal ganglia, the levels of arousal of the reticular activating and limbic systems, and the degrees of inhibition by the cerebral cortex (Panksepp, 1981; Powell, 1979).

Strictly speaking, then, the term hyperactivity should be limited to a form of hyperkinesis in which purposeful activities are overdone according to a standard for a specific task and social context, such as overtalkativeness, boisterousness, and running around. In this light most of the behaviors usually regarded as hyperactive are more accurately hyperkinetic.

The measurement of hyperkinesis is not a simple matter. The complexity of the phenomenon becomes apparent when supposedly hyperkinetic children quietly settle into sustained games and television watching (Luk, 1985). When excited all children, particularly the young, are hyperkinetic in the view of adults. For some children movement even accompanies intense concentration. For the clinician consternation results when a child described as hyperkinetic in school calmly engages with play materials in an office while receiving individualized attention. Conversely parents may have difficulty believing that a restless child at home does not show that behavior in school. Most important, the label of hyperactive or hyperkinetic can be misapplied to outgoing, energetic boys (McGuinness, 1985).

In an Isle of Wight study, only 2 percent of the children were pervasively hyperkinetic at home and in school although 16 percent were rated as hyperkinetic by either parents or teachers, but not both. Only the pervasively hyperkinetic children were found to have a high rate of disruptive behavior, cognitive impairment, and a poor prognosis (Rutter et al, 1970). In other epidemiological studies, the prevalence of hyperkinetic children in school has been reported at between 3 and 10 percent of preadolescent children (Belmont, 1980; Trites et al, 1979).

Unfortunately, the rare "organic brain drivenness" of the postencephalitic organic brain syndrome has been taken as the model for hyperkinesis, leading to the surmise that it is a putative sign of brain damage. The situation is far more complicated, as a variety of factors that contribute to

hyperkinesis can be identified (Schachar et al, 1981). They fall into two categories: hyperkinesis elicited by situational context and hyperkinesis relatively unrelated to context.

Context-Related Hyperkinesis

Hyperkinesis evoked by situational contexts may result from excitement, movement associated with intention, frustration of the motor drives, anxiety, boredom, and motor incoordination.

Excitement

The most common form of hyperkinesis is the diffuse motor response of excitement to particularly gratifying stimuli, or anticipation of them, by young children, who have not yet developed efficient prefrontal lobe inhibition. True hyperactivity in the sense of overdoing activities or overtalkativeness also may be an expression of excitement. Immature older children may continue to be overly excitable.

Movement Associated with Intention

Every intentional activity has motivational, mental, and motor aspects. Children vary in the degree to which their intentions are actually expressed in motor activity. Some can think quietly; others show movement of their lips and general bodily restlessness as their motor systems reflect their mental activity.

Frustration of the Motor Drives

In urban areas many children spend their off-school hours watching television, unable to move freely because of their crowded apartments and dangerous streets. It is too cold to play outdoors in the winter and too dangerous because of street violence in the summer. As a result the motor activity drive of these children is chronically frustrated. Consequently, they are restless and inattentive in school. They need programmed physical activity during their school hours (Mosse, 1982).

Anxiety

Another form of context-related hyperkinesis reflects anxiety evoked by the interpersonal or symbolic nature of a situation. Although adults may pace the floor and fidget, children are much more restless when anxious. In addition to impaired concentration, absentmindedness, and forgetfulness, anxious children show excessive context-related movement. Some children become anxious when interpersonal closeness is required, such as in one-to-one situations with adults in remedial tutoring, and fend off intimacy much as a prizefighter dances around a ring to avoid attack.

Many children imagine that if their weaknesses were exposed, they would be rejected by others. Classroom performance accordingly may incur humiliation. Since these moments cannot always be predicted, chronic anxiety can result in school settings. Chronic anxiety in children is described as the overanxious disorder of childhood (American Psychiatric Association, 1987) with excessive worrying and fearful behavior that are not focused on a specific situation or object, such as separation from a parent or entering a new social interaction, and that are not due to recent psychosocial stressors. Psychomotor agitation also may be an expression of depression.

Boredom

Context-related hyperkinesis also may result from boredom. A situation experienced as boring is one in which a person finds little drive satisfaction and is unable to be active. An enjoyment of fantasy may not be possible because the nature of a dull situation keeps the person in a state of frustrated expectation. Because boredom is

unpleasant, aggressive fantasies commonly emerge. There also may be regression to self-stimulating acts, because the lack of external stimulation permits the emergence of internal stimuli (Fliess, 1961). When interest flags a child's natural inclination toward motor activity emerges. This form of movement may be purposeless or purposeful and can be disruptive in school classrooms.

Some children become bored when they are not receiving the attention of others, as during the rapprochement phase of early childhood when the "radar beam" of a home base is needed. This may be expressed by disruptive intrusiveness and by touching or pushing others. Some teachers intuitively keep such a child in their peripheral attention field so that the child perceives their attention.

Motor Incoordination Disability

Another context-related form of hyperkinesis results when children with poor fine or gross motor coordination attempt tasks in which these difficulties reduce efficiency. Their clumsy efforts to perform and attendant failures produce restlessness (Silver, 1979). They appear to lack the ability to build smooth patterns of movements (Dare & Gordon, 1970; Shaw et al, 1982). Some children may attempt to compensate for this by clowning behavior.

Cerebellar inefficiency results in general motor clumsiness, which may impede classroom performance. Visual motor incoordination may interfere with manual dexterity, writing, and other fine muscle performances, such as buttoning and drawing (Gaddes, 1980). These children may be slow in learning to walk or ride a bicycle. This form of developmental clumsiness diminishes or disappears with aging and practice (Herskowitz & Rosman, 1982).

Young children with persistent primitive postural reflexes have difficulty synchronizing their motility with their mother's behavior and react to antigravity play with panic, frantic clinging, and an attempt to realign the physical orientation of their bodies with gravity (Sander et al, 1970; Condon & Sander, 1974).

Context-Unrelated Hyperkinesis

A second class of hyperkinesis is less related to context and occurs for four reasons: constitutional high energy endowment, adventitious motor discharge, hypomanic mood, physical illness, and exogenous toxic substances.

Constitutional Endowment

The most common form of hyperkinesis can be attributed to what appears to be a high energy level endowment, although it actually may result from low levels of cortical arousal and consequent inhibition. This form is evident in the fetus and newborn and persists into adult life (Korner et al, 1981). A genetic factor is suggested by the fact that with twins, identical pairs are more likely than fraternal twins to show a pattern of early-life hyperkinesis, distractibility, temper outbursts, feeding problems, and later learning difficulties.

In a study employing motion monitors that sampled and recorded movements on an hourly basis over one week's time, a group of hyperkinetic boys had significantly higher movement levels than controls regardless of the hour of the day on both school and nonschool days and during sleep. Although there was some relation to context, this study supported the concept of hyperkinesis as increased generalized body movement rather than excessive purposeful activity (Porrino et al, 1983). How these findings relate to arousal and inhibition variations in the reticular formation and extrapyramidal motor system remains an intriguing question (Powell, 1979). It may be possible to distinguish movement based upon high-energy output of the reticular activating system from that based upon adventitious random movements related to the basal ganglia.

A relationship between delayed physical development and hyperkinesis has been suggested by studies, such as one in which physical maturity as measured by bone age was significantly retarded in hyperkinetic children (Oettinger et al, 1977). A variety of minor physical malformations also have been observed in hyperkinetic children, such as fineness of hair, double hair whorls, head circumference, eye folds, eye-separation distance, set of ears, lobules of ears, palate arching, furrowing of the tongue, curvature of the fifth finger, simian palmar crease, elongated third toe, webbing of middle toes, and enlarged gap between first two toes. These minor malformations may be clinical markers for deviations in the embryogenesis of the central nervous system; however, the number of false positives and false negatives is too great to give them significance in screening for kyperkinesis. For example, a simian palmar crease occurs in 50 percent of children with Down syndrome and in 10 percent of normal subjects. Since normals vastly outnumber children with Down syndrome, in screening 10,000 children there would be seven true positives, 8987 true negatives, seven false negatives, and 999 false positives (Accardo, 1980).

More relevant to the ultimate appearance of clinically significant hyperkinesis is the nature of the unfolding relationship between child and parent. The quality of early parent–infant interaction is influenced by an infant's attentional and movement characteristics. Some infants are much more difficult to nurture than others. For example, a demanding infant who is hyperalert and restless, who orients and habituates poorly, and who does not permit a mutual gaze experience is frustrating for the parent. Rather than a rhythmic, peaceful interaction, such a parent–infant dyad is characterized by discomfort and irritability.

When the parent of a hyperkinetic infant can tune in well and provide a nurturing experience, that infant can establish basic rhythms and, with further maturation of the central nervous system, becomes capable of a better fit with the parent. Dynamic patterns that have been set in motion, however, may prevent this potential engagement from occurring. The parent may be perceived by the child as the source of the child's rage and lack of control through the mechanism of projection. Consequently anxiety stimulated by the child's wishes to destroy the parent and the consequent fear of being abandoned may be added to the constitutional movement level as a source of hyperkinetic behavior (Greenspan, 1979b).

The role of learning in the fate of constitutional hyperkinesis is further illustrated by the influence of parental expectations on the ways in which energy is to be expended and the amounts of energy tolerated in activities. When a child demands what is regarded arbitrarily as excessive attention, adults may react with annoyance, punitiveness, and avoidance (Kronick, 1981). This once again adds anxiety as a magnifier of the child's hyperkinesis.

Some hyperkinetic children may never have been taught how to sit in a classroom, listen to instructions, follow directions, or obey rules (Willis & Lovaas, 1977). Conversely some hyperkinetic children have been taught to behave in objectional ways, because they received attention for undesirable behavior from adults. Another possibility is that disturbing behaviors may be used to avoid responsibility. For example, when a teacher asks a child to complete an assignment, the child becomes fidgety and restless and does not accomplish the task at hand. If the teacher subsequently expects less, the child learns to avoid work by behaving in a restless, inattentive way.

The families of hyperkinetic children tend to have histories of impulse disorders in the form of the flightiness of the hysteric, the lack of self-control of the alcoholic, and the impulse-ridden characteristics of the antisocial character. This pattern suggests a combination of social, environmental, and genetic factors in the backgrounds of some hyperkinetic children (Cantwell, 1979).

Adventitious Motor Discharge Disabilities

A second frequently overlooked form of hyperkinesis relatively independent of context is the result of fluctuations in body movements resulting from cerebral palsy and subclinical epilepsy without manifest seizures (de Quiros & Shrager, 1978).

Basal ganglia diseases in adults produce postural changes, involuntary movements, gait disturbances, and articulatory disorders. They also are associated with forgetfulness, apathy, irritability, and lability of emotions (Mayeux, 1983). The expression of functional disabilities arising from the basal ganglia in children is unclear but worthy of consideration. The Tourette syndrome will be described later as a specific example.

Cerebral Palsy. When injury to the brain before, during, or soon after birth impairs neural control over muscular movement, a child is said to have cerebral palsy. Damage to a specific area of the brain usually results in characteristic signs,—for example, lesions in the basal ganglia result in athetosis, in the motor cortex in spasticity, and in the cerebellum in ataxia. Mild dyskinesias and ataxias may reflect individual differences in maturation of those centers. Even though cerebral palsy often is regarded as a fixed disorder, early minimal signs frequently disappear during later development (Schain, 1977).

Mild forms of the cerebral palsy syndromes may be found in children with learning problems. The most frequently encountered forms of unrecognized cerebral palsy in children with learning difficulties are mild dyskinesias and ataxias.

DYSKINESIAS. An extrapyramidal source of hyperkinesis is suggested by the dyskinesias, of which jerking, chorealike adventitious movements of the extremities are the most frequent (Marsden, 1982; Prechtl & Stemmer, 1962). These fluctuations in muscle tone may be accompanied by tremors, clumsiness, and difficulty with fine motor coordination, all of which contribute to an apparent restlessness. Tremors cause the hands, arms, or neck to shake in a rhythmical manner and occur at rest or with intentional movements. Athetoid children are in writhing motion and have difficulty controlling muscle movements; these athetoid movements are absent during sleep.

Children may attempt to compensate for dyskinesias by clowning behavior or by incorporating involuntary movements into seemingly purposeful activities (Silver, 1979).

A steadiness tester can be used to detect motor impersistence, resting tremors, choreiform movements, and anxiety. The steadiness tester also is a sensitive measuring device for the effects of stimulant medication (Gardner, 1979).

SPASTICITY. Spastic children's motions are accurate but made slowly and with great effort. They may be unable to enunciate properly or use words and sentences. Children with extrapyramidal rigidity, such as cogwheeling, move slowly and tend to be mentally retarded. They have difficulty in extending their arms and legs fully because their muscles are partially contracted most of the time.

ATAXIAS. Ataxic children are poorly coordinated. Of the ataxias generalized clumsiness is the most common and is related to difficulty in maintaining one's posture. The cerebellar vermis and flocculonodular lobes have a modulating, coordinating effect on general behavior patterns, as do the lateral cerebellar lobes on specific motor acts. Thus dysfunctions of these areas can cause impulsive, disorganized, purposeless, inefficient behavior in affected children (Berntson & Torello, 1982).

When vestibulo-cerebellar modulation is not fully developed, the primitive tonic neck reflex and the neck righting response exert their tonic force and make posture less responsive to volition. A child, therefore, may have difficulty maintaining spatial orientation and muscle tone relative to posture. The resulting disturbance in posture and equilibrium, as seen typically in the physical clinging of a young child, creates a precarious orientation to space, which contributes to a biological substrate of anxiety (Bhatara et al, 1981).

Subclinical Epilepsy. Children with subclinical thalamic, limbic, or temporal lobe dysrhythmias may suffer from restless behavior without having observable seizures. An abnormal electroencephalogram and a positive response to anticonvulsant medication confirm this diagnosis (Holdsworth & Whitmore, 1974).

Hypomanic Mood

Because they include hyperactivity, the manifestations of a hypomanic mood state should be noted. Subjectively a hypomanic mood is experienced as inflated self-confidence, exaggerated optimism, grandiosity, high energy, expansive enthusiasm, and low tolerance of frustration. The objective manifestations of a hypomanic mood are irritability, hyperactivity, infectious cheerfulness, overtalkativeness, decreased need for sleep, poor judgment, distractibility, intrusiveness, domineering behavior, and flamboyance.

Chronic Illness

The onset of the symptoms of hyperthyroidism often is insidious with behavioral and personality features prominent, such as irritability and hyperactivity. Appetite increases although weight does not increase or it decreases. Sweating and fatiguability increase, and heat is poorly tolerated. Schoolwork may suffer because of diminished attention and hasty, disorderly performance. Physical examination discloses tachycardia, exophthalmos, lid lag, fine tremor, exaggerated reflexes, and an enlarged thyroid gland.

The role of rebound hypoglycemia in hyperkinesis has been suggested by reports that children with learning difficulties show abnormal carbohydrate metabolism, particularly of glucose (Dunn, 1976). Children with allergic disorders have not been reported to show a higher incidence of hyperkinesis. An allergic tension-fatigue syndrome, however, makes sense clinically (Accardo, 1980).

Sydenham chorea may begin with hyperkinesis and emotional lability of recent onset in a school-age child. Antecedent streptococcal infection, rheumatic fever, or a choreic syndrome itself usually precede the motor disturbance.

A number of rare degenerative disorders with onsets in middle childhood affect the nervous system. The early symptoms may be most prominent in coordination functions. These children often first reveal signs of their disease through their inability to function in school. Dystonia musculorum deformans, juvenile cerebromacular degeneration, Schilder's syndrome, Friedreich's ataxia, sclerosing panencephalitis, and brain tumors are examples.

Huntington chorea is an uncommon hereditary disorder manifested by clumsiness, emotional lability, and restlessness before the presence of the progressive disorder is recognized. Wilson disease, or hepatolenticular degeneration, is a rare autosomal-recessive condition that presents with liver disease rather than neurological symptoms. Occasionally its onset with clumsiness, dysgraphia, tremors, slurred speech, and behavior disorders may be noted late in grade school. This disease is treatable with D-penicillamine (Accardo, 1980).

Exogenous Toxic Substances

The possibility that exogenous toxins and medications adversely affect brain functioning has attracted widespread lay and professional attention. There is legitimate concern that one of the hazards of modern living is chemical pollution that affects the vulnerable brains of children.

Food Additives. Feingold linked the increasing use of food additives in recent decades with an apparent increase in learning and behavior disorders in children and devised a special diet. A review of the literature concluded that 50 percent of parents rated their children as improved on the Feingold diet (Conners, 1980). These changes, however, appeared to be due largely to the placebo phenomenon or to its value as a concrete plan of action. This explanation was supported by a double-blind crossover study of children who were reported by their parents to be improved on the Feingold diet. These children, when given a mixture of food colorings in proportions thought to reflect normal patterns of consumption, showed no evidence of its effect on their behavior (Mattes & Gittelman, 1981).

In another study, however, two of 22 hyperkinetic children showed a discernible response of aggressive and overactive behavior to challenges by artificial colors at moderate dosages (Weiss et al, 1980). Still another laboratory study disclosed that hyperkinetic children given high doses of food dyes exhibited a loss in learning test performances whereas nonhyperkinetic children did not. At the same time, no changes in activity level were noted on the Conners Rating Scale of school behavior in any of the children (Swanson & Kinsbourne, 1980).

Thus no studies have clearly demonstrated the value of diets without food additives; the numbers of children affected by artificial colors are probably much smaller than originally claimed. It also is apparent that some children are helped by the Feingold diet, for whatever reason.

Monosodium glutamate has been implicated as a cause of central nervous system effects in children. It is used in foods to stimulate the gustatory sense and undoubtedly has an impact on other systems as well (Mosse, 1982).

In general a natural foods emphasis is an appropriate response to the encroachment of artificial substances with as yet unknown consequences on our lives (Varley, 1984). From the public-health point of view, all potentially harmful substances should be omitted from children's diets unless the chemicals serve an overriding dietary purpose (Rimland, 1983).

Lead. Toxic chemicals, such as lead and mercury (to which the "Mad Hatter" of *Alice in Wonderland* was exposed), can produce learning and behavior problems for children. A study of 2000 Boston children showed that as their lead levels increased, problems with learning, behavior, attention, and schoolwork also increased (Needleman et al, 1979). In another study elevated lead and cadmium levels were found in children with learning disabilities (Pihl & Parkes, 1977).

Lead also has been reported to produce hyperkinesis that is decreased by stimulant drugs in rats (Accardo, 1980). In humans the greatest effects of lead intoxication appear to be manifested in attentional problems (Gittelman & Eskenazi, 1983; Needleman & Bellinger, 1981; Rutter, 1980). The levels of lead exposure needed to produce behavioral effects have not been clearly established, in part because of confounding socioeconomic variables (Smith, 1985).

Medication Side Effects. Hyperkinetic behavior may be the unintended result of medication for physical illnesses. The most commonly encountered medication-induced hyperkinesis is found in the treatment of seizure disorders and asthma. Phenobarbitol, clonazepam (Clonopin), and primidine (Mysoline) are agents with this potential that are used in the treatment of seizures (O'Donohoe, 1979). Medications containing ephedrine and theophylline are used in the treatment of asthma and may cause or aggravate hyperkinesis. Anticonvulsant medications in therapeutic dosage ranges can impair schoolwork performance (Reynolds & Trimble, 1976). One of the common side effects of the phenothiazines is akathisia.

In general the possible role of any medication employed in the treatment of a chronic disease in a child's hyperkinetic behavior should be considered.

ATTENTION DEFICIT DISORDER

The *Diagnostic and Statistical Manual (DSM-III-R)* of the American Psychiatric Association (1987) employs the diagnostic category of attention-deficit hyperactivity disorder.

The diagnosis of attention deficit disorder is based upon the criteria of developmentally inappropriate inattention and impulsivity. Inattention refers to failing to finish tasks, not listening, easy distractibility, difficulty sustaining concentration, and difficulty staying with tasks. Impulsivity refers to acting before thinking, carelessness, shifting between activities, difficulty organizing work, inappropriate speaking in class, and difficulty taking turns. When two of the following are present, the diagnosis of hyeractivity is added: runs or climbs excessively, fidgets excessively, has difficulty remaining seated, excessive movement during sleep, and always on the go.

It is important in making this diagnosis to establish that the manifestations of hyperkinesis—short attention span, distractibility, emotional liability, and impulsivity —occur when a child can be compared with other children under similar environmental circumstances. It is difficult to evaluate these manifestations when they take place only at home. When that is the case, the parent–child relationship bears close examination. In situations in which high levels of motor activity are appropriate, such as during recreation, hyperkinesis may not be obvious. When a child's behavior is appropriate on a one-to-one basis but chaotic in a group situation, immaturity of managerial functions is suggested.

Attention deficit disorders occur in 5 percent of prepubertal children with a male:female ratio of about five to one. The onset is usually by age three, although professional help may not be sought until the child enters school. *DSM-III-R* identifies three characteristic courses for the disorder. In the first all of the symptoms persist into adolescence and adulthood. In the second the disorder is self-limited, and all the symptoms completely disappear at puberty. Finally, the hyperkinesis may disappear with puberty while the attention difficulties and impulsiveness persist into adolescence and adulthood.

In one study children with the diagnosis of attention deficit disorder were found to have deficient metabolic activity in the central frontal lobes and the caudate nuclei in regional-blood-flow studies (Lou et al, 1983). More specifically dysfunction of frontal-neostraital dopamine systems has been suggested (Hicks & Gualtieri, 1986).

These children especially need recognition of their successes. When they manage to do something difficult, they need praise for their efforts and encouragement to try more. They need help in order to organize and start tasks. They are easily confused by more than one request and should be given only one thing to do at a time.

Morning, mealtime, and bedtime are especially stressful for these children. Rou-

tines can help to reduce stress. The morning routine can be anticipated by setting out clothing the night before so that the child does not have to hunt for clothes or decide what to wear. Then the child can follow a written list of steps for getting ready for school in the morning, checking each step if necessary. Serving meals at the same time each day corresponding to the child's hunger cycle is important. An atmosphere of quiet relaxation at mealtime can be fostered by having children seated between adults. At bedtime relinquishing the waking state is difficult so that a comforting transition is needed, such as by the telling of a story and the presence of a favorite toy. If possible, the child should have a separate room or a clearly defined space in the same room with an older child rather than with one closer in age or younger. Furniture in the room can be used to separate the children as much as possible.

These children need firm limit setting. Scolding or belittling engenders their resentment. Bribery, threats, or giving in to their whims invites their manipulation of adults. Temper outbursts can be handled by the time-out removal of the child from the situation to a quiet place until self-control has been restored. Then a discussion of what upset the child can lead to better coping the next time.

Such children need to learn how to get along with others. They need help in finding playmates. At first the child may need supervision of play with another child.

Prospective and retrospective follow-up studies of children who have received a clinical diagnosis of the hyperkinetic syndrome indicate that they are prone to significant psychiatric and social problems in later life. During adolescence most effectively treated hyperkinetic boys and girls tend to have favorable outcomes, except for somewhat less success in school. In one series 31 percent continued to show the full syndrome of attention deficit disorder with hyperactivity (Gittelman et al, 1985). Alcoholism, sociopathy, hysteria, and psychosis appear to be psychiatric outcomes in adulthood of ineffectively treated children (Cantwell, 1975; 1978). A 1980 review of the literature, however, did not find more than randomly expected delinquent, sociopathic, and psychopathic behavior in adults who had been hyperkinetic children (McMahon, 1980). As adults some become narcissistic, borderline personalities with emotional instability, depression, vulnerability, and low self-esteem.

Most follow-up studies of these children suggest that they do significantly worse than their peers in adult educational attainment and degree of social adjustment. The antisocial behavior reported in follow-up studies of hyperkinetic boys, however, may be linked to childhood aggressive unsocialized conduct disorders rather than attention deficit disorders per se (August et al, 1983).

The evidence suggests that 40 percent of hyperkinetic children have fairly normal adult outcomes. Another 50 percent have significant social, emotional, substance abuse, and impulse control problems, and 10 percent are seriously disturbed (Borland & Heckman, 1976; Cantwell, 1985; Menkes et al, 1967; Hechtman & Weiss, 1983; Weiss et al, 1985). The adult outcome of hyperkinetic children is influenced by socioeconomic class, mental health of family members, intelligence, aggressiveness, emotional stability, and frustration tolerance (Hechtman et al, 1984a; 1984b). The following is a case example of a young adult who had been treated as a hyperkinetic child, and who responded favorably to psychotherapy as a young adult:

As an infant Sean was irritable and fussy. His stimulus regulation system was erratic, and his mother did not feel comfortable with him. As a young child, he was hyperkinetic, oppositional, fearful, and immature. At the age of five, he was placed on Atarax, and school entry was delayed for one year. During his elementary school years, he was excitable, anxious, unpopular with peers, and nocturnally enuretic. He was on Ritalin from the age of nine to 15. In high school he avoided athletics and devoted all of his energies to attaining the school honor roll. In college he was homesick, unable to concentrate, and overwhelmed by the pressures of schoolwork. He sought psychiatric treatment at the age of 21, when he realized that he could not continue a train of thought and feared he was losing his mind. Through intensive psychotherapy he achieved sufficient self-confidence and insight to graduate from professional school and embark upon his career.

Characteristics of adults retrospectively diagnosed as having attention deficit disorders as children include impulsive character disorders, aggressive destructiveness, alcoholism, explosive personality, depression, and certain subgroups of schizophrenia. Those who still have hyperkinetic symptoms may respond to stimulant medication (Mattes et al, 1984; Wender et al, 1981). Moreover, residual manifestations of an attention deficit disorder were found in 35 percent of a population of adult male alcoholics (Wood et al, 1983). In one study adults who had been hyperkinetic children were more field dependent and less able to inhibit responses to irrelevant and focus on relevant stimuli than controls (Hopkins, 1979).

Although clinically useful, the attention deficit disorder diagnosis oversimplifies a complicated situation that requires consideration of a number of possible factors that influence mood, stimulus regulation, attention, movement levels, impulse control, and thinking (Douglas, 1975; 1981).

AFFECTIVE DISORDERS

Affective, or bipolar, disorders are extreme, sustained, recurrent elevations or depressions in mood states. They may be expressed predominantly through depression, mania, or alternations between them.

Various forms of depression are recognized commonly in adults and are responsive to antidepressant medication. The diagnosis of depression in children had not been made commonly until recently, however, and the implication of therapeutic responsiveness to antidepressants is a controversial issue (Cantwell & Carlson, 1983; French & Berlin, 1979; Kashani et al, 1981; Schulterbrandt & Raskin, 1977). The prevalence of clinically significant depression in elementary-school children appears to be 1.5–2.0 percent (Brumback & Stanton, 1983).

The phenomenology of depression is associated with either psychomotor retardation, which is an inhibition of mental and physical activity in the form of melancholia, or agitation, which appears to be anxiety mingled with depression (Gray, 1971). Depression in childhood is not as easily recognized as in adulthood. Although depressed children express discouragement and feelings of inadequacy, they may not appear to be sad or show psychomotor retardation or agitation. They do hold perfectionistic expectations of themselves and react to discouragement by giving up on schoolwork. Characteristically they do not show joy in activities with other children.

Subjectively a depressive mood is described as sadness, discouragement, dejection, low spirits, apathy, somatic complaints, loss of interest, an inability to experience pleasure, indecisiveness, inability to concentrate, poor memory, fatiguability, and loss of appetite and sex drive. There is duirnal variation in depressive mood, often the worst in the early morning. The thoughts of a depressed person are of helplessness, hopelessness, guilt, worthlessness, inability to carry on, and suicide. The most salient psychological symptom of depression is the negative view of self, the world, and the future. Depressed persons are preoccupied with unflattering and self-castigating themes, evident in both their self-reports and dreams.

The objective manifestations of depression typically are withdrawal from people and activities, early-morning awakening, insomnia and weight loss. Psychomotor retardation may take the form of slowed, low, or monotonous speech and body movements. On the other hand, depressed persons may show psychomotor agitation which takes the form of pacing, handwringing, inability to sit still, pulling or rubbing on things, outbursts of complaining, irritability, and talking incessantly.

Childhood depression is a useful concept if limited to an identifiable, although incompletely understood, group (Lefkowitz & Burton, 1978). The American Psychiatric Association (1987) DSM-III-R criteria include dysphoric mood, often worse in the morning, in addition to at least five of the following symptoms: (1) change in appetite, (2) sleep difficulty, (3) psychomotor agitation or retardation, (4) loss of interest or pleasure in school and usual activities, (5) loss of energy, (6) feelings of self-reporach or guilt, (7) complaints or evidence of diminished ability to concentrate, and (8) recurrent thoughts of death or suicide. The Children's Depression Rating Scale is useful in this clinical assessment (Poznanski et al, 1979; 1984).

The associated features of depression vary according to age. Irritability, poor frustration tolerance, temper outbursts, and separation anxiety may be seen in the prepubertal child. Restlessness is associated with depression in adolescence, often with sulkiness, withdrawal from social activities, and reluctance to cooperate in family activities. Lack of attention to schoolwork as well as personal appearance may also be seen in adolescent depression.

In general systems terms, depression is a system dysfunction rather than a unitary disease. The central nervous system is an open system, which means that it sets its own goals on the basis of processing incoming stimuli and extracting their informational value. The disturbance indicating that the central nervous system is converting from an open, transactional state to a closed, reactive system may be called depression. Self-esteem indicating efficient central nervous system functioning is lowered or lost. This view makes it possible to understand that multiple etiologies may precipitate depressive phenomenology (Basch, 1975).

Reversal and turning against the self are phychological defense mechanisms seen in depression. Reversal is the defense in which emotions are turned into less threatening opposites. For example, affectional longings that might evoke the pain of rejection are converted into hostile emotions, as when a child avoids close relationships by experiencing irrational anger toward others. When that anger is turned against the self, depression may result. As a depressed 13-year-old girl said:

> I loved my parents so that rather than hate them, I hated myself and imagined that I was dead. Then everyone would be sorry.

Depression also can stem from a sense of loss of ability as schoolwork becomes progressively more difficult as the school years advance, and as a child loses the hope of attaining one's aspirations (Cohen, 1985).

Biochemical explanations of depression postulate low serotonin and norepinephrine levels in monoamine-related metabolic pathways of the central nervous system (Kashani et al, 1981). This is based upon the observation that antidepressant medications result in marked improvement in adult depressive symptomatology (Brumback & Stanton, 1983). Thus a subgroup of depressed patients can be identified clinically, biochemically, and pharmacologically. They may be vulnerable to depression because of inefficient regulation of norepinephrine metabolism (Siever & Davis, 1985). In a similar vein, variations in do-

pamine metabolism may predispose individuals to intense suspicion and anger. Genetically determined variations in the biogenic amines and their physiological regulation may be the basis for significant individual differences in emotional and endocrine responses to stressful situations (Hamburg et al, 1975).

The concept of masked depression as an explanation for chronic hyperactivity, aggressiveness, school failure, delinquency, and psychosomatic symptoms has proved to be of limited clinical usefulness. The most widely accepted view of childhood depression is an acute state that is characterized by a shift from a relatively healthy level of adaptation to clinically significant inefficient functioning. This may be reflected in a loss of interest and an inability to concentrate upon work in school (Ney et al, 1986).

When hyperactivity is episodic and associated with rapidly shifting moods, the question of the juvenile manifestations of a hypomanic state reflecting a manic-depressive tendency is raised (Feinstein, 1982). A manic mood is characterized by expansiveness, grandiosity, pressured speech, flight of ideas, distractibility, irritability, and sleep disturbance (Weinberg & Brumback, 1976). Unlike other forms of hyperkinesis, manic behavior tends to be reflected in excessive activity while maintaining emotional contact with other persons (Potter, 1983). Lithium compounds are used in the treatment of manic states.

TOURETTE SYNDROME

Although it was first reported by Gilles de la Tourette in 1885, the syndrome is still poorly understood and diagnosed (Friedhoff & Chase, 1982). It affects between 0.05 and 1.6 percent of the population (Shapiro & Shapiro, 1982). Under the Education for All Handicapped Children Act (PL 94-142), children with this syndrome are eligible for special education and related services, because some 60 percent of them experience learning difficulties in school (Comings & Comings, 1984).

The Tourette syndrome is characterized by recurrent involuntary, repetitive, purposeless movements of multiple muscle groups and explosive vocal sounds. With voluntary effort these tics can be suppressed for minutes to hours. Their onset is between the ages of two and 16 years, with greatest prominence during adolescence and possible lifelong duration. The symptoms wax and wane over time, with new ones replacing old ones and added to existing symptoms. While motor and vocal tics are the most obvious symptoms, deficits in attention, hyperkinesis, compulsions, obsessions, low frustration tolerance, and impulsive behavior also may be present.

In the mild form of the Tourette syndrome, a person may have a few twitches of the face or eyes, arm flapping, foot stamping, or abdominal jerks. Children elaborate means to camouflage symptoms by brushing hair out of their faces, dancing movements, and hitting themselves after socially unacceptable tics. They describe an inner tension that is almost continuous and is released by a tic.

The most socially distressing vocal symptom is the explosive utterance of obscene words, or copralalia, which occurs in about one-third of cases. Vocal tics can take place while one is watching television at home, playing with other children, or sitting at a desk in school. Compulsive behaviors are illustrated by a need to arrange objects neatly, to do, redo, or undo the same action before beginning to write, to push a chair into a certain position, and to make a sound until it feels right. These compulsions may greatly impair schoolwork, as when a child must scribble over a letter just written or go over the same sentence so many times that the assignment is not completed. Some children appear to perseverate in actions.

The most common behavioral problems involve the regulation of attention and activity. Approximately 50 percent of the children have difficulty in concentrating, poor focusing of attention, distractibility, impulsivity, and hyperkinesis, all of which may be evident in the preschool years and precede the onset of noticeable tics.

Language difficulties occur in both understanding and production but may not become apparent until the complicated vocabulary and sentences of the upper elementary grades. Mathematics can be especially difficult. Handwriting may be illegible because of difficulty in copying notes from a blackboard, which involves shifting attention from a near to far distance repeatedly.

Stress makes tics worse. Time limits are a common source of stress, especially during written tests. In addition, holding back symptoms absorbs effort and diverts attention from classroom activities, with the impairment of performance. For this reason these children need a safe place where they may release their symptoms without disturbing others. In school this can be an empty classroom or a nurse's office.

The cause of Tourette syndrome is not known, although current research suggests abnormalities in basal ganglia and cerebral cortex systems related to significant genetic factors, as proposed by Mahler and Rangell in 1943. Stimulant medications can precipitate the syndrome in predisposed children. These children may perceive internal and external stimuli more vividly than do nonafflicted individuals so that they are disturbed by loud sounds or bright lights, sensitive to touch or the feel of clothing, and distracted by events. The profane expletives, anger, irritability, attentional, and personality problems of the Tourette syndrome appear to reflect underlying impulse-control problems.

The treatment of the syndrome includes medication, behavior therapy, specialized educational services, support groups, and psychotherapy. There are several effective medications, but none eliminate all of the symptoms. Many older persons do not feel that they are successfully medicated until their internal tension is alleviated.

Haloperidol (Haldol) has been used for the longest time and is the most effective at low dosage levels. Some children experience improvement in their symptoms with as little as 0.5 mg per day. A useful schedule is to start with 0.25–0.5 mg a day and raise the dose no more than 0.5 mg a week until maximum benefit with minimum side effects is obtained (Bruun, 1984). The side effects of haloperidol sometimes outweigh the benefits. They include dysphoria, depression, phobias, sedation, cognitive blunting, excessive weight gain, acute dystonic reactions, parkinsonian symptoms, and akathisia. Extrapyramidal side effects may be treated with antiparkinsonian medications such as benztropine (Cogentin).

Clonidine (Catapres), an antihypertensive agent, is another important agent in the treatment of the Tourette syndrome. A favorable response to clonidine usually takes several weeks to months to become evident. Clonidine is started at low doses of 0.05 mg per day and slowly increased by 0.05-mg increments every one or two weeks. The effective daily dose ranges from 0.1 to 0.8 mg, with the average being 0.3 mg in multiple doses throughout the day (Bruun, 1984). The child may experience a reduction in tension before a reduction in tics is noticed. Side effects are minimal and may include transient sedation, and occasionally dry mouth. At high doses reduced blood pressure upon standing may be seen. Clonidine should be withdrawn slowly when the decision to discontinue the medication is made, to avoid rebound hypertension and anxiety. A combination of clonidine and haloperidol may be required. While tic reduction has been less than with haloperidol, clonidine offers the advantage of fewer potentially harmful side effects. Pimozide is a newly approved drug for the treatment of the syndrome. Although most patients report fewer side effects, they are similar to those of haloperidol.

Behavior therapy can be useful in training persons to substitute less obvious symptoms for those that are socially objectionable. For example, coughing can be substituted for copralalia and toe wiggling for facial movements. Psychotherapy is not an effective treatment for the symptoms of the Tourette syndrome. However, it can be very helpful in assisting children and their families to understand and cope with the effects of the syndrome. For example, distinguishing between behavior that cannot be controlled and that which is manipulative is a significant issue. Parents also need help in avoiding overprotecting affected children and sorting reasonable from unreasonable expectations. They may feel that children are deliberately exaggerating symptoms when tics actually are released in the privacy of the home. Another issue is how much stress is caused by inhibiting rather than freely expressing the symptoms. Family psychotherapy can be helpful in handling these issues.

A nine-year-old boy, Pat, told his school nurse, "Johnny called me "mental" and made fun of me." "How did Johnny make fun of you?" the nurse inquired. "Well, you see, I have these habits and sometimes I make movements with my face like I have to squeeze my mouth or my eyes. Sometimes I move my arms, and I hit kids when I don't mean to."

The nurse observed that Pat, indeed, was showing eye blinking, mouth grimacing, and tensing of his shoulders and upper chest muscles. She noticed that he also was sniffing and clearing his throat frequently. She wondered if he had a cold, a habit, or perhaps a tic. She decided to review Pat's medical record and have a conference with his teacher.

Pat's fourth-grade teacher reported that she had noticed Pat's facial and arm movements; in fact, she recently changed his seating assignment to the back of the room, because he was unable to sit quietly. He was falling behind in his arithmetic assignments, and she had just requested a conference with Pat's mother, because he had just received a detention for fighting on the bus.

Pat's school record revealed average intelligence. There had been some concern in the lower grades, and additional testing had been performed to determine if he was ready to move from kindergarten to first grade because of "immaturity." The first-grade teacher had commented on excessive eye blinking, and a referral for an eye examination was noted in the record. Pat had received unsatisfactory marks for behavior and effort throughout his school years.

Pat's medical record revealed no major illnesses or hospitalizations, other than occasional otitis media treated with antibiotics, antihistamines, and decongestants. Eye blinking and facial movements had been noted on physical examination prior to entry to school, but were thought to be nervous mannerisms.

On the basis of these findings, the school nurse encouraged Pat's parents to seek medical consultation, and the diagnosis of Tourette syndrome was established.

SUMMARY

Variations in the expression of temperament strongly influence the attention, movement, and moods of children in school, in addition to playing a key role in their motivation to perform schoolwork.

Although seemingly a simple matter, paying attention to a task proves to be an extremely complex phenomenon. For this reason it is useful to examine the involuntary and voluntary forms of attention in detail. Involuntary attention largely is a function of the state regulating system and takes place in the form of vigilance, the orienting, startle, and defensive responses, and the threshold of responsiveness. Voluntary attention brings the managerial system into play upon the state regulating system in the form of scanning, focusing, and concentration.

Vigilant attention is influenced by individual variations, seizure disorders, chemicals, sleep disorders, and physical illness. The orienting and startle responses are subject to the same influences in addition to the sympathetic-parasympathetic tonus of the autonomic nervous system.

Thresholds of responsiveness vary with sensory modality properties and involve both external and internal stimuli. Individual variations, maturational immaturity, psychological defenses, and chemicals, in addition to parenting styles, influence these thresholds.

Scanning attention is optimal when there is a free interchange of external and internal perceptions and imagery. Focused attention requires sufficient maturation to permit the filtering and channeling of stimuli relevant to interest or task at hand. Concentration is the most complex attentional function and requires sustained motivation and the engagement of the managerial system. The sublimation of drives unimpeded by neurotic conflicts is important to the ability to concentrate, which consequently is easily disrupted by distressing emotions.

The term kyperkinesis is preferable to hyperactivity because it more accurately describes the restless, fidgety, purposeless movements characteristic of children with attention, movement, and impulse-control problems. Hyperkinesis occurs in both context-related and context-unrelated forms.

Excitement is the most common form

of context-related hyperkinesis in young children. Children of all ages also are hyperkinetic when anxious in contrast with adults who show less external evidence of anxiety. Some children make body movements when concentrating intently. Frustration of the motor drives may result in the release of excessive activity in school. Boredom is a common reaction in children and adults in situations with little active involvement and drive satisfaction. Motor incoordination may cause excessive movement in some children when they are confronted with tasks or activities that are difficult for them because of vestibulo-cerebellar variations.

Constitutionally high energy endowment levels are the most common form of context-unrelated hyperkinesis in children. Even then parent–child interactions play a key role in determining whether or not clinically significant hyperkinesis develops. Adventitious motor discharges cause hyperkinesis directly and indirectly through compensatory movements. They may occur in the forms of dyskinesias, ataxias, and subclinical epilepsy. A hypomanic mood is characterized by exuberant hyperactivity.

Physical illnesses are another cause of hyperkinesis, particularly hyperthyroidism, hypoglycemia, and multiple allergies. Exogenous toxic substances, such as food additives and lead, may contribute to hyperkinetic behavior. The side effects of medications used in the treatment of chronic illness include hyperkinesis.

The attention deficit disorder with and without hyperactivity is a clinically useful diagnosis; however, it oversimplifies a complex situation in which children show the manifestations of a variety of problems with the large number of factors that influence attention, movement levels, mood, impulse control, and thinking. The Tourette syndrome includes motor and vocal tics, attention deficits, hyperkinesis, compulsions, obsessions, and impulsive behavior. Affective disorders include depressions with psychomotor retardation or agitation and manic states.

All of these factors interact in varying degrees to produce children who are temperamentally sanguine–cheerful, choleric–moody, phlegmatic–calm, or melancholy–gloomy in their relationships with people and their performance in school.

22

Cognitive Disabilities

Every man has reminiscences which he would not tell to everyone but only to his friends. He has other matters in his mind which he would not reveal even to his friends, but only to himself, and that in secret. But there are other things which a man is afraid to tell even to himself, and every decent man has a number of such things stored away in his mind.

Fyodor Dostoyevsky, 1864

Once children concentrate on material to be learned, the next essential step is accurately perceiving and understanding it. At this stage some children do not process information efficiently. The most extreme examples result from hearing and vision defects in the sensory organs themselves. Short of defects in organs and central nervous system components are a range of cognitive variations that impede didactic learning. For example, some children prefer either the auditory or visual processing and remembering of information. Others have difficulty integrating auditory and visual information.

An important task of the information processing system is to control the flow of information in order to avoid anxiety. Thus every act of perception is an act of selection. In evolution our survival as a species hinged in part on our ability to select shrewdly. Consequently, there is an optimal equilibrium between denying and facing distressing facts. There is a fundamental difference, however, between selection for the purpose of self-protection and selection that springs from self-defeating col-

lusions. Because this faculty for self-deception regularly protects us from anxiety, we fall prey to blind spots, remaining ignorant of zones of information we would be better off perceiving even if the elicited knowledge brings some distress (Goleman, 1985).

This chapter is devoted to the problems that children experience in the following key information processing system functions: (1) visual and auditory reception, (2) visual and auditory perception and spatial orientation, (3) intermodal sensory integration, (4) imagery, (5) symbolization, and (6) conceptualization. Difficulty with memory can occur with imagery, symbols, and concepts. Arithmetic disabilities are described in this chapter. Because they represent two extremes in cognitive variability, the specific problems of autistic and gifted children also are included in this chapter.

RECEPTIVE DISABILITIES

The most important sensory modalities for learning in school are vision and hearing.

Visual problems are more common than auditory problems, which are more likely to be undetected.

Visual Disabilities

Visual problems can occur in the form of acuity deficits, inefficient accommodation, and inefficient eye–movement coordination. They reduce the efficiency of reading by causing discomfort and fatigue, particularly around the fourth grade when the print in books becomes smaller. For this reason visual problems usually interfere with the later refinement of reading skills rather than their initial acquisition (Seiderman, 1976).

Visual Acuity Deficits

Myopia results when light is focused in front of the retina with resulting impairment of distance vision. Myopic children squint at the blackboard and show discomfort when looking at distant objects. Ordinarily their reading is unimpaired, and actually may be a contributing factor to their myopia. The treatment of myopia should consider reading, however, because the visual correction for distance may be stronger than a child needs for reading. In most instances the accommodation mechanism can easily compensate for this. Occasionally bifocal lenses are needed, but more often because of overconvergence rather than underaccommodation.

Hyperopia results when light is focused behind the retina with resulting impairment of near vision. Hyperopia may not be readily detected in children, because the lens automatically corrects for it. The energy expended in accommodation, however, causes eye rubbing, headaches, fatigue, and avoidance of prolonged reading. The correction of significant hyperopia, therefore, is important for reading (Grisham & Simons, 1986).

Astigmatism results when light is fo-cused in different planes before or behind the retina and causes blurring of vision. Some forms of astigmatism may be insignificant in reading; however, greater degrees, especially if combined with other visual problems, require correction.

Anisometropia refers to a condition in which the visual defect in one eye is significantly different than in the other eye. Each eye sends a different configuration to the brain. A significant discrepancy between the eyes may lead to suppression of one eye's vision, which may not affect school performance, but should be corrected to relieve strain on the binocular system.

Aniseikonia is a rare condition in which the optical percepts from each eye in the brain are significantly different in size or shape. Trying to fuse unequal images in reading may cause a child visual stress in the form of headaches and discomfort in reading. An eikonometer is required to make the diagnosis of aniseikonia, which requires careful diagnosis and correction.

Accommodation Inefficiency

Accommodation is the ability of the lens of the eye to focus on a stimulus point. It enables the eyes to focus by contraction or relaxation of the ciliary muscles, which vary the convexity of the lens to produce a clear image on the retina. The properly functioning eyes of children are able to focus from at least six inches to optical infinity with little effort. Accommodation wanes with age, tending to break down in the fourth decade of life and causing presbyopia in older persons.

A child's accommodation powers underlie the entire process of visual learning. Developmentally the first level of accommodation is at the distance of the hand and permits the infant to see, hear, and grasp objects, moving them toward the mouth for tactile, gustatory, and olfactory verification. Next the visual righting reflex permits the gaze of a child to fixate on objects and people.

Accommodation takes place involuntarily through the parasympathetic nervous system so that medications, such as antihistamines, may interfere with it. The heightened sympathetic discharge accompanying anxiety also may suppress accommodation, as when some children report that "the hard words blur."

There is a direct linkage between accommodation and convergence so that convergence increases with increasing accommodation. A proper balance between the two is necessary for comfortable reading.

Inefficient Eye-Movement Coordination

Binocular convergence is the rotation of the eye by the extraocular muscles inwardly to point both eyes at an object; it permits stereoscopic fusion of images from both eyes at varying distances.

Direct fixation is the ability to aim the eyes at an object so that stimuli fall on the fovea. Motor fusion is the ability of the eyes to follow a moving object smoothly, and it requires the complex coordination of six eye muscles. Saccadic fixation is the ability to move the eyes accurately and smoothly from one point to another and stop precisely at each point as in reading; it follows a maturational course at varying rates in different individuals. For example, young children's large saccadic movements do not efficiently keep visual stimuli focused on the central macula where acuity is the best (Kowler & Martius, 1982).

Children with poor vestibular sensory processing have difficulty following an object moving in front of their eyes. Instead of moving smoothly in following the object, their eyes may lag behind and then jerk to catch up. This interferes with playing ball, drawing a line, or reading a line of print (Ayres, 1979).

There are three stages of sensory fusion, which is the ability to unite the signals from two eyes into a single percept. The first stage is simultaneous perception and refers to the ability to form percepts from each eye at the same time. The next is fusion, in which both percepts are fused in the brain as a single percept. The third is stereopsis, which is perception of depth based on differences between the percepts from the two eyes and is more pertinent for distant than close vision.

Strabismus, or crossed eyes, results from binocular inefficiency. If there is simultaneous binocular vision, a strabismic child may see double unless cortical adaptation occurs. Otherwise the brain suppresses vision in one eye. If prolonged, suppression may lead to amblyopia, in which the acuity of one eye is irreparably damaged. When one eye stops functioning, it may wander off-center because the brain no longer yokes both eyes together. A child with intermittent loss of binocular fusion may be able to function for a short period of time, but ultimately will be overcome by visual stress and will avoid visual tasks.

Heterophorias are tendencies of the eyes to turn relative to each other under binocular conditions. Exophoria is the tendency for the eyes to turn outward; esophoria is the tendency for the eyes to turn inward. Hyperphoria exists when one of the eyes tends to point upward, and may result in head tilt, loss of place from line to line in reading, headaches, nausea while reading in a moving vehicle, neck and shoulder strain, and vague but disturbing discomfort in a visually overstimulating environment, such as a supermarket. Proper eyeglass prescription and, in some instances, orthoptics alleviate most heterophorias.

Stereoscopic vision is most efficient for activities at intermediate ranges between far distances, as in driving a car, and close, as in reading. In fact reading does not depend upon binocular vision and can be impaired because of it. For example, if the eyes are not perfectly synchronized in convergence, fatigue results from reading. When there is a significant discrepancy in synchronization between the eyes, vision in one eye is suppressed.

The ability to read depends upon the automatic and proper working together of accommodation and convergence. When accommodation or convergence is impaired, headaches, fatigue, losing one's place, double vision, and holding one's head close to a working surface may result. For some children accommodation is weak so that when they read, they experience a vicious circle in which failing accommodation stimulates greater convergence of the eyes, which, in turn, demands greater accommodation, with resulting fatigue. This can be suspected in children who move the page closer to and then away from their eyes and develop headaches when reading. Lens corrections and orthoptic exercises usually are helpful.

But faulty eye movements may be the result, rather than the cause, of poor comprehension in reading. When children have difficulty understanding a word, they show regressive eye movements or prolonged fixation as they attempt to decipher it (Goldberg & Schiffman, 1983). Consequently, the role of eye movements themselves in perceptual and language processes must be carefully evaluated (Rayner, 1983).

Parenthetically, eye-tracking dysfunctions have been suggested as possible familial markers of vulnerability to schizophrenia (Holzman et al, 1984).

Hearing Disabilities

Peripheral hearing losses are more commonly unrecognized sources of learning difficulty than are visual problems. For this reason impaired auditory acuity should be considered in all children with learning difficulties (Accardo, 1980).

Chronic otitis media before two years of age may cause a significant loss of auditory discrimination that affects receptive language. An increased incidence of recurrent middle-ear infections has been reported in the histories of children with learning difficulties in school. The typical history in these children is a delay in acquiring speech, auditory processing deficits, inefficient auditory-visual integration, and later reading and spelling disorders (Accardo, 1980; Masters & Marsh, 1978).

Congenitally deaf children are retarded in language development in comparison with hearing children. Many deaf children, therefore, fall behind their hearing counterparts in educational achievement, especially in reading in which they must decode written materials without the benefit of auditory cues (Brooks, 1978; Friedman & Gillooley, 1977; Furth, 1966; Wells, 1942). They can learn intelligible speech from vibratory feedback and can use sign language to acquire reading skills. Via these routes they can be taught to read through the combined efforts of teachers and family (Henderson, 1976).

PERCEPTIVE DISABILITIES

Much sensory information is routinely excluded through stimulus modulation so that one's cognitive capacities are not overloaded. Other forms of selective exclusion can have maladaptive consequences, however (Bowlby, 1980). Extreme examples of pathological causes of selective perception are cortical blindness and central hearing impairment, which result from dysfunction of the primary visual and auditory cortices. More typically, variations in perception result from individual differences in the perceptual apparatus and psychological defense mechanisms. A common defense mechanism is seeking external perceptual stimulation in order to prevent unconscious internal stimuli from gaining access to conscious awareness.

One of the most common reasons that children do not learn in school is that they do not perceive task-related information. Learning cannot take place because information is not registered. When the imaging mechanism is preoccupied with internally generated imagery of distressing bodily sensations in the form of anxiety and depression, external stimuli are received but not perceived as images susceptible to storage in long-term memory. The same failure to register external information occurs when the imaging mechanism is preempted by the imagery of daydreams.

Defense mechanisms also can be means for ignoring or repudiating aspects of situations, as does sleep. The exclusion of stimuli from conscious awareness by psychological defense mechanisms is called selective inattention (Sullivan, 1953). This is based upon the principle that anxiety evokes defenses that tend to exclude from awareness situations that provoke it. Sensory input may trigger anxiety in a vast continuum of mental activity that operates at the margin of conscious awareness where perception takes place without emergence of percepts into conscious awareness (Tauber & Green, 1959). That process permits subliminal recognition and response but wards off conscious awareness of a perception (Bruner, 1983).

Denial is a defense that negates external perceptions. It is a refusal to accept things as they are. It is rooted in the young child's syncretic tendency to abolish unwelcome facts by denying them in words, fantasies, and actions. Thus denying reality is a strong motive in young children's play through which a pleasant world of fantasy takes the place of unpleasant reality (Sandler, 1985).

The fight–flight responses prepare the individual for reducing awareness of external input. These mechanisms employ assimilation rather than accommodation and insulate the individual from external input. In they are are chronically activated the individual becomes inflexible and divorced from reality, ultimately breaking down under prolonged stress. In contrast excessive reliance upon accommodation can lead to dependency upon external events, with the sacrifice of continuity and stability of internal systems. The individual then becomes hyperreactive and distractible (Pribram, 1981).

Visual Perception Disabilities

Problems in visual perception occur in discrimination, foreground–background differentiation, part–whole relationships, spatial relationships, sequencing visual stimuli, revisualization, and recognition. Disturbed function of the visual association cortex may be the result of local or more remote influences, such as from the frontal lobe (Calanchini & Trout, 1971).

Cortical blindness is an example of impairment at the level of perception in which there is a complete loss of all visual sensations, including appreciation of light and dark. In another vein the light patterns of television may induce epileptic seizures. In fact flicker produced by stroboscopic lights is used as a method of provoking epileptiform discharges on the electroencephalogram (Mosse, 1982).

Lesions of the dominant visual associative areas cause difficulty with the visual recognition of objects. If the impairment is incomplete, a child may attempt to identify objects by selecting one visual cue and then use associations to reach the correct conclusion. For example, a pencil may be seen as a slender object, but with the opportunity to feel it or hear it scratching on paper, it can be identified as a pencil. Abstract qualities and symbols, such as colors and the letters of the alphabet, have only visual cues. For the verbal identification of a color or letters, the visual input must arouse the appropriate auditory verbal associations in the inferior temporal cortex. The inability to name colors thus may be present in a child who can visually match colors. In a similar vein, the reading difficulty of some children is due to difficulty in recognizing the two-dimensional configuration of letters of the alphabet; they can identify three-dimensional letters more readily.

Reading involves spatial perception over time. Since reading necessitates the coding of ordered information as in *was* and *saw*, *loin* and *lion*, some poor readers may be deficient in perceiving temporal order in visual stimuli (Bakker, 1979). They require greater contrasts in visual stimuli in order to recognize them (Lovegrove et al, 1980; Rudel, 1980). Psychological defense mechanisms probably do not create reversals of letters and words; however, neurotic conflicts may exaggerate them.

Impaired voluntary oculomotor function at the sensorimotor cortical level can affect scanning movements of the eyes. The inability of a child to perceive more than one object at a time suggests interference with the influence of the frontal association cortex upon visual input. Eye-tracking problems at this level usually are the result of a failure to interpret an object and its parts correctly. Children with inefficient scanning have difficulty interpreting thematic pictures, because they fixate on one aspect and fail to survey a picture as a whole. Consequently, they do not learn to move their eye muscles systematically. Such children become confused when their visual field contains several essential features. Because they can perceive only one feature at a time, they attend to a part and fail to gain meaning from a whole picture (Calanchini & Trout, 1971).

Auditory Perception Disabilities

Because hearing requires focused attention over time, the opportunities for misper-ception are greater than for vision, which is a better source of objective facts from the external world. The connections of the auditory system to the reticular activating and autonomic nervous systems based upon its basic function of alerting to danger link sound to the affective system. Hearing provides a rich source of emotional stimulation, as in pleasing music. Hearing thus is more sensitive than vision in communicating emotional states, as is evident in the sensitivity of children to an adult's tone of voice.

Auditory intensity and tonal discrimination take place at the subcortical level. The cortical auditory association area is located in the superior temporal gyrus, whose projections connect to the motor areas for speech and to the limbic and visual analyzer systems and which is concerned with the recognition of the temporal sequential patterns and the direction of frequency change of sounds, as involved in speech (Calanchini & Trout, 1971).

Since the brain recognizes speech sounds on the basis of probability, similar input signals can trigger erroneous identification. This accounts for the universal tendency to mishear and misspeak. Disruption in auditory development also may be seen clinically as errors in auditory discrimination, auditory analysis and synthesis, auditory sequential memory, reauditorization, articulation, or some combination of these. A child may have difficulty hearing the differences between sounds and so, mishear and misarticulate words. There may be difficulty in understanding that a word is made up of a series of sounds that must be ordered in the correct sequence and so the child will mishear or mispronounce multisyllable words. Because the speech motor analyzer is a necessary participant in the initial development of speech, as is evident when young children repeat or mouth words as they are heard, the failure to grasp sound blending may result in a later inability to learn word-attack skills in reading and oral and written spelling. A child also may be unable either to store or to retrieve the sounds of a word but be able to recognize them visually. Reauditorization problems may affect expressive language, as when a child is unable to recall specific words, grammatical structures, or word orders.

Written language may show the same kind of errors, because a child writes as the child speaks. A child may be unable to write a word or a sentence because one cannot first auditorily analyze whole words into their component parts, attach sounds to the visual letters, or remember or reauditorize the sounds of the letters within the words or words within the sentence. Such a child's spelling, therefore, may show little relationship to the sound of a word.

The relatively slow development of auditory discrimination is responsible for inaccuracies in pronunciation and reading in the early grades of school. Some children do not develop accurate auditory discrimination until the age of eight, and so lose interest in classroom activities when they cannot sustain the effort required to hear the teacher over the background noise of the classroom. Audiological appraisal, therefore, should include not only sensitivity to frequency and intensity as measured by the audiogram but also the efficiency of auditory discrimination with background noise (Accardo, 1980). When there is a disparity between audiometric hearing levels and the interpretation of speech, the possibility of a central hearing loss should be considered (Sataloff et al, 1980).

The phrase *central auditory processing* deficit refers to an interference with listening beyond the level of hearing acuity. Interference may occur at the level of integration of input from each ear (Willeford & Burleigh, 1985). It also may occur at the level of distinguishing internal and external imagery so that internal images compete with and contaminate external verbal images. For example, one teenager

described the way in which his mind went off on internal images, which were triggered while listening to another person. He then was distracted from, and "tuned out," the words of the other person. Because of his underlying paranoid tendency, he also misinterpreted the words of others as bearing unwarranted personal implications for him.

Spatial Orientation Disabilities

Understanding the external spatial world depends on grasping the consistency of relationships between things in the context of fluid, changing patterns. This fluidity presents infinite possibilities, like a face seen from different angles. But the grasp of the relationship through the development of perceptual constancy, which includes form and directional constancy, holds this infinity together to accomplish two things (Dixon, 1983).

Perceptual constancy allows a child to recognize that different instances of the same thing are seen within the infinite possibilities of a pattern because the relationships remain consistent (Money, 1966). By playing with objects of the world, a young child finds that a given thing may look different depending on the angle from which it is seen, and yet is the same thing. Perceptual constancy also allows a person to anticipate instances in the infinite flow of possibilities, even though the person may never actually have observed that given instance before.

The spatial orientation functions include the spatial location of one's body and its parts, the location of external objects in space, and the directional relationship of one's body to external objects in space. Vision is particularly involved in the spatial sense so that developmental variations in vision affect spatial orientation (Potegal, 1982). Yet visual and spatial memory are distinct functions (Koestler, 1978). The awareness of personal and extrapersonal space is based upon neural models in the parietal and frontal lobes (Calanchini & Trout, 1971). Children who lack clear discrimination between personal and extrapersonal spatial features are inattentive to body space in relationship to objects in their environment, and clumsily trip over chairs, run into doorways, or back into furniture.

The maintenance of an appropriate position of the body in space depends upon visual stimuli; proprioception from the ocular muscles; stimuli from the labyrinth in which the otoliths respond to orientation with reference to gravity and the semicircular canals to movement; proprioception from the joints and neck muscles, which relates labyrinthine impulses to the position of the head; and proprioception from the lower limbs and trunk concerned with position of the body in relation to the acts of sitting, standing, and walking. There are wide variations in the degree to which individuals achieve mastery over the motions of their bodies, as epitomized by dancers and athletes, and in the use of their hands to manipulate objects, as seen with artisans or instrumentalists (Gardner, 1983).

The spatial definition of one's body is formed in one's body image. The formation of one's body image depends upon the basic sensory spatial mechanisms of touch, proprioception, and vision. Vestibular information orients the body image to surrounding space. Parietal lobe integration of these sensations permits the recognition of such spatial attributes as figures drawn upon the skin and right and left parts of the body.

Impairment of the recognition of figures drawn upon the skin (agraphesthesia), difficulty in identifying one's fingers (agnosia), and right–left confusion have been reported in boys with learning difficulties (Adams, 1974; Peters et al, 1975). Weakness in proprioceptive feedback causes problems in tasks that require keen awareness of finger position, such as writing. Because learning numbers through finger counting links arithmetic with the orientation of the fingers and hand in space, finger agnosia also may interfere with learning numbers in arithmetic (Geschwind, 1965).

The uncommon and controversial developmental Gerstmann's syndrome is defined by handwriting problems of a characteristic type with spelling errors of letter sequence, right–left confusion, arithmetical errors in columns of digits, poor finger localization, and poor spatial and constructional ability, but ordinarily does not affect reading (Benson & Geschwind, 1970; Denckla, 1972; Kinsbourne & Warrington, 1966; Mosse, 1982).

The brain may underreact or overreact to vestibular input. Children with underreactive vestibular systems show reduced nystagmus following rotation, difficulty in visually following a moving object, gross motor clumsiness, and reduced awareness of falling. Children with overreactive vestibular systems tend to have increased postrotary nystagmus, fear of falling and sudden movements, and motion sickness (Ayres, 1979).

The role of the vestibular system in distortions of spatial perception may be indicated by the persistence of primitive neck-righting responses, which drive the body into tonic rotary motion with a tendency for sensation to flow from centripetal forces, emphasizing the periphery of the body and setting the stage for distorted sensations within the body (Silver, 1985). Sensations of elongation of the periphery of the body or fears of body parts flying away from the remainder of the body may occur. In addition the lack of bodily stability in space contributes to body-image distortions, as seen in children with schizophrenia. Milder forms of primitive neck-righting responses have been reported in learning-disabled children (Peters et al, 1975). In another study 50 percent of the children with learning problems had histories of ear infections, 40 percent had motion sickness, and 35 percent reported positional or spontaneous vertigo (Levinson, 1980).

The interplay of the vestibular system with other systems must be recognized (Polatajko, 1985). Faulty eye movements, postural coordination, balance, and spatial orientation are often regarded as symptoms of vestibular dysfunction. These symptoms also reflect functioning of the senses of proprioception and vision in addition to the controlling influences of the cerebellum, reticular formation, and parietal cortex. The most objective sign of vestibular dysfunction is nystagmus, an involuntary oscillation of the eyes characterized by alternating slow and rapid excursions of the eyes.

The spatial functions may be subdivided into the ability to perceive spatial patterns accurately and to compare them with each other, the ability to remain unconfused by the varying orientations in which a spatial pattern may be presented, and the ability to visualize imaginary movement in three-dimensional space.

Telling time from the face of a clock taps a child's ability to perceive and compare the spatial relationship of the hands on the clock. This may be impaired by visual agnosia so that a child has difficulty perceiving a clock as a whole. Such a child knows that the position of numbers on a clock has meaning in telling time, but cannot grasp how it does so (Mosse, 1982).

Confusion in spatial orientation is seen in the difficulty some children show when copying forms, such as a diamond, as a result of uncertain right-to-left orientation. These children reach the first directional change, begin to draw a line the wrong way, realize this and reverse the direction, resulting in a "tail" in the drawing (Fadely & Hosler, 1979). Directional orientation difficulty also is illustrated by a young adult who could not do turns properly in skiing until a lefthanded instructor demonstrated a pattern opposite from the usual direction.

Difficulty in visualizing imaginary movement in three-dimensional space is illustrated by a child could not copy a dancing teacher's movements when the teacher was facing her but could do so if the teacher stood by her side before a mirror as she looked at their reflections.

The directional confusion Orton noted in the reading and spelling errors of children now described as visual-spatial dyslexics has been found by subsequent investigators to have an even wider range. These dyslexic children also have impaired time and space relationships; they confuse the terms before and after, and above and below. They may be slow in learning to distinguish right and left. Consequently, drawings of their own body images may be distorted.

In a rare instance, a college student with corpus callosum agenesis performed well in courses that involved language and verbal facility but had difficulty with geometry, geography, and subjects that involved spatial and nonverbal faculties (Saul & Sperry, 1968). Spatial and directional disorientation without reading difficulty also is seen in the Turner syndrome (Alexander & Money, 196). These females with a sex chromosome defect have difficulty perceiving and manipulating spatial representations, as in figure drawing, map reading, and geometry (Hynes & Phillips, 1984).

One's spatial conception of the world must be distinguished from one's ability to communicate that conception to others. For example, a child's inability to draw a map of a room may be because of a poor spatial sense or because of a constructional apraxia expressed in the faulty transposition of conceptions of space into manual drawing without the conception of space itself being disordered. Constructional apraxia is manifested by difficulty in copying designs, putting jigsaw puzzles together, and drawing (Mosse, 1982).

INTERMODAL SENSORY INTEGRATION PROBLEMS

Intermodal sensory integration is first seen in the way infants rely upon seeing, touching, and mouthing things that are heard. With the maturation of cortical association areas, this dependency on direct external multisensory integration usually disappears as a child develops discrete sensory modality channels, which are internally integrated in most children by the age of nine.

Some children require redundant multisensory stimuli longer than others. An understanding of their different abilities to learn by eye, ear, or even by touch can be helpful in capitalizing on the strengths inherent in the dominant modality to balance weaknesses in other modalities (McWhirter, 1977). Variations in brain efficiency also can arise when information received through one sensory avenue impedes that received through another. This is seen in children who have to shut their eyes so that they can comprehend more efficiently what is being said about a visual stimulus. These children are confused by multiple sensory stimuli.

Visual and Auditory Integration

The neural structures for visual and auditory skills develop at different rates in children, depending upon genetic predisposition and environmental stimulation (Wepman, 1964). Variations in the ways children integrate auditory and visual information can be demonstrated by evoking electroencephalographic activity in the different visual and auditory parts of the brain (Shipley, 1980). Through this procedure a visually evoked occipitogram, an auditorially evoked temporogram, and an intersensory pattern evoked between those areas can be obtained.

Difficulty in integrating visual, auditory, and haptic stimuli and overriding visual reflexes may create problems in relating a visual symbol to its spoken-language counterpart. When a word is heard, the sound is initially decoded in the primary auditory cortex, but the signal must pass through the adjacent Wernicke's area if it is to be understood as a verbal message. When a word is read, the visual pattern from the primary visual cortex is transmitted to the angular gyrus of the parietal lobe, which elicits the auditory form of the word from Wernicke's area. Reading thereby involves an integration of the visual and auditory centers of the brain (Ingvar & Swartz, 1974).

Reading also involves communication between the two hemispheres via the corpus callosum so that the spatial configurations of the right hemisphere are processed by the language center in the left hemisphere (Geschwind, 1979a). The right hemisphere can recognize written words and understand spoken words by recognizing their visual-spatial or acoustic patterns, but not through phonetic analysis of the sounds. Sounding out a word is beyond the right hemisphere, which works directly from pattern to meaning (Zaidel, 1979).

Intrapsychic conflict can interfere with the synthesis of auditory and visual information. Reading difficulty may result from a failure to synthesize the auditory with the visual elements of words when the precocious maturation of visual and auditory perceptual processes is involved in the oedipal conflict before the managerial system's synthetic function has matured. A case has been described in which reading inhibition arose from a neurotic conflict in which the father was associated with visual and the mother with auditory functions as two separate, unloving human beings. As a result there was symbolic interference with the integration of auditory and visual information. Psychoanalytic treatment of that patient improved reading ability, but spelling difficulty persisted (Rosen, 1955).

Visual, Proprioceptive, and Auditory Integration

Another example of intermodal integration is the compensation for the motion in relation to the environment created by our own movements by the comparison of visual inputs with proprioceptive data that represent body movement. There are distinct mechanisms that convey perceptions of the external world that remain reassuringly stable in spite of our own movements (Wallach, 1985). The clinical implications of variations in these mechanisms are not clear, but deserve consideration.

Tactile Integration with Other Modalities

The integration of different sensory modalities also can be a problem for the hearing and visually impaired. Deficits in transfer between vision and touch were found in a study of congenitally deaf slow readers. They performed well, however, on tasks that involved either touch or vision (Allen, 1973). For the blind integration of the tactile and auditory modalities is involved in learning braille, which poses problems for some.

Tactile, somesthetic, and affective stimuli are not well integrated in tactually defensive children, who react negatively to light touch sensations that are usually perceived as neutral or sensually pleasant (Ayres, 1979). The sensation of clothes on one's body, the gentle stroke of another person, or a napkin wiping the mouth may cause a reaction of alarm or withdrawal. Thus tactual defensiveness interferes with the development of social relationships, from early parent–infant relationships to later peer relationships. Cuddling and caressing are uncomfortable for the tactually defensive child, who also overreacts to light touch sensations that cause distractibility and make schoolwork difficult.

Firm touch pressure appears to lessen reactions in tactually defensive children and light touch or stroking increases them. Firm touch that moves slowly down the body in the direction of hair growth on arms and legs is preferable to touch moving in the opposite direction, and may have a calming effect. They generally prefer wearing soft, nonscratching clothes that cover arms, legs, and feet. At school they may need to have physical space clearly defined, such as by standing on tile squares or at either end of a line to minimize bumping and jostling. It may be helpful to have a desk away from the aisle to avoid brushing by other children.

Intersensory Integration and Reading Disabilities

Reading success has been thought to be correlated with the ability to integrate auditory and visual information (Muehl & Kremenak, 1966). However, intersensory deficit as an important factor in reading disabilities has been questioned.

In a study controlled for short-term memory, attention, and intramodal processing, poor readers performed as well as normal readers on material devoid of linguistic structure presented between the various sensory modalities. They did not perform as well, however, on learning tasks involving a verbal component, pointing to a linguistic rather than a sensory intermodal problem (Vellutino, 1979). Thus the fluent reader is a verbal gymnast who employs a variety of linguistic devices for word identification and for extracting the messages embedded in a text. Poor readers tend to be insensitive to the internal structure of spoken and printed words, which leads them to attend inefficiently to visual stimuli.

A review of 60 studies that related attainment in reading and arithmetic to visual discrimination, spatial relations, visual memory, and auditory-visual integration revealed that none of them actually produced significant correlations (Larsen & Hammill, 1975). The reviewers concluded that measured intersensory modality integration was not sufficiently related to academic achievement to be diagnostically useful.

Intersensory Integration and Character Development

In another vein there are intriguing efforts to relate the integration of early sensory patterns of parenting to later behavior. The importance of the peripheral sensory systems and the vestibulocerebellar system in parent–infant bonding is suggested by the discovery of connections between the pleasure–distress centers and the cerebellum. A psychobiological theory has been proposed that human violence can originate from a developmental defect in the pleasure centers secondary to inadequate early sensory parenting experiences (Restak, 1979). In this view an infant deprived of the multiple modality sensory stimulation involved in cuddling may not fully develop the brain pathways that mediate pleasure.

At the same time, a child with motor coordination and sensory integration difficulties may show greater dependency on a parent and other adults. As a toddler such a child may be unusually active, awkward, aggressive, impulsive, and prone to mishaps. Without special understanding of the child, a parent may become exasper-

ated and punitive. This, in turn, increases the child's aggressiveness, and a sadomasochistic cycle may ensue (Weil, 1977).

Interhemispheric Integration

At this time the significance of individual variations in interhemispheric integration is not clear; however, differences between children on this dimension can be detected. At the level of interhemispheric integration a classification of disability has been based upon weaknesses in either left- or right-hemisphere functioning (Brumback & Stanton, 1983). Although probably an oversimplification, it is a testable hypothesis.

In this view left-hemisphere dysfunction in children may result in the delayed development and poor articulation of speech. On careful examination these children may be found to manifest impaired naming of colors, numbers, letters, and geometric shapes; difficulty in finding the correct words to describe objects, places, and names; substitution of verbs for nouns; difficulty with reading; difficulty in word-attack skills; difficulty in spelling because of phonemic substitutions; and difficulty with arithmetic because of symbol substitutions. If severely affected, such children may have difficulty understanding direct questions or directions. They rely upon nonverbal means to express themselves, such as pointing. Neurological examination may reveal impaired motor function of the right arm or leg and an inability to coordinate leg movements, as in skipping. Speech, even if sparse or poorly articulated, may be emotionally rich, with varied pitch and tone. Constructional abilities and ordering functions are intact.

Right-hemisphere dysfunction may vary from mild delay of motor milestones to marked clumsiness. Play with puzzles, coloring books, constructional toys, and balls is avoided because of poor spatial imagery and orientation. School skills that require

COGNITIVE DISABILITIES   473

spatial perception, such as art, penmanship, sewing, and telling time, are particularly difficult. Paper-and-pencil tasks are variably disorganized, with poorly differentiated geometric shapes, and crowding and reversals of letters, words, and numbers. Arithmetic performance is characteristically poor when problem solving requires that the relative position of digits be maintained, as in vertical columns for addition and subtraction and diagonal columns in multidigit multiplication and division. Letter reversal and loss of orientation on printed pages impair reading ability. Persistent confusion of right versus left beyond the age of seven years leads to difficulties in dressing, especially with gloves and shoes. Impaired ability to order and retain serial items makes the completion of a series of tasks very difficult. These children may disrupt classroom routines in their attempts to avoid having to perform paperwork. Neurological examination reveals impairment of left-sided motor functions. Such children usually have adequate language skills, but their speech may be monotonous and lack emotional coloring of tone and pitch.

IMAGERY PROBLEMS

Marked individual differences in mental imagery were reported by Fechner in 1860. Twenty years later Galton described differences in the vividness of visual imagery among people (Galton, 1883). In 1886 Binet described persons whose mental imagery was predominantly in words or in movement (Binet, 1899). Unfortunately, experimental psychologists lost interest in subjective imagery and became occupied with observable behavior, so that only recently has there been a resurgence of interest in imagery.

Many highly accomplished people are specialized in either visual or verbal imagery. For example, biologists and physicists tend to use visual imagery, whereas psychologists and anthropologists tend to use verbal imagery (Roe, 1950–51). On the other hand, intense visual imagery apparently provides memory for details, but does not facilitate thought. Luria studied the abilities of a person who possessed a photographic memory and found the person to be unable to perform intellectual work. The ever-present visual images made abstract thought virtually impossible for him (Dixon, 1983). Galton (1883) even concluded that vivid visual imagery was antagonistic to abstract thinking, which often involves words.

Alexithymia

Important questions need to be answered about the neural mechanisms and interactional experiences in early life that account for the transformation of neural impulses into images and result in the capacity for the symbolic expression of emotions through language. The concept of alexithymia refers to difficulty in the ability to verbalize emotions and imagery (Taylor, 1984). This is seen in children who are overinvested in external, impersonal percepts to avoid evoking anxiety-laden imagery and are unable to describe their feelings and fantasies, as if they do not have them.

Imagery Modality Memory Preference

Although most persons do not show a distinct preference for the imagery of one sensory modality over the other, some do prefer the visual modality and are inclined to remember information read in books or seen in pictures. Others prefer the auditory modality and are inclined to remember better what they have heard in discussions, lectures, and music. Those who prefer the kinesthetic modality are inclined to remember movement and texture patterns, as in underlining and writing. One's imagery preference is suggested by recalling whether visual or auditory elements are remembered from a television or movie scene. Some children form vivid images in several modes; others seldom have clear images in any sensory modality (Horowitz, 1983).

Visual and auditory percepts differ significantly. Visual stimuli are light frequencies that occur simultaneously in complex patterns; only iconic and precategorical storage are needed to distinguish a recognizable pattern. The capacity to retain visual images after viewing pictorial stimuli varies widely. Of a group of elementary-school students, 55 percent could do so but only 8 percent could reproduce details from them (Haber, 1969). In contrast to visual imagery, sound stimuli occur successively in time and rely upon forming distinct perceptions of each sound so that short-term memory for digits, for example, generally is superior to visual short-term memory (Atwood, 1971).

Our verbally communicative culture expects that all children will learn to talk and share their thoughts through the medium of spoken and written symbols. A fundamental error is made in assuming that because children can hear, they know how to listen.

Children who are visually oriented give predominant attention to the general imagery of feelings (Kuffler, 1969). They tend to do well in the first and second grades, when their imaginative abilities are significant in achievement, but from the third grade on, they appear to be less able students because they lack the words to state their responses. This makes it difficult to gauge the extent of their learning. Though they can hear, they do not listen; they have little recall of sound imagery.

The special visual, imaginative, and manipulative capacities of the visually oriented child are not recognized and developed in elementary school (Kuffler, 1969).

School is geared to the verbal child whose learning gives predominant attention to what is heard and who can immediately and clearly demonstrate what has been learned. The verbal child usually does less well in the first and second grades, where the correlation between imagination and achievement is high, but from the third grade on grasps concepts and organizational principles more quickly; however, the price paid for superior conceptualizing is a conventionalizing of memory. By the third grade, verbally oriented children are in command of more clearly demonstrable facts, since, as verbal memorizers, they can give back a clear and immediate account of their comprehension, whereas the verbally slow, visually oriented children have fallen behind in their ability to demonstrate their knowledge.

In spatial, mechanical, and other nonverbal activities, the visually oriented child can perceive and hold in mind the structure and proportions of a form or figure grasped as a whole. Perception of form is a general characteristic of the abstract thinking involved in mathematics and science, as distinct from the verbal thinking involved in most school subjects. Visual-spatial-oriented individuals also have a tolerance for ambiguity, expressed in an acceptance of untidyness and in their creativity.

Daydreaming

Eidetic images, imaginary companions, hallucinations, night terrors, and daydreaming imagery experiences are frequent in childhood but diminish by adolescence. Thus, monotony and boredom readily foster daydreaming in children, which is both a refuge for wishes that are not being fulfilled and a source of distracting worries (Horowitz, 1983). Daydreaming usually is a substitute for direct sublimations in work and play that transform forbidden wishes into socially acceptable and personally satisfying activities. When children have limited sublimation capacities, daydreaming may preempt time and seriously impair a child's capacity for work and social relationships.

There are three fairly stable patterns of daydreaming. One is a guilty and dysphoric style characterized by imagery involving self-recrimination, hostile, aggressive wishes, and fears of failure (Pope & Singer, 1978).

A second pattern is associated with positive contents, vivid visual and auditory imagery, and future-oriented, playful fantasies. This form of daydreaming is enjoyable. Some children are underinvested in external perceptions because of preoccupation with internal imagery in which they mentally transport themselves elsewhere, as one boy did through the imagery of racing in the Indianapolis 500.

A third pattern is characterized more by anxious, fleeting, uncontrollable fantasies that divert attention from external events. There is considerable mind wandering, with an inability to pursue thoughts, as illustrated by a nine-year-old boy:

> In the classroom Kevin appeared scatterbrained, spacey, and lazy. His daydreams took precedence over schoolwork and obliterated awareness that he was two grade levels below his classmates. His mind was busy with many thoughts waiting like animals to jostle through gates. He wondered what was going to push through next. Sometimes he mentally chased tigers, trying to catch them by their stripes and put them in cages.

Visual perception and visual imagery cannot take place at the same time. However, auditory perception and visual imagery can, as when listening to music while reading. Thus visual daydreaming diverts attention from schoolwork and auditory perceptions. An irrelevant visual perception or image interferes more with learning than does an irrelevant auditory percept or image.

Ideational Dyspraxia

Spontaneous writing requires the formation of kinesthetic-motor images in addition to auditory and visual images. In ideational dyspraxia the formation of kinesthetic-motor images is defective. Children with this kind of dyspraxia can trace and copy figures, but have difficulty drawing spontaneously.

SYMBOLIZATION PROBLEMS

The internally generated forms of imagery—the dream, the daydream, the extrasensory perception, the insight, the creative inspiration, the hunch—interplay with the images of external percepts and bring inner experience together with the external world in a far wider sense than is usually appreciated (Tauber & Green, 1959; Rothstein et al, 1988). Both the appropriate and irrational symbolic meaning of images and percepts may trigger pleasure or distress. When distress is evoked, the learning process can be blocked.

Symbolic Blocking of Perception and Activities

The registration of percepts in short-term memory images may be obstructed when the symbolic meaning of a percept evokes anxiety-provoking memories. For example, some children report somatic symptoms and strange sensations in their heads when they encounter unfamiliar words. As one child put it:

> A big shadow comes over me when I see
> a word I don't know. I don't want to try.
> I can't do it and just try to forget it.

Anxiety thus prevents the accommodation of schemes to a percept that ordinarily would produce retention in long-term memory.

The process of reading can be blocked by the anxiety-provoking symbolic and conceptual meaning of letters and words. For example, the nonsense word *yethl* evokes no symbolic or conceptual imagery. In contrast the word *father* evokes symbolic imagery of the properties associated with the concept father, specifically one's own father. Thus the faulty perceptions of words may actually be due to defensive alterations in their imagery that interfere with comprehension.

The activities of reading and calculating in themselves also may trigger unconscious forbidden wishes and produce phobic responses that interfere with the process of taking in information or recognizing and manipulating printed words or numbers (Blau, 1946). Conscious attention to reading may be deflected by anxiety evoked by the act of reading itself in the form of forbidden aggressive wishes that equate looking with "devouring with the eyes" and erotic wishes that equate looking with voyeurism (Schwartz & Schiller, 1970). On the other hand, the defense of isolation may separate emotion from perception and permit reading to take place.

Traumatic experiences in early reading lessons may be followed by conditioned aversive emotional responses of fear and panic. Children so exposed often cannot remember how these feelings started and cannot suppress them by conscious effort. A phobic response to reading and to school tasks results (Dean & Rattan, 1987). In psychotherapy one such child reported that when he tried to read, he felt panicky, as though he was in school and being humiliated for his mistakes.

A similarity between a percept and anxiety-provoking imagery may interfere with the retrieval of memories. Thus children may forget obviously known information.

Repressed hostile wishes toward one's father, for instance, may interfere with the recall of memories related to male authority figures. Short-term memory difficulty also may be evidence that schoolwork has become so acutely painful that a child cannot bear to keep attending to the learning task (Stott, 1978). As an illustration a boy developed such consistent forgetting of his wrongdoings that his memory became unreliable for other things as well. He became a generally forgetful person (Freud, 1981b).

The Amnesiac Syndrome

The amnesiac syndrome in adults has been used as evidence for the structural distinction between short- and intermediate-term memory and has important implications for the understanding of normal episodic memory processes (Deutsch & Deutsch, 1975).

Clinically the amnesiac syndrome manifests itself after damage to a system that consists of the hippocampus and diencephalic structures, including the medial dorsal nucleus of the thalamus. These patients suffer a profound impairment of their ability to recover a wide range of memories and to learn new information. Amnesaics can hold material within the focus of their immediate awareness, and so characteristically have unimpaired short-term memory and experience no difficulty in following normal conversation. They retain the ability to hold information pending the conclusion of the spoken thought. However, once information has been displaced from immediate awareness, they are unable to retrieve it. They sometimes confabulate, offering spurious information in place of that which they fail to retrieve.

Amnesiacs also have difficulty remembering information both about events that followed the onset of their disease and about events that occurred well before that time. Occasionally this retrograde amnesia gradually diminishes in severity. The fact that some memories then become available shows that this information must have been held intact in storage, but was inaccessible because of defective retrieval processes. Finally, amnesiacs are described as lethargic in personality. Furthermore, in the amnesia of Korsakoff's dementia episodic, but not semantic, memory is impaired (Weingartner et al, 1983).

Specific memory disorders are associated with unilateral loss of medial temporal lobe tissue. Verbal memory is selectively lost with left medial temporal damage and visual memory with right. Should these medial temporal lesions extend bilaterally, however, the memory defect becomes severe, and the classic amnesiac syndrome results. The significance of these adult clinical phenomena in childhood remains to be determined but deserves consideration.

Symbolic Distortion of Perceptions and Behavior

The meaning of images can be distorted, misinterpreted, or forgotten, because of unconscious conflicts based upon instinctual strivings, as in parapraxes (Rapaport, 1971). The configuration of a percept may be altered so as to become less threatening and more assimilable. In this way words may be misread to avoid painful connotations.

Parapraxes are transient errors in receptive and expressive language, which are immediately recognized as incorrect when attention is called to them. Examples on the receptive side are to misinterpret, misjudge, misperceive, misread, and misunderstand, and on the expressive side, to misremember, missay, misspell, misuse, and miswrite. They may have roots in repressed unconscious wishes that enter consciousness disguised as fortuitous accidents (Freud, S., 1965). For example, conflicts between curiosity and disgust about invis-

ible body orifices may interfere with their incorporation into the body image and subsequently interfere with the enterprise of knowing things completely. Conflicts over exhibitionistic and voyeuristic wishes also can lead to systematic blocking of acquiring knowledge (Allen, 1967).

All parapraxes do not have symbolic determinants, however. Individuals vary in their proneness to random, minor cognitive errors (Reason & Mycielska, 1982). This may be related to differences in the amount of attentional resource available to monitor and control routine mental and physical processes at critical moments. Consciously intended actions also may be usurped by habits based upon schemes that are appropriate most of the time, but are unsuitable under changed circumstances. The vagaries of the state regulating and managerial systems influence the efficiency of information processing.

A variety of adjustment processes in the form of psychological defense mechanisms can distort images (see Figure 22-1). Even subliminal perception is influenced by defensive operations stimulated by anxiety from unconscious sources (Kepecs & Wolman, 1972). The psychological defense mechanisms entail some degree of repression. They are tricks of self-deception to avoid painful emotions. In so doing, however, each creates perceptual blind spots.

Repression and displacement can be seen as classification and reclassification processes (Hamilton, 1983). In repression a stimulus, whether externally or internally generated, is classified and assigned to a "not-to-be-processed-as-imagery" class of experience by comparator structures, which can recognize stimuli as belonging to classes of experiences previously labeled as having aversive attributes. In this model repression keeps painful emotions out of conscious awareness by forgetting that one has forgotten. It produces forbidden zones that shield consciousness from painful memories grouped in sets of schemes ar-

THE DEFENSIVE ALTERATION OF IMAGERY	
Defense Mechanism	**Effect on Imagery**
Sublimation	modify it into socially acceptable form
Fantasy	pretend it is true
Repression	forget it
Displacement	shift it to another person or thing
Intellectualization	explain it away
Rationalization	make excuses for it
Compensation	make up for it
Introjection	take it in from someone else
Indentification	become like someone else
Regression	cry for it
Reaction formation	make it the opposite
Isolation	separate emotions from it
Undoing	cancel it
Projection	make it come from someone else
Denial	it did not happen

Figure 22-1.

ranged like layers of an onion around a forbidden core (Goleman, 1985). The superficial layers are accessible to consciousness but the deeper layers are difficult to activate. Thus schoolwork may trigger anxiety through the activation of forbidden wishes related to oral incorporation, anal production, or phallic potency. Frightened by these drives, a child may be unable to permit the free flow of imagery, and repress it.

Displacement, on the other hand, occurs when comparator structures recognize the danger of the direct expression of drive stimuli and reclassify the object by substituting a safe image of a different object in an act of self-deception. At the same time, displacement inappropriately invests percepts of that different object with the qualities of the original percept that provoked anxiety.

Projection can be regarded as an extreme example of displacement in which imagery of the drive derivatives of emotion, thought, and intention are displaced from oneself to other persons. Awareness of who is the actual possessor of the forbidden characteristics is prevented because ownership of that which is projected might lead to self-criticism or guilt. When the behavior and intentions of the other persons are attacked and produce various forms of counterattack, justification for the projection is reinforced (Hamilton, 1983). Projection takes place readily in persons who generally perceive an external locus of control and externalize responsibility for their intentions and actions.

Displacement and projection can cause academic tasks and teachers to be seen as threatening and result in irrational hostility toward and avoidance of them on the part of a child. Through projection dangers within a child also can be perceived as coming from the external world.

Every defense against a drive derivative or self-evaluation demand is a way of saying "no" to some aspect of it (Brenner, 1981). Repression, for example, can be a defense against a young boy's wish to re-

---

place his father and be his mother's husband. The wish expressed by the words "I want to marry Mommy" is excluded from awareness. As far as the boy himself is concerned, he does not want to marry Mommy or remember that he ever did want to marry her. If asked, "Do you want to marry your mother?" he would answer quite sincerely, "No, I don't." If asked, "Did you ever want to marry her?" he would answer "Never" just as sincerely, despite the fact that the wish to marry her persists in an unconscious conflicted form. Along with repressing his incestuous wishes for his mother, the boy may displace them onto an aunt or a schoolteacher; his conscious conviction then becomes, "I want to marry Aunt Jane, not Mommy."

Another defense is reaction formation through which behavior opposite to the underlying wish is expressed. Quarreling with his mother could be a defense against a boy's incestuous wishes for her, expressed by the words, "I don't love her, I hate her!" In addition, reaction formation can lead to scholarly preoccupation through which forbidden destructive wishes can be undone by compliant, constructive performance as a model student. Because this behavior is defensive, however, the destructive wishes may gain expression by trying too hard, with resulting sabotage of productive schoolwork.

Identification can be used defensively, as when a boy imagines himself to be his younger sibling in order to ward off incestuous wishes for his mother; the defensive aspect of his identification has the meaning, "I don't want to marry Mommy, I want to be her baby instead." Through identification with the aggressor, a child transforms oneself from the person threatened into the threatening person (Sandler, 1985). Thus a boy physically abused by his father becomes a bully himself. In this way a child changes a painful, passive experience into an active one as a means of mastering anxiety.

The characteristic defenses we use shape our characters so that one who relies on projection will perceive and react differently than one who favors reaction formation. Our favored defenses become habitual mental maneuvers, an armor plating imposed on experience called character armoring by Wilhelm Reich (Goleman, 1985; Reich, 1972).

CONCEPTUALIZATION PROBLEMS

Even under optimal circumstances, children develop misconceptions from erroneous, misunderstood, and incomplete information. This may be strengthened by pressure upon young children to accept adult concepts in school and to conceal their lack of understanding.

Deficient Conceptualization

Some learning difficulties may be characterized by an inability to conceptualize the learning process, so that images formed from incoming information are not linked to symbols and concepts. In this way a child can accumulate information but not convert it into knowledge (Rudel, 1980). To be unable to gain meaning from information is to be limited to the concrete observable, to be unable to deduce, infer, and profit from connotation. In contrast to be able to abstract is to detach oneself from the immediate and observable by categorizing information on the basis of commonalities and principles via inner language that permits conceptualization (Mykelbust, 1978).

When words are not linked to concepts, they remain at a syncretic level in which sensations, images, and actions closely approximate primitive, unconscious schemes that can cause anxiety. Once these images are transformed through development or psychotherapy into conscious verbal forms, verbalization of them becomes increasingly possible. Instead of words being used as things, they become used as representations of things.

There are additional ways in which conceptualization can be inadequately developed. The most obvious in school are difficulties in concepts that involve two-dimensional space, such as numbers, quantity, weight, and area (Goldschmid & Bentler, 1968). More subtle problems can be found in conceptualizing three-dimensional perspectives of things (Laurendeau & Pinard, 1970) and social situations (Chandler, 1973).

Anxiety-Laden Concepts

Reading words may bring forth concepts that have denotative and both conscious and unconscious connotations, which may trigger anxiety (Shapiro, 1979). The affective significance of these concepts blocks perceptions and activities in the same way as described for symbols in the preceding section.

Inaccurate Concepts

Persons with lesions of the frontal lobes show subtle disturbances of concept formation. Although they readily recognize simple pictures, letters or numbers, simple words, and elementary sentences, the situation changes if they encounter complicated situations that require the inhibition of initial impressions. They show pathological inertia of a perceived image; for example, they are unable to distinguish a figure against a homogeneous background. They lack the capacity to shift readily and efficiently the meaning of images in accord with the connotations of underlying concepts.

Examples of the opposite kind of problem are the "verbalisms" seen in blind children, who learn verbal concepts without an appropriate foundation in concrete visual experience. They then build abstraction upon abstraction with resulting hazy and inaccurate concepts of environmental surroundings. Their reliance upon borrowed descriptions may cause them to lose faith in the worth of their own experiences and to feel devalued. Consequently blind children should be taught words while they are in sensory contact with the objects (Harley, 1963).

ARITHMETIC DISABILITIES

The New Math method of teaching mathematics had an adverse impact on many children comparable to the look–say method of teaching reading. Because it neglected the basic principles of learning arithmetic, it did not teach practical computational skills (Kline, 1973; Mosse, 1982).

A child's ability to learn and perform arithmetic is complicated by difficulty with the conditioned process of memorization needed for arithmetic. Children, who tend to solve all problems in the same way, experience anxiety when confronted with new levels of arithmetical operations. Arithmetic is fraught with difficulties for perseverative children. They cannot easily shift from the number 5, for instance, to think of it in terms of 3 plus 2.

Numbers also may have unpleasant conscious or unconscious associations and symbolize traumatic experiences. Therefore, they may evoke anxiety, which interferes with their mental manipulation, as may letters and words. Unconscious conflicts regarding money also can emerge as inhibitions to learning arithmetic. Money plays a special role in a child's life and is an important initial shaper of attitudes toward arithmetic. The unconscious link between bodily products and giving or receiving presents and money may give rise to neurotic conflicts that affect the learning of arithmetic (Mosse, 1982).

There is evidence of a spatial type of development dyscalculia exhibited by both horizontal and vertical spatial confusion in written addition and subtraction. Developmental anarithmetria refers to mixing procedures involved in addition, subtraction, and multiplication, and confusion in carrying out the operations of written arithmetic. Children with attentional-sequential dyscalculia add and subtract inaccurately by omitting figures in adding, forgetting to carry figures, and omitting decimal points and dollar signs. Among a group of children with difficulty learning arithmetic, 24 percent were spatial, 14 percent anarithmetria, 42 percent attentional-sequential, and 20 percent mixed (Badian, 1983).

Four forms of acalculia have been described in adults (Mosse, 1982). No such studies exist concerning children; however, the arithmetical symptoms of these adult patients may be helpful in evaluating children's arithmetical difficulties.

Parietal Acalculia

Malfunctioning of parts of the parietal lobes may lead to an arithmetic disorder, with or without a reading and writing disorder. These patients have trouble with the spatial and structural aspects of arithmetic; they suffer from constructional apraxia, or the specific arithmetic disorder of the Gerstmann syndrome.

Occipital Acalculia

Malfunctioning of the part of the arithmetic apparatus located in the occipital lobes interferes with visualization, which is of crucial importance for arithmetic, especially mental arithmetic, although persons with this problem are able to solve problems by writing them down.

Frontal Acalculia

Frontal lobe lesions sometimes cause a severe arithmetic disorder in adults. These patients may be able to perform elementary addition and subtraction with concrete objects and numbers. However, they cannot do multiplication or division, because they cannot understand the more complicated underlying thought processes.

Temporal Acalculia

Malfunctioning in the temporal lobes can cause a special form of arithmetic disorder. These patients frequently know the word for the number, but not the number symbol. They have retention difficulties with calculations in which number symbols are involved.

INFANTILE AUTISM

Infantile autism is a pervasive developmental disorder accompanied by severe and enduring cognitive, language, behavioral, and social deficits. It is viewed as a distinct entity without a relationship to adult psychoses (De Myer et al, 1981; Coleman & Gillberg, 1985).

The diagnosis of infantile autism is based upon three essential criteria: failure of normal speech and language development, gross and sustained impairment of interpersonal relations, and the onset of symptoms before 30 months of age. The typical autistic child is aloof and unresponsive to others, preoccupied with objects, resistant to change, prone to distorted movement patterns, relatively insensitive to pain, provoked to anxiety by commonplace phenomena, and likely to have islands of normal functioning. If speech is present, peculiar speech patterns may be seen, such as echolalia, metaphorical language, and pronominal reversal. A Childhood Autism Rating Scale is available for facilitating diagnosis and following the course of treatment (Schopler et al, 1986).

The differential diagnosis includes deafness, degenerative neurological disorder, mental retardation, and, most important, developmental dysphasia. In contrast to dysphasia, early infantile autism is evident during infancy and is characterized by a paucity of gesture and imitation and a much greater disturbance in social attachment and the regulation of anxiety. There may be mixed dysphasic—autistic syndromes, however, and family clusterings of both types of disorders (Cohen et al, 1976). Epilepsy appears in one out of three autistic children in later life.

The prevalence rate of infantile autism is probably between four and five per 10,000 population under 15 years of age. It occurs in 5–8 percent of children with congenital rubella and mental retardation, and is found as a subgroup in the fragile-X chromosome syndrome and metabolic diseases. The ratio of males to females is about four to one.

Most autistic children score in the mentally retarded range of intelligence. Their intelligence scores tend to be predictors of ultimate outcome, with a more favorable prognosis for those with initial intelligence quotients above 70 and the onset of speech prior to the age of five. Follow-up studies show that, as adults, about 70 percent remain dependent on relatives or in institutions; 2 percent achieve normal independent status and 28 percent reach a marginally normal status (DeMyer et al, 1981).

In infantile autism congenital disturbances of both social orientation and cognition play mutually compounding roles. In neither sphere are these children able to move flexibly and intuitively with zestful problem solving (Cohen, 1978). They show a dissociation in the normal pattern of development: mild to moderate impairment of postural-motor development, moderate to severe impairments in the development of holistic processing skills, and very severe impairments in the development of language and sequential processing skills. The need for sameness could be a result of extreme language impairment coupled with limited holistic processing skills, leading to an inability to understand an otherwise chaotic environment except through limited routines and visual-spatial maps. The motor stereotypies could represent immature sensorimotor reflexes or persistence of primitive pleasure-giving activity (Tanguay, 1984). The cognitive deficits involve language, as well as sequencing and abstraction. The deficits probably do not lie in the processing of stimuli of any particular sensory modality but rather with the systems subserving attachment and affiliative instincts that process stimuli carrying emotional and social meaning (Bartak et al, 1975; Fein et al, 1986).

The relationships between disturbances in sensory modulation and motility in infantile autism are especially noteworthy (Ornitz, 1983). The abnormal motility may be evoked by sensory input in all sensory modalities; it appears to be compensatory self-stimulation of some kind. Thus these children induce sensory stimuli by scratching surfaces, flicking their ears, grinding their teeth, watching their own writhing finger and hand movements, vigorously flapping their arms and hands, and whirling and rocking their bodies. All of these abnormal movements may be evoked by unexpected sounds, flickering light displays, or spinning objects, such as tops. In contrast they may underreact to visual, auditory, or painful stimuli. The faulty modulation of sensory input also is suggested by an echolike auditory response (Ornitz, 1978).

Where the structural cellular or physiological bases of infantile autism lie is not known (DeMyer et al, 1981; Coleman & Gillberg, 1985). Autistic children appear to be more lacking in the functions of the left than the right hemisphere (Rimland, 1978). The brainstem, including the vestibular nuclei, and related nonspecific thalamic centers have been implicated (Ornitz, 1983; 1985). An inability to discern meaning from social exchanges which are thus perceived as chaotic and confusing has been proposed as the basic defect in infant autism (Bemporad et al, 1987).

Twin and other sibling studies lend weak support to genetic inheritance of the complete syndrome, although specific deficits in language and cognitive components may be more strongly genetically linked. Further evidence for an anatomical component basis for infantile autism comes from an increased incidence of prenatal and perinatal complications, abnormal electroencephalographic signs, seizures, abnormal neurological signs, frequency of mixed handedness, abnormalities of eye movements, and abnormal vestibular functions (Herskowitz & Rosman, 1982).

The treatment of infantile autism involves a long, arduous course of establishing rapport with the child and developing social and academic skills (Kramer, Anderson, & Westman, 1984; Simons & Oishi, 1987).

The Asperger syndrome refers to a group of children who lack the ability to understand and use the conventions governing social behavior (Wing, 1981). The content of their speech is sterotyped, pedantic, and uncommunicative. Their facial expression, tone of voice, and gestures are unexpressive, and their ability to receive nonverbal communication is limited. The result is impairment of two-way social interactions. In other respects they resemble mildly autistic children.

GIFTED UNDERACHIEVERS

The plight of many gifted children who underachieve in school illustrates a form of school problem related to a surfeit rather than lack of cognitive abilities. Although Plato advocated selecting the "gold" children when young and preparing them for leadership through education, an ambivalence toward gifted children has been expressed over the years in prizing the fruits of their abilities but giving them little encouragement (Whitmore, 1980).

About 3 percent of the schoolchildren in the United States are thought to be gifted, and many experience adjustment problems (Torrance, 1962). The majority learn how to handle them, but for about 25 percent life-long struggles ensue. Gifted children are vulnerable, because they may perceive themselves as having failed to meet the expectations of others, and because of their sensitivity to feedback from others, as dramatically illustrated by the following instance:

> A disadvantaged first-grader had an IQ of 177. Her teachers and parents disparaged her, because she had an imaginary playmate. By the time she reached the fifth grade, she had fallen below average in IQ. She dropped out of school in the tenth grade. As an adult, married and with three children, she said, "I know I'm not very smart, but I would still like to finish high school."

A long and dedicated learning process is necessary to develop great talent, which does not inevitably emerge as an early gift (Bloom, 1985). That long and arduous road may begin with a child's playful delight in learning followed by a more disciplined commitment and finally an individual's total immerison in a field.

Like other underachievers gifted children may have poor work habits, lack concentration, and require prodding. Their parents, sensing their talent, often are confused by their children's negative school reports, with resulting tension between parents, teachers, and administrators. These negative feelings may create disruptive behavior at home. Meanwhile the children develop low self-esteem and negative attitudes toward school and their peers. They are frustrated by the gap between their performance and the level of perfection they wish to achieve.

Gifted underachievers are frustrated, particularly in schools in which curriculum and instruction are unduly rigid, unchallenging, and irrelevant to their interests. They notably lack motivation and effort if a task, course, or opportunity is not related to their particular interests or goals. They tended to overreact if teachers seemed unfair, incompetent, or negative toward them personally, as illustrated by the following case (*Time*, April 23, 1979):

> From the day he entered first grade, Tommy was regarded as a disobedient pupil, who did shoddy work. After his third-grade teacher told his parent that their son had a learning disability, they had a psychologist test him. His IQ was 169. "He was frustrated and bored to tears," observed his father. At home Tommy's gifts seemed evident enough. He memorized advanced charts of human anatomy and could beat his grandfather at chess at the age of four. But at school Tommy produced conflicting test results, once scoring low in mathematical ability and later achieving a very high score. Teachers complained about his short attention span and removed him from the room to keep him from distracting the other children. Furthermore, because of his undisciplined behavior, he was denied admittance to the school's program for gifted children.

Boredom is the rarely noted, but deadly, enemy of education. Not just the gifted, but many children become misfits and school dropouts if they have no alternatives to the traditional curriculum. Moreover very bright children with educational disabilities may elude detection, because they can function at an average level, keep up with the class, and so not arouse suspicion that they could achieve at higher levels.

Fortunately knowledge about meeting the needs of gifted children through acceleration and enrichment programs is growing (Benbow & Stanley, 1984).

SUMMARY

The cognitive problems children encounter in schoolwork primarily involve the reception of visual and auditory stimuli; visual, auditory, and spatial perception; intermodal sensory integration; mental imagery; symbolization; and conceptualization.

Sensory receptive problems in vision occur in visual acuity, accommodation inefficiency, and impaired coordination of movements of the eyes. For the most part, however, faulty eye movements are the result, not the cause, of reading difficulties.

Hearing losses are more commonly unrecognized problems for children than are visual problems. Recurrent middle-ear infections during early life may cause delayed speech, auditory discrimination deficits, and secondary reading and spelling difficulties. Deaf children require intensive special education and have difficulty achieving educationally, when compared with hearing children.

Perceptual exclusion through stimulus modulation is essential in order to prevent sensory overload, but it also can reflect selective inattention as a psychological defense mechanism, so that conscious awareness of perceptions is blocked by anxiety. Some children have difficulty in perceiving the temporal order of information in the form of letters and words. Auditory perception can pose problems when the maturation of auditory discrimination ability is delayed. Hearing also is less accurate than vision, and sounds carry significant emotional connotations that can interfere with rapport between adults and children.

Spatial orientation difficulties can occur

in the position sense of one's body, geographical directions, and right–left discrimination. Although these manifestations may occur with visual-spatial dyslexias, spatial problems are more typically related to problems in mathematics.

Intermodal sensory integration difficulties may not be as critical in causing reading difficulties as previously thought. Still distinct differences in individual preferences for the visual, auditory, or haptic modalities are seen. Children also vary in rates of maturation in which these modalities are integrated through the interplay of the cerebral hemispheres.

There are significant individual differences in the vividness of visual, auditory, and motor imagery. Varying degrees of ability to verbalize imagery are found; alexithymia is the inability to do so. Differences also are found in modality memory capacities, which play a role in preferences for visual, auditory, and multisensory modes of learning. Anxiety-producing situations and stimuli can be responsible for immersion in internal imagery in the form of daydreaming that often distracts children from schoolwork.

The symbolic meaning of external and internal imagery can trigger anxiety because of spoken or written words or the acts of learning and reading themselves. Perceptions and images can be blocked, distorted, or forgotten by the operation of psychological defense mechanisms, such as repression, displacement, and projection. The correspondence of perceptions and the imagery of unconscious conflicts also can cause misperception and the failure of short-term memory. On the other hand, the defenses of isolation and undoing can lead to scholarly preoccupation, even though it may be inefficient.

An inability to conceptualize the learning process and material to be learned may lead to inefficiency in schoolwork so that information is not linked to personalized symbols and concepts. Children must be able to abstract meaning from information in order to understand the nature of the educational enterprise and personalize information as knowledge. The prefrontal lobe syndrome includes subtle deficits in concept formation. The amnesiac syndrome is an adult model of short-term memory loss. Children's memory problems occur at the imaging, symbolization, and conceptualization levels.

The types of arithmetic difficulties tend to involve the language aspects, visual–spatial relationships, sequential ordering, and flexibility in problem solving. Since facility in arithmetic is less crucial in society than reading, arithmetic difficulties receive less attention.

Because they represent two extremes in cognitive variability, the problems of autistic and gifted children are described in this chapter. Infantile autism is a developmental disorder of unknown origin accompanied by severe and enduring cognitive, language, behavioral, and social deficits. Gifted underachievers constitute a vulnerable population in spite of the general tendency to assume that they will flourish on their own. Misunderstanding of their boredom in school, coupled with poor work habits and low self-esteem, conspire to produce adjustment problems for 25 percent of these children.

Cognitive problems range from those involving the intactness of the sensory organs themselves to obscure distortions and blocks caused by psychological defense mechanisms. The manipulaton of imagery from internal and external sources is the crucible within which each child constructs personal knowledge in the form of concepts of the self and the world. The capacity for symbolization enriches and expedites that process, but also can introduce phantoms into the classroom.

23

Verbal Language Disabilities

Language knowledge never disappears totally; only its normal function and its use are disarranged.

Eric H. Lenneberg, 1973

Verbal language disabilities usually are classified as disorders of speech or of receptive and expressive language. This pragmatic distinction is clinically useful, however, it is important to recognize that they all are interconnected difficulties in the understanding and production of speech (Hersov & Berger, 1980; Rieber, 1981; Rousey, 1979; Yule & Rutter, 1988). Because 7 to 10 percent of school-age children exhibit verbal language disorders, they merit attention as factors contributing to problems with schoolwork (Wren, 1983).

Speech disabilities reflect frontal lobe motor functions manifested in the external aspects of expressive verbal language. They are usually described in terms of (1) variations in pronouncing words (articulation disorders), (2) variations in speaking resonance (voice disorders), and (3) variations in speaking fluency (stuttering).

Receptive and expressive disabilities involve several cortical areas and are usually described in terms of delays and variations in the use of spoken language as manifestions of (1) general developmental disabilities, (2) specific developmental language delays, (3) interpersonal speech delays, (4) developmental dysphasias, and (5) hearing deficits.

SPEECH DISABILITIES

Speech disorders are found in children of all levels of intelligence and cultural backgrounds. At least 50 percent of children with clinically diagnosed speech disorders also have psychiatric diagnoses (Cantwell et al, 1979; Stevenson & Richman, 1978). Conversely 60 percent of one series of psychiatric patients of all ages were found to have speech problems (Rousey & Toussing, 1964), as well as 24 percent of a child psychiatric population (Chess & Rosenberg, 1974).

Articulation Disabilities

The prevalence of articulation problems depends upon age, because the ability to pronounce word sounds improves with growth. Five percent of children entering school have difficulty speaking understandably to persons who are not familiar with their enunciation (Milisen, 1971; Rutherford, 1977).

Articulation disorders are classified as (1) dyslalias, which are habitual distortions without a physical basis, such as "baby talk"; (2) dysaudias, which are errors because of hearing loss; (3) dysglossias, which are distortions from structural defects in oral structures; (4) dyspraxias, which are disturbances in formulating speech; and (5) dysarthrias, which are imperfections in speech because of incoordination of the speech muscles (Emerick & Hatten, 1979).

Vowel and consonant sounds are influenced by emotions, neurotic conflicts, and self-esteem (Rousey, 1979). Thus variations is sound production other than dialect may be based upon psychological factors, situational stress, or developmental complications.

Voice Disabilities

The incidence of voice disorders has been reported as 0.5 to 2 percent of the general population, with little age or sex variation. A laryngeal examination is indicated in all voice disorders because of the possibility of diseases of the vocal cords. Nasality and harshness of the voice may result from structural abnormalities of the nasopharynx and larynx.

Psychological gender-identity conflicts may be reflected in hoarseness, which begins in boys in the late preschool years, and in breathiness in girls with an onset in early adolescence. An unusually high or low pitch of voice in boys and girls may be based upon endocrine disorders or neurotic conflicts.

Fluency Disabilities

Approximately 1 percent of the school population appears to stutter compared with a prevalence of 4 percent during the preschool years, indicating that stuttering decreases with advancing age.

Stuttering usually begins around the age of three. Generally the more a child feels under pressure to talk, the greater the repetitions or prolongations of syllables, words, or phrases. The child has difficulty coordinating the movements of the lips, tongue, and chest with sounds originating from the larynx.

The treatment of stuttering draws upon a combination of behavioral and psychotherapeutic principles. The aim is to minimize variability of speech sounds by modulating the voice and slowing down the rate of speech (Conture, 1982; Speech Foundation of America). The successful mastery of stuttering enhances one's self-evaluation and promotes self-confidence; however, underlying intrapsychic conflicts may remain and be an indication for intensive psychotherapy (Glauber, 1983).

RECEPTIVE AND EXPRESSIVE LANGUAGE DISABILITIES

Approximately 4 percent of children manifest significant delays in the onset of talking. The inner verbal language disorders of childhood include difficulties with the form, content, and use of language (Bloom & Lahey, 1978).

General Developmental Disabilities

The developmental disability syndromes are obvious explanations for the delayed onset of speech. The diagnosis is made on the basis of the other manifestations of developmental disabilities.

Specific Developmental Language Delays

The warning signs of specific language problems in acquiring the linguistic rules for word and sentence formation usually are overlooked in young children. Often it is not until a child fails to acquire skills in reading, spelling, and writing that the question of deficits in verbal language arises (Wiig & Semel, 1980).

Language delays may signal both underlying structural factors in the brain and problems in a child's social and emotional development. Lags in the appearance of language functions usually reflect delays in central nervous system maturation (Bender, 1975). Most of these problems spontaneously disappear at the age of seven or eight because of maturation or compensatory functions in the brain; however, about 20 percent of the children continue to have language, intellectual, and educational disabilities (Fundudis et al, 1980).

A relationship exists between babbling in infancy and later language development, as seen in children who fail to acquire normal language. Autistic children, for example, rarely produce normal patterns of babble. Developmentally disabled children exhibit immature patterns of babble and are delayed in acquiring speech inflections. Deaf children may babble without the development of speech inflections until the age of about nine months, so that by 12 months only primitive sounds remain (Howlin, 1981).

Environmental experience plays a key role in the development of language. The integration of auditory and visual stimuli is influenced by an infant's parenting experience between the ages of two and six months. Children who do not have adequate auditory and verbal stimulation during this period may not develop efficient auditory discrimination. Children with slowly developing auditory discrimination are slow to acquire speech accuracy. Thus children who have not been encouraged to talk or exposed to new words may be understimulated in speech development (Kaluger & Kolson, 1969). Upon entering school these children have difficulty in discriminating, sequencing, and manipulating sounds of words. They also may have difficulty in differentiating and expressing the subtle distinctions in emotion and intention conveyed by the prosody of speech.

Verbal language enriches imagery and fosters problem-solving thought. It also furthers self-awareness and introspection. It aids in achieving distance from the immediacy of external and internal stimuli, and thereby in the control of drives and the modulation of emotions. It permits trial actions in thinking. Because of language's central role in development, a significant defect in any of its multiple, interactive aspects has an effect on a child's character development. An aberration in language development affects the style and adequacy of thought, communication, and learning (Hassibi & Breuer, 1980). Individual variations in these functions are wide. Thus some children may understand spoken words well but express them poorly, as some may express them well but understand them poorly.

Children with delayed language development may use motor outlets to a greater degree than other children. Their temper outbursts tend to be frustration tantrums rather than phase-specific self-assertive tantrums. These children are frustrated by their confused, relatively disorganized inner worlds, when language is not understood. Delayed language development, therefore, may promote isolation and withdrawal (Weil, 1978).

Children raised in different social classes are exposed to a range of degrees to which words are used for communication in their homes. These language differences may create problems in classrooms, which rely upon verbal expression. Furthermore, middle-class children are more likely to have been encouraged to take the initiative, ask questions, and aspire to achievement than lower-class children, and so lower-class children who are not verbally inclined may not lack basic linguistic competence but simply be reflecting their social backgrounds (Wood, 1981).

Delays in verbal language reception, formulation, and expression may affect school achievement in all areas. To process the complex materials used in school, a child must be able to analyze and synthesize the letter-sound, syntactic, semantic, and logical ingredients of verbal language. At first learning to read and later spelling are affected. From the fourth grade on, there usually is little or no skill building in phonics, vocabulary, number concepts, or language concepts. As a result, during the adolescent years, unrecognized verbal and nonverbal communication variations continue to influence the quality of the individual's interpersonal relationships negatively. They limit sensitivity to social situations, the potential for self-realization, and identity formation (Wiig & Semel, 1980).

Verbal language is a vehicle of, but not necessary for, logical thinking, as seen in deaf persons (Furth, 1966). In fact words can create problems in logical thinking when they assume a reality of their own. Words are ideal for describing the seemingly solid, touchable aspects of the world, but problems arise when words used to describe the intangible are presumed to represent reality. Bertrand Russell (1925) pointed out that words describing solids were applied to the universe by early astronomers. In so doing the universe was oversimplified until Einstein introduced a totally new viewpoint. Much of what was supposed previously had to be rejected in order to gain a true picture of the universe. Thus a word may be construed erroneously to mean that what it represents really exists. For children with verbal language delays, misunderstandings of word meanings affect their grasps of reality.

Interpersonal Speech Delays

Another possibility to consider in the delayed onset of speech is that an older sibling or a parent may speak for a child. In these situations children do not have to speak, because their wishes are fulfilled by an intermediary. The interpersonal nature of delayed speech development also is evident when speech delays occur in the context of oppositional behavior.

The incomplete individuation of a mother and child may delay a child's self-definition and speech development (Filippi & Rousey, 1968; Rubin, 1982). In many of these families, the history discloses intense angry displays between the parents during the child's first two years of life. The family interaction is characterized by the predominant use of voices in violent arguments and stern commands. Otherwise there are angry silences and little verbal communication between the parents, and even less between them and the child.

In some instances the inhibition of speech resembles a classic conversion reaction, which wards off the intolerable anxiety a child would suffer from the expression of anger, because a parent is particularly intolerant of aggressive words and likely to retaliate. For these children adequate verbal stimulation was not forthcoming in parenting, so that their capacity for talking is impaired, leading to feelings of helplessness because of their inability to communicate. They then experience anxiety based upon the inability to express destructive wishes toward the parent, in addition to fear of parental retaliation.

Children who exhibit the syndrome of elective mutism generally do not speak to adults in school (Hayden, 1980). They can be mistakenly regarded as failing, because academic performance may be evaluated on the basis of oral productions. Special attention should be devoted to ascertaining the true abilities of the electively mute child, who usually does well in academic learning.

Developmental Dysphasias

Congenital, developmental, and acquired expressive and receptive dysphasias represent a small group of children characterized by significant disturbances in verbal language expression and comprehension (Deuel, 1983).

Approximately six children per 1000 show expressive dysphasias not associated with general developmental retardation (Stevenson & Richman, 1976). Two distinctly different aspects of spoken language have been identified (Bartak, 1975). One is the ability to select words for appropriate patterns of meaning; interference with this function is called a semantic dysphasia. The other expressive language function is the ability to organize words in coherent grammatical form; interference with this function is called a syntactical dysphasia (Luria & Wertsch, 1982).

The essential feature of an expressive dysphasia is a failure to develop vocal expression of language. The children understand language but cannot express themselves spontaneously in words. Articulation is generally immature, and the child's vocabulary is restricted. Although most of these children have the inherent capacity to respond with appropriate ideas and behavior, they are hampered in expressing them. Some are more successful than others in getting around communication obstacles, but all are subject to a sense of frustration (Hassibi, 1980). One boy revealed:

> I have trouble remembering words . . . Nobody believes me . . . I know what to say, but I forget the words.

There may be associated lags in other developmental milestones. Children with focal brain lesions that occur after the acquisition of language commonly have expressive and articulation problems but rarely comprehension difficulties (Rieber, 1980).

The essential feature of a receptive dysphasia, which may occur in one of 2000 children, is the failure to develop language-comprehension skills. In the secondary associational zones of the temporal cortex lie the fundamental apparatuses for the analysis and synthesis of the sounds of speech (Luria, 1973). To distinguish them speech sounds must be coded in accordance with different language systems, each of which differs markedly from the other. Problems occur in the auditory arousal threshold, the ability to localize sounds, the sequencing of sounds, the recognition of auditory symbols, and the integration of auditory symbols.

"Cluttering" is a language disorder characterized by rapid, indistinct speech, especially under the pressure of excitement. Children with this problem are thought to have word-finding difficulties, to not hear speech sounds clearly, including their own, and to have poor auditory memory. They think faster than they speak. They appear to be borderline cases of receptive dysphasia and may be unaware of their disability. When they do become aware of it, they may stutter. They also may have difficulty learning to read and spell (Mosse, 1982).

Although receptive and expressive features can be distinguished, as in Figure 23-1, most dysphasic children have mixtures of both (deHirsch, 1982). In the typical clinical picture, dysphasic children first show a lack of response to spoken words, and then a delay in the developmental milestones of language. Although they may not babble or use single words at the expected times, they usually seek social relatedness by establishing eye contact, playing pattycake, and peek-a-boo. They do not evince the expected onset of speech and may be slow in motor development, have articulation problems, and be clumsy. Simple words may appear at age three or four, although there may be a history of regression from greater verbal language ability. They may appear not to be listening to what is said to them. They are unable to find words to express their thoughts, and comprehension of speech is usually below age expectancy.

FEATURE	RECEPTIVE	EXPRESSIVE
Family history of language difficulties	X	X
Delayed onset of speech	X	X
History of recurrent ear infections prior to the age of 4	X	X
Delays in other developmental milestones	X	X
Limited speech vocabulary	X	X
Immature speech articulation		X
Garrulous jargon	X	
Limited flow of speech		X
Hesitancy in speaking		X
Limited attention to speech	X	
Confusion of similar sounding words	X	
Difficulty understanding speech	X	
Difficulty with grammar	X	
Difficulty finding words		X
Difficulty naming objects		X
Difficulty describing events and telling stories	X	X
Reluctance to volunteer known answers in school		X
Excessive reliance upon circumlocutions and substitution of words		X
Auditory-linguistic dyslexia	X	X

Figure 23-1. Features of developmental dysphasias.

For these children the capacity for inner language, imaginative play, gesture, and mime are limited (Cohen et al, 1976). They may try to communicate through gestures, such as by pointing at objects. Their use of toys and objects is usually appropriate. Their speech is limited, although it can be an inconsistent garrulous jargon. They may echo words in an effort to understand them. Words associated in meaning and function are substituted for each other. They may forget spoken instructions and have short auditory memory spans. They may show syntactical confusion, so that parts of speech are missing or underutilized. Visual cues may help them find the appropriate word for an object.

These children lack verbal tools to discharge emotions through words, leading to a tendency to act impulsively (deHirsch, 1967). Their limited vocabulary impairs their ability to shift from internal imagery to problem-solving thinking. Their capacity for eidetic thinking thus may be limited.

There may be difficulties in remembering, categorizing, feature scanning, organizing, sequencing, and coding, indicating a more pervasive information processing disorder in addition to language. They also may show immature postural reflexes, awkward fine motor control, fragmented human figure drawings, and fluid Bender-Gestalt drawings (deHirsch, 1967).

Educational problems are consequences of these children's difficulties in communication and behavior. They may be withdrawn and shy, irritable, or aggressive, and may show a clinical picture resembling psychotic disorganization or neurotic behavior (Chess & Hassibi, 1978). When raised by parents who did not stress verbal communication, they may use nonverbal communication and be regarded as mentally retarded. If their parents tried to force verbal communication, they may exhibit withdrawal and panic reactions in a clinical picture resembling early infantile autism (Mosse, 1982). Unlike children with early infantile autism who are mechanical and manneristic, these children make communicative efforts, as reflected in their facial expressions and voices.

Less affected dysphasic children usually show academic backwardness and interpersonal difficulties. They may have reading or writing deficits of the auditory-linguistic dysphasic type. They have little understanding of why they are hindered in expressing themselves. Thus their self-concepts tend to be defined as they appear in the eyes of others—as stupid, stubborn, bad, or even bizarre. To the degree that dysphasic children and their parents understand the reasons for their communication shortcomings, their compensatory stratagies can be successful. The symptoms of older children are more specific than those of young children, and compensatory mechanisms are more subtle and complicated. Sometimes bluffing is used to cover the deficit through purposeful bungling. Word loss, poor immediate auditory recall, grammatical errors, and missequencing and elisions of word sounds are seen. The lexical, semantic, and syntactic language difficulties tend to persist into adolescence (Caparulo & Cohen, 1977).

The importance of the early diagnosis of dysphasia is illustrated by a follow-up study that revealed that 50 percent of the children evidenced autistic features, 61 percent showed attention and behavior disorders, and 50 percent tested in the mentally retarded range. Their response to intensive language therapy and special education was limited, with prognosis relating to the level of social development and language comprehension (Paul et al, 1983).

Alexithymia, or the absence of words for feelings, is described in Chapter 21 as the limited availability of verbal and emotional imagery (Smith, 1983). The parents of some children with learning difficulties present this picture, as do their children.

Dysphasic children may have significant paroxysmal electroencephalographic ab-

normalities, and one-quarter show cortical anomalies on computerized tomography (Caparulo & Cohen, 1977; 1981). Children with delayed speech tend to have larger right posterior cortical regions than do most children. These children may have an unusual pattern of neurological organization based on hereditary, intrauterine, birth, or neonatal factors (Geschwind, 1979b). Unilateral temporal lobe defects are found in some children with delayed acquisition of speech (Hier & Rosenberger, 1980; Rapin & Wilson, 1978). Furthermore brain-stem auditory evoked responses found in children with central language disturbances suggest that there may be auditory transmission disturbances below the level of the olivary nuclei (Piggott & Anderson, 1983).

From experience with adults, it is evident that hemispheric lateralization plays a significant role in the aphasias. Right-handed adults, who sustain lesions in the lateral convexity of the left hemisphere, usually lose some of their language capacity (Pirozzolo, 1979). There is a higher incidence of aphasia reported in left-handed than in right-handed persons after unilateral injury to the adult brain, but there also is a more dramatic remission of aphasia in the left-handed. Approximately 85 percent of left-handed persons have at least partial representation of speech in the left hemisphere. This atypical organization spares them the more severe and prolonged effects of unilateral lesions that would be seen in a right-handed person, whose speech mechanisms are more exclusively in the left hemisphere (Satz, 1979).

About half of cerebral palsied children suffer speech or language problems that impair their ability to communicate (Howlin, 1981). An acquired aphasia with convulsive disorder, described as the Landau syndrome, is an unusual condition in childhood characterized by a loss of language function associated with a paroxysmal electroencephalogram. It usually has a favorable prognosis for recovery after varying lengths of time (Mantovani & Landau, 1980).

A situation analogous to the aphasias exists in processing musical information. Two forms of neurological musical ability disorder, or amusia, can be distinguished. Receptive amusia consists of disorders of musical perception, recognition, memory, evaluation, and enjoyment. Expressive amusia consists of difficulties in singing, whistling, playing musical instruments, and producing rhythmic patterns. These manifestations are most evident in adults with brain lesions, but probably occur more frequently than is recognized as individual differences in children (Kurth & Heinrichs, 1976; Mosse, 1982).

Hearing Disabilities

Delayed verbal language development also may be a function of both peripheral and central hearing loss. Lasting impairment in language function is less likely or pronounced if the hearing loss occurs after a child has begun talking.

Children who have word-sound deafness, known as an auditory agnosia, can hear, but the integration of hearing with the speech areas of the cortex is defective (Willeford & Burleigh, 1985). The lesion presumably lies in the inferior colliculi and has a relationship to maternal rubella during early pregnancy. These children cannot learn to speak by listening but can do so by kinesthetic and visual methods. They cannot analyze speech sounds and repeat them (Mosse, 1982).

Providing profoundly deaf children with amplification and alternate means of communication helps but does not eliminate basic differences in academic functioning, which grow more pronounced as the years pass (Meadow, 1975). Deaf children who rely upon signing offer a unique opportunity for research regarding the nonauditory aspects of language (Liben, 1978).

SUMMARY

Verbal language disabilities merit attention as factors contributing to problems in schoolwork. They are generally classified as disorders of speech or of receptive and expressive language.

Speech disorders involve articulation in the form of variations in pronouncing words, the voice in speaking resonance, and speaking fluency in stuttering. Those involving receptive and expressive language are usually described as delays or variations in the processing of language as manifestations of general developmental disabilities, specific developmental language delays, interpersonal delays, developmental dysphasias, or hearing deficits.

Delays in language development may signal underlying variations in language system components and hearing organs in addition to social and emotional developmental factors. Specific developmental delays primarily reflect variations in brain maturational rates. Interpersonal delays result from family interactions, ranging from those that relieve a child of the need to speak to oppositional dynamics. The developmental dysphasias are the result of variations in the receptive and expressive language centers of the central nervous system. They vary in severity from syndromes that resemble infantile autism to minor difficulties in speech comprehension and word finding. Delayed verbal language development also may result from both central and peripheral hearing losses.

Histories of delayed developmental milestones in language and recurrent infections or allergies in children with learning problems in school are particular indications for considering the possibility of underlying verbal language disabilities.

24

Written Language Disabilities

The list of dyslexic persons includes Thomas Alva Edison, Harvey Cushing, George Patton, Woodrow Wilson, William James, Auguste Rodin, Niels Bohr, Lauretta Bender, Nelson Rockefeller, and Hans Christian Andersen.

From the voluminous literature on childhood dyslexia, two points are clear. First, the many forms of dyslexia are components of broader syndromes that are not completely understood (Duane, 1984; Eisenberg, 1979; Naidoo, 1972); second, dyslexia is not simply difficulty in reading, but includes spelling and writing (Critchley, 1981). Moreover the usual definitions of reading disability do not recognize the interactive development of language and cognition in learning to read (Doehring et al, 1981).

Most definitions of developmental dyslexia are limited to reading and resemble the one proposed in 1968 by the World Federation of Neurology:

Developmental dyslexia is a disorder manifested by difficulty in learning to read, despite conventional instruction, adequate intelligence, and socio-cultural opportunities. It is dependent upon fundamental cognitive disabilities which are frequently of constitutional origin.

Later definitions recognize characteristics in addition to reading difficulty. For example, Duane (1977) offered the following definition of dyslexia:

A constitutional and often genetically determined disparate reduction in the rate and quality of the acquisition of written language skills which may or may not be associated with other problems of symbolic manipulation and disordered development of concepts of time and space.

The term dyslexia signifies difficulty in the use of written words, how they are identified, what they mean, how they are used, how they are pronounced, how they are spelled, and how they are written. To recognize its importance, an interdisciplinary field of dyslexiology has been proposed to complement aphasiology so that there would be two language pathology subspecialties, one for written and one for verbal language (Myklebust, 1978).

Since learning to read means associating print with spoken language, the language system plays a dominant role in reading. Trying to string sounds and clusters of letters together without understanding the structure of language is as frustrating as trying to assemble a jigsaw puzzle without a vision of the whole picture. Thus, when children have difficulty acquiring speech, they may have later problems in reading, spelling, and writing skills (Accardo, 1980; Cole & Walker, 1969). In contrast to speech, which usually proceeds automatically from the beginning of life, learning written language is a conscious, effortful activity that depends upon motivation and educational opportunities.

The term dyslexia still does not take into account accompanying broader sensory, interpretive, and expressive manifestations in the form of problems in spatial orientation, figure–ground discrimination, directional sense, tactile localization, and motor coordination. These more pervasive problems were vividly described by Eileen Simpson in her personal account of dyslexia in her book *Reversals* (1979). She regards dyslexia as a part of a syndrome consisting of a cluster of symptoms including physical awkwardness, poor penmanship, overactivity, stuttering, directional disorientation, weak visual memory, spelling errors, and arithmetical difficulties. She also highlights the psychological aspects:

> As a child her inability to control what she wanted to say and to write was humiliating and made her feel that her "skull housed an unruly brain," which she handled by becoming the class clown. Her secret shame over her difficulties led her to attempt to conceal her ignorance at all costs. Of particular interest is her description of "good" and "bad" days with times and circumstances under which she could function normally and others when her difficulties were accentuated.

This chapter will focus on paradigms of dyslexia syndromes with the caveat that the situation for each person is uniquely more complex. Because of the variety of factors that interfere with learning written language, it is important first to examine critically the population of children who are educationally handicapped because of retardation in reading skills.

READING RETARDATION

As does an elevation in body temperature, reading retardation signals a child's distress, but it does not indicate why.

Reading retardation usually is defined as a reading level at least two years below learning abilities in other areas in addition to a similar discrepancy between an individual's performance and that of other children of the same age exposed to the same educational opportunities. This definition covers impaired reading ability at all levels of intelligence, including the mildly retarded (Fildes, 1921). It lacks precision, however. For example, it overlooks children who manage to achieve at or near expected levels in reading through extreme effort in addition to children during the first two grades of school. As for mental retardation, reading retardation should be a clinical rather than test-based judgment. When properly diagnosed reading retardation constitutes the most common educational handicap.

As so defined, reading retardation cannot be explained on the basis of general intelligence. This distinction is critical, because many children are regarded as retarded readers, when their reading level actually reflects their general intelligence. If children with reading scores more than two standard deviations below prediction on a Gaussian distribution curve were simply the tail end of a statistical distribution, the expected rate would be 2.28 percent. The Isle of Wight study found 3.5 percent among 10 year olds and 4.5 percent among 14 year olds. This gives statistical support for an entity of reading retardation with determinants beyond that of intelligence (Eisenberg, 1979). That study is particularly significant because the Isle of Wight is relatively free from the socioeconomic and educational elements of urban areas that contribute to even higher rates of reading retardation.

An extensive international survey disclosed that in every country considered there was awareness of the existence of reading problems (Tarnopol & Tarnopol, 1981). Moreover, the relationships between spoken and written forms of a language seem to influence the degree of difficulty encountered by children learning to read it. Of the languages investigated in that survey, it appeared that the older Chinese pictographs were the easiest to learn to read, followed by the newer ideographs. The low incidence of reading disabilities in Japan may be related to the simplicity of the Japanese language, as compared with English written symbols, in addition to a high degree of parent involvement with young children in reading and a general cultural support of early reading (Sakamoto, 1981; Sheridan, 1983). English appears to be one of the most difficult languages for beginners. The closer phoneme–grapheme association in Spanish does not seem to make Spanish easier than English for dyslexics, however. Dyslexia occurs in Spanish just as frequently as in English. It also tends to be aggravated in schools that teach both Spanish and English simultaneously.

Two basic categories of reading retardation have been described in the literature. Rabinovitch (1968) classified children as having primary reading retardation related to developmental factors and secondary reading retardation related to temperamental, personality, and educational interferences with learning to read. More recent epidemiological studies (Rutter & Yule, 1975) confirm this picture in which children appear to have either specific or more general difficulties in learning to read.

As is evident from the multiple barriers to learning described in other chapters of this book, the primary, or specific, and secondary, or general, categories are oversimplifications. Nonetheless they have led to widespread use of the concept of specific reading disabilities. In contrast with children whose low reading levels correspond to intelligence levels, children with specific reading retardation are predominantly male in a 3-4 to 1 ratio, and have higher IQs but make less progress in reading and spelling than in arithmetic (Rutter & Yule, 1975). Although general sociogenic, educational, and psychogenic factors are more common than specific developmental factors in producing reading retardation (Mosse, 1982), this chapter is limited to the developmental dyslexias that are the principal forms of specific reading disorders.

PARADIGMS OF THE DEVELOPMENTAL DYSLEXIAS

There is an obvious need for more precise, reliable, and researchable markers for defining the dyslexias (Childs & Finucci, 1979; Shallice, 1981; Rourke, 1985). To this end the classification of specific reading disabilities has advanced significantly in recent years (Watson & Goldgar, 1983). The confluence of evidence resulting from both deductive and inductive approaches to the problem has brought clinical and experimental investigators into a position in which interdisciplinary communication can be of immense value in understanding the dyslexias (Doehring, 1984).

The deductive approach moves from global concepts of central nervous system (CNS) functioning to more specific details as knowledge has advanced. Thus the fields of child neurology and child psychiatry have provided clinical contexts within which the dyslexias have been studied. The term dyslexia itself is a product of these disciplines.

The neurological language for describing CNS functions has the advantage of an established clinical basis without particular etiological implications. Neurological terminology is specific enough to permit accurate communication and broad enough to accommodate revision.

The relevant neurological concepts are dysmetria, dysgnosia, dysphasia, and dyspraxia. Dysmetria refers to disturbances in the control of the range of muscle actions. It conveniently covers the variety of possible dyslexic perceptual variations resulting from the control of tracking eye movements in reading. Dysgnosia refers to interferences with the recognition of sensory stimuli and includes dyslexic problems in recognizing letters and words. Dysphasia refers to interferences with the comprehension and expression of language generally and includes dyslexic reading, spelling, and writing. Dyspraxia refers to interferences with carrying out purposeful

movements and encompasses dyslexic encoding of spelling and writing.

In this conceptual framework, a dyslexia may be a manifestation of a dysmetria, dysgnosia, dysphasia, or dyspraxia (see Figure 24-1). These more general functional categories are helpful in explaining the nature of a particular child's problem. They imply a coherent linkage of CNS functions and behavior. They also reflect the interplay of both cerebral hemisperes. Most important, they encourage looking beyond the obvious difficulties in reading to the subtle, but in the long range more revealing, underlying mechanisms in language and cognitive functions. For example, the reading and spatial difficulties of a child with a visual-spatial dyslexia reflect as yet poorly understood underlying proc-

THE DEVELOPMENTAL DYSLEXIAS		
Type	**Mechanism**	**Manifestations**
Vestibulo-Cerebellar Dysmetria	Incoordination of range of oculomotor movements interferes with visual perception (Extrapyramidal tremors)	Blurring of words Jumping around page Omission of words Loses place in paragraph
Visual-Spatial Dysgnosia	Interference with recognition of visual-spatial stimuli patterns	Cannot recognize familiar words Can sound out and recognize words Phonetic spelling errors Mislocates and reverses letters May be dyscalculia
Auditory-Linguistic Dysphasia	Interference with comprehension and expression of written language in addition to visual symbol-sound integration	Can recognize familiar words Cannot recall meaning Cannot sound out words Confuses small abstract words Bizarre spelling errors History of delayed speech
Articulo-Graphic Dyspraxia	Interference with exposition of written language	Can read silently but not orally Dysgraphia, omission, and perseveration of letters in spelling Motor incoordination

Figure 24-1.

esses (Benton, 1984). We do know that the problem is not simply with visual memory but with remembering visual symbols (Brady, 1986).

More recently the inductive approach to specific reading difficulties has empirically defined groups of children who share common characteristics by the use of multivariate statistical techniques, such as cluster analysis. In this way both encompassing groups and differentiated subgroups have been identified in order to establish the validity and reliability of classification (Satz & Morris, 1980). Thus far the evidence emerging from inductive research confirms the existence of a variety of dyslexias and differentiates dysgnostic and dysphasic types and mixtures of them (Satz & Morris, 1981; Fletcher & Satz, 1983).

Both the deductive and inductive evidence points toward at least four dyslexia paradigms that can be identified for heuristic purposes in establishing researchable markers and instructional strategies (see Figure 24-2). Some children encounter difficulty in the perception of words while reading because of variable visual tracking at the vestibulo-cerebellar dysmetric level. Other children show a visual-spatial dysgnostic form of difficulty in recognizing words and may have associated spatial orientation confusion. Others manifest an auditory-linguistic dysphasic inability to recall the meaning of words. Still others show an articulographic dyspraxic inability to spell and write accurately. These types are not clearly separated in clinical practice; however, a particular child's reading difficulty can be understood more precisely by analyzing it in terms of these motor, cognitive, and language functions of the CNS (see Figure 20-6).

Children tend to show predominantly one or a mixture of each paradigm. Epidemiological data based on this classification are not yet available; however, in Boder's series 13 percent showed a dysgnostic type, 62 percent a dysphasic type, 19 percent a mixture, and 6 percent an undetermined type (Boder & Jarrice, 1982). Similar proportions were reported by Satz and Morris (1981) and Thomson (1982).

Vestibulo-Cerebellar Dysmetria

The role of faulty eye movements in reading problems has been both exaggerated and too readily dismissed. Although the mechanisms and the relative importance still are unclear, the existence of a dysmetric form of dyslexia merits serious consideration. The ocular fixation required for reading does depend upon a background of harmonious, integrated motor activity of the eye and neck muscles coordinated by the vestibulo-cerebellar system.

One of the factors contributing to confusion about this issue is that the eye movements of children with reading difficulties appear to be abnormal, whether or not eye-movement control is a problem. When readers have difficulty understanding a text, they tend to fixate longer, make smaller saccadic movements and have more regressions. Motivation and attentional factors also are critical when evaluating the eye movements of readers; therefore, it is essential to take into account the state of the child and the difficulty of the text. Although erratic eye movements have been reported in dyslexic children on nonreading tasks (Pavlidis, 1981), there are facile readers who show the same abnormal eye fixation patterns (Pollatsek, 1983).

Linear Dyslexia

Many children have persistent difficulty keeping their places in reading paragraphs. Faltering concentration is the most likely explanation. Some children, however, may have difficulty making the return sweep from the end of a line to the beginning of the next in both reading and in nonreading tracking tests. As a result their eyes wander about the page. They can

CHARACTERISTICS OF DYSLEXIA SUBGROUPS

	Vestibulo-Cerebellar	Visual-Spatial	Auditory-Linguistic	Articulo-Graphic
Reading				
Familiar Word		X		
cannot recognize				
cannot name			X	
cannot pronounce				X
Unfamiliar Word				
can sound out	X	X		
cannot sound out			X	X
Errors				
omit letters and syllables				X
omit words	X	X		
mutilate words			X	
alter sequence of letters		X		
confuse similar words		X		
confuse small words			X	
lose place in line	X	X		
words blur	X			
perseveration of syllables and words				X
grammatical errors			X	
Handwriting				
legibility impaired				X
spatial orientation errors		X		
spontaneous writing impaired			X	X
copy inaccurately	X	X		
Spelling				
alter letter sequences		X		
spell phonetically		X		
nonphonetic spelling errors			X	
letter omission and perseveration				X
Arithmetic Problems		X		
Visual-Spatial Problems		X		
Auditory Discrimination and Memory Problems			X	
Oculomotor Problems	X			
Primitive Neck-righting Response	X			
Motor Coordination Problems				X

Figure 24-2. Characteristics of dyslexia subgroups.

read words but not integrate them in paragraphs (Mosse, 1982).

Linear dyslexia may result from faulty reading habits acquired at an early age, such as from reliance on comic books, whose prose does not follow regular lines. The whole-word method of teaching reading also can lead to excessive dependency upon picture clues rather than linear reading (Mosse, 1982).

The concept of linear dyslexia is supported by the finding that visual-spatial dyslexic persons, to be described later, may show faulty scanning strategies, such as leftward tendencies and return sweep inaccuracies during reading. They also may have longer saccadic movement reaction times to stimuli appearing in the right visual field than to those in the left visual field, when compared with normal and auditory-linguistic dyslexic persons (Pirozzolo, 1979, 1983). This may result from inefficient visual-spatial programming of saccadic eye movements rather than impairment of oculomotor mechanisms.

In any event reading is facilitated for these children by following a line with a finger or straight edge. A corrective aid for linear dyslexia is to hold an unlined card above the line the child is reading with the left corner slightly lower than the right so that, by pushing the card down while reading, the child steadies the gaze of the eyes from left to right and downward to a return sweep from one line to the next (Mosse, 1982). A card with a window exposing appropriate lengths of a line also can be useful.

Ocular Fixation

Some children complain that words seem blurred, merge with each other, or jump around because of ocular fixation, tracking, and optokinetic nystagmus dysfunctions (Mosse, 1982). Heterophorias are excessive tendencies of the eyes to turn relative to each other and may place stress on the binocular system in order to maintain ocular fixation in reading, with resulting headaches, neck, and shoulder strain and aversion to reading. Even in nonreading oculomotor sequencing, dyslexic persons tend to have inefficient eye movements (Bettman et al, 1967; Pavlidis, 1981).

Although not strictly dysmetric, other possible interferences with eye movements are the extrapyramidal choreiform tremors related to basal ganglia dysfunction. These tremors are fine, erratic, dysrhythmic movements involving the muscles of the tongue, eyes, face, neck, trunk, arms, and legs. They may interfere with movements of the eye muscles and retinal fixation. They also may interfere with the smooth flow of handwriting (Prechtl & Stemmer, 1962).

Dysrhythmic Reading

Rhythmic ability is an integral part of musical talent and can be impaired while other musical abilities are not. A lack of rhythmic ability also may interfere with reading and speaking. Some children do not sense the rhythmic patterns integral to reading, and so do not alter their speed appropriately. They may rush through a text or read so slowly that they lose comprehension. The fundamental problem may be with cerebellar sequencing functioning, although there are other more likely explanations. Focusing on a rhythmic beat while reading may be useful for these children (Mosse, 1982).

In this vein a significantly greater incidence of dysdiadokokinesis, or difficulty with rhythmical, alternating movements, has been reported in boys with learning disabilities when compared with controls (Adams et al, 1974; Peters et al, 1975).

Foreground–Background Blurring

Some children experience difficulty in coordinating, integrating, and harmonizing visual foreground–background dimensions. It has been suggested that the movement of the eye's fixation point against a stationary printed background may merge the various spatial-temporal dimensions, resulting in blurring of words (Levinson, 1980). This might be related to inefficient sensory processing of visual information by the cerebellum.

Psychophysiological Dysmetria

The complex interplay of psychological and neurological factors at the dysmetric level is illustrated by Levinson's account of his reaction to reading Eccle's book *Facing Reality*. He was shocked by Eccle's religious philosophy regarding the mind, mental events, and soul:

> My mind began spinning, and I developed what clinically might be considered "psychological dyslexia." My readings became dysmetric. I found myself scanning the content rapidly, and merely catching, or almost catching, the gist rather than the sequential details . . . I felt anxious, upset, disappointed, and "neurophysiologically betrayed." It was difficult and even impossible to slow down and study what was read. I just wanted to finish and get the book over with . . . Blocking was intense. My concentration kept drifting away, and an extreme effort was needed to refocus and fixate the content in a sequential fashion . . . (Levinson, 1980)

Anatomical Evidence

Tentative anatomical evidence supporting the existence of cerebellar involvement in dyslexia is suggested by the cerebellar atrophy or aplasia reported on neuroradiological examinations of learning disabled children. Parenthetically, structural cerebellar abnormalities also have been reported from computerized tomography and autopsy studies of adult schizophrenic persons (Weinberger et al, 1980).

All of these sensorimotor manifestations expressed in directional, coordination, rhythm, and foreground–background difficulties in addition to anatomical findings suggest that vestibulo-cerebellar mechanisms in conjunction with higher brain levels play a role in reading problems (Pavlidis, 1981).

Visual-Spatial Dysgnosia

The visual-spatial form of dyslexia has been well established in the literature and corresponds to the following types: dyseidetic (Boder, 1973), agnosic dyslexia (Critchley, 1970), visual-perceptual (Mattis et al, 1975; Mattis, 1981), visual dyslexia (Gaddes, 1980; Spraings, 1969), visual-spatial (Pirozzolo, 1979), left-hemisphere strategy—type L (Bakker, 1979; 1984), surface (Hynd & Hynd, 1984), and type S (Doehring et al, 1981).

Adult Syndromes

The acquired adult dyslexias resulting from lesions in the visual association cortex or the corpus callosum provide a useful background for understanding similar phenomena in children. At the same time, extrapolation from adult dyslexias to childhood reading difficulty is risky, because in the former a mature brain loses an existing function, and in the latter a function is not acquired well by a changing brain. There is evidence, however, that the developmental dyslexias may not be neuropsychologically distinct from acquired dyslexias (Mattis, 1975). For this reason adult-acquired dyslexias can be useful models for those in children, because the relationships between CNS function and structure can be explicated through known lesions in adults (Benton, 1978; Marshall, 1982).

The two adult conditions of posterior alexia and dysgnosia have a bearing on visual-spatial dyslexias in children.

Posterior Alexia. The syndrome of posterior alexia was initially described by Dejerine in 1892 in an adult who could write but not read following a lesion involving the medial and inferior aspects of the left occipital lobe and the splenium of the corpus callosum. Dejerine concluded that the lesion had destroyed visual pathways of the left occipital area and had severed the connection between the right-hemisphere visual area and the left-hemisphere language area. The patient, therefore, could see adequately, copy written material that he could not understand, and had no problems with spoken language or written language. Dejerine conjectured that the dominant angular gyrus was the center for the interpretation of the visual images of written language. If this area was intact but isolated from visual information, the patient could retain normal language, including the ability to write, but still be unable to read (Benson, 1977; 1985).

An optic alexia has been described in adults associated with occipital lesions in which letters similar in configuration are confused, for example, m and n or k and x. A verbal alexia associated with occipital lesions also has been described in which patients could easily recognize letters but could not grasp whole words. They must put words together letter by letter. Parenthetically, this was accompanied by a gaze disturbance in which patients easily lost their place in lines and picked out fragments from different lines (Luria, 1980).

Dysgnosia. The concept of agnosia was introduced by Sigmund Freud in 1891 and means loss of the ability to recognize objects. Dysgnosia means inefficient recognition.

An agnosic dyslexia characteristically remains after a more generalized agnosia in adults with brain lesions. Such patients read through slow, letter-by-letter analysis of a word. Word misidentification can be induced easily in this form of dyslexia by brief tachistoscopic exposure. Errors in reading tend to reflect distortions of words rather than meanings. There is awareness

of errors and resulting frustration (Brown, 1977).

Just as slips of the tongue may be cues to an individual's unconscious concerns, children's misreadings may have psychodynamic significance (Bettelheim & Zelan, 1981). When seen as subjectively meaningful, reading errors may reflect a conflict between what is printed on a page and a child's own concerns. There may be inadequate separation of internal fantasy and external stimuli. For example, one boy said:

I'll be reading about riding on a bike, and I slip away to thinking about riding out-of-doors.

Another boy revealed:

I get spaced out on words and daydream.

The interpretation of reading errors offers an opportunity similar to the interpretation of dreams in psychotherapy.

Symptoms

Visual-spatial dyslexic persons have problems at the early stages of information processing involving attentional mechanisms, decoding, and associator functions. They approach familiar words as if they are new each time and fail to build a useful sight vocabulary (Marshall, 1985). A word recognized yesterday, or even a few minutes before, evades them at a particular moment.

These persons have difficulty reading because they cannot recognize the visual-spatial configuration of letters and words. As a form of visual dysgnosia, they have difficulty discriminating and analyzing the visual gestalts for words and nonalphabetical configurations (Stanley, 1975). They confuse similar letters, alter the sequence of letters in words and reverse letters; b and d are copied correctly but confused when read. Words and letters with similar configurations or meanings are confused. For example, deference is read as difference, house as have, and phenomena as pneumonia. They may recognize mirror or reversed letters or words more readily than correct ones. They may show atypical eye movement patterns and lose their place on lines.

These persons lack a stable set of expectancies with which perceptions are compared. They are not deficient in visual memory per se but in a framework for visual memory of word configurations (Cherry, 1957). They can recognize words by sound, if a framework is provided by sounding out letters and syllables by breaking words down into their components and then blending the sounds together:

> I can read the words but not comprehend them unless I concentrate very hard and sound them out either silently or out loud so that I can hear their sounds.

They respond well to phonetic teaching methods supplemented by kinesthetic associations. They also can remember spoken phrases of spelling and pronunciation rules to assist them in visual reading and spelling (Lyon, 1983; Smith, 1980).

Their handwriting is legible, and they can write spontaneously but may copy inaccurately. Their handwriting may not be correctly oriented in space. They make spelling errors in sequences of letters (hte for the) and reversals (b for d) and may spell phonetically (sez for says).

They have other visual-spatial problems as reflected in lower performance than verbal scores on the WISC. They may have difficulty with arithmetic. They also may exhibit finger agnosia, directional problems, and difficulties in visual construction and spatial relationships. For some the letters p, q, d and b are more easily recognized in three-dimensional than two-dimensional form.

Auditory-Linguistic Dysphasia

An auditory-linguistic dyslexia results from comprehension difficulties at later stages in information processing than a visual-spatial dyslexia. This type corresponds to the following types: audiophonic (Ingram et al, 1970), dysphonetic (Boder, 1973), language disordered (Kinsbourne & Warrington, 1964; Mattis et al, 1975; Mattis, 1981), aphasiological (Critchley, 1970), auditory dyslexia (Gaddes, 1980; Spraings, 1969), auditory-linguistic (Pirozzolo, 1979), right-hemisphere strategy—type P (Bakker, 1979; 1984), phonological and deep (Hynd & Hynd, 1984), and type A (Doehring et al, 1981).

Adult Syndromes

Both expressive and receptive language deficits are present in aphasic adults, although one or the other may predominate. In either form reading, writing, and naming deficits are components of most aphasias (Reitan, 1964).

Central Alexia (Conduction Aphasia). In adults central alexia resulting from lesions of the angular gyrus region of the parietal lobe appears to be related to auditory-linguistic dyslexia in children. These lesions have the effect of disconnecting systems involved in auditory and written language and interrupting communication between the visual cortex and Wernicke's area of the temporal lobe (Benson, 1985).

Dejerine first reported a patient in 1891 in whom the abilities to read and write were lost. Subsequently reported cases of adults with angular gyrus lesions showed a loss of the meaning of words without the loss of the meaning of objects, pictures, places, and diagrams. They know that letters and words are graphic entities. They cannot write spontaneously but can copy. Spelling is very difficult (Orton, 1937).

Native Japanese speakers show left-hemisphere superiority for recognizing alphabetical kana script and right-hemisphere superiority for recognizing pictorial kanji script (Tseng & Wang, 1983). A Japanese woman with a conduction aphasia could write ideographic kanji characters much better than phonetic kana (Yamadori & Ikumura, 1975). This deficit may have been due to disruption of auditory images, resulting in an inability to remember phonemic features of words. Similar grammatical reading errors can be evoked by stimulating sites with specialized language functions between the peri-Sylvian system and the more peripheral memory system (Ojeman & Mateer, 1979a).

The characteristics of the auditory-linguistic type of dyslexia are suggestive of a conduction dysphasia in which auditory stimuli are not channeled well enough to direct the frontal cortex mechanisms for speech and writing output. The dominant parietal lobe is thereby implicated in the reading and writing problems of these children (Benson, 1977).

Dysnomia. Dysnomia is a specific form of dysphasia in which a person can recognize, but has difficulty in correctly naming, an object. Since the naming of an object depends upon the convergence of various associations evoked by sensory stimuli, a breakdown in word retrieval results in incorrectly chosen or altered words. There is a failure of association between the word meanings and phonological forms. The response may be semantically related, for example, whisper for a picture of a whistle; or only remotely related, for example, thermometer for telescope; or functionally related, heartbeater for a picture of a stethoscope.

Auditory-linguistic dyslexic persons appear to be subtly dysnomic, tending to substitute the name of another word in the same class (Denckla et al, 1981; Wolf, 1985). They have deficits in their fund of knowledge of words and the ability to use those words appropriately and fluently. They also have difficulty with syntactic sentence structure and organizing verbal concepts categorically (Vellutino, 1979).

Adults with acquired dyslexia may have difficulty naming words and colors that involve linking a purely visual configuration with a name but not in naming numbers and objects that involve multisensory associations, such as tactile, kinesthetic, and mental manipulation. Concrete words representing multisensory experienced physical objects, such as ball and spoon, are more readily recalled than abstract words, which do not have tangible features, such as hall and cloud.

The clinical criterion for dysnomia is that a person shows clear evidence of difficulty in naming objects or pictures that previously were named successfully. Persons who are unable to name correctly 20 or more of 30 items presented on second exposure are regarded as showing dysnomia (Rutherford, 1977).

Although less severe forms of word-finding difficulty may be unrecognized, they hamper verbal expression. A person settles for words that are available at the moment, though they may not reflect thought content accurately. Everyone is familiar with dysnomia when reciting in class under stress: "I knew the answer, but I just couldn't say it." Unstable word-retrieval skills, experienced day after day, are an insidious source of frustration and anxiety associated with the act of speaking. As one young adult with a residual dysnomia said:

> I'm afraid to talk to people. I'm so self-conscious. I've got to be careful not to mispronounce my words. I can't stand to feel the way I do when I'm around people. I don't have any friends.

One study suggests that Orton's hypothesis may hold for auditory-linguistic dyslexia in which the lack of greater word-evoked potential response differences over the left than right hemisphere implied inadequate cerebral dominance. This was not true for visual-spatial dyslexic persons (Fried, 1979).

The psychological defenses involved in preventing the association of perceptions and images with long-term-memory storage are described in Chapter 22.

Symptoms

Auditory-linguistic dyslexic persons have difficulty reading because they have difficulty retrieving the verbal sound of familiar words; however, they usually can retrieve the spoken words for pictures and objects.

Their dysnomia is predominantly with visual symbols in the form of alphabetical words, since they may be able to name numbers and objects because of their multisensory associations. Since they have difficulty sounding out words, their reading contains errors that predominantly involve the sight–sound relationships of letters and words in grapheme to phoneme conversion. They misread words by guessing based on first letters, adding extraneous letters and substituting similar word forms. They can read better in context.

These persons see words as gestalts and have difficulty breaking them down. They read words instantaneously as wholes rather than analytically. They misread related words, such as stool for chair (Marshall, 1985). They particularly confuse small words without concrete meaning, such as conjunctions. They make grammatical errors, such as in the use of tense, articles, prepositions, conjunctions, possessive inflections, prefixes, suffixes, and personal pronouns.

These persons may lack ideas and have difficulty writing spontaneously; they may copy accurately. Their handwriting may be legible and correctly oriented. Their spelling errors are gross mutilations and poor phonetic approximations similar to their misreading, such as lag for laugh. They may omit punctuation and capitalization.

The role of attention is important be-cause such people appear not to have learned how to listen carefully or to hear subtle differences in sounds. Accordingly they may have difficulty discriminating similar sounds and remembering spoken instructions. Note taking is especially difficult, as illustrated by Simpson's description:

> Note taking made my brain ache. Dividing attention between listening and writing was as demanding as hitting my head with one hand and making circles on my stomach with the other. I also never learned to read and eat at the same time. (Simpson, 1979)

These persons tend to have histories of delayed language development and speech problems. On the WISC their verbal level is lower than the performance IQ. They also may show linguistic immaturity in the form of limited vocabularies, lack of verbal fluency, and limited knowledge of syntax.

Albert Einstein's situation may be relevant. He struggled with marked difficulty in verbal thinking and in the use of language (Patten, 1973). This was evident in his lack of speech before the age of three, his subsequent need as a child to repeat words silently to himself, his poor performance in school, including failure in foreign languages, and his laborious and awkward use of language in later life, including the necessity for "hearing words I read." He had extraordinary abilities, however, in constructing with building blocks, working puzzles, and manipulating geometrical diagrams. In his early, verbally oriented school environment, the young Einstein seemed retarded. He blossomed, however, at a special school founded by Pestalozzi in which visual imagery was considered the key to knowledge.

The auditory-linguistic type of dyslexia can be seen as a form of language disorder characterized by a history of delayed language development, dysnomia, and deficits in auditory-verbal ability. The late maturation of the pathways involved in left-hemisphere language functions may contribute to this form of dyslexia so that the transmission of auditory-verbal information is not fully established in these children (Pirozzolo, 1979).

These persons do not respond well to phonetic instruction. They learn better through meaning or "look–say" methods, particularly by associating words with pictures and objects. After they have developed sufficient sight vocabulary to provide an adequate foundation, phonetic skills can be developed to a degree. Initial remedial efforts to improve their spelling can be directed toward converting them from dysphonetic to phonetic spellers so that they and others can at least understand the words they write (Boder, 1973).

Articulo-graphic Dyspraxia

A fourth form of dyslexia has been described as an articulation and graphomotor dyscoordination syndrome (Mattis et al, 1975) and as a subtype of an oral reading disability—type O (Doehring et al, 1981). Articulo-graphic dyslexic persons have problems at the encoding and output transducer levels of information processing.

Adult Syndromes

Broca's Aphasia. Broca's area is adjacent to the area of the frontal motor cortex that controls the muscles of the face, tongue, jaw, and throat. In adults anterior alexia, or Broca's aphasia with alexia, results from lesions of Broca's posterior– inferior frontal cortex. Motor apraxia interfering with the movements of the articulatory apparatus frequently accompanies anterior alexia (Benson, 1977; 1985). Because the output transducer for speech articulation is not functioning properly, these patients typically show nonfluent aphasia and agraphia; however, there is no loss of understanding of spoken words, and they can sing with ease.

Experimental oral reading errors with word substitution are evoked by stimulating sites in parts of the inferior frontal, superior temporal, and parietal peri-Sylvian cortex surrounding the final motor pathway for speech (Ojemann & Mateer, 1979a).

Dyspraxic Speech. Speech errors resulting from anterior speech zone lesions are typified by mispronouncing, as in the omission of initial consonants or syllables and the simplification of consonant clusters (e.g., air for chair, seep for sleep) and occur in the context of generally awkward articulation. Errors arising because of posterior speech zone lesions tend to be transpositions of the order of sounds and missequencing of syllables (e.g., zokiad for zodiac).

Symptoms

Persons with articulographic dyspraxia have difficulty reading orally, but not silently, because of problems in enunciating and blending phonemes when reading words. They have intact linguistic skills, but, encoding speech is difficult for them (Vellutino, 1979).

Their reading contains consonant and syllable omissions and perseverations or confusion of letters. The critical problem for these persons is a buccal-lingual dyspraxia at the output transducer stage of information processing. They accordingly mispronounce and misspeak words because of the lack of smooth coordination of speech musculature.

Reading follows the course of words to thoughts, and writing reverses the path from thoughts to words. Writing is one of the most sophisticated activities of the brain. It involves encoding by selecting a series of visual symbols with sounds attached to them, putting them in the correct order from left to right to produce the desired word, then putting several words in the proper order, also left to right, to convey the desired message. Expressive writing takes more organization, more differentiation, more remembering, more sequencing, and more integration than reading. Whereas a child may be able to read well as early as the third grade, few children can write well with precision, clarity, and expression before the seventh grade (Smith, 1980). Although spelling is usually seen as a function of writing, a complete assessment of spelling, should include oral expression.

The handwriting of persons with articulographic dyspraxia tends to be illegible and contains spelling errors often in the form of fragmented, incomplete, and misplaced letters and syllables. They may not dot i's and cross t's. They have difficulty writing to dictation and spontaneously and copying accurately. They have ideas but find it difficult to put them down on paper.

These persons have intact visual-spatial perceptual skills. Their verbal and performance IQ levels tend to be equivalent. They may show a variety of fine or gross motor coordination problems, although visual-motor coordination ordinarily is not affected. In contrast children with frank organic brain syndromes are clumsy and show neurological signs, particularly difficulty in coordinating their eyes and hands.

Some children in the late elementary and middle school grades begin to show evidence of difficulties in academic learning because of the increasing demands for rapid and high-volume schoolwork (Levine et al, 1981). They have difficulty organizing their time efficiently and writing themes. This appears to be related to previously latent expressive language, fine motor, attention, and memory weaknesses that are brought to light by the increasing pressures of schoolwork.

THE DYSLEXIAS IN ADULTHOOD

The literature has vacillated between regarding dyslexia as a maturational lag subject to improvement with aging and as a reflection of permanent anomalies of brain components (Hermann, 1970; Silver, 1978; Thompson, 1973). Moreover the manifestations of dyslexia in individuals vary widely. Some are not aware of the impact of an underlying dyslexia on their emotional and behavioral problems (Kafka, 1984). Some are severely educationally handicapped. At the other extreme are a host of eminently successful persons with dyslexic symptoms (Thompson, 1969). The age at which one's dyslexia becomes evident also varies widely. Some people may not become aware of their mild dyslexias until college, when their disorganization surfaces away from home and under unprecedented demands for reading. Others may not until they see themselves in their children.

A follow-up study of treated dyslexic children disclosed that over half became adequate readers as adults. They continued to show evidence of figure–background problems; however, directional discrimination improved. This study indicated that these children outgrew some, but not all, of their difficulties, suggesting that both maturation and persistent variations play roles (Silver & Hagin, 1964). Long-term follow-up studies of dyslexic children disclose that with remedial education most overcome their difficulties, develop adequate reading skills, and become accomplished persons as adults. Reading and spelling continue to be troublesome for most of them, however (Bruck, 1987; Rawson, 1968; Finucci et al, 1985).

Dyslexic adults may feel inferiority and despair. Consequently, they may resort to a number of defenses, often echoed by professionals who deal with their problems. The defenses vary from rationalization in the form of "being dyslexic is good" to concealing their problem. Some also may use dyslexia as a rationalization for broader personal failures. Most prominent, however, is a feeling of generalized anger (Mautner, 1984). They may be angry at themselves, because they are unable to read and write as effectively as others. They also may be angry at their parents for not recognizing and dealing with their problem, at their teachers for putting them down, at peers for ridiculing them, and at society and employers because they have difficulty competing with others. The nagging question remains: Why did adults not recognize that they had trouble reading earlier? They may feel misunderstood by all.

Of great concern to adults with dyslexia is differentiating what is "organic" and what is "neurotic" in their clinical pictures. When that quandary is resolved, however, self-concept and self-evaluation issues loom as more important. Because they do not have obvious external manifestations of a handicap, they may find themselves in a dilemma as to whether to tell others of their situation. If they tell others they are dyslexic, they may encounter rejection, inordinate sympathy, or perplexity.

The growing recognition of the dyslexias in adults and the following of dyslexic children into adulthood reveal that we are dealing with a complex situation that includes both temporary maturational and permanent structural elements in the brain. The impact of this complicated state on individuals depends upon their awareness, acceptance, and remediation of their difficulties (Arkell, 1974). For those who adapt to their reading, writing, and spelling problems, self-discipline is the key. They work harder to compete with eulexic peers. The outcome is strongly influenced by their families, schools, access to knowledgeable professionals' resources, and socioeconomic circumstances.

THE CAUSES OF THE DYSLEXIAS

The accumulating evidence validates the clinical usefulness of the concept of the dyslexias, when precisely defined, and continues to shed increasing light on their relationships to multiple factors, including cerebral dominance, familial patterns, and structural variations in the CNS (Hynd & Cohen, 1983). Still our understanding of the multifaceted dyslexia syndromes is just beginning to unfold and awaits the multisystem approach described in this book.

Cerebral Dominance and the Dyslexias

Orton's concept of incomplete cerebral dominance in dyslexia suggested that the left-hemisphere language mechanisms were not fully established so that poor readers were inadequately lateralized for language functions.

Earlier research appeared to discredit Orton's theory, because neither mixed cerebral dominance nor left-handedness per se seemed to be related consistently to retarded reading (Levinson, 1980; Schain, 1977; Tjossem et al, 1962). The simple association of handedness and reading problems has not proved to be significant; however, more sophisticated analyses of cerebral lateralization in language support Orton's ideas (Geschwind, 1982; Geschwind & Masland, 1981; Rawson, 1986). At the same time, a higher incidence of autoimmune disorders, migraine headaches, and dyslexias have been reported in the left-handed population (Geschwind & Behan, 1983).

We now have developmental and clinical evidence that interhemispheric communication is important in reading (Rourke et al, 1983). The time at which children learn to read is related to myelinization of the corpus callosum. The beginning reader relies upon the spatial functions of the right hemishpere for processing the lines and shapes of letters and words. At the same time, the verbal functions of the left hemisphere are involved in connecting these visual-spatial stimuli with spoken words. Alexia resulting from lesions of the corpus callosum has been described in adults (Geschwind, 1965).

The more advanced reader relies upon the automatically integrated visual-phonetic images mediated by the left hemisphere (Bakker, 1979). Thus word recognition is superior in the right visual field because of its direct, contralateral connection with the language mechanisms of the left hemisphere. Words presented to the left visual field are not recognized with the same degree of accuracy, presumably because there is a lag in the time necessary for the information to cross the corpus callosum to reach the language-dominant hemisphere.

Facile readers show a greater right visual field superiority than normal readers, whereas poor readers show no asymmetry at all (Pirozzolo, 1979). Children with the auditory-linguistic form of dyslexia show no right visual field superiority for words as do eulexics and visual-spatial dyslexics, although they have left field advantage for the nonverbal task of facial recognition. Thus auditory-linguistic dysphasic dyslexics may exhibit failure of left-hemisphere mechanisms. In contrast visual-spatial dysgnosic children may lack adequate right-hemisphere mechanisms (Fried, 1979). All of this suggests that facile reading is related to the lateralization of language functions.

Developmental dyslexia may be associated with bihemispheric representation of spatial abilities (Witelson, 1977). When nonverbal functions are unduly represented in both hemispheres, there may be interference with the development of specialized functions usually found on the left, compelling a child to read by a spatial-cognitive strategy instead of a phonetic-sequential strategy.

In another vein reading problems are reported less with the kanji ideographic (spatial) than the kana phonetic (verbal) script of the Japanese language (Makita, 1968). Ideographic characters are processed by the right cerebral hemisphere and, therefore, are less dependent upon interplay between the verbally oriented left and the spatially oriented right hemispheres. Typically the processing of verbally based kana symbols is adversely affected in the context of Broca's aphasia, a disorder that disrupts speech. In contrast interference with processing spatial kanji characters is found in Gogi aphasia (Sasanuma, 1974). These characteristics may be more related to involvement of anterior and posterior parts of the brain than lateralization, however, since lesions in the temporal cortex are associated with greater impairment of reading phonetic scripts, whereas lesions in the posterior occipito-parietal areas are associated with greater impairment of pictorial scripts (Hung & Tzeng, 1981).

Laboratory and neurological signs point to hemispheric factors as well. Electroencephalograms show greater interhemisphere coherence in controls than in dyslexic and hyperkinetic children (Accardo, 1980). Computerized brain tomography reveals a disproportionately large number of brains with a wider right than left parieto-occipital region in children with developmental dyslexia and infantile autism (Hier et al, 1978; 1979). This has led to the hypothesis that if the right hemisphere has too many cells, the left hemisphere is shut out of connection sites. The neurological finding that retarded readers show more mirror movements of their hands than other children of the same age suggests interhemispheric dysfunction (Wolff, 1982).

On the other hand, most people who show little evidence of hemispheric asymmetry on dichotic listening tests and other measures of lateralization do not have reading problems. Conversely many people with reading difficulty have apparently normal lateralization. Thus reduced lateralization may be neither a necessary nor a sufficient condition for reading problems (Springer & Deutsch, 1981). The role of cerebral lateralization in reading problems remains controversial and is not susceptible to simple analysis (Hiscock & Kinsbourne, 1982). It is likely that greater precision in diagnosis will permit identification of subgroups in which specific lateralization factors are important. For example, visual-spatial dyslexia appears to relate to right hemisphere and auditory-linguistic to left hemisphere dysfunctions. Since language is not a single function, it is likely that lateralization may occur differently for each language component (Herron et al, 1979).

The vulnerability of boys to language problems may be the result of a genetic predisposition to lesser hemispheric asymmetry of the language areas, the inhibitory effect of fetal testosterone on left hemispheric maturation, and possible fetal chemical influences on neurobiotaxis between 16 and 24 weeks' gestation. There is evidence that male dyslexics may have more difficulty than female, because the latter are able both to compensate more efficiently through right-hemisphere functions and to have milder left-hemisphere dysfunctions (Fried et al, 1981).

Familial Factors in the Dyslexias

Twin, family, and pedigree studies convincingly demonstrate the familial nature of dyslexia. For example, Hallgren (1950) found 80 percent of his dyslexic sample in Stockholm to have a history of at least one affected parent. Backwin found an 84 percent concordance for dyslexia in monozygotic twins and 29 percent concordance in dyzygotic twins. No single pattern of genetic transmission has been found, however (Bannatyne, 1971; Finucci, 1978; Rutter, 1978). More precise biological and behavioral markers are needed for further genetic progress (McClearn, 1978). A step in this direction was the finding that chromosome-15 markers were linked to inheritance from a dyslexic parent (Smith et al, 1983; Pennington, 1989).

A genetic pattern of dyslexia (De Fries et al, 1978) probably is characteristic of a hard-core group of 4 percent homozygous dyslexics in the general population. Thirty-six percent of the population have alleles for dyslexia and show varying degrees of expression, depending upon other genetic and environmental factors, with a four-to-one weighting toward males. Caution should be exercised, however, in explaining male–female ratios among poor readers, which increase as a function of the age at which initial diagnosis is made and may reflect referral rather than true incidence ratios. Boys with reading difficulties may be more significantly affected emotionally than girls and so appear in greater proportion clinically (Levinson, 1980).

An intriguing evolutionary possibility is that the dyslexic syndrome may reflect survival advantages. Dyslexia itself would not have been a handicap before reading and writing became universal. It actually may be a sign of developmental plasticity. The dyslexic's ability to recognize the reverse of a pattern and to register everything that is going on may be a nuisance in the classroom but could have been an advantage during previous evolutionary stages (Sladen, 1970).

Anatomical Findings in the Dyslexias

Postmortem anatomical evidence is beginning to illuminate the neuroanatomical basis of dyslexia and to confirm Hinshelwood's conception of congenital structural CNS variations. The findings reflect embryologically deviant cellular migration patterns rather than disease or injury.

A boy who died of a vascular malformation of the cerebellum at the age of 12 had a history of marked mood swings, dizziness, blackout spells, and reading and arithmetic retardation. Postmortem examination of his brain disclosed bilateral abnormal growth of the parietal cortices and poor development of parts of the corpus callosum (Drake, 1968). There also were unusual cortical gyri patterns, abnormal blood vessel patterns, and ectopic displacement of neurons in subcortical white matter.

The brain of a dyslexic 20-year-old accident victim, who had male relatives with reading difficulties, showed an area of polymicrogyria and abnormal cellular structures in the left temporal speech region, and neurons in atypical places in the limbic, primary, and association cortices and white matter of the left hemisphere. The left planum temporale was not asymmetrical (Galaburda & Kemper, 1979).

Three additional postmortem examinations have been performed in 14-, 20-, and 32-year-old males with a history of dyslexia. Non-right-handedness and several autoimmune and atopic illnesses also were present in the personal and family histories. All of these brains showed developmental anomalies of the cerebral cortex, consisting of neuronal ectopias and architechtonic dysplasias located mainly in perisylvian regions and predominantly affecting the left hemisphere. Furthermore, all of the brains deviated from the standard pattern of assymmetry of the planum temporale (Galaburda, 1989).

Brain electrical activity mapping procedures have demonstrated regional differences between dyslexic and eulexic boys in the medial frontal lobes (supplementary motor area), the left anterolateral frontal lobe (Broca's area), and the left posterior quadrant speech-associated areas, with minor differences in the right parietal lobe (Duffy, 1985). In general the dyslexic boys showed relative inactivity of these left hemispheric areas.

Thus both subtle and obvious distortions of cerebral cortical architecture have been demonstrated in the left hemisphere of dyslexic brains, probably related to anomalous neuronal migration between the 16th and 24th week of gestation. The impaired development of the left cortex could allow successful competition for available connection sites by neurons arising in the right hemisphere. This might explain the disproportionately large number of dyslexic persons with special talents in music and visual spatial abilities in addition to left-handedness (Galaburda, 1983).

HYPERLEXIA

Hyperlexia is a rare symptom seen in psychotic and mentally retarded children. These children can read aloud at advanced levels, but they do not comprehend the meaning of words. They also may have language disorders, such as echolalia, idioglossia, and pronoun reversal (Aram et al, 1982; Huttonlocker & Huttonlocker, 1973; Whitehouse & Harris, 1984). The relationship of hyperlexia and dyslexia is unclear (Healy & Aram, 1986).

These children may show the onset of word pronunciation as early as the age of two (Elliott & Needleman, 1976; Graziani et al, 1983). This ability usually is not used for the purpose of communication and may be an isolated acceleration of a normal developmental function in word recognition accompanied by varying levels of meaning (Healy, 1982). Occasionally these children are nonverbal, but can point to words that are sounded out.

A phenomenon that may be related to

hyperlexia in children was described in a study of teaching amnesic adults mirror-reading skills. This could be done even though the subjects could not remember what had been read. This suggests that acquiring reading skills involves the learning of encoding operations, since amnesic adults can learn the encoding skill without associated knowledge. This distinction between rule-based information and data-based information is reminiscent of the classical distinction between "knowing how," which is preserved in amnesics, and "knowing that," which is lost in amnesics (Cohen & Squire, 1980).

MIRROR WRITING

Mirror writing runs in an opposite direction to the usual, and individual letters are reversed (Critchley, 1928). It is legible when held up to a mirror. It is seen largely in left-handed adults and children and may occur involuntarily or deliberately. One may not be able to read one's own mirror writing. Mirror writing takes place when most people write upon their forehead or on the under surface of a table. Anyone can acquire the ability with practice.

Mirror writing appears to be the natural mode of writing with the left hand and is seen in young children's first writing efforts. It has been described in states of partial dissociation of consciousness or attention and in hysterical dissociative states and hypnosis. It may be an isolated enduring or transient phenomenon and may be associated with dyslexia, hemiplegias, or aphasias. It was reported in 30 percent of left-handed mentally retarded persons (Gordon, 1920).

In itself mirror writing usually is not of clinical or educational significance. Leonardo da Vinci apparently preferred mirror writing for his personal notes. When it is a significant problem, the individual usually can learn to write in the usual fashion (Lund & Kampik, 1978).

SUMMARY

In contrast with the hyperkinetic syndrome in which immaturity, developmental lags, and temperamental and managerial style variations are prominent characteristics, the dyslexias involve congenital variations with genetic elements in brain tissue that persist into adult life as features of more general cognitive and language styles.

Four paradigms of dyslexias can be described at this time. These are vestibulo-cerebellar dysmetria, visual-spatial dysgnosia, auditory-linguistic dysphasia, and articulographic dyspraxia. An individual may show manifestations largely within one of these domains, or mixtures of each. The value of this classification is that it permits a relatively precise means of describing individuals for diagnostic, therapeutic, and research purposes. These characteristics provide the phenotypic descriptors that are essential for further identification of subtypes that can lead to discoveries of etiological factors.

The hallmarks of each of these subgroups can be detected by reading with a person; having the person write to dictation, write spontaneously, and copy words; testing for agnosias, directional orientation, and fine and gross motor coordination; and obtaining information from a child's parents and school regarding achievement in reading and arithmetic.

Persons with vestibulo-cerebellar dysmetric dyslexia report perceptual blurring of words and the illusion of movement of letters and words. They omit words and lose their places in paragraphs. They may show dysdiadochokinesis and primitive neck-righting responses.

Oral reading with visual-spatial dyslexic

persons discloses that they cannot recognize familiar words, but can sound them out. They can write legibly spontaneously and in copying, but may not orient lines properly. Their spelling errors are in mislocating letters, reversals, and phonetic spelling. They may show finger agnosia and directional uncertainty. They also may have difficulty with arithmetic.

Persons with an auditory-linguistic dyslexia know that words are familiar but cannot recall their sounds and meanings. They have difficulty writing spontaneously and copying, but write legibly and in proper spatial orientation. Their spelling errors are gross mutilations of words.

Articulographic dyslexic persons can read words silently, but have difficulty pronouncing them orally. They have difficulty writing legibly spontaneously and when copying, but have proper line orientation. Their spelling errors are letter omissions and perseverations. They also tend to show motor coordination problems.

The weight of the evidence points to dyslexia as a disability for many persons who have difficulty in learning to read, spell, and write. The extent of this difficulty ranges from a severe form in which even a highly motivated, competent, and confident child cannot master reading early in school to a mild form that is discovered only during college under the pressures of intense reading requirements. In between are children who possess a variety of cognitive, temperamental, language, and managerial styles, and for whom the fortunes of education, family life, and professional intervention determine the degree to which a particular child is handicapped by retardation in reading and, on occasion, in arithmetic skills as well. The treatment of persons with dyslexias is described in Chapter 32.

The prominence of manifestations outside of the language system indicates that the term dyslexia refers to a symptom picture rather than causative factors. The failure to take into account the multiple system levels beyond language involved in the dyslexias is responsible for much of the contradictory research findings, professional controversy, and faddism in this area. Dyslexia is a useful concept, however, because of the significance of reading in our society, and because it offers an arresting catchword that flags significant barriers to learning in school.

25

Managerial Disabilities

Society cannot exist unless a controlling power upon will and appetite be placed somewhere, and the less of it there is within, the more there must be without. People of intemperate minds cannot be free. Their passions forge their fetters.

Edmund Burke, 1779

Our knowledge of the causes of problems in managerial functions is far from complete. In addressing them I first consider variations in specific managerial functions. Then I describe syndromes that result from clusters of managerial function disabilities.

SPECIFIC MANAGERIAL FUNCTION PROBLEMS

For a child to work efficiently in school, the child's managerial system must be sufficiently developed to permit engaging in a task, tolerating frustration, analyzing perceptions, and thinking rationally, in addition to organizing, carrying out, and monitoring the task. Children with incomplete development of managerial functions, therefore, have difficulty doing their schoolwork and relating to adults and peers.

Impulse Control Disabilities

The processes of impulse control include delaying drive gratification, flexibly adapting to change, tolerating frustration, modulating emotions, and selectively regressing in the expression of drives. Children who have difficulty with all of these processes will be described later as having impulsive characters. Their limited attention spans are the result of distraction by internal stimuli.

Drive Gratification Delay

Children without the capacity to delay drive gratification are at the mercy of their impulses, which may conflict with performing schoolwork. They act without forethought upon the first idea that occurs to them. They are impatient and easily bored by schoolwork when it interferes with the immediate gratification of their desires.

Children who are erratically impulsive may be employing strong repression so that drives and associated emotions that are

514

generally unavailable to conscious awareness abruptly break through. The defense of acting out is particularly troublesome in that through this mechanism a child may act directly upon unconscious urges without conscious awareness that the action is occurring. For example, self-destructive urges may be acted out through accident proneness. Weakness in the ability to delay unacceptable impulses also may result in chronic anxiety against which obsessive-compulsive defenses are erected. In contrast a strong drive delay capacity promotes self-esteem through a sense of mastery of one's internal urges.

The following case illustrates how genetically mediated individual differences in temperament and language interacted with parental conflict to impede learning impulse control and work skills:

> As an infant seven-year-old Billy disliked cuddling and rocking and was extremely active, climbing out of his crib regularly. In school he required reminding to carry out daily routines, as if "he only does what he wants to do." Other children avoided him because he always had to have his own way. He had received trials of stimulant therapy without benefit.
>
> In the clinic Billy was insensitive to the presence of others, flitting from one intriguing object to another. He described his devil and angel parts, one telling him to do as he wished, and the other telling him to be good. His reading and ciphering abilities were at grade levels; however, his speech, spelling, and handwriting were consistent with an articulo-graphic dyslexia.
>
> During the course of family psychotherapy, both parents revealed their own unhappy childhoods in which neither felt accepted and valued by their parents. The mother felt empty, and the father felt worthless, but neither had been able to show their vulnerability to the other. Billy had moved into the vaccuum that their inability to show affection to each other

and bickering had created. He had successfully sabotaged their efforts to set limits for him by pitting them against each other through disagreements over leniency and strictness. Billy also was turning anger against himself through impulsive, dangerous actions, such as sticking a nail in a light socket. As psychotherapy progressed Billy directly revealed his wish to stab his father so that he could be alone with his mother. As the parents came to terms with their own personal guilt and low self-esteem, they began to depend upon, rather than fight with, each other. They could then be firm with Billy and also pleasurably interact with him. The key to developing Billy's ability to delay gratification of impulses was freeing his parents from their blocks to maintaining limits for him.

Inflexibility

Some children are intolerant of change and have difficulty shifting the direction of their activities and thinking and are especially frustrated by group schoolwork. They rigidly persist in their behavior and may have temper outbursts in response to change. They are unable to accept alternative ways of doing things. They also may show perseveration in their imagery.

> For example, one boy misread goal as gloa. In spite of awareness that he had translocated the "l," he continued to be preoccupied with his misspelling of gloa and found himself thinking of gloo, which he pronounced as glue, moving farther away from his tutor's effort to teach him how to pronounce and spell goal.

Rigid defensive and coping strategies may result from an effort to avoid the experience of losing control and being helpless (Cohen, 1985). This rigidity surfaces in exaggerated and tense deliberateness of behavior. This purposiveness is intense and does not allow for deviation, flexibility, or spontaneity. It is an effort to control oneself and others as a means of avoiding losing control of situations.

Tolerating Frustration

A low tolerance for the inevitable distress produced by schoolwork leads to frustration, discouragement, and giving up on tasks. When anxious or depressed, a child is unable to tolerate frustration. More subtly for compulsive children, making mistakes arouses shame. Their harsh self-evaluation leads to mortification when they do not meet the perfectionism they impose upon themselves. As one child said,

> When I see a word I don't know, I get panicky. Making a mistake is terrible. I wish I could disappear so that no one would see me.

Other children use rationalization to relieve their frustration through excuses, such as disdain for the task, pleading exception, or claiming inability. As one child put it:

> Schoolwork doesn't mean anything. It won't do me any good anyway. A big shadow comes over me when I can't read something. I don't want to try. I say I can't do it and just forget it.

Modulating Emotions

Emotionally labile children have not adequately developed the psychological defense mechanisms of repression and sublimation and experience emotions triggered by minor events as catastrophic. Young children may unintentionally push, pull, or press on objects too hard, too long.

For these irritable children, trivial frustrations may trigger a startle reaction followed by sudden rage. Defining such a child's mood as a "crabby time" is helpful in signaling that the child needs distance from others. These children also need explanations that necessary frustrations are not deliberate intents to harm them in order to minimize the possibility of a shift into a paranoid stance in which the child feels unfairly treated.

The catastrophic reaction described by Goldstein in adults with brain lesions may underlie episodes of rage in children (Gardner, 1979). This reaction consists of outbursts of emotion, such as anger, cursing, and crying. These reactions in children also may spring from difficulty in controlling body movements because of unevenness of muscle tone, posture, and equilibrium (Silver, 1977).

Outbursts of rage should be distinguished from panic attacks, which also are precipitated by frustrations but consist of sudden crying, screaming, hitting oneself, running off, and ultimate unresponsiveness (Mosse, 1982). Gentle holding and quietly talking to a child in panic may be helpful, followed by rest in a quiet place.

As a reaction to their lack of emotional control and subsequent anger at themselves, some children become dependent upon adults (Leventhal, 1968). Their pervasive fear of losing control of their emotions leads to behavior that vacillates from submissiveness to hostile outbursts.

Selective Drive Regression

There are times and places for play and unbridled emotional expression. Some children are unable to wait for recreational opportunities and behave immaturely at inappropriate times. When playtime comes their immaturity is further expressed through an inability to share and take turns, with resulting difficulty in following the rules of games and adjusting to inevitable disappointments. As a result they are unpopular with their peers, because they are disruptive both in the classroom and on the playground.

Information Analysis Disabilities

A blurred distinction between external percepts and internal imagery interferes with a child's grasp of reality. For the young child, internal images are readily confused with external percepts so that subtle differences are not registered. With aging sharper images are constructed, and similarities and differences between past and present information are noticed (Santostefano, 1980). Problems in learning result when immature children persist in syncretically merging internally generated images and external percepts. A teenage boy lucidly described this state:

> I can't tell whether thoughts and feelings are coming from outside or inside of me. I don't know how I feel or what to think. I'm afraid others are going to call me names. I can hear my mother telling me everything will be all right, and I will get over this. I can hear my father angrily telling me that I can't do anything right and that I am hyperactive.

The ability to identify and sense reality accurately is imperative for performing schoolwork and interacting with people. Children who have difficulty in recognizing external reality clearly live in a world of their own and are not easily reached by the efforts of adults and peers to engage them. They lack an intuitive understanding of situations and the emotional climate surrounding them. They also have difficulty distinguishing a central idea from details in schoolwork.

Disturbances in one's sense of reality may be manifestations of the impingement of unconscious conflicts that result in derealization in which objects in the external world do not seem to be real (Abend, 1982). Some adults with visual-spatial dyslexias report difficulty in evaluating the accuracy of their perceptions of spatial and time relationships (Mykelbust, 1978). Intriguingly, lesions of the parietal lobes in adults are reflected in an impaired capacity to analyze perceptions.

Thinking Disabilities

Problems in thinking are ubiquitous in children with learning difficulties. It is possible, however, to identify degrees of thinking disabilities. To do schoolwork children must have effectively passed beyond the thinking modes of the sensorimotor and symbolic levels of development. Maladaptive patterns of thinking can result from developmental arrests at these immature stages (Malerstein & Ahern, 1982).

Psychotic Interferences with Thinking

Children who remain at the sensorimotor developmental level are incapable of participating in schoolwork. They are unable to concentrate, because they have not achieved comfortable integration of their bodily functions. They are capable of operant conditioning learning, but are unable to follow sequential instructions. They are unable to anticipate the consequences of their actions and to plan ahead. These children must directly experience through seeing, hearing, touching, and feeling. They lack a sense of humor. Their disabilities will be described later as pervasive developmental disorders.

Children who remain at the symbolic developmental level are dominated by magical thinking and approach schoolwork with highly emotionally toned personalized symbols of letters, numbers, and spoken words. Consequently they have difficulty with the abstract concepts involved in learning to read and cipher. They are unable to follow the sequential events of educational instruction. They are easily frustrated because they are unable to understand events and resolve problems accurately. The following case illustrates fixation at the symbolic level related to brain disease and traumatic psychosocial factors:

Twelve year old Diane was born into a strife-ridden home in which her mother was physically abused by her alcoholic father. Diane was an excitable infant, easily frightened by strangers but quiet and withdrawn during violent episodes in the home. At the age of 18 months, she contracted encephalitis, and thereafter began to have psychomotor and occasional grand mal seizures. Her mother obtained a divorce when Diane was four, after her father was discovered sexually stimulating Diane.

In school Diane dropped farther behind as time passed so that by the fourth grade she was preoccupied with daydreaming and was unproductive. She failed to answer questions, typically with "I don't know." She was unable to express emotions of any kind.

Three critical issues were addressed in Diane's treatment that ultimately brought her to grade-level academic functioning and appropriate levels of emotional expression and communication. First, individual psychotherapy was employed to release the developmental fixation of her thinking from the symbolic, magical level. She was immersed in daydreaming about reunion with and keeping house for her father, had a limited vocabulary, still believed in Santa Claus and thought her grandmother died by falling into a hole in the cemetery. Second, family psychotherapy was used to expose her mother's overprotectiveness together with Diane's subtle expression of resentment toward her mother through clinging dependency. Her mother acted as Diane's mouthpiece, permitting her to retreat into shy unexpressiveness. Third, careful adjustment of Diane's anticonvulsant regimen was required to achieve a tolerable balance between seizure control and side effects. As Diane became more interested

in success in school and making friends, she also could absorb factual information about her seizure disorder. When her school principal arranged a movie on epilepsy for the school, and her teacher enlisted her classmates' support in responding to her occasional seizures, Diane found herself with peer status for the first time in her life.

Children who remain at the sensorimotor or symbolic levels also show impairment of learning automatic mechanisms of thinking. This constitutes a grave disability that interferes with freeing attention from trivial details. Daily activities consist of automatic behavior in dressing, eating, washing, climbing stairs, locking and unlocking doors, tying and untying shoelaces, catching a ball, reading, writing, and calculating. Whenever these activities cannot be completed automatically, conscious awareness of them returns. Children with inefficient automatic mechanisms must pay deliberate attention to details. When their attention is diverted, they cannot proceed with an activity. These children have particular difficulty with learning that builds upon repetition of underlying facts, such as the alphabet, arithmetic tables, and calendar events (Mosse, 1982).

As a further clinical example, a study of severely reading handicapped, incarcerated delinquents revealed their paranoid ideation, illogical thought processes, problems with calculations, and impaired short-term memory. They appeared to have the loose, rambling, illogical thought processes of young children at the symbolic level (Lewis et al, 1980; Lewis, 1981).

Neurotic Interferences with Thinking

Information received during a state of distress may be stored as a frozen, unintegrated memory pattern. As distress experiences accumulate, one's flexibility of thinking may be compromised. Memories stored in this way are revived in similar situations, as if they were a literal recording of the distressing experience (Jackins, 1978). One then feels compelled to attempt reenactment of reactions to old distressing experiences. Thus the person says things that are not relevant, does things that do not work, fails to cope effectively, and endures painful emotions that have nothing to do with the present situation. Defense mechanisms erected by intrapsychic conflicts, therefore, may interfere with rational thinking, when logical thoughts imply distressing irrational consequences. Then some children use intellectualization as a defense that employs fallacious reasoning in order to explain away this distressing imagery.

Problem-solving thinking arises developmentally from resolving conflicts between the external world and internal drives. It involves blending effortless primary process and effortful secondary process thinking. In the process the potent competence associated with rational problem solving may evoke anxiety and block thinking. A 17-year-old boy explained how competent thinking evoked self-defeating sensations:

> Sometimes when I hear myself talking well and have clear thoughts, a sweeping feeling comes down from my head and into my groin so that I lose the point like static on a TV screen, blank out, and feel sick in my stomach. This feeling cuts off my mind, and then I torture myself. I force myself to be nervous and to worry. I feel naked and as if I have no genitals. Then I act like a giggling, helpless little boy. I act weak and feel that I'm not strong enough to do college work. Nobody will take me seriously then.

A 16-year-old girl vividly described how dangerous thoughts interfered with her thinking:

> "I hold on tightly so that I won't lose control of my mind. I hate to feel confused

and have mixed-up thoughts so I try to make my mind think exactly the I want it to. I chase mixed-up thoughts away to get rid of a depressed feeling like being chained in a pit." In psychotherapy Mary permitted herself to become aware of the hostile imagery of her confused thinking with a flood of tears of relief. She was then able to relinquish covering her head with a "security blanket" when she slept at night. Her repressed rage at her mother emerged in the transference, as she ridiculed and felt superior to the therapist. Her defiance of, and declaration of independence from, the therapist became the first step in expressing her wish and subsequent ability to assert her independence from her mother.

Cultural Interferences with Thinking

When the values of a school collide with the values of a child's family and culture, that child may lack motivation to adapt to educational goals.

Some children have little or no support from their parents for achievement in school because they live in cultures that do not value planning for the future and are oriented to the pleasures of the present. Abstracting ability may not be encouraged or required in their homes (Neill & Sandifer, 1982). These children lack motivation for problem-solving thinking in school, which aims to prepare them for a distant, seemingly unattainable future. Consequently they may not develop capacities for synthesizing spatial, temporal, and conceptual relationships, with resulting avoidance of schoolwork (Gardner & Sperry, 1974).

The lack of a cultural value that stresses personal responsibility also leads to an inability to accept responsibility for the consequences of one's actions.

Reading Epilepsy

Reading epilepsy is a dramatic illustration of the relationship between electrical activity of the brain and thinking. In most people with reading epilepsy, the seizures appear to be evoked by imagery or thinking while reading quietly, reading aloud to others, or writing. Moreover seizures may be triggered by braille and musical notes. The evoking stimulus apparently is not the printed word itself but the process of thinking stimulated by the word symbols (Forster, 1975).

Disabilities in Implementing Actions

The posterior sensory cortex and the anterior frontal cortex are referred to as the sensorimotor analyzer (Calanchini & Trout, 1971). A motor act is not just an efferent phenomenon, but depends upon afferent information from all the major sensory modalities. Thus the entire central nervous system is involved in movement. This explains why most children with functional disabilities have motor involvement.

The sensorimotor cortex brings information into play from all of the sensory analyzers. The various afferent signals unite in the premotor frontal cortex, where a temporal sequence of potential movements forms as a single "kinetic melody." This "melody" requires a continuing series of smoothly integrated excitatory and inhibitory messages sent to and received from muscles. This proprioceptive feedback allows the brain to compare the position and movements of the joints and muscles with the intended "melody." Fine motor incoordination is due to the sensorimotor inability to perform the smooth selection of individual movements, such as those needed to tie shoelaces, buckle a belt, or manipulate puzzle pieces.

Many children lack the ability to carry out intentions into actions. They fail to follow directions, complete tasks, and turn in assignments in school. Motor planning, or praxis, is the ability to carry out an intentional action. This is impaired in dyspraxias

in which one cannot accomplish a simple activity, such as blowing out a match (Goldstein, 1963). A dyspraxic child may try over and over to learn a game, but be unable to do so. Putting on clothing, using zippers, and tying shoes are particularly difficult. Such a child must consciously and deliberately plan actions that flow spontaneously for most children (Ayres, 1979).

Some children have inhibitions of the pleasures derived from producing things originating in early-life conflicts over urination or defecation. Inhibitions of these bodily pleasures may be expressed by withholding knowledge. A defense that may be used is projection through which hostile wishes are attributed to others, who then are perceived as bad or unfair. Guilt over exhibitionistic wishes to show one's talent in schoolwork also may inhibit productivity. Conflicts over seeing and being seen related to forbidden voyeuristic and exhibitionistic wishes can interfere with a child's ability to show what one has learned (Allen, 1967). Other children show phobic reactions to making errors and avoid difficult schoolwork, making excuses and concealing their mistakes.

Guilt evoked by assertiveness and competitiveness can hinder a child's use of knowledge and skills. As one child with learning problems tearfully discovered in psychotherapy:

> I really can be somebody and let teachers know that I can do things. I can be good in school. I always thought that I did not deserve to do what I wanted to or have what I wanted.

Castration dread and sibling rivalry can cause unconscious conflicts that lead to avoidance of competition and masochistic seeking of failure rather than success (Liss, 1944).

Anxiety stimulated by examinations and public performances can cause a temporary loss of knowledge, resembling an aphasia, and a paralysis in skills, resembling an apraxia. The following reports illustrate these phenomena:

> When people ask me a question, suddenly my mind goes blank. I'm so afraid I'll make a mistake.
> I can read it to myself, but when I have to read it aloud, I can't say it.

Provocative, angry behavior based upon identification with the aggressor also can block the school performance of delinquent children (Gardner & Sperry, 1974).

Restriction of a child's range of activities is a means of escaping painful external situations. When a child cannot tolerate comparing one's performance with that of others, the child may give up competitive activities and become preoccupied with activities in which one can feel superior. Avoidance of anxiety-provoking situations is a natural tendency; only when it is too marked does it result in warped development. Anna Freud suggested that giving a child too much freedom in choosing activities and interests could be misguided, because a child can make choices based on avoiding unpleasant situations with resulting impoverishment of character development (Sandler, 1985).

Disabilities in Verifying Actions

Some children appear to be unable to recognize their mistakes and unaware of the impact of their behavior upon others. Other children may organize and begin their work well, but thereafter respond impulsively and guess at answers, because they are unwilling to reflect on the accuracy of their actions. They rush through tasks to get them out of the way and so produce slipshod, inaccurate work.

Although the implications for children are not clear, adults with the prefrontal

lobe syndrome show an impaired ability to profit from experience. They often do not respond appropriately to reinforcers because of impaired ability to interpret feedback from their behavior. Differences between positive and negative feedback may be blurred and cause confusion leading to inertia. Perseverative behavior may occur because of impaired feedback suppression of ongoing activities. Monkeys with prefrontal lobe resections also do not react to the consequences of their behavior.

The following case illustrates disabilities in verifying actions based upon both brain damage and interpersonal factors:

> Dale was first seen at the age of 15 while in residential psychiatric placement because of episodic minor thefts. His clinical picture included poor judgment, poor planning ability, an inability to anticipate the consequences of his actions, a lack of awareness of the impact of his behavior upon others, lack of motivation for academic or recreational activities, perseverative actions, and unexpressiveness. The diagnosis of prefrontal lobe syndrome was made.
> At the age of 13, Dale sustained massive brain injury followed by coma and gradual recovery of motor and verbal capacities. Prior to the accident, Dale was incompletely individuated from his mother. During psychotherapy with him and his family, evidence emerged that, although he and his mother assumed they knew what the other was thinking and feeling, there was a little direct verbal and emotional exchange between them. The most frequent facial expression of his mother was an inscrutable Mona Lisa-like smile. As a result Dale lacked feedback regarding the actual impact of his behavior on others. The members of his family feared rebuff from exposure of vulnerability and interacted with distancing and blame-externalizing bickering.
> In psychotherapy Dale discovered that his stealing was aimed at punishing his

parents by hurting himself. Because it often followed successes, theft also was a means of spoiling his own assertive accomplishments, which evoked guilt over murderous rage toward his parents. Dale began to experience the range of emotions leading to direct expressions of explosive rage at his parents.

With the lifting of the repression of painful emotions, Dale began to act more assertively by pursuing training and obtaining employment as a computer operator. He trained himself to pay attention to the reactions of other persons to his behavior by asking himself, "How am I coming off now?" He also learned to structure his life through the use of a detailed daily schedule book to remind him of the things he wished to do to carry out his intentions for the day.

MANAGERIAL SYSTEM SYNDROMES

Several clinical syndromes reflect general difficulties in managerial system functions. They are expressed in behaviors that lead to major interferences with schoolwork and compliance with classroom expectations. The variations center around the limbic system in the impulsive character and around the prefrontal cortex in the prefrontal lobe syndrome. Many CNS levels are involved in children with pervasive developmental disorders.

The Impulsive Character

There are wide variations in the degree to which children are impulsive. Some children have pervasive problems with impulse control and can be described as having impulsive characters (Wishnie, 1977). They generally are unable to delay gratification, adapt to change, tolerate displeasure, modulate their emotions, and appropriately re-

gress in play. These children have difficulty concentrating, are easily bored, and may have constitutionally high movement levels. They react to those aspects of a situation that are the most obvious and compelling (Douglas, 1981).

Impulsive children tend to be field independent and to perceive an internal locus of control. They tend to lack automatic thinking and foresight, and show inadequate verification of their actions. Their self-evaluations tend to be high and self-esteems low. They are split into good and bad selves. Consequently, they judge themselves and others in black and white terms. Their primary orientation is gratifying their immediate urges (Malerstein & Ahern, 1982).

The impulsive character is whimsical. These children lack active interests, values, and goals beyond their immediate concerns. Their capacities for concentration, abstraction, and reflectiveness are all impaired, resulting in reckless judgments (Shapiro, 1965). Their attention-seeking behavior, camouflaging, and dissembling may result from a diminished sensitivity to negative and positive external rewards (Wender, 1971).

These children do not comply with social values nor desire to change themselves. They lack social awareness and have chronic difficulty communicating with other people (Tarnopol & Tarnopol, 1981). They fail to recognize danger signals in human relationships and pose problems for other children because of their intrusiveness and emotional lability. They exhaust their parents, fight with siblings, and become the scapegoats of peers. Their parents may experience guilt, fear, and confusion and fluctuate between rejection and overprotection. Their households revolve around these children, leaving other family members frustrated and angry.

Some impulsive children have not had the opportunity to learn to express their emotions verbally and think. They act blindly on their emotions. These children often have lived in loveless, inconsistent, neglectful, and disorganized environments. Their lives have been filled with intense hostilities, frustrations, and deprivations. The prevalence of hostile aggression in their environments necessitates that their energy be devoted to protecting themselves (Weil, 1977). Having been denied or falsely promised so much in the past, they are afraid that if they do not act quickly, they will lose out entirely. Since they have little capacity to wait, schoolwork is difficult for them (Kotkov, 1965).

The favorable response of some children with impulsive characters to stimulant medication suggests that they know the relationships between acts and consequences, but are unable to connect them effectively. This has led to the hypothesis that defective monoamine metabolism might result in defective conditioned learning (Wender, 1971).

Although the effort to find a single underlying deficit in clinical conditions is unrealistic, there is evidence to support "disinhibitory psychopathology" in adults with the diagnosis of impulsive personality, hysteria, antisocial personality, and alcoholism (Gorenstein & Newman, 1980). The common characteristic is the irresistible and exaggerated hold that immediate drive gratification has upon these persons. An animal model of this deficit has been suggested by lesions in the septal-hippocampal-frontal system.

The Prefrontal Lobe Syndrome

The frontal lobe syndrome has been described in both adults and children with known brain lesions and with neuroleptic medication side effects. Although generalizations from this adult syndrome to children are risky, it stands as a useful heuristic model (Pribram & Luria, 1973; Mattes,

1980; McCaffrey & Isaac, 1985). Many of the features of this syndrome are evident developmentally in young children as the frontal lobes mature and appear to persist longer in some children than others. For this reason there appear to be forms of the syndrome that are outgrown and that are relatively permanent. Since the motor and speech areas of the frontal lobes are not involved, the term prefrontal is more precise than frontal in describing this syndrome.

Because the prefrontal areas have a variety of complex functions, there are many variations of the prefrontal syndrome, depending upon the areas affected. For example, the dominant prefrontal area proposes action plans, while the nondominant prefrontal areas assess their progress (Harris, 1986). Impairment of these functions makes it difficult for children to initiate actions without external guidance. They lack the ability to decide what to do and accurately to assess their progress. The medial aspects of both prefrontal areas integrate imagery of internal bodily sensations, while the lateral aspects integrate imagery of the body as a tool of action. Impairment of these functions produces inefficient awareness of and concentration upon messages from their bodies as objects in the external world.

Although not the seat of intelligence as measured by psychometric tests, the prefrontal lobes are essential for the use of intelligence (Stuss & Benson, 1986). The prefrontal cortex generally is responsible for focused attention, organizational ability, and the verification of actions. The prefrontal areas combine and balance the often irrational input of the internal world from the limbic system with the rational input of the external world from the parietal lobes (Gardner, 1976). The ability of the prefrontal areas to facilitate the storage and recall of information of many types simultaneously from different parts of the brain makes possible: (1) maintaining a steadfastness of purpose against distracting stimuli by delaying action until the most adaptive response is decided, (2) considering the consequences of actions before they are performed, (3) planning for the future, (4) solving abstract problems, (5) initiating and organizing serial actions, and (6) controlling activities in accord with social values (Guyton, 1977).

The impairment of prefrontal lobe functions in itself does not affect intellect, memory, or consciousness as much as do dysfunctions of other parts of the brain, but it does interfere with the ability to respond appropriately in the emotional and social spheres. It lessens sensitivity to other persons and the capacity to reconcile the pressures of ever-changing internal and external stimuli. Adults who have lost prefrontal lobe functions are less likely to persevere in an activity in the face of distraction, discomfort, or pain. On the other hand they have difficulty shifting their strategies in the face of changing conditions. They may do well in recognizing the initial strategy, but when it is changed, they become confused. Goals are not forgotten, but are blurred, put out of correct order, or set aside (Cotman & McGaugh, 1980). They can verbally define and apparently understand an expected action, but not carry it out. In sum there may be an inability to put items in an organized sequence; an impaired ability to change set, resulting in perseverative behavior; an impaired ability to maintain a set in the face of interference; and an impaired ability to monitor personal behavior (Stuss & Benson, 1984).

Children with the prefrontal lobe syndrome do not feel like actors in the world and are continually frustrated by dissonance, both because of their inability to work effectively and of being misunderstood by others. These children do not pay attention well, but paradoxically may become perseveratively involved in tasks with an inability to shift out of them. They are field dependent and perceive an external locus of control, leading to an excessive dependency upon external events from which they cannot disengage. Their impulse control is erratic, with inertia and apathy alternating with socially unacceptable behavior and emotional outbursts. Their behavior in school suffers from a lack of sensitivity to others and a slovenly, disorganized approach to work. They give the impression that they are not listening. Careless errors, omissions, oversights, or misinterpretation of items occur even when they seem motivated to work. For these children the very appearance of unfamiliar words may trigger distress.

Such children must be taught slowly and patiently so that new material eventually takes on a familiar and orderly form. They function better on a one-to-one basis, when their managerial functions are guided for them. At home they fail to follow through on parental requests and are unable to stick to activities, including play, for periods of time appropriate to their ages. To others they appear to be apathetic, lacking in comprehension of people and events, and socially inept.

A 14-year-old boy described his mild prefrontal lobe syndrome as a frustration that kept him from doing as well as he wanted to in schoolwork and with peers. He found it difficult to follow teachers when they changed the subject, because his "brain was stuck in one track." He had to take time to plan out his day by writing down his schedule and assignments. "I have to sit down and just collect my thoughts." He was prone to be irritable, to laugh to loudly, and to cry too readily. At times he had to explain why he was laughing at his "funny thoughts," when he realized that others could not understand them. He also was insensitive to the nuances of others' reactions to him. As a younger child, he had difficulty pronouncing words and learning handwriting. He had outstanding knowledge of baseball statistics, but had difficulty composing themes and taking time-limited tests. He had to tell himself to do his homework, otherwise he would spend all of his free time watching television or "just sitting around doing nothing."

The prefrontal lobe syndrome can be more specifically characterized by varying degrees of impairment of abstracting ability, stimulus-bound inertia, lack of empathy and social awareness, a concrete view of space and time, impaired thinking, and impaired concentration.

Impairment of Abstracting Ability

Persons with the prefrontal lobe syndrome can perform well when the present context relates to past situations. However, they have difficulty generalizing to new similar situations. This may explain why they can be taught the same thing over and over again without appearing to retain it (Rudel, 1980). For example, they can learn numbers, syllables, or movements, but only reproduce them in the same situations in which they were learned. They may be unable to recite a series of numbers on request, but can do so if prompted (Goldstein, 1963).

Thus the ability to derive abstract concepts that are not of immediate personal significance is impaired, resulting in a concrete approach to life. Concrete responses may appear to be impulsive, because they are determined directly by stimuli perceived at the moment. In contrast abstract responses are determined by reflection upon and synthesis of perceptions. The failure to synthesize life experiences as organized wholes is accompanied by an inability to give an account of one's own acting or thinking, an inability to separate the self from the external world, and difficulty in relating throughts to each other (Goldstein, 1963).

Abstracting difficulty impedes formulating working strategies that (1) focus on

essential information, (2) categorize incoming information so that it can be associated with the purpose of a task, (3) develop mnemonic aids for remembering associations, and (4) classify information for storage in an orderly, retrievable fashion (Rudel, 1980).

Stimulus-Bound Inertia

In contrast with those having impulsive characters, persons with the prefrontal lobe syndrome have difficulty initiating actions that are not in direct response to external stimuli or internal instinctual urges. They lack spontaneity and initiative and act largely when stimulated by the external world. At the same time, they may be restless and impatient when external stimuli they depend upon are lacking. Thus they may be quietly absorbed in watching television or in one-to-one activities and otherwise be hyperkinetic.

Inertia is reflected in the perseverative behavior of these children when they persist in the same activity. They have difficulty shifting their set and freeing themselves from what they are doing or thinking. They continue doing or thinking the same thing over and over again and are easily disturbed by change (Mosse, 1982). They may reread words or sentences, continue adding when they should be subtracting, and persist in asking the same question. They usually are aware of their inability to stop an activity and are frustrated by it.

Slow Reaction Time

What appears to be slowness of reaction time affects the ability to learn reading, writing, and arithmetic. For example, difficulty in responding fast enough to each single letter while sounding out a word to blend letters into words impedes learning to read. These children tend to read each word slowly and pause too long to grasp the meaning of the entire text. Their slow reaction time causes a pause before they can answer questions. They can answer only one question, carry out only one instruction, or remember only one errand at a time. Too many stimuli confuse them. As a result they may be unable to complete tests within the required time.

These children may be painfully aware of the inability to do or say things quickly. They may be able to verbalize what should be done but are unable to carry it out. In their effort to be as fast as other children, they may become tense, anxious, and angry. This increases their rigidity so that they find it difficult to make any move intellectually or physically. Their entire body may become tense and their hands tremble, as they are unable to act. They may complain of headaches based upon their tenseness and feel they cannot go on with their work. They need a relaxing pause between activities (Mosse, 1982).

Lack of Empathy

Persons with the prefrontal lobe syndrome have difficulty placing themselves in the situation of others. They lack social perceptiveness, and only a concrete situation in which they are affected brings them into emotional contact with others (Goldstein, 1963). They are unable to grasp social situations and react to concrete aspects of them. Their resulting socially inappropriate behavior may appear to be because of the lack of social inhibitions. Consequently, they have difficulty forming social relationships. For example, one boy had seen a movie before, but still felt slighted when his companion went to that movie with another person; his subsequent angry outburst alienated that potential friend.

Concrete View of Space and Time

Because of their concrete approach to space, these persons may be unable to do such things as reproduce the position of two sticks forming an obtuse angle pointing upward, but can do so when the angle is underneath, because it evokes the idea of a roof. The same person may be able to reconstruct a complicated spatial design of a house, because it is related to their personal concrete image of a house. Thus they may be unable to imitate or copy anything that is not a part of their immediate concrete experience.

In a similar way, their concrete view of time might enable them to use a watch to gauge their actions, but they would be unable to describe the time by the position of the hands. Disorientation in time relationships creates problems with temporal-sequential organization. Prepositions such as "before" and "after" are elusive, and multistep instructions are confusing, so that only one or two steps can be processed. In late elementary and junior high school, children with temporal-sequential disorganization may have serious problems organizing thoughts, remembering the sequence of classes, logically ordering sections of a composition, and scheduling phases of projects.

Impaired Thinking

Because they are stimulus bound, persons with the prefrontal lobe syndrome single out random fragments of a problem and perform partial logical operations without attempting to formulate a general strategy (Mattes, 1980). They accordingly have difficulty in problem-solving thinking because of confusing associations, erratic behavior, and excessive responsiveness to extraneous stimuli (Zeigarnik, 1965).

When functioning well the prefrontal cortex organizes mental functions toward goals so that in a manageable task a child is untouched by distracting stimuli (Guyton, 1977). When a task is not understood because the prefrontal cortex is not functioning well, a child may overreact and become dazed, agitated, evasive, and irritable, presenting a picture of disorganization and fright. Such children need the predictability and certainty of orderly daily routines. Uncertainty interferes with their efficiency so that they function best in structured situations in which they know in advance exactly what will be the sequence of familiar activities (Mosse, 1982).

Impaired Concentration

These children are able to employ scanning and focusing attention but encounter difficulty in concentrating on tasks. This is a reflection of their general inability to organize and sequence their behavior appropriately and to bring percepts into interaction with the imagery of memories and emotions. Except under stimulus-bound circumstances, they cannot maintain a steadfastness of purpose because of their inability to inhibit competing impulses. The resulting clinical picture is one of a distractible child who cannot concentrate effectively and is easily frustrated by difficult tasks.

The prefrontal lobe appears to function inadequately in many children regarded as having attention deficit disorders (Mattes, 1980; Hicks & Gualtieri, 1986). Generally the prefrontal lobe is involved in the inhibition of socially inappropriate behavior (Chelune et al, 1986). More specifically the medial prefrontal areas are involved in drive motivations and self-esteem.

Childhood-Onset Pervasive Developmental Disorders

Many developmentally disordered young children do not readily fit current diagnostic categories. The term "childhood-onset pervasive developmental disorder" employed in *DSM-III-R* describes children in whom multiple developmental functions are severely distorted (American Psychiatric Association, 1987). They have qualitative distortions that are not seen in any stage of development, in contrast with specific developmental disorders, which reflect delays in usual development. These children have been described as psychotic, atypical, symbiotic, and childhood schizophrenic.

The essential features of pervasive developmental disorders are profound disturbances in social relations and multiple oddities in behavior, all developing after 30 months and before 12 years of age. Oddities of behavior include sudden excessive anxiety, constricted or inappropriate emotions, resistance to change, perseveration, motor and speech abnormalities, hyper- and hyposensitivity to sensory stimuli, and self-mutilation.

Most of these children are regarded as psychotic because they are impaired in all areas of brain functioning. Their threshold of responsiveness is low. Their movement levels may be high and unrelated to context. They may have spatial orientation difficulty and inefficient processing of sensory information. They usually are field independent and appear to have internal loci of control.

The language of psychotic children may be severely distorted. Their speech ranges from mutism through echolalia to well-formed sentences; however, it is not goal directed. When their language is well developed, the content of their speech may be irrelevant, inappropriate, or without communicative goals (Caparulo & Cohen, 1977). The distinction between thinking and language is clearly seen in psychotic children, who cannot fit words appropriately to ideas. Consequently, these children are not able to structure their world with the aid of language. Individual words and phrases seem locked into rigid recording mechanisms that do not permit reshuffling for use in varied contexts. Their speech is stilted, foreshortened, and inappropriate to context or noncommunicative (Shapiro, 1975).

Psychotic children are unable to regress appropriately in play and exhibit erratic impulse-control problems. Play materials are not used appropriately. They are not able to function in ordinary school routines and may not be able to learn academic skills (Hassibi & Breuer, 1980). They may have long auditory memories, but use words as concrete entities, not as symbols. As one said, "K is not nice, it has too many spikes" (deHirsch, 1967). They may not learn through accommodation generally, so that memorization may occur without true understanding (Christ, 1976). Their analysis of stimuli is poor, as are their synthesizing, problem solving, and automatic thinking functions. They cannot synthesize their experiences into amalgamated identifications so that images of the external world remain discrete as though literally "swallowed whole." They implement and verify their actions ineffectively. Their self-consciousness, self-esteem, self-concept, and self-evaluation functions are distorted. They do not develop coherent, integrated selves.

Most critically, psychotic children have not developed social and language skills necessary for functioning in the routines of group living (Sherman et al, 1983). They show withdrawal from, indifference to, or rejection of interpersonal relationships, most obviously with peers.

In later childhood the onset of psychosis can be recognized as schizophrenia and is characterized by deterioration from a previous level of functioning in the form of decline in school performance, social withdrawal, and impaired performance of goal-directed tasks (Cantor, 1988). At the core are disturbances of thought, cognition, emotions, volition, and self-concept. Characteristic disturbances in thinking may be in the form and content of thought, such as loosening of associations, false beliefs or delusions, ideas of reference, thought broadcasting, thought insertion, thought control, and auditory hallucinations. Motor behavior may show diminution in reactivity, posturing, purposelessness, or stereotyped actions. A vivid account of the life of a schizophrenic girl was provided by Sechehaye (1951).

Schizophrenic psychosis should be distinguished from situational reactions, anxiety states, affective disorders, temporal lobe epilepsy, and chronic drug intoxication. It appears to be a complex developmental disorder based on a genetically determined vulnerability acted upon by an aggravating psychosocial environment. Many schizophrenic children become schizophrenic adults.

In one study of children with pervasive developmental disorders, 59 percent had abnormal computerized tomography scans, as did 44 percent of a language-impaired group and 38 percent of a Tourette syndrome group (Caparulo et al, 1981). The prognosis ranges from chronic hospitalization to community functioning. Persistently disturbed interpersonal relationships are especially unfavorable prognostic signs.

Psychotropic medication may be of value, in addition to individual and family psychotherapy. When an older child or adolescent responds to treatment, mainstream education is possible with tutoring to make up for deficient academic skills.

SUMMARY

Because of the incomplete development of managerial functions, many children need special assistance in learning how to work in school and relate effectively to adults and peers.

Some children have specific difficulty with delaying gratification, adapting to change, tolerating distress, modulating their emotions, and regressing selectively in play. Children who have difficulty in analyzing internal and external perceptions and images are unable to grasp reality and are dominated by subjectivity. They may live in a world of their own and be limited in their awareness of the expectations of teachers and peers.

Problems in thinking are ubiquitous in children with learning difficulties. Developmental immaturity can be responsible for thinking limitations, particularly in the capacity for abstraction. Neurotic conflicts also can arise so that logical thinking is impaired, and even is distressing. Cultural factors play an important role in the educational values of children and, together with the influences of economic disadvantage, can result in a lack of a sense of personal responsibility for their actions.

The ability to implement intentions through productivity in school can be inhibited by a variety of neurotic and attitudinal factors. The ability to verify one's actions is compromised for children who are unaware of the impact of their behavior upon others. This function also is critical for monitoring the accuracy of schoolwork. Others have general difficulty with all of these impulse control functions and have impulsive characters. Because of the critical role of the prefrontal cortex in thinking and exercising values, the prefrontal lobe syndrome is a useful paradigm for understanding children who find it difficult to organize their lives. This syndrome is char-

acterized by limitations in abstracting ability, inertia and apathy, slow reaction time, lack of empathy and social awareness, a concrete view of time and space, impaired problem-solving thinking, and impaired concentration.

The most extreme learning problems are seen in children with pervasive developmental disorders, who have severe limitations in language, managerial, and self-system functions. Thus a progression in extent of involvement can be seen from impulsive characters with variations at the level of the limbic system, to the prefrontal lobe syndrome with variations at the prefrontal cortical level, to pervasive developmental disorders with variations at all levels of brain functioning.

Because they have not been the focus of behavioral, psychological, and educational testing, managerial functions have not been given sufficient consideration in most approaches to children with learning problems. The integrity of managerial functions can be evaluated by observing children in school and assembling information about them from a variety of sources. Intact and appropriately mature managerial functions are essential for work in school.

26

Self System Problems

Selfhood implies a personal history, friends, family, a sense
of place. Under siege, the self contracts to a defensive core,
armed against adversity.

Christopher Lasch, 1984

Disturbances in the self system
commonly affect the behavior
of children in school. For some
aberrations in the self are at the
root of their problems. For most self system
difficulties aggravate those of other systems. Knowledge of the self system is just
beginning to accumulate, because the self
is a relatively recent clinical concept.

This chapter deals with problems in
self-awareness, low self-esteem, defects and
distortions in self-concepts, and self-evaluation discrepancies, in addition to syndromes based upon them that cause
difficulties in interpersonal role relationships.

PROBLEMS IN SELF-AWARENESS

Self-awareness involves both public awareness of oneself in the presence of other
persons and private awareness of the various aspects of oneself (Buss, 1980). When
children are anxious in social situations,
they are in a state of distressing public self-
awareness.

Distressing emotions of public self-
awareness are embarrassment, marked by
blushing, nervous laughter, and a feeling
of foolishness; shame, characterized by
feelings of self-disgust and self-abasement;
audience anxiety, revealed by the presence
of tension and sometimes panic; and shyness, inferred from inhibited social behavior, and experienced as feelings of tension
and awkwardness (see Figure 26-1).

Shame and embarrassment are similar.
Common to both are gaze aversion, covering of the eyes or face, discomfort, and
parasympathetic reactions. Both emotions
may be caused by a person's own acts or by
the scrutiny of others. The actions causing
shame and embarrassment can be aligned
on a dimension of severity. A person's own
acts are more unacceptable in shame than
in embarrassment. The actions of others
also are of greater intensity in causing
shame, such as by scorn, than in embarrassment, such as by teasing. Moreover the
ensuing drop in self-esteem is greater in
shame than in embarrassment. On the
other hand, blushing, smiling, or giggling

	Embarrassment	Shame	Audience anxiety	Shyness
Reactions				
Cover face	Yes	Yes	No	No
Parasympathetic dominance	Yes	Yes	No	No
Sympathetic dominance	No	No	Yes	Sometimes
Self-blame	Yes	Yes	No	Sometimes
Trait	No	No	Yes	Yes
Causes				
Conspicuous	Sometimes	No	Yes	Yes
Novelty	No	No	Yes	Yes
Disclosure	Yes	Yes	No	No
Evaluation anxiety	No	No	Yes	Sometimes

Figure 26-1. Features that link embarrassment with shame and audience anxiety with shyness. (From A. H. Buss, *Self-Consciousness and Social Anxiety,* copyright 1980 by W. H. Freeman and Co., New York. Reproduced with permission.)

are part of embarrassment, but not of shame. The embarrassed person feels foolish or silly; the ashamed person, regretful and depressed. There also is a difference in self-evaluation: in embarrassment, a mistake has been made; in shame, a personal defect is experienced.

Embarrassment has many immediate causes, and so occurs more frequently than shame. A breach of etiquette may cause embarrassment, but not shame. Being teased, overpraised, or merely scrutinized by others cause embarrassment, but not shame. On the other hand, letting one's group down or being caught in an immoral or cowardly act cause shame, but not embarrassment. The consequences of shame and embarrassment also are different. There merely is a temporary loss of self-esteem in embarrassment, but an enduring loss in shame. Moreover an embarrassed person is likely to be accepted and consoled, whereas an ashamed person is likely to be rejected and scorned.

Since shame is the only social anxiety to involve morality, it is important to distinguish it from the other major moral emotion, guilt (Buss, 1980). In guilt the feeling is of sin or evil: "I am bad; I have

transgressed." In shame the feeling is one of exposure: "I am ugly; I have failed; I have been caught cheating." Guilt involves self-hatred. It is a private matter of one's own conscience, and so there is no escape. Thus guilt is more effective than shame in ensuring self-control. Shame is a social anxiety and is essentially public; if no one else knows, there is no basis for shame. Since one's action is seen, shame can be diminished by running away or avoiding looking at others. Therefore, shame may not lead to self-control but does cause compliance in group situations.

The conscious experience of a smoothly functioning self is taken for granted and easily entered and left. However, a fragmented or disintegrating self may experience ill-defined but intense and pervasive anxiety when leaving self-awareness (Kohut, 1977). This is seen in some children who have difficulty going to sleep. Other children have similar difficulty in relinquishing self-awareness of the act of reading, which entails losing self-awareness as one becomes absorbed in the imagery stimulated by the printed word. They have difficulty developing sufficient automatization of reading to permit moving beyond preoccupation with awareness of the act itself. This impedes learning to read for meaning (Schwartz & Schiller, 1970). This phenomenon was described in an adult patient who avoided reading because, if he allowed himself to become absorbed in what he read, he feared he would be engulfed by the printed page, and his own self would disappear (Devereaux, 1966).

LOW SELF-ESTEEM

The self-esteem of young children is exceedingly vulnerable and is influenced by the attitudes of adults toward their bodies, bodily functions, and personal mastery attempts. The development of self-esteem, therefore, can be impeded by parents who force control of a child's bodily functions and deprive the child of the experience of "doing it for myself," rather than permit the child to acquire a sense of personal mastery of them.

Conversely others cannot build a child's self-esteem simply through praise. More important is to create an atmosphere in which a child is willing to try something that is unfamiliar. Some children need encouragement to take risks and to learn through making mistakes in order to develop self-esteem that can buffer the fear that accompanies the unknown during early life. This occurs when adults accept a child's clumsiness and errors. Adults facilitate the development of self-esteem by respecting a child for trying and empathizing with fear of the unknown, rather than criticizing the child for inevitable errors. During the early school years, children discover how easily they learn how to read and to cipher. They are willing to face this novelty, if they have self-esteem earned by mastering the obstacles and fear inherent in life (Seligman, 1975).

The modeling of mastery of errors and the unknown by adults encourages children to do the same. A child also needs guidance in distinguishing between having and acting upon fantasies and emotions. An adult's acceptance of a child's feelings as the adult guides and limits their behavioral expressions helps a child to learn that unacceptable feelings can be experienced without acting upon or fearing them. When a child is forbidden the expression of feelings, the wellspring of motivation is shut off. Children need to learn that it is acceptable to have and express feelings, but it may not be acceptable to act upon them.

A child who does not fully develop self-esteem remains more or less dependent upon the approval of others. The child is easily shamed or hurt when that approval is not forthcoming. In its mature form, self-esteem frees one from dependency upon the approval of others. Some children with low self-esteem tend to withdraw from difficult academic tasks. Others provoke teachers as a means of avoiding the pain of failure in schoolwork and seeking the admiration of peers, who latently resist adult influence in school.

Children with low self-esteem may show anhedonia, depression, irritability, moodiness, and explosive tempers. Research with depressed adults suggests a separation between the state of depression and self-evaluation because antidepressant chemotherapy may improve emotional well-being without altering one's self-evaluation (Rush, 1982). Depression, therefore, may be more related to loss of self-esteem than negative self-evaluation.

DISABILITIES IN SELF-CONCEPT

One's self-concept is deeply ingrained. People behave in a fashion consistent with their own pictures of themselves and interpret contradictions of their self-concept as threats. Furthermore, one's actions are based on what one believes one is, not what one actually is. One's assumptions about oneself may be true or false and vary in stability, clarity, accuracy, and verifiability—but they are decisive (Rosenberg, 1979). A self-concept that accurately reflects one's capacities and limitations makes it possible to accept the frustrations that accompany the inevitable errors involved in schoolwork. In contrast an unrealistic self-concept impedes dealing with these challenges.

Disturbances in self-concept are related to defects in self-image and to distortions in the concept of one's disability.

Defects in Self-Image

A child's capacity to view oneself as a coherent person depends upon developing a body image as a whole body in space and as invariant in time. Four patterns can be identified in which this has not occurred. The first consists of children who lack a self-image of continuity in time, because they have experienced multiple separations from attachment figures. The second consists of children whose self-images are split into good and bad parts, because they were accepted when they were good and rejected when bad. The third is comprised of children who have been conditioned to be compliant replicas of their parents' expectations of them. The fourth consists of children with borderline character disorders whose self-images are incomplete and fragmented.

Lack of Self-Image Continuity

Through the bonds of attachment, young children turn to their parents for protection when helpless in the face of the dangers of the external world and from their drives, especially hostility (Solnit, 1982). When an attachment bond is disrupted, however, helplessness is evoked as the loved parent becomes a fading memory, and a part of the child's self-image is lost. The loss of an attachment figure may then produce aggressive behavior that demands limit setting. Only later with reattachment is affection possible. When separations are repeated as through multiple foster-home placements, each subsequent opportunity for attachment is less promising and leaves the child more vulnerable and less able to develop and sustain the previous level of attachment.

After several attachment bond disruptions and efforts to reattach, a young child may lose the capacity to trust adults and depend upon the stability of their environments. Such a child can only count on immediate gratifications and attention. Repression of the painful past, lack of complete integration in the present family, and fear of the future prevent the development of a stable self-image that bridges the past and the future. These children may be restless and unable to concentrate. They provoke responses of any kind from their environments in order to obtain the attention they need to feel like a coherent whole person.

More specifically children vary in the continuity and differentiation of their body images, with resulting variations in their ability to regulate body movements smoothly. There is a continuum of relating the body image to tempos of body actions. The developmentally immature end is illustrated by the child who has only global images of the body in static or dynamic postures. When the body is in motion, this child perceives little differentiation between slow and fast body movements and does not regulate them appropriately. At the developmentally mature end is the child who has highly differentiated images of the body and its parts and can differentiate body tempos and show the capacity for delay of movement (Santostefano, 1978).

Split Self-Image

If children are treated inconsistently and capriciously and are not experienced by their parents as the same person both when obedient and when disobedient, they do not develop a consistent, unified self-image, but are split into good and bad parts. For example, a child may be unable to recognize that one is the same person when one behaves badly and when one is good (Horowitz & Zilberg, 1983).

A split in a child's self-image can take the form of experiencing the imagery of conflicting voices. For example, children may hear one part of them encourage them to "goof off" and another part urge them to apply themselves in schoolwork. In extreme cases the parts may be perceived as hallucinated voices. Such children may experience their bad part as the devil and their good part as an angel. As a result they are unable to construct coherent configurations of themselves or the external world (Devereaux, 1966). They lack self-confidence, fear failure, and anticipate rejection. Some react defensively with an indifferent attitude and others retreat into "Walter Mitty" daydreams (Stewart et al, 1973).

When distressing emotions are overwhelming, they may be split off from conscious awareness by the defense mechanism of repression. The state in which an individual generally is not able to experience consciously emotions and imagery is referred to as alexithymia. More specifically conscious awareness of anxiety-laden internal stimuli from body organs may be repressed, so that all or parts of the body image may be split off from consciousness awareness. The sequestered part of the self-image may then distort character development.

Through the defense mechanism of reaction formation, overt behavior becomes the opposite of unconscious dispositions. The overt behavior may be disguised, as in the moralist who draws upon absolute standards of propriety, and the compulsive checker who is dominated by rigid lists of behaviors. In these instances gross, undifferentiated, and highly aversive hostile unconscious attributes are repressed with a consequent polarized split between overt socially acceptable and covert socially unacceptable dispositions (Hamilton, 1983).

The "false" self described by Winnicott is another example in which the "true" self is buried by a compliant "false" superstructure (Davis & Wallbridge, 1981). Some parents fail to respond to an infant's needs and instead substitute their own expectations with which the infant must comply. This compliance is the earliest stage of the "false self" through which an infant builds a false self-image reflected in literal compliance with parental demands. The deferred "true self" remains primitive and unintegrated. These children may be successful in school because of their compliance. They have learned only to be reactive, however, and have not developed well-grounded self-images. These children may have an intellectual awareness, but not a conviction, of their existence (Lichtenstein, 1977). Their compliance with a world that is solely to be fitted into results in a sense of futility, and their "true selves" remain underdeveloped. In school they may be driven overachievers.

Fragmented Self-Image

Children with "borderline" characters fluctuate between neurotic and psychotic states, depending upon the degree of stress experienced (Robson, 1983). They have difficulty tolerating anxiety, controlling anger, delaying gratification, containing frightening imagery, and channeling impulses appropriately. Their interpersonal behavior varies from superficial sociability to withdrawal (Bemporad, 1982).

An integrated self is experienced as confidence in one's continuity over time and between different role interactions. In contrast a child with a poorly integrated self experiences fluctuating states of being that depend upon current environmental input with little carryover betwen them. Such a child also has difficulty empathizing with others, who are regarded alternately as good or bad rather than as consistent persons who may be rewarding or frustrating (Kernberg, 1975).

These children have character structures fixated at the symbolic-representational level, between the ages of 18 months and three and a half years, so that their critical unresolved issues revolve around individuation, reality analysis, and self-image formation. Emotions are experienced as diffuse and overwhelming in the form of distress, depression, rage, or terror. They have not progressed to automatic levels of functioning, so that symbols must be consciously understood and manipulated. Psychological defenses are brittle, sweeping, or absent, resulting in psychotic decompensations.

Thus borderline children are erratic in most functional areas. Their thresholds of responsiveness are low, focusing of attention is weak, and concentration is poor. Their movement levels are high because of anxiety and boredom, which may accentuate a constitutional tendency in that direction. Their cognitive styles fluctuate between field dependence and independence and internal and external loci of control. Specific deficits in auditory-temporal processing, visual processing, and directional orientation may be present, in addition to inadequate concepts of conservation and classification. They fix on superficial aspects of perception and fail to extract essential categorical characteristics. They are attracted to the irrelevant, reflecting an inability to organize precepts and concepts hierarchically. As a consequence, they have difficulty generalizing from one situation to another.

Borderline children's inpulse control is generally weak, and their analytic function is erratic, producing lapses in reality testing. Their thinking is impaired by poor synthesis, so that they have difficulty integrating parts into wholes. Their time sense may be unreliable so that they experience situations as disconnected rather than cumulative (Greenspan, 1979b). Their syncretic thinking precludes engaging adequately with learning basic work skills and inhibits curiosity and creativity. They have difficulty in making decisions and solving problems. They lack automatic thinking, and their implementation and verification of their actions are erratic.

Most significantly these children have not formed distinct self-images and remain incompletely differentiated from their parents. They are uncertain about who they are and what they want. As their self-images are not completely separate from other persons, loss of the approval of others means complete loss of their selves (Malerstein & Ahern, 1982). It is difficult for them to establish and maintain a sense of inner cohesiveness, causing vulnerability to regression (Meissner, 1978).

When early parent–child relationships are not pleasurable, as when a parent is unable to respond to an infant's internal drives and rhythms, the internal and external stimuli of the nurturing and feeding process can become sources of distress. Because an infant remains dependent on the parent for survival, a negatively charged parent image is incorporated, but not integrated, into the self, and a schism exists between imagery of the child's internal urges and the externally generated negative mother image.

These children are torn between ambivalent feelings and attitudes that lead them to relate alternately to and withdraw from reality. There is a conflicting wish for, and fear of, merging with others. The resulting behavior may vary from autistic withdrawal to provocative demanding (Silver, 1979). Their self-evaluation rises and falls quickly, and they lack self-esteem.

Borderline children experience major problems in school. The dependent learning role in school activates distressing infantile helplessness, which leads to rejection of the submission implied in instruction. They are dominated by their own distorted version of relations with people and events. The inadequate development of the synthetic managerial function leads to bewilderment in learning tasks because of difficulty in organizing work. They are scattered in their attention, because they lack the ability to organize what they see, hear, touch, feel, smell, and taste in order to make sense of their environments (Smith, 1980). They must be taught what to look for, what to ignore, and how to put things together. They are uneven, inconsistent, unpredictable, and a puzzle to adults around them.

A state of acute identity confusion may result during postadolescence from the demands to achieve intimacy, make an occupational choice, energetically compete, and define one's self (Erikson, 1959). Rather than reflecting underlying defects in one's self-image, this relatively common state is an exaggeration of the vicissitudes of normal development.

Distorted Concept of Disability

A realistic self-concept for children with disabilities is particularly crucial to their success in school (Osman, 1982). A confused, unclear, or frightening concept of one's disability may cause a variety of defensive reactions.

A child's sense of defect may or may not correspond to the actual mental or physical defect (Coen, 1986). For example, some children exaggerate their sense of being defective in order to reassure their parents that they indeed are the cause of parental anxiety or depression.

A common concept of one's disability is that it means one is helpless or incompetent (Aleksandrowicz & Aleksandrowicz, 1987; Jones, 1983). This may be expressed directly through dependency or indirectly

through withdrawal and avoidance of responsibility. A child who regards oneself as helpless is likely to be seen as helpless by others, confirming that self-concept.

A poorly defined concept of one's body and its capabilities not only hinders the control of the body but also awareness of others. For example, a cerebral palsied boy with a distorted concept of his body in space may have difficulty finding his classroom, his desk, or his locker, and bump into people or objects in the process. When he also is anxious about becoming lost or appearing clumsy or foolish, he must devote additional attention to the functioning of his body in space and consequently less attention to the expectations of others (Kronick, 1981).

A young adult revealed in psychotherapy the impact on his self-concept of having been treated with stimulant medication through much of his childhood:

> I was enraged at my parents for giving me Ritalin to push down my feelings and make me sedated. I also was angry at my mother for not comforting me and my father for not encouraging me. Now one part of me wants to do well, but another part of me tells me I am hyperactive. Then I say to myself that I'm hyperactive, and I can't do it.

On the other hand, a realistic self-concept of disability can help a child adapt. As one boy put it:

> I used to cry when kids made fun of me, and I hadn't done anything to hurt them. Now I view my disability as a hurdle to get over. I used to feel sorry for myself. Then I noticed other people more closely. They dropped pencils, too. The kids made fun of that other boy who got low grades, too. He tried to laugh it off. I didn't laugh at him. Instead of sitting in special education and pitying myself, now I want to be out there in a regular class with everyone else.

Children react to dyslexias in a variety of ways. An adult recalled feeling as a child that her skull housed an unruly brain because she had difficulty controlling what she wanted to say, read, and write (Simpson, 1979). She also tried to conceal her difficulty by acting as the class clown. She described the phenomenon of "passing," which is concealing one's dyslexia but with a fear of being exposed. Shame and embarrassment are common consequences of dyslexia (Kris, 1983). This often is related to confusion and misunderstanding in the family and school of the child with dyslexia as illustrated by the following case:

During her psychiatric evaluation at the age of 22, Mary discovered that her father and a paternal uncle had spelling and writing difficulties similar to her's. Her mother appeared to be discovering for the first time that Mary was dyslexic.

Further inquiry revealed a longstanding conspiracy of silence in which Mary was taken to a reading clinic in the fourth grade because of her teacher's concern about her poor schoolwork. She was found to be reading at grade level, but her spelling and writing were deficient. This was not discussed with Mary. Later she could recall herself at the blackboard feeling humiliated, scared, and caught, because she could not remember the words on the spelling list. A voice was saying "but you just knew it." She felt angry at herself for not knowing. Then she felt helpless, stupid, panicky, and like crying—but she did not. Some days she could remember how to spell words and other days not. She recalled writing a story intently. Her teacher told her that she was not neat, and her spelling was bad. Since then she felt she could not write. She pretended that her hand that was having trouble writing was not her's. If she realized it was her's, she felt sad and angry, because she couldn't make it do what she wanted it to do.

When Mary came home in tears because of her frustrations in school, her mother told her that she had nothing wrong with her, but behind the scenes talked with teachers about getting tutoring, which never materialized. Instead she elegantly decorated Mary's bedroom. Retrospectively Mary felt that her mother put a wall around her. She knew that she was not normal but did not know if she could trust her perceptions.

At the age of 22, Mary felt like she was disconnected from everyone living in a glass bubble. She was afraid to expose her feelings. She could hear a voice telling her patronizingly to "sit down in that chair and don't cry. You can do what everyone else does."

A child who has difficulty understanding abstract concepts has difficulty conceptualizing a self that presents different faces in different situations. The child may feel, for instance, that displaying socially acceptable behavior is duplicity because it does not reflect one's true beliefs. That child also may construe failure in school as obliterating successes in other areas.

Children with seizure disorders need help in developing realistic self-concepts. Almost half of school-age children with seizure disorders have significant learning or behavior problems related in part to defensive reactions caused by an inadequate understanding of their seizures, compounded by adult reluctance to encourage their independence (Holdsworth & Whitmore, 1974). Some children with seizures become defensively preoccupied with bodily functioning because of their fear of sudden death (Nordan, 1976). Others may think that their seizures are contagious, feel personally responsible for them, be embarrassed by being seen having them, fear recurrences, and fear losing their minds.

Each child with a seizure disorder should receive objective explanations of the condition, together with realistic reassurance. At the same time, appropriate precautions should be advised, such as avoiding heights and sleeping in upper bunks, and using the buddy system in potentially dangerous activities, such as swimming and bicycle riding. Family members, caretakers, teachers, and school nurses should be advised about the nature of a child's seizures. For grand mal seizures, first aid is nonintervention except to assist the child to a lying position on one side to prevent aspiration of vomited material and gently extending the neck to maximize opening of the airway. A medical information bracelet or card also is indicated (Herskowitz & Rosman, 1982).

SELF-EVALUATION DISTORTIONS

The schemes of self-images are constructed through accommodation to, or identification with, significant adults during one's childhood. Children's feelings toward these externally influenced self-images are influenced by their attitudes toward the persons whom they represent (Cotton, 1983). Thus identifications based upon love tend to create self-images with positive evaluations, whereas identifications based upon fear tend to have negative self-evaluations. Furthermore other significant people in children's immediate school and community environments influence their evaluation of self-images (Rosenberg, 1979).

When desired self-concepts are realized, positive self-evaluation results and opens the way to further modification of the self-concepts. In general children who believe they can control their lives and are self-confident outperform peers who lack such a belief (Eisenberg, 1979). When desired self-concepts are unattainable, however, negative self-evaluation results, tending to close off modification of their actual self-concepts. This tendency is illustrated even in the classical behavioral conditioning of animals in which failure produces an internal inhibition, as if the animal learns to expect failure and helplessness (Seligman, 1975).

A negative self-evaluation may unrealistically exaggerate the difference between the ideal and actual self, so that actual characteristics may be much closer to the ideal than the child realizes because of self-depreciation. This is particularly the case with compulsive children who are prone to depression. Other children may actively provoke disapproval in order to confirm their negative self-evaluations. They feel that they are bad persons, so that they might as well act that way. These children block, discourage, or openly attack kindness or praise as undeserved. Some abused children vividly illustrate this picture. Low self-evaluations in these children results from parental devaluation of them through abuse and from identification with their violent, often ineffective parents (Cotton, 1983).

Negative self-evaluations that underlie self-defeating behavior can be seen as having three fundamental determinants when masochism becomes a character trait. First, masochism may originate in an infantile painful state of helplessness in which the child is unable to relieve tension. Second, there is injury to the child's narcissism by a repetitively enraged, sadistic parent figure. Third, an attempt is made to control the sadistic parent by incorporating the parent into the self-as-actor through identification with the aggressor. In this way the child's self-as-actor negatively evaluates the self-as-object, as the parent did the child (Rothstein, 1983).

Children's attitudes toward failure influence whether they seek or avoid challenges and persist in the face of obstacles. Children who believe they are irrevocably inept, clumsy, or dumb may attribute their failures to themselves and their successes to others. When convinced of their inability to perform, they expect to fail, so that failure comes to be predictable. Their failures reinforce their evaluation of themselves as incompetent, which results in further failure. Then they react to difficulties as though they were insurmountable, interpret their errors as reflecting insufficient ability, and show increasing impairment of their problem-solving abilities. They question their ability in the face of obstacles, down-play past successes, and perceive future effort as futile (Dweck & Bempechat, 1983). Parents, peers, and teachers also hold decreasing expectations of success for them (Kronick, 1981).

The following case illustrates how a family situation was the major factor in exaggerating the impact of individual differences in written language functions on the self-evaluation of a young boy:

> A nine-year-old fourth-grade student was referred to a child psychiatrist because of underachievement, failing to turn in assignments, unhappiness, lack of friends, and a mild visual-spatial dyslexia.
>
> Brad's parents divorced when he was two years old. Over the years he had occasional visits with his father, whom he idealized even though his father did not show consistent interest in him. Brad felt that he was not good enough to deserve his father's attention; this fostered his negative self-evaluations.
>
> In psychotherapy the focus was on helping Brad to accept the relationship with his father as it really was rather than as he imagined it to be. Brad revealed that he actually despised his father. His idealized father image concealed hatred and resentment, which he had turned against himself. He also discovered that his father and a paternal uncle had reading difficulty. More comfortable acceptance of his visual-spatial distortions resulting from a more realistic self-evaluation made it possible for him to overcome his academic difficulties.

Schools play an important role in determining children's self-evaluations. Chil-

dren learn how helpless or how effective they are in school. During the early grades, children form evaluations of themselves as students. Because reading is pivotal in the early school years, a child's reading ability strongly influences that child's self-evaluation. A child with difficulty reading can handle it in various ways. For example, a boy may strain prodigiously so that simply by sitting in class, listening to other children read, and paying careful attention to the printed page, he can read the whole page by memory. If confronted by similar words arranged in a slightly different order, however, he may be unable to read them. More commonly a child confronted with failure in reading becomes disinterested in all schoolwork. Other children, although troubled by their academic misadventures, manage to sustain positive self-evaluations and compensate for their disabilities. When they stimulate the development of character strengths and talents, functional disabilities even can contribute to an individual's accelerated or precocious development.

Some children believe that intelligence is displayed through performance so that judgments of their schoolwork indicate their intelligence. They are inclined toward seeking positive judgments and avoiding negative ones and toward performance goals that involve "looking smart." Other children are mastery oriented and intensify effort in the face of difficulty. They view the skill required by a task as one they can acquire by applying themselves and giving themselves the time to do so. They regard intelligence as something that is increased through their own efforts. They are inclined toward seeking to increase their skills and "becoming smarter" rather than "looking smarter" (Dweck & Bempechat, 1983).

Neurotic children have achieved the concrete-work operational stage of development and have autonomous, inner-directed selves. They tend to be concerned with more than immediate goals and to be trusting and trustworthy. Their psychopathology results from guilt that interferes with their potent mastery of schoolwork (Malerstein & Ahern, 1982).

Whereas shame and disgust are easily recognized, this is not so with guilt, which appears in numerous forms, such as a feeling of dull inner tension, that may lead to a courting of the favor of others and exaggerated helpfulness. It also may appear as an anticipation of impending disaster, a feeling of inferiority, a wish to be punished, or a wish to sacrifice oneself (Nunberg, 1955).

Guilt may be a reaction to the fear of punishment, when primitive aggressive instinctual demands are not renounced. The internal source of guilt grows on the basis of ambivalence, so that the more intense a child's attachment is to a person, the greater is the fear of losing the love of that person and the greater the guilt. Guilt appears to be one of the products of the ongoing struggle between the affiliative and aggressive instincts. Guilty children suffer inhibitions in the performance of schoolwork under stress, such as recitation and test taking. Neurotic symptoms appear in the form of phobias, obsessions, and compulsions, although there also may be diffuse anxiety that has not been transformed into a specific symptom.

In another vein the lack of experience in coping with failure contributes to low self-evaluations. An overindulged existence during early childhood preserves infantile omnipotence that leads to inordinate frustration by failure. Unless children confront and master frustration by their personal actions, they have an impoverished evaluation of their own competence. It is only when children successfully match their abilities to higher standards that their strengths emerge. Children with high self-evaluations tend to come from backgrounds with explicit, attainable standards, whereas children with low self-evaluations may not have had such standards to measure themselves against (Seligman, 1975). At the same time, a child learns more through success than error, more through pleasure than pain, more through experience than suggestion, and more through suggestion than direction.

Self-evaluations develop reciprocally between baby and parent as a baby relinquishes infantile omnipotence by accepting nurturance and patterning from the parent. When a parent smiles in response to a baby's smile, the gleam in the parent's eye signals acceptance and positive evaluation to the baby. When the baby sees a blank expression, there is no reciprocity and no sense of acceptance. In this situation reciprocal interaction may be sought through any means that will evoke it. When the only way of achieving parental attention is through a baby's distress, the conditioned result is an uncomfortable, ambivalent parent–child interaction. The baby's reaction is as if "I wish you would think I am the best. Since you do not, I will make you pay attention to me." Since that kind of parent is unlikely to reward the actual capacities of the child, the child remains fixed in a position of omnipotently demanding attention and eliciting punishment, even though distressing. The omnipotence and omniscience of infancy then is not tempered by the give and take of reciprocity between parent and child. These children later may use lying, self-deception, and grandiose tales of achievement to gain attention without responding to deterrence by punishment. Similarly, stealing within a home may be a means of gaining parental attention even though punitive.

The experience of inadequacy and helplessness may give rise to a wish to become competent in realistic areas. On the other hand, the self-evaluation of being "dumb, damaged, and inadequate" may alternate with the opposite feelings of mastery and power in exaggerated grandiose form (Cohen, 1985). The following case example of a 13-year-old boy illustrates how omnipotence can be a defense against helplessness:

> Most of the time I try to perform in a way to look normal. I watch myself from within my head. I want to feel safe. I don't want everyone to call me names and make me feel self-conscious, helpless, weak, and like crawling home to mother. Sometimes I imagine that I'm better than everyone else. I know what everyone else should do and try to boss them. I even think I can control the minds of others.

A variety of studies have been devoted to sibling order as a factor in one's self-evaluation. For example, one study suggested that middle-born children, especially if spaced apart by two years from adjacent siblings, had significantly lower self-evaluations (Kidwell, 1982). Thus a child's siblings may contribute to a self-concept of ineptitude and a negative self-evaluation. For example, a five-year-old boy who could not pump a swing as well as his three-year-old sister could felt inferior to her. As time went on, the boy shunned learning tasks and preserved infantile omnipotence by avoiding comparisons with other children through the distracting power of his passive–aggressive behavior (Weil, 1977).

MANIPULATIVE INTERPERSONAL SYNDROMES

The self system is the interface between the person and others. To the extent that the self is differentiated from but retains an investment in others, empathy is possible. The capacity for empathy is an important prerequisite for rewarding personal relationships. If one is unable to appreciate another person's viewpoint and feelings, inevitable clashes, misunderstandings, and disappointments result. Other persons are then regarded as objects to be manipulated rather than as collaborators in life. In turn these children are regarded by others as "lazy," "putting on," and "pulling my leg."

In developing interpersonal relationships, a child must learn to use three fundamental forms of relating (Feiring, 1983): (1) moving toward people and the ability to want and give affection, (2) moving against people and the ability to fight, and (3) moving away from people and the ability to keep to oneself. While most children can use all three modes in dealing with stressful situations, others cannot because of conflict between dependency upon and rebelling against authority figures. Such children have repressed hostility toward their parents because of their dependency and fear of retaliation. The manner in which these hostile and dependent strivings are handled influences the character development of these children through fantasies that hover just beneath conscious awareness, like phantoms. These inappropriate illusions shape behavior that evokes corresponding responses from other people and actualizes underlying hostile and dependent wishes (Sandler, 1981). Thus children may act out unconscious illusions from the past, or elsewhere in the present, in current life situations. This preoccupation with the manipulation of other persons can seriously interfere with the performance of schoolwork.

Character structures bind anxiety in the same sense as do neurotic symptoms. Through their roots in bodily functions, character structures can form armoring against both unconscious drives and the outside world (Reich, 1972). The armoring of character structures takes place by the repression of bodily sensations and is expressed through rigid tension in the body musculature of erogenous zones. Thus chronic muscular tension inhibits bodily sensations of pleasure and distress.

The character armoring of oral eroticism may be expressed through personality traits based upon passivity and the expectation of entitlement to personal gratification. The armoring of anal eroticism may produce an exaggerated external locus of control and leads to personality traits involving struggles for power with others. The armoring of urethral eroticism may inhibit focused aggressiveness and lead to personality traits that avoid competitiveness. Fantasies associated with these repressed drives shape behavior that reenacts infantile relationships in current situations and evokes corresponding responses from other people. The resulting personality traits are compromises between underlying drives and the fear of expressing them. These personality traits are like neurotic symptoms, because they permit the disguised appearance of forbidden unconscious wishes, but the discomfort is perceived by others rather than by the child.

Fixation can be defined as a repetitive yearning that recapitulates an earlier period of intense drive satisfaction. Acting out is behavior that expresses a fixation without conscious awareness. Trauma can be defined as a distressing experience that has not been mastered by operative accommodation; instead the distressing imagery appears to be sequested in memory through figurative accommodation. The repetition compulsion is the tendency to seek the reenactment of traumatic experiences in attenuated forms in response to present-day situations. Both fixation through acting out and trauma through repetition compulsion rivet the past to the present and influence character development.

Immature character structures are reflected in habitual patterns of reacting based upon degrees of fixation and trauma at early stages of development. Their behavioral manifestations are persistent caricatures of behavior seen at a particular earlier stage of development. Because their character structures limit flexibility and prevent the age-appropriate sublimation of

drives, the children engage in patterns of behavior that are self-defeating, even though producing pyrrhic victories in the manipulations of other persons. Furthermore the capacity for empathy is impaired by these interpersonal maneuvers in which other persons are regarded as objects to be manipulated rather than as collaborators in life. As a consequence, these children fall short of assuming age-appropriate responsibility for their lives.

Thus there is an important interpersonal manipulative element in many school learning problems, especially for children with narcissistic, dependent, oppositional, and passive–aggressive personalities. The narcissistic child feels entitled to complete effortless gratification. The dependent child helplessly clings to adults. The oppositional child openly resists adult influence. The passive–aggressive child overtly complies, while covertly sabotaging adult authority.

The Narcissistic Personality

As self love narcissism in itself is not pathological (Rothstein, 1983). Preadolescent children in particular show narcissism in the form of cognitive conceit, as they gradually relinquish the egocentric omniscience of earlier life. This is reflected in their preference for their own views over those held by adults. A much more intense investment in the veracity of their own ideas, however, is seen in children with narcissistic personality disorders that may result from a failure to resolve the rapprochement crisis of the toddler by realizing that parents are imperfect separate individuals with their own interests and gradually giving up the delusion of one's own grandiosity.

The immature state of narcissistic children's character development is reflected in their persistent syncretic merging of ideas, emotions, and actions. Their incomplete individuation leads them to assume that others are extensions of themselves.

If their ideas do not prevail through action, painful insult is experienced. They feel entitled to the adulation of others and to have their wishes granted. Because they believe that they are omnipotent and omniscient, they deny their weaknesses and lack of knowledge. They cannot bear to make mistakes, are intolerant of frustration, and are enraged by criticism. School may have little to offer them because they "know it all." Through the defense of projection, responsibility for their personal failures or unhappiness is attributed to others.

Older narcissistic children are conceited, self-centered, vain, and admiration seeking. At the same time they lack self-respect. Because love tends to overestimate the loved one, love and respect are different. One can love another person but not respect that person. The same applies to love of oneself. The narcissistic child may love, and consequently overestimate, oneself, however, that child lacks self-respect and seeks the adulation of others. When they do obtain the attention of others, they find an empty victory, because their own self-respect is not enhanced, and they feel that they have "fooled another one."

The grandiose lives of these children are on a collision course with the people around them (Noshpitz, 1984). They pursue self-destructive life courses based upon guilt, stimulated by their murderous rage at frustrating persons upon whom they also depend. Angry demandingness, prolonged screaming, and occasional violence mark them as exceptional from their earliest years. Narcissistic children can tolerate neither their own weaknesses nor the less than ideal nature of others of whom they are hypercritical. They feel entitled to the presence of ideal persons. Consequently, they are easily slighted and attack others as deficient or unfair. They show hostile behavior in school by reacting to authority with egocentric defiance, temper outbursts, and continual testing of limits. In addition to academic underachievement because of their uncooperative attitudes, they may be feared by teachers and other children when they lose control of their emotions.

The overall aim of treatment for the narcissistic child is achieving a capacity for empathy, so that awareness of the reciprocity of human relationships becomes possible. The specific targets of treatment are the child's omnipotence, omniscience, sense of entitlement, and attention seeking. The parents can be helped to recognize their adulating use of the child for their own aggrandizement. Behavioral interventions can be employed that set limits, teach frustration tolerance, and sensitize the child to the consequences of one's behavior upon others. This can be accompanied by efforts to help the child accept the realistic limitations of oneself and others. Psychotherapy with the child can expose the painful vulnerability that underlies the defenses of denial and projection.

A nine-year-old boy was initially referred because of underachievement in school, temper tantrums, and arrogant behavior. He refused to do schoolwork, which he regarded as boring. His parents regarded him as a gifted child and blamed the school for failing to stimulate him. He dominated two younger siblings.

In this case the treatment strategy over the course of two years emphasized family therapy, which exposed parental idolization of their son and subtle support of his arrogance with teachers and peers. When they became aware of the way in which their attitudes were backfiring and that their son actually was lagging in reading skills, the parents began to set firm limits, penalize failure to perform schoolwork, and arranged for reading tutoring because he had not applied himself in earlier reading instruction.

In family therapy the boy came to grips with his intolerance of making mistakes and exposing his vulnerability. Repeated, gentle confrontations by his therapist helped him to recognize the impact of his behavior upon others. He discovered that his behavior impeded fulfillment of his own selfish interests. His growing ability to acknowledge his lack of knowledge and skill made it possible for him to assume the role of student in school and accept the assistance of teachers and peers in reaching his goals. The recognition of his realistic role as an older brother permitted him to relinquish exercising illegitimate power over his younger siblings.

The Dependent Personality

The essential feature of the dependent personality is passively manipulating others into assuming responsibility for major areas of one's life. These children depend upon others in order to avoid having to be self-reliant. Such children behave immaturely and resort to clinging demanding of attention from adults. They abdicate responsibility for making decisions about how to dress, what to eat, what to do, and with whom to associate. They fear taking the initiative and assuming responsibility for themselves.

These children show a conspicuous absence of deliberate intention and sustained activities. They lead unplanned lives and drift with the prevailing current (Shapiro, 1965). For them knowing signifies independence, and thinking for themselves signifies growing up and assuming responsibility. Both of these are perceived as dangers that stimulate anxiety and block the learning process. There is an obvious pattern of parental overprotection in many of these families. The parents also inappropriately may regard the child as damaged because of physical defect.

A particular type of dependent personality has been described in the literature as "pseudoimbecility," pseudobackwardness," "pseudostupidity," and "learning impotence." The children manifesting the syndrome conceal knowledge through ineptitude in schoolwork, but appear to be indifferent to their failures and actually wield power over adults by their dependent behavior (Westman & Bennett, 1985). These children wish to return to an earlier age, when the satisfaction of their needs was the responsibility of parents. At the core of the child's clinical picture is a vivid fantasy life epitomized by the Peter Pan theme, which enables the child to resolve internal and external conflicts through imagined magical powers. These children depend upon others for direction. For example, one boy had to be reminded to get up in the morning, get dressed, catch the bus, take out his pencil in class, work on his lesson, take books home, do his homework, take a shower, and go to bed. None of these things would be done without prompting. In spite of all this, he failed in school.

In the typical family pattern of learning-impotent boys, the mother exercises covert power in the family and is controlling and seductive and unwittingly rewards the child's failure (Peck & Stackhouse, 1973). The father does not participate in growth-producing experiences with his child and depreciates the child's abilities. Although appearing dominant and threatening, he typically lacks self-confidence and is easily manipulated by his wife and children. The boys are in competition with their father for their mother's attention. The sons submit helplessly to their mothers and sacrifice themselves to their fathers by appearing nonthreatening, but they covertly achieve an "oedipal victory" by shaming their fathers. By destroying themselves, they also may be attempting to destroy a parasitic mother image within them. A reverse family pattern is seen with girls. The girls are in competition with their mothers, whom they shame, for their father's attention through helplessness.

The aim of treatment with the dependent child is achieving independent responsibility for oneself. The principal target is the infantile magical fantasy that permits the child to expect smugly the care of others. Marital couple therapy usually is necessary in order to unravel the parental dynamics that contribute to the child's oedipal victory. When the parents relinquish their overprotectiveness and reduce the rewards of helplessness and the fear of assuming age-appropriate responsibility, behavioral techniques that desensitize the child to feared activities and places and produce rewards for asssuming personal responsibility can be used. A useful aphorism is that to become responsible as an adult at 21, a child should be one-third responsible at age seven and two-thirds responsible at age 14 (Finch & Green, 1979). Psychotherapy can focus on exposing the child's fears of aggressive impulses and growing up.

> An eight-year-old girl was referred because of her failure to turn in schoolwork, forgetfulness, tardiness, general ineptitude, and enuresis. Although she was of high average intelligence, her teachers thought that she performed academically as though she were mildly mentally retarded.
>
> The overall course of treatment encompassed three years and involved family therapy, marital couple therapy, and individual psychotherapy with the girl. Family therapy disclosed a pattern in which the child literally had to be reminded to carry out each routine of daily living. Her parents believed that if they did not prod her and do things for her, she would be incapable of doing anything. They believed that she was brain damaged because of febrile seizures during infancy. Her father dominated the household, and her mother curried his favor while overprotecting her daughter.
>
> An intervening four-month course of marital couple therapy was necessary in order to shift the parents' displacement of their own marital problems upon their daughter. Family therapy then could deal

> with the self-fulfilling prophesy in which the child was realizing her parents' picture of her as helpless and ineffective. The parents began to permit their daughter to experience the consequences of their relinquishing control over her life. She kept her own record of her achievements, at first at the level of simply dressing and toileting. Bell and pad biofeedback training eliminated her enuresis. In psychotherapy she revealed her wish to remain a young child, because she feared growing up and assuming responsibility for herself. As she overcame her fear of success, she began to experience satisfaction in personal mastery and achievement in school. By the fifth grade, she was able to perform at grade level in school.

The Oppositional Personality

The essential feature of the oppositional personality is a pattern of disobedient, negativistic, and provocative opposition to authority figures, especially parents and teachers. It has been regarded as a precursor of the passive–aggressive personality, although it is seen in its characteristic form throughout childhood.

These children display an oppositional attitude, even when contrary to their own interests and well-being. For example, if there is a rule, it is violated; if a suggestion is made, the child is against it; if asked to do something, the child refuses or becomes argumentative; and if asked to refrain from an act, the child feels obligated to carry it out. The children do not regard themselves as oppositional but see others as making unreasonable demands upon them. When thwarted they may have temper tantrums.

During the first year of life, developmental oppositional behavior in response to painful situations protects an infant through recoiling from noxious influence and gaining time for recovery, such as in passive resistance to being awakened and active resistance to being fed. In the process of later individuation, the capacity to resist external influence enables a child to develop inner resources. Thus developmental oppositional behavior prior to the third year of life actually is not hostile, but protective and self-defining (Levy, 1955).

When personality traits are oriented around opposition, however, a child negativistically defines the self in terms of what one is against rather than what one is for. As a characterological defense negativism spawns contrariness, rigidity, and social isolation rather than independent self-control and self-esteem. Interpersonal relationships for these children consequently revolve around issues of control.

Rousseau eloquently described the genesis of the oppositional personality:

> At some point a child may recognize that tears have the effect of bringing adult attention. At this point the child's interest in getting things which others provide is transformed into a desire to control the person who provides those things. Concern with physical needs is transformed into a passion to control the will of adults. Tears become commands and frequently no longer are related to real needs but only to testing power. The child becomes aware of will and knows that wills, as opposed to necessity, are subject to command. Some children quickly learn that control over people is more useful than adaptation to things. Every wish that is not fulfilled could, in the child's imagination, be fulfilled if the adult only willed it that way. These children, therefore, seek power over people rather than the use of things. The children learn to see intention to do wrong in what opposes them. They become avengers. If they get what they want, they are masters. If they fail, they are angry, resentful, and likely to become slavish. In either event they enter into a dialectic of mastery and slavery which will occupy them for their whole lives. Their natural and healthy self-love and self-esteem give way to a self-love relative to other people's opinions of them; henceforth they can esteem themselves only if others esteem them. Ultimately they make the impossible demand that others care for them more than they care for themselves. This is one of the few distinctively human phenomena (no animal can be insulted); and from it flow anger, pride, vanity, resentment, revenge, jealousy, indignation, rebelliousness, and almost all the other passions that give poets their themes (Bloom, 1978).

The principal aim of treatment for the oppositional child is achieving individuation as an autonomous person. The therapeutic targets are the child's power-seeking contrariness and defiance. Through family therapy the parents can identify their own ambivalence, which embroils them in fruitless power struggles with the child. The parent–child struggles can be defused through behavioral techniques that place responsibility upon the child for decision making. This can be done by giving the child options from which to choose and minimizing confrontations. Ignoring oppositional behavior and rewarding cooperative behavior also are helpful in defusing interpersonal conflict, as are framing statements that provide rationales and consequences for behavioral expectations. Psychotherapy with the child can focus on the development of self-boundaries and exposure of underlying indecisiveness and self-doubting.

> A seven-year-old boy was referred because of failing grades in school, uncooperativeness, negativism, and fighting with peers. At home he was argumentative and defiant. As a young child, he showed excessive separation reactions from his parents, but habitually opposed their authority.

After the initiation of family therapy, a longstanding pattern of parental arguments was disclosed. It became evident that the parents were generally critical of their son, constantly correcting and attempting to change him. After several months of therapy focused on parent–child relationships, the parents could see that they were reacting to the unacceptable parts of themselves reflected in their son. By monitoring each other, they then altered their approach to him from one of making demands to one of providing options from which he could choose. They also framed their expectations of him so that the rationale for his compliance would be clear to him.

The format of treatment then shifted to marital couple therapy and individual psychotherapy for the boy. Over the next year, the parents worked on resolving their own tendencies to project their unacceptable self-concepts upon each other. In his psychotherapy the boy revealed his own indecisiveness and lack of individuation from his mother. He divulged his fear that he would lose a battle of wills, and his own identity, if he submitted to her. As he acknowledged his appropriate dependency upon the therapist in the transference, he more appropriately accepted the influence of his parents and teachers. The overall course of treatment was two years, including a gradual termination phase. At that time he achieved at grade level in school. The family style of disagreement continued at a tolerable level consistent with the skepticism of his scientist parents.

The Passive–Aggressive Personality

The essential feature of the passive–aggressive personality is indirect resistance to the expectations of others, particularly authority figures. These children habitually resent demands to increase or maintain a given level of functioning. They usually are overtly compliant, while sabotaging adult expectations. This occurs most clearly in schoolwork in which their aim is to fail, a subtle but effective expression of their hostility toward adults.

These children react to the expectations of others by an automatic negative inner response. They tend to magnify the coercive aspect of situations and erroneously feel endangered by external demands. When they perceive an external expectation that they do something, conscious reluctance is experienced. Usually there is outward compliance but progressive inner resentment or annoyance grows. For example, leaving something undone represents a refusal to yield completely to a perceived demand. Boredom, fatigue, loss of interest, resentment, and fantasies about other activities that seem more desirable are experienced (Mallinger, 1982).

These children feel unfairly treated and habitually resent demands to perform schoolwork and resist indirectly through such maneuvers as procrastination, dawdling, stubbornness, deliberate inefficiency, and forgetfulness. They are late for classes, do not keep promises, forget to bring schoolwork, and do not complete tasks. They claim self-sufficiency but lack independent self-reliance. Their grades in school progressively slip downward.

Passive–aggressive behavior is self-defeating because it impairs productivity and interpersonal relationships and obliterates a sense of ownership of one's endeavors, culminating in a feeling of estrangement from running one's own life and a loss of a sense of volition. Life is experienced as a perpetual exertion of one's autonomy by undercutting others (Mallinger, 1982).

These children may have been confused by their own parents' sabotage of their performance through lack of confidence in them (McIntyre, 1964). As young children they may have been subjected to a barrage of prohibitions, warnings of danger, cautions, critical judgments, and discouragement of risk taking, exploration, and self-expression. Their own acceptability depended upon adhering to parental prohibitions and expectations. Thus their passive–aggressive behavior may have been the only safe way to express discontentment or hostility within a suppressive hierarchical family (Parsons & Wicks, 1983).

The overall aim in treating the passive–aggressive child is achieving sublimated channels for the expression of aggressive drives. The principal targets are the child's revenge-seeking behaviors that express underlying martyr and superhero fantasies. When the parents have been able to recognize and manage their own suppressive tendencies with their child, they can employ behavioral techniques that award progressively increasing responsibility to the child. Specifically they can foster personal successes for the child and sublimate aggressiveness by supporting the child in personally attractive activities, such as athletics or music. Psychotherapy with the child aims to expose underlying hostility and promote insight regarding the self-defeating nature of the child's sabotage of adult authority.

A ten-year-old boy was referred because he did not work in school and at home. His forgetfullness, stubbornness, procrastination, and carelessness frustrated his parents and teachers, who knew he could obtain high grades if he only would try to do so. As a young child, toilet training was prolonged, and he showed little interest in playing with other children.

Family therapy over the course of six months disclosed that the parents had held high expectations for their son and criticized his shortcomings from the time of school entry. His father had been a poor student in school and wanted his son to excell. Parental efforts to punish their son were unsuccessful and only resulted in further deterioration in school per-

formance. When the parents could see that their son was sabotaging their goals for him, they shifted their emphasis to realistic rewards for his achievements. Then family therapy sessions were held at monthly intervals and a reporting system was implemented in which the boy carried feedback between his teachers and parents on a day-by-day, subject-by-subject basis. This permitted recognition of achievements and more detailed knowledge of the aspects of schoolwork that were difficult, so that the parents became aware of the frustrations in their son's daily life, including those with peers.

During a subsequent 18-month course of psychotherapy, the boy revealed his paranoid stance, in which he felt that others were against him, thereby justifying his vengence. As he felt the support of his parents and teachers, he could acknowledge that he had fallen behind in academic skills and accept tutoring with the school's resource teacher to remedy them. He ultimately obtained passing grades in school and devoted himself to athletics.

SUMMARY

Because the self system is the essence of a person, it is taken for granted when functioning harmoniously. Disturbances in its functioning are reflected in distressing feelings of and about oneself. Moreover failures in its development can have devastating effects on one's ability to relate to other people as well.

Self-awareness extends consciousness to awareness of the self. Embarrassment, shame, and shyness are distressing emotional states of self-awareness. Relinquishing self-awareness can be anxiety provoking and impede immersion in schoolwork, especially reading.

Self-esteem is vulnerable during the early years of life and is undermined by parenting experiences that deprive children of a sense of personal mastery of themselves and the world. Children with low self-esteem have difficulty facing the challenges and frustrations of unfamiliar experiences inherent in schoolwork. Depression results from the interruption or loss of self-esteem.

An essential foundation for relating to oneself and the world is an accurate and stable self-concept that synthesizes knowledge of one's social and bodily characteristics. Self-concepts, however distorted, are tenaciously held in the face of challenge, even to one's own detriment. A child's self-image may lack continuity, be split into separate parts, be falsely compliant, or be fragmented. A child's concept of one's disability often is distorted. A specific issue for children with learning problems is forming an adaptive self-concept of disability. The syndrome of the borderline character illustrates the devastating effect of a fragmented self-image that results from incomplete individuation of a child from a parent with consequent unstable, fluctuating, and ambivalent self-evaluations.

Because one's self-evaluations have the power of emotions behind them, it is important that they be realistic. When one's self-evaluation is unrealistically high, the resulting omnipotence and omniscience may interfere with accepting instruction in school. When unrealistically low, helplessness may interfere with assuming responsibility for schoolwork. Negative self-evaluations that produce guilt can be responsible for neurotic symptoms that inhibit school performance or can motivate overachievement. Self-respect and self-confidence are important signs of maturity denied to many children who fail in schoolwork, because of what they both bring to and experience in school.

In addition to applying learning skills, schoolwork involves relationships with adults in authority and peers. Children who are preoccupied with interpersonal manipulations are diverted from effective performance in school. Children with narcissistic personalities seek attention and self-centered gratification. Dependent children with learning impotence conceal their knowledge and skills through their ineptitude based upon an underlying commitment to remaining a helpless, young child. Oppositional children dissipate their energies in struggles for control that preempt productivity in schoolwork. Passive–aggressive children are motivated to fail in school as a means of sabotaging adults.

Our knowledge of the influence of self-system problems in children's schoolwork is just beginning to have an impact on education and clinical practice. In the final analysis, for successful living in our complex society, the self is the most important of all functional systems of the central nervous system, because accurate self-knowledge is the key to overcoming barriers to learning in school.

VII

The Origins of Educational Disabilities and Handicaps

Each ego is endowed from the first with individual dispositions and trends . . .

Sigmund Freud, 1937

THE CONCEPT OF individual differences in children has a long history in psychology and education. It particularly is applicable to children who founder in school, when it is not possible to assign pathological causes to their problems. A child's self-concept then can be shaped around an understanding of the variety of ways in which people differ. By the same token, a pathological syndrome can be identified by characteristic symptoms, definable onset, clinical course, and prognosis. The implications of the syndrome can be incorporated in a child's self-concept and parental expectations. Knowledge of individual differences and pathologies is important in helping children in difficulty answer the question: "Why me?"

The prevention and management of children's learning problems in school depend upon an understanding of the ways in which dispositions in central nervous system functions are transformed into problems in school. Linking these dispositions to functional disabilities, educational disabilities, and educational handicaps can be facilitated by identifying the intermediate factors of learning style, level of self-development, and personality pattern, which altogether are expressed in children's work styles. By taking into account variations in children's learning styles early in their school careers and by ameliorating maladaptive personality patterns, inefficient work styles can be avoided. After school problems have appeared, an understanding of the origins of disabilities and handicaps offers clues to remedies for them.

27

Individual Differences and Pathology

What we call a white horse is not a white horse. It has grey
and black hairs. And a black horse has red and brown hairs.
Nothing is completely pure in nature.

Jean Renoir, 1954

Each brain is as unique as a fingerprint; no two are exactly alike. Each child also grows up under a unique set of circumstances that hold true for no other human being (Westman, 1973). With this potential for variability, it is remarkable that human beings have so much in common.

At the turn of the century, psychologists were concerned with individual differences in children. In 1908 Huey pointed out that reading was a skilled act like playing the piano and varied with the talent of the performer. People differ greatly in their feel for music, just as they differ in their interest in using words expressively. In 1911 Thorndike stated that there was no typical mind and that individuality is clearly manifest in children of school age. He pointed out that the same situation evokes widely differing responses in different children; the same task is done at differing speeds and with different degrees of success; and the same education produces different results.

In 1917 Bronner noted that children enter school without their teachers' awareness of their particular characteristics or idiosyncracies. Except when deviance from the rest of the class is so extreme as to attract attention, differences among members of the group remained largely unrecognized. Bronner then acknowledged that whatever information had been garnered about a child was lost the next year, as the class passed on to the next teacher. Seventy years later the situation has changed little, although psychological research has steadily increased our knowledge of individual differences (Royce & Powell, 1983).

In the light of the burdens imposed by taking individual differences into account, it is necessary to consider why they are important. In the broadest sense, differences between individuals are essential for the survival of species that provide parental care for their offspring. Individual characteristics permit parent and offspring to recognize each other, so that a lamb can find its own mother in a flock. Furthermore most species with bonding between its members show group-dominance hierarchies in which individuals must be able to recognize other individuals.

Humans have an additional advantage in their diversity of individual skills and social responses (Burnet, 1978). In the early hunting and gathering community, there was a leader, who could control the group, and deputies to take control in emergencies. The survival of the group was enhanced by members who had special skills in weapon making and use. For the rest the requirement was loyalty and obedience, courage in combat, and self-reliance in handling personal emergencies. A genetically based diversity in individuals, therefore, favored a group's survival.

The recognition of individuals is primarily by facial structure, but is reinforced by quality of voice, personality, and behavior. The combination defines the individual (Burnet, 1978). Even the external appearances of brains vary as much as people's faces. More precisely, the uniqueness of each individual can be identified not only in fingerprints but in profiles of biochemical constituents in the blood (Robertson et al, 1980)

Innate individual differences in humans are the most evident at the beginning and end of the life cycle. The strongest evidence for individual differences in newborns has been found in feeding patterns, sensory thresholds, autonomic responsiveness, distress states, and vigilance levels (Stratton, 1982b). Later children walk, talk, ride bicycles, and read at differing times related to variations in the rates of maturation of their brains. These variations persist throughout life, but are not as obvious until aging makes them evident again in the form of differing rates of memory loss, word-finding difficulty, and fragility in motor coordination. Most significantly these variations in aging adults are accepted as personal foibles, whereas in children they tend to be regarded as pathological.

The standards by which variations in human qualities are defined are an important issue. This raises the elusive question of normality, which can be viewed from at least four perspectives. Defining normality as the absence of pathology, discomfort, or disability has appeal because this is comparatively easy to measure. Defining normality as optimal functioning is more difficult because it necessitates a model of health. Normality as an average based on a statistical distribution curve of qualities has appeal for research purposes. Finally normality as the successful mastery of developmental stages offers the advantage of a changing concept that emphasizes adaptive strengths appropriate to one's age (Offer & Sabshin, 1984).

Actually standards of normality are not needed to define differences between persons, if we recognize the fact that each individual naturally differs from others (Westman, 1973). We can then simply describe an individual in terms of position on a continuum of a particular dimension without becoming entangled in ambiguous questions about normality. For example, Figure 27-1 illustrates the likely distribution of a population on the dimensions of IQ and energy-output level.

A useful conception of individual differences then is to describe a child on a particular dimension, such as threshold of responsiveness to tactile stimulation. The functional significance of that dimension can be determined by its relationship to adaptation through mastery of developmental tasks at particular stages. The judgments of adaptive or maladaptive can then be substituted for normal or abnormal. As an example, this was done with infants with high tactile thresholds, who were found to function more smoothly later in goal-oriented, frustrating situtations in nursery school than did infants with low thresholds. The implication was that high tactile thresholds had adaptive value for young children (Bell, 1971).

THE CONCEPTS OF INDIVIDUAL DIFFERENCES AND PATHLOGY

A conceptual problem arises when individual differences lead to maladaptive behav-

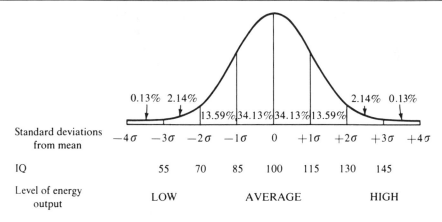

0.13%	2.14%	13.59%	34.13%	34.13%	13.59%		2.14%	0.13%

Standard deviations from mean -4σ -3σ -2σ -1σ 0 $+1\sigma$ $+2\sigma$ $+3\sigma$ $+4\sigma$

IQ   55   70   85   100   115   130   145

Level of energy output   LOW   AVERAGE   HIGH

Figure 27-1. Normal curve of distribution showing standard deviations from the mean, percentage of population in each area of the normal curve, and corresponding IQs and levels of energy output. (From *Human Development and Learning,* 2nd ed., by Hugh V. Perkins, © 1974 by Wadsworth Publishing Co., Inc. Used by permission of the publisher.)

ior at particular developmental stages. At that point the temptation is strong to think in terms of abnormality or pathology. Consequently, labels without scientific validity and with significant psychological impact are easily applied to children. The issues of normal–abnormal, variance–deviance, and intactness–defectiveness have implications for the attitudes of adults toward a particular child and that child's self-concept. Dealing with a self-concept of variance because of individual difference differs markedly from that of a self-concept of defect because of pathology. The distinction between individual differences and pathology in children, therefore, is important for scientific and psychological reasons (see Figure 27-2).

Individual differences are personal characteristics reflecting the cellular and chemical composition of the brain. They color development and are subject to change through learning. They are the results of interaction between maturation of the brain and environmental experience (Hartlage & Telzrow, 1985). In contrast pathology occurs in the form of discrete acute or chronic syndromes that stand out as disruptions in the developmental process with characteristic symptoms and signs, onset, clinical course, treatment, and prognosis. In addition the rhythms of body functions have pathologies in which oscillations in functions become irregular, such as heart arrhythmias, menstrual and other endocrine dysrhythmias, epileptic seizures, and dyskinesias (Garfinkel, 1984).

In the pathological model, maladaptive behavior that is not typically found in the course of development results from damage to brain tissue. The pathological model is best illustrated by a child with "hard" neurological signs that reflect demonstrable brain lesions. A genetically mediated cause of brain damage is seen in phenylketonuria in which there is a phenylalanine metabolic defect.

When one area of the brain is damaged subsequent to the acquisition of a skill, performance of that skill is impaired, and an acquired deficit results. The residues of brain lesions during early life, however, may be found later in "soft" neurological signs, or may not be manifest at all. As the

INDIVIDUAL DIFFERENCES	PATHOLOGY
Variations in universal characteristics	Disruptive characteristics as symptoms and signs
Emerge in course of development	Onset in time with clinical course and prognosis
Persistent	Change in clinical course

Caused by interplay of:
1) Heredity
  a) maturational rate
  b) intelligence
  c) specific mental qualities
  d) sexual dimorphism
2) Developmental Factors
  a) Prenatal
    i) neurobiotaxis
    ii) maternal diseases
    iii) maternal smoking
    iv) maternal alcoholic consumption
  b) Prematurity
  c) Tissue Destruciton
    i) birth trauma
    ii) head injuries
    iii) brain infection
  d) Malnutrition
  e) Experiential Usage
	Caused by events in time:
	1) genetic expression affecting brain
	2) disease
	3) trauma
	4) toxicants
	5) nutritional deficiencies
	6) psychic trauma and conflict
	7) irregular oscillations

Change through: 1) training 2) education 2) treatment of pathology 3) personal decision	Change through: 1) prevention 2) treatment of pathology
Self-concept of variance	Self-concept of defect

Figure 27-2. Individual differences and pathology as causes of functional disabilities.

brain matures, different areas take control over specific aspects of behavior in a predictable sequence and timing. When the damage is early and affects an area that has not yet begun to function, a child's behavior may not change at the time of the insult. Later, however, a delay, altered sequence, or deficit of a function may appear related to the earlier damage. Whereas adults with brain damage lose abilities they had prior to the insult, brain-damaged newborns may not demonstrably lose anything, but may fail to develop abilities related to the affected areas of the brain. All of this clouds application of the pathological model to specific children. Whether some have mild forms, or *formes frustes*, of clinical syndromes, thus, may be difficult to determine.

Many internal and external events interact to determine the effects of a brain lesion. The genetic endowment, past experience, motivation to learn new responses, and structural change in various parts of the brain before and after lesions all contribute to the central nervous system (CNS) functions observed at any given moment. The symptoms of brain damage do not necessarily reveal the functions of the damaged tissue, but more accurately reflect what the remaining areas of the brain can do after injury to a part. Furthermore electrical stimulation or neurotransmitter infusion of a particular area does not reveal the function of that area; it only causes responses of the system as a whole to abnormal conditions at that point.

The individual-difference model treats maladaptive behavior as arising from individual variations in the pattern and timing of the development of CNS functions typically seen during the course of development. These variations are maladaptive in the face of the demands schooling imposes upon the child (Levine, 1987). Individual variations of genetic, random, and developmental origin may be reflected in "soft" neurological signs. Neurological systems, other than the one in which signs are found, may be affected as well. For example, sensorimotor neurological signs may be accompanied by more general developmental immaturity that affects a child's performance in school.

In some instances it is not possible to establish that either the individual difference or the pathological model is more applicable. Whereas the presence of hard neurological signs supports the pathological model, a proponent of that model might conclude that their absence only means that the structural damage did not generate hard signs. A proponent of the individual-difference model might regard the presence of neurological signs as coincidental, or that a pathological condition produced individual differences by altering the course of brain development. Just as scarring of the face from smallpox may produce a permanent individual differ-

ence in physical appearance and no longer be pathological, scarring of the brain may produce variations in its functions and no longer be a pathological condition, unless it contributes to specific symptoms, such as seizures. Moreover cell death is an inherent part of brain maturation. Conversely individual differences may constitute the foundation for pathological conditions in later life, as do oncogenes that ultimately direct cancerous cell growth. All of this explains the confusion that exists if definitions of pathology and individual differences are not clearly stated as in Figure 27-2. Indeed there are not separate biological theories for healthy and unhealthy organisms, because healthy and pathological states are conceptualized in the same theoretical terms (Parsons, 1977).

Individual variations in the cellular and chemical components of the brain can be attributed to two basic types of influence: genetic and developmental. Genetic influences link individuals to the protoplasmic stream of life and determine the form, sequence, and rates at which CNS structures unfold at prescribed times and under enabling circumstances. Pathology also can be genetically determined in the form of degenerative diseases that can even cause death. Developmental influences result from the interaction at given moments of the genetically prescribed maturation of the brain and life events, thus blending internal and external factors.

The remarkable complexity of CNS development is described in Chapter 10. The plastic nature of the growing brain is illustrated by the fact that most brain-damaged children functionally improve to some extent. Theories on the mechanisms involved in the brain's plasticity can be divided in two approaches: those that postulate the growth of fresh neural tissue to subserve the acquisition of lost or poorly developed functions and those that postulate the reorganization of existing functions. The rate and degree of improvement appear to depend upon a number of factors, including the adequacy of remedial interventions (Rourke et al, 1983).

The CNS teems with redundant centers with a reorganizational capacity that results in a protective plasticity against the effects of brain damage. The research evidence emphasizes the remarkable degree to which the CNS can compensate for structures affected by injury, disease, or congenital malformation. Many studies show that brain injury to animals in infancy may make little difference in adult behavior, whereas similar injury to adults has profound effects (Rourke et al, 1983).

> An astonishing case that demonstrates the resiliency of the brain is that of a thirty-five year old man, who died of an abdominal malignancy. At autopsy he was found to have a congenital absence of the hippocampal fimbria, the fornix, septum pellucidum, and the mass intermedia of the thalamus in addition to small hippocampal and dentate gyri. In spite of these remarkable anatomical deficits, he had displayed an easygoing personality and even had led his class in school academically (Nathan & Smith, 1950).

The brain is most apt to be exposed to influences that alter brain components and their maturational courses during the middle and last trimester of pregnancy, the perinatal period, and early childhood (Harel & Anastasiow, 1984). During these stages trauma, infection, vascular insult, and degenerative disease can alter the cellular components of the brain. Nutritional deficiencies, noxious chemicals, and deficient environmental stimulation also can alter cellular components, but are more likely to affect chemical components. However, extreme sensory deprivation in early life also can alter cellular components, as light deprivation does the cells of the visual system in cases of amblyopia.

The interplay of the components of the brain and experiential factors is illustrated by the improvement in subsequent development of malnourished children with retarded brain maturation who were raised in affluent adoptive homes after the second year of life, where they received adequate nutrition and parenting (Winick et al, 1975). Furthermore even the adverse effects of malnutrition are influenced by parenting (Lloyd-Still, 1976).

In sum the growing nervous system can compensate for gross anatomical variations by following other developmental paths that utilize intact tissue. In adults this is much less likely than in children. The timing and strategic placement of tissue damage can lead to particular pathological syndromes (Rodier, 1980). Genetic and developmental influences on brain components may be transient and only delay maturation, or they may be permanent and alter the course of brain maturation. In most instances, however, an altered developmental course is determined by both inherent and environmentally induced compensatory reactions to cellular and chemical component changes. For these reasons it usually is not possible to think in terms of brain-tissue destruction as the sole cause of a change in CNS functioning. A more realistic approach is to conceive of the panorama of insults to brain components as playing a role in altering the course of brain maturation, and thereby as manifested in individual variations. This view leaves the door open to the discovery of a range of currently unknown ecological influences that affect CNS development.

The remainder of this chapter will detail the determinants of significant individual differences and pathological conditions. When these variations are maladaptive under certain conditions, they constitute disabilities. When a disability impairs a critical physical, social, or educational skill, a handicap exists. Thus hereditary or developmental individual differences, in addition to pathological conditions, may cause disabilities. Specific pathological conditions are described in greater detail in other chapters.

Individual differences and pathologies with important implications for children's learning problems in school are found in rates of maturation and variations in the components, structures, and processes of the CNS based upon: (1) heredity and (2) development in the form of (a) prenatal events, (b) prematurity, (c) tissue destruction, (d) brain allergies, (e) malnutrition, and (f) experiential usage of CNS functions.

HEREDITARY FACTORS

The relationship of genes to behavior is extremely complex. In essence a gene is the self-reproducing biological mechanism of heredity located at a definite position on a particular chromosome; as a *genotype* it is a potential instruction to the body. When activated a gene alone, or in combination with other genes, is indirectly expressed in behavior through an observable biological or behavioral *phenotype*. Different environments may evoke different phenotypes from the same gene, and a particular phenotype can be produced by different genes. Thus there is an immense range of variability in phenotypes. Most individual differences are due to the effect of many combined genes, together with many environmental factors, on phenotypes. For each of us, a unique combination of genes functions in a unique environment to produce an individual who has never existed before and will never exist again.

Genes do not carry on their work in a vacuum, nor does the environment shape an organism without interaction with genes. In the complex metamorphosis from the fertilized ovum to the newborn infant, chemical processes within the body operate

at every stage to bring about the expression of genetic programs. Environmental factors also play key roles in genetic expression. All of this demonstrates the fallacy of a dualistic viewpoint of causation based upon either nature or nurture.

In a larger sense, genetic evolution interacts with culture in transmitting information from one generation to the next. Genetic transmission is by reproduction. Cultural transmission is both by subtle influences on genes and by learning from others.

Genetic variation is highly desirable from an evolutionary point of view. Completely homogeneous genes would mean a dead end for a species, because without variation natural selection has nothing to choose between. When a given gene survives the weeding-out process of natural selection, it is propagated in the species. Darwinian natural selection through survival of the fittest, however, is not the most important cause of evolutionary change (Fishbein, 1979; Motoo, 1983). Modern evolutionary theory adds mutations of genes and chromosomes as minor sources of genetic variability; the major source is genetic recombination, which occurs when two individuals mate. In humans there are 246 possible combinations of chromosomes for each offspring; these combinations contain more possibilities for variability than the total number of people who have ever lived on the earth (Burnet, 1978).

The cultural transmission of information evolves rapidly through the mixing of cultures. Frequent communication between cultures has a homogenizing effect that reduces cultural diversity. The historical spreading of cultures by conquest, and more recently by rapid transportation and communication, has facilitated the worldwide spread of innovations. The loss of diversity, however, means the loss of definitive cultures in which people can continue unique paths of cultural evolution. It also means that both constructive and destructive influences can sweep across the planet (Pulliam & Dunford, 1980).

Since every human characteristic ultimately depends on the complex interaction of genetic and environmental inputs, it may seem futile to try to disentangle them. Nonetheless it is possible to differentiate them partially by seeing how much an influence contributes to the variance in a particular characteristic. For example, a genetically determined brain mechanism preordains the emergence of speech; however, the language one speaks is culturally determined. In another vein a genetic disorder, such as phenyketonuria, requires a specific external dietary condition to bring it out. At a more complex level, twin studies disclosed that for scholastic achievement, genetic and life-experience factors have similar degrees of influence. On the specific dimensions of neuroticism and extroversion, however, genetic factors appeared to be stronger than home-based factors (Fulker, 1981). Most human characteristics cannot be understood as easily as these; they fall somewhere between the extremes of genetic and environmental influences (Plomin & DeFries, 1985).

In the late 1950s, Watson and Crick made the discoveries that led to a new understanding of the role of the nucleic acids deoxyribonucleic acid (DNA) and ribonucleic acid (RNA) in fundamental life processes. We now know that DNA, which is found in cell nuclei, directs the synthesis of proteins and forms the genetic code that determines the characteristics an organism will have when it matures. RNA carries on the day-to-day job of complying with the directions of that genetic code. The genes regulate the operation of specific enzymes by switching their production on and off. In this way genes exert a major control on development, speeding up one process, slowing down another, or waiting until the environment triggers it. The genes exert their influence at all stages of life from conception onward. For example, they influence not only the color of one's hair, but when it turns gray and grows thin.

Genetic inheritance is transmitted in several characteristic patterns. Dominant inheritance is when a gene from one parent results in a trait that then is found in half of the offspring of that individual. In recessive inheritance both parents' genes must contain the trait for its expression in an offspring. That trait may then appear in one-fourth of the offspring's children. In sex-linked inheritance, genes are carried primarily on the X chromosome, and may be either recessive or dominant in a female but only dominant in a male.

The study of genetic diseases has revealed that, paradoxically, the advantages conferred upon a population that carries the predisposition to these conditions may outweigh the disadvantages for an individual. Sickle cell anemia, for example, is caused by the inheritance of a gene from each parent. Those who carry only a single gene are less likely to contract malaria. In this case the benefit to the greater number of people, those who carry one gene, outweighs the disadvantage to those who coincidentally carry a double dose of the gene (Geschwind, 1982).

In a similar way, the genetic picture of certain forms of dyslexia may have produced evolutionary superiority in other functions. Only when literacy became important to success did these dyslexic individuals become disadvantaged. This may explain why they frequently are talented in areas other than reading.

Another example is the intriguing association between creative intelligence and myopia, alcoholism, and schizophrenia found in a study of foster and biological parent-reared children in Iceland (Karlsson, 1978). This study suggested that creative intelligence may have socially maladaptive consequences in modern society.

A word of caution about genetic causation is in order. Because a family shares ecological, cultural, and interpersonal environmental influences, as well as genetic ones, the fact that a disease runs in families does not reveal its etiology. For example, pellagra in the early decades of this century accounted for a significant number of the mentally ill in the United States. Because it occurred in families, it was thought to be genetically determined. The true explanation became apparent when the cause of pellagra was discovered to be a niacin-deficient diet. Since members of the family ate the same foods, the disease ran in families.

Inasmuch as behavior depends on the architecture of the CNS, it is reasonable to assume that inheritance is an important determinant of all forms of human behavior and the aging process itself. The genetic factors in aging may be the progressive accumulation of genetic errors in the immune system, which are responsible for many of the manifestations of aging, rather than wear and tear or some form of poisoning (Burnet, 1978). The incredible challenge is to understand how genes, which evolved simply for the survival of primitive humans in hostile environments, could on occasion produce Newton, Beethoven, and Einstein.

Individual Differences in Rates of Maturation

Children differ in the rates of growth of their organ systems. Often referred to as delays or lags, these variations in developmental rates usually reflect genetically different maturational timetables. Within individuals the parallel maturation of different cognitive abilities may not take place at the same rate. For example, the visual, auditory, cross-modal, and language structures mature at strikingly different rates (Kinsbourne & Caplan, 1979; Nelson, 1977a). Differences in rates of development of the CNS substystems responsible

for impulse control also arise (Brown, 1973). When the abilities that lag relate to academic learning, failure in schoolwork may result.

Inborn individual differences in the intensity and rhythm of instinctual patterns play an important role in learning processes beginning with the sucking response, which may occur reflexively at birth or require some learning (Sylvester, 1949).

Variations in developmental timetables thus contribute to some learning problems. The fact that many delayed readers who respond to treatment continue as adults to have spelling and writing difficulties, however, indicates that maturational delay is not the only factor in their reading difficulties.

The Inheritance of Intelligence

One of the strongest manifestations of heredity is in intelligence. A summary of 111 studies on familial intelligence revealed a profile remarkably consistent with a polygenic mode of inheritance. This does not discount the importance of environmental factors, however. Monozygotic twins reared apart are far from perfectly correlated in intelligence, and adoptive parents' intelligence test scores demonstrate consistent correlations with the scores of their adopted offspring (Bouchard & McGue, 1981). Also, at the first-grade level, there typically is a spread of four years between the intelligence test scores of children. By the time the sixth grade has been reached, this range has increased to almost seven years, most likely reflecting degrees of success in academic performance (Kaluger & Kolson, 1969).

The role of family factors is further highlighted by studies that have shown that first-born children are overrepresented among students with high intelligence test scores. In five-child families, the first-born constitute 52 percent of the National Merit

Scholarship finalists, whereas the fifth-born constitute 6 percent. This disparity points to the importance of family and psychological dynamics in school achievement. Intelligence test scores also have been shown to increase with decreasing family size, with longer spacing of children, and with earlier position in a sibship (Zajonc, 1976).

Research on the genetic basis for intelligence tends to be controversial, because of its susceptibility to racist interpretations. This occurred as a reaction to the publication of *Genetics and Education* by Arthur Jensen. The black educator Thomas Sowell pointed out, however, that Jensen actually found that the educational performance of black children was related to both their social-class-determined school experiences and their intrinsic capabilities (Sowell, 1973). Jensen's explication of bias in mental testing has since appeared (Jensen, 1980).

More fundamentally, resistance to accepting the influence of heredity on intelligence arises from the unexpressed modern version of Locke's naive view that each person enters the world as a blank page on which society writes what it will. It also may be based on the false assumption that behavior determined by genetic influences inherently is less changeable than environmentally determined behavior.

The Inheritance of Specific Mental Characteristics

The most clear-cut evidence for genetic influences lies in defects in specific metabolic processes that underlie known pathological syndromes. For example, metabolic diseases of the nervous system, such as phenylketonuria, constitute an uncommon group of genetically determined disorders often associated with mental retardation. Many rare neurological disorders also are genetically transmitted, and tend to involve one or more specific areas of the brain: (1) the

basal ganglia, such as Huntington chorea; 2) the cerebellum, brainstem, and spinal cord, such as Friedrich ataxia; (3) the autonomic peripheral and cranial nerves, such as familial dysautonomia, and (4) diffuse cerebral areas, such as Alper disease (Menkes, 1980).

Evidence of a genetic etiology for schizophrenia and for the manic-depressive disorders lies in studies of identical twins, who have a much higher concordance rate when compared with fraternal twins. This has been confirmed by studies of adopted individuals. whose genetic background can be investigated through their biological relatives and whose environmental influences can be examined through their adoptive relatives.

Manfred Bleuler cautioned, however, that schizophrenia as a phenotype is not directly inherited, but that genetic factors operate through underlying CNS structures and processes. Thus the inheritance of individual differences on specific character dimensions comes closer to the facts than the general inheritance of schizophrenia, or of manic-depressive disorders and of dyslexia for that matter. For this reason specific information-processing characteristics are being studied in schizophrenic persons; for example, at the usual rates of information input they make omissions and errors and are more readily overloaded than others. They may be unable to filter irrelevant information efficiently and appear to have lowered channel capacities (Miller, 1978).

An example of an effort to relate a biochemical marker to brain processes and thence behavior can be seen in studies of monoamine oxidase (MAO) levels (Buck, 1984). Individual differences in blood platelet MAO levels are related to the availability of norepinephrine, dopamine, and serotonin at synaptic junctions in the brain. In rhesus monkeys and humans, high platelet MAO levels have been associated with passivity, inactivity, and reduced social interaction, whereas low MAO levels are associated with high activity and social interaction. Low MAO persons tend to be sensation seekers with high needs for stimulation.

Still the complexity of genetic contributions to clinical syndromes is illustrated by the seemingly simple matter of color blindness, which is based upon the absence or insufficient functioning of one or all of three different types of retinal cones, each of which responds to either red, green, or blue. Color blindness is of two major types: protanopia, or red blindness, and deuteranopia, or green blindness. These differences are caused by two different recessive sex-linked genes (Guyton, 1977). Thus, even with color blindness, a single gene is not involved. This suggests that for far more complicated mental and behavioral conditions, genetic research would be most profitably directed toward the most precisely defined underlying factors, such as the subtypes of memory, impulse control, and attentional mechanisms.

Sexual Dimorphism

The differences in brain functions between the sexes have received critical attention in the social and biological sciences (Gilligan, 1982; Fausto-Sterling, 1985). In most instances they are of only mild statistical significance, and the stereotypes of femininity and masculinity are socially conditioned. Still they have significant implications for the mass programming of children, particularly in schools (Maccoby & Jacklin, 1974; Maccoby, 1980). Sex differences are especially prominent in children with academic difficulties (McGuinness, 1985). To ignore them runs the risk of misunderstanding, and even oppressing, certain children.

Except for the distinct anatomical differences of the genitalia, sexual dimorphism is not absolute, but relative. In terms of psychological characteristics, the sexes are more alike than different. However, sex differences tend to favor the female in terms of life span and adaptation in schools.

Different features have evolved in the CNS structures of male and female mammals in order to perform different biological functions (Kolata, 1979). For females these qualities promote bearing and nurturing the young, and for males, driving off intruders, maintaining a food supply, and dispersing populations over available terrain.

The growth of mammalian males and females is programmed differently from the moment of conception. When conception occurs and cell division begins, an immensely complicated architectural scheme is commissioned by the genes and follows a distinctively male or female plan. Every cell nucleus has 46 paired chromosomes (23 from the mother and 23 from the father). Twenty-two of these pairs are called autosomes, because they govern the general structure of the body. The 23rd pair is the sex chromosomes. The female sex chromosome is designated X and the male Y.

Mammalian development probably proceeds in a feminine direction unless androgens are present at sufficient levels during fetal development (Goy & McEwen, 1980). Males shift during fetal growth from a female to a male pattern, thereby increasing the chance of variations in development. A critical stage in the development of the embryo occurs with the formation of the ovaries in the female and the testes in the male, because from there onward the fetus manufactures its own sex hormones. If the embryo develops functioning testes or is subjected to high concentrations of testosterone in the maternal bloodstream, the result is masculine appearance and behavior tendencies.

A variety of conjectures have been made about the effects of sex hormones during early life. Fetal androgens have been implicated in cerebral lateralization to explain why the left hemisphere in males matures later and leads to a greater frequency of left-handedness in males. Testosterone also might interfere with neuronal migration and result in aberrations in the left hemisphere (Geschwind & Behan, 1982). An intriguing relationship between male left-handness, immune system disorders, and mathematical ability has been proposed (Kolata, 1983).

From studies of surgically treated lesions of adults, males show strong left-hemisphere specialization for verbal processing and strong right-hemisphere specialization for spatial processing, whereas females show greater bihemispheric participation in both verbal and spatial abilities. In one study males with left-sided brain lesions had a deficit in verbal-scale IQ and with right-sided lesions a performance-scale deficit. This was not found with females, suggesting their greater functional symmetry (Inglis & Lawson, 1981). Apparently women have language representation in both the left and the right hemispheres, whereas men are limited to the left hemisphere, and women have a more efficient organization of language on the left side than men (McGuinness, 1985). The greater hemispheric specialization observed in males may reduce their potential for shifting language to the right hemisphere after early life left hemisphere injury and their diminished capacity to compensate for unfavorable left–right anatomic asymmetries (Hier, 1979). The female splenium of the corpus collosum also tends to be larger than in males (De la Coste-Utamsing & Holloway, 1982).

Furthermore sensorimotor differences between groups of male and female infants are apparent long before they could possibly be induced by social conditioning. At a few weeks of age, boys attend more readily to visual patterns and girls to auditory sequences. The bodily movements of male infants are more vigorous and global than those of females. Newborn males tend to

be stronger than females. On the whole female infants are quieter and more placid, and males are more fretful and irritable. Later three- and four-year-old boys tend to be more active than girls in group environments (Hutt, 1972).

Sex differences are reflected in groups of intelligence test scores. Males tend to score higher on arithmetical, design, and visual-spatial tests. Females tend to obtain higher scores on verbal, short-term memory, and fine motor speed items. These higher female scores correlate with the observation that girls tend to exceed boys in verbal fluency. No sex distinction is found in overall intelligence test scores except in the distribution of subtest scores, in which male scores are spread out over a wider range. This greater variability applies to height, weight, muscular development, and strength as well. Males thus tend to be more variable in basic physical characteristics than females (Tyler, 1965).

Females tend to surpass males in language skills, including articulation, comprehensibility, fluency, the use of verbal information in learning tasks, and the rapid production of symbolic codes or names. Men are less skillful than women in translating visual information into verbal responses and in creating visual images of words they hear (McGuinness, 1985). Females also tend to show greater sensitivity than males to nonverbal dimensions of communication, such as gesture or facial expression (Marx, 1983).

On the other hand, males tend to exceed females in performance on a variety of visual-spatial tasks, for example, copying intricate geometrical block designs, solving mazes, disembedding geometric figures from complex backgrounds, labeling one's left and right movements through a spatial layout, and mentally rotating representations of two- and three-dimensional shapes in order to compare them with standard figures (Liben et al, 1981). Males also tend to exceed females in mechanical and mathematical skills with visual-spatial components (Wittig & Peterson, 1979; Peterson & Crockett, 1987).

Sex differences in mathematical ability have been cast in terms of excelling rather than difficulties. Thus boys have been found to excel more than girls in mathematical subjects in school (McGuinness, 1985). In attempting to explain this phenomenon, particular attention has been devoted to the hypothesis that boys are more apt than girls in spatial visualization skills. In addition to training and socialization, the empirical evidence generally implicates genetically determined factors favoring males in spatial task performance (McGee, 1979).

Within each sex cognitive differences have been reported in early and late maturing persons. Early maturing boys and girls show a cognitive pattern with higher verbal than spatial abilities, as compared with late maturing boys and girls, who show a cognitive pattern with higher spatial than verbal abilities (Goy & McEwen, 1980).

We know that male fetuses are more vulnerable to mishaps of pregnancy and childbirth. A higher proportion of males than females are spontaneously aborted; the approximately equal sex ratio at birth exists only because more males than females are conceived. The incidence of congenital defects and anoxia at birth are higher for males than females. Febrile convulsions during the first year of life tend to have a greater effect on boys than girls (Geschwind & Behan, 1982). Even experimental neonatal frontal lobe lesions in rhesus monkeys are less devastating for females than for males (Goldman et al, 1974).

In the early school years, girls adapt to the world of school learning more successfully than boys, especially when schoolwork is largely concerned with learning verbal skills and conforming to adult directions (Bardwick, 1971). The general language facility of females tends to facilitate their learning to read more readily than males (Ansara et al, 1981).

Sex differences sharpen in clinical populations in which stuttering, reading disabilities, and other language-related problems are far more common in males than in females. Males outnumber females in the following disorders: infantile autism, 3.8 to one; delayed speech, four to one; stuttering, 3.8 to one; and developmental dyslexia, 3.5 to one (Anastas & Reinherz, 1984; Hier, 1979; Marx, 1983). At the same time dyslexic females may be overlooked, because they do not have behavior problems. There is a greater probability of conduct disorders, psychopathology, and schizophrenia in males and of dysphoric moods and depression in females (Flor-Henry, 1983).

In a more general sense, a tendency has been described for males to be oriented toward conceptualizing relationships in a hierarchical manner of dominance, in contrast with a female orientation toward interacting networks (Bleier, 1983). Males thus tend to value individual achievement and ideals of perfection by which they measure themselves. In contrast females tend to value attachments and measure themselves by interpersonal activities and empathy. Males also tend to emphasize individual rights and females responsibilities. It is as if males are imbued with the Greek ideal of mind and form as knowledge, whereas females are steeped in the Judaic conception of knowing as a product of human relationships (Gilligan, 1982).

Cultural definitions of gender roles draw upon these biological sex differences, so that explanations of sex differences have ranged between the poles of biology and socialization. These biological predispositions only represent statistical tendencies that vary widely in expression between individuals. Consequently, they have more value in understanding groups of children than individuals.

DEVELOPMENTAL FACTORS

Developmental influences range from the effect of chemicals upon a fetus in the uterus to the sensory interchange between parent and infant. These events occur in an actively changing, maturing brain. The developmental factors include the prenatal events of neurobiotaxis, maternal diseases, maternal smoking, maternal alcohol consumption, maternal substance abuse, and maternal medications; prematurity; tissue destruction from birth trauma, head injuries and brain infections; brain allergies; malnutrition and experiential usage.

Prenatal Events

Gestation is a developmental period of unequaled hazard to human life and health. The mortality rate is 20 percent, largely during the first trimester; however, the rate from the fifth month of gestation to the end of the first postnatal month remains as high as 3.5 percent, which is eight times the general mortality rate after birth (Menolascino et al, 1983). It is evident that many critical events take place in the brain prior to birth. As will be seen, the evidence points to the prenatal period as having a greater developmental impact than the perinatal.

Research in molecular genetics is beginning to clarify how the genetic code results in brain maturation. During each phase of fetal development, genetic messages result in chemicals that attach to specific receptor sites in the brain, stimulating growth of that particular area. Each day different sites are stimulated in sequence and for a period of time. This process continues beyond birth and into early childhood, and perhaps beyond. If something interferes with these neurochemical messengers on a particular day, so that the neuronal tracks scheduled for that phase of development are not laid down, this would affect the functioning of specific brain sites and later circuitry that was to connect with these sites. We know little about this molecular genetic-neuroendocrine process. Not only will such knowledge clarify why some individuals develop brains that are "wired" differently, but it might point to prevention opportunities. For example, it is likely that medications taken during pregnancy result in consequences depending on the stage of gestation and amount and length of time they circulate in the fetus (Silver, 1983). Behavioral teratology is the study of behavior resulting from abnormalities arising during prenatal development, particularly during late pregnancy (Yanai, 1984).

Neurobiotaxis

The migration of neurons in the brain through neurobiotaxis during fetal maturation provides the opportunity for numerous and significant variations in the anatomical structure of the brain. The hormone nerve-growth factor (NGF) influences the growth of nerve cells, so that they know which cells they must connect with in order to deliver appropriate signals. There also is a precise time at which the nerve axon grows out from the nerve cell to make the connections under the influence of NGF (Mobley et al, 1977).

The possibility of errors in the timing and place of neuronal migration is significant, as seen in the dyslexias. This process is described in greater detail in Chapter 10.

Maternal Disorders

Many forms of cerebral palsy and mental retardation owe their origin to fetal environment influences. Some maternal infections affect the fetal brain and produce a continuum of sensory and motor functional disabilities. Although most common are cytomegalovirus and rubella, herpes simplex, varicella, syphilis, and toxoplasmosis also may do so (Sever, 1982). For example, if rubella is transmitted from the mother to the fetus in the first trimester of pregnancy, the disease can cause mental retardation and possibly infantile autism.

Kernicterus, a form of fetal jaundice resulting from the blood Rh factor incompatibility between the mother and fetus, can cause hearing loss, cerebral palsy, and mental retardation, although the incidence of such complications has been greatly reduced by preventive intervention.

Hormonal disorders in the mother and her exposure to certain drugs and other foreign substances have been shown to give rise to abnormalities in the fetus. The role of maternal emotional states in fetal development is only beginning to be explored (Lederman, 1984).

Maternal Smoking

Babies born to women who smoke during pregnancy are an average of 200 grams lighter than those of comparable nonsmokers (USDHHS, 1981). A slight effect of maternal smoking during pregnancy on fetal brain development and subsequent intelligence was suggested by a prospective study that demonstrated significant differences in school behavior ratings in favor of children whose mothers did not smoke (Dunn et al, 1977).

In laboratory animals nicotine has a direct effect on developing neurons and probably causes reduced birthweight, hyperactivity, and reproductive abnormalities (Yanai, 1984).

Maternal Alcohol Consumption

One-third of the babies born to chronic alcoholic mothers show evidence of the fetal alcohol syndrome, which is characterized in childhood by at least one sign in each of the following categories: postnatal growth retardation; signs of neurological abnormality, developmental delay, or in-

tellectual impairment; and facial characteristics in the form of small eyes, narrow eyelid fissures, poorly developed upper lip vertical groove, thin upper lip, or flattening of the cheekbones (Abel, 1984). Lesser degrees of the syndrome undoubtedly occur and may account for learning and behavior disorders in affected children (Rosett, 1980; Smith, D.W., 1980). The extent of functional disability appears to be directly related to the structural effects (Steinhausen et al, 1982).

Maternal Substance Abuse

The evidence for harmful developmental effects from the maternal consumption of chemicals other than alcohol generally described under the rubric of "substance abuse" is derived from laboratory animals and limited experience with human infants and children (Yanai, 1984).

The greatest body of evidence is with children born of mothers addicted to opiates and cocaine. Well over 50 percent of the infants born to mothers who continue narcotic abuse during pregnancy show symptoms of the neonatal narcotic abstinence syndrome. Later behavioral disturbances also often develop, including hyperkinesis and attentional deficits.

Maternal marijuana and tetrahydrocannabinol use during pregnancy has been shown to result in behavioral disturbances in offspring in experimental animals and at high doses with regular use in humans. Attention deficits seem to be the major developmental finding in human infants.

The consequences of maternal lysergic acid (LSD) use have been difficult to separate from other drugs used concomitantly. LSD exposure in experimental animals does produce long-lasting changes in brain biochemistry, although their functional correlates have not yet been established.

In pregnant experimental animals, high doses of amphetamines have resulted in hyperkinesis and growth retardation in offspring (Yanai, 1984). High doses of caffeine also have been found to interfere with postnatal myelination of brain tissue in animals, however, there is little evidence of adverse effect on fetal development. Because of the widespread consumption of the methylxanthines (caffeine, theophylline, and theobromine), research on their teratogenic effects is needed.

Maternal Medications

Certain medications taken by the mother during pregnancy can adversely affect the development of the CNS. They include anticonvulsants, anticoagulants, and antimetabolites (Moore, 1982). Barbiturates also may have an adverse effect on fetal brain development (Reinisch & Sander, 1982). There is suggestive evidence in experimental animals that tricyclic antidepressants, neuroleptics, benzodiazepines, steroid hormones, and even aspirin have teratogenic effects (Yanai, 1984).

Prematurity

A premature infant is defined as one born before the 38th week of gestation with a weight below the tenth percentile for the gestational age (see Figure 27-3). There are three different methods of estimating gestational age: menstrual dates, obstetrical examination, and direct examination of the physical characteristics of the baby (Schreiner, 1981).

Premature birth may be the result of factors in the mother or infant or both. Infants born too small are at risk for a number of problems. They have more difficulty than full-term infants in adapting to the postnatal environment, because their body organs are less mature. Their overall growth potential may be restricted, as was intrauterine growth. Finally they may have biochemical and physical disturbances in the newborn period that place them at greater risk for brain damage than full-term infants (Batshaw & Perret, 1981; Holmes et al, 1984).

Premature babies have incompletely developed information-processing and arousal-modulating abilities. The range of stimulation to which they attend and respond may be narrower than that of full-term infants. Their parents walk a fine line to avoid overstimulating them because of their narrow range of stimulation tolerance. By imitating them rather than initiating activity, parents can better engage and hold their attention (Field, 1981).

Substantial evidence has accumulated suggesting that premature infants, particularly under three and a half pounds, are at risk for later development problems (Schain, 1977). Premature infants followed from three months to five years were unusually sensitive to sounds and keenly aware of ephemeral visual phenomena, like shadows and reflections. Their period of baby talk was prolonged, and they tended to be clumsy, distractable, and emotionally volatile (Shirley, 1939). Abnormal neurological signs, hyperkinetic behavior, neuropsychological findings of encephalopathy, and abnormal electroencephalograms were found in 18 percent of premature compared with 6.5 percent of normal-birthweight controls followed in a 15-year prospective study (Dunn et al, 1980). The psychological abnormalities increased and the neurological features decreased over the years. Complicating the interpretation of these studies is the likelihood that 12–19 percent of children without these psychological and educational characteristics also are overactive or clumsy and have abnormal electroencephalograms.

Another study compared infants requiring intensive nursery care because of prematurity with controls over the first year of life. The premature infants showed divergent brainstem auditory-evoked-potential (BAEP) amplitude trajectories from

Grams

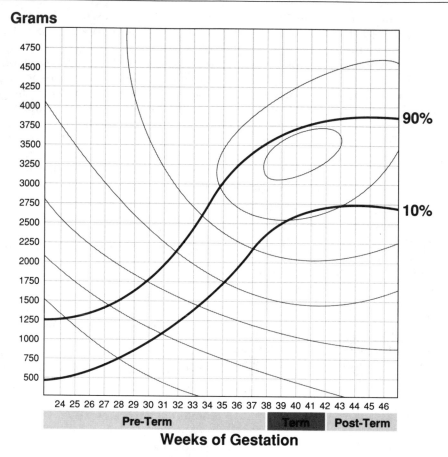

Figure 27-3. Neonatal mortality risk as a function of birth weight and gestational age. The area between the 10th and 90th percentiles represents the appropriate weight for gestational age. Prematurity is defined as an infant born before 38 weeks gestation below the 10th percentile in weight. (Adapted from D. L. Holmes, J. N. Reich, and J. F. Pasternak, *The Development of Infants Born at Risk,* Lawrence Erlbaum, Hillsdale NJ, 1984.)

the full-term infants. Abnormal BAEP trajectories also have been reported in children manifesting autistic traits, attention deficits, hyperkinesis, and psychomotor retardation (Salamy et al, 1980).

Dysmaturity refers to infants who are born smaller than expected for gestational age, with absent vernix caseosa, dry desquammating skin, and a meconium staining of the amniotic fluid, presumably related to premature degeneration of the placenta that interferes with fetal nutrition in the last weeks of pregnancy. Follow-up of a population of these children at the age of seven, however, disclosed no differences between them and controls on psychological, achievement, and behavioral assessments (Ting et al, 1977).

Brain Tissue Destruction

Lower vertebrates possess a remarkable capacity for regeneration within the CNS. Even recovery from damage to the motor system in immature monkeys is rapid and virtually complete, in contrast to similar damage in adult animals. Whereas neuroscientists previously thought that brain neurons in humans could not regenerate, now they are looking for factors that inhibit axon regrowth after injury in humans (Menolascino et al, 1983). Another line of animal research suggests that, through compensatory mechanisms, infants who sustain brain injury may develop brains that are structurally different from the way in which they were genetically programmed (Prechtl, 1978).

Michael Rutter considered the postulate that "minimal brain dysfunction" is a lesser variant of gross brain injury (Rutter, 1981b; 1982). He pointed out that five complications must be considered in any study of brain injury in children. First, rates of disorder in children with brain injury must be compared with rates in the general population, because psychiatric disorders have many causes, including psychosocial, and constitutional factors. Second, children with brain injury frequently have additional physical handicaps from which psychological sequelae could stem. Third, psychiatric disorder could be the result of intellectual impairment, which may be due to reasons other than brain injury. Fourth, children with psychological and intellectual difficulties are more prone to receive head injuries so that changes clearly related to the head injury must be documented. Fifth, children with brain injuries often are economically disadvantaged with its attendant complicating factors.

With these factors in mind, Rutter studied children with demonstrated severe brain damage. They showed intellectual impairment directly proportional to the overall severity of brain damage. Psychiatric disorder appeared to be an indirect result, substantially influenced by the child's preinjury behavior, psychosocial circumstances, and cognitive factors. Hyperkinesis was not one of the regular sequelae, which were related more to visual-spatial-motor functioning and social disinhibition (Rutter, 1981b).

Social disinhibition, reminiscent of Still's defects of moral control, refers to a general lack of social conventions manifested by outspokenness, forgetfulness, overtalkativeness, carelessness in personal hygiene and dress, and impulsiveness. These symptoms resemble those seen in the prefrontal lobe syndrome. Rutter concluded that the continuum of brain injury concept has some validity in association with uncommon severe brain injuries, but does not result in a particular psychiatric syndrome. Research in this area is complicated by the large number of variables and the degree of precision with which they are measured.

Birth Trauma

The major impact of birth is the abrupt transition from a "water-living" to a "land-living" existence. Cerebral insult resulting from this sudden change is more common than supposed. Almost every baby born through the birth canal, especially the first-born, suffers some disturbance of cerebral circulation as a result of the sudden release effect from compression of the cranium. Up to 14 percent of newborns have blood in their cerebrospinal fluid (Menkes, 1980; Schwartz, 1957).

It has been said that everyone has more or less a touch of mental retardation, cerebral palsy, or other blight as a sequel to gestation and birth (Towbin, 1971). Biologically the maternal–placental–fetal relationship is delicately balanced so that maternal disease and intrauterine disturbances reverberate in the fetus. Even under

	POINTS		
	0	**1**	**2**
Heart rate	Absent	100	100
Respiratory effort	Absent	Slow, irregular	Normal respiration; crying
Muscle tone	Limp	Some flexion	Active motion
Gag reflex	No response	Grimace	Sneeze; cough
Color	Blue all over; pale	Blue extremities	Pink all over

Figure 27-4. The Apgar rating system for newborns. (Adapted from M. L. Batshaw and Y. M. Perret, *Children with Handicaps: A Medical Primer*, Paul H. Brookes Publishing Co., Baltimore MD, 1981.)

optimal conditions, the birth process is traumatic, so that hypoxic and mechanical injury to the CNS in some measure is inescapable.

The Apgar scores are a useful means of evaluating an infant's status at birth (Batshaw & Perret, 1981). They reflect the effect of oxygen deficiency on the circulation in the newborn infant (see Figure 27-4). They range from 0 to 10 and are taken at one minute and five minutes after birth. At one minute the Apgar score may reflect the effect of anesthesia and can be low even in normal babies; however, the five-minute score may predict future developmental progress. Scores above six are associated with an excellent prognosis. Infants with scores of three to five have a 20 percent incidence of neurodevelopmental problems. Those with scores of zero to two have a poor prognosis.

From observations of large cerebral lesions in the newborn and chronic lesions in children with cerebral palsy, mental retardation, and other brain disorders, the conclusion is inescapable that lesser lesions due to hypoxia and other causes in the perinatal period could be correspondingly responsible for the appearance of more subtle forms of developmental malformations and attenuated brain functioning (Rorke, 1982).

Birth causes enormous changes for a baby because of the sudden increase in total sensory stimulation in the setting of limited opportunity for motor response. Expulsion from the uterus also interrupts the rhythms, such as the maternal heartbeat, to which the fetus has adapted (Salk, 1973). Phyllis Greenacre (1952) proposed that the intense suffering and frustration of birth leave a baby with an "organic stamp" consisting of physiological sensitivity, which heightens the anxiety potential and gives greater resonance to the anxieties of later life, constituting a predisposition to anxiety in the form of the amorphous threat of imminent disorder.

Children delivered by cesarean section, however, apparently do not differ from birth canal delivered children in their later developmental courses. The evidence is that children spared the trauma of birth canal delivery through cesarean section are not developmentally favored. In the absence of other complicating factors, such as a poor antenatal history, prematurity, and disorganized home environments, delivery complications do not appear to be significant early-risk factors (Broman et al, 1975; McBride et al, 1979; Ounsted et al, 1980; & Silva et al, 1979).

The concept of graded brain insult originating in early life was expanded from

Gesell's minimal brain damage by Lilien-feld and Parkhurst (1951), who postulated a continuum of reproductive wastage extending from perinatal deaths to the consequences of subtle perinatal injuries that might underlie educational disabilities. In 1966 Pasamanik and Knobloch suggested a continuum of reproductive casualty that included such entities as perceptual, learning, and behavioral difficulties. They called attention to prenatal abnormalities in the histories of educationally handicapped children. Their anterospective study of children with reading retardation and controls suggested a weak relation between perinatal factors and reading disorder. Of special interest was the finding that circumstances associated with cerebral hemorrhage and anoxia did not appear to be significantly associated with reading disorders (Kawi & Pasamick, 1959).

A carefully devised study followed children with transient perinatal distress and found them to be more intellectually impaired than controls at the age of 11 (Mednick, 1977). Another study found that neonates with perinatal distress did not visually fixate as long as normal newborns and accordingly were less likely to learn from their environments (Denhoff, 1973). This points to the critical interaction between brain structures and learning.

Another study found that otherwise unremarkable five-year old boys who were asphyxiated at birth differed from age mates in their heightened degree of sensitivity to changes in the environment and in emotional lability and difficulty adapting (Leventhal, 1968). On the other hand, another controlled study of infants subjected to perinatal anoxia revealed little impairment of functioning at seven years of age (Corah, 1965).

The discrepancies between studies of perinatal factors may be explained by Sameroff and Chandler's finding that infants whose perinatal environments increased their risk for developmental problems did not show a greater incidence of developmental deviations if lower socioeconomic infants were excluded from the group. They proposed a continuum of caretaking casualty to emphasize the potent impact of social and environment factors on the ultimate outcome of biologically vulnerable children (Levine et al, 1980; Sameroff & Chandler, 1975). This corresponds to the position that children cannot be studied apart from their parents and the concept of parent–child vulnerability (Westman, 1979a).

The British National Study and the Kauai study also found that social and family factors were more contributory to school and behavior problems than perinatal trauma (Davie & Butler, 1975; Werner et al, 1971). After reviewing the literature, Shaffer (1978) concluded that there is no clear evidence that children with a history of early perinatal complications without evidence of persistent neurological abnormalities are predisposed to later social or psychological difficulties.

Head Injuries

One third of children with severe head injuries develop posttraumatic syndromes, and one-fifth show behavioral symptoms, the most common being decreased attention span, difficulty controlling anger, and headaches (Accardo, 1980).

In one study of children who had a history of compound depressed skull fractures with surgical confirmation of gross brain damage, one-third had a reading level at least two years below their chronological age at follow-up two years later. This was related to the length of coma and complications (Schaffer et al, 1980). In another study the hyperkinetic syndrome was not the typical picture in a heterogeneous group of preschool children with demonstrated brain injury due to trauma, infection, and intoxication. In comparison with controls, the brain-injured children showed impairment in perceptual-motor, conceptual, and language functions, but not behavior (Ernhart et al, 1963).

Brain Infections

Up to three and a half years of age, febrile seizures occur in at least 50 percent of children with a family history of convulsions in contrast with only 25 percent of those with a negative family history (Solomon & Plum, 1976). They usually last less than five minutes, consist of generalized tonic and clonic convulsions and occur with a variable frequency. The electroencephalogram at least one week after the seizure usually is normal. Childhood diseases, such as shigellosis and roseola infantum, often produce seizures associated with fever. Clues that suggest that future epilepsy will occur in a child with febrile seizures include prolonged repetitive convulsions over 20 to 30 minutes, focal seizures, a lack of family history of febrile seizures, previous suspicion of neurological disorder, and an abnormal electroencephalogram recorded more than one week after the seizure. There apparently is no higher incidence of mental retardation or other difficulties in children with than without febrile seizures.

In contrast bacterial and viral meningitis and encepthalitis frequently have devastating effects on the brain, but milder cases of these infections have been thought to cause later behavioral and cognitive disorders. Measles, German measles, chicken pox, and mumps before the age of three have been related to reading and arithmetic problems in later childhood (Accardo, 1980). Chess et al (1971) found that almost 75 percent of children with congenital German measles were deaf, 37 percent were mentally retarded, and 7 percent were autistic.

Rey syndrome, which has been increasingly recognized in recent years, is second only to acute infectious encephalitis as a virus-associated cause of death from CNS disease in children. Most cases occur four to seven days after an influenzal illness or chicken pox. They present with recurring vomiting and rapidly developing confusion, delirium, and coma. Their recovery depends upon the stage of encephalopathy at the time hospital treatment begins. The long-range effects on recovered cases is not known; however, the possibility of a postencephalitic organic brain syndrome exists (Corey, 1977).

Children with postencephalitic organic brain syndromes tend to be destructive and impulsive. They apparently lack fear of punishment and make little effort to evade detection. Their mood changes in response to slight stimuli. They are restless, overactive, and hurry from one form of mischief to another, such as stealing, destroying property, setting fires, and defying rules (Ford, 1966).

Brain Allergies

Allergies are exaggerated reactions to a foreign substance that result from a combination of the molecules of that substance with antibodies characteristic of the affected individual. The exposure of a person to an allergen may sensitize that person, so that on later exposure to the allergen an abnormal response occurs. Some allergies undoubtedly involve the brain (Philpott & Kalita, 1980). How and when this takes place is not well understood and merits study because of our growing awareness of the importance of histamine in the brain.

The allergic tension–fatigue syndrome has been described as a source of emotional symptoms that could interfere with a child's performance in school (Speer, 1970). The syndrome is characterized by fatigability, irritability, pallor, circles under the eyes, and nasal congestion. There is some evidence that reversible localized edema occurs in the brain as a result of allergies to inhalants, drugs, and foods.

Malnutrition

Brain development may be affected by the lack of essential nutritional elements. Whether or not they are most appropriately regarded as producing individual differences or pathological conditions is an open question and depends upon the degree to which the manifestations have a discrete clinical course. We know about the effects of extreme deficiencies, but have little understanding of the benefits of optimal nutrition for the mental and emotional states of children.

The incidence of fetal malnutrition varies from 3 to 10 percent of all live births in developed societies (Metcoff et al, 1981). Fetal malnutrition may result in small size for gestational age. In one study children whose head growth began to slow before 26 weeks of gestation showed delayed cognitive development at the age of five (Harvey et al, 1982). Animal research shows marked reduction in cell division in the brain and endocrine glands as a result of maternal malnutrition at critical periods in fetal development (Wurtman & Wurtman, 1977). Thus malnutrition has been implicated as a factor in maldevelopment of the CNS (Lloyd-Still, 1976).

Nutrition is of great importance in the first three years of life, and poor socioeconomic conditions exacerbate the effects of early malnutrition. Vitamins of the B complex are particularly important (Hallahan & Cruickshank, 1973). Children with moderate to severe protein malnutrition in the first year of life showed more attention deficits, restlessness, memory difficulty, reduced social skills, poorer physical appearance, and emotional instability than controls during the elementary-school years in one study (Galler et al, 1983).

The implications of the evidence for malnourished children in underdeveloped countries are grave. The reversibility of some early malnutrition effects, however, was suggested by previously malnourished foreign children adopted and raised in the United States who showed improvement in their development with adequate parenting and nutrition (Winick et al, 1975).

Experiential Usage

In addition to serving as releasers for innate mechanisms, life experiences have a significant effect on CNS development. Sensory stimulation is an absolute requirement for normal development of the CNS. The evidence also suggests that the lack of the use of CNS functions contributes to individual differences based upon consequent variations in CNS structures (Rosenfeld, 1981).

The fact that there are biological concomitants of mental disorders in itself does not mean that they are genetically based. Much of the maturation of the central nervous system occurs after birth and is strongly influenced by the social matrix, particularly by the quality of parental attachments. The brains of neonates are plastic enough to permit compensation for gross abnormalities provided that parental care is adequate. By the same token early social deprivation may cause lasting changes in neuronal structures and function.

The most fundamental life experience is infant–parent bonding. Experimental animals have been used to demonstrate the behavioral results of mother–infant separation (Harlow, 1974). The possible effect of maternal bonding on the brain is suggested by the finding that separation of a rat pup from its mother for a period as brief as one hour disrupted brain enzyme activity and, therefore, might affect synaptic maturation (Butler & Schanberg, 1977).

A significant aspect of infant–parent

interactions is body movement which activates the cerebellum. Since its cell multiplication continues long after birth, the cerebellum is susceptible to structural modification by experience. An infant with little proprioceptive and tactile stimuli from cuddling and playful movements has few impulses associating pleasure and body stimulation passing between the growing cerebellum and the limbic system. As a result fewer connections may be made between the cerebellum and the affective system. Later that person may have difficulty being satisfied by pleasure, develop an insatiable need for it, and become violent when frustrated. The rocking behavior of isolation-reared monkeys and institutionalized children may result from a background of insufficient body stimulation and movement (Restak, 1979).

A relationship was suggested between the complex experiential factors surrounding breast and bottle feeding and later learning difficulties in a study that found 13.8 percent of the children with learning disorders and 47.2 percent of the control children were breast fed (Menkes, 1977).

An illustration of the effect of training on a presumably innate incapacity was seen in a group of children, who could not learn to sing despite prolonged attempts at instruction (Leontiev, 1957). At the beginning they were unable to match vocally the pitch of a continuously sounding tone. However, with training in vocal matching, they learned to match a given pitch. Then the sounds were turned off, and they learned to continue singing the tones independently. Next they learned to match tones from memory, starting to sing only after the tones were turned off. When they finally became proficient at matching tones after a brief interval had elapsed, training in reproducing simple melodies was begun. Using this series of steps, progress was rapid, and all of the children learned to sing. The relevance of this model to stepwise learning to read is striking.

SUMMARY

Individual differences in appearance, skills, and behavior are essential for successful group living. They are most apparent in early and late life; however, because of agism, they tend to be regarded as personal foibles in adults and as pathological in children.

Because of the psychological differences between developing variant in contrast with defective self-concepts, it is important to distinguish between individual variations and pathology in children whenever possible. Individual differences can be defined as persistent variations in universal human characteristics that emerge during the course of development; they are caused by the interplay of genetic and experiential factors and can be changed through training, education, and personal decision. In contrast pathology can be defined as disruptive human characteristics with an onset, clinical course, and prognosis that are caused by events, such as genetic expression, disease, trauma, toxicants, nutritional deficiencies, and intrapsychic conflict, and that can be changed through preventive measures and treatment of the disorder.

Individual differences may occur in rates of brain maturation and variations in the cellular and chemical components of the brain based upon heredity and development. Hereditary factors are expressed in brain maturational rates, intelligence, specific mental qualities, and sexual dimosphism. Developmental factors relate to prenatal influences, prematurity, brain tissue destruction, brain allergies, malnutrition, and experiential usage.

Heredity is expressed through genes that influence evolution by mutation and recombination under the process of natural selection. Heredity plays a significant role in all personal characteristics, especially in intelligence, and specific mental characteristics that may result in mental, affective, metabolic, and neurological disorders. Familial inheritance also takes place in the form of the transmission of cultural, ecological, and interpersonal influences.

Sexual dimorphism occurs in distinct genital anatomy and in relatively small statistical differences in CNS functions. Males shift from a female to a male pattern prenatally and tend to be more vulnerable to developmental mishaps than females. Females tend to be more facile in language and males in visual-spatial skills. Males significantly outnumber females in clinical populations, such as infantile autism, speech disorders, and the developmental dyslexias. Explanation of sex differences shift between the poles of biology and socialization. The importance of sex differences lies in understanding the needs of groups of children more than individuals.

Prenatal factors that influence development during the most hazardous period of life include the vagaries of neurobiotaxis and maternal disorders, smoking, alcohol consumption, substance abuse, and medications.

Premature birth may result from factors in an infant or mother, or both. Premature babies are at risk for later neurological, educational, and behavioral problems.

Tissue destruction can occur in the brain because of birth trauma, head injuries, and brain infections. The concept of a continuum of reproductive casualty has validity, but is more completely expressed by a continuum of parent–child vulnerability, because the parent–child unit is the most fundamental form of early life and allows for the inclusion of social, economic, and interpersonal influences.

The relationship of brain allergies to behavior is not well understood and merits study. Malnutrition during fetal life and early childhood affects the development of the CNS in ways that appear to be susceptible to varying degrees of reversibility.

The releasing of innate mechanisms and the development of the CNS depend upon life experiences in the form of the stimulation and training of infants and young children.

Behavioral scientists and educators have long known that teaching is more effective when individual differences in students' personal characteristics, prior knowledge, and level of development are taken into account. The educational system, however, has been unable to accommodate to the needs of individual children because of its basic orientation toward dealing with groups. The question is whether sufficient accommodations can be made to each child's individuality so that school becomes a resource for growth, rather than convert an individual into something less than at the beginning. The health-care worker with knowledge of individual differences and pathologies is in a unique position to create an individual focus as a child's advocate in the schools. Understanding how we can be similar but not identical, and how we can be biologically different but politically equal, is difficult but necessary, if we are to maintain our pluralistic way of life.

28

From Functional Disabilities to Educational Disabilities and Handicaps

Every drive and need in us . . . is secondary to the search
for something to fill up the inner emptiness and loneliness
of life. We search for ultimate meaning.

Viktor Frankl, 1962

Success or failure in school—the workplace of children—can enhance or diminish the meaning of their lives. Unlike the work of adults, difficulty in school affects a child's character development and interest in the widening world, just as a child's character development and interest in the world influence schoolwork. More specifically many factors interacting over extended periods determine whether or not central nervous system (CNS) functional disabilities become educational disabilities and handicaps. The most important of these additional disposing factors are variant learning styles, immature levels of self-development, and maladaptive personality patterns, all of which affect children's work styles in school.

As this book has unfolded, a series of system levels that extends from the schemes of the CNS to a child's social roles in the external world has been identified as illustrated in Figure 28-1. The series begins with the cellular structures and electrochemical processes of schemes. At the organ level, the schemes are organized within the anatomical structures of the component subsystems of the CNS.

A person's *character* can be defined as being composed of the functions of the CNS listed in Figure 28-2. The nature of the imaging and imagination subsystems of the information processing system determines one's basic *learning style,* as these subsystems place differing emphases on the external or internal worlds and upon events occurring in time or space. In the context of the level of self-development, a child's *learning style* shapes, and in turn is shaped by, the development of the CNS functions comprising that child's character. At the individual level, one's personality consists of the output of the organism through externally manifested behavioral and bodily expressions that typify an individual in the eyes of others. For our purposes the most important ingredients of a child's personality are *work style* and functional disabilities. A child's *character* and *learning style* determine a child's *work style* and thereby the quality of schoolwork. At the interpersonal level, the sustained intrusion of func-

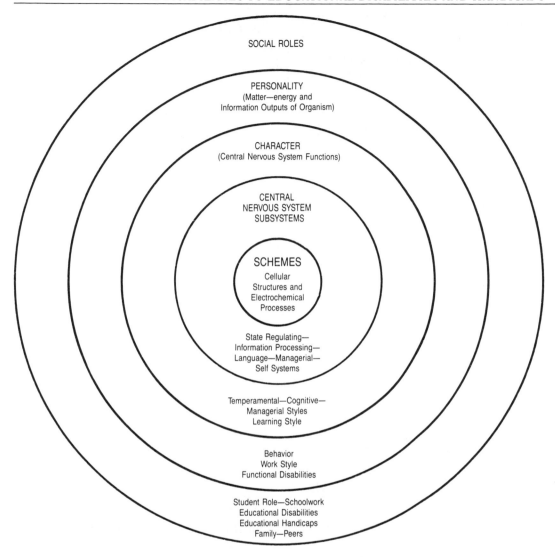

Figure 28-1. Organ, individual, and interpersonal system levels involved in schoolwork.

tional disabilities on a child's performance of schoolwork in the social role of student leads to educational disabilities. The relative intensity of these factors, interacting with the particular interpersonal and ecological characteristics of a child's family, school, and classroom, determines the degree of educational disability and handicap experienced by that child.

In this chapter I have assembled available evidence in order to construct theoretical models of learning styles, work styles, levels of self-development, personality patterns, and functional disabilities, all of which contribute to children's educational disabilities and handicaps. I have drawn upon the work of a number of authors who devised typologies of character

TEMPERAMENT

Disposition
  Rhythmicity of Appetitive Instincts
  Adaptability of Affective System

Attention
  Involuntary Arousal
    Vigilance
    Orienting Response
    Stimulus Modulation
  Voluntary
    Scanning
    Focusing
    Concentration

Movement Level
  Constitutional Energy Level
  Excitability
  Drive Intensity
  Motor Control

COGNITION

Learning Style
  Imaging
  Imagination
  Time and Space Orientation
  Memory

Cognitive Style
  Automatization
  Sensory Modality Preference
  Intermodal Integration
  Flexibility—Rigidity
  Field Dependent vs. Independent
  Locus of Control

LANGUAGE

  Verbal and Written
  Understanding
  Formulating
  Expressing

MANAGERIAL SYSTEM

Impulse Control
  Drive Gratification Delay
  Distress Tolerance
  Modulation of Emotions
  Selective Drive Regression

Information Analysis
  External-Internal
    Discrimination
  Relevance of Perceptions

Thinking
  Synthesis
  Decision Making
  Planning
  Style
    Automatic
    Problem Solving
    Creative

Implementing Actions
  Time Sequencing
  Efficiency

Verifying Actions

SELF SYSTEM

  Self-Awareness
  Self-Esteem
  Self-Concept
  Self-Evaluation

Figure 28-2. Central nervous system functions comprising character.

based largely upon its manifestations in personality (Dixon, 1983; Eysenck, 1977; Fadely & Hosler, 1979; Flor-Henry, 1983; Forisha, 1983; Gregorc, 1979; Lawrence, 1982; Lowen, 1982; Myers, 1975; Plutchik, 1979, 1980; Shapiro, 1965; & Welsh, 1975). Although there are speculative elements in this effort, it is useful for heuristic purposes to relate the CNS to character and learning styles and then to personality and work styles.

First I will describe four basic learning styles to which general classroom instruction can be profitably adapted. Then for children who have particular difficulty with schoolwork, I will show how their learning styles and their levels of self-development can be related to maladaptive personality patterns that underlie their difficulties. Next I will describe how functional disabilities interfere with the performance of schoolwork, and thus become educational disabilities, and ultimately educational handicaps. Last I will

		IMAGINATION STYLE	
		Left Hemisphere Analytic-verbal-sequential Functions	Right Hemisphere Intuitive-visual gestalt Functions
I M A G E R Y	External Imagery	Analytic-extrovert	Intuitive-extrovert
E M P H A S I S	Internal Imagery	Analytic-introvert	Intuitive-introvert

Figure 28-3. Learning styles.

summarize the epidemiological evidence on the prevalence of the major categories of school learning problems.

LEARNING STYLES

The evidence from the studies I have drawn upon points to *imaging* as the center stage of relating to the external and internal worlds and to *imagination* as the symbolic and conceptual means through which knowledge is gained. There are fundamental individual differences, first, in one's relative emphasis upon external and internal imagery, and second, in one's style of imagination through which imagery is handled. The nature of subcortical imaging and cortical imagination together make up one's learning style (see Figure 28-3).

External Versus Internal Imagery

Individual differences can be observed in the relative orientation of infants toward

stimuli arising from their external and internal worlds (Escalona, 1968). Throughout life a composite of subcortical CNS functions influences an individual's relative orientation toward internal or external imagery, particularly the relative strength of the drives, impulse control, and the characteristics of the imaging apparatus itself. Psychological defense mechanisms also play a role.

The relative orientation of an individual's imagery can be described on an extrovert–introvert continuum. *Extroverts* are more "other directed" and oriented to externally generated imagery; *introverts* are more "inner directed" and oriented to internally generated imagery (Eysenck, 1971; Jung, 1959; Riesman et al, 1950).

Extroversion refers to an individual's predominant emphasis on perceptions arising from the external world through the special senses. The stimulus modulation of extroverts tends to reduce the intensity of stimuli, and consequently they seek additional novel external stimulation. This appears to be related to their low cortical arousal and generally refractory central nervous systems, in which reactive inhibition is generated readily and dissipated slowly (Powell, 1979).

Introversion refers to a reflective emphasis upon the internal world of imagery arising from the viscera and from memories. Introverts subjectively augment the intensity of stimuli and thereby tend to avoid novel external stimulation. Background sound, such as music, may enhance their concentration. This incremental modulation of stimuli may be related to their high cortical arousal and general facilitory central nervous systems in which reactive inhibition develops slowly, but is dissipated quickly (Powell, 1979).

Analytic Versus Intuitive Imagination

In addition to their relative emphasis on external or internal imagery, individuals can be characterized by their relative orientation toward time or space. As the process through which symbol and concept formation take place, imagination is the vehicle of instrumental and didactic learning (see Chapter 13). One's imagination can be predominantly *analytic* with an emphasis on time or *intuitive* with an emphasis on space.

There are two fundamentally different sources from which knowledge can be acquired through the process of imagination. The first is from meaning derived from an event occurring over time, as with music, and the second is from the meaning of an event in space, as with a picture. Thus the sequence of stimuli in time and the configuration of stimuli in space convey different forms of meaning. Temporal events are understood by analyzing sequential stimuli, which is the modus operandi of the auditory system. Spatial events are understood from the intuitive grasp of meaning, which is the primary mode of the visual system.

The interaction of the cerebral hemispheres influences the temporal and spatial ways imagery is handled through imagination. How the hemispheres relate to each other depends upon the degree of each hemisphere's activation, the communication between them, and the inhibition of one by the other (Flor-Henry, 1983). As detailed in Chapter 9, at the broadest levels in most persons the left hemisphere is associated with analytic and verbal-sequential-time functions and the right hemisphere with intuitive and visual-gestalt-space functions (Pribram, 1977).

Through the different functions of the two hemispheres, therefore, *analytic* and *intuitive* forms of imagination can be distinguished. Analytically inclined children scrutinize imagery from the internal and external worlds deductively and inductively. They are oriented toward verbal symbols and orderly, sequential processes. On the other hand, intuitive children are oriented toward holistic visual-spatial impressions. In psychoanalytic terms the analytic mode reflects secondary process activity whereas the intuitive mode reflects primary process activity.

At the analytic end of the continuum of imagination is orderly, sequential, verbally based, problem-solving thinking, which follows a step-by-step sequence of operations that moves forward to a solution. Analytic persons tend to remember parts rather than wholes. They tend to talk themselves through, and precisely carry out, tasks without needing awareness of their general purposes.

At the intuitive end of the continuum is a spontaneous, global, visually-based imagination. Intuitive children are impatient with step-by-step procedures and likely to make mistakes while doing them. They are adept at guessing and may spontaneously give a correct answer to a problem without knowing how it was derived. At the same time, their performance is enhanced by knowing the overall purpose of what they are doing.

Basic Learning Styles

Different learning styles can be derived from the interplay of imaging orientation and imagination styles. Interest in doing this is growing in educational circles. As a result instruments have appeared for defining learning styles. Several of them can be mentioned as examples of the work being done in this area.

The Edmonds Learning Style Identification Exercise (ELSIE) is a method of detecting the perceptual modes through which students internalize individual words. It provides a profile of cognitive style based on the individual's responses to common English words on the dimensions of visual imagery, auditory imagery, and the emotional coloration of words (Keefe, 1982). The Gregorc Style Delineator assesses four learning patterns by scoring on an instrument on which a child ranks impressions of words (Gregorc, 1979). Cognitive Style Mapping is done through observation and recording information on the various cognitive-style elements ordinarily used by younger children and by the self-reporting of older children (Hills, 1976). The Learning Style Inventory is a widely used assessment instrument in elementary and secondary schools (Dunn & Dunn, 1978). The Productivity Environmental Preference Survey is used to analyze individual differences in adults under working conditions, but has implications for children as well. It reveals such things as preferred sound levels, optimal times of day for working, visual or auditory information processing, and solitary versus group work (Dunn, 1982).

These efforts to detect learning styles can be enhanced by an understanding of underlying mechanisms. In so doing four basic learning styles can be defined in terms of the relative prominence of left or right cerebral hemisphere imagination and the relative prominence of the external and internal worlds in one's imagery. These basic orientations to imagination and imaging are depicted in Figure 28-3.

Persons who show dominant left-hemisphere imagination and an orientation toward outer-world imagery can be called *analytic-extroverts*. Those who show dominant right-hemisphere imagination and an orientation toward outer-world imagery can be called *intuitive-extroverts*. Persons who show dominant left-hemisphere imagination and an orientation toward inner-world imagery can be called *analytic-introverts*. Those who show dominant right-hemisphere imagination and an orientation toward inner-world imagery then are *intuitive-introverts*.

Most children do not fall clearly into one of these groups. Furthermore there are endless possibilities for differential dominance in a variety of CNS functions, making each individual's learning style as unique as the person's fingerprints. Children with learning problems in school, however, are likely to prefer one of these four learning styles.

Learning and Work Styles

These four *learning styles* are expressed through children's personality *work styles* in school. A child's work style reflects the preferred learning style, in addition to the way in which that child's character sublimates drives in work. It also is embedded in a child's self-concept as a student and is influenced by one's self-evaluation as a productive person. Thus a child's schoolwork is a product of the social role relationships among student, teacher, and peers. A teacher sees a particular child's work style expressed in personality traits exhibited during the performance of tasks. A child's success in school depends upon a reasonable fit between that child's work style and the teacher's expectations. It also depends

Learning Style (Character)	Analytic-Extrovert	Intuitive-Extrovert	Intuitive-Introvert	Analytic-Introvert
Work Style (Personality)	Take initiative Organized, respond to directions Perfectionistic, fear ambiguity, overreact to errors and blame themselves, conformist Productive	Erratic initiative Disorganized Impulsive, distractible, discouraged by errors, actor Unproductive	Lack initiative Disorganized Apathetic, preoccupied, indifferent to errors, loner Unproductive	Self-serving initiative Organized if interested Wary, irritable, overreact to errors and blame others, rebel Erratically productive
Optimal Schoolwork Conditions	Work at own pace independently	Supervised structured routines with limit setting Detailed instructions, short and limited number of tasks Quiet, undistracting atmosphere	Inspiring attention of teacher Novel, challenging tasks with specific goals and time limits Work with hands	Can work at own pace with goals set by teacher Explain practical purposes of tasks
Optimal Teaching Methods	Didactic classroom techniques Textbooks Audiotapes	Individual attention in tutoring area Workbooks Games and simulations	Resource areas Demonstrations Field trips Microcomputers	Special projects Library resources Audio-visual aids

Figure 28-4. The relationship of basic learning styles to work styles and teaching methods.

upon the child's assumption of the role of student in the classroom, rather than another role with peers, such as "class clown."

The Socratic method of ancient Greece sought to foster the personal involvement of students in learning. At the beginning of the 20th century, John Dewey popularized individually oriented education. Since then much research has been devoted to developing individualized instruction methods as a means of promoting learning and preventing failure in school. The idea of individualization has been around for a long time, but the necessity of dealing with children in groups in schools has prevented its application. Fortunately, there are two practical ways of meeting the needs of individual children in the context of group instruction. The first is through modifying mainstream education so as to reach the most common variations in learning styles. The second is through programming specialized educational services for a particular child.

Under optimal circumstances main-stream schooling can be adapted to meet the needs of children with the four basic learning styles described in this chapter. Working conditions and teaching methods can be adjusted to meet their differing needs (see Figure 28-4). Schooling ordinarily favors children with analytic-extroverted learning styles. Even these children can suffer, however, from excessively embracing educational goals and values. For children with the other learning styles, the usual forms of classroom education pose significant barriers.

Children with an analytic-extrovert learning style can take the initiative in organizing their time in schoolwork. They are productive, but tend to be perfectionistic and are threatened by ambiguity. They also overreact to errors, for which they may blame themselves excessively. They respect authority and can work at their own paces. They respond to didactic educational techniques in the classroom and can use textbooks effectively.

Intuitive-extroverted children show

spontaneous initiative that must be directed in order to be applied to schoolwork. They are disorganized in their approach to work and manage time poorly. As a result they are unproductive unless their distractibility and impulsivity are channeled through structured supervision. Because they are easily discouraged by errors, they need the reinforcement of a teacher for performing short tasks in limited numbers in addition to detailed instructions. They respond to work books, games, and simulations. They need undistracted areas for tutored work.

Intuitive-introverted children lack initiative and are disorganized in their approach to work and the management of time. They are unproductive, preoccupied, and apparently indifferent to errors. They need stimulation from novel, challenging tasks that draw upon their creativity. In addition they need specific time goals that can be reached and reinforced immediately by the teacher. Demonstrations, field trips, and microcomputers aid in attracting their interest.

Children with analytic-introverted learning styles demonstrate initiative, if they can see a personally useful value in schoolwork. Their productivity and the management of time, therefore, are erratic. They are wary, preoccupied, and overreactive to errors, for which they tend to blame others. They respond to interesting projects with goals set by the teacher within which they can work at their own paces. They must, however, understand the practical value of the schoolwork to them. They can use audiovisual aids, library resources, and experiments in carrying out special projects that attract their interest.

The foregoing learning styles are recognized implicitly in some modern elementary classrooms through the limitation of class size, the inclusion of a tutoring area, and the availability of microcomputers and audiovisual aids, in addition to the use of demonstrations, field trips, and in-

structional materials centers. An example of such a classroom is shown in Figure 30-5. For these classrooms the ideas expressed here provide a validating rationale. For those that do not have these resources, this exposition offers an important justification for adapting classrooms to major differences in learning styles. If classroom teaching can be adapted to these learning styles, it is not necessary to determine specifically children's preferred learning conditions. They will gravitate to them. Individual assessment can be reserved for those who still have academic problems.

LEARNING STYLES, LEVELS OF SELF-DEVELOPMENT, AND MALADAPTIVE PERSONALITY PATTERNS

Although the primary determinants of children's maladaptive personality patterns lie elsewhere, the schools play significant roles in both exaggerating and ameliorating them. If a child with functional disabilities has a favorable school experience, the likelihood of successful adaptation in later life is enhanced. Conversely failure in school not only produces educational disabilities but reinforces maladaptive personality patterns. Thus a child's experiences in school play important roles in the translation of dispositions into problems.

One of the key factors in determining the extent to which a particular learning style contributes to difficulty in school is the degree to which children have successfully passed through the stages of self-development as reflected in the maturity of their personality patterns. The interaction of learning style and level of self-development is illustrated in Figure 28-5.

Adolescents who have successfully achieved an integrative-achievement level of self-development exhibit adaptive per-

Learning Style (Character)		Analytic-Extrovert	Intuitive-Extrovert	Intuitive-Introvert	Analytic-Introvert
L E V E L O F S E L F D E V E L O P M E N T	**I M M A T U R E P R E A D O L E S C E N T S** (Level 1, 2, 3) / **A D O L E S C E N T S** (Level 4)				
Level 1 — **Symbolic-Impulsive Self**		Control of impulses key issue Catastrophic reaction to distress Obsessive-compulsive personality	Attention seeking key issue Emotional lability Impulsive Demanding Impulsive personality	Unlovability key issue Emotionally inhibited Withdrawn Schizoid personality	Power key issue Omnipotent Omniscient Selfish Petulant Narcissistic personality (Internally preoccupied) Oppositional personality (Externally preoccupied)
Level 2 — **Conceptual-Imperial Self**		Fear unknown and ambiguity Overconforming Worrisome Preoccupied with details Compulsive personality	Helpless Forgetful Manipulatively helpless and pseudostupid Dependent personality	Aloof Apathetic	Distrustful Suspicious Blames others Paranoid personality
Level 3 — **Evaluative-Affiliative Self**		Perfectionistic Self-blaming Authoritarian	Uninhibited Dramatic Role playing Conversion and dissociative symptoms Hysterical personality	Slow to warm-up Indifferent	Sensitive to injustice Resists and sabotages authority Passive-aggressive personality
Level 4 — **Integrative-Achievement Self**		Orderly Organized Rational Affiliative	Flexible Enthusiastic Impressionistic Affiliative	Innovative Mechanically oriented Vivid imagery Reserved	Sensitive Verbal Creative Self-reliant

Figure 28-5. Personality patterns of mature adolescents and immature children whose levels of self-development remain fixated at earlier levels.

sonality patterns. The analytic extrovert is organized, rational, and affiliative. The intuitive extrovert is enthusiastic, flexible, and affiliative. The intuitive introvert is innovative, mechanically inclined, and self-reliant. The analytic introvert is sensitive, verbally expressive, and creative. Adolescents with mature levels of self-development are depicted at level 4 in Figure 28-5.

At the present time, preadolescent children compose the age group most frequently identified as having school learning problems. The first three levels in Figure 28-5 show the possible personality patterns of preadolescent children whose self-development remains at earlier levels.

Children who have successfully mastered the sensorimotor, symbolic-impulsive, and conceptual-imperial stages but are not successfully experiencing the evaluative-affiliative stage, may have the following characteristics (level 3; Figure 28-5). Analytic extroverts may be perfectionistic, authoritarian, and fear the unknown and ambiguity; they still may be regarded as "model" children. Intuitive-extroverts may have uninhibited, dramatic, and egocentric hysterical personalities; they may be regarded as "actors" or "actresses." Intuitive-introverts may be indifferent, disinterested, and hesitant; they may be regarded as "loners." Analytic-introverts are sensitive to injustice and may openly resist or sabotage authority as "rebels" or passive-aggressive personalities.

Preadolescent children who have successfully mastered the sensorimotor and symbolic-impulsive stages but remain at the conceptual-imperial stage may show the following (level 2; Figure 28-5). Analytic extroverts may have compulsive personalities and be ineffective in schoolwork because of their preoccupation with details. Intuitive extroverts may have helpless, forgetful dependent personalities. Intuitive introverts may be aloof and apathetic. Analytic introverts may have distrustful, suspicious paranoid personalities.

Preadolescent children who have passed the sensorimotor stage of self-development but remain at the symbolic-impulsive level may appear as follows (level 1; Figure 28-5). The analytic extrovert may be obsessive-compulsive and be paralyzed in schoolwork by obsessional imagery and compulsive rituals. Intuitive extroverts may have impulsive personalities manifested by emotional lability and erratic productivity. Intuitive introverts may be isolated and unproductive and have schizoid personalities. Analytic introverts may have narcissistic or oppositional personalities.

Many factors are involved in determining the appearance of personality patterns that are academically and socially maladaptive. We lack a complete understanding of how these patterns emerge. Even so we need a theoretical framework within which we can place the knowledge that is available. When basic personality patterns are related to temperament, cognition, language, managerial functions, and levels of self-development, an impressive picture emerges. Figures 28-6(a) and 28-6(b) are offered as a hypothetical framework within which maladaptive personality patterns of varying degrees of severity can be defined by an analysis of the basic CNS functions that make up one's character. Because it identifies the array of variables that need to be taken into account in understanding learning problems at school, this model is a tool for relating clinical and educational phenomena to the neural sciences.

For research purposes this model identifies critical CNS functions that must be taken into account in understanding behavior. With these variables in mind, syndromes can be compared with each other on specific dimensions, such as the dimensions of attention or impulse control. It also is possible to trace developmental lines on specific CNS functions through the successive stages of development. Ultimately testable hypotheses about CNS functions could be derived from this approach.

From the clinical point of view, this comprehensive model for relating CNS functions to behavior provides a degree of conceptual clarity that is not possible in anecdotal and single-discipline approaches. This model ensures that the range of pertinent factors are considered in the evaluation of a particular child. It also points toward underlying processes and functions rather than surface behavior as the targets for treatment. Most important, it provides a language for communication between the various professional disciplines.

To give them vitality, a series of hypothetical descriptions of the four basic learning styles and their associated maladaptive personality patterns related to levels of self-development follows.

The Analytic-Extroverted Child

> I make good school grades, which my parents tell me will help when I go to college. I play all sports and have many friends. I try hard to do the right thing and get upset with people who do not. I wish that all children in the world could live like I do.

Analytic-extroverted children reflect the logical and orderly behavior prized by

MALADAPTIVE PERSONALITY PATTERNS (CNS Output)

CHARACTER (CNS Functions)	COMPULSIVE	IMPULSIVE	DEPENDENT	HYSTERICAL	SCHIZOID	OPPOSITIONAL
Learning Style (Imaging & Imagination)	Analytic-extrovert	Intuitive-extrovert	Intuitive-extrovert	Intuitive-extrovert	Intuitive-introvert	Analytic-introvert
SELF-SYSTEM						
Self-awareness	High	Low	High	High	High	Low
Self-evaluation	Perfectionist, guilty	Distrusts, dislikes self	Helpless, assumed disability	Vacillating	Negative	Ambivalent
Self-concept	Compliant, perfect child	Insatiable, demanding	Infantile, Peter Pan, failure-seeking	Insatiable, attention-seeking, imitating	Pariah, unlovable, withdrawn	Contrary, attacked victim, power-seeking
Self-esteem	Variable	Low	Low	Variable	Low	Low
Self-development Level	Conceptual-imperial	Symbolic-impulsive	Conceptual-imperial	Evaluative-affiliative	Symbolic-impulsive	Symbolic-impulsive
TEMPERAMENT						
Disposition (Mood)	Phlegmatic	Choleric	Sanguine	Sanguine	Phlegmatic	Melancholic
Attention						
Involuntary						
Vigilant	High	Low	Low	Low	High	Variable
Orienting	Keen	Blunt	Variable	Intense	Sluggish	Rebuffing
Stimulus Modulation	Low threshold	Low threshold	Variable	High threshold	Low threshold	Low threshold
Voluntary						
Scanning	Narrow	Narrow	Narrow	Narrow	Broad	Broad
Focusing	Precise	Imprecise	Imprecise	Imprecise	Precise	Precise
Concentration	Intense	Distractible	Distractible	Variable	Variable	Distractible
Motivation-Movement						
Context Related						
Excitement	Low	High	Low	High	Low	Variable
Investment in Work	High	Low	Low	Variable	Low	Variable
Motor Incoordination	Non-specific	Related to impulsiveness	Non-specific	Non-specific	Non-specific	Non-specific
Context Unrelated						
Constitutional	Non-specific	Hyperkinetic	Variable	Variable	Hypo-kinetic	Variable
Adventitious Movements	Non-specific	Non-specific	Non-specific	Non-specific	Non-specific	Non-specific

Category / Attribute	1	2	3	4	5	6
COGNITION						
Flexible-rigid	Rigid	Rigid	Flexible	Flexible	Rigid	Rigid
Automatization	High	Low	Low	Variable	High	Variable
Field Dependent vs. Independent	Field independent	Field independent	Field dependent	Field dependent	Field independent	Field dependent
Visual or Auditory Preference	Auditory	Variable	Variable	Visual	Variable	Variable
Intermodal Integration	Non-specific	Non-specific	Non-specific	Non-specific	Non-specific	Non-specific
Locus of Control	Internal	Internal	External	Internal	Internal	External
Imagery	Strong verbal	Weak	Strong	Weak	Strong	Weak
Spatial Orientation	Indistinct	Indistinct	Distinct	Distinct	Variable	Variable
Memory	Keen	Variable	Forgetful	Variable	Keen	Variable
LANGUAGE						
Receptive	Keen	Restricted	Restricted	Restricted	Blocked	Variable
Inner	Highly developed	Primitive	Limited	Well developed	Constricted	Limited
Expressive	Facile	Variable	Variable	Variable	Blocked	Limited
MANAGERIAL SYSTEM						
Impulse Control						
Drive Gratification Delay	Strong	Weak	Variable	Weak	Strong	Weak
Tolerance of Distress	High	Low	Variable	Low	Low	Low
Modulation of Emotions	Strong	Weak	Variable	Weak	Strong	Weak
Selective Drive Regression	Restrained	Faulty	Excessive	Variable	Blocked	Variable
Information Analysis						
External vs. Internal Discrimination	Accurate	Variable	Accurate	Accurate	Variable	Variable
Relevance of Perceptions	Discerning, good	Variable	Discerning	Variable	Misinterprets	Variable
Thinking						
Synthesis	Logical	Weak	Variable	Global, impressionistic	Erroneous impressionistic	Variable
Decision Making	Indecisive	Abruptly decisive	Indecisive	Variable	Decisive	Decisive in opposing
Planning	Preoccupied with future	Poor	Poor	Variable	Variable	Poor
Thinking Style						
Automatic	Strong	Weak	Weak	Weak	Variable	Weak
Problem Solving	Strong	Weak	Weak	Variable	Variable	Weak
Creative	Low	Low	Low	High	High innovative	Low
Implementing Actions						
Time Sequencing	Preoccupied	Poor	Poor	Variable	Variable	Poor
Efficiency	Variable	Low	Low	Variable	Variable	Low
Verifying Actions	Perfectionistic	Careless	Careless	Variable	Variable	Variable

Figure 28-6a.

587

MALADAPTIVE PERSONALITY PATTERNS (CNS Output)

CHARACTER (CNS Functions)	NARCISSISTIC	PARANOID	PASSIVE-AGGRESSIVE	PREFRONTAL LOBE SYNDROME	BORDERLINE	INFANTILE AUTISM
Learning Style (Imaging & Imagination)	Analytic-extrovert	Analytic-introvert	Analytic-introvert	Intuitive-introvert	Erratic	Intuitive-introvert
SELF-SYSTEM						
Self-awareness	High	High	Low	Erratic	Low	Low
Self-evaluation	Omnipotent, omniscient	Grandiose, omniscient	Omnipotent	Defective	Ambivalent	Lacking
Self-concept	Entitlement to attention and power	Ill-fated, rejected, persecuted	Martyr, superhero, revenge-seeking	Frustrated, acted-upon	Fragmented, empty	Lacking, brittle
Self-esteem	High	Low	High	Low	Low	Variable
Self-development Level	Symbolic-impulsive	Conceptual-imperial	Evaluative-affiliative	Low	Symbolic-impulsive	Sensorimotor
TEMPERAMENT						
Disposition (Mood)	Choleric	Choleric	Melancholic	Phlegmatic	Choleric	Phlegmatic
Attention						
Involuntary						
Vigilant	Variable	High	Variable	Low	Variable	High
Orienting	Variable	Keen	Variable	Sluggish	Variable	Avoidant
Stimulus Modulation	High threshold	Low threshold	High threshold	Low threshold	Low threshold	High threshold
Voluntary						
Scanning	Narrow	Broad	Narrow	Narrow	Broad	Narrow
Focusing	Variable	Precise	Precise	Imprecise	Imprecise	Precise
Concentration	Variable	Variable	Variable	Perseverative	Distractible	Intense
Motivation-Movement						
Context Related						
Excitement	Variable	Low	Low	Low	High	Low
Investment in Work	Variable	Variable	Low	Low	Erratic	Erratic
Motor Incoordination	Non-specific	Non-specific	Non-specific	Variable	Variable	Variable
Context Unrelated						
Constitutional	Variable	Hypokinetic	Variable	Hypokinetic	Hyperkinetic	Hypokinetic
Adventitious Movements	Non-specific	Non-specific	Non-specific	Non-specific	Variable	Motor stereotopies

588

COGNITION						
Flexible-rigid	Rigid	Rigid	Flexible	Rigid	Erratic	Rigid
Automatization	Variable	High	Variable	Low	Low	Erratic
Field Dependent vs. Independent	Field independent	Field dependent	Field independent	Field dependent	Ambivalent	Field independent
Visual or Auditory Preference	Variable	Auditory	Auditory	Variable	Variable	Visual
Intermodal Integration	Non-specific	Non-specific	Non-specific	Variable	Poor	Poor
Locus of Control	Internal	External	External	External	Ambivalent	Internal
Imagery	Weak	Strong verbal	Strong	Weak	Poor	Poor
Spatial Orientation	Variable	Variable	Variable	Variable	Poor	Variable
Memory	Keen	Keen	Forgetful	Erratic	Erratic	Erratic
LANGUAGE						
Receptive	Variable	Keen	Keen	Variable	Erratic	Blocked
Inner	Well developed	Well-developed	Well-developed	Sluggish	Primitive	Defective
Expressive	Facile	Facile	Facile	Erratic	Erratic	Idiosyncratic
MANAGERIAL SYSTEM						
Impulse Control						
Drive Gratification Delay	Weak	Strong	Strong	Weak	Weak	Strong
Tolerance of Distress	Low	Low	Variable	Low	Low	Low
Modulation of Emotions	Weak	Variable	Variable	Weak	Weak	Weak
Selective Drive Regression	Variable	Restrained	Variable	Indiscriminant	Volatile	Blocked
Information Analysis						
External vs. Internal Discrimination	Accurate	Variable	Accurate	Variable	Erratic	Erratic
Relevance of Perceptions	Discerning	Misinterprets, poor	Discerning	Variable	Poor	Erratic
Thinking						
Synthesis	Global	Erroneous-logical	Variable	Weak	Weak	Weak
Decision Making	Decisive	Decisive	Indecisive	Indecisive	Erratic	Abruptly decisive
Planning	Variable	Variable	Variable	Poor	Poor	Poor
Thinking Style						
Automatic	Strong	Variable	Variable	Weak	Weak	Variable
Problem Solving	Strong	Variable	Variable	Weak	Weak	Variable
Creative	High	Variable	Variable	Low	Low	Erratic
Implementing Actions						
Time Sequencing	Variable	Variable	Variable	Poor	Poor	Erratic
Efficiency	Variable	Variable	Low	Low	Low	Erratically high
Verifying Actions	Variable	Variable	Variable	Careless	Erratic	Erratically perfectionistic

Figure 28-6b.

589

Western cultures (Fadely & Hosler, 1979). At the integrative-achievement level of self-development, they fit experience into categories, persevere in tasks, and have good long-term memories (Eysenck, 1977). They readily link verbal descriptions with visual pictures (Hunt, 1983). They are rational, field independent, and in control of themselves (Goldstein & Blackman, 1978). With other persons these children tend to be affiliative, respond to the reasoning of adults, learn from others, and deferentially submit to authority. They may be students, however, who take in and give out information with little useful integration into their own lives (Kubie, 1962).

This type resembles the rationally oriented personality described by Jung (Myers, 1962) and the sensible-judicious type described by Keirsey and Bates (1978). It also resembles the intellective type found in professionals in the physical sciences (Welsh, 1975; 1980) and in undergraduate engineering students (Forisha, 1983).

Evaluative-Affiliative Level Fixation

At the evaluative-affiliative level of self-development, analytic-extroverted children need to fit experience into logical systems, and are distressed if it does not. Consequently, they dislike the liberal arts and the social sciences. If they do not find logical orderliness in either the material or the teacher, they cannot bring their best energies and effort to academic tasks (Buss, 1980).

The analytic-extroverted child is disposed to become an authoritarian personality who thinks in terms of rigid categories and stereotypes, believes in oversimplified explanations for phenomena, and exhibits an intolerance of ambiguity (Goldstein & Blackman, 1978; Messick, 1976). Because of the tendency to focus attention outward, these children rarely examine their emotions or motives (Buss, 1980). Their highly developed verbal skills tend to protect them from having to deal with their internal worlds (Blank, 1972).

Verbal memory is often highly developed in these children, who easily absorb what they hear. Should their memorized information prove insufficient, however, they may become paralyzed when confronted with the unknown. They have difficulty visualizing future events and recoil from contemplation beyond the immediate present.

These children tend to learn in school from lectures, texts, readings, and audiotapes (Kolb et al, 1971). They are likely to work best in situations in which they know what is expected of them. They can work independently at a steady speed with accuracy and attention to details. They do not respond well to the unexpected or to stressors, however (Buss, 1980).

Conceptual-Imperial Level Fixation

Although a degree of concern about orderliness and precision are important ingredients of successful performance in school, analytic-extroverted children may be overfocused (Kinsbourne & Caplan, 1979) and develop compulsive personalities, if self-development remains at the conceptual-imperial level.

The compulsive personality revolves around the dominant self-image of being a compliant child who is continually frustrated by guilt because of perceived imperfections. Children with compulsive personalities tend to be perfectionistic, rigid, ruminative, doubting, righteous, intellectualizing, and unsentimental (Flor-Henry, 1983). Such children like to do one thing at a time and become disorganized if compelled to attend to several things at once. Their field independence and internal locus of control may cause them to feel an inordinate sense of responsibility for their actions. Their strong impulse control minimizes the possibility of behavior problems and, coupled with cognitive rigidity, inhibits selective drive regression. They restrict their personal involvements, and as older children or adults, they may be pedantic list-makers, who exhaust the patience of associates.

Compulsive children are alert, focused in attention, and capable of prolonged concentration. They are verbally oriented and fit into didactic educational methods and may not conflict with usual school standards except when it is time to switch tasks. Rather from the vantage point of others, they are conforming caricatures of what schools expect of pupils. They work carefully, check their work, stick to tasks, and do not disrupt their classmates. For this reason the compulsive child has been overlooked as prone to school failure.

Compulsive children's performance of schoolwork may suffer, however, because of preoccupation with details, worry, and examination anxiety. Compulsive rituals, such as pencil sharpening and continual erasing, may thwart productivity. They may be unable to finish their schoolwork on time. They tend to hesitate unduly before committing themselves to an answer, which they check and recheck even when they recognize that it is correct. At home rituals devoted to cleanliness may interfere with doing homework.

At least three kinds of pressures contribute to the development of a compulsive personality. One is anxiety because of guilt aroused by hostile impulses leading to punitive, inflexible self-evaluations (Shapiro, 1965). This may result from strong parental suppression of a child's anger, especially by threatening the child with loss of love (Hoffman, 1970). A second source of pressure that might prepare the way for a compulsive personality is an overload of demands from the family or school for achievement or religious conduct. Third, a child who lives in an environment in which there is little interaction with peers or parents may adopt a compulsive style as an adaptation.

Symbolic-Impulsive Level Fixation

At the symbolic-impulsive level of self development, analytic-extroverted children may have obsessive-compulsive neuroses (Adams, 1973). Their mental life is cluttered with irrelevant thoughts separated from emotions by the psychological defense of isolation. In contrast to the child with a hysterical character in whom only emotions are conscious and the mind is empty because of the repression of internal imagery, these children are dispassionately plagued with internal imagery that would be frightening to others. Their attention is narrowed, preoccupied with detail, and missing the flavor of conviction. They vacillate between doubt and dogma. Because their minds are cluttered with irrelevant details, they become anxious when required to make decisions, with resulting paralysis of actions and confusion.

The Intuitive-Extroverted Child

> I love the feeling of running and lying on the grass. I dream of racing to distant places in a moment and living in tomorrow and yesterday as if they were today. I can sense things before they happen. I learn about the world without reading or going to school. I am determined to do what I will, and I am full of love and hate all at once. I love to be touched and to touch back. I get into trouble because I forget what time it is. Everyone worries about my school grades, except me.

Imaginative, creative, intuitive-extroverted children with their predominantly nonverbal, impulsive style of life contrast sharply with analytic-extroverted children, who adhere to convention and logic (Fadely & Hosler, 1979). Intuitive-extroverted children seek new experiences and relish thrills. They plunge into friendly expanses and wish to conquer the world. These qualities were admired and successful in earlier

America, but are less adaptive today, particularly in schools (Raeithel, 1979).

At the integrative-achievement level of self-development, these happy-go-lucky children approach others enthusiastically. They jauntily embrace life with unedited comments and gestures. Their friendliness and open, guileless remarks enchant strangers. They are the ones who discover the path to a hermit's cottage, uncover a nest of eggs, find attic treasures, and duck under a barrier to shake a politician's hand. Their free spirits may be regarded by others as laziness, however (Smith, S.L., 1980).

The world of these children resembles the mysticism of Eastern religions. They are field dependent and direct their senses toward external sources of stimulation as a means of increasing arousal (Eysenck, 1977; Gale, 1983). They relate to the world according to their moods and immediate sensory experiences. They are extremely sensitive to the feelings of others. They perceive obscure connections, think divergently, and are creative. They resemble Jung's feeling-oriented person, who is dominated by seeking pleasure and avoiding distress (Myers, 1962). They resemble the intuitive-feeling type of Keirsey and Bates (1978). They are oriented toward an internal locus of control, which may assume magical proportions. They are adept in recognizing spatial patterns as reflected in the ability to rotate mental visual images (Hunt, 1983).

In one study the intuitive-extroverted type was heavily represented in psychology and business undergraduate students (Forisha, 1983). In another typology it resembles the imaginative type, also heavily represented in creative sales and business persons (Welsh, 1975; 1980).

Some of these children may have the strong right-hemisphere powers of the "mirrored" person or the "Leonardo syndrome" seen in the creative natures of persons who otherwise might be regarded mistakenly as dyslexic. Leonardo da Vinci was left-handed, and his notebooks were inscribed with mirror writing. He studied flowers, anatomy, and the flight of birds. He conceived of the flywheel, the machine gun, the parachute, and the machine lathe. He did all of this with a matchless immediacy and penetration, and almost without a word, simply by drawing what he imagined (Hart, 1962; Rawson, 1982).

Intuitive-extroverted children are strongly influenced by the attention of a teacher and the interest of an activity. A caring relationship with a teacher can carry them through many school tasks that do not interest them. When stimulated both by a teacher and the content of school subjects, these children produce the most. When both conditions are absent, they lose interest in instructional procedures (Blackman & Goldstein, 1982).

Mature intuitive-extroverted children tend to learn best in school from workbooks, games, and simulations (Kolb et al, 1971). They profit from trying out their ideas to see if they work and from opportunities to discover new ways of doing things. They are not able to provide a detailed accounting of how they use their time, however.

Evaluative-Affiliative Level Fixation

At the evaluative-affiliative level of self development, the intuitive-extroverted style is the global, relatively diffusely focused, impressionistic hysterical personality (Flor-Henry, 1983).

The hysterical personality is based upon an insatiable attention-seeking self-image that seeks to imitate others. Children with hysterical personalities live in romantic, fantasy-dominated worlds and lack intellectual curiosity and persistent concentration powers. They do not have solid self-images and are easily carried away by impressions. They tend to be naive, emotionally labile, impulsive, dramatic, histrionic, and suggestible. These children do not attend well and both miss and misinterpret material, although they are capable of intense concentration. Repression is facilitated by their impressionistic style, because their attention is not sharply focused and logically coordinated with external facts (Shapiro, 1965).

These children are field dependent and aware of ongoing events, but they participate in them largely when personal wishes and interests are involved because of their internal locus of control. Their weak impulse control and fragile emotional modulation produce erratic and exaggerated responses to urges and emotions. Their performance of schoolwork ranges from creative enthusiastic accomplishments to lapses of boredom with routines. From the vantage point of others, they are seen as charming but unreliable.

These children may show conversion reaction symptoms in the form of impairment in or loss of voluntary functions. For example, seizurelike conversion symptoms were reported in adolescents who had unrecognized visual imagery interference with their school performances (Silver, 1982). Their symptoms disappeared once their underlying cognitive problems and an associated lack of self-confidence were identified and treated. Another example is a child who became paralyzed when asked to read in front of a group (Simpson, 1979). As she gripped the lecturn to steady herself, a white light, like a flashbulb, went off in front of her eyes. As the light cleared, she saw the words on the page rise, fall, twist, and turn, as if the page were a paper floating under water.

Chronic invalidism and hypochondriasis may be a response to academic pressures when a physical illness is simulated by histrionic teenagers. The physical incapacity may be the result of a fantasy converted into body language. The stress of prolonged excitement and fear also may precipitate psychophysiological somatic symptoms (Kotkov, 1965).

An adult with dyslexia described having psychophysiological symptoms when she was tutored as a child (Simpson, 1979). She recalled admonishing herself to keep calm as she tried to read words; however, a panic, opaque as fog and numbing as ether, settled into her brain. At other times she felt as though her brain had turned to ice and ached. When asked to look up a word in a dictionary, she felt as though a flying tile had hit her in the temple, dealing a stunning blow. When facing a dictionary, she felt like an impotent, stupid little girl, and a giant ball of stone formed in her throat. Note taking made her brain ache. Dividing her attention between listening and writing was like patting her head with one hand while making circles on her abdomen with the other.

A person with a hysterical personality may resort to pathological lying, which means that the person believes in the reality of internal images and acts upon them (Prelinger & Zimet, 1964). When confronted pathological liars usually acknowledge their fabrications; however, it is difficult to determine whether their falsehoods are intended to deceive or are circumscribed distortions of reality. Their behavior usually is self-defeating and provokes punishment from their outraged victims (Kaplan & Sadock, 1985).

Conceptual-Imperial Stage Fixation

The dependent personality, more fully described in Chapter 26, revolves around a self-image of an infantile person with magical powers who seeks attention through helpless dependency. The child appears to be aware of ongoing events and participating in classroom activities. Field dependency and an external locus of control heighten the appearance of involvement with others and interest in school. The child's apparent strong impulse control actually is based upon defensive passivity that is responsible for the appearance of high frustration tolerance and emotional bland-ness. The child fails in schoolwork because of numerous errors, the failure to complete and turn in work, and forgetfulness. From the vantage point of others, the child is seen as compliant, and even charming, but as a hopeless student.

Symbolic-Impulsive Stage Fixation

The impulsive personality has a dominant self-image of an insatiable attention-seek-ing person who must have one's own way, as described in detail in Chapter 25. The child does not pay attention to others and cannot concentrate in the classroom, lead-ing to boredom and impulsive behavior. The child is field independent and ori-ented to an internal locus of control with little resulting concern for routines or the interests of others. The child's weak im-pulse control results in disruptive behavior determined by momentary urges. Per-formance in school is impaired by an ina-bility to carry out the sequential routines of schoolwork, the failure to listen to in-structions, and poor planning. From the vantage point of others, the child is seen as emotionally labile, willful, and disrup-tive.

The Intuitive-Introverted Child

> I like to make things with my hands. I like to work alone and don't like to have others telling me what to do or checking up on me. I get frustrated when I try to explain things to other people, and they don't understand what I am trying to say. I can find my way around strange places easily. I can't remember names very well and do not need many friends.

Intuitive-introverted children enjoy making things but not talking about them. They are fascinated by taking apart and reassembling machinery from visual and spatial memory. They readily improvise

repairs and may devise mechanical inven-tions. They are self-reliant and field in-dependent. They use visual imagery in problem solving and have difficulty ex-plaining their ideas verbally to others. They have excellent orientation in space and direction.

Intuitive-introverted children become fully engaged in schoolwork when their imaginations are fired with intriguing ideas and plans. Unless a teacher or the material inspires them, however, boredom with rou-tines drives them to seek out something else, such as daydreaming or reading off-task material. These children tend to ex-plore their moods, ambitions, and beliefs (Buss, 1980). Their consciousness is filled with associations and imagined possibilities that do not depend directly on their senses. They rely upon intuitive insights. These children resemble Jung's intuitive kind of adult, who relies upon hunches (Myers, 1962), and the intuitive-thinking type of Keirsey and Bates (1978). They also resem-ble the intuitive type described in profes-sionals in the arts and humanities (Welsh, 1975; 1980).

These children are likely to do their best in situations that let them work with their own ideas in their own ways. They respond to chances to be creative, follow their cur-iosity, set their own standards, and work hard when they feel like it. They need time to think out their ideas before acting upon them. These children tend to learn most effectively in school through the use of demonstrations, field trips, computer-as-sisted instruction, and hands-on material (Kolb et al, 1971).

Evaluative-Affiliative Level Fixation

At the evaluative-affiliative level of self-de-velopment, the children resemble the "slow-to-warm-up" child (Thomas & Chess, 1977). They initially show mildly negative re-sponses to new stimuli and are not verbally expressive. They accordingly may appear to be apathetic, disinterested, and even of low intelligence. The integration of new information requires time and effort, so that they can easily be overburdened by stimuli and shun external stimulation (Gale, 1983). Communicating ideas to other people also tends to be laborious (Dixon, 1983).

Conceptual-Imperial Level Fixation

At the conceptual-imperial level of self-development, the children tend to withdraw from others by ignoring and escaping. They tend to be absorbed in fantasy and their own activities. They prefer to be alone and fail to develop social skills, increasing the tug toward social isolation. They may conjure up imaginary companions as substitutes for social relationships with other children. They may be frightened by strangers and stimulating environments. Consequently, they perform schoolwork best in situations with minimal distractions.

Whereas extroverts tend to perform at a higher level when they feel aroused, introverts tend to perform at a lower level. Introverted children tend to have memory problems, especially for detailed information under pressured conditions. When they acquire information under less pressured circumstances, their memory is unimpaired (Eysenck, 1977).

Symbolic-Impulsive Level Fixation

At the symbolic-impulsive level of self-development, intuitive-introverted children may have schizoid characters centering around a self-image of being unlovable. The schizoid child lacks warm, tender feelings for others and is indifferent to praise, criticism, and the feelings of others. Field independency and an internal locus of control result in a lack of participation in classroom activities and a preoccupation with internal imagery.

The schizoid child's strong impulse control generally produces a lack of emotional responsiveness, however, a low tolerance for distress leads to readily giving up on difficult schoolwork. The child's performance in school is impaired by a lack of productivity and misinterpretation of material. An idiosyncratic form of creativity may appear on occasions.

Schizoid children are loners, humorless, and aloof. They are vague about their goals, indecisive in their actions, self-absorbed, absentminded, and detached from their environments. To others they appear withdrawn, isolated, and odd.

The Analytic-Introverted Child

> I like to write poetry and do a lot of different things, but my teachers say I don't stick with one thing very long. They say I jump to conclusions, but I really know a lot about why things happen. I can tell what people are thinking about me and am very sensitive to injustice. If my feelings have been hurt by people I wanted to trust, I don't trust anyone.

At the integrative-achievement level of self development, analytic-introverted children are inclined toward the verbal expression of ideas and feelings. They are creative and like to play with solutions to problems. They enjoy talking, writing, and improvising. They seek music and other mood-setting sensory stimuli, but are not well oriented in space and direction. They tend to be field dependent, but to be inflexible in cognitive discrimination and to have low stimulus thresholds. Although sensitive to external stimuli, they tend to make inaccurate inferences from wide conceptual categories. They are weak in automatized behavior and lack perseverance in repetitive learning tasks. They tend to perceive an external locus of control, such as being dominated by fate.

This character type resembles the sensing, practical kind of person described by Jung (Myers, 1962) and the sensible–playful type of Keirsey and Bates (1978). In one study it was heavily represented in undergraduate education students (Forisha, 1983). It also resembles the industrious type described in service-oriented persons (Welsh, 1975; 1980).

Analytic-introverted children need logical order and harmonious working relationships (Buss, 1980). They respond to what their senses can master and put to use. They are likely to do their best work in situations that produce practical results and have goals toward which they can progress in an orderly way. They learn from first-hand experience and work with concrete hands-on projects. They can learn from others in group discussions and from audiovisual aids, such as television and movies (Kolb et al, 1971).

Evaluative-Affiliative Level Fixation

At the evaluative-affiliative level, these children may have passive-aggressive personalities with the dominant self-image of being a martyred hero, who seeks revenge by underachieving in school. Their attention is distracted from classroom activities by daydreaming. They are bored, forgetful, and resistant to schedules. Although they are field independent, an external locus of control leads to a feeling of being controlled by others, which they resist through sabotage. Their strong impulse control favors the expression of hostility by passive means. They are wary and fearful when under stress and tend to blame others for their difficulties. Still they comply with rules while acting put-upon and sulking. They are attuned to the subjective world of feelings and values and are alert to injustices. Their performance in schoolwork is marred by poor decision making, and their planning is careless and inefficient. From the vantage point of others, the child is seen as stubborn, procrastinating, and forgetful.

Conceptual-Imperial Level Fixation

When self-development remains at the conceptual-imperial level, the children may have paranoid personalities. The paranoid personality is based upon a self-image of being an ill-fated, persecuted person who expects, and even provokes, rejection. Because of their sensitivity and suspiciousness, they are disliked by others. This adds actual to imagined rejections and intensifies their suspiciousness, sometimes leading to delusions of persecution. Their pattern of interpersonal relations is one of withdrawal, although they may explode in rage when their suspiciousness is extreme (Shapiro, 1965).

Paranoid children are preoccupied with what they imagine are the attitudes and feelings of others toward them. Because of their perception of an external locus of control, they interpret actions and events as personally intended and make intuitive, unwarranted generalizations from random events. They are extremely sensitive to traces of hostility in others. Their inefficient analysis of internal and external imagery gives rise to inaccurate interpretations of reality. Suspiciousness and guardedness may follow, in addition to a general contraction of emotional experience and loss of spontaneity. Their verification of their own actions also tends to be faulty. Their self-evaluation tends to be high and self-esteem low.

The paranoid child's strong, but brittle, impulse control produces a generally implacable appearance punctuated by hostile outbursts in which others are blamed for personal shortcomings and frustrations. The child's performance in school is marred by erroneous logic in schoolwork and social isolation. The child's productivity varies and is inhibited when authority figures are seen as hostile and persecutory. To others the child appears touchy, hostile, and irresponsible.

The common assumption that the paranoid child needs affection is well-meaning but naive. For them tenderness initially is a frightening thing. D. H. Lawrence (1922) provided a clear illustration of the way in which a distrustful person avoids tender feelings:

> I don't want kindness or love. I don't believe in harmony and people loving one another. I believe in the fight and nothing else . . . I want the world to hate me, because I can't bear the thought that it might love me, and especially from such a repulsive world as I think it is. . . .

Symbolic-Impulsive Level Fixation

At the symbolic-impulsive level, analytic-introverted children may have an oppositional personality, if they have not fully individuated from their parents, and a narcissitic personality, if they have not fully attached to their parents. These personality types are described in detail in Chapter 26.

The oppositional personality is based upon an underlying self-image of being an attacked victim, who counteracts by seeking to control others. The child's attentiveness is impaired by distractibility and an automatic tendency to oppose the influence of authority figures. An exaggerated field-independent orientation is a reflection of an effort to establish oneself as an independent person. Such children's external locus of control, however, leads to continual embroilment with others, who are perceived as trying to dominate them. Their weak impulse control is manifested in a low tolerance of frustration. Their performance of schoolwork is blocked by authority conflicts through open defiance or sulking withdrawal. They lack the ability to solve problems independently and responsibly to follow through on tasks. To others they appear irritable, defiant, and irresponsible.

The child with a narcissistic personality holds a self-image of omnipotence and omniscience with a sense of entitlement to power and the admiration of others. The child has a high capacity for attention and concentration on interesting activities, but becomes bored readily by those that are not personally rewarding. Field independence and an internal locus of control make the child unresponsive to others but capable of creative acts. The child's weak impulse control leads to emotional displays and a low tolerance of frustration. The child's schoolwork may be exceedingly productive in creative activities but unproductive in uninteresting areas. If the child values excellence in school, however, achievement may be high. To others the child appears selfish, conceited, and, perhaps, brilliant.

SPECIFIC FUNCTIONAL DISABILITIES AND SCHOOLWORK PERFORMANCE

The distinction between disability and handicap made by vocational rehabilitation specialists has relevance to education, as pointed out in Chapter 2. In the health field, the term *disability* refers to the condition of a person, whereas *handicap* refers to interference with a person's activity.

More specifically a disability is the functioning of an organ system that departs from a particular health standard. The diagnosis of the existence and degree of a disability lies within the province of professionals trained to diagnose disabilities. For example, cerebral palsy can be expressed in the disability of paralysis of an arm, and a lens cataract can cause the disability of blindness.

A handicap exists when a disability significantly interferes with the performance of an activity and requires special consideration or compensatory advantage. The degree and salience of a disability determine whether it constitutes a handicap. The judgment of the existence and degree of a handicap lies with professionals equipped to evaluate social, educational, vocational, and recreational functional abilities. For example, a cerebral palsied child with a paralyzed arm may not be handicapped in walking but be handicapped in riding a bicycle. A blind person may be handicapped in traveling alone but not when assisted by a guide dog in familiar places. Moreover color blindness is a disability but not a handicap, unless one wishes to be an interior decorator.

A disability then is a distinguishing characteristic of an individual that is susceptible to objective study. A handicap is a judgment of the effect a disability has upon a specific activity. The judgment of handicap has social, legal, political, and educational implications through determining whether an individual qualifies for exemption, compensatory programming, or financial assistance.

The concepts of disability and handicap can help to clarify the learning problems of children in school. To adapt these health concepts to education, a further distinction should be made between educational handicaps and educational and functional disabilities.

Children who cannot read or cipher well enough to participate in academic activities are handicapped in schoolwork and require special consideration. Thus educational handicap is a useful concept for identifying and programming for children who definitely require specialized educational services. The assessment of educational handicaps is based upon academic achievement levels.

In contrast children who founder in acquiring basic academic skills because of educational disabilities but have not progressed sufficiently to be handicapped in schoolwork can be managed through adaptation of academic tasks to their learning styles and by tutoring. Parenthetically, when children cannot carry a tune, we do not say they have a singing disability. To be sure they can learn to sing better with practice, but some people sing well and others do not. Yet we regard children who have difficulty reading as having disabilities because their personal characteristics constitute disabilities in educational settings. For complicated reasons we accept individual differences in arts and athletics more readily than in academic learning. Thus the assessment of educational disability focuses upon reading and ciphering skills. However, if performance in music or athletics were viewed as critical, similar disabilities could be identified in those areas.

A further distinction can be made between educational and functional disabilities. Kirk and Chalfant (1984) make a parallel distinction between academic and developmental disabilities. Educational disabilities are based upon underlying personal characteristics in the form of disabilities in CNS functions. In fact an educational disability usually is but one manifestation of more generalized functional disabilities. For example, a visual-spatial dyslexia may be one manifestation of a dysgnosia that is also reflected in right–left confusion and spatial disorientation. Conversely functional disabilities may be present and not be manifested in educational disabilities, as illustrated by partial color blindness or gross motor incoordination. Functional disability has the advantage over developmental disability in that specific CNS functions can be described without implying a developmental or pathological etiology. Clinical techniques are useful in detecting functional disabilities in people who are currently described as having learning or developmental disabilities.

From the perspective of a child's external world, CNS dysfunctions can be seen as functional disabilities that can become educational disabilities and educational handicaps. From the perspective of a child's internal world, functional disabilities can be analyzed in terms of deficits in the components, structures, and processes of the subsystems whose output they represent. In a particular child, these deficits, in turn, point to the interaction between the subsystems of the CNS and ultimately to the group, organization, and societal variables that influence that child. The challenge of considering all of these variables may seem to be overwhelming at this time. Unless they are taken into account, however, the scientific validity of research is questionable. Fortunately the management of specific children need not await research on the precise causes of their problems.

An advantage of the concept of functional disability is that it focuses attention on variables in a child that underlie performance in school. It provides a framework for explaining behavior beyond laziness or lack of motivation. Another advantage is that it opens up an understanding of a child in terms of individual differences and pathological conditions. Moreover it brings into play examination of the multiple societal, organizational, interpersonal, individual, organ, and cellular system levels in understanding the origins of a particular child's functional disabilities.

The relationship of specific disabilities in CNS functions to schoolwork can be demonstrated by relating the behavioral manifestations of variations in these functions to each component of schoolwork and then to educational disabilities and handicaps, as illustrated in Figure 28-7. To work effectively in school, children must be able to accept the influence of a teacher; be motivated and able to pay attention and concentrate quietly; be able to communicate verbally and in writing; and be able to organize, begin, carry out, finish, and correct academic tasks.

The level of development of a child's self-system affects that child's ability to accept and use the influence of a teacher. A child's self-awareness includes both private and public awareness of the self in social contexts. A child who is unaware of one's appearance and behavior has difficulty relating to others. A child who is excessively self-aware in public is susceptible to shame, embarrassment, and shyness. A child with a fragmented self-image lacks continuity in time and space. Exaggerations in both negative or positive self-evaluations lead to unrealistic self-deprecation or grandiosity, with resulting failure to draw upon, or the ignoring of, a teacher's influence. Low self-esteem may be expressed through depression and loss of interest in schoolwork.

One's temperament influences one's motivation and ability to pay attention and concentrate. The sanguine temperament is expressed in cheerful optimism, the phlegmatic in sluggishness, the choleric in irritability, and the melancholic in moodiness. Vigilant attention can be alert or diverted, as in daydreaming. Absence seizures are specific disabilities in vigilance. Orienting responses vary from slow to quick reaction times. Stimulus modulation may produce a high or low threshold of responsiveness. Scanning attention may be broad or narrow and affect a child's awareness of surroundings. The precision of attention focusing affects whether or not a child notices details. Powers of concentration may be weak or strong, resulting in distractibility or perseveration.

Easily excited children exuberantly react to stimuli and have difficulty settling down to schoolwork. The various forms of hyperkinesis are specific movement disabilities. Poorly coordinated children are clumsy in handwriting and at sports. Children with constitutionally high energy levels are hyperkinetic, as are those with adventitious movements. Anxious children are hyperkinetic and cannot sit still. Specific mood disabilities are depression and hypomania. Depressed children lose interest in school-

Dimensions of Functional Disabilities Individual Differences—Pathology	Schoolwork Performance	Dimensions of Educational Disabilities	Dimensions of Educational Handicaps
SELF SYSTEM **Self-Awareness** **Self-Evaluation** **Self-Concept**	**Accepting Influence of Teacher**	Self-awareness of appearance and behavior in social context: shyness, shame, embarrassment Accuracy of judgments of self-concepts: self-deprecation—discouragement; self-aggrandizement—omnipotence, omniscience Dominant self-concept: attention seeking (hysterical, narcissistic, impulsive); power seeking (oppositional, narcissistic—conceited, bully, impudent, quarrelsome, defiant); revenge seeking (passive-aggressive—stubborn); helplessness (passive-dependent—submissive, easily led, pseudostupid); paranoid (sensitive to criticism); compulsive (perfectionistic); schizoid (withdrawn)	**Deficient Social Skills** **Authority Relations** **Peer Relations**
Self-Esteem **TEMPERAMENT** **Disposition (Mood)** **Attention** INVOLUNTARY Vigilant Orienting Stimulus Modulation VOLUNTARY (Interest) Scanning Focusing Concentration **Motivation-Movement-Affect** CONTEXT RELATED Excitement Anxiety Drive Investment Motor Incoordination CONTEXT UNRELATED Constitutional Adventitious Hypomanic Depression	**Ability and Motivation to Pay Attention and Concentrate Quietly**	Low self-confidence and despair Sanguine (cheerful), phlegmatic (calm), choleric (irritable), melancholic (morose) moods Level of consciousness and alertness: lapses in attention, daydreaming Variations in reaction time: sluggishness—misses instructions Over and under responsiveness: confused, unresponsive Readiness to pay attention to stimuli of external world Distinctness in noticing details Ability to engage and sustain interest in tasks: perseveration, distractibility Overreaction to stimuli: exuberant, cannot settle down Mobilization for fight or flight: hyperkinetic, cannot sit still or concentrate Disinterest, boredom: hyperkinetic, fails to concentrate upon and complete school work Clumsy fine or gross motor coordination: messy handwriting, inept in athletics Low or high energy level: continuously hypoactive and sluggish or hyperactive Erratic tremors: continually hyperkinetic; covering movements; cannot sit still; handwriting erratic Exaggerated euphoria: continually hyperactive, flits from one activity to another Psychomotor retardation, loss of interest in school work, poor concentration, sadness	**Inability to Initiate and Sustain Effort In School Work**
COGNITION **Flexible-Rigid** **Automatization** **Field Independent vs. Dependent** **Visual Preference** **Auditory Preference** **Intermodal Integration** **Imagery** **Spatial Orientation**	**Ability to See, Hear, Interpret and Understand as Does Teacher**	Cognitive shifting between foreground and background and different stimulus fields: loses place in work, misses connections between lectures and book Conditioned, rote learning inefficient Degree of reliance upon external and internal referents: excessively swayed by distractions in context, impervious to external influence Recognizes and remembers visual stimuli best Recognizes and remembers auditory stimuli best Ability to relate visual and auditory stimuli: sounds and words Ability to imagine sights and sounds: may facilitate or impede schoolwork Orientation to direction and geographical location: use of space on paper, drawing figures, awareness of shapes	**Lack of Knowledge** **Time and Space Confusion** **Memory Deficits** **Arithmetic Retardation**

Function	Description	Ability	Outcome
Time Orientation	Sense of time: ability to sequence stimuli		
Memory	Short- and long-term memory: for information, where things are, when and what to do		
Imagination	Ability to form and use symbols and concepts		
Locus of Control	Sense of self-control or being excessively controlled by others		
LANGUAGE		**Ability to Communicate Verbally and in Writing**	**Reading Retardation**
Speech Disorders	Articulation, voice and fluence difficulty: dyslalia, dysphonia, stuttering; embarrassment, shyness		
Written Language Vulnerabilities			
Vestibulo-cerebellar dysmetria	Focusing difficulty in reading-vestibulo-cerebellar dyslexia		
Visual-spatial dysgnosia	Recognition difficulty in reading and spelling-visual-spatial dyslexia		
Auditory-linguistic dysphasia	Dysnomia in reading and spelling-auditory-linguistic dyslexia		
Articulo-graphic dyspraxia	Spelling and writing difficulty-articulo-graphic dyslexia		
Dysphasias			
Receptive	Difficulty understanding speech: jargon speech, does not respond appropriately to verbal instructions		
Expressive	Difficulty expressing ideas in speech: reduced, halting speech flow; frustration		
MANAGERIAL		**Ability to Organize, Begin, Carry Out, Finish, and Correct Academic Tasks**	**Inability to Solve Problems in Schoolwork**
Impulse Control			
Drive Gratification Delay	Degree of restraint of urges low		
Tolerance of Distress	Frustration level low		
Modulation of Emotions	Tempering of emotional responses lacking		
Selective Drive Regression	Appropriately, freely express urges in play infrequently		
Information Analysis			
External-Internal Stimulus Discrimination	Distinguishing external and internal percepts and images inefficient		
Relevance of Perceptions	Inaccurately assesses percepts and images		
Thinking			
Synthesis	Classifying and blending related images inefficient		
Decision Making	Choosing between alternatives and arriving at decisions difficult		
Planning	Arranging activities in relation to future consequences inefficient		
Style			
Automatic	Learning automatic patterns for problem solving inefficient		
Problem Solving	Rational and logical inductive and deductive problem solving ineffective		
Creative	Drawing internal imagery for problem solving activities difficult		
Implementing Actions	Carrying out ideas in actions ineffective		
Time Sequencing	Sense of time: ability to follow instructions and schedules		
Efficiency	Effectiveness in carrying out actions		
Verifying Actions	Inefficient monitoring and correcting of actions		

Figure 28-7.

work, are sluggish, and concentrate poorly. Hypomanic children are hyperactive and flit from one activity to another.

Individual variations in cognition affect the ways in which children process information. Specific cognitive disabilities occur in the sensory modalities, spatial orientation, and memory. Cognitively rigid children cannot easily shift back and forth between foreground and background in their perception of a teacher, a blackboard, their desktops, and other children. Children who are weak in automatization do not condition easily in rote tasks, such as in learning the alphabet or multiplication tables. Children who are extremely field independent do not rely upon external information sufficiently; those who are extremely field dependent do not use their own resources effectively. Some children discriminate and retain what they see better than what is heard; others are the opposite. Many children do not relate sounds and printed words easily. A strongly perceived external locus of control deprives a child of a sense of being in control of the self and leads to inappropriate reactions to authority. Children with rich imagery may daydream or be creative. Those with impoverished imagery may be unable to visualize or auditorize problems. Children with poor spatial orientation have difficulty with directions, shapes, finding their way to places, and efficiently organizing their work on a sheet of paper. Difficulties are commonly seen in short-term and long-term memory for information, where things are, and when and what to do. A poor sense of time makes it difficult to follow step-by-step instructions and schedules.

Specific disabilities in language interfere with verbal and written communication. Speech disorders take the form of articulation, voice, and fluency difficulties that make it difficult to understand what a child is trying to say. A receptive dysphasia interferes with understanding others' speech and an expressive dysphasia with speaking ideas. A vestibulo-cerebellar dyslexia causes discomfort in reading. A visual-spatial dyslexia interferes with recognizing words and spelling. An auditory-linguistic dyslexia results in word- and meaning-finding difficulty in reading and spelling. An articulo-graphic dyslexia causes oral reading, spelling, and writing errors.

Variations in managerial functions affect a child's ability to organize, begin, carry out, finish, and correct schoolwork. Specific disabilities occur in impulse control, the analysis of perceptions, planning, organization, and thinking. The inability to delay the gratification of wishes is expressed through impulsivity. The inability to tolerate distress produces continual frustration with the inherently unpleasant aspects of schoolwork. Inefficient modulation of emotions is expressed through intense emotional displays. The inability to express drives selectively inhibits their release in play at appropriate times and places.

Difficulty in distinguishing internal from external stimuli interferes with dealing accurately with reality. Poor assessment of the relevance of perceptions causes inappropriate and confused behavior. When the ability to classify and blend information accurately is weak, decision making is difficult, and planning is poor, children have difficulty with problem-solving thinking. Weakness in automatic learning also interferes with developing conditioned responses that form the basis for unconscious automatic thinking. At times creative children encounter difficulty because of their novel ideas and behaviors. Children who lack the ability to implement their actions do not finish their schoolwork. Children who do not verify their actions produce erroneous and slipshod work.

When any of these CNS functions consistently interfere with schoolwork, a specific disability in that function can be said to exist. Disabilities can be temporary, as with depression, or enduring, as with dyslexias. Instead of resorting to the vague generalization of learning disability, we can be more precise about a particular child's underlying functional disabilities. When this is done, we usually find that, rather than having a single disability, a child shows a cluster of disabilities. The clinical process identifies them and emphasizes their treatability, so that the child can be helped appropriately. As knowledge progresses, we will be able to identify more specific disabilities with greater precision.

Figure 28-8 illustrates the way in which the detailed evaluation of a 15-year-old boy's character, or profile of specific CNS functions as expressed in his personality traits, provides a basis for understanding his underachievement in school. This boy's temperament is characterized by a sanguine disposition, sensitivity to stimuli, poor concentration, bodily tension, and a high energy level. His cognition is impaired because of his poor rote memory, distracting auditory imagery, lack of time sense, predominantly symbolic imagination, and dependency upon others for direction and advice. His ability to postpone drive gratification is strong; however, his tolerance of distress is low. It is difficult for him to plan, make decisions, and think clearly. He has an intuitive-extroverted learning style. His self-esteem is low, and his view of himself is split between that of a helpless child and an omnipotent, controlling master. His self-development is at the conceptual-imperial level, and his personality has a maladaptive dependent pattern. In school he regards himself as mentally incompetent to do the work. With this profile it is no wonder that he is unsuccessful in school.

THE PREVALENCE OF EDUCATIONAL DISABILITIES AND HANDICAPS

The types of problems that result when dispositions become educational disabilities and then handicaps are only beginning to be appreciated. At this point, we lack definitive information about the prevalence of the various forms of educational disabilities and handicaps in the general population of schoolchildren. Epidemiological studies in this area are fraught with definitional and methodological questions. It is particularly difficult to take into account cultural, educational, and family factors. Still the evidence is sufficient to provide an impression of the prevalence of types of children's learning problems in school.

In the United States and Great Britain, 17 percent of the school-age population shows evidence of some form of educational problem. Reasonable estimates of the general forms of underlying causative factors are depicted in Figure 28-9 as follows: dyslexias—2 percent (Critchley, 1974); hyperkinetic-impulsive behavior—5½ percent; lack of educational opportunity—4 percent (Adelman & Taylor, 1983; Nichols & Chen, 1981); other personality disorders—2½ percent; mental retardation—2¼ percent; childhood psychosis—¼ percent; and epilepsy—½ percent (Rutter, 1970; Holdsworth & Whitmore, 1974).

In the school year 1984–1985, the U.S. Department of Education reported that 7.5 percent of the children between the ages of three and 21 received services designated for the learning disabled, mentally retarded, and emotionally disturbed (U.S. Department of Education, 1986).

From this overview it is evident that consideration of the lack of opportunity for an adequate education must be in the foreground in approaching more than half of the over 8,000,000 children with learning problems in school. The largest group of 3,500,000 children show impulsive-hyperkinetic behavior. 1,500,000 children with various personality disorders, 1,300,000 with dyslexias, and 1,400,000 with mental retardation are of about equal prevalence. Of the children with epilepsy, 300,000 have school learning problems. Significant because of the severity of their difficulties are the 150,000 children with childhood psychoses.

CENTRAL NERVOUS SYSTEM FUNCTIONS (Character)	PERSONALITY TRAITS
TEMPERAMENT	
Disposition	Sanguine
Attention	
Vigilant	Alert, no seizures
Orienting	Quickly responsive
Stimulus Modulation	Easily overloaded
Scanning	Unobservant
Focusing	Does not notice details
Concentration	Cannot keep mind on subject
Movement	
Excitement	High with gestures and agitation
Anxiety	Apprehensive, tense
Drive Investment	Lack of interest in schoolwork
Motor Coordination	Fine and gross motor coordination intact
Constitutional	High energy level
Adventitious	No adventitious movements
COGNITION	
Flexible-rigid	Perceptual flexibility
Automatic	Poor conditioned responses
Field Indep. vs Dep.	Field dependent
Visual or Auditory Preference	Auditory preference
Intermodality Integration	Integrates sounds and visual symbols well
Imagery	Internal voice cuts off thoughts
Spatial Orientation	Excellent—visual artist
Time Orientation	Lacks time sense in present
Memory	Forgetful
Imagination	Global—predominantly symbolic
Locus of Control	External—looks to others for direction and advice
LANGUAGE	
Receptive	Intact
Inner	Occasional dysphasia—loses thought
Expressive	Occasional dyspraxia—misspeaks
MANAGERIAL SYSTEM	
Impulse Control	
Drive Gratification Delay	Very strong
Distress Tolerance	Low—"freaks out" easily
Modulation of Emotions	Weak—variable intensity
Selective Drive Regression	Acts like young child inappropriately
Information Analysis	
External vs Internal	Accurately distinguishes external and internal stimuli
Relevance of Perceptions	Appropriately weighs significance
Thinking	
Synthesis	Difficulty organizing thoughts
Decision Making	Indecisive
Planning	Difficulty setting steps to goal
Style	Automatic weak; problem solving—weak; creative—strong
Implementing Actions	Procrastinates; inefficient
Verifying Actions	Accurate
Learning Style	Intuitive-extrovert
SELF SYSTEM	
Self-awareness	Acutely self-conscious; must appear "normal"
Self-esteem	Low: feels "like crawling home to Mom"
Self-concept	Split: infantile silliness vs domineering gradiosity; mental disability excuse
Self-evaluation	Ambivalent: self-denigrating or inflating

Figure 28-8. Character structure analysis of 15-year-old boy with dependent personality pattern.

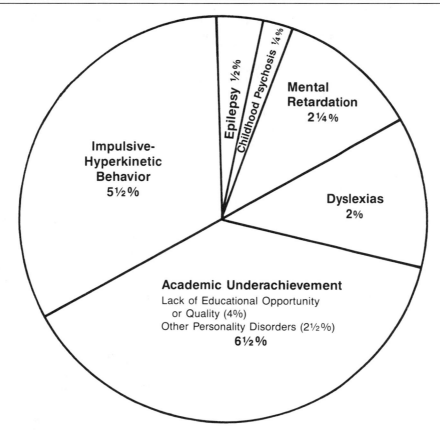

Figure 28-9. Prevalence of types of educational problems.

SUMMARY

Whether a child has difficulty in school depends upon the transformation of dispositions in that child's learning style, level of self-development, personality pattern, and specific CNS functions into educational disabilities and handicaps.

This chapter first related CNS functions to learning style, which underlies the development of a child's character and the acquisition of knowledge and skills. The proposal was made that learning styles could be defined according to a child's orientation toward external and internal imagery, in addition to a preference for analytic or intuitive imagination. Then the expression of these learning styles in work styles was delineated.

Four learning styles were identified as common predisposing factors to problems in school, especially when specific dispositions are present and neurotic processes elaborate upon them to produce maladaptive personality patterns. The level of maturity of self-development influences the degree to which each personality pattern becomes maladaptive in school.

Analytic-extroverts are conventionally oriented in school and appreciated by adults; however, they are disposed to develop obsessive-compulsive neurotic symptoms and compulsive personalities under adverse circumstances.

The second learning style is seen in the intuitive extrovert. These children are predominantly nonverbal, impulsive, creative free spirits, who contrast with the conventional verbal analytic-extroverted children. Their behavior may be readily regarded as problematic by adults. When exaggerated by defenses, this learning style may result in hysterical personality traits and symptoms.

The third learning style is found in the intuitive-introvert, who may be mechanically oriented and enjoy working with material things. The inward-directed nature of these children, coupled with their limited capacities for verbal communication, disposes them under pathogenic circumstances toward the formation of schizoid personalities.

The fourth learning style is typical of the analytic-introvert, who can be creative and interpersonally stimulating. If life experience produces mistrustful attitudes toward other people, however, the sensitivity of these children to external stimuli can lead to paranoid suspiciousness and withdrawal. In the extreme paranoid delusions and explosive rage may appear.

Analytic-extroverted children pursue logical order, intuitive-extroverted children follow their hearts, intuitive-introverted children follow whatever inspires them, and analytic-introverted children strive to engage their senses in practical matters. General awareness and acceptance of these varieties of learning styles before maladaptive personality patterns develop would contribute substantially to public and personal tolerance of valid differences in children's ways of thinking and behaving and reduce the number of children with problems in school.

Several maladaptive personality patterns, or clinical syndromes, can be defined by their characteristic variations on specific dimensions of CNS functions. Compulsive children are perfectionistically paralyzed in their work. Attention seeking is a dominant motive of children with hysterical, dependent, and impulsive personalities. Schizoid children shun and withdraw from interaction with others. Power-seeking behavior is characteristic of children with narcissistic and oppositional personalities. Revenge seeking motivates the passive-aggressive child. Paranoid children are mistrustful, suspicious, and sensitive to criticism.

Disabilities in CNS functions both shape character development and interfere with schoolwork. These factors constitute barriers to accepting the influence of teachers; to paying attention and concentrating; to the ability to see, hear, interpret, and understand stimuli as does the teacher; to the ability to communicate verbally and in writing; and to the capacity to organize, begin, carry out, finish, and correct schoolwork.

Seventeen percent of school children have educational handicaps. Although necessarily impressionistic, an estimate of the prevalence of underlying causative factors is as follows: underachievement because of lack of opportunity for adequate education and personality disorders, 6 ½ percent; impulsive-hyperkinetic behavior, 5 ½ percent; dyslexias, 2 percent; mental retardation, 2 ¼ percent; childhood psychosis, ¼ percent; and epilepsy, ½ percent.

All of the factors involved in the transition from dispositions to school learning problems make for an exceedingly complex situation. Appreciating this complexity, however, is essential to realistic and effective research, clinical practice, and education. This chapter has traced this developmental course through the expression of learning styles in work styles in school. The roles of specific disabilities in CNS functions and of the level of self-development also have been described, as they influence learning styles and character development. Thus the interplay of learning style, level of self-development, personality pattern, specific CNS functional disabilities, and work style, in addition to the interpersonal and ecological characteristics of one's family, school, and classroom, determine a child's success or failure in schoolwork.

VIII

Treatment

We have not mastered the art of stimulating rather than
repressing the human tendency toward learning, growing,
expanding, experimenting and developing.

Sidney Harris

E ach chapter in this section
is primarily addressed to
a particular professional
orientation. Familiarity
with all of the approaches described, however, will enrich each profession and facilitate teamwork. The lack of understanding and communication between professional disciplines contributes heavily to the
fragmentation and deficient coordination of services for children.

For children with educational disabilities and handicaps, the
health-care principles of prevention and treatment can usefully supplement the episodic and curriculum-focused practices of education.
These health-care principles emphasize group-level adjustments that
can prevent, and individual interventions that can treat, educational
disabilities and handicaps.

Social policies that support the provision of effective education for
children are especially important for those who have difficulty in
school. More specifically legislated public policies are needed to ensure
the availability of funding for special educational services. At this time
the Education for All Handicapped Children Act provides a mandate
for educating children with special needs. This act was the result of
the intense efforts of professional and lay organizations whose continued vigilance will be required to ensure implementation and refinement of this federal mandate.

As specialized educational services grow, it is imperative that they
be guided by rational strategies. There is a great risk that programs
intended to benefit children can be used to reduce stress within schools
themselves and be harmful for the children. This danger can be minimized by following the principles of preventing educational disabilities, the early detection and treatment of educational disabilities, and
the amelioration of existing educational handicaps. This can be accomplished through a hierarchy of special services within which chil-

dren can move readily from one level to another, as their treatment needs require. These services are most appropriate when designed to respond to educational disabilities and handicaps rather than to abstract diagnostic categories. To work effectively with schools, clinicians should have a general knowledge of special education practices and specific awareness of local resources.

Because of the importance of mainstream educational experiences for most children with educational disabilities and handicaps, a variety of teaching techniques are useful for them in both special and regular classes. These techniques recognize the importance of teachers as models as they manage their classrooms. Teachers can enhance the motivation of children in learning how to work in prescribed methods that fit each child's needs. The importance of the peer group in supporting rather than undermining educational goals also should be recognized. In addition the arts, crafts, and recreation can support the development of work skills.

The tutoring model is especially useful in meeting the need of educationally disabled and handicapped children for continuous individualized service. It is the antidote to the failure of fragmented, discontinuous special education offerings. Effective remedial tutoring programs are available for basic reading, spelling, writing, and arithmetical skill development. They can be supplemented by training programs in sensorimotor integration, attention, and thinking. In addition programs are available for developing speech, communication, an social skills.

Although its full application lies in the hands of mental health professionals, intensive child psychotherapy is a resource that has indirect application in educational settings. The purpose of psychotherapy is to expose and resolve intrapsychic and interpersonal conflicts that interfere with motivation for, and the performance of, schoolwork. The principles of psychotherapy can be useful for educators in establishing working alliances with children and understanding the sources of their seemingly irrational behavior.

The use of psychoactive medications with children can be beneficial, but is fraught with ethical and psychological issues. For this reason, medications should not be used as instruments of behavioral control but as adjuncts to an overall treatment program in which their purposes are clear to the children, their parents, and teachers. The most commonly used medications are the stimulants, which can enhance the performance of school work and build self-esteem and a sense of mastery through resulting academic successes. Their administration should be carefully designed and monitored, as is necessary with other long-term medications, such as anticonvulsants and insulin. Further clinical research offers the possibility of additional medications for the improvement of memory and the alleviation of debilitating mood disorders.

The effective involvement of families is essential to the successful treatment of children. The readiness of parents to participate as members of a therapeutic team varies. For this reason family therapy may be required in order to establish a foundation for teamwork through the formation of a parent–professional alliance. The technology of family therapy is the province of clinical professionals; however, knowledge of the principles of family diagnosis and therapy is important for educators. The cooperation of school and clinical personnel is enhanced by a mutual appreciation of each other's perspectives. The overall aim is to establish parents as knowledgeable advocates for their children.

29

Social and Public Policy

An educational system and the society in which it flourishes
are reciprocal. You cannot improve a society without changing its education; but you cannot lift the educational system
above the level of the society in which it exists.

Mortimer Adler, 1977

ocial policy is the crystallization of popular sentiment around major social issues. As such it is the articulation of a society's wishes for itself and influences priorities throughout society. An example of a social policy is the expectation of quality in goods and services. This has resulted in a variety of forms of standard setting, ranging from informal consumer rejection of products in the marketplace to formal governmental, professional, and consumer organization standards of quality.

Social policy guides democratic governments in formulating public policies through governmental action. Because of the checks and balances of the constitutional government of the United States, public policy varies with the times and is formed slowly through an elaborate feedback system comprised of the interaction of social policy with the agendas of the legislative, executive, and judicial arms of government. Public policy, in turn, influences social policy, as have the actions of the Supreme Court and the executive branch of the federal government in civil rights matters.

Developing social policies to guide public policies for children with educational disabillities and handicaps has been an arduous task. Questions about what to call these children, why they have problems, and what to do about them have been difficult to answer. Even the question of whether they are worth doing anything about exists.

The first challenge has been to find an acceptable designation for children with learning problems in school. As discussed in Chapter 2, this issue remains confused, but could be clarified pragmatically by first defining the children who are educationally handicapped. This step is comparatively simple in that these children already exhibit school failure and have identifiable skill deficiencies. The next step is more complicated, but still attainable. It is identifying the educational disabilities of the handicapped children and of those children who have not yet become handicapped. Of great social importance is describing these children in ways that do not stigmatize them or impute inferiority. For this reason the concepts of educational disability and handicap are appealing because they clearly place the problems in proper context: the learning of academic skills in school. They do not imply more than that.

The greatest problems lie at the next level of cause. Not only do we lack knowledge of causes, but it is unlikely that linear questions of causation are answerable in the light of the multisystem nature of the problems, as this book makes evident. Furthermore, for the purposes of public policy in the United States, the manifest designations of causes should not imply wrongdoing or responsibility on the part of an individual or others. This means that either causes must be framed in terms of factors beyond human control, such as disease or destiny, or suitable language must be found for describing realistic knowledge of causation. The latter can be achieved through the concept of functional disabilities that reflect multisystem individual difference and pathological determinants of temperamental, cognitive, language, managerial, and self functions. The concept of functional disability employs scientific knowledge in assigning causes and is not pejorative.

The next question of what to do about these children once they are identified hinges on whether there is social support for doing anything at all, whether there is anything that can be done, and how much what is done will cost. On the first point, the United States has recognized the need to prepare all citizens for as productive adult lives as is possible. The second point is answered affirmatively by our existing knowledge and the array of potential services (Rapoport & Ismond, 1982). The last point of cost remains unanswered, but clearly lies within the realm of the capabilities of the United States. The evidence supports the existence of a social policy that all children should receive the benefits of a socializing education. (National Commission on Excellence in Education, 1983.)

Parenthetically, as we have learned from public planning for the developmentally handicapped, the population of educationally disabled and handicapped includes both children and adults. Indeed the view of these problems as limited to childhood is not in accord with the facts. Thus whatever is done during childhood must be in a framework that makes the transition from childhood into adulthood.

Through the efforts of professional and citizen organizations, the social policy that all children are entitled to an education has been translated into a series of public policies (Weintraub et al, 1976). The expansion of services for the handicapped over the last two decades is due largely to federal legislation.

FEDERAL SPECIAL EDUCATION LEGISLATION

In 1965 the Elementary and Secondary Education Act included the handicapped in its general education provisions, and through its Title VI Amendments established the Bureau of Education for the Handicapped within the U.S. Office of Education in 1966.

The Developmental Disabilities Act of 1970 (P.L. 91-517) emphasized the federal government's efforts to provide a better life for the developmentally disabled through direct assistance at the state and local levels. In 1971 Title VI of the Elementary and Secondary Education Act was replaced by the Education of the Handicapped Act. In 1973 Section 504 of the Vocational Rehabilitation Act guaranteed the rights of the handicapped in employment and educational institutions that receive federal money.

The passage of P.L. 94-142, the Education for All Handicapped Children Act of 1975, brought together these partial commitments and established as public policy the right of all handicapped children to an appropriate education (Ballard et al, 1982; Weintraub et al, 1985). The essence of Public Law 94-142 is its mandate that every educationally handicapped child must have an Individual Education Plan (IEP) that satisfactorily addresses each child's needs in the least restrictive environment regardless of who provides the services (Martin, 1979). Public Law 99-457 reauthorized P.L. 94-142 in 1989 with greater emphasis on young children with special needs (Gallagher et al, 1989).

The IEP specifies what a school will provide for a child with the approval of the parents and the child. The IEP must include the following: a child's level of functioning, long- and short-range goals, specific services to be provided, extent of involvement in regular and special education classes, and the date of initiation and proposed duration of services. Also included are criteria for evaluation procedures and a schedule for applying them, at least on an annual basis (Meade, 1978; Lidz, 1981). The IEP includes a prevocational or vocational component at the secondary educational level. Experience has shown that the participation of the children themselves and their parents is vital to the success of IEPs (Valletutti & Salpino, 1979).

Public Law 94-142 and Section 504 of the 1973 Vocational Rehabilitation Act (P.L. 93-112) provide the following due process rights for children and their parents to (McCarthy, 1981):

1. Adequate notice of meetings and plans.
2. Present evidence and testimony.
3. Obtain an independent professional evaluation of the child.
4. Examine all school records.
5. Determine whether hearings are open or closed.
6. Be represented by counsel at hearings.
7. Have children present at the hearing.
8. Maintain the existing placement of the child until due process has been completed.
9. Prohibit inclusion of information at a hearing if not disclosed five days before.
10. Cross-examine and challenge evidence at a hearing.
11. Receive a verbatim transcript of hearing at reasonable cost.

If parents are not satisfied with the outcome of these procedures, Public Law 94-142 provides that parents may take their cases to courts. Similarly, schools may initiate the court process, if parents obstruct obtaining needed services for their children (Green, 1981; Smith, S.L., 1980).

Public Law 94-142 offers an unprecedented opportunity for cooperation between the educational, mental health, and health systems. The intent of the act was to provide all of the services required in order to educate a handicapped child, including psychiatric and medical diagnostic services, occupational therapy, physical therapy, psychological services, speech and hearing services, and other adjunctive services. To provide for these multidisciplinary facets, interagency agreements are needed in order to draw fully upon local resources.

P.L. 94-142 does not state explicitly the manner or degree to which physicians should participate in the diagnosis or treatment of handicapped children; however, medical services are included, as related to the evaluation process. State regulations may specify the manner in which physicians are involved in these processes, including the following:

1. Evaluating children and communicating findings to a multidisciplinary team, teachers, and parents.
2. Treating children and coordinating the treatment plan with the school district.
3. Evaluating a child's progress.
4. Providing a second opinion when appropriate.

5. Conducting inservice workshops for educators about child development and medically related topics.

6. Including educators in medical facility conferences.

Thus physicians can play a significant role in the treatment and management of children with disabilities and handicaps. They should familiarize themselves with P.L. 94-142 so that they can discuss it knowledgeably with parents and work effectively with school personnel.

In addition to its direct application to children, Public Law 94-142 outlines a plan for a comprehensive system of educational personnel development. Accordingly each state plan must include training related to handicapped children for regular teachers, special education teachers, and other professionals, including physicians. As an aid in carrying out this mandate, the American Academy of Pediatrics has developed inservice training modules for pediatricians.

The Education of the Handicapped Act Amendments of 1986 (P.L. 99-457) expanded federally funded services to handicapped infants and toddlers and their families. It also strengthened aid to preschool and postsecondary education programs.

The most important accomplishment of Public Law 94-142 is the interdisciplinary cooperation that takes place in designing treatment programs that meet the needs of specific children for the extended period of time required to resolve their problems (McCarthy, 1981). We know today that when the knowledge of relevant professional disciplines is brought to bear upon a specific child, the nature of that child's problems can be identified, and effective interventions made (Kinsbourne & Caplan, 1979). Many educationally foundering children do not receive help today, not because we lack knowledge of how to help them, but simply because services are not available or utilized.

MATERNAL AND CHILD HEALTH AND CRIPPLED CHILDREN'S PROGRAMS

In the early 1930s, Title V of the Social Security Law made federal grants available to the states for maternal and child health services and for services to crippled children (Gobel & Erickson, 1980).

Maternal and child health program funds can be used by the states to support services that improve the health of mothers and children. Such funds have been used largely to support prenatal and well-baby clinics. They also have been used to help fund diagnostic clinics for developmentally disabled children. Crippled children's program funds can be used for services for children with neurological, visual, and hearing impairments. Most states have added substantial funding to the federal funds they receive, and a few states have comprehensive programs for the treatment and rehabilitation of children with a variety of handicapping conditions. Little use has been made, however, of a provision in the law that makes funds available for the prevention of handicapping conditions.

In 1965 the Social Security Act was amended to allow grants under Title V for special demonstration projects in maternal and infant care and comprehensive care for children and youth. These projects provided comprehensive preventive and treatment services for families and children who live in a high-risk area covered by a project.

MEDICAID

The Medicaid legislation (Title XIX, Social Security Act Amendments of 1965) provides federal funds to match funds that a state expends for medical, dental, and hospital care to low-income persons (Gobel & Erickson, 1980). Developmentally disabled persons who need care in residential institutions for medical reasons may have this form of care financed by Medicaid.

Amendments to the Social Security Act in 1967 urged that early and periodic screening, diagnosis, and treatment (EPSDT) be made available to all persons under 21 years of age who are eligible for Medicaid. Each state is required to develop a program that would provide screening evaluations to identify and treat children with medical and developmental disabilities that might otherwise go unnoticed. This has significant implications for the early detection of educational disabilities as well. The content, periodicity, and eligibility for EPSDT; the providers eligible to be paid for evaluations and treatment; and the reporting and payment regulations are determined by each state within broad federal guidelines.

The Supplemental Security Income (SSI) amendments (1976) to the Social Security Act provide income-maintenance payments and automatic eligibility for Medicaid benefits to low-income persons with documented long-term handicaps. Regulations under this law call for coordination of medical, educational, and rehabilitative services in each state.

OTHER FEDERAL PROGRAMS

The Economic Opportunity Act of 1965 provided for the establishment of neighborhood health centers and Project Head Start. Neighborhood health centers provide a broad array of preventive and treatment services to children and adults living within defined low-income areas. Project Head Start established grants to a variety of agencies for child development centers in which disadvantaged preschool children were offered developmental education, along with nutritional, psychological, social, medical, and dental services. Many centers offer day care. After 1970 all Head Start centers also were required to enroll handicapped children and to offer appropriate educational and medical services to them. Since then Head Start has become the largest provider of preschool education to handicapped children (Gobel & Erickson, 1980).

University-affiliated facilities for the care of developmentally disabled children were authorized in the 1965 amendments to Title V of the Social Security Act. These facilities train professional personnel in skills largely related to the care of developmentally handicapped children and their families.

Federal support of community mental health clinics was authorized in the early 1960s. Although such centers can include a full range of preventive and habilitative services for children, most devote their efforts to adult mental illness and provide limited children's services.

The Developmental Disabilities Act of 1970 urged the states to coordinate all services for developmentally disabled children and adults and provided funding for developmental disabilities councils in each state.

PROBLEMS IN PUBLIC PROGRAMS FOR THE EDUCATIONALLY HANDICAPPED

As an expression of the civil rights movement, Public Law 94-142 encountered predictable resistance in many schools, and so its implementation has lagged behind its promise. The law also has resulted too often in the use of special education classes as repositories for minority and disadvantaged children (Sarason & Doris, 1979).

More significantly the limited interpretation of Public Law 94-142 has led to the belief that educational disabilities and handicaps can be resolved through education alone. As a result of the neglect of the spectrum of functional disabilities, many children grow into adulthood academically remediated, but remain friendless, lonely, and unproductive. The experience of special education tracking also may instill a negative self-concept of disability that later fosters dependency. In the long range, these social disabilities can be more handicapping than academic skill disabilities (Kronick, 1981). This is not taken into account by a rehabilitation ideology that provides only for training in a work skill and finding a willing employer. Overlooked is the often more important need to develop a work personality (Neff, 1968). Thus many adults with educational disabilities and handicaps also experience difficulties in their personal, social, and emotional adjustments and are unable to work productively.

A related problem is the lack of appreciation of the persistence of educational disabilities, their heterogeneity, and their changing manifestations throughout the life span of an individual. It is important to prepare young persons with educational handicaps for transition to postsecondary programs or vocational training from the elementary level on. Furthermore, consistent with the Rehabilitation Act of 1973 and the regulations implementing Section 504 of that Act, postsecondary and vocational training programs, as well as appropriate federal, state, and local agencies, need to continue their efforts to develop effective programs for adults with educational handicaps. At this time there is little advocacy for adults with educational disabilities and handicaps in business, industry, unions, and government agencies, including the armed forces.

Most important, professionals need education and training in the nature and management of educational disabilities and handicaps. Appropriate curricula must be developed in the fields of special education, vocational and rehabilitative counseling, pediatrics, psychiatry, psychology, social work, and law. In particular mental health professionals need to be more aware of the unique personal, social, and emotional difficulties that individuals with educational handicaps experience. Throughout their lives some individuals with educational disabilities have been exposed to teachers, parents, peers, and other mentors, who were not prepared or willing to understand their needs or to help them cope with their problems. Mental health professionals must be prepared to prevent and treat the psychological and emotional aspects of persistent educational disabilities and handicaps.

In another vein, in the treatment of children with medications, there are significant ethical issues colored by social attitudes that range from magical expectations to irrational fears. The use of medications for relieving adults' tensions and changing the behavior of children are popular solutions to life stressors. How the use of medication as a chemical restraint fits into the concept of least restrictive treatment, however, has not been addressed. Pressure to use the least costly method of handling a child's behavior may lead to medicating that child. The right to refuse treatment and the right to treatment raise additional considerations relating to the age of a child and how to determine a child's interests. The matter of informed consent also must be considered as it applies to children (Whalen & Henker, 1980).

CITIZEN AND PROFESSIONAL ORGANIZATIONS

Parents have the greatest investment in their own children's development, problems, and futures. Only parents have a personal interest in the total development of their own children. They are acutely aware of the problems faced by their children and are in a position to articulate them effectively. Experience indicates that professionals need the support of parents to obtain new services. Moreover, both legislators and school boards tend to be more responsive to parents than to professionals. Parents, therefore, can exert powerful influences in the political arena.

As the culmination of the efforts of many others, the Association for Children with Learning Disabilities prevailed upon Congress to pass the Education for All Handicapped Children Act in 1975. Since then the National Joint Committee on Learning Disabilities has been formed to facilitate the cooperation of organizations concerned with individuals considered to have disabilities. These organizations include the Association for Children and Adults with Learning Disabilities, the American Speech-Language Hearing Association's Division for Children with Communication Disorders, the Council for Learning Disabilities, the Council for Exceptional Children, the International Reading Association, and the Orton Dyslexia Society.

An example of the institutional impact of citizen organizations is the National Institute of Dyslexia, which was established in Chevy Chase, Maryland, in 1987 as an interdisciplinary division of TRI-Services, Incorporated, for the study of learning disabilities.

SUMMARY

Society cannot afford to ignore children with educational disabilities, because of the expense it assumes in looking after its educationally handicapped adult citizens in welfare, correctional, and mental health services.

Professional and lay organizations have been successful in shaping social policy that expects that all children, regardless of disability or handicap, shall receive an appropriate education. This has been implemented in public policies through a series of legislative actions for developmentally and educationally disabled children, culminating in the federal Education for All Handicapped Children Act of 1975, Public Law 94-142.

Parents cannot assume that the existence of Public Law 94-142 means that their children's needs will be served appropriately, however. Even though a legal basis for educating all children exists in the United States, most educators, parents, and children are dissatisfied, because adequate special education is far from realization. Furthermore the resolution of many learning problems in school requires more than the educational system can offer.

As was the case for the parents of the developmentally handicapped, the parents of educationally disabled and handicapped children constitute a significant political force to press for further improvements. Thus far citizen groups have attracted the parents of severely handicapped children. More parental political involvement is needed to ensure that their children's needs are met.

The appropriate public response to these problems is not to yield in a grudging, piecemeal fashion but to design and cost-account steps to assist all affected children. Unfortunately, the generation of legislation usually has been in response to the pressures of a particular era rather than an overall strategy. As a result the remedies are incomplete. And even incomplete implementation of existing legislative intent often results from the fact that responsibility is diffused among many different agencies at federal, state, and community levels. Agencies are asked to coordinate their efforts but none has sufficient control of resources to effect such coordination. In most states the responsibilities for helping children are separated by barriers between educational, social service, and mental health bureaucracies.

Public schools have the largest financial stake in the prevention of developmental and educational disabilities. Special education adds thousands of dollars each year to the cost of educating even a mildly impaired child. At a broader level, society is burdened with the loss of productive citizens and the costs of caring for them. Because of federal laws and court orders, schools no longer can avoid their responsibilities by excluding children. With this large financial vulnerability, schools have an incentive to concern themselves with the prevention and early amelioration of the conditions that underlie developmental and educational disabilities.

C H A P T E R

30

Special Education Programs

> Someday, maybe, there will exist a well-informed, well-considered, and yet fervent public conviction that the most deadly of all possible sins is the mutiliation of a child's spirit; for such mutilation undercuts the life principle of trust, without which every human act, may it feel ever so good and seem ever so right, is prone to perversion. . . .
>
> *Erik Erikson, 1959*

Special education programs are particularly vulnerable to the social, economic, and political pressures that influence education generally (Ford et al, 1982). In their efforts to provide education for handicapped children, school administrators must respond to parents who want new services, boards of education that must balance budgets, teaching staffs that seek relief, and special educators themselves (Bryan & Bryan, 1975).

An ever-present hazard is that special educational placement can be used as an instrument of social control for segregating children who pose educational challenges (Ford et al, 1982). This possibility is encouraged by the implication in teacher training that children who show puzzling learning and behavior styles should be in special education programs (Apter, 1982). It is reinforced by the desire of overburdened teachers for undisrupted classrooms.

Special education financial aids to local districts create incentives for segregation, when funds are allotted only to programs for exceptional children in separate school settings and not to special instruction conducted in regular class settings. Special education programs also usually are administratively segregated from general education. In addition they usually do not function as a continuum of services from the preschool, elementary, and secondary level to vocational schools, colleges, and lifelong learning programs (Cohen, 1983; Vogel, 1982). Another problem is that the placements of children in special education often are made on the basis of fixed categories of handicapping conditions rather than the current educational needs of the children and so lack appropriate flexibility.

For all of these reasons, there is a wide gap between existing and optimal special education services. Rational special education strategies, therefore, are urgently needed.

This chapter discusses special education strategy, the evaluation of special education programs, the responses of school sys-

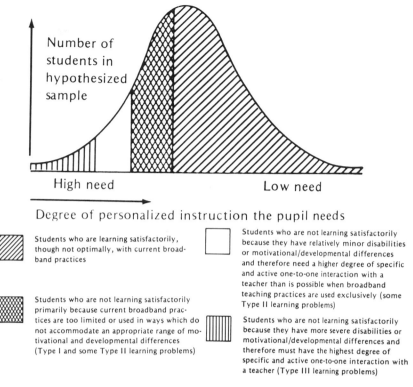

Number of
students in
hypothesized
sample

High need   Low need

Degree of personalized instruction the pupil needs

Students who are learning satisfactorily, though not optimally, with current broad-band practices

Students who are not learning satisfactorily primarily because current broadband practices are too limited or used in ways which do not accommodate an appropriate range of motivational and developmental differences (Type I and some Type II learning problems)

Students who are not learning satisfactorily because they have relatively minor disabilities or motivational/developmental differences and therefore need a higher degree of specific and active one-to-one interaction with a teacher than is possible when broadband teaching practices are used exclusively (some Type II learning problems)

Students who are not learning satisfactorily because they have more severe disabilities or motivational/developmental differences and therefore must have the highest degree of specific and active one-to-one interaction with a teacher (Type III learning problems)

Figure 30-1. A hypothetical representation of the population of children with learning problems. (Source unknown.)

tems to children with academic problems, and relationships between school and community professionals.

SPECIAL EDUCATION PROGRAM STRATEGY

Public health conceptions of preventing handicaps can be applied profitably to the learning problems of children in school. In public health terms, the primary prevention of educational handicaps involves ensuring optimal early developmental and educational experiences that minimize functional disabilities. Secondary preven-

tion is the prevention of educational handicaps through the early identification and treatment of educational disabilities. Tertiary prevention is reducing the handicapping effect of existing disabilities.

In the light of all these considerations, an overall strategy for individualizing education for all children is needed. As a background the population of children with learning problems in school can be described as in Figure 30-1 (Adelman & Taylor, 1983). The largest group consists of children who are learning satisfactorily, but not optimally, in the mainstream of schooling. The next group of children is not learning satisfactorily, because mainstream education is not accommodating to their needs. The third group of children

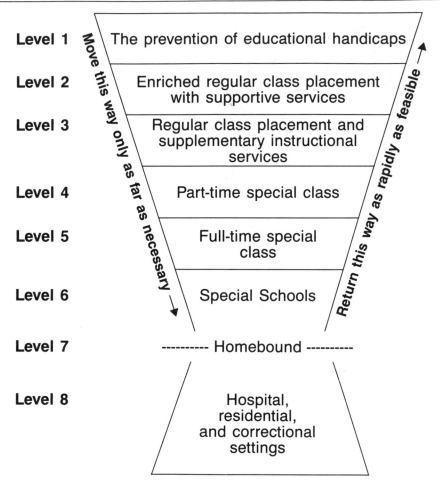

Level 1 — The prevention of educational handicaps

Level 2 — Enriched regular class placement with supportive services

Level 3 — Regular class placement and supplementary instructional services

Level 4 — Part-time special class

Level 5 — Full-time special class

Level 6 — Special Schools

Level 7 — ---------- Homebound ----------

Level 8 — Hospital, residential, and correctional settings

Move this way only as far as necessary →

Return this way as rapidly as feasible →

Figure 30-2. The cascade system of special education service. (Adapted from S. J. Apter, *Troubled Children: Troubled Systems,* Pergamon Press, Inc., New York, 1982. Used with permission.)

need more individualized attention than can be given by classroom teachers. The fourth group comprises children who have severe heterogeneous educational disabilities and handicaps that require major educational and clinical interventions, although they show similar behavioral and learning patterns.

In accord with these varied educational needs of children, the cascade model depicted in Figure 30-2 presents a strategy for providing a range of special educa-

tional services (Apter, 1982). Many special education programs have been much more restrictive. In some a child is classified as mentally retarded or emotionally disturbed and sent to a special class and may remain there throughout the child's school career. That approach exacerbates negative attitudes about educational handicaps and results in the mislabeling and inappropriate placement of many children. In contrast the cascade model enables the flexible movement of children between levels as indicated by the needs of each child. It involves the placement and monitoring of each child through a child-centered interdisciplinary team composed of appropriate educational and clinical professionals (Golin & Ducanis, 1981). The following case illustrates a common problem resulting from inflexible special education policies:

> Since entering the first grade, Jerry had difficulty mastering the sounds of written words and spelling them. He received tutoring in reading for the first three grades, but on moving to another school system was placed in a series of special education classes. Because his academic skills were close to grade level, he was totally mainstreamed in the sixth grade. On entering junior high school in the seventh grade, he failed all of his courses. He was not found to be eligible for learning disabilities programming because his skills were not two years below grade level. He was not eligible for emotionally disturbed instruction because he did not present behavior problems. In spite of school failure as a result of auditory-linguistic dyslexia and severe right-left confusion, Jerry was not eligible for specialized educational services.

This chapter is organized according to the eight levels in Figure 30-2. Level 1 is the most important and has received the least attention because of the crisis-recoil nature of organizational and social systems, whose inherent responses are reacting to immediate problems rather than their underlying causes (Rhodes, 1972). This orientation toward short-range rather than long-range advantage continually undermines prevention planning. Level 2 is a regular classroom in which the teacher receives consultative assistance. Level 3 is a regular classroom with specialist consultation for the teacher and tutoring for a child from specialized personnel. Level 4 is primary placement in a specialized education program. Level 5 is placement in a self-

contained classroom. Level 6 is placement in a day or residential educational facility. Level 7 is transitional education for a child temporarily unable to function in school. Finally, level 8 is special education in residential institutions or psychiatric hospitals.

Level 1—The Prevention of Educational Handicaps

The public health concepts of primary and secondary prevention apply to the prevention of educational handicaps, the former by removing their causes and the latter by the early detection and remediation of educational disabilities.

Primary Prevention

Primary prevention aims to prevent functional disabilities by ensuring each child's optimal development through education for responsible parenthood, support during pregnancy and labor, counseling parents in helping their children develop self-control, and helping parents and teachers to model problem-solving skills (Joffe et al, 1983). For example, the cognitive development of disadvantaged young children can be improved by parent training in emotional and educational areas, as shown by the Milwaukee Study Project (Garber, 1988). All of these measures help children develop skills in motor control, speech, self-care, and self-discipline (Kozloff, 1974).

Preschool education of high quality has value in cost-benefit and humanistic terms, particularly for disadvantaged children (Consortium for Longitudinal Studies, 1983). High-quality programs are those with supervision, in-service training, teamwork, and evaluation procedures. Although the initial gains of children in Operation Head Start may be attenuated by later educational experiences, significant reductions in special education requirements have been reported in later years for such children (Cookson, 1978; House et al, 1978; Lewin, 1977).

A well-controlled study of children with preschool experience disclosed that they had higher scores on achievement tests, they were more strongly committed to schooling, and their parents were more satisfied with their school performance. As adults they were better able to avoid unemployment, the need for welfare assistance, dropping out of high school, and prison. The preschool program also reduced the need for special education placement by one-half and the incidence of juvenile delinquency by six-sevenths (Schweinhart & Weikart, 1980).

The most important means for preventing educational handicaps is a greater range of alternatives for the education of children with a broad range of individual differences so that functional disabilities do not become educational disabilities. A model for this approach is described in Chapter 28. The education and inservice training of teachers in child development and individual differences are important steps in this direction (Norris & Boucher, 1980; Wright, 1984).

A simple example of primary prevention is arriving at a judicious decision as to when a child should enter school. Within the normative range of development, some five-year-olds are ready for kindergarten and others are not. Children who are prematurely committed to their educational courses are predisposed to academic problems (Di Pasquale et al, 1980).

Another example of primary prevention at the curriculum level is the use of the phonic method for beginning readers and teaching writing first or simultaneously with reading as ways of accommodating to children who require these methods in order to learn to read with their age mates (Mosse, 1982). Another curricular example of primary prevention in elementary health education is using the concept of individual differences to ex-

plain differences in the ways people think, feel, and act (Cummings, 1981). This stimulates awareness of the fact that each person can do some things well, but has difficulty with others. It is one thing to feel that one is in the lowest reading group because one is "dumb" and another to know that reading comes more easily for some other children. This promotes evaluating oneself on a variety of dimensions, some weak and some strong, rather than on a single one, such as reading skill or grades in school (Kinsbourne & Caplan, 1979).

Secondary Prevention

The secondary prevention of handicap by the early detection of functional disabilities is dramatically illustrated by the modern approach to Down syndrome. Two decades ago Down syndrome, then called mongolism, was regarded as a hopeless condition with intelligence in the moderate to severely retarded range. Now we know that when infants with Down syndrome have the benefit of early stimulation, as well as early entry into developmentally oriented educational programs, they can attain mildly retarded functional levels (Menolascino et al, 1983; Pueschel, 1984).

For children with obvious developmental disabilities, early childhood intervention programs can be useful (Lerner et al, 1987; Regional Interventional Program, 1976). Still the false prediction of educational disabilities by early diagnostic testing that presumably reveals functional disabilities has serious repercussions. Like a self-fulfilling prophecy, a prediction can influence parents' and teachers' expectations and attitudes and a child's self-concept, and so generate the very failure it is intended to forestall.

The variability in the rates of children's mental development clouds the long-range determination of a child's learning capacities. Therefore, preschool testing in itself does not predict later learning failures

(Lindequist, 1982). The shorter the interval between the assessment and the scheduled time for deciding on educational placement, the more reliable is the assessment in guiding that placement. Pending major advances in prediction, the only responsible policy is to defer the diagnosis of educational disability until it can be directly related to academics. Preschool assessment should be handled in a multidisciplinary framework (Karnes & Stoneburner, 1983). Inappropriate early childhood educational placement can seal a child's fate in a special education track.

The readiness of children, particularly boys, for kindergarten cannot be based simply upon age or tests of intelligence. According to Louise Bates Ames, one child out of three may be in a grade level too high for that child's ability (Ames, 1978). Moreover children who fall behind in school generally do not catch up. The evidence points to delaying school entry for immature children as an important and simple means of preventing later school problems.

In making the decision for first-grade entry, a review of kindergarten performance and school readiness testing during the summer before the first grade can most reliably guide a decision to have a mature child enter the first grade, give an immature child an additional year in kindergarten, place a mentally retarded child in a special education class, and provide a child with selective unreadiness for first grade with appropriate support from the start. A repetition of kindergarten is preferable to failure in later grades (Weil, 1977). In these ways the likelihood of later failure is minimized.

Children enter school with certain expectations of personal success shared by parents, teachers, siblings, and peers. Failure to meet these expectations results in a cycle of unfavorable consequences. Most children comfortably engage with the first years of school, as they begin to ascend the ladder of socialization. Too frequently, however, the initial encounter is distasteful for both child and teacher. A child bewildered by failure is beset by the reactions of others. Teachers, frustrated in their attempts to teach the child, may suspect idleness or hostility. Parents may vacillate between blaming the teacher, their child for disappointing and embarrassing them, and themselves for their part in the genesis of the problem. Peers may be derogatory, and siblings may resent the spotlight of parental attention being focused on the child in difficulty. The child's self-evaluation is lowered by failure, evoking an attitude of hopelessness, often masked by indifference or denial that problems exist. Eventually that child is labeled educationally handicapped, and expectations are lowered, often at the price of accepting the inevitability of limited achievement.

For obvious reasons the early detection of incompatibility between a child and school is essential for the prevention of educational handicaps. The early years of school can bring to the surface previously unrecognized variances in children. The rationale is compelling for identifying educational disabilities during these years in which they can be remediated. At the same time, when children are identified as vulnerable, there is an ethical obligation to provide treatment (Ohlson, 1978).

One of the most tangible academic skills is the ability to learn to read. Because reading is essential to independent living in our complex society, persons who cannot read are socially and vocationally handicapped. Children who have difficulty learning to read have educational disabilities, and their chances for academic later success are greatly reduced (Wallach & Wallach, 1976). Thus a child's response to reading instruction is an important indicator of impending difficulties in school. Behavioral indicators of the lack of academic readiness skills are inappropriate relations with peers and teachers, parents, and other authority figures (Santostefano, 1978; Wallace & Kauffman, 1973).

The gravity of early educational disabilities is illustrated by the finding that without effective interventions only 6 percent of children with serious reading retardation in the second grade improve by the end of the fifth grade (Satz et al, 1978). Furthermore in that study 30 percent of average readers in the third grade became problem readers by the end of the fifth grade, indicating the latent period before the appearance of most educational disabilities.

Reading readiness was first used in the 1920s to describe the maturational stage in which children are able to learn to read. In the 1930s teachers were advised to wait until children had a mental age of 6.6 years before beginning reading instruction. Later studies, however, revealed that the methods used to teach reading were more crucial to reading success than was mental age (Chall, 1983a).

The evidence is growing that children who lack reading readiness skills can be identified during kindergarten (Silver, 1981b). Those children need reading readiness training rather than formal reading instruction, which results in failure for them (Pflaum, 1974; Smith & Johnson, 1976). They need to develop attention capacities, awareness of time, language abilities, visual motor skills, conceptualization ability, and an integration of body image with behavior. Unfortunately, conventional school programs force these vulnerable children to suffer from years of failure before receiving remedial aid. With the aim of secondary prevention, efforts have been made to develop both group and individually administered test batteries that can efficiently assess children on these dimensions (see Figure 30-3).

The Pupil Rating Scale tests auditory comprehension and memory, spoken language, orientation, motor coordination, and personal social behavior (Myklebust,

1981; 1983). It assists teachers in identifying difficulties in auditory language between kindergarten and the sixth grade. More generally five factors have been found to be predictors of reading problems: (1) finger localization, (2) visual recognition discrimination, (3) performance on the Beery Visual-Motor Integration Test, (4) alphabet recitation, and (5) performance on the Peabody Picture Vocabulary Test (Satz & Friel, 1978).

Jansky's battery of letter-naming, picture-naming, Gates word-matching, the Bender motor gestalt, and sentence memory tests administered in kindergarten correctly identified 79 percent of failing readers in the second grade (Jansky & deHirsch, 1972). Teachers' impressions in combination with a battery such as this reinforce its strength (Goldberg et al, 1983).

Another example of secondary prevention is the New York University Program SEARCH (Silver et al, 1980). It consists of an individually administered test for five- to six-year-old children (Silver & Hagin, 1976). It has visual discrimination, visual recall, visual-motor, auditory discrimination, auditory sequencing, visual-auditory intermodal, dictation, articulation, and body image (direction, pencil-grip finger scheme) tests. The program's second element is formulating a prescriptive teaching plan (TEACH) based on a child's weaknesses as identified by SEARCH. This step includes interdisciplinary psychological, neurological, and psychiatric evaluations. The program's third element is implementing the TEACH prescription to build neurological and psychological skills basic to progress in reading, writing, and spelling (Hagin et al, 1976). Learning tasks are followed through three stages: a recognition state, a same–difference response; a copying stage, which adds a motor response; and finally a recall stage. The children are seen three to five times a week for 30-minute sessions over a two-year period. Follow-up studies in different localities have demonstrated

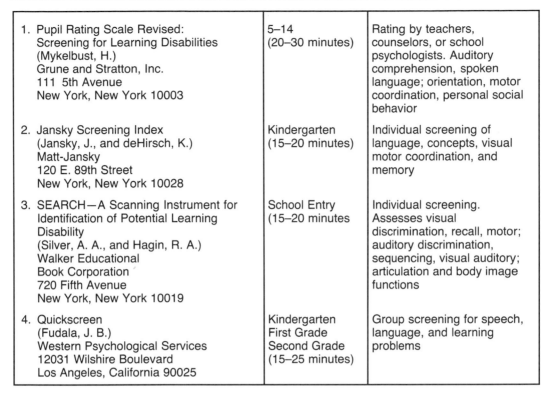

1. Pupil Rating Scale Revised: Screening for Learning Disabilities (Mykelbust, H.) Grune and Stratton, Inc. 111 5th Avenue New York, New York 10003	5–14 (20–30 minutes)	Rating by teachers, counselors, or school psychologists. Auditory comprehension, spoken language; orientation, motor coordination, personal social behavior
2. Jansky Screening Index (Jansky, J., and deHirsch, K.) Matt-Jansky 120 E. 89th Street New York, New York 10028	Kindergarten (15–20 minutes)	Individual screening of language, concepts, visual motor coordination, and memory
3. SEARCH—A Scanning Instrument for Identification of Potential Learning Disability (Silver, A. A., and Hagin, R. A.) Walker Educational Book Corporation 720 Fifth Avenue New York, New York 10019	School Entry (15–20 minutes	Individual screening. Assesses visual discrimination, recall, motor; auditory discrimination, sequencing, visual auditory; articulation and body image functions
4. Quickscreen (Fudala, J. B.) Western Psychological Services 12031 Wilshire Boulevard Los Angeles, California 90025	Kindergarten First Grade Second Grade (15–25 minutes)	Group screening for speech, language, and learning problems

Figure 30-3. Functional disability screening instruments.

that lasting benefit in learning reading skills through the fifth grade follows the TEACH (Arnold et al, 1977; Silver et al, 1980).

A number of screening batteries have been developed by drawing upon subtests of standardized tests that are the most selective in identifying academic learning problems (see Figure 30-4). All of these batteries aid the initial detection of vulnerability to problems in learning in school. The judgment of the professional person using them is critical in evaluating their significance (Ohlson, 1978).

Teachers themselves play a key role as screening agents for large numbers of children. The availability of questionnaires and behavior rating scales has permitted teachers' judgments to equal those of standardized instruments (Bower, 1981;

Ohlson, 1978). The importance of including teachers in the assessment process is illustrated by the finding that even without formal assessment, 80 percent of later educationally handicapped children can be predicted by kindergarten teachers (Satz & Friel, 1978).

A fundamentally different approach particularly suitable to schools in disadvantaged areas is to adapt the kindergarten and first-grade curricula to compensate for missing basic skills, owing to a child's lack of previous experience. This approach does not test individual children, but assumes that disadvantaged children may not have learned such skills as recognizing and manipulating the sounds of letters and counting. The Flying Start Project and the Wallach and Wallach method are examples.

INSTRUMENT	AGE & ADMINISTRATION	EMPHASIS
1. Developmental Indicators for Assessment of Learning (Mandell, C. D., and Goldenberg, D. S.) Dial, Inc. 6 Jennifer Lane DeKalb, Illinois 60115	Ages 2$^1/_2$–5$^1/_2$ (20–30 minutes) Individual	Gross motor, fine motor, concepts, communication
2. Meeting Street School Screening Test (Hainsworth, P. K., and Signeland, M. L.) Crippled Children and Adults of Rhode Island, Inc. 667 Waterman Avenue East Providence, Rhode Island 02914	Kindergarten and 1st grade (15–20 minutes) Individual	Motor patterning, visual-perceptual-motor, language
3. Basic School Skills Inventory (Hammill, D. D., and Leigh, J.) PRO-ED 5341 Industrial Oaks Blvd. Austin, Texas 78735	Ages 4–6 (30 minutes) Individual	Observational rating and performance test items. Basic information, oral communication, reading and number readiness, classroom behavior
4. Survey of Basic Competencies (Som Waru, J. P.) Scolastic Testing Service 480 Meyer Road Beusenville, Illinois 60106	Ages 3–15 (15–20 minutes) Individual	Rapid screening for potential school learning problems. Information processing, language reading, mathematics,
5. Wide Range Achievement Test—Revised Edition (WRAT) Jastak, J., Bijou, S., and Jastak, S.) The Psychological Corporation 757 Third Avenue New York, New York 10017	Kindergarten to 12th grade (20–30 minutes) Individual	Commonly used screening assessment of reading, spelling and arithmetic skills
6. Peabody Individual Achievement Test (PIAT) American Guidance Service Publishers Building Circle Pines, Minnesota 55014	Ages 5 to 18 (30–40 minutes) Individual	Well-standardized screening test of reading, spelling, and arithmetic skills and general information

Figure 30-4. Academic skills screening instruments.

The Toronto Flying Start Project was designed to prevent high-risk children from having academic problems by motivating them to think and learn (Stott, 1978). The project groups consisted of four to six children, who were taught puzzle and card-matching games for 12 half-hour biweekly sessions over six weeks. Success in the games and the ignoring of unproductive behavior gave the project children a feeling of competence by observing the results of their own and their partners' responses.

The Wallach and Wallach method addresses reading-readiness skills and is described in Chapter 31. The key person is the community tutor, who provides the individual attention required for the success of the program. A child and a responsive adult working together constitute a social experience that is especially important in a society drifting toward greater automation; in the long range it may be more desirable for children to learn initially from people than machines.

Level 2—Mainstream Programming

The trend in American education toward more individualized instruction has provided a means for handling many children with educational disabilities in regular classrooms with the support of teachers' aides, team teachers, and lay volunteers, all of whom increase the resources of regular classrooms. The availability of programmed materials and individual study carrels also helps (Wallace & Kaufman, 1973).

The concept of mainstreaming is based upon the assumption that children should not be withdrawn from their regular educational setting and from their peers more than is required by their needs for individual attention. The degree to which mainstreaming can be successful is related directly to the ability of a school to respond to all children in all curricular areas (Apter, 1982; Lewis & Doorlag, 1983).

Mainstreaming means enlarging the scope of regular education to accommodate a wide variety of children. It means providing an appropriate education for each child in the least restrictive setting by uniting the skills of general teachers and special educators to develop an educational prescription for each child. It means training regular teachers in special education techniques and training special educators for collaboration with classroom teachers.

But, mainstream classrooms are not the optimal environments for some children. Although diversity in peer relationships helps children understand the greater diversity encountered in adult life, it is important that they have access to compatible peers. However profound an educational disability may be, a child should be able to interact with other children of comparable abilities. Simply being in the mainstream does not ensure acceptance by others and experiences that build self-confidence. In fact it often produces the opposite.

The more difficulty a child has with learning in school, the more likely that the child's anxiety will result in inappropriate behavior, such as self-defeating actions, withdrawal, disinterest, interpersonal difficulties, and hyperkinesis (Gardner, 1978). Children with learning problems in school need constructive experiences on emotional, social, motivational, and attitudinal levels as well as in the more basic academic areas. They usually require a consistent and supportive educational environment in which specific behavioral expectations are set for them. Unstructured educational approaches have not been successful for them as they are for easy-to-teach children (Hammill & Bartel, 1978).

Classroom Teacher Support

Most classroom teachers have not been trained to individualize instruction with so-

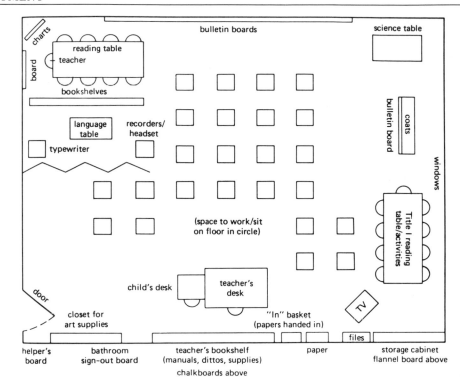

Figure 30-5. Floor plan for self-contained elementary classroom. (From C. Morsink, *Mainstreaming: Making It Work in Your Classroom*, University of Kentucky, College of Education, Lexington, 1981. Reproduced with permission.)

phistication. They must be able to handle children with special needs, because their management of the entire class depends upon their control of the situation. In-service opportunities for teachers are needed, such as workshops on Public Law 94-142 and the various facets of mainstreaming. There have been a number of formal and informal efforts to modify teacher training curricula in line with the mainstreaming philosophy.

The following attitudes and skills needed for mainstreaming were compiled by teachers in one school (Apter, 1982):

1. Knowing how to talk to children about disabilities and handicaps
2. Teaching impulsive children self-discipline

3. Learning how to support parents of children with special needs
4. Learning how to work with parents who deny their children's limitations

In addition adequate instructional supplies and materials are needed in order to improve teachers' abilities to accommodate to individual differences in children.

Special attention to physical and social environments is important (Adelman & Taylor, 1983). Physical-environment variables include architectural design, furnishings, and equipment—as well as proximity, privacy, distractions, access, traffic patterns, visibility, types and range of workspace and material, cleanliness, and esthetic features. Figure 30-5 illustrates an elementary classroom that contains a tutoring and assessment area, learning centers, incentive areas, and a small-group instructional area (Morsink, 1981; Stephens et al, 1982). Social-environment variables that can be rearranged include sex, age, social class, ethnic status, noise levels, behavioral groupings of children, and relationships between teachers and children. Children also can learn from each other in peer-assisted instruction (Allen, 1976; Haring & Schiefelbusch, 1976).

The range of individual differences mainstream classrooms can accommodate varies considerably. However, that range can be significantly increased when alternatives to traditional instructional approaches, tailored staffing patterns, and inservice training are used (Adelman & Taylor, 1983). An example is the Adaptive Learning Environments Model, which includes prescriptive teaching for children in the mainstream of early grades (Wang & Birch, 1984).

Personalized classroom programs based upon the following principles are promising approaches to minimizing learning problems:

1. The importance of how a child perceives what is being done is acknowledged in relation to the environment and program.

2. Each child takes an active role in making choices related to major intervention decisions as a way to increase commitment to, and personal responsibility for, achievement through contractual agreements.

3. A continuum of structure is provided to ensure communication support, direction, and limits, including periods during which children work either independently or in small groups without adult supervision.

4. Informal and formal conferences are held regularly for communication about and enhancing a child's perceptions of options, decisions, and commitments.

Mixing Grade Levels

Another approach consistent with maintaining children in the mainstream relies upon flexibility in the levels at which they are taught, as in the one-room schoolhouse. Thus they might be taught at a third-grade level in mathematics and a second-grade level in reading, or vice versa. This approach is applicable to younger children who are not too far behind, but it is cumbersome if it means the humiliating shuttling of a child between different classrooms. The approach is most useful in mixed-grade situations within a single classroom so that children are working at different levels for different subjects over several years. It makes sense in developmental terms, because an educationally disabled child may be at the same achievement level in a particular subject as a younger child.

Retention

In the past the educational response to individual differences in children has been primarily administrative rather than pedagogical (Messick, 1976). The earliest method of dealing with individual differences was to fail students until educational requirements were mastered. More recently, however, many children have been passed from grade to grade as social promotions. The pressures to retain or not to retain often have little to do with a child's interests.

There is considerable disagreement about the wisdom of retaining chidren in a particular grade because of slow learning, and there is a dearth of data to substantiate most of the arguments. The term immaturity sometimes is applied with little critical scrutiny, because of the belief that ultimately a child will catch up if kept in a holding pattern. Unfortunately, such intentions may constitute thinly disguised excuses for inaction, so that retention replaces needed interventions. It is all too easy to regard a child as immature, when maladaptive behaviors really reflect underlying educational disabilities.

If a child is to be retained, there should be evidence of developmental immaturity. Such data as retarded bone age, delayed dentition, and short stature combined with confirmatory findings on psychological assessment can be used to determine developmental immaturity. Such a child may be unable to keep up with peers and may reach puberty late. When there also is a clear lag in the acquisition of academic skills, the argument for retention is strengthened. Thus when a child is physically, emotionally, and socially immature, a repetition of a grade may be advisable, with a change in schools, if peer-group considerations warrant.

Level 3—Mainstream and Supplemental Programming

At level 3 a special education resource teacher or tutor is required to provide academic skill building for a child as formulated in an individual education plan. The resource teacher is a full-time teacher who specializes in educational diagnosis and programming for children who present problems in academic learning and behavior (see Figure 30-5). There must be no retreat from the hard-won principle that children with unusual learning requirements need individual instruction. Unless an educational disability is mild or a teacher in the regular classroom is exceptionally skilled and energetic, mainstreaming such a child without individual instruction only perpetuates the problem.

Remedial work should be scheduled during periods of the day that will not deprive children of enjoyable activities, ideally at the time of the subject in the regular classroom, so that children can avoid daily confirmation of their inadequacies and missing other subjects.

Microcomputer-based education offers the advantages of a one-to-one learning environment free of exposure of errors to others. The individualization and immediate feedback can stimulate the initiative of a child through the child's control of a program (Boettcher, 1983). The role of microcomputers in special education is promising for many children (Watkins & Webb, 1981).

Level 4—Part-Time Special Class

Children with severe academic learning problems cannot be accommodated conveniently in a regular class without doing injustice to other children. In such instances a resource class with special groupings and appropriate methodologies can be used. At this level the resource teacher takes over classroom subjects in which a child needs more than supportive tutoring so that the advantage of a self-contained and mainstream classroom are combined. Rather than being with the resource teacher for brief tutoring meetings, a child spends varying portions of the day in the resource room, as a support to mainstreaming. This approach has the specificity needed to go to the heart of a particular child's academic problems, and at the same time it can help many children throughout a school building.

A resource teacher ideally incorporates several models, as depicted in Figure 30-6 (Apter, 1982). Consultation is based upon the premise that classroom teachers would be more willing to deal with children with behavioral and learning problems, if they knew how to do so. The resource teacher can consult with teachers in adjusting to children's individual needs through prescriptive techniques.

Crisis intervention is a role that utilizes the principles of life-space interviewing as a tool in the school setting (Redl, 1966). The major goals of crisis intervention are

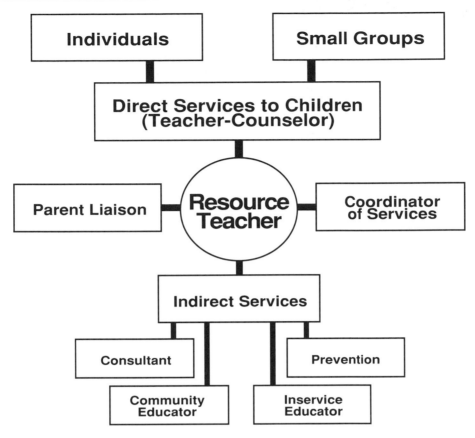

Figure 30-6. Roles of the resource teacher. (From S. J. Apter, *Troubled Children: Troubled Systems,* copyright 1982 by Pergamon Press, Inc., New York. Reproduced with permission.)

to provide a child with conceptual training and to teach coping. A crisis can involve fighting, aggression, or withdrawal. Once a crisis is targeted, a teacher can use an episode to promote insight by talking issues through and helping the youngster to understand one's own behavior.

When children are overwhelmed by events, particularly those leading to loss of emotional control, life-space interviewing can be a timely and useful intervention. Life-space interviewing attempts to pull out of an experience ideas that will help a child understand what is going on and to develop coping skills. It also provides emo-tional first aid on the spot. The technique involves empathetically establishing communication with a child in any way possible and permitting venting of emotions with the continued presence of an adult. By being with a child immediately after the excitement of a crisis abates, an adult can help the child put the event into perspective by recognizing the factors both external to and within the child that precipitated the crisis. By encouraging the analysis of reality and self-evaluation, life events can be used to learn adaptive ways of coping with frustrations. Because the classroom teacher usually lacks time for such interventions, the resource teacher can either take the class while the teacher handles the life-space interview or handle the crisis directly.

The resource teacher also functions as a coordinator of school and community resources in planning for children and providing individualized tutoring or small-group instruction in a resource room or in the regular classroom (Lerner, 1985). The resource teacher can play a key role in bridging the school and family by working with parents and supporting their efforts to help their children (Michaelis, 1980; Marion, 1981).

No resource class should have a greater number of children than a teacher can instruct individually. How large that number is depends not only on the skill, experience, and energy of the teacher, but also on the nature of the children's problems. Because each child requires an individualized program, most resource teachers do not have the energy to achieve this with more than six to eight children. A compensating administrative consideration is that some of the special education expense can be absorbed by assigning a counterbalancing larger number of easy-to-teach children to regular classroom teachers (Rosner, 1979).

Another important consideration is that placing underachievers together in one class tends to reinforce negative behavior and block the progress of the group (Perkins, 1974). If children are placed together in a special classroom without recognizing their different educational requirements, their needs will not be met better than in a regular classroom.

Level 5—Full-Time Special Class

Some youngsters are served most effectively in self-contained settings, when regular classes with appropriate supplemental assistance are not sufficient to meet their needs. Mainstreaming may not be the least restrictive environment for children who need the consistent individualized attention possible in smaller groups (Accardo, 1980). Still these children should have the opportunity to interact with peers at recess, mealtimes, and after school, as well as in regular classrooms when appropriate subjects are being taught.

There essentially are four kinds of educationally handicapped children who need full-time special educational programming—those who need help in learning to care for themselves, who need help in preparing for vocational lives, who need help in learning social and working skills, and who need to learn basic academic skills. Classification should be based upon these educational objectives, so that specialized services can be directed to the nature of the educational handicap. Thus rather than classifying children as mentally retarded, emotionally disturbed, or learning disabled, it is more realistic to identify those who are handicapped educationally in learning self-care, vocational, social and working, and basic academic skills. Such an approach avoids labeling the children and instead bases classification on their educational needs.

The curricula of separate special classes for children permanently unable to function in the mainstream differ from other curricula in their emphasis on teaching practical self-care, daily living skills, and practical reading and arithmetic skills. They concentrate on fostering vocational skills and increasing a child's level of independence. In these classes units should be divided into small teachable components with explicit objectives and criteria prerequisite for the next level (Rumanoff-Simonson, 1979).

The hope for most children, however, is that full-time special-class placement is a preparatory stage for mainstream functioning. The array of structured transi-

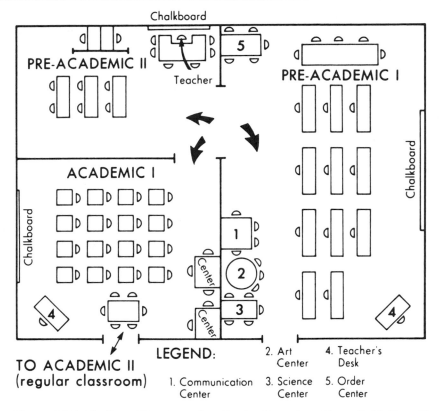

Figure 30-7. Madison Plan Learning Center floorplan. (From F. M. Hewett and S. R. Forness, *Education of Exceptional Learners,* 3rd ed., copyright 1984 by Allyn and Bacon, Boston. Reproduced with permission.)

tional educational approaches based upon the teachability of children with learning problems in school is illustrated by the Madison Plan of the Santa Monica school system (Hewett, 1972, 1974; Hewett & Forness, 1984). It is described as a broad administrative and instructional framework for preparing children who are educationally handicapped in social, working, and academic skills for participation in regular classrooms by concentrating upon improvement of their levels of learning competence through a series of settings that progressively increase in both behavioral and academic expectations.

Educable mentally retarded and edu-

cationally handicapped children are combined into a single population, which also includes some visually impaired and hearing-impaired children. The plan assumes that most of these children can profit from some time spent in a regular classroom, provided proper scheduling and support are given.

The Learning Center of the Madison Plan (see Figure 30-7) consists of three areas. Preacademic I is a classroom of eight or so pupils who work with a teacher and aide at individual desks with an emphasis on paying attention, following directions, and exploring basic knowledge. There is no group instruction and a check-mark system with tangible rewards is employed.

The Preacademic I mastery-achievement center includes the student desk area and study booths, where work may be undertaken free from visual distraction. The exploratory-social center is in one corner of the room and consists of equipment necessary for simple science experiments, as well as a fish tank, animals in cages, arts and crafts projects, and an area for communication tasks. Thus emphasis is given to building basic academic skills by involving children in orderly and exploratory experiences.

Central to the engineered Precademic I design is adjusting assignments to assure each child's continued success. For example, when a boy is having difficulty with an assignment, the teacher may send him to the study booth with the original assignment, change the assignment and have him continue at his desk, send him to the exploratory center for a science or art task, take him outside the room and negotiate a task for which he can earn checkmarks, or give him one-to-one tutoring.

Preacademic II is a classroom of six or so pupils who can begin to handle the more formal demands of a classroom. Here the emphasis shifts to remedial academic work and social and language training through group participation under a teacher or an aide. There still are merit check marks, but they may be exchanged for free-choice activities rather than tangible objects.

Academic I provides a simulated regular classroom experience with a teacher instructing 16 or so pupils seated at desks. Pupils use basic curricular materials of regular classes, and a grading system providing immediate feedback replaces the merit marks. Academic II is the regular classroom in which children in Preacademic II and Academic I spend as much time as possible. The Learning Center teachers aid regular classroom teachers in designing plans for individual children in addition to working with them directly.

Level 6—Special School Placement

Special schools operate either as day or boarding schools and provide controlled environments for children who need them.

Day programs tend to be educationally or mental health oriented. For example, Re-Ed programs operating since 1961 provide systematically structured educational day environments for children who need to learn basic social, working, and academic skills (Hobbs, 1982). Therapeutic day programs are associated with mental health services and short-term psychiatric hospitals in which the goal is mainstreaming after academic, social, and working skills have been acquired (Westman, 1979b; Zimet & Farley, 1985). A therapeutic day program usually offers specialized education, occupational therapy and recreational therapy, group and individual therapy, and family therapy. The setting provides structure, so that a child derives security from a predictable, dependable environment.

Boarding schools are used for children who may benefit from intensive specialized education and an environment away from their homes and communities. A completely new environment may offer some older children the opportunities and incentives needed to draw out additional effort in school.

When a child returns to a regular classroom from full time in a special class or school, placement with younger children may be indicated. Even if a child is achieving at a level comparable to classmates, this may be so because of individual attention and extra effort in the special setting. Thus the grade-level placement should be carefully adjusted as indicated.

Level 7—Homebound Instruction

Although usually regarded as a service for the physically incapacitated, homebound instruction is a resource to be considered under certain circumstances for the educationally handicapped. As a transition between placements, homebound tutoring can take advantage of a child's available time with beneficial results. Away from the stimulating and frustrating school environment, remedial tutoring also can be highly focused for an individual child. Homebound programming is contraindicated for school-phobic children, however. It also can be used inappropriately as an excuse for excluding a child from school.

When judiciously employed, homebound instruction programs offer an alternative that has only begun to be explored. As an example of one school's program, the Phoenix Union High School District has intensive homebound instruction for which the two most frequent indications are teenage pregnancy and behavior problems with underachievement (Arizona Research Services, 1981).

Level 8—Residential Placement

Last are special education programs in residential facilities for children, training schools, and psychiatric hospitals (Wolins & Wozner, 1982). These facilities emphasize learning social and adaptive skills necessary for helping children cope with life situations.

Residential treatment is indicated when community treatment programs for children and their families are unsuccessful, insufficient, or unavailable. Although offering the advantage of total care, residential treatment has drawbacks that vary with the quality of the program. The most important is the limited opportunity to involve the child's family therapeutically in

order to prepare them for the child's return. Relinquishing a child's care also may add burdens of guilt to already overburdened and ambivalent parents and siblings. Separation from home may add new stresses that further impede a child's tenuous coping ability, so that a child comes to depend upon an institutional setting and is unable to function in community schools. Furthermore residential facilities lack peer models of competence and so may promote regressive tendencies in children.

EVALUATION OF SPECIAL EDUCATIONAL PROGRAMS

The evaluation of special education programs has been fraught with difficulties. Accumulating the ultimate evidence of a child's progress in school requires the passage of time and continuity of follow-up.

The judgment of success or failure of special education is related to the rationale that underlies an intervention in the first place and who sets the criteria for determining progress. The enthusiasm for special education programs may come from considerations unrelated to the welfare of the children. Simply removing troublesome children from regular classrooms may be regarded as success by classroom teachers and administrators. Reducing the school dropout rate might be another gross indication of success. More insidiously, however, the slow progress of children who remain in special education programs throughout their school careers may be seen as success, when return to the mainstream and greater progress would have been possible.

If special education is to serve the interests of a child, then improvement in the child's skill levels is critical. If it was instigated to remove a disruptive influence from a classroom, a change in both the child's behavior and educational handicaps is important. Underusage of the special education system itself may increase the likelihood of the placement of a child, just as may premature termination of special education services. In most instances factors in both children and educational systems actually influence judgments of success (Adelman & Taylor, 1983).

A particular problem in evaluating improvement is the shifting baseline of maturation through which children gain skills with aging. Also children may not be able to generalize what they have learned in special education to other subjects, so that gains may not be maintained after special education is discontinued.

Also the favorable response of children to any intervention may be due to the Hawthorne, or placebo, effect. The Hawthorne effect was described years ago when productivity rose in a group of factory workers because of the esprit de corps resulting from the fact that they were being studied (Roethlisberger & Dickson, 1939). Thereafter the fact that motivation has profound effects on workers' style and output spurred the human relations movement in industry (Neff, 1968). The Hawthorne effect is an important aspect of all successful educational programs for children. Irrespective of method the fact that something novel is being done harnesses the enthusiasm of teachers and children so that improvement results. This enthusiasm particularly is conveyed by those who market special education materials and programs (Kinsbourne & Caplan, 1979).

With all of these obstacles, study of the long-range effectiveness of special education programs is only beginning to bear fruit. Large-scale studies suffer because samples are ill defined and the criteria are too general. One follow-up study of educationally handicapped children revealed that only one in four was able to be mainstreamed within five years. Although they made 1.1 years of reading progress in the first year of special education, this rating dropped to 0.5 year by the fourth year, to give them an overall gain of 2.9 years over four years (Koppitz, 1971). In addition to lagging skill levels, the "closed ranks" pnenomenon is a well-establlished social reaction to persons removed from the mainstream of society and constitutes a powerful resistance to their return (Cumming & Cumming, 1957). The earlier predictions that special education separate from the mainstream could harm children may well be fulfilled (Morse, 1974).

THE RESPONSE OF SCHOOL SYSTEMS TO CHILDREN WITH ACADEMIC PROBLEMS

Around children and teachers swirl many diverging forces. There are teachers' unions that are devoted to improving the working conditions of teachers and children, including their rights to classrooms conducive to learning. Parents have their expectations. And administrators may be more concerned about administrative design than the actual service it produces for children (Morse, 1974).

Schools are complex systems in which a central administration plans, implements, and evaluates the system's programs. Curriculum specialists develop systemwide curricula and select books and materials. The building principal is responsible for the operation of a particular school. Teachers deliver the critical service. Special service personnel provide special education and consultation to teachers.

The tone of a school is set by its administrators through how open they are to feedback and how they maintain school discipline (Furtwengler & Konnert, 1982). The building principal has the greatest need for system management skills at all levels (Comer, 1980). When teachers and principals think dynamically and respond to student feelings and needs, potentially serious problems can be averted. The naturalistic study methods used in anthropology, dynamic interviewing, and case studies as used in business and system analysis are helpful in approaching the interacting forces at play in a school. For example, a dynamic case study revealed that a recently transferred student misbehaved in school because of anxiety. At a system level, it followed that the school should examine how its transfer procedures can increase or decrease anxiety for affected children (Comer, 1980).

Unfortunately, administrators and teachers usually are not trained to manage systems and adequately address the social and psychological development of children. Educators are as much victims of systems as are students (Parelius & Parelius, 1978). Human systems management, child development, and relationship skills should be taught at the teacher training level and through inservice training (Comer, 1980). This training for classroom teachers is essential, if they are to recognize children with learning difficulties and help make suitable provisions for them (Ainscow & Tweddle, 1979).

The Family Educational Rights and Privacy Act of 1976 gives parents the right to inspect and review all records used by schools for the identification, evaluation, and placement of their children in special education programs. In spite of this fundamental recognition of the importance of parents, the impact upon parents of school procedures, such as multidisciplinary team meetings, often is not appreciated by school personnel. Because they usually are the result of the school's frustration with a child, special education plans are efforts to cope with problematic behavior rather than to enhance that child's education. The special education decision-making process, therefore, involves many subjective elements and often lacks an adequate informational basis (Smith, 1982).

With this background it is understandable that meetings with school personnel can be frightening, and even overwhelming, for parents. As vividly reported by one parent:

> There we were sitting before nine people, who were not saying one good thing about Jimmie. They slapped us in the face with "learning disability." I couldn't believe it. They didn't mention anything good. Our Jimmie can't be all bad!

A powerful antidote to professional meetings that tend to be denigrating is to include the child in them, so that a truly child-centered team is formed.

Although school staffs, parents, and students may feel that others do not care sufficiently, most really want to be effective and successful. The low expectations school personnel have for many students can be defenses against their own sense of failure as professionals. Similarly the lack of interest in schools shown by parents may be defensive, as it is with students. Most teachers and parents would make the personal changes necessary to be successful, if the support for doing so existed in and outside of schools (Comer, 1980).

When children see parents and school staffs as congenial and supportive, they work more effectively than if they perceive tension and conflict. This is possible when trust and openness within a faculty help teachers feel like participants in setting school policy and decision making under the leadership of the principal. Faculty members also can help each other by constructive criticism and support (Schmuck & Schmuck, 1971). In particular social performance and learning can be improved among economically disadvantaged students by a school staff's modeling of successful problem solving within the school itself. This potential power of schools is frequently overlooked.

When behavior problems arise, a child-centered team effort, including special service personnel, the teacher, the principal, the parents, and the child offers the greatest potential for change. Omitting any of these elements invites conflict and misunderstanding.

THE ALLIANCE OF SCHOOL AND COMMUNITY PROFESSIONALS

Nicholas Hobbs (1975) suggested that public schools coordinate the delivery of comprehensive services to all children with special needs. He listed five reasons for this proposal:

1. The school is responsible for helping families to socialize children.
2. Schools already are responsible for providing educational services to exceptional children.
3. The most important problems of children with functional disabilities are educational, and schools are the most competent educational agency.
4. Schools are geographically dispersed to serve the total population.
5. Schools have a state and local tax base that can provide funds to add to federal or private support in the service of children with special educational needs.

The realization of Hobbs' suggestion would resemble the "total school" conceptualized as a comprehensive educational resource for all the children and adults of its community (Apter, 1982).

The "total school" philosophy assumes that children live and learn within the context of their environments. Parents, siblings, neighborhood peer groups, church, school, and playground are all potentially supportive elements of a particular child's world. Each element has an impact on a child and, through the child, on each other, as depicted in Figure 30-8 (Apter, 1982). This view assumes that a youngster's difficulty in one part of this system can have serious repercussions in another part. Dramatic environmental examples in urban areas are lead poisoning at the brain-system level and antisocial gangs at the peer-system level.

Because the central nervous system (CNS) is the organ of learning, knowledge of CNS functions offers a viable, coherent, and useful theoretical basis for education. Thus knowledge about learning styles and the CNS is a fundamental tool for teachers and schools. It can be used both to alter the learning environment to fit the learner and to help the learner develop learning styles that are more responsive to existing learning environments (Keefe, 1982).

As this book illustrates, the management of educational disabilities actually goes beyond the boundaries of the schools because of the relevance of many systems that impinge upon children. Health and mental health professionals can be helpful, and often essential, collaborators with school personnel in meeting the needs of children with learning problems as members of interdisciplinary teams organized around each child (Golin & Ducanis, 1981). In particular mental health consultation has evolved as a useful tool through individual and group vehicles for teachers, special education personnel, and administrators (Berlin, 1977; Lawrence, 1971; Parsons & Meyers, 1984).

School personnel and clinicians can enhance their value to children by establishing ongoing alliances. Opportunities should be taken by clinicians to discuss learning problems and other relevant issues with school personnel, as through inservice training activities. Those clinicians fortunate enough to relate to a relatively small number of schools can become personally familiar with personnel and resources. Thus they can both support individual chil-

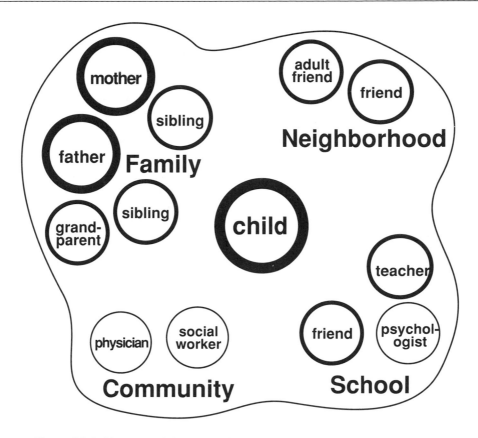

Figure 30-8. Diagram of the ecological system of a child. (From S. J. Apter, *Troubled Children: Troubled Systems*, copyright 1982 by Pergamon Press, Inc., New York. Reproduced with permission.)

dren and school personnel (Levine et al, 1980).

Clinicians should be aware of a school's need to establish priorities in service allocation. A clinician may feel strongly that a child should receive intensive individual services, and, in fact, a physician's influence may be necessary to obtain such a program. On the other hand, services for one child may displace those for children who are in greater need but whose parents are not resourceful enough to seek professional influence. Furthermore a school system may not have the community mandate to provide optimal services for a particular problem. For example, a child with severe attentional problems might benefit from one-to-one teaching. Most school systems cannot afford to offer this. While the clinician cannot abandon advocacy for a child, treatment recommendations should be made with a school's resource allocation in mind.

At times clinicians can help defuse an adversarial stance between parents and schools. Parents may be angry at an individual teacher, a particular school, or an entire school system, and wish to engage a clinician as an ally in a frontal assault against them. Such alliances are likely to be counterproductive and damaging to the child. It is important for the clinician to help balance the needs of a child and the resources of a school. When a school appears not to be offering appropriate services or supports for a youngster, the problem may be at higher administrative levels. This is particularly the case when federal and state statutes and regulations are changing. Special education teachers need help rather than criticism in working within their constraints. To effect change for a particular child, a nonadversarial cooperative approach by clinicians is most likely to yield results.

Clinicians should be aware, however, of defensive postures in school personnel. School personnel may feel that they are being assessed and harbor feelings of guilt. Excessive defensiveness on the part of school personnel may be intensified by accusations from parents. The heat can be diminished with well-placed support for teachers from clinicians. This can go a long way toward strengthening school–clinician–family alliances and toward focusing on the needs of a child.

At the same time, clinicians should not permit themselves to be placed in positions of ultimate authority. Sometimes health professionals are given an inordinately important role by school personnel and parents. Beneath the veneer of adulation, however, school personnel and parents may harbor resentment, jealousy, and anger. To be optimally effective and form an alliance with school personnel, clinicians should decline the seduction of imputed omniscience.

A particular problem exists when one-sided emphasis is placed upon the legal rights of children (Adelman & Taylor, 1983). This only adds to the responsibilities of their parents and may sacrifice the welfare of children to their presumed rights. The following principles of child advocacy should not be overlooked (Westman, 1979a). Children gradually acquire the ability to assume responsibility for themselves in specific areas as they pass from one stage of development to the next. Children are less competent than adults and require protection. Independence and self-reliance in adulthood are products of adult authority having been constructively exercised during childhood.

For many educationally disabled and handicapped children, the child psychiatrist is in a unique position to function as a diagnostician, therapist, and advocate in ensuring the coordination of services and the continuity of care. Initially the focus of a child psychiatrist is on helping a child and parents gain an understanding of the child's problems with schoolwork. The typical course of child psychiatric treatment includes family counseling, child psychotherapy, educational consultation and, when indicated, pharmacotherapy. Intensive family therapy and marital couple therapy for the parents also can be used. Individual psychotherapy with a child follows or parallels therapeutic work with the family. Collaboration between child psychiatrists and educators through parents is important in ensuring the most effective therapeutic outcome.

In some cases the advocacy role of the child psychiatrist is useful in working out legal custody and placement issues that are essential in order to provide a stable family life for children who lack the home foundation essential to the success of psychiatric and educational interventions. A school social worker or psychologist can be an advocate for a child by mustering the necessary services and acting as an intermediary for parents, school, and professional services.

SUMMARY

The operations of school systems both contribute to and alleviate children's problems with schoolwork. The school system has powerful mechanisms at its disposal to relieve its stress at the peril of affected children. One of the undesirable outcomes is extrusion of children from school; another is molding children to fit into special education tracks in order to isolate deviants from the mainstream. These possibilities must be borne in mind, because dispositions presumably arranged for the benefit of children can deliberately and unwittingly be used to reduce stress in the school system itself.

To maximize the ability of schools to help children with learning problems, the public health concepts of primary, secondary, and tertiary prevention are useful. Primary prevention in education aims to reduce the appearance of educational disabilities through social, health, and educational measures for parents and ensuring the optimal character and intellectual development of children. Secondary prevention takes place through early identification of children with educational disabilities and provision of corrective interventions. Tertiary prevention programs are interventions designed to reduce the levels of educational handicaps.

The largest group of children with learning problems in school are those who are performing satisfactorily, but not optimally, in the mainstream of schooling. The next group of children are those with academic problems, because mainstream education is not accommodating to their individual needs. The third group requires more individualized attention than can be given by classroom teachers. The fourth group has severe heterogeneous educational disabilities and handicaps and requires major educational and clinical interventions.

The cascade system of special education services provides a model that outlines the required levels of service and places them in a framework within which flexible movement between them can take place based upon the needs of each child. The eight levels in this model are prevention programs, enriched regular class placement,

regular class and supplementary instructional services, part-time special class, full-time special class, special schools, homebound instruction, and residential placement. The resource teacher is the central figure in providing both mainstream and special-class individualized tutoring and crisis-intervention services in a school building.

The evaluation of special education programs is hampered by the lack of long-range prospective follow-up; the Hawthorne effect, which produces favorable effects for any special intervention; and the closed ranks phenomenon, which impedes the reentry of persons separated from a social mainstream.

The administrative context within which special educational services are provided shapes their form and influences their effectiveness. The school system has developed specialists to handle various aspects of the special education programs, and their integration through child-centered multidisciplinary teams has been developed under Public Law 94-142.

The key to adapting school systems to children with learning problems is identifying easy, average, and difficult-to-teach children. In the last group are children with educational handicaps in academic, social, working, and self-care skills. In helping these children, the interdependence of the school, social service, health, and mental health systems is evident. The schools can be supported particularly by community health and mental health professionals, who can play advocacy roles for children through system-bridging, development-enhancing, conflict-resolving, family-supporting, and collaborative therapeutic roles.

For children, youth, and adults with educational disabilities and handicaps to receive appropriate educations, alternative and modified instruction is necessary, as well as a diverse range of professional services. Parents should be given opportunities for involvement in educational programs, because their success depends upon the commitment of both parents and affected children. Special education programs should be integrated with a school system's total instructional program and not regarded as an administratively separate system. Special education teachers should not be assigned more children than they can handle effectively.

For persons with educational disabilities and handicaps, the emphasis should be upon instruction directly related to enhancing functioning in the areas of manifest disabilities in addition to clinical treatment. The long-term nature of educational handicaps necessitates a continuity of services at all age levels from preschool through college.

C H A P T E R

31

Teaching Techniques

I hear and I forget
I see and I remember
I do and I understand
—*Chinese Proverb*

The aims of both education and psychotherapy are to prepare children for independent living. The word pedagogue is derived from roots meaning to lead children. In so doing education emphasizes acquiring knowledge and skills, while psychotherapy emphasizes self-awareness and personal relationships. Thus the differences between education and psychotherapy are in emphasis rather than purpose, since both foster the development of a child.

In teaching knowledge and skills, a successful teacher employs psychotherapeutic techniques to find out how each child learns best. Talking with children about what happens when they try to do their schoolwork can reveal reasons for their failures. Talking with parents also can provide helpful information from their observations of their children (Stevens, 1984).

Although written with children with learning problems in mind, this chapter deals with issues common to all forms of teaching. It includes discussions of the teacher–child relationship, classroom management policies, motivating children for schoolwork, teaching organizational skills, prescriptive teaching for individual children, and the importance of the arts and recreation in education.

More than for most children, a teacher is a role model for children with educational disabilities and handicaps. These children particularly need relationships of mutual trust and respect fostered by sympathetic communication with their teachers in order to face the frustrations of schoolwork. Because the process of schooling is carried out in groups, the management of classrooms, whether large or small, involves attention to self-discipline, curriculum, scheduling, and space utilization. Many children with educational problems require specific training in organizational skills. They also need prescriptive teaching based upon knowledge of their strengths and weaknesses. In addition the arts and recreation can be used purposefully to help children with problems, as can the influence of the peer group.

THE TEACHER AS A MODEL

Schoolwork requires motivated effort and sustained activity based upon self-control and self-direction. Accordingly children need teachers as models in the learning process rather than simply as judges of performance. Some teachers are too strict, some unwittingly foster students' nonconformity, and some cannot face their own weaknesses. Permissive teachers may be perceived by children as disinterested and uninvolved. Other teachers may overprotect children, who then are regarded as teachers' pets and rejected by peers (Smith, 1980). The ways teachers approach situations, solve problems, handle their emotions, and treat others, therefore, are important influences upon children (Carew & Lightfoot, 1979).

The central question is how the behavior of teachers can convey the message that they want their students to succeed in schoolwork. Since many children have difficulty handling conflicting emotions, the challenge for teachers is handling their own mixed feelings about their work in such a way that acknowledging their own frustrations permits enthusiasm for teaching to prevail. Troubled children are like insatiable sponges that absorb adults' efforts. As a result teachers feel frustrated or guilty because they do not have enough time to give these children the extra attention they incessantly demand. For all of these reasons, teachers find themselves feeling inadequate in frustrating situations, just as do their students (Greenberg, 1984; Greenstein, 1983). If they can see troubled children's anger, irritability, and defensiveness as expressions of frustration in school, teachers need not take the reactions of these children personally. What appears to be frustration with others often is frustration with oneself. The fact that teachers resolve their mixed emotions about their work constructively models the same for children.

Children benefit from a teacher's acknowledgment that tasks are difficult, the teacher's acceptance of their frustration and discouragement, the teacher's words of encouragement, and the teacher's assurance that it is all right to make mistakes. Thus a teacher's personal failings can be used profitably. By acknowledging and coping with their own mistakes, teachers can model adaptive techniques for children (Shane, 1980). For example, one teacher asked a class to discuss the meaning of failure in their lives based upon the following list (Ginott, 1972):

1. In this class it is permissible to make mistakes.
2. An error is not a terror.
3. Goofs are lessons.
4. Mistakes are for correcting.
5. Value your correction—not your error.
6. Don't let failure go to your head.

THE TEACHER–CHILD RELATIONSHIP

Because their relationship takes place in groups, the opportunities for personal interaction between teacher and child often are fleeting and colored by authority issues. Thus the nature of schooling places a high premium upon each exchange between teacher and child.

Since teacher and child do not choose each other, a relationship of mutual trust cannot be assumed initially, but it can be earned. A teacher's empathic ability to take the position of children and listen to them facilitates their trust (Lovitt, 1982). When a child is understood by an adult, the experience affirms that child's sense of importance. Teachers need a language of compassion that lingers warmly. They need words that convey goodwill and radiate respect. Eye contact is particularly important with attention-seeking children, as through the subtleties of a glance that appeals, a nod that affirms, and a look that conveys firmness. When appropriate the nuances of annoyance can be helpful as well (Ginott, 1972).

The teachers of children with educational disabilities and handicaps particularly require sensitivity to children's feelings about schoolwork. These children are attempting tasks that are difficult for them and fraught with the threat of failure and social condemnation. Thus they depend heavily on realistic encouragement. For example, appreciative comments about the amount of effort a child has put into schoolwork can be made, regardless of whether that work was done correctly. Conversely, if a child keeps failing, it is useful to switch to another task in which the teacher knows the child can succeed, so that the child can find relief and the teacher can legitimately praise successful performance (Kinsbourne & Caplan, 1979).

In making requests of children, an uncritical message invites cooperation; a critical one engenders resistance. Talking to the situation is helpful in minimizing the consequences of hurting a child's feelings. Abstract questions can trigger failure and reinforce a sense of inadequacy, if they are beyond a child's grasp (Blank et al, 1982). Teachers frequently ask terse questions with no elaboration or context. It is important to take the extra moments needed to ascertain whether a child understood what was said in order to prevent misunderstandings (Burke, 1981). When a richer verbal framework is supplied, misunderstanding is less likely.

Teachers can use their own emotional reactions as clues to a child's emotional state. Often a teacher's feelings toward a child reflect how the student is feeling. The way in which attitudes are inappropriately transferred from one person to another is explained in Chapter 33. In addition the personal frustrations of these children extend to parents and teachers, who in turn may feel helpless, guilty, or infuriated themselves. These reactions in adults often reflect a child's feeling state. As one teacher said, "The moment I'm with Brian I feel anger; perhaps it is because he feels so angry." When confronted by failure, children react in a variety of ways—avoidance, anger, giggling, clowning, fatigue, restlessness, complaining, talking, and provoking peers. It is easier for some children to say "I won't" than to say "I can't," since seeing oneself as defiantly self-assertive is preferable to feeling dumb.

In special education a teacher's ability to establish rapport with a student is so crucial that it may outweigh the importance of the teacher's technical training. Special education personnel can be drawn not only from qualified educators but also from teachers-in-training, teacher's aides, and even from older students. Such flexibility in using available resources is justified in principle and essential in practice. When a teacher is unsympathetic to children's needs or is incompetent, an entire class may underachieve unless the parents and principals are alert to the situation. We know that some children respond to one teacher and not another, yet the matching of teachers and students remains haphazard. This is an area that needs exploration.

CLASSROOM MANAGEMENT

In a harmonious classroom expectations are synchronized between teacher and children (Hewett & Taylor, 1980). This favorable climate for learning based upon mutual respect between teachers and pupils is particularly critical in special education settings. Unfortunately, in recent years teachers have been encouraged to find their own teaching methods and styles suited to their personalities and have not received training in controlling classrooms (Rinne, 1984).

Even well planned lessons are not always successful with students. Application of the principles of classroom control also is needed.

Learning to live within a classroom regulated for the welfare of the children provides an important means of developing self-discipline (Jones & Jones, 1982; Wolfgang & Glickman, 1980). As children mature they demonstrate their independence when they do not need to have controls established by others. They shift from relying upon external controls to relying on internal controls (Redl, 1965).

Although essential for optimal learning and the principal concern of beginning teachers, classroom discipline still has received insufficient attention in teacher education (Hollingsworth et al, 1984; Wayson et al, 1982). In recent decades, social policy has shifted from the control of children by chastisement to control by rewards. The word discipline still has a punitive connotation, however.

Actually discipline means training that develops self-control. Democratic discipline is not permissiveness, which actually is the absence of discipline, democratic or otherwise. In 1939 Lewin, Lippitt, and White conducted the well-known and still valid experiments on autocratic, permissive, and democratic classrooms. They found that both the autocratic and the permissive teachers fostered regression in their children. The democratic teacher, however, asked for and received the assistance of the children without abdicating responsibility for them and produced more learning achievement and mature behavior in the class. Unfortunately, the democratic middle ground staked out by this research has been ignored in the specious debate over "traditional" autocratic versus "progressive" permissive education.

There are a variety of ways of handling misbehavior that reflect a teacher's personality and style. The details are less important than the teacher's attitude toward rules. Class rules based upon the right of the children to have a comfortable learning environment, therefore, are needed. Framing classroom expectations for the benefit of children's schoolwork allows students to recognize that rules are not simply for the convenience of the teacher. Whether classroom rules are seen as guidelines for the purpose of enhancing learning opportunities for all or to maintain the authority of adults determines the children's attitude toward them. This point draws upon the core of a teacher's and society's attitude toward them. Since classroom rules inevitably are imperfectly formulated and cannot anticipate all exceptions, minor infractions usually can be overlooked, if their purpose of preserving the learning climate is not jeopardized so that observing the "letter of the law" is irrelevant. Disruptive behavior is most likely to occur when children do not understand the reasons for teachers' expectations. When necessary teachers simply can point out that they need to be the bosses so that they can help children learn how to boss themselves (Smith, S.L., 1980).

In general it is wise to deal as expeditiously as possible with situations that interfere with class activities. Since attention seeking lies behind most disruptive behavior and punishment seeking behind some, a teacher should avoid arguing with a student or taking class time to discuss a conflict situation (Anthony, 1965). A teacher can find ways to avoid confrontations and allow a child to save face (Smith, S.L., 1980). Emotionally charged situations, for example, often can be defused with humor. Threats of punishment are likely to be counterproductive, as is the escalation of any conflict to the level of a contest between teacher and child. When circumstances warrant, however, it is not oppressive to reprove or penalize children for misconduct or to ask them to apologize for offensive behavior. Young children may require external control in the form of a holding environment both psychologically and physically in order to regain internal control. After dealing with a conflict with a student, a conference can be held when tempers have cooled, so that the teacher can renew rapport with that child.

A common source of misunderstanding between teachers and children can be explained by "attribution theory" (Jones, 1979). Persons with problems tend to blame the environment, while those observing the problem see the cause as based in the person with the problem. Thus adults naturally tend to see variables in a child as causes of misbehavior and overlook indications that the environment might be a contributing cause.

When a situation is beyond a teacher's control, outside help should be used. The teacher must decide when the group is sufficiently threatened by one child to justify such an intervention. Every teacher encounters children whose needs require the involvement of their parents, school administrators, and specialized services.

There are ways of helping troubled children through selective scheduling and modification of curriculum content (Perkins, 1974). As a foundation for learning to cope with the ambiguities of life, they first need to have the stability of dependable structure. Because of brief attention spans, intolerance, and emotional instability, pacing and sequencing of their activities are important. The use of repetition and routines is especially important for stabilizing the world of a troubled child. Some children have vague perceptions of time and have difficulty working within broad time limits. They need brief attainable tasks with clear beginnings and ends and advance notice of changes. Abrupt transitions from one activity to another is a source of tension for some children, who have difficulty detaching from an ongoing activity. Providing simple, nonchallenging, repetitive activities and maintaining eye contact with them while shifting activities helps to

smooth transitions between learning activities.

Excessive sensitivity to auditory or visual stimulation is characteristic of some children. Thus as a means of controlling children's sensory input, a teacher can minimize distractions by placing a distractible child in the front row away from areas of heavy traffic. On the other hand, an overly active child may disturb the class in that position and be placed in the back of the room with a clear definition of the boundaries within which the child may move, so that the teacher need only intervene when those boundaries are exceeded and not be distracted by minor movements. Moreover choosing a neighbor for a child who can provide constructive support within agreed-upon limits can establish a "good neighbor policy" that can meet the needs of the child for keeping up with classroom activities (Stevens, 1984). Children also are more likely to remain attentive if a teacher moves around the classroom, encouraging, and helping them.

Recognition of children's fatigue cycles permits reserving the most intense teaching for the times when they are the most receptive. Alternating energetic and restful activities also may be useful. For example, introducing a quiet, structured activity after an active lunch period helps to reduce tension in the classroom. Unfortunately, however, in many classrooms the timing of special teaching tends to dictate when subjects are taught.

Children who have difficulty in distinguishing between reality and fantasy can be helped by curriculum materials that clearly distinguish between the likely and the unlikely. For example, science activities related to immediate life experience rather than events of destruction can be grasped without undue confusion. The study of the seasons is more appropriate for this kind of child than of lightning, earthquakes, and volcanoes. On the other hand, another child might use the scientific study of nature's violence as a means for sublimating personal violent fantasies.

MOTIVATING CHILDREN FOR SCHOOLWORK

The differences between deep and superficial approaches to learning are supported by many studies. Interest, relevance, humor, and paradox enhance internal motivation and favor deep, lasting learning, while external motivation, such as by testing, favors superficial, transient learning.

Knowledge of the role of reinforcement in learning is useful in understanding externally and internally generated motivation. A reinforcer is an event that either increases behavior through a reward or decreases it through a penalty. A positive reinforcer is a pleasurable or desirable event, as expressed in the Premack principle: anything a child likes to do more can be used to reinforce any behavior the child likes to do less (Premack, 1979). Conversely a behavior can be decreased by withdrawing a positive reinforcer. A negative reinforcer usually decreases behavior as does a distressing event experienced as punishment, although behavior can be increased in order to avoid a negative reinforcer.

External Reinforcement

External, positive, concrete reinforcers, such as candy, and symbolic reinforcers, such as tokens, provide immediate gratification and may be useful initially with severely disturbed children; however, they usually do not promote the development of enduring skills.

Token rewards provide tangible evidence that something has been achieved. They can be used after steps toward a goal in order to divide time into short, meaningful segments. The rewards should be for the achievement of specific tasks or goals, not merely because the child pleases the teacher or is well behaved. Tokens then can be used to develop self-discipline through the child's own evaluation of achievement (Friedling & O'Leary, 1979).

Except when used judiciously, praise actually can sabotage learning in school. Praise can induce children to depend upon external rewards and weaken self-motivation. It also can be used patronizingly with low achieving children and perpetuate unequal treatment of racial and ethnic groups (Rowe, 1973). In a similar way, success may be used with the intent of building self-confidence, so that children are shielded from errors in the hope that the accumulation of successes untarnished by failure would lead them to conclude that they are competent. The result, however, may be that children thus protected tend to interpret setbacks as failures, and may even see themselves as less bright, because they are assigned easy work and praised for work that does not seem particularly noteworthy. Most important, they do not learn how to tolerate frustration and overcome obstacles (Dweck & Bempechat, 1983).

Transition from External to Internal Reinforcement

Developmentally children learn to accept and like themselves by first experiencing the acceptance and adulation of others. Building upon a background of parental support, teachers also influence children through approval and attention. A teacher's pleasure in a child's spontaneous actions is external reinforcement for actions that also are internally satisfying to the child. This is what makes children educable. They are ready to renounce other satisfactions if the reward of affection is promised or if withdrawal of affection is threatened (Fenichel, 1945; Marcus, 1971).

Parents and teachers can foster a shift from external to internal motivation by working together in providing a child with personal responsibility for measuring the degree to which expectations are met. For children who have difficulty organizing their lives or are engaged in responsibility-avoiding maneuvers, a reporting system that bridges the school and home can be helpful. A variety of arrangements can be made, depending upon the ages of children. The key is having the child obtain feedback from the teachers regarding behavior and schoolwork assignments each day with acknowledgment that it has been monitored by a parent. A useful technique is to have a daily checklist of work kept by the child and signed by both parents and teachers, so that each knows what is expected and what has been done. For the child this is like a personal appointment book as used by busy adults. It unites the teachers and parents through shared knowledge of what a child is expected to be doing. It also makes evident the areas in which the child is having difficulty. Lapses in the communication system flag issues related to the child's ability to assume responsibility. And most important, the system reduces opportunities for the child to manipulate adults.

By observing the events preceding and following disturbing behavior, a teacher can gain an understanding of what methods might work in the classroom (Hammill & Bartel, 1978; Warm, 1978). What happens immediately after a behavior occurs serves to reinforce it positively or negatively. A common positive reinforcer for inappropriate behavior is the attention of another person. If attention is removed, the behavior may be diminished. Another technique is positively reinforcing desired behaviors. For example, a child may not only be ignored when out of the seat without permission, but be positively reinforced by attention when sitting in the seat. Thus attention to appropriate behavior

and ignoring inappropriate behavior may be useful techniques in setting the stage for stimulating a child's internal motivation.

Internal Reinforcement

The children most likely to succeed in school are those who enjoy schoolwork. Their behavior reflects confidence, organization, initiative, persistence, self-discipline, and pride in accomplishment (Wallace & Kauffman, 1973).

From the first day of school, children are made aware that the key to success is through doing schoolwork. No one knows this more than the child who experiences academic difficulties. The frustration and agony of school failure are all too apparent for children who encounter difficulties in learning to read, write, or calculate (Wallace & Kauffman, 1973). It follows then that the progress of children in school depends upon building a repertoire of academic, social, and emotional skills that permit a child to find satisfaction and pleasure in schoolwork.

Pleasure in mastery is the most potent internal reinforcer of learning (Sanders, 1979). The gratification experienced by feeling competent surpasses that of external reinforcers. "I did it" is one of the happiest phrases a struggling student utters, and it is among the most gratifying a teacher hears (Gardner, 1978).

The motivation to be competent is the strongest and most enduring for achievement in school. Even for younger children, approval and praise from others are not sufficient explanations of the efforts children make to master their environments. They find satisfaction in doing things for themselves. The crushing repetition of failures, however, can dispel the pleasure of performing effectively for its own sake. Then, no longer self-motivated, the child may become dependent upon external rewards. Restoring self-motivation cannot be accomplished by sympathy and praise alone. It can happen when children succeed by their own efforts.

A focus on internal motivation can increase self-determination and self-confidence in addition to self-discipline (Dorr et al, 1983; Phillips et al, 1960; Ruble & Boggiano, 1980). Self-monitoring by having children keep track of their own achievements and self-reinforcement is useful in building a sense of responsibility for themselves (Smith, S. L., 1980; Workman, 1982). Visible proof of progress through graphs and stars may appeal to young children. These techniques have the drawbacks of setting up opportunities for cheating; however, if that occurs, it can be used as another kind of learning experience with the child.

Two examples of building upon internal motivation with children posing two different forms of behavior are:

A Hyperactive Child

The minds of hyperactive children, like butterflies, skip so rapidly from one thing to another that it seems impossible to capture their attention. Once the energy that propelled the hyperactivity becomes zest for learning, however, they can be delightful students (Blank, 1972).

One young boy's predominant characteristic was a rapid succession of intense, but logically unconnected, bits of behavior. He was attracted to a toy—so he ran to it; on his way, he saw a different toy and decided to take that instead; after a moment he dropped it and looked for something else; and so on ad infinitum. For him the most effective reward for sustained attention was an integral part of the task. Thus in a cooking lesson the reward was taking food with him to his class and eating the final product; in a reading lesson, the reward was taking home a certificate of reading achievement to show his parents. In each case the reward was

the direct and immediate result of the child's effort in completing an activity. The reward symbolizes "I can do it." At first the reward can be earned after each step, such as a series of stars that then validate an achievement certificate. With progress the reward becomes receiving the certificate without having to validate each step.

A Withdrawn Child

A withdrawn child presents an opposite picture from that of the hyperactive child (Blank, 1972). Withdrawn children show massive inhibition of activity when under stress. They are unsure of themselves and cannot face situations that have the potential for failure. In effect their reward is the absence of failure and its attendant humiliation. This goal requires that the child initially be presented with simple tasks in which success can occur.

The withdrawn child's defense is simply to be silent in the face of demands. The silence is amazingly effective; nothing is more disconcerting than to talk with a person who does not respond. If one feels compassion for the child's fragility and retreats from futile efforts at interchange, the pattern of withdrawal becomes even more firmly ingrained. In effect the child trains the teacher to become as silent as is the child. The resistance may be overcome, if the teacher proceeds as if it does not exist. This approach is most effective when combined with attractive, nonthreatening materials that lower the child's resistance to participation. The teacher confidently proceeds in an activity with the child, as if all were well. The child's comfort with the material and the teacher's confident attitude takes the child off guard. The teacher then can make simple requests in a matter-of-fact way without looking at the child, thereby inducing the child to respond.

As withdrawn children discover their competencies and gain confidence, they often show an attraction to aggressive behavior once their initial fear is lessened. This can be handled by encouraging them to engage in physically aggressive activities.

One of the barriers to success in schoolwork is an ambivalent attitude toward practice and drill. On the one hand, drill is regarded as mechanical, old-fashioned, and antithetical to meaningful learning. On the other hand, we know that practice is essential for skill development so that proficiency in athletics obviously depends upon tedious practice. The upshot of this ambiguity is that drill often is half-heartedly and apologetically employed in classrooms. Many difficulties in arithmetic, reading, spelling, and grammar can be attributed to insufficient practice to ensure a child's mastery of basic skills. When drill in school is compared to the practice of a musical or athletic skill, children can appreciate its necessity. Without an adequate skill foundation, the study of science, the arts, and social subjects cannot be appreciated, and certainly not enjoyed.

In another vein underachievement can be related to a student's failure to acquire values supporting education. For this reason helping older students clarify their beliefs, interests, and aspirations can promote open embracing of education objectives that otherwise are frustrated by unexpressed, irrational, and emotionally tinged attitudes (Raths, 1961). The opportunity to talk about the purposes of education and the range of later choices available to each individual promotes a sense of control over life and internal motivation to work toward those opportunities.

Instrumentation in Education

Mechanical devices have motivating potential for many children (Behrmann, 1984). They offer an engaging form of activity in which children are intrigued by gadgetry and the sense of control that flows from the successful mastery of a machine. Auditory tapes with headsets and microcomputers, therefore, can be invaluable aids in absorbing a child's attention, promoting concentration, and reducing fear of failure.

Microcomputers cannot directly teach thinking or interpersonal skills; however, they are useful for drills in which they provide immediate feedback, which is not possible in the delayed correcting of paperwork. Children who are easily bored in classroom groups may find themselves deeply absorbed in relating to a machine that can be controlled rather than to a teacher, who may be perceived as a controlling authority figure. As one child put it, "With the computer, nobody bothers me; I know when I'm right and wrong; I like its colors and sounds, and it makes me smarter!" Thus the microcomputer may enhance academic learning by bypassing interpersonal conflicts.

Word processors also offer the advantages of circumventing the panic some children feel when confronted with a pencil and blank sheet of paper and removing the element of potential criticism by teachers and peers. They involve a child on four sensory levels: visual, auditory, kinesthetic, and tactile. They offer novelty and permit the correction of errors neatly with the easy production of a printed draft (Stevens, 1984).

The anthropomorphizing capability of microcomputers offers children an engaging sense of personal power, such as through the turtles used in the LOGO project (McCorduck, 1979). This technique can be employed to help children gain a sense of power by playfully applying knowledge. In this sense microcomputers offer tools to help children learn how to solve problems. On the other hand, microcomputers exclude human interactions and may control their users (Weizenbaum, 1976). When this is not desirable, software can be created to encourage cooperative learning situations in which children are required to interact in order to reach mutual goals.

TEACHING WORK SKILLS

Children learn how to learn in school by assuming the roles of students (Boocock, 1972). The ultimate goal in any type of learning cannot be the retention of large amounts of information, most of which will be forgotten. What can be retained are techniques for acquiring new information, for attending to relevant and ignoring irrelevant cues, and for testing hypotheses and strategies. Teaching children how to be students is a more lasting contribution to their education than the accumulation of facts (Stevenson, 1972). In the higher grades, independent study and test-taking skills are essential. For many children learning how to approach a task is as important as the task itself. They need to learn how to work.

Some children tend to be lost in space and time. They do not view a room as an organized space to be entered and used in relation to what is going on in it and who is there. They do not plan to have pencil and paper, sit in a certain place, and accommodate to the activities of other people in the room. They do not organize what they do during a given time period and pace themselves to finish a task on time. They do not know when to begin and when to stop a task. These children need to learn how to organize themselves for schoolwork and for study (Devine, 1983). They must learn how to sit in a classroom, organize materials, and start working.

Clues to how each child learns best can be found through observation and discussion of that child's approach to work. Moreover patterns of learning can be discerned by reviewing formal and informal test re-

sults, past teachers' records, and information from parents. Experimentation also helps to determine what will be successful (Smith, S. L., 1980). In general regular routines, familiar procedures, and prescribed ways of behaving are helpful for children who have difficulty working.

While the adult brain can absorb about 300 words a minute, normal speech plods along at as little as one-third that rate. Thus spoken information is inefficiently slow, and the unchallenged mind wanders off into other thoughts, as college students well know during some lectures. Effective listening is a basic skill that requires self-discipline. In order to listen, a child must be able to sit still and pay attention, hear all of the directions and understand a sequence of details in the proper order, remember what is heard, and carry out instructions.

Before starting a task, some children need help in focusing their attention so as to discriminate between what is important and what is not. They can be asked first to look at the teacher, then to stop and think about what is going to be done and then to look at what is to be done. They need to be told the purpose of the task, what is expected of them, and what to look for. They need to be shown explicitly how and where to begin a task. It also may be useful to draw the child's attention to how long it takes to perform a particular task. To ensure initial success and maintain enthusiasm, the place to begin teaching is at a familiar level, just below a child's point of mastery. The child must master one learning task before being expected to comprehend and learn the next (Bloom, 1964). New material then can be introduced as a manageable challenge. If a task is too difficult, children become discouraged or disinterested.

Some children may be capable of comprehending a problem but be unable to remember what is needed. The material given to such a child should be broken down into parts and limited in amount so that the child learns each part before moving on. Each step can be structured into a lesson plan and taught systematically, one step at a time; then it can be reintroduced and repeated until the goal is reached. The child can be asked to repeat directions to ensure that they have been understood. A teacher can act as an external memory aid, literally or metaphorically holding constant aspects of the task that have been done and aspects that will need to be done later (Wood, 1981). Talking or whispering to oneself is a useful way for some children to keep themselves on a task (Kendall & Wilcox, 1980).

Mental imagery is one of the oldest and most effective means for assisting memory. Recent research on memory adds that people are most helped by imagery that is interactive. For example, learning the words dog and broom can be more efficient by creating an image of a dog sweeping with a broom than to have images of the two separate objects. The crucial element in this linking process is to teach children to take separate pieces of information and connect them into meaningful images. After this has been accomplished, the interconnectedness of the imagery causes the various parts to imply each other, allowing mental reconstruction of the image and the recall of details (Dixon, 1983).

The organization of thinking skills is an essential foundation for academic learning (Sternberg, 1986). The thinking styles of children may be either overly abstract or overly concrete so that a child needs help to become more flexible. Whenever possible linking what is unknown to children to their own experience and knowledge is helpful. They need to be introduced to abstract ideas through their bodies, familiar objects, and pictures. Furthermore, in rote learning, the introduction of unrelated material just before or after a task inter-

feres with learning (Ausubel, 1969). When new material is preceded and followed by related material, the new material is more solidly anchored. Review on the same day of learning has a consolidating effect. In addition delayed review before a test permits the recall and reinforcement of material. Combining the two does both.

Children need help in becoming aware of the aspects of learning that are difficult and those that are easy for them. This can be done by asking them what they dislike and like about schoolwork. Just as a tennis player must learn the feel of an effective as compared with a less effective stroke, these children must distinguish between when they are headed for trouble and when they are on the right track. Without this self-awareness, they cannot become personally involved in their schoolwork. They do not perceive academic learning as something they are doing for themselves, and they remain dependent upon someone else for guidance, criticism, and rewards. By involving children in finding out how they learn best, they can discover their strengths and accept and compensate for their weaknesses. The answers lie in a child, but none are useful unless they are known to and employed by that child. Many failures in working with these children result from turning to others for insight about a child rather than asking the child.

An example of the importance of personal awareness of the specifics of learning how one learns is seen in mentally retarded persons, who can be taught to think abstractly. When this is done, transfer to generalized problem solving is exceedingly limited, however, unless the retarded persons pay close attention to whether the skills learned are useful to them (Menolascino et al, 1983).

An Instructional Paradigm
Buzan cites an experiment to demonstrate instruction in thinking through fos-

tering self-awareness (Buzan & Dixon, 1977).

Ten-year-old children were asked to write a paper as a basis for giving talks to their class. As might be expected, very little came of this. Buzan then provided success for the children by asking them to raise their hands, if they knew any of a long list of words. Every child, needless to say, scored 100 percent. For the next ten minutes, the children worked on the list in pairs, taking turns to say words to each other and list how many they knew.

Buzan then explained that each word has many hooks for building up ideas, sentences, books, and even libraries. The children were asked to write the word "fist" in the middle of a blank page and to put their own hooks around it. The result was that the children virtually ignored each other and, during the next ten-minute exercise, each child thought of many associations. They were then shown that they could use the multihook nature of words to overcome their fear of formal sentences and grammar.

Then the children were asked to write down ten sentences containing words that they remembered from any source. After ten minutes, no child had more than two sentences. In the next exercise, they were asked to think about the way they thought. Each child sat for a few minutes thinking about and observing the way in which thoughts were formed and discovering that they did not come in ordered grammar, but in ideas like they found stimulated by the word "fist." Through this exercise the children learned that grammar and spelling are only useful cosmetics after ideas are flowing, rather than the essential natures of an idea.

Finally the children once again were asked to prepare a talk for the class. During the half hour available, each child built up a striking pattern of words, ideas, images, and linked thoughts, using the multihook method. The children were totally engrossed and disappointed when the time was up. Their fear of spelling mistakes disappeared. Throughout the round of talks, their level of attention was high, as reflected in their enthusiasm for the genuine exchange of information that took place.

PRESCRIPTIVE TEACHING

The Education for All Handicapped Children Act (Public Law 94-142) requires schools to develop an individualized program for each child receiving special education services (Fiscus & Mandell, 1983). In so doing specific information about how children learn is more relevant than diagnostic categories unrelated to teaching techniques (Gardner, 1978).

At the broadest level, children tend to learn most effectively in either an analytic or an intuitive manner. The analytic children learn sequentially, inductively, verbally, and reflectively. Intuitive children are holistic, deductive, visually oriented, and impressionistic. Developmentally until the age of seven, most children favor intuitive learning. To reach all students in a typical classroom, therefore, teaching should be done both inductively for analytic children and deductively for intuitive children. Mathematics is an analytical subject that can be taught holistically; similarly, holistic social studies can be taught analytically.

More specifically, prescriptive teaching depends upon the following principles: (1) determining existing skill levels, (2) formulating instructional goals for specific abilities, (3) structuring steps of instruction, (4) providing learners with feedback on task performance, and (5) keeping evaluative records so that teachers can benefit from previous experience (Wallace & Kauffman, 1973).

Instructional formats that generate curiosity and in turn lead to pleasure in being competent are needed (Olson & Dillner, 1976; Stott, 1978). They must be related to practical academic skills, however, because training in specific components of learning, such as memory, do not generalize. For example, a college student memorized an eighty digit number with 230 hours of practice, but this did not improve his memory for other things (Ericsson & Chase, 1982).

One approach is to match a child's abilities and interests to an array of program alternatives such as follows (Messick, 1976):

1. *Corrective matches* are those that rectify deficiencies in basic skills and knowledge that jeopardize further progress in academic learning. The deficit is attacked directly by having the child engage in the difficult activity. Teaching deaf children to speak and comprehend vocal language is based on this philosophy. Generally this approach employs the usual methods of programmed learning with gradually increasing expectations of the child. Particularly useful with disadvantaged children, this approach aims to develop the same skills that most children possess.

2. *Compensatory matches* are those that circumvent skill deficiencies by providing alternatives, such as substituting typing for handwriting. The deficit is bypassed by the development of compensatory devices. For example, one adult dyslexic, who was a company president, reported that he had so arranged his life through the use of tape recorders, secretaries, and an acute memory that the demands for him to read were minimized.

This method in inappropriate for disadvantaged children, since it would leave them in a permanently underdeveloped state. On the other hand, attempts to make a withdrawn child engage in the activities in which the child is deficient only serve to reinforce anxiety and withdrawal. The child must first gain confidence in oneself. To this end allowing the child to rehearse those skills in which one is proficient provides a measure of security. Then the child

can be placed in situations that require developing deficient skills.

Another example of the temporary use of a compensatory tactic is a child who was not promoted because the child did not demonstrate her reading ability through reading aloud in school, although she could read at home. The teacher was asked by the mother to listen to tape recordings of the child reading aloud at home. The teacher, probably reasoning that the child should master her fear and not become dependent upon "crutches," refused this accommodation to the child's avoidance of confronting weaknesses. Still permitting a temporary compensatory adjustment could have prevented failing a grade in school, which should only be based upon the actual achievement level of a child.

3. *Preferential matching* draws upon the strengths of the learner, allowing exercise of the strongest mode of functioning, such as using a tape recorder for children whose auditory memory is superior to visual. A variation of this approach is to channel a difficulty so that it becomes a strength. For instance, a boy's bossiness can be turned to advantage by giving him classroom responsibility. The hope is not to reinforce the maladaptive behavior, but rather to convert it to an acceptable and constructive form. The secondary reward of approval may serve as an impetus to help the child develop more adaptive personality traits (Blank, 1972).

4. *Challenge matches* make a deliberate attempt to create conflict between task components and learner characteristics in order to challenge the learner to become more flexible. An example is using the "look–say" method in reading tutoring of a child with visual-spatial dyslexia.

5. *Combination matches* include ingredients of the corrective, compensatory, and preferential treatments.

Efforts are being made to collate specific teaching techniques that can be applied to special learning problems. An example is the *Educator's Desk Reference* (Weller & Buchanan, 1987).

The risk of prescriptive teaching is that an exclusive focus on teaching a child may distract attention from school, parental, and societal factors in a child's school problems (Accardo, 1980).

THE ARTS AND RECREATION

As schools seek new ways to help children achieve satisfaction in learning, the importance of the arts and recreation has become increasingly evident. The arts are universal languages in which gestures, movements, sounds, rhythms, and figures carry symbolic meanings that can be understood without words. Organizational skills also can be learned through crafts, drama, puppetry, and film making. Thus the creative arts can be useful adjuncts to academic education (Eddy, 1983; Remer, 1983).

Visual arts teachers can develop basic work skills as do classroom teachers in different and captivating ways (Hausman, 1983). Music can stimulate children's esthetic needs and develop awareness of their heritage. Moreover, the enjoyment of artistic and musical activities also can improve performance in other areas of a child's life by enhancing self-confidence. In addition to playing instruments, singing, listening, and moving to music, children can be encouraged to make discoveries about music through the exploration of sound, playing the roles of composer, performer, conductor, listener, and critic, as they discover concepts about the structure of music (Land and Vaughan, 1973).

The movement dialogue in dance is an expression of nonverbal communication and a creative enactment of issues important to children. Dance also provides a climate in which a child is free to risk new behaviors and release the restraints of inhibiting self-consciousness (Schmais & Orleans, 1981).

The academic club is a means of involving older children in special education by combining all of the arts (Smith, S.L., 1980). Drama, which adapts well to a club organization, screens out distractions and focuses on the child through the use of props and decorations that hold attention upon the particular subject under study. Examples of clubs are a secret agent club with agent rules run by a captain; an Indian tribe with respect for its elders; a storekeeper's club run by a manager; and a renaissance councillor's club using the knights' code of chivalry. Children can accept discipline and also muster courage to experiment and risk failure in the club format, because it is not the child who might fail but the character being portrayed. The club idea also conveys an atmosphere of fun in learning.

In general the physical fitness of school children has been neglected (President's Council on Physical Fitness and Sports, 1980). All children, but particularly the educationally handicapped, profit from physical conditioning. Many children with learning problems have not had the opportunity to discover their athletic strengths, and the poor physical condition of some has aggravated their temperamental problems.

Systematic physical exercises in the form of gymnastics or calisthenics are helpful in the treatment as well as the prevention of learning difficulties in school. They improve motor control, body image, sensory attention, kinesthetic imagery, and self-confidence, in addition to benefiting physical development. Their effects depend upon their regularity, cohesiveness, and involvement of all muscle groups. Free play, games, and competitive sports in themselves do not provide these benefits, which are of particular value for children with attention and movement problems.

To be effective therapeutic exercises should be done daily for enough time to combine energetic exercise, meditation, and rest (Prudden, 1979). Exercise of this nature has been compatible with European and Far Eastern cultures, but it has been neglected in the United States, in part because of an inherent resistance to the group- and self-discipline involved in these activities. The result has been to the disadvantage of children with temperamental and impulse control problems.

INFLUENCING THE PEER GROUP

Since a child's behavior is greatly influenced by peers whose attitudes may be at variance with the goals of schooling, any educational design that does not involve the peer group overlooks an important teaching channel (Strain, 1981). The hidden world of attraction and hostility between peers especially influences the schoolwork of children with learning problems. Moreover classes can be disrupted by vicious circles of negativism. Without adult guidance peer influences foster cliques and the isolation of vulnerable children. Thus children have the potential for influencing each other through disruptive acts.

Although children's prosocial influences on their companions are less dramatically brought to adult attention than are negative influences, peers can be significant socializers of altruism and reciprocity (Rubin & Ross, 1982). Adults can promote the constructive influence of peers by accepting and working with peer groups instead of trying to control them. The influence of adults is needed particularly because of strong pressures for conformity within the group (Perkins, 1974). When teaching involves small groups, a teacher has a mentor role and an opportunity to influence positively peer attitudes toward children who need special help.

The experience of the some 1000 one-room schools in the United States continues to show that younger children can learn both academic skills and more mature behavior from older children. Classroom working groups in which most students have a degree of influence over other students have higher morale than groups dominated by particular students. For example, in one study a teacher divided a class into subgroups that met one hour each day. Each student was the leader of the group for one week. The leaders drew up lesson plans for each week with the teacher's help. They also reported on the progress of their group that week. This approach brought out leadership qualities in all of the children (Schmuck & Schmuck, 1971). Another technique is encouraging each child to develop an area of expertise and help the child demonstrate that knowledge to others (Cooper et al, 1982).

Leadership in a classroom lies in the actions by group members, most prominently the teacher, that aid in setting and implementing group goals. Largely untapped are the possibilities of promoting supportive interactions between peers (Bryan & Bryan, 1983). One possibility for accomplishing this is by working directly with high-power children who influence the social structure of the classroom. A teacher who is aware of informal interactions among peers may be able to win over influential students so that they feel involved in classwork, and thus influence the entire group (Schmuck & Schmuck, 1971). Older students can be used effectively to tutor or counsel younger students. Children also can learn effectively in self-chosen mutual tutoring pairs.

A teacher can assist in improving the acceptance of students rejected by their peers and promote constructive interactions between varying combinations of children through small group projects, such as interviewing each other to write biographies and role playing. A useful technique is drawing a "pal for a week" and structuring activities for each pairing. There are academic games and team projects designed to enhance peer relations and promote positive attitudes toward learning (Millman et al, 1980). In addition to academic goals, some children need assistance in cultivating a social life by developing talents and coaching in social skills or through creating social groups with similar interests (Smith, S.L., 1980). Encouraging children to develop their talents in the arts and athletics helps them to enhance their value and status in their peer groups.

More attention should be devoted to helping teachers develop curriculum content and training procedures that directly influence the peer group. The individual-difference approach is an example of what can be done at the elementary level to influence student attitudes toward differences in children's backgrounds and appearances (Cummings, 1981).

SUMMARY

The aim of both education and psychotherapy is fostering the optimal development of children for independent living through mastery of themselves and life situations. To this end the teacher is an important agent of change in the lives of children.

The importance of the teacher as a model cannot be underestimated. To the extent that teachers are palpable persons with satisfactions and frustrations, children and teachers can build mutually trusting relationships. The experience of being heard, accepted, and understood by a teacher affirms a child's sense of importance. It also helps children to accept their errors and cope with failures. Through empathy teachers also can use their reac-

tions to children as diagnostic clues to the inner state of a child.

Classroom management is critical to maintaining an atmosphere conducive to didactic learning. When rules are seen as guidelines for facilitating schoolwork, they are more readily accepted by children than if they are seen as arbitrary expressions of adult authority. Children with learning difficulties particularly need structure, predictable routines, the pacing of high- and low-activity periods, the minimizing of distracting stimuli, and the modulation of exciting elements in instructional content.

At the core of a child's success in school is motivation to learn successfully. Internally generated motivation promotes lasting learning, and externally generated motivation results in superficial learning. Although external reinforcement is a useful initial motivating technique with some children, internal reinforcement from the satisfactions of success and competence is more desirable. The transition from external to internal reinforcement can take place most expeditiously through a teacher's approval of actions that also are internally satisfying to a child. This can be facilitated by shifting from teacher and parent monitoring of progress in schoolwork to including a child's self-monitoring.

Children with learning difficulties often need to learn how to work in school through specific assistance in approaching tasks, focusing attention, following manageable steps, repetition, and review until mastery is evident. Personalizing the content of material, identifying one's own weaknesses and strengths, and becoming aware of the usefulness of didactic knowledge and skills enhances the value of schoolwork for children.

Prescriptive teaching is a means of matching instructional methods with the strengths and weaknesses of children. Diagnostic information about a child can be used to formulate instructional goals. Then corrective, compensatory, preferential, or challenge matches can be made between methods and learner characteristics. The pace of instruction can be gauged through ongoing feedback to the learner. Annotative record keeping preserves information about the most effective approaches and methods for each child. The matching concept also can be extended profitably to matching children and teachers.

Children with difficulties in academic learning often can be reached by drawing upon the creative arts, particularly crafts, music, visual art, dance, and drama, all of which offer means of acquiring self-discipline, interpersonal skills, and self-confidence. Physical education and athletic skills are particularly important. These modalities offer important complements to academic learning.

The peer group has obvious detrimental effects when distracting children from educational goals. At the same time, peer modeling and pressure can be important incentives for acceptance of, and adherence to, classroom values. Teachers need help in learning how to use peer group influence in creating classroom atmospheres conducive to academic learning, the acceptance of children with special needs, and positive peer support.

Above all teachers need working conditions that acknowledge their professionalism and foster qualities of wisdom, zeal, kindness, patience, firmness, and humor. Although important for all children, the teacher–child relationship is particularly crucial for children who have difficulty working in school. One of the most important barriers to learning in school is the inability of teachers to apply their teaching skills because of the lack of time, materials, and support.

32

Remedial Techniques

I am a very poor visualizer, and find that I can seldom call to mind even a single letter of the alphabet in purely retinal terms. I must trace the letter by running my mental eye over its contours in order that the image of it shall leave any distinctness at all.

William James, 1842–1910

Tutoring is academic training carried out with an individual student as one of the roles of a teacher, as a full-time occupation, or as a part-time activity. In addition to supporting school subjects, tutoring can be provided in specific reading and mathematical skills, most commonly in reading.

The intent of this chapter is to assemble systematically information about remedial techniques that have been found to be useful. Because its effectiveness depends upon individual attention and continuity over extended periods, many practical obstacles prevent children from receiving the well-demonstrated benefits of tutoring.

First of all the relationship between a child and tutor is the key to the success of any tutoring endeavor (Pflaum, 1974; Sapir, 1985; Spache, 1981a), even in the rehabilitation of severely brain-damaged persons (Pirozzolo, 1979). The importance of building self-confidence through the tutoring relationship is illustrated by the following statements:

I am still very ashamed of my inability to read. I carry this dreadful secret always. I live in fear of having to read aloud. At all costs I must conceal my ignorance (Simpson, 1979).

One teacher helped me to ask questions so that I forgot to worry about being stupid.

In addition to the support and imagination of the tutor, special techniques are needed beyond those used in classroom teaching. Non-English-speaking children require special consideration (Chinn, 1984). Parents can help work on drills between tutoring sessions, and when appropriate carry out tutoring themselves. At the least, through insight into their children's tutoring requirements, parents are better equipped to obtain the kind of help their children need. Tutors from a child's community also can be trained (Wallach & Wallach, 1976). In some instances peer tutoring can be useful (Spache, 1981a).

REMEDIAL READING TUTORING

Many techniques have been devised to teach reading (Kaluger & Kolson, 1969; Spache, 1976, 1981a). At this time the experience of educators, clinicians, and researchers is converging around common principles. In general whatever is done must have significance to the child. The chief task of the reading tutor, therefore, is conveying the purpose of reading as a source of information and pleasure, as if the child were an apprentice to the tutor (Smith & Johnson, 1976).

Remedial reading programs generally emphasize multisensory techniques, phonics, rules of pronounciation and spelling, and drills in the context of a painstaking, step-by-step approach over the required number of years (Naidoo, 1972). In designing a treatment approach for a child, it is essential to establish why a child is making reading errors. A diagnostic method allows the tutor to determine exactly where the child is functioning and begin instruction at or slightly below that point (Traub, 1975). This usually results in the indentification of patterns rather than a single specific problem. As a joint endeavor with the child, the discovery of these idiosyncrasies helps to explain the child's difficulties and to guide improving the child's skills. Some children initially are curious about their specific problems (Cohen, 1983). Most need time and help to develop this interest. An explanation of the nature of the difficulties to parents and teachers with the child's participation is the first step in successful treatment. The moment of illumination about the importance of tutoring is illustrated by a 13-year-old boy, who exclaimed:

> Now I understand how people can read. They have to think about it.

When a child knows why effort must be mobilized to acquire the desired skills, an instructional program that proceeds from the simple to the complex and allows continual feedback on progress should be used. The most useful tutoring concentrates upon the components of reading, such as word analysis and comprehension skills, rather than underlying information processing, such as auditory discrimination (Vellutino, 1979). An example of a comprehensive method is Goodman's system of miscue analysis (Goodman, 1982). The task of reading is reduced to basic units after which meaning can be related to words in reading, writing, spelling, and speaking. The tutor must experiment with each pupil to find the most effective procedures so that techniques can be fitted to the child. Initial success is important to a child in enhancing willingness to pursue a difficult undertaking.

The commonly used tutoring programs draw upon three general approaches (Kinsbourne & Caplan, 1979; Thomson, 1984). The first is by providing phonetic renderings of the language as an intermediate step that serves as a foundation for reading conventional letters and words. Examples are the Initial Teaching Alphabet, in which 42 symbols represent English phonemes and the Peabody Rebus, which is a set of picture words. These intermediate steps are used to facilitate reading and to defer the more difficult orthography until fear of the reading process has been overcome. Even braille has been suggested as an intermediate language for the severely dyslexic child (McCoy, 1975; Fishbein, 1979).

The second approach is to capitalize on a child's preferred sensory modality supplemented by other modalities. The diagrams in Figure 32-1 represent three of the many possible individual sensory modality learning styles (Williams, 1983). The individual represented as A is competent in all

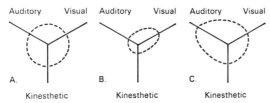

Figure 32-1. In these diagrams each line represents one learning modality. The dotted circle indicates how much the learner uses each modality. If the circle crosses the modality line close to the point where the three lines join, the learner uses that modality so little that it must be considered underdeveloped or impaired. If the dotted circle crosses at the center of the line, the modality is functional; and if it crosses near the far end of the line, it is preferred. (From *Teaching for the Two-Sided Mind*, by Linda Verlee Williams, copyright 1983 Linda Verlee Williams. Reprinted by permission of the publisher, Prentice Hall, Inc.)

modes. B is poor in auditory and kinesthetic but competent in visual. C is competent is kinesthetic and visual but outstanding in auditory. According to this scheme, A will function well in any classroom, B will be more successful when material is presented visually, and C will be able to learn in any classroom but will do so more quickly when allowed to function in the auditory mode. For children who have trouble remembering spoken instructions but can follow written directions, it can be a relief to discover that for a particular task their visual system works better than their auditory system. With that information a child can develop strategies that use the stronger system, and also practice strengthening the weaker one. Thus a child with poor word-recognition ability initially can be taught to read by an auditory method and a child with poor word-sounding ability can be taught by a visual and haptic method. Empirically it has been shown that increasing print size in itself facilitates reading for many types of readers (Laurinen & Nyman, 1982).

The third approach is to teach grammatical and spelling rules (Hanna et al, 1971; Rak, 1979). Up to the third-grade level in reading, the emphasis is upon recognition skills. To read beyond that level, additional understanding of language structure is needed (Kinsbourne & Caplan, 1979). Whenever possible reading materials should be gleaned from those used in mainstream classrooms.

The *Corrective Reading Program* (Science Research Associates, 1984) is an example of a broad-gauged approach that begins with phonic word attack skills, proceeds to visual decoding of letters and words, and then builds up words from their components. Next it emphasizes basic thinking skills, reading comprehension, and reading for specific purposes. *Reading from Scratch* is a multisensory reading and spelling program in an adult format (Van den Honert, 1985).

Beyond teaching the general principles of intermediate languages, capitalizing on preferred sensory modalities, and teaching grammatical and spelling rules, the dyslexia paradigms described in Chapter 24 can be useful tools for remedying specific problems in reading, writing, and spelling. They have implications for emphasis in tutoring as a particular child shows difficulties in one or more of these areas.

Vestibulo-cerebellar Dyslexia

Binocular coordination, focusing, and visual-motor integration abilities are compromised in some children with learning problems and may be improved by orthoptic training (Hoffman, 1980). Constant strabismus, however, requires careful study and may respond to orthoptic training, surgery, glasses, medication, or a combination of these.

Oculomotor pursuit and tracking training may enhance the basic visual skills involved in reading, but in itself does not improve reading ability. (American Academy of Ophthalmology and the American Association for Pediatric Ophthalmology and Strabismus, 1981; American Academy of Pediatrics, 1972; Flax et al, 1984). On the other hand, children receiving concomitant visual training may profit more from reading tutoring than those who did not (Seiderman, 1980). A report that antimotion medication might enhance the effects of reading tutoring has not been confirmed (Levinson, 1980).

Several practical suggestions for detecting and treating problems in this area are described in Chapter 24. At this point, the practical therapeutic contributions of oculomotor and vestibular coordination training are unclear but merit further clinical research.

Visual-spatial Dyslexia

In this paradigm children have intact spoken language and writing skills. They can recite the alphabet and correctly sound out letters and syllables but cannot discriminate letters and letter patterns in words, because their visual processing of language symbols is inefficient.

The treatment strategy addresses a child's visual-spatial weakness by capitalizing on intact auditory-linguistic abilities and adding haptic and kinesthetic and three-dimensional visual associations, through such aids as sandpaper, flannel, and block letters. Visual imagery can be used to stimulate the weak function. With these multisensory aids, a child can be asked to look at a letter, then hear it, repeat it, feel muscle movements while tracing it, and feel its surface tactually. This can be combined with learning sounds of syllables and then synthesizing words from blending sounds (Lyon, 1983; Mattis, 1981; Smith, S.L., 1980).

The Orton-Gillingham technique is an established phonic approach that takes advantage of multimodal practicing and is particularly adaptable to the needs of an individual (Gillingham & Stillman, 1960; Orton, 1976). Slingerland adapted this method to classroom use (Slingerland, 1981). Because of its extensive usage in tutoring, the Orton-Gillingham technique will be described.

Anna Gillingham stressed the need for sympathetic understanding of the unique plight of the child. She also understood the importance of explaining the reasons for the training not only in terms of the child's own difficulty but by reviewing with the child the history of the development of the English language itself and its inconsistencies in pronounciation and spelling. She explained the advantages of the alphabetic method over pictographs and ideographs to each child.

The basic principles of the Orton-Gillingham method are introducing the kinesthetic element to reinforce the visual-auditory language associations and to establish left-to-right habits of progression; teaching the phonetic units in isolation, then in blending; introducing consonants and short sounds of the vowels first and building three-letter words with them for reading and spelling and programming the material in easy, orderly, cumulative steps of drill. The method teaches the sounds of letters, which are built into words through association of visual, auditory, and kinesthetic elements. Basic vowel-consonant units and syllables are used to construct words from smaller units. Phoneme sequences are pronounced quickly for blending, but words are pronounced slowly for analysis of their sounds.

The Orton-Gillingham technique is based upon the constant association of all of the following: how a letter or word looks, how it sounds, and how the speech organs and the writing hand feel when producing it. First the child is shown the printed letter symbol and asked to repeat its name after the tutor. When this has been, the letter's sound is made by the tutor and repeated by the child. The child's own speech organs provide a kinesthetic element.

Next the child watches while the tutor writes the letter and explains its form, orientation, starting point, and direction of strokes; then the child traces over the tutor's model. A verbal description of the letter helps, such as T is a line going up and down and a line going across on top. The next step is to copy, then to write from memory and finally to write with one's eyes closed.

Visualization can be fostered by forming a visual mental image through tracing letters and words in the air with a finger, first with eyes open, then with eyes shut. The child can try to "read" the traced word image letter-by-letter. The visual image associated with the physical movement and verbalization serves to fix the word in memory.

After these fundamental associations are established, the linkages are strengthened by drills repeated with substitution of the letter sound for the letter name. The most important linkages in reading and spelling are those that enable a child to translate the printed letter into its sound as the basis for reading and to give the letter name from its sound as the basis for spelling.

After the child has learned the names for the letters, their sounds, and how to write them all with the linkages well established, the process of blending is started by using phonic cards. A consonant, a vowel, and another consonant card are laid out on a table, and the child is taught to give their sounds in succession rapidly and smoothly until the child knows a word is being produced. The concept of syllables is carefully worked out with the child before two-syllable words are introduced for reading and spelling.

After blending is started, the analysis of words into their component sounds begins. A word's sound structure is dissected to foster meticulous symbol-sound and sound-symbol association. The tutor pronounces the word slowly, separating the sounds, and asks the child to repeat each sound in turn, name the letter, select its card on the table, and then write it. Later the rules for syllable division are taught according to the maturity of the child; for example, the rule that when two consonants stand between two vowels the syllable division usually occurs between the consonants. The child then is shown how to attack words with one consonant between two vowels, with digraphs, and with diphthongs. Learning how to hunt out the many decoding units larger than single letters can help a child remember words, such as an, ack and tion (Rosner, 1979).

Learning the rules of pronunciation, such as that a vowel has a long sound if followed by a consonant and an e, is of great importance. Teaching the differences and similarities in spelling and oral pronunciation allow relating a child's spoken vocabulary to words (Vellutino, 1979). With an understanding of the historical development of the English language, a child can see why certain phonograms have more than one possible sound and that certain phonemes can be spelled in more than one way.

Through persistent drills much as a musician practices scales, a child can master these fundamental skills. When ready the child is encouraged to select books for independent reading. Such reading should be limited to carefully selected and prepared material to ensure successes and build self-confidence.

Simultaneous oral and written spelling were used extensively by Orton and Gillingham in remedial spelling. They believed that severe spelling handicaps could be improved at least to the extent of becoming correct phonetically and, therefore, intelligible. There is some evidence that the best strategy for spelling is visual, since expert spellers "see" a mental image of the word. The strategy of visualizing spelling words by seeing the image of a word in the mind and copying it from there can be taught by spelling words aloud in a rhythmic pattern and by kinesthetically writing or tracing the words repeatedly. Later work on spelling can be taught in the context of creative writing, so that the words have personal meaning to the child.

The *Progressive Choice Reading Method* (Woolman, 1966) is a graduated approach to both auditory and visual aspects of reading in which letter discrimination is taught by matching and letter writing by tracing. When letter sounds are learned, they are blended in meaningless letter pairings to teach blending; then words are introduced. A similar program was designed for teaching youths and adults beginning reading (Woolman, 1964). The related *Laubach Way to Reading* has been augmented in phonics (Rice, 1984).

Auditory-linguistic Dyslexia

In this paradigm children have intact visual-spatial and writing skills but have difficulty sounding out and remembering the meaning of words. The sound referents for letters are anchored in the name of the letter or a word that begins with this letter. The language-disordered auditory-linguistic child is unable to retrieve these cue sounds reliably and arrives at faulty letter–sound associations. These children produce neologisms without recognizing that they are doing so.

Such children have a language disorder in which anomia is a critical factor (Mattis, 1981; Wolf, 1984). They misname letters and words, as they misname objects, colors, and body parts. They have difficulty recognizing the symbolic meaning of letters and words related to their degree of abstraction. Thus the problem is not with the recognition of words per se but with symbolism and conceptual categorization. Words with rich meanings are easier to remember through associations to them than are abstract words devoid of associations, such as "the."

The treatment strategy addresses a child's auditory-linguistic weaknesses by capitalizing on the visual imagery of words, symbols, and concepts in addition to reinforcement by kinesthetic sensations from the hands in writing and in the oral-facial muscles in speech.

To build a recognition vocabulary, a child with this syndrome can begin by learning the sight recognition of short, concrete words by elaborating upon a new word verbally, creating visual images, drawing pictures, constructing inferences, applying analogies, and associating the word with higher-order concepts. The objective is to induce a relationship between the word and the child's knowledge and experience (Wittrock, 1981). For example, it may be helpful to diagram the levels of relationships from the concrete to the abstract, as from Lassie, to collie, to dog, to animal, and to living thing.

Conceptual abilities can be enhanced by presenting dissimilar objects or pictures and asking a child to categorize them, such as pictures typifying eating utensils, animals, musical instruments, or parts of the body. Similarly younger children can be helped to distinguish appropriate and inappropriate objects for placement in a doll house. Parents can enhance conceptual ability in their everyday interactions with their child by pointing out similarities between objects, for example, house–umbrella—they both keep you dry; cat–truck—they both make sounds; and grass–tree—they both grow in the ground.

Next a direct approach to the auditory-linguistic weaknesses can be made with techniques, such as the Fernald method, that rely upon linking sounds with letter and word configurations in addition to kinesthetic reinforcement (Fernald, 1943; Myers & Hammill, 1976; Miccinati, 1979). In contrast to the similar Orton-Gillingham method, the first step is teaching the sounds of syllables and words without letter names but with word meaning. The child traces a word with a finger, pronouncing each part aloud until it can be written without copying. The same is done with letters, which can be ultimately blended to form words. With practice the child learns to look at a word, pronounce it, write it, and thereby recognize it. Finally the child learns new words by generalizing from known words.

Some children do not consciously perceive movements of the oral-facial muscles involved in speech. This deprives them of kinesthetic reinforcement for associating sounds with words. For them training in becoming consciously aware of the sensations of muscle movements by watching mouth and tongue positions in a mirror can be useful. For children with difficulty remembering sound word associations, the Lindamood method stresses auditory conceptualization, oral-motor feedback, and matching phonemes to written symbols. It has been used with the educationally handicapped and as a preventive supplement in the teaching of reading in the primary grades (Lindamood & Lindamood, 1979; McGuinness, 1985).

Once the initial hurdle of learning the sounds of letters and blending them is surmounted, the language-disordered dyslexic may make rapid gains in oral reading, but poor comprehension impedes further achievement. Because the content of the basal readers that accompany most programs appropriate for lower levels of reading competence is inappropriate for an older child's interests, stories written with words known to the child can be created to provide material for enlarging the recognition vocabulary. Developmental reading texts and novels are available for older children (Quercus). Reading materials at the second-grade level also are available in science, social studies, home economics, career education, and practical living skills for high-school-age students (Janus).

In summary, the treatment program for the language-disorder syndrome emphasizes developing letter-sound-kinesthetic associations without regard for letter naming. It employs sight recognition of simple concrete words and the reinforcement of word meaning through conceptual linkages. Once this word-attack skill has been gained, phonic readers are used concurrently with ongoing phonic training. To draw upon known words, present more age-appropriate content, and augment comprehension, stories dictated by a child can be introduced, once third-grade material has been reached (Mattis, 1981). The following case illustrates this approach:

> Following a cerebral infarct an adolescent boy had a mild oral verbal apraxia in addition to a mild aphasia with a prominent dyslexic component. At the initiation of therapy, a whole-word, visual-kinesthetic approach was the method of choice. His ability to identify several familiar words established sufficient self-confidence to enable tackling phonics. Then attention to the individual phonic components of words reduced visual confusion of similar word shapes. When using phonic word-attack skills, he was encouraged to reduce impulsive errors. Then phrases and sentences could be used to enhance his reading rate (Wiegel-Crump, 1979).

Auditory-linguistic dyslexic children have particular difficulty with spelling. English spelling patterns are so varied that a good speller must have not only a clear-cut auditory pattern of the spoken word and adequate handwriting to reproduce it but also a dependable visual memory of the particular letters and their sequence in their graphic counterparts. Nearly one-half of the words in ordinary usage can be spelled correctly solely on the basis of the relationship between spoken sound and written symbol. About 85 percent of the words in common usage can be spelled correctly with additional knowledge of the fundamental rules of spelling. Less than 3 percent defy these rules. Thus learning the rules of pronouncing and spelling English is essential for these children (Hanna et al, 1971; Rak, 1977). The use of adapted dictionaries, such as *The Bad Speller's Dictionary* (Krevisky & Linfield, 1967), is helpful as well.

Articulo-graphic Dyslexia

In this paradigm children have intact visual-spatial language and comprehension skills. They may have gross and fine motor coordination problems; however the crucial difficulties are a buccolingual dyspraxia that causes speech errors and a graphomotor dyscoordination that affects handwriting and causes spelling errors. They have difficulties in speech, oral reading, and spelling because of difficulty pronouncing phonemes and writing graphemes reliably. Some are unable to produce a consonant that ends word without uttering an associated vowel; when "cat" is spoken, such a child responds "catuh." The attempt to blend letter sounds may result in perseveration of a phoneme, substitution of irrelevant phonemes, and omission or transposition of vowels and consonants (Mattis, 1981). Although adolescents and adults with this syndrome usually have a large sight vocabulary, their silent reading may be tedious because it remains at the subvocalizing level, and their spelling is impaired.

The treatment program capitalizes on a child's intact visual-spatial, language, and word-meaning skills and initially minimizes oral phonic reading. Reading is approached by developing a sight-recognition vocabulary in order to bolster self-confidence. A "whole-word" program with an initial emphasis on meaning and appreciation of story line can be used.

A word-analysis approach to teach word-attack skills that will enable comprehension of unfamiliar words is introduced once a modest lexicon of sight words has been learned. In contrast to word synthesis, which is employed in phonic methods, word analysis breaks words down into recognizable segments representing a prefix, root, and suffix. The Bank Street Readers and the Swain Beginning Reading Program (Swain, 1985) introduce phonics through the analysis of known sight-learned words.

A sustained effort on the part of a child is required to improve handwriting, which suffers from illegibility and spelling errors, but there usually is less motivation to work on handwriting than reading. Frequently settling for a personalized form of printing is more realistic than demanding traditional cursive writing. Indeed many older children show dramatic differences between their illegible cursive script and more legible printed letters. In severe cases typing and using word processors can be useful alternatives to handwriting.

Before starting handwriting training with a child, it is important to determine which hand should be used. This decision involves observation of laterality patterns as well as the history of hand preference for various activities. Similarly the optimal slant for the individual to use in writing should be ascertained by experimentation with different slants to determine a natural angle. After the tutor and child have agreed upon the hand and slant to be used, the child may need to be shown a better way to hold a pencil and the proper placement of the paper. For example, for the left-hander the top of the paper is on the right.

Training initially consists of copying letters and words and taking dictation. The actions for forming letters are taught through copying movements and by sounding or naming the letter as it is being copied or written. If visualization is vivid, a child can be encouraged to copy from imagery. When visual imagery is poor, a child can be encouraged to imitate the tutor's writing, to copy writing through transparencies, and to sound or name letters as they are written. The tutor also can guide the child's hand (Chalfant & Scheffelin, 1969). In handwriting drills less attention is paid to the neatness of the product and more to the consistency with which a given letter is drawn. Chalkboards are useful for this purpose.

In summary, children with the articulographic syndrome have a buccolingual dyspraxia that limits development of phonic attack skills in addition to handwriting dyscoordination. The treatment program initially emphasizes the development of a whole-word vocabulary and handwriting training with attention to consistency of letter production rather than neatness. At a later phase, word-analysis skills are introduced in reading.

When a child with articulo-graphic difficulty also has significant clumsiness, training should extent beyond the language area to include equilibrium and motor coordination. Finding a skill in which the child can acquire enough proficiency for successful competition with schoolmates is useful. The techniques for training such children are most promising when based upon the analysis of complex activities into the simplest component parts. For example, one cannot teach children how to pitch a baseball until they are taught how to stand properly, how to balance their weight, and how to swing their arms. For some hemiplegic children, the addition of visual control in training can improve their limbs' functioning; otherwise they tend to ignore their affected limbs (Connolly, 1969).

REMEDIAL ARITHMETICAL TUTORING

A fundamental understanding of quantity and space is essential to learning mathematics, just as spoken language is the foundation of reading. The teaching of mathematics usually skips concrete quantitative and spatial relationships and begins with the rote memory of symbols, such as in counting, adding, and subtracting. Consequently programs for tutoring in arithmetic generally stress the manipulation of concrete objects as preliminary to abstract symbols and include the following (Kinsbourne & Caplan, 1979).

Montessori Arithmetic Readiness Materials

This method relies on materials designed to be self-teaching of arithmetic readiness operations. They are concrete geometric shapes, counting boxes, sandpaper numbers, arithmetic frames, counting frames, and bead chains.

The Cuisenaire-Gattegno Method

Through this method children discover arithmetical principles by using 291 rods that vary in length and color independently. The tutor observes and asks questions about what the child discovers. Then directed activities are undertaken in the course of which number values are assigned to the rods. The Davidson approach moves from concrete Cuisenaire rods to the pictorial to the abstract (Davidson & Wilcutt, 1983; Davidson & Marolda, 1986). This method enlists a child's active participation and enthusiasm.

Rosner's Arithmetic Program

This is a custom-tailored arithmetic program utilizing 100 numbered chips and a 100-square map. Initial number concepts can be developed by the use of blocks and counting boards. This method provides a basis for memorizing essential number facts and stresses drill (Rosner, 1979).

Direct Instruction Mathematics

This program deals with procedures for evaluating, selecting, and modifying techniques for each skill area in addition to procedures for pacing tasks, motivating students, and correcting errors (Silbert et al, 1982).

In the remediation of arithmetic difficulties, verbal rules are helpful in highly structured routines (Strang & Rourke, 1985). The calculation steps should be broken down to their simplest forms and described in words, which the child can write down and repeat with comprehension. When the verbal steps have been mastered, graph paper can be used to ensure the correct use of space and number alignment, as the child begins simple written calculations. A hand calculator can be used to check answers. In the process the child's specific error types can be identified for particular emphasis, such as misaligning columns, misreading signs and numbers, omitting steps, failing to shift from addition to subtraction, and miswriting numbers.

MATH "21"—A Multisensory Approach to Multiplication

This program concentrates on 21 difficult-to-remember multiplication facts that are taught through slow, repetitive, multisensory practice with three sets of rough surfaced cards (Callahan, 1976).

Training in Math Facts

This is a flexible teaching tool to supplement any mathematics curriculum in the primary grades and for remedial use in higher grades (Kingston, 1985).

Programmed Mathematics

For a child who already has mastered mathematical concepts, there are a variety of instructional packages that are useful for developing facility in computation by means of feedback and self-correction.

ELIGIBILITY CRITERIA

Schools face practical considerations in determining eligibility for special education services by a rising number of students (Lerner, 1985). The discrepancy between actual and potential achievement levels in reading often is employed as an eligibility criterion.

Four methods for determining discrepancy scores are used commonly in schools. The simplest compares achievement scores with current grade placement.

The three most frequently used methods assess the discrepancy between a child's actual achievement and expected levels related to intelligence and exposure to school. The first is the mental grade method, which determines the expected reading grade level by deducting five years from a student's mental age and then subtracting the reading achievement level from that.

The second method takes into account the years of teaching exposure by adjusting the expected reading grade level to the child's years in school and intelligence:

$$\text{Expected reading level} = \frac{\text{Years in school} \times \text{IQ}}{100}$$

The discrepancy score is obtained once again by subtracting the actual reading achievement level from the expected reading level.

The third method takes into consideration mental age (MA), chronological age (CA), and grade age (GA) in order to minimize the variations in determining the expected reading age factor. The grade age is established by adding the child's age at kindergarten entry to the present grade placement:

Expected reading age =
$$\frac{MA + CA + GA}{3}$$

A learning quotient is then obtained by dividing the actual reading achievement age, which is obtained by adding the age at school entry to the reading achievement grade level, by the expected reading age:

Learning quotient (LQ) =
$$\frac{Achievement\ age}{Expected\ age}$$

A learning quotient of 89 or below frequently is used as the eligibility threshold.

There are a variety of more complicated methods for determining discrepancy scores, such as by converting data to standardized scores and employing standard deviation criteria and by the technique of regression analysis. Unfortunately, these complicated statistical techniques are being used on imprecise measures and consequently imply a false sense of objectivity. Moreover, discrepancy measurements only identify handicaps and do not reveal educational disabilities at earlier stages, when they can be more effectively remedied.

PROGNOSIS FOR REMEDIAL TUTORING

A critical review of follow-up studies revealed that 75 percent of children who had mild reading disabilities early in grade school had become handicapped in reading by the end of grade school. It also concluded that unsystematic episodic remedial reading tutoring relieved reading difficulties temporarily but produced no long-range benefits (Spache, 1981a). On the other hand, therapeutic remedial tutoring carried out over sufficient time has been successful with long-term benefits (Raw-

son, 1968; Smith, 1978; Silver & Hagin, 1985). Seldom can a child be successfully treated if sessions occur less than three times per week (Spache, 1981a). A controlled study found that children who received Orton-Gillingham therapy from trained tutors in a community mental health center made impressive gains as a result of two to three years of reading therapy (Kline & Kline, 1975). A multimodality approach to treatment can be especially effective for children with behavioral and academic problems (Satterfield et al, 1979b). The evidence suggests that episodic remedial reading efforts are much less effective than coordinated clinical multimodality programs.

Favorable prognostic factors for remedial tutoring are (Critchey, 1981; Duane, 1979): high intelligence; early diagnosis; sympathetic, enlightened, and encouraging attitudes of teachers and parents; individual coaching by a trained tutor; compensating social or athletic skills; and courage. The monumental achievements of persons with stroke-induced aphasias and dyslexias demonstrate that perseverance can overcome even severe handicaps.

ADJUSTMENTS IN ACADEMIC EXPECTATIONS

An important temporary or permanent alternative in the education of children with academic learning problems entails the adjustment of educational expectations by permitting a child to bypass a deficient skill entirely or partially. The following steps can rescue certain children from inevitable failure situations when carried out with respect for a child's dignity: reduced expectations of output volume; increased time for completing written examinations; and the adjustment of grading criteria, such as for punctuation, capitalizing, and spelling in the written themes of dyslexic children. Bypass adjustments are particularly useful in managing handwriting problems by allowing printing instead of cursive writing and the use of a typewriter or a word processor.

These modifications in expectations are relevant to other subject areas as well. The use of a calculator for arithmetic is another example of a temporary or permanent bypass maneuver. In practice optimal special education depends upon a balance between intervention and circumvention.

TRAINING IN CENTRAL NERVOUS SYSTEM FUNCTIONS

All learning obviously involves training the CNS. Specific brain function training techniques, however, focus on functions rather than skills (Powell, 1981). These methods are based upon the assumption that training a disabled CNS function is useful in preventing and overcoming educational disabilities. Furthermore direct CNS function training methods may produce results that could not be achieved through other forms of training. They are directed at underlying functions rather than skills (Powell, 1981). These methods are based upon the assumption that training a disabled CNS function is useful in preventing and overcoming educational disabilities. Furthermore direct CNS function training methods may produce results that could not be achieved through other forms of training. They are directed at underlying functions rather than specific academic skills (Kirk & Chalfant, 1984). The CNS function training methods also may be less anxiety provoking than academic skill tutoring, because they do not involve judgments about one's skills.

In approaching remediation, however, a functional disability must be established as a causative, rather than simply correlated, factor in producing an educational disability. Many efforts to train specific brain functions often have not improved educational disabilities, because they have not been direct causes of the educational disability.

Sensorimotor Training

A number of sensorimotor techniques are employed by occupational therapists. Among them are proprioceptive neuromuscular facilitation (Knott & Voss, 1968) and sensory integration therapy (Ayres, 1972; 1979).

Sensory integration therapy is based upon the theory that higher cortical functions depend upon neural organization at more primitive brain levels (Bhatara et al, 1981). Beyond six months of age, primitive brainstem reflexes become integrated into sensorimotor patterns that maintain muscle tone, balance, posture, walking, and the body image (Morrison et al, 1978). They provide the background for both automatic and intentional motor activities. The persistence of primitive neck and labyrinthine reflexes interferes with sensorimotor integration and a young child's exploration and control of body and environment. A variety of techniques have been developed to aid parents in the habilitation of their children with these problems. They center around the interaction of caregiver and child in playful, purposeful coordinated activities and offer both the possibility of training in fine and gross motor functions and the benefits of adult–child play. These techniques include passive and active vestibular and somatosensory stimulation through such activities as swinging, rolling, climbing, crawling, spinning, riding a scooterboard down a ramp, and working with manual puzzles (Ayres, 1979). A direct relationship, however, between sensory integration therapy and improvement in academic skills has not been established (Carte et al, 1984).

In another vein clinical neuropsychological techniques are thought to train the CNS directly (Diller & Gordon, 1981). Among the techniques are methods of training visual-field neglect, especially for persons with lesions of the right cerebral hemisphere who exhibit left-visual-field neglect (Bakker, 1983). Encouraging effects have been reported on the reading performance of dyslexic children who received specialized stimulation delivered to either the right or the left visual field, depending on the type of reading problem (Bakker, 1984).

It has been suggested that it may be possible to train a child's CNS through the employment of apparatuses that alter the visual or auditory stimuli received by the brain (Tomatis, 1972). For example, a child who relies on auditory-verbal feedback for orientation and direction may benefit from the systematic suppression of auditory-verbal feedback in carefully engineered social situations. This may encourage the child to become more aware of nonverbal cues in these situations.

In general, however, literature reviews have concluded that sensorimotor training per se is not effective in improving academic skills (American Academy of Pediatrics, 1972; Benton, 1978; Kavale & Mattson, 1983). The reported success of perceptual-motor training in children with learning problems may result from improvement in conceptual strategies rather than in perception itself (Pierce, 1977). Furthermore ineffective perceptual motor training that bypasses reading tutoring can be harmful to children (Kline & Kline, 1973). The matching of instructional materials and methods to presumed auditory, visual, tactile, or kinesthetic deficits is at the least premature. Although sensorimotor approaches may benefit some children, the efficacy of these treatment approaches has yet to be determined (Rourke et al, 1983).

Concentration Training

When children cannot adequately attend to school work, training in focusing and concentrating attention may be appropriate (Wittrock, 1981).

Learning how to focus attention is the most important step in memorization. It is possible to train oneself to notice objects at the periphery of one's vision and hearing. One can learn to notice marginal objects without moving one's eyes or head while concentrating one's attention on objects in the center of one's visual field. Many classroom teachers acquire this ability by necessity. The greater clarity and intensity of sensory impressions provided by focused peripheral attention make objects more exciting and interesting as well.

Another approach for assisting children to learn how to focus attention is emerging from parapsychology and biofeedback research (Ostrander & Schroeder, 1979). Learning methods based upon relaxation techniques, imagery, and the introduction of information in synchronized rhythms have been used successfully in teaching factual material, particularly languages. As an example, when relaxation methods are used to bring one's body into a relaxed state, baroque music of about 60 beats per minute can be used to synchronize bodily rhythms. Spoken information with varied voice intonation is introduced at eight-second intervals corresponding with the rhythm of breathing. Thus information, voice intonations, music, breathing, and heart rhythms are synchronized to a specific cycle with remarkable effects reported upon learning. This technique has been developed for group use and may be particularly valuable for children with learning problems (Prichard & Taylor, 1980).

For activities that require high levels of proficiency, a considerable amount of time must be spent in concentrating upon the practice of skills. Music students and athletes repeatedly practice in order to develop automatic skills. The same need for practice in beginning reading is often overlooked, however. Although the goals in both music and reading are accuracy and fluency, the beginning reader is seldom encouraged to reread a passage until these goals are achieved. Instead teachers tend to move many students through reading texts before the mastery of basic reading skills have been reached. In this way children without brain function disabilities become educationally disabled in reading.

Some children are so attentive to the act of reading that they miss the meaning of words. For these children whose attention is on decoding rather than on comprehension, practice is required to move beyond accurate recognition to concentration upon the meaning of words. A technique of repeated readings can improve a child's reading speed (Samuels & Eisenberg, 1981):

1. A chart for recording word recognition errors and a stopwatch for timing reading are needed.

2. The child selects a short reading of moderate difficulty and reads the selection aloud to a helper who counts the number of errors and records the time in seconds.

3. The child then studies the words missed in addition to rereading the selection silently.

4. The oral reading cycle is repeated until the student can read the selection with fluency within the desired time. When this goal is reached, a new selection is chosen, and the process is repeated. The charts provide feedback to the child to indicate the rate of progress.

5. A useful modification of this technique is to have the child listen to a story on a tape recorder while silently reading it and then practice rereading it silently without the tape recorder. This progression from reading with auditory support to reading without support is continued until the child can fluently read the selection orally.

A similar problem commonly arises when skilled readers cannot remember what they read. For them decoding words takes place without attention to paragraph meaning. Instead of focusing attention on understanding the text, the child's attention wanders to matters entirely unrelated to the material. The poor recall is not due to memory deficit but to lack of attention to the meaning of the text. To help focus attention on text meaning, that child can be taught to test oneself by asking what ideas are expressed in each paragraph. Concentration and memory also can be improved by visual imagery, with the eyes open or closed, of letters, numbers, and the spelling of words (Mosse, 1982).

One technique for increasing concentration span is to increase progressively periods of task performance as measured by an attractive timing device, such as a mechanical timer or hourglass. By beginning with short, easily manageable spans, a child can be motivated to achieve longer spans of concentration as measured by the timer.

Memory Training

Although there are no ways of generally improving memory at this time, memory for specific things can be significantly improved by associating a new piece of information with existing concepts. Examples are associating a famous name with that person's accomplishment, a city with a product manufactured there, and a foreign word with its English equivalent. This keyword strategy is based upon the use of imagery to associate items to be remembered (Kail, 1984).

Additional techniques can be used to enhance memory by broadening the associations of the items to be remembered (Kirk & Chalfant, 1984). To remember events and places, mnemonic devices can be used, such as by forming the word CAN'T from the first letters of the four southwestern states and by rhyming: "I feel a great elation, I confess, when I can spell occasion with two c's and one s." Lists of items can be linked around an activity, such as recalling the courses of a meal in remembering groceries and visualizing oneself in forthcoming activities indoors and outdoors in varieties of weather in packing for a trip.

Thinking Training

Although an implicit goal of education is teaching children to think for themselves, little attention is devoted to learning the tools for doing so. Thus most children do not develop their thinking potential (McKim, 1980). Children who are impulsive, narrowly focused on immediate stimuli, judgmental, and concrete particularly need specific training in how to think. For this reason there is a growing literature on teaching cognitive strategies (Pressley et al, 1985).

Imagery Stimulation

The first step in helping children learn how to think more effectively is to stimulate their imaging capacities as the vehicles for conscious thinking (Sheikh & Sheikh, 1985). So-called right-hemisphere teaching emphasizes intuitive multisensory imagery as a means of connecting categories and classifications to discover new relationships (Williams, 1983).

Fantasy is imagination that generates and manipulates imagery and can be used as a teaching technique. Guided fantasy is particularly useful for explaining a phenomenon one cannot experience first-hand; for example, a verbal explanation of osmosis may be too abstract and technical for a student to master. That child can grasp the concept by imagining oneself as a molecule passing through a membrane like a net. Thus ideas are more easily understood through pictures, maps, and diagrams than through words.

Furthermore textbooks usually present information in a linear manner that emphasizes details, leaving students with a fragmented rather than an integrated sense of a subject. In contrast direct experience presents students with an opportunity to approach a subject with all their senses and to develop sensorimotor images of the whole before trying to master specific pieces of information. With the imagery of direct experience as background, detailed facts and concepts have enhanced meaning.

Visualization is a useful technique for poor spellers. It can be employed together with speaking and drawing the letters of a word. Looking at the whole word and speaking the letters aloud can be followed by closing one's eyes and attempting to see the letters of the word in one's mind. Next the letters of the word can be traced with a finger or pencil. Then the letters of the word can be seen in one's mind with eyes closed again with simultaneous writing of the word in the air. Last, the word can be written on paper from the visual image and checked against the correct spelling. With ten to 15 minutes' practice each day, the capacity for visualization can be learned by most persons.

A number of accomplished competitive athletes attribute their sensorimotor successes to imagery rehearsal. Jack Nicklaus described improving his accuracy in golf by first visualizing a ball landing on a green and seeing the bounce and then visualizing the arc of the ball in flight back to the swing and the ball leaving the ground (Suinn, 1983). Imagining throwing a basketball also has been found to be as effective as actual practice (Vandell et al, 1943). Moreover imagery rehearsal can be used to desensitize one to anxiety-producing situations (Sheikh, 1983).

Developing Conceptualization

Learning to think involves learning how to conceptualize (Bourne, 1982). One program for accomplishing this is called CoRT, for Cognitive Research Trust (de Bono, 1976). The program consists of six sections, each of which has ten lessons and covers a general theme, such as breadth, organization, interaction, creativity, information, feeling, and action. This method widens the field of attention by setting up attention directing aids, such as the following:

1. The north–south method of setting up an external reference grid for classifying the location of things.
2. The bird-watching method of spotting patterns in arrays.
3. The apple-boxing method of sorting things into categories.
4. The isolation method of separating certain obvious areas in an array as a start for analyzing patterns.
5. The framework method of setting up a checklist for identifying common features of things.
6. The process model of analyzing and comparing different logical approaches.

In addition to these attention-directing methods, tactics for solving problems are included in CoRT: techniques for considering other people's viewpoints; examining the plus and minus points of an issue; considering all factors; anticipating consequences and sequelae; and choosing between alternatives.

Problem-Solving Training

Daily living involves problem solving that everyone can learn to do more successfully (Bransford & Stein, 1984). The processes underlying problem solving are identifying potential problems, defining them appropriately, exploring a variety of possible approaches, acting on one's ideas, and looking at the effects of these actions. For many children learning something new at first seems overwhelming, and people who can already perform the task seem almost superhuman. They go through a period of feeling and being awkward. With the courage to risk mistakes, one comes to perform the task automatically without conscious attention. Problem solving, therefore, is a self-correcting activity that requires the acceptance of errors and risks.

Impulsive and concrete children particularly need training in the steps of problem-solving thinking as a means of developing self-control (Blackman & Goldstein, 1982; Kendall & Wilcox, 1980). The verbal imagery of talking to oneself silently or aloud is a means of facilitating this, so that a child can be encouraged to speak to oneself about what is to be done, about focusing attention, about each step of the task and about checking the work when it is finished. Thus an internal narration by the child of the child's own activities, including praising oneself when a task is completed, can be useful (Meichembaum & Goodman, 1971). Self-control can be promoted by encouraging self-assessment, self-recording, self-determination of reinforcement, and self-administration of reinforcement (Glynn et al, 1973; Kirk & Chalfant, 1984).

De Bono also distinguishes different modes of thinking (de Bono, 1983; 1984). He assigns a black hat to negative thinking: "This won't work because." The red hat is purely emotional and gives one permission to like or dislike something without having to justify one's judgment. The yellow hat is for when one wears rose-colored glasses. The white hat is for pure facts and figures a computer might put out. The green hat is creative. The blue hat looks at thinking itself and might say, "We need to look at priorities."

The Instrumental Enrichment Program is a training package designed to develop the capacities involved in schoolwork through the correction of deficient cognitive functions; the acquisition of basic concepts, symbols, and work habits; the production of reflective, insightful problem solving; the inherent attractiveness of the tasks; and the favorable impact of success with the instruments on a child's self-evaluation and self-concept (Feuerstein, 1980; Chance, 1981). The program consists of more than 500 pages of paper-and-pencil exercises divided into 15 instruments. Each instrument focuses on a specific cognitive function but addresses the acquisition of other prerequisites of learning as well. The instruments include nonverbal organization of dots, analytic perception, and illustrations. The instruments that do not depend upon reading are orientation in space, comparisons, family relations, numerical progressions, and syllogisms. The instruments requiring independent reading comprehension are categorization, instructions, temporal relations, transitive relations, and representative stencil designs.

Creative writing can be used to enhance conceptualization and problem-solving thinking (Moulton & Bader, 1985). The stages of writing can be explicitly taught as a means of helping students explore and organize their knowledge through expressive writing. The prewriting stage consists of brainstorming and listing facts and events. The planning stage involves logically arranging these ideas in time sequence. The drafting stage is a trial of writing with corrections and editing. The next stage is revising the draft in response to questions, such as its relevance to the topic, organization, and choice of words. Finally, proofreading is done for grammatical accuracy.

Further exploration of practical ways to cultivate thinking hold promise for both general and special education.

INTERPERSONAL SKILL TRAINING

Many children can profit from training in the interpersonal skills of speech, communication, and social interaction.

Speech Therapy

A variety of methods are employed by speech therapists in the remediation of voice and articulation problems. Breathing and voice exercises together with specific training in mouth and tongue movements are used to develop accurate pronunciation (Howlin, 1981).

Some children's difficulties in pronunciation and comprehension result from poor auditory discrimination. For them systematic training in recognizing differences between word sounds and in the use of visual cues such as lip movements can be helpful. Other children have no difficulty in auditory discrimination but need help to build confidence in self-expression, descriptive language skills, and vocabulary.

For children who lack a spontaneous desire to communicate, operant conditioning methods can be employed to reward and reinforce the child's production of desired sounds and words. Mute children with little apparent comprehension are less responsive than children who already are using words and possess some of the cognitive prerequisites for language (Howlin, 1981).

Training in Communication Skills

Interest in helping children develop communication skills has been high in the teaching of second languages (Savignon, 1983). The basic priniciples also apply to efforts to teach children how to use language as a tool in social relationships.

Broadly defined interpersonal communication is the process of exchanging meaning between people. The essential ingredients of competent communication are mastery of a spoken language and the ability to carry on an intelligible conversation in all social contexts. It depends upon verbal clarity, sensitivity to nonverbal signals, self-assertion, and active listening. In essence communication competence is the goal of all language learning. Knowing words is only a step to learning how to use them so that people can share information and feelings accurately with each other. Formats have been devised for training in communication skills (Pearson, 1983). Listening skills are particularly important (Robinson & Smith, 1983).

The explanation and modeling of listening and verbal assertiveness skills by adults can be helpful in assisting children to communicate effectively with others. These methods are used in Parent Effectiveness Training (Gordon, 1978). Specific teaching of oral communication skills also can be done with children (Dickson, 1982).

Children who have difficulty understanding verbal language under less than optimal sound conditions may appear to be distractible and limited in listening skills. In noisy environments sound-reducing ear devices may be useful (Willeford & Burleigh, 1985). When the children are aware of their auditory function disability, they also can learn to ask for the repetition or clarification of the speech of others and to avoid trying to communicate verbally in noisy environments.

Social Skills Training

The responsiveness of the peer group may have profound implications for a child's later social, emotional, and academic adjustment.

Social skills training has been directed in particular to withdrawn children with low levels of peer popularity and social interaction (Hops, 1982). This has included adult coaching, modeling, films and videotapes, assertiveness training, interpersonal problem-solving training, peer assisted tutoring, instruction in specific social skills, and stress management training (Pfohl, 1980; Schultz & Heuchert, 1983). Cooperative learning games have been devised for stimulating sharing information and ideas among children. Microcomputers also hold promise as learning centers for creating structured interactions between children.

Children who act impulsively and aggressively with peers, as well as children with limited experience in social interaction, need help in learning how to cope with social situations (Clabby & Elias, 1986; Pelligrini, 1985). Training in Interpersonal Cognitive Problem Solving is designed to develop four skills: 1) the ability to recognize that a problem exists; 2) the ability to generate alternative solutions to an interpersonal problem situation; 3) the ability to foresee the immediate and long-range consequences of a particular alternative and to use this information in decision making; and 4) the ability to plan a series of actions to attain a goal, to recognize and devise ways around potential obstacles, and to use a realistic time framework for achieving a goal.

For example, in a dispute between two children, the first step is to have the child express one's feelings (I'm mad at Billy); describe the problem in words (I'm mad because Billy teased me); identify a goal (I want Billy to stop picking on me); list possible solutions (I could hit Billy or yell at him or ignore him); focus on the possible consequences of these actions and pick the one that will achieve the goal; and, last, try out the solution and report back in order to evaluate its effect.

Children often have difficulty distinguishing and describing their emotions. They need to learn to attend to internal emotional cues that they are becoming angry or sad so that they can "stop, look, and listen" in order to gain better control over their behavior. Relaxation training can be helpful in learning how to cope with anxiety-producing situations (Carter & Cheesman, 1988).

CLASSROOM TUTORIAL PROGRAMS

When children lack exposure to fundamental reading skills on school entry, they need to learn these skills first. Examples of systematic ways of doing this for disadvantaged children are the Wallach and Wallach and DISTAR programs.

The Wallach and Wallach Program

The Wallach and Wallach program automatically adapts itself to each child's situation through tutoring designed to supplement the classroom work of low reading readiness first-graders (Wallach & Wallach, 1976). Lay tutors need three weeks of practice to learn the routines.

The Wallach and Wallach program has three parts. In part I a child learns to recognize letter sounds at the start of words and to connect letter shapes with the sounds. Part I starts with sounding out each letter, looking at pictures of objects whose names begin with the sound of each letter, naming the picture and saying whether the name starts with the sound, tracing the letter embedded in a picture of the object beginning with the letter's sound, drawing the letter with only horizontal guidelines, and matching pictures with letters in a variety of ways. It takes one to two weeks for a child to get through the five steps of the letters a and b; thereafter, a letter is the focus of each session.

In part II a child gains skill at recognizing and manipulating the sounds and letters in short, regularly spelled words. Part II involves three steps, each of which is repeated a number of times with different sets of words before going on to the next step. In the first step, the tutor sounds out the name in broken down letter component sounds with an object picture. The child is asked to sound out the word by blending the sounds. In step two the child is given letter cards and builds words with the letters to match the pictures by sounding them out. In step three, instead of building and reading the names of object pictures, the building and reading are done with short spoken words. Part II typically takes about two or three weeks.

Part III utilizes the child's classroom reading materials. In part III a child finally begins work with whatever materials are in use in the child's classroom. Four steps are involved. Larger words are broken down into component words. The tutor tells the child the sound of any letter or set of letters when the sound is different from what the child has learned before. Then the tutor points to the letters in turn from left to right. When a child has made all of the sounds, the child is helped to pronounce the whole word by blending.

The DISTAR Program

Another instructional method applicable to language and arithmetic as well as reading is DISTAR (Meyer et al, 1983). This method was designed for small-group instruction and includes observing the responses of individual children. Provision is made for a graduated exposure to information at a pace that minimizes overload and for the repetition of explanations when mistakes occur. The emphasis is on conceptual rather than rote learning. The approach to reading is highly structured phonics and deals with decoding prior to comprehension of words.

Follow-up studies have credited DIS-

TAR with impressive success in work with disadvantaged children (Gersten et al, 1985). The emphasis on stimuli stripped of irrelevant attributes so that children can focus on the essentials of concepts contributes to its success. Also, this method does not take preexisting knowledge for granted, so that the children do not founder because they are too shy or disorganized to ask for the specific information they lack. These features are important for children with academic learning problems.

SUMMARY

Children with specific educational disabilities and handicaps need extended tutoring in order to catch up with and maintain their position with classmates. Intensive individual tutoring may be a role of special education teachers or a full- or part-time activity for professionals and laypersons.

The most common forms of tutoring are in reading, spelling, and writing through methods that may utilize an intermediate alphabet, multimodal learning of letters and words, and learning the grammatical and spelling rules. An individually tailored tutoring program can be based most effectively on the nature of a child's educational disabilities. Different emphases are required for the vestibulo-cerebellar, visual-spatial, auditory-linguistic, and articulo-graphic dyslexias. A variety of approaches to tutoring in arithmetic also have been devised. They generally begin with the manipulation of concrete objects and progress to abstract symbols. The efficacy of remedial tutoring in written language and arithmetic depends upon its specificity, intensity, duration, and integration with other therapeutic interventions and with a child's general education. Most tutoring efforts have not met these criteria and have been fragmented and episodic. Consequently, they have been ineffective.

Efforts have been made to train the brain in basic functions that underlie academic skills. Although they do not improve schoolwork in themselves, they may have value as adjuncts to tutoring in academic skills. These training techniques focus on sensorimotor integration, concentration, and thinking. Training in interpersonal skills can be provided in the form of speech therapy, communication skills, and social skills.

For young disadvantaged children who lack a background of exposure to fundamental reading skills, the principles of reading tutoring can be applied to teaching groups of children. More generally, however, the lack of appreciation that many children can respond to systematic tutoring in academic skills has deprived them of the opportunity to participate in classroom education with their age mates. Tutoring is one of the most neglected educational resources.

CHAPTER
33

Individual Psychotherapy

Every adult was once a small child. A sense of smallness forms an ineradicable substratus of the adult's mind. The question of who is bigger and who can do this or that and to whom—these questions fill the adult's inner life beyond necessity and desirability.

Erik Erikson, 1959

Children with educational difficulties pose particular challenges for psychotherapists, because of the need to attend to functional and educational disabilities in the process of psychotherapy. The clarification of unalterable individual differences and pathology is essential in order to shift embarrassment and shame about them to realistic self-acceptance (Christ, 1978; 1981). This chapter is devoted to the process of intensive child psychotherapy adapted to the temperamental and cognitive styles of children with learning problems in school. It is written with awareness that an appreciation of psychotherapy can be helpful for educators in understanding the seemingly irrational behavior of children.

Children who have attained the concrete or formal operational levels of development can profit from intensive insight-oriented psychotherapy. The purpose of psychotherapy is to free a child from self-defeating neurotic barriers to learning, so that the course of character development can proceed and permit the expression of the child's abilities. In the process both child and parents need help in learning life roles in which these abilities can be developed and realistic expectations established.

The unfolding course of psychotherapy helps children to accept what they already know about themselves in addition to troublesome parts of themselves, previously hidden from their awarenesses.

STYLES OF CHILD PSYCHOTHERAPY

Unlike adults children do not possess a complete vocabulary for describing their own feelings and ideas. Consequently, they need help in self-expression, without imposition of the psychotherapist's ideas upon them. Although conversation with a child is the key to ultimate self-discovery, verbal exchange, in itself, is not sufficient to lead to self-discovery and understanding. For this reason indirect routes to a child's inner life are used that involve play and creative expressions with their metaphorical and displaced meanings (Adams, 1974; Coppolillo, 1985; Group for the Advancement of Psychiatry, 1982).

The point is that children differ from adults in their use of language, and these differences affect both the validity and reliability of verbal communication with them. Talking with children, therefore, is an insufficient basis for depth interviewing, so that other routes to their inner lives are needed. What they do is more important than what they say. In fact with young children the most important information is derived from their behavior, specifically their play.

Just as the royal road to the unconscious of adults is through dreams, entry to the fantasies of children is through their play. It is quite possible for a child to be consciously unaware of hostile wishes toward a parent and to provide no clue of this in a verbal interview, other than, perhaps, by too readily denying it. The same child's play, however, may be infused with violence and hostility. For example, hostile feelings toward a father become quite clear when male dolls come to grievous ends in a child's play. In a similar fashion, children's feelings and attitudes toward their own bodies can be inferred from the way they avoid or approach nude anatomical dolls. Youngsters' attitudes toward the world also are expressed in the manner in which they use creative materials. A painting of an idyllic house with trees, sky, and sun says something about a child's fantasy life when this next becomes the scene of a tornado.

Verbal communication with a child is not completely replaced by play or other interactions. Conversation is used to facilitate children's play, clarify their actions, aid them in formulating their expressions, and, ultimately, confirm attitudes and feelings that are expressed through their behavior. The use of words is helpful for both the discharge of emotions and the transformation of experience from an emotional to a symbolic level where it can be subjected to examination. Emotions can be expressed in words rather than being acted upon. For example, hostile emotions can be expressed through the muscles of phonation, allowing for motor discharge, along with verbal symbols, which can express wishes without actual harm to the sender or receiver (Adamson & Adamson, 1979). Thus spoken words, while ideas are displaced upon play materials, are vehicles of intensive psychotherapy. The potential for insight follows from separating ideas, emotions, and actions, so that forbidden ideas are rendered less threatening and manageable when put into words while harmlessly acting upon them in play (Shapiro, 1979).

The desirable elements common to most psychotherapies with children include a properly qualified, sensitive, and empathic psychotherapist, who operates in a therapeutic atmosphere and orients a child to a healing rationale that the child and parents implement. The stages of psychotherapy involve establishing a working relationship, analyzing the causes of problems, and implementing formulas for change and termination (McDermott & Char, 1984).

No two experienced therapists work in the same way. A psychotherapist's preferences determine the setting, materials, and styles of psychotherapy. Variations include having parents present during all or parts of therapy sessions or behind a one-way window with another therapist. At the least an alliance with parents is fostered by including them for a few minutes at the beginning of each session. The approach described here emphasizes the use of the evolving relationship between a child and psychotherapist as a vital source of information about the child's distorted attitudes and misconceptions.

Although changes in location can occur without basically disrupting therapeutic work, a familiar place for meeting is desirable. Unlike adults, who are comfortable with chairs and desks, children of all ages are more comfortable in places where they can be active and in which there are objects of interest to them. A playroom or an office can invite activity when stocked with materials, such as the following: a furnished dollhouse with a doll family, a baby doll, anatomical dolls, hand puppets, cars, trucks, paper and crayons, an easel, paints, clay, blocks, and dart guns.

Some therapists find that playing two-person games can be a tool for learning more about the behavior and thoughts of a youngster. In fact games have been specifically designed to elicit feelings and thoughts from children (Gardner, R.A., 1971). The mutual story-telling technique can be used to help children communicate their experiences and describe behavior imaginatively. The child tells a story and is encouraged to speculate about its meaning. The therapist then tells a story that introduces alternative coping strategies appropriate to the child's situation.

On the other hand, games are notoriously utilized by children, and sometimes therapists, as resistances to progress in psychotherapy. Simply being with a child at play as an observer is sufficient for developing a therapeutic relationship. For example, sitting beside a child painting or drawing and assisting in the mechanical aspects of the activity are particularly valuable interactions in that the therapist's personality and skill at games are not injected in the process. Activities really are tools for self-disclosure rather than ends in themselves.

By virtue of their size, adults ordinarily look down upon children in interactions. The simple maneuver of positioning oneself at a child's height and alongside, rather than in front of, a child creates an implied willingness to enter the child's world. It is helpful for the therapist to move around the room with a child and remain at the child's side rather than above or in front of the child.

Individual psychotherapy can be adapted to special populations, such as delinquent adolescents, who see becoming socialized as capitulation to society's norms. One successful program for that group hinged on the therapist providing remedial education, psychotherapy, and assistance in vocational placement. This counteracted the tendency of these youths to pit different professionals providing these separate services against each other (Shore et al, 1966).

THE STRATEGY OF CHILD PSYCHOTHERAPY

In many ways the work of a psychotherapist resembles that of a detective. Both look for clues to discover explanations for mysterious events and actions. The psychotherapist and detective bear responsibility for the process of their work. The patient and the subject bear responsibility for the content of what is done and discovered.

As Hercule Poirot, the Belgian detective of Agatha Christie fame, pointed out, there are two kinds of detectives. One tediously searches for fingerprints and fragments of evidence. The other is the master detective (referring, of course, to himself) who uses "gray cells" to reconstruct mentally the drama that led up to a crime.

Although the footwork of gathering facts about a child aids the process of psychotherapy, the approach of the "master detective" is more fruitful. In so doing the psychotherapist approaches a youngster and family with the expectation that the plot will thicken as more evidence emerges. One expects that what is seen at the beginning is the visible tip of an iceberg and that explanations making sense at one level may be drastically revised as further information is obtained. One expects that learning more about the youngster will yield different versions of the same events. One expects that efforts to unravel the child's difficulties and to uncover their secret roots will encounter resistance. One also expects that the work of uncovering will take time, and that as the therapist pursues facts, people significant to the child may be threatened by exposure, as accessories to the child's "crimes."

The basic conceptions of the conscious, preconscious, and unconscious aspects of the human mind make it possible to respect what people say about themselves, but at the same time to recognize that there may be verbal and behavioral clues that signal contradictory aspects of themselves beyond consciousness awareness. In addition knowledge of the functional systems of the brain is useful. One part of a child is comprised of basic urges that arise within the state regulating system. Another part, the managerial system, handles relationships with the world and the other parts of the self. The self system is another sector of the person that represents internalized images of significant people in the form of values and ideas about the self. With this conceptual framework, it is possible to see that not only can children be in conflict with people in their external worlds, but they also can have conflicts between parts of themselves.

In psychotherapy happenings that appear to be irrational or coincidental on the surface assume a logical, understandable character when the themes that lie behind them are uncovered. In the solution of a crime, one looks for the plot. In unraveling a troubled child's life, one looks for organizing beliefs that explain puzzling behavior. Just as the plot lying behind a crime is inaccessible because it is hidden by the perpetrators, forbidden imagery that lies

beneath a child's behavior is hidden from a child's awareness by defense mechanisms. The psychotherapist then operates at two levels: the manifest, through observing that which can be seen or heard, and the latent, through uncovering ideas and themes. A commonly encountered example is a child who at the manifest level regularly fails at simple tasks; at the latent level, the idea of being successful is so frightening that failing is less dangerous. Thus the child's self-defeating behavior fulfills an unconscious need to fail.

The strategy of child psychotherapy, then, is searching for explanations of behavior that lie in conflicts within a child. The value of this procedure is that self-awareness provides one with the power to choose between alternative actions rather than being blindly driven into one of them. Also, through the creativity implicit in the psychotherapeutic process, new relations can be formed between images and memories, enhancing the synthesis of isolated unconscious experiences that have been split off from each other. Increased maturity results when conflicts that have impeded developmental progression are resolved, thereby permitting movement upward from a lower developmental stage. To put it another way, intellectual insight is helpful but it does not result in behavioral change unless a child masters and dissipates the anxiety created by internal conflict. The work of psychotherapy, therefore, leads to the identification of false ideas and fears, linking these fears with a child's behavior and releasing the child from them, thereby providing relief and promoting health growth. Thus both self-awareness and working through, or the "corrective emotional experience" through which painful inner feelings are exposed and defused, are the objectives of psychotherapy. The detective's story has a happy ending when the innocent are vindicated and the guilty indicted. Psychotherapy results in a happy ending when the child is vindicated and false beliefs are exposed.

ESTABLISHING A CHILD–PSYCHOTHERAPIST ALLIANCE

The first step in initiating psychotherapy is to establish a supportive relationship in which a child can experience the therapist as an ally with special offerings within a nonjudgmental and hopeful atmosphere. In contrast with other adults who have been disappointed, critical, disparaging, and even accusatory, the psychotherapist can be experienced by the child as a refreshing change. Time is needed to earn a child's trust and awareness of the therapist's usefulness. In fact the success of psychotherapy does not depend solely on trust, which can be shared in any relationship, but on a child's gradual discovery that the therapist is a person with interesting ideas and special ways, although sometimes painful, of relating to the child. Against the background of a positive therapeutic alliance, the unrealistic attitudes and emotions experienced by a child toward the therapist can be seen as neurotic distortions.

Care must be taken so that the psychotherapist is not regarded as a parent surrogate by a child. This is a particular risk when a parent or parents are not immediately available. In addition to a psychotherapist, each child needs a parent or parent surrogate of the therapist's sex in order to provide a realistic model for identification purposes outside of the context of psychotherapy.

Establishing an alliance with a child then depends more on demonstrating one's usefulness to the child than it does on becoming a friend. In fact it is through the elaboration and understanding of emotional reactions between the child and therapist that progress occurs. Without the mutual trust and a sense of usefulness of the therapeutic alliance, the intense emotions generated during the course of psychotherapy can dislocate the therapeutic process and serve to reinforce, rather than unravel, the forces leading to the child's problems.

Establishing rapport with a child includes explaining that the psychotherapist and child will be working together in order to achieve a better life for the child. The therapist is well advised to establish a contract with the child at the beginning of treatment. It is essential to discuss the specific difficulties that led to undertaking psychotherapy. This consists of drawing out the child's own view of the troubles and establishing an understanding that the psychotherapist's role is to assist the child in resolving them. At the least the child can appreciate that psychotherapy may help one to get along better in school. When appropriate this can be more sharply focused, such as on learning to read.

The basic elements of the psychotherapy process bear explanation to the child, specifically that there will be meetings at a predetermined frequency for a certain amount of time, such as a weekly meeting of 50 minutes' duration. When the psychotherapist is working with other family members, has contact with the youngster in other settings, and is involved in decision making regarding the child, the youngster should be aware of these parameters.

Most psychotherapists find that words describing psychotherapy with a connotion of "working together" rather than "playing together" help children understand the therapeutic intent of the process. Adhering also to the time factors and the simple limits of psychotherapy provides a living opportunity to interpret continuously the fact that an important, purposeful process is taking place in the youngster's life. It is useful for children to understand that they are free to express themselves and that the limits encountered are different than in their schools and homes. They are free to do and say as they wish, with the understanding that they will not be permitted to hurt themselves, the therapists, or objects that are not intended to be destructable. Playrooms contain some items that can be damaged without creating problems. However, others, including walls and furniture, must be protected. The equipment is meant for the use of others and, therefore, is not available for personal possession by a child. Cleaning up the playroom is a realistic return to the "outside world" in the same way that entering the playroom and doing as the child wishes is entering the special world of psychotherapy.

The task for the therapist is to develop an attitude and behavioral style that will permit children to reveal themselves and their inner worlds. Parenthetically, it is reassuring to note that even those who converse with children regularly find that their knowledge of a particular child may be superficial and inaccurate. There is a difference between conversing with children and gaining access to their inner lives. For developmental reasons it is difficult for children to know at a given moment what they are thinking or feeling. It also is understandable that children may be reluctant to disclose inner experiences. They may withhold facts, responding with an "I don't know" to even the most skilled inquiry. Consequently, information conveyed verbally should be evaluated in the light of each child's developmental level, powers of observation, dominant feelings, and desire to please the interviewer. Many children quickly discover that the simplest way to minimize their own anxiety is to agree with interviewers and provide what they believe are desired answers.

It is important to consider several general principles that influence adult–child interactions. The beginning therapist inevitably holds stereotyped attitudes toward children, such as feeling a need to direct, guide, or in some way assume a position of authority over them. In addition the therapist also often feels a responsibility to be doing something actively. Unless talking or managing situations, beginning therapists may feel they are not doing their job. Actually, by minimizing their own activity and adopting an accepting, catalyzing attitude, therapists encourage children to expose and to face the frightening aspects of themselves.

Children tend to expect that adults will ask questions in order to check their knowledge, much as they have encountered with teachers in school. Therefore, there is an initial imbalance in child–adult encounters that leads adults to act as interrogators and children to feel that they are being judged. If a therapist is not aware of the natural tendency for adults and children to engage in an interrogation, the door may be closed to a child's inner life.

Another commonly encountered reaction of children to interaction with adults is interpreting questioning as intended to expose wrongdoing. "Whys?" from adults often have been in the context of "Why did you do" something wrong or has been a prelude to an accusation. Since many children hold beliefs that their own fantasies, at the least, are personal secrets and, at the most, "crimes" in themselves, children naturally fear that open disclosure of their thoughts may be incriminating. The presence of troubling, forbidden wishes in children often leads them to resist disclosure to an adult, because they fear the consequences of doing so. This is a major consideration for some children, who are aware of circumstances, actions of others, or things they have done that actually could lead to retribution if disclosed. For example, a child who has been physically beaten by a parent may not only conceal the fact but also deny anger toward that parent.

Another point is that the significance of what is said differs for adults and children, varying considerably with the age of the child. For example, the magical thinking of young children leads to a child's belief that to say something means that it is true. This causes many children in good faith to say things that they wish were true by "pretending," which does not mean "lying." Some older children skillfully use words to conceal, rather than to convey, meaning to adults whom they regard as intrusive in their lives.

Another factor related to developmental stage is the difference between a child's and an adult's perception of the same events. The cognition of children is colored by their own abilities to understand what is going on and their own emotional state. For example, children's interpretations of arguments between divorcing parents may leave them with the conviction that they caused their parents to separate. In other instances children whose behavior is disruptive in school may feel anger toward their teachers or school situations, rather than recognize their own contribution to the problems. The reporting and memories of children ordinarily are influenced to a greater degree by personal distortions than those of adults.

Another consideration is that children have had limited experience in formulating and expressing their thoughts. They often literally do not know what to say to adults. Young children in particular are accustomed to being with each other and with adults without talking. Whereas it would be unusual for two adults to sit in a room and face each other without saying something, children tend to find things to do in an office or playroom without engaging in conversation. Children also frequently do not know how to respond to open-ended questions, because they are not accustomed to unstructured situations. They can recite the alphabet or give answers to mathematical problems, but to express their own thoughts directly is difficult. Prior to the early adolescent years, even the

capacity to think and talk about oneself is limited. This means that children need help in formulating their ideas and in understanding the meaning of words that are used to express thoughts and emotions.

These general principles explain some of the barriers that stand in the way of communication with children. There also is a wide range of individual variation, so that some older children may be more difficult to interview than some younger children who are more articulate. Quiet observation as a participant observer is characteristic of the skillful psychotherapist who is responsive, but not overcontrolling. Because of their difficulty in focusing attention and regulating their internal states, some children invite an overcontrolling or rejecting style in others. This is grist for interpreting the transference aspect of the child's relationship, as will be shown later. In sum the enticing combination of a supportive relationship and useful insights forms the foundation of the child–therapist alliance.

TECHNIQUES OF PSYCHOTHERAPY

Psychotherapy has important educational elements. These take place indirectly through identification of the child with the therapist and directly through self knowledge garnered by the child. Still the techniques of psychotherapy differ considerably from those employed in educational settings. The objective is not to present information to the child or to teach skills, with the exception of the skill of self-observation.

The events that transpire in child psychotherapy differ dramatically from those in an educational setting. In psychotherapy the child is in the role of "teacher" and the psychotherapist in the role of "student." The thread running through the various techniques of child psychotherapy is learning from the child and tactfully inserting influence. Thus the child is the center of attention in the arena of psychotherapy.

In a typical psychotherapy session, the vast majority of the words and behaviors emanate from the child. Although the psychotherapist certainly is not a "blank screen," the therapist's contributions are low in quantity and high in impact. The emphasis, therefore, is upon the accuracy and the timing of the psychotherapist's words and actions. As noted by Sigmund Freud, "the voice of reason is soft, but persistent." There are three basic techniques for offering useful ideas to children at times when they can absorb them.

The first technique is called *confrontation,* or describing behavior. It is based upon the principle that helping youngsters to see themselves as seen by the psychotherapist lays the foundation for improved self-awareness and self-understanding. It is a simply stated description of an action or words produced by the child. For example, as a seven-year-old bangs trucks together in collisions, the therapist can simply observe that "the trucks are crashing together." At first such a statement might seem inane; however, it achieves several things for the child. First of all it focuses attention upon describing what is going on in the session. Second, it identifies the action as a shared experience between the child and the therapist. Third, it shifts behavior from the level of action to symbolic expression through words. Last, it gives a manifest idea prominence so that latent undercurrents can be released. In this particular example, the boy immediately began banging the trucks together more loudly, while smiling with delight. This permitted the therapist to proceed with further descriptions of the obvious: "Tommy, crashing those trucks together seems to be fun for you." This simple step then led to Tommy's exclamation, "Yes, I love to see people get hurt."

Confrontation does not imply echoing a child's words or rigidly adhering to a literal description of actions. An analog of this technique is a radio announcer describing a ballgame. In the same way, the therapist offers a running commentary on the child's behavior, words, and play themes. In fact it is desirable to focus on things said or done without emphasis upon the fact that the child is doing them. The aim is to promote self-awareness without precipitating awkward self-consciousness. Just as the therapist's spatial position alongside a child promotes a participant observer interaction, verbal comments about the play or objects, rather than directly about a child, blend into the easy interaction of play rather than appearing as critical comments. One of the difficulties beginning therapists have in developing this technique arises from the tendency to usurp the child's right to personal thoughts and reactions. Beginning therapists, for example, find themselves foundering with youngsters through comments such as, "Wouldn't you like to play with the dolls? It's fun in here, isn't it? Let's use the paints."

The second level of technical emphasis is *clarification,* which is connecting a series of previously described events to form a pattern or theme. It is relating several actions or ideas that seem to be the expression of underlying fantasies, or beliefs. Clarification remains descriptive in the sense of limiting itself to observations made of manifest behavior and expressed ideas. It does not extend to exposing underlying fantasies. If, for example, Tommy is preoccupied with crashing trucks together during several sessions and later shows similar delight when a male doll falls from the table to the floor, the therapist can call attention to a possible underlying fantasy by saying, "Tommy, you get a kick out of crashing cars together. Last time you said that you love to see people getting hurt. Today that man fell off the table." The purpose of clarification is to link together for the child a series of consciously and preconsciously remembered and perceived events. Through this example of clarification, Tommy became aware of the fact that he was preoccupied with destruction and that a man was involved. Tommy's response came somewhat later in the same session when he caused the man to drop to the floor again, but this time he gleefully crushed the man into the floor with his foot. During the next session, he placed male dolls in dangerous positions and pretended they were decapitated or otherwise maimed, inviting the psychotherapist to progress to a deeper level.

The third technical concept is *interpretation*. This term is widely misunderstood. It is helpful to restrict its technical use to that step at which unconscious urges become conscius, rather than to use it when confrontation or clarification would be more appropriate (Lewis, 1974). Interpretation is the ultimate tool of psychotherapy and depends upon timing based upon a child's readiness to receive an idea. When a theme is repeated and called to the attention of the child through clarification, a time comes when a link can be made between the conscious and the unconscious aspects of the theme. For Tommy this occurred when he repeatedly injured a number of dolls, but chose one in particular that he really wanted to smash and kill. At that point reminding him of his pleasure in hurting the dolls and calling his attention to the fact that one particular man seemed to be the special target, and that this man stood for the therapist, was enough to bring Tommy's rage at the therapist in the transference into conscious awareness.

A successful interpretation may not produce an evident response in the child. However, the repetitive behavior leading to the interpretation usually disappears, and the child shifts to another theme, signaling a deeper more troublesome fantasy. For Tommy the next step was the discovery that his rage at the therapist actually was displaced from his father.

THE STAGES OF PSYCHOTHERAPY

The overall course of psychotherapy can be divided into early, middle, and late phases. It also is useful to understand each psychotherapy session in terms of its beginning, middle, and ending segments. At the beginning of a session defenses predominate, and the ending activates separation issues. The middle of the session is the working ground. In each session the route to the inner life of the child is through unraveling fantasies that have to do with everyday life, past experience, and the transference relationship with the psychotherapist. The relatively constant structure of treatment permits the emergence of these ingredients of psychotherapy.

Since a child is in difficulty because of misperceiving and misunderstanding the motives, actions, and responses of others, the initial purpose of psychotherapy is to bring these distortions into the context of the child's relationship with the therapist in what is called the transference (Sandler et al, 1975). Children grow up with a range of attitudes toward and expectations of others and hold these with psychotherapists, as with anyone else. For example, if children have assumed that no one loves them, they transfer, or generalize, this assumption to their therapists as well. A child's distortions, therefore, become focused on the person and place of psychotherapy in the transference relationship, where they can be analyzed.

Early Psychotherapy

During the initial phase of psychotherapy, the aim is to discover a child's existing fantasies and views of the world. But progress cannot be made unless children feel that their viewpoints are understood. The thrust of early psychotherapy then is acceptance of a child's expressions within the time, space, and behavioral boundaries of the psychotherapeutic process. The undivided attention and interest of the therapist facilitate a child's positive attitude toward the process.

In early sessions the therapist does not utilize interpretation or expect to carry out dramatic interventions. During this phase education of the youngster to the therapeutic process, the description of observed behavior and clarification take place. This phase may occupy weeks or months. If the child does not progress beyond this phase after a reasonable period of time, one looks for explanations either in the therapeutic technique or in other aspects of the child's life.

Exploring Functional Disabilities

At the outset of psychotherapy with children with educational problems, it is helpful to explore learning tasks, such as reading, in order to link psychotherapy to the child's academic problems. More important, however, this provides the therapist with an opportunity to explore a child's subjective experience in schoolwork and elicit associated emotions and imagery. The early focus on academic learning tasks reproduces the child's symptoms in the treatment process and sets the stage for exploring their intertwining roots (Prentice & Sperry, 1965; Templeton et al, 1967). It helps further to define the reasons for and purpose of psychotherapy. Along with demonstrating the benign supportive nature of the psychotherapist, the learning tasks provide stimuli for unfolding of transference manifestations with the therapist. They also offer the child an opportunity to bring out personal reactions to failure in schoolwork, thereby shifting the emphasis from the complaints of adults about the child to the distress of the child.

Children profit from exploration of their cognitive, temperamental, and adaptive styles. For example, if a child is hyperreactive to stimulation or has difficulty focusing attention, these qualities can be described as they become evident in a manner that stimulates the child's awareness of and curiosity about them. Premature attempts to search for psychodynamic causes of these basic processing difficulties, however, only may entangle the child in further self-recriminations.

A child's functional disabilities should be identified and described in as simple and realistic terms as is possible, such as reversing letters and difficulty paying attention. Explanations in euphemisms may result in a child imagining that a disability is too terrible to talk about (Gardner, 1968). As much as possible, these difficulties should be pointed out as they can be directly observed in the psychotherapeutic process and easily discussed in other sectors of the child's life. Children with established brain injury and seizure disorders must cope with persistent functional disabilities and related traumatic experiences that occur during their school years. Gradual exposure of children's reading difficulties, memory defects, short attention spans, distractibility, and emotional lability can take place. Their pervasive self-concepts of being brain damaged, retarded, or "creeps" begin to emerge. Their distortions of life experiences in the light of these self-perceptions as defective and rejected by peers then can be exposed and realistically handled (Christ, 1981).

Thus the child is given tangible evidence that the psychotherapist's aims are to discover the roots of the child's difficulties. The therapist's interest, for example, in a child's reaction of feeling dumb and having "butterflies in my stomach" when making reading errors demonstrates to the child that the psychotherapist brings a new approach to the problem and can accept and help clarify the child's inner experiences.

Fostering the Transference

After the initial exploration of academic tasks that may be accomplished in one or a few meetings, the essential nature of psychotherapy is brought home to a child through the opportunity to freely engage with expressive play materials. Unless brought up by the child, the therapist now need not refer to schoolwork. The aim of early therapy is to support a child's right to have and express feelings and to assist in finding ways of doing so.

When a child is maintained in an intensive therapeutic relationship, a transference configuration organizes itself. The configuration has its roots in various development levels of childhood and may be dealt with through transference interpretations and reconstructions and optimally through recollections of past emotions and experiences during middle psychotherapy.

During early psychotherapy a child may be inappropriately angry at the therapist, may be cold and distant, may be overly friendly, and may unload a "bag of tricks" of accustomed ways of dealing with people. The child even may show symptomatic cure in the sense that behavior dramatically changes elsewhere, as the transference develops in psychotherapy. This phenomenon is responsible for unrealistic optimism at the beginning of treatment, and also may account for reported cures of patients followed over a brief period of time. On the other hand, during the early phase, little change may be observed in the youngster.

Children who have not fully achieved psychological individuation may be afraid of interacting with the psychotherapist and revealing feelings because of the underlying fear that they will lose control of themselves and merge with or destroy the therapist. The surface arrogance and fearlessness of these children conceals an underlying panic. For example, one seven-year-old jumped around the room, declaring that he could fly like superman, in order to avoid quiet interaction with the therapist.

Thus the initial phase may be experienced by the beginning therapist as a wondrous testimony to a therapist's gifts or as a horrible encounter, proving that the therapist ought to find something more constructive to do. In either case the truth lies elsewhere. One can be deceived through early enthusiasm as much as through early pessimism. Whatever reaction occurs, the essential point is that the psychotherapist move through it by maintaining objectivity and concentrating on the application of therapeutic techniques.

As an illustration of transference formation, a girl revealed her fantasy that she wished to be a hermit. This emerged during play when she regularly isolated a doll at the top of the playhouse far away from other people. As time went on, she said the doll felt that no one loved her and, later, that everyone should love the doll. She further described a wish that the doll would be the only girl in the world, so that everyone would pay attention to her. It did not take long for her to identify directly the doll as herself, and also to express her disbelief that the therapist could really care about her, even though the behavior and availability of the therapist demonstrated the opposite. It emerged that her transferred expectation was that the therapist's friendliness merely was window dressing, covering disinterest in her, as she had previously experienced from her mother.

Early Psychotherapy Adaptations

There are specific techniques that can be used in early psychotherapy to provide corrective experiences that restructure a particular functional disability. Cognitive control therapy is an example of such an approach devised for use with children with difficulties with attention, imagery formation, perceptual discrimination, memory, and conceptualization (Santostefano, 1978; 1985). These children lack the capacities needed to sublimate physical activity, express themselves through play, and bring their attention to bear on their conflicts. In essence the technique of desensitization is integrated with the techniques of psychodynamic psychotherapy.

A series of seven specific programs have been developed to be used during the initial stage of psychotherapy with three- to nine-year-old children in order to build the cognitive skills needed for further psychodynamic psychotherapy (Santostefano, 1978). They may be systematically applied, or aspects of them may be infused into an individually tailored course of psychotherapy.

The first two programs foster the shift of focused attention from the body to the external world. The program *Follow Me* provides experiences in sustaining attention on information that moves through space through passive visual tracking of a target, such as an interesting toy, while walking and following it. The program *Which is Big, Which is Small?* trains a child to focus attention on articulating and registering the properties of objects, such as by comparing the quantitative aspects of wooden rods.

The third program, *Find the Shapes*, emphasizes selective deployment of focused attention by withholding attention from irrelevant information while sustaining attention to relevant information, such as through identifying all of the green triangles in an array of different colored geometric forms.

The fourth and fifth programs promote imagery of body sensory experiences and the regulation of motility. The first, *Who is Me? Where is Me?*, is designed to train a child to become more perceptive of body sensations during simple movements, ranging from lying down to hopping, and more articulate in describing them in order to build imagery of the body. The second, *Moving Fast and Slow*, is designed to train a child to differentiate various tempos of moving the body and objects through space, ranging from walking to moving a pencil across a sheet of paper at different rates of speed and describing the imagery experienced. This program essentially promotes mastery of one's body through greater awareness and conceptualization of it.

The sixth program, *Remember Me*, was designed to promote the construction of stable memory images as a basis for sharpening cognitive differentiation by changing an array of geometric forms in progressively complex ways and asking the child to determine how the array has been altered. Training in conceptualization is provided by the seventh program, *Where Does it Belong?*, which arranges objects according to progressively more complex classifications of physical and functional properties.

In these cognitive training programs, the therapist initiates a systematic sequence of kinesthetic and perceptual experiences through the use of materials and activities aimed at retracing the stages of cognitive development. These therapeutic experiences are designed to stimulate constructing a body image; regulating motility and delaying action and impulse; scanning information actively; deploying attention selectively in terms of relevance; constructing stable, articulate memory images of information; and manipulating information conceptually.

Another adaptation in early psychotherapy useful with some older children is to enhance the experiencing of imagery. Imagery may be the main access to important preverbal memories or to memories encoded at developmental stages at which language was not predominant (Sheikh, 1983). Images have a greater capacity than speech for the attraction and focusing of emotionally loaded associations. Words are linear abstractions whereas images are spatial and consonant with the concrete qualities of perceptions. Thus free imagery is effective in circumventing defenses and uncovering repressed material. Three-dimensional eidetic images in which vision is accompanied by bodily sensations and by experiential meaning are particularly useful.

Middle Psychotherapy

The middle phase of psychotherapy appears when the transference has developed. It is during this period of time that the work of self-discovery by the child involves more participation on the part of the therapist. By this time the child has begun to show repetitive, stereotyped patterns of behavior, which are direct clues to defense mechanisms and underlying conflicts.

Because temperamental and cognitive styles are involved in the structuring and the maintenance of defenses, their analysis should prepare the ground for the analysis of defenses. Accordingly it is helpful to identify defensive styles that are elaborations upon individual temperamental differences (Santostefano, 1980). For example, children vary in styles of focusing attention and movement levels. Children who have difficulty focusing attention on internal stimuli and who have high movement levels tend not to experience fear and to act in bold, potentially dangerous ways. These temperamental qualities predispose them to denial and counterphobic behavior. On the other hand, children who are excessively sensitive to internal stimuli and have low movement levels tend to fear loss of self-control and to develop inhibiting obsessive-compulsive defenses.

Moreover a particular style of processing internal and external experience can be caught up with dynamic issues (Greenspan, 1979b). An example is a child's emotional lability, which leads to sudden shifts in emotional state. The tendency to displace one feeling by another is the defense of reversal in which one emotion is replaced by another. Helping a child recognize that attention, movement, and emotions can be used defensively permits the child to develop alternative styles for processing internal experience.

Concomitant with psychotherapeutic work on a child's temperamental and cognitive styles, the content of children's play and their behavior toward the therapist progressively reveal the various forms of transference (Sandler, 1975). The repetition of themes with play materials and the misunderstandings and distortions of the therapist's behavior and role reflect transference phenomena. It is during this time that the psychotherapist introduces doubt about the child's system of beliefs. When this is done, resistance usually is encountered as children make strong efforts to validate their distortions before discarding them.

As an illustration, with her therapist's aid, the girl with the hermit fantasy began to realize that not only had she been rejected by her mother, but she also had promoted and produced the very rejection that she complained about from other people. This was happening with the therapist whom she attempted to alienate by ignoring him, threatening to refuse to come to therapy sessions, and talking against him to her parents. Because of her underlying trust of the therapist, however, she could expose objectionable, monstrous parts of herself to him and depend upon continued respect and acceptance. It is during this phase that the therapist's soft, but persistent, voice of reason can prevail.

For each child individual differences in temperament interact with wishes and powerful feeling states to form a central-core configuration from which defensive and adaptive functions emerge (Greenspan, 1979b). This core configuration, as well as the secondary defensive and adaptive functions, can be dealt with in treatment. The secondary feelings of defectiveness and loss of control are relatively easy to deal with in comparison with underlying core primitive aggressive and sexual yearnings that may exist in undifferentiated forms and frighten both the patient and the therapist. Because they often involve painful and frightening feeling states and fantasies that stimulate countertransference reactions in therapists, these primitive core fantasies may be overlooked.

A preverbal transference configuration derived from the first year and a half of life and based upon temperamental factors is particularly difficult for psychotherapists to handle (Greenspan, 1979b). As infants children showing this configuration were hyperreactive to stimuli, had difficulty focusing attention, and were frequently in a state of panic. They had difficulty developing a homeostatic relationship with their primary caregivers. Because they did not have a peaceful homeostatic experience in infancy, they react to frustration with irritability, rage, and a recurrent sense of losing control of themselves. There also is an unrequited, deep-seated longing for a peaceful dyadic equilibrium that was at best attained only intermittently in the past. Thus, together with irritability, rage, and fear of being out of control, they have strong dependent longings. Because this transference configuration emanates from the earliest time of life, the rage and passive longings tend to be global and undifferentiated and almost defy verbal description. In the transference these feeling states need to be reconstructed and experienced through the psychotherapist's empathic responses to the patient's feeling states, since both the therapist and the patient may not find words that adequately describe them. However, nonverbal communication, such as touching and holding, may be useful in conveying an empathic conviction of accepting the feeling tone.

As these feelings states develop in the transference, a child often becomes frightened of destroying the therapist, either because of the intensity of the longings to literally swallow up the therapist or because of the intensity of the rage the child feels toward the much needed but frustrating therapist. Sometimes at this juncture, the child attempts either to escape treatment or to find an outlet for these painful feeling states with other people.

By maintaining a respectful, noncontrolling posture and facilitating the associative process, the psychotherapist can allow this early transference configuration to manifest itself. When the child talks about feeling out of control, the therapist can empathetically inquire further about related feelings, rather than attempt closure with premature interpretations or reassuring comments. Because they are of a primitive, undifferentiated preverbal nature, the rage and passive longing tend to frighten both child and therapist. The child needs to learn how to bear them. These early dependent longings may take on sexual coloring in older children in the form of bizarre, primitive fantasies. Similarly the rage may take on highly frightening characteristics, such as bloody, gory images. It is important for the therapist to tolerate and facilitate the full development of these primitive emotional states and their verbal approximations.

Even these constitutionally influenced temperamental styles can be altered in the process of working through transference configurations that stem from the period of life when character structures were organizing around that particular style. For example, just as an infant whose mother provides an appropriate environment can be helped to develop compensatory mechanisms to better focus attention and regulate activity in the first year of life, working through transference distortions can lead to a more mature level of compensatory adaptation in children.

During the middle phase of psychotherapy, self-knowledge grows as a child becomes aware of the misunderstandings and misinterpretations of the therapist and the realities of the playroom. After the child discovers distortions in the transference toward the therapist, the shift can be made to discovery of distorted perceptions of parents and other significant adults. Next the child can move to becoming aware of defensive distortions of bodily impulses, sensations, and urges. Defenses reduce stress associated with forbidden wishes. The most commonly encountered defenses are projection, denial, reversal, displacement, and repression (Brenner, 1981). Defenses also can serve drive gratification, self-evaluations, and adaptation alternately or simultaneously. Projection, for example, can be used to further drive gratification, as when one's own sexual desire is attributed to another for oneself.

The distinction between psychopathology that stems from defenses against anxiety and that which is rooted in an arrest at a prestage of defense has important therapeutic consequences. While the approach to the former is to interpret the forbidden wishes, which are being warded off by defensive maneuvers, the approach to the latter is to focus empathically on the state of arrested development (Stolorow & Lachmann, 1978). For example, an arrest at a generalized infantile state of externalizing responsibility for one's life should be identified and exposed before dealing with specific projections of one's anger onto other people. In this way there are developmental lines with prestages for defense mechanisms.

The psychosexual roots of neurotic symptoms become apparent as youngsters implicate urination, spitting, defecation, and flatus production in the expression of deep-seated wishes and conflicts through body language. For example, a boy with bitter hatred of the world, which he perceived as excessively oppressive, expressed this directly by passing flatus and ultimately by abruptly leaving the playroom to defecate, illustrating the relationship of destructive rage and anally based hostility. Indeed if a degree of expression through body language does not take place during the middle phase, the therapeutic process has not progressed deeply enough.

The middle phase of therapy can be prolonged and characterized by mercurial ups and downs. A youngster may need to work through the same insight from several directions, before it becomes usefully integrated. The anxiety created by therapy may be so intense that the youngster shows resistance to treatment, as expressed through boredom on the part of the child, which, in turn, is experienced by the therapist as an appropriate counterreaction to the child's behavior. Middle therapy is the heartland of the therapeutic process, and it is during this period that the therapist's mettle is tested.

Children with learning problems in school have reservoirs of hurt and angry feelings because of repeated failures in school work and relationships with peers (Adamson & Adamson, 1979). The years of failure often foster passively resistant or oppositional personality patterns that avoid conscious awareness of hurt and anger. Counterphobic denial and grandiosity may cover painfully low self-esteem. When helped to see relationships between hurt pride, resulting anger, and expressions of resentment, a child can recognize that satisfaction from needling teachers has been an expression of anger that has covered feeling hurt. Once the stopper is removed, the bottled-up feelings may shift a child from a "sluggish" to a "slugging" form of behavior. The course of child psychotherapy may then be punctuated by more direct expressions of anger that could be interpreted as becoming worse.

During middle therapy aggressive behavior may result from identification with the aggressor or from guilt. In the former a child may attack the therapist as a transference figure who represents a feared parent or sibling. The rage accompanying the attacks may evoke fear in the therapist. This is in contrast to aggressive misbehavior due to guilt, which is not directed at the person of the therapist and evokes a counterreaction on the therapist's part to scold or punish the child (Keith, 1981). When a child believes that to think and to feel and to wish are equated with acting, the angrier the child, the more dangerous the child is, and the greater the fear of imagined retribution. Thus a child's own fearsome rage produces guilt that leads the child to seek punishment. When parents tend toward violent behavior, the child has an added external reason for fearing the worst (Bloch, 1978). The resolution of these focal conflicts over anxiety engendered by aggressive wishes can lead to direct improvement in school performance (Pareus & Weech, 1966).

The fear that children have of their parents has roots in parental infanticidal wishes that have been glossed over by omission of the parental abandonment aspect of the oedipal complex. This dimly experienced terror of infanticide underlies a child's physical and psychological vulnerability and the inevitably threatening character of the outer world. These fears usually are ameliorated by the psyche's resourcefulness as well as the predominantly positive character of parenting. When uncertain of parental support, some children idealize their parents and devalue themselves in seeking to be loved. These children convince themselves that their parents want to and are capable of loving them, but their own worthlessness makes them hateful. Because of their depreciated self-evaluation, these children pursue a life of self-defeating behavior, fulfilling the fantasy of worthlessness. The fantasy of one's own worthlessness serves to preserve an ideal-

ized parental image that obscures the underlying fear of being killed or abandoned by that parent (Bloch, 1978).

At the other extreme are narcissistic children with omnipotent fantasies of being the best, so that they are easily angered by the frustration and delay of gratification of their wishes. Their externalization of responsibility by blaming others, also, often provokes others to control them.

In another vein the distortion of symbols involved in schoolwork is illustrated by a dyslexic adult who failed to synthesize the auditory and visual aspects of a word in order to symbolically keep mother and father images apart in their sexual aspects. Developmentally the auditory comprehension of spoken and written words has roots in the pregenital period. The visual aspects of written words tend to be associated with emotions and memory traces from later oedipal relationships. The core of this man's reading problem was conflict between the auditory components of words, representing his relationship with his mother, and the visual component, which was associated with his father. Through psychotherapy he became freer in verbal expression and showed dramatic improvement in reading ability; his spelling difficulties did not completely abate, however (Walsh, 1966).

Late Psychotherapy

Gradually the termination phase of psychotherapy is entered, sometimes heralded by glimmers of maturity and sometimes seeming to result from a truce between the battle worn child and therapist. At this point the child is aware of the usefulness of the therapeutic relationship and is confronted with the dilemma of wishing to be free from dependency upon the now much needed therapist. In addition to projecting images and feelings upon the therapist, the child also has used the therapist as a developmentally appropriate figure for identification. Having become freed from distorted expectations of the therapist, the child begins to understand appropriate to one's age the actual role of the psychotherapist. Most important the child discovers that one can control aspects of one's life. As an illustration this may occur in the form of reparative motifs in play in which helpful figures save victims (Clegg, 1984).

When fixations at the pregenital level from which fears of annihilation and loss dominate have been released, progress to later developmental stages brings advancing cognitive and managerial capacities. For example, rational problem-solving thinking is not possible for a child who has not achieved full individuation and is preoccupied with irrational fears of separation. The successful interpretation and working through of the child's distorted relationships with people, however, permits the child to assume a more mature level of perceiving and thinking about others.

As a child masters painful emotions and as self-awareness and self-responsibility emerge, self-confidence heightens. When painful emotions and their underlying drives have been exposed, their taming through sublimation can take place as the managerial synthetic function becomes stronger. The emphasis then is on helping a child accept ownership of, and responsibility for, the disowned parts of the self (Pine, 1982).

During this phase the emphasis of psychotherapy shifts from that which goes on within the session to the child's life elsewhere. The child may talk for the first time with the therapist about "problems," as the child's interests shift to problem solving and developing skills. Although regressions to manipulative, responsibility escaping behavior recur, the child basically assumes more personal responsibility for

the pleasant and unpleasant aspects of life. The child may be attracted to the idea of assuming responsibility for oneself and becoming one's own "boss" instead of living in the fear and resentment of being "bossed."

With greater maturity and the desire to relinquish self-defeating behavior, a child is in a position to undertake the arduous work of catching up on lagging academic skills. At this point the child and psychotherapist can refine their understanding of the cognitive, temperamental, self-system, adaptive, and thinking characteristics of the child. The emphasis is upon helping the child to develop compensatory mechanisms and add new skills. Just as in academic work, the child needs help in learning how to make friends by reducing repelling and adding attracting social behaviors. For example, an 11-year-old girl was elated by the discovery that if she showed interest in other children, they responded in a friendly way to her, whereas if she attracted attention to herself, they turned away.

When a child's learning skills are markedly retarded, major efforts must be devoted to tutoring. Tutoring is most successful when a child understands its value and is motivated to use it as an opportunity rather than dread it as an unpleasant burden (Prentice & Sperry, 1965).

During the termination phase, the sessions are progressively spaced out so that ultimately six months might elapse between them. Regressions or "curtain calls" of symptoms may occur during the termination phase. If medication has been employed adjunctively, the focus is on reducing or discontinuing its use.

The ultimate improvement in the child can only take place after psychotherapy has been discontinued. By definition a child cannot be fully independent until the relationship has been terminated with the therapist. Forces set in motion by the psychotherapeutic process continue to operate after therapy and produce further maturation and growth. The option of returning is open to the child and family at a later developmental stage.

THE CHILD PSYCHOTHERAPIST

The psychotherapist obviously determines the style and process of psychotherapy. Factors related to the personality, motivation, skill, and maturity of the therapist, therefore, can both facilitate and frustrate the psychotherapeutic process.

It is important to differentiate between therapists' counterreactions and countertransference to children in psychotherapy (Schowalter, 1984). Counterreactions are any reactions stimulated by the clinical situation. Some children bring out similar reactions from everyone who works with them. For example, when a therapist feels bored with a child, the boredom is a counterreaction whose source may be appropriately or inappropriately related to the child's behavior.

Countertransference reactions are inappropriate counterreactions in the psychotherapist triggered by the psychopathology of the child or some other element of the situation. They are more likely to arise in work with children than with adults and are especially likely when a child is the same age as, or has problems similar to, members of the psychotherapist's family. They are subjective counterreactions that are not solely based upon the patient's influence and at least partially arise from the therapist. Most counterreactions of therapists have a countertransference component, so that the degree is the crucial question. Excessive countertransference results in repetitive, unhelpful responses that prevent therapists from being objective with particular types of patients.

Countertransference is unconscious, but hints are usually discernible from the clinical work. Countertransference reactions most likely to be noticed are those involving anger, hate, or fear, because they cause anxiety in the therapist or disruption in the therapeutic process. Positive feelings, such as affection, admiration, or identification, are generally less disruptive and, therefore, are less likely to be recognized. Competitive feelings, especially with parents and adolescents, also often go unnoticed.

All psychotherapists bring to their work a number of rational and irrational motives that merit discussion as countertransference possibilities. First of all, the therapist has a rational conscious wish to help the child. This is necessary for one to devote all the time and energy, often with little obvious reward, required by psychotherapeutic work. At an unconscious, irrational level, this constructive desire may arise from a "rescue fantasy," which in exaggerated form can lead a therapist to wish to save the child from the clutches of incompetent, cruel parents, or to usurp the child's parents' roles. In this way a conscious, rational wish to help can be a derivative of a more basic "save the world" fantasy. When limited to the wish to heal, it is the source of energy for the therapist; when openly acted upon, it can be the reason for blind overinvolvement with a child and resulting frustration for the therapist.

The therapist at a conscious, rational level desires to display professional competence in the practice of psychotherapy. On the other hand, this can reflect an unconscious need for omnipotently proving that one is better than someone else, so that the course of psychotherapy is contaminated by competition between the therapist and the child, each trying to prove respective superiority. Conversely a therapist can maintain personal omnipotence through fostering a helpless, dependent position in patients. An omniscient therapist may wish to prove personal theories through a youngster's productions. A child learns very quickly that the way to pacify or please a therapist is through agreement or producing material that seems to attract the therapist's interest and attention. This fantasy also can result in despair on the part of the therapist when early improvement does not occur with a child.

At a rational, conscious level a therapist desires to assume responsibility for the course of treatment. At an unconscious level, this may stem from a wish to control others, leading the therapist to dominate the child. There is satisfaction for a therapist through participating in producing change in a child, in facilitating growth, and in seeing the development of useful values. On the other hand, this can result in self-aggrandizement, so that the therapist acts upon the feeling that nothing could have happened to the child without the therapist.

At a conscious, rational level, a therapist accepts hostility and destructiveness from a child so that the youngster is able to learn over time that this is misdirected and is a result of transferred rather than appropriate hostility toward the therapist. On the other hand, therapists may act upon masochistic fantasies and induce children to provoke and injure them. Sometimes a therapist adopts the posture of being "long suffering" with a child and impedes the child's progress and uses the child's failure to satisfy a personal need to suffer.

A therapist obviously is interested in obtaining knowledge about the child and understanding the youngster's psychodynamic patterns. At a conscious, rational level curiosity about a child's life is appropriate and needed in order to sustain therapeutic interest. This may, however, be an expression of a therapist's unconscious voyeuristic wishes.

A therapist at a conscious, rational level does respond to children in supportive and nurturant ways. In so doing, however, the therapist runs the risk of parenting and taking care of the child, so that a child is surrounded with aid and encouraged to be helpless and dependent.

On the positive side, psychotherapists grow through work with children who contribute to a therapist's maturity. On the negative side, a therapist may be struggling with immaturity and use a child in the service of personal needs by seeking emotional support from the child. This can lead to an inappropriate attachment to the child or to disappointment in the child for not satisfying the therapist, as through a sense of personal injury when the child does not improve as expected.

A strong positive force in psychotherapy at a conscious level is empathy. At the same time, this can be associated with identification with the child, which impairs a therapist's objectivity. Therapists may find themselves taking the children's sides in controversies with parents or other professionals. An advocacy position for a child is one of the appropriate roles for a therapist to assume, however, when a youngster's distortions of the world are shared by the therapist, improvement in the child may be stymied.

In order for psychotherapy to progress, therapists must believe that they can be useful to children. When a therapist does not expect the work to be effective, a similar attitude develops in the child. Thus a therapist's lack of belief in oneself can be contagious.

Just as it is true that parents experience grief with the maturing diminution of the child's dependency on them, a psychotherapist also may perceive the maturation and growing independence of a child as a loss. The termination phase of psychotherapy can contain an element of grief for both a child and therapist. Strong feelings of loss or depression, however, signal unresolved issues on either side.

The regressive pull on psychotherapists

faced with children's continual sexual and aggressive provocations is a factor in the tendency of many psychotherapists to avoid children and of child psychotherapists to gradually shift toward adults. This means that training in child psychotherapy is particularly critical to recruiting professionals and preventing burn out. Child psychotherapists need the support of other professionals and need to continually refine their skills.

The giving, succoring aspects of the mature adult and the child within the psychotherapist are the wellsprings of interest in child psychotherapy. More than in other life endeavors, a short supply of patience can lead to disaster in work with children. Individuals who are oriented strongly toward competition or producing tangible products often find psychotherapy with children to be boring and unfruitful. Child psychotherapists, therefore, tend to have succoring qualities in addition to patience. Most importantly, participating in the lives of children gives psychotherapists rejuvenating contact with the young.

SUMMARY

Individual child psychotherapy can be a useful component of the treatment of children with learning problems in school. In preparing for individual psychotherapy, therapeutic work with the child's family is needed to reverse pathogenic forces, enlist the parents as allies in the therapeutic endeavor, alleviate parent-school communication problems, and identify sibling conflicts, so that they are susceptible to parental management. Intensive individual psychotherapy is most useful with children who are able accurately to analyze reality and form relationships.

The styles of child psychotherapy vary widely, however, intensive psychotherapy involves a process within which the relationship between child and therapist is the fulcrum for relieving anxiety based upon distorted perceptions of people and unconscious intrapsychic conflicts.

Because of the centrality of the child–psychotherapist relationship, establishing rapport with the child is the first task. Then the techniques of confrontation, clarification, and interpretation can be progressively employed during the early, middle, and late stages of psychotherapy.

Children with learning problems in school often have temperamental and cognitive style variations that can be dealt with in psychotherapy before, and concomitant with, the interpretation of defenses and transference phenomena. These children have difficulty processing and organizing experiences in terms of interrelationships with people and emotional states. The transference issues can be challenging for therapists, because they evoke passive longings from unmet early dependency needs and fears of loss of control of primitive rage.

Child psychotherapists require training in order to develop the technical skill and perspective needed to handle the challenges of intensive psychotherapy. An interest in children and the basic qualities of succorance and patience are important personal attributes for child psychotherapists.

The process of intensive psychotherapy with children is a valuable tool for unraveling the complex interplay between character styles, specific functional disabilities, emotions, and psychological defense mechanisms.

34

Medications

Because of his hyperactivity Winston Churchill's teachers let him leave the classroom at regular intervals to run around the school grounds.

Ross & Ross, 1976

The use of psychoactive medications with children poses challenging questions for physicians. The temptation to prescribe a medication when a physician can offer little else is great, particularly when parents and teachers are grateful when a medicated child's behavior becomes manageable (Schain, 1977). As a result about 20 percent of the children in special education programs receive psychoactive medications (Safer & Kruger, 1983). Stimulant medications are the most commonly used. Since the indications for tranquilizers and antidepressants are less clear-cut, and research on their efficacy is incomplete (Campbell et al, 1985), stimulants will be the major focus of this chapter. Sroufe (1975) summarized well the issues involved in treating children with psychoactive medications.

Ethical issues are raised when medications are used to change the behavior of children, who usually do not participate in the decision to use them. One of the most significant is that medication may reinforce scapegoating of a child by connoting that there is something wrong with the child.

Adults thus may be relieved of the responsibility to deal with their contributions to a child's problems at home and in school. The continued use of drugs also may set in motion a subtle dependence on them for the social adjustment of a child. Furthermore their use may imply that children are unable to control, or even that they are not responsible for, their own behavior (Kronick, 1981).

Intense feelings have been aroused generally by the widespread use of psychoactive medications (Breggin, 1983). Underlying these feelings are the complicated personal and social repercussions of giving psychoactive medications to children, as depicted in Figure 34-1 (Whalen & Henker, 1980). The use of medications to modify the personal characteristics of children affects the social system as a whole. Children whose school performance improves with stimulant medication (circle 1) may think of themselves as learning because of the pills (circle 2). Their parents and teachers may interpret improvement as proof that the children have brain chemical imbalances (circle 3). This supports society's

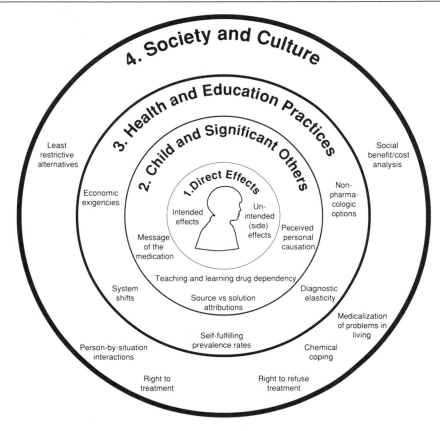

Figure 34-1. The direct and emanative effects of psychostimulant treatments. (Adapted from C. K. Whalen and B. Henker, "The Social Ecology of Psychostimulant Treatment," in C. K. Whalen and B. Henker, eds., *Hyperactive Children: The Social Ecology of Identification and Treatment,* Academic Press, New York.)

quest for chemical solutions to the problems of daily life and pills to enhance memory and learning (circle 4). Thus the initial positive impact of a medication may have unexpected long-range effects on the social issue of using drugs to enhance mood, intelligence, and even athletic performance. Ironically the more positive the immediate impact of a medication on a child, the more unfavorable may be the ultimate outcome for society in its preference for short-term relief over more difficult long-term problem solving.

STIMULANT MEDICATION

The personal, family, and social potential for abuse notwithstanding, stimulant medication has been used for over 50 years to enhance learning and social experiences in school for children with attention and movement problems (Bradley, 1937).

The importance of viewing stimulant medication as an adjunct to psychotherapy and educational management is supported by evidence that a favorable response to medication does not in itself improve school performance (Barkley & Cunningham, 1978; McGuinness, 1985).

The Indications for Stimulant Therapy

Stimulants should not be used for behavior that is not manifested in school, since strained interpersonal relations may be the source of these symptoms when seen only at home. They should not be employed to change a child's consciousness or constrain freedom of expression, but rather to enlarge the range of possible actions from which a child may choose. When properly used a medication enables children to accomplish what they set out to do, but does not suppress the exercise of initiative.

The clinical evaluation of a child for the purpose of determining the indications for a medication is described in Chapter 20 and includes a detailed interview with the parents, a mental status examination of the child, information from the school, physical and neurologic examinations, and appropriate laboratory studies. A psychoeducational assessment of the child is essential to detect specific deficits in intellectual, sensory, perceptual, motor, and academic skills. Behavior rating scales completed by both parents and teachers should be obtained as baseline assessments of a child. Examples include the Conner's Parent Symptoms Questionnaire, and the Conner's Abbreviated Symptoms Questionnaire. The last is especially useful for follow-up assessments by parents and teachers.

A multimodality treatment plan commensurate with a child's functional disabilities then can combine medication with appropriate family and individual psychotherapy and remedial education (Accardo, 1980; Barkley, 1981; Satterfield et al, 1979b; Wiener, 1985; Werry, 1982). The various treatment options should not be regarded as alternatives but as resources

to be used in the combination that will best meet the needs of a particular child.

Stimulants appear to increase a child's abilities to focus on meaningful stimuli and to organize bodily movements more purposefully. A major action of methylphenidate, for example, is diminution of distractibility through enhanced focusing of attention (Ackerman et al, 1982). Children receiving stimulants usually demonstrate increased attention spans, concentration ability, and alertness along with decreased movement levels and impulsivity.

The therapeutic goal of stimulant medication is to improve functioning throughout the waking day in the classroom, home, and community. The continuous administration of medication during a child's waking hours, therefore, is preferable to intermittent dosages. Children on intermittent medication may have difficulty developing stable self-images and may be frightened by shifts in their ability to control their own behavior produced by intermittent medication effects. Consequently, their relationships with siblings, peers, and parents may be adversely affected. Furthermore the medication is needed to assist them with their homework.

When a child finds it possible to work in school while taking a medication and receives positive instead of negative feedback, self-esteem and coping skills profit (Hechtman et al, 1984b). Children also become capable of the reflectiveness needed to participate in psychotherapy. Stimulant therapy, therefore, usually does not mask underlying psychopathology, but makes it more accessible.

Mechanisms of Action of Stimulants

The most commonly used stimulants are methylphenidate (Ritalin), dextroamphetamine (Dexedrine), and pemoline (Cylert), as described in Figure 34-2. The first

Generic Name	Brand Name	Preparations	Range of Daily Dose (Average)	Onset of Action	Benign Side Effects	Serious Side Effects
Methylphenidate	Ritalin	Tablets: 5, 10, 20 mg Sustained release tablet: 20 mg	10–60 mg (10–30) 0.6 to 1.7 mg/kg	30 minutes Half-life: 2–4 hours	Insomnia, appetite loss, abdominal pain, headaches, skin rash	Growth retardation, hypersensitivity reactions, leukopenia, anemia
Dextroamphetamine	Dexedrine	Spans and Tablets: 5, 10, 15 mg, Elixir	5–40 mg (5–20) 0.3 to 1.25 mg/kg	30 minutes Half-life: 6–10 hours	Appetite loss, insomnia, headache, diarrhea or constipation, pinched facial expression	Growth retardation
Pemoline	Cylert	Tablets: 18.75, 37.5, 75 mg Chewable tablets: 37.5 mg	18.75–112.5 (56.25–75) 0.5 to 3.0 mg/kg	2–4 hours (maybe after 3–4 weeks) Half-life: 4–16 hours	Insomnia, appetite loss, nausea, abdominal pain, dizziness, skin rash	Weight loss, liver dysfunction, extra-pyramidal signs, seizures

Figure 34-2. The commonly used stimulant medications.

agent used effectively was the racemic form of amphetamine (Benzedrine).

Although their exact mechanism of action is not know, much has been made of the "paradoxical" sedative effect of stimulants. The term is inappropriate, however, because stimulants do not have sedative properties in children. They actually increase the activity of catecholamine synapses in the brain, probably by blocking the uptake of norepinephrine and dopamine at the presynaptic membrane or by blocking degradation of catecholamines by monoamine oxidase, thereby increasing catecholamine levels in the synapses (Cooper et al, 1986).

Norepinephrine is an important neurotransmitter in the reticular formation which determines the general arousal of the nervous system. Dopamine transmission is concentrated in the limbic system, which relates to learning, and the striatonigral system, which relates to movement and attention control. These considerations raise the possibility that children who respond favorably to stimulants have low levels of central nervous system arousal, as suggested by electroencephalographic (EEG) and pupillographic indications of underarousal (Kinsbourne & Caplan, 1979). They are inattentive or hyperkinetic because of insufficient arousal of central nervous system inhibitory activity.

Stimulants may have two different physiological actions. Their faster acting but short-lived enhancement of attention could reflect their excitation of thalamic, limbic, and reticular arousal systems. Their longer acting reduction of hyperkinesis could reflect their enhancement of frontal lobe inhibition systems (Conners & Wells, 1986).

One group of favorable responders to stimulants may be comprised of those who respond more on account of the norepinephrine effect and another group may consist of those who respond favorably because of the medication's dopamine effects

(Kinsborne & Caplan, 1979). Following this rationale those hyperkinetic children who are highly aroused and still have low cortical inhibition may be those who do not respond to or become worse with stimulants (Powell, 1979). According to the Law of Initial Values, the higher the initial level of autonomic functioning, the smaller will be the response to function raising and the larger the response to function lowering stimuli. Thus beyond medium values, reversals of the usual type of response occur. Applied to children with highly aroused sympathetic nervous systems, this means that a stimulant would have no effect (Mosse, 1982).

Regional blood-flow studies suggest that methylphenidate increases metabolic activity in the mesencephalon and basal ganglia and decreases it in the motor and sensory cortical areas. The former effect may heighten the ability to focus attention, and the latter may decrease distractibility and movement levels (Lou et al, 1983).

Adults also may show individual differences in responses to stimulants, as do children. For example, many adults use caffeine to increase concentration because the stimulant drugs are powerful attention-focusing agents (Kinsbourne & Caplan, 1979). For people who are impulsive, a certain amount of stimulant might make them more focused by raising the arousal of the underaroused cortex to render performance more efficient. But the same amount of stimulant with normally focused people may make them unduly so; and the same amount given to overfocused people may cause them to become withdrawn (Powell, 1979). The same principle holds for barbiturates and alcohol. The same amount of barbiturate and alcohol that beneficially unlocks the attention of the overly focused individual disorganizes an impulsive person (Kinsbourne & Caplan, 1979). The favorable responder to stimulants then becomes impulsive when given a barbiturate or alcohol.

Another factor to consider is that children may differ from adults in the characteristics of their brain electrical activity. When conditions of rest and effort were compared in one study, while exerting effort children showed changes in EEG patterns, which would indicate drowsiness in adults (Elliot, 1964). Thus, adults tend to show decreases in EEG amplitude with increasing motivation and activity, whereas children may respond with increased amplitudes.

The Administration of Stimulants

The indications for a therapeutic trial of a stimulant should be discussed with parents, many of whom are likely to have mixed feelings about medications. The initial purpose is to determine whether or not a stimulant will be effective. When parents, teachers, and clinicians agree that a significant beneficial effect is obtained, the matter of long-term stimulant management can be broached. Parents also should be assured of regular review, so that an opportunity to discontinue therapy will not be missed.

A child's cooperation can be enlisted by explaining the purpose and action of the medication. This can be done in terms of helping the child to settle down, pay attention, and work more effectively. The child may wonder why it is necessary to take pills when siblings and classmates do not. It is crucial to explain that the pills will not magically result in better grades in school. Improvement will come from both increased concentration induced by medication and increased effort. In this way a child bears responsibility for working in school, as the pills make it easier to concentrate.

The initial titration of dosage and adjustment of administration times are important in determining whether or not a stimulant will be effective and how to provide maximum duration of benefit (Dulcan, 1985). Unfortunately many children do not receive optimal benefit from medication because of improper dosage, intermittent administration, and mishandling of side effects.

When available laboratory tests can be used to determine the behavioral effects of a stimulant (Kinsbourne & Caplan, 1979). Prior to the time of administration and at half-hourly intervals thereafter, a child's behavior can be sampled by presenting various performance tests. At an effective stimulant dose level, performance steadily improves, reaching maximum improvement between two and three hours after administration with the beneficial effect decreasing by four hours.

Laboratory tests of performance to gauge the proper level of stimulant administration are beginning to be developed for general use. The Gordon Diagnostic System illustrates the efforts being made to develop objective instrument testing of behaviors essential to the performance of schoolwork. It measures a child's ability to maintain attention in the absence of reinforcement and to delay responding in the presence of distractions (Gordon, 1984; McClure & Gordon, 1985).

Still the clinician should rely on the actual trial of the medication with monitoring by parents and teachers. The teacher often is the only person to see the child regularly in a group setting in which the child can be compared with peers from one day to the next (Okolo et al, 1978). Several weeks may be required to determine the optimal dosage, although this is usually evident during the first week.

The first stage is to determine the dosage of a stimulant required to produce a behavioral effect. Every three days an initial small dose can be increased until evidence of improvement is reported. If a child becomes withdrawn, tearful, or dulled from overdosage, scaling down of the dose is required. An initial exaggeration of hyperkinesis is a favorable sign, and continuation of the same dosage usually produces the desired result.

Once a therapeutic dosage level has been established, a second stage of double-blind assessment is desirable in order to be sure that the chemical effect of the medication is the beneficial variable. One approach is to prepare identical capsules containing the therapeutic stimulant dosage and a placebo. Each is given on alternate weeks. At the end of each school day, the same teacher fills out a Conner's Teacher Rating Scale. The same parent also rates the child's behavior at 7:00 p.m. on the Conner's Parent Rating Scale. A score of 25 percent improvement on the mean score of the Conner's rating forms for a week represents a positive response to the medication (Varley & Trupin, 1983).

The objective evaluation of medication effects is important. Many failures of stimulant therapy have been related to distorted assessments. For example, one mother complained that the drug was producing adverse effects. When she was carefully questioned, it became evident that her son's hyperkinetic behavior had lessened, and the child no longer was at his mother's side, but was quietly reading books, working on projects, and pursuing his own interests. In this particular situation, one of the important factors in this child's hyperkinesis was the mother's covert gratification from his need for her attention. In another instance a teacher first was annoyed by a hyperkinetic child and then complained that he appeared drugged, when he simply sat quietly at his desk. Discrepancies between the assessments of teachers and parents may occur and require careful analysis. When this is done, the desired effect of the drug often has been attained, but the behavioral changes were being interpreted differently by adults.

The evaluation of the effectiveness of a medication extends to the administration pattern needed to cover a child's waking hours. Many hyperkinetic children experience difficulty going to sleep, awakening during the night or early in the morning (Kinsbourne & Caplan, 1979). These complaints may emerge after stimulant therapy is instituted, or if already present, exacerbate at that time. When the effect of a stimulant has worn off by late afternoon, the return of impulsive behavior and distractibility may interfere with going to sleep and result in the effects of sleep deprivation the next day.

A late afternoon or early evening supplementary stimulant dose can be timed, so that the duration of the agent's effectiveness includes the child's bedtime and the sleep problem is minimized. A lower dose usually is sufficient, because the morning dosage level may cause a child to ruminate and be unable to go to sleep. Occasionally a tricyclic agent, such as imipramine, or a sedative, such as benedryl, may be combined at night with a stimulant during the day, if sleep problems are persistent. Attention to a child's sleep pattern may in itself reveal the need for changes in sleep routine, such as reducing excessive television viewing (Mosse, 1982).

Persistent bed wetting is common in hyperkinetic children. It may be relieved by the stimulant program in itself. If not, biofeedback conditioning or imipramine can be employed. The use of stimulants usually does not lower the seizure threshold in children who are epileptic.

There does not appear to be an association between the medical use of stimulants in children and later drug abuse (Accardo, 1980). Children take stimulants in doses many orders of magnitude lower than those taken by addicts. Since even a slight increase in these moderate doses induces adverse effects that are quite unpleasant, the kind of children who receive stimulants are unlikely to want to repeat such an experience. Furthermore children treated with stimulants apparently do not experience the pleasurable subjective effects that would encourage misuse. They also do not show the rapid tolerance that develops when such drugs are taken in much larger doses by addicts.

When stimulant therapy is instituted, a child's appetite may decrease. There may be some weight loss, although this usually is temporary. Still the subsequent rate of weight gain may follow a curve lower than that previously observed. This can be assessed through weekly weighings (Greenhill et al, 1981). A daily multiple vitamin should be prescribed, and dietary supplements can be provided when appetite loss is significant. Stimulant therapy is contraindicated in cardiovascular disease and for persons receiving monoamine-oxidase inhibitors.

Stimulants should be viewed as agents that will be needed over an extended period of time, if they are beneficial for a child. The administration of stimulant medication, therefore, is comparable to anticonvulsant therapy. Occasionally, in the first month or two of therapy, a tolerance develops that quickly responds to a minor dose increase. Cumulative tolerance reducing a stimulant's effect, however, is uncommon. Increases in dosage usually are not required until a child undergoes an appreciable change in body size. If habituation does develop, different stimulants can be alternated.

The continued need for stimulant therapy should be regularly reviewed. The periodic interruption of stimulant therapy on weekends and during vacations is advisable to minimize the development of tolerance; to minimize the possibility of side effects; to keep the focus on the medication as an educational aid and not as a behavioral control; to minimize growth retardation; and, particularly, to permit evaluation of the medication's effectiveness. There is no critical age at which stimulant therapy can be expected to become unnecessary, although most children appear to outgrow the need for stimulant medication in adolescence.

Methylphenidate

The most commonly used stimulant is methylphenidate (Ritalin), which is available in 5-, 10- and 20 mg-tablets in addition to a sustained-release form. The sustained release form of Ritalin in 20-mg SR tablets is useful, because its duration of action is eight hours in contrast with four hours for the regular tablet. The sustained-release form eliminates the need for the inconvenience and disruption of a noon dosage in school, where taking medication may subject a child to the special attention of other children.

Methylphenidate takes effect one half hour after administration and has a duration of action of approximately four hours. The initial dose of methylphenidate for children between five and 12 years is 5 mg at least 30 minutes before breakfast and lunch. Methylphenidate is decomposed by digestive juices, if taken during or soon after meals. The dose can be increased in 5- to 10-mg increments weekly to a daily maximum of 60 mg. The dosage should be kept at the minimum level required to facilitate schoolwork. It is not known whether variations in dose requirements are related to individual responsiveness or vagaries in the absorption of the drug.

The effects of methylphenidate on short-term learning have been studied as a function of dosage (Sprague et al, 1974). The optimal effect of methylphenidate on behavior was obtained at the level of 1 mg/kg. However, when performances on the short-term learning task was used as the criterion, an optimal effect was seen in the neighborhood of 0.3 mg/kg. This relatively minute dose indicates a differential dosage level for learning and behavioral responses.

The side effects of methylphenidate at therapeutic dosage levels occur in 10 to 20 percent of children in the following order of frequency: insomnia, decreased appetite, weight loss, abdominal pain, and headaches. Minor growth retardation, skin rash, hypersensitivity reactions, palpitations, diastolic hypertension, leukopenia, anemia, and hair loss, also, have been reported in patients taking methylphenidate. Periodic blood counts, therefore, are advisable during prolonged therapy. Methylphenidate can interfere with the enzymatic degradation of a number of anticonvulsants and cause their serum levels to rise to toxic levels (Accardo, 1980). Tourette syndrome has been reported as a complication of stimulant therapy (Lowe et al, 1982).

An indication of mild methylphenidate overdose is an increased flow of speech and hypersensitivity. At higher doses children act withdrawn and tearful, as if sedated; at still higher doses, multiple tics appear, and heavy overdoses can precipitate psychotic behavior. Signs and symptoms of acute overdosage result principally from overstimulation of the central nervous system and from excessive sympathomimetic effects. They include vomiting, agitation, tremors, hyperreflexia, muscle twitching, convulsions, confusion, hallucinations, delirium, sweating, flushing, headache, hyperpyrexia, tachycardia, palpitations, cardiac arrhythmia, hypertension, mydriasis, and dryness of mucous membranes. The tics and other involuntary movements resulting from an acute overdose are reminiscent of Parkinsonian patients overdosed with levodopa. Some children show overdose effects without showing the beneficial effects that other children achieve at lower doses.

In a study of hyperkinetic boys treated for over two years, methylphenidate had a minor retarding effect on growth in height and in weight in the first year of treatment, but not in the second year; the first year height deficit was offset in the second year by an increased growth rate. Height growth retardation was not related to dosage or summer drug holidays, as were lags in weight gain (Satterfield et al, 1979a). Another study reported a 2 percent dosage related growth suppressant effect in children receiving methylphenidate after two to four years of treatment (Mattes & Gittelman, 1983).

Dextroamphetamine

The stimulant with the longest history of use with children is dextroamphetamine (Dexedrine). It has the advantage of having fewer significant side effects and more vivid clinical effects than methylphenidate. It is available in 5-mg tablets; elixir form; and 5-mg, 10-mg, and 15-mg spansules.

For a typical nine-year-old, the initial dose might be a 10-mg spansule on arising. This dosage is continued for three days. If no effect is seen, either in the direction of increased or decreased hyperkinesis, the dosage should be doubled. If there is an initial period of excitement, a later favorable response usually ensues. Occasionally as much as 60 mg a day is required. It is likely that dextroamphetamine will be effective in eight out of ten cases, if administered in this fashion.

The side effects of dextroamphetamine at the therapeutic dosage levels are largely a result of its sympathomimetic activity: appetite loss, insomnia, headache, diarrhea, constipation, urticaria, increased heart rate, and elevations of systolic blood pressure. Occasionally children may develop an "amphetamine facies," a pale, pinched, serious facial expression with dark hollows under their eyes.

The signs and symptoms of overdosage include dryness of mucous membranes, difficulty swallowing, thirst, blurred vision, dilated pupils, light sensitivity, fever, rapid pulse and respiration, and disorientation. Hallucinations, delirium, ataxia, dyskinesia, and psychosis from extremely high dosages disappear upon withdrawal of the drug.

Pemoline

Pemoline (Cylert) has a longer duration of action than methylphenidate and dextroamphetamine and can be given in single daily doses. It is available in 18.75-mg, 37.5-mg, and 75-mg tablets in addition to 37.5-mg chewable tablets. Its serum half-life is approximately 12 hours with peak levels within two to four hours and steady serum levels with daily doses in two to three days. Significant clinical benefit, however, may not be evident until the third or fourth week.

Pemoline is not recommended for children less than six years of age. It may exacerbate the symptoms of psychotic children. Its side effects at therapeutic dosage levels include insomnia, appetite and weight loss, liver dysfunction, dyskinesia, nystagmus, and convulsive seizures. Stomachache, skin rashes, irritability, depression, nausea, dizziness, headache, drowsiness, and hallucinations, also, have been reported. Mild adverse reactions appearing early in the course of pemoline administration often disappear with continuing therapy. There has been insufficient experience with pemoline to assess its influence on growth. Liver function tests should be performed prior to and during therapy. The signs and symptoms of overdosage include agitation, restlessness, hallucinations, increased pulse rate, and abnormal movements.

MEMORY MEDICATIONS

The search for drugs to alter learning and memory has its roots in mythology as well as the history of medicine (Essman, 1983). The facilitation of learning and the improvement of memory have been claimed for a number of plant-derived substances, including coca, chat, caffeine, and nicotine. In Germany in the 1860s the role of phosphorous in the brain gave rise to the suggestion that foods high in phosphorous content, such as fish, were good for brain functioning.

In the light of contemporary studies of drug effects on learning and memory, it is evident that the premise for using a given drug based upon its effect on the central nervous system may be sound, but its actual effect unimpressive. In the context of the other neurotransmitter systems, the cholinergic systems, particularly the muscarinic aspect, is involved in a variety of learning and memory processes. In contrast, serotonin appears to negatively influence the acquisition or processing of information by the central nervous system. Still few clinically useful results have emerged from this knowledge as yet.

The biochemical aspects of memory are being extensively investigated. Scopolomine is known to interfere with short-term memory. As a result physostigmine, a cholinesterase inhibitor, has been used to improve memory in organic brain syndromes with some success. Naturally occurring and synthetic peptides, such as vasopressin, also, have been reported to improve memory. In the treatment of senile dementias of the Alzheimer type, improvements in memory may be possible with polypharmaceutical regimens consisting of normal tissue constituents, such as vitamins, acetylcholine, antidiuretic hormone, and coenzyme Q, or drugs such as piracetam, anticonvulsants, and local anesthetics (Menolascino et al, 1983; Roberts, 1982).

A variety of individual differences undoubtedly play an important role in the effect of drugs on the central nervous system. For example, physostigmine impaired the performance of skilled chess players, but improved it in low-performance-level players. On the other hand, scopolomine impaired the performance of all players (Liljequist & Mattila, 1979).

The clinical application of these findings to children who have memory problems remains to be seen (Herskowitz & Rosman, 1982). Piracetam is related to gamma-aminobutyric acid and appears to facilitate the memory, reading and writing efficiency of dyslexic children (Chase et al, 1984; Rudel & Helfgott, 1984; Wilsher, 1986).

ANTICONVULSANT MEDICATIONS

The diagnosis and prescription of treatment for seizure disorders in children require the expertise of a child neurologist. However, the monitoring of a medication program can be carried out by other physicians. The administration of anticonvulsant medications requires careful selection, combining, and adjustment in order to achieve an optimal balance. Periodic blood levels of an anticonvulsant are needed to ensure that the dosage of medication is neither too low nor too high.

Phenobarbital is widely used for seizure control. Unfortunately its efficacy may be impaired by side effects in the form of sedation or agitation. Dilantin (phenytoin) is the most commonly employed medication for the control of grand mal and psychomotor seizures. Mysoline (primidone) is used to treat grand mal, psychomotor, and focal seizures.

Celontin (methsuximide), Milontin (phensuximide), and Zarontin (ethosuximide) are used in the treatment of absence seizures. Because of its greater toxicity, Tridione (trimethadione) is reserved for absence seizures unresponsive to the preceding medications. Clonopin (clonazepam) is used to treat absence, akinetic, and myoclonic seizures.

Three additional anticonvulsants are used when the preceding medications are ineffective; however, their toxic properties must be carefully weighed against their potential benefits. Mesantoin (mephenytoin) is effective with grand mal, focal, and psychomotor seizures. Tegretol (carbamazepine) is used for mixed seizure types. Depakane (valproic acid) may be useful with refractory absence and multiple seizures.

In some situations an optimal control of seizure activity is not possible and the cooperation of school personnel, parents, and clinicians is needed to assess the tolerable frequency of seizures in order to avoid deleterious anticonvulsant side effects.

SUMMARY

Psychoactive medications can be useful adjuncts in the treatment of certain children with learning problems in school. The use of medications with children has ethical and psychological implications, however, for a child, family, and society that relate to controlling the behavior of children and short-term rather than long-range solutions to human problems.

The most clear-cut indication for psychoactive medications with children is the use of stimulants to improve a child's capacity to function in school. Stimulant medications operate through the reticular activating and extrapyramidal systems to increase the efficiency of attention and body movements.

Dextroamphetamine and methylphenidate are the most commonly used stimulants with children. They both are most effectively used as a part of a treatment program involving the child, family, school, and physician. Full understanding by the child and parents of the indications for and the administration, actions, and side effects of a medication is important to the success of treatment. Careful monitoring of the medication by parents and school personnel in addition to clinical procedures are needed in order to determine optimal dosage and administration patterns.

The role of other psychoactive medications, such as antidepressants, neuroleptics, and memory enhancing agents, has yet to be clearly defined with children. At this time, however, properly managed stimulant and anticonvulsant medications can play a significant role in the treatment of some children.

35

The Role of Families

If there is anything that we wish to change in a child, we should first examine it and see whether it is not something that could better be changed in ourselves.

Carl Gustav Jung, 1935

Parents know their own children better than anyone else. When learning problems arise in school they can become knowledgeable team members in dealing with their child and other systems (Smith, S. L., 1980).

Most parents feel at some level, however, that educational problems in their children reflect upon their parenting. Often this attitude is reinforced by professionals, family members, and friends who offer child-rearing advice that results in further doubt about their parenting abilities. In addition the complexity of school learning problems precludes precise diagnoses and treatment plans and adds to parental frustrations.

All of these factors emphasize the importance of forming a parent–professional alliance (Gargiulo, 1985). Such an alliance sensitizes professionals to the reactions of parents who are actively involved in helping their children.

THE PARENT–PROFESSIONAL ALLIANCE

Increasingly parents approach professionals with their own formulations of a child's problem and treatment expectations, such as a particular diet or medication for hyperactivity. They also tend to seek a point of view that confirms their own. Consequently, professionals find themselves in the position of helping parents both to understand and to accept information about their children. In so doing care should be taken to explain professional terms with concrete examples. Clinicians frequently overlook the fact that parents and children are unfamiliar with their technical jargon. Parents and children should receive the same consideration that clinicians would desire were they in the same position.

Clinicians err on the side of sharing too little rather than too much information with parents and children. They tend to assume that parents know more than they do. For disadvantaged parents in particular, a negative image of professionals is reinforced by ineffective communication. It is the clinician's responsibility to bridge that gap. Even when this is done, parents may, or may not, be inclined to join in the resolution of their children's problems.

At the outset parents show varying levels of availability for a working alliance often related to the level of family functioning (Swift, 1981). The classification of families as *healthy, faltering, dominated, conflicted,* and *chaotic* is useful for our purposes (Lewis, 1979).

At the first level in a *healthy* family, parents realize the complicated nature of their child's problem and ask for a working alliance. They both realistically and unrealistically assume they are responsible for their child's problems or for their inability to solve them. This offers a basis for exploration of the family's role in contributing to and resolving their child's problems. In a healthy family, the family members are relatively free from individual psychopathology, and the family ambience promotes the autonomy and self-actualization of its members. Healthy families vary immensely in their surface appearances, reflecting the interests and personalities of their members. They have in common, however, power invested in the parents; open, intelligible communication; individuating family members; resilient coping abilities; and successful engagement with stage-appropriate developmental tasks.

A second, less available, state is found in a *faltering* family, in which parents are wary of professionals and appear to be hesitant to accept their child's problems because of the fear that their child's failures are their fault. They may be protecting themselves from painful personal or marital problems which are too intense to reveal to professionals. If they expressed feelings about their child's problems, they might express other more painful feelings about themselves. An example of this common pattern are parents who prefer to see their child's problems as the result of laziness rather than limitations in abilities.

In faltering families there is dissatisfaction in the marriage, but the family generally is coping well. Coalitions may exist outside of the family with grandparents, friends, or lovers. Neither the parents nor the children are seriously troubled by emotional or behavioral symptoms, but their unhappiness makes the future un-

certain. An understanding of the facts regarding their children and a forthright acknowledgement of distracting tensions in the family can help these parents gain the perspective needed for a working alliance.

A third level of availability is found in *dominated* families, in which there is acknowledgement of a problem in a child; however, making the shift from a linear focus on the child to the family system is difficult. These parents hold preconceived ideas about the cause of their child's problems and reject opinions to the contrary. As a result they take the child from one clinic to another until they find satisfaction. Their aim is to change the child to fit their expectations. This message amounts to a crushing rejection of the child, who is made to feel unloved and unwanted.

Dominated families are troubled families in which one parent wields the power. Some dominated families have a relatively stable structure with little open conflict, whereas others are in evident strife with attempts by other family members to rebel and maneuver against the heavy-handed control of the dominant member. There is diminished closeness in the family with suppression of feelings but clear communication. These families are rigidly controlled and have little flexibility to deal effectively with change. Achieving autonomy is difficult for family members, who may leave at an early age or cling dependently to the powerful parent. There is a strong tendency to avoid individual responsibility so that the family selects a scapegoat.

These parents prefer not to confront their own sadness over their failing child and may focus their energies upon time-consuming treatment methods and diets. The periodic influxes of new esoteric methods attract these parents. These parents may be reserved, even cold, persons who relate more comfortably to impersonal rituals than relaxed affectionate interactions with their child. They need the sympathetic respect of professionals for their desire to take every reasonable step possible to help the child and to seek more than one professional opinion. Clinicians should demonstrate the level of competence involved in a diagnostic study and solicit the parents' wishes for further investigations so that there is no rational basis for feeling that a stone has been left unturned. The clinician can then assist these parents to place the diagnostic findings in perspective. Thereafter the emphasis can be placed upon their feelings toward the child so that the child's behavior can be recognized as a reaction to forces within the family.

At the least accessible level are parents in conflicted and chaotic families that overtly deny problems. They rarely seek help themselves and are usually referred under pressure. Their frequent anger at the school personnel is a by-product of their own covert feelings of helplessness and hopelessness.

Conflicted families are characterized by power struggles and warfare between the parents. Manipulation results throughout the family, often in shifting coalitions. Anger is freely expressed, but feelings of affection and sadness are not. Parental values tend to be intensely competitive. Communications are usually clear, but efficiency in problem solving is diminished, because disagreements become escalating counterattacks between the parents.

Chaotic families involve either a fused relationship between the parents, so that neither functions as an individual, or an emotional divorce with little interaction between the parents. These families often are disorganized and isolated from the outside world. They may appear bizarre to others. The family lacks structure and control because of parental impotence. Communication is confused, and family members experience pain and misery. Chaotic families have difficulty dealing with change, particularly the advancing ages of their

children, and discourage individuality and independence. As a result the children do not have solid parental figures with whom to identify. They sense their parents' confusion and vulnerability. They may assert their own willfulness to gain power in this vacuum or resort to withdrawal. In either case they resent their parents for leaving them at the mercy of their impulses and for the resulting confusion.

Thus the levels of parental readiness to form a working alliance may pass through denial, preoccupation with the child, and wariness in order to attain open involvement of the family system. It is helpful to recognize these levels so that treatment of the family can be employed to help parents work through them, as it is difficult to help fully a child if a working parent–professional alliance is not established.

REFRAMING ATTITUDES TOWARD THE CHILD

The first step in establishing the foundation for treatment based upon a working parent–professional alliance is reframing parental attitudes toward their child's school problem.

Parents need help in developing confidence in their own observations and judgment. It is all too easy for professionals to find fault with parenting practices. A sensitive, nonjudgmental attitude on the part of professionals facilitates gaining the trust of parents. Reframing parental attitudes toward authority, their child, and the school can be helpful (Klein et al, 1981). Even though it may not be evident on the surface, parents need to temper their image of themselves as bad or inadequate. For instance, unwarranted parental guilt can be addressed by correcting distortions, such as when a parent felt that striking a two-year-old child caused brain damage and subsequent learning problems. Without being oversolicitous the professionals can acknowledge that parenting is a difficult venture made even more problematic when a child has problems in school.

Parents often are preoccupied with what has gone wrong. Professionals can point out areas of strength in a child and parents, who need to hear positive things about themselves. Such statements can counteract pessimism, while nurturing the parents' sense of competence. Emphasizing the positive can begin early in contacts with the family and remain a guiding principle.

Many parents find themselves evaluating their children on the basis of school achievement, so that report card time becomes judgment day for the children. These children come to believe that they are valued for what they do. For them life is success or failure in the eyes of others. Love, relaxation, imagination, and enjoyment have little value in their lives. Their parents need help in recognizing that their children are reflecting their own discontentment with themselves.

Parents often attribute their children's failure in school to lack of motivation. Although this may be the case at some level in each child, it overlooks the realistic difficulties that a child encounters in handling schoolwork and the child's own discouragement because of failure. That discouragement spawns giving up on schoolwork, deceitful behavior around schoolwork, and apparent indifference or laziness. Furthermore the accusation of laziness may frustrate and embitter children who have been trying. They become confused about themselves when they hear they "can do it if you try harder." This drastically distorts their self-evaluations. If their best effort is far from sufficient, how can lesser efforts be worthy? This confusion may produce unrealistic overachieving or giving up completely. In these instances parental and child awareness of the details of a child's abilities and skills can be helpful in distinguishing between motivational lacks and particular difficulties in a child's cognitive, language, and managerial functions. Parental blame of a child based upon lack of understanding, thereby, can be alleviated. The situation is more complicated when scapegoating of the child occurs in the family, however.

Many parents lack holistic conceptualizing ability in the sense that their lives are lived as parts rather than as wholes so that it is difficult for them to see the relationships between phenomena. They need help in shifting from a linear search for single causes to a systems level of thinking. These parents also tend to be unintuitive, so that they have difficulty empathizing with the plight of their children, who accordingly may perceive them as not really understanding or caring about them. They are unable to trust their own judgments with resulting insecurity, indecisiveness, doubting, and ambivalence. Thus they are excessively dependent upon professionals to tell them what to do.

An essential element in reframing parental attitudes toward a child is exposing and dealing with their understandable guilt. Parents need help to see that they really are partly responsible without stimulating immobilizing guilt feelings or defensive denials. For example, observations of the interactions between child and parent may capture whaat is going on: "I notice when you feel uncomfortable about an issue being discussed, Johnny completely clams up. He seems very sensitive to your feelings." Furthermore, parents need to know the positives first; then they can more clearly hear the negatives. Not infrequently one parent invites blame, and the other tacitly agrees. In these instances the passive parent needs help in sharing the responsibility for what has gone wrong. It may be helpful to alleviate one parent's guilt and stimulate the others to promote involvement.

Some parents are immersed in self-

blame that borders on self-pity. They ruminate about what they have done or not
done to cause a child's learning problems.
This may be reinforced by a familial tendency toward educational problems. There
also are inevitable instances in which an
incident or illness may have related to a
degree of parental negligence. Indeed the
ambivalence all parents and children feel
toward each other provides many reasons
for feeling responsible for the misfortune
of a loved one. The effect of parental self-
blame on a child, however, may be guilt in
the child for causing parental unhappiness
and result in a vicious circle of reinforcing
guilt in parent and child. A useful approach with parental guilt is to first affirm
the way in which parents inevitably hurt
their children, and vice versa. By providing
confirmation of universal ambivalent love
and hate in family relationships, the stage
can be set for the discovery that the parents' own anger toward their child has been
turned against themselves. In the process
they can be helped to see that their guilt
actually has a destructive effect on their
child.

Honesty with parents, however, should
not be confused with bluntness. It is better
to say, "You're trying too hard to be a good
mother," than "Get off his back!" If a
mother can say herself, "You mean I
should get off his back," she can then be
pleased with her ability to contribute to
ways of solving her son's problems. The
aim is to help parents find their own solutions. As a result, professionals may not
receive credit for their insights, but their
rewards come later in the form of improvement in the family and child, as in the following example:

When Jerry entered the fourth grade, he
needed to improve in neatness, prompt-
ness, and schoolwork.

At his first school conference, Jerry's
parents decided to move in on the situation. They put him on a supervised home-

work schedule and pointed out to him
whenever possible that at the rate he was
going he would never amount to anything. This concentration on Jerry lasted
for only two weeks. Then in January
Jerry's parents were warned that he would
be required to repeat the fourth grade
unless there was marked improvement in
his schoolwork. His parents felt angry,
ashamed, guilty, and disgraced. They
wondered how they would explain this to
their friends whose children were winning awards. As a result Jerry's father
turned on him with a tongue lashing.
Later, still furious, his father tore up
Jerry's homework because it was messy.

Several days later, as they looked back
at the hurtful things they had said to him
and each other, the parents were amazed
that it never once occurred to them to try
to get at the reasons why Jerry was failing.
Jerry's mother then went to see his teacher.
By that time she had convinced herself
that it was the school's fault. What kind
of place was it, she was primed to ask, that
could not get a bright nine-year-old
through fourth grade? The teacher anticipated her, however, by showing that
Jerry was resisting school every inch of
the way. He lost his assignments on his
way home from school, heard the teacher
wrong when he took tests, and forgot
arithmetic that he had known since second grade.

Worried now that there might be
something seriously wrong with Jerry, his
parents saw the school psychologist, much
as they disliked discussing a family problem with a stranger. The psychologist
shared her impression that the parents
were busy people and asked if their children were as busy as their parents. She
then asked if they ever get into a jam when
they plan to do too much in an afternoon
and run late, get a frantic feeling, and
then find that everything goes wrong.
Suddenly his parents saw Jerry in a new
light—a child spinning hopelessly in the
frenzied life they had created for him.

Thereafter his parents continued to

work with Jerry on his homework but in a different atmosphere. They were no longer fighting but helping him. Their impatience and irritation were gone. They no longer pushed goals they had set for themselves, pretending they were for Jerry. Instead they gave him support to find his own strengths and build upon them. They set off a chain reaction. As Jerry saw he was valued for himself and not for grades in school, he began to feel more confident about himself. Soon his grades improved, and his parents could relax about him and themselves. They did not change their own lives in any major way, but somehow they no longer felt harrassed. Jerry was promoted to the fifth grade.

FAMILY THERAPY

A child's poor schoolwork may be a cry for help in family relationships. If the family's request for help is ignored, the school may be left with a refractory educational problem and an angry child, who may continue to fail until someone finally gets the message. In most instances, when children fail in school, some form of family therapy is warranted.

The goal of family therapy is to change structures and processes in the family or in its environment so as to relieve existing strains (Miller & Miller, 1980). Family diagnosis based on living systems theory makes it possible to determine whether pathology lies in a family as a whole, in one or more individual members, or in a suprasystem, such as an economically disadvantaged neighborhood or a school with limited resources.

The range of interventions available to families is considerable. The health, mental health, social service, pastoral care, and educational systems all deal with family problems. The field of marriage counseling has specifically focused on one aspect of the family, and family service agencies handle all aspects of the family. For faltering families the marital relationship is the most important focus; marriage counseling or marital couple therapy may be useful. For families with more serious problems, self-help groups such as Alcoholics Anonymous, Parents Without Partners, and Parents Anonymous are available in most communities. Child psychiatrists deal with the range of child, adolescent, and family problems.

The fit between clinical resource and a family is critical. Ethnic and economic factors may override psychological issues. Every clinical resource sets some limit on the range of factors it can work with in both diagnosis and therapy. These limits evolve out of the history peculiar to a given clinical setting, the training backgrounds of professionals, the socioeconomic surroundings, and the nature of the social pressures.

Motivating Families for Therapy

Professionals should be sensitive to the misunderstanding, hesitation, and fear in family members as they approach help.

Each family member's level of sophistication about psychological problems and openness to using a mental health resource varies. At the least education of the members of the family is required so that an intellectual understanding of the reasons for working with the family can be achieved. This step often is omitted, with resulting misunderstandings.

Troubled families are the most likely to lack insight and even the strength to engage in family therapy. Their defensive maneuvers may be so extreme that engaging the family in therapy may depend upon equally skillful maneuvering by the therapist or the external pressure of agencies, such as the schools and the courts. If given a choice, many of these families would either drop out or limit their involvement to supporting treatment of the identified patient. Their denial and projection are particularly difficult to handle.

Ferreting out the family's expectations of therapy is an important step toward assessing their motivation for change. For example, because *dominated* families involve both family and individual psychopathology, they often lodge their concerns upon a single identified patient. The other family members may not be disposed to see themselves as a part of that person's problem and certainly not as the focus of therapy. When an attempt is made to involve the family, the parents may withdraw and look for someone who will "help" the family member identified as a patient. As a strategy the therapist may need to appear to join the family in its efforts to change the symptom bearer as a means of involving the entire family with the passage of time (Becvar & Becvar, 1982).

Conflicted families usually require intensive family therapy in addition to consultation to other systems, such as the schools, social services, and law enforcement agencies. *Chaotic* families are the most difficult to engage in family therapy because their views of reality are not congruent with their social milieu. Hospitalization, medication, and consultation to other agencies may be necessary in order to provide a foundation for family therapy. Several authors have written in greater detail about engaging these families in therapy (Karpel & Strauss, 1983; Minuchin, 1974; Wynne, 1965; Swift, 1981).

A delicate issue in motivating families for treatment is how to separate a clinician's responsibility to assist the family from the family's responsibility for change. This is a problem especially when other agencies are involved with the family. For example, both school personnel and parents may look to a clinician for answers about a child. In these circumstances the clinician must carefully keep the child and the family in the position of responsibility and work through them for intersystem negotiations. Unsuccessful management of this issue can make the clinician a scapegoat by permitting both the parents and school personnel to expect that the therapist is responsible for changing the child.

From the educator's point of view, it is important to be aware of the complicated role of the family in a child's school problems over which educators and parents find themselves in conflict. Some parents obtain satisfaction from this fight, because they were embittered by their own past unhappy school experience and find this opportunity to retaliate. The child has an especially important role to play in this manipulative struggle. In the battle over who will control the helping process, if the school and clinical team are not coordinated, a family can find a weak link and defeat both. An effective position for school personnel in these situations is to recognize that no one can help the child until everyone works together.

The Techniques of Family Therapy

The theories and techniques employed by family therapists vary widely (Gurman & Kniskern, 1981; Nichols, 1984). The growing use of general systems theory, however, is providing a rationale for integrating them.

The aims of family therapy are to promote the basic functions of the family (Westman, 1984). Forming a family unit assists adults in appropriately disengaging from their families of origin. The functions of a family relate to intimacy between family members in the form of attachment bonds and empathic communication, which can be fostered through increasing sensitivity to others and risking exposure of one's personal vulnerability. As the heart of the socialization process, the family is the vehicle for imparting cultural customs and values through the process of identification and through learning coping skills. The family also is the forum for safely expressing transient irrational emotions and accepting them from others. In the family the irrationality of life can be accepted by acknowledging the differences between the way things should be and the way they are, between expectations and reality, and between verbalizing socially unacceptable emotions and wishes and acting upon them.

The barriers to healthy family functioning are stereotyped roles enacted by family members based upon covert scripts that are incongruent with family functions. Examples of these roles are victim, martyr, hero, tyrant, scapegoat, saint, rebel, fool, and genius. These roles are played out from ritualized scripts that maintain immature, destructive relationships and frustrate the individuation and development of family members. Family therapy creates awareness of these counterproductive scripts and roles through confrontation, interpretation, playfulness, and humor in order to foster flexibility in family members within legitimate family roles.

The techniques of family therapy include behavioral (Willis & Lovaas, 1977; Barkley, 1981), structural (Horewitz, 1979; Minuchin, 1974), and intuitive methods (Neill & Kniskern, 1982). The accumulation of clinical experience is demonstrating the usefulness of employing a range of techniques in an integrated style of therapy (Lebow, 1984). The family therapist can assist families to more realistically function by acting as a catalyst, who facilitates interaction; a critic, who describes behavior; a teacher, who shows new ways; a supporter, who gives license and hope; an interpreter, who offers explanations of behavior; a provocateur, who stimulates interaction; and a model, who demonstrates solving problems.

Because of its highly structured nature, the Milan method of family therapy has been employed for training purposes (Selvini Palazzoli et al, 1978; Tomm, 1984). It involves a therapeutic team that helps families through confronting them with more realistic views of their family interactions while encouraging family members to achieve more adaptive levels of relating to each other.

The Process of Family Therapy

Once a family becomes engaged in the therapeutic process, a varied and exciting course of growth may ensue, or the process itself may be impeded by resistance that must be worked through in order to achieve the aims of therapy.

Family members usually have linear cause-and-effect views of what goes on in the family. For example, "Jimmy's restlessness gets us all upset." The aim of family therapy is to shift the level of understanding from this simplistic and partially correct view to an interactional system level. An important technique for accomplishing this is through encouraging family members to comment on each other's relationships in the family. This both opens up communication and focuses attention on interactions within the family.

Through a variety of reframing statements additional information can be given to a family to encourage more accurate interactional and psychodynamic understandings of the determinants of symptoms in family members. For example, the success that a child achieves through failing in school and sabotaging adults can be contrasted with the view of the child's behavior as simply negative. As a family grapples with a child's problem, their frustrations and discomforts become evident and permit redefinition of the problem in terms of family members' personal sufferings rather than the problem child's behavior. New communication lines can be opened, so that an awareness of the family's role in a child's educational difficulties can add a crucial dimension to helping the child. The family can then realistically support the educational program for their child and assume a parent–professional alliance with school personnel (Kline & Kline, 1973).

Some parents, however, remain involved in the genesis and perpetuation of their children's school problems (Peck, 1971; Ziegler & Holden, 1988). Handicapped by inflexibility, this kind of family is stable and inclined to deny the educational problem and becomes upset when the severity of the problem diminishes (Miller & Westman, 1966).

In troubled families the *double bind* is a frequently encountered interactional pattern that can have devastating consequences for family members enmeshed in it. In essence the double bind is a covert relationship in which one person has power over the other, who cannot escape. It has two important components. The first consists of paradoxical injunctions in which the less powerful member of the dyad is given conflicting messages either through impossible injunctions, for example, "be spontaneous," or through the nonverbal contradiction of verbal messages, for example, a parent's statement "don't worry about me" in an anxious tone of voice. The second component occurs over time in which the paradoxical injunctions lead to repetitive behavior patterns. The participants provoke the very behavior from each other that they deplore through incongruous behavior. For example, a mother criticized her silent daughter and encouraged here to express her feelings. When she did, however, the mother broke into tears with, "How can you feel that way after all I have done for you?" Then the daughter became silent, eliciting her mother's criticism again, because she was not speaking.

During therapy these resistant families act like well-drilled teams. When interviewed together family members may feel persecuted, become confused, find it hard to think of anything to say, be preoccupied with and silent about the same secret, agree on a fabricated version of a touchy incident, or start arguing with one another and then blame the therapist for upsetting them.

These families typically employ power plays that maintain the status quo. For example, one set of parents nagged their adolescent son into being a "good boy." To qualify he had to be passive, compliant, infantile, and sexless. When he rebelled his mother histrionically went to bed with intense heart pains, presumably induced by the son, and the father expressed the horror of one who had sired a homicidal son. Another mother coached her son in reading even though the drills ended with both in tears and obviously impeded her son's motivation to learn. Other parents are so punitive when their children get poor grades that the children retaliate by failing even more.

A specific aim of one family script is to maintain the symptom. As an illustration one family with a retarded reader convinced their son that he was doing as well as might be expected in view of his presumed limited intelligence. They denied clinical reports that his intelligence was normal and disparaged the validity of the tests. Another aim of a family script is to maintain the acceptability of the family's public image. For example, a family maintained the image of cheerful cooperativeness with no problems apart from their son's retardation in reading.

Scripts also protect a family's secrets. For example, when one son began to talk about the "skeleton in the closet" in a family session, the others started conversations on unrelated subjects. If he persisted, they continued to divert the discussion to peripheral topics or tried to talk him out of his opinion.

Some children improve in schoolwork while acquiring a new emotional or behavioral problem. In this maneuver the children maintain their scapegoat functions in their families and do not have to deal with upsets, which would follow relinquishing their problem roles. Thus they help keep their families from become unstable. If the new problem is addressed therapeutically, the members of these families close ranks. They offer carefully reasoned excuses for missing appointments. They accuse therapists of using ineffectual treatment methods and may discontinue therapy. One parent simply said, "I can't stand any more talk about me. If we have to do that, I would rather have Bryan stay in special ed."

PARENT EDUCATION

Parents benefit from insight into their children's problems, but insight alone is not enough. They need help in learning to change the emotional climate in the home (Missildine, 1975; Kozloff, 1979).

Parent-guidance materials are important means of assisting parents to understand and to cope with a child's characteristics (Cameron, 1978; Miezio, 1983). Training in parenting skills also is useful (Forehand et al, 1984). This is particularly needed in developing communication skills through listening, talking with children, and verbal problem solving as employed in Parent Effectiveness Training (Gordon, 1978). Effective communication is basic to the survival of all groups including families. More specific behavioral management techniques have been developed for hyperkinetic children (Barkley, 1981). Literature is available to help parents play a more significant role in their children's schoolwork (Miller, 1981; Rich, 1988).

Fostering communication between parent and child through early parent training can produce substantial gains in the competencies of children (Garber & Garber, 1988; Shearer & Shearer, 1976). This confirms earlier demonstrations of the superior performance of foster home compared to institutionally raised children (Skodak & Skeels, 1949; Skeels, 1966). Another example is in the early diagnosis of blindness and teaching a parent how to stimulate a blind baby through other sensory channels. The blind infant in turn responds, and a parent child dialogue is established reducing the risk of complicating autism (Freedman, 1979).

Infants and young children with difficult temperamental styles may cause their parents to feel threatened and inadequate with resulting unconscious rejection or scapegoating of the child. A difficult child and threatened parents, therefore, can set in motion a cyclic interaction that makes the child increasingly vulnerable (Lambert, 1982). With older children parents need help in examining their child-rearing techniques. Viewing themselves interacting with their children on videotapes can be particularly useful (Bernal, 1969). They may unwittingly reinforce behavior problems through attention to misbehavior, double messages, failing to set limits, ignoring desired behaviors, and inappropriate punishment, all of which result in losing a child's respect. Although striving for consistancy is a laudable objective, still there are times when parental authority must be arbitrary and so acknowledged with children.

To effect a climate of communication, parents can motivate their children by helping them to analyze their own behavior and select target behaviors for change (Patterson, 1976). Family meetings are useful for exercising the democratic process, so that each member participates in decision making within appropriately defined limits. When the atmosphere in family meetings is conducive to discussion of problems with openness and dignity, parents can appreciate the importance of changing their own attitudes and listening to their children more carefully. Parent modeling of self-discipline, forgiveness, and a willingness to acknowledge mistakes promotes similar qualities in their children.

Motivating a child toward making a commitment to change depends on age, level of development, and a child's desires. When children have not yet become self-motivating, they need feedback to assist them in developing adaptive behavior. Negative feedback is a message that the output has reached some predetermined level and is an indication to cut off or reduce inputs. For example, limit setting is negative feedback when it stops disruptive behavior. Conversely positive feedback is the signal that output is less than desired as when a parent stimulates a child to do more homework through praise. Feed-forward is increasing output by gratifying the underlying motivation, for example, finding activities a child likes (Becvar & Becvar, 1982). Older children react favorably to rewards that symbolize greater maturity and merit respect. Younger children need more tangible reinforcements. Whatever form rewards take, they should be given only after attaining agreed-upon specific objectives.

Parents can profit from an understanding of the dynamics of sibling relationships in which a mixture of pleasure, affection, hostility, aggression, jealousy, rivalry, and frustration is freely expressed. The rivalrous aspects often are emphasized, however, the warmth of a close relationship between siblings is an important source of strength throughout life (Dunn & Kendrick, 1982). The sibling relationship can be profoundly important in shaping the development of social skills. It is a relationship of poignancy and power that has been underestimated.

Children who have siblings with educational problems need support to deal with their own feelings that arise as a consequence of their sibling's functional and educational disabilities. Many siblings experience anger and frustration at a brother or sister who takes so long to do things, demands and receives so much attention, is a pest, seems to get away with many things, and does not seem to share in household chores. Siblings also may experience guilt over the anger they feel, because they are not the one with the problem. Shame and embarrassment arise in response to hearing others calling their sibling "mental" or "retard." Then they must deal with their own feelings of hurt and anger; they also must decide whether to defind their siblings or join in condemnation.

Professionals are in a strategic position to help if there is ongoing contact with siblings of a particular child. Siblings can be assisted in managing their feelings, discussing how to deal with an affected brother or sister, and responding to what other children say and do.

PARENTS AS CHILD ADVOCATES

All children require advocates, and most have them in the form of their parents, who assume the responsibility to act on behalf of their children (Westman, 1979a). When this is done in an organized fashion for a general group of children, class advocacy takes place.

Under optimal circumstances the parents of children with problems in school should be sufficiently well informed and assertive to ensure that their children's needs are met in their schools and communities. Professionals can be helpful in producing and supporting this level of parental advocacy. Parents need varying degrees of assistance in achieving this result. Thus parents can play a key role in helping schools to understand the special education needs of their children (Lillie & Place,

1983). They also can participate directly through obtaining supplementary tutoring (Rosner, 1979).

Unfortunately many school administrators and teachers are limited in time and professional knowledge. They must respond to the needs of most children and cannot devote the time required by children with special needs. Consequently, parents may be reluctant to insist upon adequate help for their child. Still parents must keep in close touch with their child's teacher and may need to make the first move in establishing communication in order to minimize the consequences of compounding frustration for their child when school difficulties are reported to them through routine channels late in the school year (Stevens, 1980). Coordinating the management of children's behavior at home and in school is critical (Kozloff, 1974; 1979).

Parents should be prepared for a long and sometimes frustrating struggle, but one that can be won through persistence and drawing upon community resources, including organizations such as the Association for Children with Learning Disabilities and the Orton Dyslexia Society. Mental health professionals, including psychiatrists, social workers, psychologists, and public health nurses, also can be asked to help.

SUMMARY

The aim of professional work with families should be to form a parent–professional alliance and assist parents to be effective advocates for their children with educational problems. This can be carried out by establishing a working alliance through which child and family can effectively utilize educational interventions.

Parents vary in their states of readiness to form an alliance with professionals. They may deny the existence of a problem, focus exclusively on an aspect of their child's behavior, mistrust professionals, or be ready to enter collaborative teamwork. The readiness of families for a working alliance is related to the family's level of functioning, which may be *healthy* or *faltering* and open to alliance formation. Family therapy usually is required to form alliances with troubled families, which can be described as *dominated, conflicted,* or *chaotic.* For these families therapy can unravel pathological patterns and promote successful child-rearing techniques, open communication, and healthy family functioning. Just as do children, families can resist professional efforts to help them for reasons that may not be evident, except as uncovered and dealt with through the process of family therapy.

When a working alliance has been established, education of the family members can be carried out so that they become knowledgeable team members in managing their child's problem. The form of parent education indicated ranges from basic child rearing to sophisticated knowledge of a child's particular barriers to learning in school. After a parent–professional alliance has been formed, a child's problems can be dealt with in the light of objective knowledge of their nature, origins, and treatment needs.

To a greater or lesser degree, all children with learning problems in school rely upon their parents to be advocates for them. Parents are in a key position to gain the expertise needed as knowledgeable team members to interpret their children's needs to the various professionals encountered by their children over the years. They are crucial in helping their children explain their difficulties to others as well.

IX

Conclusion

We are still waiting for the revolution in educational technique that will make children willing collaborators instead
of grudging accomplices in the marshalling and structuring
of their intellectual powers. How can something so natural
as learning be made to seem so hostile?

Sydney Harris, 1985

The quest for a button to push to resolve a child's learning problems in school propels parents, teachers, and researchers to seek simple causes and remedies. Although occasionally rewarding, the search for a pill, diet, computer technique, or the right words to say usually is disappointing.

However, when the efforts of children match the efforts of adults to help them in school, excitement and hope result. This occurs when children understand their functional and educational disabilities, so that they can draw upon the enormous reserves of power for learning that lie in their adaptive instincts.

We know that some children with special talents and opportunities are unsuccessful students but later become successful, even eminent, adults. But most children who fail in school face discouraged, and even embittered, lives; some become burdens on society. Because the tendency of schools is to wait for failure and disruptive behavior before addressing their learning problems, many children must endure frustration and despair until they break down.

Achieving a hopeful outlook for educationally vulnerable children has much to do with social values. Society is managed by adults, who are naturally preoccupied with their own interests. The welfare of the next generation, and even the planet, is not their central concern. In addition the subtle prejudice of agism fosters ignoring the needs of children. Agism makes it possible to place devastating labels on children and to segregate them in ways that adults would not tolerate. In disguised revenge some young people view failure in school and thwarting adult expectations as successes. Children also are prone to misinterpret society's emphasis on pleasure, consumerism, and in-

725

dependence as meaning work is onerous and unfulfilling. Economic disadvantage and differences in cultural values restrict educational opportunities for many children. Thus a child's performance of schoolwork depends upon supportive social values that encourage cooperation with authority figures, that hold out a hopeful future, and that place importance on that child's achievement.

The dominant orientation of society toward linear cause and effect thinking obcures the complexity of problems. This is accompanied by a tendency to attribute responsibility for unpleasant conditions to others and to confuse responsibility with the causes of behavior. As a consequence when children have difficulty in school, there is a readiness to blame children, parents, teachers, clinicians, and the brain itself and to assume that one of them is the cause of the problem. The implication often is that someone else bears the responsibility for changing the child. Furthermore the greater the guilt of any of these persons, the greater is the tendency to seek simple expiating causes. For many the issue of "organic" versus "psychological" causation is crucial. The former appears to absolve them of responsibility and the latter to signify their fault. In fact the multifactorial nature of children's academic learning problems defies single cause explanations. Accordingly there is a great need to elevate research, clinical practice, and education to a multisystem level at which there is no place for single-factor causation and blame.

Fortunately public policy in the United States has been gradually shifting toward a commitment to educating all children. This was signaled by the Education for All Handicapped Children Act of 1975, which encouraged a nationwide focus on children with educational handicaps and reflected the impact of the learning disabilities movement.

In spite of its political value, however, the term learning disability is misleading from the scientific point of view. Whether because of individual differences or pathology, the disabilities actually are in the temperamental, cognitive, language, managerial, and self functions of the central nervous system related to their underlying components, structures, and processes, not learning itself. If we look closely, each of us has strengths and weaknesses in these functions. Moreover, education is essential for optimal central nervouse system (CNS) development and can compensate for damage to brain tissue, when instructional methods are matched to central nervous system functions. Thus the term functional disability has both scientific and pragmatic advantages over learning disability. It calls attention to the possibility of identifying specific functions of the CNS for research, clinical, and educational purposes.

The model of the CNS described in this book facilitates the identification of functional disabilities, as they influence learning and work styles. As such functional disabilities often are responsive to change, because the redundancy of the brain's resources permits strengthening of, and compensation for, weak functions. When this is not possible, they can be accepted as limitations to acquiring a particular skill. Functional disabilities vary in severity and duration and may have intermittent rhythms. They are affected by stress as well.

When it interferes with schoolwork, a functional disability becomes an educational disability. Educational disabilities can be viewed as psychophysiological disorders, because they involve a vulnerable target organ, personality factors, and stressors. Their underlying functional disabilities reflect the vulnerability of the target organ, the brain; the levels of character and self development contribute to the personality factors; and social, classroom, and family pressures constitute the stressors.

Unlike learning disability, the concept of educational disability places a child's problems squarely within the context of school. Children who fail in school often do so because they do not successfully assume the roles of students. The capacity for work is an essential component of the student role. Since the capacity to work has strong genetic and cultural supports, we are dealing largely with interferences with, rather than the absence of, the ingredients of the ability to work. This perspective sharply contrasts with a view of vulnerable children as incapable of academic learning. It emphasizes the potential for alleviating their inhibitions and cultivating compensatory abilities.

Self-defeating attitudes are major barriers to learning in school. Children who lack a sense of purpose and self-discipline avoid work and seek easy gratification. Children who "know it all" lack curiosity and are threatened by criticism. Children who fear ridicule for mistakes shun schoolwork. Children preoccupied with family problems lose interest in school. In contrast industrious and creative children succeed in spite of their disabilities.

The term educational disability applies to a child's difficulty in acquiring academic skills. An educational handicap exists when an educational disability results in a child's inability to perform academic tasks in the educational mainstream. The concept of educational handicap invokes the possibilities of minimizing the handicap or of adjusting expectations of that child. It also directs attention to the educational task as distinct from the social and ecological atmosphere of the classroom. Many children are regarded spuriously as educationally handicapped, because their performance of schoolwork is adversely affected by the nature of their classrooms rather than their inability to perform the academic tasks themselves.

The concept of educational handicap also is useful, because it brings to bear all that we know about the psychologically damaging effects of the handicap label and encourages caution in applying it. As we know from the experience of the blind and the physically disabled, the term handicap should be used precisely and with respect for its impact on a person's self-concept.

As is society generally, schools continually are confronted with conflicts between the interests of an individual and the group. Schools obviously cannot accommodate to each child in all respects, but much can be done to help children with special needs. First of all mainstream education can be provided in classrooms that recognize common variations in learning and work styles. This in itself reduces the adverse effect of schooling on children who do not have analytic-extrovert learning styles. Second, children who still have problems with school-work can be provided specialized educational services, optimally in the form of academic skill tutoring and in the form of small-group teaching for work style and social skill development.

It is crucial that educational practitioners and researchers have the benefit of contributions from all of the disciplines concerned with children with academic difficulties and of relevant knowledge from the biological, psychological, and social sciences. Increasingly sophisticated techniques offer promise, such as split-brain studies of cerebral hemisphere specialization, computerized cortical-evoked potentials, biochemical research on neurotransmitters, postmortem anatomical studies, computerized radiology of the brain, psychological studies of time and space, and the systematic analysis of interpersonal transactions.

The guidelines for defining functional and educational disabilities described in this book offer a language for communication between professional disciplines and for characterizing research samples. At the present time, our diagnostic understanding of children is based largely on their behavioral characteristics. Progress in our knowledge of CNS functions can bring more etiologically based classifications. Furthermore, because of the interplay of CNS substems, it is not necessary to specify primary causation. We do not need to conclude that emotional symptoms or behavioral signs are secondary to a particular disability or to conclude that a disability is the result of primary psychological conflicts. The motives for assigning primary causation to a specific factor are political, administrative, and psychologically defensive, not scientific.

There is reason to be optimistic about future advances in research, but we need not wait for breakthroughs. The facts that the brain is the organ of the mind and that behavior is based upon the cellular and chemical components of the brain have been known for years. More importantly, the tools already are available for effective treatment. There also is sufficient knowledge of epidemiological risk, psychosocial strategies, and prevention for effective action. Unfortunately, professionals have not used existing knowledge. Clinicians and educators suffer from the lack of the common framework exemplified by this book and have not taken advantage of the principles and procedures of the clinical process. It they do so, their cooperative efforts can be more efficient and fruitful.

The clinical process is a developmentally based diagnostic understanding of an individual child and that child's family with a treatment plan monitored over time. It creates a therapeutic team in which the child is the central participant by drawing upon the multiple systems impinging upon that child. This integration provides maximum leverage for change in the child's performance of schoolwork and personal growth. The child-centered team operates for as long as needed with the expectation that parents will continue in strengthened advocacy roles for their children.

The barriers to learning in school exist at many levels within and outside of children. However, the failure to develop a child-centered team involving family, school personnel, and professionals in the health, mental health, social service, and, occasionally, legal systems has been the most important barrier. Training in the multisystem approach and the clinical process is needed for all professionals who work with children, and even could reduce the number of professionals needed in schools.

The child-centered team offers an understanding of the nature of a child's assets and vulnerabilities. The clinical process can identify functional disabilities in temperament, cognition, language, personal management, and the self. The ambiguous term learning disability then can be replaced by descriptions of specific functional disabilities in one or more of these areas. The clinical process also can help make judgments about when a functional disability constitutes an educational disability or handicap. The goal is to discover what a child can and cannot do easily in order to capitalize on strengths and shore up weaknesses. When a child knows these things and others understand and support that child, changes can occur through the child's sustained efforts. The aim is not determining what adults should do to a child, but what a child can do for oneself with adult guidance and support.

We are moving into a new age in which the learning potentials of even the most handicapped individuals are being recognized. We know that children vary in reading and ciphering talents, as they do in musical and athletic aptitude. We can help children who encounter difficulty working in school by identifying their functional and educational disabilities before they become educational handicaps. We have paid too much attention to what children cannot do and not enough to what they can do. We must convert their presently insurmountable barriers into surmountable hurdles.

Glossary

Abstract Having a quality that cannot be perceived by the senses.

Acalculia The inability to do arithmetical calculations.

Achievement level The grade level of performance on standardized tests of basic academic skills.

Accommodation Eyes: focusing by the lens; Piaget: restructuring of schemes for processing new information.

Acting out A defense mechanism through which repressed impulses are expressed without conscious awareness.

Acuity The discrimination accuracy of a sensory modality.

Adrenergic Pertaining to the action of epinephrine (adrenalin) or norepinephrine (noradrenalin).

Affect The current state of the affective system; mood.

Afferent From the peripheral nerves to the central nervous system and from the axon to the cell body.

Agenesis The failure of a body structure to appear in embryonic development.

Agnosia The inability to recognize the meaning of perceptions.

Agraphia The inability to write.

Akathisia Uncontrollable bodily restlessness; an extrapyramidal side effect of psychoactive medications.

Alexia The inability to read.

Allele Alternative forms of a gene, such as for determining blue or brown eyes.

Alimentary Pertaining to the organs that process food.

Ambivalence The simultaneous existence of conflicting emotions, as of love and hate toward the same person or activity.

Amblyopia Loss of vision from disuse of an eye, as from strabismus.

Amnesia Loss of the ability to retrieve memories.

Amniocentesis The removal of fluid surrounding a fetus by a hypodermic needle for testing purposes.

Amphetamines Stimulant drugs similar to epinephrine.

Amusica The inability to produce or recognize musical sounds.

Analog measurement Measurement by using a form of output that indirectly reflects another form of input, as in a mercury thermometer or a pointer meter.

Androgens Hormones that stimulate the male sex organs, such as testosterone.

Angiogram (cerebral) The x-ray study of blood distribution in the brain by injecting radiopaque die.

Angular gyrus A visual memory center in the patietal lobe that forms and stores associations between words and sounds.

Anhedonia Diminished ability to experience pain and pleasure.

Animism Magically attributing life to inanimate objects.

Anoxia Oxygen content of the blood below the level needed to maintain cellular functioning.

Antibody An immunoglobulin molecule that interacts only with the antigen that induced its production by lymphoid tissue.

Anticholinergic Antagonistic to the action of acetylcholine.

Antigen A substance that induces the formation of antibodies that may produce allergic reactions.

Aphasia The inability to comprehend (receptive or Wernicke's) or express (expressive or Broca's) words.

Apraxia The inability to perform purposeful movements: kinetic—fine motor actions; ideomotor—acting spontaneously; ideational—putting together the steps of an activity; constructional —reproducing figures by drawing.

Apnea Cessation of breathing.

Articulation The enunciation of words.

Assimilation Piaget: processing information in terms of existing knowledge.

Associated movements Involuntary movements that accompany the movements of other muscles, such as swinging the arms while walking.

Association cortex The major portion of the cerebral cortex that is neither sensory nor motor in which symbolization and conceptualization take place.

Astereognosis The inability to recognize objects by touching or holding them.

Atavistic Resembling a primitive type.

Ataxia Impaired coordination of muscular movements.

Athetoid Slow, writhing involuntary muscle movements.

Atonia Deficient muscular tone.

Atrophy Wasting in size of a cell, organ, or body part.

Audiogram A graphic representation of the weakest sounds heards at different frequency levels.

Auditory Pertaining to the sense of hearing.

Aura The imagery that precedes a seizure.

Aural Pertaining to hearing speech.

Autistic Extreme preoccupation with internal imagery.

Autoimmune An immune response to the body's own tissue.

Autonomy Functioning independently.

Autosome A chromosome other than the X and Y sex chromosomes.

Avoidance Conscious or unconscious defensive action to escape distress.

Babbling Speech sounds that do not convey meaning to the listener.

Barbiturates A class of drugs that act as central nervous system depressants; in street parlance: "downers."

Basal ganglia The collective term for the nuclei overlying the thalamus that modulate movement and sensory information, including the caudate nucleus, putamen, globus pallidus, and substantia nigra.

Basal metabolic rate (BMR) The calories per kilogram of body weight per hour produced at rest.

Behavior Any externally observable action of a living system.

Behavior modification A systematic method for altering behavior.

Benign Favorable prognosis.

Biofeedback Utilizing information about a body function to aid modifying it, for example, heart rate and urination.

Biopsy The excision of a piece of tissue for diagnostic purposes.

Bipolar disorder Manic-depressive affective disorder.

Blindisms Repetitive, stereotyped movements observed in blind children, such as eye rubbing and rocking.

Brainstem The lowest portion of the brain that regulates visceral, arousal, and reflexive sensorimotor functions.

Brain waves Fluctuating electrical potentials recorded from the brain by surgery or from the scalp by an electroencephalogram.

Buccolingual Pertaining to the cheek and tongue.

Bureaucrat A government official who carries out policies through regulations and routines.

Canalization An innate process in which genes create brain functions that serve instincts.

Catastrophic reaction The disorganized panic response to overwhelming stressors.

Catecholamines A class of chemicals having sympathomimetic actions, including dopamine, epinephrine, and norepinephrine.

Cenesthesia The mass of visceral sensations that make one aware of one's affective state, as in the feeling of health, illness, and discomfort.

Cerebellum The portion of the brain

consisting of two hemispheres above and behind the medulla that maintains postural and sensorimotor coordination.

Cerebral cortex The convoluted outer layer of gray matter of the cerebral hemispheres.

Cerebral dominance When one cerebral hemisphere leads the other in governing a brain function.

Cerebral palsy A persisting motor disorder appearing before the age of three due to nonprogressive damage to the brain.

Cerebrospinal fluid The fluid that fills the spaces in and around the brain and spinal cord.

Cerebrum The two cerebral hemispheres and the corpus callosum.

Character The relatively enduring central nervous system functions that make up the infrastructures of personality.

Cholinergic Relating to the action of acetylcholine.

Choreiform Involuntary, jerking muscle movements.

Chromosome A filament in a cell nucleus that contains the genes; a normal human cell contains 46.

Chronic brain syndrome A relatively irreversible disorder resulting from damage to brain tissue manifested by memory loss, disorientation, and emotional lability.

Chronological age (CA) Age of an individual based upon birthdate.

Circadian Occurring approximately every 24 hours.

Class action Litigation on behalf of a group of individuals with common interests.

Clonic Involuntary rapid muscular contractions and relaxations.

Cluttering Rapid, erratic, indistinct speech.

Compensation A defense mechanism that devises a substitute for a real or imagined inadequacy.

Compulsion Repetitive, stereotyped actions that express obsessions.

Concrete Having a form that can be perceived by the senses.

Concrete thinking Thinking based upon the imagery of perceptions without symbolization or conceptualization.

Condensation The fusion of symbols and concepts to produce a new symbol or concept.

Conditioning Learning in which a response is elicited by a neutral stimulus that previously had been repeatedly presented with another stimulus that originally elicited the response.

Congenital Present at birth.

Consent (informed) Freely given consent for a specific completely described procedure given by a person capable of understanding the information.

Contralateral The opposite side.

Control group A group of subjects comparable in every possible respect to an experimental group except that an intervention is not applied to it.

Conversion The defense mechanism through which neurotic conflict is resolved by the alteration of voluntary motor or sensory functions.

Cortical Pertaining to the cerebral cortex.

Cortical-evoked potential The electroencephalographic response to a sensory stimulus.

Cortisol A glucocorticoid hormone of the adrenal cortex.

Counterphobic Behavior through which feared situations or objects are sought.

Countertransference Inappropriate personal reactions in a psychotherapist to a patient's psychopathology or behavior.

Cranial circumference The external measurement of head size that averages 48 centimeters at age two and 55 centimeters at age 18.

Cretinism Mental retardation resulting from hypothyroidism in early life.

Criterion referenced test A test that compares performance with predetermined objectives rather than other persons.

Culture The values and customs that communicate, perpetuate, and evolve attitudes toward life.

Culture-fair Minimizing biases resulting from socioeconomic and cultural factors.

Curriculum A specific course of study or all of the courses in a school.

Cybernetic Pertaining to systems that control information processing in organisms and machines.

Decibel A unit of sound intensity.

Decoding Deciphering symbols.

Deduction Drawing specific conclusions from general principles.

Defense mechanism An unconscious operation that achieves a compromise between instinctual demands and the restrictions of the external world.

Déjà vu The feeling that one has had a new experience before.

Delusion A fixed false belief.

Dementia General structural mental deterioration.

Demographic Statistics on human geographical, environmental, community, and personal events and places.

Denial A defense mechanism through which past or present perceptions are blocked from conscious awareness.

Deoxyribonucleic acid (DNA) The chemical that forms the genetic code in cell nuclei and directs the synthesis of proteins.

Depersonalization A feeling of unreality and estrangement from one's self, body, or surroundings.

Development The process of growth resulting from the interaction of brain maturation and environmental experience.

Developmental delay A disparity in the rate of development in a particular function compared with a norm.

Dexamethasone A synthetic analog of cortisol used in a test for major depression.

Dichotic Input to each ear separately.

Didactic Formal classroom teaching.

Digital measurement Directly representing information through extension or magnification, such as an electroencephalographic tracing.

Digraph Two letters that represent a single sound, for example, *ea* in read and *sh* in show.

Dimorphism Physical or behavioral differences associated with sex.

Diphthong Two vowel sounds as a single phoneme, for example, *ou*.

Discrimination The detection of differences between stimuli.

Disadvantaged Deprived of material resources or education by lack of opportunity.

Displacement A defense in which the aim of a drive is shifted to a substitute object.

Dissociation A defense mechanism in which subsystems of the self are separated from each other without conscious awareness.

Distractibility An inability to fix attention on a sequence of stimuli.

Dorsal The top of the brain or the back of the body.

Double-blind The alternation of a placebo with a drug without the awareness of the investigator and patient in order to compare their effects.

Down syndrome (mongolism, trisomy 21) A syndrome resulting from a chromosomal abnormality manifested by varying degrees of mental retardation, a mongoloid physical appearance, muscular hypotonia, and often congenital heart disease.

Dysarthria Articulation defect due to inadequate control of the speech muscles.

Dyscalculia Difficulty with arithmetic.

Dysdiadochokinesis Impaired ability to perform rapid alternating movements.

Dysgenesis Partial failure of parts of the body to develop.

Dysgraphesthesia Difficulty in recognizing symbols traced on the skin.

Dyskinesia Impaired coordination of voluntary movements.

Dyslalia Immature articulation.

Dyslexia Difficulty in reading, writing, and spelling words.

Dysnomia Difficulty in naming objects.

Dysphasia Difficulty in finding and expressing words in their proper sequence.

Dysphonia Impaired voice quality.

Dyspraxia Difficulty performing purposeful movements.

Echolalia The imitation of the speech of another.

Echopraxia The imitation of the movements or gestures of others.

Ecology The relations between living organisms and their material environments.

Ectoderm The preembryonic tissue from which the skin and the nervous system are derived.

Efferent Away from the cell body or from the brain to the peripheral nervous system.

Ego The psychoanalytic conception of the executive functions of one's character herein referred to as the information-processing (autonomous ego functions) and managerial systems.

Electrochemical The interplay of chemical and electrical charges.

Elision In pronunciation: the cutting off of a vowel at the end of a word. In neurophysiology: the inhibition of one component of a brain function by another, usually between the cerebral hemispheres.

Embryo The human organism from about the second to the eighth week after conception.

Emotion A more or less genetically programmed transient neural response of the voluntary and autonomic nervous systems reflected in imagery.

Emotional lability The easy arousal and instability of emotions.

Encephalitis Inflammation of brain tissue.

Encoding Translating information into a communicable form.

Encopresis Incontinence of feces without structural defect or illness.

Endocrine glands Ductless glands that secrete hormones directly into the bloodstream.

Endoderm The preembryonic tissue from which the epithelium of the viscera is derived.

Endogenous Originating from within an individual.

Engram The structural basis of memory herein referred to as a scheme.

Entropy That part of energy in a system that is not available to perform work and is irreversibly increasing in the universe according to the second law of thermodynamics.

Enuresis The involuntary discharge of urine during the day (diurnal) and at night (nocturnal).

Epidemiology The relationships of factors that determine the frequency and distribution of characteristics, particularly diseases, in human communities.

Epigenetic The theory of development in which each stage builds anew upon preceding stages.

Ethology The study of animal behavior under natural conditions.

Etiology Cause of a pathological condition.

Excitation In neurophysiology: the stimulation of nerve activity.

Exogenous Originating outside of the individual.

Extrapyramidal The motor aspects of the central nervous system outside of those controlled by the pyramidal cells of the frontal lobe.

Familial Occurring in blood relatives and implying a genetic basis.

Fantasy The use of imagery in the service of defense mechanisms.

Feedback The process by which a system is controlled by its output. Positive feedback is when a fraction of the output increases the activity of the system; negative feedback is the opposite.

Feed forward A type of connection in a system in which information from within the system in addition to input increases the output.

Feral Refers to children raised by animals.

Figure–ground discrimination The ability to attend to one aspect of a visual field and perceive its relationship to the rest of the field.

Finger agnosia The inability to identify the individual fingers of one's hand.

Fixation An arrest of an aspect of development at an earlier stage.

Functional Refers to a definable function of the central nervous system.

Gait The manner of walking or running.

Galvanic skin response Electrical changes of the skin following stressor stimuli.

Gene The fundamental chromosomal unit of inheritance composed of DNA.

Genotype The underlying genetic make-up of an individual.

Gestalt The unified whole whose properties cannot be derived simply by adding up the parts.

Gifted Intellectually talented children sometimes defined as having an IQ above 130.

Grapheme The alphabetical unit that represents a particular spoken sound.

Gray matter Regions of the brain comprised of nerve cell bodies with relatively little myelin so that they have darker appearance.

Guardian ad litem An individual who has the authority to make decisions on behalf of another person in legal actions, particularly in protecting the interests of a child.

Gyrus A convolution of the cerebral cortex.

Habituation Learning not to respond to a stimulus which by meaningless repetition loses significance to the organism.

Hallucination A false perception in which an internal image assumes the vividness of a perception.

Haptic The combined tactile and proprioceptive sense of position involved in writing and stereognosis.

Hemiparesis Partial paralysis of one side of the body.

Heterogeneous Composed of dissimilar members.

Heterozygous Possessing different alleles at a given gene locus on a chromosome.

Heuristic Conducive to discovery particularly through scientific investigation.

Holistic Taking all the parts of a system together.

Homeostasis Maintaining the steady state or an equilibrium in the internal environment of a system through negative feedback.

Homogeneous Composed of similar members.

Homolateral On the same side.

Homozygous A pair of identical alleles at a given gene locus on a chromosome.

Homunculus A figurative representation of the human body in the frontal and parietal lobes.

Hormone A complex chemical substance formed in one body organ and circulated in the bloodstream.

Hydrocephalus Enlargement of the head and compression of the brain due to the excessive pressure of cerebrospinal fluid.

Hypertrophy Enlargement due to an increase in size of constituent cells.

Hyperventilation Prolonged, rapid, deep breathing resulting in the reduction of carbon dioxide tension in the blood and the symptoms of anxiety.

Hypnagogic The partially awake state preceding sleep.

Hypnopompic The partially awake state that follows sleep.

Hypoglycemia An inadequate concentration of glucose in the blood.

Hypoplasia Incomplete cellular proliferation so that an organ fails to reach adult size.

Hypoxic The deficiency of oxygen in inspired air.

Hysterical Neurotic symptoms and behavior based upon conversion, impulsivity, the exaggeration of perceptions, and the simulation of various disorders.

Ictal Pertaining to seizures.

Incidence The number of cases occurring in a population during a certain time period.

Identification The assumption of other person's qualities through the process of accommodation.

Ideograph A written symbol that represents an idea or a thing, as Chinese characters.

Idiopathic Of unknown cause.

Imprinting A species specific rapid form of learning during a critical period of early life in which social bonding is established.

Incestuous Pertaining to sexual intercourse between two persons too closely related to marry legally.

Infanticidal An impulse to kill an infant or child.

Inheritance The acquisition of qualities by transmission from parent to offspring, usually construed as genetic.

Inhibition The restraint of lower centers by excitatory activity of higher centers.

Innate A genetically inherited quality.

Instinct A genetically determined cyclic tendency toward behavior that serves individual or species preservation through canalized sensorimotor schemes.

Instrument A test or inventory for measuring mentation or behavior.

Intellectualization The psychological process in which reasoning is used as a defense against signal anxiety.

Interaction The interplay between variables in which each acts upon the other without changing it.

Introjection The mental operation through which the qualities of other people are internalized.

Ion A charged atom resulting from the gain or loss of electrons.

Isolation The defense mechanism through which emotions are separated from imagery.

Junction The synapse between neurons.

Kernicterus Yellow staining of parts of a newborn's brain because of excessive bilirubin in the blood.

Kindling The gradual buildup of central nervous system activity from repeated subliminal stimuli.

Kinesthetic The proprioceptive muscular sense of movement, weight, and position.

Klinefelter syndrome An abnormality in males in which the sex chromosome is XXY and characterized by small testes.

Korsakoff psychosis An alcoholic chronic brain syndrome characterized by the loss of recent memory, hallucinations, and confabulation.

Lateral Toward the side.

Laterality The ability to discriminate between the two sides of a midline; cerebral hemispheric dominance in a particular function.

Learned helplessness A response to repeated frustration observed in animals and humans in which the individual gives up and withdraws.

Least restrictive environment The legal concept of providing treatment or education that restricts a person's freedom the least of available alternatives.

Lesion Pathological tissue because of trauma, infection, tumor, or anoxia.

Leukopenia Reduction in the white blood cell count below 5000.

Lexicon A person's vocabulary store.

Linear thinking Simple unidirectional cause and effect thinking; contrasts with transactional system thinking.

Linguistic   Pertaining to the study of the structure and development of a language and its relationships to other languages.

Locomotion   Movement from one place to another.

Macula   The central region of the retina that contains the fovea which is the point on which the lens of the eye focuses light.

Marker   An objectively verifiable characteristic used to identify a syndrome.

Masochistic   Sexual gratification from painful or humiliating experiences.

Maturation   The progressive growth of nerve tissue that underlies the development of character.

Medial   Toward the midline.

Meningitis   An infection of the tissues covering the brain and spinal cord.

Meningocele   A protrusion of the membranes of the brain or spinal cord through a defect in the skull or spinal column.

Mental age   The adjusted chronological age level at which an individual performs on intelligence tests; for example, an IQ of 120 for a ten-year-old yields a mental age of 12.

Mesoderm   The preembryonic tissue from which the bone, muscle, circulatory, and connective tissue of the body are derived.

Microcephaly   A head circumference which is more than two standard deviations below the mean for age, sex, and race.

Mixed dominance   A discrepancy between the preferred lateralization of different functions.

Mirror movements   The duplication of voluntary movements of one side of the body by the other.

Modality   A particular form or method, as of sensation or treatment.

Monozygotic   Pertaining to derivation from one egg, as with identical twins.

Morpheme   The smallest meaningful sound of a written language.

Motor   Producing a subserving motion.

Motor impersistence   The inability to sustain a posture or a motor activity.

Motor planning   The ability to conceive, organize, and carry out a sequence of unfamiliar actions; praxis.

Multimodal   Including several methods of treatment.

Multisensory   Employing more than one sensory modality.

Mutism   A refusal or inability to talk.

Myelination   The deposition of the insulating substance myelin around nerve fibers.

Neurobiotaxis   The tendency of nerve cell bodies to move toward their sources of excitation in the process of maturation.

Neuroglia   The supporting and nourishing tissue of neurons.

Neuroleptic drugs   Antipsychotic medications.

Neurosis   An emotional disorder due to unresolved unconscious conflicts with various manifestations related to the predominant defense mechanisms.

Nonverbal ability   Skills that do not involve verbal language, particularly as measured by psychometric subtests.

Norm referenced tests   Measurement of an individual's performance in relation to the performance of others.

Nystagmus   Rapid jerking movement of the eyes.

Object   In psychoanalytic terminology: a person or thing of emotional significance to an individual.

Object permanence   The ability to know that an object continues to exist even when removed from the visual field.

Obsession   Preoccupation with an idea that morbidly dominates the mind, continually suggesting irrational actions.

Occipital   Relating to the back of the head.

Ocular   Pertaining to the eye.

Olfactory   Pertaining to the sense of smell.

Omnipotence   The state of being all powerful, especially the belief that one's wishes will be fulfilled as soon as they are expressed.

Omniscience   All knowing, especially knowing better than everyone else.

Ontogeny   The developmental history of an individual.

Operant conditioning   Learning through positively reinforcing an individual's ongoing behavior.

Operation (Piaget)   The functioning of a scheme, such as adding or classifying.

Orienting response   The initial automatic response to a novel stimulus.

Organic brain syndrome   An identifiable psychiatric disorder caused by temporary or permanent alteration in the cellular (chronic) or electrochemical (acute) structure of the brain.

Orthography   The rules, principles, and conventions by which spoken forms of language are transcribed into written forms.

Otitis media   Inflammation of the middle ear.

Paranoid   Suspicious, persecutory, grandiose attitudes.

Parapsychology   The branch of psychology that deals with experiences that appear to fall outside the scope of physical laws, such as extrasensory perception.

Paroxysmal   Sudden recurrence or intensification of a phenomenon.

Pathognomonic   Characteristic of a disease.

Pathway   In neuroanatomy: a functional route of nerve fibers.

Performance test   A test comprised of items that do not involve verbal language.

Perinatal   Pertaining to the period shortly before and after birth from 28 weeks of gestation to one to four weeks after birth.

Perseveration   Continuation of an activity after cessation of the causative stimulus.

Personality   The behavioral expression of character that differentiates one individual from another.

Pharmacologic   Pertaining to the properties and reactions of drugs in living systems.

Phenotype   An expressed trait resulting from genetic–environmental transaction.

Phobia   A persistent, irrational fear.

Phoneme   The smallest unit of sound in speech.

Phonetics   The study of the production, transmission, and reception of speech sounds.

Phonics   The application of phonetics to teaching reading by sounding out of graphemes.

Phylogenetic   The evolutionary history of a species.

Physiological   The functions of a living organism.

Placebo   An inactive preparation used in controlled studies for comparison with an active preparation.

Plasticity   The capacity of the central nervous system to alter itself in conformity with the environment.

Postnatal   The period immediately following birth.

Postterm (postmature)   Infants born after more than 42 weeks of gestation.

Praxis   The process through which motor acts are planned and carried out.

Prematurity   An infant born after the 27th week and before the 40th week of gestation and weighing between 2.2 and 5.5 pounds.

Prenatal   Existing or occurring prior to birth.

Presynaptic   Parts of the neuron or events before a synapse.

Prevalence   The total number of cases in existence at a certain time in a designated population.

Primary process   A psychoanalytic term for the primitive mode of mental activity characteristic of subcortical processes and the imagery and symbolic stages of development.

Primordial Of the most undeveloped nature.

Prognosis The prediction of the duration, course, and outcome of a certain condition.

Projection A defense mechanism in which one's unacceptable thoughts, traits, or wishes are attributed to other persons.

Prolactin A hormone secreted by the anterior pituitary gland that stimulates the production of milk.

Proprioceptive Sensory information from the muscles, tendons, and the labyrinth concerning movements and position of the body.

Psychoactive Medications that affect the mind and behavior.

Psychopathology A general term that refers to identifiable psychiatric disorder.

Psychoses Any major psychiatric disorder in which the analysis of reality is impaired with varying degrees of social, vocational, and educational disabilities.

Psychotropic Exerting an effect on the mind, usually applied to drugs.

Punishment An aversive stimulus that decreases the frequency of a response.

Pyramidal The motor aspect of the central nervous system controlled by the pyramidal cells of the frontal lobe.

Rationalization The mental process in which a plausible explanation or justification is used as a defense against awareness of forbidden wishes.

Raw score The actual number of items scored as correct on a test; in contrast with a scaled score that is adjusted to norms.

Reaction formation The defense mechanism through which unacceptable wishes are expressed through the opposite attitudes and personality traits.

Reauditorization The ability to retrieve the auditory images of previous perceptions.

Receptor A cell or part of a cell specialized to convert stimuli into responses.

Reflex Automatic, stereotyped, simple behavior elicited by stimuli and independent of volition.

Regimen A procedure intended to produce beneficial effects through specific steps.

Regression Return to the behavior of an earlier stage of development.

Regression effect Tendency for a retest score to be closer to the mean than an initial test score.

Reinforcement Positive: a stimulus that increases or maintains a response. Negative: an aversive stimulus that increases or maintains a response when removed.

Releaser A structure, chemical, sound or action that triggers specific behavior patterns.

Reliability The degree to which a test is consistent in its measurements.

Repression The exclusion from consciousness of images that stimulate anxiety.

Revisualization The ability to retrieve a visual image of a previous perception.

Ribonucleic acid (RNA) The chemical that carries out the instructions of the genetic code in cells.

Role A set of prescribed behavioral expectations within which a person is an actor.

Saccadic The rapid involuntary movements of both eyes simultaneously in changing the point of fixation on a visualized object.

Schizoid Resembling schizophrenia in withdrawn behavior and introspection.

Schizophrenia A group of psychiatric disorders characterized by ambivalence, inappropriate emotions, and the misinterpretation of reality resulting in withdrawn, bizarre, and regressive behavior in addition to delusions and hallucinations.

Screening The use of brief assessments to identify functional and educational disabilities.

Secondary process A psychoanalytic term for the adaptive mode of mental activity characteristic of higher cortical processes and the conceptual and theoretical stages of development.

Semantics   The relation of word meanings to language symbols.

Sensorimotor   Both sensory and motor.

Shaping   A systematic plan of reinforcement to develop new behavior.

Simian   Apelike.

Society   The organization of human activities in the concrete conditions of the environment through social roles.

Somatic   Pertaining to the body exclusive of the visceral organs.

Somatotropic   Having an influence on all of the cells of the body.

Somesthetic   Pertaining to the sensations of pain, touch, pressure, cold, and warmth arising from the skin, muscles, and viscera that produce conscious awareness of one's body.

Spastic   The involuntary contraction of muscles.

Splitting   A psychological term for the splitting off of parts of the self from each other.

Standardized test   A test with empirically selected items, definite directions for administration and scoring, the conversion of raw to normative scores, and demonstrated reliability and validity.

Stereognosis   The ability to recognize the shapes of solids grasped in a hand without vision.

Stereotyped behavior   Complex, repetitive, nonfunctional movements, such as hand movements, rocking, twirling, and head banging.

Stimulus   In physiology: any external agent, state, or change capable of influencing the activity of a cell.

Stimulus bound   An inability to shift away from an ongoing stimulus set.

Strabismus   Failure of the eyes to focus properly on the same point; squint or cross-eye.

Structuralism   The scientific approach that analyzes the basic relatively stable structural elements of systems.

Sublimation   The process of refining instinctual aims to permit their expression in socially acceptable ways.

Subliminal   Below the threshold of conscious sensory awareness.

Substrate   An underlying foundation.

Suppression   Conscious avoidance of unacceptable sensations or images.

Syndrome   A constellation of symptoms and signs that characterize a particular disorder.

Synesthesia   The evoking of imagery of one sensory mode by a stimulus received by another mode, as when a picture evokes sounds.

Synkinesia   Mirror movements.

Syntax   The system of grammar of a particular language, including word order and sentences.

Tachistoscopic   A type of stereoscope in which a movable diaphragm permits brief exposures to visual stimuli.

Tactile   Pertaining to the sense of touch.

Tachycardia   Excessively rapid action of the heart.

Temporal   Pertaining to time; also to near the temples of the skull.

Temporal-sequential   An orientation to the order in which stimuli appear on the dimension of time.

Territoriality   The marking and defense of a particular area against intruders.

Therapeutic milieu   An environment in which interpersonal relationships and events are employed psychotherapeutically.

Time out   A period of time during which an individual is removed from or denied the opportunity to obtain reinforcers; a cooling-off period until a specific state is achieved.

Token reinforcement   The use of attractive rewards to produce desired behavior.

Trait A physical, mental, or behavioral characteristic that distinguishes one person from another.

Transaction The interplay between variables in which each changes the other.

Transduce The transformation of information from one modality to another.

Transference In psychotherapy: the displacement of attitudes, perceptions, and emotions from personally significant persons to the psychotherapist.

Trauma Physical or mental injury that inflicts damage to an individual.

Tremor Continual involuntary, rhythmic, muscular movements.

Unconscious In psychoanalytic terminology: that part of mental activity inaccessible to conscious awareness, except under certain circumstances.

Undoing A defense mechanism through which behavior or images cancel out unacceptable behavior or imagery.

Unilateral One-sided.

Validity The degree of accuracy with which a test measures what it is intended to measure.

Ventral Toward the base of the brain or the underside of an animal.

Verbal test A test in which the ability to understand and use words plays a crucial role in determining a subject's performance.

Visceral Pertaining to the internal organs of the body.

Visual Pertaining to the sense of sight.

Visual-motor coordination The performance of skills involving visual and haptic perception and motor responses.

Visual tracking The ability to follow visual stimuli through space with the eyes.

Vocalization Speaking or singing.

Volition The exercise of intention.

Voyeuristic Sexual gratification from watching or looking at others.

Wernicke's aphasia Abundant nonsensical speech and inability to comprehend the speech of others caused by damage to the posterior language area of the left hemisphere.

White matter The portion of the brain composed principally of neuron fiber tracts that are lighter in color than neuron bodies.

Word attack Analyzing unfamiliar words by sounding them out.

Word finding The ability to associate an image with the correct word at an appropriate rate.

Suggested Readings

FOR STUDENTS

Anatomy and Physiology

Cotman, C. W. & McGaugh, J. L. (1980) *Behavioral Neuroscience: An Introduction.* New York: Academic Press.
> An engaging basic textbook that relates neuroanatomy and neurophysiology to behavior.

Ottoson, D. (1983) *Physiology of the Nervous System.* New York: Oxford University Press.
> An advanced textbook of neurophysiology in the context of the anatomical structure of the brain.

Brain and Mind

Eccles, J. & Robinson, D. N. (1984) *The Wonder of Being Human: Our Brain and Our Mind.* New York: Free Press.
> An eloquent discussion of the brain–mind relationship.

Gedo, J. E. & Goldberg, A. (1973) *Models of the Mind: A Psychoanalytic Theory.* Chicago: University of Chicago Press.
> A concise description of psychoanalytic theory.

Goleman, D. (1985) *Vital Lies, Simple Truths: The Psychology of Self Deception.* New York: Simon & Schuster.
> A vivid description of the role of emotion in information processing.

Hunt, M. (1982) *The Universe Within: A New Science Explores the Human Mind.* New York: Simon & Schuster.
> A clearly written review of the evidence that the brain has characteristics of a computer.

Child Development Theory

Boden, M. A. (1979) *Jean Piaget.* New York: Viking Press.
> A lucid, engaging perspective on Piaget.

Fishbein, H. D. (1976). *Evolution, Development and Children's Learning.* Santa Monica, CA: Goodyear Publishing Co.
> An intriguing approach to the biological and cultural roots of learning.

FOR CLINICIANS AND SPECIAL EDUCATORS

Child Development

Greenspan, S. I. (1979) *Intelligence and Adaptation: An Integration of Psychoanalytic and Piagetian Developmental Psychology.* New York: International Universities Press.
> An integration of Piagetian and psychoanalytic theories.

Kronick, D. (1981) *Social Development of Learning Disabled Persons.* San Francisco: Jossey-Bass Publishers.
> A humane approach to the critical social factors in the lives of educationally disabled and handicapped persons.

Maccoby, E. E. (1980) *Social Development: Psychological Growth and the Parent–Child Relationship.* New York: Harcourt Brace Jovanovich.
> A review of child development in the context of families.

Rosen, H. (1985) *Piagetian Dimensions of Clinical Relevance*. New York: Columbia University Press.

A brief summary of Piaget's key concepts and a review of the literature relating them to psychopathology and psychotherapy.

Shafii, M. & Shafii, S. L. (1982) *Pathways of Human Development: Normal Growth and Emotional Disorders in Infancy, Childhood and Adolescence*. New York: Thieme-Stratton.

A comprehensive overview of child development and psychopathology for clinicians and educators.

Sandler, J., with Freud, A. (1985) *The Analysis of Defense: The Ego and the Mechanisms of Defense Revisited*. New York: International Universities Press.

An update on Anna Freud's seminal formulation of psychological defense mechanisms.

Shaffer, D., Ehrhardt, A. A., & Greenhill, L. L. (Eds.) (1984) *The Clinical Guide to Child Psychiatry*. New York: Free Press.

A reference for the full spectrum of childhood psychiatric disorders.

Clinical Practice

Kinsbourne, D. M. & Caplan, P. J. (1979) *Children's Learning and Attention Problems*. Boston: Little Brown & Co.

A general introduction for clinicians to children's learning problems as seen in medical clinics.

Levine, M. D., Brooks, R., & Shonkoff, J. P. (1980) *A Pediatric Approach to Learning Disorders*. New York: John Wiley & Sons.

A textbook for pediatricians with diagnostic and treatment methods.

Rourke, B. P., Bakker, D. J., Fisk, J. L., & Strang, J. D. (1983) *Child Neuropsychology: An Introduction to Theory, Research and Clinical Practice*. New York: Guilford Press.

An introductory textbook to child neuropsychology.

Rutter, M. (Ed.) (1981) *Scientific Foundations of Child Psychiatry*. Baltimore, MD: University Park Press.

An overview of the basic and clinical sciences upon which child psychiatric practice is based.

Psychoeducational Assessment

Lidz, C. S. (1981) *Improving Assessment of School Children*. San Francisco: Jossey-Bass Publishers.

A guide to the comprehensive assessment of children for school-based professionals.

Mitchell, J. V. (1983) *Tests in Print III*. Lincoln, NB: Buros Institute of Mental Measurements.

A periodically revised comprehensive listing and evaluation of psychological and educational tests.

Sattler, J. M. (1988) *Assessment of Children's Intelligence and Special Abilities* (3rd ed.). San Diego: Jerome M. Sattler.

A basic textbook of psychometric assessment.

Swanson, H. L. & Watson, B. L. (1982) *Educational and Psychological Assessment of Exceptional Children*. St. Louis, MO: C. V. Mosby Company.

A general textbook of psychological and achievement testing; it includes screening tests for teachers and school psychologists.

Special Education

Kavale, K.A., Forness, S.R. & Bender, M. (1987) *Handbook of Learning Disabilities*. Boston, MA: College-Hill Press.

Kirk, S. A. & Chalfant, J. C. (1984) *Academic and Developmental Learning Disabilities*. Denver, CO: Cove Publishing Company.

A practical introduction to techniques in specialized education.

Lerner, J. (1985) *Learning Disabilities: Theories, Diagnosis and Teaching Strategies* (2nd ed.). Boston: Houghton-Mifflin Company.

A useful introductory text to the learning disabilities field.

Pernecke, R. B. & Schreiner, S. M. (1983) (Eds.) *Schooling for the Learning Disabled: A Selective Guide to LD Programs in Elementary and Secondary Education Throughout the United States*. Brookfield, CT: SMS Publishing.

A listing of the various kinds of special education programs for the educationally disabled and handicapped.

Special Problems

Barkley, R. A. (1981) *Hyperactive Children: A Handbook for Diagnosis and Treatment*. New York: Guilford Press.

A description of the behavioral management of hyperkinetic children for professionals and parents.

Thomson, M. (1984) *Developmental Dyslexia*. London: Edward Arnold.

A practical textbook on the developmental dyslexias.

Yule, W. & Rutter, M. (Eds.) (1987) *Language Development and Disorders*. London: MacKeith Press.

A comprehensive coverage of both language development and pathology.

FOR CLASSROOM TEACHERS AND PARENTS

Child Development

Norris, D. & Boucher, J. (1980) *Observing Children*. Toronto: The Board of Education for the City of Toronto, 155 College St., Toronto, Ont. M5T 1P6, Canada.

A concise, readable overview of child development related to elementary- and middle-school curricula.

Perkins, H. V. (1974) *Human Development and Learning* (2nd ed.). Belmont, CA: Wadsworth Publishing Co.

A general introduction to child development written particularly for educators.

Wright, O. M. (1984) *Observing Adolescents*. Toronto: Board of Education for the City of Toronto, 155 College St., Toronto, Ont. M5T 1P6, Canada.

An overview of adolescent development related to the high-school curriculum.

Educational Disabilities in the Classroom

Jordan, D. R. (1977) *Dyslexia in the Classroom* (2nd ed.). Columbus, Ohio: Charles E. Merrill Publishing Company.

A practical guide for the diagnosis and remediation of dyslexias in the classroom.

Stevens, S. H. (1984) *Classroom Success for the Learning Disabled*. Winston-Salem, NC: John F. Blair, Publisher.

A practical guide for making mainstream classroom adjustments for children with learning problems and for creative child management techniques.

Preventive Classroom Teaching

Gordon, T. (1974) *Teacher Effectiveness Training*. New York: Peter H. Wyden.

A practical guide to classroom management and parent relationships.

Greenstein, J. (1983) *What the Children Taught Me*. Chicago: University of Chicago Press.

A highly readable and wise report from the educational trenches.

Hanna, P. R., Hodges, R. E., & Hanna, J. S. (1971) *Spelling: Structure and Strategies*. Washington, D.C.: University Press of America.

A useful reference for learning the principles and rules of spelling English.

Wallach, M. A. & Wallach, L. (1976) *Teaching All Children to Read*. Chicago: University of Chicago Press.

A model for the successful introduction to reading of children with different learning styles.

Williams, L. V. (1983) *Teaching for the Two-Sided Mind*. Englewood Cliffs, NJ: Prentice-Hall.

A practical description of teaching methods for the right brain.

Teacher–Parent Alliance

Gargiulo, R. M. (1985) *Working with Parents of Exceptioal Children*. Boston: Houghton-Mifflin Company.

A practical guide for professionals in their work with parents.

Ginott, H. G. (1972) *Teacher and Child: A Book for Parents and Teachers*. New York: Macmillan.

An anecdotal description of typical problems encountered by teachers, children, and parents.

McWhirter, J. J. (1977) *The Learning Disabled Child: A School and Family Concern*. Champaign, IL: Research Press Company.

A practical guide for managing the behavior of children in the classroom and at home.

Help in the Home

Osman, B. B. (1982) *No One to Play With: The Social Side of Learning Disabilities*. New York: Random House.

A down-to-earth description for older children and parents of the social attitudes children with learning problems face in school and with peers.

Rich, D. (1988) *Megaskills: How Families Can Help Children Succeed in School and Beyond*. Boston: Houghton-Mifflin.

A useful exposition of the basic work skills that underlie academic learning.

Rosner, J. (1979) *Helping Children Overcome Learning Difficulties*. New York: Walker & Company.

A practical guide for parents in understanding and helping children with learning problems in school.

Stevens, S. H. (1980) *The Learning Disabled Child: Ways That Parents Can Help*. Winston-Salem, NC: John F. Blair, Publisher.

A practical guide for parents in meeting the needs of their children with school learning problems.

FOR RESEARCHERS

Furth, H. F. (1981) *Piaget and Knowledge: Theoretical Foundations* (2nd ed.). Chicago: University of Chicago Press.
  An authoritative discussion of Piaget's ideas.

Harris, J. E. (1986) *Clinical Neuroscience: From Neuroanatomy to Psychodynamics.* New York: Human Sciences Press.
  A bold and coherent effort to link current knowledge of the neural sciences with psychoanalytic concepts.

Lowen, W. (1982) *Dichotomies of the Mind: A Systems Science Model of the Mind and Personality.* New York: John Wiley & Sons.
  An ingenious model that employs sophisticated technology to describe brain functions.

Luria, A. R. (1973) *The Working Brain: An Introduction to Neuropsychology.* New York: Basic Books.
  A comprehensive exposition of Luria's conceptions of brain functions in addition to a description of the field of neuropsychology.

Menolascino, F. J., Neman, R., & Stark, J. A. (Eds.) (1983) *Curative Aspects of Mental Retardation: Biomedical and Behavioral Advances.* Baltimore, MD: Brookes Publishing Co.
  An intriguing view of the prospects for the field of developmental disabilities.

Miller, J. G. (1978) *Living Systems.* New York: McGraw-Hill Book Company.
  A monumental, broad-gauged presentation of the general theory of living systems.

Pirozzolo, F. J. (1979) *The Neuropsychology of Developmental Reading Disorders.* New York: Praeger Publishing.
  A detailed description of the neuropsychological findings in dyslexic children.

Sternberg, R. J. (1985) *Human Abilities: An Information-Processing Approach.* New York: W. H. Freeman & Company.
  A broad overview of current knowledge of individual differences in intelligence and thinking based upon information processing theory.

References

Abel, E. L. (1984) *Fetal Alcohol Syndrome and Fetal Alcohol Effects*. New York: Plenum.

Abend, S. M. (1982) Some Observations on Reality Testing as a Clinical Concept. *Psychoanalytic Quarterly* 51:218–238.

Accardo, P. J. (1980) *A Neurodevelopmental Perspective on Specific Learning Disabilities*. Baltimore, MD: University Park Press.

Ackerman, P. T., Holcomb, P. J., McCray, D. S., & Dykman, R. A. (1982) Studies of Nervous System Sensitivity in Children with Learning and Attention Disorders. *Pavlovian Journal of Biological Science* 17:30–41.

Adams, P. L. (1973) *Obsessive Children: A Sociopsychiatric Study*. New York: Brunner/Mazel.

Adams, P. L. (1974) *A Primer of Child Psychotherapy*. Boston: Little, Brown.

Adams, R. M., Kocsis, J. J., & Estes, R. L. (1974) Soft Neurological Signs in Learning-Disabled Children and Controls. *American Journal of Diseases of Children* 128:267–277.

Adamson, W. C. & Adamson, K. K. (1979) *A Handbook for Specific Learning Disabilities*. New York: Gardner Press.

Adelman, H. S. (1978) Diagnostic Classification of Learning Problems: Some Data. *American Journal of Orthopsychiatry* 48:717–726.

Adelman, H. S. & Taylor, L. (1983) *Learning Disabilities in Perspective*. Glenview, IL: Scott, Foresman.

Adelman, H. S., Taylor, L., & Nelson, P. (1982) Prevalence and Treatment of Learning Problems in Upper and Lower Income Areas. *American Journal of Orthopsychiatry* 52:719–724.

Adler, M. J. (1977) *Reforming Education*. Boulder, CO: Westview Press.

Adler, S. (1983) *The Non-Verbal Child: An Introduction to Pediatric Language Pathology* (3rd ed.). Springfield, IL: Charles C. Thomas.

Ahearn, G. L. & Schwartz, G. E. (1979) Differential Lateralization for Positive vs Negative Emotion. *Neuropsychologia* 17:693–698.

Ainscow, M. & Tweddle, D. A. (1979) *Preventing Classroom Failure: An Objective Approach*. New York: Wiley.

Akiskal, H. S. (1979) A Biobehavioral Approach to Depression. In Depue, R. (Ed.), *The Psychobiology of Depressive Disorders: Implications for the Effects of Stress*. New York: Academic Press.

Akiskal, H. S. & McKinney, W. J. (1975) Overview of Recent Research in Depression. *Archives of General Psychiatry* 32:285–305.

Aleksandrowicz, D. R. & Aleksandrowicz, M. K. (1987) Psychodynamic Approach to Low Self-Esteem Related to Developmental Deviations: Growing Up Incompetent. *Journal of Child and Adolescent Psychiatry* 26:583–585.

Alexander, D. & Money, J. (1966) Turner's Syndrome: Neuropsychological Comparisons. *Neuropsychologia* 4:265–273.

Allen, D. W. (1967) Exhibitionistic and Voyeuristic Conflicts in Learning and Functioning. *Psychoanalytic Quarterly* 36:546–570.

Allen, D. W. & Rothman, R. K. (1973) Intersensory Integration and Reading Ability in the Deaf. *Bulletin of the Psychoneurological Society* 1:199–201.

Allen, V. L. (Ed.) (1976) *Children as Teachers: Theory and Research on Tutoring*. New York: Academic Press.

Alloway, T., Pliner, P., & Krames, L. (1977) *Attachment Behavior*. New York: Plenum.

Alpert, J. E., Cohen, D. J., Shaywitz, B. A., Piccarillo, M., & Shaywitz, S. E. (1978) Animal Models and Childhood Behavioral Disturbances: Dopamine Depletion in the Newborn Rat Pup. *Journal of Child Psychiatry* 17:239–251.

Als, H. (1985) Patterns of Infant Behavior: Analogues of Later Organizational Difficulties. In Duffy, F. H. & Geschwind, N. (Eds.), *Dyslexia: A Neuroscientific Approach to Clinical Evaluation*. Boston: Little, Brown.

Amabile, T. M. (1983) *The Social Psychology of Creativity*. New York: Springer-Verlag.

American Academy of Ophthalmology and the American Association for Pediatric Ophthalmology and Strabismus (1981). Approved by Board of Directors, AAPOS, 5-7-81 and AAO 6-27-81.

American Academy of Pediatrics (1972) Report of Ad Hoc Committee of the American Academy of Pediatrics, American Academy of Ophthalmology and Otolaryngology, American Association of Ophthalmology. *Pediatrics* 49:454–455.

American Psychiatric Association (1987) *Diagnostic and Statistical Manual—III-R*. Washington, DC: American Psychiatric Association.

Ames, L. B. (1978) *Is Your Child in the Wrong Grade?* Lumberville, PA: Modern Learning Press.

Amosov, N. M. (1967) *Modeling of Thinking and the Mind*. New York: Spartan.

Amsterdam, B. K. & Levitt, M. (1980) Consciousness of Self and Painful Self-Consciousness. *The Psychoanalytic Study of the Child* 35:67–83.

Anastas, J. W. & Reinherz, H. (1984) Gender Differences in Learning and Adjustment Problems in School; Results of a Longitudinal Study. *American Journal of Orthopsychiatry* 54:110–122.

Anders, T. F. (1978) State and Rhythmic Processes. *Journal of Child Psychiatry* 17:401–420.

Anderson, J. R. (1983a) Retrieval of Information from Long-Term Memory. *Science* 220:25–30.

Anderson, J. R. (1983b) *The Architecture of Cognition*. Cambridge, MA: Harvard University Press.

Anderson, N. (1964) *Dimensions of Work: The Sociology of a Work Culture*. New York: McKay.

Anderson, S. B. (1973) Educational Compensation and Evaluation: A Critique. In Stanley, J. C. (Ed.), *Compensatory Education for Children Ages Two to Eight*. Baltimore, MD: Johns Hopkins University Press.

Ansara, A., Geschwind, N., Galaburda, A., Albert, M., & Gartrell, N. (1981) *Sex Differences in Dyslexia*. Towson, MD: The Orton Dyslexia Society.

Anthony, B. J. & Graham, F. K. (1983) Evidence for Sensory-Selective Set in Young Infants. *Science* 220: 742–744.

Anthony, E. J. (1965) It Hurts Me More Than It Hurts You—An Approach to Discipline as a Two-Way Process. *The Reiss-Davis Clinic Bulletin* 2:7–22.

Anthony, E. J. (1982) Normal Adolescent Development from a Cognitive Point of View. *Journal of Child Psychiatry* 21:318–327.

Anthony, E. J. & Koupernick, C. (Eds.) (1973) *The Child in His Family: The Impact of Disease and Death*. New York: Wiley.

Apter, S. J. (1982) *Troubled Children —Troubled Systems*. New York: Pergamon.

Aram, D. M., Rose, D. F., & Horwitz, S. J.

(1982) Hyperlexia: Developmental Reading without Meaning. In Malatesha, R. N. & Whitaker, H. A. (Eds.), *Dyslexia: A Global Issue*. The Hague, Netherlands: Martinus Nijhoff.

Arend, R., Gove, F. L., & Sroufe, L. A. (1979) Continuity of Individual Adaptation from Infancy to Kindergarten: A Predictive Study of Ego-Resilience and Curiosity in Preschoolers. *Child Development* 50:950–959.

Arieti, S. (1976) *Creativity: The Magic Synthesis*. New York: Basic Books.

Arizona Research Services (1981) *Phoenix Union High School District Homebound Program. Report No. 33-08-80/81-007*. Phoenix, AZ.

Arkell, H. (1974) *Dyslexia: Introduction—A Dyslexic's Eye View*. London: Helen Arkell Dyslexia Centre.

Armstrong, E. (1983) Relative Brain Size and Metabolism in Mammals. *Science* 220:1302–1306.

Arnold, L. E., Barneby, N., McManus, J., Smelzer, D. J., Conrad, A., Winer, G., & Desgranges, L. (1977) Prevention by Specific Perceptual Remediation for Vulnerable First-graders. *Archives of General Psychiatry* 34:1279–1294.

Asher, S. R. & Gottman, J. M. (1981) *The Development of Children's Friendships*. Cambridge, England: Cambridge University Press.

Aston-Jones, G. & Bloom, F. E. (1981) Norepinephrine-containing Locus Coeruleus Neurons in Behaving Rats Exhibit Pronounced Responses to Non-noxious Environmental Stimuli. *Journal of Neuroscience* 8:887–900.

Atwood, G. (1971) An Experimental Study of Visual Imagination and Memory. *Cognitive Psychology* 2:290–299.

August, G. J., Stewart, M. A., & Holmes, C. S. (1983) A Four-year Follow-up of Hyperactive Boys with and without Conduct Disorder. *British Journal of Psychiatry* 143:192–198.

Ausubel, D. P. (1969) *Readings in School Learning*. New York: Holt, Rinehart & Winston.

Averill, J. R. (1976) Emotion and Anxiety: Sociocultural, Biological and Psychological Determinants. In Zuckerman, M. & Spielberger, C. D. (Eds.), *Emotions and Anxiety: New Concepts, Methods and Applications*. Hillsdale, NJ: Erlbaum.

Axelrod, R. (1984) *The Evolution of Cooperation*. New York: Basic Books.

Ayres, A. J. (1972) *Sensory Integration and Learning Disabilities*. Los Angeles: Western Psychological Services.

Backer, W. (1973) *Motivating Black Workers*. Johannesburg, South Africa: Mc-Graw-Hill.

Backwin, H. (1973) Reading Disability in Twins. *Developmental Medicine and Child Neurology* 15:184–187.

Bakwin, H. & Bakwin, R. M. (1960) *Clinical Management of Behavior Disorders in Children*. Philadelphia, PA: Saunders.

Badian, N. (1983) Dyscalculia and Nonverbal Disorders of Learning. In Myklebust, H. R. (Ed.), *Progress in Learning Disabilities. Volume 5*. New York: Grune & Stratton.

Baird, H. W., John E. R., Ahn, H., & Maisel, E. (1980) Neurometric Evaluation of Epileptic Children Who Do Well and Poorly in School. *Electroencephalography and Neurophysiology* 48:683–693.

Bakan, P. (1978) Dreaming, REM Sleep and the Right Hemisphere: A Theoretical Integration. *Journal of Altered States of Consciousness* 3:285–307.

Bakker, D. J. (1979) Hemispheric Differences and Reading Strategies: Two Dyslexias? *Bulletin of the Orton Society* 29: Reprint no. 82.

Bakker, D. J. (1983) Hemispheric Specialization and Specific Reading Retardation. In Rutter, M. (Ed.), *Developmental Neuropsychiatry*. New York: Guilford.

Bakker, D. J. (1984) The Brain as a Dependent Variable. *Journal of Clinical Neuropsychology* 6:1–16.

Ballard, J., Ramirez, J., & Weintraub, F. J. (Eds.) (1982) *Special Education in America: Its Legal and Governmental Foundations*. Reston, VA: Council for Exceptional Children.

Baloh, R. W. & Honrubia, V. (1979) *Clinical Neurophysiology of the Vestibular System*. Philadelphia, PA: Davis.

Bank, S. P. & Kahn, M. D. (1982) *The Sibling Bond*. New York: Basic Books.

Bannatyne, A. (1971) *Language, Reading and Learning Disabilities*. Springfield, IL: Charles C. Thomas.

Bannatyne, A. (1974) Diagnosis: A Note on Recategorization of the WISC Scales Scores. *Journal of Learning Disabilities* 7:272–274.

Barchas, J. D., Berger, P. A., Ciaranello, R. D., & Elliott, G. R. (Eds.) (1977a) *Psychopharmacology from Theory to Practice*. New York: Oxford University Press.

Barchas, J. D., Patrick, R. L., Raese, J., & Berger, P. A. (1977b) Neuropharmacological Aspects of Affective Disorders. In Usdin, G. (Ed.), *Depression: Clinical, Biological and Psychological Perspectives*. New York: Brunner/Mazel.

Bardwick, J. M. (1971) *Psychology of Women: A Study of Biocultural Conflicts*. New York: Harper & Row.

Baribeau-Braun, J., Picton, T. W., & Gosselin, J. (1983) Schizophrenia: A Neurophysiological Evaluation of Abnormal Information Processing. *Science* 219:874–876.

Barkley, R. A. (1981) *Hyperactive Children: A Handbook for Diagnosis and Treatment*. New York: Guilford.

Barkley, R. A. & Cunningham, C. E. (1978) Do Stimulant Drugs Improve the Academic Performance of Hyperkinetic Children? *Clinical Pediatrics* 17:85–92.

Bartak, L., Rutter, M., & Cox, A. (1975) A Comparative Study of Infantile Autism and Specific Developmental Receptive Language Disorder. *British Journal of Psychiatry* 126:127–145.

Bartlett, F. C. (1932) *Remembering*. Cambridge, England: Cambridge University Press.

Barzun, J. (1983) *A Stroll with Henry James*. New York: Harper & Row.

Basch, M. F. (1975) Toward a Theory That Encompasses Depression: A Revision of Existing Causal Hypotheses in Psychoanalysis. In Anthony, E. J. & Benedek, T. (Eds.), *Depression and Human Existence*. Boston: Little, Brown.

Basch, M. F. (1976a) Psychoanalysis and Communication Science. *The Annual of Psychoanalysis* 4:385–421.

Basch, M. F. (1976b) The Concept of Affect: A Reexamination. *Journal of the American Psychoanalytic Association* 24:759–777.

Basch, M. F. (1977) Developmental Psychology and Explanatory Theory in Psychoanalysis. *Annual of Psychoanalysis* 5:229–263.

Basch, M. F. (1979) Mind, Self and Dreamer. In Stoller, R. J. (Ed.), *Sexual Excitement: Dynamics of Erotic Life*. New York: Pantheon.

Bateman, B. (1969) A Reading on a Controversial View of Research and Rationale. In Tarnapol, L. (Ed.), *Learning Disabilities—Introduction to Educational and Medical Management.* Springfield, IL: Charles C. Thomas.

Bateson, G. (1972) *Steps to An Ecology of Mind.* New York: Ballantine.

Bateson, P. P. G. (1974) The Nature of Early Learning. *Science* 183:740–741.

Batshaw, M. L. & Perret, Y. M. (1981) *Children with Handicaps: A Medical Primer.* Baltimore, MD: Brookes.

Becker, W. C., Engelmann, S., Carnine, D. W., & Maggs, A. (1982) Direct Instruction Technology: Making it Happen. In Karoly, P. & Steffan, J. J. (Eds.), *Improving Children's Competence.* Lexington, MA: Lexington Books.

Beckman, L. (1970) Effect of Student's Performance on Teacher's and Observer's Attributions of Causality. *Journal of Educational Psychology* 6:76–82.

Becvar, R. J. & Becvar, D. S. (1982) *Systems Theory and Family Therapy: A Primer.* Washington, D.C.: University Press of America.

Begg, I. (1983) Imagery and Language. In Sheikh, A. A. (Ed.), *Imagery: Current Theory, Research and Application.* New York: Wiley.

Behrmann, M. M. (Ed.) (1984) *Handbook of Microcomputers in Special Education.* Reston, VA: Council for Exceptional Children.

Bell, R. Q., Weller, G. M., & Waldrop, M. R. (1971) Newborns and Preschoolers: Organization of Behavior and Relations between Periods. *Monograph of the Society for Research in Child Development.* Serial No. 142, Vol. 36, Nos. 1–2.

Bellak, L. (Ed.) (1979) *Psychiatric Aspects of Minimal Brain Dysfunction in Adults.* New York: Grune & Stratton.

Belmont, L. (1980) Epidemiology. In Rie, H. E. & Rie, E. D. (Eds.), *Handbook of Minimal Brain Dysfunction: A Critical Review.* New York: Wiley.

Bemporad, J. R. (1982) Borderline Syndromes in Childhood: Criteria for Diagnosis. *American Journal of Psychiatry* 139:596–602.

Bemporad, J. R. (1984) From Attachment to Affiliation. *American Journal of Psychoanalysis* 44:79–97.

Bemporad, J. R., Ratey, J. J., & O'Driscoll, G. (1987) Autism and Emotion: An Ethological Theory. *American Journal of Orthopsychiatry* 57: 477–484.

Benbow, C. P. & Stanley, J. C. (Eds.) (1984) *Academic Precocity: Aspects of Its Development.* Baltimore, MD: Johns Hopkins University Press.

Bender, L. (1975) A Fifty-year Review of Experiences with Dyslexia. *Bulletin of the Orton Society* 25:5–22.

Benjamin, L. S. (1981) A Psychosocial Competence Classification System. In Wine, J. D. & Smye, M. D. (Eds.), *Social Competence.* New York: Guilford Press.

Benjamin, L. S. (1988) *Interpersonal Diagnosis and Treatment: The SASB Approach.* New York: Guilford Press.

Bennett, T. L. (1977) *Brain and Behavior.* Monterey, CA: Brooks/Cole.

Benowitz, L. I. (1980) Cerebral Lateralization in the Perception of Nonverbal Emotional Cues. *McLean Hospital Journal* 5:146–167.

Benson, D. F. (1977) The Third Alexia. *Archives of Neurology* 34:327–331.

Benson, D. F. (1984) Alexia and the Neural Basis of Reading. *Annals of Dyslexia* 34:3–13.

Benson, D. F. (1985) Alexia. In Frederiks, J. A. M. (Ed.), *Handbook of Clinical Neurology. Volume I.* New York: Elsevier.

Benson, D. F. & Geschwind, N. (1970) Developmental Gerstmann Syndrome. *Neurology* 20:293–298.

Benson, D. F. & Zaidel, E. (Eds.) (1985) *The Dual Brain*. New York: Guilford Press.

Benton, A. L. (1978) Some Conclusions about Dyslexia. In Benton, A. L. & Pearl, D. (Eds.), *Dyslexia: An Appraisal of Current Knowledge*. New York: Oxford University Press.

Benton, A. L. (1984) Dyslexia and Spatial Thinking. *Annals of Dyslexia* 34:69–85.

Bergland, R. (1986) *The Fabric of the Mind*. New York: Viking.

Berenberg, R. A. et al (1977) Lumping or Splitting? Ophthalmoplegia—Plus or Kearns-Sayre Syndrome? *Annals of Neurology* 1:37–54.

Beres, D. (1981) Self, Identity and Narcissism. *Psychoanalytic Quarterly* 50:515–534.

Bergstrom, R. A. M. (1963) On the Physiology of the Meso-diencephalic Extrapyramidal System, with Special Reference to the Pathogenesis of Involuntary Movements. *Acta Neurologica Scandinavia* 39:Supplementum 4:52–60.

Berkson, W. & Wettersten, J. (1984) *Learning from Error: Karl Popper's Psychology of Learning*. LaSalle, IL: Open Court Publications.

Berlin, I. N. (1977) Some Lessons Learned in 25 Years of Mental Health Consultation to Schools. In Plog, S. C. and Ahmed, P. I. (Eds.), *Principles and Techniques of Mental Health Consultation*. New York: Plenum.

Berlin, I. N. (1981) Psychotherapy with MBD Children and Their Parents. In Ochroch, R. (Ed.), *The Diagnosis and Treatment of Minimal Brain Dysfunction in Children: A Clinical Approach*. New York: Human Sciences Press.

Berlyne, D. E. (Ed.) (1974) *Studies in the New Experimental Asthetics*. New York: Wiley.

Bernal, M. E. (1969) Behavioral Feedback in the Modification of Brat Behaviors. *Journal of Nervous and Mental Disease* 148:375–385.

Bernstein, N. R. & Menolascino, F. J. (1970) Apparent and Relative Mental Retardation: Their Challenges to Psychiatric Treatment. In Menolascino, F. J. (Ed.), *Psychiatric Approaches to Mental Retardation*. New York: Basic Books.

Berntson, G. G. & Micco, D. J. (1976) Theoretical Review: Organization of Brainstem Behavioral Systems. *Brain Research Bulletin* 1:471–483.

Berntson, G. G. & Torello, M. W. (1982) Paleocerebellum in the Integration of Behavioral Function. *Physiological Psychology* 10:2–12.

Berrien, F. K. (1968) *General and Social Systems*. New Brunswick, NJ: Rutgers University Press.

Berry, G. L. & Mitchell-Kernan, C. (Eds.) (1982) *Television and the Socialization of the Minority Child*. New York: Academic Press.

Berthoz, A. & Jones, G. M. (Eds.) (1985) *Adaptive Mechanisms in Gaze Control*. New York: Elsevier.

Bettelheim, B. (1976) *The Uses of Enchantment: The Meaning and Importance of Fairy Tales*. New York: Knopf.

Bettelheim, B. & Zelan, K. (1981) *The Child's Fascination with Meaning*. New York: Knopf.

Bettman, J. W., Stern, E. L., Whitsell, L. J., & Gofman, H. F. (1967) Cerebral Dominance in Developmental Dyslexia: Role of Ophthalmology. *Archives of Ophthalmology* 78:722–730.

Betz, B. J. (1979) Some Neurophysiological Aspects of Individual Behavior.

American Journal of Psychiatry 136:1251–1256.

Bhatara, V., Clark, D., Arnold, L. E., Gansett, R., & Smeltzer, D. J. (1981) Hyperkinesis Treated by Vestibular Stimulation: An Exploratory Study. *Biological Psychiatry* 16:269–279.

Bicknell, J. (1983) The Psychopathology of Handicap. *British Journal of Medical Psychology* 56:167–178.

Binet, A. (1899) *The Psychology of Reasoning, Based on Experimental Researches in Hypnotism.* Chicago: Open Court.

Birch, H. G., Richardson, S. A., Baird, D., Horobin, G., & Illsley, R. (1970) *Mental Subnormality in the Community. A Clinical and Epidemiological Study.* Baltimore, MD: Williams & Wilkins.

Birdwhistell, R. L. (1970) *Kinesics and Context: Essays on Body Motion Communication.* Philadelphia, PA: University of Pennsylvania Press.

Bjorklund, G. (1978) *Planning for Play, A Developmental Approach.* Columbus, Ohio: Merrill.

Black, I. B., Adler, J. E., Dreyfus, C. F., Friedman, W. F., LaGamma, E. F., & Roach, A. H. (1987) Biochemistry of Information Storage in the Nervous System. *Science* 236:1263–1268.

Blackman, S. & Goldstein, M. (1982) Cognitive Styles and Learning Disabilities. *Journal of Learning Disabilities* 15:106–115.

Blanchard, P. (1946) Psychoanalytic Contributions to the Problems of Reading Disabilities. *The Psychoanalytic Study of the Child* 2:163–187.

Blank, M. (1972) The Treatment of Personality Variables in a Preschool Cognitive Program. In Stanley, J. C. (Ed.), *Preschool Programs for the Disadvantaged.* Baltimore, MD: Johns Hopkins Press.

Blank, M., Berlin, L. J., & Rose, S. A. (1982) Classroom Dialogue. Abilities and Disabilities of Learning Disabled Children. In McKinney, J. D. & Feagans, L. (Eds.), *Current Topics in Learning Disabilities.* Piscataway, NJ: Department of Psychiatry, Institute of Mental Health Sciences.

Blau, A. (1946) The Master Hand: A Study of the Origin and Meaning of Right and Left Sidedness and Its Relation to Personality and Language. *Research Monograph—No. 5.* New York: American Orthopsychiatric Association.

Bleier, R. (1983) *Science and Gender: A Critique of Biology and Its Theories on Women.* New York: Pergamon.

Bloch, A. M. (1978) Combat Neurosis in Inner City Schools. *American Journal of Psychiatry* 135:1189–1192.

Block, J. & Block, J. (1979) The Role of Ego-Control and Ego-Resiliency in the Organization of Behavior. In Collins, W. A. (Ed.), *Minnesota Symposia on Child Psychology 13.* Hillsdale, NJ: Erlbaum.

Block, N. (1981) *Imagery.* Cambridge, MA: MIT Press.

Blom, G. E. & Jones, A. W. (1970) Bases of Classification of Reading Disorders. *Journal of Learning Disabilities* 3:606–617.

Bloom, A. (1978) The Education of Democratic Man. *Daedelus* 109:135–153.

Bloom, B. (1964) *Stability and Change in Human Characteristics.* New York: Wiley.

Bloom, B. (1985) *Developing Talent in Young People.* New York: Ballantine Books.

Bloom, F. E. & Henrikson, S. J. (1981) Endorphin Studies: Electrophysiological Effects. *Modern Problems of Psychopharmacology* 17:19–37.

Bloom, L. & Lahey, M. (1978) *Language Development and Language Disorders.* New York: Wiley.

Boden, M. A. (1977) *Artificial Intelligence*

and Natural Man. New York: Basic Books.

Boden, M. A. (1979) *Jean Piaget*. New York: Viking Press.

Boden, M. A. (1981) *Minds and Mechanisms: Philosophical Psychology and Computational Models*. Brighton, England: Harvester Press.

Boder, E. (1973) Developmental Dyslexia: A Diagnostic Approach Based on Three Atypical Reading-spelling Patterns. *Developmental Medicine and Child Neurology* 15:663–687.

Boder, E. & Jarrice, S. (1982) *The Boder Test of Reading-Spelling Patterns: A Diagnostic Screening Test for Subtypes of Reading Disability*. New York: Grune & Stratton.

Boettcher, J. V. (1983) Computer-Based Education: Classroom Application and Benefits for the Learning-Disabled Student. *Annals of Dyslexia* 33:203–219.

Bohm, D. (1980) *Wholeness and the Implicate Order*. London: Routledge & Kegan Paul.

Boll, T. J. & Barth, J. T. (1981) Neuropsychology of Brain Damage in Children. In Filskov, S. B. & Boll, T. J. (Eds.), *Handbook of Clinical Neuropsychology*. New York: Wiley-Interscience.

Boocock, S. S. (1972) *An Introduction to the Sociology of Learning*. Boston, MA: Houghton-Mifflin.

Bootzin, R. R. & Max, D. (1980) Learning and Behavioral Theories. In Kutash, I. L., Schlesinger, L. B., & Associates (Eds.), *Handbook on Stress and Anxiety*. San Francisco: Jossey-Bass.

Borland, B. L. & Heckman, H. K. (1976) Hyperactive Boys and Their Brothers. *Archives of General Psychiatry* 33:669–675.

Bosco, J. J. & Robin, S. S. (1980) Hyperkinesis: Prevalence and Treatment. In Whalen, C. K. & Henker, B. *Hyperactive Children: The Social Ecology of Identification and Treatment*. New York: Academic Press.

Bouchard, T. J. & McGue, M. (1981) Familial Studies of Intelligence: A Review. *Science* 212:1055–1059.

Bourne, L. E. (1982) Typicality Effects in Logically Defined Categories. *Memory and Cognition* 10:3–9.

Bowen, F. P. (1976) Behavioral Alterations in Patients with Basal Ganglia Lesions. In Yahr, M. D. (Ed.), *The Basal Ganglia*. New York: Raven.

Bower, E. M. (1981) *Early Identification of Emotionally Handicapped Children in School*. Springfield, IL: Charles C. Thomas.

Bower, E. M. & Hollister, W. G. (Eds.) (1967) *Behavioral Science, Frontiers in Education*. New York: Wiley.

Bower, T. G. R. (1979) *Human Development*. San Francisco: Freeman.

Bowlby, J. (1958) The Nature of the Child's Tie to the Mother. *International Journal of Psychoanalysis* 39:350–373.

Bowlby, J. (1980) *Attachment and Loss. Volume III: Loss*. New York: Basic Books.

Boyd, R. & Richerson, P. J. (1985) *Culture and the Evolutionary Process*. Chicago: University of Chicago Press.

Bradley, C. (1937) The Behavior of Children Receiving Benzedrine. *American Journal of Psychiatry* 94:577–585.

Brady, S. (1986) Short-Term Memory, Phonological Processing and Reading Ability. *Annals of Dyslexia* 36:138–153.

Branden, N. (1969) *The Psychology of Self-esteem*. New York: Bantam.

Bransford, J. D. & Stein, B. S. (1984) *The Ideal Problem Solver*. New York: Freeman.

Brazelton, T. B. (1973) *Neonatal Behavioral Assessment Scale*. London: Heinemann.

Brazelton, T. B., Koslowski, B., & Main, M. (1980) The Origins of Reciprocity: The Early Mother–Infant Interaction. In Harrison, S. I. & McDermott, J. (Eds.), *New Directions in Childhood Psychopathology. Volume I.* New York: International Universities Press.

Breggin, P. R. (1983) *Psychiatric Drugs: Hazards to the Brain.* New York: Springer.

Brenner, C. (1981) Defense and Defense Mechanisms. *Psychoanalytic Quarterly* 50:557–569.

Brenner, C. (1982) *The Mind in Conflict.* New York: International Universities Press.

Briggs, D. C. (1975) *Your Child's Self-Esteem.* Garden City, NY: Doubleday.

Brim, O. (1975) Macro-Structural Influences on Child Development and the Need for Childhood Social Indicators. *American Journal of Orthopsychiatry* 45:516–524.

Brodal, A. (1963) Some Data and Perspectives on the Anatomy of the So-called 'Extrapyramidal System.' *Acta Neurologica Scandinavica* 39-Supplementum 4:17–38.

Broman, S. H., Nichols, P. L., & Kennedy, W. A. (1975) *Preschool I.Q.: Prenatal and Early Developmental Correlates.* Hillsdale, NJ: Erlbaum.

Bronner, A. F. (1917) *The Psychology of Special Abilities and Disabilities.* Boston: Little, Brown.

Bronson, G. (1965) The Hierarchical Organization of the Central Nervous System: Implications for Learning Processes and Critical Periods in Early Development. *Behavioral Science* 10:7–25.

Brooks, P. H. (1978) Some Speculations Concerning Deafness and Learning to Read. In Liben, L. S. (Ed.), *Deaf Children: Developmental Perspectives.* New York: Academic Press.

Brooks, V. W. (1956) *Helen Keller: Sketch for a Portrait.* New York: Dutton.

Brophy, J. E. & Evertson, C. M. (1976) *Learning from Teaching: A Developmental Perspective.* Boston: Allyn & Bacon.

Brothers, L. (1989) A Biological Perspective on Empathy. *American Journal of Psychiatry* 146: 10–19.

Brown, E. R. (1980) Theories of Reading and Language Development. In Rieber, R. W. (Ed.), *Language Development and Aphasia in Children.* New York: Academic Press.

Brown, H. (1976) *Brain and Behavior.* New York: Oxford University Press.

Brown, J. (1977) *Mind, Brain and Consciousness: The Neuropsychology of Cognition.* New York: Academic Press.

Brown, R. (1973) *A First Language: The Early Stages.* Cambridge, MA: Harvard University Press.

Brown, R. T. (1982) Hyperactivity: Assessment and Evaluation of Rating Instruments. *Journal of Psychiatric Treatment and Evaluation* 4:359–369.

Brown, S. L. (1980) Developmental Cycle of Families. In Christ, A. & Flomenhart, D. (Eds.), *The Challenge of Family Therapy.* New York: Plenum.

Brownell, G. L., Budinger, T. F., Lauterbur, P. C., & McGeer, P. L. (1982) Positron Tomography and Nuclear Resonance Imaging. *Science* 215:619–626.

Brownowski, J. (1972) *The Identity of Man.* Garden City, NJ: Doubleday.

Bruck, M. (1987) The Adult Outcomes of Children with Learning Disabilities. *Annals of Dyslexia* 37: 252–263.

Brumback, R. A. & Stanton, R. D. (1983)

Learning Disability and Childhood Depression. *American Journal of Orthopsychiatry* 53:269–281.

Bruner, J. S. (1980) Thought, Language and Interaction in Infancy. *Presented at the First World Congress on Infant Psychiatry, Cascais, Portugal.*

Bruner, J. S. (1983) *In Search of Mind: Essays in Autobiography.* New York: Harper & Row.

Bruner, J. S., Goodnow, J. J., & Austin, G. A. (1956) *A Study of Thinking.* New York: Wiley.

Bruun, R. D. (1984) Gilles de la Tourette's Syndrome: An Overview of Clinical Experience. *Journal of Child Psychiatry* 23:126–133.

Bryan, J. H. & Bryan, T. H. (1983) The Social Life of the Learning Disabled Youngster. In McKinney, J. D. & Feagans, L. (Eds.), *Current Topics in Learning Disabilities. Volume I.* Norwood, NJ: Ablex.

Bryan, T. H. (1974) Peer Popularity of Learning Disabled Children. *Journal of Learning Disabilities* 7:261–268.

Bryan, T. H. (1978) Social Relationships and Verbal Interactions of Learning Disabled Children. *Journal of Learning Disabilities* 11:107–123.

Bryan, T. H. & Bryan, J. H. (1975) *Understanding Learning Disabilities.* Port Washington, NY: Alfred.

Bryan, T. H., Wheeler, R., & Felcan, J. (1976) Come On Dummy: An Observational View of Children's Communication. *Journal of Learning Disabilities* 9:661–669.

Bryant, J. & Anderson, D. R. (Eds.) (1983) *Children's Understanding of Television: Research on Attention and Comprehension.* New York: Academic Press.

Bryden, M. P. (1982) *Laterality: Functional Asymmetry in the Intact Brain.* New York: Academic Press.

Buchsbaum, M. (1976). Self-regulation of Stimulus Intensity. In Schwartz, G. E. & Shapiro, D. (Eds.), *Consciousness and Self-regulation: Advances in Research. Volume I.* New York: Plenum.

Buchtel, H. A. (Ed.) (1982) *The Conceptual Nervous System.* Oxford, England: Pergamon.

Buck, Ross (1984) *The Communication of Emotion.* New York: Guilford Press.

Bugelski, B. R. (1971) The Definition of the Image. In Segal, S. J. (Ed.), *Imagery: Current Cognitive Approaches.* New York: Academic Press.

Bugelski, B. R. (1983) Imagery and the Thought Processes. In Sheikh, A. A. (Ed.), *Imagery: Current Theory, Research and Application.* New York: Wiley.

Burke, R. R. (1981) *Communicating with Students in Schools: A Workbook for Practitioners and Teachers in Training.* Washington, DC: University Press of America.

Burnet, M. (1978) *Endurance of Life.* Cambridge, England: Cambridge University Press.

Buss, A. H. (1980) *Self-consciousness and Social Anxiety.* San Francisco: Freeman.

Buss, A. H. & Plomin, R. (1975) *A Temperament theory of Personality Development.* New York: Wiley.

Butler, S. R. & Schanberg, S. M. (1977) Effect of Maternal Deprivation on Polyamine Metabolism in Preweanling Rat Brain and Heart. *Life Sciences* 21:877–884.

Buzan, T. & Dixon, T. (1977) *The Evolving Brain.* New York: Holt, Rinehart & Winston.

Calanchini, P. R. & Trout, S. S. (1971) The Neurology of Learning Disabilities. In Tarnopol, L. (Ed.), *Learning Disorders in Children: Diagnosis, Medica-*

tion and Education. Boston: Little, Brown.

Calfee, R. (1983) The Mind of the Dyslexic. *Annals of Dyslexia* 33:9–28.

Callahan, C. (1976) *Math '21'—A Multisensory Approach to Multiplication*. Cambridge, MA: Educators Publishing Service.

Cameron, J. (1978) Parental Treatment, Children's Temperament and the Risk of Childhood Behavioral Problems. *American Journal of Orthopsychiatry* 48:140–147.

Campbell, M., Green, W. H., & Deutsch, S. I. (1985) *Child and Adolescent Psychopharmacology*. Beverly Hills, CA: Sage Publications.

Campbell, S. B. & Cluss, P. (1982) Peer Relationships of Young Children with Behavior Problems. In Rubin, K. H. & Ross, H. S. (Eds.), *Peer Relationships and Social Skills in Childhood*. New York: Springer-Verlag.

Campione, J. C., Brown, A. L., & Bryant, N. R. (1985) Individual Differences in Learning and Memory. In Sternberg, R. J. (Ed.), *Human Abilities: An Information-Processing Approach*. New York: Freeman.

Candland, D. K. (1977) The Persistent Problems of Education. In Candland, D. K. et al (Eds.), *Emotions*. Monterey, CA: Brooks/Cole.

Cannon, W. B. (1927) The James-Lange Theory of Emotion. *American Journal of Psychology* 39:106.

Cantor, S. (1988) *Childhood Schizophrenia*. New York: Guilford Press.

Cantwell, D. P. (Ed.) (1975) *The Hyperactive Child: Diagnosis Management, Current Research*. New York: Spectrum.

Cantwell, D. P. (1978) Hyperactivity and Antisocial Behavior. *Journal of Child Psychiatry* 11:252–262.

Cantwell, D. P. (1979) Minimal Brain Dys-

function in Adults: Evidence from Studies of Psychiatric Illness in the Families of Hyperactive Children. In Bellak, L. (Ed.), *Psychiatric Aspects of Minimal Brain Dysfunction in Adults*. New York: Grune & Stratton.

Cantwell, D. P. (1985) Hyperactive Children Have Grown Up. *Archives of General Psychiatry* 42:1026–1028.

Cantwell, D. P., Baker, L., & Mattison, R. E. (1979) The Prevalence of Psychiatric Disorder in Children with Speech and Language Disorder. *Journal of Child Psychiatry* 18:450–461.

Cantwell, D. P. & Carlson, G. A. (Eds.) (1983) *Affective Disorders in Childhood and Adolescence: An Update*. New York: SP Medical and Scientific Books.

Cantwell, D. P. & Forness, S. R. (1982) Learning Disorders. *Journal of Child Psychiatry* 21:417–419.

Caparulo, B. K. & Cohen, D. J. (1977) Cognitive Structures, Language, and Emerging Social Competence in Autistic and Aphasic Children. *Journal of Child Psychiatry* 16:620–645.

Caparulo, B. K., Cohen, D. J., Rothman, S.L., Young, J.G., Katz, J.D., Shaywitz, S.E., & Shaywitz, B.A. (1981) Computed Tomographic Brain Scanning in Children with Developmental Neuropsychiatric Disorders. *Journal of Child Psychiatry* 20:338–357.

Capra, F. (1982) *The Turning Point: Science, Society and the Rising Culture*. New York: Simon & Schuster.

Capute, A. J. & Palmer, F. B. (1980) A Pediatric Overview of the Spectrum of Developmental Disabilities. *Developmental and Behavioral Pediatrics* 1:66–69.

Carbo, M. (1982) Reading Styles: Key to Preventing Reading Failure. In *Student Learning Styles and Brain Behav-*

ior. Reston, VA: National Association of Secondary School Principals.

Carew, J. V. & Lightfoot, S. L. (1979) *Beyond Bias: Perspectives on Classrooms*. Cambridge, MA: Harvard University Press.

Carey, W. B., McDevitt, S. C., & Baker, D. (1979) Differentiating Minimal Brain Dysfunction and Temperament. *Developmental Medicine and Child Neurology* 21:765–772.

Carroll, J. B. (Ed.) (1956) *Language, Thought and Reality: Selected Writings of Benjamin Lee Whorf*. Cambridge, MA: MIT Press.

Carte, E., Morrison, D., Sublett, J., Uenura, A., & Setrakian, W. (1984) Sensory Integration Therapy: A Trial of a Specific Neurodevelopmental Therapy for the Remediation of Learning Disabilities. *Developmental and Behavioral Pediatrics* 5:189–194.

Carter, P., Pazak, B., & Kahl, R. (1983) Algorithms for Processing Spatial Information. *Journal of Experimental Child Psychology* 36:284–304.

Carter, F. & Cheesman, P. (1988) *Anxiety in Childhood and Adolescence: Encouraging Self-Help through Relaxation Training*. London: Croom Helm.

Case, R. (1985) *Intellectual Development: Birth to Adulthood*. Orlando, FL: Academic Press.

Cattell, R. B. (1972) The Nature and Genesis of Mood States: A Theoretical Model with Experimental Measurements Concerning Anxiety, Depression, Arousal and Other Mood States. In Spielberger, C. D. (Ed.), *Anxiety: Current Trends in Theory and Research*. New York: Academic Press.

Cattell, R. B. (1980) *Personality and Learning Theory: A Systems Theory of Maturation and Structured Learning. Volume 2*. New York: Springer.

Chalfant, J. C. & Scheffelin, M. A. (1969) *Central Processing Dysfunctions in Children: A Review of Research*. NINDS Monograph No. 9. Washington, DC: U.S. Department of Health, Education and Welfare.

Chall, J. S. (1979) On Reading: Some Thoughts on the Old and the New. *Bulletin of the Orton Society* 29:6–16.

Chall, J. S. (1983a) *Learning to Read: The Great Debate*. New York: McGraw-Hill.

Chall, J. S. (1983b) *Stages of Reading Development*. New York: McGraw-Hill.

Chall, J. S. & Mirsky, A. F. (Eds.) (1978) *Education and the Brain*. Chicago: University of Chicago Press.

Chance, P. (1979) *Learning Through Play*. New York: Gardner Press.

Chandler, M. J. (1973) Egocentrism and Antisocial Behavior. *Developmental Psychology* 9:326–332.

Chase, C. H., Schmitt, R. L., Russell, G., & Tallal, P. (1984) A New Chemotherapeutic Investigation: Piracetam Effects on Dyslexia. *Annals of Dyslexia* 34:29–48.

Chase, R. A. (1965) An Information-Flow Model of the Organization of Motor Activity: II. Sampling, Central Processing and Utilization of Sensory Information. *Journal of Nervous and Mental Disease* 140:334–350.

Chasseguet-Smirgel, J. (1976) Some Thoughts on the Ego Ideal: A Contribution to the Study of the Illness of Ideality. *Psychoanalytic Quarterly* 45:345–373.

Chaudhari, N. & Hahn, W. E. (1983) Genetic Expression in the Developing Brain. *Science* 220:924–928.

Chelune, G. J. & Baer, R. A. (1986) Developmental Norms for the Wisconsin Card Sorting Test. *Journal of Clinical and Experimental Neuropsychology* 8:219–228.

Chelune, G. J., Ferguson, W., Koon, R.,

& Dickey, T. O. (1986) Frontal Lobe Disinhibition in Attention Deficit Disorder. *Child Psychiatry and Human Development* 16:221–234.

Cherry, Colin (1957) *On Human Communication*. New York: Science Editions.

Chess, S. & Hassibi, M. (1978) *Principles and Practice of Child Psychiatry*. New York: Plenum.

Chess, S. & Thomas, A. (1986) *Temperament in Clinical Practice*. New York: Guilford Press.

Chess, S., Korn, S. J., & Fernandez, P. B. (1971) *Psychiatric Disorders of Children with Congenital Rubella*. New York: Brunner/Mazel.

Chess, S. & Rosenberg, M. (1974) Clinical Differentiation Among Children with Initial Language Complaints. *Journal of Autism and Child Schizophrenia* 4:99–109.

Childs, B. & Finucci, J. (1979) The Genetics of Learning Disabilities. In Porter, R. & O'Connor, M. (Eds.), *Human Genetics: Possibilities and Realities*. New York: Excerpta Medica.

Chinn, P. C. (1984) *Education of Culturally and Linguistically Different Exceptional Children*. Reston, VA: Council for Exceptional Children.

Chomsky, N. (1968) *Language and Mind*. New York: Harcourt, Brace & World.

Chomsky, N. (1970) Phonology and Reading. In Levin, H. & Wiliams, J. P. (Eds.), *Basic Studies on Reading*. New York: Basic Books.

Christ, A. E. (1976) Cognitive Assessment of the Psychotic Child: A Piagetian Framework. *Journal of Child Psychiatry* 15:227–237.

Christ, A. E. (1978) Psychotherapy of the Child with True Brain Damage. *American Journal of Orthopsychiatry* 48:505–515.

Christ, A. E. (1981). Psychotherapy of the Adolescent with True Brain Damage. In Ochroch, R. (Ed.), *The Diagnosis and Treatment of Minimal Brain Dysfunction in Children: A Clinical Approach*. New York: Human Sciences Press.

Churchland, P. S. (1986) *Neurophilosophy: Toward a Unified Science of the Mind-Brain*. Cambridge, MA: MIT Press.

Clabby, J. F. & Elias, M. J. (1986) *Teach Your Child Decision Making*. Garden City, NY: Doubleday.

Clegg, H. G. (1984) *The Reparative Motif in Child and Adult Therapy*. New York: Aronson.

Clynes, M. (1973) Sentics: Biocybernetics of Emotion Communication. *Annals of the New York Academy of Sciences* 220:55–131.

Clynes, M. (1977) *Sentics: The Touch of Emotions*. Garden City, NY: Anchor.

Cobb, E. (1977) *The Ecology of Imagination in Childhood*. New York: Columbia University Press.

Coen, S. J. (1986) The Sense of Defect. *Journal of the American Psychoanalytic Association* 34:47–67.

Cohen, D. J., Caparulo, B., & Shaywitz, B. (1976) Primary Childhood Aphasia and Autism. *Journal of Child Psychiatry* 15:604–645.

Cohen, D. J., Caparulo, B., & Shaywitz, B. (1978) Neurochemical and Developmental Models of Childhood Autism. In Serban, G. (Ed.), *Cognitive Defects in the Development of Mental Illness*. New York: Brunner/Mazel.

Cohen, J. (1983) Learning Disabilities and the College Student: Identification and Diagnosis. *Adolescent Psychiatry* 11:177–198.

Cohen, J. (1985) Learning Disabilities and Adolescence: Developmental Considerations. *Adolescent Psychiatry* 12:177–196.

Cohen, N. J. & Squire, L. R. (1980) Preserved Learning and Retention of Pattern-Analyzing Skill in Amnesia: Dissociation of Knowing How and Knowing That. *Science* 210:207–210.

Cohen, R. L. (1983) Reading Disabled Children are Aware of Their Cognitive Deficits. *Journal of Learning Disabilities* 16:286–289.

Cole, E. J. & Walker, L. (1969) Reading and Speech Problems as Expressions of a Specific Language Disability. *Disorders of Communication*. New York: Hafner.

Coleman, J. S., Hoffer, T., & Kilgore, S. (1982) *High School Achievement: Public, Catholic and Private Schools Compared*. New York: Basic Books.

Coleman, M. & Gillberg, C. (1985) *The Biology of Autistic Syndromes*. New York: Praeger.

Coles, G. S. (1983) The Use of Soviet Psychological Theory in Understanding Learning Dysfunctions. *American Journal of Orthopsychiatry* 53:619–628.

Coles, G. S. (1987) *The Learning Mystique: A Critical Look at "Learning Disabilities."* New York: Pantheon Books.

Coltheart, M. (1979) When Can Children Learn to Read—and When Should They Be Taught? In Waller, T. G. & MacKinnon, G. E. (Eds.), *Reading Research: Advances in Theory and Practice. Volume I*. New York: Academic Press.

Comer, J. P. (1980) *School Power*. New York: Free Press.

Comings, D. E. & Comings, B. G. (1984) Tourette's Syndrome and Attention Deficit Disorder with Hyperactivity. *Journal of Child Psychiatry* 23:138–146.

Compton, A. (1983) The Current Status of Psychoanalytic Theory of Instinctual Drives. *Psychoanalytic Quarterly* 52:364–426.

Compton, A. (1980) A Study of the Psychoanalytic Theory of Anxiety, III·

A Preliminary Formulation of the Anxiety Response. *Journal of the American Psychoanalytic Association* 28:739–773.

Compton, A. (1983) The Current Status of Psychoanalytic Theory of Instinctual Drives. *Psychoanalytic Quarterly* 52:364–426.

Condon, W. S. (1985) Sound-Film Microanalysis: A Means for Correlating Brain and Behavior. In Duffy, F. H. & Geschwind, N. (Eds.), *Dyslexia: A Neuroscientific Approach to Clinical Evaluation*. Boston: Little, Brown.

Condon, W. S. & Sander, L. W. (1974) Neonate Movement is Synchronized with Adult Speech: Interactional Participation in Language Acquisition. *Science* 183:99–101.

Conners, C. K. (1980) *Food Additives and Hyperactive Children*. New York: Plenum.

Conners, C. K. & Wells, K. C. (1986) *Hyperkinetic Children: A Neuropsychosocial Approach*. Beverly Hills, CA: Sage Publications.

Connolly, J. A. (1978) Intelligence Levels of Down's Syndrome Children. *American Journal of Mental Deficiency* 83:193–196.

Connolly, K. (1969) Sensory-Motor Coordination: Mechanisms and Plans. In Wolff, P. H. & MacKeith, R. (Eds.), *Planning for Better Learning*. London: Heinemann.

Consortium for Longitudinal Studies (1983) *As the Twig is Bent . . . Lasting Effects of Preschool Programs*. Hillsdale, NJ: Erlbaum.

Constantine-Paton, M. & Law, M. I. (1982) The Development of Maps and Stripes in the Brain. *Scientific American* 247:62–70.

Conture, E. G. (1982) *Stuttering*. Englewood Cliffs, NJ: Prentice-Hall.

Cookson, C. (1978) Teenagers Begin to Reap the Benefits of Head Start. *Time Educational Supplement* 9:6–78.

Cooper, A. M. (1985) Will Neurobiology Influence Psychoanalysis? *American Journal of Psychiatry* 142:1395–1402.

Cooper, C. R., Marquis, A., & Ayers-Lopez, S. (1982) Peer Learning in the Classroom: Tracing Developmental Patterns and Consequences of Children's Spontaneous Interactions. In Wilkinson, L. C. (Ed.), *Communicating in the Classroom*. New York: Academic Press.

Cooper, J. R., Bloom, F. E., & Roth, R. H. (1978) *The Biochemical Basics of Neuropharmacology* (3rd ed.). New York: Oxford University Press.

Cooper, L. A. & Shepard, R. N. (1984) Turning Something Over in the Mind. *Scientific American* 251:106–114.

Cooper, L. N. & Imbert, M. (1981) Seat of Memory. *The Sciences* 2:10–29.

Coopersmith, S. (1967) *The Antecedents of Self-Esteem*. San Francisco: Freeman.

Coppolillo, H. P. (1985) *Psychoanalytic Psychotherapy of Children*. New York: International Universities Press.

Corah, N. L., Anthony, E. J., Painter, P., Stern, J. A., & Thurston, D. (1965) Effects of Perinatal Anoxia After Seven Years. *Psychological Monographs* (Gen. Appl.) 79, no. 596.

Corballis, M. C. (1982) Mental Rotation: Anatomy of a Paradigm. In Potegal, M. (Ed.), *Spatial Abilities: Development and Physiological Foundations*. New York: Academic Press.

Corballis, M. C. (1983) *Human Laterality*. New York: Academic Press.

Corey, L., Rubin, R. J., & Hattwick, A. W. (1977) Reye's Syndrome: Clinical Progression and Evaluation of Therapy. *Pediatrics* 60:708.

Costa, E. & Greengard, P. (1983) *Molecular Pharmacology of Neurotransmitter Receptors*. New York: Raven.

Cotman, C. W. & McGaugh, J. L. (1980) *Behavioral Neuroscience*. New York: Academic Press.

Cotton, N. S. (1983) The Development of Self-Esteem and Self-Esteem Regulation. In Mack, J. & Ablon, S. (Eds.), *The Development and Sustenance of Self-Esteem*. New York: International Universities Press.

Cotton, N. S. (1984) Childhood Play as an Analog to Adult Capacity to Work. *Child Psychiatry and Human Development* 14:135–144.

Cowan, W. M. (1979) The Development of the Brain. *Scientific American* 241:113–133.

Cowan, W. M., Fawcett, J. W., O'Leary, D. D. M., & Stanfield, B. B. (1984) Regressive Events in Neurogenesis. *Science* 225:1258–1265.

Cox, T. (1978) *Stress*. Baltimore, MD: University Park Press.

Crick, F. H. C. (1979) Thinking About the Brain. *Scientific American* 241:219–232.

Critchley, M. (1928) *Mirror-Writing*. London: Kegan-Paul.

Critchley, M. (1970a) *Aphasiology*. London: Edward Arnold.

Critchley, M. (1970b) *The Dyslexic Child, Second Edition of Developmental Dyslexia*. London: Heinemann.

Critchley, M. (1974) Developmental Dyslexia: Its History, Nature and Prospects. In Duane, D. D. (Ed.), *Reading, Perception and Language*. Baltimore, MD: York.

Critchley, M. (1981) Dyslexia: An Overview. In Pavlides, G. Th. & Miles, T. R. *Dyslexia Research and Its Application to Education*. New York: Wiley.

Cruickshank, W. M. (1967) *Teaching the*

Brain-Injured Child. Syracuse, NY: Syracuse University Press.

Cruickshank, W. M. (1977) *Learning Disabilities in Home, School and Community.* Syracuse, NY: Syracuse University Press.

Cruickshank, W. M. (1979) Learning Disabilities: A Definitional Statement. In Polak, E. (Ed.), *Issues and Initiatives in Learning Disabilities: Selected Papers from the First National Conference on Learning Disabilities.* Ottawa, Canada: Canadian Association for Children with Learning Disabilities.

Cumming, E. & Cumming, J. (1957) *Closed Ranks.* Cambridge, MA: Harvard University Press.

Cummings, M. (1981) *Individual Differences: A Program for Elementary School Age Children.* New York: Anti-defamation League of B'nai B'rith.

Curtiss, S. (1977) *Genie: A Psycholinguistic Study of a Modern-Day "Wild Child."* New York: Academic Press.

Daehler, M. W. & Greco, C. (1985) Memory in Very Young Children. In Pressley, M. & Brainerd, C. J. (Eds.), *Cognitive Learning and Memory in Children.* New York: Springer-Verlag.

Dai, B. (1952) A Socio-psychiatric Approach to Personality Organization. *American Sociological Review* 17:44–49.

Daniels, M. (1964) The Dynamics of Morbid Envy in the Etiology and Treatment of Chronic Learning Disability. *Psychoanalytic Review* 51:586–596.

Dare, M. T. & Gordon, N. (1970) Clumsy Children: A Disorder of Perception and Motor Organization. *Developmental Medicine and Child Neurology* 12:178–185.

Davidson, P. S. & Marolda, M. R. (1986) *The Neuropsychology of Mathematics Learning.* Menlo Park, CA: Addison-Wesley.

Davidson, P. S. & Wilcutt, R. E. (1983) *Spatial Problem Solving with Cuisenaire Rods.* New Rochelle, NY: Cuisenaire Co. of America.

Davidson, R. J. & Fox, N. A. (1982) Asymmetrical Brain Activity Discriminates Between Positive and Negative Affective Stimuli in Human Infants. *Science* 218:1235–1237.

Davidson, R. J., Schwartz, G. E., & Shapiro, D. (Eds.) (1983) *Consciousness and Self-Regulation Advances in Research and Theory.* New York: Plenum.

Davie, R. & Butler, N. R. (1975) *From Birth to Seven: The Second Report of the National Child Development Survey.* London: Humanities.

Davis, M. & Wallbridge, D. (1981) *Boundary and Space: An Introduction to the Work of D. W. Winnicott.* New York: Brunner/Mazel.

Davis, R. C., Buchwald, A. M., & Frankmann, R. W. (1955) Autonomic and Muscular Response and Their Relation to Simple Stimuli. *Psychological Monographs, General and Applied.* Whole No. 405:1–71.

Dean, R.S. & Rattan, A.I. (1987) Measuring the Effects of Failure with Learning Disabled Children. *International Journal of Neuroscience* 37:27–30.

De Bono, E. (1969) *The Mechanism of the Mind.* New York: Simon & Schuster.

De Bono, E. (1976) *Teaching Thinking.* New York: Penguin.

De Casper, A. J. & Fifer, W. P. (1980) Fetal Auditory Learning. *Science* 208:1174.

De Charms, R. (1976) *Enhancing Motivation: Change in the Classroom.* New York: Irvington.

De Feudis, F. V. & Mandel, P. (Eds.) (1981) *Amino Acid Neurotransmitters.* New York: Raven.

De Fries, J. C., Singer, S. M., Foch, T. T., & Lewitter, F. I. (1978) Familial Nature of Reading Disability. *British Journal of Psychiatry* 132:361–367.

De Hirsch, K. (1966) *Predicting Reading Failure.* New York: Harper & Row.

De Hirsch, K. (1967) Differential Diagnosis Between Aphasic and Schizophrenic Language in Children. *Journal of Speech and Hearing Disorders* 32:3–10.

De Hirsch, K. (1982) Dysphasia-Autism. *Annals of Dyslexia* 32:305–320.

Deich, R. F. & Hodges, P. M. (1978) *Language Without Speech.* New York: Brunner/Mazel.

De la coste-Utamsing, C. & Holloway, R. L. (1982) Sexual Dimorphism in the Human Corpus Callosum. *Science* 216:1431–1432.

Delgado, J. M. R. (1975) Inhibitory Systems and Emotions. In Levi, L. (Ed.), *Emotions—Their Parameters and Measurement.* New York: Raven.

Demos, E. V. (1982a) Facial Expression in Young Children: A Descriptive Analysis. In Field, T. & Fegel, A. (Eds.), *Emotion and Early Interaction.* Hillsdale, NJ: Erlbaum.

Demos, E. V. (1982b) The Role of Affect in Early Childhood: An Exploratory Study. In Trenick, E. (Ed.), *Social Interchange in Infancy, Affect, Cognition and Communication.* Baltimore, MD: University Park Press.

Demos, E. V. (1984) Empathy and Affect: Reflections on Infant Experience. In Lichtenberg, J., Bornstein, M., & Silver, D. (Eds.), *Empathy I and II.* New York: Analytic Press.

De Myer, M. K., Hingtgen, J. N., & Jackson, R. K. (1981) Infantile Autism Reviewed: A Decade of Research. *Schizophrenia Bulletin* 7:388–45.

Denckla, M. B. (1972) Clinical Syndromes in Learning Disabilities: The Case for "Splitting" vs "Lumping." *Journal of Learning Disabilities* 5:26–32.

Denckla, M. B., Rudel, R. G., & Broman, M. (1981) Tests that Discriminate between Dyslexic and Other Learning-Disabled Boys. *Brain and Language* 13:118–129.

Denhoff, E. (1973) Natural Life History of Children with MBD. *Annals of the New York Academy of Sciences* 205:188–205.

Denny-Brown, D. & Yanagisawa, N. (1976) The Role of the Basal Ganglia in the Initiation of Movement. In Yahr, M. D. (Ed.), *The Basal Ganglia.* New York: Raven.

Deno, E. (1970) Special Education as Development Capital. *Exceptional Children* 37:229–237.

DeQuiros, J. B. & Schrager, O. L. (1978) *Neuropsychological Fundamentals in Learning Disabilities.* San Rafael, CA: Academic Therapy Publications.

Deri, S. K. (1984) *Symbolization and Creativity.* New York: International Universities Press.

De Saint-Exupery, A. (1943) *The Little Prince.* New York: Harcourt, Brace & World.

Deuel, R. K. (1983) Aphasia in Childhood. In Mykelbust, H. R. (Ed.), *Progress in Learning Disabilities. Volume V.* New York: Grune & Stratton.

Deutsch, D. & Deutsch, J. A. (Eds.) (1975) *Short-Term Memory.* New York: Academic Press.

Devereux, G. (1966) Loss of Identity, Impairment of Relationships, Reading Disability. *Psychoanalytic Quarterly* 35:18–39.

Devine, T. G. (1983) *Teaching Study Skills: A Guide for Teachers.* Rockleigh, NJ: Allyn & Bacon.

Diamond, M. (1988) *Enriching Heredity: The Impact of the Environment on the Anat-*

omy of the Brain. New York: Free Press.

Diamond, S. J. (1971) Hemisphere Function and Word Registration. *Journal of Experimental Psychology* 87:183–186.

Dickson, W. P. (1982) Creating Communication-Rich Classrooms: Insights from the Sociolinguistic and Referential Traditions. In Wilkinson, L. C. (Ed.), *Communicating in the Classroom.* New York: Academic Press.

Diller, L. & Gordon, W. (1981) Rehabilitation and Clinical Neuropsychology. In Filskov, S. G. & Boll, T. J. (Eds.), *Handbook of Clinical Neuropsychology.* New York: Wiley.

Di Pasquale, G. W., Moule, A. D., & Flewelling, R. W. (1980) The Birthdate Effect. *Journal of Learning Disabilities* 13:234–238.

Dixon, J. P. (1983) *The Spatial Child.* Springfield, IL: Charles C. Thomas.

Dixon, N. F. (1981) *Preconscious Processing.* New York: Wiley.

Dixon, S. D., Yogman, M., Tronick, E., Adamson, L., Als, H., & Brazelton, T. B. (1981) Early Infant Social Interaction with Parents and Strangers. *Journal of Child Psychiatry* 20:32–52.

Dobson, R. & Dobson, J. (1981) *The Language of Schooling.* Washington, DC: University Press of America.

Doehring, D. G. (1984) Subtyping of Reading Disorders: Implications for Remediation. *Annals of Dyslexia* 34:205–216.

Doehring, D. G., Trites, R. L., Patel, P. G., & Fiedorowicz, C. A. M. (1981) *Reading Disabilities: The Interaction of Reading, Language and Neuropsychological Deficits.* New York: Academic Press.

Donaldson, M. & Reid, J. F. (1982) Language Skills and Reading: A Developmental Perspective. In Hendry,

A. (Ed.), *Teaching Reading: The Key Issues.* London: Heinemann.

Dorr, D., Zax, M., & Bonner, III, J. W. (Eds.) (1982) *The Psychology of Discipline.* New York: International Universities Press.

Douglas, V. I. (1975) Are Drugs Enough? —To Treat or to Train the Hyperactive Child. *International Journal of Mental Health* 4:199–212.

Douglas, V. I. (1981) Attentional and Cognitive Problems. In Rutter, M. (Eds.), *Scientific Foundations of Developmental Psychiatry.* Baltimore, MD: University Park Press.

Downing, J. (1979) *Reading and Reasoning.* New York: Springer-Verlag.

Drake, W. E. (1968) Clinical and Pathological Findings in a Child with a Developmental Learning Disability. *Journal of Learning Disabilities* 9:486–502.

Dreeben, R. (1976) The Organizational Structure of Schools and School Systems. In Loubser, J. J., Baum, R. C., Effrat, A., & Lidz, V. M. (Eds.), *Explorations in General Theory in Social Sciences, Volume II.* New York: Free Press.

Dreikurs, R., Grunwald, B. B., & Pepper, F. C. (1971) *Maintaining Sanity in the Classroom.* New York: Harper & Row.

Dretske, F. I. (1981) *Knowledge and the Flow of Information.* Boston: MIT Press.

Drew, A. L. (1956) A Neurological Appraisal of Familial Congenital Word-Blindness. *Brain* 79:440–460.

Dreyfus, H. & Dreyfus, S. (1986) *Mind Over Machine.* New York: Free Press.

Duane, D. D. (1977) Developmental Dyslexia: Etiologic Theories and Therapeutic Implications. *Psychiatric Annals* 7:448–453.

Duane, D. D. (1984) Underachievement in

Written Language: Auditory Aspects. In Myklebust, H. R. (Ed.), *Progress in Learning Disabilities. Volume 5.* New York: Grune & Stratton.

Duffy, F. H. & McAnulty, G. B. (1985) Brain Electrical Activity Mapping (BEAM). In Duffy, F. H. (Ed.), *Dyslexia: A Neuroscientific Approach to Clinical Evaluation.* Boston: Little, Brown.

Dulcan, M. K. (1985) Attention Deficit Disorder: Evaluation and Treatment. *Pediatric Annals* 14:383–400.

Dunn, H. G., Crichton, J. V., Grunau, R. V. E., McBurney, A. K., McCormick, A. Q., Robertson, A. M., & Schulzer, M. (1980) Neurological, Psychological and Educational Sequelae of Low Birth Weight. *Brain and Development* 2:57–67.

Dunn, H. G., McBurney, A. K., Ingram, S., & Hunter, C. M. (1977) Maternal Cigarette Smoking during Pregnancy and the Child's Subsequent Development: II. Neurological and Intellectual Maturation to the Age of 6½ Years. *Canadian Journal of Public Health* 68:43–50.

Dunn, J. (1981) Individual Differences in Temperament. In Rutter, M. (Ed.), *Scientific Foundations of Developmental Psychiatry.* Baltimore, MD: University Park Press.

Dunn, J. & Kendrick, C. (1982) *Siblings: Love, Envy and Understanding.* London: Grant McIntyre.

Dunn, K. J. (1982) Measuring Productivity Preferences in Adults. In *Student Learning Styles and Brain Behavior.* Reston, VA: National Association of Secondary School Principals.

Dunn, P. (1976) Orthomolecular Therapy: Implications for Learning Disability. In Leisman, G. (Ed.), *Basic Visual Processes and Learning Disability.* Springfield, IL: Charles C. Thomas.

Dunn, R. & Dunn, K. (1978) *Teaching Students Through Their Individual Learning Styles: A Practical Approach.* Reston, VA: Reston Publishing.

Duplaix, J. (1950) Is Learning to Read an Abstract Process; Notes on "Experiences, Concepts and Reading." *Quarterly Journal of Child Behavior* 1:465–471.

Dusek, J. B. (1975) Do Teachers Bias Children's Learning? *Review of Educational Research* 45:661–684.

Dweck, C. S. & Bempechat, J. (1983) Children's Theories of Intelligence: Consequences for Learning. In Paris, S. G., Olson, G. M., & Stevenson, H. W. (Eds.), *Learning and Motivation in the Classroom.* Hillsdale, NJ: Erlbaum.

Dykman, R. A., Walls, R. C. Suzuki, T., Ackerman, P. T., & Peters, J. E. (1970) Children with Learning Disabilities: Conditioning, Differentiation and the Effect of Distraction. *American Journal of Orthopsychiatry* 40:766–782.

Eastwood, M. R., Whitton, J. C., Kramer, P. M., & Peter, A. M. (1985) Infradian Rhythms. *Archives of General Psychiatry* 42:295–299.

Ebaugh, F. G. (1923) Neuropsychiatric Sequelae of Acute Epidemic Encephalitis in Children. *American Journal of Diseases of Children* 25:89–97.

Ebels, E. J. (1981) Maturation of the Central Nervous System. In Rutter, M. (Ed.), *Scientific Foundations of Developmental Psychiatry.* Baltimore, MD: University Park Press.

Ebling, F. J. G. (1981) The Role of Odour in Mammalian Aggression. In Brain, P. F. & Benton, D. (Eds.), *The Biology of Aggression.* Rockville, MD: Sijthogg & Noordhoff.

Eccles, J. C. (1970) *Facing Reality: Philosophical Adventures by a Brain Scientist.* New York: Springer-Verlag.

Eccles, J. C. (1973) *The Understanding of the Brain.* New York: McGraw-Hill.

Eccles, J. C. (1989) *Evolution of the Brain: Creation of the Self.* London: Routledge.

Eccles, J. C. & Robinson, D. N. (1984) *The Wonder of Being Human.* New York: Free Press.

Eckblad, G. (1981) *Scheme Theory: A Conceptual Framework for Cognitive-Motivational Processes.* New York: Academic Press.

Eco, U. (1983) *Semiotics and the Philosophy of Language.* Bloomington, IN: Indiana University Press.

Eddy, J. (1983) *The Music Came from Deep Inside: A Story of Artists and Severely Handicapped Children.* New York: McGraw-Hill.

Edelheit, H. (1972) Mythopoiesis and the Primal Scene. *Psychoanalytic Study of Society* 5:212–233.

Edelman, G. M. & Finkel, L. (1984) Neuronal Group Selection in the Cerebral Cortex. In Edelman, G. M., Cowan, W. M., & Gall, W. E. (Eds.), *Dynamic Aspects of Neocortical Function.* New York: Wiley.

Edgerton, R. B., Bollinger, M., & Herr, B. (1984) The Cloak of Competence: After Two Decades. *American Journal of Mental Deficiency* 88:345–351.

Educational Utility Group. 8150 Leesburg Pike, Vienna, VA 22180.

Eeg-Olafsson, O. (1970) The Development of the Electroencephalogram in Normal Children and Adolescents from the Age of 1 through 21 Years. *Acta Paediatrica Scandinavica.* Supplementum 208.

Efron, R. (1957) The Conditioned Inhibition of Uncinate Fits. *Brain* 80:251–262.

Egan, K. (1983) *Education and Psychology: Plato, Piaget and Scientific Psychology.* New York: Teacher's College Press, Columbia University.

Eichorn, D. H. (1970) Physiological Development. In Mussen, P. H. (Ed.), *Carmichael's Manual of Child Psychology. Volume I.* New York: Wiley.

Eidelberg, D. & Galaburda, A. M. (1982) Symmetry and Asymmetry in the Human Posterior Thalamus. *Archives of Neurology* 39:325–332.

Eisenberg, L. (1979) Reading Disorders: Strategies for Recognition and Management. *Bulletin of the Orton Society* 29:39–55.

Eisnitz, A. J. (1980) The Organization of the Self-Representation and Its Influence on Pathology. *Psychoanalytic Quarterly* 49:361–392.

Ekman, P. (1980) Biological and Cultural Contributions to Body and Facial Movement in the Expression of Emotions. In Rorty, A. O. (Ed.), *Explaining Emotions.* Berkeley, CA: University of California Press.

Ekman, P., Levenson, R. W., & Friesen, W. V. (1983) Autonomic Nervous System Activity Distinguishes Among Emotions. *Science* 221:1208–1210.

Elkind, D. (1981) *The Hurried Child: Growing Up Too Fast Too Soon.* Reading, MA: Addison-Wesley.

Elkind, D. (1982) Piagetian Psychology and the Practice of Child Psychiatry. *Journal of Child Psychiatry* 21:435–445.

Elkind, D. (1983) The Curriculum-Disabled Child. *Topics in Learning and Learning Disabilities* 31:71–78.

Eliot, J. (1975) The Spatial World of the Child. In Myklebust, H. R. (Ed.), *Progress in Learning Disabilities. Volume III.* New York: Grune & Stratton.

Elliott, E. & Needleman, R. (1976) The

Syndrome of Hyperlexia. *Brain and Language* 3:339–349.

Elliott, R. (1964) Physiological Activity and Performance: A Comparison of Kindergarten Children with Young Adults. *Psychological Monographs: General and Applied* 781(10):1–31.

Emde, R. N., Gaensbauer, T. J., & Harmon, R. J. (1976) Emotional Expression in Infancy: A Biobehavioral Study. *Psychological Issues.* Monograph 37, Volume 10, No. 1. New York: International Universities Press.

Emde, R. N., Harmon, R. J., & Good, W. V. (1986) Depressive Feelings in Children: A Transactional Model for Research. In Rutter, M., Izard, C. E., & Rud, P. B. (Eds.), *Depression in Young People: Developmental and Clinical Perspectives.* New York: Guilford.

Emerick, L. L. & Hatten, J. T. (1979) *Diagnosis and Evaluation in Speech Pathology* (2nd ed.). Englewood Cliffs, NJ: Prentice-Hall.

Engel, G. L. (1963) Toward a Classification of Affects. In Knapp, P. H. (Ed.), *Expression of the Emotions in Man.* New York: International Universities Press.

English, O. S. & Pearson, G. H. J. (1963) *Emotional Problems of Living.* New York: W. W. Norton.

Entwisle, D. R. (1979) The Child's Social Environment and Learning to Read. In Waller, T. G. & MacKinnon, G. E. (Eds.), *Reading Research: Advances in Theory and Practice. Volume I.* New York: Academic Press.

Epstein, H. T. (1978) Growth Spurts During Brain Development: Implications for Educational Policy Practice. In Chall, J. S. & Mirsky, A. F. (Eds.), *Education and the Brain.* Chicago: University of Chicago Press.

Epstein, H. T. (1980) Some Biological Bases of Cognitive Development. *Bulletin of the Orton Society* 30:46–62.

Epstein, S. (1982) Conflict and Stress. In Goldberger, L. & Bregnitz, S. (Eds.), *Handbook of Stress: Theoretical and Clinical Aspects.* New York: Free Press.

Ericsson, K. A. & Chase, W. G. (1982) Exceptional Memory. *American Scientist* 70:607–615.

Erikson, E. H. (1950) Growth and Crises of the Healthy Personality. *Psychological Issues. Monograph 1* pp. 50–100. New York: International Universities Press.

Erikson, E. H. (1959) *Identity and the Life Cycle: Selected Papers.* New York: International Universities Press.

Erikson, E. H. (1968) *Identity: Youth and Crisis.* New York: Norton.

Erikson, K. (1966) *Wayward Puritans.* New York: Wiley.

Ernhart, C. B., Graham, F. K., Eichman, P. L., Marshall, J. M., & Thurston, D. (1963) Brain Injury in the Preschool Child: Some Developmental Considerations: II. Comparison of Brain Injured and Normal Children. *Psychological Monographs, General and Applied* 77(10):17–33.

Escalona, S. K. (1968) *The Roots of Individuality.* Chicago: Aldine.

Esman, A. H. (1983) The Stimulus Barrier: A Review and Reconsideration. *Psychoanalytic Study of the Child* 38:193–207.

Essman, W. B. (1983) *Clinical Pharmacology of Learning and Memory.* New York: SP Medical & Scientific Books.

Etzioni, A. (1982) *An Immodest Agenda: Rebuilding America Before the 21st Century.* New York: McGraw-Hill.

Evarts, E. V. (1962) A Neurophysiologic Theory of Hallucinations. In West, L. J. (Ed.), *Hallucinations.* New York: Grune & Stratton.

Evarts, E. V., Shinoda, Y., & Wise, S. P. (1984) *Neurophysiological Approaches to Higher Brain Functions*. New York: Wiley-Interscience.

Everhart, R. B. (1983) *Reading, Writing and Resistance: Adolescence and Labor in a Junior High School*. Boston: Routledge & Kegan Paul.

Everly, G. S. & Rosenfeld, R. (1981) *The Nature and Treatment of the Stress Response*. New York: Plenum.

Eyetech Vision Screening System, Levolar Lorentzen, Inc., 1280 Wall Street West, Lyndhurst, NJ 07071.

Eysenck, H. J. (Ed.) (1971) *Readings in Extraversion-Introversion. Volume 3*. London: Staples.

Eysenck, M. W. (1977) *Human Memory: Theory, Research and Individual Differences*. Oxford, England: Pergamon Press.

Fadely, J. L. & Hosler, V. N. (1979) *Understanding the Alpha Child at Home and School: Left and Right Hemispheric Function and Relation to Personality and Learning*. Springfield, IL: Charles C. Thomas.

Faerstein, L. M. (1981) Stress and Coping in Families of Learning Disabled Children: A Literature Review. *Journal of Learning Disabilities* 14:420–423.

Fagen, J. W. & Rovee-Collier, C. (1983) Memory Retrieval: A Time-locked Process in Infancy. *Science* 222:1349–1351.

Family, The, Educational Rights and Privacy Act (1976) 20, V.S.C. 1232g.

Farnham-Diggory, S. (1980) Learning Disabilities: A View from Cognitive Science. *Journal of Child Psychiatry* 19:570–578.

Fausto-Sterling, A. (1985) *Myths of Gender: Biological Theories about Men and Women*. New York: Basic Books.

Fein, D., Pennington, B., Markowitz, P.,

Braverman, M., & Waterhouse, L. (1986) Toward a Neuropsychological Model of Infantile Autism: Are the Social Deficits Primary? *Journal of Child Psychiatry* 25:198–212.

Feinberg, I. (1987) Adolescence and Mental Illness. *Science* 236:507–508.

Feinstein, S. C. (1982) Manic-Depressive Disorder in Children and Adolescents. *Adolescent Psychiatry* 10: 256–272.

Feiring, C. (1983) Behavioral Styles in Infancy and Adulthood: The Work of Karen Horney and Attachment Theorists Collaterally Considered. *Journal of Child Psychiatry* 22:1–7.

Fenichel, C. (1974) Development of the League School. In Kauffman, J. M. & Lewis, C. D. (Eds.), *Teaching Children with Behavior Disorders: Personal Perspectives*. Columbus, OH: Merrill.

Fenichel, O. (1945) *the Psychoanalytic Theory of Neurosis*. New York: Norton.

Fernald, G. (1943) *Remedial Techniques in Basic School Subjects*. New York: McGraw-Hill.

Festinger, L. (1962) *Theory of Cognitive Dissonance*. Stanford, CA: Stanford University Press.

Feuerstein, R. (1980) *Instrumental Enrichment: An Intervention Program for Cognitive Modifiability*. Baltimore, MD: University Park Press.

Field, T. (1979) Differential Behavior and Cardiac Responses of 3-Month-Old Infants to a Mirror and a Peer. *Infant Behavior and Development* 2:179–184.

Field, T. (1981) Gaze Behavior of Normal and High-risk Infants During Early Interactions. *Journal of Child Psychiatry* 20:308–317.

Field, T. (1982) Affective Displays of High-Risk Infants during Early Interactions. In Field, T. & Fogel, A. (Eds.),

Emotion and Early Interaction. Hillsdale, NJ: Erlbaum.

Field, T. (1983) Infant Arousal, Attention and Affect During Early Interaction. In Lipsitt, L. (Ed.), *Advances in Infant Behavior and Development.* Hillsdale, NJ: Erlbaum.

Field, T. M., Woodson, R., Greenberg, R., & Cohen, D. (1982) Discrimination and Imitation of Facial Expressions by Neonates. *Science* 218:179–181.

Field, T. W. (1980) Preschool Play: Effects of Teacher/Child Ratios and Organization of Classroom Space. *Child Study Journal* 10:191–205.

Fields, W. S. & Willis, W. D. (1970) *The Cerebellum in Health and Disease.* St. Louis, MO: Warren H. Green.

Fildes, L. G. (1921) A Psychological Inquiry Into the Nature of the Condition Known as Congenital Word Blindness. *Brain* 44:286–307.

Filer, L. J., Garattine, S., Kare, M. F., Reynolds, W. A., & Wurtman, R. J. (1979) *Glutamic Acid: Advances in Biochemistry and Physiology.* New York: Raven Press.

Filippi, R. & Rousey, C. L. (1968) Delayed Onset of Talking. A Symptom of Interpersonal Disturbance. *Journal of Child Psychiatry* 7:316–328.

Finch, S. M. & Green, J. M. (1979) Personality Disorders. In Noshpitz, J. D. (Ed.), *Basic Handbook of Child Psychiatry.* New York: Basic Books.

Finger, S. & Stein, D. G. (1982) *Brain Damage and Recovery: Research and Clinical Perspectives.* New York: Academic Press.

Finucci, J. M. (1978) Genetic Considerations in Dyslexia. In Mykelbust, H. R. (Ed.), *Progress in Learning Disabilities. Volume IV.* New York: Grune & Stratton.

Finucci, J. M., Gottfredson, L. S., & Childs, B. (1985) A Follow-up Study of Dyslexic Boys. *Annals of Dyslexia* 35:117–136.

Fischer, W. F. (1982) An Empirical-Phenomenological Approach to the Psychology of Anxiety. In DeKoning, A. J. J. & Jenner, F. A. (Eds.), *Phenomenology and Psychiatry.* New York: Academic Press.

Fiscus, E. D. & Mandell, C. J. (1983) *Developing Individualized Education Programs.* St. Paul, MN: West Publishing.

Fish, B. (1976) The Maturation of Arousal and Attention in the First Months of Life. In Rexford, E. N., Sander, L. W., & Shapiro, T. (Eds.), *Infant Psychiatry: A New Synthesis.* New Haven, CT: Yale University Press.

Fishbein, H. D. (1976) *Evolution, Development and Children's Learning.* Santa Monica, CA: Goodyear Publishing.

Fishbein, H. D. (1979) Braille-Phonics: A New Technique for Aiding the Reading Disabled. *Journal of Learning Disabilities* 12:69–73.

Fisher, S. & Greenberg, R. P. (1977) *The Scientific Credibility of Freud's Theories and Therapy.* New York: Basic Books.

Flavell, J. H. (1963) *The Developmental Psychology of Jean Piaget.* New York: D. Van Nostrand.

Flax, N., Mozlui, R., & Solan, H. A. (1984) Learning Disabilities, Dyslexia and Vision. *Journal of the American Optometric Association* 55:399–403.

Flesch, R. (1981) *Why Johnny Still Can't Read: A New Look at the Scandal of Our Schools.* New York: Harper & Row.

Fletcher, J. M. & Satz, P. (1983) Cluster Analysis and the Search for Learning Disability Subtypes. In Rourke, B. (Ed.), *Learning Disabilities in Children: Advances in Subtype Analysis.* New York: Guilford Press.

Fletcher, J. M. & Taylor, H. G. (1984) Neuropsychological Approaches to Children: Towards a Developmetal Neuropsychology. *Journal of Clinical Neuropsychology* 6:39–56.

Fliess, R. (1961) *Ego and Body Ego; Contributions to Their Psychoanalytic Psychology*. New York: International Universities Press.

Flor-Henry, P. (1976) Lateralized Temporal-limbic Dysfunction and Psychopathology. *Annals of the New York Academy of Sciences* 380:777–797.

Flor-Henry, P. (1983) *Cerebral Basis of Psychopathology*. Boston: John Wright-PSG Inc.

Fogel, A. (1982) Affect Dynamics in Early Infancy: Affective Tolerance. In Field, T. & Fogel, A. (Eds.), *Emotion and Early Interaction*. Hillsdale, NJ: Erlbaum.

Ford, F. (1966) *Diseases of Nervous System in Infancy*. Springfield, IL: Charles C. Thomas.

Ford, J., Mongon, D., & Whelan, M. (1982) *Special Education and Social Control: Invisible Disasters*. London: Routledge & Kegan Paul.

Forehand, R., Rogers, T., Steffe, M., & Middlebrook, J. (1984) Helping Parents Help Their Non-Compliant Child. *Child and Adolescent Psychotherapy* 1:6–10.

Forisha, B. L. (1983) Relationship Between Creativity and Mental Imagery. In Sheikh, H. A. (Ed.), *Imagery: Current Theory, Research and Application*. New York: Wiley.

Forness, S. R., Sinclair, E., & Russell, A. T. (1984) Serving Children with Emotional or Behavior Disorders: Implications for Educational Policy. *American Journal of Orthopsychiatry* 54:22–32.

Forster, F. M. (1975) Reading Epilepsy, Musicogenic Epilepsy and Related Disorders. In Mykelbust, H. (Ed.), *Progress in Learning Disabilities. Volume 3*. New York: Grunc & Stratton.

Fraiberg, S. (1969) Libidinal Object Constancy and Mental Representation. *The Psychoanalytic Study of the Child* 24:9–47. New York: International Universities Press.

Freedman, D. A. (1979) The Sensory Deprivations. *Bulletin of the Menninger Clinic* 43:29–68.

Freedman, D. G., Loring, C. B., & Martin, R. M. (1967) Emotional Behavior and Personality Development. In Brackbill, Y. (Ed.), *Infancy and Early Childhood*. New York: Free Press.

Freedman, R. R. (1986) E.E.G. Power Spectra in Sleep-Onset Insomnia. *Electroencephalography and Clinical Neurophysiology* 63:408–413.

Freeman, R. D., Carbin, C. F., & Boese, R. J. (1981) *Can't Your Child Hear? A Guide for Those Who Care about Deaf Children*. Baltimore, MD: University Park Press.

French, A. & Berlin, A. (1979) *Depression in Children and Adolescents*. New York: Human Sciences Press.

Freud, A. (1976) *The Concept of Developmental Lines*. In Neubauer, P. (Ed.), *The Process of Child Development*. New York: Jason Aronson.

Freud, A. (1981a) Insight: Its Presence and Absence as a Factor in Normal Development. In *Psychoanalytic Psychology of Normal Development*. New York: International Universities Press.

Freud, A. (1981b) *The Writings of Anna Freud. Volume VIII*. New York: International Universities Press.

Freud, S. (1910) Leonardo da Vinci and a Memory of His Childhood. In Strachey, J. (Ed.), *Collected Works of Sigmund Freud. Volume 11* (1958). London: Hogarth Press.

Freud, S. (1912) The Dynamics of Transference. *Complete Psychological Works* of Sigmund Freud. Volume 12 (1958). London: Hogarth.

Freud, S. (1937) Analysis Terminable and Interminable. In Strachey, J. (Ed.), *Collected Papers. Volume V* (1956). London: Hogarth Press.

Freud, S. (1938) *The Basic Writings of Sigmund Freud.* Brill, A. A. (Ed.). New York: Random House.

Freud, S. (1965) *The Psychopathology of Everyday Life.* New York: Norton.

Freyberg, J. (1973) Increasing the Imaginative Play of Urban Disadvantaged Kindergarten Children through Systematic Training. In Singer, J. L. (Ed.), *Child's World of Make-Believe.* New York: Academic Press.

Frick, R. B. (1982) The Ego and the Vestibulocerebellar System: Some Theoretical Perspectives. *The Psychoanalytic Quarterly* 51:93–122.

Fried, I. (1979) Cerebral Dominance and Subtypes of Developmental Dyslexia. *Bulletin of the Orton Society* 29:101–112.

Fried, I., Tanguay, P. E., Boder, E., Doubleday, C., & Greensite, M. (1981) Developmental Dyslexia Electrophysiological Evidence of Clinical Subgroups. *Brain and Language* 12:14–22.

Friedhoff, A. J. & Chase, T. N. (Eds.) (1982) *Gilles de la Tourette Syndrome.* New York: Raven.

Friedlander, S., Pothier, P., Morrison, D., & Herman, L. (1982) The Role of Neurological-Developmental Delay in Childhood Psychopathology. *American Journal of Orthopsychiatry* 52:102–107.

Friedling, C. & O'Leary, S. G. (1979) Teaching Self-instruction to Hyperactive Children: A Replication. *Journal of Applied Behavioral Analysis* 12:211–219.

Friedman, J. B. & Gillooley, W. B. (1977) Perceptual Development in the Profoundly Deaf as Related to Early Reading. *Journal of Special Education* 11:347–354.

Friedman, R. (Ed.) (1973) *Family Roots of School Learning and Behavior Disorders.* Springfield, IL: Charles C. Thomas.

Frostig, M., Lefever, W., & Whittlesey, J. (1964) *Developmental Test of Visual Perception.* Palo Alto, CA: Consulting Psychologists Press.

Fulker, D. W. (1981) Biometrical Genetics and Individual Differences. *British Medical Bulletin* 37:115–120.

Fundudis, T., Kolvin, I., & Garside, R. G. (1980) A Follow-up of Speech Retarded Children. In Hersov, L. A. & Berger, M. (Eds.), *Language and Language Disorders in Childhood.* Oxford, England: Pergamon.

Furth, H. G. (1966) *Thinking Without Language: Psychological Implications of Deafness.* New York: Free Press.

Furth, H. G. (1981) *Piaget and Knowledge: Theoretical Foundations* (2nd ed.). Chicago: University of Chicago Press.

Furtwengler, W. J. & Konnert, W. (1982) *Improving School Discipline: An Administrator's Guide.* Rockleigh, NJ: Allyn & Bacon.

Gabel, S. & Erickson, M. T. (Eds.) (1980) *Child Development and Developmental Disabilities.* Boston: Little, Brown.

Gaddes, W. H. (1980) *Learning Disabilities and Brain Functions: A Neuropsychological Approach.* New York: Springer-Verlag.

Gagne, R. M. (1959) Problem-Solving and Thinking. *Annual Review of Psychology* 10:147–172.

Galaburda, A. M. (1989) Ordinary and Extraordinary Brain Development: Anatomical Variation in Developmental Dyslexia. *Annals of Dyslexia* 39:67–80.

Galaburda, A. M. & Kemper, T. L. (1979) Cytoarchitectonic Abnormalities in Developmental Dyslexia: A Case Study. *Annals of Neurology* 6:94–100.

Galaburda, A. M., Sherman, G. F., Rosen, G. D., Aboitiz, F., & Geschwind, H. (1985) Developmental Dyslexia: Four Consecutive Patients with Cortical Anomalies. *Annals of Neurology* 18:222–233.

Gale, A. (1983) Electroencephalographic Correlates of Extraversion-Introversion. In Sinz, R. & Rosenzweig, M. R. (Eds.), *Psychophysiology*. New York: Elsevier.

Galin, D., Johnstone, J., Nakell, L., & Herron, J. (1979) Development of the Capacity for Tactile Information Transfer between Hemispheres in Normal Children. *Science* 204:1330–1332.

Gallagher, J. J., Trohanis, P. L., & Clifford, R. M. (1989) *Policy Implementation and P.L. 99-457: Planning for Young Children with Special Needs*. Baltimore, MD: Paul H. Brooks.

Galler, J. R., Ramsey, F., Solimano, G., & Lowell, W. E. (1983) The Influence of Early Malnutrition on Subsequent Behavioral Development. II. Classroom Behavior. *Journal of Child Psychiatry* 22:16–22.

Galton, F. (1883) *Inquiries Into Human Faculty and Its Development*. New York: Macmillan.

Garber, H. L. (1988) *The Milwaukee Project: Preventing Mental Retardation in Children at Risk*. Washington, D.C.: American Association on Mental Retardation.

Garber, J., Miller, W. R., & Seaman, S. F. (1979) Learned Helplessness, Stress and the Depressive Disorders. In Depue, R. A. (Ed.), *The Psychobiology of the Depressive Disorders: Implications for the Effects of Stress*. New York: Academic Press.

Gardner, G. E. (1971) Aggression and Violence—The Enemies of Precision Learning in Children. *American Journal of Psychiatry* 128:445–450.

Gardner, G. E. & Sperry, B. M. (1974) School Problems—Learning Disabilities and School Phobia. In Arieti, S., *American Handbook of Psychiatry. Vol. 2*. New York: Basic Books.

Gardner, H. (1976) *The Shattered Mind: The Person After Brain Damage*. New York: Knopf.

Gardner, H. (1981) *The Quest for Mind* (2nd ed.). Chicago: University of Chicago Press.

Gardner, H. (1983) *Frames of Mind: The Theory of Multiple Intelligences*. New York: Basic Books.

Gardner, R. A. (1968) Psychogenic Problems of Brain-Injured Children and Their Parents. *Journal of Child Psychiatry* 7:471–491.

Gardner, R. A. (1971) *Therapeutic Communication with Children*. New York: Science House.

Gardner, R. A. (1979) *The Objective Diagnosis of Minimal Brain Dysfunction*. Cresskill, NJ: Creative Therapeutics.

Gardner, R. A. & Gardner, D. T. (1969) Teaching Sign Language to a Chimpanzee. *Science* 165:664–672.

Gardner, W. I. (1978) *Children with Learning and Behavior Problems: A Behavior Management Approach* (2nd ed.). Boston: Allyn & Bacon.

Garfinkel, A. (1984) A Mathematics for Physiology. *American Journal of Physiology* 245:R455-466.

Gargiulo, R. M. (1984) *Working with Parents of Exceptional Children: A Guide for Professionals*. Boston: Houghton-Mifflin.

Garvey, C. (1977) *Play*. Cambridge, MA: Harvard University Press.

Gates, A. I. (1922) Psychology of Reading and Spelling with Special Reference to Disability. *Contributions to Education, No. 129.* New York: Bureau of Publications, Teachers College, Columbia University.

Gaylin, W. (Ed.) (1968) *The Meaning of Despair.* New York: Human Sciences House.

Gazzaniga, M. S., Steen, D., & Volpe, B. (1979) *Functional Neuroscience.* New York: Harper & Row.

Gazzara, R. A. & Altman, J. (1981) Early Postnatal X-irradiation of the Hippocampus and Discrimination Learning in Adult Rats. *Journal of Comparative and Physiological Psychology* 95:484–495.

Gedimen, H. K. (1971) The Concept of Stimulus Barrier. *International Journal of Psychoanalysis* 52:243–257.

Gedo, J. E. & Goldberg, A. (1973) *Models of the Mind: A Psychoanalytic Theory.* Chicago: University of Chicago Press.

Gersten, R., Carnine, E., & White, W. A. T. (1985) The Pursuit of Clarity: Direct Instruction and Applied Behavioral Analysis. In Heward, W. L., Heron, T. E., Hill, D. S., & Trap-Porter, J. (Eds.), *Focus on Behavior Analysis in Education.* Columbus, OH: Merrill.

Geschwind, N. (1965) Disconnexion Syndromes in Animals and Man. *Brain* 88:237–294.

Geschwind, N. (1979a) Specializations of the Human Brain. *Scientific American* 241:180–199.

Geschwind, N. (1979b) Asymmetries of the Brain. *Bulletin of the Orton Society* 29: Reprint No. 80.

Geschwind, N. (1982) Why Orton Was Right. *Annals of Dyslexia* 32:13–30.

Geschwind, N. (1985a) Biological Foundations of Reading. In Duffy, F. H. & Geschwind, N. (Eds.), *Dyslexia: A Neuroscientific Approach to Clinical Evaluation.* Boston: Little, Brown.

Geschwind, N. (1985b) Mechanism of Change after Brain Lesions. *Annals of the New York Academy of Sciences* 457:1–11.

Geschwind, N. & Behan, P. (1982) Left-Handedness: Association with Immune Disease, Migraine and Developmental Learning Disorder. *Proceedings of the National Academy of Sciences* 79:5097–5100.

Geschwind, N. & Behan, P. (1984) Autoimmune Disorders, Migraine and Dyslexia. In Geschwind, N. & Galaburda, A. M. (Eds.), *Cerebral Dominance: The Biological Foundations.* Cambridge, MA: Harvard University Press.

Gesell, A. & Armatruda, C. S. (1974) *Developmental Diagnosis* (3rd ed.). New York: Harper & Row.

Getty, B. M. & Dubay, I. S. (1983) *Italic Handwriting Series.* Portland, OR: Portland State University.

Getzels, J. W. & Jackson, P. W. (1962) *Creativity and Intelligence.* New York: Wiley.

Ghiselin, B. (Ed.) (1952) *The Creative Process.* Berkeley, CA: University of California Press.

Gholson, B. (1980) *The Cognitive-Developmental Basis of Human Learning.* New York: Academic Press.

Giannitrapani, D. (1985) *The Electrophysiology of Intellectual Functions.* New York: S. Karger.

Gibson, D. (1978) *Down's Syndrome.* Cambridge, England: Cambridge University Press.

Gibson, E. J. (1966) Experimental Psychology of Learning to Read. In Money, J. (Ed.), *The Disabled Reader.* Baltimore, MD: Johns Hopkins Press.

Gibson, E. J. (1970) Development of Perception: Discrimination of Depth Compared with Discrimination of Graphic Symbols. In Brown, R. (Ed.), *Cognitive Development in Children.* Chicago: University of Chicago Press.

Gibson, E. J. (1971) Perceptual Learning

and Theory of Work Perception. *Cognitive Psychology* 2:351–368.

Gibson, E. J. & Levin, H. (1975) *The Psychology of Reading*. Cambridge, MA: MIT Press.

Gilligan, C. (1982) *In a Different Voice: Psychological Theory and Women's Development*. Cambridge, MA: Harvard University Press.

Gillingham, A. & Stillman, B. (1960) *Remedial Training for Children with Specific Disability in Reading, Spelling and Penmanship*. Cambridge, MA: Educators Publishing Service.

Ginott, H. G. (1972) *Teacher and Child: A Book for Parents and Teachers*. New York: Macmillan.

Gittelman, R. & Eskenazi, B. (1983) Lead and Hyperactivity Revisited. *Archives of General Psychiatry* 40:827–833.

Gittelman, R., Mannuzza, S., Shenker, R., & Bonagura, N. (1985) Hyperactive Boys Almost Grown Up. *Archives of General Psychiatry* 42:937–947.

Glauber, I. P. (1983) *Stuttering—A Psychoanalytic Study*. New York: Human Science Press.

Glick, J. (1975) Cognitive Development in Cross-cultural Perspective. In Horowitz, F. D. (Ed.), *Review of Child Development Research. Volume 4*. Chicago: University of Chicago Press.

Glynn, E. L., Thomas, J. D., & Shee, S. K. (1973) Behavioral Self-control of On-Task Behavior in an Elementary Classroom. *Journal of Applied Behavioral Analysis* 6:105–113.

Gobel, S. & Erikson, M. T. (Eds.) (1980) *Child Development and Developmental Disabilities*. Boston: Little, Brown.

Goertzel, M. G., Goertzel, V., & Goertzel, T. G. (1978) *300 Eminent Personalities*. San Francisco: Jossey-Bass.

Goffman, E. (1959) *The Presentation of Self in Everyday Life*. Garden City, NY: Doubleday Anchor Books.

Goffman, E. (1974) *Frame Analysis: An Essay on the Organization of Experience*. Cambridge, MA: Harvard University Press.

Gold, P. E. (1987) Sweet Memories. *American Scientist* 75:151–155.

Goldberg, G. (1985) Supplementary Motor Area Structure and Function: Review & Hypothesis. *The Behavioral and Brain Sciences* 8:567–616.

Goldberg, H. K. & Schiffman, G. B. (1983) *Dyslexia*. New York: Grune & Stratton.

Goldberg, R. J. (1982) *Anxiety: A Guide to Biobehavioral Diagnoses and Therapy for Physicians and Mental Health Clinicians*. Garden City, NY: Medical Examination Publishing.

Goldings, C. R. (1968) Some New Trends in Children's Literature from the Perspective of the Child Psychiatrist. *Journal of Child Psychiatry* 7:377–397.

Goldman, J., Stein, C. L., & Guerry, S. (1984) *Psychological Methods of Child Assessment*. New York: Brunner/Mazel.

Goldman, P. S., Crawford, H. T., Stokes, L. P., Golkin, T. W., & Rosvold, H. E. (1974) Sex-Dependent Behavioral Effects of Cerebral Cortical Lesions in the Development Rhesus Monkey. *Science* 186:540–542.

Goldmeier, E. (1972) Similarity in Visually Perceived Forms. *Psychological Issues* Monograph 29, Vol. VIII, No. 1. New York: International Universities Press.

Goldschmid, M. L. & Bentler, P. M. (1968) The Dimensions and Measurement of Conservation. *Child Development* 39:787–802.

Goldstein, K. (1954) The Brain Injured Child. In Michael-Smith, H. (Ed.), *Pediatric Problems in Clinical Practice*. New York: Grune & Stratton.

Goldstein, K. (1963) *Human Nature in the*

Light of Psychopathology. New York: Schocken Books.

Goldstein, K. N. & Blackman, S. (1978) *Cognitive Style: Five Approaches and Relevant Research*. New York: Wiley.

Goleman, D. (1985) *Vital Lies, Simple Truths*. New York: Simon & Schuster.

Golin, A. K. & Ducanis, A. J. (1981) *The Interdisciplinary Team: A Handbook for the Education of Exceptional Children*. Rockville, MD: Aspen Systems.

Goodman, J. D. & Sours, J. A. (1967) *The Child Mental Status Examination*. New York: Basic Books.

Goodman, K. S. (1982) *Language and Literacy: The Selected Writings of Kenneth S. Goodman. Vols. I & II*. Boston: Routledge & Kegan Paul.

Goody, W. & Reinhold, M. (1961) Congenital Dyslexia and Asymmetry of Cerebral Function. *Brain* 84:231–242.

Gordon, H. (1920) Left-Handedness and Mirror Writing, Especially Among Defective Children. *Brain* 43:313–336.

Gordon, M. (1984) The Gordon Diagnostic System. Clinical Diagnostics. Golden, CO.

Gordon, T. (1978) *P.E.T.: Parent Effectiveness Training: The Tested New Way to Raise Responsible Children*. New York: Wyden.

Gorenstein, E. E. & Newman, J. P. (1980) Disinhibitory Psychopathology: A New Perspective and a Model for Research. *Psychological Review* 87:301–315.

Gough, P. B. (1974) The Structure of Language. In Duane, D. D. (Ed.), *Reading, Perception and Language*. Baltimore, MD: York Press.

Gould, J. L. & Gould, C. G. (1981) The Instinct to Learn. *Science* 81:44–50.

Gould, R. (1972) *Child Studies Through Fantasy: Cognitive-Affective Patterns in Development*. New York: Quadrangle Books.

Gould, S. J. (1976) Human Babies as Embryos. *Natural History* 84:22–26.

Gould, S. J. (1980) *The Mismeasure of Man*. New York: Norton.

Goy, R. W. & McEwen, B. S. (1980) *Sexual Differentiation of the Brain*. Cambridge, MA: MIT Press.

Goyette, C. H., Conners, C. K., & Ulrich, R. F. (1978) Normative Data on Revised Conners Parent and Teacher Rating Scales. *Journal of Abnormal Child Psychology* 8:33–50.

Graffagnino, P. (1966) The Brain-Damaged Child: A Misconception? *Connecticut Medicine* 30:115–118.

Graham, F. K. (1979) Distinguishing Among Orienting, Defensive and Startle Reflexes. In Kimmel, H. D., Van Olst, D. H., & Orlebeke, J. F. (Eds.), *The Orienting Response in Humans*. Hillsdale, NJ: Erlbaum.

Graham, P. A. (1980) Whither Equality of Educational Opportunity. *Daedelus* 109:115–132.

Graham, P. A. (1984) Cacophony About Practice, Silence About Purpose. *Daedelus* 113:29–57.

Grahame-Smith, D. G. (1978) Animal Hyperactivity Syndromes: Do They Have Any Relevance to Minimal Brain Dysfunction? In Kalverboer, A. F., van Praag, H. M., & Mendlewicz, J. (Eds.), *Advances in Biological Psychiatry. Vol. 1: Minimal Brain Dysfunction: Fact or Fiction*. Basel, Switzerland: Karger.

Graubard, S. R. (1981) Preface to the Issue—America's Schools: Portraits and Perspectives. *Daedelus* 110(4): v–xvi.

Gray, J. A. (1971) *The Psychology of Fear and Stress*. New York: McGraw-Hill.

Gray, J. A. (1982) *The Neuropsychology of Anxiety: An Enquiry into the Functions of the Septo-Hippocampal System.* Oxford, England: Oxford University Press.

Gray, W. S. (1922) Remedial Cases in Reading: Their Diagnosis and Treatment. *Supplementary Educational Monographs No. 22.* Chicago: University of Chicago Press.

Graziani, L. J., Brodsky, K., Mason, J. C., & Zager, R. P. (1983) Variability in IQ Scores and Prognosis of Children with Hyperlexia. *Journal of Child Psychiatry* 22:441–443.

Green, K. (1981) *Complete Special Education Handbook.* New York: Parker.

Greenacre, P. (1952) *Trauma, Growth and Personality.* New York: Norton.

Greenberg, S. F. (1984) *Stress and The Teaching Profession.* Baltimore, MD: Brookes.

Greenberg, S., Kadowitz, P. J., & Burks, T. F. (Eds.) (1982) *Prostaglandins: Organ and Tissue Specific Actions.* New York: Marcel Dekker.

Greenhill, L. L., Puig-Antich, J., Chambers, W., Rubenstein, B., Halpern, F., & Sachar, E. J. (1981) Growth Hormone, Prolactin and Growth Responses in Hyperkinetic Males Treated with D-Amphetamine. *Journal of Child Psychiatry* 20:84–103.

Greenspan, S. I. (1979a) *Intelligence and Adaptation: An Integration of Psychoanalytic and Piagetian Developmental Psychology.* New York: International Universities Press.

Greenspan, S. I. (1979b) Principles of Intensive Psychotherapy of Neurotic Adults with Minimal Brain Dysfunction. In Bellak, L. (Ed.), *Psychiatric Aspects of Minimal Brain Dysfunction in Adults.* New York: Grune & Stratton.

Greenspan, S. I. (1981) *The Clinical Interview of the Child.* New York: McGraw-Hill.

Greenspan, S. & Lourie, R. W. (1981) Developmental Structuralist Approach to the Classification of Adaptive and Pathologic Personality Organizations: Infancy and Early Childhood. *American Journal of Psychiatry* 138:725–735.

Greenstein, J. (1983) *What the Children Taught Me.* Chicago: University of Chicago Press.

Gregorc, A. F. (1979) Learning/Teaching Styles: Potent Forces Behind Them. *Educational Leadership.* January 1979:234–236.

Gregory, R. L. (1981) *Mind in Science: A History of Explanations in Psychology and Physics.* Cambridge, England: Cambridge University Press.

Griffin, D. R. (1984) Animal Thinking. *American Scientist* 72:456–464.

Grisham, J. D. & Simons, H. D. (1986) Refractive Errors and the Reading Process. A Literature Analysis. *Journal of the American Optometric Association* 57:44–55.

Gross, M. (Ed.) (1983) *Pseudoepilepsy: The Clinical Aspects of False Seizures.* Lexington, MA: Lexington Books.

Grossman, H. J. (Ed.) (1983) *Classification in Mental Retardation.* Washington, D.C.: American Association on Mental Deficiency.

Group for the Advancement of Psychiatry (1982) *The Process of Child Therapy.* New York: Brunner/Mazel.

Gruner, C. R. (1978) *Understanding Laughter: The Workings of Wit and Humor.* Chicago: Nelson-Hall.

Guardo, C. J. & Bohan, J. B. (1971) Development of a Sense of Self-Identity in Children. *Child Development* 42:1909–1921.

Guilford, J. P. (1980) Cognitive Styles. What are They? *Education and Psychological Measurement* 40:715–735.

Guilford, J. P. (1982) Cognitive Psychology's Ambiguities: Some Suggested Remedies. *Psychological Review* 89:48–59.

Guntrip, H. (1973) *Psychoanalytic Theory, Therapy, and the Self.* New York: Basic Books.

Gur, R. C. et al (1982) Sex and Handedness Differences in Cerebral Blood Flow during Rest and Cognitive Activity. *Science* 217:659–661.

Gurman, A. S. & Kniskern, D. P. (1981) *Handbook of Family Therapy.* New York: Brunner/Mazel.

Guyton, A. C. (1977) *Basic Human Physiology: Normal Function and Mechanisms of Disease.* Philadelphia, PA: W. B. Saunders.

Haber, R. N. (1969) Eidetic Images. *Scientific American* 220:36.

Haber, R. N. (1971) Where are the Visions in Visual Perception? In Segal, S. J. (Ed.), *Imagery: Current Cognitive Approaches.* New York: Academic Press.

Haber, L. R. & Haber, R. N. (1981) Preceptual Processes in Reading: An Analysis-by-Synthesis Model. In Pirozzolo, F. J. & Wittrock, M. C. (Eds.), *Neuropsychological and Cognitive Processes in Reading.* New York: Academic Press.

Hagerman, R. & McBogg, P.M. (1983) *The Fragile X Syndrome: Diagnosis, Biochemistry and Intervention.* Dillon, CO: Spectra.

Hagen, R. A., Silver, A. A., & Kreeger (1976) *TEACH: A Preventive Approach for Potential Reading Disability.* New York: Walter Educational Book.

Hall, D. M. B. (1984) *The Child with a Handicap.* London: Blackwell Scientific Publications.

Hallahan, D. P. & Cruickshank, W. M. (1973) *Psychoeducational Foundations of Learning Disabilities.* Englewood Cliffs, NJ: Prentice-Hall.

Hallgren, B. (1950) Specific Dyslexia (Congenital Word-Blindness): A Clinical and Genetic Study. *Acta Psychiatrica and Neurologica,* Supplementum 65:1–287. Copenhagen: Ejnar-Munksgaard.

Halliday, M. (1975) *Learning How to Mean.* London: Edward Arnold.

Hamburg, D. A., Hamburg, B. A., & Barchas, J. D. (1975) Anger and Depression in Perspective of Behavioral Biology. In Levi, L. (Ed.), *Emotions—Their Parameters and Measurement.* New York: Raven.

Hamilton, V. (1983) *The Cognitive Structures and Processes of Human Motivation and Personality.* Chichester, England: Wiley.

Hammill, D. D. & Bartel, N. (1978) *Teaching Children with Learning and Behavior Problems.* Boston: Allyn & Bacon.

Hammill, D. D., Leigh, J. E., McNutt, G., & Larsen, S. C. (1981) A New Definition of Learning Disabilities. *Learning Disabilities Quarterly* 4:336–342.

Hanna, P. R., Hodges, R. E., & Hanna, J. S. (1971) *Spelling: Structure and Strategies.* Washington, DC: University Press of America.

Hardy, W. G. (1978) *Language, Thought and Experience: A Tapestry of the Dimensions of Meaning.* Baltimore, MD: University Park Press.

Harel, S. & Anastasiow, N. J. (1984) *The At-Risk Infant: Psycho-Socio-Medical Aspects.* Baltimore, MD: Brookes.

Haring, N. G. & Schiefelbusch, R. L. (1976) *Teaching Special Children.* New York: McGraw-Hill.

Harley, R. K. (1963) *Verbalism Among Blind Children.* New York: American Foundation for the Blind.

Harlow, H. F. (1974) *Learning to Love.* New York: Jason Aronson.

Harman, D. W. & Ray, W. J. (1977) Hemispheric Activity During Affective

Verbal Stimuli: An EEG Study. *Neuropsychologia* 15:457–460.

Harris, J. E. (1986) *Clinical Neuroscience: From Neuroanatomy to Psychodynamics.* New York: Human Sciences Press.

Hart, I. B. (1962) *The World of Leonardo da Vinci: Man of Science, Engineer and Dreamer of Flight.* New York: Viking.

Hart, L. A. (1975) *How the Brain Works.* New York: Basic Books.

Hart, Z., Rennick, P. M., Klinge, V., & Schwartz, M. (1974) A Pediatric Neurologist's Contribution to Evaluations of School Underachievers. *American Journal of Diseases of Children* 128:319–323.

Hartmann, E. (1982) From the Biology of Dreaming to the Biology of the Mind. *Psychoanalytic Study of the Child* 37:302–335.

Hartlage, L. C. & Telzrow, C. F. (1985) *The Neuropsychology of Individual Differences.* New York: Plenum.

Hartrup, W. W. (1981) Peer Relations and Family Relations: Two Social Worlds. In Rutter, M. (Ed.), *Scientific Foundations of Developmental Psychiatry.* Baltimore, MD: University Park Press.

Hartwig, L. J. (1984) Living with Dyslexia: One Parent's Experience. *Annals of Dyslexia* 34:313–318.

Harvey, D., Prince, J., Bunton, J. B., Partkinson, C., & Campbell, S. (1982) Abilities of Children Who Were Small-for-Gestational-Age Babies. *Pediatrics* 69:296–300.

Haskins, V. L. (1981) *Individual and Gender Differences in the Orienting and Defensive Responses.* Doctoral Thesis. Madison, WI: University of Wisconsin, Madison.

Hassibi, M. & Breuer, H. (1980) *Disordered Thinking and Communication in Children.* New York: Plenum.

Hausman, J. J. (1983) *Arts and the Schools.* New York: McGraw-Hill.

Hawkridge, D. G. (1983) *New Information Technology in Education.* Baltimore, MD: Johns Hopkins University Press.

Hayden, T. L. (1980) Classification of Elective Mutism. *Journal of Child Psychiatry* 19:118–133.

Healy, J. M. (1982) The Enigma of Hyperlexia. *Reading Research Quarterly* 17:319–338.

Healy, J. M. & Aram, D. M. (1986) Hyperlexia and Dyslexia: A Family Study. *Annals of Dyslexia* 36:237–252.

Hearnshaw, L. S. (1979) *Cyril Burt, Psychologist.* Ithaca, NY: Cornell University Press.

Heath, R. (Ed.) (1964) *The Role of Pleasure in Behavior.* New York: Hoeber Medical Division, Harper & Row.

Hebb, D. O. (1949) *The Organization of Behavior.* New York: Wiley.

Hechtman, L. & Weiss, G. (1983) Long-Term Outcome of Hyperactive Children. *American Journal of Orthopsychiatry* 53:532–541.

Hechtman, L., Weiss, G., & Perlman, T. (1984a) Young Adult Outcome of Hyperactive Children Who Received Long-Term Stimulant Treatment. *Journal of Child Psychiatry* 23:261–269.

Hechtman, L., Weiss, G., Perlman, T., & Amsel, R. (1984b) Hyperactives as Young Adults: Initial Predictors of Adult Outcome. *Journal of Child Psychiatry* 23:250–260.

Heilbrunn, G. (1979) Biological Correlates of Psychoanalytic Concepts. *Journal of the American Psychoanalytic Association* 27:597–626.

Heilman, K. M. & Satz, P. (Eds.) (1983) *Neuropsychology of Human Emotion.* New York: Guilford Press.

Henderson, J. M. (1976) Learning to Read:

A Case Study of a Deaf Child. *American Annals of the Deaf* 121:502–506.

Hendrick, I. (1943) The Discussion of the "Instinct to Master" *Psychoanalytic Quarterly* 12:561–565.

Henry, J. P. (1980) Present Concept of Stress Theory. In Usdin, E., Kvetnansky, R., & Kopin, I. J. (Eds.), *Catecholamines and Stress: Recent Advances*. New York: Elsevier/North-Holland.

Henry, J. P. & Ely, D. L. (1980) Ethological and Physiological Theories. In Kutash, I. C., Schlesinger, L. B., & Associates (Eds.), *Handbook on Stress and Anxiety*. San Francisco: Jossey-Bass.

Hermann, K. (1970) *Reading Disability*. Copenhagen: Munksgaard.

Herron, J., Galin, D., Johnstone, J., & Ornstein, R. E. (1979) Cerebral Specialization, Writing Posture and Motor Control of Writing in Left-handers. *Science* 205:1285–1289.

Herskowitz, J. & Rosman, N. P. (1982) *Pediatrics, Neurology and Psychiatry —Common Ground*. New York: Macmillan.

Hersov, L. A. & Berger, M. (Eds.) (1980) *Language and Language Disorders in Childhood*. Oxford, England: Pergamon.

Hertzig, M. E. (1982) Stability and Change in Nonfocal Neurological Signs. *Journal of Child Psychiatry* 21:231–236.

Herzberg, F., Mausner, B., & Snyderman, B. B. (1959) *The Motivation to Work* (2nd ed.). New York: Wiley.

Hess, E. H. (1964) Imprinting in Birds. *Science* 146:1128–1130.

Hess, E. H. (1973) *Imprinting: Early Experience and the Developmental Psychobiology of Attachment*. New York: Van Nostrand Reinhold.

Hewett, F. M. (1972) Educational Programs for Children with Behavior Disorders. In Quay, H. C. & Werry, J. S. (Eds.), *Psychopathological Disorders of Childhood*. New York: Wiley.

Hewett, F. M. (1974) The Field Today. In Kauffman, J. M. & Lewis, C. D. (Eds.), *Teaching Children with Behavior Disorders: Personal Perspectives*. Columbus, Ohio: Merrill.

Hewett, F. M. & Forness, S. R. (1984) *Education of Exceptional Learners* (3rd ed.). Boston: Allyn & Bacon.

Hewett, F. M. & Taylor, F. D. (1980) *The Emotionally Disturbed Child in the Classroom: The Orchestration of Success* (2nd ed.). Boston: Allyn & Bacon.

Hicks, R. E. & Gualtieri, C. T. (1986) Differential Psychopharmacology of Methylphenidate and the Neuropsychology of Childhood Hyperactivity. In Bloomingdale, L. (Ed.), *Attention Deficit Disorder—III*. New York: Spectrum.

Hier, D. B. (1979) Sex Differences on Hemispheric Specialization: Hypothesis for the Excess of Dyslexia in Boys. *Bulletin of the Orton Society* 29:74–83.

Hier, D. B., LeMay, M., & Rosenberger, P. B. (1979) Autism and Unfavorable Left-Right Asymmetrics of the Brain. *Journal of Autism and Developmental Disorders* 9:153–159.

Hier, D. B., LeMay, M., Rosenberger, P. B., & Perlo, V. P. (1978) Developmental Dyslexia: Evidence for a Sub-group with a Reversal of Cerebral Asymmetry. *Archives of Neurology* 35:90–92.

Hier, D. B. & Rosenberger, P. B. (1980) Focal Left Temporal Lobe Lesions and Delayed Speech Acquisition. *Developmental and Behavioral Pediatrics* 1:54–57.

Higgins, P. C. (1980) *Outsiders in a Hearing*

World. A Sociology of Deafness. Beverly Hills, CA: Sage Publications.

Hildreth, G. (1950) Individual Differences. In Monroe, W. S. (Ed.), *Encyclopedia of Educational Research.* New York: Macmillan.

Hillner, K. B. (1978) *Psychology of Learning.* Oxford, England: Pergamon.

Hills, J. E. (1976) *The Educational Sciences.* Bloomfield Hills, MI: Oakland Community College.

Hills, R. J. (1976) The Public School as a Type of Organization. In Loubser, J. J., Baum, R. C., Effrat, A., & Lidz, V. M. (Eds.), *Explorations in General Theory in Social Science. Volume II.* New York: Free Press.

Hinshelwood, J. (1917) *Congenital Word Blindness.* London: H. K. Lewis.

Hintzman, D. L. (1978) *The Psychology of Learning and Memory.* San Francisco: W. H. Freeman.

Hiscock, M. & Kinsbourne, M. (1982) Laterality and Dyslexia: A Critical View. *Annals of Dyslexia* 32:177–228.

Hobbs, N. (1975) *The Futures of Children.* San Francisco: Jossey-Bass.

Hobbs, N. (1982) *The Troubled and Troubling Child: Reeducation in Mental Health, Education and Human Services Programs for Children and Youth.* San Francisco: Jossey-Bass.

Hobson, J. A. & McCarley, R. W. (1977) The Brain as a Dream State Generator: An Activation-Synthesis Hypothesis of the Dream Process. *American Journal of Psychiatry* 134:1335–1348.

Hoehn-Saric, R. (1982) Neurotransmitters in Anxiety. *Archives of General Psychiatry* 39:735–742.

Hoffman, L. G. (1980) Incidence of Vision Difficulties in Children with Learning Disabilities. *Journal of the American Optometric Association* 51:447–451.

Hoffman, M. L. (1970) Moral Develop-ment. In Mussen, P. H. (Ed.), *Carmichael's Manual of Child Psychology. Volume 2.* New York: Wiley.

Hofstadter, D. R. (1981) Prelude . . . Ant Fugue. In Hofstadter, D. R. & Dennett, D. C. (Eds.), *The Mind's I.* New York: Basic Books.

Hohman, L. B. (1922) Postencephalitic Behavior Disorders in Children. *Johns Hopkins Hospital Bulletin* 33:372–375.

Holcomb, P. J., Ackerman, P. T., & Dykman, R. A. (1985) Cognitive Event-Related Brain Potentials in Children with Attention and Reading Deficits. *Psychophysiology* 22:656–667.

Holdsworth, L. & Whitmore, K. (1974) A Study of Children with Epilepsy Attending Ordinary Schools. *Developmental Medicine and Child Neurology* 16:746–758.

Hollingsworth, E. J., Lufler, H. S., & Clune, W. H. (1984) *School Discipline: Order and Autonomy.* New York: Praeger.

Hollingworth, L. S. (1923) *Special Talents and Defects.* New York: Macmillan.

Holmes, D. L., Reich, J. N., & Pasternak, J. F. (1984) *The Development of Infants Born at Risk.* Hillsdale, NJ: Erlbaum.

Holt, R. R. (1976) Drive or Wish? A Reconsideration of the Psychoanalytic Theory of Motivation. *Psychological Issues* 9:158–198.

Holzman, P. S., Solomon, C. M., Levin, S., & Waternaux, C. S. (1984) Pursuit Eye Movement Dysfunctions in Schizophrenia. *Archives of General Psychiatry* 41:136–139.

Hopkins, J. (1979) Cognitive Style in Adults Originally Diagnosed as Hyperactives. *Journal of Child Psychology and Psychiatry* 20:209–216.

Hops, H. (1982) Social-Skills Training for Socially Withdrawn/Isolate Children. In Karoly, P. & Steffan, J. J. (Eds.), *Improving Children's Compe-*

tence. Lexington, MA: Lexington Books.

Horewitz, J. S. (1979) *Family Therapy and Transactional Analysis.* New York: Aronson.

Horowitz, M. J. (1983a) *Image Formation and Psychotherapy.* New York: Aronson.

Horowtiz, M. J. (1983b) Psychological Responses to Serious Life Events. In Breznitz, S. (Ed.), *The Denial of Stress.* New York: International Universities Press.

Horowitz, M. J. & Zilberg, N. (1983) Regressive Alterations of the Self Concept. *American Journal of Psychiatry* 140:284–295.

House, E. R., Glass, G. V., McLean, L. D., & Walker, D. F. (1978) No Simple Answer: A Critique of the Follow Through Evaluation. *Harvard Educational Review* 48:128–160.

Howe, M. J. A. (Ed.) (1983) *Learning from Television: Psychological and Educational Research.* New York: Academic Press.

Howlin, P. (1981) Language. In Rutter, M. (Ed.), *Scientific Foundations of Developmental Psychiatry.* Baltimore, MD: University Park Press.

Hubbard, D. C. & Wright, C. G. (1985) The Emotion of Motion. In Shaskan, D. A. & Roller, W. L. (Eds.), *Paul Schilder: Mind Explorer.* New York: Human Sciences Press.

Hubel, D. H. (1979) The Brain. *Scientific American* 241:45–53.

Hudson, L. (1967) *Contrary Imaginations.* Baltimore, MD: Penguin.

Huey, E. B. (1908) *The Psychology and Pedagogy of Reading.* New York: Macmillan. New Edition: 1968. Cambridge, MA: MIT Press.

Hughes, M. & Grieve, R. (1983) On Asking Children Bizarre Questions. In Donaldson, M., Grieve, R., & Pratt, C. (Eds.), *Early Childhood Development and Education.* New York: Guilford Press.

Huizinga, J. (1944) *Homo Ludens.* New York: Beacon Press, 1950.

Hung, D. L. & Tzeng, O. J. L. (1981) Orthographic Variation and Visual Information Processing. *Psychological Bulletin* 90:377–414.

Hunt, E. (1983) On the Nature of Intelligence. *Science* 219:141–146.

Hunt, E. B. (1962) *Concept Learning: An Information Processing Problem.* New York: Wiley.

Hunt, M. (1982) *The Universe Within: A New Science Explores the Mind.* New York: Simon & Schuster.

Hunt, N. (1967) *The World of Nigel Hunt: The Diary of a Mongoloid Youth.* New York: Garrett.

Hurwitz, I., Bibace, R., Wolff, P. H., & Rowbotham, B. M. (1972) Neuropsychological Functions of Normal Boys, Delinquent Boys and Boys with Learning Problems. *Perceptual Motor Skills* 35:387–394.

Hutt, C. (1972) *Males and Females.* New York: Harmondsworth, Penguin.

Huttenlocher, J., Smiley, P., & Charney, R. (1983) Emergence of Action Categories in the Child: Evidence from Verb Meanings. *Psychological Review* 90:72–93.

Huttenlocher, P. R. & Huttenlocher, J. (1973) A Study of Children with Hyperlexia. *Neurology* 23:1107–1116.

Hynd, G. & Cohen, M. (1983) *Dyslexia: Neuropsychological Theory, Research and Clinical Differentiation.* New York: Grune & Stratton.

Hynd, G. W. & Hynd, C. R. (1984) Dyslexia: Neuroanatomical/Neurolinguistic Perspective. *Reading Research Quarterly* 19:482–498.

Hynes, P. & Phillips, W. (1984) Turner's Syndrome: Assessment and Treatment for Adult Psychiatric Patients. *American Journal of Psychotherapy* 38:558–565.

Inglis, J. & Lawson, J. S. (1981) Sex Differences in the Effects of Unilateral Brain Damage on Intelligence. *Science* 212:693–695.

Ingram, T. T. S., Mason, A. W., & Blackburn, I. (1970) A Retrospective Study of 82 Children with Reading Disability. *Developmental Medicine and Child Neurology* 40:1–23.

Ingvar, D. H. & Schwartz, M. S. (1974) Blood Flow Patterns Induced in the Dominant Hemisphere by Speech and Reading. *Brain* 97:273–288.

Inhelder, B., Sinclair, H., & Bovet, M. (1974) *Learning and the Development of Cognition.* Cambridge, MA: Harvard University Press.

Insel, T. R., Ninan, P. T., Aloi, J., Jimerson, D. C., Skolnick, P., & Paul, S. J. (1984) A Benzodiazepine Receptor—Mediated Model of Anxiety. *Archives of General Psychiatry* 41:741–750.

Irwin, O. C. (1932) The Amount of Motility of Seventy-three Newborn Infants. *Journal of Comparative Psychology* 14:415–428.

Isaacson, R. L. (1975) Memory Processes and the Hippocampus. In Deutsch, D. & Deutsch, J. A. (Eds.), *Short-Term Memory.* New York: Academic Press.

Itard, J. M. C. (1962) *The Wild Boy of Aveyron* (translated by George & Muriel Humphrey). New York: Appleton-Century-Crofts.

Izard, C. E. (1972) Anxiety: A Variable Combination of Interacting Fundamental Emotions. In Spielberger, C. D. (Ed.), *Anxiety: Current Trends in Theory and Research. Volume I.* New York: Academic Press.

Jackins, H. (1978) *The Human Side of Human Beings.* Seattle, WA: Rational Island Publishers.

Jackson, J. H. (1958) Evolution and Dissolution of the Nervous System. In Taylor, J. (Ed.), *Selected Writings of John Hughlings Jackson* (Croonian Lectures, 1884). New York: Basic Books.

Jacobson, E. (1967) *Biology of Emotions: New Understanding Derived from Biological Multidisciplinary Measurements.* Springfield, IL: Charles C. Thomas.

James, W. (1892) *Principles of Psychology.* Cleveland, OH: World.

Jansky, J. & de Hirsch, K. (1972) *Preventing Reading Failure: Prediction, Diagnosis, Intervention.* New York: Harper & Row.

JANUS Curriculum. Hayward, CA: Janus.

Jaynes, J. (1976) *The Origin of Consciousness in the Breakdown of the Bicameral Mind.* Boston: Houghton-Mifflin.

Jensen, A. R. (1980) *Bias in Mental Testing.* New York: Free Press.

Joffe, J. M., Albee, G. W., & Kelly, C. D. (Eds.) (1983) *Readings in Primary Prevention of Psychopathology: Basic Concepts.* Hanover, NH: University Press of New England.

John, E. R. (1976) A Model of Consciousness. In Schwartz, G. E. & Shapiro, D. (Eds.), *Consciousness and Self-regulation: Advances in Research. Volume I.* New York: Plenum.

John, E. R. & Schwartz, E. L. (1978) The Neuropsychology of Information Processing and Cognition. *Annual Review of Psychology* 29:1–29.

Johnson, D. J. & Mykelbust, H. R. (1967) *Learning Disabilities: Educational Principles and Practices.* New York: Grune & Stratton.

Johnson-Laird, P. N. (1985) Deductive Reasoning Ability. In Sternberg, R. J. (Ed.), *Human Abilities: An Infor-*

mation-processing Approach. New York: Freeman.

Jones, E. E. (1979) The Rocky Road from Acts to Dispositions. *American Psychologist* 34:107–117.

Jones, R. L. (Ed.) (1983) *Reflections on Growing Up Disabled*. Reston, VA: Council for Exceptional Children.

Jones, V. F. & Jones, L. S. (1982) *Responsible Classroom Discipline: Creating Positive Learning Environments and Solving Problems*. Rockleigh, NJ: Longwood Division. Allyn & Bacon.

Joyce, B., Hersh, R. H., & McKibbin, M. (1983) *The Structure of School Improvement*. New York: Longman.

Joynt, R. J. (1974) Neuroanatomy Underlying the Language Function. In Duane, D. D. (Ed.), *Reading Perception and Language*. Baltimore, MD: York.

Jung, C. G. (1959) *The Structure and Dynamics of the Psyche*. New York: Pantheon.

Kafka, E. (1984) Cognitive Difficulties in Psychoanalysis. *Psychoanalytic Quarterly* 53:533–550.

Kagan, J. (1965) Reflection—Impulsivity and Reading Ability in Primary Grade Children. *Child Development* 36:609–628.

Kagan, J. (1971) *Change and Continuity in Infancy*. New York: Wiley.

Kagan, J. (1979) The Form of Early Development. *Archives of General Psychiatry* 36:1047–1054.

Kagan, J. (1981) The Moral Function of the School. *Daedalus* 110(3):151–165.

Kagan, J. (1982) The Emergence of Self. *Journal of Child Psychology and Psychiatry* 23:363–381.

Kahn, E. & Cohen, L. H. (1934) Organic Drivenness: A Brain-Stem Syndrome and an Experience. *New England Journal of Medicine* 210:748–756.

Kail, R. (1984) *The Development of Memory in Children* (2nd ed.). New York: Freeman.

Kaluger, G. & Kolson, C. J. (1969) *Reading and Learning Disabilities*. Columbus, OH: Merrill.

Kalverboer, A. F., van Praag, H. M., & Mendlewicz, J. (Eds.) (1978) *Advances in Biological Psychiatry. Volume 1: Minimal Brain Dysfunction: Fact or Fiction*. Basel, Switzerland: Karger.

Kandel, E. R. (1979) Psychotherapy and the Single Synapse: The Impact of Psychiatric Thought on Neurobiological Research. *New England Journal of Medicine* 301:1028–1037.

Kandel, E. R. (1983) From Metapsychology to Molecular Biology: Explorations Into the Nature of Anxiety. *American Journal of Psychiatry* 140:1277–1293.

Kant, I. (1979) *Inaugural Dissertation on Early Writings on Space*. Translated by Handyside, J. Westport, CT: Hyperion.

Kaplan, H. I. & Sadock, B. J. (1985) *Comprehensive Textbook of Psychiatry—IV*. Baltimore, MD: Williams & Wilkins.

Karli, P. (1981) Conceptual and Methodological Problems Associated with the Study of Brain Mechanisms Underlying Behavior. In Brain, P. F. & Benton, D. (Eds.), *The Biology of Aggression*. Rockville, MD: Sijthoff & Noordhoff.

Karlsson, J. L. (1978) *Inheritance of Creative Intelligence*. Chicago: Nelson-Hall, Chapter 19.

Karnes, M. B. & Stoneburner, R. L. (1983) Prevention of Learning Disabilities: Preschool Assessment and Intervention. In McKinney, J. D. & Feagans, L. (Eds.), *Current Topics in Learning Disabilities. Volume 1*. Norwood, NJ: Ablex.

Karpel, M. A. & Strauss, E. S. (1983) *Family*

Evaluation. New York: Brunner /Mazel.

Kashani, J. H., Husain, A., Shekim, W. O., Hodges, K. K., Cytryn, L., & McKnew, D. H. (1981) Current Perspectives on Childhood Depression: An Overview. *American Journal of Psychiatry* 138:143–153.

Kavale, K. & Forness, S. (1985) *The Science of Learning Disabilities*. San Diego, CA: College-Hill.

Kavale, K. & Mattson, P. D. (1983) One Jumped Off the Balance Beam: Meta-analysis of Perceptual-Motor Training. *Journal of Learning Disabilities* 16:165–173.

Kawi, A. A. & Pasamanick, B. (1959) Prenatal and Paranatal Factors in the Development of Childhood Reading Disorders. *Monograph of the Society for Research in Child Development*. Volume 24, No. 4.

Keefe, J. W. (1982) Assessing Student Learning Styles: An Overview. In *Student Learning Styles and Brain Behavior*. Reston, VA: National Association of Secondary School Principals.

Kegan, R. (1982) *The Evolving Self*. Cambridge, MA: Harvard University Press.

Keirsey, D. & Bates, M. (1978) *Please Understand Me: Character and Temperament Types*. Del Mar, CA: Prometheus-Nemesis Books.

Keith, C. R. (1981) A Paradoxical Effect of Guilt in the Psychotherapy of Children. *American Journal of Psychotherapy* 35:16–26.

Keller, Helen (1908) *The World I Live In*. London: Hodder & Stoughton.

Kendall, P. C. & Wilcox, L. E. (1980) Cognitive-Behavioral Treatment for Impulsivity. *Journal of Consulting and Clinical Psychology* 48:80–91.

Keogh, B. (1977) Current Issues in Educational Methods. In Millichap, J. G. (Ed.), *Learning Disabilities and Related Disorders*. Chicago: Year Book Medical Publishers.

Keogh, B. K. (1983) Individual Differences in Temperament—A Contribution to the Personal, Social and Educational Competence of Learning Disabled Children. In McKinney, J. D. & Feagans, L. (Eds.), *Current Topics in Learning Disabilities*. *Volume 1*. Norwood, NJ: Ablex.

Kepecs, J.G. & Wolman, R. (1972) Preconscious Perception of the Transference. *Psychoanalytic Quarterly* 41:172–194.

Kernberg, O. F. (1975) *Borderline Conditions and Pathological Narcissism*. New York: Aronson.

Key, E. (1909) *The Century of the Child*. New York: Putnam.

Kidwell, J. S. (1982) The Neglected Birth Order: Middleborns. *Journal of Marriage and Family* 44:225.

Killen, J. R. (1975) A Learning Systems Approach to Intervention. In Myklebust, H. R. (Ed.), *Progress in Learning Disabilities*. *Volume III*. New York: Grune & Stratton.

Kimmel, H. D., Van Olst, E. H., & Orlebeke, J. F. (1979) *The Orienting Reflex in Humans*. Hillsdale, NJ: Erlbaum.

Kinder, J. A. (1978) *Decision Making in Public Education*. Washington, DC: Capitol Publications.

King, S. H. (1973) *Five Lives at Harvard: Personality Change during College*. Cambridge, MA: Harvard University Press.

Kingston, N. D. (1985) *Training in Math Facts: Addition, Subtraction, Multiplication, and Division*. Allen, TX: DLM Teaching Resources.

Kinsbourne, M. (1977) Selective Difficulties in Learning to Read, Write and Calculate. In Millichap, J. G. (Ed.),

Learning Disabilities and Related Disorders. Chicago: Year Book Medical Publishers.

Kinsbourne, M. (1980) Disorders of Mental Development. In Menkes, J. H., *Textbook of Child Neurology.* Philadelphia, PA: Lea & Febiger.

Kinsbourne, M. & Caplan, P.J. (1979) *Children's Learning and Attention Problems.* Boston: Little, Brown.

Kinsbourne, M. & Warrington, E. K. (1964) Disorders of Spelling. *Journal of Neurology, Neurosurgery and Psychiatry* 27:224–228.

Kirk, S. A. & Chalfant, J. C. (1984) *Academic and Developmental Learning Disabilities.* Denver, CO: Love.

Kirk, S. A. & Gallagher, J. J. (1983) *Educating Exceptional Children* (4th ed.). Boston: Houghton-Mifflin.

Kirk, S. A. & Kirk, W. D. (1983) On Defining Learning Disabilities. *Journal of Learning Disabilities* 16:20–21.

Klein, R. S., Altman, S. D., Dreizen, K., Friedman, R., & Powers, L. (1981) Restructuring Dysfunctional Parental Attitudes toward Children's Learning and Behavior in School: Family-Oriented Psychoeducational Therapy. Parts I and II. *Journal of Learning Disabilities* 14:15–19, 99–101.

Kline, C. L. & Kline, C. L. (1973) Severe Reading Disabilities: The Family's Dilemmas. *Bulletin of the Orton Society* 23:146–159.

Kline, C. L. & Kline, C. L. (1975) Follow-up Story of 216 Dyslexic Children. *Bulletin of the Orton Society* 25:127–145.

Kline, C. L. & Lee, N. (1972) A Transcultural Study of Dyslexia: Analysis of Language Disabilities in 277 Chinese Children Simultaneously Learning to Read and Write in English and in Chinese. *Journal of Special Education* 6:9–26.

Kline, M. (1973) *Why Johnny Can't Add: The Failure of the New Math.* New York: St. Martin's Press.

Knapp, H. D. & Kaye, S. (1980) Family Patterns Leading to Learning Disability: A Cognitive Approach. *Journal of Contemporary Psychotherapy* 11:167–177.

Knapp, P. H. (Ed.) (1963) *Expression of the Emotions in Man.* New York: International Universities Press.

Knight, R. A. & Bell, J. D. (1983) Childhood and Young Adult Predictors of Schizophrenic Outcome. In Ricks, D. F. & Dohrenhend, B. S. (Eds.), *Origins of Psychopathology: Problems in Research and Public Policy.* New York: Cambridge University Press.

Knott, M. & Voss, D. E. (1968) *Proprioceptive Neuromuscular Facilitation: Patterns and Techniques* (2nd ed.). New York: Hoeber.

Koch, R., Azen, C. G., Friedman, E. G., & Williamson, M. L. (1982) Preliminary Report on the Effects of Diet Discontinuation in PKU. *Journal of Pediatrics* 100:870–874.

Koestler, A. (1978) *Janus: A Summing Up.* New York: Random House.

Kogan, N. (1976) *Cognitive Styles in Infancy and Early Childhood.* Hillsdale, NJ: Erlbaum.

Kohlberg, L. (1977) *Assessing Moral Judgment Stages: A Manual.* New York: Humanities Press.

Kohlberg, L., Levine, C., & Hewer, A. (1983) *Moral Stages: A Current Formulation and a Response to Critics.* New York: Karger.

Kohut, H. (1971) *The Analysis of the Self.* New York: International Universities Press.

Kohut, H. (1977) *The Restoration of Self.* New York: International Universities Press.

Kolata, G. B. (1979) Sex Hormones and

Brain Development. *Science* 205:985–987.

Kolata, G. (1983) Math Genius May Have a Hormonal Basis. *Science* 222:1312.

Kolb, D. A., Irwin, M. R., & McIntyre, J. M. (1971) *Organizational Psychology; An Experimental Approach.* Chicago: Prentice-Hall.

Kolb, L. (1973) *Modern Clinical Psychiatry.* (8th ed.). Philadelphia: Saunders.

Koppitz, E. M. (1971) *Children with Learning Disabilities: A Five Year Followup Study.* New York: Grune & Stratton.

Korchin, S. J. et al (1958) Experience of Perceptual Distortion as a Source of Anxiety. *Archives of Neurology and Psychiatry* 80:98–113.

Korner, A. F., Hutchinson, C. A., Koperski, J. A., Kraemer, H. C., & Schneider, P. A. (1981) Stability of Individual Differences of Neonatal Motor and Crying Patterns. *Child Development* 52:83–90.

Korner, A. F., Zeanah, C. H., Linden, J., Berkowitz, R. I., Kraemer, H. C., & Agras, W. S. (1985) Relation Between Neonatal and Later Activity and Temperament. *Child Development* 56:38–42.

Korzybski, A. (1933) *Science and Sanity.* Lakeville, CT: Institute of General Semantics.

Kosslyn, S. M. (1985) Mental Imagery Ability. In Sternberg, R. J. (Ed.), *Human Abilities: An Information-Processing Approach.* New York: Freeman.

Kotkov, B. (1965) Emotional Syndromes Associated with Learning Failure. *Diseases of the Nervous System* 25:48–55.

Kowler, E. & Martius, A. J. (1982) Eye Movements of Preschool Children. *Science* 215:997–999.

Kozloff, M. A. (1974) *Educating Children with Learning and Behavior Problems.* New York: Wiley.

Kozloff, M. A. (1979) *A Program for Families of Children with Learning and Behavior Problems.* New York: Wiley.

Kozol, J. (1967) *Death at an Early Age.* Boston: Houghton-Mifflin.

Kramer, D.A., Anderson, R.B., & Westman, J.C. (1984) The Corrective Autistic Experience: An Application of the Models of Tinbergen and Mahler. *Childs Psychiatry and Human Development.* 15:104–120

Kramer, Y. (1977) Work Compulsion—A Psychoanalytic Study. *The Psychoanalytic Quarterly* 46:361–385.

Krasner, L. & Krasner, M. (1987) The Classroom of the Future. *Annals of the New York Academy of Sciences* 517: 139–152

Krause, E. A. (1976) The Political Sociology of Rehabilitation. In Albrecht, G. L. (Ed.), *The Sociology of Physical Disability ánd Rehabilitation.* Pittsburgh, PA: University of Pittsburgh Press.

Krevisky, J. & Linfield, J. L. (1967) *The Bad Speller's Dictionary.* New York: Random House.

Krieger, D. T. & Martin, J. B. (1981) Brain Peptides. *New England Journal of Medicine* 340:876–885, 944–951.

Krieger, D. T. (1983) Brain Peptides: What, Where and Why? *Science* 222:975–985.

Kris, K. (1983) A 70-Year Follow-up of a Childhood Learning Disability: The Case of Fanny Burney. *Psychoanalytic Study of the Child* 38:637–652.

Krogsgaard-Larsen, P., Scheel-Kruger, J., & Kofod, H. (Eds.) (1979) *GABA— Neurotransmitters: Physiological, Biochemical and Pharmacological Aspects.* Copenhagen: Munksgaard.

Kronick, D. (1981) *Social Development of Learning Disabled Persons.* San Francisco: Jossey-Bass.

Kronick, D. (1985) Divorce and Learning Disabilities. *Academic Therapy* 20:369–375.

Kubie, L. S. (1962) The Fostering of Creative Scientific Productivity. *Daedalus* 91:294–309.

Kuffler, P. (1969) Modal Preference: A Key to Idiosyncratic Learning. In Wolff, P. H. & MacKeith, R. (Eds.), *Planning for Better Learning.* London: Heinemann.

Kurth, E. & Heinrichs, M. (1976) Contribution to the Question of the Ability of Children with Reading and Writing Disorders to Differentiate and Remember Music and Rhythms. *Psychiatrie, Neurologie und Medizinische Psychologie* 28:559–564.

Kutash, I. L. (1980) Prevention and Equilibrium-disequilibrium Theory. In Kutash, I. L., Schlesinger, L. B., & Associates (Eds.), *Handbook on Stress and Anxiety.* San Francisco: Jossey-Bass.

Laddington, C. H. (1962) *The Ethical Animal.* London: Allen & Unwin.

Lader, M. (1975) Psychophysiological Parameters and Methods. In Levi. L. (Ed.), *Emotions—Their Parameters and Measurement.* New York: Raven.

Lader, M. (1980) Psychophysiological Studies in Anxiety. In Burrows, G. D. & Davies, B. (Eds.), *Handbook of Studies on Anxiety.* Amsterdam, Holland: Elsevier/North-Holland.

Lader, M. & Tyrer, P. (1975) Vegetative System and Emotion. In Levi, L. (Ed.), *Emotions—Their Parameters and Measurement.* New York: Raven.

Lambert, N. M. (1982) Temperament Profiles of Hyperactive Children. *American Journal of Orthopsychiatry* 52:458–467.

Lamble, J. W. (1981) *Towards Understanding Receptors.* Amsterdam: Elsevier/North-Holland.

Land, L. R. & Vaughan, M. A. (1973) *Music in Today's Classroom: Creating, Listening, Performing.* New York: Harcourt, Brace, Jovanovich.

Lane, H. & Pillard, R. (1978) *The Wild Boy of Burundi.* New York: Random House.

Lane, R. D. & Schwartz, G. E. (1987) Levels of Emotional Awareness. *American Journal of Psychiatry* 144:133–143.

Lang, P. J. (1979) Language, Image and Emotion. In Pliner, P., Blankstein, K. R., & Spigel, I. M. (Eds.), *Perception of Emotion in Self and Others.* New York: Plenum.

Lange, C. G. & James, W. (1967) *The Emotions.* New York: Hafner.

Langer, J. (1986) *The Origins of Logic.* Orlando, FL: Academic Press.

Langer, S. (1967) *Mind: An Essay on Human Feeling. Vol. 1.* Baltimore, MD: Johns Hopkins Press.

Larsen, S. C. & Hammill, D. D. (1975) The Relationship of Selected Visual-Perceptual Abilities to School Learning. *Journal of Special Education* 9:281–291.

Lashley, K. S. (1951) The Problem of Serial Order in Behavior. In Jeffress, L. A. (Ed.), *Cerebral Mechanisms in Behavior, the Hixon Symposium.* New York: Wiley.

Lasky, E. Z. (1985) Perspectives on Language Development. In Hartlage, L. C. & Telzrow, C. F. (Eds.), *The Neuropsychology of Individual Differences.* New York: Plenum.

Laszlo, E. (1972) *The Systems View of the World.* New York: Braziller.

Latham, C., Holzman, P. S., Manschreck, T. C., & Tole, J. (1981) Optokinetic Nystagmus and Pursuit Eye Movements in Schizophrenia. *Archives of General Psychiatry* 38:997–1003.

Laufer, M. W. (1975) In Osler's Day It Was Syphilis. In Anthony, E. J. (Ed.), *Explorations in Child Psychiatry*. New York: Plenum.

Laurendeau, M. & Pinard, A. (1970) *The Development of the Concept of Space in the Child*. New York: International Universities Press.

Laurinen, P. & Nyman, G. (1982) Information Value of Print Size on Reading Performance. In Malatesha, R. N. & Whitaker, H. A. (Eds.), *Dyslexia: A Global Issue*. The Hague, Netherlands: Nijhoff.

Lawrence, D. H. (1922) *Aaron's Rod*. New York: Seltzer.

Lawrence, G. (1982) Personality Structure and Learning Style: Uses of the Myers-Briggs Type Indicator. In *Student Learning Styles and Brain Behavior*. Reston, VA: National Association of Secondary School Principals.

Lawrence, M. M. (1971) *The Mental Health Team in the Schools*. New York: Behavioral Publications.

Lax, R. F., Bach, S., & Burland, J. A. (1980) *Rapprochement: The Critical Subphase of Separation-Individuation*. New York: Jason Aronson.

Leach, E. (1970) *Claude Levi-Strauss*. New York: Viking.

Lebow, J. L. (1984) On the Value of Integrating Approaches to Family Therapy. *Journal of Marital and Family Therapy* 10:127–138.

Lederman, R. P. (1984) *Psychosocial Adaptation in Pregnancy*. Englewood Cliffs, NJ: Prentice-Hall.

Lee, R. G. (1984) Physiology of the Basal Ganglia: An Overview. *Canadian Journal of Neurological Sciences* 11:124–128.

Lefkowitz, M. M. & Burton, N. (1978) Childhood Depression: A Critique of the Concept. *Psychological Bulletin* 85:716–726.

Lenneberg, E. H. (1964) *New Directions in the Study of Language*. Cambridge, MA: MIT Press.

Lenneberg, E. H. (1967) *Biological Foundations of Language*. New York: Wiley.

Leontiev, A. N. (1957) The Nature and Formation of Human Psychic Properties. In Simon, B. (Ed.), *Psychology in the Soviet Union*. London: Routledge & Kegan Paul.

Lerner, J. W. (1985) *Learning Disabilities: Theories, Diagnosis and Teaching Strategies* (4th ed.). Boston: Houghton-Mifflin.

Lerner, J. W., Mandell-Czudnowski, C., & Goldenberg, D. (1987) *Special Education for the Early Childhood Years*. (2nd ed.). Englewood Cliffs, NJ: Prentice-Hall.

Leshner, A. I. (1977) Hormones and Emotions. In Candland, D. K. et al (Eds.), *Emotion*. Monterey, CA: Brooks/Cole.

Leshner, A. I. (1978) *An Introduction to Behavioral Endocrinology*. New York: Oxford University Press.

Lester, D. (1974) *A Physiological Basis for Personality Traits*. Springfield, IL: Charles C. Thomas.

Leventhal, D. S. (1968) The Significance of Ego Psychology for the Concept of Minimal Brain Dysfunction in Children. *Journal of Child Psychiatry* 7:242–251.

Leventhal, H. (1979) A Perceptual-Motor Processing Model of Emotion. In Pliner, P., Blankstein, K. R., & Spigel, I. M. (Eds.), *Perception of Emotion in Self and Others*. New York: Plenum.

Levine, M. D. (1983) *Pediatric Early Elementary Examination (PEEX)*. Cambridge, MA: Educators Publishing Service.

Levine, M.D. (1987) *Developmental Variation*

and Learning Disorders. Cambridge, MA: Educators Publishing Service.

Levine, M. D., Brooks, R., & Shonkoff, J. P. (1980) *A Pediatric Approach to Learning Disorders.* New York: Wiley.

Levine, M. D. & Melmed, R. (1982) The Unhappy Wanderers: Children with Attention Deficits. *Pediatric Clinics of North America* 29:105–110.

Levine, M. D., Oberklaid, F., & Meltzer, L. (1981) Developmental Output Failure: A Study of Low Productivity in School-Aged Children. *Pediatrics* 67:18–25.

Levine, M. D. & Schneider, E. A. (1982) *Pediatric Examination of Educational Readiness.* Cambridge, MA: Educators Publishing Service.

Levinson, H. N. (1980) *A Solution to the Riddle of Dyslexia.* New York: Springer-Verlag.

Leviton, A. (1980) Otitis Media and Learning Disorders. *Developmental and Behavioral Pediatrics* 1:58–63.

Levy, D. (1955) Oppositional Syndromes and Oppositional Behavior. In Hoch, P. H. & Zubin, J. (Eds.), *Psychopathology of Childhood.* New York: Grune & Stratton.

Levy, F. & Hobbes, G. (1981) The Diagnosis of Attention Deficit Disorder (Hyperkinesis) in Children. *Journal of Child Psychiatry* 20:376–384.

Lewin, K. (1951) *Field Theory in Social Science.* New York: Harper Torchbooks.

Lewin, K., Lippitt, R. L., & White, R. K. (1939) Patterns of Aggressive Behavior in Experimentally Created "Social Climates." *Journal of Social Psychology* 10:271–299.

Lewin, R. (1977) Head Start Pays Off. *New Scientist* 73:508–509.

Lewis, A. (1980) Problems Presented by the Ambiguous Word "Anxiety" as Used in Psychopathology. In Burrows, G. D. & Davies, B. (Eds.), *Handbook of Studies on Anxiety.* Amsterdam, Holland: Elsevier/North Holland.

Lewis, C. D. (1975) Introduction: Landmarks. In Kauffman, J. M. & Lewis, C. D. (Eds.), *Teaching Children with Behavior Disorders: Personal Perspectives.* Columbus, OH: Merrill.

Lewis, D. O. (1981) *Vulnerabilities to Delinquency.* New York: SP Medical & Scientific Books.

Lewis, D. O., Shanok, S. S., Balla, D. A., & Bard, B. (1980) Psychiatric Correlates of Severe Reading Disabilities in an Incarcerated Delinquent Population. *Journal of Child Psychiatry* 19:611–622.

Lewis, D. O., Shanok, S. S., Balla, D. A., & Bard, B. (1981) Delinquency and Reading Disabilities. In Lewis, D. O. (Ed.), *Vulnerabilities to Delinquency.* New York: SP Medical and Scientific Books.

Lewis, J. M. (1979) *How's Your Family?* New York: Brunner/Mazel.

Lewis, M. (1977) Language, Cognitive Development and Personality: A Synthesis. *Journal of Child Psychiatry* 16:646–660.

Lewis, M. (1982) *Clinical Aspects of Child Development.* Philadelphia, PA: Lea & Febiger.

Lewis, M. & Brooks, J. (1975) Infant's Social Perception: A Constructivist View. In Cohen, L. & Salapetek, S. (Eds.), *Infant Perception: From Sensation to Cognition. Volume 2: Perception of Space, Speech and Sound.* New York: Academic Press.

Lewis, M. & Michalson, L. (1983) *Children's Emotions and Moods: Developmental Theory and Measurement.* New York: Plenum.

Lewis, R. B. & Doorlag, D. H. (1983) *Teach-*

ing Special Students in the Mainstream. Columbus, OH: Merrill.

Lewis, W. C. (1965) Structural Aspects of the Psychoanalytic Theory of Instinctual Drives, Affects and Time. In Greenfield, N. W. & Lewis, W. C. (Eds.), *Psychoanalysis and Current Biological Thought.* Madison, WI: University of Wisconsin Press.

Lewis, W. C. (1972) *Why People Change: The Psychology of Influence.* New York: Holt, Rinehart & Winston.

Lewis, W. C., Wolman, R. N., & King, M. (1971) The Development of the Language of Emotions. *American Journal of Psychiatry* 127:1491–1497.

Ley, R. G. (1983) Cerebral Laterality and Imagery. In Sheikh, A. A. (Ed.), *Imagary: Current Theory, Research and Application.* New York: Wiley.

Liben, L. S. (1978) *Deaf Children: Developmental Perspectives.* New York: Academic Press.

Liben, L. S., Patterson, A. H., & Newcombe, N. (Eds.) (1981) *Spatial Representation and Behavior Across the Life Span.* New York: Academic Press.

Liberman, I. Y. (1983) A Language-Oriented View of Reading and Its Disabilities. In Myklebust, H. R. (Ed.), *Progress in Learning Disabilities. Volume 5.* New York: Grune & Stratton.

Libet, B. (1989) Neural Destiny, *The Sciences* March/April: 32–35.

Libet, B., Gleason, C. A., Wright, E. W., & Pearl, D. K. (1983) Time of Conscious Intention to Act in Relation to Onset of Cerebral Activity/ Readiness-Potential. *Brain* 106:623–642.

Lichtenstein, H. (1977) *The Dilemma of Human Identity.* New York: Jason Aronson.

Lidz, C. & Lidz, V. (1973) The Psychology of Intelligence of Jean Piaget and Its Place in the Theory of Action. In

Parsons, T. & Platt, G. M. (Eds.), *The American University.* Cambridge, MA: Harvard University Press.

Lidz, C. & Lidz, V. (1975) The Psychology of Intelligence of Jean Piaget and its Place in the Theory of Action. In Loubser, J., Baum, R., Effrat, A., & Lidz, V. (Eds.), *Explorations in General Theory in Social Science, Essays in Honor of Talcott Parsons. Volume 1.* New York: Free Press.

Lidz, C. S. (1981) *Improving Assessment of Schoolchildren.* San Francisco, CA: Jossey-Bass.

Lillie, D. L. & Place, P. A. (1983) *Partners: A Guide to Working with Schools for Parents of Children with Special Instructional Needs.* Glenview, IL: Scott, Foresman.

Lilienfeld, A. & Parkhurst, E. (1951) A Study of the Association of Factors of Pregnancy and Parturition with the Development of Cerebral Palsy: A Preliminary Report. *American Journal of Hygiene* 53:262.

Liljequist, R. & Mattila, M. J. (1979) Effect of Physostigmine and Scopolomine on the Memory Functions of Chess Players. *Medical Biology* 57:402–405.

Lindal, R. E. & Venables, P. H. (1983) Factor Dimensions of the Child Nowicki-Strickland Internal-External Scale. *Journal of Personality and Individual Differences* 4:645–649.

Lindamood, P. & Lindamood, C. (1979) *LAC Test Manual.* Allen, TX: DLM Teaching Resources.

Lindequist, G. T. (1982) Preschool Screening as a Means of Predicting Later Reading Achievement. *Journal of Learning Disabilities* 15:331–332.

Lipe, H. P. (1980) The Function of Weeping in the Adult. *Nursing Forum* 19:26–44.

Lipowski, Z. J. (1975) Sensory and Information Inputs Overload: Behavioral Effects. *Comprehensive Psychiatry* 16:199–221.

Lippitt, R. L. & Gold, M. (1959) Classroom Social Structure as a Mental Health Problem. *Journal of Social Issues* 15:40–49.

Liss, E. (1944) Examination Anxiety. *American Journal of Orthopsychiatry* 14:345–348.

Livanov, M. (1977) *Spatial Organization of Cerebral Processes.* New York: Wiley.

Livingstone, R. L. (1978) *Sensory Processing, Perception and Behavior.* New York: Raven.

Lloyd-Still, J. D. (1976) *Malnutrition and Intellectual Development.* Littleton, MA: Publishing Sciences Group.

Locke, J. (1959) *An Essay Concerning Human Understanding. 2 Volumes, 1690.* Frazer, A. C. (Ed.). New York: Dover.

Long, N. J. (1974) Future Trends in Special Education. In Kauffman, J. M. & Lewis, C. D. (Eds.), *Teaching Children with Behavior Disorders: Personal Perspectives.* Columbus, OH: Merrill.

Lou, H. C., Henriksen, L., & Bruhn, P. (1983) Focal Cerebral Hypoperfusion in Children with Dysphasia and/or Attention Deficit Disorders. *Archives of Neurology* 41:825–829.

Loubser, J. (1976) General Introduction. In Loubser, J. J., Baum, R. C., Effrat, A., & Lidz, V. M. (Eds.), *Explorations in General Theory in Social Science. Volume 1.* New York: Free Press.

Lovegrove, W. J., Bowling, A., Babcock, D., & Blackwood, M. (1980) Specific Reading Disability: Differences in Contrast Sensitivity as a Function of Spatial Frequency. *Science* 210:439–440.

Lovitt, T. C. (1982) *Because of My Persistance, I've Learned from Children: Comments on Issues in Special Education.* Columbus, OH: Merrill.

Lowe, M. (1975) Trends in the Development of Representational Play in Infants from One to Three Years—An Observational Study. *Journal of Child Psychology and Psychiatry* 16:33–47.

Lowe, T. L., Cohen, D. J., Detlor, J., Kemenitzer, M. W., & Shaywitz, B. A. (1982) Stimulant Medications Precipitate Tourette's Syndrome. *Journal of the American Medical Association* 247:1729–1731.

Lowe, V. (1962) *Understanding Whitehead.* Baltimore: Johns Hopkins Press.

Lowen, W. (1982) *Dichotomies of the Mind: A Systems Science Model of the Mind and Personality.* New York: Wiley.

Loye, D. (1983) *The Sphinx and the Rainbow.* Boulder, CO: New Science Library.

Luk, S. (1985) Direct Observation Studies of Hyperactive Behaviors. *Journal of Child Psychiatry* 24:338–344.

Lund, O. E. & Kampik, A. (1978) The Phenomenon of Mirror Writing in Children. *Bericht Uber die Zusammenkunst der Deutschen Ophthalmologischen Gesellshaft* 75:599–600.

Luria, A. & Yudovich, F. (1959) *Speech and the Development of Mental Processes in the Child.* New York: Staples.

Luria, A. (1961) *The Role of Speech in the Regulation of Normal and Abnormal Behavior.* (Translated by Tizard, J.) New York: Liveright.

Luria, A. R. (1973) *The Working Brain: An Introduction to Neuropsychology.* New York: Basic Books.

Luria, A. R. (1980) *Higher Cortical Functions in Man.* (2nd ed.). New York: Basic Books.

Luria, A. R. & Wertsch, J. V. (Eds.) (1982) *Language and Cognition.* New York: Wiley-Interscience.

Lynch, G. & Baudry, M. (1984) The Biochemistry of Memory: A New and Specific Hypothesis. *Science* 224:1057–1063.

Lyon, G. R. (1983) Learning-Disabled Readers: Identification of Subgroups. In Myklebust, H. R. (Ed.), *Progress in Learning Disabilities. Volume V.* New York: Grune & Stratton.

McBride, W. G., Black, B. P., Brown, C. J., Dolby, R. M., Murray, A. D., & Thomas, D. B. (1979) Method of Delivery and Developmental Outcome at Five Years of Age. *Medical Journal of Australia* 1:301–304.

McCaffrey, R. J. & Isaac, W. (1985) Preliminary Data on the Presence of Neuropsychological Deficits in Adults Who Are Mentally Retarded. *Mental Retardation* 23:63–66.

McCall, R. B., Applebaum, M. I., & Hogarty, P. S. (1973) Developmental Changes in Mental Performance. *Monographs of the Society for Research in Child Development.* No. 150, 38(3).

McCarthy, M. M. (1981) *Public School Law: Teachers' and Students' Rights.* New York: Longwood Division, Allyn & Bacon.

McClearn, G. E. (1978) Review of Dyslexia-Genetic Aspects. In Benton, A. L. & Pearl, D. (Eds.) *Dyslexia: An Appraisal of Current Knowledge.* New York: Oxford University Press.

McClelland, J. L. (1985) Distributed Models of Cognitive Processes. *Annals of the New York Academy of Sciences* 444:1–9.

McClure, F. D. & Gordon, M. (1984) Performance of Disturbed Hyperactive and Nonhyperactive Children on an Objective Measure of Hyperactivity. *Journal of Abnormal Child Psychology* 12:561–572.

McCorduck, P. (1979) *Machines Who Think.* New York: Freeman.

McCoy, L. E. (1975) Braille: A Language for Severe Dyslexics. *Journal of Learning Disabilities* 8:32–36.

McDermott, J. F. & Char, W. F. (1984) Stage-Related Models of Psychotherapy with Children. *Journal of Child Psychiatry* 23:537–543.

McDougall, J. (1985) Reflections on Affect: A Psychoanalytic View of Alexithymia. In McDougall, J. *Theaters of the Mind: Illusion and Truth on the Psychoanalytic Stage.* New York: Basic Books.

McGee, M. G. (1979) *Human Spatial Abilities.* New York: Praeger.

McGuigan, F. J. (1978) Imagery and Thinking: Covert Functioning of the Motor System. In Schwartz, G. E. & Shapiro, D. (Eds.), *Consciousness and Self-Regulation: Advances in Research and Theory. Volume 2.* New York: Plenum.

McGuinness, D. (1985) *When Children Don't Learn.* New York: Basic Books.

McIntyre, P. M. (1964) Dynamics and Treatment of the Passive-Aggressive Underachiever. *American Journal of Psychotherapy* 28:95–108.

McKellar, P. (1957) *Imagination and Thinking.* London: Cohen & West.

McKellar, P. (1968) *Experience and Behavior.* London: Penguin.

McKenzie, J. S., Kemm, R. E., & Wilcock, L. N. (1984) *The Basal Ganglia: Structure and Function.* New York: Plenum.

McKim, R. H. (1980) *Experiences in Visual Thinking* (2nd ed.). Monterey, CA: Brooke/Cole.

McLeod, J. (1978) *Psychometric Identification of Children with Learning Disabilities.* Saskatoon, Canada: University of Saskatchewan.

McMahon, R. C. (1980) Genetic Etiology in the Hyperactive Child Syndrome: A Critical Review. *American Journal of Orthopsychiatry* 50:145–150.

McReynolds, W. I. (1976) Anxiety as Fear: A Behavioral Approach to One Emotion. In Zuckerman, M. Spielberger, C. D. (Eds.), *Emotions and Anxiety: New Concepts, Methods and Applications*. Hillsdale, NJ: Erlbaum.

McWhirter, J. J. (1977) *The Learning Disabled Child: A School and Family Concern*. Champaign, IL: Research Press.

Mabry, C. C. & Podoll, E. (1963) Above Average Intelligence in Untreated Phenylketonuria. *Journal of Pediatrics* 63:1038–1040.

Maccoby, E. E. (1980) *Social Development: Psychological Growth and the Parent–Child Relationship*. New York: Harcourt, Brace, Jovanovich.

Maccoby, E. E. & Jacklin, C. N. (1974) *The Psychology of Sex Differences. Volume I*. Stanford, CA: Stanford University Press.

Mack, J. E. & Ablon, S. L. (1983) *The Development and Sustaining of Self-Esteem*. New York: International Universities Press.

MacKinnon, D. W. (1965) Personality and the Realization of Creative Potential. *American Psychologist* 20:273–281.

MacLean, P. D. (1970) The Limbic Brain in Relation to the Psychoses. In Black, P. H. (Ed.), *Physiological Correlates of Emotion*. New York: Academic Press.

MacLean, P. D. (1980) Sensory and Perceptive Factors in Emotional Functions of the Triune Brain. In Rorty, A. O. (Ed.), *Explaining Emotions*. Berkeley, CA: University of California Press.

MacNamara, J. (1982) *Names for Things: A Study of Human Learning*. Cambridge, MA: MIT Press.

Madge, N. & Tizard, J. (1981) Intelligence. In Rutter, M. (Ed.), *Scientific Foundations of Developmental Psychiatry*.

Baltimore, MD: University Park Press.

Madow, L. (1972) *Anger*. New York: Scribner.

Mahler, M. S., Pine, F., & Bergman, A. (1975) *The Psychological Birth of the Human Infant*. New York: Basic Books.

Mahler, M. S. & Rangell, L. (1943) A Psychosomatic Study of Maladie des Tics. *Psychoanalytic Quarterly* 17:579–603.

Mahoney, M. J. (1974) *Cognition and Behavior Modification*. Cambridge, MA: Ballinger.

Makita, K. (1968) The Rarity of Reading Disability in Japanese Children. *American Journal of Orthopsychiatry* 38:599–614.

Malatesta, C. Z. (1982) The Expression and Regulation of Emotion: A Lifespan Perspective. In Field, T. & Fogel, A. (Eds.), *Emotion and Early Interaction*. Hillsdale, NJ: Erlbaum.

Malerstein, A. J. & Ahern, M. (1982) *A Piagetian Model of Character Structure*. New York: Human Sciences Press.

Malick, J. B. & Bell, R. M. S. (Eds.) (1982) *Endorphins: Chemistry, Physiology, Pharmacology and Clinical Relevance*. New York: Marcel Dekker.

Mallet, C-H. (1984) *Fairy Tales and Children*. New York: Schocken.

Mallinger, A. E. (1982) Demand-Sensitive Obsessionals. *Journal of the American Academy of Psychoanalysis* 10:407–426.

Mandler, G. (1969) Acceptance of Things Past and Present. A Look at the Mind and the Brain. In MacLeod, R. B. (Ed.), *William James: Unfinished Business*. Washington, D.C.: American Psychological Association.

Mandler, G. (1975) The Search for Emotion. In Levi, L. (Ed.), *Emotions—Their Parameters and Measurement*. New York: Raven.

Mangan, G. L. (1982) *The Biology of Human Conduct: East-West Models of Temperament and Personality.* Oxford: Pergamon.

Mantovani, J. F. & Landau, W. M. (1980) Acquired Aphasia with Convulsive Disorder: Course and Prognosis. *Neurology* 30:524–529.

Marcell, M. M. & Armstrong, V. (1982) Auditory and Visual Sequential Memory of Down Syndrome and Non-Retarded Children. *American Journal of Mental Deficiency* 87:86–95.

Marcus, I. M. (1967) Learning Problems. In Usdin, G. L. (Ed.), *Adolescence.* Philadelphia, PA: Lippincott.

Marcus, I. M. (1971) The Influence of Teacher–Child Interaction on the Learning Process. *Journal of Child Psychiatry* 10:481–500.

Marion, R. L. (1981) *Educators, Parents and Exceptional Children.* Rockville, MD: Aspen.

Marjoribanks, K. (1979) *Families and Their Learning Environments: An Empirical Analysis.* London: Routledge & Kegan Paul.

Marks, D. F (1983) Mental Imagery and Consciousness: A Theoretical Review. In Sheikh, A. A. (Ed.), *Imagery: Current Theory, Research and Application.* New York: Wiley.

Marmor, J. (1983) Systems Thinking in Psychiatry: Some Theoretical and Clinical Implications. *American Journal of Psychiatry* 140:833–838.

Marono, H. E. (1981) Biology Is One Key to the Bonding of Mothers and Babies. *Smithsonian* 11:60–68.

Marsden, C. D. (1982) Neurotransmitters and CNS Disease. *Lancet. Volume II for 1982* 1141–1146.

Marshall, J. C. (1982) Toward a Rational Taxonomy of the Developmental Dyslexias. In Malatesha, R. N. &

Whitaker, H. A. (Eds.), *Dyslexia: A Global Issue.* The Hague, Netherlands: Nijhoff.

Marshall, J. C. (1985) On Some Relationships between Acquired and Developmental Dyslexia. In Duffy, F. H. & Geschwind, N. (Eds.), *Dyslexia, A Neuroscientific Approach to Clinical Evaluation.* Boston: Little, Brown.

Martin, J. H. & Harrison, C. H. (1972) *Free to Learn.* Englewood Cliffs, NJ: Prentice-Hall.

Martin, J. H. & Friedberg, A. (1985) *Writing to Read.* New York: Warner Books.

Martin, R. (1979) *Educating Handicapped Children: The Legal Mandate.* Champaign, IL: Research Press.

Marx, R. W., Winne, P. H., & Walsh, J. (1985) Studying Student Cognition During Classroom Learning. In Pressley, M. & Brainerd, C. J. (Eds.), *Cognitive Learning and Memory in Children.* New York: Springer-Verlag.

Marz, J. L. (1983) The Two Sides of the Brain. *Science* 220:488–490.

Marzollo, J. & Lloyd, J. (1976) *Child Learning Through Child Play.* New York: St. Martin Press.

Masland, R. L. (1981) Neurological Aspects of Dyslexia. In Pavlides, G. Th & Miles, T. R. *Dyslexia Research and its Application to Education.* New York: Wiley.

Masters, L. & Marsh, II, G. E. (1978) Middle Ear Pathology as a Factor in Learning Disabilities. *Journal of Learning Disabilities* 11:103–106.

Mattes, J. A. (1980) The Role of Frontal Lobe Dysfunction in Childhood Hyperkinesis. *Comprehensive Psychiatry* 21:358–367.

Mattes, J. A., Boswell, L., & Oliver, H. (1984) Methylphenidate Effects on

Symptoms of Attention Deficit Disorder in Adults. *Archives of General Psychiatry* 41:1059–1063.

Mattes, J. A. & Gittelman, R. (1981) Effects of Artificial Food Colorings in Children with Hyperactive Symptoms: A Critical Review and Results of a Controlled Study. *Archives of General Psychiatry* 38:714–718.

Mattes, J. A. & Gittelman, R. (1983) Growth of Hyperactive Children on Maintenance Regimen of Methylphenidate. *Archives of General Psychiatry* 40:317–321.

Matthews, C. G. (1985) Personal Communication.

Matthews, C. G. (1981) Neuropsychology Practice in a Hospital Setting. In Filskov, S. B. & Boll, T. J. (Eds.), *Handbook of Clinical Neuropsychology*. New York: Wiley-Interscience.

Mattis, S. (1981) Dyslexia Syndromes in Children: Toward the Development of Syndrome-Specific Treatment Programs. In Pirozzolo, F. J. & Wittrock, M. C. (Eds.), *Neuropsychological and Cognitive Processes in Reading*. New York: Academic Press.

Mattis, S., French, J. H., & Rapin, I. (1975) Dyslexia in Children and Young Adults: Three Independent Neuropsychological Syndromes. *Developmental Medicine and Child Neurology* 17:150.

Mautner, T. S. (1984) Dyslexia—My "Invisible" Handicap. *Annals of Dyslexia* 34:299–311.

May, F. B. (1973) *To Help Children Read: Mastery Performance Modules for Teachers in Training*. Columbus, OH: Merrill.

Mayer, D. J. & Price, D. D. (1982) A Physiological and Psychological Analysis of Pain: A Potential Model of Motivation. In Pfaff, D. W. (Ed.), *The Physiological Mechanisms of Motivation*. New York: Springer-Verlag.

Mayer, R. E. (1985) Mathematical Ability. In Sternberg, R. J. (Ed.), *Human Abilities: An Information-Processing Approach*. New York: Freeman.

Mayeux, R.(1983) Emotional Changes Associated with Basal Ganglia Disorders. In Heilman, K. M. & Satz, P. (Eds.), *Neuropsychology of Human Emotion*. New York: Guilford Press.

Mayr, E. (1982) *The Growth of Biological Thought*. Cambridge, MA: The Belknap Press of Harvard University Press.

Mead, G. H. (1936) *Mind, Self and Society*. Chicago: University of Chicago Press.

Meade, J. G. (1978) *The Rights of Parents and the Responsibilities of Schools*. Cambridge, MA: Educators Publishing Service.

Meadow, K. P. (1975) The Development of Deaf Children. In Hetherington, E. M. (Ed.), *Review of Child Development Research. Volume 5*. Chicago: University of Chicago Press.

Mednick, B. R. (1977) Intellectual and Behavioral Functioning of Ten-to-Twelve-year-old Children who Showed Certain Transient Symptoms in the Neonatal Period. *Child Development* 48:844–853.

Meichembaum, D. H. & Goodman, J. (1971) Training Impulsive Children to Talk to Themselves: A Means of Developing Self Control. *Journal of Abnormal Psychology* 77:115–126.

Meissner, W. W. (1978) Narcissistic Personality and Borderline Conditions: A Differential Diagnosis. *The Annual of Psychoanalysis* 7:171–202.

Mencius, V. (1970) *Mencius* (D. C. Lau, trans.). Baltimore, MD: Penguin.

Mendelowitz, D. M. (1963) *Children Are Artists* (2nd ed.). Stanford, CA: Stanford University Press.

Menkes, J. H. (1977) Early Feeding History of Children with Learning Disorders. *Developmental Medicine and Child Neurology* 19:169–171.

Menkes, J. H. (1980) *Textbook of Child Neurology* (2nd ed.). Philadelphia, PA: Lea & Febiger.

Menkes, M. M., Rowe, J. S., & Menkes, J. H. (1967) A Twenty Five Year Followup Study on the Hyperkinetic Child with Minimal Brain Dysfunction. *Pediatrics* 39:393–399.

Menolascino, F. J., Neman, R., & Stark, J. A. (Eds.) (1983) *Curative Aspects of Mental Retardation: Biomedical and Behavioral Advances*. Baltimore, MD: Brookes.

Mercer, G. E. (1980) *Theoretical Frameworks in the Sociology of Education*. Cambridge, MA: Schenkman.

Mercer, J. (1979) *System of Multicultural Pluralistic Assessment: Technical Manual*. New York: Psychological Corporation.

Merry, F. K. (1932) *Touch Readings of the Blind*. New York: American Foundation for the Blind.

Messick, S. (1976) *Individuality in Learning*. San Francisco: Jossey-Bass.

Messick, S. (1984) The Nature of Cognitive Styles: Problems and Promise in Educational Practice. *Educational Psychologist* 19:59–74.

Metcoff, J., Klein, E. R., & Nichols, B. L. (Eds.) (1981) Nutrition of the Child: Maternal Nutritional Status and Fetal Outcome. *American Journal of Nutrition* 34:653–817 (Supplement).

Meyer, L. A., Gersten, R. M., & Gutkin, J. (1983) Direct Instruction: A Project Follow Through Success Story in an Inner City School. *Elementary School Journal* 84:241–252.

Meyer-Bahlburg, H. F. L. (1981) Sex Chromosomes and Aggression in Humans. In Brain, P. F. & Benton, D. (Eds.), *The Biology of Aggression*. Rockville, MD: Sijthoff & Noordhoff.

Miccinati, J. (1979) The Fernald Tracing Technique: Modifications Increase the Probability of Success. *Journal of Learning Disabilities* 13:3.

Michaelis, C. T. (1980) *Home and School Partnerships in Exceptional Education*. Rockville, MD: Aspen Systems.

Miezio, P. G. (1983) *Parenting Children with Disabilities: A Professional Source for Physicians and Guide for Parents*. New York: Marcel Dekker.

Milisen, R. (1971) The Incidence of Speech Disorders. In Travis, L. E. (Ed.), *Handbook of Speech Pathology and Audiology*. New York: Appleton-Century-Crofts.

Miller, D. R. & Westman, J. C. (1964) Readily Disability as a Condition of Family Stability. *Family Process* 3:66–76.

Miller, D. R. & Swanson, G. E. (1960) *Inner Conflict and Defense*. New York: Henry Holt.

Miller, D. R. & Westman, J. C. (1966) Family Teamwork and Psychotherapy. *Family Process* 5:49–59.

Miller, J. G. (1978) *Living Systems*. New York: McGraw-Hill.

Miller, J. G. (1986) Can Systems Theory Generate Testable Hypotheses? *Systems Research* 3:73–84.

Miller, J. G. & Miller, J. L. (1980) The Family as a System. In Hofling, C. K. & Lewis, J. M. (Eds.), *The Family: Evaluation and Treatment*. New York: Brunner/Mazel.

Miller, M. S. (1981) *Bringing Learning Home: How Parents Can Play a More Active and Effective Role in the Children's Education*. New York: Harper & Row.

Miller, T. L. & Davis, E. E. (1982) *The Mildly Handicapped Student*. New York: Academic Press.

Millman, H. L., Schaefer, C. E., & Cohen, J. J. (1980) *Therapies for School Be-*

havior Problems. San Francisco: Jossey-Bass.

Milner, B. (1972) Disorders of Learning and Memory After Temporal Lobe Lesions in Man. In *Proceedings of the Congress of Neurological Surgeons, 1971.* Baltimore, MD: Williams & Wilkins.

Minde, K. (1974) Study Problems of Ugandan Students. *British Journal of Psychiatry.* 125:131–137.

Minkowski, A. (Ed.) (1976) *Regional Development of the Brain in Early Life.* Philadelphia, PA: Davis.

Minuchin, S. (1974) *Families and Family Therapy.* Cambridge, MA: Harvard University Press.

Mishkin, M., Malamut, B., & Bachevalier, J. (1984) Memories and Habits: Two Neural Systems. In McGaugh, J. L., Lynch, G., & Weinberger, N. M. (Eds.), *The Neurobiology of Learning in Memory.* New York: Guilford Press.

Mishkin, M. & Petri, (1984) Memories and Habits: Some Implications for the Analysis of Learning and Retention. In Butters, N. & Squire, L. (Eds.), *Neuropsychology of Memory.* New York: Guilford.

Miskimins, R. W. (1972) *Manual: MSGO-II.* Fort Collins, CO: Rocky Mountain Behavioral Science Research Institute.

Missildine, W. H. (1963) The Emotional Background of Thirty Children with Reading Disabilities with Emphasis on its Coercive Elements. *Nervous Child* 5:263–272.

Missildine, W. H. (1975) *Your Inner Conflicts—How To Solve Them.* New York: Simon & Schuster.

Mitchell, D. C. (1982) *The Process of Reading: A Cognitive Analysis of Fluent Reading and Learning to Read.* New York: Wiley.

Mitchell, G. (1975) What Monkeys Can Tell Us About Human Violence. *The Futurist,* April:75–80.

Miyoshi, T., Hiwatashi, S., Kishimoto, S., & Tamada, A. (1981) Dissociation of the Eyes in Saccadic Movement. *Annals of the New York Academy of Sciences* 374:731–743.

Mobley, W. C., Server, A. C., Ishii, D. N., Riopelle, R. J., & Shooter, E. M. (1977) Nerve Growth Factor. *New England Journal of Medicine* 297:1096–1104, 1149–1158, 1211–1218.

Money, J. (1966) On Learning and Not Learning to Read. In Money, J. (Ed.), *The Disabled Reader.* Baltimore, MD: Johns Hopkins University Press.

Monroe, M. (1932) *Children Who Cannot Read.* Chicago: The University of Chicago Press.

Montagu, A. (1976) *The Nature of Human Aggression.* New York: Oxford University Press.

Montagu, A. (Ed.) (1980) *Sociobiology Examined.* New York: Oxford University Press.

Montessori, M. (1974) *Childhood Education.* Chicago: Regnery.

Moore, K. (1982) *The Developing Human.* (3rd ed.). New York: Saunders.

Morgan, G. A. & Harmon, R. J. (1984) Developmental Transformations in Mastery Motivation. In Emde, R. N. & Harmon, R. J. (Eds.), *Continuities and Discontinuities in Development.* New York: Plenum.

Morgan, W. P. (1896) A Case of Congenital Word Blindness. *British Medical Journal* 2:1378–1379.

Morrison, D. (1985) *Neurobehavioral and Perceptual Dysfunction in Learning Disabled Children.* Toronto: Hogrefe.

Morrison, D., Pothier, P., & Horr, K. (1978) *Sensory-Motor Dysfunction and Therapy in Infancy and Early Childhood.* Springfield, IL: Charles C. Thomas.

Morse, W. C. (1964) Intervention Techniques for the Classroom Teacher of the Emotionally Disturbed. In Knoblock, P. (Ed.), *Educational Programming for Emotionally Disturbed Children: the Decade Ahead.* Syracuse, NY: Syracuse University Press.

Morse, W. C. (1974) The Future. In Kauffman, J. M. & Lewis, C. D. (Eds.), *Teaching Children with Behavior Disorders: Personal Perspectives.* Columbus, OH: Merrill.

Morse, W. C. & Wingo, G. M. (1955) *Psychology and Teaching.* Glenview, IL: Scott, Foresman.

Morsink, C. (1981) *Mainstreaming: Making It Work in Your Classroom.* Lexington, KY: College of Education, University of Kentucky.

Moscovitch, M. (1985) Memory from Infancy to Old Age. *Annals of the New York Academy of Sciences* 444:78–96.

Moser, H. W., Moser, A. B., Frayer, K. K., Chen, W., Schulman, J. D., O'Neill, B. P., & Kishimoto, Y. (1981) Adrenoleukodystrophy: Increased Plasma Content of Saturated Very Long Chain Fatty Acids. *Neurology* 31:1241–1249.

Mosse, H. L. (1982) *The Complete Handbook of Children's Reading Disorders: A Critical Evaluation of their Clinical, Educational and Social Dimensions. Volumes I & II.* New York: Human Sciences Press.

Motoo, K. (1983) *The Neutral Theory of Molecular Evolution.* Cambridge, England: Cambridge University Press.

Moulton, J. R. & Bader, M. S. (1985) The Writing Process: A Powerful Approach for the Language-Disabled Student. *Annals of Dyslexia* 35:161–173.

Mountcastle, V. B. et al (1975) Posterior Parietal Association Cortex of the Monkey: Command Functions for Operations within Extrapersonal Space. *Journal of Neurophysiology* 38:871–908.

Moyer, K. E. (1976) *The Psychobiology of Aggression.* New York: Harper & Row.

Muehl, S. & Kremenak, S. (1966) Ability to Match Information Within and Between Auditory and Visual Sense Modalities and Subsequent Reading Achievement. *Journal of Educational Psychology* 57:230–238.

Muller, E. E. & Genazzani, A. R. (1984) *Central and Peripheral Endorphins: Basic and Clinical Aspects.* New York: Raven.

Muller, J. P. (1983) Cognitive Psychology and the Ego: Lacanian Theory and Empirical Research. *Psychoanalysis and Contemporary Thought* 5:257–291. New York: International Universities Press.

Murphy, L. B. & Moriarty, A. E. (1976) *Vulnerability, Coping and Growth from Infancy to Adolescence.* New Haven, CT: Yale University Press.

Myers, I. B. (1962) *Myers-Briggs Type Indicator Manual.* Princeton, NJ: Educational Testing Service.

Myers, I. B. (1975) *Myers-Briggs Type Indicator Manual.* Palo Alto, CA: Consulting Psychologists Press.

Myers, P. I. & Hammill, D. D. (1976) *Methods for Learning Disorders.* (2nd ed.). New York: Wiley.

Myklebust, H. R. (Ed.) (1978) *Progress in Learning Disabilities. Volume IV.* New York: Grune & Stratton.

Mykelbust, H. R. (1981) *The Pupil Rating Scale Revised.* New York: Grune & Stratton.

Mykelbust, H. R. (1983) Disorders of Auditory Language. In Mykelbust, H. R. (Ed.), *Progress in Learning Disabilities. Volume V.* New York: Grune & Stratton.

Nadi, N. S., Nurnberger, J. I., & Gershon, E. S. (1984) Muscarinic Cholinergic Receptors on Skin Fibroblasts in Familial Affective Disorders. *New England Journal of Medicine* 311:225–230.

Naidoo, S. (1972) *Specific Dyslexia*. London: Pitman.

Namnum, A. & Prelinger, E. (1961) On the Psychology of the Reading Process. *The American Journal of Orthopsychiatry* 31:820–828.

Nathan, P. W. & Smith, M. C. (1950) Normal Mentality Associated with a Maldeveloped Rhinecephalon. *Journal of Neurology, Neurosurgery and Psychiatry* 13:191–197.

National Center for Educational Statistics (1981) *National Assessment of Educational Progress*. Washington, D.C.: U.S. Department of Commerce.

National Commission on Excellence in Education (1983) *A Nation at Risk: The Imperative for Educational Reform*. Washington, D.C.: U.S. Government Printing Office.

Nauta, W. J. H. & Feirtag, M. (1979) The Organization of the Brain. *Scientific American* 241:88–111.

Needleman, H. L. & Bellinger, D. C. (1981) The Epidemiology of Low-level Lead Exposure in Childhood. *Journal of Child Psychiatry* 20:496–512.

Needleman, H. L., Gannoe, C., Leviton, A., Reed, R., Peresie, H., Maher, C., & Barrett, P. (1979) Deficits in Psychologic and Classroom Performance of Children with Elevated Dentine Lead Levels. *New England Journal of Medicine* 300:689–695.

Neff, W. S. (1968) *Work and Human Behavior*. New York: Atherton.

Neill, J. R. & Kniskern, D. P. (1982) *From Psyche to System: The Evolving Therapy of Carl Whitaker*. New York: Guilford Press.

Neill, J. R. & Sandifer, M. G. (1982) The Clinical Approach to Alexithymia: A Review. *Psychosomatics* 23:1223–1231.

Nelson, K. & Ross, G. (1980) The Generalities and Specifics of Long-term Memory in Infants and Young Children. In Perlmutter, M. (Ed.), *New Directions for Child Development: Children's Memory*. San Francisco: Jossey-Bass.

Nelson, K. E. (1977a) First Steps in Language Acquisition. *Journal of Child Psychiatry* 16:563–583.

Nelson, K. E. (1977b) Aspects of Language Acquisition and Use from Age 2 to Age 20. *Journal of Child Psychiatry* 16:584–607.

Nestoros, J. N. (1981) Anxiety as a State of Diminished GABA-ergic Neurotransmission Resulting from Too Frequent Recruitment of GABA-ergic Neurons: A Neurophysiological Model. *Progress in Neuropsychopharmacology* 5:591–594.

Neubauer, P. B. (1982) Rivalry and Jealousy. *Psychoanalytic Study of the Child*. 37:121–142.

Neubauer, P. B. (1983) The Importance of the Sibling Experience. *Psychoanalytic Study of the Child* 38:325–336.

Newman, R. G. (1974) *Groups in Schools*. New York: Simon & Schuster.

Ney, P., Colbert, P., Newman, B., & Young, J. (1986) Aggressive Behavior and Learning Difficulties as Symptoms of Depression in Children. *Child Psychiatry and Human Development* 17:3–14).

Nichols, M. (1984) *Family Therapy: Concepts and Methods*. New York: Gardner.

Nichols, P. L. & Chen, T. (1981) *Minimal Brain Dysfunction: A Prospective Study*. Hillsdale, NJ: Erlbaum.

Noda, H. (1981) Visual Mossy Fiber Inputs

to the Flocculus of the Monkey. *Annals of the New York Academy of Sciences* 374:465–475.

Norbeck, E. (1978) The Study of Play. In Lancey, D. F. & Tindall, B. A. (Eds.), *The Anthropological Study of Play*. New York: Leisure Press.

Nordan, R. (1976) The Psychological Reactions of Children with Neurological Problems. *Child Psychiatry and Human Development* 6:214–223.

Norman, D. A. (Ed.) (1981) *Perspectives on Cognitive Science*. Hillsdale, NJ: Erlbaum; Norwood, NJ: Ablex.

Norman, D. A. & Bobrow, D. G. (1976) On the Role of Active Memory Processes in Perception and Cognition. In Cofer, C. N. (Ed.), *The Structure of Human Memory*. San Francisco: Freeman.

Norris, D. & Boucher, J. (1980) *Observing Children*. Toronto: Board of Education.

Noshpitz, J. D. (1982) Reality Testing: A Neurophysiological Fantasy. *Comprehensive Psychiatry* 23:25–32.

Noshpitz, J. D. (1984) Narcissism and Aggression. *American Journal of Psychotherapy* 38:17–34.

Novak, J. & Gowin, R. (1984) *Learning How To Learn*. New Rochelle, NY: Cambridge University Press.

Noy, P. (1979) The Psychoanalytic Theory of Cognitive Development. *Psychoanalytic Study of the Child* 34:169–216.

Nunberg, H. (1955) *Principles of Psychoanalysis*. New York: International Universities Press.

Nyberg, D. & Egan, K. (1981) *The Erosion of Education: Socialization and the Schools*. New York: Teachers College Press.

O'Donohoe, N. V. (1979) *Epilepsies of Childhood*. London: Butterworths.

Oettinger, L., Gauch, R. R., & Majovski, L. V. (1977) Maturity and Growth in Children with MBD. In Millichap, J. G. (Ed.), *Learning Disabilities and Related Disorders*. Chicago: Year Book Medical Publishers.

Offer, D. & Sabshin, M. (Eds.) (1984) *Normality and the Life Cycle*. New York: Basic Books.

Ogg, S. T. (1948) *The 26 Letters*. New York: Crowell.

Ohlson, E. L. (1978) *Identification of Specific Learning Disabilities*. Champaign, IL: Research Press.

Ohrman, A. (1979) The Orienting Response, Attention and Learning: An Information-Processing Perspective. In Kimmel, H. D., Van Olst, E. H., & Orlebeke, J. F. (Eds.), *The Orienting Reflex in Humans*. Hillsdale, NJ: Erlbaum.

Ojemann, G. A. & Mateer, C. (1979a) Human Language Cortex: Localization of Memory, Syntax, and Sequential Motor-Phoneme Identification Systems. *Science* 205:1401–1403.

Ojemann, G. A. & Mateer, C. (1979b) Cortical and Subcortical Organization of Human Communication. In Steklis, H. D. & Raleigh, M. J. (Eds.), *Neurobiology of Social Communication in Primates: An Evolutionary Perspective*. New York: Academic Press.

O'Keefe, J. & Nadel, L. (1978) *The Hippocampus as a Cognitive Map*. New York: Clarenden Oxford University Press.

Okolo, C., Bartlett, A., & Shaw, F. (1978) Communication Between Professionals Concerning Medication for the Hyperactive Child. *Journal of Learning Disabilities* 11:647–650.

Olds, J. & Olds, M. E. (1964) The Mechanisms of Voluntary Behavior. In Heath, R. G. (Ed.), *The Role of Pleasure in Behavior*. New York: Hoeber Medical Division, Harper & Row.

Olson, D. R. & Bialystok, E. (1983) *Spatial*

Cognition: The Structure and Development of Mental Representations of Spatial Relations. Hillsdale, NJ: Erlbaum.

Olson, J. P. & Dillner, M. H. (1976) *Learning to Teach Reading in the Elementary School Utilizing a Competency-Based Instructional System.* New York: Macmillan.

Omwake, E. G. (1963) The Child's Estate. In Solnit, A. J. & Provence, S. A. (Eds.), *Modern Perspectives in Child Development.* New York: International Universities Press.

O'Neil, Jr., H. F. (Ed.) (1981) *Computer-Based Instruction: A State-of-the-Art Assessment.* New York: Academic Press.

Orbach, J. (1982) *Neuropsychology after Lashley—Fifty Years Since Publication of Brain Mechanisms and Intelligence.* New York: Erlbaum.

Ornitz, E. M. (1983) The Functional Neuroanatomy of Infantile Autism. *International Journal of Neuroscience* 19:85–124.

Ornitz, E. M. (1985) Neurophysiology of Infantile Autism. *Journal of Child Psychiatry* 24:251–262.

Ornitz, E. M., Guthrie, D., & Farley, A. J. (1978) The Early Symptoms of Childhood Autism. In Serban, G. (Ed.), *Cognitive Defects in the Development of Mental Illness.* New York: Brunner/Mazel.

Ornstein, R. E. (1972) *The Psychology of Consciousness.* New York: Viking.

Ornstein, R. E. (1986) *Multimind.* Boston: Houghton Mifflin.

Ornstein, R. E. & Galin, D. (1977) Physiological Studies of Consciousness. In Lee, P. R., Ornstein, R. E., Galin, D., Deikman, A., & Tart, C. T. (Eds.), *Symposium on Consciousness.* New York: Harmondsworth, Penguin.

Ornstein, R. E. & Thompson, R. F. (1984) *The Amazing Brain.* Boston: Houghton-Mifflin.

Orton, J. L. (1976) *A Guide to Teaching Phonics.* Cambridge, MA: Educators Publishing Service.

Orton, S. T. (1928) Specific Reading Disability—Strephosymbolia. *Journal of the American Medical Association* 90:1095–1099.

Orton, S. T. (1937) *Reading, Writing and Speech Problems in Children.* New York: Norton.

Osler, W. (1930) *Aequanimitas* (3rd ed.). New York: McGraw-Hill.

Osman, B. B. (1982) *No One to Play With: The Social Side of Learning Disabilities.* New York: Random House.

Ostrander, S. & Schroeder, L. (1979) *Super-Learning.* New York: Delta/Confucian Press.

Ottoson, D. (1983) *Physiology of the Nervous System.* New York: Oxford University Press.

Ounsted, M., Scott, A., & Moar, V. (1980) Delivery and Development: To What Extent Can One Associate Cause and Effect? *Journal of the Royal Society of Medicine* 73:786–792.

Paivio, A. (1971) Imagery and Language. In Segal, S. J. (Ed.), *Imagery: Current Cognitive Approaches.* New York: Academic Press.

Palfrey, J., Levine, M. D., & Oberklaid, F. (1981) An Analysis of Observed Activity and Attention Patterns in Preschool Children. *Journal of Pediatrics* 98:1006–1011.

Palmer, J. O. (1983) *The Psychological Assessment of Children* (2nd ed.). New York: Wiley.

Panksepp, J. (1981) Hypothalamic Integration of Behavior. In Morgane, P. J. & Panksepp, J. (Eds.), *Behavioral Studies of the Hypothalamus.* New York: Marcel Dekker.

Pardes, H. (1986) Neuroscience and Psychiatry: Marriage or Coexistence? *American Journal of Psychiatry* 143:1205–1212.

Parelius, A. P. & Parelius, R. J. (1978) *The Sociology of Education.* Englewood Cliffs, NJ: Prentice-Hall.

Pareus, H. & Weech, Jr., A. A. (1966) Accelerated Learning Responses in Young Patients with School Problems. *Journal of Child Psychiatry* 5:75–92.

Parrill-Burnstein, M. (1981) *Problem Solving and Learning Disabilities: An Information Processing Approach.* New York: Grune & Stratton.

Parsons, R. D. & Meyers, J. (1984) *Developing Consultation Skills.* San Francisco: Jossey-Bass.

Parsons, R. D. & Wicks, R. J. (Eds.) (1983) *Passive-aggressiveness: Theory and Practice.* New York: Brunner/Mazel.

Parsons, T. (1964) *Social Structure and Personality.* New York: Free Press.

Parsons, T. (1977) *Social Systems and the Evolution of Action Theory.* New York: Free Press.

Parsons, T. (1978) *Action Theory and the Human Condition.* New York: Free Press. pp. 381–383.

Pasamanick, B. & Knobloch, H. (1966) Retrospective Studies on the Epidemiology of Reproductive Casualty: Old and New. *Merrill-Palmer Quarterly* 12:7–26.

Patten, B. M. (1973) Visually Mediated Thinking: A Report of the Case of Albert Einstein. *Journal of Learning Disabilities* 6:15–20.

Patterson, G. R. (1976) *Families: Applications of Social Learning to Family Life.* Champaign, IL: Research Press.

Paul, R., Cohen, D. J., & Caparulo, B. K. (1983) A Longitudinal Study of Patients with Severe Developmental Disorders of Language Learning. *Journal of Child Psychiatry* 22:525–534.

Pavlidis, G. T. (1981) Sequencing, Eye Movements and the Early Objective Diagnosis of Dyslexia. In Pavlidis, G. T. & Miles, T. R. (Eds.), *Dyslexia Research and Its Application to Education.* New York: Wiley.

Pearson, J. C. (1983) *Interpersonal Communication.* Glenview, IL: Scott, Foresman.

Peck, B. B. (1971) Reading Disorders: Have We Overlooked Something? *Journal of School Psychology* 9:182–191.

Peck, B. B. & Stackhouse, T. W. (1973) Reading Problems and Family Dynamics. *Journal of Learning Disabilities* 6:43–48.

Pellegrini, D. S. (1985) Training in Social Problem-solving. In Rutter, M. & Hersov, L. (Eds.), *Child and Adolescent Psychiatry.* Oxford, England: Blackwell Scientific Publications.

Pellegrino, J. W. (1985) Inductive Reasoning Ability. In Sternberg, R. J. (Ed.), *Human Abilities: An Information-Processing Approach.* New York: Freeman.

Penfield, W. (1956) The Permanent Record of the Stream of Consciousness. *Acta Psychologica* 11:47–69.

Penfield, W. (1975) *The Mystery of the Mind: A Critical Study of Consciousness and the Human Brain.* Princeton, NJ: Princeton University Press.

Pennington, B. F. (1989) Using Genetics to Understand Dyslexia. *Annals of Dyslexia* 39:81–93.

Perkins, H. V. (1974) *Human Development and Learning* (2nd ed.). Belmont, CA: Wadsworth.

Perosa, L. M. & Perosa, S. L. (1982) Structural Interaction Patterns in Families with Learning Disabled Children. *Family Therapy* 9:175–187.

Perry, S. E. (1966) Notes for a Sociology

of Prevention in Mental Retardation. In Phillips, I. (Ed.), *Prevention and Treatment of Mental Retardation.* New York: Basic Books.

Peters, J., Romine, J., & Dykman, R. (1975) A Special Neurological Examination of Children with Learning Disabilities. *Developmental Medicine and Child Neurology* 17:63–78.

Petersen, A.C. & Crockett, L.J. (1987) Biological Correlates of Spatial Ability and Mathematical Performance. *Annals of New York Academy of Sciences* 517: 69–86.

Petit, T. L., Milgram, N. W., & MacLeod, C. (Eds.) (1987) *Neuroplasticity: Learning and Memory.* New York: Alan R. Liss.

Pflaum, S. W. (1974) *The Development of Language and Reading in the Young Child.* Columbus, OH: Merrill.

Pfohl, W. (1980) Children's Anxiety Management Program. *Dissertation Abstracts International* 41:3424-A.

Phillips, E. L., Wiener, D. N., & Haring, N. G. (1960) *Discipline, Achievement and Mental Health.* Englewood Cliffs, NJ: Prentice-Hall.

Philpott, W. H. & Kalita, D. K. (1980) *Brain Allergies: The Psycho-Nutrient Connection.* New Canaan, CT: Keats.

Piaget, J. (1950) *Psychology of Intelligence.* London: Routledge & Kegan Paul.

Piaget, J. (1959) *The Language and Thought of the Child.* London: Routledge & Kegan Paul.

Piaget, J. (1974) *Experiments in Contradiction.* Chicago: University of Chicago Press.

Piaget, J. (1976) *The Grasp of Consciousness: Action and Concept in the Young Child.* Cambridge, MA: Harvard University Press.

Piaget, J. (1978) *Success and Understanding.* Cambridge, MA: Harvard University Press.

Piaget, J. & Inhelder, B. (1969) *The Psychology of the Child.* London: Routledge & Kegan Paul.

Piaget, J. & Inhelder, B. (1973) *Memory and Intelligence.* New York: Basic Books.

Pickering, G. (1976) Creativity and Psychoneurosis. In *Creative Psychiatry Series.* Ardsley, NY: Geigy Pharmaceuticals.

Pierce, J. R. (1977) Is There a Relationship Between Vision Therapy and Academic Achievement? *Review of Optometry* June 1977:48–63.

Piggott, L. R. & Anderson, T. (1983) Brainstem Auditory Evoked Responses in Children with Central Language Disturbance. *Journal of Child Psychiatry* 22:535–540.

Pihl, R. O. & Parkes, M. (1977) Hair Element Content in Learning Disabled Children. *Science* 198:204–206.

Pine, F. (1982) The Experience of Self: Aspects of its Formation, Expansion and Vulnerability. *Psychoanalytic Study of the Child* 37:143–167.

Pirozzolo, F. J. (1979) *The Neuropsychology of Developmental Reading Disorders.* New York: Praeger.

Pirozzolo, F. J. (1983) Eye Movements and Reading Disability. In Rayner, K. (Ed.), *Eye Movements in Reading: Perceptual and Language Processes.* New York: Academic Press.

Plant, E. A. (1979) Play and Adaptation. *Psychoanalytic Study of the Child* 34: 217–232.

Plomin, R. & DeFries, J. C. (1985) *The Origins of Individual Differences in Infancy.* Orlando, FL: Academic Press.

Plutchik, R. (1977) Cognitions in the Services of Emotions. In Candland, D. K. et al (Eds.), *Emotion.* Monterey, CA: Brooks/Cole.

Plutchik, R. (1980) *Emotions in Humans and Animals: A Psychoevolutionary Synthesis.* New York: Harper & Row.

Plutchik, R., Kellerman, H., & Conte, H. R. (1979) A Structural Theory of Ego Defenses and Emotions. In Izard, C. E. (Ed.), *Emotions in Personality and Psychopathology*. New York: Plenum.

Polatajko, H. J. (1985) A Critical Look at Vestibular Dysfunction in Learning-Disabled Children. *Developmental Medicine and Child Neurology* 27:283–292.

Pollack, C. & Branden, A. (1982) Odyssey of a 'Mirrored' Personality. *Annals of Dyslexia* 32:275–288.

Pollatsek, A. (1983) What Can Eye Movements Tell Us About Dyslexia? In Rayner, K. (Ed.), *Eye Movements in Reading: Perceptual and Language Processes*. New York: Academic Press.

Pond, D. (1960) Is There a Syndrome of "Brain Damage" of Children? *Cerebral Palsy Bulletin* 2:296–297.

Pope, K. S. & Singer, J. L. (1978) Regulation of the Stream of Consciousness. In Schwartz, G. E. & Shapiro, D. (Eds.), *Consciousness and Self-Regulation: Advances in Research and Theory*. New York: Plenum.

Popkewitz, T. S., Tabachnick, B. R., & Wehlage, G. (1982) *The Myth of Educational Reform: A Study of School Response to a Program Change*. Madison, WI: University of Wisconsin Press.

Popper, K. R. & Eccles, J. C. (1977) *The Self and Its Brain*. New York: Springer International.

Porrino, L. J., Rapoport, J. L., Behar, D., Sceery, W., Ismond, D. R., & Bunney, Jr., W. E. (1983) A Naturalistic Assessment of the Motor Activity of Hyperactive Boys: I. Comparison with Normal Controls. *Archives of General Psychiatry* 40:681–687.

Potegal, M. (1982) *Spatial Abilities: Development and Physiological Foundations*. New York: Academic Press.

Pothier, P. C., Friedlander, S., Morrison, D. C., & Herman, L. (1983) Procedure for Assessment of Neurodevelopmental Delay in Young Children. *Child: Care, Health and Development* 9:73–83.

Potter, R. L. (1983) Manic-Depressive Variant Syndrome of Childhood. *Clinical Pediatrics* 22:495–499.

Powell, G. E. (1981) *Brain and Personality*. Farnborough, England: Saxon House.

Powell, G. E. (1981) *Brain Function Therapy*. Aldershot, England: Gower.

Poznanski, E., Cook, S. C., & Carroll, B. J. (1979) A Depression Rating Scale for Children. *Pediatrics* 64:442–450.

Poznanski, E. O., Grossman, J. A., Buchsbaum, Y., Banegas, M., Freeman, L., & Gibbons, R. (1984) Preliminary Studies of the Reliability and Validity of the Children's Depression Rating Scale. *Journal of Child Psychiatry* 23:191–197.

Prechtl, H. F. R. (1978) Minimal Brain Dysfunction Syndrome and Plasticity of the Nervous System. In Kalverboer, A. F., van Praag, H. M., & Mendlewicz, J. (Eds.), *Advances in Biological Psychiatry, Volume I: Minimal Brain Dysfunction: Fact or Fiction*. Basel, Switzerland: Karger.

Prechtl, H. F. R. & Stemmer, C. J. (1962) The Choreiform Syndrome in Children. *Developmental Medicine and Child Neurology* 4:119–127.

Prelinger, E. & Zimet, C. N. (1964) *An Ego-Psychological Approach to Character Assessment*. New York: Free Press.

Premack, A. J. & Premack, D. (1972) Teaching Language to an Ape. *Scientific American* 227:92–99.

Premack, D. (1979) Toward Empirical Behavior: Law I, Positive Reinforcement. *Psychological Review* 66:219–233.

Prentice, N. M. & Sperry, B. M. (1965) Therapeutically Oriented Tutoring of Children with Primary Neurotic Learning Inhibitions. *American Journal of Orthopsychiatry* 35:521–530.

Prescott, J. W. (1975) Body Pleasure and the Origins of Violence. *The Futurist.* April 64–74.

President's Council on Physical Fitness and Sports (1980) *Youth Physical Fitness.* Washington, DC: U.S. Government Printing Office.

Pressley, M., Forrest-Pressley, D. L., Elliot-Faust, D., & Miller, G. (1985) Children's Use of Cognitive Strategies. In Pressley, M. & Brainerd, C. J. (Eds.), *Cognitive Learning and Memory in Children.* New York: Springer-Verlag.

Pribram, K. H. (1971) *Languages of the Brain.* Englewood Cliffs, NJ: Prentice-Hall.

Pribram, K. H. (1976) Self-Consciousness and Intentionality. In Schwartz, G. E. & Shapiro, D. (Eds.), *Consciousness and Self-regulation. Volume I.* New York: Plenum.

Pribram, K. H. (1977) *Languages of the Brain: Experimental Paradoxes and Principles in Neuropsychology.* Monterey, CA: Wadsworth.

Pribram, K. H. (1979) The Orienting Reaction: Key to Brain Re-presentational Mechanisms. In Kimmel, H. D., Val Olst, E. H., & Orlebeke, J. F. (Eds.), *The Orienting Reflex in Humans.* Hillsdale, NJ: Erlbaum.

Pribram, K. H. (1980) The Role of Analogy in Transcending Limits in the Brain Sciences. *Daedelus* 109:19–38.

Pribram, K. H. (1981) Emotions. In Filskov, S. B. & Boll, T. J. (Eds.), *Handbook of Clinical Neuropsychology.* New York: Wiley-Interscience.

Pribram, K. H. & Gill, M. M. (1976) *Freud's "Project" Re-assessed.* New York: Basic Books.

Pribram, K. H. & Luria, A. R. (1973) *Psychophysiology of the Frontal Lobes.* New York: Academic Press.

Pribram, K. H., Nuwer, M., & Baron, R. J. (1974) The Holographic Hypothesis of Memory Structure in Brain Function and Perception. In Atkinson, R. C., Krantz, D. H., Luce, R. C., & Suppes, P. (Eds.), *Contemporary Developments in Mathematical Psychology.* San Francisco: Freeman.

Price, G. E., Dunn, R., & Sanders, W. (1980) Reading Achievement and Learning Style Characteristics. *The Clearing House* 54:223–226.

Prichard, A. & Taylor, J. (1980) *Accelerating Learning: The Use of Suggestion in the Classroom.* Novato, CA: Academic Therapy Publications.

Prince, R. (1960) The "Brain Fag" Syndrome in Nigerian Students. *Journal of Mental Science* 106:559–570.

Prudden, S. (1979) *Suzy Prudden's Family Fitness Book.* New York: Grosset & Dunlap.

Pueschel, S. M. (Ed.) (1984) *The Young Child with Down Syndrome.* New York: Human Sciences Press.

Pugh, G. E. (1977) *The Biological Origin of Human Values.* New York: Basic Books.

Pulliam, H. R. & Dunford, C. (1980) *Programmed to Learn: An Essay on the Evolution of Culture.* New York: Columbia University Press.

Quercus Corporation. *Caught Reading Program.* Castro Valley, CA: Quercus.

Rabinovitch, R. D. (1968) Reading Problems in Children: Definition and Classification. In Keeney, A. H. & Keeney, V. T. (Eds.), *Dyslexia, Diagnosis and Treatment of Reading Disorders.* St. Louis, MO: Mosby.

Radilova, J. & Radil-Weiss, T. (1983) *Some EEG Correlates of Perception and Cognition.* In Sinz, R. & Rosenzweig, M. R. (Eds.), *Psychophysiology.* New York: Elsevier.

Rado, S. (1956, 1962) *Psychoanalysis of Behavior. Volumes I & II.* New York: Grune & Stratton.

Raeithel, G. (1979) Philobatism and American Culture. *Journal of Psychohistory* 6:491–496.

Rajecki, D. W. (1983) (Ed.) *Comparing Behavior: Studying Man Studying Animals.* Hillsdale, NJ: Erlbaum.

Rak, E. T. (1977) *Spellbound.* Cambridge, MA: Educators Publishing Service.

Rak, E. T. (1979) *The Spell of Words.* Cambridge, MA: Educators Publishing Service.

Rakic, P. (1985) Limits of Neurogenesis in Primates. *Science* 227:1054–1056.

Randall, J. H. (1926) *The Making of the Modern Mind.* Cambridge, MA: Riverside Press.

Rapaport, D. (1951) *Organization and Pathology of Thought.* New York: Columbia University Press.

Rapaport, D. (1971) *Emotions and Memory.* New York: International Universities Press.

Rapin, I. (1982) *Children with Brain Dysfunction: Neurology, Cognition, Language and Behavior.* New York: Raven.

Rapin, I. & Wilson, B. C. (1978) Children with Developmental Language Disability: Neurological Aspects and Assessment. In Wyke, M. D. (Ed.), *Developmental Aphasia.* New York: Academic Press.

Rapoport, J. L. & Ismond, D. R. (1982) Biological Research in Child Psy-

chiatry. *Journal of Child Psychiatry* 21:543–548.

Raths, J. D. (1961) Underachievement and a Search for Values. *Journal of Educational Sociology* 14:423–424.

Rauschecker, J.P. & Marier, P. (1987) *Imprinting and Cortical Plasticity.* New York: Wiley.

Rawson, M. B. (1968) *Developmental Language Disability: Adult Accomplishment of Dyslexic Children.* Baltimore, MD: Johns Hopkins Press.

Rawson, M. B. (1982) Louise Baker and the Leonardo Syndrome. *Annals of Dyslexia* 32:289–304.

Rawson, M. B. (1986) The Many Faces of Dyslexia. *Annals of Dyslexia* 36:179–191.

Rayner, K. (Ed.) (1983) *Eye Movements in Reading: Perceptual and Language Processes.* New York: Academic Press.

Read, C. (1986) *Children's Creative Spelling.* London: Routledge & Kegan Paul.

Reason, J. & Mycielska, K. (1982) *Absentminded? The Psychology of Mental Lapses and Everyday Errors.* Englewood Cliffs, NJ: Prentice-Hall.

Redl, F. & Wineman, D. (1960) *Children Who Hate* (2nd ed.). New York: Free Press.

Redl, F. (1965) Management of Discipline Problems in Normal Students. *The Reiss-Davis Clinic Bulletin* 2:38–46.

Redl, F. (1966) *When We Deal With Children.* New York: Free Press.

Reed, S. (1980) *Counseling in Medical Genetics* (3rd ed.). New York: Liss.

Regional Intervention Program (1976) A Parent-Implemented Early Intervention Program for Preschool Children. *Hospital and Community Psychiatry* 27:728–731.

Reich, W. (1972) *Character Analysis.* New York: Farrar, Straus & Giroux.

Reinhardt, J. B. & Brash, A. L. (1969) Psychosocial Dwarfism: Environmentally Induced Recovery. *Psychosomatic Medicine* 31:165–172.

Reinisch, J. M. & Sander, S. A. (1982) Early Barbiturate Exposure: The Brain, Sexually Dimorphic Behavior and Learning. *Neuroscience and Biobehavioral Reviews* 6:311–319.

Reiser, M. F. (1984) *Mind, Brain, Body: Toward a Convergence of Psychoanalysis and Neurobiology.* New York: Basic Books.

Reitan, R. M. (1964) Relationships Between Neurological and Psychological Variables and Their Implication for Reading Instruction. In Robinson, H. A. (Ed.), *Meeting Individual Differences in Reading.* Chicago: University of Chicago Press.

Remer, J. (1983) *Changing Schools Through the Arts.* New York: McGraw-Hill.

Renshaw, P. D. & Asher, S. R. (1982) Social Competence and Peer Status. In Rubin, K. H. & Ross, H. S. (Eds.), *Peer Relationships and Social Skills in Childhood.* New York: Springer-Verlag.

Restak, R. M. (1979) *The Brain; The Last Frontier.* New York: Doubleday.

Reyna, V. F. (1985) Figure and Fantasy in Children's Language. In Pressley, M. & Brainerd, C. J. (Eds.), *Cognitive Learning and Memory in Children.* New York: Springer-Verlag.

Reynolds, E. & Trimble, M. (1976) Anticonvulsant Drugs and Mental Symptoms. *Psychological Medicine* 6:169–178.

Rhine, W. R. (1981) *Making Schools More Effective: New Directions from Follow Through.* New York: Academic Press.

Rhodes, W. C. (1972) *BehaviorThreat and Community Response.* New York: Behavioral Publications.

Rice, G. V. (1984) *Focus on Phonics.* Syracuse, NY: New Readers Press.

Rich, D. (1988) *Megaskills: How Families Can Help Children Succeed in School and Beyond.* Boston, MA: Houghton Mifflin.

Richardson, A. (1983) Imagery: Definition and Types. In Sheikh, A. A. (Ed.), *Imagery: Current Theory, Research and Application.* New York: Wiley.

Richmond, G. (1973) *The Micro-Society School: A Real World in Miniature.* New York: Harper & Row.

Rieber, R. W. (Ed.) (1980) *Language Development and Aphasia in Children.* New York: Academic Press.

Riesman, D., Glazer, N., & Denney, R. (1950) *The Lonely Crowd.* New Haven, CT: Yale University Press.

Rifkin, J. (1980) *Entropy: A New World View.* New York: Viking.

Rimland, B. (1983) The Feingold Diet. *Journal of Learning Disabilities* 16:331–333.

Rinne, C. H. (1984) *Attention: The Fundamentals of Classroom Control.* Columbus, OH: Merrill.

Rist, R. C. & Harrell, J. E. (1982) Labeling the Learning Disabled Child: The Social Ecology of Educational Practice. *American Journal of Orthopsychiatry* 52:146–160.

Robbins, D. M., Beck, J. C., Pries, R., Jacobs, D., & Smith, C. (1983) Learning Disability and Neuropsychological Impairment in Adjudicated, Unincarcerated Male Delinquents. *Journal of the American Academy of Child Psychiatry* 22:40–46.

Roberts, E. (1982) Potential Therapies in Aging and Senile Dementias. *Annals of the New York Academy of Sciences* 396:165–178.

Robertson, E. A., Van Steirteghem, A. C., Byrkit, J. E., & Young, D. S. (1980) Biochemical Individuality and the Recognition of Personal Profiles with a Computer. *Clinical Chemistry* 26:30–36.

Robinson, H. M. (1966) The Major Aspects of Reading. In Robinson, H. A. (Ed.), *Reading: Seventy-five Years of Progress*. Chicago: University of Chicago Press.

Robinson, S. & Smith, D. D. (1983) Listening Skills: Teaching Learning Disabled Students to Be Better Listeners. In Meyen, E. L., Vergason, G. A., & Whelan, R. J. (Eds.), *Promising Practices for Exceptional Children: Cirriculum Implications*. Denver, CO: Love.

Robson, K. S. (Ed.) (1983) *The Borderline Child: Approaches to Etiology, Diagnosis and Treatment*. New York: McGraw-Hill.

Rockefeller, D. (1983) *Coming to Our Senses: The Significance of the Arts for American Education*. New York: McGraw-Hill.

Rodier, P. M. (1980) Chronology of Neuron Development: Animal Studies and Their Clinical Implication. *Developmental Medicine and Child Neurology* 22:525–545.

Roe, A. (1950–1951) A Study of Imagery in Research Scientists. *Journal of Personality* 19:464.

Roethlisberger, F. J. & Dickson, W. J. (1939) *Management and the Worker*. Cambridge, MA: Harvard University Press.

Rolls, E. T. (1981) Central Nervous Mechanisms Related to Feeding and Appetite. *British Medical Bulletin* 37:131–134.

Rorke, L. B. (1982) *Pathology of Perinatal Brain Injury*. New York: Raven.

Rosen, V. H. (1955) Strephosymbolia: An Intrasystemic Disturbance of the Synthetic Function of the Ego. *Psychoanalytic Study of the Child* 10:83–99.

Rosenberg, M. (1979) *Conceiving the Self*. New York: Basic Books.

Rosenblatt, D. B. (1981) Play. In Rutter, M. (Ed.), *Scientific Foundations of Developmental Psychiatry*. Baltimore, MD: University Park Press.

Rosenfeld, A. (1981) Teaching the Body to Program the Brain in Moshe Feldenkrais' Miracle—A Technique That Stimulates Mind and Muscle. *Smithsonian* 11:52–58.

Rosenthal, J. H. (1977) *The Neuropsychopathology of Written Language*. Chicago, IL: Nelson-Hall.

Rosenthal, R. & Fode, K. L. (1963) The Effect of Experimenter Bias in the Performance of the Albino Rat. *Behavioral Science* 8:183–189.

Rosenthal, R. & Jacobson, L. (1968) *Pygmalion in the Classroom*. New York: Holt, Rinehart & Winston.

Rosenzweig, M. R., Bennett, E. L., & Diamond, M. C. (1972) Brain Changes in Response to Experience. *Scientific American* 226:22–29.

Rosett, H. L. (1980) A Clinical Perspective of the Fetal Alcohol Syndrome. *Alcoholism: Clinical and Experimental Research* 4:119.

Rosner, J. (1979) *Helping Children Overcome Learning Difficulties. A Step-by-Step Guide for Parents and Teachers* (2nd ed.). New York: Walker.

Ross, A. O. (1977) *Learning Disability: The Unrealized Potential*. New York: McGraw-Hill.

Ross, D. M. & Ross, S. A. (1976) *Hyperactivity, Research, Theory, Action*. New York: Wiley.

Ross, E. D. (1982) The Divided Self: Contrary to Convential Wisdom, Not All Language Is Commanded by the Brain's Left Side. *The Sciences* 22:8–12.

Rossi, I. (1983) *From the Sociology of Symbols to the Sociology of Signs*. New York: Columbia University Press.

Roth, B. (1978) Narcolepsy and Hypersomnia. In Williams, R. L. & Karacan, I. (Eds.), *Sleep Disorders: Diagnosis and Treatment.* New York: Wiley.

Rothenberg, A. (1979) *The Emerging Goddess: The Creative Process in Art, Science and Other Fields.* Chicago: University of Chicago Press.

Rothenberg, A. (1983) Psychopathology and Creative Cognition. *Archives of General Psychiatry* 40:937–942.

Rothstein, A. (1983) *The Structural Hypothesis: An Evolutionary Perspective.* New York: International Universities Press.

Rothstein, A.R., Benjamin, L., Crosby, M. & Einstadt, K. (1988) *Learning Disorders: An Integration of Neuropsychological and Psychoanalytic Considerations.* New York: International Universities Press.

Rotter, J. B. (1966) Generalized Expectancies for Internal Versus External Control of Reinforcement. *Psychological Monographs* 80:1.

Rourke, B. P. (1978) Neuropsychological Research in Reading Retardation: A Review. In Benton, A. L. & Pearl, D. (Eds.), *Dyslexia: An Appraisal of Current Knowledge.* New York: Oxford University Press.

Rourke, B. P. (Ed.) (1985) *Neuropsychology of Learning Disabilities: Essentials of Subtype Analysis.* New York: Guilford Press.

Rourke, B. P., Bakker, D. J., Fisk, J. L., & Strang, J. D. (1983) *Child Neuropsychology: An Introduction to Theory, Research and Clinical Practice.* New York: Guilford Press.

Rousey, C. (1979) Disorders of Speech. In Noshpitz, J. E. (Ed.), *Basic Handbook of Child Psychiatry.* New York: Basic Books.

Rousey, C. & Toussieng, P. (1964) Contributions of a Speech Pathologist to the Psychiatric Examination of Children. *Mental Hygiene* 48:566–575.

Routtenberg, A. (1968) The Two-Arousal Hypothesis: Reticular Formation and Limbic System. *Psychological Review* 75:51–80.

Rowe, M. B. (1973) *Teaching Science as a Continuous Enquiry.* New York: McGraw-Hill.

Royce, J. R. & Powell, A. (1983) *Theory of Personality and Individual Differences: Factors, Systems and Processes.* Englewood Cliffs, NJ: Prentice-Hall.

Rubin, K. H. & Ross, H. S. (Eds.) (1982) *Peer Relationships and Social Skills in Childhood.* New York: Springer-Verlag.

Rubin, R. T. & Kendler, K. S. (1977) Psychoneuroendocrinology: Fundamental Concepts and Correlates in Depression. In Usdin, G. (Ed.), *Depression: Clinical, Biological and Psychological Perspectives.* New York: Brunner/Mazel.

Rubin, S. S. (1982) Expressive Language Deficits in Preschool Children and Faulty Development of the Self: Description and Case Study. *American Journal of Orthopsychiatry* 52:58–64.

Rubin, Z. (1980) *Children's Friendships.* Cambridge, MA: Harvard University Press.

Rubin, Z. (1983) The Skills of Friendship. In Donaldson, M., Grieve, R., & Pratt, C. (Eds.), *Early Childhood Development and Education.* New York: Guilford Press.

Ruble, D. N. & Boggiano, A. K. (1980) Optimizing Motivation in an Achievement Context. In Keogh, B. (Ed.), *Advances in Special Education: Basic Constructs and Theoretical Orientation.* Greenwich, CT: JAI Press.

Rudel, R. G. (1980) Learning Disability: Diagnosis by Exclusion and Discrepancy. *Journal of Child Psychiatry* 19:547–569.

Rudel, R. G. & Helfgott, E. (1984) Effect

of Piracetam on Verbal Memory of Dyslexic Boys. *Journal of Child Psychiatry* 23:695–699.

Rumanoff-Simonson, L. (1979) *A Curriculum Model for Individuals with Severe Learning and Behavior Disorders.* Baltimore, MD: University Park Press.

Rumelhart, D. (1978) *Schemata: The Building Blocks of Cognition.* San Diego, CA: Center for Human Information Processing, University of California.

Rush, A. J., Beck, A. T., Kovacs, M., Weissenburger, J., & Hollon, S. D. (1982) Comparison of the Effects of Cognitive Therapy and Pharmacotherapy on Hopelessness and Self Concept. *American Journal of Psychiatry* 139:862–866.

Russell, B. (1925) *The ABC of Relativity.* New York: New American Library, 1969.

Rutherford, D. (1977) Speech and Language Disorders and MBD. In Millichap, J. G. (Ed.), *Learning Disabilities and Related Disorders.* Chicago: Year Book Medical Publishers.

Rutter, M. (1978) Prevalence and Types of Dyslexia. In Benton, A. L. & Pearl, D. (Eds.), *Dyslexia: An Appraisal of Current Knowledge.* New York: Oxford University Press.

Rutter, M. (1980) Raised Lead Levels and Impaired Cognitive Behavioral Functioning. *Developmental Medicine and Child Neurology* 22:1–26.

Rutter, M. (1981a) *Scientific Foundations of Developmental Psychiatry.* Baltimore, MD: University Park Press.

Rutter, M. (1981b) Psychological Sequelae of Brain Damage in Children. *American Journal of Psychiatry* 138:1533–1544.

Rutter, M. (1982) Syndromes Attributed to "Minimal Brain Dysfunction" in Childhood. *American Journal of Psychiatry* 139:21–33.

Rutter, M. & Hersov, L. (Eds.) *Child and Adolescent Psychiatry.* Oxford, England: Blackwell Scientific Publications.

Rutter, M., Maughan, B., Mortimore, P., & Ouston, J. (1979) *Fifteen Thousand Hours: Secondary Schools and Their Effects on Children.* Cambridge, MA: Harvard University Press.

Rutter, M., Tizard, J., & Whitmore, K. (1970) *Education, Health and Behavior.* London: Longmans.

Rutter, M. & Yule, W. (1975) The Concept of Specific Reading Retardation. *Journal of Child Psychology and Psychiatry* 16:161–197.

Saccuzzo, D. P. & Braff, D. L. (1981) Early Information Processing Deficit in Schizophrenia. *Archives of General Psychiatry* 36:175–179.

Safer, D. J. & Kruger, J. M. (1983) Trends in Medication Treatment of Hyperactive School Children. *Clinical Pediatrics* 22:501–504.

Sahakian, B. J. (1981) The Neuro-chemical Basis of Hyperactivity and Aggression Induced by Social Deprivation. In Lewis, D. O. (Ed.), *Vulnerabilities to Delinquency.* New York: SP Medical and Scientific Books.

Sakamoto, T. (1981) Beginning Reading in Japan. In Ollila, L. (Ed.), *Beginning Reading Instruction in Different Countries.* Newark, DL: International Reading Association.

Salamy, A. (1978) Commissural Transmission: Maturational Changes in Humans. *Science* 200:1409–1411.

Salk, L. (1973) The Role of Heartbeat in the Relations between Mother and Infant. *Scientific American* 228:24.

Sameroff, A. J. (1982) The Environmental Context of Development Disabilities. In Bricker, D. (Ed.), *Intervention with At-Risk and Handicapped Infants: From Research to Application.* Baltimore, MD: University Park Press.

Sameroff, A. J. & Chandler, M. G. (1975)

Reproductive Risk and the Continuum of Caretaker Casuality. In Horowitz, F. D., Hetherington, M., Scarr-Salapatek, S. & Siegel, G. (Eds.), *Review of Child Development Research. Volume 4.* Chicago: University of Chicago Press.

Samuels, S. J. & Eisenberg, P. (1981) A Framework for Understanding the Reading Process. In Pirozzolo, F. J. & Wittrock, M. C. (Eds.), *Neuropsychological and Cognitive Processes in Reading.* New York: Academic Press.

Sander, L. W. (1983) Polarity Paradox and the Organizing Process in Development. In Call, J. & Galenson, R. T. (Eds.), *Frontiers of Infant Psychiatry.* New York: Basic Books.

Sander, L. W., Stechler, G., Burns, P., & Julia, H. (1970) Early Mother-Infant Interaction and 14-Hour Patterns of Sleep and Activity. *Journal of Child Psychiatry* 9:103–123.

Sanders, M. (1979) *Clinical Assessment of Learning Problems: Model, Process and Remedial Planning.* Boston: Allyn & Bacon.

Sandler, J. (1981) Character Traits and Object Relationships. *Psychoanalytic Quarterly* 50:694–708.

Sandler, J. with Freud, A. (1985) *The Analysis of Defense: The Ego and the Mechanism of Defense Revisited.* New York: International Universities Press.

Sandler, J., Kennedy, H., & Tyson, R. I. (1975) Discussion on Transference. *The Psychoanalytic Study of the Child* 30:409–441.

Sandler, M. (1983) Monoamineoxidase Inhibitors and Their Pharmacological Significance. *Acta Neurologica Scandinavica.* (Suppl.) 95:37–41.

Santostefano, S. (1978) *A Biodevelopmental Approach to Clinical Child Psychology: Cognitive Controls and Cognitive Control Therapy.* New York: Wiley-Interscience.

Santostefano, S. (1980) Cognition in Personality and the Treatment Process: A Psychoanalytic View. *Psychoanalytic Study of the Child* 35:41–66.

Santostefano, S. (1985) *Cognitive Control Therapy with Children and Adolescents.* New York: Pergamon.

Sapir, S. G. (1985) *The Clinical Teaching Model.* New York: Brunner/Mazel.

Sapir, S. G. & Nitzburg, A. C. (Eds.) (1973) *Children with Learning Problems.* New York: Brunner/Mazel.

Sarason, S. B. (1971) *The Culture of the School and the Problem of Change.* Boston: Allyn & Bacon.

Sarason, S. B. & Doris, J. (1979) *Educational Handicap, Public Policy and Social History: A Broadened Perspective on Mental Retardation.* New York: Free Press.

Sasanuma, S. (1974) Impairment of Written Language in Japanese Aphasics. *Journal of Chinese Linguistics* 2:141–157.

Sataloff, J., Sataloff, R. T., & Vassallo, L. A. (1980) *Hearing Loss* (2nd ed.). Philadelphia, PA: Lippincott.

Satterfield, J. H., Cantwell, D. P., & Satterfield, B. T. (1979a) Multimodal Treatment: A One Year Followup of 84 Hyperactive Boys. *Archives of General Psychiatry* 36:965–974.

Satterfield, J. H., Cantwell, D. P., Schell, A., & Blaschke, T. (1979b) Growth of Hyperactive Children Treated with Methylphenidate. *Archives of General Psychiatry* 36:212–217.

Sattler, J. M. (1988) *Assessment of Children's Intelligence and Special Abilities* (3rd ed.). San Diego, CA: Jerome M. Sattler.

Satz, P. (1979) A Test of Some Models of Hemispheric Speech Organization on the Left and Right Handed. *Science* 203:1131–1133.

Satz, P. & Friel, J. (1978) Predictive Validity of an Abbreviated Screening Battery. *Journal of Learning Disabilities* 11:347–351.

Satz, P. & Morris, R. (1980) The Search for Subtype Classification in Learning Disabled Children. In Tartar, R. E. (Ed.), *The Child at Risk*. New York: Oxford University Press.

Satz, P. & Morris, R. (1981) Learning Disability Subtypes: A Review. In Pirozzolo, F. J. & Wittrock, M. C. (Eds.), *Neuropsychological and Cognitive Processes in Reading*. New York: Academic Press.

Satz, P., Taylor, H. G., Friel, J., & Fletcher, J. M. (1978) Some Developmental and Predictive Precursors of Reading Disabilities: A Six Year Followup. In Benton, A. L. & Pearl, D. (Eds.), *Dyslexia: An Appraisal of Current Knowledge*. New York: Oxford University Press.

Saul, R. & Sperry, R. W. (1968) A Case of Congenitally Lacking a Corpus Callosum. *Neurology* 18:307.

Savignon, S. J. (1983) *Communicative Competence: Theory and Classroom Practice*. Reading, MA: Addison-Wesley.

Saxon, D. S. (1982) Liberal Education in a Technological Age. *Science* 218:845.

Schachar, R., Rutter, M., & Smith, A. (1981) The Characteristics of Situationally and Pervasively Hyperactive Children: Implications for Syndrome Definition. *Journal of Child Psychology and Psychiatry* 22:375–382.

Schacter, S.C. & Galaburda, A.M. (1986) Development and Biological Association of Cerebral Dominance. *Journal of Child Psychiatry* 25: 741–750.

Schachter, S. S. (1964) The Interaction of Cognitive and Physiological Determinants of Emotional State. In Berkowitz, L. (Ed.), *Advances in Experimental Social Psychology Volume I*. New York: Academic Press.

Schachter, S. S. (1971) *Emotion, Obesity and Crime*. New York: Academic Press.

Schafer, R. (1968) *Aspects of Internalization*. New York: International Universities Press.

Schain, R. J. (1977) *Neurology of Childhood Learning Disorders* (2nd ed.). Baltimore, MD: Williams & Wilkins.

Schalling, D., Cronholm, B., & Asberg, M. (1975) Components of State and Trait Anxiety as Related to Personality and Arousal. In Levi, L. (Ed.), *Emotions—Their Parameters and Measurement*. New York: Raven.

Scheder, J. A., Folstein, S. E., Geiger, E. H., & Murvis, D. F. (1977) Effects of Neonatal Disconnection in Kittens. In Harnard, S., Doty, D. W. P., Goldstein, L., Jaynes, J., & Caruthamer, G. (Eds.), *Lateralization in the Nervous System*. New York: Academic Press.

Scheinfeld, D. R. (1983) Family Relationships and School Achievement Among Boys of Lower-Income Urban Black Families. *American Journal of Orthopsychiatry* 53:127–143.

Schmais, C. & Orleans, F. (1981) Dance/Movement Therapy with MBD Children. In Ochrock, R. (Ed.), *The Diagnosis and Treatment of Minimal Brain Dysfunction in Children: A Clinical Approach*. New York: Human Sciences Press.

Schmuck, R. A. & Schmuck, P. A. (1971) *Group Processes in the Classroom*. Dubuque, IO: Brown.

Schopler, E., Reichler, R. J., & Renner, B. R. (1986) *The Childhood Autism Rating Scale*. New York: Irvington.

Schowalter, J. E. (1986) Countertransference in Work with Children: Review of a Neglected Concept. *Journal of Child Psychiatry* 25:40–45.

Schreiner, R. L. (1981) *Care of the Newborn*. New York: Raven.

Schrier, M. (1979) Ocular Dysfunction in MBS. In Gardner, R. A., *The Objective Diagnosis of Minimal Brain Dys-*

function. Creskill, NJ: Creative Therapeutics.

Schulterbrandt, J. G. & Raskin, A. (Eds.) (1977) *Depression in Childhood*. New York: Raven.

Schultz, E. W. & Heuchert, C. M. (1983) *Child Stress and the School Experience*. New York: Human Sciences Press.

Schwartz, F. & Schiller, P. H.(1970) *A Psychoanalytic Model of Attention and Learning Psychological Issues*. Monograph 23, Volume VI, No. 3. New York: International Universities Press.

Schwartz, G. E., Brown, S. L., & Ahern, G. L. (1980) Facial Muscle Patterning and Subjective Experience During Affective Imagery: Sex Differences. *Psychophysiology* 17:75–82.

Schwartz, J., Pollard, H., & Quach, T. T. (1980) Histamine as a Neurotransmitter in Mammalian Brain: Neurochemical Evidence. *Journal of Neurochemistry* 35:26–33.

Schwartz, P. (1957) Birth Trauma as a Cause of Mental Deficiency. Exhibition at APA Annual Meeting, Chicago, 1957.

Schwartz, M. A. & Wiggins, O. P. (1986) Systems and the Structure of Meaning: Contributions to a Biopsychosocial Medicine. *American Journal of Psychiatry* 143:1213–1221.

Schweinhart, L. J. & Weikart, D. P. (1980) *Young Children Grow Up: The Effects of the Perry Preschool Program on Youths Through Age 15*. Ypsilanti, MI: High/Scope Press.

Science Research Associates (1984) *Corrective Reading Program*. 155 North Wacker Drive, Chicago, IL 60606.

Scott, D. F. (1970) *The Psychology of Work*. London: Duckworth.

Scott, R. A. (1969) *The Making of Blind Men: A Study of Adult Socialization*. New York: Russell Sage Foundation.

Scott, W. A., Osgood, D. W., & Peterson, C. (1979) *Cognitive Structure: Theory and Measurement of Individual Differences*. New York: Wiley.

Scribner, S. & Cole, M. (1981) *The Psychology of Literacy*. Cambridge, MA: Harvard University Press.

Scruton, R. (1980) Humane Education. *The American Scholar* 49:489–498.

Secheheye, M. (1951) *Autobiography of a Schizophrenic Girl*. New York: Grune & Stratton; Signet, 1968.

Segal, S. J. (1971) Processing of the Stimulus in Imagery and Perception. In Segal, S. J. (Ed.), *Imagery: Current Cognitive Approaches*. New York: Academic Press.

Seiderman, A. S. (1976) An Optometric Approach to the Diagnosis of Visually Based Problems in Learning. In Leisman, G. (Ed.), *Basic Visual Processes and Learning Disability*. Springfield, IL: Thomas.

Seiderman, A. S. (1980) Optometric Vision Therapy—Results of a Demonstration Project with a Learning-Disabled Population. *Journal of the American Optometric Association* 51:5.

Selakovich, D. (1984) *Schooling in America: Social Foundations of Education*. New York: Longman.

Seligman, M. E. P. (1975) *Helplessness: On Depression, Development and Death*. San Francisco: Freeman.

Selman, R. L. (1981) What Children Understand of Intrapsychic Processes: The Child as a Budding Personality Theorist. In Shapiro, E. K. & Weber, E. (Eds.), *Cognitive and Affective Growth: Developmental Interaction*. Hillsdale, NJ: Erlbaum.

Selvini Palazzoli, M., Boscolo, L., Cecchin, G., & Prata, G. (1978) *Paradox and Counterparadox*. New York: Aronson.

Selye, H. (1976a) *The Stress of Life.* New York: McGraw-Hill.

Selye, H. (1976b) *Stress in Health and Disease.* Boston: Butterworths.

Selye, H. (1980) The Stress Concept Today. In Kutash, I. L., Schlesinger, L. B. & Associates (Eds.), *Handbook on Stress and Anxiety.* San Francisco: Jossey-Bass.

Sem-Jacobsen, C. W. & Styri, O. B. (1975) Manipulation of Emotion: Electrophysiological and Surgical Methods. In Levi, L. (Ed.), *Emotions—Their Parameters and Measurement.* New York: Raven.

Serban, G. (Ed.) *Cognitive Defects in the Development of Mental Illness.* New York: Brunner/Mazel.

Sever, J. L. (1982) Infections in Pregnancy: Highlights from the Collaborative Perinatal Project. *Teratology* 25:227–237.

Shaffer, D. (1978) Longitudinal Research and the Minimal Brain Damage Syndrome. In Kalverboer, A. F., van Praag, H. M., & Mendlewicz, J. (Eds.), *Advances in Biological Psychiatry. Volume I: Minimal Brain Dysfunction: Fact of Fiction.* Basel, Switzerland: Karger.

Shaffer, D., Bijur, P., Chadwick, O. F. D., & Rutter, M. L. (1980) Head Injury and Later Reading Disability. *Journal of Child Psychiatry* 19:592–610.

Shaffer, D., Meyer-Bahlburg, H. F. L., & Stokman, C. L. J. (1981) The Development of Aggression. In Rutter, M. (Ed.), *Scientific Foundations of Developmental Psychiatry.* Baltimore, MD: University Park Press.

Shaffer, D., Schonfeld, I., O'Connor, P. A., Stokman, C., Troutman, P., Shafer, S., & Ng, S. (1985) Neurological Soft Signs: Their Relationship to Psychiatric Disorder and Intelligence in Childhood and Adolescence. *Archives of General Psychiatry* 42:342–351.

Shafii, M. & Shafii, S. L. (1982) *Pathways of Human Development: Normal Growth and Emotional Disorders in Infancy, Childhood and Adolescence.* New York: Thieme-Stratton.

Shallice, T. (1981) Neurological Impairment of Cognitive Processes. *British Medical Bulletin* 37:187–192.

Shane, P. (1980) Shame and Learning. *American Journal of Orthopsychiatry* 50:348–355.

Shantz, C. V. (1975) The Development of Social Cognition. In Heatherington, E. M. (Ed.), *Review of Child Development Research. Volume 5.* Chicago: University of Chicago Press.

Shapiro, A. K. & Shapiro, E. (1982) An Update on Tourette Syndrome. *American Journal of Psychotherapy* 36:379–390.

Shapiro, D. (1965) *Neurotic Styles.* New York: Basic Books.

Shapiro, E. K. & Weber, E. (Eds.) (1981) *Cognitive and Affective Growth: Developmental Interaction.* Hillsdale, NJ: Erlbaum.

Shapiro, T. (1975) Language and Ego Function of Young Psychotic Children. In Anthony, E. J. (Ed.), *Explorations in Child Psychiatry.* New York: Plenum.

Shapiro, T. (1979) *Clinical Psycholinguistics.* New York: Plenum.

Shapiro, T., Burkes, L., Pettit, T. A., & Ranz, J. (1978) Consistency of "Nonfocal" Neurological Signs. *Journal of Child Psychiatry* 17:70–79.

Shaw, L., Levine, M. D., & Belfer, M. (1982) Developmental Double Jeopardy: A Study of Clumsiness and Self-esteem in Learning Disabled Children. *Journal of Developmental and Behavioral Pediatrics* 3:191–196.

Shearer, D. E. & Shearer, M. S. (1976) The Portage Project: A Model for Early Childhood Intervention. In Tjossem, T. D. (Ed.), *Intervention Strate-*

gies for High Risk Infants and Young Children. Baltimore, MD: University Park Press.

Sheehan, P. W., Ashton, R., & White, K. (1983) Assessment of Mental Imagery. In Sheikh, A. A. (Ed.), *Imagery: Current Theory, Research and Application.* New York: Wiley.

Sheikh, A. A. (Ed.) (1983) *Imagery: Current Theory, Research and Application.* New York: Wiley.

Sheikh, A. A. & Sheikh, K. S. (1985) *Imagery and Education.* Farmingdale, NY: Baywood.

Sheridan, E. M. (1983) Reading Disabilities: Can We Blame the Written Language? *Journal of Learning Disabilities* 16:81–86.

Sherman, M., Shapiro, T., & Glassman, M. (1983) Play and Language in Developmentally Disordered Preschoolers: A New Approach to Classification. *Journal of Child Psychiatry* 22:511–524.

Shipley, T. (1980) *Sensory Integration in Children: Evoked Potentials and Intersensory Functions in Pediatrics and Psychology.* Springfield, IL: Charles C. Thomas.

Shirley, M. (1939) A Behavior Syndrome Characterizing Prematurely Born Children. *Child Development* 10, No. 2.

Shontz, F. C. (1969) *Perceptual and Cognitive Aspects of Body Experience.* New York: Academic Press.

Shore, M. F., Massimo, J. L., Kisielewski, J., & Moran, J. K. (1966) Object Relations Changes Resulting from Successful Psychotherapy with Adolescent Delinquents and Their Relationship to Academic Performance. *Journal of Child Psychiatry* 5:93–104.

Shure, M. B. & Spivak, G. (1978) *Problem-Solving Techniques in Child Rearing.* San Francisco: Jossey-Bass.

Shweder, R. A. & LeVine, R. A. (Eds.) (1984) *Culture Theory: Essays on Mind, Self and Emotion.* New York: Cambridge University Press.

Siegler, R. S. (1983) How Knowledge Influences Learning. *American Scientist* 71:631–638.

Siever, L. J. & Davis, K. L. (1985) Overview: Toward a Dysregulation Hypothesis of Depression. *American Journal of Psychiatry* 142:1017–1031.

Sigg, E. B. (1975) The Organization and Functions of the Central Sympathetic System. In Levi, L. (Ed.), *Emotions—Their Parameters and Measurement.* New York: Raven.

Silbermann, I. (1979) Mental Transitional Spheres. *Psychoanalytic Quarterly* 48:85–105.

Silbert, J., Carnine, D., & Stein, M. (1982) *Direct Instruction Mathematics.* Columbus, OH: Merrill.

Silva, P. A., Buckfield, P., & Spears, G. F. (1979) Mode of Delivery and Developmental Characteristics in a Thousand Dunedin Three Year Olds. *New Zealand Medical Journal* 89(629):79–81.

Silver, A. A. (1977) Anxiety and Defense in Children with Central Nervous System Dysfunction. *Audio Digest* 6:10.

Silver, A. A. (1978) Prevention. In Benton, A. & Pearl, D. (Eds.), *Dyslexia, an Appraisal of Current Knowledge.* New York: Oxford University Press.

Silver, A. A. (1979) Early Signs of Delay in Learning. In Noshpitz, J. D. (Ed.), *Basic Handbook of Child Psychiatry.* New York: Basic Books.

Silver, A. A. (1981) The Prediction of Reading Failure: A Review and Critique. In Cruickshank, W. & Silver, A. A. (Eds.), *Bridges to Tomorrow. Volume II. The Best of ACLD.* Syracuse, NY: Syracuse University Press.

Silver, A. A. (1985) The Influence of Primitive Postural Responses on Body Image of Children with Schizophrenia. In Shaskin, D. A. & Roller, W. L. (Eds.), *Paul Schilder, Mind Explorer*. New York: Human Sciences Press.

Silver, A. A. & Hagin, R. A. (1964) Specific Reading Disability: Follow-up Studies. *American Journal of Orthopsychiatry* 34:95–102.

Silver, A. A. & Hagin, R. A. (1976) *SEARCH: A Scanning Instrument for the Identification of Potential Learning Disability*. New York: Walker.

Silver, A. A. & Hagin, R. A. (1985) Outcomes of Learning Disabilities in Adolescence. *Adolescent Psychiatry* 12:197–213.

Silver, A. A., Hagin, R. A., Thackery, S., Angel, R., Liles, A. B., Barnaby, N., & Williams, M. (1980) Models for the Dissemination of a Program for the Prevention of Reading Disability: The New York-Edgemont-Gastonia-Columbus Connection. In Cruickshank, W. (Ed.), *Approaches to Learning. Volume I. The Best of ACLD*. Syracuse, NY: Syracuse University Press.

Silver, L. B. (1982) Conversion Disorder with Pseudo-Seizures in Adolescence: A Stress Reaction to Unrecognized and Untreated Learning Disabilities. *Journal of Child Psychiatry* 21:508–512.

Silver, L. B. (1983) Introduction. In Brown, C. C. (Ed.), *Childhood Learning Disabilities and Prenatal Risk*. Skillman, NJ: Johnson & Johnson.

Silverman, M. A. (1985) Progression, Regression and Child Analytic Techniques. *Psychoanalytic Quarterly* 54:1–19.

Silverstein, A. B., Legutki, G., Friedman, S. L., & Takayama, D. L. (1982) Performance of Down Syndrome In-dividuals on the Stanford-Binet Intelligence Scale. *American Journal of Mental Deficiency* 86:548–551.

Simmons, J. E. (1981) *Psychiatric Examination of Children* (3rd ed.). Philadelphia, PA: Lea & Febiger.

Simonov, P. V. (1975) Parameters of Action and Measuring Emotions. In Levi, L. (Ed.), *Emotions—Their Parameters and Measurement*. New York: Raven.

Simons, J. & Oislii, S. (1987) *The Hidden Child: The Linwood Method for Reaching the Autistic Child*. Kensington, MD: Woodbine Press.

Simpson, E. (1979) *Reversals*. Boston: Houghton-Mifflin.

Simpson, G. G. (1949) *The Meaning of Evolution*. New Haven, CT: Yale University Press.

Singer, B. & Benassi, V. A. (1981) Occult Beliefs. *American Scientist* 69:49–55.

Singer, J. L. (1976) Affect and Imagination in Play and Fantasy. In Izard, C. E. (Ed.), *Emotions in Personality and Psychopathology*. New York: Plenum.

Sinz, R. & Rosenzweig, M. R.(Eds.) (1983) *Psychophysiology: Memory, Motivation and Event-Related Potentials in Mental Operations*. New York: Elsevier.

Sizer, T. R. (1973) *Places for Learning, Places for Joy: Speculations on American School Reform*. Cambridge, MA: Harvard University Press.

Skeels, H. M. (1966) Adult Status of Children with Contrasting Early Life Experience. *Monographs Society Research Child Development* 31:1–65.

Skinner, B. F. (1953) *Science and Human Behavior*. New York: Free Press.

Skodak, M. & Skeels, H. M. (1949) A Final Followup of One Hundred Adopted Children. *Journal of Genetic Psychology* 75:85–125.

Sladen, B. K. (1970) Inheritance of Dyslexia. *Bulletin of the Orton Society* 20:30–40.

Slingerland, B. H. (1981) *A Multi-sensory Approach to Language Arts for Specific Language Disability Children*. Cambridge, MA: Educators Publishing Service.

Sloboda, J. A. (1985) *The Musical Mind: The Cognitive Psychology of Music*. New York: Clarendon.

Smith, D. W. (1980) Alcohol Effects on the Fetus. In Schwartz, R. H. & Yaffe, S. J. (Eds.), *Drug and Chemical Risks to the Fetus and Newborn*. New York: Alan R. Liss.

Smith, Jr., G. R. (1983) Alexithymia in Medical Patients Referred to a Consultation Liaison Service. *American Journal of Psychiatry* 140:99–101.

Smith, L. C. (1978) An Evaluation of Studies of Long Term Effects of Remedial Reading Programs. Unpublished Thesis. Harvard University Graduate School of Education.

Smith, M. (1985) Recent Work on Low Level Lead Exposure and its Impact on Behavior, Intelligence and Learning: A Review. *Journal of Child Psychiatry* 24:24–32.

Smith, M. L. (1982) *How Educators Decide Who is Learning Disabled*. Springfield, IL: Thomas.

Smith, R. J. & Johnson, O. D. (1976) *Teaching Children to Read*. Reading, MA: Addison-Wesley.

Smith, S. D., Kimberling, W. J., Pennington, B. F., & Lubs, H. A. (1983) Specific Reading Disability: Identification of an Inherited Form through Linkage Analysis. *Science* 219:1345–1347.

Smith, S. L. (1980) *No Easy Answers: The Learning Disabled Child at Home and at School*. New York: Bantam Books.

Snowdon, C. T., Brown, C. H., & Peterson, M. R. (Eds.) (1983) *Primate Communication*. New York: Cambridge University Press.

Snyder, S. H. (1984a) Drug and Neurotransmitter Receptors in the Brain. *Science* 224:22–31.

Snyder, S. H. (1984b) Neurosciences: an Integrative Discipline. *Science* 225:1255–1257.

Sokolov, E. N. & Vinogradova, O. S. (Eds.) (1975) *Neuronal Mechanisms of the Orienting Reflex*. New York: Wiley.

Solnit, A. J. & Neubauer, P. B. (1986) Object Constancy and Early Triadic Relationships. *Journal of Child Psychiatry*. 25:23–29.

Solomon, G. E. & Plum, F. (1976) *Clinical Management of Seizures*. Philadelphia, PA: Saunders.

Sonis, W. A. & Costello, A. J. (1981) Evaluation of Differential Data Sources: Application of the Diagnostic Process in Child Psychiatry. *Journal of Child Psychiatry* 20:597–610.

Sowell, T. (1973) Arthur Jensen and His Critics. In *On Learning and Change*. New Rochell, NY: Change Magazine.

Sowell, T. (Ed.) (1980) *Essays and Data on American Ethnic Groups*. Washington, D.C.: Urban Institute.

Spache, G. D. (1976) *Investigating the Issues in Reading Disabilities*. Boston: Allyn & Bacon.

Spache, G. D. (1981a) *Diagnosing and Correcting Reading Disabilities* (2nd ed.). Boston: Allyn & Bacon.

Spache, G. D. (1981b) *Diagnostic Reading Scales*. Monterey, CA: Test Bureau.

Spalding, R. B. & Spalding, W. T. (1969) *The Writing Road to Reading* (2nd ed.). New York: Morrow.

Speech Foundation of America. *Self-Therapy for the Stutterer*. Memphis, TN: Speech Foundation of America.

Speer, F. (Ed.) (1970) *Allergy of the Nervous System*. Springfield, IL: Thomas.

Sperry, R. W. (1982) Some Effects of Disconnecting the Cerebral Hemispheres. *Science* 217:1223–1226.

Spiegel, J. (1971) *Transactions: The Interplay between Individual Family and Society.* New York: Science House.

Spitz, R. A. (1963) Ontogenesis: The Proleptic Function of Emotion. In Knapp, P. H. (Ed.), *Expression of Emotions in Man.* New York: International Universities Press.

Sprague, R. L., Christensen, D. E., & Werry, J. S. (1974) Experimental Psychology and Stimulant Drugs. In Conners, C. K. (Ed.), *Clinical Use of Stimulant Drugs in Children.* New York: Elsevier.

Spraings, V. E. (1969) The Dyslexias, a Psychoeducational and Physiological Approach. In Tarnopol, L., *Learning Disabilities.* Springfield, IL: Thomas.

Springer, S. P. & Deutsch, G. (1981) *Left Brain, Right Brain.* San Francisco: Freeman.

Spruiell, V. (1975) Three Strands of Narcissism. *Psychoanalytic Quarterly* 44:577–595.

Spruiell, V. (1981) The Self and the Ego. *Psychoanalytic Quarterly* 50:319–344.

Spruiell, V. (1983) The Rules and Frames of the Psychoanalytic Situation. *Psychoanalytic Quarterly* 52:1–33.

Sroufe, L. A. (1975) Drug Treatment of Children with Behavior Problems. In Horowitz, F. D. (Ed.), *Review of Child Development Research.* Chicago: University of Chicago Press.

Sroufe, L.A. (1979) Socioemotional Development. In Osofky, J.D. (Ed.), *The Handbook of Infant Development.* New York: Wiley.

Staats, A. W. & Staats, C. K. (1962) A Comparison of the Development of Speech and Reading Behavior with Implications for Research. *Child Development* 33:831–846.

Stanley, G. (1975) Visual Memory Processes in Dyslexia. In Deutsch, D. & Deutsch, J. A. (Eds.), *Short-Term Memory.* New York: Academic Press.

Stanley-Jones, D. (1970) *Kybernetics of Mind and Brain.* Springfield, IL: Thomas.

Stechler, G. & Kaplan, S. (1980) The Development of the Self: A Psychoanalytic Perspective. *Psychoanalytic Study of the Child* 35:85–105.

Stein, M. I. (1975) Creativity: The Process and its Stimulation. *Creative Psychiatry 3.* Ardsley, NY: Geigy Pharmaceuticals.

Stein, M. & Schleifer, S. J. (1985) Frontiers of Stress Research: Stress and Immunity. In Zales, M. R. (Ed.), *Stress in Health and Disease.* New York: Brunner/Mazel.

Steinhausen, H. C., Nestler, V., & Spohr, H. L. (1982) Development and Psychopathology of Children with the Fetal Alcohol Syndrome. *Developmental and Behavioral Pediatrics* 2:49–54.

Stephens, T. M., Blackhurst, A. E., & Magliocca, L. A. (1982) *Teaching Mainstreamed Students.* New York: Wiley.

Stern, D. N. (1985) *The Interpersonal World of the Infant: A View from Psychoanalysis and Developmental Psychology.* New York: Basic Books.

Sternberg, R. J. (Ed.) (1982) *The Handbook of Human Intelligence.* New York: Cambridge University Press.

Sternberg, R. J. (Ed.) (1984) *Mechanisms of Cognitive Development.* New York: Freeman.

Sternberg, R. J. (1985) *Beyond I.Q.: A Triarchic Theory of Human Intelligence.* Cambridge, England: Cambridge University Press.

Sternberg, J. (1986) *Intelligence Applied: Understanding and Increasing Your Intellectual Skills.* San Diego, CA: Harcourt, Brace, Jovanovich.

Stevens, A. (1982) *Archetypes: A Natural*

History of the Self. New York: Morrow.

Stevens, S. H. (1980) *The Learning Disabled Child: Ways That Parents Can Help*. Winston-Salem, NC: John F. Blair.

Stevens, S. H. (1984) *Classroom Success for the Learning Disabled*. Winston-Salem, NC: John F. Blair.

Stevenson, H. W. (1972) *Children's Learning*. New York: Appleton-Century-Crofts.

Stevenson, H. W., Lee, S., & Stigler, J. W. (1986) Mathematics Achievement of Chinese, Japanese and American Children. *Science* 231:693–699.

Stevenson, J. & Richman, N. (1976) The Prevalence of Language Delay in a Population of Three Year Old Children and its Association with General Retardation. *Developmental Medicine and Child Neurology* 18:431–441.

Stewart, M. A., Mendelson, W. B., & Johnson, N. E. (1973) Hyperactive Children as Adolescents: How They Describe Themselves. *Child Psychiatry and Human Development* 4:3–11.

Still, G. F. (1902) The Coulstonian Lectures on Some Abnormal Psychical Conditions in Children. *Lancet* 1:1008–1012, 1077–1082, 1163–1168.

Stokes, M. C. (1968) Heraclitus of Ephesus. In Edwards, P. (Ed.), *Encyclopedia of Philosophy. Volume 3*. New York: Macmillan.

Stone, C. R. & Selman, R. L. (1982) A Structural Approach to Research. In Rubin, K. H. & Ross, H. S. (Eds.), *Peer Relationships and Social Skills in Childhood*. New York: Springer-Verlag.

Storlorow, R. D. & Lachmann, F. M. (1978) The Developmental Prestages of Defenses: Diagnostic and Therapeutic Implications. *Psychoanalytic Quarterly* 47:73–102.

Stott, D. H. (1978) *The Hard-to-Teach Child:*

A Diagnostic-Remedial Approach. Baltimore, MD: University Park Press.

Strachey, J. (1930) Some Unconscious Factors in Reading. *International Journal of Psychoanalysis* 11:322–331.

Strain, P. S. (Ed.) (1981) *The Utilization of Classroom Peers as Behavior Change Agents*. New York: Plenum.

Strang, J. D. & Rourke, B. P. (1985) Arithmetic Disability Subtypes. In Rourke, B. P. (Ed.), *Neuropsychology of Learning Disabilities*. New York: Guilford Press.

Strang, R. (1962) *Helping Your Child Improve His Reading*. New York: Dutton.

Stratton, P. (1982a) *Psychobiology of the Human Newborn*. New York: Wiley.

Stratton, P. (1982b) Newborn Individuality. In Stratton, P. (Ed.), *Psychobiology of the Human Newborn*. New York: Wiley.

Strauss, A. A. & Kephart, N. C. (1955) *Psychopathology and Education of the Brain Injured Child*. New York: Grune & Stratton.

Strickler, E. (1969) Family Interaction Factors in Psychogenic Learning Disturbance. *Journal of Learning Disabilities* 2:31–38.

Strong, L. (1973) Language Disability in the Hispano-American Child. *Bulletin of the Orton Society* 23:30–38.

Stuss, D. T. & Benson, D. F. (1984) Neuropsychological Studies of the Frontal Lobes. *Psychological Bulletin* 95:3–28.

Stuss, D. T. & Benson, D. F. (1986) *The Frontal Lobes*. New York: Raven.

Sugarman, B. (1973) *The School and Moral Development*. London: Croom Helm.

Suinn, R. M. (1983) Imagery and Sports. In Sheikh, A. A. (Ed.), *Imagery: Current Theory, Research and Application*. New York: Wiley.

Sullivan, H. S. (1953) *Conceptions of Modern Psychiatry*. New York: Norton.

Summers, J. A. (1981) The Definition of

Developmental Disabilities: A Concept in Transition. *Mental Retardation* 19:259–265.

Suomi, S. J. (1979) Peers, Play and Primary Prevention in Primates. In Kent, M. W. & Rolf, J. E. (Eds.), *The Primary Prevention of Psychopathology: Promoting Social Competence and Coping in Children*. Hanover, NH: University Press of New England.

Suomi, S. J. & Harlow, H. F. (1976) The Facts and Functions of Fear. In Zuckerman, M. & Spielberger, C. D. (Eds.), *Emotions and Anxiety: New Concepts, Methods and Applications*. Hillsdale, NJ: Erlbaum.

Suomi, S. J., Seaman, S. F., Lewis, J. K., De Lizio, R. D., & McKinney, W. T. (1978) Effects of Imipramine Treatment on Separation Induced Social Disorders in Rhesus Monkeys. *Archives of General Psychiatry* 35:321–325.

Sussman, G. J. (1975) *A Computer Model of Skill Acquisition*. New York: Elsevier.

Swain, E. H. (1985) *Swain Beginning Reading Program*. Allen, TX: DLM Teaching Resources.

Swanson, D. W. (1984) Chronic Pain as a Third Pathological Emotion. *American Journal of Psychiatry* 141:210–214.

Swanson, H. L. & Watson, B. L. (1982) *Educational and Psychological Assessment of Exceptional Children*. St. Louis, MO: Mosby.

Swanson, J. M. & Kinsbourne, M. (1980) Food Dyes Impair Performance of Hyperactive Children on a Laboratory Learning Test. *Science* 207:1485–1487.

Sweeney, D. R., Gold, M. S., Pottash, A. L. C., & Davies, R. K. (1980) Neurobiological Theories. In Kutash, I. L., Schlesinger, L. B., & Associates (Eds.), *Handbook on Stress and Anxiety*. San Francisco: Jossey-Bass.

Swift, W. J. (1981) Family Availability for the Working Alliance: A Neglected Area in Child Psychiatry Training. *Journal of Child Psychiatry* 20:810–821.

Sylvester, E. (1949) Emotional Aspects of Learning. *Quarterly Journal of Child Behavior* 1:133–139.

Szasz, T. S. (1957) *Pain and Pleasure: A Study of Bodily Feelings*. London: Tavistock.

Tanguay, P. E. (1984) Toward a New Classification of Serious Psychopathology in Children. *Journal of Child Psychiatry* 23:373–384.

Tarnopol, L. & Tarnopol, M. (1981) *Comparative Reading and Learning Difficulties*. Lexington, MA: Lexington Books.

Tarpy, R. M. (1977) The Nervous System and Emotion. In Candland, D. K. et al (Eds.), *Emotion*. Monterey, CA: Brooks/Cole.

Tauber, E. S. & Green, M. R. (1959) *Prelogical Experience: An Inquiry into Dreams and Other Creative Processes*. New York: Basic Books.

Taylor, E. A. (1966) *The Fundamental Reading Skill: As Related to Eye-Movement Photography and Visual Anomalies*. Springfield, IL: Thomas.

Taylor, E. (1981) Development of Attention. In Rutter, M.(Ed.), *Scientific Foundations of Developmental Psychiatry*. Baltimore, MD: University Park Press.

Taylor, G. J. (1984) Alexithymia: Concept, Measurement and Implications for Treatment. *American Journal of Psychiatry* 141:725–732.

Taylor, J. (Ed.) (1932) *Selected Writings of John Hughlings Jackson. Volume 2*. London: Hodder & Stoughton.

Templeton, R. G., Sperry, B. M., & Prentice, N. M. (1967) Theoretical and Technical Issues in Therapeutic Tutoring of Children with Psychogenic

Learning Problems. *Journal of Child Psychiatry* 6:464–477.

Tenzer, A. (1983) Piaget and Psychoanalysis. Some Reflections on Insight. *Contemporary Psychanalysis* 19:319–339.

Ter-Pogossian, M. M., Raichle, M. E., & Sobel, B. E. (1980) Positron Emission Tomography. *Scientific American* 243:139–155.

Thatcher, R. W., Walker, R. A., & Guidice, S. (1987) Human Cerebral Hemispheres Develop at Different Rates and Ages. *Science* 236:1110–1113.

Thomas, A. (1981) Current Trends in Developmental Theory. *American Journal of Orthopsychiatry* 51:580–609.

Thomas, A., Birch, H. G., Chess, S., Hertzig, M. E., & Korn, S. (1963) *Behavioral Individuality in Early Childhood*. New York: New York University Press.

Thomas, A. & Chess, S. (1977) *Temperament and Development*. New York: Brunner/Mazel.

Thomas, A. & Chess, S. (1980) *The Dynamics of Psychological Development*. New York: Brunner/Mazel.

Thomas, A. & Chess, S. (1984) Genesis and Evolution of Behavioral Disorders: From Infancy to Early Adult Life. *American Journal of Psychiatry* 141:1–9.

Thompson, L. J. (1969) Language Disabilities in Men of Eminence. *Bulletin of the Orton Society* 19:113–120.

Thomson, M. E. (1982) The Assessment of Children with Specific Reading Difficulties (Dyslexia) Using the British Ability Scales. *British Journal of Psychology* 73:461–478.

Thomson, M. (1984) *Developmental Dyslexia*. London: Edward Arnold.

Thorley, G. (1984) Hyperkinetic Syndrome of Childhood: Clinical Characteristics. *British Journal of Psychiatry* 144:16–24.

Tilson, H.A. & Crammer, J.M. (Eds) (1986) *Neurotoxicology in the Fetus and Child*. Roland, AR: Intox Press.

Ting, R. Y., Wang, M. H., & Scott, T. F. M. (1977) The Dysmature Infant: Associated Factors and Outcome at 7 Years of Age. *Pediatrics* 90:943–948.

Tjossem, T. D., Hansen, T. J., & Ripley, H. S. (1962) An Investigation of Reading Difficulty in Young Children. *American Journal of Psychiatry* 118:1104–1113.

Tomatis, A. A. (1972) *Education and Dyslexia*. Fribourg, Switzerland: AIAPP.

Tomkins, S. S. (1962) *Affect, Imagery, Consciousness. Volume I. The Positive Affects*. New York: Springer.

Tomkins, S. S. (1968) Affects: Primary Motives of Man. *Humanitas* 3:321–346.

Tomkins, S. S. (1970) Affect as the Primary Motivational System. In Arnold, M. B. (Ed.), *Feelings and Emotions*. New York: Academic Press.

Tomkins, S. S. (1980) Affects as Amplifications: Some Modification in Theory. In Plutchik, R. & Kellerman, H. (Eds.), *Emotions: Theory, Research and Experience*. New York: Academic Press.

Tomkins, S. (1981) The Quest for Primary Motives: Biography and Autobiography of an Idea. *Journal of Personality and Social Psychology* 41:306–326.

Tomlinson, T.M. (1987) A Nation at Risk: Towards Excellence for All. *Annals of the New York Academy of Sciences* 517: 7–27.

Tomm, K. (1984) One Perspective on the Milan Systemic Approach Parts I and II. *Journal of Marital and Family Therapy* 10:113–125, 253–271.

Torgesen, J. (1975) Problems and Prospects in the Study of Learning Disabilities. In Hetherington, M. (Ed.), *Review of Child Development Research*.

Volume 5. Chicago: University of Chicago Press.

Torrance, E. P. (1962) *Guiding Creative Talent*. Englewood Cliffs, NJ: Prentice-Hall.

Torrance, E. P. (1963) *Education and the Creative Potential*. Minneapolis, MN: University of Minnesota Press.

Torrance, E. P. & Myers, R. E. (1972) *Creative Learning and Teaching*. New York: Dodd, Mead.

Torrey, J. W. (1979) Reading that Comes Naturally: The Early Reader. In Waller, T. G. & MacKinnon, G. E. (Eds.), *Reading Research: Advances in Theory and Practice. Volume I*. New York: Academic Press.

Touwen, B. C. L. & Sporrel, T. (1979) Soft Signs and MBD. *Developmental Medicine and Child Neurology* 21:528–530.

Towbin, A. (1971) Organic Causes of Minimal Brain Dysfunction: Perinatal Origin of Minimal Cerebral Lesion. *Journal of the American Medical Association* 217:1207–1214.

Tower, R. B. (1983) Imagery: Its Role in Development. In Sheikh, A. A. (Ed.), *Imagery: Current Theory, Research and Application*. New York: Wiley.

Traub, N. (1975) *Recipe for Reading*. Cambridge, MA: Educators Publishing Service.

Trites, R. L., Sprague, R. L., & Conners, K. (1979) Prevalence of Hyperactivity in Ottawa, Canada. In Trites, R. L. (Ed.), *Hyperactivity in Children: Etiology, Measurement and Treatment Implication*. Baltimore, MD: University Park Press.

Tseng, O. J. L. & Wang, W. S.-Y. (1983) The First Two R's. *American Scientist* 71:238–243.

Turvey, M. T. (1974) Perspectives in Vision: Conception or Perception? In Duane, D. D. & Rawson, M. B. (Eds.), *Reading, Perception and Language*. Baltimore, MD: York.

Tyler, L. (1965) *The Psychology of Human Differences*. New York: Appleton-Century-Crofts.

Urbano, R. C., Borness, S. R., Lynch, E. W., Bender, M., Rotberg, J. M., & Gardner, T. P. (1984) Interdisciplinary Evaluation: Types of Children Referred to UAF Clinics and Hospitals. *Mental Retardation* 22:117–120.

U.S. Department of Education (1985) *National Enrollment Statistics, 1979–1984*. Washington, D.C.: National Center for Education Statistics.

U.S.D.H.S.S. (1981) *The Health Consequences of Smoking for Women—A Report of the Surgeon General*. Rockville, MD: U.S. Department of Health and Social Services, Public Health Service.

U.S. Office of Education (1979) *Definition of Learning Disabilities*. Washington, D.C.: U.S. Office of Education.

U.S. Supreme Court (1988) *Honig v. Doe et al*, No 86–728, Decided January 20, 1988. Washington, D.C.

Valentine, C. A. & Valentine, B. (1975) Brain Damage and the Intellectual Defense of Inequality. *Current Anthropology* 16:117–150.

Valletutti, P. J. & Salpino, A. O. (1979) *Individualizing Educational Objectives and Programs: A Modular Approach*. Baltimore, MD: University Park Press.

Valzelli, L. (1981) *Psychobiology of Aggression and Violence*. New York: Raven.

Vandell, R. A., Davis, R. A., & Clugston, H. (1943) The Function of Mental Practice in the Acquisition of Motor Skills. *Journal of General Psychology* 29:243–260.

Van den Honert, D. (1985) *Reading from Scratch/RFS*. Cambridge, MA: Educators Publishing Service.

van der Velde, C. D. (1985) Body Images

of One's Self and of Others: Developmental and Clinical Significance. *American Journal of Psychiatry* 142:527–537.

Varley, C. K. (1984) Diet and the Behavior of Children with Attention Deficit Disorder. *Journal of Child Psychiatry* 23:182–185.

Varley, C. K. & Trupin, E. W. (1983) Double-Blind Assessment of Stimulant Medication for Attention Deficit Disorder: A Model for Clinical Application. *American Journal of Orthopsychiatry* 53:542–547.

Vellutino, F. R. (1979) *Dyslexia: Theory and Research*. Cambridge, MA: MIT Press.

Vernon, P. A. (1985) Individual Differences in Cognitive Ability. In Hartlage, L. C. & Telzrow, C. F. (Eds.), *The Neuropsychology of Individual Differences*. New York: Plenum.

Vickers, G. (1959) Is Adaptability Enough? *Behavioral Science* 4:223.

Vigas, M. (1980) Contribution to the Understanding of the Stress Concept. In Usdin, E., Kvetnansky, R., & Kopin, I. J. (Eds.), *Catecholamines and Stress: Recent Advances*. New York: Elsevier/North Holland.

Vinogradova, O. S. (1975) Functional Organization of the Limbic System in the Process of Registration of Information: Facts and Hypotheses. In Isaacson, R. L. & Pribram, K. H. (Eds.), *The Hippocampus. Volume 2*. New York: Plenum.

Vogel, S. A. (1982) On Developing LD College Programs. *Journal of Learning Disabilities* 15:518–528.

von Neumann, J. (1958) *The Computer and the Brain*. New Haven, CT: Yale University Press.

Vygotsky, L. S. (1962) *Thought and Language*. Cambridge, MA: MIT Press, Wiley.

Vygotsky, L. S. (1978) *Mind in Society: The Development of Higher Psychological Processes*. Cambridge, MA: Harvard University Press.

Walk, R. D. (1981) Perception. In Rutter, M. (Ed.), *Scientific Foundations of Developmental Psychiatry*. Baltimore, MD: University Park Press.

Wallace, G. & Kauffman, J. M. (1973) *Teaching Children with Learning Problems*. Columbus, OH: Merrill.

Wallach, H. (1985) Perceiving a Stable Environment. *Scientific American* 252:118–124.

Wallach, M. A. & Wallach, L. (1976) *Teaching All Children to Read*. Chicago: University of Chicago Press.

Walsh, M. N. (1966) Strephosymbolia Reconsidered: A Re-study of a Specific Inhibition of the Use of Visual and Auditory Verbal Symbols. *International Journal of Psychoanalysis* 48:584–595.

Walsh, M. N. (1968) Explosives and Spirants: Primitive Sounds in Cathected Words. *Psychoanalytic Quarterly* 37:199–211.

Walton, J. N., Ellis, E., & Court, S. D. M. (1962) Clumsy Children: A Study of Developmental Apraxia and Agnosia. *Brain* 85:603–612.

Wang, M. C. & Birch, J. W. (1984) Effective Special Education in Regular Classes. *Exceptional Children* 50:391–398.

Warburton, D. M. (1981) Neurochemistry of Behavior. *British Medical Bulletin* 37:121–125.

Warm, T. R. (1978) An Approach to Psychiatric School Consultation: What's Good About Bad Behavior. *Journal of Child Psychiatry* 17:708–716.

Watkins, M. & Webb, C. (1981) Computer Assisted Instruction with Learning Disabled Students. *Educational Computer Magazine* Sept.–Oct.

Watson, B. V. & Goldgar, D. E. (1983) Subtypes of Reading Disabilities. *Journal of Clinical Neuropsychology* 5:377–399.

Watts, G. O. (1975) *Dynamic Neuroscience: Its Application to Brain Disorders.* Hagerstorm, MD: Harper & Row.

Waxman, S. G. & Geschwind, N. (1975) The Interictal Behavior Syndrome of Temporal Lobe Epilepsy. *Archives of General Psychiatry* 32:1580–1586.

Wayson, W. W., DeVoss, G. G., Kaeser, S. C., Lasley, T., & Pinnell, G. S. (1982) *Handbook for Developing Schools with Good Discipline.* Bloomington, IN: Phi Delta Kappa.

Webster, T. G. (1970) Unique Aspects of Emotional Development in Mentally Retarded Children. In Menolascino, F. J. (Ed.), *Psychiatric Approaches to Mental Retardation.* New York: Basic Books.

Weil, A. P. (1977) Learning Disturbances with Special Consideration of Dyslexia. *Issues in Child Mental Health* 5:52–66.

Weil, A. P. (1978) Maturational Variations and Genetic-Dynamic Issues. *Journal of the American Psychoanalytic Association* 26:461–491.

Weil, J. L. (1974) *A Neurophysiological Model of Emotional and Intentional Behavior.* Springfield, IL: Thomas.

Weinberg, W. A. & Brumback, R. A. (1976) Mania in Childhood: Case Studies and Literature Review. *American Journal of Diseases of Children* 130:380–385.

Weinberger, D. R. Kleinman, J.E., Luchins D.J., Bigelow, L.B., & Wyatt, R.J. (1980) Cerebellar Pathology in Schizophrenia: A Controlled Postmortem Study. *American Journal of Psychiatry* 137:359–361.

Weingartner, H., Grafman, J., Boutelle, W., Kaye, W., & Martin, P. R. (1983) Forms of Memory Failure. *Science* 221:380–382.

Weintraub, F. J., Abson, A., Ballard, J., & LaVor, M. L. (Eds.) (1976) *Public Policy and the Education of Exceptional Children.* Reston, VA: Council for Exceptional Children.

Weintraub, F. J. & Ramirez, B.A. (Eds.) (1985) *Progress in the Education of the Handicapped and Analysis of P. L. 98–199, The Education of the Handicapped Amendments of 1983.* Reston, VA: Council for Exceptional Children.

Weiss, B. et al (1980) Behavioral Responses to Artificial Food Colors. *Science* 207:1487–1489.

Weiss, G., Hechtman, L., & Trokenberg, L. (1986) *Hyperactive Children Grown Up.* New York: Guilford Press.

Weizenbaum, J. (1976) *Computer Power and Human Reason.* San Francisco: Freeman.

Weller, D. & Buchanan, M. (1987) *Educators' Desk Reference.* Boston, MA: Allyn & Bacon.

Wells, C. O. (1942) *The Development of Abstract Language Concepts in Normal and in Deaf Children.* Chicago: University of Chicago Libraries.

Wells, G. (1983) Talking with Children: The Complementary Roles of Parents and Teachers. In Donaldson, M., Grieve, R., & Pratt, C. (Eds.), *Early Childhood Development and Education.* New York: Guilford Press.

Welsh, G. (1975) *Creativity and Intelligence: A Personality Approach.* Chapel Hill, NC: Institute for Research in Social Science.

Welsh, G. (1980) *Manual: Welsh Figure Preference Test.* Palo Alto, CA: Consulting Psychologists' Press.

Welsh, P. (1986) *Tales Out of School.* New York: Viking.

Wender, P. H. (1971) *Minimal Brain Dysfunction in Children*. New York: Wiley-Interscience.

Wender, P. H., Reimherr, F. W., & Wood, D. R. (1981) Attention Deficit Disorder ("Minimal Brain Dysfunction") in Adults: A Replication Study of Diagnosis and Drug Treatment. *Archives of General Psychiatry* 38:449–456.

Wepman, J. M. (1964) The Perceptual Basis for Learning. In Robinson, H. A. (Ed.), *Meeting Individual Differences in Reading*. Chicago: University of Chicago Press.

Werkman, S. L. (1965) The Psychiatric Diagnostic Interview with Children. *American Journal of Orthopsychiatry* 35:764–771.

Werner, E. E., Bierman, J. M., & French, F. E. (1971) *The Children of Kauai*. Honolulu: University of Hawaii Press.

Werner, E. E. & Smith, R. S. (1979) An Epidemiological Perspective on Some Antecedents and Consequences of Childhood Mental Health Problems and Learning Disabilities. *Journal of Child Psychiatry* 18:292–306.

Werner, H. (1948) *Comparative Psychology of Mental Development*. New York: International Universities Press.

Werry, J. S. (1982) An Overview of Pediatric Psychopharmacology. *Journal of Child Psychiatry* 21:3–9.

West, J. (1967) The Psychobiology of Racial Violence. *Archives of General Psychiatry* 16:645–651.

Westman, J. C. (1973) *Individual Differences in Children*. New York: Wiley.

Westman, J. C. (1979a) *Child Advocacy: New Professional Roles for Helping Families*. New York: Free Press.

Westman, J. C. (1979b) Psychiatric Day Treatment. In Noshpitz, J. D. (Ed.), *Basic Handbook of Child Psychiatry*. New York: Basic Books.

Westman, J. C. (1984) Family Assessment. In Bernstein, N. R. & Sussex, J. (Eds.), *Handbook of Psychiatric Consultation with Children and Youth*. New York: SP Medical & Scientific Books.

Westman, J. C., Arthur, B., & Scheidler, E. P. (1965) Reading Retardation: An Overview. *American Journal of Diseases of the Child* 109:359–369.

Westman, J. C. & Bennett, T. M. (1985) Learning Impotence and the Peter Pan Fantasy. *Child Psychiatry and Human Development* 15:153–166.

Westman, J.C., Miller, D. R., & Arthur, B. (1966) Psychiatric Symptoms and Family Dynamics as Illustrated by the Retarded Reader. *Psychiatric Research Report 20*. Washington, D.C.: American Psychiatric Association.

Westman, J. C., Ownby, R. L., & Smith, S. (1987) An Analysis of 180 Children Referred to a University Hospital Learning Disabilities Service. *Child Psychiatry and Human Development* 17:275–282.

Westman, J. C. & Walters, J. R. (1981) Noise and Stress: A Comprehensive Approach. *Environmental Health Perspectives* 41:291–309.

Wexler, B. E. (1980) Cerebral Laterality and Psychiatry: A Review of the Literature. *American Journal of Psychiatry* 137:279–291.

Whalen, C. K. & Henker, B. (Eds.) (1980) The Social Ecology of Psychostimulant Treatment: A Model for Conceptual and Empirical Analysis. In Whalen, C. K. & Henker, B., *Hyperactive Children: The Social Ecology of Identification and Treatment*. New York: Academic Press.

White, A. R. (1982) *The Nature of Knowledge*. Totowa, NJ: Rowman & Littlefield.

White, B. L., Kaban, B. T., & Attanucci, J. S. (1979) *The Origins of Human Competence.* Lexington, MA: D. C. Heath.

White, R. B., Davis, H. K., & Cantrell, W. A. (1977) Psychodynamics of Depression: Implications for Treatment. In Usdin, G. (Ed.), *Depression: Clinical, Biological and Psychological Perspectives.* New York: Brunner /Mazel.

White, R. K. & Lippitt, R. (1960) *Autocracy and Democracy.* New York: Harper.

White, R. W. (1959) Motivation Reconsidered: The Concept of Competence. *Psychological Review* 66:297–333.

Whitehouse, D. & Harris, J. C. (1984) *Journal of Autism and Developmental Disorders* 14:281–289.

Whitford, E. M., Chapman, J. W., & Boersma, F. J. (1982) Family Stability and Mothers' Perceptions of Elementary Learning Disabled Children. *Canadian Counsellor* 16:237–244.

Whitmore, J. R. (1980) *Giftedness, Conflict, and Achievement.* Boston: Allyn & Bacon.

Whybrow, P. C., Akiskal, H. S., & McKinney, Jr., W. T. (1984) *Mood Disorders: Toward a New Psychobiology.* New York: Plenum.

Wickelgren, W. A. (1975) More on the Long and Short of Memory. In Deutsch, D. & Deutsch, J. A. (Eds.), *Short-Term Memory.* New York: Academic Press.

Wickens, D. D. (1970a) Processes in Wood Recognition. *Cognitive Psychology* 1:59–85.

Wickens, D. D. (1970b) Encoding Categories of Words: An Empirical Approach to Meaning. *Psychological Review* 77:1–15.

Wiegel-Crump, C. A. (1979) Rehabilitation of Acquired Dyslexia in Adolescence. In Waller, T. G. & MacKinnon, G. E. (Eds.), *Reading Research: Advances in Theory and Practice. Volume I.* New York: Academic Press.

Wiener, J. M. (Ed.) (1985) *Diagnosis and Psychopharmacology of Childhood and Adolescent Disorders.* New York: Wiley.

Wiig, E. H. & Semel, E. M. (1980) *Language Assessment and Intervention for the Learning Disabled.* Columbus, OH: Merrill.

Wilder, J. (1957) The Law of Initial Values in Neurology and Psychiatry. Facts and Problems. *Journal of Nervous and Mental Disease* 125:73–86.

Willeford, J. A. & Burleigh, J. M. (1985) *Handbook of Central Auditory Processing Disorders in Children.* Orlando, FL: Grune & Stratton.

Williams, L. (1977) *Challenge to Survival.* New York: New York University Press.

Williams, L. V. (1983) *Teaching for the Two-Sided Mind.* Englewood Cliffs, NJ: Prentice-Hall.

Williams, M. (1979) *Brain Damage, Behavior and the Mind.* New York: Wiley.

Willis, T. J. & Lovaas, I. (1977) A Behavioral Approach to Treating Hyperactive Children: The Parent's Role. In Millichap, J. G. (Ed.), *Learning Disabilities and Related Disorders.* Chicago: Year Book Medical Publishers.

Wilsher, C. R. (1986) The Nootropic Concept and Dyslexia. *Annals of Dyslexia* 36:118–137.

Wilson, E. O. (1980) *Sociobiology: The Abridged Edition.* Cambridge, MA: Harvard University Press.

Wilson, M. R. & Calistro, P. F. (1977) Adolescent Psychosis: A Holistic Syndrome. *Psychiatric Annals* 7:5.

Wilson, S. C. & Barber, T. X. (1983) The

Fantasy-prone Personality: Implications for Understanding Imagery, Hypnosis and Parapsychological Phenomena. In Sheikh, A. A. (Ed.), *Imagery: Current Theory, Research and Application.* New York: Wiley.

Wing, L. (1981) Asperger Syndrome. *Journal of Psychological Medicine* 11:115–129.

Winick, M., Katchadurian, K., & Harris, R. C. (1975) Malnutrition and Environmental Enrichment by Early Adoption. *Science* 190:1173–1175.

Winston, J. (1985) *Brain and Psyche. The Biology of the Unconscious.* Garden City, NY: Anchor Press/Doubleday.

Wishnie, H. (1977) *The Impulsive Personality.* New York: Plenum.

Witelson, S. (1977) Developmental Dyslexia: Two Right Hemispheres and None Left. *Science* 195:309–311.

Witelson, S. F. (1985) The Brain Connection: The Corpus Callosum Is Larger in Left-Handers. *Science* 229:665–668.

Witkin, H. A. & Goodenough, D. R. (1981) *Cognitive Styles: Essence and Origins; Field Dependence and Field Independence.* New York: International Universities Press.

Witmer, L. (1920) Orthogenic Cases 14. Don: A Curable Case of Arrested Development Due to Fear Psychosis: the Result of Shock in a Three Year Old Infant. *Psychological Clinics* 13:97–111.

Wittig, M. A. & Petersen, A. C. (Eds.) (1979) *Sex-Related Differences in Cognitive Functioning: Developmental Issues.* New York: Academic Press.

Wittrock, M. C. (1981) Reading Comprehension. In Pirozzolo, F. J. & Wittrock, M. C. (Eds.), *Neuropsychological and Cognitive Processes in Reading.* New York: Academic Press.

Woerner, M. G., Pollack, M., Rogalski, C., Pollack, Y., & Klein, D. F. (1974) A Comparison of the School Records of Personality Disorders, Schizophrenia and Their Sibs. In Rogg, M., Robins, L. N., & Pollack, M. (Eds.), *Life History Research in Psychopathology.* Minneapolis, MN: University of Minnesota Press.

Wolf, M. (1984) Naming, Reading and the Dyslexias: A Longitudinal Overview. *Annals of Dyslexia* 34:87–115.

Wolf, M. (1985) When Words Fail: Insights for Psychopathology from Developmental Cognitive Sciences. *McLean Hospital Journal* 10:15–36.

Wolf, S. G. (1965) *The Stomach.* New York: Oxford University Press.

Wolff, P. (1982) Brain Hemispheres Function as Unit in Complex Tasks. *Psychiatric News* August 6:26–29.

Wolff, P. H. (1969) The Natural History of Crying and Other Vocalizations in Early Infancy. In Foss, B. M. (Ed.), *Determinants of Infant Behavior.* London: Methuen.

Wolfgang, C. H. & Glickman, C. D. (1980) *Solving Discipline Problems: Strategies for Classroom Teachers.* Boston: Allyn & Bacon.

Wolins, M. & Wozner, Y. (1982) *Revitalizing Residential Settings: Problems and Potential in Education, Health, Rehabilitation and Social Service.* San Francisco: Jossey-Bass.

Wood, D. J. (1981) Cognitive Development. In Rutter, M. (Ed.), *Scientific Foundations of Developmental Psychiatry.* Baltimore, MD: University Park Press.

Wood, D., Wender, P. H., & Reimherr, F. W. (1983) The Prevalence of Attention Deficit Disorder, Residual Type, or Minimal Brain Dysfunction in a Population of Male Alcoholic Patients. *American Journal of Psychiatry* 140:95–98.

Woolman, M. (1964) *Reading in High Gear*. Chicago: Science Research Associates.

Woolman, M. (1966) *Lift Off to Reading*. Chicago: Science Research Associates.

Workman, E. A. (1982) *Teaching Behavioral Self-Control to Students*. Austin, TX: PRO-ED.

Wren, C. T. (Ed.) (1983) *Language Learning Disabilities*. Rockville, MD: Aspen Systems.

Wright, O. M. (1984) *Observing Adolescents*. Toronto: Board of Education.

Wright, R. V. S. (1972) Imitative Learning of a Flaked Stone Technology—The Case of an Orangutan. *Mankind* 8:296–306.

Wright, S. (1978) *Variability Within and Among Natural Populations*. Chicago: University of Chicago Press.

Wurtman, R. J. & Wurtman, J. J. (1977) *Nutrition and the Brain. Volume 2*. New York: Basic Books.

Wylie, R. C. (1979) *The Self-Concept, Revised Edition. Volume Two*. Lincoln, NB: University of Nebraska Press.

Wynne, L. C. (1958) Pseudomutuality in Family Relationships of Schizophrenics. *Psychiatry* 21:205–220.

Wynne, L. C. (1965) Some Indications and Contraindications for Exploratory Family Therapy. In Boszormenyi-Nagy, I. & Framo, J. L. (Eds.), *Intensive Family Therapy*. New York: Hoeber Medical Division, Harper & Row.

Yakovlev, P. I. (1948) Motility, Behavior and the Brain. *Journal of Nervous and Mental Disease* 107:313–335.

Yakovlev, P. I. (1972) A Proposed Definition of the Limbic System. In Hock-man, D. H. (Ed.), *Limbic System Mechanisms and Autonomic Functions*. Springfield, IL: Charles C. Thomas.

Yakovlev, P. I. & Lecours, A. R. (1967) The Myelogenetic Cycles of Regional Maturation of the Brain. In Minkowski, A. (Ed.), *Regional Development of the Brain*. Oxford, England: Blackwell.

Yamadori, A. & Ikumura, G. (1975) Central (or Conduction) Aphasia in a Japanese Patient. *Cortex* 11:73–82.

Yanai, J. (1984) *Neurobehavioral Teratology*. New York: Elsevier.

Yorke, C. & Wiseberg, S. (1976) A Developmental View of Anxiety. *Psychoanalytic Study of the Child* 31:107–135.

Young, J. Z. (1978) *Programs of the Brain*. Oxford, England: Oxford University Press.

Yule, W. (1978) Diagnosis: Developmental Psychological Assessment. In Kalverboer, A. F., van Praag, H. M., & Mendlewicz, J. (Eds.), *Advances in Biological Psychiatry. Volume I; Minimal Brain Dysfunction: Fact or Fiction*. Basel, Switzerland: Karger.

Yule, W. & Rutter, M. (Eds.) (1987) *Language Development and Disorders*. Philadelphia, PA: J. B. Lippincott.

Zaidel, E. (1979) The Split and Half Brains as Models of Congenital Language Disability. In Ludlow, C. L. & Doran-Quine, M. E. (Eds.), *The Neurological Bases of Language Disorders in Children: Methods and Directions for Research*. Washington, D.C.: National Institute of Neurological and Communicative Disorders and Stroke, U.S. Department of Health, Education and Welfare.

Zajonc, R. B. (1976) Family Configuration and Intelligence. *Science* 192: 227–236.

Zajonc, R. B. (1985) Emotion and Facial Efference: A Theory Reclaimed. *Science* 228:15–21.

Zales, M. R. (Ed.) (1982) *Eating, Sleeping and Sexuality: Treatment of Disorders in Basic Life Functions.* New York: Brunner/Mazel.

Zeigarnik, B. V. (1965) *The Pathology of Thinking.* New York: Consultants Bureau.

Zelazo, P. R. (1972) Smiling and Vocalizing: A Cognitive Emphasis. *Merrill-Palmer Quarterly* 18:349–365.

Zelnicker, T. & Jeffrey, W. E. (1976) Reflective and Impulsive Children: Strategies of Information Processing Underlying Differences in Problem Solving. *Monographs of the Society for Research in Child Development* 41:1–59.

Ziegler, R. & Holden, L. (1988) Family Therapy for Learning Disabled and Attention-Deficit Disordered Children. *American Journal of Orthopsychiatry.* 58: 196–210.

Zillman, D. (1979) *Hostility and Aggression.* Hillsdale, NJ: Erlbaum.

Zimet, S. G., & Farley, G. K. (1985) Day Treatment for Children in the United States. *Journal of Child Psychiatry* 24:732–738.

Zola-Morgan, S., Squire, L. R., & Mishkin, M. (1982) The Neuroanatomy of Amnesia: Amygdala-Hippocampus versus Temporal Stem. *Science* 218:1337–1339.

Zuckerman, M. (1983) Sensation Seeking: Optimal Levels of Arousal or Reward Systems Neurotransmitters. In Sinz, R., & Rosenzweig, M. R. (Eds.), *Psychophysiology.* New York: Elsevier Biomedical Press.

AUTHOR INDEX

SUBJECT INDEX

Absence seizures, 175
Acalculia, 147
Accommodation:
 defined, 304–306, 730
 figurative:
  as information processing, 238
  in learning, 307
  in object permanence, 350
  in perception, 241, 242, 243
 operative:
  in conceptualization, 254, 255
  imagination in, 251
  as information processing, 238
  in learning, 307
  in operations of schemes, 49
  in perception, 242
 under stress, 465
 visual, 462–463
Acetylcholine, 110, 224, 229
 in development, 161
Activity level:
 conceptual stage, 360, 364
 as instinct, 201
 sensorimotor stage, 346, 348
 symbolic stage, 354
 theoretical stage, 368
Adaptive instinctual systems, 201–205
Adaptive Learning Environments Model, 629
Adolescence, 367–371
Adrenal cortical axis, 230
Adrenal medulla, 218, 219
Adrenergic, 129–131
Adrenocorticotrophic hormone, 230
Adrenoleukodystrophy, 419
Adventitious movements, 414
Affective disorders, 454–456
Affective system:
 defined, 203
 development of, 232–235
 functions, 206–212
 processes, 212–232
Affiliative instincts, 201–202, 280, 283
After images, 246
Aggression:
 fear-induced, 203
 frustration-induced, 203
 instincts, 202–203, 280–281

maternal, 203
predatory, 202
sex-related, 203
status-related, 202
Aggressive instincts, 202–203, 280–281
Agism:
 defined, 55
 in handicaps, 424
 in individual differences, 574
 in labeling, 725
 in schools, 71
Agraphia, 147, 249, 730
Agnosia, 10, 730
Akathesia, 452, 730
Alcoholics Anonymous, 717
Alexia:
 anterior, 506
 central, 503–504
 defined, 730
 left-hemisphere damage, 147
 posterior, 501–502
 and writing, 249
Alexithymia, 473, 492, 534
Alimentary instinct, 200
Allergies:
 brain, 572–573
 food dyes, 451
Alliance:
 child-therapist, 684–686
 parent-professional, 712–714
Alper disease, 561
Alzheimer disease, 709
Amblyopia, 463
American Academy of Ophthalmology, 663
American Academy of Pediatrics, 663, 672
American Association for Pediatric Ophthalmology and Strabismus, 663
American Orthopsychiatric Association, 12
American Psychiatric Association, 447, 452, 455, 527
Amino acids, 111
Amnesia:
 defined, 730
 and memory system, 302
 in organic brain syndromes, 10
Amnesia syndrome, 476–477, 512
Amusia, 493

Amygdala:
 anatomy of, 131–134
 fear, 216
 fight-flight response, 176, 201, 223, 227, 330
 kindling in, 307
 memory, 179, 302
Anencephaly, 159
Anger:
 as arouser, 209
 development of, 233–234
 as signal, 211
Angular gyrus:
 congenital dyslexia, 6, 15
 Gerstmann syndrome, 398
 maturation of, 161
 reading, 267, 470, 502
 visual memory, 181, 262
Aniseikonia, 328, 462
Anisometropia, 462
Anosognosia, 147
Anticonvulsants, 710
Antidepressants:
 action of, 222
 in depression, 455
 in grief, 223
 in panic attacks, 220
Anxiety, 217–221
 anticipatory, 220
 behavioral manifestations, 217–218, 383
 castration, 363
 chronic, 220
 as compound emotion, 207
 defined, 217–218
 development of, 233
 fight-flight response, 230
 physiology, 218
 predisposition, 235
 psychic, 217
 signal, 219–220, 289, 354
 somatic, 217
Aphasia:
 Broca's, 164, 506, 509
 defined, 730
 Gogi, 164, 509
 left hemisphere, 147
 organic brain syndromes, 10
 Wernicke's, 741
Appetitive instinctual systems, 199–201
Approach-withdrawal, 279–280
Apraxia, 10, 147
Aprosody, 147